AN INTRODUCTION TO LITERATURE

D0170104

AN INTRODUCTION TO LITERATURE

WILLIAM M. CHACE
Stanford University

PETER COLLIER

HARCOURT BRACE JOVANOVICH, PUBLISHERS
San Diego   New York   Chicago   Atlanta   Washington, D.C.
London   Sydney   Toronto

ABOUT THE COVER: *Santa Fe Studio* by Frank Harmon Myers. Gift of Mr. and Mrs. Frank P. Myers from the collection of the San Diego Museum of Art.

ISBN: 0-15-543034-3
Library of Congress Catalog Card Number: 84-81487
Printed in the United States of America

To Ralph Rader
Small payment on a large debt

PREFACE

T his book is based on two assumptions—first, that literature matters; and, second, that literature can and should be taught and studied. Learning to understand and appreciate literary works helps strengthen our critical faculties and other skills useful elsewhere in our lives. In addition to this very practical dividend, literature can also make us aware of the rich complexity of our own experience. It is no exaggeration to say that literature can make us more fully human.

In designing this book, we have tried to establish conditions for a creative collaboration between teacher and student. We want not only to introduce students to literary works, but also to help them begin making the critical judgments that can give literature—and life itself—greater meaning. We have begun with the three major genres—fiction, poetry, and drama—and with a detailed discussion of the elements of composition a reader must master to understand them. After studying these introductions, the student should be able to approach a literary work on its own terms and to begin grappling with such questions as how plot and character interact in a short story; how the meaning of a poem can be determined by the poet's choice of meter and rhythm; and how a dramatist uses the physical stage to reinforce the themes of his or her work. Indeed, because close analysis is an entry point for understanding literature, we have tried to reinforce the points made in our introductions to each genre with a series of study questions. These questions seek no single "right" answer; rather, they try to promote discriminating insights into form and meaning, and into the creative process itself.

Although we believe that careful textual analysis is centrally important in understanding a literary work, we also feel students should understand that writers do not work from operating manuals, nor exist in social isolation. They are part of the real world, which dramatically influences what and how they write. As an acknowledgment of this fact, we have organized the contents of this book to lead the student from the compositional elements of a work toward the social and biographical facts that also contribute to its final form. In the fiction section, for instance, we have included a section on Southern writers showing the importance of a sense of history and regional identity to the work they have produced. We have concluded the poetry section by focusing on Robert Lowell and Sylvia Plath, two contemporary American writers whose poems reflect the pressures that personal experience can exert on art. And in the drama section we have concluded with a chapter on classic American theater showing the common national themes expressed by writers otherwise greatly different in outlook and background.

The advantage of the approach we have chosen is clear. It demonstrates that what takes place in the writer's study is crucial, but it also emphasizes the importance of what takes place in the larger world. Moreover, by concluding each of the three genres with a section on American writers—some of the best writing in fiction, poetry, and drama produced in this country during the last fifty years—we have sought to give the book a coherence and a depth of subject matter that anthologies often lack. Ideally, students will emerge from their reading with a knowledge of the compositional tools a writer uses, with an understanding of the role large social and historical forces play in the creative act, *and* with a basic appreciation for the distinctive strengths of the literature of the country in which they live.

While this book has been designed as a teaching text, we hope that it also has its own literary integrity. Proceeding from the poet Ezra Pound's shrewd observation that literature is "news that stays new," we have tried to present a solid sampling of great writers of the past—writers like Tolstoy, Shakespeare, and Emily Dickinson, who continue to address us with undiminished urgency today. We have also included the work of Lillian Hellman, John Updike, Anne Sexton, and other writers some future generation may regard as having produced the classics of our own age. In this distinctive blend of many voices, we have tried to find the common motifs, the subtle harmonies, that exist in all great writing. We hope the result is a book that students can use to discover the great riches of literature and, after their classroom experience is over, keep with them as a reminder that the enterprise they have embarked on will last the rest of their lives.

We have had considerable help in this work. We offer special thanks to Bill Barnett, Carolyn Viola-John, Eleanor Garner, and Helen Triller of Harcourt Brace Jovanovich; and to Susan Lansdale and Cristy Juencke of Stanford University. More than anyone else, Matt Milan helped initiate this project and made sure that it was finished. Our families supported us not by any actual involvement in this project, but by simply being themselves.

William Chace
Peter Collier

CONTENTS

POETRY

7   POEMS FOR FURTHER READING   514

DRAMA

AN INTRODUCTION TO LITERATURE

FICTION

1
AN INTRODUCTION TO FICTION

Modern storytelling occurs in a clean, well-lighted place rather than beside a fire casting shadows onto the walls of a cave. It is a solitary experience, not a communal one. What we hear is not the booming voice of a bard or shaman, but an inaudible narrator, a voice whose sound extends no further than our own mind. The subject matter of modern storytelling is not the familiar tale whose repetition reassures us about the truths that make up our world; it is the trials and tribulations of isolated characters whose relationship to our own destinies is not always readily apparent.

Modern storytelling, in short, is far different for us than it was for our ancestors, so different, in fact, that we have another, more technical term for it—*fiction*. The advent of the printing press, the manufacture of paper, the ability of authors to make a living from their work, the rise of the publishing industry—much has changed from the time when the storyteller's function was to reveal and consolidate the myths that helped explain the way things work. Modern writers invent the world as they go, groping for small truths and private insight; their subject matter is not the formation of a people nor the epic of their history, but at best an illuminating moment between two individuals or the understanding of that instant when an isolated person captures a fleeting truth about his life. What hasn't changed is that modern fiction, like ancient myth, helps us discover who we are. It takes us out of ourselves, and at the same time forces us deeper into ourselves. We emerge from the experience of reading a story the way that our ancestors emerged from listening to a tale—the same, but somehow different; our view of the world is enlarged and our imaginations are enhanced.

Asked why they read, of course, most people wouldn't respond in such abstract or metaphysical terms. They would probably say, quite rightly, that they read because reading gives them pleasure. Pressed for specifics, they might say that reading allows them to participate vicariously in other, more exciting worlds—the distant galaxies of science fiction; the intellectual chess games of the detective story; the global intrigue of espionage novels; the fairy-tale morality of the paperback romance.

Popular fiction does allow us to escape the confines of our mundane lives. And there is nothing wrong with that unless it creates an exclusive appetite for standardized writing with its predictable heroes and villains, its contrived surprises, and its happy endings; unless, in short, it makes us impatient with literature that is not only pleasurable but also instructive and broadening. Lasting fiction allows us not only to "lose" ourselves but to "find" ourselves as well. It entertains, but it also sharpens our awareness of the complexities of our own experiences. It may take us into the drawing rooms of Jane Austen's *Pride and Prejudice* or along on the wild philosophical quest of Herman Melville's *Moby Dick*; what it leaves us with is a broadened understanding of the human condition. It may be more demanding than popular fiction, but the rewards it offers are greater too.

The question "why read?" probably doesn't need to be asked because the answers are so obvious. The question "why study what we read?" is a little more difficult. Many readers are protective of their reading experiences. They feel that analyzing fiction drains it of its mystery and reduces it to a set of sterile ideas about form and content. While it is indeed possible to analyze a work "to death," dissecting what should be a living experience as if it were a laboratory object, it is also possible, through what we will distinguish as "creative" analysis, to breathe added life into literature and deepen its impact on us.

Why do we feel more sympathy toward one character than another? Why do the themes of one story touch us while those of another leave us cold? What are the principles of artistic selection at work in a given piece of fiction? Why, given the many alternatives available, did the writer choose the particular techniques he employed? These are valid questions. Readers who pursue them faithfully and honestly will find that, if anything, their awe for the finished work is augmented. Reading should not be an academic exercise. But it should be more than the passive reception of what appears on the printed page. Reading can be an active collaboration in which the reader brings something to the relationship and helps make it work. By trying to discover how and why a piece of fiction works, we come upon hidden aspects of ourselves as well.

The stories that make up this collection have been chosen with an eye toward strengthening the collaboration between writer and reader. Some of you may have studied fiction before and found the contents of the anthology you were using divided into a number of "elements of composition." Such a mechanical arrangement suggests that a writer is like a cook following a recipe that calls for specified ingredients. ("Take a pinch of setting, stir in some characters, add a dollop of dialogue, and simmer in a plot.") The truth, as we have tried to suggest in the following pages, is both simpler and more complex. A writer begins with initial ideas about *plot and character*—what a story is about. He makes crucial technical decisions, most importantly those regarding *point of view*—how the story will be told. And if a writer succeeds, the ultimate result are *themes* that make fiction different from fact—not just a recounting of events, but a fabric of meanings.

Yet we believe that fiction is the result of something larger than the decisions writers make in the solitude of their studies. Writers and the literature they produce are part of a specific *time and place*, a system of values and a distinctive way of seeing things. Hence we have included a section on Southern writing, some of the strongest and most lasting fiction to come out of America in the last half century. We have done so to show, in a specific way, the relationship between the work and the social world that helps create it.

We conclude by observing that short stories are not just abbreviated or "quick" novels. They are part of a form with its own integrity. Unable to use the digressions, leisurely development, and extensive circumstantial data that go into the making of most novels, short stories compensate with a compression and clarity that is in many ways similar to poetry. Edgar Allan Poe, one of the early masters of the form, said that short fiction achieves a "unity of effect or impression" because it can be read in one sitting. A contemporary short story writer and critic, V. S. Pritchett, put it this way: "The novel tells everything, whereas the short story tends to tell us only one thing and that intensely."

We have included classic stories like "The Secret Sharer" by Joseph Conrad and "The Lady with the Pet Dog" by Anton Chekhov. We have also included the work of Ann Beattie, Barry Hannah, Raymond Carver, and John Gardner, and other young writers whose fiction may someday attain that stature. Most of the stories are straightforward in subject and approach, although some, such as Franz Kafka's "A Hunger Artist," have unusual themes, and others, such as "Unmailed, Unwritten Letters" by Joyce Carol Oates, employ unusual techniques. While we have appended questions we hope will help students in their attempt to understand these works, we have not insisted on any one interpretation. Henry James was right when he said that "nothing will ever take the place of the good old fashion of 'liking' a work or not liking it."

2
ELEMENTS OF SHORT FICTION

PLOT AND CHARACTER

We have all noticed the way an excited child tells a story—a hasty sequence of facts connected by one "and then" after another. It is hard to keep from interrupting the child's account with adult questions. What, we want to ask, were the motives of the people involved? What were the underlying causes that determined the outcome of events? Which of the incidents were important and which subordinate? Our desire for answers suggests that *what* happens in any incident is to a large degree determined by *why* things happened as they did. The child's way is storytelling without art. What we want instead are the discriminations that give events significance—in other words, a satisfying *plot*.

Plot is more than chronology or the sum of a sequence of events. It is *the action of a narrative*, the inner logic that gives a story its meaning. As such, it is the most basic aspect of fiction. Plots of myths and parables can be told over and over again without diminishing their power to move and instruct us. The plots of some novels are so compelling that a reader can exist imaginatively within their grasp for days on end, feeling that the life found there is more intense than the reality of the daily world. Plots can be long and incredibly complex. The Old Testament, for instance, written over thousands of years by many authors, has essentially a single elaborate plot concerning the vexed relationship between God and the Chosen People. But plots can also exist in stories so short and compact that they seem almost to be epigrams. Consider Enrique Anderson-Imbert's *short* short story "Taboo":

> His guardian angel whispered to Fabian, behind his shoulder.
> "Careful, Fabian! It is decreed that you will die the minute you pronounce the word *doyen*."
> "*Doyen?*" asks Fabian, intrigued.
> And he died.

In some popular fiction—novels of intrigue and espionage, detective stories and science fiction—an ingenious plot is sometimes almost the sole source of pleasure. If a boorish reader decides to tell a friend what happens in this sort of book, it is certain that the friend won't bother to read the book (and probably won't remain a friend for long). But to know in advance what

6

Leopold Bloom does on his day of days in Joyce's *Ulysses* or to receive a summary of Marcel's imaginative reconstruction of his life and that of his family and friends in Proust's *Remembrance of Things Past* does not give away what makes either of these novels worth reading. In these works and others acknowledged as great, plot is more than a network of suspenseful happenings; it is the skeleton that writers flesh out with wisdom and insight, creating the enduring truths which the finest writing is all about.

Novels customarily acquire their power from the sheer accumulation of data about characters and the dilemmas in which they find themselves. Short stories, on the other hand, are compressed—more often evoking a critical moment in the life of a character than a detailed biography. To use Ernest Hemingway's phrase, short stories have plots that show "the tip of the iceberg"; such stories hint at a bulkier shape below but do not describe that shape in detail. Yet like novels, short stories have *plot structure*—a pattern of conflict and its resolution which leads to what V. S. Pritchett calls *disclosure:* "An event, a complete revelation of character, the close of a mood, the changing of an emotion, the clinching of an idea, the statement of a situation now completed."

In William Carlos Williams's "The Use of Force," the conflict is more subtle than may appear on first reading. It is announced at the onset of the story when the narrator says that he could see that his new patients "were all very nervous" and that they eyed him "with distrust." In other words, there is an adversarial situation from the very beginning, a conflict which gradually focuses on the doctor and the girl. She is almost picture perfect in her beauty, yet "eating [him] up with her cold, steady eyes." Soon what has begun as simply an uncomfortable situation opens up into a ferocious battle, with the girl flailing out at the narrator and knocking his glasses off, and he prying open her throat with such force that her mouth bleeds. At the end the girl is still fighting, but the physical contest has always been subordinate to the contest of will, which she has irretrievably lost. The doctor's victory may be a "social necessity," but it also testifies to the importance of brute strength in any struggle.

Because Stephen Crane's "The Blue Hotel" is longer and more elaborate than "The Use of Force," we can see the plot structure in a more diagrammatic way. The *issue* of the story is announced in the first few paragraphs. The oddly colored Palace Hotel is described as standing alone on the flat and nondescript prairie as if it were a theatre for bizarre human dramas that spring naturally from errors such as the Swede's nervous assertion that "some of these Western communities [are] very dangerous." The story's *complication* comes when the Swede's misperception of the relatively civilized Fort Romper as an outpost of the violent frontier he has read about brings him into conflict with others in the hotel. After Pat Scully fills the Swede with liquid courage and manages to talk him out of leaving, the reader feels as though a door has clanged shut. Escape or avoidance are no longer possible; the story will now have to be worked out in terms of the Swede's initial delusion. The *climax* comes after the second card game when the violence in the air since the men arrived at the hotel erupts in the fistfight between the Swede and Johnnie Scully, and the victorious Swede stalks off to town, convinced that he is as dangerous as any hero of the dime novels from which he has taken his idea of the wild west. The *resolution* of the story takes place in the bar, when the gambler provides the deluded Swede with the sudden death he originally feared at the onset of the story. The *conclusion*, when the Easterner informs the cowboy that Johnnie Scully had indeed been cheating at cards, reinforces Crane's idea that fate is not determined by the more or less anonymous individual actors (the cowboy is merely "Bill" and the Easterner is "Mr. Blank") of any human drama but is the result of larger social forces.

There is *suspense* in both "The Use of Force" and "The Blue Hotel." It is not, however, the page-turning suspense of the pulp novel. In that sort of literature the focus is on the arrival; in these stories the focus is on getting there. In "The Use of Force" the reader is less interested in the ultimate outcome of the conflict than in the way the situation forces the doctor to lay aside his civilized professional identity in order to cope with the girl's savage will to keep her illness undiscovered. In "The Blue Hotel" we read on to discover how exactly it will all come out but even more to see how the factors present from the beginning—the moody portent of the setting, the Swede's deluded belief that he has arrived at a dangerous edge of civilization, the blood-lust his behavior causes in the others—will finally be resolved.

In both these stories a large part of our satisfaction comes from the *dramatic ironies* intrinsic in the plot, that is, from the twists and turns of fate resulting from the collision of character and event. In "The Use of Force" dramatic irony is present in the ease with which the surface civility of social transactions quickly gives way to a power struggle. "The Blue Hotel" is filled with ironies, most notably in the way that the Swede's almost willful refusal to see the reality of Fort Romper finally creates exactly the situation he had initially feared. In both stories, moreover, there is a sense of *dramatic completion* once the initial problem of the story has been explored. In "The Use of Force" the girl could (and does) continue to struggle; but the plot has been completed once the doctor looks into her throat and confirms the diagnosis of diphtheria. In "The Blue Hotel" the cowboy and Easterner presumably go on to other adventures, but the plot of the story is completed once we have received the last relevant piece of information about the Swede—that he had actually been right when he claimed he was being cheated.

Although different in form and length, these stories have plots that are chronological. In other stories in this collection, chronology will be sliced up and rearranged. In Ambrose Bierce's "Occurrence at Owl Creek Bridge," for instance, events are narrated through *flashback* (and flash-forward) that take the story far beyond the hanging party with which it begins and ends. In Joyce Carol Oates's "Unwritten, Unmailed Letters," the story of an obsessed and destructive love affair is revealed through an imaginary correspondence the heroine addresses to the other characters. As you read these and the other stories that follow, try to go beyond what seems to be the given sequence of events and see plot as a complex matter involving a *strategy of exposition.* What do authors gain from ordering the subject matter of their stories as they have? How would a different order alter the ultimate effect of the work?

As we have seen in our discussion of "The Use of Force" and "The Blue Hotel," discussion of plot inevitably involves discussion of character as well. We cannot talk about either story without also talking about motivation as well: the doctor's determination to triumph over his willful young patient; the Swede's irrational fantasy of Fort Romper and the way that it ultimately becomes true.

Fictional characters are no more separable from the plots that contain them than we are from the events that make up our lives. Like us, characters in literature have been formed by past experience; and like us, what they *are* at any given point in their lives affects what happens to them. This is exactly the plight of Dorothy Parker's Hazel Morse. Her lazy preoccupation with good times, her triviality, and her belief that women such as she have a duty to be "good sports" in the company of men turn her life into a succession of lost weekends and sordid romantic interludes, each one emptier than the last. In this sense, her character determines the plot of "Big Blonde." But it could also be said that the specific sequence of events—the fact that Hazel falls in love with and marries Herbie, that he is a heavy drinker, that he eventually leaves her, that she then takes up with Ed who happens to be married, and so on—determines the sort of person she becomes and leads her to attempt suicide.

As "Big Blonde" shows, deciding whether plot creates character or vice versa is like arguing whether the glass is half full or half empty. Henry James put the issue nicely in his famous rhetorical question: "What is character but the determination of incident? What is incident but the illustration of character?"

What makes Hazel Morse (and Emma Bovary, Anna Karenina, Isadora Wing, and countless other heroines) live in our imaginations is this chemistry between what she is and what happens to her. This is not to say that *characterization* is an unimportant consideration in the art of fiction. Some writers have a special talent for presenting a character in such a precise and insightful way that we see that individual quite vividly. Generally speaking, however, what we are reacting to is more than vital statistics—height, weight, and identifying characteristics. Appearance is, in some sense, a key to Hazel Morse's fate, perhaps more than with most characters in fiction. Dorothy Parker makes us *see* her very well; but by the end of the very first paragraph of the story we feel that we also know her because of descriptions that go deeper than what she looks like. Given her eye-catching appearance, for instance, Hazel may not be able to keep men from clicking their tongues when she passes by. But "boxing" her feet in tiny shoes is a voluntary and (as far as we are concerned) telling piece of vanity. She may not be able to do anything about "flabby" arms that are "splattered" with liver spots, but she could avoid calling attention to these defects if she had not "disfigured" her fingers with rings. There are other passages early in the story which make us see Hazel as empty-headed and vain, the "dumb blonde" of popular culture: "Men liked her, and she took it for granted that the liking of many men was a desirable thing." And: "Her ideas, or, better, her acceptances, ran right along with those of the other substantially built blondes in whom she found her friends."

By the end of the first page we have gotten the picture of someone whose limits prevent her from seeing who she is and what is happening to her— exactly the qualities which cause her downward spiral. Yet even though she is faintly unpleasant, we do identify with her—in part because we understand that she is behaving exactly as the culture that produced her expects her to behave. *Identification* involves more than mere liking. It also means conceiving *dramatic expectations* about characters and their fate. For instance, Parker writes of Hazel and Herbie: "She was completely bewildered by what happened to their marriage. First they were lovers; and then, it seemed without transition, they were enemies. She never understood it." But we understand. We have been prepared for the end of their relationship and would be surprised, and perhaps even disappointed, if they lived happily ever after. Novelist and critic E. M. Forster described the *satisfaction* of dramatic expectations this way: "a slight shock, followed by the feeling, 'Oh, that's all right.'" That is how we feel about the conclusion of "Big Blonde." We may be surprised when Hazel swallows two bottles of barbiturates, but we feel that it's "all right" when she recovers. Big blondes like her don't suffer tragic ends.

In novels we expect *character development*—changes in perception or being in response to the events that make up the plot. In most short stories there is not time or space to show a character's evolving reaction to complex circumstances. We do demand, however, that characters in short fiction be *plausible* and *consistent*. We may not have met someone like Hazel Morse, for instance, but after reading "Big Blonde" we believe that such a person could exist and that if she did she might well have experiences such as those that make up this story. Other characters in the stories in this collection may be more sympathetic than Hazel; less of their lives may be shown. The important thing to look for is how we come to know these characters and how we come to conceive certain expectations about how the conflicts in which they find themselves will be resolved.

William Carlos Williams (1883–1963)
The Use of Force

They were new patients to me, all I had was the name, Olson. Please come down as soon as you can, my daughter is very sick.

When I arrived I was met by the mother, a big startled looking woman, very clean and apologetic who merely said, Is this the doctor? and let me in.

In the back, she added. You must excuse us, doctor, we have her in the kitchen where it is warm. It is very damp here sometimes.

The child was fully dressed and sitting on her father's lap near the kitchen table. He tried to get up, but I motioned for him not to bother, took off my overcoat and started to look things over. I could see that they were all very nervous, eyeing me up and down distrustfully. As often, in such cases, they weren't telling me more than they had to, it was up to me to tell them; that's why they were spending three dollars on me.

The child was fairly eating me up with her cold, steady eyes, and no expression to her face whatever. She did not move and seemed, inwardly, quiet; an unusually attractive little thing, and as strong as a heifer in appearance. But her face was flushed, she was breathing rapidly, and I realized that she had a high fever. She had magnificent blonde hair, in profusion. One of those picture children often reproduced in advertising leaflets and the photogravure sections of the Sunday papers.

She's had a fever for three days, began the father and we don't know what it comes from. My wife has given her things, you know, like people do, but it don't do no good. And there's been a lot of sickness around. So we tho't you'd better look her over and tell us what is the matter.

As doctors often do I took a trial shot at it as a point of departure. Has she had a sore throat?

Both parents answered me together, No . . . No, she says her throat don't hurt her.

Does your throat hurt you? added the mother to the child. But the little girl's expression didn't change nor did she move her eyes from my face.

Have you looked?

I tried to, said the mother, but I couldn't see.

As it happens we had been having a number of cases of diphtheria in the school to which this child went during that month and we were all, quite apparently, thinking of that, though no one had as yet spoken of the thing.

Well, I said, suppose we take a look at the throat first. I smiled in my best professional manner and asking for the child's first name I said, come on, Mathilda, open your mouth and let's take a look at your throat.

Nothing doing.

Aw, come on, I coaxed, just open your mouth wide and let me take a look. Look, I said opening both hands wide, I haven't anything in my hands. Just open up and let me see.

Such a nice man, put in the mother. Look how kind he is to you. Come on, do what he tells you to. He won't hurt you.

At that I ground my teeth in disgust. If only they wouldn't use the word "hurt" I might be able to get somewhere. But I did not allow myself to be hurried or disturbed but speaking quietly and slowly I approached the child again.

As I moved my chair a little nearer suddenly with one catlike movement both her hands clawed instinctively for my eyes and she almost reached them too. In fact she knocked my glasses flying and they fell, though unbroken, several feet away from me on the kitchen floor.

Both the mother and father almost turned themselves inside out in embarrassment and apology. You bad girl, said the mother, taking her and shaking her by one arm. Look what you've done. The nice man . . .

For heaven's sake, I broke in. Don't call me a nice man to her. I'm here to look at her throat on the chance that she might have diphtheria and possibly die of it. But that's nothing to her. Look here, I said to the child, we're going to look at your throat. You're old enough to understand what I'm saying. Will you open it now by yourself or shall we have to open it for you?

Not a move. Even her expression hadn't changed. Her breaths however were coming faster and faster. Then the battle began. I had to do it. I had to have a throat culture for her own protection. But first I told the parents that it was entirely up to them. I explained the danger but said that I would not insist on a throat examination so long as they would take the responsibility.

If you don't do what the doctor says you'll have to go to the hospital, the mother admonished her severely.

Oh yeah? I had to smile to myself. After all, I had already fallen in love with the savage brat, the parents were contemptible to me. In the ensuing struggle they grew more and more abject, crushed, exhausted while she surely rose to magnificent heights of insane fury of effort bred of her terror of me.

The father tried his best, and he was a big man but the fact that she was his daughter, his shame at her behavior and his dread of hurting her made him release her just at the critical moment several times when I had almost achieved success, till I wanted to kill him. But his dread also that she might have diphtheria made him tell me to go on, go on though he himself was almost fainting, while the mother moved back and forth behind us raising and lowering her hands in an agony of apprehension.

Put her in front of you on your lap, I ordered, and hold both her wrists.

But as soon as he did the child let out a scream. Don't, you're hurting me. Let go of my hands. Let them go I tell you. Then she shrieked terrifyingly, hysterically. Stop it! Stop it! You're killing me!

Do you think she can stand it, doctor! said the mother.

You get out, said the husband to his wife. Do you want her to die of diphtheria?

Come on now, hold her, I said.

Then I grasped the child's head with my left hand and tried to get the wooden tongue depressor between her teeth. She fought, with clenched teeth, desperately! But now I also had grown furious—at a child. I tried to hold myself down but I couldn't. I know how to expose a throat for inspection. And I did my best. When finally I got the wooden spatula behind the last teeth and just the point of it into the mouth cavity, she opened up for an instant but before I could see anything she came down again and gripping the wooden blade between her molars she reduced it to splinters before I could get it out again.

Aren't you ashamed, the mother yelled at her. Aren't you ashamed to act like that in front of the doctor?

Get me a smooth-handled spoon of some sort, I told the mother. We're going through with this. The child's mouth was already bleeding. Her tongue was cut and she was screaming in wild hysterical shrieks. Perhaps I should have desisted and come back in an hour or more. No doubt it would have been better. But I have seen at least two children lying dead in bed of neglect in such cases, and feeling that I must get a diagnosis now or never I went at it again. But the worst of it was that I too had got beyond reason. I could have torn the child apart in my own fury and enjoyed it. It was a pleasure to attack her. My face was burning with it.

The damned little brat must be protected against her own idiocy, one says to one's self at such times. Others must be protected against her. It is social necessity. And all these things are true. But a blind fury, a feeling of adult shame, bred of a longing for muscular release are the operatives. One goes on to the end.

In a final unreasoning assault I overpowered the child's neck and jaws. I forced the heavy silver spoon back of her teeth and down her throat till she gagged. And there it was—both tonsils covered with membrane. She had fought valiantly to keep me from knowing her secret. She had been hiding that sore throat for three days at least and lying to her parents in order to escape just such an outcome as this.

Now truly she *was* furious. She had been on the defensive before but now she attacked. Tried to get off her father's lap and fly at me while tears of defeat blinded her eyes.

Stephen Crane (1871–1900)
The Blue Hotel

1

The Palace Hotel at Fort Romper was painted a light blue, a shade that is on the legs of a kind of heron, causing the bird to declare its position against any background. The Palace Hotel, then, was always screaming and howling in a way that made the dazzling winter landscape of Nebraska seem only a grey swampish hush. It stood alone on the prairie, and when the snow was falling the town two hunderd yards away was not visible. But when the traveller alighted at the railway station he was obliged to pass the Palace Hotel before he could come upon the company of low clapboard houses which composed Fort Romper, and it was not to be thought that any traveller could pass the Palace Hotel without looking at it. Pat Scully, the proprietor, had proved himself a master of strategy when he chose his paints. It is true that on clear days, when the great transcontinental expresses, long lines of swaying Pullmans, swept through Fort Romper, passengers were overcome at the sight, and the cult that knows the brown-reds and the subdivisions of the dark greens of the East expressed shame, pity, horror, in a laugh. But to the citizens of this prairie town and to the people who would naturally stop there, Pat Scully had performed a feat. With this opulence and splendour, these creeds, classes, egotisms, that streamed through Romper on the rails day after day, they had no colour in common.

As if the displayed delights of such a blue hotel were not sufficiently enticing, it was Scully's habit to go every morning and evening to meet the leisurely trains that stopped at Romper and work his seductions upon any man that he might see wavering, gripsack in hand.

One morning, when a snow-crusted engine dragged its long string of freight cars and its one passenger coach to the station, Scully performed the marvel of catching three men. One was a shaky and quick-eyed Swede, with a great shining cheap valise; one was a tall bronzed cowboy, who was on his way to a ranch near the Dakota line; one was a little silent man from the East, who didn't look it, and didn't announce it. Scully practically made them prisoners. He was so nimble and merry and kindly that each probably felt it would be the height of brutality to try to escape. They trudged off over the creaking board sidewalks in the wake of the eager little Irishman. He wore a heavy fur cap squeezed tightly down on his head. It caused his two red ears to stick out stiffly, as if they were made of tin.

At last, Scully, elaborately, with boisterous hospitality, conducted them through the portals of the blue hotel. The room which they entered was small. It seemed to be merely a proper temple for an enormous stove, which, in the centre, was humming with godlike violence. At various points on its surface the iron had become luminous and glowed yellow from the heat. Beside the stove Scully's son Johnnie was playing High-Five with an old farmer who had whiskers both grey and sandy. They were quarrelling. Frequently the old farmer turned his face toward a box of sawdust—coloured brown from tobacco juice—that was behind the stove, and spat with an air of great impatience and irritation. With a loud flourish of words Scully destroyed the game of cards, and bustled his son upstairs with part of the baggage of the new guests. He himself conducted them to three basins of the coldest water in the world. The cowboy and the Easterner burnished themselves fiery red with this water, until it seemed to be some kind of metal-polish. The Swede, however, merely dipped his fingers gingerly and with trepidation. It was notable that throughout this series of small ceremonies the three travellers were made to feel that Scully was very benevolent. He was conferring great favours upon them. He handed the towel from one to another with an air of philanthropic impulse.

Afterward they went to the first room, and, sitting about the stove, listened to Scully's officious clamour at his daughters, who were preparing the midday meal. They reflected in the silence of experienced men who tread carefully amid new people. Nevertheless, the old farmer, stationary, invincible in his chair near the warmest part of the stove, turned his face from the sawdust-box frequently and addressed a glowing commonplace to the strangers. Usually he was answered in short but adequate sentences by either the cowboy or the Easterner. The Swede said nothing. He seemed to be occupied in making furtive estimates of each man in the room. One might have thought that he had the sense of silly suspicion which comes to guilt. He resembled a badly frightened man.

Later, at dinner, he spoke a little, addressing his conversation entirely to Scully. He volunteered that he had come from New York, where for ten years he had worked as a tailor. These facts seemed to strike Scully as fascinating, and afterward he volunteered that he had lived in Romper for fourteen years. The Swede asked about the crops and the price of labour. He seemed barely to listen to Scully's extended replies. His eyes continued to rove from man to man.

Finally, with a laugh and a wink, he said that some of these Western communities were very dangerous; and after his statement he straightened his legs under the table, tilted his head, and laughed again, loudly. It was plain that the demonstration had no meaning to the others. They looked at him wondering and in silence.

2

As the men trooped heavily back into the front room, the two little windows presented views of a turmoiling sea of snow. The huge arms of the wind were making attempts—mighty, circular, futile—to embrace the flakes as they sped. A gate-post like a still man with a blanched face stood aghast amid this profligate fury. In a hearty voice Scully announced the presence of a blizzard. The guests of the blue hotel, lighting their pipes, assented with grunts of lazy masculine contentment. No island of the sea could be exempt in the degree of this little room with its humming stove. Johnnie, son of Scully, in a tone which defined his opinion of his ability as a card-player, challenged the old farmer of both grey and sandy whiskers to a game of High-Five. The farmer agreed with a contemptuous and bitter scoff. They sat close to the stove, and squared their knees under a wide board. The cowboy and the Easterner watched the game with interest. The Swede remained near the window, aloof, but with a countenance that showed signs of an inexplicable excitement.

The play of Johnnie and the grey-beard was suddenly ended by another quarrel. The old man arose while casting a look of heated scorn at his adversary. He slowly buttoned his coat, and then stalked with fabulous dignity from the room. In the discreet silence of all the other men the Swede laughed. His laughter rang somehow childish. Men by this time had begun to look at him askance, as if they wished to inquire what ailed him.

A new game was formed jocosely. The cowboy volunteered to beome the partner of Johnnie, and they all then turned to ask the Swede to throw in his lot with the little Easterner. He asked some questions about the game, and, learning that it wore many names, and that he had played it when it was under an alias, he accepted the invitation. He strode toward the men nervously, as if he expected to be assaulted. Finally, seated, he gazed from face to face and laughed shrilly. This laugh was so strange that the Easterner looked up quickly, the cowboy sat intent and with his mouth open, and Johnnie paused, holding the cards with still fingers.

Afterward there was a short silence. Then Johnnie said, "Well, let's get at it. Come on now!" They pulled their chairs forward until their knees were bunched under the board. They began to play, and their interest in the game caused the others to forget the manner of the Swede.

The cowboy was a board-whacker. Each time that he held superior cards he whanged them, one by one, with exceeding force, down upon the improvised table, and took the tricks with a glowing air of prowess and pride that sent thrills of indignation into the hearts of his opponents. A game with a board-whacker in it is sure to become intense. The countenances of the Easterner and the Swede were miserable whenever the cowboy thundered down his aces and kings, while Johnnie, his eyes gleaming with joy, chuckled and chuckled.

Because of the absorbing play none considered the strange ways of the Swede. They paid strict heed to the game. Finally, during a lull caused by a new deal, the Swede suddenly addressed Johnnie: "I suppose there have been a good many men killed in this room." The jaws of the others dropped and they looked at him.

"What in hell are you talking about?" said Johnnie.

The Swede laughed again his blatant laugh, full of a kind of false courage and defiance. "Oh, you know what I mean all right," he answered.

"I'm a liar if I do!" Johnnie protested. The card was halted, and the men stared at the Swede. Johnnie evidently felt that as the son of the proprietor he should make a direct inquiry. "Now, what might you be drivin' at, mister?" he asked. The Swede winked at him. It was a wink full of cunning. His fingers shook on the edge of the board. "Oh, maybe you think I have been to nowheres. Maybe you think I'm a tenderfoot?"

"I don't know nothin' about you," answered Johnnie, "and I don't give a damn where you've been. All I got to say is that I don't know what you're driving at. There hain't never been nobody killed in this room."

The cowboy, who had been steadily gazing at the Swede, then spoke: "What's wrong with you, mister?"

Apparently it seemed to the Swede that he was formidably menaced. He shivered and turned white near the corners of his mouth. He sent an appealing glance in the direction of the little Easterner. During these moments he did not forget to wear his air of advanced pot-valour. "They say they don't know what I mean," he remarked mockingly to the Easterner.

The latter answered after prolonged and cautious reflection. "I don't understand you," he said, impassively.

The Swede made a movement then which announced that he thought he had encountered treachery from the only quarter where he had expected sympathy, if not help. "Oh, I see you are all against me. I see——"

The cowboy was in a state of deep stupefaction. "Say," he cried, as he tumbled the deck violently down upon the board, "say, what are you gittin' at, hey?"

The Swede sprang up with the celerity of a man escaping from a snake on the floor. "I don't want to fight!" he shouted. "I don't want to fight!"

The cowboy stretched his long legs indolently and deliberately. His hands were in his pockets. He spat into the sawdust-box. "Well, who the hell thought you did?" he inquired.

The Swede backed rapidly toward a corner of the room. His hands were out protectingly in front of his chest, but he was making an obvious struggle to control his fright. "Gentlemen," he quavered, "I suppose I am going to be killed before I can leave this house! I suppose I am going to be killed before I can leave this house!" In his eyes was the dying-swan look. Through the windows could be seen the snow turning blue in the shadow of dusk. The wind tore at the house, and some loose thing beat regularly against the clapboards like a spirit tapping.

A door opened, and Scully himself entered. He paused in surprise as he noted the tragic attitude of the Swede. Then he said, "What's the matter here?"

The Swede answered him swiftly and eagerly: "These men are going to kill me."

"Kill you!" ejaculated Scully. "Kill you! What are you talkin'?"

The Swede made the gesture of a martyr.

Scully wheeled sternly upon his son. "What is this, Johnnie?"

The lad had grown sullen. "Damned if I know," he answered. "I can't make no sense to it." He began to shuffle the cards, fluttering them together with an angry snap. "He says a good many men have been killed in this room, or something like that. And he says he's goin' to be killed here too. I don't know what ails him. He's crazy, I shouldn't wonder."

Scully then looked for explanation to the cowboy, but the cowboy simply shrugged his shoulders.

"Kill you?" said Scully again to the Swede. "Kill you? Man, you're off your nut."

"Oh, I know," burst out the Swede. "I know what will happen. Yes, I'm crazy—yes. Yes, of course, I'm crazy—yes. But I know one thing—" There was a sort of sweat of misery and terror upon his face. "I know I won't get out of here alive."

The cowboy drew a deep breath, as if his mind was passing into the last stages of dissolution. "Well, I'm doggoned," he whispered to himself.

Scully wheeled suddenly and faced his son. "You've been troublin' this man!"

Johnnie's voice was loud with its burden of grievance. "Why, good Gawd, I ain't done nothin' to 'im."

The Swede broke in. "Gentlemen, do not disturb yourselves. I will leave this house. I will go away, because"—he accused them dramatically with his glance—"because I do not want to be killed."

Scully was furious with his son. "Will you tell me what is the matter, you young divil? What's the matter, anyhow? Speak out!"

"Blame it!" cried Johnnie in despair, "don't I tell you I don't know? He—he says we want to kill him, and that's all I know. I can't tell what ails him."

The Swede continued to repeat: "Never mind, Mr. Scully; never mind. I will leave this house. I will go away, because I do not wish to be killed. Yes, of course, I am crazy—yes. But I know one thing! I will go away. I will leave this house. Never mind, Mr. Scully; never mind. I will go away."

"You will not go 'way," said Scully. "You will not go 'way until I hear the reason for this business. If anybody has troubled you I will take care of him.

This is my house. You are under my roof, and I will not allow any peaceable man to be troubled here." He cast a terrible eye upon Johnnie, the cowboy, and the Easterner.

"Never mind, Mr. Scully; never mind. I will go away. I do not wish to be killed." The Swede moved toward the door which opened upon the stairs. It was evidently his intention to go at once for his baggage.

"No, no," shouted Scully peremptorily; but the white-faced man slid by him and disappeared. "Now," said Scully severely, "what does this mane?"

Johnnie and the cowboy cried together: "Why, we didn't do nothin' to 'im."

Scully's eyes were cold. "No," he said, "you didn't?"

Johnnie swore a deep oath. "Why, this is the wildest loon I ever see. We didn't do nothin' at all. We were jest sittin' here playin' cards, and he—"

The father suddenly spoke to the Easterner. "Mr. Blanc," he asked, "what has these boys been doin'?"

The Easterner reflected again. "I didn't see anything wrong at all," he said at last, slowly.

Scully began to howl. "But what does it mane?" He stared ferociously at his son. "I have a mind to lather you for this, me boy."

Johnnie was frantic. "Well, what have I done?" he bawled at his father.

3

"I think you are tongue-tied," said Scully finally to his son, the cowboy, and the Easterner; and at the end of this scornful sentence he left the room.

Upstairs the Swede was swiftly fastening the straps of his great valise. Once his back happened to be half turned toward the door, and, hearing a noise there, he wheeled and sprang up, uttering a loud cry. Scully's wrinkled visage showed grimly in the light of the small lamp he carried. This yellow effulgence, streaming upward, coloured only his prominent features, and left his eyes, for instance, in mysterious shadow. He resembled a murderer.

"Man! man!" he exclaimed, "have you gone daffy?"

"Oh, no! Oh, no!" rejoined the other. "There are people in this world who know pretty nearly as much as you do—understand?"

For a moment they stood gazing at each other. Upon the Swede's deathly pale cheeks were two spots brightly crimson and sharply edged, as if they had been carefully painted. Scully placed the light on the table and sat himself on the edge of the bed. He spoke ruminatively. "By cracky, I never heard of such a thing in my life. It's a complete muddle. I can't, for the soul of me, think how you ever got this idea into your head." Presently he lifted his eyes and asked: "And did you sure think they were going to kill you?"

The Swede scanned the old man as if he wished to see into his mind. "I did," he said at last. He obviously suspected that this answer might precipitate an outbreak. As he pulled on a strap his whole arm shook, the elbow wavering like a bit of paper.

Scully banged his hand impressively on the footboard of the bed. "Why, man, we're goin' to have a line of ilictric street-cars in this town next spring."

" 'A line of electric street-cars,' " repeated the Swede, stupidly.

"And," said Scully, "there's a new railroad goin' to be built down from Broken Arm to here. Not to mintion the four churches and the smashin' big brick school-house. Then there's the big factory, too. Why, in two years Romper'll be a met-tro-*pol*-is."

Having finished the preparation of his baggage, the Swede straightened himself. "Mr. Scully," he said, with sudden hardihood, "how much do I owe you?"

"You don't owe me anythin'," said the old man, angrily.

"Yes, I do," retorted the Swede. He took seventy-five cents from his pocket and tendered it to Scully; but the latter snapped his fingers in disdainful refusal. However, it happened that they both stood gazing in a strange fashion at three silver pieces on the Swede's open palm.

"I'll not take your money," said Scully at last. "Not after what's been goin' on here." Than a plan seemed to strike him. "Here," he cried, picking up his lamp and moving toward the door. "Here! Come with me a minute."

"No," said the Swede, in overwhelming alarm.

"Yes," urged the old man. "Come on! I want you to come and see a picter—just across the hall—in my room."

The Swede must have concluded that his hour was come. His jaw dropped and his teeth showed like a dead man's. He ultimately followed Scully across the corridor, but he had the step of one hung in chains.

Scully flashed the light high on the wall of his own chamber. There was revealed a ridiculous photograph of a little girl. She was leaning against a balustrade of gorgeous decoration, and the formidable bang to her hair was prominent. The figure was as graceful as an upright sled-stake, and, withal, it was of the hue of lead. "There," said Scully, tenderly, "that's the picter of my little girl that died. Her name was Carrie. She had the purtiest hair you ever saw! I was that fond of her, she—"

Turning then, he saw that the Swede was not contemplating the picture at all, but, instead, was keeping keen watch on the gloom in the rear.

"Look, man!" cried Scully, heartily. "That's the picter of my little gal that died. Her name was Carrie. And then here's the picter of my oldest boy, Michael. He's a lawyer in Lincoln, an' doin' well. I gave that boy a grand eddication, and I'm glad for it now. He's a fine boy. Look at 'im now. Ain't he bold as blazes, him there in Lincoln, an honoured an' respicted gintleman! An honoured and respicted gintleman," concluded Scully with a flourish. And, so saying, he smote the Swede jovially on the back.

The Swede faintly smiled.

"Now," said the old man, "there's only one more thing." He dropped suddenly to the floor and thrust his head beneath the bed. The Swede could hear his muffled voice. "I'd keep it under me piller if it wasn't for that boy Johnnie. Then there's the old woman— Where is it now? I never put it twice in the same place. Ah, now come out with you!"

Presently he backed clumsily from under the bed, dragging with him an old coat rolled into a bundle. "I've fetched him," he muttered. Kneeling on the floor, he unrolled the coat and extracted from its heart a large yellow-brown whisky-bottle.

His first manœuvre was to hold the bottle up to the light. Reassured, apparently, that nobody had been tampering with it, he thrust it with a generous movement toward the Swede.

The weak-kneed Swede was about to eagerly clutch this element of strength, but he suddenly jerked his hand away and cast a look of horror upon Scully.

"Drink," said the old man affectionately. He had risen to his feet, and now stood facing the Swede.

There was a silence. Then again Scully said: "Drink!"

The Swede laughed wildly. He grabbed the bottle, put it to his mouth; and as his lips curled absurdly around the opening and his throat worked, he kept his glance, burning with hatred, upon the old man's face.

4

After the departure of Scully the three men, with the cardboard still upon their knees, preserved for a long time an astounded silence. Then Johnnie said: "That's the doddangedest Swede I ever see."

"He ain't no Swede," said the cowboy, scornfully.

"Well, what is he then?" cried Johnnie. "What is he then?"

"It's my opinion," replied the cowboy deliberately, "he's some kind of a Dutchman." It was a venerable custom of the country to entitle as Swedes all light-haired men who spoke with a heavy tongue. In consequence the idea of the cowboy was not without its daring. "Yes, sir," he repeated. "It's my opinion this feller is some kind of a Dutchman."

"Well, he says he's a Swede, anyhow," muttered Johnnie, sulkily. He turned to the Easterner: "What do you think, Mr. Blanc?"

"Oh, I don't know," replied the Easterner.

"Well, what do you think makes him act that way?" asked the cowboy.

"Why, he's frightened." The Easterner knocked his pipe against a rim of the stove. "He's clear frightened out of his boots."

"What at?" cried Johnnie and the cowboy together.

The Easterner reflected over his answer.

"What at?" cried the others again.

"Oh, I don't know, but it seems to me this man has been reading dime novels, and he thinks he's right out in the middle of it—the shootin' and stabbin' and all."

"But," said the cowboy, deeply scandalized, "this ain't Wyoming, ner none of them places. This is Nebrasker."

"Yes," added Johnnie, "an' why don't he wait till he gits *out* West?"

The travelled Easterner laughed. "It isn't different there even—not in these days. But he thinks he's right in the middle of hell."

Johnnie and the cowboy mused long.

"It's awful funny," remarked Johnnie at last.

"Yes," said the cowboy. "This is a queer game. I hope we don't git snowed in, because then we'd have to stand this here man bein' around with us all the time. That wouldn't be no good."

"I wish pop would throw him out," said Johnnie.

Presently they heard a loud stamping on the stairs, accompanied by ringing jokes in the voice of old Scully, and laughter, evidently from the Swede. The men around the stove stared vacantly at each other. "Gosh!" said the cowboy. The door flew open, and old Scully, flushed and anecdotal, came into the room. He was jabbering at the Swede, who followed him, laughing bravely. It was the entry of two roisterers from a banquet hall.

"Come now," said Scully sharply to the three seated men, "move up and give us a chance at the stove." The cowboy and the Easterner obediently sidled their chairs to make room for the new-comers. Johnnie, however, simply arranged himself in a more indolent attitude, and then remained motionless.

"Come! Git over, there," said Scully.

"Plenty of room on the other side of the stove," said Johnnie.

"Do you think we want to sit in the draught?" roared the father.

But the Swede here interposed with a grandeur of confidence. "No, no. Let the boy sit where he likes," he cried in a bullying voice to the father.

"All right! All right!" said Scully, deferentially. The cowboy and the Easterner exchanged glances of wonder.

The five chairs were formed in a crescent about one side of the stove. The Swede began to talk; he talked arrogantly, profanely, angrily. Johnnie, the cowboy, and the Easterner maintained a morose silence, while old Scully appeared to be receptive and eager, breaking in constantly with sympathetic ejaculations.

Finally the Swede announced that he was thirsty. He moved in his chair, and said that he would go for a drink of water.

"I'll git it for you," cried Scully at once.

"No," said the Swede, contemptuously. "I'll get it for myself." He arose and stalked with the air of an owner off into the executive parts of the hotel.

As soon as the Swede was out of hearing Scully sprang to his feet and whispered intensely to the others: "Upstairs he thought I was tryin' to poison 'im."

"Say," said Johnnie, "this makes me sick. Why don't you throw 'im out in the snow?"

"Why, he's all right now," declared Scully. "It was only that he was from the East, and he thought this was a tough place. That's all. He's all right now."

The cowboy looked with admiration upon the Easterner. "You were straight," he said. "You were on to that there Dutchman."

"Well," said Johnnie to his father, "he may be all right now, but I don't see it. Other time he was scared, but now he's too fresh."

Scully's speech was always a combination of Irish brogue and idiom, Western twang and idiom, and scraps of curiously formal diction taken from the story-books and newspapers. He now hurled a strange mass of language at the head of his son. "What do I keep? What do I keep? What do I keep?" he demanded, in a voice of thunder. He slapped his knee impressively, to indicate that he himself was going to make reply, and that all should heed. "I keep a hotel," he shouted. "A hotel, do you mind? A guest under my roof has sacred privileges. He is to be intimidated by none. Not one word shall he hear that would prijudice him in favour of goin' away. I'll not have it. There's no place in this here town where they can say they iver took in a guest of mine because he was afraid to stay here." He wheeled suddenly upon the cowboy and the Easterner. "Am I right?"

"Yes, Mr. Scully," said the cowboy, "I think you're right."

"Yes, Mr. Scully," said the Easterner, "I think you're right."

5

At six-o'clock supper, the Swede fizzed like a fire-wheel. He sometimes seemed on the point of bursting into riotous song, and in all his madness he was encouraged by old Scully. The Easterner was encased in reserve; the cowboy sat in wide-mouthed amazement, forgetting to eat, while Johnnie wrathily demolished great plates of food. The daughters of the house, when they were obliged to replenish the biscuits, approached as warily as Indians, and, having succeeded in their purpose, fled with ill-concealed trepidation. The Swede domineered the whole feast, and he gave it the appearance of a cruel bacchanal. He seemed to have grown suddenly taller; he gazed, brutally disdainful, into every face. His voice rang through the room. Once when he jabbed out harpoon-fashion with his fork to pinion a biscuit, the weapon nearly impaled the hand of the Easterner, which had been stretched quietly out for the same biscuit.

After supper, as the men filed toward the other room, the Swede smote Scully ruthlessly on the shoulder. "Well, old boy, that was a good, square meal." Johnnie looked hopefully at his father; he knew that shoulder was tender from an old fall; and, indeed, it appeared for a moment as if Scully was going to flame out over the matter, but in the end he smiled a sickly smile and remained silent. The others understood from his manner that he was admitting his responsibility for the Swede's new view-point.

Johnnie, however, addressed his parent in an aside. "Why don't you license somebody to kick you downstairs?" Scully scowled darkly by way of reply.

When they were gathered about the stove, the Swede insisted on another game of High-Five. Scully gently deprecated the plan at first, but the Swede turned a wolfish glare upon him. The old man subsided, and the Swede canvassed the others. In his tone there was always a great threat. The cowboy and the Easterner both remarked indifferently that they would play. Scully said that he would presently have to go to meet the 6.58 train, and so the Swede turned menacingly upon Johnnie. For a moment their glances crossed like blades, and then Johnnie smiled and said, "Yes, I'll play."

They formed a square, with the little board on their knees. The Easterner and the Swede were again partners. As the play went on, it was noticeable that the cowboy was not board-whacking as usual. Meanwhile, Scully, near the lamp, had put on his spectacles and, with an appearance curiously like an old priest, was reading a newspaper. In time he went out to meet the 6.58 train, and, despite his precautions, a gust of polar wind whirled into the room as he opened the door. Besides scattering the cards, it chilled the players to the marrow. The Swede cursed frightfully. When Scully returned, his entrance

disturbed a cosy and friendly scene. The Swede again cursed. But presently
they were once more intent, their heads bent forward and their hands moving
swiftly. The Swede had adopted the fashion of board-whacking.

Scully took up his paper and for a long time remained immersed in
matters which were extraordinarily remote from him. The lamp burned
badly, and once he stopped to adjust the wick. The newspaper, as he turned
from page to page, rustled with a slow and comfortable sound. Then suddenly
he heard three terrible words: "You are cheatin'!"

Such scenes often prove that there can be little of dramatic import in
environment. Any room can present a tragic front; any room can be comic.
This little den was now hideous as a torture-chamber. The new faces of the
men themselves had changed it upon the instant. The Swede held a huge fist
in front of Johnnie's face, while the latter looked steadily over it into the
blazing orbs of his accuser. The Easterner had grown pallid; the cowboy's jaw
had dropped in that expression of bovine amazement which was one of his
important mannerisms. After the three words, the first sound in the room was
made by Scully's paper as it floated forgotten to his feet. His spectacles had
also fallen from his nose, but by a clutch he had saved them in air. His hand,
grasping the spectacles, now remained poised awkwardly and near his shoulder. He stared at the card-players.

Probably the silence was while a second elapsed. Then, if the floor had
been suddenly twitched out from under the men they could not have moved
quicker. The five had projected themselves headlong toward a common
point. It happened that Johnnie, in rising to hurl himself upon the Swede,
had stumbled slightly because of his curiously instinctive care for the cards
and the board. The loss of the moment allowed time for the arrival of Scully,
and also allowed the cowboy time to give the Swede a great push which sent
him staggering back. The men found tongue together, and hoarse shouts of
rage, appeal, or fear burst from every throat. The cowboy pushed and jostled
feverishly at the Swede, and the Easterner and Scully clung wildly to Johnnie;
but through the smoky air, above the swaying bodies of the peace-compellers,
the eyes of the two warriors ever sought each other in glances of challenge that
were at once hot and steely.

Of course the board had been overturned, and now the whole company of
cards was scattered over the floor, where the boots of the men trampled the fat
and painted kings and queens as they gazed with their silly eyes at the war that
was waging above them.

Scully's voice was dominating the yells. "Stop now! Stop, I say! Stop,
now—"

Johnnie, as he struggled to burst through the rank formed by Scully and
the Easterner, was crying, "Well, he says I cheated! He says I cheated! I won't
allow no man to say I cheated! If he says I cheated, he's a —— ——!"

The cowboy was telling the Swede, "Quit, now! Quit, d'ye hear—"

The screams of the Swede never ceased: "He did cheat! I saw him! I saw
him—"

As for the Easterner, he was importuning in a voice that was not heeded:
"Wait a moment, can't you? Oh, wait a moment. What's the good of a fight
over a game of cards? Wait a moment—"

In this tumult no complete sentences were clear. "Cheat"—"Quit"—"He says"—these fragments pierced the uproar and rang out sharply. It was remarkable that, whereas Scully undoubtedly made the most noise, he was the least heard of any of the riotous band.

Then suddenly there was a great cessation. It was as if each man had paused for breath; and although the room was still lighted with the anger of men, it could be seen that there was no danger of immediate conflict, and at once Johnnie, shouldering his way forward, almost succeeded in confronting the Swede. "What did you say I cheated for? What did you say I cheated for? I don't cheat, and I won't let no man say I do."

The Swede said, "I saw you! I saw you!"

"Well," cried Johnnie, "I'll fight any man what says I cheat."

"No, you won't," said the cowboy. "Not here."

"Ah, be still, can't you?" said Scully, coming between them.

The quiet was sufficient to allow the Easterner's voice to be heard. He was repeating, "Oh, wait a moment, can't you? What's the good of a fight over a game of cards? Wait a moment!"

Johnnie, his red face appearing above his father's shoulder, hailed the Swede again. "Did you say I cheated?"

The Swede showed his teeth. "Yes."

"Then," said Johnnie, "we must fight."

"Yes, fight," roared the Swede. He was like a demoniac. "Yes, fight! I'll show you what kind of a man I am! I'll show you who you want to fight! Maybe you think I can't fight! Maybe you think I can't! I'll show you, you skin, you card-sharp! Yes, you cheated! You cheated! You cheated!"

"Well, let's go at it, then, mister," said Johnnie, coolly.

The cowboy's brow was beaded with sweat from his efforts in intercepting all sorts of raids. He turned in despiar to Scully. "What are you goin' to do now?"

A change had come over the Celtic visage of the old man. He now seemed all eagerness; his eyes glowed.

"We'll let them fight," he answered, stalwartly. "I can't put up with it any longer. I've stood this damned Swede till I'm sick. We'll let them fight."

<h1 style="text-align:center">6</h1>

The men prepared to go out of doors. The Easterner was so nervous that he had great difficulty in getting his arms into the sleeves of his new leather coat. As the cowboy drew his fur cap down over his ears his hands trembled. In fact, Johnnie and old Scully were the only ones who displayed no agitation. These preliminaries were conducted without words.

Scully threw open the door. "Well, come on," he said. Instantly a terrific wind caused the flame of the lamp to struggle at its wick, while a puff of black smoke sprang from the chimney-top. The stove was in mid-current of the blast, and its voice swelled to equal the roar of the storm. Some of the scarred and bedabbled cards were caught up from the floor and dashed helplessly against the farther wall. The men lowered their heads and plunged into the tempest as into the sea.

No snow was falling, but great whirls and clouds of flakes, swept up from the ground by the frantic winds, were streaming southward with the speed of bullets. The covered land was blue with the sheen of an unearthly satin, and there was no other hue save where, at the low, black railway station—which seemed incredibly distant—one light gleamed like a tiny jewel. As the men floundered into a thigh-deep drift, it was known that the Swede was bawling out something. Scully went to him, put a hand on his shoulder, and projected an ear. "What's that you say?" he shouted.

"I say," bawled the Swede again, "I won't stand much show against this gang. I know you'll all pitch on me."

Scully smote him reproachfully on the arm. "Tut, man!" he yelled. The wind tore the words from Scully's lips and scattered them far alee.

"You are all a gang of—" boomed the Swede, but the storm also seized the remainder of this sentence.

Immediately turning their backs upon the wind, the men had swung around a corner to the sheltered side of the hotel. It was the function of the little house to preserve here, amid this great devastation of snow, an irregular V-shape of heavily encrusted grass, which crackled beneath the feet. One could imagine the great drifts piled against the windward side. When the party reached the comparative peace of this spot it was found that the Swede was still bellowing.

"Oh, I know what kind of a thing this is! I know you'll all pitch on me. I can't lick you all!"

Scully turned upon him panther-fashion. "You'll not have to whip all of us. You'll have to whip my son Johnnie. An' the man what troubles you durin' that time will have me to dale with."

The arrangements were swiftly made. The two men faced each other, obedient to the harsh commands of Scully, whose face, in the subtly luminous gloom, could be seen set in the austere impersonal lines that are pictured on the countenances of the Roman veterans. The Easterner's teeth were chattering, and he was hopping up and down like a mechanical toy. The cowboy stood rock-like.

The contestants had not stripped off any clothing. Each was in his ordinary attire. Their fists were up, and they eyed each other in a calm that had the elements of leonine cruelty in it.

During this pause, the Easterner's mind, like a film, took lasting impressions of three men—the iron-nerved master of the ceremony; the Swede, pale, motionless, terrible; and Johnnie, serene yet ferocious, brutish yet heroic. The entire prelude had in it a tragedy greater than the tragedy of action, and this aspect was accentuated by the long, mellow cry of the blizzard, as it sped the tumbling and wailing flakes into the black abyss of the south.

"Now!" said Scully.

The two combatants leaped forward and crashed together like bullocks. There was heard the cushioned sound of blows, and of a curse squeezing out from between the tight teeth of one.

As for the spectators, the Easterner's pent-up breath exploded from him with a pop of relief, absolute relief from the tension of the preliminaries. The cowboy bounded into the air with a yowl. Scully was immovable as from supreme amazement and fear at the fury of the fight which he himself had permitted and arranged.

For a time the encounter in the darkness was such a perplexity of flying arms that it presented no more detail than would a swiftly revolving wheel. Occasionally a face, as if illumined by a flash of light, would shine out, ghastly and marked with pink spots. A moment later, the men might have been known as shadows, if it were not for the involuntary utterance of oaths that came from them in whispers.

Suddenly a holocaust of warlike desire caught the cowboy, and he bolted forward with the speed of a broncho. "Go it, Johnnie! go it! Kill him! Kill him!"

Scully confronted him. "Kape back," he said; and by his glance the cowboy could tell that this man was Johnnie's father.

To the Easterner there was a monotony of unchangeable fighting that was an abomination. This confused mingling was eternal to his sense, which was concentrated in a longing for the end, the priceless end. Once the fighters lurched near him, and as he scrambled hastily backward he heard them breathe like men on the rack.

"Kill him, Johnnie! Kill him! Kill him! Kill him!" The cowboy's face was contorted like one of those agony masks in museums.

"Keep still," said Scully, icily.

Then there was a sudden loud grunt, incomplete, cut short, and Johnnie's body swung away from the Swede and fell with sickening heaviness to the grass. The cowboy was barely in time to prevent the mad Swede from flinging himself upon his prone adversary. "No, you don't," said the cowboy, interposing an arm. "Wait a second."

Scully was at his son's side. "Johnnie! Johnnie, me boy!" His voice had a quality of melancholy tenderness. "Johnnie! Can you go on with it?" He looked anxiously down into the bloody, pulpy face of his son.

There was a moment of silence, and then Johnnie answered in his ordinary voice, "Yes, I—it—yes."

Assisted by his father he struggled to his feet. "Wait a bit now till you git your wind," said the old man.

A few paces away the cowboy was lecturing the Swede. "No, you don't! Wait a second!"

The Easterner was plucking at Scully's sleeve. "Oh, this is enough," he pleaded. "This is enough! Let it go as it stands. This is enough!"

"Bill," said Scully, "git out of the road." The cowboy stepped aside. "Now." The combatants were actuated by a new caution as they advanced toward collision. They glared at each other and then the Swede aimed a lightning blow that carried with it his entire weight. Johnnie was evidently half stupid from weakness, but he miraculously dodged, and his fist sent the overbalanced Swede sprawling.

The cowboy, Scully, and the Easterner burst into a cheer that was like a chorus of triumphant soldiery, but before its conclusion the Swede had scuffled agilely to his feet and come in berserk abandon at his foe. There was another perplexity of flying arms, and Johnnie's body again swung away and fell, even as a bundle might fall from a roof. The Swede instantly staggered to a little wind-waved tree and leaned upon it, breathing like an engine, while his savage and flame-lit eyes roamed from face to face as the men bent over Johnnie. There was a splendour of isolation in his situation at this time which the Easterner felt once when, lifting his eyes from the man on the ground, he beheld that mysterious and lonely figure, waiting.

"Are you any good yet, Johnnie?" asked Scully in a broken voice.

The son gasped and opened his eyes languidly. After a moment he answered, "No—I ain't—any good—any—more." Then, from shame and bodily ill, he began to weep, the tears furrowing down through the blood-stains on his face. "He was too—too—too heavy for me."

Scully straightened and addressed the waiting figure, "Stranger," he said, evenly, "it's all up with our side." Then his voice changed into that vibrant huskiness which is commonly the tone of the most simple and deadly announcements. "Johnnie is whipped."

Without replying, the victor moved off on the route to the front door of the hotel.

The cowboy was formulating new and unspellable blasphemies. The Easterner was startled to find that they were out in a wind that seemed to come direct from the shadowed arctic floes. He heard again the wail of the snow as it was flung to its grave in the south. He knew now that all this time the cold had been sinking into him deeper and deeper, and he wondered that he had not perished. He felt indifferent to the condition of the vanquished man.

"Johnnie, can you walk?" asked Scully.

"Did I hurt—hurt him any?" asked the son.

"Can you walk, boy? Can you walk?"

Johnnie's voice was suddenly strong. There was a robust impatience in it. "I asked you whether I hurt him any!"

"Yes, yes, Johnnie," answered the cowboy, consolingly; "he's hurt a good deal."

They raised him from the ground, and as soon as he was on his feet he went tottering off, rebuffing all attempts at assistance. When the party rounded the corner they were fairly blinded by the pelting of the snow. It burned their faces like fire. The cowboy carrried Johnnie through the drift to the door. As they entered, some cards again rose from the floor and beat against the wall.

The Easterner rushed to the stove. He was so profoundly chilled that he almost dared to embrace the glowing iron. The Swede was not in the room. Johnnie sank into a chair and, folding his arms on his knees, buried his face in them. Scully, warming one foot and then the other at a rim of the stove, muttered to himself with Celtic mournfulness. The cowboy had removed his fur cap, and with a dazed and rueful air he was running one hand through his tousled locks. From overhead they could hear the creaking of boards, as the Swede tramped here and there in his room.

The sad quiet was broken by the sudden flinging open of a door that led toward the kitchen. It was instantly followed by an inrush of women. They precipitated themselves upon Johnnie amid a chorus of lamentation. Before they carried their prey off to the kitchen, there to be bathed and harangued with that mixture of sympathy and abuse which is a feat of their sex, the mother straightened herself and fixed old Scully with an eye of stern reproach. "Shame be upon you, Patrick Scully!" she cried. "Your own son, too. Shame be upon you!"

"There, now! Be quiet, now!" said the old man, weakly.

"Shame be upon you, Patrick Scully!" The girls, rallying to this slogan, sniffed disdainfully in the direction of those trembling accomplices, the cowboy and the Easterner. Presently they bore Johnnie away, and left the three men to dismal reflection.

7

"I'd like to fight this here Dutchman myself," said the cowboy, breaking a long silence.

Scully wagged his head sadly. "No, that wouldn't do. It wouldn't be right. It wouldn't be right."

"Well, why wouldn't it?" argued the cowboy. "I don't see no harm in it."

"No," answered Scully, with mournful heroism. "It wouldn't be right. It was Johnnie's fight, and now we mustn't whip the man just because he whipped Johnnie."

"Yes, that's true enough," said the cowboy; "but—he better not get fresh with me, because I couldn't stand no more of it."

"You'll not say a word to him," commanded Scully, and even then they heard the tread of the Swede on the stairs. His entrance was made theatric. He swept the door back with a bang and swaggered to the middle of the room. No one looked at him. "Well," he cried, insolently, at Scully, "I s'pose you'll tell me now how much I owe you?"

The old man remained stolid. "You don't owe me nothin'."

"Huh!" said the Swede, "huh! Don't owe 'im nothin'."

The cowboy addressed the Swede. "Stranger, I don't see how you come to be so gay around here."

Old Scully was instantly alert. "Stop!" he shouted, holding his hand forth, fingers upward. "Bill, you shut up!"

The cowboy spat carelessly into the sawdust-box. "I didn't say a word, did I?" he asked.

"Mr. Scully," called the Swede, "how much do I owe you?" It was seen that he was attired for departure, and that he had his valise in his hand.

"You don't owe me nothin'," repeated Scully in the same imperturbable way.

"Huh!" said the Swede. "I guess you're right. I guess if it was any way at all, you'd owe me somethin'. That's what I guess." He turned to the cowboy. " 'Kill him! Kill him! Kill him!' " he mimicked, and then guffawed victoriously. " 'Kill him!' " He was convulsed with ironical humour.

But he might have been jeering the dead. The three men were immovable and silent, staring with glassy eyes at the stove.

The Swede opened the door and passed into the storm, giving one derisive glance backward at the still group.

As soon as the door was closed, Scully and the cowboy leaped to their feet and began to curse. They trampled to and fro, waving their arms and smashing into the air with their fists. "Oh, but that was a hard minute!" wailed Scully. "That was a hard minute! Him there leerin' and scoffin'! One bang at his nose was worth forty dollars to me that minute! How did you stand it, Bill?"

"How did I stand it?" cried the cowboy in a quivering voice. "How did I stand it? Oh!"

The old man burst into sudden brogue. "I'd loike to take that Swade," he wailed, "and hould 'im down on a shtone flure and bate 'im to a jelly wid a shtick!"

The cowboy groaned in sympathy. "I'd like to get him by the neck and ha-ammer him"—he brought his hand down on a chair with a noise like a pistol-shot—"hammer that there Dutchman until he couldn't tell himself from a dead coyote!"

"I'd bate 'im until he—"

"I'd show *him* some things—"

And then together they raised a yearning, fanatic cry—"Oh, o-oh! if we only could—"

"Yes!"

"Yes!"

"And then I'd—"

"O-o-oh!"

8

The Swede, tightly gripping his valise, tacked across the face of the storm as if he carried sails. He was following a line of little naked, grasping trees which, he knew, must mark the way of the road. His face, fresh from the pounding of Johnnie's fists, felt more pleasure than pain in the wind and the driving snow. A number of square shapes loomed upon him finally, and he knew them as the houses of the main body of the town. He found a street and made travel along it, leaning heavily upon the wind whenever, at a corner, a terrific blast caught him.

He might have been in a deserted village. We picture the world as thick with conquering and elate humanity, but here with the bugles of the tempest pealing, it was hard to imagine a peopled earth. One viewed the existence of man then as a marvel, and conceded a glamour of wonder to these lice which were caused to cling to a whirling, fire-smitten, ice-locked, disease-stricken, space-lost bulb. The conceit of man was explained by this storm to be the very engine of life. One was a coxcomb not to die in it. However, the Swede found a saloon.

In front of it an indomitable red light was burning, and the snowflakes were made blood-colour as they flew through the circumscribed territory of the lamp's shining. The Swede pushed open the door of the saloon and entered. A sanded expanse was before him, and at the end of it four men sat about a table drinking. Down one side of the room extended a radiant bar, and its guardian was leaning upon his elbows listening to the talk of the men at the table. The Swede dropped his valise upon the floor and, smiling fraternally upon the barkeeper, said, "Gimme some whisky, will you?" The man placed a bottle, a whisky-glass, and a glass of ice-thick water upon the bar. The Swede poured himself an abnormal portion of whisky and drank it in three gulps. "Pretty bad night," remarked the bartender, indifferently. He was making the pretension of blindness which is usually a distinction of his class; but it could have been seen that he was furtively studying the half-erased blood-stains on the face of the Swede. "Bad night," he said again.

"Oh, it's good enough for me," replied the Swede, hardily, as he poured himself some more whisky. The barkeeper took his coin and manœuvred it through its reception by the highly nickelled cash-machine. A bell rang; a card labelled "20 cts." had appeared.

"No," continued the Swede, "this isn't too bad weather. It's good enough for me."

"So?" murmured the barkeeper, languidly.

The copious drams made the Swede's eyes swim, and he breathed a trifle heavier. "Yes, I like this weather. I like it. It suits me." It was apparently his design to impart a deep significance to these words.

"So?" murmured the bartender again. He turned to gaze dreamily at the scroll-like birds and bird-like scrolls which had been drawn with soap upon the mirrors in back of the bar.

"Well, I guess I'll take another drink," said the Swede, presently. "Have something?"

"No, thanks; I'm not drinkin'," answered the bartender. Afterward he asked, "How did you hurt your face?"

The Swede immediately began to boast loudly. "Why, in a fight. I thumped the soul out of a man down here at Scully's hotel."

The interest of the four men at the table was at last aroused.

"Who was it?" said one.

"Johnnie Scully," blustered the Swede. "Son of the man what runs it. He will be pretty near dead for some weeks, I can tell you. I made a nice thing of him, I did. He couldn't get up. They carried him in the house. Have a drink?"

Instantly the men in some subtle way encased themselves in reserve. "No, thanks," said one. The group was of curious formation. Two were prominent local business men; one was the district attorney; and one was a professional gambler of the kind known as "square." But a scrutiny of the group would not have enabled an observer to pick the gambler from the men of more reputable pursuits. He was, in fact, a man so delicate in manner, when among people of fair class, and so judicious in his choice of victims, that in the strictly masculine part of the town's life he had come to be explicitly trusted and admired. People called him a thoroughbred. The fear and contempt with which his craft was regarded were undoubtedly the reason why his quiet dignity shone conspicuous above the quiet dignity of men who might be merely hatters, billiard markers, or grocery clerks. Beyond an occasional unwary traveller who came by rail, this gambler was supposed to prey solely upon reckless and senile farmers, who, when flush with good crops, drove into town in all the pride and confidence of an absolutely invulnerable stupidity. Hearing at times in circuitous fashion of the despoilment of such a farmer, the important men of Romper invariably laughed in contempt of the victim, and if they thought of the wolf at all, it was with a kind of pride at the knowledge that he would never dare think of attacking their wisdom and courage. Besides, it was popular that this gambler had a real wife and two real children in a neat cottage in a suburb, where he led an exemplary home life; and when any one even suggested a discrepancy in his character, the crowd immediately vociferated descriptions of this virtuous family circle. Then men who led exemplary home lives, and men who did not lead exemplary home lives, all subsided in a bunch, remarking that there was nothing more to be said.

However, when a restriction was placed upon him—as, for instance, when a strong clique of members of the new Pollywog Club refused to permit him, even as a spectator, to appear in the rooms of the organization—the candour and gentleness with which he accepted the judgment disarmed many of his foes and made his friends more desperately partisan. He invariably distinguished between himself and a respectable Romper man so quickly and frankly that his manner actually appeared to be a continual broadcast compliment.

And one must not forget to declare the fundamental fact of his entire position in Romper. It is irrefutable that in all affairs outside his business, in all matters that occur eternally and commonly between man and man, this thieving card-player was so generous, so just, so moral, that, in a contest, he could have put to flight the consciences of nine tenths of the citizens of Romper.

And so it happened that he was seated in this saloon with the two prominent local merchants and the district attorney.

The Swede continued to drink raw whisky, meanwhile babbling at the barkeeper and trying to induce him to indulge in potations. "Come on. Have a drink. Come on. What—no? Well, have a little one, then. By gawd, I've whipped a man to-night, and I want to celebrate. I whipped him good, too. Gentlemen," the Swede cried to the men at the table, "have a drink?"

"Ssh!" said the barkeeper.

The group at the table, although furtively attentive, had been pretending to be deep in talk, but now a man lifted his eyes toward the Swede and said, shortly, "Thanks. We don't want any more."

At this reply the Swede ruffled out his chest like a rooster. "Well," he exploded, "it seems I can't get anybody to drink with me in this town. Seems so, don't it? Well!"

"Ssh!" said the barkeeper.

"Say," snarled the Swede, "don't you try to shut me up. I won't have it. I'm a gentleman, and I want people to drink with me. And I want 'em to drink with me now. Now—do you understand?" He rapped the bar with his knuckles.

Years of experience had calloused the bartender. He merely grew sulky. "I hear you," he answered.

"Well," cried the Swede, "listen hard then. See those men over there?

Well, they're going to drink with me, and don't you forget it. Now you watch."

"Hi!" yelled the barkeeper, "this won't do!"

"Why won't it?" demanded the Swede. He stalked over to the table, and by chance laid his hand upon the shoulder of the gambler. "How about this?" he asked wrathfully. "I asked you to drink with me."

The gambler simply twisted his head and spoke over his shoulder. "My friend, I don't know you."

"Oh, hell!" answered the Swede, "come and have a drink."

"Now, my boy," advised the gambler, kindly, "take your hand off my shoulder and go 'way and mind your own business." He was a little, slim man, and it seemed strange to hear him use this tone of heroic patronage to the burly Swede. The other men at the table said nothing.

"What! You won't drink with me, you little dude? I'll make you, then! I'll make you!" The Swede had grasped the gambler frenziedly at the throat, and was dragging him from his chair. The other men sprang up. The barkeeper dashed around the corner of his bar. There was a great tumult, and then was seen a long blade in the hand of the gambler. It shot forward, and a human body, this citadel of virtue, wisdom, power, was pierced as easily as if it had been a melon. The Swede fell with a cry of supreme astonishment.

The prominent merchants and the district attorney must have at once tumbled out of the place backward. The bartender found himself hanging limply to the arm of a chair and gazing into the eyes of a murderer.

"Henry," said the latter, as he wiped his knife on one of the towels that hung beneath the bar rail, "you tell 'em where to find me. I'll be home, waiting for 'em." Then he vanished. A moment afterward the barkeeper was in the street dinning through the storm for help and, moreover, companionship.

The corpse of the Swede, alone in the saloon, had its eyes fixed upon a dreadful legend that dwelt atop the cash-machine: "This registers the amount of your purchase."

9

Months later, the cowboy was frying pork over the stove of a little ranch near the Dakota line, when there was a quick thud of hoofs outside, and presently the Easterner entered with the letters and the papers.

"Well," said the Easterner at once, "the chap that killed the Swede has got three years. Wasn't much, was it?"

"He has? Three years?" The cowboy poised his pan of pork, while he ruminated upon the news. "Three years. That ain't much."

"No. It was a light sentence," replied the Easterner as he unbuckled his spurs. "Seems there was a good deal of sympathy for him in Romper."

"If the bartender had been any good," observed the cowboy, thoughtfully, "he would have gone in and cracked that there Dutchman on the head with a bottle in the beginnin' of it and stopped all this here murderin'."

"Yes, a thousand things might have happened," said the Easterner, tartly.

The cowboy returned his pan of pork to the fire, but his philosophy continued. "It's funny, ain't it? If he hadn't said Johnnie was cheatin' he'd be alive this minute. He was an awful fool. Game played for fun, too. Not for money. I believe he was crazy."

"I feel sorry for that gambler," said the Easterner.

"Oh, so do I," said the cowboy. "He don't deserve none of it for killin' who he did."

"The Swede might not have been killed if everything had been square."

"Might not have been killed?" exclaimed the cowboy. "Everythin' square? Why, when he said that Johnnie was cheatin' and acted like such a jackass? And then in the saloon he fairly walked up to git hurt?" With these arguments the cowboy browbeat the Easterner and reduced him to rage.

"You're a fool!" cried the Easterner, viciously. "You're a bigger jackass than the Swede by a million majority. Now let me tell you one thing. Let me tell you something. Listen! Johnnie *was* cheating!"

"'Johnnie,'" said the cowboy, blankly. There was a minute of silence, and then he said, robustly, "Why, no. The game was only for fun."

"Fun or not," said the Easterner, "Johnnie was cheating. I saw him. I know it. I saw him. And I refused to stand up and be a man. I let the Swede fight it out alone. And you—you were simply puffing around the place and wanting to fight. And then old Scully himself! We are all in it! This poor gambler isn't even a noun. He is kind of an adverb. Every sin is the result of a collaboration. We, five of us, have collaborated in the murder of this Swede. Usually there are from a dozen to forty women really involved in every murder, but in this case it seems to be only five men—you, I, Johnnie, old Scully; and that fool of an unfortunate gambler came merely as a culmination, the apex of a human movement, and gets all the punishment."

The cowboy, injured and rebellious, cried out blindly into this fog of mysterious theory: "Well, I didn't do anythin', did I?"

Dorothy Parker *(1893–1967)*
Big Blonde

Hazel Morse was a large, fair woman of the type that incites some men when they use the word "blonde" to click their tongues and wag their heads roguishly. She prided herself upon her small feet and suffered for her vanity, boxing them in snub-toed, high-heeled slippers of the shortest bearable size. The curious things about her were her hands, strange terminations to the flabby white arms splattered with pale tan spots—long, quivering hands with deep and convex nails. She should not have disfigured them with little jewels.

She was not a woman given to recollections. At her middle thirties, her old days were a blurred and flickering sequence, an imperfect film, dealing with the actions of strangers.

In her twenties, after the deferred death of a hazy widowed mother, she had been employed as a model in a wholesale dress establishment—it was still the day of the big woman, and she was then prettily colored and erect and high-breasted. Her job was not onerous, and she met numbers of men and spent numbers of evenings with them, laughing at their jokes and telling them she loved their neckties. Men liked her, and she took it for granted that the liking of many men was a desirable thing. Popularity seemed to her to be worth all the work that had to be put into its achievement. Men liked you because you were fun, and when they liked you they took you out, and there you were. So, and successfully, she was fun. She was a good sport. Men like a good sport.

No other form of diversion, simpler or more complicated, drew her attention. She never pondered if she might not be better occupied doing something else. Her ideas, or, better, her acceptances, ran right along with those of the other substantially built blondes in whom she found her friends.

When she had been working in the dress establishment some years she met Herbie Morse. He was thin, quick, attractive, with shifting lines about his shiny, brown eyes and a habit of fiercely biting at the skin around his finger nails. He drank largely; she found that entertaining. Her habitual greeting to him was an allusion to his state of the previous night.

"Oh, what a peach you had," she used to say, through her easy laugh. "I thought I'd die, the way you kept asking the waiter to dance with you."

She liked him immediately upon their meeting. She was enormously amused at his fast, slurred sentences, his interpolations of apt phrases from vaudeville acts and comic strips; she thrilled at the feel of his lean arm tucked firm beneath the sleeve of her coat; she wanted to touch the wet, flat surface of his hair. He was as promptly drawn to her. They were married six weeks after they had met.

She was delighted at the idea of being a bride; coquetted with it, played upon it. Other offers of marriage she had had, and not a few of them, but it happened that they were all from stout, serious men who had visited the dress establishment as buyers; men from Des Moines and Houston and Chicago and, in her phrase, even funnier places. There was always something immensely comic to her in the thought of living elsewhere than New York. She could not regard as serious proposals that she share a western residence.

She wanted to be married. She was nearing thirty now, and she did not take the years well. She spread and softened, and her darkening hair turned her to inexpert dabblings with peroxide. There were times when she had little flashes of fear about her job. And she had had a couple of thousand evenings of being a good sport among her male acquaintances. She had come to be more conscientious than spontaneous about it.

Herbie earned enough, and they took a little apartment far uptown. There was a Mission-furnished dining-room with a hanging central light globed in liver-colored glass; in the living-room were an "over-stuffed suite," a Boston fern, and a reproduction of the Henner "Magdalene" with the red hair and the blue draperies; the bedroom was in gray enamel and old rose, with Herbie's photograph on Hazel's dressing-table and Hazel's likeness on Herbie's chest of drawers.

She cooked—and she was a good cook—and marketed and chatted with the delivery boys and the colored laundress. She loved the flat, she loved her life, she loved Herbie. In the first months of their marriage, she gave him all the passion she was ever to know.

She had not realized how tired she was. It was a delight, a new game, a holiday, to give up being a good sport. If her head ached or her arches throbbed, she complained piteously, babyishly. If her mood was quiet, she did not talk. If tears came to her eyes, she let them fall.

She fell readily into the habit of tears during the first year of her marriage. Even in her good sport days, she had been known to weep lavishly and disinterestedly on occasion. Her behavior at the theater was a standing joke. She could weep at anything in a play—tiny garments, love both unrequited and mutual, seduction, purity, faithful servitors, wedlock, the triangle.

"There goes Haze," her friends would say, watching her. "She's off again."

Wedded and relaxed, she poured her tears freely. To her who had laughed so much, crying was delicious. All sorrows became her sorrows; she was Tenderness. She would cry long and softly over newspaper accounts of kidnaped babies, deserted wives, unemployed men, strayed cats, heroic dogs. Even when the paper was no longer before her, her mind revolved upon these things and the drops slipped rhythmically over her plump cheeks.

"Honestly," she would say to Herbie, "all the sadness there is in the world when you stop to think about it!"

"Yeah," Herbie would say.

She missed nobody. The old crowd, the people who had brought her and Herbie together, dropped from their lives, lingeringly at first. When she thought of this at all, it was only to consider it fitting. This was marriage. This was peace.

But the thing was that Herbie was not amused.

For a time, he had enjoyed being alone with her. He found the voluntary isolation novel and sweet. Then it palled with a ferocious suddenness. It was as if one night, sitting with her in the steam-heated living-room, he would ask no more; and the next night he was through and done with the whole thing.

He became annoyed by her misty melancholies. At first, when he came home to find her softly tired and moody, he kissed her neck and patted her shoulder and begged her to tell her Herbie what was wrong. She loved that. But time slid by, and he found that there was never anything really, personally, the matter.

"Ah, for God's sake," he would say. "Crabbing again. All right, sit here and crab your head off. I'm going out."

And he would slam out of the flat and come back late and drunk.

She was completely bewildered by what happened to their marriage. First they were lovers; and then, it seemed without transition, they were enemies. She never understood it.

There were longer and longer intervals between his leaving his office and his arrival at the apartment. She went through agonies of picturing him run over and bleeding, dead and covered with a sheet. Then she lost her fears for his safety and grew sullen and wounded. When a person wanted to be with a person, he came as soon as possible. She desperately wanted him to want to be with her; her own hours only marked the time till he would come. It was often nearly nine o'clock before he came home to dinner. Always he had had many drinks, and their effect would die in him, leaving him loud and querulous and bristling for affronts.

He was too nervous, he said, to sit and do nothing for an evening. He boasted, probably not in all truth, that he had never read a book in his life.

"What am I expected to do—sit around this dump on my tail all night?" he would ask, rhetorically. And agan he would slam out.

She did not know what to do. She could not manage him. She could not meet him.

She fought him furiously. A terrific domesticity had come upon her, and she would bite and scratch to guard it. She wanted what she called "a nice home." She wanted a sober, tender husband, prompt at dinner, punctual at work. She wanted sweet, comforting evenings. The idea of intimacy with other men was terrible to her; the thought that Herbie might be seeking entertainment in other women set her frantic.

It seemed to her that almost everything she read—novels from the drug-store lending library, magazine stories, women's pages in the papers—dealt with wives who lost their husbands' love. She could bear those, at that, better than accounts of neat, companionable marriage and living happily ever after.

She was frightened. Several times when Herbie came home in the evening, he found her determinedly dressed—she had had to alter those of her clothes that were not new, to make them fasten—and rouged.

"Let's go wild tonight, what do you say?" she would hail him. "A person's got lots of time to hang around and do nothing when they're dead."

So they would go out, to chop houses and the less expensive cabarets. But it turned out badly. She could no longer find amusement in watching Herbie drink. She could not laugh at his whimsicalities, she was so tensely counting his indulgences. And she was unable to keep back her remonstrances—"Ah, come on, Herb, you've had enough, haven't you? You'll feel something terrible in the morning."

He would be immediately enraged. All right, crab; crab, crab, crab, crab, that was all she ever did. What a lousy sport *she* was! There would be scenes, and one or the other of them would rise and stalk out in fury.

She could not recall the definite day that she started drinking, herself. There was nothing separate about her days. Like drops upon a window-pane, they ran together and trickled away. She had been married six months; then a year; then three years.

She had never needed to drink, formerly. She could sit for most of a night at a table where the others were imbibing earnestly and never droop in looks or spirits, nor be bored by the doings of those about her. If she took a cocktail, it was so unusual as to cause twenty minutes or so of jocular comment. But now anguish was in her. Frequently, after a quarrel, Herbie would stay out for the night, and she could not learn from him where the time had been spent. Her heart felt tight and sore in her breast, and her mind turned like an electric fan.

She hated the taste of liquor. Gin, plain or in mixtures, made her promptly sick. After experiment, she found that Scotch whisky was best for her. She took it without water, because that was the quickest way to its effect.

Herbie pressed it on her. He was glad to see her drink. They both felt it might restore her high spirits, and their good times together might again be possible.

"'Atta girl," he would approve her. "Let's see you get boiled, baby."

But it brought them no nearer. When she drank with him, there would be a little while of gaiety and then, strangely without beginning, they would be in a wild quarrel. They would wake in the morning not sure what it had all been about, foggy as to what had been said and done, but each deeply injured and bitterly resentful. There would be days of vengeful silence.

There had been a time when they had made up their quarrels, usually in bed. There would be kisses and little names and assurances of fresh starts. . . . "Oh, it's going to be great now, Herb. We'll have swell times. I was a crab. I guess I must have been tired. But everything's going to be swell. You'll see."

Now there were no gentle reconciliations. They resumed friendly relations only in the brief magnanimity caused by liquor, before more liquor drew them into new battles. The scenes became more violent. There were shouted invectives and pushes, and sometimes sharp slaps. Once she had a black eye. Herbie was horrified next day at sight of it. He did not go to work; he followed her about, suggesting remedies and heaping dark blame on himself. But after they had had a few drinks—"to pull themselves together"— she made so many wistful references to her bruise that he shouted at her and rushed out and was gone for two days.

Each time he left the place in a rage, he threatened never to come back. She did not believe him, nor did she consider separation. Somewhere in her head or her heart was the lazy, nebulous hope that things would change and she and Herbie settle suddenly into soothing married life. Here were her home, her furniture, her husband, her station. She summoned no alternatives.

She could no longer bustle and potter. She had no more vicarious tears; the hot drops she shed were for herself. She walked ceaselessly about the rooms, her thoughts running mechanically round and round Herbie. In those days began the hatred of being alone that she was never to overcome. You could be by yourself when things were all right, but when you were blue you got the howling horrors.

She commenced drinking alone, little, short drinks all through the day. It was only with Herbie that alcohol made her nervous and quick in offense. Alone, it blurred sharp things for her. She lived in a haze of it. Her life took on a dream-like quality. Nothing was astonishing.

A Mrs. Martin moved into the flat across the hall. She was a great blonde woman of forty, a promise in looks of what Mrs. Morse was to be. They made acquaintance, quickly became inseparable. Mrs. Morse spent her days in the opposite apartment. They drank together, to brace themselves after the drinks of the nights before.

She never confided her troubles about Herbie to Mrs. Martin. The subject was too bewildering to her to find comfort in talk. She let it be assumed that her husband's business kept him much away. It was not regarded as important; husbands, as such, played but shadowy parts in Mrs. Martin's circle.

Mrs. Martin had no visible spouse; you were left to decide for yourself whether he was or was not dead. She had an admirer, Joe, who came to see her almost nightly. Often he brought several friends with him—"The Boys," they were called. The Boys were big, red, good-humored men, perhaps forty-five, perhaps fifty. Mrs. Morse was glad of invitations to join the parties—Herbie was scarcely ever at home at night now. If he did come home, she did not visit Mrs. Martin. An evening alone with Herbie meant inevitably a quarrel, yet she would stay with him. There was always her thin and wordless idea that, maybe, this night, things would begin to be all right.

The Boys brought plenty of liquor along with them whenever they came to Mrs. Martin's. Drinking with them, Mrs. Morse became lively and good-natured and audacious. She was quickly popular. When she had drunk enough to cloud her most recent battle with Herbie, she was excited by their approbation. Crab, was she? Rotten sport, was she? Well, there were some that thought different.

Ed was one of The Boys. He lived in Utica—had "his own business" there, was the awed report—but he came to New York almost every week. He was married. He showed Mrs. Morse the then current photographs of Junior and Sister, and she praised them abundantly and sincerely. Soon it was accepted by the others that Ed was her particular friend.

He staked her when they all played poker; sat next her and occasionally rubbed his knee against hers during the game. She was rather lucky. Frequently she went home with a twenty-dollar bill or a ten-dollar bill or a handful of crumpled dollars. She was glad of them. Herbie was getting, in her words, something awful about money. To ask him for it brought an instant row.

"What the hell do you do with it?" he would say. "Shoot it all on Scotch?"

"I try to run this house half-way decent," she would retort. "Never thought of that, did you? Oh, no, his lordship couldn't be bothered with that."

Again, she could not find a definite day, to fix the beginning of Ed's proprietorship. It became his custom to kiss her on the mouth when he came in, as well as for farewell, and he gave her little quick kisses of approval all through the evening. She liked this rather more than she disliked it. She never thought of his kisses when she was not with him.

He would run his hand lingeringly over her back and shoulders.

"Some dizzy blonde, eh?" he would say. "Some doll."

One afternoon she came home from Mrs. Martin's to find Herbie in the bedroom. He had been away for several nights, evidently on a prolonged drinking bout. His face was gray, his hands jerked as if they were on wires. On the bed were two old suitcases, packed high. Only her photograph remained on his bureau, and the wide doors of his closet disclosed nothing but coat-hangers.

"I'm blowing," he said. "I'm through with the whole works. I got a job in Detroit."

She sat down on the edge of the bed. She had drunk much the night before, and the four Scotches she had had with Mrs. Martin had only increased her fogginess.

"Good job?" she said.

"Oh, yeah," he said. "Looks all right."

He closed a suitcase with difficulty, swearing at it in whispers.

"There's some dough in the bank," he said. "The bank book's in your top drawer. You can have the furniture and stuff."

He looked at her, and his forehead twitched.

"God damn it, I'm through, I'm telling you," he cried. "I'm through."

"All right, all right," she said. "I heard you, didn't I?"

She saw him as if he were at one end of a cannon and she at the other. Her head was beginning to ache bumpingly, and her voice had a dreary, tiresome tone. She could not have raised it.

"Like a drink before you go?" she asked.

Again he looked at her, and a corner of his mouth jerked up.

"Cockeyed again for a change, aren't you?" he said. "That's nice. Sure, get a couple of shots, will you?"

She went to the pantry, mixed him a stiff highball, poured herself a couple of inches of whisky and drank it. Then she gave herself another portion and brought the glasses into the bedroom. He had strapped both suitcases and had put on his hat and overcoat.

He took his highball.

"Well," he said, and he gave a sudden, uncertain laugh. "Here's mud in your eye."

"Mud in your eye," she said.

They drank. He put down his glass and took up the heavy suitcases.

"Got to get a train around six," he said.

She followed him down the hall. There was a song, a song that Mrs. Martin played doggedly on the phonograph, running loudly through her mind. She had never liked the thing.

> "Night and daytime,
> Always playtime.
> Ain't we got fun?"

At the door he put down the bags and faced her.

"Well," he said. "Well, take care of yourself. You'll be all right, will you?"

"Oh, sure," she said.

He opened the door, then came back to her, holding out his hand.

" 'By, Haze," he said. "Good luck to you."

She took his hand and shook it.

"Pardon my wet glove," she said.

When the door had closed behind him, she went back to the pantry.

She was flushed and lively when she went in to Mrs. Martin's that evening. The Boys were there, Ed among them. He was glad to be in town, frisky and loud and full of jokes. But she spoke quietly to him for a minute.

"Herbie blew today," she said. "Going to live out west."

"That so?" he said. He looked at her and played with the fountain pen clipped to his waistcoat pocket.

"Think he's gone for good, do you?" he asked.

"Yeah," she said. "I know he is. I know. Yeah."

"You going to live on across the hall just the same?" he said. "Know what you're going to do?"

"Gee, I don't know," she said. "I don't give much of a damn."

"Oh, come on, that's no way to talk," he told her. "What you need—you need a little snifter. How about it?"

"Yeah," she said. "Just straight."

She won forty-three dollars at poker. When the game broke up, Ed took her back to her apartment.

"Got a little kiss for me?" he asked.

He wrapped her in his big arms and kissed her violently. She was entirely passive. Her held her away and looked at her.

"Little tight, honey?" he asked, anxiously. "Not going to be sick, are you?"

"Me?" she said. "I'm swell."

2

When Ed left in the morning, he took her photograph with him. He said he wanted her picture to look at, up in Utica. "You can have that one on the bureau," she said.

She put Herbie's picture in a drawer, out of her sight. When she could look at it, she meant to tear it up. She was fairly successful in keeping her mind from racing around him. Whisky slowed it for her. She was almost peaceful, in her mist.

She accepted her relationship with Ed without question or enthusiasm. When he was away, she seldom thought definitely of him. He was good to her; he gave her frequent presents and a regular allowance. She was even able to save. She did not plan ahead of any day, but her wants were few, and you might as well put money in the bank as have it lying around.

When the lease of her apartment neared its end, it was Ed who suggested moving. His friendship with Mrs. Martin and Joe had become strained over a dispute at poker; a feud was impending.

"Let's get the hell out of here," Ed said. "What I want you to have is a place near the Grand Central. Make it easier for me."

So she took a little flat in the Forties. A colored maid came in every day to clean and to make coffee for her—she was "through with that housekeeping stuff," she said, and Ed, twenty years married to a passionately domestic woman, admired this romantic uselessness and felt doubly a man of the world in abetting it.

The coffee was all she had until she went out to dinner, but alcohol kept her fat. Prohibition she regarded only as a basis for jokes. You could always get all you wanted. She was never noticeably drunk and seldom nearly sober. It required a larger daily allowance to keep her misty-minded. Too little, and she was achingly melancholy.

Ed brought her to Jimmy's. He was proud, with the pride of the transient who would be mistaken for a native, in his knowledge of small, recent restaurants occupying the lower floors of shabby brownstone houses; places where, upon mentioning the name of an habitué friend, might be obtained strange whisky and fresh gin in many of their ramifications. Jimmy's place was the favorite of his acquaintances.

There, through Ed, Mrs. Morse met many men and women, formed quick friendships. The men often took her out when Ed was in Utica. He was proud of her popularity.

She fell into the habit of going to Jimmy's alone when she had no engagement. She was certain to meet some people she knew, and join them. It was a club for her friends, both men and women.

The women at Jimmy's looked remarkably alike, and this was curious, for, through feuds, removals, and opportunities of more profitable contacts, the personnel of the group changed constantly. Yet always the newcomers resembled those whom they replaced. They were all big women and stout, broad of shoulder and abundantly breasted, with faces thickly clothed in soft, high-colored flesh. They laughed loud and often, showing opaque and luster-less teeth like squares of crockery. There was about them the health of the big, yet a slight, unwholesome suggestion of stubborn preservation. They might have been thirty-six or forty-five or anywhere between.

They composed their titles of their own first names with their husbands' surnames—Mrs. Florence Miller, Mrs. Vera Riley, Mrs. Lilian Block. This gave at the same time the solidity of marriage and the glamour of freedom. Yet only one or two were actually divorced. Most of them never referred to their dimmed spouses; some, a shorter time separated, described them in terms of great biological interest. Several were mothers, each of an only child—a boy at school somewhere, or a girl being cared for by a grand-mother. Often, well on towards morning, there would be displays of kodak portraits and of tears.

They were comfortable women, cordial and friendly and irrepressibly matronly. Theirs was the quality of ease. Become fatalistic, especially about money matters, they were unworried. Whenever their funds dropped alarm-ingly, a new donor appeared; this had always happened. The aim of each was to have one man, permanently, to pay all her bills, in return for which she would have immediately given up other admirers and probably would have become exceedingly fond of him; for the affections of all of them were, by now, unexacting, tranquil, and easily arranged. This end, however, grew increasingly difficult yearly. Mrs. Morse was regarded as fortunate.

Ed had a good year, increased her allowance and gave her a sealskin coat. But she had to be careful of her moods with him. He insisted upon gaiety. He would not listen to admissions of aches or weariness.

"Hey, listen," he would say, "I got worries of my own, and plenty. Nobody wants to hear other people's troubles, sweetie. What you got to do, you got to be a sport and forget it. See? Well, slip us a little smile, then. That's my girl."

She never had enough interest to quarrel with him as she had with Herbie, but she wanted the privilege of occasional admitted sadness. It was strange. The other women she saw did not have to fight their moods. There was Mrs. Florence Miller who got regular crying jags, and the men sought only to cheer and comfort her. The others spent whole evenings in grieved recitals of worries and ills; their escorts paid them deep sympathy. But she was instantly undesirable when she was low in spirits. Once, at Jimmy's, when she could not make herself lively, Ed had walked out and left her.

"Why the hell don't you stay home and not go spoiling everybody's evening?" he had roared.

Even her slightest acquaintances seemed irritated if she were not conspicuously light-hearted.

"What's the matter with you, anyway?" they would say. "Be your age, why don't you? Have a little drink and snap out of it."

When her relationship with Ed had continued nearly three years, he moved to Florida to live. He hated leaving her; he gave her a large check and some shares of a sound stock, and his pale eyes were wet when he said good-by. She did not miss him. He came to New York infrequently, perhaps two or three times a year, and hurried directly from the train to see her. She was always pleased to have him come and never sorry to see him go.

Charley, an acquaintance of Ed's that she had met at Jimmy's, had long admired her. He had always made opportunities of touching her and leaning close to talk to her. He asked repeatedly of all their friends if they had ever heard such a fine laugh as she had. After Ed left, Charley became the main figure in her life. She classified him and spoke of him as "not so bad." There was nearly a year of Charley; then she divided her time between him and Sydney, another frequenter of Jimmy's; then Charley slipped away altogether.

Sydney was a little, brightly dressed, clever Jew. She was perhaps nearest contentment with him. He amused her always; her laughter was not forced.

He admired her completely. Her softness and size delighted him. And he thought she was great, he often told her, because she kept gay and lively when she was drunk.

"Once I had a gal," he said, "used to try and throw herself out of the window every time she got a can on. Jee-*zuss*," he added, feelingly.

Then Sydney married a rich and watchful bride, and then there was Billy. No—after Sydney came Fred, then Billy. In her haze, she never recalled how men entered her life and left it. There were no surprises. She had no thrill at their advent, nor woe at their departure. She seemed to be always able to attract men. There was never another as rich as Ed, but they were all generous to her, in their means.

Once she had news of Herbie. She met Mrs. Martin dining at Jimmy's, and the old friendship was vigorously renewed. The still admiring Joe, while on a business trip, had seen Herbie. He had settled in Chicago, he looked fine, he was living with some woman—seemed to be crazy about her. Mrs. Morse had been drinking vastly that day. She took the news with mild interest, as one hearing of the sex peccadilloes of somebody whose name is, after a moment's groping, familiar.

"Must be damn near seven years since I saw him," she commented. "Gee. Seven years."

More and more, her days lost their individuality. She never knew dates, nor was sure of the day of the week.

"My God, was that a year ago!" she would exclaim, when an event was recalled in conversation.

She was tired so much of the time. Tired and blue. Almost everything could give her the blues. Those old horses she saw on Sixth Avenue— struggling and slipping along the car-tracks, or standing at the curb, their heads dropped level with their worn knees. The tightly stored tears would squeeze from her eyes as she teetered past on her aching feet in the stubby, champagne-colored slippers.

The thought of death came and stayed with her and lent her a sort of drowsy cheer. It would be nice, nice and restful, to be dead.

There was no settled, shocked moment when she first thought of killing herself; it seemed to her as if the idea had always been with her. She pounced upon all the accounts of suicides in the newspapers. There was an epidemic of self-killings—or maybe it was just that she searched for the stories of them so eagerly that she found many. To read of them roused reassurance in her; she felt a cozy solidarity with the big company of the voluntary dead.

She slept, aided by whisky, till deep into the afternoons, then lay abed, a bottle and glass at her hand, until it was time to dress to go out for dinner. She was beginning to feel towards alcohol a little puzzled distrust, as toward an old friend who has refused a simple favor. Whisky could still soothe her for most of the time, but there were sudden, inexplicable moments when the cloud fell treacherously away from her, and she was sawed by the sorrow and be- wilderment and nuisance of all living. She played voluptuously with the thought of cool, sleepy retreat. She had never been troubled by religious belief and no vision of an after-life intimidated her. She dreamed by day of never again putting on tight shoes, of never having to laugh and listen and admire, of never more being a good sport. Never.

But how would you do it? It made her sick to think of jumping from heights. She could not stand a gun. At the theater, if one of the actors drew a revolver, she crammed her fingers into her ears and could not even look at the stage until after the shot had been fired. There was no gas in her flat. She looked long at the bright blue veins in her slim wrists—a cut with a razor blade, and there you'd be. But it would hurt, hurt like hell, and there would be blood to see. Poison—something tasteless and quick and painless—was the thing. But they wouldn't sell it to you in drugstores, because of the law.

She had few other thoughts.

There was a new man now—Art. He was short and fat and exacting and hard on her patience when he was drunk. But there had been only occasionals for some time before him, and she was glad of a little stability. Too, Art must be away for weeks at a stretch, selling silks, and that was restful. She was convincingly gay with him, though the effort shook her.

"The best sport in the world," he would murmur, deep in her neck. "The best sport in the world."

One night, when he had taken her to Jimmy's, she went into the dressing-room with Mrs. Florence Miller. There, while designing curly mouths on their faces with lip-rouge, they compared experiences of insomnia.

"Honestly," Mrs. Morse said, "I wouldn't close an eye if I didn't go to bed full of Scotch. I lie there and toss and turn and toss and turn. Blue! Does a person get blue lying awake that way!"

"Say, listen, Hazel," Mrs. Miller said, impressively, "I'm telling you I'd be awake for a year if I didn't take veronal. That stuff makes you sleep like a fool."

"Isn't it poison, or something?" Mrs. Morse asked.

"Oh, you take too much and you're out for the count," said Mrs. Miller. "I just take five grains—they come in tablets. I'd be scared to fool around with it. But five grains, and you cork off pretty."

"Can you get it anywhere?" Mrs. Morse felt superbly Machiavellian.

"Get all you want in Jersey," said Mrs. Miller. "They won't give it to you here without you have a doctor's prescription. Finished? We'd better go back and see what the boys are doing."

That night, Art left Mrs. Morse at the door of her apartment; his mother was in town. Mrs. Morse was still sober, and it happened that there was no whisky left in her cupboard. She lay in bed, looking up at the black ceiling.

She rose early, for her, and went to New Jersey. She had never taken the tube, and did not understand it. So she went to the Pennsylvania Station and bought a railroad ticket to Newark. She thought of nothing in particular on the trip out. She looked at the uninspired hats of the women about her and gazed through the smeared window at the flat, gritty scene.

In Newark, in the first drug-store she came to, she asked for a tin of talcum powder, a nailbrush, and a box of veronal tablets. The powder and the brush were to make the hypnotic seem also a casual need. The clerk was entirely unconcerned. "We only keep them in bottles," he said, and wrapped up for her a little glass vial containing ten white tablets, stacked one on another.

She went to another drug-store and bought a face-cloth, an orange-wood stick, and a bottle of veronal tablets. The clerk was also uninterested.

"Well, I guess I got enough to kill an ox," she thought, and went back to the station.

At home, she put the little vials in the drawer of her dressing-table and stood looking at them with a dreamy tenderness.

"There they are, God bless them," she said, and she kissed her finger-tip and touched each bottle.

The colored maid was busy in the living-room.

"Hey, Nettie," Mrs. Morse called. "Be an angel, will you? Run around to Jimmy's and get me a quart of Scotch."

She hummed while she awaited the girl's return.

During the next few days, whisky ministered to her as tenderly as it had done when she first turned to its aid. Alone, she was soothed and vague, at Jimmy's she was the gayest of the groups. Art was delighted with her.

Then, one night, she had an appointment to meet Art at Jimmy's for an early dinner. He was to leave afterward on a business excursion, to be away for a week. Mrs. Morse had been drinking all the afternoon; while she dressed to go out, she felt herself rising pleasurably from drowsiness to high spirits. But as she came out into the street the effects of the whisky deserted her completely, and she was filled with a slow, grinding wretchedness so horrible that she stood swaying on the pavement, unable for a moment to move forward. It was a gray night with spurts of mean, thin snow, and the streets shone with dark ice. As she slowly crossed Sixth Avenue, consciously dragging one foot past the other, a big, scarred horse pulling a rickety express-wagon crashed to his knees before her. The driver swore and screamed and lashed the beast insanely, bringing the whip back over his shoulder for every blow, while the horse struggled to get a footing on the slippery asphalt. A group gathered and watched with interest.

Art was waiting, when Mrs. Morse reached Jimmy's.

"What's the matter with you, for God's sake?" was his greeting to her.

"I saw a horse," she said. "Gee, I—a person feels sorry for horses. I—it isn't just horses. Everything's kind of terrible, isn't it? I can't help getting sunk."

"Ah, sunk, my eye," he said. "What's the idea of all the bellyaching? What have you got to be sunk about?"

"I can't help it," she said.

"Ah, help it, me eye," he said. "Pull yourself together, will you? Come on and sit down, and take that face off you."

She drank industriously and she tried hard, but she could not overcome her melancholy. Others joined them and commented on her gloom, and she could do no more for them than smile weakly. She made little dabs at her eyes with her handkerchief, trying to time her movements so they would be unnoticed, but several times Art caught her and scowled and shifted impatiently in his chair.

When it was time for him to go to his train, she said she would leave, too, and go home.

"And not a bad idea, either," he said. "See if you can't sleep yourself out of it. I'll see you Thursday. For God's sake, try and cheer up by then, will you?"

"Yeah," she said. "I will."

In her bedroom, she undressed with a tense speed wholly unlike her usual slow uncertainty. She put on her nightgown, took off her hair-net and passed the comb quickly through her dry, vari-colored hair. Then she took the two little vials from the drawer and carried them into the bathroom. The splintering misery had gone from her, and she felt the quick excitement of one who is about to receive an anticipated gift.

She uncorked the vials, filled a glass with water and stood before the mirror, a tablet between her fingers. Suddenly she bowed graciously to her reflection, and raised the glass to it.

"Well, here's mud in your eye," she said.

The tablets were unpleasant to take, dry and powdery and sticking obstinately half-way down her throat. It took her a long time to swallow all twenty of them. She stood watching her reflection with deep, impersonal interest, studying the movements of the gulping throat. Once more she spoke aloud.

"For God's sake, try and cheer up by Thursday, will you?" she said. "Well, you know what he can do. He and the whole lot of them."

She had no idea how quickly to expect effect from the veronal. When she had taken the last tablet, she stood uncertainly, wondering, still with a courteous, vicarious interest, if death would strike her down then and there. She felt in no way strange, save for a slight stirring of sickness from the effort of swallowing the tablets, nor did her reflected face look at all different. It would not be immediate, then; it might even take an hour or so.

She stretched her arms high and gave a vast yawn.

"Guess I'll go to bed," she said. "Gee, I'm nearly dead."

That struck her as comic, and she turned out the bathroom light and went in and laid herself down in her bed, chuckling softly all the time.

"Gee, I'm nearly dead," she quoted. "That's a hot one!"

3

Nettie, the colored maid, came in late the next afternoon to clean the apartment, and found Mrs. Morse in her bed. But then, that was not unusual. Usually, though, the sounds of cleaning waked her, and she did not like to wake up. Nettie, an agreeable girl, had learned to move softly about her work.

But when she had done the living-room and stolen in to tidy the little square bedroom, she could not avoid a tiny clatter as she arranged the objects on the dressing-table. Instinctively, she glanced over her shoulder at the sleeper, and without warning a sickly uneasiness crept over her. She came to the bed and stared down at the woman lying there.

Mrs. Morse lay on her back, one flabby, white arm flung up, the wrist against her forehead. Her stiff hair hung untenderly along her face. The bed covers were pushed down, exposing a deep square of soft neck and a pink nightgown, its fabric worn uneven by many launderings; her great breasts, freed from their tight confiner, sagged beneath her arm-pits. Now and then she made knotted, snoring sounds, and from the corner of her opened mouth to the blurred turn of her jaw ran a lane of crusted spittle.

"Mis' Morse," Nettie called. "Oh, Mis' Morse! It's terrible late."

Mrs. Morse made no move.

"Mis' Morse," said Nettie. "Look, Mis' Morse. How'm I goin' get this bed made?"

Panic sprang upon the girl. She shook the woman's hot shoulder.

"Ah, wake up, will yuh?" she whined. "Ah, please wake up."

Suddenly the girl turned and ran out in the hall to the elevator door, keeping her thumb firm on the black, shiny button until the elderly car and its Negro attendant stood before her. She poured a jumble of words over the boy, and led him back to the apartment. He tiptoed creakingly in to the bedside; first gingerly, then so lustily that he left marks in the soft flesh, he prodded the unconscious woman.

"Hey, there!" he cried, and listened intently, as for an echo.

"Jeez. Out like a light," he commented.

At his interest in the spectacle, Nettie's panic left her. Importance was big in both of them. They talked in quick, unfinished whispers, and it was the boy's suggestion that he fetch the young doctor who lived on the ground floor. Nettie hurried along with him. They looked forward to the limelit moment of breaking their news of something untoward, something pleasurably un-pleasant. Mrs. Morse had become the medium of drama. With no ill wish to her, they hoped that her state was serious, that she would not let them down by being awake and normal on their return. A little fear of this determined them to make the most, to the doctor, of her present condition. "Matter of life and death," returned to Nettie from her thin store of reading. She considered startling the doctor with the phrase.

The doctor was in and none too pleased at interruption. He wore a yellow and blue striped dressing-gown, and he was lying on his sofa, laughing with a dark girl, her face scaly with inexpensive powder, who perched on the arm. Half-emptied highball glasses stood beside them, and her coat and hat were neatly hung up with the comfortable implication of a long stay.

Always something, the doctor grumbled. Couldn't let anybody alone after a hard day. But he put some bottles and instruments into a case, changed his dressing-gown for his coat and started out with the Negroes.

"Snap it up there, big boy," the girl called after him. "Don't be all night."

The doctor strode loudly into Mrs. Morse's flat and on to the bedroom, Nettie and the boy right behind him. Mrs. Morse had not moved; her sleep was as deep, but soundless, now. The doctor looked sharply at her, then plunged his thumbs into the lidded pits above her eyeballs and threw his weight upon them. A high, sickened cry broke from Nettie.

"Look like he tryin' to push her right on th'ough the bed," said the boy. He chuckled.

Mrs. Morse gave no sign under the pressure. Abruptly the doctor aban-doned it, and with one quick movement swept the covers down to the foot of the bed. With another he flung her nightgown back and lifted the thick, white legs, cross-hatched with blocks of tiny, iris-colored veins. He pinched them repeatedly, with long, cruel nips, back of the knees. She did not awaken.

"What's she been drinking?" he asked Nettie, over his shoulder.

With the certain celerity of one who knows just where to lay hands on a thing, Nettie went into the bathroom, bound for the cupboard where Mrs. Morse kept her whisky. But she stopped at the sight of the two vials, with their red and white labels, lying before the mirror. She brought them to the doctor.

"Oh, for the Lord Almighty's sweet sake!" he said. He dropped Mrs. Morse's legs, and pushed them impatiently across the bed. "What did she want to go taking that tripe for? Rotten yellow trick, that's what a thing like that is. Now we'll have to pump her out, and all that stuff. Nuisance, a thing like that is; that's what it amounts to. Here, George, take me down in the elevator. You wait here, maid. She won't do aything."

"She won't die on me, will she?" cried Nettie.

"No," said the doctor. "God, no. You couldn't kill her with an ax."

4

After two days, Mrs. Morse came back to consciousness, dazed at first, then with a comprehension that brought with it the slow, saturating wretchedness.

"Oh, Lord, oh, Lord," she moaned, and tears for herself and for life striped her cheeks.

Nettie came in at the sound. For two days she had done the ugly, incessant tasks in the nursing of the unconscious, for two nights she had caught broken bits of sleep on the living-room couch. She looked coldly at the big, blown woman in the bed.

"What you been tryin' to do, Mis' Morse?" she said. "What kine o' work is that, takin' all that stuff?"

"Oh, Lord," moaned Mrs. Morse, again, and she tried to cover her eyes with her arms. But the joints felt stiff and brittle, and she cried out at their ache.

"Tha's no way to ack, takin' them pills," said Nettie. "You can thank you' stars you heah at all. How you feel now?"

"Oh, I feel great," said Mrs. Morse. "Swell, I feel."

Her hot, painful tears fell as if they would never stop.

"Tha's no way to take on, cryin' like that," Nettie said. "After what you done. The doctor, he says he could have you arrested, doin' a thing like that. He was fit to be tied, here."

"Why couldn't he let me alone?" wailed Mrs. Morse. "Why the hell couldn't he have?"

"Tha's terr'ble, Mis' Morse, swearin' an' talkin' like that," said Nettie, "after what people done for you. Here I ain' had no sleep at all for two nights, an' had to give up goin' out to my other ladies!"

"Oh, I'm sorry, Nettie," she said. "You're a peach. I'm sorry I've given you so much trouble. I couldn't help it. I just got sunk. Didn't you ever feel like doing it? When everything looks just lousy to you?"

"I wouldn' think o' no such thing," declared Nettie. "You got to cheer up. Tha's what you got to do. Everybody's got their troubles."

"Yeah," said Mrs. Morse. "I know."

"Come a pretty picture card for you," Nettie said. "Maybe that will cheer you up."

She handed Mrs. Morse a post-card. Mrs. Morse had to cover one eye with her hand, in order to read the message; her eyes were not yet focusing correctly.

It was from Art. On the back of a view of the Detroit Athletic Club he had written: "Greeting and salutations. Hope you have lost that gloom. Cheer up and don't take any rubber nickles. See you on Thursday."

She dropped the card to the floor. Misery crushed her as if she were between great smooth stones. There passed before her a slow, slow pageant of days spent lying in her flat, of evenings at Jimmy's being a good sport, making herself laugh and coo at Art and other Arts; she saw a long parade of weary horses and shivering beggars and all beaten, driven, stumbling things. Her feet throbbed as if she had crammed them into the stubby champagne-colored slippers. Her heart seemed to swell and harden.

"Nettie," she cried, "for heaven's sake pour me a drink, will you?"

The maid looked doubtful.

"Now you know, Mis' Morse," she said, "you been near daid. I don' know if the doctor he let you drink nothin' yet."

"Oh, never mind him," she said. "You get me one, and bring in the bottle. Take one yourself."

"Well," said Nettie.

She poured them each a drink, deferentially leaving hers in the bathroom to be taken in solitude, and brought Mrs. Morse's glass in to her.

Mrs. Morse looked into the liquor and shuddered back from its odor. Maybe it would help. Maybe, when you had been knocked cold for a few days, your very first drink would give you a lift. Maybe whisky would be her friend again. She prayed without addressing a God, without knowing a God. Oh, please, please, let her be able to get drunk, please keep her always drunk.

She lifted the glass.

"Thanks, Nettie," she said. "Here's mud in your eye."

The maid giggled. "Tha's the way, Mis' Morse," she said. "You cheer up, now."

Yeah," said Mrs. Morse. "Sure."

Questions

1. We have described in some detail the plot structure of "The Blue Hotel." Try to locate the issue, the complication, the climax, and the resolution of "Big Blonde."

2. In "Big Blonde," Dorothy Parker gives us a fairly well-detailed summary of Hazel Morse's background. William Carlos Williams, on the other hand, gives us almost no background for the characters in "The Use of Force." How does he make us understand those characters?

3. In "The Use of Force" the young girl is described as having "magnificent blonde hair, in profusion." She is "one of those picture children often reproduced in advertising leaflets and the photogravure sections of the Sunday papers." Why does Williams characterize her in these terms instead of as a plain or even a homely child? How would it alter the impact of the story if he did describe her in such a way?

4. Find those places in "The Blue Hotel" where Stephen Crane describes the physical appearances of the main characters. You will probably be surprised that these descriptions are brief, even sketchy. How do you account for the fact, therefore, that we see the Swede, the Cowboy, and Eastener so vividly? What devices other than physical descriptions does Crane use in characterizing these three men?

POINT OF VIEW

A reader might summarize his reaction to Stephen Crane's "The Blue Hotel" this way: "Crane is saying that tragedies such as the one that befalls the Swede are a natural outcome of conflict in a universe ruled by delusion, mischance, indifference, and alienation." He might say of "The Use of Force": "Williams is saying that even the most civilized of relationships, such as the one between doctor and patient, will under stress revert to a contest determined by superior strength and coercive power."

The authors probably have tried to lead us toward such conclusions. But it would be wrong to assume that voices advocating these views belong to Stephen Crane and William Carlos Williams. It is not *Crane* who describes the gambler's sudden attack on the Swede and then says: ". . . this citadel of virtue, wisdom, power was pierced as easily as if it had been a melon." Nor is it *Williams* who defines the doctor's reaction to the stubborn patient: "I could have torn the child apart in my own fury and enjoyed it." Between Crane and Williams and us, between all writers of fiction and their readers, stands a *narrator* who describes and interprets events, and, in ways that are sometimes obvious but more often quite subtle, controls our response to them.

After decisions about plot, those concerning narrative *perspective* and *voice* are probably the most important an author will make. The narrator provides the key for us to unlock the meaning of the plot. Think how differently we would react to "The Blue Hotel" if we saw things from the perspective of the Easterner. We might gain an insight into individual deviousness and cowardice; but we would certainly lose our sense of the larger role of collective guilt in the human tragedy that the aloof narrator gives us. In "The Use of Force," on the other hand, we are dependent for our facts on someone who is a main actor in events as well as the reporter. Think how differently we would react if we thought this narrator was self-serving; we would doubt the essential truthfulness of his account. Then the story would no longer be about a conflict of two strong wills, but about an adult's sadistic cruelty toward a child.

What we see, in other words, depends on *how* we see it. In the famous Japanese story and film *Rashomon*, for instance, a samurai warrior, his wife, a bandit, and a woodcutter each give an interpretation of a rape and murder that occurs along a highway; the result is four different stories determined by each of the narrators' "stake" in what happens. And each version, in a sense, is the truth. *Point of view*, then, involves the narrator's distance from the action, the degree to which he can intrude into the character's private thoughts, the extent to which he participates in events, and how reliable a witness we feel he is. As readers we are alert to any signal of a disparity between events and the narrator's interpretation of them. Without being told to do so, we would be inclined to agree with D. H. Lawrence: "Never trust the artist. Trust the tale."

An understanding of point of view can also draw on the analogy of optics. The perspective narrators use does resemble camera positions and lens openings: wide-angle shots, close-ups, fisheye distortions, and the like. *Voice* (which we will define a bit later) is also important in establishing a narrative stance. While the point of view of every story is distinctive, the following are narrative approaches that appear frequently in the stories in this collection.

The Omniscient Observer

The omniscient narrator stands above the story he is telling, unlimited in his knowledge of what will happen and endowed with an almost godlike ability to intrude into, and comment upon, the thoughts and feelings of all the characters. This narrative stance dominated much of the fiction written during the eighteenth and nineteenth centuries. In a novel like Henry Fielding's *Tom Jones*, for instance, the narrator chats with the reader about the unfolding events and finally decides to intervene in behalf of the hero when his prospects grow desperate. Narrators in the works of Thackeray and Dickens gossip about their characters and speak in asides to the reader about the unusually complex webs of fate which comprise the plots of their books.

This sort of *involved* narrator may seem archaic by twentieth-century standards, but omniscience itself is still a frequently used narrative stance. In the very first paragraph of "The Blue Hotel," an omniscient narrator muses about the color of the Palace Hotel and its relationship to the bleak and nondescript landscape surrounding it. He discusses the way travelers passing through Fort Romper as well as the citizens themselves feel about this odd structure. Finally he notes the way in which Pat Scully, the proprietor, makes a point of always meeting the trains to "seduce" potential customers to his establishment. The narrator also says that on this particular winter day Scully has "caught" the three men who will be the focus of the drama. A narrator who knows all this could easily tell us, for instance, that Johnnie Scully cheated the Swede at cards. But once the story has begun, the narrator voluntarily shortens his panoramic perspective and concentrates on unfolding events so that suspense will build. He returns to his prior stance only when the thematic needs of the story are served by commentary on the corrupt relationship between the "thieving card player" who kills the Swede and the town's "fair class" of people.

As "The Blue Hotel" shows, an omniscient narrator (even one who decides at times to foreshorten his omniscience) can give events scope and resonance. He can make us see the characters and their dilemma as exemplifying something archetypal in the human drama. It is also true, however, that when we are kept at arm's length from the action we don't experience an intense identification with a character. In addition, we may, at times, feel that we are being manipulated, as when the Easterner steps up at the end of the story to deliver what seems to be the moral.

The Intimate Observer

In twentieth-century literature, writers have become more and more self-conscious about their art, particularly that part of their art involving the ways in which a story is told. Henry James, for instance, said that a writer should *show* the reader an unfolding drama rather than *telling* him exactly what was happening. In making this distinction, he was suggesting that a narrator should draw the reader into intriguing ambiguities at the heart of the work, allowing him the pleasure of discovering buried meanings for himself. The best narrator in such an approach observes events from a privileged position of intimacy. He is *limited* in terms of his knowledge, but not in terms of his access to the hearts and minds of the main characters.

If the omniscient narrator can be imagined as looking down at events from high ground, the *intimate observer*, such as the one we find in John Updike's "A Sense of Shelter," should be seen as unobtrusively (sometimes almost invisibly) standing at ground level, at the shoulder of the main character, and able to enter his mind to report on and evaluate his thoughts and emotions. It is a technique that gives subtlety and depth. Because of its *psychological realism*, it has been the preferred narrative stance for writers of the present century.

A story like "A Sense of Shelter" gives us a sense of the range of resources the intimate observer offers. Because of the narrator's precise understanding of the central character's thoughts and feelings, we know William Young as well, if not better, than he knows himself. He gains credit for an honest and unsparing evaluation: "He was not popular, he never had a girl, his intense friends of childhood had drifted off into teams and gangs . . ." In fact, William's status as a "loner" is somewhat to his advantage, for we too sense the immaturity of his classmates and the silliness of high school rituals. We feel the legitimacy of William's pride at having almost outgrown this past: "Taunts no longer much frightened him; he had come late into his physical inheritance, but this summer it had arrived . . ."

But this obsolete world has one final lesson in the person of Mary Landis, whom William professes to "love." We see her too through William's eyes and appreciate the appeal for him of her lean body and "pronged chest," and her general air of sexual ripeness. Yet the narrative technique of the story forces us to construe the information about Mary somewhat differently than William does. The "wild stories" he has heard about her only make her more profoundly a sexual object for him. But we see what the romantic progress from boys a grade or so ahead of her, to football hero, to young men outside the school really means. Mary is one of those girls prematurely old, forced by circumstances beyond her control to leave quite early the world that constrains William but also comforts him and gives him a limited arena in which he can succeed.

From William's reaction to Mary, we get a feeling for the limits of his perceptions. We understand how callow and conventional, how sheltered he still is, for all his pride at growing up. When William tries to kiss her and then dismisses the gesture as a momentary "disposition of his heart, nothing permanent or expensive," and when he blurts out that he knows she is not a virgin, we understand that he is still, for all his newfound confidence in his body and mind, quite immature. (Updike's choice of a last name for his hero is not accidental.)

As Mary walks off into the snow to meet her older boyfriend and leaves William inside the school building, he has a sudden insight into his "ugly, educable self," and this makes what might have been a cruel insult of a friend into a forgivable sin committed by a naif. Because the narrator has given us information through William's eyes but has controlled this information so that we are constantly evaluating William himself, we appreciate the extent to which he is on the threshold of maturity, having outgrown a part of his life yet not quite ready for the next stage. Because he is redeemed by his exuberance and his intelligent, if still naive, approach to the world, we assume that he will someday look back at this experience with Mary Landis and recognize, as we do, exactly what it meant.

The Objective Observer

Omniscient narrators are godlike in their knowledge of everything that happens in a story, and intimate observers are privy to the deep recesses of characters' hearts and minds. The *objective observer*, however, knows absolutely nothing more than what can be seen. This stance is sometimes called the "camera technique" because the narrator's function is simply to record the surfaces of the scene—its "look" rather than its "feel"—as if he were exposing its image on a sheet of film. It is the apparently value-free quality of this narrative stance—an extreme form of *showing* as opposed to *telling*—that made it an appealing technique in the early part of this century when social science was beginning to stress the fallibility of human perception and the uncertainty about what any individual can know about other human beings. Objective observation relies on dialogue and gesture to reveal character. It is like a stage play in this regard, except that there are no soliloquies in which the protagonist tells the reader what is on his mind. It is like life itself in the way it forces us to extract meaning from an uninterpreted situation.

This narrative stance is closely identified with the work of Ernest Hemingway. Hemingway wanted to pare his short stories down to essential dramas, primal scenes of conflict unencumbered by narrative commentary. In "The Killers," a classic example of his art, the meaning of events at the diner arises out of the evidence of the scene. We learn what is happening as a result of the accumulation of detail—the two strangers' irritable reaction to the limited menu; their uniform of derby hat, bulging overcoat, and gloves; the menacing repetition of the phrase "bright boy" as they taunt George and Nick Adams. We never have to be told that these men are dangerous; we see it for ourselves.

What is interesting about his story is exactly how much we know without being told. When Nick goes to warn the killers' target, Ole Andreson, about the danger he is in, the former prize fighter makes no response except to say that he is "through with all that running around." Yet we get the picture. He has somehow, somewhere and at some time—the details really don't matter—double-crossed the killers' "friend." Now he has to pay. Other kinds of narrators might tell us what sort of person Andreson is and what in his past behavior led to his current jeopardy. But Hemingway is less interested in these psychological truths than in the documentary truth of the situation: an insight into impersonal violence that has nothing to do with scale or justice and is beyond remedy.

The objective observer is unobtrusive, almost invisible; we rarely sense his presence. But it would be wrong to assume that he is any less *there* than are other kinds of narrators. Objectivity is an uncertain quality. It could be said, for instance, that *what* a camera records is itself an act of judgment about what is important. Why some details and not others? *How* the camera records the scene also contains considerable opportunity for bias. For example, in describing Al's face, the narrator says it was "small and white and he had tight lips." How different the impression would be if the sentence read: "He was light complected, fine-featured, serious and unsmiling." We may also feel that an attempt to achieve objectivity forces the dialogue to carry too heavy a load in this story. Max volunteers rather a lot of information to George and Nick: that he and Al are in town to kill Andreson; that they've never seen the man before; that they're contract killers. To some degree, wordy arrogance may be in character for such a man; but when Al tells him he is talking too much, we are inclined to agree.

First Person Narrator
In literature, as in life, some of the best stories are those told by someone with a distinct personality, someone involved in the events at hand, an "I" (there may be a proper name as well) whose outlook and personality are at least part of what we react to in the plot.

First person narration can carry great authenticity. In "The Use of Force," for example, the narrator is the subject of the story as well as the storyteller. We have almost no biographical data about him (the absence of detail is intentional; Williams wants us to focus on the elementary conflict in the scene itself), but by admitting the extent of his fury and his growing desire to triumph over the girl—not particularly flattering qualities—he establishes himself as trustworthy and gives us grounds for believing his account.

There are times, however, when it serves an author's purpose to endow a first-person narrator with some defect—excessive emotional involvement in events, moral blindness, or perhaps simple ignorance—that makes him an *unreliable witness*. In this case we must sift through his observations and compensate for his defects by making our own judgments. This gives the story a double-edged quality: the plot not only involves events but also the narrator's misinterpretation of their significance.

"Guests of the Nation" by Frank O'Connor is a classic example of the kinds of effects available to a writer using a first person narrator. From the onset of the story we are taking in the scene through Bonaparte's eyes and also evaluating him and his reaction to it. No intellectual, he is nonetheless a sensible, feeling man; he is a person who yearns for action instead of guard duty, yet is at ease in his current setting. He is a connoisseur of the English prisoners' individuality, noting the polite silence and the contentiousness that make Belcher and Hawkins so human. He finds himself amused that they "have taken root like a native weed" in the soil of Irish custom and camaraderie. We note that Bonaparte and his friend Noble consider themselves different from the dour, duty-ridden commander Donovan.

The reader sees the developing conflict in terms of the predicament Bonaparte himself faces. It is true, as Donovan believes, that war is war and that atrocities committed against Irish prisoners not only justify but demand reprisal. But it is also true that the guards have become "chums" with the Englishmen, seeing them as human beings rather than as pawns in a political struggle. We might have no doubt about which side of the issue to line up on, but we can sympathize with the narrator's conflicting loyalties. We see the implications of the situation even though Bonaparte never goes further than accusing Donovan of being "unforseen" and though he never sees any real alternative to doing his duty.

As the story draws to a climax, we sense the probable tragic outcome before Bonaparte does. When the normally silent Belcher becomes loquacious after Hawkins has been shot, the narrator simply observes that he had "said more than in all the weeks before" as if it were an odd fact; but the reader knows that the condemned man is trying to spend all the words he's hoarded up during his life, trying to get them out before the coming dark. When the prisoners are led to the killing ground in the bog and Bonaparte hopes they'll either put up a fight or make a run for it—something to justify the act to come—we know he will not be let off so easily. When the horrible logic of his position demands that he draw his pistol and finish off the wounded Hawkins, we react as much to the spectacle of a decent man being forced to commit murder as to the death of an innocent individual. In the end, our reaction to "Guests of the Nation" is based less on what has happened than on the way it has left the narrator isolated and profoundly changed. The effect on him is summarized in one of the most memorable closing lines of short fiction: "And anything that ever happened me after I never felt the same about again."

Voice

Point of view, as is shown by the four narrative approaches outlined above, involves a wide range of considerations for a writer. How much sympathy does he want the reader to feel for a character? How involved in the character's dilemma? How attentive to the external factors in the situation? How aware of the philosophical implications of the action?

But writers have personal points of view as well, an unmistakable way of addressing the world and giving it a distinctive verbal shape and feel. If any one element serves as the indelible signature of an author, it is the *voice* he or she adopts. As you read through the stories in this collection, you will encounter many different voices and become aware that some of the most celebrated authors owe their reputations to the distinctiveness of those voices. This kind of success is obvious when one considers the stories of Hemingway, Faulkner, Kafka, Thurber, or Chekhov. Even if these writers were all to write about the same plot from the same narrative point of view not a one of them could ever be confused with any other. So decisive is their approach, the way they claim the world (and in turn the reader's imagination) that *Kafkaesque* or *Hemingwayesque* serve as useful adjectives to describe a fundamental vision of existence. Thus *voice* establishes what is immutably personal about a writer's entire being. And, like many other intimate features of an individual style of success, voice cannot be transferred from one writer to another. If the attempt is made, an uncomfortable distortion occurs. Once established, a voice seems to live and die with that writer.

This is not to declare, however, that all important voices in the short story twist ordinary patterns of prose description, narration, and dialogue into odd shapes. Not all voices are extreme deformations of everyday language. Indeed, some voices are distinctive and memorable because the author has ingeniously succeeded in mirroring exactly the cadences, the diction, and the atmosphere of everyday language. Like all apparently "easy" triumphs, this one is vastly more difficult than it seems. A voice, then, can be like a prism through which the light and the colors of the world pass and become miraculous new shapes and hues. Or it can be a perfectly transparent pane of glass whose presence is not noticed at all by the reader.

You will, for instance, immediately note the striking way that Edgar Allan Poe, in "The Fall of the House of Usher," creates a sense of place, atmosphere, and expectation with only a few phrases. Poe's story begins:

> During the whole of a dull, dark and soundless day in the autumn of the year, when the clouds hung oppressively low in the heavens, I had been passing alone, on horseback, through a singularly dreary tract of country; and at length found myself, as the shades of the evening drew on, within view of the melancholy House of Usher.

The voice in a Poe story such as this one speaks of the mysterious, the solitary, the gloomy, and the malevolent. It is not a voice we would ever expect to hear in everyday conversation. We would never employ it in a business or personal letter. We know that it is a language deflected from the paths of ordinary usage. We might even wish to call it "mannered." But we have little trouble understanding it, once we accept the patterns governing it. You will encounter other such powerful voices in this collection. They are as unforgettable as a person with a strong accent.

But other voices do not immediately strike us as so strong or mannered. Let us return for a moment to Updike's "A Sense of Shelter." The narrator's voice seems to be our own, but now returned to us. It has the ring of utter familiarity to it. When William Young grasps the fact that he is going to tell Mary Landis that he loves her, the recognition comes this way:

> . . . his long legs blocking two aisles, he felt regal even in size and, almost trembling with happiness under the high globes of light beyond whose lunar glow invisible snowflakes were drowning on the gravel roof of his castle, believed that the long delay of unpopularity had been merely a consolidation, that he was at last strong enough to make his move.

Updike's voice here speaks in an unhurried way about the kinds of things that make up the world as we customarily find it. Boys do grow up to be young men and do gather initiative. Updike's voice seems to be at home with such homely facts of existence. His language does not reach out to the eccentric phrase. Yet we would be wrong to think it is the voice of a stupid or insensitive observer. As much as the observer notes the changing physical size of the boy, he notes also his interior or psychological changes: "the long delay of unpopularity had been merely a consolidation . . . he was at last strong enough to make his move." And, here and there, Updike's narrator gently reminds us of the precision of his observations through the precision of his diction: the boy "felt regal even in size" and the invisible snowflakes were "drowning" near the "lunar glow" of the lights. The voice of Updike is more leisurely and less forced than that of Poe. It speaks to us in a less designing and coercive way. Perhaps that is because it seems to depend very little on language used for its own sake. It is not a voice rich with alliteration or assonance. It is not a voice apparently much interested in effect, but it seems to be one much interested in meaning.

Other stories in the collection that might be compared in the same way are Joseph Conrad's "The Secret Sharer" and Anton Chekhov's "The Lady with the Pet Dog." Conrad's story is richly saturated by a voice with strong rhythms and formal cadences. It calls attention to itself as the means by which the innermost significance of events may be determined. And it is a voice that rather insistently commands the attention of the reader. The voice in Chekhov's story, on the other hand, speaks quietly and seems to defer attention to the events themselves. It suggests that the meaning of those events would be apparent even if all literary effects were removed from the scene. It is a voice that suggests only its own unimportance.

Between such extremes as Poe and Conrad, on the one hand, and Updike and Chekhov, on the other, most of the stories in this collection can be located. Reading those stories will make you aware of the range, and the importance, of voices. Not the least important quality of voice is the pleasure it can afford a reader who, after having read one story by a distinctive writer, turns to another and comes upon a presence that is wholly familiar. The pleasure of such recognition issues primarily from the authority of a voice that has clearly defined itself. To talk about voice, then, is to talk about one of the chief delights that reading can give.

John Updike (b. 1932)
A Sense of Shelter

Snow fell against the high school all day, wet big-flaked snow that did not accumulate well. Sharpening two pencils, William looked down on a parking lot that was a blackboard in reverse, car tires had cut smooth arcs of black into the white, and wherever a school bus had backed around, it had left an autocratic signature of two V's. The snow, though at moments it whirled opaquely, could not quite bleach these scars away. The temperature must be exactly 32°. The window was open a crack, and a canted pane of glass lifted outdoor air into his face, coating the cedarwood scent of pencil shavings with the transparent odor of the wet window sill. With each revolution of the handle his knuckles came within a fraction of an inch of the tilted glass, and the faint chill this proximity breathed on them sharpened his already acute sense of shelter.

The sky behind the shreds of snow was stone-colored. The murk inside the high classroom gave the air a solidity that limited the overhead radiance to its own vessels; six globes of dull incandescence floated on the top of a thin sea. The feeling the gloom gave him was not gloomy but joyous: he felt they were all sealed in, safe; the colors of cloth were dyed deeper, the sound of whispers was made more distinct, the smells of tablet paper and wet shoes and varnish and face powder pierced him with a vivid sense of possession. These were his classmates sealed in, his, the stupid as well as the clever, the plain as well as the lovely, his enemies as well as his friends, his. He felt like a king and seemed to move to his seat between the bowed heads of subjects that loved him less than he loved them. His seat was sanctioned by tradition; for twelve years he had sat at the rear of classrooms, William Young, flanked by Marsha Wyckoff and Andy Zimmerman. Once there had been two Zimmermans, but one went to work in his father's greenhouse, and in some classes— Latin and Trig—there were none, and William sat at the edge of the class as if on the lip of a cliff, and Marsha Wyckoff became Marvin Wolf or Sandra Wade, but it was always the same desk, whose surface altered from hour to hour but from whose blue-stained ink-hole his mind could extract, like a chain of magicians' handkerchiefs, a continuity of years. As a senior he was a kind of king, and as a teacher's pet another kind, a puppet king, who gathered in appointive posts and even, when the moron vote split between two football heroes, some elective ones. He was not popular, he had never had a girl, his intense friends of childhood had drifted off into teams and gangs, and in large groups—when the whole school, for instance, went in the fall to the beautiful, dung-and-cotton-candy-smelling county fair—he was always an odd man, without a seat on the bus home. But exclusion is itself a form of inclusion. He even had a nickname: Mip, because he stuttered. Taunts no longer much frightened him; he had come late into his physical inheritance, but this summer it had arrived, and he at last stood equal with his enormous, boisterous parents, and had to unbutton his shirt cuffs to get his wrists through them, and discovered he could pick up a basketball with one hand. So, his long legs blocking two aisles, he felt regal even in size and, almost trembling with happiness under the high globes of light beyond whose lunar glow invisible snowflakes were drowning on the gravel roof of his castle, believed that the long delay of unpopularity had been merely a consolation, that he was at last strong enough to make his move. Today he would tell Mary Landis he loved her.

He had loved her ever since, a fat-faced tomboy with freckles and green eyes, she deftly stole his rubber-lined schoolbag on the walk back from second grade along Jewett Street and outran him—simply had better legs. The superior speed a boy was supposed to have failed to come: his kidneys burned with panic. In front of the grocery store next to her home she stopped and turned. She was willing to have him catch up. This humiliation on top of the rest was too much to bear. Tears broke in his throat; he spun around and ran home and threw himself on the floor of the front parlor, where his grandfather, feet twiddling, perused the newspaper and soliloquized all morning. In time the letter slot rustled, and the doorbell rang, and Mary gave his mother the schoolbag and the two of them politely exchanged whispers. Their voices had been to him, lying there on the carpet with his head wrapped in his arms, indistinguishable. Mother had always liked Mary. From when she had been a tiny girl dancing along the hedge on the end of an older sister's arm, Mother had liked her. Out of all the children that flocked, similar as pigeons, through the neighborhood, Mother's heart had reached out with claws and fastened on Mary. He never took the schoolbag to school again, had refused to touch it. He supposed it was still in the attic, still faintly smelling of sweet pink rubber.

Fixed high on the plaster like a wren clinging to a barn wall, the buzzer sounded the two-minute signal. In the middle of the classroom Mary Landis stood up, a Monitor badge pinned to her belly. Her broad red belt was buckled with a brass bow and arrow. She wore a lavender sweater with the sleeves pushed up to expose her forearms, a delicately cheap effect. Wild stories were told about her; perhaps it was merely his knowledge of these that put the hardness in her face. Her eyes seemed braced for squinting and their green was frosted. Her freckles had faded. William thought she laughed less this year; now that she was in the Secretarial Course and he in the College Preparatory, he saw her in only one class a day, this one, English. She stood a second, eclipsed at the thighs by Jack Stephens' zebra-striped shoulders, and looked back at the class with a stiff worn glance, as if she had seen the same faces too many times before. Her habit of perfect posture emphasized the angularity she had grown into. There was a nervous edge, a boxiness in her bones, that must have been waiting all along under the childish fat. Her eye sockets were deeply indented and her chin had a prim square set that seemed in the murky air tremulous and defiant. Her skirt was cut square and straight. Below the waist she was lean; the legs that had outrun him were still athletic; she starred at hockey and cheerleading. Above, she was abundant; so stacked her spine curved backwards to keep her body balanced. She turned and in switching up the aisle encountered a boy's leg thrown into her path. She coolly looked down until it withdrew. She was used to such attentions. Her pronged chest poised, Mary proceeded out the door, and someone she saw in the hall made her smile, a wide smile full of warmth and short white teeth, and love scooped at William's heart. He would tell her.

In another minute, the second bell rasped. Shuffling through the perfumed crowds to his next class, he crooned to himself in the slow, over-enunciated manner of the Negro vocalist who had brought the song back this year:

> "Lah-vender blue, dilly dilly,
> Lavendih gree-heen;
> *Eef* I were king, dilly dilly,
> You would: be queen."

The song gave him an exultant sliding sensation that intertwined with the pleasures of his day. He knew all the answers, he had done all the work, the teachers called upon him only to rebuke the ignorance of the others. In Trig and Soc Sci both it was this way. In gym, the fourth hour of the morning, he, who was always picked near the last, startled his side by excelling at volleyball, leaping like a madman, shouting like a bully. The ball felt light as a feather against his big bones. His hair in wet quills from the shower, he walked in the icy air to Luke's Luncheonette, where he ate three hamburgers in a booth with three juniors. There was Barry Kruppman, a tall, thyroid-eyed boy who came on the school bus from the country town of Bowsville and who was an amateur hypnotist; he told the tale of a Portland, Oregon, businessman who under hypnosis had been taken back through sixteen reincarnations to the condition of an Egyptian concubine in the household of a high priest of Isis. There was his friend Lionel Griffin, a pudgy simp whose blond hair puffed out above his ears in two slick waxed wings. He was rumored to be a fairy, and in fact did seem most excited by the transvestite aspect of the soul's transmigration. And there was Lionel's girl Virginia, a drab little mystery who chain-smoked Herbert Tareytons and never said anything. She had sallow skin and smudged eyes and Lionel kept jabbing her and shrieking, making William wince. He would rather have sat with members of his own class, who filled the other booths, but he would have had to force himself on them. These juniors admired him and welcomed his company. He asked, "Wuh-well, was he ever a c-c-c-cockroach, like Archy?"

Kruppman's face grew intense; his furry lids dropped down over the bulge of his eyes, and when they drew back, his pupils were as small and hard as BBs. "That's the really interesting thing. There was this gap, see, between his being a knight under Charlemagne and then a sailor on a ship putting out from Macedonia—that's where Yugoslavia is now—in the time of Nero; there was this gap, when the only thing the guy would do was walk around the office snarling and growling, see, like this." Kruppman worked his blotched ferret face up into a snarl and Griffin shrieked. "He tried to bite one of the assistants and they think that for six hundred years"—the uncanny, unhealthy seriousness of his whisper hushed Griffin momentarily—"for six hundred years he just was a series of wolves. Probably in the German forests. You see, when he was in Macedonia"—his whisper barely audible—"he murdered a woman."

Griffin squealed in ecstasy and cried, "Oh, Kruppman! Kruppman, how you do go on!" and jabbed Virginia in the arm so hard a Herbert Tareyton jumped from her hand and bobbled across the Formica table. William gazed over their heads in pain.

The crowds at the soda counter had thinned so that when the door to the outside opened he saw Mary come in and hesitate there for a second where the smoke inside and the snow outside swirled together. The mixture made a kind of—Kruppman's ridiculous story had put the phrase in his head—wolf-weather, and she was just a gray shadow caught in it alone. She bought a pack of cigarettes from Luke and went out again, a kerchief around her head, the pneumatic thing above the door hissing behind her. For a long time, always in fact, she had been at the center of whatever gang was the one: in the second grade the one that walked home up Jewett Street together, and in the sixth grade the one that went bicycling as far away as the quarry and the Rentschler estate and played touch football Saturday afternoons, and in the ninth grade the one that went roller-skating at Candlebridge Park with the tenth-grade boys, and in the eleventh grade the one that held parties lasting past midnight and that on Sundays drove in caravans as far as Philadelphia and back. And all the while there had been a succession of boy friends, first Jack Stephens and Fritz March in their class and then boys a grade ahead and then Barrel Lord, who was a senior when they were sophomores and whose name was in the newspapers all football season, and then this last summer someone out of the school altogether, a man she met while working as a waitress in the city of Alton. So this year her weekends were taken up, and the party gang carried on as if she had never existed, and nobody saw her much except in school and when she stopped by in Luke's to buy a pack of cigarettes. Her silhouette against the big window had looked wan, her head hooded, her face nibbled by light, her fingers fiddling on the veined counter with her coins. He yearned to reach out, to comfort her, but he was wedged deep in the shrill booths, between the jingling guts of the pinball machine and the hillbilly joy of the jukebox. The impulse left him with a disagreeable feeling. He had loved her too long to want to pity her; it endangered the investment of worship on which he had not yet realized any return.

The two hours of the school afternoon held Latin and a study hall. In study hall, while the five people at the table with him played tic-tac-toe and sucked cough drops and yawned, he did all his homework for the next day. He prepared thirty lines of Vergil, Aeneas in the Underworld. The study hall was a huge low room in the basement of the building; its coziness crept into Tartarus. On the other side of the fudge-colored wall the circular saw in the woodworking shop whined and gasped and then whined again; it bit off pieces of wood with a rising, somehow terrorized inflection—bzzzzzup! He solved ten problems in trigonometry. His mind cut neatly through their knots and separated them, neat stiff squares of answer, one by one from the long but finite plank of problems that connected Plane Geometry with Solid. Lastly, as the snow on a ragged slant drifted down into the cement pits outside the steel-mullioned windows, he read a short story by Edgar Allan Poe. He closed the book softly on the pleasing sonority of its final note of horror, gazed at the red, wet, menthol-scented inner membrane of Judy Whipple's yawn, rimmed with flaking pink lipstick, and yielded his conscience to the snug sense of his work done, of the snow falling, of the warm minutes that walked through their shelter so slowly. The perforated acoustic tiling above his head seemed the lining of a long tube that would go all the way: high school merging into college, college into graduate school, graduate school into teaching at a college—section man, assistant, associate, *full* professor, possessor of a dozen languages and a thousand books, a man brilliant in his forties, wise in his fifties, renowned in his sixties, revered in his seventies, and then retired, sitting in the study lined with acoustical books until the time came for the last transition from silence to silence, and he would die, like Tennyson, with a copy of *Cymbeline* beside him on the moon-drenched bed.

After school he had to go to Room 101 and cut a sports cartoon into a stencil for the school paper. He liked the building best when it was nearly empty, when the casual residents—the rural commuters, the do-nothings, the trash—had cleared out. Then the janitors went down the halls sowing seeds of red wax and making an immaculate harvest with broad brooms, gathering all the fluff and hairpins and wrappers and powder that the animals had dropped that day. The basketball team thumped in the hollow gymnasium; the cheerleaders rehearsed behind drawn curtains on the stage. In Room 101 two empty-headed typists with stripes bleached into their hair banged away between giggles and mistakes. At her desk Mrs. Gregory, the faculty sponsor, wearily passed her pencil through misspelled news copy on tablet paper. William took the shadow box from the top of the filing cabinet and the styluses and little square plastic shading screens from their drawer and the stencil from the closet where the typed stencils hung, like fragile scarves, on hooks. B-BALLERS BOW, 57-42, was the headline. He drew a tall b-baller bowing to a stumpy pagan idol, labelled "W" for victorious Weiserton High, and traced it in the soft blue wax with the fine loop stylus. His careful breath grazed his knuckles. His eyebrows frowned while his heart bobbed happily on the giddy prattle of the typists. The shadow box was simply a black frame holding a pane of glass and lifted at one end by two legs so the light bulb, fitted in a tin tray, could slide under; it was like a primitive lean-to sheltering a fire. As he worked, his eyes smarting, he mixed himself up with the light bulb, felt himself burning under a slanting roof upon which a huge hand scratched. The glass grew hot; the danger in the job was pulling the softened wax with your damp hand, distorting or tearing the typed letters. Sometimes the center of an o stuck to your skin like a bit of blue confetti. But he was expert and cautious. He returned the things to their places feeling airily tall, heightened by Mrs. Gregory's appreciation, which she expressed by keeping her back turned, in effect stating that other staff members were undependable but William did not need to be watched.

In the hall outside Room 101 only the shouts of a basketball scrimmage reverberated; the chant of the cheerleaders had been silenced. Though he had done everything, he felt reluctant to leave. Neither of his parents—both worked—would be home yet, and this building was as much his home. He knew all its nooks. On the second floor of the annex, beyond the art room, there was a strange, narrow boys' lavatory that no one ever seemed to use. It was here one time that Barry Kruppman tried to hypnotize him and cure his stuttering. Kruppman's voice purred and his irises turned tiny in the bulging whites and for a moment William felt himself lean backward involuntarily, but he was distracted by the bits of bloodshot pink in the corners of these portentous eyes; the folly of giving up his will to an intellectual inferior occurred to him; he refused to let go and go under, and perhaps therefore his stuttering had continued.

The frosted window at the end of the long room cast a watery light on the green floor and made the porcelain urinals shine like slices of moon. The semi-opacity of this window gave the room's air of secrecy great density. William washed his hands with exaggerated care, enjoying the lavish amount of powdered soap provided for him in this castle. He studied his face in the mirror, making infinitesimal adjustments to attain the absolutely most flattering angle, and then put his hands below his throat to get their strong, long-fingered beauty into the picture. As he walked toward the door he sang, closing his eyes and gasping as if he were a real Negro whose entire career depended upon this recording:

"Who—told me so, dilly dilly,
Who told me soho?
A*ii* told myself, dilly dilly,
I told: me so."

When he emerged into the hall it was not empty: one girl walked down its varnished perspective toward him, Mary Landis, a scarf on her head and books in her arms. Her locker was up here, on the second floor of the annex. His own was in the annex basement. A tickling sensation that existed neither in the medium of sound nor of light crowded against his throat. She flipped the scarf back from her hair and in a conversational voice that carried well down the clean planes of the hall said, "Hi, Billy." The name came from way back, when they were both children, and made him feel small but brave.

"Hi. How are you?"

"Fine." Her smile broadened out from the *F* of this word.

What was so funny? Was she really, as it seemed, pleased to see him? "Du-did you just get through cheer-cheer-cheerleading?"

"Yes. Thank God. *Oh* she's so awful. She makes us do the same stupid locomotives for every cheer; I told her, no wonder nobody cheers any more."

"This is M-M-Miss Potter?" He blushed, feeling that he made an ugly face in getting past the *M*. When he got caught in the middle of a sentence the constriction was somehow worse. He admired the way words poured up her throat, distinct and petulant.

"Yes, Potbottom Potter," she said, "she's just aching for a man and takes it out on us. I wish she would get one. Honestly, Billy, I have half a mind to quit. I'll be so glad when June comes, I'll never set foot in this idiotic building again."

Her lips, pale with the lipstick worn off, crinkled bitterly. Her face, foreshortened from the height of his eyes, looked cross as a cat's. It a little shocked him that poor Miss Potter and this kind, warm school stirred her to what he had to take as actual anger; this grittiness in her was the first abrasive texture he had struck today. Couldn't she see around teachers, into their fatigue, their poverty, their fear? It had been so long since he had spoken to her, he wasn't sure how coarse she had become. "Don't quit," he brought out of his mouth at last. "It'd be n-n-n-nuh—it'd be nothing without you."

He pushed open the door at the end of the hall for her and as she passed under his arm she looked up and said, "Why, aren't you sweet?"

The stairwell, all asphalt and iron, smelled of galoshes. It felt more secret than the hall, more specially theirs; there was something magical in its shifting multiplicity of planes as they descended that lifted the spell on his tongue, so that words came as quickly as his feet pattered on the steps.

"No I mean it," he said, "you're really a beautiful cheerleader. But then you're beautiful period."

"I've skinny legs."

"Who told you that?"

"Somebody."

"Well *he* wasn't very sweet."

"No."

"Why do you hate this poor old school?"

"Now Billy. You know you don't care about this junky place any more than I do."

"I love it. It breaks my heart to hear you say you want to get out, because then I'll never see you again."

"You don't care, do you?"

"Why sure I care; you *know*"—their feet stopped; they had reached bottom, the first-floor landing, two brass-barred doors and a grimy radiator—"I've always li-loved you."

"You don't mean that."

"I do too. It's ridiculous but there it is. I wanted to tell you today and now I have."

He expected her to laugh and go out the door, but instead she showed an unforseeable willingness to discuss this awkward matter. He should have realized before this that women enjoy being talked to. "It's a very silly thing to say," she asserted tentatively.

"I don't see why," he said, fairly bold now that he couldn't seem more ridiculous, and yet picking his words with a certain strategic care. "It's not *that* silly to love somebody, I mean what the hell. Probably what's silly is not to do anything about it for umpteen years but then I never had an opportunity, I thought."

He set his books down on the radiator and she set hers down beside his. "What kind of opportunity were you waiting for?"

"Well, see, that's it; I didn't know." He wished, in a way, she would go out the door. But she had propped herself against the wall and plainly awaited more talking. "Yuh-you were such a queen and I was such a nothing and I just didn't really want to presume." It wasn't very interesting; it puzzled him that she seemed to be interested. Her face had grown quite stern, the mouth very small and thoughtful, and he made a gesture with his hands intended to release her from the bother of thinking about it; after all, it was just a disposition of his heart, nothing permanent or expensive; perhaps it was just his mother's idea anyway. Half in impatience to close the account, he asked, "Will you marry me?"

"You don't want to marry me," she said. "You're going to go on and be a great man."

He blushed in pleasure; is this how she saw him, is this how they all saw him; as worthless now, but in time a great man? Had his hopes always been on view? He dissembled, saying, "No I'm not. But anyway, you're great now. You're so pretty, Mary."

"Oh, Billy," she said, "if you were me for just one day you'd hate it."

She said this rather blankly, watching his eyes; he wished her voice had shown more misery. In his world of closed surfaces a panel, carelessly pushed, had opened, and he hung in this openness paralyzed, unable to think what to say. Nothing he could think of quite fit the abruptly immense context. The radiator cleared its throat; its heat made, in the intimate volume just this side of the doors on whose windows thé snow beat limply, a provocative snugness; he supposed he should try, and stepped forward, his hands lifting toward her shoulders. Mary sidestepped between him and the radiator and put the scarf back on. She lifted the cloth like a broad plaid halo above her head and then wrapped it around her chin and knotted it so she looked, in her red galoshes and bulky coat, like a peasant woman in a movie of Europe. With her thick hair swathed, her face seemed pale and chunky, and when she recradled the books in her arms her back bent humbly under the point of the kerchief. "It's too hot in here," she said. "I've got to wait for somebody." The disconnectedness of the two statements seemed natural in the fragmented atmosphere his stops and starts had produced. She bucked the brass bar with her shoulder and the door slammed open; he followed her into the weather.

"For the person who thinks your legs are too skinny?"

"Uh-huh." As she looked up at him a snowflake caught on the lashes of one eye. She jerkily rubbed that cheek on the shoulder of her coat and stamped a foot, splashing slush. Cold water gathered on the back of his thin shirt. He put his hands in his pockets and pressed his arms against his sides to keep from shivering.

"Thuh-then you wo-won't marry me?" His wise instinct told him the only way back was by going forward, through absurdity.

"We don't know each other," she said.

"My God," he said. "Why not? I've known you since I was two."

"What do you know about me?"

This awful seriousness of hers; he must dissolve it. "That you're not a virgin." But instead of making her laugh this made her face go dead and turned it away. Like beginning to kiss her, it was a mistake; in part, he felt grateful for his mistakes. They were like loyal friends who are nevertheless embarrassing. "What do you know about *me?*" he asked, setting himself up for a finishing insult but dreading it. He hated the stiff feel of his smile between his cheeks; glimpsed, as if the snow were a mirror, how hateful he looked.

"That you're basically very nice."

Her returning good for evil blinded him to his physical discomfort, set him burning with regret. "Listen," he said, "I did love you. Let's at least get that straight."

"You never loved anybody," she said. "You don't know what it is."

"O.K." he said. "Pardon me."

"You're excused."

"You better wait in the school," he told her. "He's-eez-eez going to be a long time."

She didn't answer and walked a little distance, toeing out in the childish Dutch way common to the women in this county, along the slack cable that divided the parking lot from the softball field. One bicycle, rusted as if it had been there for years, leaned in the rack, its fenders supporting airy crescents of white.

The warmth inside the door felt heavy. William picked up his books and ran his pencil along the black ribs of the radiator before going down the stairs to his locker in the annex basement. The shadows were thick at the foot of the steps; suddenly it felt late, he must hurry and get home. He was seized by the irrational fear that they were going to lock him in. The cloistered odors of paper, sweat, and, from the woodshop at the far end of the basement hall, sawdust no longer flattered him. The tall green double lockers appeared to study him critically through the three air slits near their tops. When he opened his locker, and put his books on his shelf, below Marvin Wolf's, and removed his coat from his hook, his self seemed to crawl into the long dark space thus made vacant, the humiliated ugly, educable self. In answer to a flick of his great hand the steel door weightlessly floated shut and through the length of his body he felt so clean and free he smiled. Between now and the happy future predicted for him he had nothing, almost literally nothing, to do.

Ernest Hemingway (1899–1961)
The Killers

The door of Henry's lunch-room opened and two men came in. They sat down at the counter.

"What's yours?" George asked them.

"I don't know," one of the men said. "What do you want to eat, Al?"

"I don't know," said Al. "I don't know what I want to eat."

Outside it was getting dark. The street-light came on outside the window. The two men at the counter read the menu. From the other end of the counter Nick Adams watched them. He had been talking to George when they came in.

"I'll have a roast pork tenderloin with apple sauce and mashed potatoes," the first man said.

"It isn't ready yet."

"What the hell do you put it on the card for?"

"That's the dinner," George explained. "You can get that at six o'clock."

George looked at the clock on the wall behind the counter.

"It's five o'clock."

"The clock says twenty minutes past five," the second man said.

"It's twenty minutes fast."

"Oh, to hell with the clock," the first man said. "What have you got to eat?"

"I can give you any kind of sandwiches," George said. "You can have ham and eggs, bacon and eggs, liver and bacon, or a steak."

"Give me chicken croquettes with green peas and cream sauce and mashed potatoes."

"That's the dinner."

"Everything we want's the dinner, eh? That's the way you work it."

"I can give you ham and eggs, bacon and eggs, liver————"

"I'll take ham and eggs," the man called Al said. He wore a derby hat and a black overcoat buttoned across the chest. His face was small and white and he had tight lips. He wore a silk muffler and gloves.

"Give me bacon and eggs," said the other man. He was about the same size as Al. Their faces were different, but they were dressed like twins. Both wore overcoats too tight for them. They sat leaning forward, their elbows on the counter.

"Got anything to drink?" Al asked.

"Silver beer, bevo, ginger-ale," George said.

"I mean you got anything to *drink?*"

"Just those I said."

"This is a hot town," said the other. "What do they call it?"

"Summit."

"Ever hear of it?" Al asked his friend.

"No," said the friend.

"What do you do here nights?" Al asked.

"They eat the dinner," his friend said. "They all come here and eat the big dinner."

"That's right," George said.

"So you think that's right?" Al asked George.

"Sure."

"You're a pretty bright boy, aren't you?"

"Sure," said George.

"Well, you're not," said the other little man. "Is he, Al?"

"He's dumb," said Al. He turned to Nick. "What's your name?"

"Adams."

"Another bright boy," Al said. "Ain't he a bright boy, Max?"

"The town's full of bright boys," Max said.

George put the two platters, one of ham and eggs, the other of bacon and eggs, on the counter. He set down two side-dishes of fried potatoes and closed the wicket into the kitchen.

"Which is yours?" he asked Al.

"Don't you remember?"

"Ham and eggs."

"Just a bright boy," Max said. He leaned forward and took the ham and eggs. Both men ate with their gloves on. George watched them eat.

"What are *you* looking at?" Max looked at George.

"Nothing."

"The hell you were. You were looking at me."

"Maybe the boy meant it for a joke, Max," Al said.

George laughed.

"*You* don't have to laugh," Max said to him. "*You* don't have to laugh at all, see?"

"All right," said George.

"So he thinks it's all right." Max turned to Al. "He thinks it's all right. That's a good one."

"Oh, he's a thinker," Al said. They went on eating.

"What's the bright boy's name down the counter?" Al asked Max.

"Hey, bright boy," Max said to Nick. "You go around on the other side of the counter with your boy friend."

"What's the idea?" Nick asked.

"There isn't any idea."

"You better go around, bright boy," Al said. Nick went around behind the counter.

"What's the idea?" George asked.

"None of your damn business," Al said. "Who's out in the kitchen?"

"The nigger."

"What do you mean the nigger?"

"The nigger that cooks."

"Tell him to come in."

"What's the idea?"

"Tell him to come in."

"Where do you think you are?"

"We know damn well where we are," the man called Max said. "Do we look silly?"

"You talk silly," Al said to him. "What the hell do you argue with this kid for? Listen," he said to George, "tell the nigger to come out here."

"What are you going to do to him?"

"Nothing. Use your head, bright boy. What would we do to a nigger?"

George opened the slit that opened back into the kitchen. "Sam," he called. "Come in here a minute."

The door to the kitchen opened and the nigger came in. "What was it?" he asked. The two men at the counter took a look at him.

"All right, nigger. You stand right there," Al said.

Sam, the nigger, standing in his apron, looked at the two men sitting at the counter. "Yes, sir," he said. Al got down from his stool.

"I'm going back to the kitchen with the nigger and bright boy," he said. "Go on back to the kitchen, nigger. You go with him, bright boy." The little man walked after Nick and Sam, the cook, back into the kitchen. The door shut after them. The man called Max sat at the counter opposite George. He didn't look at George but looked in the mirror that ran along back of the counter. Henry's had been made over from a saloon into a lunch-counter.

"Well, bright boy," Max said, looking into the mirror, "why don't you say something?"

"What's it all about?"

"Hey, Al," Max called, "bright boy wants to know what it's all about."

"Why don't you tell him?" Al's voice came from the kitchen.

"What do you think it's all about?"

"I don't know."

"What do you think?"

Max looked into the mirror all the time he was talking.

"I wouldn't say."

"Hey, Al, bright boy says he wouldn't say what he thinks it's all about."

"I can hear you, all right," Al said from the kitchen. He had propped open the slit that dishes passed through into the kitchen with a catsup bottle. "Listen, bright boy," he said from the kitchen to George. "Stand a little further along the bar. You move a little to the left, Max." He was like a photographer arranging for a group picture.

"Talk to me, bright boy," Max said. "What do you think's going to happen?"

George did not say anything.

"I'll tell you," Max said. "We're going to kill a Swede. Do you know a big Swede named Ole Andreson?"

"Yes."

"He comes here to eat every night, don't he?"

"Sometimes he comes here."

"He comes here at six o'clock, don't he?"

"If he comes."

"We know all that, bright boy," Max said. "Talk about something else. Ever go to the movies?"

"Once in a while."

"You ought to go to the movies more. The movies are fine for a bright boy like you."

"What are you going to kill Ole Andreson for? What did he ever do to you?"

"He never had a chance to do anything to us. He never even seen us."

"And he's only going to see us once," Al said from the kitchen.

"What are you going to kill him for, then?" George asked.

"We're killing him for a friend. Just to oblige a friend, bright boy."

"Shut up," said Al from the kitchen. "You talk too goddam much."

"Well, I got to keep bright boy amused. Don't I, bright boy?"

"You talk too damn much," Al said. "The nigger and my bright boy are amused by themselves. I got them tied up like a couple of girl friends in the convent."

"I suppose you were in a convent?"

"You never know."

"You were in a kosher convent. That's where you were."

George looked up at the clock.

"If anybody comes in you tell them the cook is off, and if they keep after it, you tell them you'll go back and cook yourself. Do you get that, bright boy?"

"All right," George said. "What you going to do with us afterward?"

"That'll depend," Max said. "That's one of those things you never know at the time."

George looked up at the clock. It was a quarter past six. The door from the street opened. A street-car motorman came in.

"Hello, George," he said. "Can I get supper?"

"Sam's gone out," George said. "He'll be back in about half an hour."

"I'd better go up the street," the motorman said. George looked at the clock. It was twenty minutes past six.

"That was nice, bright boy," Max said. "You're a regular little gentleman."

"He knew I'd blow his head off," Al said from the kitchen.

"No," said Max. "It ain't that. Bright boy is nice. He's a nice boy. I like him."

At six-fifty-five George said: "He's not coming."

Two other people had been in the lunch-room. Once George had gone out to the kitchen and made a ham-and-egg sandwich "to go" that a man wanted to take with him. Inside the kitchen he saw Al, his derby hat tipped back, sitting on a stool beside the wicket with the muzzle of a sawed-off shotgun resting on the ledge. Nick and the cook were back to back in the corner, a towel tied in each of their mouths. George had cooked the sandwich, wrapped it up in oiled paper, put it in a bag, brought it in, and the man had paid for it and gone out.

"Bright boy can do everything," Max said. "He can cook and everything. You'd make some girl a nice wife, bright boy."

"Yes?" George said. "Your friend, Ole Andreson, isn't going to come."

"We'll give him ten minutes," Max said.

Max watched the mirror and the clock. The hands of the clock marked seven o'clock, and then five minutes past seven.

"Come on, Al," said Max. "We better go. He's not coming."

"Better give him five minutes," Al said from the kitchen.

In the five minutes a man came in, and George explained that the cook was sick.

"Why the hell don't you get another cook?" the man asked. "Aren't you running a lunch-counter?" He went out.

"Come on, Al," Max said.

"What about the two bright boys and the nigger?"

"They're all right."

"You think so?"

"Sure. We're through with it."

"I don't like it," said Al. "It's sloppy. You talk too much."

"Oh, what the hell," said Max. "We got to keep amused, haven't we?"

"You talk too much, all the same," Al said. He came out from the kitchen. The cut-off barrels of the shotgun made a slight bulge under the waist of his too tight-fitting overcoat. He straightened his coat with his gloved hands.

"So long, bright boy," he said to George. "You got a lot of luck."

"That's the truth," Max said. "You ought to play the races, bright boy."

The two of them went out the door. George watched them, through the window, pass under the arc-light and cross the street. In their tight overcoats and derby hats they looked like a vaudeville team. George went back through the swinging-door into the kitchen and untied Nick and the cook.

"I don't want any more of that," said Sam, the cook. "I don't want any more of that."

Nick stood up. He had never had a towel in his mouth before.

"Say," he said, "What the hell?" He was trying to swagger it off.

"They were going to kill Ole Andreson," George said. "They were going to shoot him when he came in to eat."

"Ole Andreson?"

"Sure."

The cook felt the corners of his mouth with his thumbs.

"They all gone?" he asked.

"Yeah," said George. "They're gone now."

"I don't like it," said the cook. "I don't like any of it at all."

"Listen," George said to Nick. "You better go see Ole Andreson."

"All right."

"You better not have anything to do with it at all," Sam, the cook, said. "You better stay way out of it."

"Don't go if you don't want to," George said.

"Mixing up in this ain't going to get you anywhere," the cook said. "You stay out of it."

"I'll go see him," Nick said to George. "Where does he live?"

The cook turned away.

"Little boys always know what they want to do," he said.

"He lives up at Hirsch's rooming-house," George said to Nick.

"I'll go up there."

Outside the arc-light shone through the bare branches of a tree. Nick walked up the street beside the car-tracks and turned at the next arc-light down a side-street. Three houses up the street was Hirsch's rooming-house. Nick walked up the two steps and pushed the bell. A woman came to the door.

"Is Ole Andreson here?"

"Do you want to see him?"

"Yes, if he's in."

Nick followed the woman up a flight of stairs and back to the end of a corridor. She knocked on the door.

"Who is it?"

"It's somebody to see you, Mr. Andreson," the woman said.

"It's Nick Adams."

"Come in."

Nick opened the door and went into the room. Ole Andreson was lying on the bed with all his clothes on. He had been a heavyweight prizefighter and he was too long for the bed. He lay with his head on two pillows. He did not look at Nick.

"What was it?" he asked.

"I was up at Henry's," Nick said, "and two fellows came in and tied up me and the cook, and they said they were going to kill you."

It sounded silly when he said it. Ole Andreson said nothing.

"They put us out in the kitchen," Nick went on. "They were going to shoot you when you came in to supper."

Ole Andreson looked at the wall and did not say anything.

"George thought I better come and tell you about it."

"There isn't anything I can do about it," Ole Andreson said.

"I'll tell you what they were like."

"I don't want to know what they were like," Ole Andreson said. He looked at the wall. "Thanks for coming to tell me about it."

"That's all right."

Nick looked at the big man lying on the bed.

"Don't you want me to go and see the police?"

"No," Ole Andreson said. "That wouldn't do any good."

"Isn't there something I could do?"

"No. There ain't anything to do."

"Maybe it was just a bluff."

"No. It ain't just a bluff."

Ole Andreson rolled over toward the wall.

"The only thing is," he said, talking toward the wall, "I just can't make up my mind to go out. I been in here all day."

"Couldn't you get out of town?"

"No," Ole Andreson said. "I'm through with all that running around."

He looked at the wall.

"There ain't anything to do now."

"Couldn't you fix it up some way?"

"No. I got in wrong." He talked in the same flat voice. "There ain't anything to do. After a while I'll make up my mind to go out."

"I better go back and see George," Nick said.

"So long," said Ole Andreson. He did not look toward Nick. "Thanks for coming around."

Nick went out. As he shut the door he saw Ole Andreson with all his clothes on, lying on the bed looking at the wall.

"He's been in his room all day," the landlady said down-stairs. "I guess he don't feel well. I said to him: 'Mr. Andreson, you ought to go out and take a walk on a nice fall day like this,' but he didn't feel like it."

"He doesn't want to go out."

"I'm sorry he don't feel well," the woman said. "He's an awfully nice man. He was in the ring, you know."

"I know it."

"You'd never know it except from the way his face is," the woman said. They stood talking just inside the street door. "He's just as gentle."

"Well, good-night, Mrs. Hirsch," Nick said.

"I'm not Mrs. Hirsch," the woman said. "She owns the place. I just look after it for her. I'm Mrs. Bell."

"Well, good-night, Mrs. Bell," Nick said.

"Good-night," the woman said.

Nick walked up the dark street to the corner under the arc-light, and then along the car-tracks to Henry's eating-house. George was inside, back of the counter.

"Did you see Ole?"

"Yes," said Nick. "He's in his room and he won't go out."

The cook opened the door from the kitchen when he heard Nick's voice.

"I don't even listen to it," he said and shut the door.

"Did you tell him about it?" George asked.

"Sure. I told him but he knows what it's all about."

"What's he going to do?"

"Nothing."

"They'll kill him."

"I guess they will."

"He must have got mixed up in something in Chicago."

"I guess so," said Nick.

"It's a hell of a thing."

"It's an awful thing," Nick said.

They did not say anything. George reached down for a towel and wiped the counter.

"I wonder what he did?" Nick said.

"Double-crossed somebody. That's what they kill them for."

"I'm going to get out of this town," Nick said.

"Yes," said George. "That's a good thing to do."

"I can't stand to think about him waiting in the room and knowing he's going to get it. It's too damned awful."

"Well," said George, "you better not think about it."

Frank O'Connor (1903–1966) *
Guests of the Nation

1

At dusk the big Englishman Belcher would shift his long legs out of the ashes and ask, 'Well, chums, what about it?' and Noble or me would say, 'As you please, chum' (for we had picked up some of their curious expressions), and the little Englishman 'Awkins would light the lamp and produce the cards. Sometimes Jeremiah Donovan would come up of an evening and supervise the play, and grow excited over 'Awkins's cards (which he always played badly), and shout at him as if he was one of our own, 'Ach, you divil you, why didn't you play the tray?' But, ordinarily, Jeremiah was a sober and contented poor devil like the big Englishman Belcher, and was looked up to at all only because he was a fair hand at documents, though slow enough at these, I vow. He wore a small cloth hat and big gaiters over his long pants, and seldom did I perceive his hands outside the pockets of that pants. He reddened when you talked to him, tilting from toe to heel and back and looking down all the while at his big farmer's feet. His uncommon broad accent was a great source of jest to me, I being from the town as you may recognise.

---

*Frank O'Connor is the pen name of Michael O'Donovan.

I couldn't at the time see the point of me and Noble being with Belcher and 'Awkins at all, for it was and is my fixed belief you could have planted that pair in any untended spot from this to Claregalway and they'd have stayed put and flourished like a native weed. I never seen in my short experience two men that took to the country as they did.

They were handed on to us by the Second Battalion to keep when the search for them became too hot, and Noble and myself, being young, took charge with a natural feeling of responsibility. But little 'Awkins made us look right fools when he displayed he knew the countryside as well as we did and something more. 'You're the bloke they calls Bonaparte?' he said to me. 'Well, Bonaparte, Mary Brigid Ho'Connell was arskin abaout you and said 'ow you'd a pair of socks belonging to 'er young brother.' For it seemed, as they explained it, that the Second used to have little evenings of their own, and some of the girls of the neighbourhood would turn in, and, seeing they were such decent fellows, our lads couldn't well ignore the two Englishmen, but invited them in and were hail-fellow-well-met with them. 'Awkins told me he learned to dance 'The Walls of Limerick' and 'The Siege of Ennis' and 'The Waves of Tory' in a night or two, though naturally he could not return the compliment, because our lads at that time did not dance foreign dances on principle.

So whatever privileges and favours Belcher and 'Awkins had with the Second they duly took with us, and after the first evening we gave up all pretence of keeping a close eye on their behaviour. Not that they could have got far, for they had a notable accent and wore khaki tunics and overcoats with civilian pants and boots. But it's my belief they never had an idea of escaping and were quite contented with their lot.

Now, it was a treat to see how Belcher got off with the old woman of the house we were staying in. She was a great warrant to scold, and crotchety even with us, but before ever she had a chance of giving our guests, as I may call them, a lick of her tongue, Belcher had made her his friend for life. She was breaking sticks at the time, and Belcher, who hadn't been in the house for more than ten minutes, jumped up out of his seat and went across to her.

'Allow me, madam,' he says, smiling his queer little smile; 'please allow me,' and takes the hatchet from her hand. She was struck too parlatic to speak, and ever after Belcher would be at her heels carrying a bucket, or basket, or load of turf, as the case might be. As Noble wittily remarked, he got into looking before she lept, and hot water or any little thing she wanted Belcher would have it ready before her. For such a huge man (and though I am five foot ten myself I had to look up to him) he had an uncommon shortness—or should I say lack—of speech. It took us some time to get used to him walking in and out like a ghost, without a syllable out of him. Especially because 'Awkins talked enough for a platoon, it was strange to hear big Belcher with his toes in the ashes come out with a solitary 'Excuse me, chum,' or 'That's right, chum.' His one and only abiding passion was cards, and I will say for him he was a good card-player. He could have fleeced me and Noble many a time; only if we lost to him, 'Awkins lost to us, and 'Awkins played with the money Belcher gave him.

'Awkins lost to us because he talked too much, and I think now we lost to Belcher for the same reason. 'Awkins and Noble would spit at one another about religion into the early hours of the morning; the little Englishman as you could see worrying the soul out of young Noble (whose brother was a priest) with a string of questions that would puzzle a cardinal. And to make it worse, even in treating of these holy subjects, 'Awkins had a deplorable tongue; I never in all my career struck across a man who could mix such a variety of cursing and bad language into the simplest topic. Oh, a terrible man was little 'Awkins, and a fright to argue! He never did a stroke of work, and when he had no one else to talk to he fixed his claws into the old woman.

I am glad to say that in her he met his match, for one day when he tried to get her to complain profanely of the drought she gave him a great comedown by blaming the drought upon Jupiter Pluvius (a deity neither 'Awkins nor I had ever even heard of, though Noble said among the pagans he was held to have something to do with rain). And another day the same 'Awkins was swearing at the capitalists for starting the German war, when the old dame laid down her iron, puckered up her little crab's mouth and said, 'Mr. 'Awkins, you can say what you please about the war, thinking to deceive me because I'm an ignorant old woman, but I know well what started the war. It was that Italian count that stole the heathen divinity out of the temple in Japan, for believe me, Mr. 'Awkins, nothing but sorrow and want follows them that disturbs the hidden powers!' Oh, a queer old dame, as you remark!

2

So one evening we had our tea together, and 'Awkins lit the lamp and we all sat in to cards. Jeremiah Donovan came in too, and sat down and watched us for a while. Though he was a shy man and didn't speak much, it was easy to see he had no great love for the two Englishmen, and I was surprised it hadn't struck me so clearly before. Well, like that in the story, a terrible dispute blew up late in the evening between 'Awkins and Noble, about capitalists and priests and love for your own country.

'The capitalists,' says 'Awkins, with an angry gulp, 'the capitalists pays the priests to tell you all abaout the next world, so's you waon't notice what they do in this!'

'Nonsense, man,' says Noble, losing his temper, 'before ever a capitalist was thought of people believed in the next world.'

'Awkins stood up as if he was preaching a sermon. 'Oh, they did, did they?' he says with a sneer. 'They believed all the things you believe, that's what you mean? And you believe that God created Hadam and Hadam created Shem and Shem created Jehoshophat? You believe all the silly hold fairy-tale abaout Heve and Heden and the happle? Well, listen to me, chum. If you're entitled to 'old to a silly belief like that, I'm entitled to 'old to my own silly belief—which is, that the fust thing your God created was a bleedin' capitalist with mirality and Rolls Royce complete. Am I right, chum?' he says then to Belcher.

'You're right, chum,' says Belcher, with his queer smile, and gets up from the table to stretch his long legs into the fire and stroke his moustache. So, seeing that Jeremiah Donovan was going, and there was no knowing when the conversation about religion would be over, I took my hat and went out with him. We strolled down towards the village together, and then he suddenly stopped, and blushing and mumbling, and shifting, as his way was, from toe to heel, he said I ought to be behind keeping guard on the prisoners. And I, having it put to me so suddenly, asked him what the hell he wanted a guard on the prisoners at all for, and said that so far as Noble and me were concerned we had talked it over and would rather be out with a column. 'What use is that pair to us?' I asked him.

He looked at me for a spell and said, 'I thought you knew we were keeping them as hostages.' 'Hostages——?' says I, not quite understanding. 'The enemy,' he says in his heavy way, 'have prisoners belong' to us, and now they talk of shooting them. If they shoot our prisoners we'll shoot theirs, and serve them right.' 'Shoot them?' said I, the possibility just beginning to dawn on me. 'Shoot them, exactly,' said he. 'Now,' said I, 'wasn't it very unforeseen of you not to tell me and Noble that?' 'How so?' he asks. 'Seeing that we were acting as guards upon them, of course.' 'And hadn't you reason enough to guess that much?' 'We had not, Jeremiah Donovan, we had not. How were we to know when the men were on our hands so long?' 'And what difference does it make? The enemy have our prisoners as long or longer, haven't they?' 'It makes a great difference,' said I. 'How so?' said he sharply; but I couldn't tell him the difference it made, for I was struck too silly to speak. 'And when may we expect to be released from this anyway?' said I. 'You may expect it to-night,' says he. 'Or to-morrow or the next day at latest. So if it's hanging round here that worries you, you'll be free soon enough.'

I cannot explain it even now, how sad I felt, but I went back to the cottage, a miserable man. When I arrived the discussion was still on, 'Awkins holding forth to all and sundry that there was no next world at all and Noble answering in his best canonical style that there was. But I saw 'Awkins was after having the best of it. 'Do you know what, chum?' he was saying, with his saucy smile, 'I think you're jest as big a bleedin' hunbeliever as I am. You say you believe in the next world and you know jest as much abaout the next world as I do, which is sweet damn-all. What's 'Eaven? You dunno. Where's 'Eaven? You dunno. Who's in 'Eaven? You dunno. You know sweet damn-all! I arsk you again, do they wear wings?'

'Very well then,' says Noble, 'they do; is that enough for you? They do wear wings.' 'Where do they get them then? Who makes them? 'Ave they a fact'ry for wings? 'Ave they a sort of store where you 'ands in your chit and tikes your bleedin' wings? Answer me that.'

'Oh, you're an impossible man to argue with,' says Noble. 'Now listen to me——'. And off the pair of them went again.

It was long after midnight when we locked up the Englishmen and went to bed ourselves. As I blew out the candle I told Noble what Jeremiah Donovan had told me. Noble took it very quietly. After we had been in bed about an hour he asked me did I think we ought to tell the Englishmen. I having thought of the same thing myself (among many others) said no, because it was more than likely the English wouldn't shoot our men, and anyhow it wasn't to be supposed the Brigade who were always up and down with the second battalion and knew the Englishmen well would be likely to want them bumped off. 'I think so,' says Noble. 'It would be sort of cruelty to put the wind up them now.' 'It was very unforeseen of Jeremiah Donovan anyhow,' says I, and by Noble's silence I realised he took my meaning.

So I lay there half the night, and thought and thought, and picturing myself and young Noble trying to prevent the Brigade from shooting 'Awkins and Belcher sent a cold sweat out through me. Because there were men on the Brigade you daren't let nor hinder without a gun in your hand, and at any rate, in those days disunion between brothers seemed to me an awful crime. I knew better after.

It was next morning we found it so hard to face Belcher and 'Awkins with a smile. We went about the house all day scarcely saying a word. Belcher didn't mind us much; he was stretched into the ashes as usual with his usual look of waiting in quietness for something unforeseen to happen, but little 'Awkins gave us a bad time with his audacious gibing and questioning. He was disgusted at Noble's not answering him back. 'Why can't you tike your beating like a man, chum?' he says. 'You with your Hadam and Heve! I'm a Communist—or an Anarchist. An Anarchist, that's what I am.' And for hours after he went round the house, mumbling when the fit took him 'Hadam and Heve! Hadam and Heve!'

3

I don't know clearly how we got over that day, but get over it we did, and a great relief it was when the tea-things were cleared away and Belcher said in his peaceable manner, 'Well, chums, what about it?' So we all sat round the table and 'Awkins produced the cards, and at that moment I heard Jeremiah Donovan's footsteps up the path, and a dark presentiment crossed my mind. I rose quietly from the table and laid my hand on him before he reached the door. 'What do you want?' I asked him. 'I want those two soldier friends of yours,' he says reddening. 'Is that the way it is, Jeremiah Donovan?' I ask. 'That's the way. There were four of our lads went west this morning, one of them a boy of sixteen.' 'That's bad, Jeremiah,' says I.

At that moment Noble came out, and we walked down the path together talking in whispers. Feeney, the local intelligence officer, was standing by the gate. 'What are you going to do about it?' I asked Jeremiah Donovan. 'I want you and Noble to bring them out: you can tell them they're being shifted again; that'll be the quietest way.' 'Leave me out of that,' says Noble suddenly. Jeremiah Donovan looked at him hard for a minute or two. 'All right so,' he said peaceably. 'You and Feeney collect a few tools from the shed and dig a hole by the far end of the bog. Bonaparte and I'll be after you in about twenty minutes. But whatever else you do, don't let anyone see you with the tools. No one must know but the four of ourselves.'

We saw Feeney and Noble go round to the houseen where the tools were kept, and sidled in. Everything if I can so express myself was tottering before my eyes, and I left Jeremiah Donovan to do the explaining as best he could, while I took a seat and said nothing. He told them they were to go back to the

Second. 'Awkins let a mouthful of curses out of him at that, and it was plain that Belcher, though he said nothing, was duly perturbed. The old woman was for having them stay in spite of us, and she did not shut her mouth until Jeremiah Donovan lost his temper and said some nasty things to her. Within the house by this time it was pitch dark, but no one thought of lighting the lamp, and in the darkness the two Englishmen fetched their khaki topcoats and said good-bye to the woman of the house. 'Just as a man mikes a 'ome of a bleedin' place,' mumbles 'Awkins shaking her by the hand, 'some bastard at headquarters thinks you're too cushy and shunts you off.' Belcher shakes her hand very hearty. 'A thousand thanks, madam,' he says, 'a thousand thanks for everything . . .' as though he'd made it all up.

We go round to the back of the house and down towards the fatal bog. Then Jeremiah Donovan comes out with what is in his mind. 'There were four of our lads shot by your fellows this morning so now you're to be bumped off.' 'Cut that stuff out,' says 'Awkins flaring up. 'It's bad enough to be mucked about such as we are without you plying at soldiers.' 'It's true,' says Jeremiah Donovan, 'I'm sorry, 'Awkins, but 'tis true,' and comes out with the usual rigmarole about doing our duty and obeying our superiors. 'Cut it out,' says 'Awkins irritably, 'Cut it out!'

Then, when Donovan sees he is not being believed he turns to me. 'Ask Bonaparte here,' he says. 'I don't need to arsk Bonaparte. Me and Bonaparte are chums.' 'Isn't it true, Bonaparte?' says Jeremiah Donovan solemnly to me. 'It is,' I say sadly, 'it is.' 'Awkins stops. 'Now, for Christ's sike. . . .' 'I mean it, chum,' I say. 'You daon't saound as if you mean it. You knaow well you don't mean it.' 'Well, if he don't I do,' says Jeremiah Donovan. 'Why the 'ell sh'd you want to shoot me, Jeremiah Donovan?' 'Why the hell should your people take out four prisoners and shoot them in cold blood upon a barrack square?' I perceive Jeremiah Donovan is trying to encourage himself with hot words.

Anyway, he took little 'Awkins by the arm and dragged him on, but it was impossible to make him understand that we were in earnest. From which you will perceive how difficult it was for me, as I kept feeling my Smith and Wesson and thinking what I would do if they happened to put up a fight or ran for it, and wishing in my heart they would. I knew if only they ran I would never fire on them. 'Was Noble in this?' 'Awkins wanted to know, and we said yes. He laughed. But why should Noble want to shoot him? Why should we want to shoot him? What had he done to us? Weren't we chums (the word lingers painfully in my memory)? Weren't we? Didn't we understand him and didn't he understand us? Did either of us imagine for an instant that he'd shoot us for all the so-and-so brigadiers in the so-and-so British Army? By this time I began to perceive in the dusk the desolate edges of the bog that was to be their last earthly bed, and, so great a sadness overtook my mind, I could not answer him. We walked along the edge of it in the darkness, and every now and then 'Awkins would call a halt and begin again, just as if he was wound up, about us being chums, and I was in despair that nothing but the cold and open grave made ready for his presence would convince him that we meant it all. But all the same, if you can understand, I didn't want him to be bumped off.

4

At last we saw the unsteady glint of a lantern in the distance and made towards it. Noble was carrying it, and Feeney stood somewhere in the darkness behind, and somehow the picture of the two of them so silent in the boglands was like the pain of death in my heart. Belcher, on recognising Noble, said ''Allo, chum' in his usual peaceable way, but 'Awkins flew at the poor boy immediately, and the dispute began all over again, only that Noble hadn't a word to say for himself, and stood there with the swaying lantern between his gaitered legs.

It was Jeremiah Donovan who did the answering. 'Awkins asked for the twentieth time (for it seemed to haunt his mind) if anybody thought he'd shoot Noble. 'You would,' says Jeremiah Donovan shortly. 'I wouldn't, damn you!' 'You would if you knew you'd be shot for not doing it.' 'I wouldn't, not if I was to be shot twenty times over; he's my chum. And Belcher wouldn't —isn't that right, Belcher?' 'That's right, chum,' says Belcher peaceably. 'Damned if I would. Anyway, who says Noble'd be shot if I wasn't bumped off? What d'you think I'd do if I was in Noble's place and we were out in the middle of a blasted bog?' 'What would you do?' 'I'd go with him wherever he was going. I'd share my last bob with him and stick by 'im through thick and thin.'

'We've had enough of this,' says Jeremiah Donovan, cocking his revolver. 'Is there any message you want to send before I fire?' 'No, there isn't, but . . .' 'Do you want to say your prayers?' 'Awkins came out with a cold-blooded remark that shocked even me and turned to Noble again. 'Listen to me, Noble,' he said. 'You and me are chums. You won't come over to my side, so I'll come over to your side. Is that fair? Just you give me a rifle and I'll go with you wherever you want.'

Nobody answered him.

'Do you understand?' he said. 'I'm through with it all. I'm a deserter or anything else you like, but from this on I'm one of you. Does that prove to you that I mean what I say?' Noble raised his head, but as Donovan began to speak he lowered it again without answering. 'For the last time have you any messages to send?' says Donovan in a cold and excited voice.

'Ah, shut up, you, Donovan; you don't understand me, but these fellows do. They're my chums; they stand by me and I stand by them. We're not the capitalist tools you seem to think us.'

I alone of the crowd saw Donovan raise his Webley to the back of 'Awkins's neck, and as he did so I shut my eyes and tried to say a prayer. 'Awkins had begun to say something else when Donovan let fly, and, as I opened my eyes at the bang, I saw him stagger at the knees and lie out flat at Noble's feet, slowly, and as quiet as a child, with the lantern-light falling sadly upon his lean legs and bright farmer's boots. We all stood very still for a while watching him settle out in the last agony.

Then Belcher quietly takes out a handkerchief, and begins to tie it about his own eyes (for in our excitement we had forgotten to offer the same to 'Awkins), and, seeing it is not big enough, turns and asks for a loan of mine. I give it to him and as he knots the two together he points with his foot at

'Awkins. ' 'E's not quite dead,' he says, 'better give 'im another.' Sure enough 'Awkins's left knee as we see it under the lantern is rising again. I bend down and put my gun to his ear; then, recollecting myself and the company of Belcher, I stand up again with a few hasty words. Belcher understands what is in my mind. 'Give 'im 'is first,' he says. 'I don't mind. Poor bastard, we dunno what's 'appening to 'im now.' As by this time I am beyond all feeling I kneel down again and skilfully give 'Awkins the last shot so as to put him for ever out of pain.

Belcher who is fumbling a bit awkwardly with the handkerchiefs comes out with a laugh when he hears the shot. It is the first time I have heard him laugh, and it sends a shiver down my spine, coming as it does so inappropriately upon the tragic death of his old friend. 'Poor blighter,' he says quietly, 'and last night he was so curious abaout it all. It's very queer, chums, I always think. Naow, 'e knows as much abaout it as they'll ever let 'im know, and last night 'e was all in the dark.'

Donovan helps him to tie the handkerchiefs about his eyes. 'Thanks, chum,' he says. Donovan asks him if there are any messages he would like to send. 'Naow, chum,' he says, 'none for me. If any of you likes to write to 'Awkins's mother you'll find a letter from 'er in 'is pocket. But my missus left me eight years ago. Went away with another fellow and took the kid with her. I likes the feelin' of a 'ome (as you may 'ave noticed) but I couldn't start again after that.'

We stand around like fools now that he can no longer see us. Donovan looks at Noble and Noble shakes his head. Then Donovan raises his Webley again and just at that moment Belcher laughs his queer nervous laugh again. He must think we are talking of him; anyway, Donovan lowers his gun. ' 'Scuse me, chums,' says Belcher, 'I feel I'm talking the 'ell of a lot . . . and so silly . . . abaout me being so 'andy abaout a 'ouse. But this thing come on me so sudden. You'll forgive me, I'm sure.' 'You don't want to say a prayer?' asks Jeremiah Donovan. 'No, chum,' he replies, 'I don't think that'd 'elp. I'm ready if you want to get it over.' 'You understand,' says Jeremiah Donovan, 'it's not so much our doing. It's our duty, so to speak.' Belcher's head is raised like a real blind man's, so that you can only see his nose and chin in the lamplight. 'I never could make out what duty was myself,' he said, 'but I think you're all good lads, if that's what you mean. I'm not complaining.' Noble, with a look of desperation, signals to Donovan, and in a flash Donovan raises his gun and fires. The big man goes over like a sack of meal, and this time there is no need of a second shot.

I don't remember much about the burying, but that it was worse than all the rest, because we had to carry the warm corpses a few yards before we sunk them in the windy bog. It was all mad lonely, with only a bit of lantern between ourselves and the pitch-blackness, and birds hooting and screeching all round disturbed by the guns. Noble had to search 'Awkins first to get the letter from his mother. Then having smoothed all signs of the grave away, Noble and I collected our tools, said good-bye to the others, and went back along the desolate edge of the treacherous bog without a word. We put the tools in the houseen and went into the house. The kitchen was pitch-black and cold, just as we left it, and the old woman was sitting over the hearth telling her beads. We walked past her into the room, and Noble struck a match to light the lamp. Just then she rose quietly and came to the doorway, being not at all so bold or crabbed as usual.

'What did ye do with them?' she says in a sort of whisper, and Noble took such a mortal start the match quenched in his trembling hand. 'What's that?' he asks without turning round. 'I heard ye,' she said. 'What did you hear?' asks Noble, but sure he wouldn't deceive a child the way he said it. 'I heard ye. Do you think I wasn't listening to ye putting the things back in the houseen?' Noble struck another match and this time the lamp lit for him. 'Was that what ye did with them?' she said, and Noble said nothing—after all what could he say?

So then, by God, she fell on her two knees by the door, and began telling her beads, and after a minute or two Noble went on his knees by the fireplace, so I pushed my way out past her, and stood at the door, watching the stars and listening to the damned shrieking of the birds. It is so strange what you feel at such moments, and not to be written afterwards. Noble says he felt he seen everything ten times as big, perceiving nothing around him but the little patch of black bog with the two Englishmen stiffening into it; but with me it was the other way, as though the patch of bog where the two Englishmen were was a thousand miles away from me, and even Noble mumbling just behind me and the old woman and the birds and the bloody stars were all far away, and I was somehow very small and very lonely. And anything that ever happened me after I never felt the same about again.

Edgar Allan Poe (1809–1849)
The Fall of the House of Usher

> Son cœur est un luth suspendu;
> Sitôt qu'on le touche il résonne.
>
> —De Béranger

During the whole of a dull, dark, and soundless day in the autumn of the year, when the clouds hung oppressively low in the heavens, I had been passing alone, on horseback, through a singularly dreary tract of country, and at length found myself, as the shades of the evening drew on, within view of the melancholy House of Usher. I know not how it was—but, with the first glimpse of the building, a sense of insufferable gloom pervaded my spirit. I say insufferable; for the feeling was unrelieved by any of that half-pleasurable, because poetic, sentiment with which the mind usually receives even the sternest natural images of the desolate or terrible. I looked upon the scene before me—upon the mere house, and the simple landscape features of the domain—upon the bleak walls—upon the vacant eye-like windows—upon a few rank sedges—and upon a few white trunks of decayed trees—with an utter depression of soul which I can compare to no earthly sensation more properly than to the after-dream of the reveller upon opium—the bitter lapse into every-day life—the hideous dropping off of the veil. There was an iciness, a sinking, a sickening of the heart—an unredeemed dreariness of thought which no goading of the imagination could torture into aught of the sublime. What was it—I paused to think—what was it that so unnerved me in the contemplation of the House of Usher? It was a mystery all insoluble; nor could I grapple with the shadowy fancies that crowded upon me as I pondered. I was forced to fall back upon the unsatisfactory conclusion, that while, beyond doubt, there *are* combinations of very simple natural objects which have the power of thus affecting us, still the analysis of this power lies among considerations beyond our depth. It was possible, I reflected, that a mere different arrangement of the particulars of the scene, of the details of the picture, would be sufficient to modify, or perhaps to annihilate its capacity for sorrowful impression; and, acting upon this idea, I reined my horse to the precipitous brink of a black and lurid tarn that lay in unruffled lustre by the dwelling, and gazed down—but with a shudder even more thrilling than before—upon the remodelled and inverted images of the gray sedge, and the ghastly tree-stems, and the vacant and eye-like windows.

Nevertheless, in this mansion of gloom I now proposed to myself a sojourn of some weeks. Its proprietor, Roderick Usher, had been one of my boon companions in boyhood; but many years had elapsed since our last meeting. A letter, however, had lately reached me in a distant part of the country—a letter from him—which, in its wildly importunate nature, had admitted of no other than a personal reply. The MS. gave evidence of nervous agitation. The writer spoke of acute bodily illness—of a mental disorder which oppressed him—and of an earnest desire to see me, as his best and indeed his only personal friend, with a view of attempting, by the cheerfulness of my society, some alleviation of his malady. It was the manner in which all this, and much more, was said—it was the apparent *heart* that went with his request—which allowed me no room for hesitation; and I accordingly obeyed forthwith what I still considered a very singular summons.

Although, as boys, we had been even intimate associates, yet I really knew little of my friend. His reserve had been always excessive and habitual. I was aware, however, that his very ancient family had been noted, time out of mind, for a peculiar sensibility of temperament, displaying itself, through long ages, in many works of exalted art, and manifested, of late, in repeated deeds of munificent yet unobtrusive charity, as well as in a passionate devotion to the intricacies, perhaps even more than to the orthodox and easily recognizable beauties, of musical science. I had learned, too, the very re- markable fact, that the stem of the Usher race, all time-honored as it was, had put forth, at no period, any enduring branch; in other words, that the entire family lay in the direct line of descent, and had always, with very trifling and very temporary variation, so lain. It was this deficiency, I considered, while running over in thought the perfect keeping of the character of the premises with the accredited character of the people, and while speculating upon the possible influence which the one, in the long lapse of centuries, might have exercised upon the other—it was this deficiency, perhaps, of collateral issue, and the consequent undeviating transmission, from sire to son, of the patrimony with the name, which had, at length, so identified the two as to merge the original title of the estate in the quaint and equivocal appellation of the "House of Usher"—an appellation which seemed to include, in the minds of the peasantry who used it, both the family and the family mansion.

I have said that the sole effect of my somewhat childish experiment—that of looking down within the tarn—had been to deepen the first singular impression. There can be no doubt that the consciousness of the rapid increase of my superstition—for why should I not so term it?—served mainly to accelerate the increase itself. Such, I have long known, is the paradoxical law of all sentiments having terror as a basis. And it might have been for this reason only, that, when I again uplifted my eyes to the house itself, from its image in the pool, there grew in my mind a strange fancy—a fancy so ridiculous, indeed, that I but mention it to show the vivid force of the sensations which oppressed me. I had so worked upon my imagination as really to believe that about the whole mansion and domain there hung an atmosphere peculiar to themselves and their immediate vicinity—an atmosphere which had no affinity with the air of heaven, but which had reeked up from the decayed trees, and the gray wall, and the silent tarn—a pestilent and mystic vapor, dull, sluggish, faintly discernible, and leaden-hued.

Shaking off from my spirit what *must* have been a dream, I scanned more narrowly the real aspect of the building. Its principal feature seemed to be that of an excessive antiquity. The discoloration of ages had been great. Minute fungi overspread the whole exterior, hanging in a fine tangled web-work from the eaves. Yet all this was apart from any extraordinary dilapidation. No portion of the masonry had fallen; and there appeared to be a wild inconsistency between its still perfect adaptation of parts, and the crumbling condition of the individual stones. In this there was much that reminded me of the specious totality of old wood-work which has rotted for long years in some neglected vault, with no disturbance from the breath of the external air. Beyond this indication of extensive decay, however, the fabric gave little token of instability. Perhaps the eye of a scrutinizing observer might have discovered a barely perceptible fissure, which, extending from the roof of the building in front, made its way down the wall in a zigzag direction, until it became lost in the sullen waters of the tarn.

Noticing these things, I rode over a short causeway to the house. A servant in waiting took my horse, and I entered the Gothic archway of the hall. A valet, of stealthy step, thence conducted me, in silence, through many dark and intricate passages in my progress to the *studio* of his master. Much that I encountered on the way contributed, I know not how, to heighten the vague sentiments of which I have already spoken. While the objects around me— while the carvings of the ceilings, the sombre tapestries of the walls, the ebon blackness of the floors, and the phantasmagoric armorial trophies which rattled as I strode, were but matters to which, or to such as which, I had been accustomed from my infancy—while I hesitated not to acknowledge how familiar was all this—I still wondered to find how unfamiliar were the fancies which ordinary images were stirring up. On one of the staircases, I met the physician of the family. His countenance, I thought, wore a mingled expression of low cunning and perplexity. He accosted me with trepidation and passed on. The valet now threw open a door and ushered me into the presence of his master.

The room in which I found myself was very large and lofty. The windows were long, narrow, and pointed, and at so vast a distance from the black oaken floor as to be altogether inaccessible from within. Feeble gleams of encrimsoned light made their way through the trellissed panes, and served to render sufficiently distinct the more prominent objects around; the eye, however, struggled in vain to reach the remoter angles of the chamber, or the recesses of the vaulted and fretted ceiling. Dark draperies hung upon the walls. The general furniture was profuse, comfortless, antique, and tattered. Many books and musical instruments lay scattered about, but failed to give any vitality to the scene. I felt that I breathed an atmosphere of sorrow. An air of stern, deep, and irredeemable gloom hung over and pervaded all.

Upon my entrance, Usher arose from a sofa on which he had been lying at full length, and greeted me with a vivacious warmth which had much in it, I at first thought, of an overdone cordiality—of the constrained effort of the *ennuyé* man of the world. A glance, however, at his countenance convinced me of his perfect sincerity. We sat down; and for some moments, while he spoke not, I gazed upon him with a feeling half of pity, half of awe. Surely, man had never before so terribly altered, in so brief a period, as had Roderick Usher! It was with difficulty that I could bring myself to admit the identity of the wan being before me with the companion of my early boyhood. Yet the character of his face had been at all times remarkable. A cadaverousness of complexion; an eye large, liquid, and luminous beyond comparison; lips somewhat thin and very pallid but of a surpassingly beautiful curve; a nose of a delicate Hebrew model, but with a breadth of nostril unusual in similar formations; a finely moulded chin, speaking, in its want of prominence, of a want of moral energy; hair of a more than web-like softness and tenuity;—these features, with an inordinate expansion above the regions of the temple, made up altogether a countenance not easily to be forgotten. And now in the mere exaggeration of the prevailing character of these features, and of the expression they were wont to convey, lay so much of change that I doubted to whom I spoke. The now ghastly pallor of the skin, and the now miraculous lustre of the eye, above all things startled and even awed me. The silken hair, too, had been suffered to grow all unheeded, and as, in its wild gossamer texture, it floated rather than fell about the face, I could not, even with effort, connect its Arabesque expression with any idea of simple humanity.

In the manner of my friend I was at once struck with an incoherence—an inconsistency; and I soon found this to arise from a series of feeble and futile struggles to overcome an habitual trepidancy—an excessive nervous agitation. For something of this nature I had indeed been prepared, no less by his letter, than by reminiscences of certain boyish traits, and by conclusions deduced from his peculiar physical confirmation and temperament. His action was alternately vivacious and sullen. His voice varied rapidly from a tremulous indecision (when the animal spirits seemed utterly in abeyance) to that species of energetic concision—that abrupt, weighty, unhurried, and hollow-sounding enunciation—that leaden, self-balanced, and perfectly modulated guttural utterance, which may be observed in the lost drunkard, or the irreclaimable eater of opium, during the periods of his most intense excitement.

It was thus that he spoke of the object of my visit, of his earnest desire to see me, and of the solace he expected me to afford him. He entered, at some length, into what he conceived to be the nature of his malady. It was, he said, a constitutional and a family evil, and one for which he despaired to find a remedy—a mere nervous affection, he immediately added, which would undoubtedly soon pass off. It displayed itself in a host of unnatural sensations. Some of these, as he detailed them, interested and bewildered me; although, perhaps, the terms and the general manner of their narration had their weight. He suffered much from a morbid acuteness of the senses; the most insipid food was alone endurable; he could wear only garments of certain texture; the odors of all flowers were oppressive; his eyes were tortured by even a faint light; and there were but peculiar sounds, and these from stringed instruments, which did not inspire him with horror.

To an anomalous species of terror I found him a bounden slave. "I shall perish," said he, "I *must* perish in this deplorable folly. Thus, thus, and not otherwise, shall I be lost. I dread the events of the future, not in themselves, but in their results. I shudder at the thought of any, even the most trivial, incident, which may operate upon this intolerable agitation of soul. I have, indeed, no abhorrence of danger, except in its absolute effect—in terror. In this unnerved, in this pitiable, condition I feel that the period will sooner or later arrive when I must abandon life and reason together, in some struggle with the grim phantasm, FEAR."

I learned, moreover, at intervals, and through broken and equivocal hints, another singular feature of his mental condition. He was enchained by certain superstitious impressions in regard to the dwelling which he tenanted, and whence, for many years, he had never ventured forth—in regard to an influence whose supposititious force was conveyed in terms too shadowy here to be re-stated—an influence which some peculiarities in the mere form and substance of his family mansion had, by dint of long sufferance, he said, obtained over his spirit—an effect which the *physique* of the gray walls and turrets, and of the dim tarn into which they all looked down, had, at length, brought about upon the *morale* of his existence.

He admitted, however, although with hesitation, that much of the peculiar gloom which thus afflicted him could be traced to a more natural and far more palpable origin—to the severe and long-continued illness—indeed to the evidently approaching dissolution—of a tenderly beloved sister, his sole companion for many long years, his last and only relative on earth. "Her decease," he said, with a bitterness which I can never forget, "would leave him (him, the hopeless and the frail) the last of the ancient race of the Ushers." While he spoke, the lady Madeline (for so was she called) passed through a remote portion of the apartment, and, without having noticed my presence, disappeared. I regarded her with an utter astonishment not unmingled with dread; and yet I found it impossible to account for such feelings. A sensation of stupor oppressed me as my eyes followed her retreating steps. When a door, at length, closed upon her, my glance sought instinctively and eagerly the countenance of the brother; but he had buried his faced in his hands, and I could only perceive that a far more than ordinary wanness had overspread the emaciated fingers through which trickled many passionate tears.

The disease of the lady Madeline had long baffled the skill of her physicians. A settled apathy, a gradual wasting away of the person, and frequent although transient affections of a partially cataleptical character were the unusual diagnosis. Hitherto she had steadily borne up against the pressure of her malady, and had not betaken herself finally to bed; but on the closing in of the evening of my arrival at the house, she succumbed (as her brother told me at night with inexpressible agitation) to the prostrating power of the destroyer; and I learned that the glimpse I had obtained of her person would thus probably be the last I should obtain—that the lady, at least while living, would be seen by me no more.

For several days ensuing, her name was unmentioned by either Usher or myself; and during this period I was busied in earnest endeavors to alleviate the melancholy of my friend. We painted and read together, or I listened, as if in a dream, to the wild improvisations of his speaking guitar. And thus, as a closer and still closer intimacy admitted me more unreservedly into the recesses of his spirit, the more bitterly did I perceive the futility of all attempt at cheering a mind from which darkness, as if an inherent positive quality, poured forth upon all objects of the moral and physical universe in one unceasing radiation of gloom.

I shall ever bear about me a memory of the many solemn hours I thus spent alone with the master of the House of Usher. Yet I should fail in any attempt to convey an idea of the exact character of the studies, or of the occupations, in which he involved me, or led me the way. An excited and highly distempered ideality threw a sulphureous lustre over all. His long improvised dirges will ring forever in my ears. Among other things, I hold painfully in mind a certain singular perversion and amplification of the wild air of the last waltz of Von Weber. From the paintings over which his elaborate fancy brooded, and which grew, touch by touch, into vaguenesses at which I shuddered and more thrillingly, because I shuddered knowing not why—from these paintings (vivid as their images now are before me) I would in vain endeavor to educe more than a small portion which should lie within the compass of merely written words. By the utter simplicity, by the nakedness of his designs, he arrested and overawed attention. If ever mortal painted an idea, that mortal was Roderick Usher. For me at least, in the circumstances then surrounding me, there arose out of the pure abstractions which the hypochondriac contrived to throw upon his canvas, an intensity of intolerable awe, no shadow of which felt I ever yet in the contemplation of the certainly glowing yet too concrete reveries of Fuseli.

One of the phantasmagoric conceptions of my friend, partaking not so rigidly of the spirit of abstraction, may be shadowed forth, although feebly, in words. A small picture presented the interior of an immensely long and rectangular vault or tunnel, with low walls, smooth, white, and without interruption or device. Certain accessory points of the design served well to convey the idea that this excavation lay at an exceeding depth below the surface of the earth. No outlet was observed in any portion of its vast extent, and no torch or other artificial source of light was discernible; yet a flood of intense rays rolled throughout, and bathed the whole in a ghastly and inappropriate splendor.

I have just spoken of that morbid condition of the auditory nerve which rendered all music intolerable to the sufferer, with the exception of certain effects of stringed instruments. It was, perhaps, the narrow limits to which he thus confined himself upon the guitar which gave birth, in great measure, to the fantastic character of his performances. But the fervid *facility* of his *impromptus* could not be so accounted for. They must have been, and were, in the notes, as well as in the words of his wild fantasias (for he not unfrequently accompanied himself with rhymed verbal improvisations), the result of that intense mental collectedness and concentration to which I have previously alluded as observable only in particular moments of the highest artificial excitement. The words of one of these rhapsodies I have easily remembered. I was, perhaps, the more forcibly impressed with it as he gave it, because, in the under or mystic current of its meaning, I fancied that I perceived, and for the first time, a full consciousness on the part of Usher of the tottering of his lofty reason upon her throne. The verses, which were entitled "The Haunted Palace," ran very nearly, if not accurately, thus:—

I.

In the greenest of our valleys,
　By good angels tenanted,
Once a fair and stately palace—
　Radiant palace—reared its head.
In the monarch Thought's dominion—
　It stood there!
Never seraph spread a pinion
　Over fabric half so fair.

II.

Banners yellow, glorious, golden,
　On its roof did float and flow
(This—all this—was in the olden
　Time long ago);
And every gentle air that dallied,
　In that sweet day,
Along the ramparts plumed and pallid,
　A winged odor went away.

III.

Wanderers in that happy valley
   Through two luminous windows saw
Spirits moving musically
   To a lute's well-tunèd law;
Round about a throne, where sitting
   (Porphyrogene!)
In state his glory well befitting,
   The ruler of the realm was seen.

IV.

And all with pearl and ruby glowing
   Was the fair palace door,
Through which came flowing, flowing, flowing
   And sparkling evermore,
A troop of Echoes whose sweet duty
   Was but to sing,
In voices of surpassing beauty,
   The wit and wisdom of their king.

V.

But evil things, in robes of sorrow,
   Assailed the monarch's high estate;
(Ah, let us mourn, for never morrow
   Shall dawn upon him, desolate!)
And, round about his home, the glory
   That blushed and bloomed
Is but a dim-remembered story
   Of the old time entombed.

VI.

And travellers now within that valley,
   Through the red-litten windows see
Vast forms that move fantastically
   To a discordant melody;
While, like a rapid ghastly river,
   Through the pale door;
A hideous throng rush out forever,
   And laugh—but smile no more.

I well remember that suggestions arising from this ballad led us into a train of thought wherein there became manifest an opinion of Usher's which I mention not so much on account of its novelty (for other men have thought thus), as on account of the pertinacity with which he maintained it. This opinion, in its general form, was that of the sentience of all vegetable things. But, in his disordered fancy, the idea had assumed a more daring character, and trespassed, under certain conditions, upon the kingdom of inorganization. I lack words to express the full extent, or the earnest *abandon* of his persuasion. The belief, however, was connected (as I have previously hinted) with the gray stones of the home of his forefathers. The conditions of the sentence had been here, he imagined, fulfilled in the method of collocation of these stones—in the order of their arrangement, as well as in that of the many *fungi* which overspread them, and of the decayed trees which stood around—above all, in the long undisturbed endurance of this arrangement, and in its reduplication in the still waters of the tarn. Its evidence—the evidence of the sentience—was to be seen, he said (and I here started as he spoke), in the gradual yet certain condensation of an atmosphere of their own about the waters and the walls. The result was discoverable, he added, in that silent yet importunate and terrible influence which for centuries had moulded the destinies of his family, and which made *him* what I now saw him—what he was. Such opinions need no comment, and I will make none.

Our books—books which, for years, had formed no small portion of the mental existence of the invalid—were, as might be supposed, in strict keeping with this character of phantasm. We pored together over such works as the "Ververt et Chartreuse" of Gresset; the "Belphegor" of Machiavelli; the "Heaven and Hell" of Swedenborg; the "Subterranean Voyage of Nicholas Klimm" of Holberg; the "Chiromancy" of Robert Flud, of Jean D'Indaginé, and of Dela Chambre; the "Journey into the Blue Distance of Tieck"; and the "City of the Sun of Campanella." One favorite volume was a small octavo edition of the "Directorium Inquisitorium," by the Dominican Eymeric de Gironne; and there were passages in Pomponius Mela, about the old African Satyrs and Œgipans, over which Usher would sit dreaming for hours. His chief delight, however, was found in the perusal of an exceedingly rare and curious book in quarto Gothic—the manual of a forgotten church—the *Vigiliæ Mortuorum secundum Chorum Ecclesiæ Maguntinæ.*

I could not help thinking of the wild ritual of this work, and of its probable influence upon the hypochondriac, when, one evening, having informed me abruptly that the lady Madeline was no more, he stated his intention of preserving her corpse for a fortnight (previously to its final interment), in one of the numerous vaults within the main walls of the building. The worldly reason, however, assigned for this singular proceeding, was one which I did not feel at liberty to dispute. The brother had been led to his resolution (so he told me) by consideration of the unusual character of the malady of the deceased, of certain obtrusive and eager inquiries on the part of her medical men, and of the remote and exposed situation of the burial-ground of the family. I will not deny that when I called to mind the sinister countenance of the person whom I met upon the staircase, on the day of my arrival at the house, I had no desire to oppose what I regarded as at best but a harmless, and by no means an unnatural, precaution.

At the request of Usher, I personally aided him in the arrangements for the temporary entombment. The body having been encoffined, we two alone bore it to its rest. The vault in which we placed it (and which had been so long unopened that our torches, half smothered in its oppressive atmosphere, gave us little opportunity for investigation) was small, damp, and entirely without means of admission for light; lying, at great depth, immediately beneath that portion of the building in which was my own sleeping apartment. It had been used, apparently, in remote feudal times, for the worst purposes of a donjon-keep, and, in later days, as a place of deposit for powder, or some other highly combustible substance, as a portion of its floor, and the whole interior of a long archway through which we reached it, were carefully sheathed with copper. The door, of massive iron, had been, also, similarly protected. Its immense weight caused an unusually sharp, grating sound, as it moved upon its hinges.

Having deposited our mournful burden upon tressels within this region of horror, we partially turned aside the yet unscrewed lid of the coffin, and looked upon the face of the tenant. A striking similitude between the brother and sister now first arrested my attention; and Usher, divining, perhaps, my thoughts, murmured out some few words from which I learned that the deceased and himself had been twins, and that sympathies of a scarcely intelligible nature had always existed between them. Our glances, however, rested not long upon the dead—for we could not regard her unawed. The disease which had thus entombed the lady in the maturity of youth, had left, as usual in all maladies of a strictly cataleptical character, the mockery of a faint blush upon the bosom and the face, and that suspiciously lingering smile upon the lip which is so terrible in death. We replaced and screwed down the lid, and, having secured the door of iron, made our way, with toil, into the scarcely less gloomy apartments of the upper portion of the house.

And now, some days of bitter grief having elapsed, an observable change came over the features of the mental disorder of my friend. His ordinary manner had vanished. His ordinary occupations were neglected or forgotten. He roamed from chamber to chamber with hurried, unequal, and objectless step. The pallor of his countenance had assumed, if possible, a more ghastly hue—but the luminousness of his eye had utterly gone out. The once occasional huskiness of his tone was heard no more; and a tremulous quaver, as if of extreme terror, habitually characterized his utterance. There were times, indeed, when I thought his unceasingly agitated mind was laboring with some oppressive secret, to divulge which he struggled for the necessary courage. At times, again, I was obliged to resolve all into the mere inexplicable vagaries of madness, for I beheld him gazing upon vacancy for long hours, in an attitude of the profoundest attention, as if listening to some imaginary sound. It was no wonder that his condition terrified—that it infected me. I felt creeping upon me, by slow yet certain degrees, the wild influences of his own fantastic yet impressive superstitions.

It was, especially, upon retiring to bed late in the night of the seventh or eighth day after the placing of the lady Madeline within the donjon, that I experienced the full power of such feelings. Sleep came not near my couch—while the hours waned and waned away. I struggled to reason off the nervousness which had dominion over me. I endeavored to believe that much, if not all of what I felt, was due to the bewildering influence of the gloomy furniture of the room—of the dark and tattered draperies, which, tortured into motion by the breath of a rising tempest, swayed fitfully to and fro upon the walls, and rustled uneasily about the decorations of the bed. But my efforts were fruitless. An irrepressible tremor gradually pervaded my frame; and, at length, there sat upon my very heart an incubus of utterly causeless alarm. Shaking this off with a gasp and a struggle, I uplifted myself upon the pillows, and, peering earnestly within the intense darkness of the chamber, hearkened—I know not why, except that an instinctive spirit prompted me—to certain low and indefinite sounds which came, through the pauses of the storm, at long intervals, I knew not whence. Overpowered by an intense sentiment of horror, unaccountable yet unendurable, I threw on my clothes with haste (for I felt that I should sleep no more during the night), and endeavored to arouse myself from the pitiable condition into which I had fallen, by pacing rapidly to and fro through the apartment.

I had taken but few turns in this manner, when a light step on an adjoining staircase arrested my attention. I presently recognized it as that of Usher. In an instant afterward he rapped, with a gentle touch, at my door, and entered, bearing a lamp. His countenance was, as usual, cadaverously wan—but, moreover, there was a species of mad hilarity in his eyes—an evidently restrained *hysteria* in his whole demeanor. His air appalled me—but any thing was preferable to the solitude which I had so long endured, and I even welcomed his presence as a relief.

"And you have not seen it?" he said abruptly, after having stared about him for some moments in silence—"you have not then seen it?—but, stay! you shall." Thus speaking, and having carefully shaded his lamp, he hurried to one of the casements, and threw it freely open to the storm.

The impetuous fury of the entering gust nearly lifted us from our feet. It was, indeed, a tempestuous yet sternly beautiful night, and one wildly singular in its terror and its beauty. A whirlwind had apparently collected its force in our vicinity; for there were frequent and violent alterations in the direction of the wind; and the exceeding density of the clouds (which hung so low as to press upon the turrets of the house) did not prevent our perceiving the life-like velocity with which they flew careering from all points against each other, without passing away into the distance. I say that even their exceeding density did not prevent our perceiving this—yet we had no glimpse of the moon or stars, nor was there any flashing forth of the lightning. But the under surfaces of the huge masses of agitated vapor, as well as all terrestial objects immediately around us, were glowing in the unnatural light of a faintly luminous and distinctly visible gaseous exhalation which hung about and enshrouded the mansion.

"You must not—you shall not behold this!" said I, shuddering, to Usher, as I led him, with a gentle violence, from the window to a seat. "These appearances, which bewilder you, are merely electrical phenomena not uncommon—or it may be that they have their ghastly origin in the rank miasma of the tarn. Let us close this casement;—the air is chilling and dangerous to your frame. Here is one of your favorite romances. I will read, and you shall listen:—and so we will pass away this terrible night together."

The antique volume which I had taken up was the "Mad Trist" of Sir Launcelot Canning; but I had called it a favorite of Usher's more in sad jest that in earnest; for, in truth, there is little in its uncouth and unimaginative prolixity which could have had interest for the lofty and spiritual ideality of my friend. It was, however, the only book immediately at hand; and I indulged a vague hope that the excitement which now agitated the hypochondriac, might find relief (for the history of mental disorder is full of similar anomalies) even in the extremeness of the folly which I should read. Could I have judged, indeed, by the wild overstrained air of vivacity with which he hearkened, or apparently hearkened, to the words of the tale, I might well have congratulated myself upon the success of my design.

I had arrived at that well-known portion of the story where Ethelred, the hero of the Trist, having sought in vain for peaceable admission into the dwelling of the hermit, proceeds to make good an entrance by force. Here, it will be remembered, the words of the narrative run thus:

"And Ethelred, who was by nature of a doughty heart, and who was now mighty withal, on account of the powerfulness of the wine which he had drunken, waited no longer to hold parley with the hermit, who, in sooth, was of an obstinate and maliceful turn, but, feeling the rain upon his shoulders, and fearing the rising of the tempest, uplifted his mace outright, and, with blows, made quickly room in the plankings of the door for his gauntleted hand; and now pulling therewith sturdily, he so cracked, and ripped, and tore all asunder, that the noise of the dry and hollow-sounding wood alarumed and reverberated throughout the forest."

At the termination of this sentence I started and, for a moment, paused; for it appeared to me (although I at once concluded that my excited fancy had deceived me)—it appeared to me that, from some very remote portion of the mansion, there came, indistinctly to my ears, what might have been, in its exact similarity of character, the echo (but a stifled and dull one certainly) of the very cracking and ripping sound which Sir Launcelot had so particularly described. It was, beyond doubt, the coincidence alone which had arrested my attention; for, amid the rattling of the sashes of the casements, and the ordinary commingled noises of the still increasing storm, the sound, in itself, had nothing, surely, which should have interested or disturbed me. I continued the story:

"But the good champion Ethelred, now entering within the door, was sore enraged and amazed to perceive no signal of the maliceful hermit; but, in the stead thereof, a dragon of a scaly and prodigious demeanor, and of a fiery tongue, which sate in guard before a palace of gold, with a floor of silver; and upon the wall there hung a shield of shining brass with this legend enwritten—

Who entereth herein, a conqueror hath bin;
Who slayeth the dragon, the shield he shall win.

And Ethelred uplifted his mace, and struck upon the head of the dragon, which fell before him, and gave up his pesty breath, with a shriek so horrid and harsh, and withal so piercing, that Ethelred had fain to close his ears with his hands against the dreadful noise of it, the like whereof was never before heard."

Here again I paused abruptly, and now with a feeling of wild amazement—for there could be no doubt whatever that, in this instance, I did actually hear (although from what direction it proceeded I found it impossible to say) a low and apparently distant, but harsh, protracted, and most unusual screaming or grating sound—the exact counterpart of what my fancy had already conjured up for the dragon's unnatural shriek as described by the romancer.

Oppressed, as I certainly was, upon the occurrence of this second and most extraordinary coincidence, by a thousand conflicting sensations, in which wonder and extreme terror were predominant, I still retained sufficient presence of mind to avoid exciting, by any observation, the sensitive nervousness of my companion. I was by no means certain that he had noticed the sounds in question; although, assuredly, a strange alteration had, during the last few minutes, taken place in his demeanor. From a position fronting my own, he had gradually brought round his chair, so as to sit with his face to the door of the chamber; and thus I could but partially perceive his features, although I saw that his lips trembled as if he were murmuring inaudibly. His head had dropped upon his breast—yet I knew that he was not asleep, from the wide and rigid opening of the eye as I caught a glance of it in profile. The motion of his body, too, was at variance with this idea—for he rocked from side to side with a gentle yet constant and uniform sway. Having rapidly taken notice of all this, I resumed the narrative of Sir Launcelot, which thus proceeded:

"And now, the champion, having escaped from the terrible fury of the dragon, bethinking himself of the brazen shield, and of the breaking up of the enchantment which was upon it, removed the carcass from out of the way before him, and approached valorously over the silver pavement of the castle to where the shield was upon the wall; which in sooth tarried not for his full coming, but fell down at his feet upon the silver floor, with a mighty great and terrible ringing sound."

No sooner had these syllables passed my lips, than—as if a shield of brass had indeed, at the moment, fallen heavily upon a floor of silver—I became aware of a distinct, hollow, metallic, and clangorous, yet apparently muffled, reverberation. Completely unnerved, I leaped to my feet; but the measured rocking movement of Usher was undisturbed. I rushed to the chair in which he sat. His eyes were bent fixedly before him, and throughout his whole countenance there reigned a stony rigidity. But, as I placed my hand upon his shoulder, there came a strong shudder over his whole person; a sickly smile quivered about his lips; and I saw that he spoke in a low, hurried, and gibbering murmur, as if unconscious of my presence. Bending closely over him, I at length drank in the hideous import of his words.

"Now hear it?—yes, I hear it, and *have* heard it. Long—long—long— many minutes, many hours, many days, have I heard it—yet I dared not— oh, pity me, miserable wretch that I am!—I dared not— I *dared* not speak! *We have put her living in the tomb!* Said I not that my senses were acute? I *now* tell you that I heard her first feeble movements in the hollow coffin, I heard them—many, many days ago—yet I dared not—*I dared not speak!* And now—to-night—Ethelred—ha! ha!—the breaking of the hermit's door, and the death-cry of the dragon, and the clangor of the shield—say, rather, the rending of her coffin, and the grating of the iron hinges of her prison, and her struggles within the coppered archway of the vault! Oh! whither shall I fly? Will she not be here anon? Is she not hurrying to upbraid me for my haste? Have I not heard her footstep on the stair? Do I not distinguish that heavy and horrible beating of her heart? Madman!"—here he sprang furiously to his feet, and shrieked out his syllables, as if in the effort he were giving up his soul—"*Madman! I tell you that she now stands without the door!*"

As if in the superhuman energy of his utterance there had been found the potency of a spell, the huge antique panels to which the speaker pointed threw slowly back, upon the instant, their ponderous and ebony jaws. It was the work of the rushing gust—but then without those doors there *did* stand the lofty and enshrouded figure of the lady Madeline of Usher. There was blood upon her white robes, and the evidence of some bitter struggle upon every portion of her emaciated frame. For a moment she remained trembling and reeling to and fro upon the threshold—then, with a low moaning cry, fell heavily inward upon the person of her brother, and in her violent and now final death-agonies, bore him to the floor a corpse, and a victim to the terrors he had anticipated.

From that chamber, and from that mansion, I fled aghast. The storm was still abroad in all its wrath as I found myself crossing the old causeway. Suddenly there shot along the path a wild light, and I turned to see whence a gleam so unusual could have issued; for the vast house and its shadows were alone behind me. The radiance was that of the full, setting, and blood-red moon, which now shone vividly through that once barely discernible fissure, of which I have before spoken as extending from the roof of the building, in a zigzag direction, to the base. While I gazed, this fissure rapidly widened— there came a fierce breath of the whirlwind—the entire orb of the satellite burst at once upon my sight—my brain reeled as I saw the mighty walls rushing asunder—there was a long tumultuous shouting sound like the voice of a thousand waters—and the deep and dank tarn at my feet closed sullenly and silently over the fragments of the "*House of Usher.*"

QUESTIONS

1. What might our reactions be to "The Blue Hotel" if it were told from the perspective of the Easterner? Could the story gain any greater force if such a major change were made?

2. What new elements in our reaction to "The Use of Force" would be introduced if, in a brief aside, the narrator were to disclose that he had always nourished a quiet dislike for children?

3. As you read "The Killers," do you feel that Hemingway would have weakened, or strengthened, the story if the narrator had provided an explicit description of Nick's reaction to Ole Andreson's passive statement, "There ain't anything to do"? Nick seems at first to have no reaction to the statement. Why not? Does the narrative perspective somehow limit our understanding of Nick?

4. In "A Sense of Shelter," what do you know about Mary Landis? How do you know it? Do you feel that the picture drawn of her is a trustworthy one? Why or why not? How can you go about judging if William's perceptions of her make sense?

5. Can you imagine how another writer, for example Hemingway, might go about telling the story in "The Fall of the House of Usher"? What elements crucial to Poe's sensibility would be surrendered? Might anything be gained?

6. Rewrite, in your own mind, "Guests of the Nation" in third person narration. What kind of a story would it then be? As a story composed in the first person, what are its most important subjects of attention? As third person narration, what elements of the story would probably elicit your attention?

THEME

The *theme* of any story might seem to be its most important and obvious element. We do catch ourselves, after having read a story, immediately asking: "What was this all about?" Or, if a friend enthusiastically recommends that we read something, we expect him to say: "It's a really wonderful story about . . . ." And he will go on to say that it is about someone falling in love, or being crushed in defeat, or getting revenge, or acting courageously.

Yet, when we think more exactly about this, we know our curiosity isn't going to be satisfied if we learn just what the *subject* of a story is. The subject could involve love, or defeat, or revenge. But what we find ourselves asking, once we define the subject, is: To what *use* is this subject being put? What is *made* of it? Once we grasp the fact that our minds do work this way, we know that what we are ultimately interested in is if there is some *idea* or *thesis* controlling the story.

For such a controlling idea to do its work well, it has to make its effect on every part of the story, both large and small. Part of the attractiveness and strength of short stories is that they are not what Henry James thought certain novels were—"loose and baggy monsters." They are shaped in such a way that digressions and side issues are stripped from them. Left exposed to view is only the essential action itself, an action governed by the theme. This theme need not be dramatically announced at the outset, or at the conclusion, or even at all. But it is nonetheless present, giving unity to the story and reassuring the reader that he has encountered something more than a chronicle of events or a mere collection of descriptive passages. Both events and description are governed by the values of the writer and by his conception of how the world—at least his part of it—works.

This does not mean, however, that the theme of a story can effortlessly be translated into a handy one- or two-sentence slogan. Fiction is not a work of philosophy, history, or sociology. We do not expect, or want, a set of schematic ideas presented in an expository style. If you attempt to paraphrase the meaning of any story, even one whose implications seem unmistakably clear to you, something odd will happen. The theme that has seemed so complex in context will suddenly seem utterly flat or commonplace: "All men are brothers" or "Guilt is a collective sin" or something like that. Once separated from the rich and unique environment of a memorable short story, a theme starts looking like just another platitudinous idea or notion, or, even worse, the sort of banal formulation found inside fortune cookies. Since most ideas, as ideas, can be conquered by better or bigger ideas, the exposed theme of almost any story can be made to appear quite vulnerable, or even silly.

This danger does not seem to have bothered short-story writers. Few of them are first preoccupied with a theme, seeking thereafter to put it into a story. Not being philosophers or formal social thinkers, their designs do not begin with abstractions. Instead, the authors might begin with an old-fashioned yarn, or with the picture of an event in their minds, or with the startling complexities of a certain human situation worrying them. Whatever the point of origin, however, a short-story writer will, if successful, allow his impulses and his craftsmanship to be guided by the power of a theme. The result will be a residue that remains after the excitement of reading the story has faded, a resonance that gives the events that have been narrated a continuing weight and relevance.

One additional observation is in order: certain themes can inform a great many stories. When any such theme is extracted from stories that are otherwise apparently dissimilar, the reader should not conclude that the stories are essentially the same. They are not. The character of stories is not given primary definition by thematic considerations. (Many writers have been surprised by the themes ingenious readers have discovered in their work.) Other considerations we have already mentioned, such as plot and character and point of view, probably have a combined effect more powerful than that exerted by theme alone. Theme is crucial; it is unmistakable, but it is not wholly decisive in making discriminations among stories.

In both Nathaniel Hawthorne's "My Kinsman, Major Molineux" and in Philip Roth's "The Conversion of the Jews" the theme of a young person's struggle with adult authority makes itself felt. A reader would be right in thinking that Hawthorne and Roth have both recognized the power of this fundamental relationship and all its associated problems. The kinsman in the one story and the rabbi in the other both represent the kind of authority that is at first absolutely imposing and then becomes oddly vulnerable. In two strikingly different idioms, one of colonial New England and the other of modern urban life, the authors expose us to the recurring drama of a young man's self-assertion against a community of knowledge, mystery, and ritual practice. The world of adults appears at first a conspiracy under whose rule the young are made to suffer in fumbling ignorance. But in time the tables are turned. What was once implacable becomes weak. The kinsman, a symbol of aloof and unattainable majesty, is reduced: "mighty no more, but majestic still in his agony." The rabbi, a mighty figure of learning and doctrine, is forced to fall to his knees, "exhausted, and with his hands curled together in front of his chest like a little dome." Characters who once suffered under the weight of the adult world now feel free to move. One is told that he "may rise in the world without the help of your kinsman." In Roth's story the other feels perfectly secure in falling freely "into the center of the yellow net" that guarantees his safety.

A common thematic consideration is very strong in the two stories. It would be impossible to talk about "My Kinsman" or "The Conversion of the Jews" without discussing this theme. At the same time, it would be impossible to reproduce the stories were one to be told nothing more than the theme. Another way of putting this fundamental proposition about the theme of a short story is to say that theme is a *necessary*, but not a *sufficient*, component of a story's existence. Theme is, in a sense, one of the extra dividends a sophisticated reader draws out of a fictional work.

In reading the stories in this book, you might find some profit and pleasure in perceiving how thematic considerations are treated by the various authors. Specifically, you might wish to study how *explicitly* the themes are registered. Are they ever flatly stated? Or is the art of thematic statement an art of hints and suggestions? How much effort is asked of the reader in making inferences about a buried theme? Another line of inquiry is to examine the point in the story at which you feel the theme emerges. Can that emergence come early in the story, or is it likely to be an element of the story's conclusion? Another question to consider is the range of themes in fiction. Is there a rich variety of themes, all rather distinct, or is there only a small family of themes, each member of that family put vigorously to work by a wide variety of authors? And a general question useful to ask is if the themes you discover can be classified: Are there "moral," "political," "historical," or "social" themes? What other types of themes strike you as present in the stories included in this anthology?

Nathaniel Hawthorne (1804–1864)
My Kinsman, Major Molineux

After the kings of Great Britain had assumed the right of appointing the colonial governors, the measures of the latter seldom met with the ready and general approbation which had been paid to those of their predecessors, under the original charters. The people looked with most jealous scrutiny to the exercise of power which did not emanate from themselves, and they usually rewarded their rulers with slender gratitude for the compliances by which, in softening their instructions from beyond the sea, they had incurred the reprehension of those who gave them. The annals of Massachusetts Bay will inform us, that of six governors in the space of about forty years from the surrender of the old charter, under James II., two were imprisoned by a popular insurrection; a third, as Hutchinson inclines to believe, was driven from the province by the whizzing of a musket-ball; a fourth, in the opinion of the same historian, was hastened to his grave by continual bickerings with the House of Representatives; and the remaining two, as well as their successors, till the Revolution, were favored with few and brief intervals of peaceful sway. The inferior members of the court party, in times of high political excitement, led scarcely a more desirable life. These remarks may serve as a preface to the following adventures, which chanced upon a summer night, not far from a hundred years ago. The reader, in order to avoid a long and dry detail of colonial affairs, is requested to dispense with an account of the train of circumstances that had caused much temporary inflammation of the popular mind.

It was near nine o'clock of a moonlight evening, when a boat crossed the ferry with a single passenger, who had obtained his conveyance at that unusual hour by the promise of an extra fare. While he stood on the landing-place, searching in either pocket for the means of fulfilling his agreement, the ferryman lifted a lantern, by the aid of which, and the newly risen moon, he took a very accurate survey of the stranger's figure. He was a youth of barely eighteen years, evidently country-bred, and now, as it should seem, upon his first visit to town. He was clad in a coarse gray coat, well worn, but in excellent repair; his under garments were durably constructed of leather, and fitted tight to a pair of serviceable and well-shaped limbs; his stockings of blue yarn were the incontrovertible work of a mother or a sister; and on his head was a three-cornered hat, which in its better days had perhaps sheltered the graver brow of the lad's father. Under his left arm was a heavy cudgel formed of an oak sapling, and retaining a part of the hardened root; and his equipment was completed by a wallet, not so abundantly stocked as to incommode the vigorous shoulders on which it hung. Brown, curly hair, well-shaped features, and bright, cheerful eyes were nature's gifts, and worth all that art could have done for his adornment.

The youth, one of whose names was Robin, finally drew from his pocket the half of a little province bill of five shillings, which, in the depreciation of that sort of currency, did but satisfy the ferryman's demand, with the surplus of a sexangular piece of parchment, valued at three pence. He then walked forward into the town, with as light a step as if his day's journey had not already exceeded thirty miles, and with as eager an eye as if he were entering London city, instead of the little metropolis of a New England colony. Before Robin had proceeded far, however, it occurred to him that he knew not whither to direct his steps; so he paused, and looked up and down the narrow street, scrutinizing the small and mean wooden buildings that were scattered on either side.

"This low hovel cannot be my kinsman's dwelling," thought he, "nor yonder old house, where the moonlight enters at the broken casement; and truly I see none hereabouts that might be worthy of him. It would have been wise to inquire my way of the ferryman, and doubtless he would have gone with me, and earned a shilling from the Major for his pains. But the next man I meet will do as well."

He resumed his walk, and was glad to perceive that the street now became wider, and the houses more respectable in their appearance. He soon discerned a figure moving on moderately in advance, and hastened his steps to overtake it. As Robin drew nigh, he saw that the passenger was a man in years, with a full periwig of gray hair, a wide-skirted coat of dark cloth, and silk stockings rolled above his knees. He carried a long and polished cane, which he struck down perpendicularly before him at every step; and at regular intervals he uttered two successive hems, of a peculiarly solemn and sepulchral intonation. Having made these observations, Robin laid hold of the skirt of the old man's coat, just when the light from the open door and windows of a barber's shop fell upon both their figures.

"Good evening to you," honored sir, said he, making a low bow, and still retaining his hold of the skirt. "I pray you tell me whereabouts is the dwelling of my kinsman, Major Molineux."

The youth's question was uttered very loudly; and one of the barbers, whose razor was descending on a well-soaped chin, and another who was dressing a Ramillies wig, left their occupations, and came to the door. The citizen, in the mean time, turned a long-favored countenance upon Robin, and answered him in a tone of excessive anger and annoyance. His two sepulchral hems, however, broke into the very centre of his rebuke, with most singular effect, like a thought of the cold grave obtruding among wrathful passions.

"Let go my garment, fellow! I tell you, I know not the man you speak of. What! I have authority, I have—hem, hem—authority; and if this be the respect you show for your betters, your feet shall be brought acquainted with the stocks by daylight, tomorrow morning!"

Robin released the old man's skirt, and hastened away, pursued by an ill-mannered roar of laughter from the barber's shop. He was at first considerably surprised by the result of his question, but, being a shrewd youth, soon thought himself able to account for the mystery.

"This is some country representative," was his conclusion, "who has never seen the inside of my kinsman's door, and lacks the breeding to answer a stranger civilly. The man is old, or verily—I might be tempted to turn back and smite him on the nose. Ah, Robin, Robin! even the barber's boys laugh at you for choosing such a guide! You will be wiser in time, friend Robin."

He now became entangled in a succession of crooked and narrow streets, which crossed each other, and meandered at no great distance from the water-side. The smell of tar was obvious to his nostrils, the masts of vessels pierced the moonlight above the tops of the buildings, and the numerous signs, which Robin paused to read, informed him that he was near the centre of business. But the streets were empty, the shops were closed, and lights were visible only in the second stories of a few dwelling-houses. At length, on the corner of a narrow lane, through which he was passing, he beheld the broad countenance of a British hero swinging before the door of an inn, whence proceeded the voices of many guests. The casement of one of the lower windows was thrown back, and a very thin curtain permitted Robin to distinguish a party at supper, round a well-furnished table. The fragrance of the good cheer steamed forth into the outer air, and the youth could not fail to recollect that the last remnant of his travelling stock of provision had yielded to his morning appetite, and that noon had found and left him dinnerless.

"Oh, that a parchment three-penny might give me a right to sit down at yonder table!" said Robin, with a sigh. "But the Major will make me welcome to the best of his victuals; so I will even step boldly in, and inquire my way to his dwelling."

He entered the tavern, and was guided by the murmur of voices and the fumes of tobacco to the public-room. It was a long and low apartment, with oaken walls, grown dark in the continual smoke, and a floor which was thickly sanded, but of no immaculate purity. A number of persons—the larger part of whom appeared to be mariners, or in some way connected with the sea—occupied the wooden benches, or leather-bottomed chairs, conversing on various matters, and occasionally lending their attention to some topic of general interest. Three or four little groups were draining as many bowls of punch, which the West India trade had long since made a familiar drink in the colony. Others, who had the appearance of men who lived by regular and laborious handicraft, preferred the insulated bliss of an unshared potation, and became more taciturn under its influence. Nearly all, in short, evinced a predilection for the Good Creature in some of its various shapes, for this is a vice to which, as Fast Day sermons of a hundred years ago will testify, we have a long heriditary claim. The only guests to whom Robin's sympathies inclined him were two or three sheepish countrymen, who were using the inn somewhat after the fashion of a Turkish caravansary; they had gotten themselves into the darkest corner of the room, and heedless of the Nicotian atmosphere, were supping on the bread of their own ovens, and the bacon cured in their own chimney-smoke. But though Robin felt a sort of brotherhood with these strangers, his eyes were attracted from them to a person who stood near the door, holding whispered conversation with a group of ill-dressed associates. His features were separately striking almost to grotesqueness, and the whole face left a deep impression on the memory. The forehead bulged out into a double prominence, with a vale between; the nose came boldly forth in an irregular curve, and its bridge was of more than a finger's breadth; the eyebrows were deep and shaggy, and the eyes glowed beneath them like fire in a cave.

While Robin deliberated of whom to inquire respecting his kinsman's dwelling, he was accosted by the innkeeper, a little man in a stained white apron, who had come to pay his professional welcome to the stranger. Being in the second generation from a French Protestant, he seemed to have inherited the courtesy of his parent nation; but no variety of circumstances was ever known to change his voice from the one shrill note in which he now addressed Robin.

"From the country, I presume, sir?" said he, with a profound bow. "Beg leave to congratulate you on your arrival, and trust you intend a long stay with us. Fine town here, sir, beautiful buildings, and much that may interest a stranger. May I hope for the honor of your commands in respect to supper?"

"The man sees a family likeness! the rogue has guessed that I am related to the Major!" thought Robin, who had hitherto experienced little superfluous civility.

All eyes were now turned on the country lad, standing at the door, in his worn three-cornered hat, gray coat, leather breeches, and blue yarn stockings, leaning on an oaken cudgel, and bearing a wallet on his back.

Robin replied to the courteous innkeeper, with such an assumption of confidence as befitted the Major's relative. "My honest friend," he said, "I shall make it a point to patronize your house on some occasion, when"—here he could not help lowering his voice—"when I may have more than a parchment three-pence in my pocket. My present business," continued he, speaking with lofty confidence, "is merely to inquire my way to the dwelling of my kinsman, Major Molineux."

There was a sudden and general movement in the room, which Robin interpreted as expressing the eagerness of each individual to become his guide. But the innkeeper turned his eyes to a written paper on the wall, which he read, or seemed to read, with occasional recurrences to the young man's figure.

"What have we here?" said he, breaking his speech into little dry fragments. "'Left the house of the subscriber, bounden servant, Hezekiah Mudge,—had on, when he went away, gray coat, leather breeches, master's third-best hat. One pound currency reward to whosoever shall lodge him in any jail of the province.' Better trudge, boy; better trudge!"

Robin had begun to draw his hand towards the lighter end of the oak cudgel, but a strange hostility in every countenance induced him to relinquish his purpose of breaking the courteous innkeeper's head. As he turned to leave the room, he encountered a sneering glance from the bold-featured personage whom he had before noticed; and no sooner was he beyond the door, than he heard a general laugh, in which the innkeeper's voice might be distinguished, like the dropping of small stones into a kettle.

"Now, is it not strange," thought Robin, with his usual shrewdness,—"is it not strange that the confession of an empty pocket should outweigh the name of my kinsman, Major Molineux? Oh, if I had one of those grinning rascals in the woods, where I and my oak sapling grew up together, I would teach him that my arm is heavy though my purse be light!"

On turning the corner of the narrow lane, Robin found himself in a spacious street, with an unbroken line of lofty houses on each side, and a steepled building at the upper end, whence the ringing of a bell announced the hour of nine. The light of the moon, and the lamps from the numerous shop-windows, discovered people promenading on the pavement, and amongst them Robin hoped to recognize his hitherto inscrutable relative. The result of his former inquiries made him unwilling to hazard another, in a scene of such publicity, and he determined to walk slowly and silently up the street, thrusting his face close to that of every elderly gentleman, in search of the Major's lineaments. In his progress, Robin encountered many gay and gallant figures. Embroidered garments of showy colors, enormous periwigs, gold-laced hats, and silver-hilted swords glided past him and dazzled his optics. Travelled youths, imitators of the European fine gentlemen of the period, trod jauntily along, half dancing to the fashionable tunes which they hummed, and making poor Robin ashamed of his quiet and natural gait. At length, after many pauses to examine the gorgeous display of goods in the shop-windows, and after suffering some rebukes for the impertinence of his scrutiny into people's faces, the Major's kinsman found himself near the steepled building, still unsuccessful in his search. As yet, however, he had seen only one side of the thronged street; so Robin crossed, and continued the same sort of inquisition down the opposite pavement, with stronger hopes than the philosopher seeking an honest man, but with no better fortune. He had arrived about midway towards the lower end, from which his course began, when he overheard the approach of some one who struck down a cane on the flag-stones at every step, uttering, at regular intervals, two sepulchral hems.

"Mercy on us!" quoth Robin, recognizing the sound.

Turning a corner, which chanced to be close at his right hand, he hastened to pursue his researches in some other part of the town. His patience now was wearing low, and he seemed to feel more fatigue from his rambles since he crossed the ferry, than from his journey of several days on the other side. Hunger also pleaded loudly within him, and Robin began to balance the propriety of demanding, violently, and with lifted cudgel, the necessary guidance from the first solitary passenger whom he should meet. While a resolution to this effect was gaining strength, he entered a street of mean appearance, on either side of which a row of ill-built houses was straggling towards the harbor. The moonlight fell upon no passenger along the whole extent, but in the third domicile which Robin passed there was a half-opened door, and his keen glance detected a woman's garment within.

"My luck may be better here," said he to himself.

Accordingly, he approached the door, and beheld it shut closer as he did so; yet an open space remained, sufficing for the fair occupant to observe the stranger, without a corresponding display on her part. All that Robin could discern was a strip of scarlet petticoat, and the occasional sparkle of an eye, as if the moonbeams were trembling on some bright thing.

"Pretty mistress," for I may call her so with a good conscience, thought the shrewd youth, since I know nothing to the contrary,—"my sweet pretty mistress, will you be kind enough to tell me whereabouts I must seek the dwelling of my kinsman, Major Molineux?"

Robin's voice was plaintive and winning, and the female, seeing nothing to be shunned in the handsome country youth, thrust open the door, and came forth into the moonlight. She was a dainty little figure, with a white neck, round arms, and a slender waist, at the extremity of which her scarlet petticoat jutted out over a hoop, as if she were standing in a balloon. Moreover, her face was oval and pretty, her hair dark beneath the little cap, and her bright eyes possessed a sly freedom, which triumphed over those of Robin.

"Major Molineux dwells here," said this fair woman.

Now, her voice was the sweetest Robin had heard that night, the airy counterpart of a stream of melted silver; yet he could not help doubting whether that sweet voice spoke Gospel truth. He looked up and down the mean street, and then surveyed the house before which they stood. It was a small, dark edifice of two stories, the second of which projected over the lower floor, and the front apartment had the aspect of a shop for petty commodities.

"Now, truly, I am in luck," replied Robin, cunningly, "and so indeed is my kinsman, the Major, in having so pretty a housekeeper. But I prithee trouble him to step to the door; I will deliver him a message from his friends in the country, and then go back to my lodgings at the inn."

"Nay, the Major has been abed this hour or more," said the lady of the scarlet petticoat; "and it would be to little purpose to disturb him to-night, seeing his evening draught was of the strongest. But he is a kind-hearted man, and it would be as much as my life's worth to let a kinsman of his turn away from the door. You are the good old gentleman's very picture, and I could swear that was his rainy-weather hat. Also he has garments very much resembling those leather small-clothes. But come in, I pray, for I bid you hearty welcome in his name."

So saying, the fair and hospitable dame took our hero by the hand; and the touch was light, and the force was gentleness, and though Robin read in her eyes what he did not hear in her words, yet the slender-waisted woman in the scarlet petticoat proved stronger than the athletic country youth. She had drawn his half-willing footsteps nearly to the threshold, when the opening of a door in the neighborhood startled the Major's housekeeper, and, leaving the Major's kinsman, she vanished speedily into her own domicile. A heavy yawn preceded the appearance of a man, who, like the Moonshine of Pyramus and Thisbe, carried a lantern, needlessly aiding his sister luminary in the heavens. As he walked sleepily up the street, he turned his broad, dull face on Robin, and displayed a long staff, spiked at the end.

"Home, vagabond, home!" said the watchman, in accents that seemed to fall asleep as soon as they were uttered. "Home, or we'll set you in the stocks by peep of day!"

"This is the second hint of the kind," thought Robin. "I wish they would end my difficulties, by setting me there to-night."

Nevertheless, the youth felt an instinctive antipathy towards the guardian of midnight order, which at first prevented him from asking his usual question. But just when the man was about to vanish behind the corner, Robin resolved not to lose the opportunity, and shouted lustily after him,—

"I say, friend! will you guide me to the house of my kinsman, Major Molineux?"

The watchman made no reply, but turned the corner and was gone; yet Robin seemed to hear the sound of drowsy laughter stealing along the solitary street. At that moment, also, a pleasant titter saluted him from the open window above his head; he looked up, and caught the sparkle of a saucy eye; a round arm beckoned to him, and next he heard light footsteps descending the staircase within. But Robin, being of the household of a New England clergyman, was a good youth, as well as a shrewd one; so he resisted temptation, and fled away.

He now roamed desperately, and at random, through the town, almost ready to believe that a spell was on him, like that by which a wizard of his country had once kept three pursuers wandering, a whole winter night, within twenty paces of the cottage which they sought. The streets lay before him, strange and desolate, and the lights were extinguished in almost every house. Twice, however, little parties of men, among whom Robin distinguished individuals in outlandish attire, came hurrying along; but, though on both occasions they paused to address him, such intercourse did not at all enlighten his perplexity. They did but utter a few words in some language of which Robin knew nothing, and perceiving his inability to answer, bestowed a curse upon him in plain English and hastened away. Finally, the lad determined to knock at the door of every mansion that might appear worthy to be occupied by his kinsman, trusting that perseverance would overcome the fatality that had hitherto thwarted him. Firm in this resolve, he was passing beneath the walls of a church, which formed the corner of two streets, when, as he turned into the shade of its steeple, he encountered a bulky stranger, muffled in a cloak. The man was proceeding with the speed of earnest business, but Robin planted himself full before him, holding the oak cudgel with both hands across his body as a bar to further passage.

"Halt, honest man, and answer me a question," said he, very resolutely.

"Tell me, this instant, whereabouts is the dwelling of my kinsman, Major Molineux!"

"Keep your tongue between your teeth, fool, and let me pass!" said a deep, gruff voice, which Robin partly remembered. "Let me pass, I say, or I'll strike you to the earth!"

"No, no, neighbor!" cried Robin, flourishing his cudgel, and then thrusting its larger end close to the man's muffled face. "No, no, I'm not the fool you take me for, nor do you pass till I have an answer to my question. Whereabouts is the dwelling of my kinsman, Major Molineux?"

The stranger, instead of attempting to force his passage, stepped back into the moonlight, unmuffled his face, and stared full into that of Robin.

"Watch here an hour, and Major Molineux will pass by," said he.

Robin gazed with dismay and astonishment on the unprecedented physiognomy of the speaker. The forehead with its double prominence, the broad hooked nose, the shaggy eyebrows, and fiery eyes were those which he had noticed at the inn, but the man's complexion had undergone a singular, or, more properly, a twofold change. One side of the face blazed an intense red, while the other was black as midnight, the division line being in the broad bridge of the nose; and a mouth which seemed to extend from ear to ear was black or red, in contrast to the color of the cheek. The effect was as if two individual devils, a fiend of fire and a fiend of darkness, had united themselves to form this infernal visage. The stranger grinned in Robin's face, muffled his party-colored features, and was out of sight in a moment.

"Strange things we travellers see!" ejaculated Robin.

He seated himself, however, upon the steps of the church-door, resolving to wait the appointed time for his kinsman. A few moments were consumed in philosophical speculations upon the species of man who had just left him; but having settled this point shrewdly, rationally, and satisfactorily, he was compelled to look elsewhere for his amusement. And first he threw his eyes along the street. It was of more respectable appearance than most of those into which he had wandered; and the moon, creating, like the imaginative power, a beautiful strangeness in familiar objects, gave something of romance to a scene that might not have possessed it in the light of day. The irregular and often quaint architecture of the houses, some of whose roofs were broken into numerous little peaks, while others ascended, steep and narrow, into a single point, and others again were square; the pure snow-white of some of their complexions, the aged darkness of others, and the thousand sparklings, reflected from bright substances in the walls of many; these matters engaged Robin's attention for a while, and then began to grow wearisome. Next he endeavored to define the forms of distant objects, starting away, with almost ghostly indistinctness, just as his eye appeared to grasp them; and finally he took a minute survey of an edifice which stood on the opposite side of the street, directly in front of the church-door, where he was stationed. It was a large, square mansion, distinguished from its neighbors by a balcony, which rested on tall pillars, and by an elaborate Gothic window, communicating therewith.

"Perhaps this is the very house I have been seeking," thought Robin.

Then he strove to speed away the time, by listening to a murmur which swept continually along the street, yet was scarcely audible, except to an unaccustomed ear like his; it was a low, dull, dreamy sound, compounded of many noises, each of which was at too great a distance to be separately heard. Robin marvelled at this snore of a sleeping town, and marvelled more whenever its continuity was broken by now and then a distant shout, apparently loud where it originated. But altogether it was a sleep-inspiring sound, and, to shake off its drowsy influence, Robin arose, and climbed a window-frame, that he might view the interior of the church. There the moonbeams came trembling in, and fell down upon the deserted pews, and extended along the quiet aisles. A fainter yet more awful radiance was hovering around the pulpit, and one solitary ray had dared to rest upon the open page of the great Bible. Had nature, in that deep hour, become a worshipper in the house which man had builded? Or was that heavenly light the visible sanctity of the place,—visible because no earthly and impure feet were within the walls? The scene made Robin's heart shiver with a sensation of loneliness stronger than he had ever felt in the remotest depths of his native woods; so he turned away and sat down again before the door. There were graves around the church, and now an uneasy thought obtruded into Robin's breast. What if the object of his search, which had been so often and so strangely thwarted, were all the time mouldering in his shroud? What if his kinsman should glide through yonder gate, and nod and smile to him in dimly passing by?

"Oh that any breathing thing were here with me!" said Robin.

Recalling his thoughts from this uncomfortable track, he sent them over forest, hill, and stream, and attempted to imagine how that evening of ambiguity and weariness had been spent by his father's household. He pictured them assembled at the door, beneath the tree, the great old tree, which had been spared for its huge twisted trunk and venerable shade, when a thousand leafy brethren fell. There, at the going down of the summer sun, it was his father's custom to perform domestic worship, that the neighbors might come and join with him like brothers of the family, and that the wayfaring man might pause to drink at that fountain, and keep his heart pure by freshening the memory of home. Robin distinguished the seat of every individual of the little audience; he saw the good man in the midst, holding the Scriptures in the golden light that fell from the western clouds; he beheld him close the book and all rise up to pray. He heard the old thanksgivings for daily mercies, the old supplications for their continuance, to which he had so often listened in weariness, but which were now among his dear remembrances. He perceived the slight inequality of his father's voice when he came to speak of the absent one; he noted how his mother turned her face to the broad and knotted trunk; how his elder brother scorned, because the beard was rough upon his upper lip, to permit his features to be moved; how the younger sister drew down a low hanging branch before her eyes; and how the little one of all, whose sports had hitherto broken the decorum of the scene, understood the prayer for her playmate, and burst into clamorous grief. Then he saw them go in at the door; and when Robin would have entered also, the latch tinkled into its place, and he was excluded from his home.

"Am I here, or there?" cried Robin, starting: for all at once, when his thoughts had become visible and audible in a dream, the long, wide, solitary street shone out before him.

He aroused himself, and endeavored to fix his attention steadily upon the large edifice which he had surveyed before. But still his mind kept vibrating between fancy and reality; by turns, the pillars of the balcony lengthened into the tall, bare stems of pines, dwindled down to human figures, settled again into their true shape and size, and then commenced a new succession of changes. For a single moment, when he deemed himself awake, he could have sworn that a visage—one which he seemed to remember, yet could not absolutely name as his kinsman's—was looking towards him from the Gothic window. A deeper sleep wrestled with and nearly overcame him, but fled at the sound of footsteps along the opposite pavement. Robin rubbed his eyes, discerned a man passing at the foot of the balcony, and addressed him in a loud, peevish, and lamentable cry.

"Hallo, friend! must I wait here all night for my kinsman, Major Molineux?"

The sleeping echoes awoke, and answered the voice: and the passenger, barely able to discern a figure sitting in the oblique shade of the steeple, traversed the street to obtain a nearer view. He was himself a gentleman in his prime, of open, intelligent, cheerful, and altogether prepossessing countenance. Perceiving a country youth, apparently homeless and without friends, he accosted him in a tone of real kindness, which had become strange to Robin's ears.

"Well, my good lad, who are you sitting here?" inquired he. "Can I be of service to you in any way?"

"I am afraid not, sir," replied Robin, despondingly; "yet I shall take it kindly, if you'll answer me a single question. I've been searching, half the night, for one Major Molineux; now, sir, is there really such a person in these parts, or am I dreaming?"

"Major Molineux! The name is not altogether strange to me," said the gentleman, smiling. "Have you any objection to telling me the nature of your business with him?"

Then Robin briefly related that his father was a clergyman, settled on a small salary, at a long distance back in the country, and that he and Major Molineux were brother's children. The Major, having inherited riches, and acquired civil and military rank, had visited his cousin, in great pomp, a year or two before; had manifested much interest in Robin and an elder brother, and, being childless himself, had thrown out hints respecting the future establishment of one of them in life. The elder brother was destined to succeed to the farm which his father cultivated in the interval of sacred duties; it was therefore determined that Robin should profit by his kinsman's generous intentions, especially as he seemed to be rather the favorite, and was thought to possess other necessary endowments.

"For I have the name of being a shrewd youth," observed Robin, in this part of his story.

"I doubt not you deserve it," replied his new friend, good-naturedly; "but pray proceed."

"Well, sir, being nearly eighteen years old, and well grown, as you see," continued Robin, drawing himself up to his full height, "I thought it high time to begin the world. So my mother and sister put me in handsome trim, and my father gave me half the remnant of his last year's salary, and five days ago I started for this place, to pay the Major a visit. But, would you believe it, sir! I crossed the ferry a little after dark, and have yet found nobody that would show me the way to his dwelling; only, an hour or two since, I was told to wait here, and Major Molineux would pass by."

"Can you describe the man who told you this?" inquired the gentleman.

"Oh, he was a very ill-favored fellow, sir," replied Robin, "with two great bumps on his forehead, a hook nose, fiery eyes; and, what struck me as the strangest, his face was of two different colors. Do you happen to know such a man, sir?"

"Not intimately," answered the stranger, "but I chanced to meet him a little time previous to your stopping me. I believe you may trust his word, and that the Major will very shortly pass through this street. In the mean time, as I have a singular curiosity to witness your meeting, I will sit down here upon the steps and bear you company."

He seated himself accordingly, and soon engaged his companion in animated discourse. It was but of brief continuance, however, for a noise of shouting, which had long been remotely audible, drew so much nearer that Robin inquired its cause.

"What may be the meaning of this uproar?" asked he. "Truly, if your town be always as noisy, I shall find little sleep while I am an inhabitant."

"Why, indeed, friend Robin, there do appear to be three or four riotous fellows abroad to-night," replied the gentleman. "You must not expect all the stillness of your native woods here in our streets. But the watch will shortly be at the heels of these lads and"—

"Ay, and set them in the stocks by peep of day," interrupted Robin, recollecting his own encounter with the drowsy lantern-bearer. "But, dear sir, if I may trust my ears, an army of watchmen would never make head against such a multitude of rioters. There were at least a thousand voices went up to make that one shout."

"May not a man have several voices, Robin, as well as two complexions?" said his friend.

"Perhaps a man may; but Heaven forbid that a woman should!" responded the shrewd youth, thinking of the seductive tones of the Major's housekeeper.

The sounds of a trumpet in some neighboring street now became so evident and continual, that Robin's curiosity was strongly excited. In addition to the shouts, he heard frequent bursts from many instruments of discord, and a wild and confused laughter filled up the intervals. Robin rose from the steps, and looked wistfully towards a point whither people seemed to be hastening.

"Surely some prodigious merry-making is going on," exclaimed he. "I have laughed very little since I left home, sir, and should be sorry to lose an opportunity. Shall we step round the corner by that darkish house, and take our share of the fun?"

"Sit down again, sit down, good Robin," replied the gentleman, laying his hand on the skirt of the gray coat. "You forget that we must wait here for your kinsman; and there is reason to believe that he will pass by, in the course of a very few moments."

The near approach of the uproar had now disturbed the neighborhood; windows flew open on all sides; and many heads, in the attire of the pillow, and confused by sleep suddenly broken, were protruded to the gaze of whoever had leisure to observe them. Eager voices hailed each other from house to house, all demanding the explanation, which not a soul could give. Half-dressed men hurried towards the unknown commotion, stumbling as they went over the stone steps that thrust themselves into the narrow footwalk. The shouts, the laughter, and the tuneless bray, the antipodes of music, came onwards with increasing din, till scattered individuals, and then denser bodies, began to appear round a corner at the distance of a hundred yards.

"Will you recognize your kinsman, if he passes in this crowd?" inquired the gentleman.

"Indeed, I can't warrant it, sir; but I'll take my stand here, and keep a bright lookout," answered Robin, descending to the outer edge of the pavement.

A mighty stream of people now emptied into the street, and came rolling slowly towards the church. A single horseman wheeled the corner in the midst of them, and close behind him came a band of fearful wind-instruments, sending forth a fresher discord now that no intervening buildings kept it from the ear. Then a redder light disturbed the moonbeams, and a dense multitude of torches shone along the street, concealing, by their glare, whatever object they illuminated. The single horseman, clad in a military dress, and bearing a drawn sword, rode onward as the leader, and, by his fierce and variegated countenance, appeared like war personified; the red of one cheek was an emblem of fire and sword; the blackness of the other betokened the mourning that attends them. In his train were wild figures in the Indian dress, and many fantastic shapes without a model, giving the whole march a visionary air, as if a dream had broken forth from some feverish brain, and were sweeping visibly through the midnight streets. A mass of people, inactive, except as applauding spectators, hemmed the procession in; and several women ran along the sidewalk, piercing the confusion of heavier sounds with their shrill voices of mirth or terror.

"The double-faced fellow has his eye upon me," muttered Robin, with an indefinite but an uncomfortable idea that he was himself to bear a part in the pageantry.

The leader turned himself in the saddle, and fixed his glance full upon the country youth, as the steed went slowly by. When Robin had freed his eyes from those fiery ones, the musicians were passing before him, and the torches were close at hand; but the unsteady brightness of the latter formed a veil which he could not penetrate. The rattling of wheels over the stones sometimes found its way to his ear, and confused traces of a human face appeared at intervals, and then melted into the vivid light. A moment more, and the leader thundered a command to halt: the trumpets vomited a horrid breath, and then held their peace; the shouts and laughter of the people died away, and there remained only a universal hum, allied to silence. Right before

Robin's eyes was an uncovered cart. There the torches blazed the brightest, there the moon shone out like day, and there, in tar-and-feathery dignity, sat his kinsman, Major Molineux!

He was an elderly man, of large and majestic person, and strong, square features, betokening a steady soul; but steady as it was, his enemies had found means to shake it. His face was pale as death, and far more ghastly; the broad forehead was contracted in his agony, so that his eyebrows formed one grizzled line; his eyes were red and wild, and the foam hung white upon his quivering lip. His whole frame was agitated by a quick and continual tremor, which his pride strove to quell, even in those circumstances of overwhelming humiliation. But perhaps the bitterest pang of all was when his eyes met those of Robin; for he evidently knew him on the instant, as the youth stood witnessing the foul disgrace of a head grown gray in honor. They stared at each other in silence, and Robin's knees shook, and his hair bristled, with a mixture of pity and terror. Soon, however, a bewildering excitement began to seize upon his mind; the preceding adventures of the night, the unexpected appearance of the crowd, the torches, the confused din and the hush that followed, the spectre of his kinsman reviled by that great multitude,—all this, and, more than all, a perception of tremendous ridicule in the whole scene, affected him with a sort of mental inebrity. At that moment a voice of sluggish merriment saluted Robin's ears; he turned instinctively, and just behind the corner of the church stood the lantern-bearer, rubbing his eyes, and drowsily enjoying the lad's amazement. Then he heard a peal of laughter like the ringing of silvery bells; a woman twitched his arm, a saucy eye met his, and he saw the lady of the scarlet petticoat. A sharp, dry cachinnation appealed to his memory, and, standing on tiptoe in the crowd, with his white apron over his head, he beheld the courteous little innkeeper. And lastly, there sailed over the heads of the multitude a great, broad laugh, broken in the midst by two sepulchral hems; thus, "Haw, haw, haw,—hem, hem,—haw, haw, haw, haw!"

The sound proceeded from the balcony of the opposite edifice, and thither Robin turned his eyes. In front of the Gothic window stood the old citizen, wrapped in a wide gown, his gray periwig exchanged for a nightcap, which was thrust back from his forehead, and his silk stockings, hanging about his legs. He supported himself on his polished cane in a fit of convulsive merriment, which manifested itself on his solemn old features like a funny inscription on a tombstone. Then Robin seemed to hear the voices of the barbers, of the guests of the inn, and of all who had made sport of him that night. The contagion was spreading among the multitude, when all at once, it seized upon Robin, and he sent forth a shout of laughter that echoed through the street,— every man shook his sides, every man emptied his lungs, but Robin's shout was the loudest there. The cloud-spirits peeped from their silvery islands, as the congregated mirth went roaring up the sky! The Man in the Moon heard the far bellow. "Oho," quoth he, "the old earth is frolicsome to-night!"

When there was a momentary calm in that tempestuous sea of sound, the leader gave the sign, the procession resumed its march. On they went, like fiends that throng in mockery around some dead potentate, mighty no more, but majestic still in his agony. On they went, in counterfeited pomp, in senseless uproar, in frenzied merriment, trampling all on an old man's heart. On swept the tumult, and left a silent street behind.

"Well, Robin, are you dreaming?" inquired the gentleman, laying his hand on the youth's shoulder.

Robin started, and withdrew his arm from the stone post to which he had instinctively clung, as the living stream rolled by him. His cheek was some-what pale, and his eye not quite as lively as in the earlier part of the evening.

"Will you be kind enough to show me the way to the ferry?" said he, after a moment's pause.

"You have, then, adopted a new subject of inquiry?" observed his com-panion, with a smile.

"Why, yes, sir," replied Robin, rather dryly. "Thanks to you, and to my other friends, I have at last met my kinsman, and he will scarce desire to see my face again. I begin to grow weary of a town life, sir. Will you show me the way to the ferry?"

"No, my good friend Robin,—not to-night, at least," said the gentleman. "Some few days hence, if you wish it, I will speed you on your journey. Or, if you prefer to remain with us, perhaps, as you are a shrewd youth, you may rise in the world without the help of your kinsman, Major Molineux."

Philip Roth (b. 1933)
The Conversion of the Jews

"You're a real one for opening your mouth in the first place," Itzie said. "What do you open your mouth all the time for?"

"I didn't bring it up, Itz, I didn't," Ozzie said.

"What do you care about Jesus Christ for anyway?"

"I didn't bring up Jesus Christ. He did. I didn't even know what he was talking about. Jesus is historical, he kept saying. Jesus is historical." Ozzie mimicked the monumental voice of Rabbi Binder.

"Jesus was a person that lived like you and me," Ozzie continued. "That's what Binder said—"

"Yeah? . . . So what! What do I give two cents whether he lived or not. And what do you gotta open your mouth!" Itzie Lieberman favored closed-mouthedness, especially when it came to Ozzie Freedman's questions. Mrs. Freedman had to see Rabbi Binder twice before about Ozzie's questions and this Wednesday at four-thirty would be the third time. Itzie preferred to keep *his* mother in the kitchen; he settled for behind-the-back subtleties such as gestures, faces, snarls and other less delicate barnyard noises.

"He was a real person, Jesus, but he wasn't like God, and we don't believe he is God." Slowly, Ozzie was explaining Rabbi Binder's position to Itzie, who had been absent from Hebrew School the previous afternoon.

"The Catholics," Itzie said helpfully, "they believe in Jesus Christ, that he's God." Itzie Lieberman used "the Catholics" in its broadest sense—to include the Protestants.

Ozzie received Itzie's remark with a tiny head bob, as though it were a footnote, and went on. "His mother was Mary, and his father probably was Joseph," Ozzie said. "But the New Testament says his real father was God."

"His *real* father?"

"Yeah," Ozzie said, "that's the big thing, his father's supposed to be God."

"Bull."

"That's what Rabbi Binder says, that it's impossible—"

"Sure it's impossible. That stuff's all bull. To have a baby you gotta get laid," Itzie theologized. "Mary hadda get laid."

"That's what Binder says: 'The only way a woman can have a baby is to have intercourse with a man.' "

"He said *that*, Ozz?" For a moment it appeared that Itzie had put the theological question aside. "He said that, intercourse?" A little curled smile shaped itself in the lower half of Itzic's face like a pink mustache. "What you guys do, Ozz, you laugh or something?"

"I raised my hand."

"Yeah? Whatja say?"

"That's when I asked the question."

Itzie's face lit up. "Whatja ask about—intercourse?"

"No, I asked the question about God, how if He could create the heaven and earth in six days, and make all the animals and the fish and the light in six days—the light especially, that's what always gets me, that He could make the light. Making fish and animals, that's pretty good—"

"That's damn good." Itzie's appreciation was honest but unimaginative: it was as though God had just pitched a one-hitter.

"But making light . . . I mean when you think about it, it's really something," Ozzie said. "Anyway, I asked Binder if He could make all that in six days, and He could *pick* the six days he wanted right out of nowhere, why couldn't He let a woman have a baby without having intercourse."

"You said intercourse, Ozz, to Binder?"

"Yeah."

"Right in class?"

"Yeah."

Itzie smacked the side of his head.

"I mean, no kidding around," Ozzie said, "that'd really be nothing. After all that other stuff, that'd practically be nothing."

Itzie considered a moment. "What'd Binder say?"

"He started all over again explaining how Jesus was historical and how he lived like you and me but he wasn't God. So I said I under*stood* that. What I wanted to know was different."

What Ozzie wanted to know was always different. The first time he had
wanted to know how Rabbi Binder could call the Jews "The Chosen People" if
the Declaration of Independence claimed all men to be created equal. Rabbi
Binder tried to distinguish for him between political equality and spiritual
legitimacy, but what Ozzie wanted to know, he insisted vehemently, was
different. That was the first time his mother had to come.

Then there was the plane crash. Fifty-eight people had been killed in a
plane crash at La Guardia. In studying a casualty list in the newspaper his
mother had discovered among the list of those dead eight Jewish names (his
grandmother had nine but she counted Miller as a Jewish name); because of
the eight she said the plane crash was "a tragedy." During free-discussion time
on Wednesday Ozzie had brought to Rabbi Binder's attention this matter of
"some of his relations" always picking out the Jewish names. Rabbi Binder
had begun to explain cultural unity and some other things when Ozzie stood
up at his seat and said that what he wanted to know was different. Rabbi
Binder insisted that he sit down and it was then that Ozzie shouted that he
wished all fifty-eight were Jews. That was the second time his mother came.

"And he kept explaining about Jesus being historical, and so I kept asking
him. No kidding, Itz, he was trying to make me look stupid."

"So what he finally do?"

"Finally he starts screaming that I was deliberately simple-minded and a
wise guy, and that my mother had to come, and this was the last time. And
that I'd never get bar-mitzvahed if he could help it. Then, Itz, then he starts
talking in that voice like a statue, real slow and deep, and he says that I better
think over what I said about the Lord. He told me to go to his office and think
it over." Ozzie leaned his body towards Itzie. "Itz, I thought it over for a solid
hour, and now I'm convinced God could do it."

Ozzie had planned to confess his latest transgression to his mother as soon
as she came home from work. But it was a Friday night in November and
already dark, and when Mrs. Freedman came through the door she tossed off
her coat, kissed Ozzie quickly on the face, and went to the kitchen table to
light the three yellow candles, two for the Sabbath and one for Ozzie's father.

When his mother lit the candles she would move her two arms slowly
towards her, dragging them through the air, as though persuading people
whose minds were half made up. And her eyes would get glassy with tears.
Even when his father was alive Ozzie remembered that her eyes had gotten
glassy, so it didn't have anything to do with his dying. It had something to do
with lighting the candles.

As she touched the flaming match to the unlit wick of a Sabbath candle,
the phone rang, and Ozzie, standing only a foot from it, plucked it off the
receiver and held it muffled to his chest. When his mother lit candles Ozzie
felt there should be no noise; even breathing, if you could manage it, should
be softened. Ozzie pressed the phone to his breast and watched his mother
dragging whatever she was dragging, and he felt his own eyes get glassy. His
mother was a round, tired, gray-haired penguin of a woman whose gray skin
had begun to feel the tug of gravity and the weight of her own history. Even

when she was dressed up she didn't look like a chosen person. But when she lit candles she looked like something better; like a woman who knew momentarily that God could do anything.

After a few mysterious minutes she was finished. Ozzie hung up the phone and walked to the kitchen table where she was beginning to lay the two places for the four-course Sabbath meal. He told her that she would have to see Rabbi Binder next Wednesday at four-thirty, and then he told her why. For the first time in their life together she hit Ozzie across the face with her hand.

All through the chopped liver and chicken soup part of the dinner Ozzie cried; he didn't have any appetite for the rest.

On Wednesday, in the largest of the three basement classrooms of the synagogue, Rabbi Marvin Binder, a tall, handsome, broad-shouldered man of thirty with thick strong-fibered black hair, removed his watch from his pocket and saw that it was four o'clock. At the rear of the room Yakov Blotnik, the seventy-one-year-old custodian, slowly polished the large window, mumbling to himself, unaware that it was four o'clock or six o'clock, Monday or Wednesday. To most of the students Yakov Blotnik's mumbling, along with his brown curly beard, scythe nose, and two heel-trailing black cats, made of him an object of wonder, a foreigner, a relic, towards whom they were alternately fearful and disrespectful. To Ozzie the mumbling had always seemed a monotonous, curious prayer; what made it curious was that old Blotnik had been mumbling so steadily for so many years, Ozzie suspected he had memorized the prayers and forgotten all about God.

"It is now free-discussion time," Rabbi Binder said. "Feel free to talk about any Jewish matter at all—religion, family, politics, sports—"

There was silence. It was a gusty, clouded November afternoon and it did not seem as though there ever was or could be a thing called baseball. So nobody this week said a word about that hero from the past, Hank Greenberg—which limited free discussion considerably.

And the soul-battering Ozzie Freedman had just received from Rabbi Binder had imposed its limitation. When it was Ozzie's turn to read aloud from the Hebrew book the rabbi had asked him petulantly why he didn't read more rapidly. He was showing no progress. Ozzie said he could read faster but that if he did he was sure not to understand what he was reading. Nevertheless, at the rabbi's repeated suggestion Ozzie tried, and showed a great talent, but in the midst of a long passage he stopped short and said he didn't understand a word he was reading, and started in again at a drag-footed pace. Then came the soul-battering.

Consequently when free-discussion time rolled around none of the students felt too free. The rabbi's invitation was answered only by the mumbling of feeble old Blotnik.

"Isn't there anything at all you would like to discuss?" Rabbi Binder asked again, looking at his watch. "No questions or comments?"

There was a small grumble from the third row. The rabbi requested that Ozzie rise and give the rest of the class the advantage of his thought.

Ozzie rose. "I forget it now," he said, and sat down in his place.

Rabbi Binder advanced a seat towards Ozzie and poised himself on the edge of the desk. It was Itzie's desk and the rabbi's frame only a dagger's-length away from his face snapped him to sitting attention.

"Stand up again, Oscar," Rabbi Binder said calmly, "and try to assemble your thoughts."

Ozzie stood up. All his classmates turned in their seats and watched as he gave an unconvincing scratch to his forehead.

"I can't assemble any," he announced, and plunked himself down.

"Stand up!" Rabbi Binder advanced from Itzie's desk to the one directly in front of Ozzie; when the rabbinical back was turned Itzie gave it five-fingers off the tip of his nose, causing a small titter in the room. Rabbi Binder was too absorbed in squelching Ozzie's nonsense once and for all to bother with titters. "Stand up, Oscar. What's your question about?"

Ozzie pulled a word out of the air. It was the handiest word. "Religion."

"Oh, now you remember?"

"Yes."

"What is it?"

Trapped, Ozzie blurted the first thing that came to him. "Why can't He make anything He wants to make!"

As Rabbi Binder prepared an answer, a final answer, Itzie, ten feet behind him, raised one finger on his left hand, gestured it meaningfully towards the rabbi's back, and brought the house down.

Binder twisted quickly to see what had happened and in the midst of the commotion Ozzie shouted into the rabbi's back what he couldn't have shouted to his face. It was a loud, toneless sound that had the timbre of something stored inside for about six days.

"You don't know! You don't know anything about God!"

The rabbi spun back towards Ozzie. "What?"

"You don't know—you don't—"

"Apologize, Oscar, apologize!" It was a threat.

"You don't—"

Rabbi Binder's hand flicked out at Ozzie's cheek. Perhaps it had only been meant to clamp the boy's mouth shut, but Ozzie ducked and the palm caught him squarely on the nose.

The blood came in a short, red spurt on to Ozzie's shirt front.

The next moment was all confusion. Ozzie screamed, "You bastard, you bastard!" and broke for the classroom door. Rabbi Binder lurched a step backwards, as though his own blood had started flowing violently in the opposite direction, then gave a clumsy lurch forward and bolted out the door after Ozzie. The class followed after the rabbi's huge blue-suited back, and before old Blotnik could turn from his window, the room was empty and everyone was headed full speed up the three flights leading to the roof.

If one should compare the light of day to the life of man: sunrise to birth; sunset—the dropping down over the edge—to death; then as Ozzie Freedman wiggled through the trapdoor of the synagogue roof, his feet kicking backwards bronco-style at Rabbi Binder's outstretched arms—at that moment the day was fifty years old. As a rule, fifty or fifty-five reflects accurately the age of late afternoons in November, for it is in that month, during those hours, that one's awareness of light seems no longer a matter of seeing, but of hearing: light begins clicking away. In fact, as Ozzie locked shut the trapdoor in the rabbi's face, the sharp click of the bolt into the lock might momentarily have been mistaken for the sound of the heavier gray that had just throbbed through the sky.

With all his weight Ozzie kneeled on the locked door; any instant he was certain that Rabbi Binder's shoulder would fling it open, splintering the wood into shrapnel and catapulting his body into the sky. But the door did not move and below him he heard only the rumble of feet, first loud then dim, like thunder rolling away.

A question shot through his brain. "Can this be *me?*" For a thirteen-year-old who had just labeled his religious leader a bastard, twice, it was not an improper question. Louder and louder the question came to him—"Is it me? It is me?"—until he discovered himself no longer kneeling, but racing crazily towards the edge of the roof, his eyes crying, his throat screaming, and his arms flying every-whichway as though not his own.

"Is it me? Is it me Me ME ME ME! It has to be me—but is it!"

It is the question a thief must ask himself the night he jimmies open his first window, and it is said to be the question with which bridegrooms quiz themselves before the altar.

In the few wild seconds it took Ozzie's body to propel him to the edge of the roof, his self-examination began to grow fuzzy. Gazing down at the street, he became confused as to the problem beneath the question: was it, is-it-me-who-called-Binder-a-bastard? or, is-it-me-prancing-around-on-the-roof? However, the scene below settled all, for there is an instant in any action when whether it is you or somebody else is academic. The thief crams the money in his pockets and scoots out the window. The bridegroom signs the hotel register for two. And the boy on the roof finds a streetful of people gaping at him, necks stretched backwards, faces up, as though he were the ceiling of the Hayden Planetarium. Suddenly you know it's you.

"Oscar! Oscar Freedman!" A voice rose from the center of the crowd, a voice that, could it have been seen, would have looked like the writing on scroll. "Oscar Freedman, get down from there. Immediately!" Rabbi Binder was pointing one arm stiffly up at him; and at the end of that arm, one finger aimed menacingly. It was the attitude of a dictator, but one—the eyes confessed all—whose personal valet had spit neatly in his face.

Ozzie didn't answer. Only for a blink's length did he look towards Rabbi Binder. Instead his eyes began to fit together the world beneath him, to sort out people from places, friends from enemies, participants from spectators. In little jagged starlike clusters his friends stood around Rabbi Binder, who was still pointing. The topmost point on a star compounded not of angels but of five adolescent boys was Itzie. What a world it was, with those stars below, Rabbi Binder below . . . Ozzie, who a moment earlier hadn't been able to control his own body, started to feel the meaning of the word control: he felt Peace and he felt Power.

"Oscar Freedman, I'll give you three to come down."

Few dictators give their subjects three to do anything; but, as always, Rabbi Binder only looked dictatorial.

"Are you ready, Oscar?"

Ozzie nodded his head yes, although he had no intention in the world— the lower one of the celestial one he'd just entered—of coming down even if Rabbi Binder should give him a million.

"All right then," said Rabbi Binder. He ran a hand through his black Samson hair as though it were the gesture prescribed for uttering the first digit. Then, with his other hand cutting a circle out of the small piece of sky around him, he spoke. "One!"

There was no thunder. On the contrary, at that moment, as though "one" was the cue for which he had been waiting, the world's least thunderous person appeared on the synagogue steps. He did not so much come out the synagogue door as lean out, onto the darkening air. He clutched at the doorknob with one hand and looked up at the roof.

"Oy!"

Yakov Blotnik's old mind hobbled slowly, as if on crutches, and though he couldn't decide precisely what the boy was doing on the roof, he knew it wasn't good—that is, it wasn't-good-for-the-Jews. For Yakov Blotnik life had fractionated itself simply: things were either good-for-the-Jews or no-good-for-the-Jews.

He smacked his free hand to his in-sucked cheek, gently. "Oy, Gut!" And then quickly as he was able, he jacked down his head and surveyed the street. There was Rabbi Binder (like a man at an auction with only three dollars in his pocket, he had just delivered a shaky "Two!"); there were the students, and that was all. So far it-wasn't-so-bad-for-the-Jews. But the boy had to come down immediately, before anybody saw. The problem: how to get the boy off the roof?

Anybody who has ever had a cat on the roof knows how to get him down. You call the fire department. Or first you call the operator and you ask her for the fire department. And the next thing there is great jamming of brakes and clanging of bells and shouting of instructions. And then the cat is off the roof. You do the same thing to get a boy off the roof.

That is, you do the same thing if you are Yakov Blotnik and you once had a cat on the roof.

When the engines, all four of them, arrived, Rabbi Binder had four times given Ozzie the count of three. The big hook-and-ladder swung around the corner and one of the firemen leaped from it, plunging headlong towards the yellow fire hydrant in front of the synagogue. With a huge wrench he began to unscrew the top nozzle. Rabbi Binder raced over to him and pulled at his shoulder.

"There's no fire . . ."

The fireman mumbled back over his shoulder and, heatedly, continued working at the nozzle.

"But there's no fire, there's no fire . . ." Binder shouted. When the fireman mumbled again, the rabbi grasped his face with both his hands and pointed it up at the roof.

To Ozzie it looked as though Rabbi Binder was trying to tug the fireman's head out of his body, like a cork from a bottle. He had to giggle at the picture they made: it was a family portrait—rabbi in black skullcap, fireman in red fire hat, and the little yellow hydrant squatting beside like a kid brother, bareheaded. From the edge of the roof Ozzie waved at the portrait, a one-handed, flapping, mocking wave; in doing it his right foot slipped from under him. Rabbi Binder covered his eyes with his hands.

Firemen work fast. Before Ozzie had even regained his balance, a big, round, yellowed net was being held on the synagogue lawn. The firemen who held it looked up at Ozzie with stern, feelingless faces.

One of the firemen turned his head towards Rabbi Binder. "What, is the kid nuts or something?"

Rabbi Binder unpeeled his hands from his eyes, slowly, painfully, as if they were tape. Then he checked: nothing on the sidewalk, no dents in the net.

"Is he gonna jump, or what?" the fireman shouted.

In a voice not at all like a statue, Rabbi Binder finally answered. "Yes, Yes, I think so . . . He's been threatening to . . ."

Threatening to? Why, the reason he was on the roof, Ozzie remembered, was to get away; he hadn't even thought about jumping. He had just run to get away, and the truth was that he hadn't really headed for the roof as much as he'd been chased there.

"What's his name, the kid?"

"Freedman," Rabbi Binder answered. "Oscar Freedman."

The fireman looked up at Ozzie. "What is it with you, Oscar? You gonna jump, or what?"

Ozzie did not answer. Frankly, the question had just arisen.

"Look, Oscar, if you're gonna jump, jump—and if you're not gonna jump, don't jump. But don't waste our time, willya?"

Ozzie looked at the fireman and then at Rabbi Binder. He wanted to see Rabbi Binder cover his eyes one more time.

"I'm going to jump."

And then he scampered around the edge of the roof to the corner, where there was no net below, and he flapped his arms at his sides, swishing the air and smacking his palms to his trousers on the downbeat. He began screaming like some kind of engine, "Wheeeee . . . wheeeeee," and leaning way out over the edge with the upper half of his body. The firemen whipped around to cover the ground with the net. Rabbi Binder mumbled a few words to Somebody and covered his eyes. Everything happened quickly, jerkily, as in a silent movie. The crowd, which had arrived with the fire engines, gave out a long, Fourth-of-July fireworks oooh-aahhh. In the excitement no one had paid the crowd much heed, except, of course, Yakov Blotnik, who swung from the doorknob counting heads. "Fier und tsvansik . . . finf und tsvantsik . . . Oy, Gut!" It wasn't like this with the cat.

Rabbi Binder peeked through his fingers, checked the sidewalk and net. Empty. But there was Ozzie racing to the other corner. The firemen raced with him but were unable to keep up. Whenever Ozzie wanted to he might jump and splatter himself upon the sidewalk, and by the time the firemen scooted to the spot all they could do with their net would be to cover the mess.

"Wheeeee . . . wheeeee . . ."

"Hey, Oscar," the winded fireman yelled, "What the hell is this, a game or something?"

"Wheeeee . . . wheeeee . . ."

"Hey, Oscar—"

But he was off now to the other corner, flapping his wings fiercely. Rabbi Binder couldn't take it any longer—the fire engines from nowhere, the screaming suicidal boy, the net. He fell to his knees, exhausted, and with his hands curled together in front of his chest like a little dome, he pleaded, "Oscar, stop it, Oscar. Don't jump, Oscar. Please come down . . . Please don't jump."

And further back in the crowd a single voice, a single young voice, shouted a lone word to the boy on the roof.

"Jump!"

It was Itzie. Ozzie momentarily stopped flapping.

"Go ahead, Ozz—jump!" Itzie broke off his point of the star and courageously, with the inspiration not of a wise-guy but of a disciple, stood alone. "Jump, Ozz, jump!"

Still on his knees, his hands still curled, Rabbi Binder twisted his body back. He looked at Itzie, then, agonizingly, back to Ozzie.

"Oscar, Don't jump! Please, Don't Jump . . . please please . . ."

"Jump!" This time it wasn't Itzie but another point of the star. By the time Mrs. Freedman arrived to keep her four-thirty appointment with Rabbi Binder, the whole little upside down heaven was shouting and pleading for Ozzie to jump, and Rabbi Binder no longer was pleading with him not to jump, but was crying into the dome of his hands.

Understandably Mrs. Freedman couldn't figure out what her son was doing on the roof. So she asked.

"Ozzie, my Ozzie, what are you doing? My Ozzie, what is it?"

Ozzie stopped wheeeeeing and slowed his arms down to a cruising flap, the kind birds use in soft winds, but he did not answer. He stood against the low, clouded, darkening sky—light clicked down swiftly now, as on a small gear—flapping softly and gazing down at the small bundle of a woman who was his mother.

"What are you doing, Ozzie?" She turned towards the kneeling Rabbi Binder and rushed so close that only a paper-thickness of dusk lay between her stomach and his shoulders.

"What is my baby doing?"

Rabbi Binder gaped up at her but he too was mute. All that moved was the dome of his hands; it shook back and forth like a weak pulse.

"Rabbi, get him down! He'll kill himself. Get him down, my only baby . . ."

"I can't," Rabbi Binder said, "I can't . . ." and he turned his handsome head towards the crowd of boys behind him. "It's them. Listen to them."

And for the first time Mrs. Freedman saw the crowd of boys, and she heard what they were yelling.

"He's doing it for them. He won't listen to me. It's them." Rabbi Binder spoke like one in a trance.

"For them?"

"Yes."

"Why for them?"

"They want him to . . ."

Mrs. Freedman raised her two arms upward as though she were conducting the sky. "For them he's doing it!" And then in a gesture older than pyramids, older than prophets and floods, her arms came slapping down to her sides. "A martyr I have. Look!" She tilted her head to the roof. Ozzie was still flapping softly. "My martyr."

"Oscar, come down, *please*," Rabbi Binder groaned.

In a startlingly even voice Mrs. Freedman called to the boy on the roof. "Ozzie, come down, Ozzie. Don't be a martyr, my baby."

As though it were a litany, Rabbi Binder repeated her words. "Don't be a martyr, my baby. Don't be a martyr."

"Gawhead, Ozz—*be* a Martin!" It was Itzie. "Be a Martin, be a Martin," and all the voices joined in singing for Martindom, whatever *it* was. "Be a Martin, be a Martin . . ."

Somehow when you're on a roof the darker it gets the less you can hear. All Ozzie knew was that two groups wanted two new things: his friends were spirited and musical about what they wanted; his mother and the rabbi were even-toned, chanting, about what they didn't want. The rabbi's voice was without tears now and so was his mother's.

The big net stared up at Ozzie like a sightless eye. The big, clouded sky pushed down. From beneath it looked like a gray corrugated board. Suddenly, looking up into that unsympathetic sky, Ozzie realized all the strangeness of what these people, his friends, were asking: they wanted him to jump, to kill himself; they were singing about it now—it made them that happy. And there was an even greater strangeness: Rabbi Binder was on his knees, trembling. If there was a question to be asked now it was not "Is it me?" but rather "Is it us? . . . Is it us?"

Being on the roof, it turned out, was a serious thing. If he jumped would the singing become dancing? Would it? What would jumping stop? Yearningly, Ozzie wished he could rip open the sky, plunge his hands through, and pull out the sun; and on the sun, like a coin, would be stamped JUMP or DON'T JUMP.

Ozzie's knees rocked and sagged a little under him as though they were setting him for a dive. His arms tightened, stiffened, froze, from shoulders to fingernails. He felt as if each part of his body were going to vote as to whether he should kill himself or not—and each part as though it were independent of *him*.

The light took an unexpected click down and the new darkness, like a gag, hushed the friends singing for this and the mother and rabbi chanting for that.

Ozzie stopped counting votes, and in a curiously high voice, like one who wasn't prepared for speech, he spoke.

"Mamma?"

"Yes, Oscar."

"Mamma, get down on your knees, like Rabbi Binder."

"Oscar—"

"Get down on your knees," he said, "or I'll jump."

Ozzie heard a whimper, then a quick rustling, and when he looked down where his mother had stood he saw the top of a head and beneath that a circle of dress. She was kneeling beside Rabbi Binder.

He spoke again. "Everybody kneel." There was the sound of everbody kneeling.

Ozzie looked around. With one hand he pointed towards the synagogue entrance. "Make *him* kneel."

There was a noise, not of kneeling, but of body-and-cloth stretching. Ozzie could hear Rabbi Binder saying in a gruff whisper, ". . . or he'll *kill* himself," and when next he looked there was Yakov Blotnik off the doorknob and for the first time in his life upon his knees in the Gentile posture of prayer.

As for the firemen—it is not as difficult as one might imagine to hold a net taut while you are kneeling.

Ozzie looked around again; and then he called to Rabbi Binder.

"Rabbi?"

"Yes, Oscar."

"Rabbi Binder, do you believe in God."

"Yes."

"Do you believe God can do Anything?" Ozzie leaned his head out into the darkness. "Anything?"

"Oscar, I think—"

"Tell me you believe God can do Anything."

There was a second's hesitation. Then: "God can do Anything."

"Tell me you believe God can make a child without intercourse."

"He can."

"Tell me!"

"God," Rabbi Binder admitted, "can make a child without intercourse."

"Mamma, you tell me."

"God can make a child without intercourse," his mother said.

"Make *him* tell me." There was no doubt who *him* was.

In a few moments Ozzie heard an old comical voice say something to the increasing darkness about God.

Next, Ozzie made everybody say it. And then he made them all say they believed in Jesus Christ—first one at a time, then all together.

When the catechizing was through it was the beginning of evening. From the street it sounded as if the boy on the roof might have sighed.

"Ozzie?" A woman's voice dared to speak. "You'll come down now?"

There was no answer, but the woman waited, and when a voice finally did speak it was thin and crying, and exhausted as that of an old man who has just finished pulling the bells.

"Mamma, don't you see—you shouldn't hit me. He shouldn't hit me. You shouldn't hit me about God, Mamma. You should never hit anybody about God—"

"Ozzie, please come down now."

"Promise me, promise me you'll never hit anybody about God."

He had asked only his mother, but for some reason everyone kneeling in the street promised he would never hit anybody about God.

Once again there was silence.

"I can come down now, Mamma," the boy on the roof finally said. He turned his head both ways as though checking the traffic lights. "Now I can come down . . ."

And he did, right into the center of the yellow net that glowed in the evening's edge like an overgrown halo.

QUESTIONS

1. Is "The Conversion of the Jews" a story about religion? Or is it a story about schoolboys? About parents? Could it be a story about the difficulties of being a rabbi? If an author like Philip Roth does not formally declare the theme of one of his stories, how do we go about deciding *which* theme, among many possibilities, is the central one?

2. Of what thematic importance is the opening paragraph of "My Kinsman, Major Molineux"? Would the story be better or worse if the theme of that paragraph were brought up several more times before the story's end?

3. As Hawthorne's story comes to its conclusion, we learn that the boy might have been dreaming the experiences he has had. Amid such ambiguity, what are you to make of the importance of theme in the story? Can themes be important in a story which may be just a dream?

4. What difference to the theme (as you define it) of "The Conversion of the Jews" is the outcome of Ozzie's fall from the roof? What thematic difference would be involved in a fatal fall?

3
SOUTHERN WRITERS: A WORLD OF FICTION

C oncentrating as we have on plot, point of view, theme, and other elements of composition might suggest that writing successful fiction is a mechanical process. Nothing could be further from the truth. A great piece of fiction is ultimately a great mystery: after all the words of criticism and appreciation have been written and said, there is no way of understanding exactly how the story or novel evolved. But we do know that in addition to perfecting the art of composition—making the right artistic choices—authors must deal with tradition, building on (and often distinguishing themselves from) the achievement of previous generations. As well as being creative artists, authors are also social beings who live in a concrete world and react concretely in their lives and work to its crises, moral dilemmas, hopes, and fears.

The importance of *time and place* in creating a world of fiction is shown by the literature of the American South. No geographical area of the United States has been richer in literary talent. This talent is alive in every form: poetry, drama, the novel, literary criticism. And in the genre of the short story, Southern writing has often revealed a stunning genius, as the pieces that follow demonsrate.

Many speculations have been offered as to why this region has produced such literary riches. One explanation focuses on the paradox of the defeat once visited upon the South. The minds and memories of many Southerners are still preoccupied with the defeat their forebears suffered in the Civil War and the desolation that followed. After 1865, the rest of America experienced progress, confidence, industrial growth, and material prosperity. The South alone felt disadvantaged—a land apart—in a nation that was otherwise strong and confident. The writers of the South, so this argument goes, turned inward to themselves and to their intimate traditions of folktales, familiar stories of family and region, and the idealized conceptions of a prewar society that had vanished. The sense of regional uniqueness, intensified by defeat, gave support and encouragement to writers. The South had the particularity, the self-consciousness, and the distinctive history in which writing could flourish. The critic and Southerner John Crowe Ransom once described the paradox of a luxuriant growth thriving in a damaged land:

There was an apple tree which dropped its limbs one by one as the seasons went by, and finally crashed to earth in a storm. But its apples seemed to grow finer every year to the end, and to be much superior to the apples of the other and healthier trees. I had the feeling that the flavor was better even though the apples tended to be faulty, and could not always be eaten. Are the works of art like those apples, reaching their best when the society behind them is under sentence of death?

This analogy should also remind us that Southern fiction has been marked by its attention to the past, to its sense of loss, and to its awareness of the importance of fate in human affairs. For instance, in William Faulkner's "A Rose for Emily," the attachment to the past is so powerful that it wholly consumes a life. Much has been taken from Miss Emily, and little returned. Her mind becomes riveted upon her losses and, as the townspeople watch her disintegration as a person, they say: "We remembered all the young men her father had driven away, and we knew that with nothing left, she would have to cling to that which had robbed her, as people will." Miss Emily seems fated to devote heself to macabre rituals and strangely gothic ceremonies, "as people will," while the world around her moves rapidly into the future.

The progression into the future has been seen as a mixed blessing by many Southern writers. The future promises the means by which the legacy of the past, with all its cruel disappointments, can be escaped. But still the past, despite all its tragic reminders, seems to represent a security that is given up only at considerable cost. In either case, Southern writing is preoccupied with "the backward glance." The past is seen by some writers as a heavy burden, and by others as a subject for nostalgic reflection. In Robert Penn Warren's "Blackberry Winter," the two attitudes are combined to produce a story that is a meditation on both the pleasurable and the painful aspects of the past. The young boy thinks back to a time in rural Tennessee when he was suddenly made aware of his vulnerability to the threatening elements of society and to the change of his own natural development. On his boyhood farm, with his father momentarily absent, he becomes the protector of his mother and of their black workers. A malevolent man who abruptly wanders onto the property stands for all of the dangers to which the family is prey should the customary order of things be altered. The boy is too young to know what these changes might specifically be, but he is old enough to fear them. When the servant Big Jebb tells him that there are changes "of life and time," he adds that "time come and you find out everything." And the boy does: the future brings with it the death of his mother and of his father, the latter in a terrible accident. Big Jebb's family is also transformed by death and violence. And the boy, having become a man, cannot escape from thinking about the malevolent figure whose earlier appearance in his life seemed to foreshadow all the disastrous later changes. The boy was told not to "follow" the figure, but the last sentence in the story reads: "I did follow him, all the years." Thus Robert Penn Warren perceives the ambivalence with which the South surveys its own past, an ambivalence mixing fascination with pain.

Pain and violence are constants in the fiction of Richard Wright. His stories as well as his novels lay forth in the starkest of terms the oppressive realities, both physical and mental, through which black people have histori-cally been forced to move in the South. In "Big Boy Leaves Home," Wright fastens his attention on the facts, semi-autobiographical in kind, of one young black man's sense of total entrapment. While it is certainly true that many Southern white writers have concerned themselves with the terrible hold that the South as a region can have on Southerners as people, Wright's vision of things is vastly more claustrophobic than theirs. He makes his readers see that his native Mississippi was a place where it was impossible to be black and also a free human being. He also portrays the sudden violence that has been a part of the lives of blacks and rural whites as well.

The story races at a dizzying speed from its early moments, when Big Boy Morrison and his friends frolic easily in the midday sun, to its later moments when only Big Boy is alive, his friends shot or burned alive. Wright's art consists in mapping the journey from innocence to terror. He shows the isolated individual's descent into a nightmarish world where, just to live, he must kill. Big Boy kills not only the enraged soldier, but a coiled snake and a vicious dog as well. "He had to kill this snake. Just had t kill im!" Like the snake, so the white man with the gun and the dog. More importantly, Big Boy has to "kill" his past, to extinguish his connections with his family and all his ties with the only world he has ever known. He has to move north, to Chicago, to a world about which he knows nothing save what his imagination prompts him to dream about when he hears the mournful sound of the train whistles. The trains move northward to something called "freedom," but Big Boy Morrison is caught in the here and now. He must, at any cost, flee it. Richard Wright is a Southern writer in his concern, not just with the weight of the past, but also with the dilemmas that occur when one escapes into the terrible burden of the present.

If Wright's world is flat and stark, with a line of narrative action that drives straight to shocking outcomes, the world of Eudora Welty is magically alive to the mysterious and to the beauty of the implausible, and filled with a pro-found sense of nature that is a hallmark of much Southern writing. The response to a sudden emergency—the disappearance of a pregnant and angry wife—becomes a leisurely pilgrimage. What might have been a desperate search is turned instead into an oddly patient and stately journey, on the part of a small community, to the fascinating Pearl River. The net that is to be used to discover the drowned woman becomes instead a means to adorn the beauty of the river: "the river was glimmering, narrow, soft, and skin-colored, and slowed nearly to stillness. . . . The net that was being drawn out, so old and so long-used, it too looked golden, strung and tied with golden threads." The searchers find no woman, but instead fish, flowers, plants, snakes, and an alligator. The enterprise is communal, intense, and wholly pleasurable. "I've never been on a better river-dragging," says one participant, "or seen better behavior." And in the end, man and wife are reconciled, she never having drowned, and he somewhat wiser and more loving for the experience. Eudora Welty takes her readers to a world somewhat similar to the one they know, but one with conventions, beauties, and surprises wholly its own. She seems gracefully at home with the unexpected.

Ritual and ceremony are also crucial in the work of Flannery O'Connor, now recognized as one of the best writers of short fiction to come out of the South—and of the country as a whole—in this century. Her art consists in part of taking careful notice of the many formalities, conventions, and rules, spoken and unspoken, that people employ to make sense of their lives. Mr. Head, "a suitable guide for the young," arranges a trip to the city for his grandson Nelson. He does so because he believes that, once having seen the city, the boy "would be content to stay at home for the rest of his life." The entire experience is planned as the means by which Mr. Head's authority will be vindicated and "the boy would at last find out that he was not as smart as he thought he was." In the end, after a day of overwhelming surprises and defeats, Nelson does affirm that he wishes never to return to the city. But the changes in Mr. Head are vastly more profound than those befalling Nelson. Mr. Head comes to understand how little he grasps of life or of himself. The world beyond him, he recognizes, is made up of the grotesque and the unknowable. He can do little more than acknowledge his inadequacy in the presence of that world. But when he does so, he also acknowledges his closeness to Nelson, "as if they were faced with some great mystery, some monument to another's victory that brought them together in their common defeat." As provincial Southerners, but also as representatives of the tragically inadequate human race, they are "kin." Flannery O'Connor owes some of her absorption in the formal and the fated to her own Roman Catholicism; but she also must be seen as a Southerner to whom the awareness of kinship, of convention, and of being overrun by life is familiar.

The fast-moving adventures—the violent action and flamboyant talk—of Barry Hannah's "Testimony of Pilot" originate in the same strong energy that has driven many Southern writers. When, at the end of the events that have led to the death of his friend and of the girl they both loved, and after we have been led through everything from pranks to wars and hijackings, Hannah abruptly tells us: "That is why I told this story and will never tell another." In being "just" a *story*, "Testimony of Pilot" shares in the rich traditions of the Southern fable or tall tale. We read to be surprised, to be shocked, to be challenged by an imagination stronger and more reckless than our own. We watch to see how Hannah will twist and shape the narrative line. What will Quadberry do? To whom *will* Lilian extend her favors?

In telling his story, Hannah displays the strength that all compelling narrators have: he masters the art of compressing a great deal of time in a very small space. We move at breakneck speed from the time when the narrator was ten or twelve years old to the time when, the friends of his past destroyed, his own life seems empty of meaning. The narrator's attitude toward such tumultuous activity is a mixture of comic elation and stoic despair. He loves his past but he knows that it is fated to wind up being his sorry present. Hannah thus shares with his fellow Southern writers an historical awareness. When once as a boy he filled his days with leisurely delinquencies, he now faces a present that, as he says, "hurts me every day." The town he was once so lazy in now embraces "aluminum subdivisions, cigar boxes with four thin columns in front, thick as a hive. We got a turquoise water tank; got a shopping center, a monster Jitney Jungle, fifth-rate teenyboppers covering the place like ants." In making reflections like this, Hannah reminds us of many Southern writers of earlier generations. He witnesses, as did they, the ruination of an environment that once provided intimacy and security. The friends that once made his private life so intense have left to be killed in public affairs. Once again the peculiar strengths of the South seem threatened. And, once again, in the face of such disadvantage, the Southern imagination reacts with sudden power, comic energies, and a love of surprising event.

Six stories, no matter how good, cannot do justice to the variety, the wealth, and the power of the Southern imagination as it has been distilled into the short story. Just as the South itself is a region of many different parts, so Southern writing is a richness of many different voices. What these stories do suggest, however, is the way that the strong identity of the South—with the continuing preoccupations of memory of place, the violence of the historical past and present, and a strong vernacular tradition—continues to shape the work of the writers who have been born there.

William Faulkner (1897–1962)
A Rose for Emily

1

When Miss Emily Grierson died, our whole town went to her funeral: the men through a sort of respectful affection for a fallen monument, the women mostly out of curiosity to see the inside of her house, which no one save an old man-servant—a combined gardener and cook—had seen in at least ten years.

It was a big, squarish frame house that had once been white, decorated with cupolas and spires and scrolled balconies in the heavily lightsome style of the seventies, set on what had once been our most select street. But garages and cotton gins had encroached and obliterated even the august names of that neighborhood; only Miss Emily's house was left, lifting its stubborn and coquettish decay above the cotton wagons and the gasoline pumps—an eyesore among eyesores. And now Miss Emily had gone to join the representatives of those august names where they lay in the cedar-bemused cemetery among the ranked and anonymous graves of Union and Confederate soldiers who fell at the battle of Jefferson.

Alive, Miss Emily had been a tradition, a duty, and a care; a sort of hereditary obligation upon the town, dating from that day in 1894 when Colonel Sartoris, the mayor—he who fathered the edict that no Negro woman should appear on the streets without an apron—remitted her taxes, the dispensation dating from the death of her father on into perpetuity. Not that Miss Emily would have accepted charity. Colonel Sartoris invented an involved tale to the effect that Miss Emily's father had loaned money to the town, which the town, as a matter of business, preferred this way of repaying. Only a man of Colonel Sartoris' generation and thought could have invented it, and only a woman could have believed it.

When the next generation, with its more modern ideas, became mayors and aldermen, this arrangement created some little dissatisfaction. On the first of the year they mailed her a tax notice. February came, and there was no reply. They wrote her a formal letter, asking her to call at the sheriff's office at her convenience. A week later the mayor wrote her himself, offering to call or to send his car for her, and received in reply a note on paper of an archaic shape, in a thin, flowing calligraphy in faded ink, to the effect that she no longer went out at all. The tax notice was also enclosed, without comment.

They called a special meeting of the Board of Aldermen. A deputation waited upon her, knocked at the door through which no visitor had passed since she ceased giving china-painting lessons eight or ten years earlier. They were admitted by the old Negro into a dim hall from which a stairway mounted into still more shadow. It smelled of dust and disuse—a close, dank smell. The Negro led them into the parlor. It was furnished in heavy, leather-covered furniture. When the Negro opened the blinds of one window, they could see that the leather was cracked; and when they sat down, a faint dust rose sluggishly about their thighs, spinning with slow motes in the single sun-ray. On a tarnished gilt easel before the fireplace stood a crayon portrait of Miss Emily's father.

They rose when she entered—a small, fat woman in black, with a thin gold chain descending to her waist and vanishing into her belt, leaning on an ebony cane with a tarnished gold head. Her skeleton was small and spare; perhaps that was why what would have been merely plumpness in another was obesity in her. She looked bloated, like a body long submerged in motionless water, and of that pallid hue. Her eyes, lost in the fatty ridges of her face, looked like two small pieces of coal pressed into a lump of dough as they moved from one face to another while the visitors stated their errand.

She did not ask them to sit. She just stood in the door and listened quietly until the spokesman came to a stumbling halt. Then they could hear the invisible watch ticking at the end of the gold chain.

Her voice was dry and cold. "I have no taxes in Jefferson. Colonel Sartoris explained it to me. Perhaps one of you can gain access to the city records and satisfy yourselves."

"But we have. We are the city authorities, Miss Emily. Didn't you get a notice from the sheriff, signed by him?"

"I received a paper, yes," Miss Emily said. "Perhaps he considers himself the sheriff . . . I have no taxes in Jefferson."

"But there is nothing on the books to show that, you see. We must go by the—"

"See Colonel Sartoris. I have no taxes in Jefferson."

"But, Miss Emily—"

"See Colonel Sartoris." (Colonel Sartoris had been dead almost ten years.) "I have no taxes in Jefferson. Tobe!" The Negro appeared. "Show these gentlemen out."

2

So she vanquished them, horse and foot, just as she had vanquished their fathers thirty years before about the smell. That was two years after her father's death and a short time after her sweetheart—the one we believed would marry her—had deserted her. After her father's death she went out very little; after her sweetheart went away, people hardly saw her at all. A few of the ladies had the temerity to call, but were not received, and the only sign of life about the place was the Negro man—a young man then—going in and out with a market basket.

"Just as if a man—any man—could keep a kitchen properly," the ladies said; so they were not surprised when the smell developed. It was another link between the gross, teeming world and the high and mighty Griersons.

A neighbor, a woman, complained to the mayor, Judge Stevens, eighty years old.

"But what will you have me do about it, madam?" he said.

"Why, send her word to stop it," the woman said. "Isn't there a law?"

"I'm sure that won't be necessary," Judge Stevens said. "It's probably just a snake or a rat that nigger of hers killed in the yard. I'll speak to him about it."

The next day he received two more complaints, one from a man who came in diffident deprecation. "We really must do something about it, Judge. I'd be the last one in the world to bother Miss Emily, but we've got to do something." That night the Board of Aldermen met—three graybeards and one younger man, a member of the rising generation.

"It's simple enough," he said. "Send her word to have her place cleaned up. Give her a certain time to do it in, and if she don't . . ."

"Dammit, sir," Judge Stevens said, "will you accuse a lady to her face of smelling bad?"

So the next night, after midnight, four men crossed Miss Emily's lawn and slunk about the house like burglars, sniffing along the base of the brick-work and at the cellar openings while one of them performed a regular sowing motion with his hand out of a sack slung from his shoulder. They broke open the cellar door and sprinkled lime there, and in all the outbuildings. As they recrossed the lawn, a window that had been dark was lighted and Miss Emily sat in it, the light behind her, and her upright torso motionless as that of an idol. They crept quietly across the lawn and into the shadow of the locusts that lined the street. After a week or two the smell went away.

That was when people had begun to feel really sorry for her. People in our town, remembering how old lady Wyatt, her great-aunt, had gone completely crazy at last, believed that the Griersons held themselves a little too high for what they really were. None of the young men were quite good enough for Miss Emily and such. We had long thought of them as a tableau, Miss Emily a slender figure in white in the background, her father a spraddled silhouette in the foreground, his back to her and clutching a horsewhip, the two of them framed by the back-flung front door. So when she got to be thirty and was still single, we were not pleased exactly, but vindicated; even with insanity in the family she wouldn't have turned down all of her chances if they had really materialized.

When her father died, it got about that the house was all that was left to her; and in a way, people were glad. At last they could pity Miss Emily. Being left alone, and a pauper, she had become humanized. Now she too would know the old thrill and the old despair of a penny more or less.

The day after his death all the ladies prepared to call at the house and offer condolence and aid, as is our custom. Miss Emily met them at the door, dressed as usual and with no trace of grief on her face. She told them that her father was not dead. She did that for three days, with the ministers calling on her, and the doctors, trying to persuade her to let them dispose of the body. Just as they were about to resort to law and force, she broke down, and they buried her father quickly.

We did not say she was crazy then. We believed she had to do that. We remembered all the young men her father had driven away, and we knew that with nothing left, she would have to cling to that which had robbed her, as people will.

3

She was sick for a long time. When we saw her again, her hair was cut short, making her look like a girl, with a vague resemblance to those angels in colored church windows—sort of tragic and serene.

The town had just let the contracts for paving the sidewalks, and in the summer after her father's death they began the work. The construction company came with niggers and mules and machinery, and a foreman named Homer Barron, a Yankee—a big, dark, ready man, with a big voice and eyes lighter than his face. The little boys would follow in groups to hear him cuss the niggers, and the niggers singing in time to the rise and fall of picks. Pretty soon he knew everybody in town. Whenever you heard a lot of laughing anywhere about the square, Homer Barron would be in the center of the group. Presently we began to see him and Miss Emily on Sunday afternoons driving in the yellow-wheeled buggy and the matched team of bays from the livery stable.

At first we were glad that Miss Emily would have an interest, because the ladies all said, "Of course a Grierson would not think seriously of a Northerner, a day laborer." But there were still others, older people, who said that even grief could not cause a real lady to forget *noblesse oblige*—without calling it *noblesse oblige*. They just said, "Poor Emily. Her kinsfolk should come to her." She had some kin in Alabama; but years ago her father had fallen out with them over the estate of old lady Wyatt, the crazy woman, and there was no communication between the two families. They had not even been represented at the funeral.

And as soon as the old people said, "Poor Emily," the whispering began. "Do you suppose it's really so?" they said to one another. "Of course it is. What else could . . ." This behind their hands; rustling of craned silk and satin behind jalousies closed upon the sun of Sunday afternoon as the thin, swift clop-clop-clop of the matched team passed: "Poor Emily."

She carried her head high enough—even when we believed that she was fallen. It was as if she demanded more than ever the recognition of her dignity as the last Grierson; as if it had wanted that touch of earthiness to reaffirm her imperviousness. Like when she bought the rat poison, the arsenic. That was over a year after they had begun to say "Poor Emily," and while the two female cousins were visiting her.

"I want some poison," she said to the druggist. She was over thirty then, still a slight woman, though thinner than usual, with cold, haughty black eyes in a face the flesh of which was strained across the temples and about the eye-sockets as you imagine a lighthouse-keeper's face ought to look. "I want some poison," she said.

"Yes, Miss Emily. What kind? For rats and such? I'd recom—"

"I want the best you have. I don't care what kind."

The druggist named several. "They'll kill anything up to an elephant. But what you want is—"

"Arsenic," Miss Emily said. "Is that a good one?"

"Is . . . arsenic? Yes, ma'am. But what you want—"

"I want arsenic."

The druggist looked down at her. She looked back at him, erect, her face like a strained flag. "Why, of course," the druggist said. "If that's what you want. But the law requires you to tell what you are going to use it for."

Miss Emily just stared at him, her head tilted back in order to look him eye for eye, until he looked away and went and got the arsenic and wrapped it up. The Negro delivery boy brought her the package; the druggist didn't come back. When she opened the package at home there was written on the box, under the skull and bones: "For rats."

4

So the next day we all said, "She will kill herself"; and we said it would be the best thing. When she had first begun to be seen with Homer Barron, we had said, "She will marry him." Then we said, "She will persuade him yet," because Homer himself had remarked—he liked men, and it was known that he drank with the younger men in the Elks' Club—that he was not a marrying man. Later we said, "Poor Emily" behind the jalousies as they passed on Sunday afternoon in the glittering buggy, Miss Emily with her head high and Homer Barron with his hat cocked and a cigar in his teeth, reins and whip in a yellow glove.

Then some of the ladies began to say that it was a disgrace to the town and a bad example to the young people. The men did not want to interfere, but at last the ladies forced the Baptist minister—Miss Emily's people were Episcopal—to call upon her. He would never divulge what happened during that interview, but he refused to go back again. The next Sunday they again drove about the streets, and the following day the minister's wife wrote to Miss Emily's relations in Alabama.

So she had blood-kin under her roof again and we sat back to watch developments. At first nothing happened. Then we were sure that they were to be married. We learned that Miss Emily had been to the jeweler's and ordered a man's toilet set in silver, with the letters H.B. on each piece. Two days later we learned that she had bought a complete outfit of men's clothing, including a nightshirt, and we said, "They are married." We were really glad. We were glad because the two female cousins were even more Grierson than Miss Emily had ever been.

So we were not surprised when Homer Barron—the streets had been finished some time since—was gone. We were a little disappointed that there was not a public blowing-off, but we believed that he had gone on to prepare for Miss Emily's coming, or to give her a chance to get rid of the cousins. (By that time it was a cabal, and we were all Miss Emily's allies to help circumvent the cousins.) Sure enough, after another week they departed. And, as we had expected all along, within three days Homer Barron was back in town. A neighbor saw the Negro man admit him at the kitchen door at dusk one evening.

And that was the last we saw of Homer Barron. And of Miss Emily for some time. The Negro man went in and out with the market basket, but the front door remained closed. Now and then we would see her at a window for a moment, as the men did that night when they sprinkled the lime, but for almost six months she did not appear on the streets. Then we knew that this was to be expected too; as if that quality of her father which had thwarted her woman's life so many times had been too virulent and too furious to die.

When we next saw Miss Emily, she had grown fat and her hair was turning gray. During the next few years it grew grayer and grayer until it attained an even pepper-and-salt iron-gray, when it ceased turning. Up to the day of her death at seventy-four it was still that vigorous iron-gray, like the hair of an active man.

From that time on her front door remained closed, save for a period of six or seven years, when she was about forty, during which she gave lessons in china-painting. She fitted up a studio in one of the downstairs rooms, where the daughters and granddaughters of Colonel Sartoris' contemporaries were sent to her with the same regularity and in the same spirit that they were sent to church on Sundays with a twenty-five-cent piece for the collection plate. Meanwhile her taxes had been remitted.

Then the newer generation became the backbone and the spirit of the town, and the painting pupils grew up and fell away and did not send their children to her with boxes of color and tedious brushes and pictures cut from the ladies' magazines. The front door closed upon the last one and remained closed for good. When the town got free postal delivery, Miss Emily alone refused to let them fasten the metal numbers above her door and attach a mailbox to it. She would not listen to them.

Daily, monthly, yearly we watched the Negro grow grayer and more stooped, going in and out with the market basket. Each December we sent her a tax notice, which would be returned by the post office a week later, unclaimed. Now and then we would see her in one of the downstairs windows—she had evidently shut up the top floor of the house—like the carven torso of an idol in a niche, looking or not looking at us, we could never tell which. Thus she passed from generation to generation—dear, inescapable, impervious, tranquil, and perverse.

And so she died. Fell ill in the house filled with dust and shadows, with only a doddering Negro man to wait on her. We did not even know she was sick; we had long since given up trying to get information from the Negro. He talked to no one, probably not even to her, for his voice had grown harsh and rusty, as if from disuse.

She died in one of the downstairs rooms, in a heavy walnut bed with a curtain, her gray head propped on a pillow yellow and moldy with age and lack of sunlight.

5

The Negro met the first of the ladies at the front door and let them in, with their hushed, sibilant voices and their quick, curious glances, and then he disappeared. He walked right through the house and out the back and was not seen again.

The two female cousins came at once. They held the funeral on the second day, with the town coming to look at Miss Emily beneath a mass of bought flowers, with the crayon face of her father musing profoundly above the bier and the ladies sibilant and macabre; and the very old men—some in their brushed Confederate uniforms—on the porch and the lawn, talking of Miss Emily as if she had been a contemporary of theirs, believing that they had danced with her and courted her perhaps, confusing time with its mathematical progression, as the old do, to whom all the past is not a diminishing road but, instead, a huge meadow which no winter ever quite touches, divided from them now by the narrow bottle-neck of the most recent decade of years.

Already we knew that there was one room in that region above stairs which no one had seen in forty years, and which would have to be forced. They waited until Miss Emily was decently in the ground before they opened it.

The violence of breaking down the door seemed to fill this room with pervading dust. A thin, acrid pall as of the tomb seemed to lie everywhere upon this room decked and furnished as for a bridal: upon the valance curtains of faded rose color, upon the rose-shaded lights, upon the dressing table, upon the delicate array of crystal and the man's toilet things backed with tarnished silver, silver so tarnished that the monogram was obscured. Among them lay a collar and tie, as if they had just been removed, which, lifted, left upon the surface a pale crescent in the dust. Upon a chair hung the suit, carefully folded; beneath it the two mute shoes and the discarded socks.

The man himself lay in the bed.

For a long while we just stood there, looking down at the profound and fleshless grin. The body had apparently once lain in the attitude of an embrace, but now the long sleep that outlasts love, that conquers even the grimace of love, had cuckolded him. What was left of him, rotted beneath what was left of the nightshirt, had become inextricable from the bed in which he lay; and upon him and upon the pillow beside him lay that even coating of the patient and biding dust.

Then we noticed that in the second pillow was the indentation of a head. One of us lifted something from it, and leaning forward, that faint and invisible dust dry and acrid in the nostrils, we saw a long strand of iron-gray hair.

Robert Penn Warren (b. 1905)
Blackberry Winter

It was getting into June and past eight o'clock in the morning, but there was a fire—even if it wasn't a big fire, just a fire of chunks—on the hearth of the big stone fireplace in the living room. I was standing on the hearth, almost into the chimney, hunched over the fire, working my bare toes slowly on the warm stone. I relished the heat which made the skin of my bare legs warp and creep and tingle, even as I called to my mother, who was somewhere back in the dining room or kitchen, and said: "But it's June, I don't have to put them on!"

"You put them on if you are going out," she called.

I tried to assess the degree of authority and conviction in the tone, but at that distance it was hard to decide. I tried to analyze the tone, and then I thought what a fool I had been to start out the back door and let her see that I was barefoot. If I had gone out the front door or the side door she would never have known, not till dinner time anyway, and by then the day would have been half gone and I would have been all over the farm to see what the storm had done and down to the creek to see the flood. But it had never crossed my mind that they would try to stop you from going barefoot in June, no matter if there had been a gully-washer and a cold spell.

Nobody had ever tried to stop me in June as long as I could remember, and when you are nine years old, what you remember seems forever; for you remember everything and everything is important and stands big and full and fills up Time and is so solid that you can walk around and around it like a tree and look at it. You are aware that time passes, that there is a movement in time, but that is not what Time is. Time is not a movement, a flowing, a wind then, but is, rather, a kind of climate in which things are, and when a thing happens it begins to live and keeps on living and stands solid in Time like the tree that you can walk around. And if there is a movement, the movement is not Time itself, any more than a breeze is climate, and all the breeze does is to shake a little the leaves on the tree which is alive and solid. When you are nine, you know that there are things that you don't know, but you know that when you know something you know it. You know how a thing has been and you know that you can go barefoot in June. You do not understand that voice from back in the kitchen which says that you cannot go barefoot outdoors and run to see what has happened and rub your feet over the wet shivery grass and make the perfect mark of your foot in the smooth, creamy, red mud and then muse upon it as though you had suddenly come upon that single mark on the glistening auroral beach of the world. You have never seen a beach, but you have read the book and how the footprint was there.

The voice had said what it had said, and I looked savagely at the black stockings and the strong, scuffed brown shoes which I had brought from my closet as far as the hearth rug. I called once more, "But it's June," and waited.

"It's June," the voice replied from far away, "but it's blackberry winter."

I had lifted my head to reply to that, to make one more test of what was in that tone, when I happened to see the man.

The fireplace in the living room was at the end; for the stone chimney was built, as in so many of the farmhouses in Tennessee, at the end of a gable, and there was a window on each side of the chimney. Out of the window on the north side of the fireplace I could see the man. When I saw the man I did not call out what I had intended, but, engrossed by the strangeness of the sight, watched him, still far off, come along the path by the edge of the woods.

What was strange was that there should be a man there at all. That path went along the yard fence, between the fence and the woods which came right down to the yard, and then on back past the chicken runs and on by the woods until it was lost to sight where the woods bulged out and cut off the back field. There the path disappeared into the woods. It led on back, I knew, through the woods and to the swamp, skirted the swamp where the big trees gave way to sycamores and water oaks and willows and tangled cane, and then led on to the river. Nobody ever went back there except people who wanted to gig frogs in the swamp or to fish in the river or to hunt in the woods, and those people, if they didn't have a standing permission from my father, always stopped to ask permission to cross the farm. But the man whom I now saw wasn't, I could tell even at that distance, a sportsman. And what would a sportsman have been doing down there after a storm? Besides, he was coming from the river, and nobody had gone down there that morning. I knew that for a fact, because if anybody had passed, certainly if a stranger had passed, the dogs would have made a racket and would have been out on him. But this man was coming up from the river and had come up through the woods. I suddenly had a vision of him moving up the grassy path in the woods, in the green twilight under the big trees, not making any sound on the path, while now and then, like drops off the eaves, a big drop of water would fall from a leaf or bough and strike a stiff oak leaf lower down with a small, hollow sound like a drop of water hitting tin. That sound, in the silence of the woods, would be very significant.

When you are a boy and stand in the stillness of woods, which can be so still that your heart almost stops beating and makes you want to stand there in the green twilight until you feel your very feet sinking into and clutching the earth like roots and your body breathing slow through its pores like the leaves—when you stand there and wait for the next drop to drop with its small, flat sound to a lower leaf, that sound seems to measure out something, to put an end to something, to begin something, and you cannot wait for it to happen and are afraid it will not happen, and then when it has happened, you are waiting again, almost afraid.

But the man whom I saw coming through the woods in my mind's eye did not pause and wait, growing into the ground and breathing with the enormous, soundless breathing of the leaves. Instead, I saw him moving in the green twilight inside my head as he was moving at that very moment along the path by the edge of the woods, coming toward the house. He was moving steadily, but not fast, with his shoulders hunched a little and his head thrust forward, like a man who has come a long way and has a long way to go. I shut my eyes for a couple of seconds, thinking that when I opened them he would not be there at all. There was no place for him to have come from, and there was no reason for him to come where he was coming, toward our house. But I opened my eyes, and there he was, and he was coming steadily along the side of the woods. He was not yet even with the back chicken yard.

"Mama," I called.

"You put them on," the voice said.

"There's a man coming," I called, "out back."

She did not reply to that, and I guessed that she had gone to the kitchen window to look. She would be looking at the man and wondering who he was and what he wanted, the way you always do in the country, and if I went back there now she would not notice right off whether or not I was barefoot. So I went back to the kitchen.

She was standing by the window. "I don't recognize him," she said, not looking around at me.

"Where could he be coming from?" I asked.

"I don't know," she said.

"What would he be doing down at the river? At night? In the storm?"

She studied the figure out the window, then said, "Oh, I reckon maybe he cut across from the Dunbar place."

That was, I realized, a perfectly rational explanation. He had not been down at the river in the storm, at night. He had come over this morning. You could cut across from the Dunbar place if you didn't mind breaking through a lot of elder and sassafras and blackberry bushes which had about taken over the old cross path, which nobody ever used any more. That satisfied me for a moment, but only for a moment. "Mama," I asked, "what would he be doing over at the Dunbar place last night?"

Then she looked at me, and I knew I had made a mistake, for she was looking at my bare feet. "You haven't got your shoes on," she said.

But I was saved by the dogs. That instant there was a bark which I recognized as Sam, the collie, and then a heavier, churning kind of bark which was Bully, and I saw a streak of white as Bully tore round the corner of the back porch and headed out for the man. Bully was a big, bone-white bull dog, the kind of dog that they used to call a farm bull dog but that you don't see any more, heavy chested and heavy headed, but with pretty long legs. He could take a fence as light as a hound. He had just cleared the white paling fence toward the woods when my mother ran out to the back porch and began calling, "Here you, Bully! Here you!"

Bully stopped in the path, waiting for the man, but he gave a few more of those deep, gargling, savage barks that reminded you of something down a stone-lined well. The red clay mud, I saw, was splashed up over his white chest and looked exciting, like blood.

The man, however, had not stopped walking even when Bully took the fence and started at him. He had kept right on coming. All he had done was to switch a little paper parcel which he carried from the right hand to the left, and then reach into his pants pocket to get something. Then I saw the glitter and knew that he had a knife in his hand, probably the kind of mean knife just made for devilment and nothing else, with a blade as long as the blade of a frog-sticker, which will snap out ready when you press a button in the handle. That knife must have had a button in the handle, or else how could he have had the blade out glittering so quick and with just one hand?

Pulling his knife against the dogs was a funny thing to do, for Bully was a big, powerful brute and fast, and Sam was all right. If those dogs had meant business, they might have knocked him down and ripped him before he got a stroke in. He ought to have picked up a heavy stick, something to take a swipe at them with and something which they could see and respect when they came at him. But he apparently did not know much about dogs. He just held the knife blade close against the right leg, low down, and kept on moving down the path.

Then my mother had called, and Bully had stopped. So the man let the blade of the knife snap back into the handle, and dropped it into his pocket, and kept on coming. Many women would have been afraid with the strange man who they knew had that knife in his pocket. That is, if they were alone in the house with nobody but a nine-year-old boy. And my mother was alone, for my father had gone off, and Dellie, the cook, was down at her cabin because she wasn't feeling well. But my mother wasn't afraid. She wasn't a big woman, but she was clear and brisk about everything she did and looked everybody and everything right in the eye from her own blue eyes in her tanned face. She had been the first woman in the county to ride a horse astride (that was back when she was a girl and long before I was born), and I have seen her snatch up a pump gun and go out and knock a chicken hawk out of the air like a busted skeet when he came over her chicken yard. She was a steady and self-reliant woman, and when I think of her now after all the years she has been dead, I think of her brown hands, not big, but somewhat square for a woman's hands, with square-cut nails. They looked, as a matter of fact, more like a young boy's hands than a grown woman's. But back then it never crossed my mind that she would ever be dead.

She stood on the back porch and watched the man enter the back gate, where the dogs (Bully had leaped back into the yard) were dancing and muttering and giving sidelong glances back to my mother to see if she meant what she had said. The man walked right by the dogs, almost brushing them, and didn't pay them any attention. I could see now that he wore old khaki pants, and a dark wool coat with stripes in it, and a gray felt hat. He had on a gray shirt with blue stripes in it, and no tie. But I could see a tie, blue and reddish, sticking in his side coat-pocket. Everything was wrong about what he wore. He ought to have been wearing blue jeans or overalls, and a straw hat or an old black felt hat, and the coat, granting that he might have been wearing a wool coat and not a jumper, ought not to have had those stripes. Those clothes, despite the fact that they were old enough and dirty enough for any tramp, didn't belong there in our back yard, coming down the path, in Middle Tennessee, miles away from any big town, and even a mile off the pike.

When he got almost to the steps, without having said anything, my mother, very matter-of-factly, said, "Good morning."

"Good morning," he said, and stopped and looked her over. He did not take off his hat, and under the brim you could see the perfectly unmemorable face, which wasn't old and wasn't young, or thick or thin. It was grayish and covered with about three days of stubble. The eyes were a kind of nondescript, muddy hazel, or something like that, rather bloodshot. His teeth, when he opened his mouth, showed yellow and uneven. A couple of them had been knocked out. You knew that they had been knocked out, because there was a scar, not very old, there on the lower lip just beneath the gap.

"Are you hunting work?" my mother asked him.

"Yes," he said—not "yes, mam"—and still did not take off his hat.

"I don't know about my husband, for he isn't here," she said, and didn't mind a bit telling the tramp, or whoever he was, with the mean knife in his pocket, that no man was around, "but I can give you a few things to do. The storm has drowned a lot of my chicks. Three coops of them. You can gather them up and bury them. Bury them deep so the dogs won't get at them. In the woods. And fix the coops the wind blew over. And down yonder beyond that pen by the edge of the woods are some drowned poults. They got out and I couldn't get them in. Even after it started to rain hard. Poults haven't got any sense."

"What are them things—poults?" he demanded, and spat on the brick walk. He rubbed his foot over the spot, and I saw that he wore a black, pointed-toe low shoe, all cracked and broken. It was a crazy kind of shoe to be wearing in the country.

"Oh, they're young turkeys," my mother was saying. "And they haven't got any sense. I oughtn't to try to raise them around here with so many chickens, anyway. They don't thrive near chickens, even in separate pens. And I won't give up my chickens." Then she stopped herself and resumed briskly on the note of business. "When you finish that, you can fix my flower beds. A lot of trash and mud and gravel has washed down. Maybe you can save some of my flowers if you are careful."

"Flowers," the man said, in a low, impersonal voice which seemed to have a wealth of meaning, but a meaning which I could not fathom. As I think back on it, it probably was not pure contempt. Rather, it was a kind of impersonal and distant marveling that he should be on the verge of grubbing in a flower bed. He said the word, and then looked off across the yard.

"Yes, flowers," my mother replied with some asperity, as though she would have nothing said or implied against flowers. "And they were very fine this year." Then she stopped and looked at the man. "Are you hungry?" she demanded.

"Yeah," he said.

"I'll fix you something," she said, "before you get started." She turned to me. "Show him where he can wash up," she commanded, and went into the house.

I took the man to the end of the porch where a pump was and where a couple of wash pans sat on a low shelf for people to use before they went into the house. I stood there while he laid down his little parcel wrapped in newspaper and took off his hat and looked around for a nail to hang it on. He poured the water and plunged his hands into it. They were big hands, and strong looking, but they did not have the creases and the earth-color of the hands of men who work outdoors. But they were dirty, with black dirt ground into the skin and under the nails. After he had washed his hands, he poured another basin of water and washed his face. He dried his face, and with the towel still dangling in his grasp, stepped over to the mirror on the house wall. He rubbed one hand over the stubble on his face. Then he carefully inspected his face, turning first one side and then the other, and stepped back and settled his striped coat down on his shoulders. He had the movements of a man who has just dressed up to go to church or a party—the way he settled his coat and smoothed it and scanned himself in the mirror.

Then he caught my glance on him. He glared at me for an instant out of the bloodshot eyes, then demanded in a low, harsh voice, "What you looking at?"

"Nothing," I managed to say, and stepped back a step from him.

He flung the towel down, crumpled, on the shelf, and went toward the kitchen door and entered without knocking.

My mother said something to him which I could not catch. I started to go in again, then thought about my bare feet, and decided to go back of the chicken yard, where the man would have to come to pick up the dead chicks. I hung around behind the chicken house until he came out.

He moved across the chicken yard with a fastidious, not quite finicking motion, looking down at the curdled mud flecked with bits of chicken-droppings. The mud curled up over the soles of his black shoes. I stood back from him some six feet and watched him pick up the first of the drowned chicks. He held it up by one foot and inspected it.

There is nothing deader looking than a drowned chick. The feet curl in that feeble, empty way which back when I was a boy, even if I was a country boy who did not mind hog-killing or frog-gigging, made me feel hollow in the stomach. Instead of looking plump and fluffy, the body is stringy and limp with the fluff plastered to it, and the neck is long and loose like a little string of rag. And the eyes have that bluish membrane over them which makes you think of a very old man who is sick about to die.

The man stood there and inspected the chick. Then he looked all around as though he didn't know what to do with it.

"There's a great big old basket in the shed," I said, and pointed to the shed attached to the chicken house.

He inspected me as though he had just discovered my presence, and moved toward the shed.

"There's a spade there, too," I added.

He got the basket and began to pick up the other chicks, picking each one up slowly by a foot and then flinging it into the basket with a nasty, snapping motion. Now and then he would look at me out of the blood-shot eyes. Every time he seemed on the verge of saying something, but he did not. Perhaps he was building up to say something to me, but I did not wait that long. His way of looking at me made me so uncomfortable that I left the chicken yard.

Besides, I had just remembered that the creek was in flood, over the bridge, and that people were down there watching it. So I cut across the farm toward the creek. When I got to the big tobacco field I saw that it had not suffered much. The land lay right and not many tobacco plants had washed out of the ground. But I knew that a lot of tobacco round the country had been washed right out. My father had said so at breakfast.

My father was down at the bridge. When I came out of the gap in the osage hedge into the road, I saw him sitting on his mare over the heads of the other men who were standing around, admiring the flood. The creek was big here, even in low water; for only a couple of miles away it ran into the river, and when a real flood came, the red water got over the pike where it dipped down to the bridge, which was an iron bridge, and high over the floor and even the side railings of the bridge. Only the upper iron work would show, with the water boiling and frothing red and white around it. That creek rose so fast and so heavy because a few miles back it came down out of the hills, where the gorges filled up with water in no time when a rain came. The creek ran in a deep bed with limestone bluffs along both sides until it got within three quarters of a mile of the bridge, and when it came out from between those bluffs in flood it was boiling and hissing and steaming like water from a fire hose.

Whenever there was a flood, people from half the county would come down to see the sight. After a gully-washer there would not be any work to do anyway. If it didn't ruin your crop, you couldn't plow and you felt like taking a holiday to celebrate. If it did ruin your crop, there wasn't anything to do except to try to take your mind off the mortgage, if you were rich enough to have a mortgage, and if you couldn't afford a mortgage you needed something to take your mind off how hungry you would be by Christmas. So people would come down to the bridge and look at the flood. It made something different from the run of days.

There would not be much talking after the first few minutes of trying to guess how high the water was this time. The men and kids just stood around, or sat their horses or mules, as the case might be, or stood up in the wagon beds. They looked at the strangeness of the flood for an hour or two, and then somebody would say that he had better be getting on home to dinner and would start walking down the gray, puddled limestone pike, or would touch heel to his mount and start off. Everybody always knew what it would be like when he got down to the bridge, but people always came. It was like church or a funeral. They always came, that is, if it was summer and the flood unexpected. Nobody ever came down in winter to see high water.

When I came out of the gap in the bodock hedge, I saw the crowd, perhaps fifteen or twenty men and a lot of kids, and saw my father sitting his mare, Nellie Gray. He was a tall, limber man and carried himself well. I was always proud to see him sit a horse, he was so quiet and straight, and when I stepped through the gap of the hedge that morning, the first thing that happened was, I remember, the warm feeling I always had when I saw him up on a horse, just sitting. I did not go toward him, but skirted the crowd on the far side, to get a look at the creek. For one thing, I was not sure what he would say about the fact that I was barefoot. But the first thing I knew, I heard his voice calling, "Seth!"

I went toward him, moving apologetically past the men, who bent their large, red or thin, sallow faces above me. I knew some of the men, and knew their names, but because those I knew were there in a crowd, mixed with the strange faces, they seemed foreign to me, and not friendly. I did not look up at my father until I was almost within touching distance of his heel. Then I looked up and tried to read his face, to see if he was angry about my being barefoot. Before I could decide anything from that impassive, high-boned face, he had leaned over and reached a hand to me. "Grab on," he commanded.

I grabbed on and gave a little jump, and he said, "Up-see-daisy!" and whisked me, light as a feather, up to the pommel of his McClellan saddle.

"You can see better up here," he said, slid back on the cantle a little to make me more comfortable, and then, looking over my head at the swollen, tumbling water, seemed to forget all about me. But his right hand was laid on my side, just above my thigh, to steady me.

I was sitting there as quiet as I could, feeling the faint stir of my father's chest against my shoulders as it rose and fell with his breath, when I saw the cow. At first, looking up the creek, I thought it was just another big piece of driftwood steaming down the creek in the ruck of water, but all at once a pretty good-size boy who had climbed part way up a telephone pole by the pike so that he could see better yelled out, "Golly-damn, look at that-air cow!"

Everybody looked. It was a cow all right, but it might just as well have been driftwood; for it was dead as a chunk, rolling and roiling down the creek, appearing and disappearing, feet up or head up, it didn't matter which.

The cow started up the talk again. Somebody wondered whether it would hit one of the clear places under the top girder of the bridge and get through or whether it would get tangled in the drift and trash that had piled against the upright girders and braces. Somebody remembered how about ten years before so much driftwood had piled up on the bridge that it was knocked off its foundations. Then the cow hit. It hit the edge of the drift against one of the girders, and hung there. For a few seconds it seemed as though it might tear loose, but then we saw that it was really caught. It bobbed and heaved on its side there in a slow, grinding, uneasy fashion. It had a yoke around its neck, the kind made out of a forked limb to keep a jumper behind fence.

"She shore jumped one fence," one of the men said.

And another: "Well, she done jumped her last one, fer a fack."

Then they began to wonder about whose cow it might be. They decided it must belong to Milt Alley. They said that he had a cow that was a jumper, and kept her in a fenced-in piece of ground up the creek. I had never seen Milt Alley, but I knew who he was. He was a squatter and lived up the hills a way, on a shirt-tail patch of set-on-edge land, in a cabin. He was pore white trash. He had lots of children. I had seen the children at school, when they came. They were thin-faced, with straight, sticky-looking, dough-colored hair, and they smelled something like old sour buttermilk, not because they drank so much buttermilk but because that is the sort of smell which children out of those cabins tend to have. The big Alley boy drew dirty pictures and showed them to the little boys at school.

That was Milt Alley's cow. It looked like the kind of cow he would have, a scrawny, old, sway-backed cow, with a yoke around her neck. I wondered if Milt Alley had another cow.

"Poppa," I said, "do you think Milt Alley has got another cow?"

"You say 'Mr. Alley,' " my father said quietly.

"Do you think he has?"

"No telling," my father said.

Then a big gangly boy, about fifteen, who was sitting on a scraggly little old mule with a piece of croker sack thrown across the saw-tooth spine, and who had been staring at the cow, suddenly said to nobody in particular, "Reckin anybody ever et drownt cow?"

He was the kind of boy who might just as well as not have been the son of Milt Alley, with his faded and patched overalls ragged at the bottom of the pants and the mud-stiff brogans hanging off his skinny, bare ankles at the level of the mule's belly. He had said what he did, and then looked embarrassed and sullen when all the eyes swung at him. He hadn't meant to say it, I am pretty sure now. He would have been too proud to say it, just as Milt Alley would have been too proud. He had just been thinking out loud, and the words had popped out.

There was an old man standing there on the pike, an old man with a white beard. "Son," he said to the embarrassed and sullen boy on the mule, "you live long enough and you'll find a man will eat anything when the time comes."

"Time gonna come fer some folks this year," another man said.

"Son," the old man said, "in my time I et things a man don't like to think on. I was a sojer and I rode with Gin'l Forrest, and them things we et when the time come. I tell you. I et meat what got up and run when you taken out yore knife to cut a slice to put on the fire. You had to knock it down with a carbeen butt, it was so active. That-air meat would jump like a bullfrog, it was so full of skippers."

But nobody was listening to the old man. The boy on the mule turned his sullen sharp face from him, dug a heel into the side of the mule and went off up the pike with a motion which made you think that any second you would hear mule bones clashing inside that lank and scrofulous hide.

"Cy Dundee's boy," a man said, and nodded toward the figure going up the pike on the mule.

"Reckin Cy Dundee's young-uns seen times they'd settle fer drownt cow," another man said.

The old man with the beard peered at them both from his weak, slow eyes, first at one and then at the other. "Live long enough," he said, "and a man will settle fer what he kin git."

Then there was silence again, with the people looking at the red, foam-flecked water.

My father lifted the bridle rein in his left hand, and the mare turned and walked around the group and up the pike. We rode on up to our big gate, where my father dismounted to open it and let me myself ride Nellie Gray through. When he got to the lane that led off from the drive about two hundred yards from our house, my father said, "Grab on." I grabbed on, and he let me down to the ground. "I'm going to ride down and look at my corn," he said. "You go on." He took the lane, and I stood there on the drive and watched him ride off. He was wearing cowhide boots and an old hunting coat, and I thought that that made him look very military, like a picture. That and the way he rode.

I did not go to the house. Instead, I went by the vegetable garden and crossed behind the stables, and headed down for Dellie's cabin. I wanted to go down and play with Jebb, who was Dellie's little boy about two years older than I was. Besides, I was cold. I shivered as I walked, and I had goose-flesh. The mud which crawled up between my toes with every step I took was like ice. Dellie would have a fire, but she wouldn't make me put on shoes and stockings.

Dellie's cabin was of logs, with one side, because it was on a slope, set on limestone chunks, with a little porch attached to it, and had a little white-washed fence around it and a gate with plow-points on a wire to clink when somebody came in, and had two big white oaks in the yard and some flowers and a nice privy in the back with some honeysuckle growing over it. Dellie and Old Jebb, who was Jebb's father and who lived with Dellie and had lived with her for twenty-five years even if they never had got married, were careful to keep everything nice around their cabin. They had the name all over the community for being clean and clever Negroes. Dellie and Jebb were what they used to call "white-folks' niggers." There was a big difference between their cabin and the other two cabins farther down where the other tenants lived. My father kept the other cabins weatherproof, but he couldn't undertake to go down and pick up after the litter they strewed. They didn't take the trouble to have a vegetable patch like Dellie and Jebb or to make preserves from wild plum, and jelly from crab apple the way Dellie did. They were shiftless, and my father was always threatening to get shed of them. But he never did. When they finally left, they just up and left on their own, for no reason, to go and be shiftless somewhere else. Then some more came. But meanwhile they lived down there, Matt Rawson and his family, and Sid Turner and his, and I played with their children all over the farm when they weren't working. But when I wasn't around they were mean sometimes to Little Jebb. That was because the other tenants down there were jealous of Dellie and Jebb.

I was so cold that I ran the last fifty yards to Dellie's gate. As soon as I had entered the yard, I saw that the storm had been hard on Dellie's flowers. The yard was, as I have said, on a slight slope, and the water running across had gutted the flower beds and washed out all the good black woods-earth which Dellie had brought in. What little grass there was in the yard was plastered sparsely down on the ground, the way the drainage water had left it. It reminded me of the way the fluff was plastered down on the skin of the drowned chicks that the strange man had been picking up, up in my mother's chicken yard.

I took a few steps up the path to the cabin, and then I saw that the drainage water had washed a lot of trash and filth out from under Dellie's house. Up toward the porch, the ground was not clean any more. Old pieces of rag, two or three rusted cans, pieces of rotten rope, some hunks of old dog dung, broken glass, old paper, and all sorts of things like that had washed out from under Dellie's house to foul her clean yard. It looked just as bad as the yards of the other cabins, or worse. It was worse, as a matter of fact, because it was a surprise. I had never thought of all that filth being under Dellie's house. It was not anything against Dellie that the stuff had been under the cabin. Trash will get under any house. But I did not think of that when I saw the foulness which had washed out on the ground which Dellie sometimes used to sweep with a twig broom to make nice and clean.

I picked my way past the filth, being careful not to get my bare feet on it, and mounted to Dellie's door. When I knocked, I heard her voice telling me to come in.

It was dark inside the cabin, after the daylight, but I could make out Dellie piled up in bed under a quilt, and Little Jebb crouched by the hearth, where a low fire simmered. "Howdy," I said to Dellie, "how you feeling?"

Her big eyes, the whites surprising and glaring in the black face, fixed on me as I stood there, but she did not reply. It did not look like Dellie, or act like Dellie, who would grumble and bustle around our kitchen, talking to herself, scolding me or Little Jebb, clanking pans, making all sorts of unneccessary noises and mutterings like an old-fashioned black steam thrasher engine when it has got up an extra head of steam and keeps popping the governor and rumbling and shaking on its wheels. But now Dellie just lay up there on the bed, under the patch-work quilt, and turned the black face, which I scarcely recognized, and the glaring white eyes to me.

"How you feeling?" I repeated.

"I'se sick," the voice said croakingly out of the strange black face which was not attached to Dellie's big, squat body, but stuck out from under a pile of tangled bedclothes. Then the voice added: "Mighty sick."

"I'm sorry," I managed to say.

The eyes remained fixed on me for a moment, then they left me and the head rolled back on the pillow. "Sorry," the voice said, in a flat way which wasn't question or statement of anything. It was just the empty word put into the air with no meaning or expression, to float off like a feather or a puff of smoke, while the big eyes, with the whites like the peeled white of hard-boiled eggs, stared at the ceiling.

"Dellie," I said after a minute, "there's a tramp up at the house. He's got a knife."

She was not listening. She closed her eyes.

I tiptoed over to the hearth where Jebb was and crouched beside him. We began to talk in low voices. I was asking him to get out his train and play train. Old Jebb had put spool wheels on three cigar boxes and put wire links between the boxes to make a train for Jebb. The box that was the locomotive had the top closed and a length of broom stick for a smoke stack. Jebb didn't want to get the train out, but I told him I would go home if he didn't. So he got out the train, and the colored rocks, and fossils of crinoid stems, and other junk he used for the load, and we began to push it around, talking the way we thought trainmen talked, making a chuck-chucking sound under the breath for the noise of the locomotive and now and then uttering low, cautious toots for the whistle. We got so interested in playing train that the toots got louder. Then, before he thought, Jebb gave a good, loud *toot-toot*, blowing for a crossing.

"Come here," the voice said from the bed.

Jebb got up slow from his hands and knees, giving me a sudden, naked, inimical look.

"Come here!" the voice said.

Jebb went to the bed. Dellie propped herself weakly up on one arm, muttering, "Come closer."

Jebb stood closer.

"Last thing I do, I'm gonna do it," Dellie said. "Done tole you to be quiet."

Then she slapped him. It was an awful slap, more awful for the kind of weakness which it came from and brought to focus. I had seen her slap Jebb before, but the slapping had always been the kind of easy slap you would expect from a good-natured, grumbling Negro woman like Dellie. But this was different. It was awful. It was so awful that Jebb didn't make a sound. The tears just popped out and ran down his face, and his breath came sharp, like gasps.

Dellie fell back. "Cain't even be sick," she said to the ceiling. "Git sick and they won't even let you lay. They tromp all over you. Cain't even be sick." Then she closed her eyes.

I went out of the room. I almost ran getting to the door, and I did run across the porch and down the steps and across the yard, not caring whether or not I stepped on the filth which had washed out from under the cabin. I ran almost all the way home. Then I thought about my mother catching me with the bare feet. So I went down to the stables.

I heard a noise in the crib, and opened the door. There was Big Jebb, sitting on an old nail keg, shelling corn into a bushel basket. I went in, pulling the door shut behind me, and crouched on the floor near him. I crouched there for a couple of minutes before either of us spoke, and watched him shelling the corn.

He had very big hands, knotted and grayish at the joints, with calloused palms which seemed to be streaked with rust with the rust coming up between the fingers to show from the back. His hands were so strong and tough that he could take a big ear of corn and rip the grains right off the cob with the palm of his hand, all in one motion, like a machine. "Work long as me," he would say, "and the good Lawd'll give you a hand lak cass-ion won't nuthin' hurt." And his hands did look like cast iron, old cast iron streaked with rust.

He was an old man, up in his seventies, thirty years or more older than Dellie, but he was strong as a bull. He was a squat sort of man, heavy in the shoulders, with remarkably long arms, the kind of build they say the river natives have on the Congo from paddling so much in their boats. He had a round bullet-head, set on powerful shoulders. His skin was very black, and the thin hair on his head was now grizzled like tufts of old cotton batting. He had small eyes and a flat nose, not big, and the kindest and wisest old face in the world, the blunt, sad, wise face of an old animal peering tolerantly out on the goings-on of the merely human creatures before him. He was a good man, and I loved him next to my mother and father. I crouched there on the floor of the crib and watched him shell corn with the rusty cast-iron hands, while he looked down at me out of the little eyes set in the blunt face.

"Dellie says she's might sick," I said.

"Yeah," he said.

"What's she sick from?"

"Woman-mizry," he said.

"What's woman-mizry?"

"Hit comes on 'em," he said. "Hit just comes on 'em when the time comes."

"What is it?"

"Hit is the change," he said. "Hit is the change of life and time."

"What changes?"

"You too young to know."

"Tell me."

"Time come and you find out everthing."

I knew that there was no use in asking him any more. When I asked him things and he said that, I always knew that he would not tell me. So I continued to crouch there and watch him. Now that I had sat there a little while, I was cold again.

"What you shiver fer?" he asked me.

"I'm cold. I'm cold because it's blackberry winter," I said.

"Maybe 'tis and maybe 'tain't," he said.

"My mother says it is."

"Ain't sayen Miss Sallie doan know and ain't sayen she do. But folks doan know everthing."

"Why isn't it blackberry winter?"

"Too late fer blackberry winter. Blackberries done bloomed."

"She said it was."

"Blackberry winter just a leetle cold spell. Hit come and then hit go away, and hit is growed summer of a sudden lak a gunshot. Ain't no tellen hit will go way this time."

"It's June," I said.

"June," he replied with great contempt. "That what folks say. What June mean? Maybe hit is come cold to stay."

"Why?"

"Cause this-here old yearth is tahrd. Hit is tahrd and ain't gonna perduce. Lawd let hit come rain one time forty days and forty nights, 'cause He wus tahrd of sinful folks. Maybe this-here old yearth say to the Lawd, Lawd, I done plum tahrd, Lawd, lemme rest. And Lawd say, Yearth, you done yore best, you give 'em cawn and you give 'em taters, and all they think on is they gut, and, Yearth, you kin take a rest."

"What will happen?"

"Folks will eat up everthing. The yearth won't perduce no more. Folks cut down all the trees and burn 'em cause they cold, and the yearth won't grow no more. I been tellen 'em. I been tellen folks. Sayen, maybe this year, hit is the time. But they doan listen to me, how the yearth is tahrd. Maybe this year they find out."

"Will everything die?"

"Everthing and everbody, hit will be so."

"This year?"

"Ain't no tellen. Maybe this year."

"My mother said it is blackberry winter," I said confidently, and got up.

"Ain't sayen nuthin' agin Miss Sallie," he said.

I went to the door of the crib. I was really cold now. Running, I had got up a sweat and now I was worse.

I hung on the door, looking at Jebb, who was shelling corn again.

"There's a tramp came to the house," I said. I had almost forgotten the tramp.

"Yeah."

"He came by the back way. What was he doing down there in the storm?"

"They comes and they goes," he said, "and ain't no tellen."

"He had a mean knife."

"The good ones and the bad ones, they comes and they goes. Storm or sun, light or dark. They is folks and they comes and they goes lak folks."

I hung on the door, shivering.

He studied me a moment, then said, "You git on to the house. You ketch yore death. Then what yore mammy say?"

I hesitated.

"You git," he said.

When I came to the back yard, I saw that my father was standing by the back porch and the tramp was walking toward him. They began talking before I reached them, but I got there just as my father was saying, "I'm sorry, but I haven't got any work. I got all the hands on the place I need now. I won't need any extra until wheat thrashing."

The stranger made no reply, just looked at my father.

My father took out his leather coin purse, and got out a half-dollar. He held it toward the man. "This is for half a day," he said.

The man looked at the coin, and then at my father, making no motion to take the money. But that was the right amount. A dollar a day was what you paid them back in 1910. And the man hadn't even worked half a day.

Then the man reached out and took the coin. He dropped it into the right side pocket of his coat. Then he said, very slowly and without feeling: "I didn't want to work on your——farm."

He used the word which they would have frailed me to death for using.

I looked at my father's face and it was streaked white under the sunburn. Then he said, "Get off this place. Get off this place or I won't be responsible."

The man dropped his right hand into his pants pocket. It was the pocket where he kept the knife. I was just about to yell to my father about the knife when the hand came back out with nothing in it. The man gave a kind of twisted grin, showing where the teeth had been knocked out above the new scar. I thought that instant how maybe he had tried before to pull a knife on somebody else and had got his teeth knocked out.

So now he just gave that twisted, sickish grin out of the unmemorable, grayish face, and then spat on the brick path. The glob landed just about six inches from the toe of my father's right boot. My father looked down at it, and so did I. I thought that if the glob had hit my father's boot something would have happened. I looked down and saw the bright glob, and on one side of it my father's strong cowhide boots, with the brass eyelets and the leather thongs, heavy boots splashed with good red mud and set solid on the bricks, and on the other side the pointed-toe, broken, black shoes, on which the mud looked so sad and out of place. Then I saw one of the black shoes move a little, just a twitch first, then a real step backward.

The man moved in a quarter circle to the end of the porch, with my father's steady gaze upon him all the while. At the end of the porch, the man reached up to the shelf where the wash pans were to get his little newspaper-wrapped parcel. Then he disappeared around the corner of the house and my father mounted the porch and went into the kitchen without a word.

I followed around the house to see what the man would do. I wasn't afraid of him now, no matter if he did have the knife. When I got around in front, I saw him going out the yard gate and starting up the drive toward the pike. So I ran to catch up with him. He was sixty yards or so up the drive before I caught up.

I did not walk right up even with him at first, but trailed him, the way a kid will, about seven or eight feet behind, now and then running two or three steps in order to hold my place against his longer stride. When I first came up behind him, he turned to give me a look, just a meaningless look, and then fixed his eyes up the drive and kept on walking.

When we had got around the bend in the drive which cut the house from sight, and were going along by the edge of the woods, I decided to come up even with him. I ran a few steps, and was by his side, or almost, but some feet off to the right. I walked along in this position for a while, and he never noticed me. I walked along until we got within sight of the big gate that let on the pike.

Then I said: "Where did you come from?"

He looked at me then with a look which seemed almost surprised that I was there. Then he said, "It ain't none of yore business."

We went on another fifty feet.

Then I said, "Where are you going?"

He stopped, studied me dispassionately for a moment, then suddenly took a step toward me and leaned his face down at me. The lips jerked back, but not in any grin, to show where the teeth were knocked out and to make the scar on the lower lip come white with the tension.

He said: "Stop following me. You don't stop following me and I cut yore throat, you little son-of-a-bitch."

Then he went on to the gate, and up the pike.

That was thirty-five years ago. Since that time my father and mother have died. I was still a boy, but a big boy, when my father got cut on the blade of a mowing machine and died of lockjaw. My mother sold the place and went to town to live with her sister. But she never took hold after my father's death, and she died within three years, right in middle life. My aunt always said, "Sallie just died of a broken heart, she was so devoted." Dellie is dead, too, but she died, I heard, quite a long time after we sold the farm.

As for Little Jebb, he grew up to be a mean and ficey Negro. He killed another Negro in a fight and got sent to the penitentiary, where he is yet, the last I heard tell. He probably grew up to be mean and ficey from just being picked on so much by the children of the other tenants, who were jealous of Jebb and Dellie for being thrifty and clever and being white-folks' niggers.

Old Jebb lived forever. I saw him ten years ago and he was about a hundred then, and not looking much different. He was living in town then, on relief—that was back in the Depression—when I went to see him. He said to me: "Too strong to die. When I was a young feller just comen on and seen how things wuz, I prayed the Lawd. I said, Oh, Lawd, gimme strength and meke me strong fer to do and to in-dure. The Lawd hearkened to my prayer. He give me strength. I was in-duren proud fer being strong and me much man. The Lawd give me my prayer and my strength. But now He done gone off and fergot me and left me alone with my strength. A man doan know what to pray fer, and him mortal."

Jebb is probably living yet, as far as I know.

That is what has happened since the morning when the tramp leaned his face down at me and showed his teeth and said: "Stop following me. You don't stop following me and I cut yore throat, you little son-of-a-bitch." That was what he said, for me not to follow him. But I did follow him, all the years.

Richard Wright (1908–1960)
Big Boy Leaves Home 1934

1

Yo mama don wear no drawers . . .

Clearly, the voice rose out of the woods, and died away. Like an echo another voice caught it up:

Ah seena when she pulled em off . . .

Another, shrill, cracking, adolescent:

N she washed 'em in alcohol . . .

Then a quartet of voices, blending in harmony, floated high above the tree tops:

N she hung 'em out in the hall . . .

Laughing easily, four black boys came out of the woods into cleared pasture. They walked lollingly in bare feet, beating tangled vines and bushes with long sticks.

"Ah wished Ah knowed some mo lines t tha song."

"Me too."

"Yeah, when yuh gits t where she hangs em out in the hall yuh has t stop."

"Shucks, whut goes wid *hall?*"

"*Call.*"

"*Fall.*"

"*Wall.*"

"*Quall.*"

They threw themselves on the grass, laughing.

"Big Boy?"

"Huh?"

"Yuh know one thing?"

"Whut?"

"Yuh sho is crazy!"

"Crazy?"

"Yeah, yuh crazys a bed-bug!"

"Crazy bout whut?"

"Man, whoever hearda *quall?*"

"Yuh said yuh wanted something to go wid *hall*, didn't yuh?"

"Yeah, but whuts a *quall?*"

"Nigger, a *qualls* a *quall.*"

They laughed easily, catching and pulling long green blades of grass with their toes.

"Waal, ef a *qualls* a *quall*, whut IS a *quall?*"

"Oh, Ah know."

"Whut?"

"Tha ol song goes something like this:

> Yo mama don wear no drawers,
>   Ah seena when she pulled em off,
> N she washed em in alcohol,
>   N she hung em out in the hall,
>   N then she put em back on her QUALL!"

They laughed again. Their shoulders were flat to the earth, their knees propped up, and their faces square to the sun.

"Big Boy, yuhs CRAZY!"

"Don ax me nothin else."

"Nigger, yuhs CRAZY!"

They fell silent, smiling, dropping the lids of their eyes softly against the sunlight.

"Man, don the groun feel warm?"

"Jus lika bed."

"Jeeesus, Ah could stay here ferever."

"Me too."

"Ah kin feel tha ol sun goin all thu me."

"Feels like mah bones is warm."

In the distance a train whistled mournfully.

"There goes number fo!"

"Hittin on all six!"

"Highballin it down the line!"

"Boun fer up Noth, Lawd, bound fer up Noth!"

They began to chant, pounding bare heels in the grass.

> Dis train bound fo Glory
> Dis train, Oh Hallelujah
> Dis train bound fo Glory
> Dis train, Oh Hallelujah
> Dis train bound fo Glory
> Ef yuh ride no need fer fret er worry
> Dis train, Oh Hallelujah
> Dis train . . .
> Dis train don carry no gambler
> Dis train, Oh Hallelujah
> Dis train don carry no gambler
> Dis train, Oh Hallelujah
> Dis train don carry no gambler
> No fo day creeper er midnight rambler
> Dis train, Oh Hallelujah
> Dis train . . .

When the song ended they burst out laughing, thinking of a train bound for Glory.

"Gee, thas a good ol song!"

"Huuuuummmmmmmmman . . ."

"Whut?"

"Geeee whiiiiiiz . . ."

"Whut?"

"Somebody done let win! Das whut!"

Buck, Bobo and Lester jumped up. Big Boy stayed on the ground, feigning sleep.

"Jeeesus, tha sho stinks!"

"Big Boy!"

Big Boy feigned to snore.

"Big Boy!"

Big Boy stirred as though in sleep.

"Big Boy!"

"Hunh?"

"Yuh rotten inside!"

"Rotten?"

"Lawd, cant yuh smell it?"

"Smell whut?"

"Nigger, yuh mus gotta bad col!"

"Smell what?"

"NIGGER, YUH BROKE WIN!"

Big Boy laughed and fell back on the grass, closing his eyes.

"The hen whut cackles is the hen whut laid the egg."

"We ain no hens."

"Yuh cackled, didnt yuh?"

The three moved off with noses turned up.

"C mon!"

"Where yuh-all goin?"

"T the creek fer a swim."

"Yeah, les swim."

"Naw buddy naw!" said Big Boy, slapping the air with a scornful palm.

"Aa, c mon! Don be a heel!"

"N git *lynched?* Hell naw!"

"He ain gonna see us."

"How yuh know?"

"Cause he ain."

"Yuh-all go on. Ahma stay right here," said Big Boy.

"Hell, let im stay! C mon, les go," said Buck.

The three walked off, swishing at grass and bushes with sticks. Big Boy looked lazily at their backs.

"Hey!"

Walking on, they glanced over their shoulders.

"Hey, niggers!"

"C mon!"

Big Boy grunted, picked up his stick, pulled to his feet, and stumbled off.

"Wait!"

"C mon!"

He ran, caught up with them, leaped upon their backs, bearing them to the ground.

"Quit, Big Boy!"

"Gawddam, nigger!"

"Git t hell offa me!"

Big Boy sprawled in the grass beside them, laughing and pounding his heels in the ground.

"Nigger, whut yuh think we is, hosses?"

"How come yuh awways hoppin on us?"

"Lissen, wes gonna doubt-team on yuh one of these days n beat yo ol ass good."

Big Boy smiled.

"Sho nough?"

"Yeah, don yuh like it?"

"We gonna beat yuh sos yuh cant walk!"

"N dare yuh to do nothin erbout it!"

Big Boy bared his teeth.

"C mon! Try it now!"

The three circled around him.

"Say, Buck, yuh grab his feets!"

"N yuh git his head, Lester!"

"N Bobo, yuh get berhin n grab his arms!"

Keeping more than arm's length, they circled round and round Big Boy.

"C mon!" said Big Boy, feinting at one and then the other.

Round and round they circled, but could not seem to get any closer. Big Boy stopped and braced his hands on his hips.

"Is all three of yuh-all scareda me?"

"Les git im some other time," said Bobo, grinning.

"Yeah, we kin ketch yuh when yuh ain thinkin," said Lester.

"We kin trick yuh," said Buck.

They laughed and walked together.

Big Boy belched.

"Ahm hongry," he said.

"Me too."

"Ah wished Ah hada big hot pota belly-busters!"

"Cooked wid some good ol saltry ribs . . ."

"N some good ol egg cornbread . . ."

"N some buttermilk . . ."

"N some hot peach cobbler swimmin in juice . . ."

"Nigger, hush!"

They began to chant, emphasizing the rhythm by cutting at grass with sticks.

> Bye n bye
> Ah wanna piece of pie
> Pies too sweet
> Ah wanna piece of meat
> Meats too red
> Ah wanna piece of bread
> Breads too brown
> Ah wanna go t town
> Towns too far

Ah wanna ketch a car
Cars too fas
Ah fall n break mah ass
Ahll understan it better bye n bye . . .

They climbed over a barbed-wire fence and entered a stretch of thick woods. Big Boy was whistling softly, his eyes half-closed.

"LES GIT IM!"

Buck, Lester, and Bobo whirled, grabbed Big Boy about the neck, arms, and legs, bearing him to the ground. He grunted and kicked wildly as he went back into weeds.

"Hol im tight!"

"Git his arms! Git his arms!"

"Set on his legs so he cant kick!"

Big Boy puffed heavily, trying to get loose.

"WE GOT YUH NOW, GAWDDAMMIT, WE GOT YUH NOW!"

"Thas a Gawddam lie!" said Big Boy. He kicked, twisted, and clutched for a hold on one and then the other.

"Say, yuh-all hep me hol his arms!" said Bobo.

"Aw, we got this bastard now!" said Lester.

"Thas a Gawddam lie!" said Big Boy again.

"Say, yuh-all hep me hol his arms!" called Bobo.

Big Boy managed to encircle the neck of Bobo with his left arm. He tightened his elbow scissors-like and hissed through his teeth:

"Yuh got me, ain yuh?"

"Hol im!"

"Les beat this bastard's ass!"

"Say, hep me hol his *arms!* Hes got aholda mah *neck!*" cried Bobo.

Big Boy squeezed Bobo's neck and twisted his head to the ground.

"Yuh got me, ain yuh?"

"Quit, Big Boy, yuh chokin me! Yuh hurtin mah neck!" cried Bobo.

"Turn me loose!" said Big Boy.

"Ah ain got yuh! Its the others whut got yuh!" pleaded Bobo.

"Tell them others t git t hell offa me or Ahma break yo neck," said Big Boy.

"Ssssay, yyyuh-al gggit ooooffa Bbig Boy. Hhhes got me," gurgled Bobo.

"Cant yuh hol im?"

"Nnaw, hhes ggot mmah nneck . . ."

Bib Boy squeezed tighter.

"N Ahma break it too les yuh tell em t git t hell offa me!"

"Ttturn mmmeee llloose," panted Bobo, tears gushing.

"Cant yuh hol im, Bobo?" asked Buck.

"Nnaw, yuh-all tturn im lloose; hhhes got mah nnneck . . ."

"Grab his neck, Bobo . . ."

"Ah cant; yugurgur . . ."

To save Bobo, Lester and Buck got up and ran to a safe distance. Big Boy released Bobo, who staggered to his feet, slobbering and trying to stretch a crick out of his neck.

"Shucks, nigger, yuh almos broke mah neck," whimpered Bobo.
"Ahm gonna break yo ass nex time," said Big Boy.
"Ef Bobo coulda hel yuh we woulda had yuh," yelled Lester.
"Ah waznt gonna let im do that," said Big Boy.
They walked together again, swishing sticks.
"Yuh see," began Big Boy, "when a ganga guys jump on yuh, all yuh gotta do is put the heat on one of them n make im tell the others t let up, see?"
"Gee, thas a good idee!"
"Yeah, thas a good idee!"
"But yuh almos broke mah neck, man," said Bobo.
"Ahma smart nigger," said Big Boy, thrusting out his chest.

2

They came to the swimming hole.
"Ah ain goin in," said Bobo.
"Done got scared?" asked Big Boy.
"Naw, Ah ain scared . . ."
"How come yuh ain goin in?"
"Yuh know ol man Harvey don erllow no niggers t swim in this hole."
"N jus las year he took a shot at Bob fer swimming in here," said Lester.
"Shucks, ol man Harvey ain studyin bout us niggers," said Big Boy.
"Hes at home thinking about his jelly-roll," said Buck.
They laughed.
"Buck, yo mins lowern a snakes belly," said Lester.
"Ol man Harveys too doggone ol t think erbout jelly-roll," said Big Boy.
"Hes dried up; all the saps done lef im," said Bobo.
"C mon, les go!" said Big Boy.
Bobo pointed.
"See tha sign over yonder?"
"Yeah."
"Whut it say?"
"NO TRESPASSIN," read Lester.
"Know whut tha mean?"
"Mean ain no dogs n niggers erllowed," said Buck.
"Waal, wes here now," said Big Boy. "Ef he ketched us even like this thered be trouble, so we just as waal go on in . . ."
"Ahm wid the nex one!"
"Ahll go ef anybody else goes!"
Big Boy looked carefully in all directions. Seeing nobody, he began jerking off his overalls.
"LAS ONE INS A OL DEAD DOG!"
"THAS YO MA!"
"THAS YO PA!"
"THAS BOTH YO MA N YO PA!"
They jerked off their clothes and threw them in a pile under a tree. Thirty seconds later they stood, black and naked, on the edge of the hole under a sloping embankment. Gingerly Big Boy touched the water with his foot.

"Man, this waters col," he said.

"Ahm gonna put mah cloes back on," said Bobo, withdrawing his foot.

Big Boy grabbed him about the waist.

"Like hell yuh is!"

"Git outta the way, nigger!" Bobo yelled.

"Throw im in!" said Lester.

"Duck im!"

Bobo crouched, spread his legs, and braced himself against Big Boy's body. Locked in each other's arms, they tussled on the edge of the hole, neither able to throw the other.

"C mon, les me n yuh push em in."

"O.K."

Laughing, Lester and Buck gave the two locked bodies a running push. Big Boy and Bobo splashed, sending up silver spray in the sunlight. When Big Boy's head came up he yelled:

"Yuh bastard!"

"Tha wuz yo ma yuh pushed!" said Bobo, shaking his head to clear the water from his eyes.

They did a surface dive, came up and struck out across the creek. The muddy water foamed. They swam back, waded into shallow water, breathing heavily and blinking eyes.

"C mon in!"

"Man, the water's fine!"

Lester and Buck hesitated.

"Les wet em," Big Boy whispered to Bobo.

Before Lester and Buck could back away, they were dripping wet from handfuls of scooped water.

"Hey, quit!"

"Gawddam, nigger; tha waters col!"

"C mon in!" called Big Boy.

"We just as waal go on in now," said Buck.

"Look n see ef anybody's comin."

Kneeling, they squinted among the trees.

"Ain nobody."

"C mon, les go."

They waded in slowly, pausing each few steps to catch their breath. A desperate water battle began. Closing eyes and backing away, they shunted water into one another's faces with the flat palms of hands.

"Hey, cut it out!"

"Yeah, Ahm bout drownin!"

They came together in water up to their navels, blowing and blinking. Big Boy ducked, upsetting Bobo.

"Look out, nigger!"

"Don holler so loud!"

"Yeah, they kin hear yo ol big mouth a mile erway."

"This waters too col fer me."

"Thas cause it rained yistiddy."

They swam across and back again.

"Ah wish we hada bigger place t swim in."

"The white folks got plenty swimming pools n we ain got none."

"Ah useta swim in the ol Missippi when we lived in Vicksburg."

Big Boy put his head under the water and blew his breath. A sound came like that of a hippopotamus.

"C mon, les be hippos."

Each went to a corner of the creek and put his mouth just below the surface and blew like a hippopotamus. Tiring, they came and sat under the embankment.

"Look like Ah gotta chill."

"Me too."

"Les stay here n dry off."

"Jeeesus, Ahm col!"

They kept still in the sun, suppressing shivers. After some of the water had dried off their bodies they began to talk through clattering teeth.

"Whut would yuh do ef ol man Harveyd come erlong right now?"

"Run like hell!"

"Man, Ahd run so fas hed thinka black streaka lightnin shot pass im."

"But spose he hada gun?"

"Aw, nigger, shut up!"

They were silent. They ran their hands over wet, trembling legs, brushing water away. Then their eyes watched the sun sparkling on the restless creek.

Far away a train whistled.

"There goes number seven!"

"Headin fer up Noth!"

"Blazin it down the line!"

"Lawd, Ahm goin Noth some day."

"Me too, man."

"They say colored folks up Noth is got ekual rights."

They grew pensive. A black winged butterfly hovered at the water's edge. A bee droned. From somewhere came the sweet scent of honeysuckles. Dimly they could hear sparrows twittering in the woods. They rolled from side to side, letting sunshine dry their skins and warm their blood. They plucked blades of grass and chewed them.

"Oh!"

They looked up, their lips parting.

"Oh!"

A white woman, poised on the edge of the opposite embankment, stood directly in front of them, her hat in her hand and her hair lit by the sun.

"Its a woman!" whispered Big Boy in an underbreath. "A *white* woman!"

They stared, their hands instinctively covering their groins. Then they scrambled to their feet. The white woman backed slowly out of sight. They stood for a moment, looking at one another.

"Les git outta here!" Big Boy whispered.

"Wait till she goes erway."

"Les run, they'll ketch us here naked like this!"

"Mabbe theres a man wid her."

"C mon, les git our cloes," said Big Boy.

They waited a moment longer, listening.

"What t hell! Ahma git mah cloes," said Big Boy.

Grabbing at short tufts of grass, he climbed the embankment.

"Don run out there now!"

"C mon back, fool!"

Bobo hesitated. He looked at Big Boy, and then at Buck and Lester.

"Ahm goin wid Big Boy n git mah cloes," he said.

"Don run out there naked like tha, fool!" said Buck. "Yuh don know whos out there!"

Big Boy was climbing over the edge of the embankment.

"C mon," he whispered.

Bobo climbed after. Twenty-five feet away the woman stood. She had one hand over her mouth. Hanging by fingers, Buck and Lester peeped over the edge.

"C mon back; that womans scared," said Lester.

Big Boy stopped, puzzled. He looked at the woman. He looked at the bundle of clothes. Then he looked at Buck and Lester.

"C mon, les git our cloes!"

He made a step.

"Jim!" the woman screamed.

Big Boy stopped and looked around. His hands hung loosely at his side. The woman, her eyes wide, her hand over her mouth, backed away to the tree where their clothes lay in a heap.

"Big Boy, come back here n wait till shes gone!"

Bobo ran to Big Boy's side.

"Les go home! Theyll ketch us here," he urged.

Big Boy's throat felt tight.

"Lady, we wanna git our cloes," he said.

Buck and Lester climbed the embankment and stood indecisively. Big Boy ran toward the tree.

"Jim!" the woman screamed. "Jim! Jim!"

Black and naked, Big Boy stopped three feet from her.

"We wanna git our cloes," he said again, his words coming mechanically.

He made a motion.

"You go away! You go away! I tell you, you go away!"

Big Boy stopped again, afraid. Bobo ran and snatched the clothes. Buck and Lester tried to grab theirs out of his hands.

"You go away! You go away! You go away!" the woman screamed.

"Les go!" said Bobo, running toward the woods.

CRACK!

Lester grunted, stiffened, and pitched forward. His forehead struck a toe of the woman's shoes.

Bobo stopped, clutching the clothes. Buck whirled. Big Boy stared at Lester, his lips moving.

"Hes gotta gun; hes gotta gun!" yelled Buck, running wildly.

CRACK!

Buck stopped at the edge of the embankment, his head jerked backward, his body arched stiffly to one side; he toppled headlong, sending up a shower of bright spray to the sunlight. The creek bubbled.

Big Boy and Bobo backed away, their eyes fastened fearfully on a white man who was running toward them. He had a rifle and wore an army officer's uniform. He ran to the woman's side and grabbed her hand.

"You hurt, Bertha, you hurt?"

She stared at him and did not answer.

The man turned quickly. His face was red. He raised the rifle and pointed it at Bobo. Bobo ran back, holding the clothes in front of his chest.

"Don shoot me, Mistah, don shoot me . . ."

Big Boy lunged for the rifle, grabbing the barrel.

"You black sonofabitch!"

Big Boy clung desperately.

"Let go, you black bastard!"

The barrel pointed skyward.

CRACK!

The white man, taller and heavier, flung Big Boy to the ground. Bobo dropped the clothes, ran up, and jumped onto the white man's back.

"You black sonsofbitches!"

The white man released the rifle, jerked Bobo to the ground, and began to batter the naked boy with his fists. Then Big Boy swung, striking the man in the mouth with the barrel. His teeth caved in, and he fell, dazed. Bobo was on his feet.

"C mon, Big Boy, les go!"

Breathing hard, the white man got up and faced Big Boy. His lips were trembling, his neck and chin wet with blood. He spoke quietly.

"Give me that gun, boy!"

Big Boy leveled the rifle and backed away.

The white man advanced.

"Boy, I say give me that gun!"

Bobo had the clothes in his arms.

"Run, Big Boy, run!"

The man came at Big Boy.

"Ahll kill yuh; Ahll kill yuh!" said Big Boy.

His fingers fumbled for the trigger.

The man stopped, blinked, spat blood. His eyes were bewildered. His face whitened. Suddenly, he lunged for the rifle, his hands outstretched.

CRACK!

He fell forward on his face.

"Jim!"

Big Boy and Bobo turned in surprise to look at the woman.

"Jim!" she screamed again, and fell weakly at the foot of the tree.

Big Boy dropped the rifle, his eyes wide. He looked around. Bobo was crying and clutching the clothes.

"Big Boy, Big Boy . . ."

Big Boy looked at the rifle, started to pick it up, but didn't. He seemed at a loss. He looked at Lester, then at the white man; his eyes followed a thin stream of blood that seeped to the ground.

"Yuh done killed im," mumbled Bobo.

"Les go home!"

Naked, they turned and ran toward the wood. When they reached the barbed-wire fence they stopped.

"Les git our cloes on," said Big Boy.

They slipped quickly into overalls. Bobo held Lester's and Buck's clothes.

"Whut we gonna do wid these?"

Big Boy stared. His hands twitched.

"Leave em."

They climbed the fence and ran through the woods. Vines and leaves switched their faces. Once Bobo tripped and fell.

"C mon!" said Big Boy.

Bobo started crying, blood streaming from his scratches.

"Ahm scared!"

"C mon! Don cry! We wanna git home fo they ketches us!"

"Ahm scared!" said Bobo again, his eyes full of tears.

Big Boy grabbed his hand and dragged him along.

"C mon!"

3

They stopped when they got to the end of the woods. They could see the open road leading home, to ma and pa. But they hung back, afraid. The thick shadows cast from the trees were friendly and sheltering. But the wide glare of sun stretching out over the fields was pitiless. They crouched behind an old log.

"We gotta git home," said Big Boy.

"Theys gonna lynch us," said Bobo, half-questioningly.

Big Boy did not answer.

"Theys gonna lynch us," said Bobo again.

Big Boy shuddered.

"Hush!" he said. He did not want to think of it. He could not think of it; there was but one thought, and he clung to that one blindly. He had to get home, home to ma and pa.

Their heads jerked up. Their ears caught the rhythmic jingle of a wagon. They fell to the ground and clung flat to the side of a log. Over the crest of the hill came the top of a hat. A white face. Then shoulders in a blue shirt. A wagon drawn by two horses pulled into full view.

Big Boy and Bobo held their breath, waiting. Their eyes followed the wagon till it was lost in dust around a bend of the road.

"We gotta git home," said Big Boy.

"Ahm scared," said Bobo.

"C mon! Les keep t the fields."

They ran till they came to the cornfields. Then they went slower, for last year's corn stubbles bruised their feet.

They came in sight of a brickyard.

"Wait a minute," gasped Big Boy.

They stopped.

"Ahm goin on t mah home n yuh better go on t yos."

Bobo's eyes grew round.

"Ahm scared!"

"Yuh better go on!"

"Lemme go wid yuh; they'll ketch me . . ."

"Ef yuh kin git home mabbe yo folks kin hip yuh t git erway."

Big Boy started off. Bobo grabbed him.

"Lemme go wid yuh!"

Big Boy shook free.

"Ef yuh stay here theys gonna lynch yuh!" he yelled, running.

After he had gone about twenty-five yards he turned and looked; Bobo was flying through the woods like the wind.

Big Boy slowed when he came to the railroad. He wondered if he ought to go through the streets or down the track. He decided on the tracks. He could dodge a train better than a mob.

He trotted along the ties, looking ahead and back. His cheek itched, and he felt it. His hand came away smeared with blood. He wiped it nervously on his overalls.

When he came to his back fence he heaved himself over. He landed among a flock of startled chickens. A bantam rooster tried to spur him. He slipped and fell in front of the kitchen steps, grunting heavily. The ground was slick with greasy dishwater.

Panting, he stumbled through the doorway.

"Lawd, Big Boy, whuts wrong wid yuh?"

His mother stood gaping in the middle of the floor. Big Boy flopped wordlessly onto a stool, almost toppling over. Pots simmered on the stove. The kitchen smelled of food cooking.

"Whuts the matter, Big Boy?"

Mutely, he looked at her. Then he burst into tears. She came and felt the scratches on his face.

"Whut happened t yuh, Big Boy? Somebody been botherin yuh?"

"They after me, Ma! They after me . . ."

"Who!"

"Ah . . . Ah . . . We . . ."

"Big Boy, whuts wrong wid yuh?"

"He killed Lester n Buck," he muttered simply.

"Killed!"

"Yessum."

"Lester n Buck!"

"Yessum, Ma!"

"How killed?"

"He shot em, Ma!"

"Lawd Gawd in Heaven, have mercy on us all! This is mo trouble, mo trouble," she moaned, wringing her hands.

"N Ah killed im, Ma . . ."

She stared, trying to understand.

"Whut happened, Big Boy?"

"We tried t git our cloes from the tree . . ."

"Whut tree?"

"We wuz swimmin, Ma. N the white woman . . ."

"*White* woman? . . ."

"Yessum. She wuz at the swimmin hole . . ."

"Lawd have mercy! Ah knowed yuh boys wuz gonna keep on till yuh got into somethin like this!"

She ran into the hall.

"Lucy!"

"Mam?"

"C mere!"

"Mam?"

"C mere, Ah say!"

"Whutcha wan, Ma? Ahm sewin."

"Chile, will yuh c mere like Ah ast yuh?"

Lucy came to the door holding an unfinished apron in her hands. When she saw Big Boy's face she looked wildly at her mother.

"Whut's the matter?"

"Wheres Pa?"

"He's out front, Ah reckon."

"Git im, quick!"

"Whuts the matter, Ma?"

"Go git yo Pa, Ah say!"

Lucy ran out. The mother sank into a chair, holding a dish rag. Suddenly, she sat up.

"Big Boy, Ah thought yuh wuz in school?"

Big Boy looked at the floor.

"How come yuh didn't go t school?"

"We went t the woods."

She sighed.

"Ah done done all Ah kin fer yuh, Big Boy. Only Gawd kin help yuh now."

"Ma, don let em git me; don let em git me . . ."

His father came into the doorway. He stared at Big Boy, then at his wife.

"Whuts Big Boy inter now?" he asked sternly.

"Saul, Big Boys done gone n got inter trouble wid the white folks."

The old man's mouth dropped, and he looked from one to the other.

"Saul, we gotta git im erway from here."

"Open yo mouth n talk! Whut yuh been doin?" The old man gripped Big Boy's shoulders and peered at the scratches on his face.

"Me n Lester n Buck n Bobo wuz out on ol man Harveys place swimmin . . ."

"Saul, its a *white* woman!"

Big Boy winced. The old man compressed his lips and stared at his wife. Lucy gaped at her brother as though she had never seen him before.

"Whut happened? Cant yuh all talk?" the old man thundered, with a certain helplessness in his voice.

"We wuz swimmin," Big Boy began, "n then a white woman comes up t the hole. We got up right erway to git our cloes sos we could git erway, n she started screamin. Our cloes wuz right by the tree where she wuz standin, n when we started t git em she jus screamed. We told her we wanted our cloes . . . Yuh see, Pa, she was standin' right *by* our cloes; n when we went t git em she jus screamed . . . Bobo got the cloes, n then he shot Lester . . . "

"*Who* shot Lester?"

"The white man."

"Whut white man?"

"Ah dunno, Pa. He wuz a soljer, n he had a rifle."

"A soljer?"

"Yessuh."

"A *soljer?*"

"Yessuh, Pa. A soljer."

The old man frowned.

"N then what yuh-all do?"

"Waal, Buck said, 'Hes gotta gun!' N we started runnin. N then he shot Buck, n he fell in the swimmin hole. We didn't see im no mo . . . He wuz close on us then. He looked at the white woman n then he started t shoot Bobo. Ah grabbed the gun, n we started fightin. Bobo jumped on his back. He started beatin Bobo. Then Ah hit im wid the gun. Then he started at me n Ah shot im. Then we run . . ."

"Who seen?"

"Nobody."

"Wheres Bobo?"

"He went home."

"Anybody run after yuh-all?"

"Nawsuh."

"Yuh see anybody?"

"Nawsuh. Nobody but a white man. But he didnt see us."

"How long fo yuh-all lef the swimmin hole?"

"Little while ergo."

The old man nervously brushed his hand across his eyes and walked to the door. His lips moved, but no words came.

"Saul, whut we gonna do?"

"Lucy," began the old man, "go t Brother Sanders n tell im Ah said c mere; n go t Brother Jenkins n tell im Ah said c mere; n go t Elder Peters n tell im Ah said c mere. N don say nothin t nobody but whut Ah tol yuh. N when yuh git thu come straight back. Now go!"

Lucy dropped her apron across the back of a chair and ran down the steps. The mother bent over, crying and praying. The old man walked slowly over to Big Boy.

"Big Boy?"

Big Boy swallowed.

"Ahm talkin t yuh!"

"Yessuh."

"How come yuh didnt go t school this mawnin?"

"We went t the woods."

"Didnt yo ma send yuh t school?"

"Yessuh."

"How come yuh didnt go?"

"We went t the woods."

"Don yuh know thas wrong?"

"Yessuh."

"How come yuh go?"

Big Boy looked at his fingers, knotted them, and squirmed in his seat.

"AHM TALKIN T YUH!"

His wife straightened up and said reprovingly:

"Saul!"

The old man desisted, yanking nervously at the shoulder straps of his overalls.

"How long wuz the woman there?"

"Not long."

"Wuz she young?"

"Yessuh. Lika gal."

"Did yuh-all say anythin t her?"

"Nawsuh. We jes said we wanted our cloes."

"N what she say?"

"Nothin, Pa. She jus backed erway t the tree n screamed."

The old man stared, his lips trying to form a question.

"Big Boy, did yuh-all bother her?"

"Nawsuh, Pa. We didnt *touch* her."

"How long fo the white man come up?"

"Right erway."

"Whut he say?"

"Nothin. He jus cussed us."

Abruptly the old man left the kitchen.

"Ma, cant Ah go fo they ketches me?"

"Sauls doin what he kin."

"Ma, Ma, Ah don want em t ketch me . . ."

"Sauls doin what he kin. Nobody but the good Lawd kin hep us now."

The old man came back with a shotgun and leaned it in a corner. Fascinatedly, Big Boy looked at it.

There was a knock at the front door.

"Liza, see whos there."

She went. They were silent, listening. They could hear her talking.

"Whos there?"

"Me."

"Who?"

"Me, Brother Sanders."

"C mon in. Sauls waitin fer yuh."

Sanders paused in the doorway, smiling.

"Yuh sent fer me, Brother Morrison?"

"Brother Sanders, wes in deep trouble here."

Sanders came all the way into the kitchen.

"Yeah?"

"Big Boy done gone n killed a white man."

Sanders stopped short, then came forward, his face thrust out, his mouth open. His lips moved several times before he could speak.

"A *white* man?"

"They gonna kill me; they gonna kill me!" Big Boy cried, running to the old man.

"Saul, cant we git im erway somewhere?"

"Here now, take it easy; take it easy," said Sanders, holding Big Boy's wrists.

"They gonna kill me; they gonna lynch me!"

Big Boy slipped to the floor. They lifted him to a stool. His mother held him closely, pressing his head to her bosom.

"Whut we gonna do?" asked Sanders.

"Ah done sent fer Brother Jenkins n Elder Peters."

Sanders leaned his shoulders against the wall. Then, as the full meaning of it came to him, he exclaimed:

"Theys gonna git a mob! . . ." His voice broke off and his eyes fell on the shotgun.

Feet came pounding on the steps. They turned toward the door. Lucy ran in crying. Jenkins followed. The old man met him in the middle of the room, taking his hand.

"Wes in bad trouble here, Brother Jenkins. Big Boy's done gone n killed a white man. Yuh-alls gotta hep me . . ."

Jenkins looked hard at Big Boy.

"Elder Peters says hes comin," said Lucy.

"When all this happen?" asked Jenkins.

"Near bout a hour ergo, now," said the old man.

"Whut we gonna do?" asked Jenkins.

"Ah wanna wait till Elder Peters come," said the old man helplessly.

"But we gotta work fas ef we gonna do anythin," said Sanders. "We'll git in trouble jus standin here like this."

Big Boy pulled away from his mother.

"Pa, lemma go now! Lemma go now!"

"Be still, Big Boy!"

"Where kin yuh go?"

"Ah could ketch a freight!"

"Thas *sho* death!" said Jenkins. "They'll be watchin em all!"

"Kin yuh-all hep me wid some money?" the old man asked.

They shook their heads.

"Saul, whut kin we do? Big Boy cant stay here."

There was another knock at the door.

The old man backed stealthily to the shotgun.

"Lucy, go!"

Lucy looked at him, hesitating.

: 165

"Ah better go," said Jenkins.
It was Elder Peters. He came in hurriedly.
"Good evenin, everybody!"
"How yuh, Elder?"
"Good evenin."
"How yuh today?"
Peters looked around the crowded kitchen.
"Whuts the matter?"
"Elder, wes in deep trouble," began the old man. "Big Boy n some mo boys . . ."
". . . Lester n Buck n Bobo . . ."
". . . wuz over on ol man Harveys place swimmin . . ."
"N he don like us niggers *none*," said Peters emphatically. He widened his legs and put his thumbs in the armholes of his vest.
". . . n some white woman . . ."
"Yeah?" said Peters, coming closer.
". . . comes erlong n the boys tries t git their cloes where they done lef em under a tree. Waal, she started screamin n all, see? Reckon she thought the boys wuz after her. Then a white man in a soljers suit shoots two of em . . ."
". . . Lester n Buck . . ."
"Huummm," said Peters. "Tha wuz old man Harveys son."
"Harveys son?"
"Yuh mean the one that wuz in the Army?"
"Yuh mean Jim?"
"Yeah," said Peters. "The papers said he wuz here fer a vacation from his regiment. N tha woman the boys saw wuz jus erbout his wife . . ."
They stared at Peters. Now that they knew what white person had been killed, their fears became definite.
"N whut else happened?"
"Big Boy shot the man . . ."
"Harveys *son?*"
"He had t, Elder. He wuz gonna shoot im ef he didnt . . ."
"Lawd!" said Peters. He looked around and put his hat back on.
"How long ergo wuz this?"
"Mighty near an hour, now, Ah reckon."
"Do the white folks know yit?"
"Don know, Elder."
"Yuh-all better git this boy outta here right now," said Peters. "Cause ef yuh don theres gonna be a lynchin . . ."

"Where kin Ah go, Elder?" Big Boy ran up to him.
They crowded around Peters. He stood with his legs wide apart, looking up at the ceiling.
"Mabbe we kin hide im in the church till he kin git erway," said Jenkins.
Peters' lips flexed.
"Naw, Brother, thall never do! Theyll git him there sho. N anyhow, ef they ketch im there itll ruin us all. We gotta git the boy outta town . . ."
Sanders went up to the old man.

"Lissen," he said in a whisper. "Mah son, Will, the one whut drives fer the Magnolia Express Comny, is takin a truck o goods t Chicawgo in the mawnin. If we kin hide Big Boy somewhere till then, we kin put him on the truck . . ."

"Pa, please, lemme go wid Will when he goes in the mawnin," Big Boy begged.

The old man stared at Sanders.

"Yuh reckon thas safe?"

"Its the only thing yuh *kin* do," said Peters.

"But where we gonna hide im till then?"

"Whut time yo boy leavin out in the mawnin?"

"At six."

They were quiet, thinking. The water kettle on the stove sang.

"Pa, Ah knows where Will passes erlong wid the truck out on Bullards Road. Ah kin hide in one of them ol kilns . . ."

"Where?"

"In one of them kilns we built . . ."

"But they'll git yuh there," wailed the mother.

"But there ain no place else fer im t go."

"Theres some holes big enough fer me t git in n stay till Will comes erlong," said Big Boy. "Please, Pa, lemme go fo they ketches me . . ."

"Let im go!"

"Please, Pa . . ."

The old man breathed heavily.

"Lucy, git his things!"

"Saul, theyll git im out there!" wailed the mother, grabbing Big Boy.

Peters pulled her away.

"Sister Morrison, ef yuh don let im go n git erway from here hes gonna be caught shos theres a Gawd in Heaven!"

Lucy came running with Big Boy's shoes and pulled them on his feet. The old man thrust a battered hat on his head. The mother went to the stove and dumped the skillet of corn pone into her apron. She wrapped it, and un-buttoning Big Boy's overalls, pushed it into his bosom.

"Heres something fer yuh t eat; n pray, Big Boy, cause thas all anybody kin do now . . ."

Big Boy pulled to the door, his mother clinging to him.

"Let im go, Sister Morrison!"

"Run fas, Big Boy!"

Big Boy raced across the yard, scattering the chickens. He paused at the fence and hollered back:

"Tell Bobo where Ahm hidin n tell im t c mon!"

4

He made for the railroad, running straight toward the sunset. He held his left hand tightly over his heart, holding the hot pone of corn bread there. At times he stumbled over the ties, for his shoes were tight and hurt his feet. His throat burned from thirst; he had had no water since noon.

He veered off the track and trotted over the crest of a hill, following Bullard's Road. His feet slipped and slid in the dust. He kept his eyes straight ahead, fearing every clump of shrubbery, every tree. He wished it were night. If he could only get to the kilns without meeting anyone. Suddenly a thought came to him like a blow. He recalled hearing the old folks tell tales of blood-hounds, and fear made him run slower. None of them had thought of that. Spose blood-houns wuz put on his trail? Lawd! Spose a whole pack of em, foamin n howlin, tore im t pieces? He went limp and his feet dragged. Yeah, thas whut they wuz gonna send after im, blood-houns! N then thered by no way fer im t dodge! Why hadnt Pa let im take tha shotgun? He stopped. He oughta go back n git tha shotgun. And then when the mob came he would take some with him.

In the distance he heard the approach of a train. It jarred him back to a sharp sense of danger. He ran again, his big shoes sopping up and down in the dust. He was tired and his lungs were bursting from running. He wet his lips, wanting water. As he turned from the road across a plowed field he heard the train roaring at his heels. He ran faster, gripped in terror.

He was nearly there now. He could see the black clay on the sloping hillside. Once inside a kiln he would be safe. For a little while, at least. He thought of the shotgun again. If he only had something! Someone to talk to . . . Thas right! Bobo! Bobod be wid im. Hed almost fergot Bobo. Bobod bringa gun; he knowed he would. N tergether they could kill the whole mob. Then in the mawning theyd git inter Will's truck n go far erway, t Chicawgo . . .

He slowed to a walk, looking back and ahead. A light wind skipped over the grass. A beetle lit on his cheek and he brushed it off. Behind the dark pines hung a red sun. Two bats flapped against that sun. He shivered, for he was growing cold; the sweat on his body was drying.

He stopped at the foot of the hill, trying to choose between two patches of black kilns high above him. He went to the left, for there lay the ones he, Bobo, Lester, and Buck had dug only last week. He looked around again; the landscape was bare. He climbed the embankment and stood before a row of black pits sinking four and five feet deep into the earth. He went to the largest and peered in. He stiffened when his ears caught the sound of a whir. He ran back a few steps and poised on his toes. Six foot of snake slid out of the pit and went into coil. Big Boy looked around wildly for a stick. He ran down the slope, peering into the grass. He stumbled over a tree limb. He picked it up and tested it by striking it against the ground.

Warily, he crept back up the slope, his stick poised. When about seven feet from the snake he stopped and waved the stick. The coil grew tighter, the whir sounded louder, and a flat head reared to strike. He went to the right, and the flat head followed him, the blue-black tongue darting forth; he went to the left, and the flat head followed him there too.

He stopped, teeth clenched. He had to kill this snake. Jus had t kill im! This wuz the safest pit on the hillside. He waved the stick again, looking at the snake before, thinking of a mob behind. The flat head reared higher. With stick over shoulder, he jumped in, swinging. The stick sang through the air, catching the snake on the side of the head, sweeping him out of coil. There was a brown writhing mass. Then Big Boy was upon him, pounding blows home, one on top of the other. He fought viciously, his eyes red, his teeth bared in a snarl. He beat till the snake lay still; then he stomped it with his heel, grinding its head into the dirt.

He stopped, limp, wet. The corners of his lips were white with spittle. He spat and shuddered.

Cautiously, he went to the hole and peered. He longed for a match. He imagined whole nests of them in there waiting. He put the stick into the hole and waved it around. Stooping, he peered again. It mus be awright. He looked over the hillside, his eyes coming back to the dead snake. Then he got to his knees and backed slowly into the hole.

When inside he felt there must be snakes about him, ready to strike. It seemed he could see and feel them there, waiting tensely in coil. In the dark he imagined long, white fangs ready to sink into his neck, his side, his legs. He wanted to come out, but kept still. Shucks, he told himself, ef there wuz any snakes in here they sho woulda done bit me by now. Some of his fear left, and he relaxed.

With elbows on ground and chin on palms, he settled. The clay was cold to his knees and thighs, but his bosom was kept warm by the hot pone of corn bread. His thirst returned and he longed for a drink. He was hungry, too. But he did not want to eat the corn pone. Naw, not now. Mabbe after erwhile, after Bobo came. Then theyd both eat the corn pone.

The view from his hole was fringed by the long tufts of grass. He could see all the way to Bullard's Road, and even beyond. The wind was blowing, and in the east the first touch of dusk was rising. Every now and then a bird floated past, a spot of wheeling black printed against the sky. Big Boy sighed, shifted his weight, and chewed at a blade of grass. A wasp droned. He heard number nine, far away and mournful.

The train made him remember how they had dug these kilns on long hot summer days, how they had made boilers out of big tin cans, filled them with water, fixed stoppers for steam, cemented them in holes with wet clay, and built fires under them. He recalled how they had danced and yelled when a stopper blew out of a boiler, letting out a big spout of steam and a shrill whistle. There were times when they had the whole hillside blazing and smoking. Yeah, yuh see, Big Boy wuz Casey Jones n wuz speedin it down the gleamin rails of the Southern Pacific. Bobo had number two on the Santa Fe. Buck wuz on the Illinoy Central. Lester the Nickel Plate. Lawd, how they sheveled the wood in! The boiling water would almost jar the cans loose from the clay. More and more pine-knots and dry leaves would be piled under the cans. Flames would grow so tall they would have to shield their eyes. Sweat would pour off their faces. Then, suddenly, a peg would shoot high into the air, and

Pssseeeezzzzzzzzzzzzzzzzz . . .

Big Boy sighed and stretched out his arm, quenching the flames and scattering the smoke. Why didnt Bobo c mon? He looked over the fields; there was nothing but dying sunlight. His mind drifted back to the kilns. He remembered the day when Buck, jealous of his winning, had tried to smash his kiln. Yeah, that ol sonofabitch! Naw, Lawd! He didnt go t say tha! Whut wu he thinkin erbout? Cussin the dead! Yeah, po ol Buck wuz dead now. N Lester too. Yeah, it wuz awright fer Buck t smash his kiln. Sho. N he wished he hadnt socked ol Buck so hard tha day. He wuz sorry fer Buck now. N he sho wished he hadnt cussed po ol Bucks ma, neither. Tha wuz sinful! Mabbe Gawd would git im fer that? But he didnt go t do it! Po Buck! Po Lester! Hed never treat anybody like tha ergin, never . . .

Dusk was slowly deepening. Somewhere, he could not tell exactly where, a cricket took up a fitful song. The air was growing soft and heavy. He looked over the fields, longing for Bobo . . .

He shifted his body to ease the cold damp of the ground, and thought back over the day. Yeah, hed been dam right erbout not wantin t go swimmin. N ef hed followed his right min hed neverve gone n got inter all this trouble. At first hed said naw. But shucks, somehow hed jus went on wid the res. Yeah he shoulda went on t school tha mawnin, like Ma told im t do. But, hell, who wouldnt git tireda awways drivin a guy t school! Tha wuz the big trouble awways drivin a guy t school. He wouldnt be in all this trouble now if it wuznt fer that Gawddam school! Impatiently, he took the grass out of his mouth and threw it away, demolishing the little red school house . . .

Yeah, if they had all kept still n quiet when tha ol white woman showed-up, mabbe shedve went on off. But yuh never kin tell erbout these white folks. Mabbe she wouldntve went. Mabbe tha white man woulda killed all of em! All *fo* of em! Yeah, yuh never kin tell erbout white folks. Then, ergin, mabbe tha white woman woulda went on off n laffed. Yeah, mabbe tha white man woulda said: *Yuh nigger bastards git t hell outta here! Yuh know Gawdam well yuh don berlong here!* N then they woulda grabbed their cloes n run like all hell . . . He blinked the white man away. Where wuz Bobo? Why didnt he hurry up n c mon?

He jerked another blade and chewed. Yeah, ef Pa had only let im have tha shotgun! He could stan off a whole mob wid a shotgun. He looked at the ground as he turned a shotgun over in his hands. Then he leveled it at an advancing white man. *Boooom!* The man curled up. Another came. He reloaded quickly, and let him have what the other had got. He too curled up. Then another came. He got the same medicine. Then the whole mob swirled around him, and he blazed away, getting as many as he could. They closed in; but, by Gawd, he had done his part, hadnt he? N the newspapersd say: NIGGER KILLS DOZEN OF MOB BEFO LYNCHED! Er mabbe theyd say: TRAPPED NIGGER SLAYS TWENTY BEFO KILLED! He smiled a little. Tha wouldnt be so bad, would it? Blinking the newspaper away, he looked over the fields. Where wuz Bobo? Why didnt he hurry up n c mon?

He shifted, trying to get a crick out of his legs. Shucks, he wuz gettin tireda this. N it wuz almos dark now. Yeah, there wuz a little bittie star way over yonder in the eas. Mabbe tha white man wuznt dead? Mabbe they wuznt even lookin fer im? Mabbe he could go back home now? Naw, better wait erwhile. Thad be bes. But, Lawd, ef he only had some water! He could hardly swallow, his throat was so dry. Gawddam them white folks! Thas all they wuz good fer, t run a nigger down lika rabbit! Yeah, they git yuh in a corner n then they let yuh have it. A thousan of em! He shivered, for the cold of the clay was chilling his bones. Lawd, spose they found im here in this hole? N wid nobody t help im? . . . But ain no use in thinkin erbout tha; wait till trouble come fo yuh start fightin it. But if tha mob came one by one hed wipe em all out. Clean up the whole bunch. He caught one by the neck and choked him long and hard, choked him till his tongue and eyes popped out. Then he jumped upon his chest and stomped him like he had stomped that snake. When he had finished with one, another came. He choked him too. Choked till he sank slowly to the gound, gasping . . .

"Hoalo!"

Big Boy snatched his fingers from the white man's neck and looked over the fields. He saw nobody. Had someone spied him? He was sure that somebody had hollered. His heart pounded. But, shucks, nobody couldnt see im here in this hole . . . But mabbe theyd seen im when he wuz comin n had laid low n wuz now closin in on im! Praps they wuz signalin fer the others? Yeah, they wuz creepin up on im! Mabbe he oughta git up n run . . . Oh! Mabbe tha wuz Bobo! Yeah, Bobo! He oughta clim out n see if Bobo wuz lookin fer im . . . He stiffened.

"Hoalo!"

"Hoalo!"

"Wheres yuh?"

"Over here on Bullards Road!"

"C mon over!"

"Awright!"

He heard footsteps. Then voices came again, low and far away this time.

"Seen anybody?"

"Naw, Yuh?"

"Naw."

"Yuh reckon they got erway?"

"Ah dunno. Its hard t tell."

"Gawddam them sonofabitchin niggers!"

"We oughta kill ever black bastard in this country!"

"Waal, Jim got two of em, anyhow."

"But Bertha said there wuz *fo!*"

"Where in hell they hidin?"

"She said one of em wuz named Big Boy, or somethin like tha."

"We went t his shack lookin fer im."

"Yeah?"

"But we didnt fin im."

"These niggers stick tergether; they don never tell on each other."

"We looked all thu the shack n couldnt fin hide ner hair of im. Then we drove the ol woman n man out n set the shack on fire . . ."

"Jeesus! Ah wished Ah coulda been there!"

"Yuh shoulda heard the ol nigger woman howl . . ."

"Hoalo!"

"C mon over!"

Big Boy eased to the edge and peeped. He saw a white man with a gun slung over his shoulder running down the slope. Wuz they gonna search the hill? Lawd, there wuz no way fer im to git erway now; he wuz caught! He shoulda knowed theyd git im here. N he didnt hava thing, notta thing t fight wid. Yeah, soon as the blood-houns came theyd fin im. Lawd, have mercy! Theyd lynch im right here on the hill . . . Theyd git im n tie im t a stake n burn im erlive! Lawd! Nobody but the good Lawd could hep im now, nobody . . .

He heard more feet running. He nestled deeper. His chest ached. Nobody but the good Lawd could hep now. They wuz crowdn all round im n when they hada big crowd theyd close in on im. Then itd be over . . . The good Lawd would have t hep im, cause nobody could hep him now, nobody . . .

And then he went numb when he remembered Bobo. Spose Bobod come now? Hed be caught sho! Both of em would be caught! Theyd make Bobo tell where he wuz! Bobo oughta not try to come now. Somebody oughta tell im . . . But there wuz nobody; there wuz no way . . .

He eased slowly back to the opening. There was a large group of men. More wcre coming. Many had guns. Some had coils of rope slung over shoulders.

"Ah tell yuh they still here, somewhere . . ."

"But we looked all over!"

"What t hell! Wouldnt do t let em git erway!"

"Naw. Ef they git erway notta woman in this town would be safe."

"Say, whuts tha yuh got?"

"Er pillar."

"Fer whut?"

"Feathers, fool!"

"Chris! Thisll be hot if we kin ketch them niggers!"

"Ol Anderson said he wuz gonna bringa barrela tar!"

"Ah got some gasolin in mah car if yuh need it."

Big Boy had no feelings now. He was waiting. He did not wonder if they were coming after him. He just waited. He did not wonder about Bobo. He rested his cheek against the cold clay, waiting.

A dog barked. He stiffened. It barked again. He balled himself into a knot at the bottom of the hole, waiting. Then he heard the patter of dog feet.

"Look!"

"Whuts he got?"

"Its a snake!"

"Yeah, the dogs foun a snake!"

"Gee, its a big one!"

"Shucks, Ah wish he could fin one of them sonofabitchin niggers!"

The voices sank to low murmurs. Then he heard number twelve, its bell tolling and whistle crying as it slid along the rails. He flattened himself against the clay. Someone was singing:

We'll hang ever nigger t a sour apple tree . . .

When the song ended there was hard laughter. From the other side of the hill he heard the dog barking furiously. He listened. There was more than one dog now. There were many and they were barking their throats out.

"Hush. Ah hear them dogs!"

"When theys barkin like tha theys foun somethin!"

"Here they come over the hill!"

"WE GOT IM! WE GOT IM!"

There came a roar. Tha must be Bobo; tha must be Bobo . . . In spite of his fear, Big Boy looked. The road, and half of the hillside across the road, were covered with men. A few were at the top of the hill, stenciled against the sky. He could see dark forms moving up the slopes. They were yelling.

"By Gawd, we got im!"

"C mon!"

"Where is he?"

"Theyre bringin im over the hill!"

"Ah got a rope fer im!"

"Say, somebody go n git the others!"

"Where is he? Cant we see im, Mister?"

"They say Berthas comin, too."

"Jack! Jack! Don leave me! Ah wanna see im!"

"Theyre bringin im over the hill, sweetheart!"

"AH WANNA BE THE FIRST T PUT A ROPE ON THA BLACK BASTARDS NECK!"

"Les start the fire!"

"Heat the tar!"

"Ah got some chains t chain im."

"Bring im over this way!"

"Chris, Ah wished Ah hada drink . . ."

Big Boy saw men moving over the hill. Among them was a long dark spot. Tha mus be Bobo; tha must be Bobo theys carryin . . . Theyll git him here. He oughta git up n run. He clamped his teeth and ran his hand over his forehead, bringing it away wet. He tried to swallow, but could not; his throat was dry.

They had started the song again:

We'll hang ever nigger t a sour apple tree . . .

There were women singing now. Their voices made the song round and full. Song waves rolled over the top of pine trees. The sky sagged low, heavy with clouds. Wind was rising. Sometimes cricket cries cut surprisingly across the mob song. A dog had gone to the utmost top of the hill. At each lull of the song his howl floated full into the night.

Big Boy shrank when he saw the first flame light the hillside. Would they see im here? Then he remembered you could not see into the dark if you were standing in the light. As flames leaped higher he saw two men rolling a barrel up the slope.

"Say, gimme a han here, will yuh?"

"Awright, heave!"

"C mon! Straight up! Git t the other end!"

"Ah got the feathers here in this pillar!"

"BRING SOME MO WOOD!"

Big Boy could see the barrel surrounded by flames. The mob fell back, forming a dark circle. Theyd fin im here! He had a wild impulse to climb out and fly across the hills. But his legs would not move. He stared hard, trying to find Bobo. His eyes played over a long, dark spot near the fire. Fanned by wind, flames leaped higher. He jumped. That dark spot had moved. Lawd, thas Bobo; thas Bobo . . .

He smelt the scent of tar, faint at first, then stronger. The wind brought it full into his face, then blew it away. His eyes burned and he rubbed them with his knuckles. He sneezed.

"LES GIT SOURVINEERS!"

He saw the mob close in around the fire. Their faces were hard and sharp in the light of the flames. More men and women were coming over the hill. The long, dark spot was smudged out.

"Everybody git back!"

"Look! Hes gotta finger!"

"C MON! GIT THE GALS BACK FROM THE FIRE!"

"He's got one of his ears, see!"

"Whuts the matter!"

"A woman fell out! Fainted, Ah reckon . . ."

The stench of tar permeated the hillside. The sky was black and the wind was blowing hard.

"HURRY UP N BURN THE NIGGER FO IT RAINS!"

Big Boy saw the mob fall back, leaving a small knot of men about the fire. Then, for the first time, he had a full glimpse of Bobo. A black body flashed in the light. Bobo was struggling, twisting; they were binding his arms and legs.

When he saw them tilt the barrel he stiffened. A scream quivered. He knew the tar was on Bobo. The mob fell back. He saw a tar-drenched body glistening and turning.

"THE BASTARDS GOT IT!"

There was a sudden quiet. Then he shrank violently as the wind carried, like a flurry of snow, a widening spiral of white feathers into the night. The flames leaped tall as the trees. The scream came again. Big Boy trembled and looked. The mob was running down the slopes, leaving the fire clear. Then he saw a writhing white mass cradled in yellow flame, and heard screams, one on top of the other, each shriller and shorter than the last. The mob was quiet now, standing still, looking up the slopes at the writhing white mass gradually growing black, growing black in a cradle of yellow flame.

"PO ON MO GAS!"

"Gimme a lif, will yuh!"

Two men were struggling, carrying between them a heavy can. They set it down, tilted it, leaving it so that the gas would trickle down to the hollowed earth around the fire.

Big Boy slid back into the hole, his face buried in clay. He had no feelings now, no fears. He was numb, empty, as though all blood had been drawn from him. Then his muscles flexed taut when he heard a faint patter. A tiny stream of cold water seeped to his knees, making him push back to a drier spot. He looked up; rain was beating in the grass.

"It's rainin!"

"C mon, les git t town!"

". . . don worry, when the fire git thu wid im hell be gone . . ."

"Wait, Charles! Don leave me; its slippery here . . ."

"Ahll take some of yuh ladies back in mah car . . ."

Big Boy heard the dogs barking again, this time closer. Running feet pounded past. Cold water chilled his ankles. He could hear raindrops steadily hissing.

Now a dog was barking at the mouth of the hole, barking furiously, sensing a presence there. He balled himself into a knot and clung to the bottom, his knees and shins buried in water. The bark came louder. He heard paws scraping and felt the hot scent of dog breath on his face. Green eyes glowed and drew nearer as the barking, muffled by the closeness of the hole, beat upon his eardrums. Backing till his shoulders pressed against the clay, he held his breath. He pushed out his hands, his fingers stiff. The dog yawped louder, advancing, his bark rising sharp and thin. Big Boy rose to his knees, his hands before him. Then he flattened out still more against the bottom, breathing lungsful of hot dog scent, breathing it slowly, hard, but evenly. The dog came closer, bringing hotter dog scent. Big Boy could go back no more. His knees were slipping and slopping in the water. He braced himself, ready. Then, he never exactly knew how—he never knew whether he had lunged or the dog had lunged—they were together, rolling in the water. The green eyes were beneath him, between his legs. Dognails bit into his arms. His knees slipped backward and he landed full on the dog; the dog's breath left in a heavy gasp. Instinctively, he fumbled for the throat as he felt the dog twisting between his knees. The dog snarled, long and low, as though gathering strength. Big Boy's hands traveled swiftly over the dog's back, groping for the throat. He felt dognails again and saw green eyes, but his fingers had found the throat. He choked, feeling his fingers sink; he choked, throwing back his head and stiffening his arms. He felt the dog's body heave, felt dognails digging into his loins. With strength flowing from fear, he closed his fingers, pushing his full weight on the dog's throat. The dog heaved again, and lay still . . . Big Boy heard the sound of his own breathing filling the hole, and heard shouts and footsteps above him going past.

For a long time he held the dog, held it long after the last footstep had died out, long after the rain had stopped.

5

Morning found him still on his knees in a puddle of rainwater, staring at the stiff body of a dog. As the air brightened he came to himself slowly. He held still for a long time, as though waking from a dream, as though trying to remember.

The chug of a truck came over the hill. He tried to crawl to the opening. His knees were stiff and a thousand needlelike pains shot from the bottom of his feet to the calves of his legs. Giddiness made his eyes blur. He pulled up and looked. Through brackish light he saw Will's truck standing some twenty-five yards away, the engine running. Will stood on the running board, looking over the slopes of the hill.

Big Boy scuffled out, falling weakly in the wet grass. He tried to call to Will, but his dry throat would make no sound. He tried again.

"Will!"

Will heard, answering:

"Big Boy, c mon!"

He tried to run, and fell. Will came, meeting him in the tall grass.

"C mon," Will said, catching his arm.

They struggled to the truck.

"Hurry up!" said Will, pushing him onto the running board.

Will pushed back a square trapdoor which swung above the back of the driver's seat. Big Boy pulled through, landing with a thud on the bottom. On hands and knees he looked around in the semi-darkness.

"Wheres Bobo?"

Big Boy stared.

"Wheres Bobo?"

"They got im."

"When?"

"Las night."

"The mob?"

Big Boy pointed in the direction of a charred sapling on the slope of the opposite hill. Will looked. The trapdoor fell. The engine purred, the gears whined, and the truck lurched forward over the muddy road, sending Big Boy on his side.

For a while he lay as he had fallen, on his side, too weak to move. As he felt the truck swing around a curve he straightened up and rested his back against a stack of wooden boxes. Slowly, he began to make out objects in the darkness. Through two long cracks fell thin blades of daylight. The floor was of smooth steel, and cold to his thighs. Splinters and bits of sawdust danced with the rumble of the truck. Each time they swung around a curve he was pulled over the floor; he grabbed at corners of boxes to steady himself. Once he heard the crow of a rooster. It made him think of home, of ma and pa. He thought he remembered hearing somewhere that the house had burned, but could not remember where . . . It all seemed unreal now.

He was tired. He dozed, swaying with the lurch. Then he jumped awake. The truck was running smoothly, on gravel. Far away he heard two short blasts from the Buckeye Lumber Mill. Unconsciously, the thought sang through his mind: Its six erclock . . .

The trapdoor swung in. Will spoke through a corner of his mouth.

"How yuh comin?"

"Awright."

"How they git Bobo?"

"He wuz comin over the hill."

"Whut they do?"

"They burnt im . . . Will, Ah wan some water; mah throats like fire . . ."

"Well git some when we pass a filling station."

Big Boy leaned back and dozed. He jerked awake when the truck stopped. He heard Will get out. He wanted to peep through the trapdoor, but was afraid. For a moment, the wild fear he had known in the hole came back. Spose theyd search n fin im? He quieted when he heard Will's footsteps on the running board. The trapdoor pushed in. Will's hat came through, dripping.

"Take it, quick!"

Big Boy grabbed, spilling water into his face. The truck lurched. He drank. Hard cold lumps of brick rolled into his hot stomach. A dull pain made him bend over. His intestines seemed to be drawing into a tight knot. After a bit it eased, and he sat up, breathing softly.

The truck swerved. He blinked his eyes. The blades of daylight had turned brightly golden. The sun had risen.

The truck sped over the asphalt miles, sped northward, jolting him, shaking out of his bosom the crumbs of corn bread, making them dance with the splinters and sawdust in the golden blades of sunshine.

He turned on his side and slept.

Eudora Welty (b. 1909)
The Wide Net

William Wallace Jamieson's wife Hazel was going to have a baby. But this was October, and it was six months away, and she acted exactly as though it would be tomorrow. When he came in the room she would not speak to him, but would look as straight at nothing as she could, with her eyes glowing. If he only touched her she stuck out her tongue or ran around the table. So one night he went out with two of the boys down the road and stayed out all night. But that was the worst thing yet, because when he came home in the early morning Hazel had vanished. He went through the house not believing his eyes, balancing with both hands out, his yellow cowlick rising on end, and then he turned the kitchen inside out looking for her, but it did no good. Then when he got back to the front room he saw she had left him a little letter, in an envelope. That was doing something behind someone's back. He took out the letter, pushed it open, held it out at a distance from his eyes. . . . After one look he was scared to read the exact words, and he crushed the whole thing in his hand instantly, but what it had said was that she would not put up with him after that and was going to the river to drown herself.

"Drown herself. . . . But she's in mortal fear of the water!"

He ran out front, his face red like the red of the picked cotton field he ran over, and down in the road he gave a loud shout for Virgil Thomas, who was just going in his own house, to come out again. He could just see the edge of Virgil, he had almost got in, he had one foot inside the door.

They met half-way between the farms, under the shade-tree.

"Haven't you had enough of the night?" asked Virgil. There they were, their pants all covered with dust and dew, and they had had to carry the third man home flat between them.

"I've lost Hazel, she's vanished, she went to drown herself."

"Why, that ain't like Hazel," said Virgil.

William Wallace reached out and shook him. "You heard me. Don't you know we have to drag the river?"

"Right this minute?"

"You ain't got nothing to do till spring."

"Let me go set foot inside the house and speak to my mother and tell her a story, and I'll come back."

"This will take the wide net," said William Wallace. His eyebrows gathered, and he was talking to himself.

"How come Hazel to go and do that way?" asked Virgil as they started out.

William Wallace said, "I reckon she got lonesome."

"That don't argue—drown herself for getting lonesome. My mother gets lonesome."

"Well," said William Wallace. "It argues for Hazel."

"How long is it now since you and her was married?"

"Why, it's been a year."

"It don't seem that long to me. A year!"

"It was this time last year. It seems longer," said William Wallace, breaking a stick off a tree in surprise. They walked along, kicking at the flowers on the road's edge. "I remember the day I seen her first, and that seems a long time ago. She was coming along the road holding a little frying-size chicken from her grandma, under her arm, and she had it real quiet. I spoke to her with nice manners. We knowed each other's names, being bound to, just didn't know each other to speak to. I says, 'Where are you taking the fryer?' and she says, 'Mind your manners,' and I kept on till after while she says, 'If you want to walk me home, take littler steps.' So I didn't lose time. It was just four miles across the field and full of blackberries, and from the top of the hill there was Dover below, looking sizeable-like and clean, spread out between the two churches like that. When we got down, I says to her, 'What kind of water's in this well?' and she says, 'The best water in the world.' So I drew a bucket and took out a dipper and she drank and I drank. I didn't think it was that remarkable, but I didn't tell her."

"What happened that night?" asked Virgil.

"We ate the chicken," said William Wallace, "and it was tender. Of course that wasn't all they had. The night I was trying their table out, it sure had good things to eat from one end to the other. Her mama and papa sat at the head and foot and we was face to face with each other across it, with I remember a pat of butter between. They had real sweet butter, with a tree drawed down it, elegant-like. Her mama eats like a man. I had brought her a whole hat-ful of berries and she didn't even pass them to her husband. Hazel, she would leap up and take a pitcher of new milk and fill up the glasses. I had heard how they couldn't have a singing at the church without a fight over her."

"Oh, she's a pretty girl, all right," said Virgil. "It's a pity for the ones like her to grow old, and get like their mothers."

"Another thing will be that her mother will get wind of this and come after me," said William Wallace.

"Her mother will eat you alive," said Virgil.

"She's just been watching her chance," said William Wallace. "Why did I think I could stay out all night."

"Just something come over you."

"First it was just a carnival at Carthage, and I had to let them guess my weight . . . and after that . . ."

"It was nice to be sitting on your neck in a ditch singing," prompted Virgil, "in the moonlight. And playing on the harmonica like you can play."

"Even if Hazel did sit home knowing I was drunk, that wouldn't kill her," said William Wallace. "What she knows ain't ever killed her yet. . . . She's smart, too, for a girl," he said.

"She's a lot smarter than her cousins in Beula," said Virgil. "And especially Edna Earle, that never did get to be what you'd call a heavy thinker. Edna Earle could sit and ponder all day on how the little tail of the 'C' got through the 'L' in a Coca-Cola sign."

"Hazel *is* smart," said William Wallace. They walked on. "You ought to see her pantry shelf, it looks like a hundred jars when you open the door. I don't see how she could turn around and jump in the river."

"It's a woman's trick."

"I always behaved before. Till the one night—last night."

"Yes, but the one night," said Virgil. "And she was waiting to take advantage."

"She jumped in the river because she was scared to death of the water and that was to make it worse," he said. "She remembered how I used to have to pick her up and carry her over the oak-log bridge, how she'd shut her eyes and make a dead-weight and hold me round the neck, just for a little creek. I don't see how she brought herself to jump."

"Jumped backwards," said Virgil. "Didn't look."

When they turned off, it was still early in the pink and green fields. The fumes of morning, sweet and bitter, sprang up where they walked. The insects ticked softly, their strength in reserve; butterflies chopped the air, going to the east, and the birds flew carelessly and sang by fits and starts, not the way they did in the evening in sustained and drowsy songs.

"It's a pretty *day* for sure," said William Wallace. "It's a pretty *day* for it."

"I don't see a sign of her ever going along here," said Virgil.

"Well," said William Wallace. "She wouldn't have dropped anything. I never saw a girl to leave less signs of where she's been."

"Not even a plum seed," said Virgil, kicking the grass.

In the grove it was so quiet that once William Wallace gave a jump, as if he could almost hear a sound of himself wondering where she had gone. A descent of energy came down on him in the thick of the woods and he ran at a rabbit and caught it in his hands.

"Rabbit . . . Rabbit . . ." He acted as if he wanted to take it off to himself and hold it up and talk to it. He laid a palm against its pushing heart. "Now . . . There now . . ."

"Let her go, William Wallace, let her go." Virgil, chewing on an elderberry whistle he had just made, stood at his shoulder: "What do you want with a live rabbit?"

William Wallace squatted down and set the rabbit on the ground but held it under his hand. It was a little, old, brown rabbit. It did not try to move. "See there?"

"Let her go."

"She can go if she wants to, but she don't want to."

Gently he lifted his hand. The round eye was shining at him sideways in the green gloom.

"Anybody can freeze a rabbit, that wants to," said Virgil. Suddenly he gave a far-reaching blast on the whistle, and the rabbit went in a streak. "Was you out catching cotton-tails, or was you out catching your wife?" he said, taking the turn to the open fields. "I came along to keep you on the track."

"Who'll we get, now?" They stood on top of a hill and William Wallace looked critically over the countryside. "Any of the Malones?"

"I was always scared of the Malones," said Virgil. "Too many *of* them."

"This is my day with the net, and they would have to watch out," said William Wallace. "I reckon some Malones, and the Doyles, will be enough. The six Doyles and their dogs, and you and me, and two little nigger boys is enough, with just a few Malones."

"That ought to be enough," said Virgil, "no matter what."

"I'll bring the Malones, and you bring the Doyles," said William Wallace, and they separated at the spring.

When William Wallace came back, with a string of Malones just showing behind him on the hilltop, he found Virgil with the two little Rippen boys waiting behind him, solemn little towheads. As soon as he walked up, Grady, the one in front, lifted his hand to signal silence and caution to his brother Brucie who began panting merrily and untrustworthily behind him.

Brucie bent readily under William Wallace's hand-pat, and gave him a dreamy look out of the tops of his round eyes, which were pure green-and-white like clover tops. William Wallace gave him a nickel. Grady hung his head; his white hair lay in a little tail in the nape of his neck.

"Let's let them come," said Virgil.

"Well, they can come then, but if we keep letting everybody come it is going to be too many," said William Wallace.

"They'll appreciate it, those little-old boys," said Virgil. Brucie held up at arm's length a long red thread with a bent pin tied on the end; and a look of helpless and intense interest gathered Grady's face like a drawstring—his eyes, one bright with a sty, shone pleadingly under his white bangs, and he snapped his jaw and tried to speak. . . . "Their papa was drowned in the Pearl River," said Virgil.

There was a shout from the gully.

"Here come all the Malones," cried William Wallace. "I asked four of them would they come, but the rest of the family invited themselves."

"Did you ever see a time when they didn't," said Virgil. "And yonder from the other direction comes the Doyles, still with biscuit crumbs on their cheeks, I bet, now it's nothing to do but eat as their mother said."

"If two little niggers would come along now, or one big nigger," said William Wallace. And the words were hardly out of his mouth when two little Negro boys came along, going somewhere, one behind the other, stepping high and gay in their overalls, as though they waded in honeydew to the waist.

"Come here, boys. What's your names?"

"Sam and Robbie Bell."

"Come along with us, we're going to drag the river."

"You hear that, Robbie Bell?" said Sam.

They smiled.

The Doyles came noiselessly, their dogs made all the fuss. The Malones, eight giants with great long black eyelashes, were already stamping the ground and pawing each other, ready to go. Everybody went up together to see Doc.

Old Doc owned the wide net. He had a house on top of the hill and he sat and looked out from a rocker on the front porch.

"Climb the hill and come in!" he began to intone across the valley. "Harvest's over . . . slipped up on everybody . . . cotton's picked, gone to the gin . . . hay cut . . . molasses made around here . . . Big explosion's over, supervisors elected, some pleased, some not. . . . We're hearing talk of war!"

When they got closer, he was saying, "Many's been saved at revival, twenty-two last Sunday including a Doyle, ought to counted two. Hope they'll be a blessing to Dover community besides a shining star in Heaven. Now what?" he asked, for they had arrived and stood gathered in front of the steps.

"If nobody is using your wide net, could we use it?" asked William Wallace.

"You just used it a month ago," said Doc. "It ain't your turn."

Virgil jogged William Wallace's arm and cleared his throat. "This time is kind of special," he said. "We got reason to think William Wallace's wife Hazel is in the river, drowned."

"What reason have you got to think she's in the river drowned?" asked Doc. He took out his old pipe. "I'm asking the husband."

"Because she's not in the house," said William Wallace.

"Vanished?" and he knocked out the pipe.

"Plum vanished."

"Of course a thousand things could have happened to her," said Doc, and he lighted the pipe.

"Hand him up the letter, William Wallace," said Virgil. "We can't wait around till Doomsday for the net while Doc sits back thinkin'."

"I tore it up, right at the first," said William Wallace. "But I know it by heart. It said she was going to jump straight in the Pearl River and that I'd be sorry."

"Where do you come in, Virgil?" asked Doc.

"I was in the same place William Wallace sat on his neck in, all night, and done as much as he done, and come home the same time."

"You-all were out cuttin' up, so Lady Hazel has to jump in the river, is that it? Cause and effect? Anybody want to argue with me? Where do these others come in, Doyles, Malones, and what not?"

"Doc is the smartest man around," said William Wallace, turning to the solidly waiting Doyles, "but it sure takes time."

"These are the ones that's collected to drag the river for her," said Virgil.

"Of course I am not going on record to say so soon that *I* think she's drowned," Doc said, blowing out blue smoke.

"Do you think . . ." William Wallace mounted a step, and his hands both went into fists. "Do you think she was *carried off?*"

"Now that's the way to argue, see it from all sides," said Doc promptly. "But who by?"

Some Malone whistled, but not so you could tell which one.

"There's no booger around the Dover section that goes around carrying off young girls that's married," stated Doc.

"She was always scared of the Gypsies." William Wallace turned scarlet. "She'd sure turn her ring around on her finger if she passed one, and look in the other direction so they couldn't see she was pretty and carry her off. They come in the end of summer."

"Yes, there are the Gypsies, kidnappers since the world began. But was it to be you that would pay the grand ransom?" asked Doc. He pointed his finger. They all laughed then at how clever old Doc was and clapped William Wallace on the back. But that turned into a scuffle and they fell to the ground.

"Stop it, or you can't have the net," said Doc. "You're scaring my wife's chickens."

"It's time we was gone," said William Wallace.

The big barking dogs jumped to lean their front paws on the men's chests.

"My advice remains, Let well enough alone," said Doc. "Whatever this mysterious event will turn out to be, it has kept one woman from talking a while. However, Lady Hazel is the prettiest girl in Mississippi, you've never seen a prettier one and you never will. A golden-haired girl." He got to his feet with the nimbleness that was always his surprise, and said, "I'll come along with you."

The path they always followed was the Old Natchez Trace. It took them through the deep woods and led them out down below on the Pearl River, where they could begin dragging it upstream to a point near Dover. They walked in silence around William Wallace, not letting him carry anything, but the net dragged heavily and the buckets were full of clatter in a place so dim and still.

Once they went through a forest of cucumber trees and came up on a high ridge. Grady and Brucie who were running ahead all the way stopped in their tracks; a whistle had blown and far down and far away a long freight train was passing. It seemed like a little festival procession, moving with the slowness of ignorance or a dream, from distance to distance, the tiny pink and gray cars like secret boxes. Grady was counting the cars to himself, as if he could certainly see each one clearly, and Brucie watched his lips, hushed and cautious, the way he would watch a bird drinking. Tears suddenly came to Grady's eyes, but it could only be because a tiny man walked along the top of the train, walking and moving on top of the moving train.

They went down again and soon the smell of the river spread over the woods, cool and secret. Every step they took among the great walls of vines and among the passion-flowers started up a little life, a little flight.

"We're walking along in the changing-time," said Doc. "Any day now the change will come. It's going to turn from hot to cold, and we can kill the hog that's ripe and have fresh meat to eat. Come one of these nights and we can wander down here and tree a nice possum. Old Jack Frost will be pinching things up. Old Mr. Winter will be standing in the door. Hickory tree there will be yellow. Sweet-gum red, hickory yellow, dogwood red, sycamore yellow." He went along rapping the tree trunks with his knuckle. "Magnolia and live-oak never die. Remember that. Persimmons will all get fit to eat, and the nuts will be dropping like rain all through the woods here. And run, little quail, run, for we'll be after you too."

They went on and suddenly the woods opened upon light, and they had reached the river. Everyone stopped, but Doc talked on ahead as though nothing had happened. "Only today," he said, "today, in October sun, it's all gold—sky and tree and water. Everything just before it changes looks to be made of gold."

William Wallace looked down, as though he thought of Hazel with the shining eyes, sitting at home and looking straight before her, like a piece of pure gold, too precious to touch.

Below them the river was glimmering, narrow, soft, and skin-colored, and slowed nearly to stillness. The shining willow trees hung round them. The net that was being drawn out, so old and so long-used, it too looked golden, strung and tied with golden threads.

Standing still on the bank, all of a sudden William Wallace, on whose word they were waiting, spoke up in a voice of surprise. "What is the name of this river?"

They looked at him as if he were crazy not to know the name of the river he had fished in all his life. But a deep frown was on his forehead, as if he were compelled to wonder what people had come to call this river, or to think there was a mystery in the name of a river they all knew so well, the same as if it were some great far torrent of waves that dashed through the mountains somewhere, and almost as if it were a river in some dream, for they could not give him the name of that.

"Everybody knows Pearl River is named the Pearl River," said Doc.

A bird note suddenly bold was like a stone thrown into the water to sound it.

"It's deep here," said Virgil, and jogged William Wallace. "Remember?"

William Wallace stood looking down at the river as if it were still a mystery to him. There under his feet which hung over the bank it was transparent and yellow like an old bottle lying in the sun, filling with light.

Doc clattered all his paraphernalia.

Then all of a sudden all the Malones scattered jumping and tumbling down the bank. They gave their loud shout. Little Brucie started after them, and looked back.

"Do you think she jumped?" Virgil asked William Wallace.

2

Since the net was so wide, when it was all stretched it reached from bank to bank of the Pearl River, and the weights would hold it all the way to the bottom. Jug-like sounds filled the air, splashes lifted in the sun, and the party began to move upstream. The Malones with great groans swam and pulled near the shore, the Doyles swam and pushed from behind with Virgil to tell them how to do it best; Grady and Brucie with his thread and pin trotted along the sandbars hauling buckets and lines. Sam and Robbie Bell, naked and bright, guided the old oarless rowboat that always drifted at the shore, and in it, sitting up tall with his hat on, was Doc—he went along without ever touching water and without ever taking his eyes off the net. William Wallace himself did everything but most of the time he was out of sight, swimming about under water or diving, and he had nothing to say any more.

The dogs chased up and down, in and out of the water, and in and out of the woods.

"Don't let her get too heavy, boys," Doc intoned regularly, every few minutes, "and she won't let nothing through."

"She won't let nothing through, she won't let nothing through," chanted Sam and Robbie Bell, one at his front and one at his back.

The sandbars were pink or violet drifts ahead. Where the light fell on the river, in a wandering from shore to shore, it was leaf-shaped spangles that trembled softly, while the dark of the river was calm. The willow trees leaned overhead under muscadine vines, and their trailing leaves hung like waterfalls in the morning air. The thing that seemed like silence must have been the endless cry of all the crickets and locusts in the world, rising and falling.

Every time William Wallace took hold of a big eel that slipped the net, the Malones all yelled, "Rassle with him, son!"

"Don't let her get too heavy, boys," said Doc.

"This is hard on catfish," William Wallace said once.

There were big and little fishes, dark and bright, that they caught, good ones and bad ones, the same old fish.

"This is more shoes than I ever saw got together in any store," said Virgil when they emptied the net to the bottom. "Get going!" he shouted in the next breath.

The little Rippens who had stayed ahead in the woods stayed ahead on the river. Brucie, leading them all, made small jumps and hops as he went, sometimes on one foot, sometimes on the other.

The winding river looked old sometimes, when it ran wrinkled and deep under high banks where the roots of trees hung down, and sometimes it seemed to be only a young creek, shining with the colors of wildflowers. Sometimes sandbars in the shapes of fishes lay nose to nose across, without the track of even a bird.

"Here comes some alligators," said Virgil. "Let's let them by."

They drew out on the shady side of the water, and three big alligators and four middle-sized ones went by, taking their own time.

"Look at their great big old teeth!" called a shrill voice. It was Grady making his only outcry, and the alligators were not showing their teeth at all.

"The better to eat folks with," said Doc from his boat, looking at him severely.

"Doc, you are bound to declare all you know," said Virgil. "Get going!"

When they started off again the first thing they caught in the net was the baby alligator.

"That's just what we wanted!" cried the Malones.

They set the little alligator down on a sandbar and he squatted perfectly still; they could hardly tell when it was he started to move. They watched with set faces his incredible mechanics, while the dogs after one bark stood off in inquisitive humility, until he winked.

"He's ours!" shouted all the Malones. "We're taking him home with us!"

"He ain't nothing but a little-old baby," said William Wallace.

The Malones only scoffed, as if he might be only a baby but he looked like the oldest and worst lizard.

"What are you going to do with him?" asked Virgil.

"Keep him."

"I'd be more careful what I took out of this net," said Doc.

"Tie him up and throw him in the bucket," the Malones were saying to each other, while Doc was saying, "Don't come running to me and ask me what to do when he gets big."

They kept catching more and more fish, as if there was no end in sight.

"Look, a string of lady's beads," said Virgil. "Here, Sam and Robbie Bell."

Sam wore them around his head, with a knot over his forehead and loops around his ears, and Robbie Bell walked behind and stared at them.

In a shadowy place something white flew up. It was a heron, and it went away over the dark tree-tops. William Wallace followed it with his eyes and Brucie clapped his hands, but Virgil gave a sigh, as if he knew that when you go looking for what is lost, everything is a sign.

An eel slid out of the net.

"Rassle with him, son!" yelled the Malones. They swam like fiends.

"The Malones are in it for the fish," said Virgil.

It was about noon that there was a little rustle on the bank.

"Who is that yonder?" asked Virgil, and he pointed to a little undersized man with short legs and a little straw hat with a band around it, who was following along on the other side of the river.

"Never saw him and don't know his brother," said Doc.

Nobody had ever seen him before.

"Who invited you?" cried Virgil hotly. "Hi . . . !" and he made signs for the little undersized man to look at him, but he would not.

"Looks like a crazy man, from here," said the Malones.

"Just don't pay any attention to him and maybe he'll go away," advised Doc.

But Virgil had already swum across and was up on the other bank. He and the stranger could be seen exchanging a word apiece and then Virgil put out his hand the way he would pat a child and patted the stranger to the ground. The little man got up again just as quickly, lifted his shoulders, turned around, and walked away with his hat tilted over his eyes.

When Virgil came back he said, "Little-old man claimed he was harmless as a baby. I told him to just try horning in on this river and anything in it."

"What did he look like up close?" asked Doc.

"I wasn't studying how he looked," said Virgil. "But I don't like anybody to come looking at me that I am not familiar with." And he shouted, "Get going!"

"Things are moving in too great a rush," said Doc.

Brucie darted ahead and ran looking into all the bushes, lifting up their branches and looking underneath.

"Not one of the Doyles has spoke a word," said Virgil.

"That's because they're not talkers," said Doc.

All day William Wallace kept diving to the bottom. Once he dived down and down into the dark water, where it was so still that nothing stirred, not even a fish, and so dark that it was no longer the muddy world of the upper river but the dark clear world of deepness, and he must have believed this was the deepest place in the whole Pearl River, and if she was not here she would not be anywhere. He was gone such a long time that the others stared hard at the surface of the water, through which the bubbles came from below. So far down and all alone, had he found Hazel? Had he suspected down there, like some secret, the real, the true trouble that Hazel had fallen into, about which words in a letter could not speak . . . how (who knew?) she had been filled to the brim with that elation that they all remembered, like their own secret, the elation that comes of great hopes and changes, sometimes simply of the harvest time, that comes with a little course of its own like a tune to run in the head, and there was nothing she could do about it—they knew—and so it had turned into this? It could be nothing but the old trouble that William Wallace was finding out, reaching and turning in the gloom of such depths.

"Look down yonder," said Grady softly to Brucie.

He pointed to the surface, where their reflections lay colorless and still side by side. He touched his brother gently as though to impress him.

"That's you and me," he said.

Brucie swayed precariously over the edge, and Grady caught him by the seat of his overalls. Brucie looked, but showed no recognition. Instead, he backed away, and seemed all at once unconcerned and spiritless, and pressed the nickel William Wallace had given him into his palm, rubbing it into his skin. Grady's inflamed eyes rested on the brown water. Without warning he saw something . . . perhaps the image in the river seemed to be his father, the drowned man—with arms open, eyes open, mouth open. . . . Grady stared and blinked, again something wrinkled up his face.

And when William Wallace came up it was in an agony from submersion, which seemed an agony of the blood and of the very heart, so woeful he looked. He was staring and glaring around in astonishment, as if a long time had gone by, away from the pale world where the brown light of the sun and the river and the little party watching him trembled before his eyes.

"What did you bring up?" somebody called—was it Virgil?

One of his hands was holding fast to a little green ribbon of plant, root and all. He was surprised, and let it go.

It was afternoon. The trees spread softly, the clouds hung wet and tinted. A buzzard turned a few slow wheels in the sky, and drifted upwards. The dogs promenaded the banks.

"It's time we ate fish," said Virgil.

On a wide sandbar on which seashells lay they dragged up the haul and built a fire.

Then for a long time among clouds of odors and smoke, all half-naked except Doc, they cooked and ate catfish. They ate until the Malones groaned and all the Doyles stretched out on their faces, though for long after, Sam and Robbie Bell sat up to their own little table on a cypress stump and ate on and on. Then they all were silent and still, and one by one fell asleep.

"There ain't a thing better than fish," muttered William Wallace. He lay stretched on his back in the glimmer and shade of trampled sand. His sunburned forehead and cheeks seemed to glow with fire. His eyelids fell. The shadow of a willow branch dipped and moved over him. "There is nothing in the world as good as . . . fish. The fish of Pearl River." Then slowly he smiled. He was asleep.

But it seemed almost at once that he was leaping up, and one by one up sat the others in their ring and looked at him, for it was impossible to stop and sleep by the river.

"You're feeling as good as you felt last night," said Virgil, setting his head on one side.

"The excursion is the same when you go looking for your sorrow as when you go looking for your joy," said Doc.

But William Wallace answered none of them anything, for he was leaping all over the place and all, over them and the feast and the bones of the feast, trampling the sand, up and down, and doing a dance so crazy that he would die next. He took a big catfish and hooked it to his belt buckle and went up and down so that they all hollered, and the tears of laughter streaming down his cheeks made him put his hand up, and the two days' growth of beard began to jump out, bright red.

But all of a sudden there was an even louder cry, something almost like a cheer, from everybody at once, and all pointed fingers moved from William Wallace to the river. In the center of three light-gold rings across the water was lifted first an old hoary head ("It has whiskers!" a voice cried) and then in an undulation loop after loop and hump after hump of a long dark body, until there were a dozen rings of ripples, one behind the other, stretching all across the river, like a necklace.

"The King of the Snakes!" cried all the Malones at once, in high tenor voices and leaning together.

"The King of the Snakes," intoned old Doc in his profound base.

"He looked you in the eye."

William Wallace stared back at the King of the Snakes with all his might.

It was Brucie that darted forward, dangling his little thread with the pin tied to it, going toward the water.

"That's the King of the Snakes!" cried Grady, who always looked after him.

Then the snake went down.

The little boy stopped with one leg in the air, spun around on the other, and sank to the ground.

"Git up," Grady whispered. "It was just the King of the Snakes. He went off whistling. Git up. It wasn't a thing but the King of the Snakes."

Brucie's green eyes opened, his tongue darted out, and he sprang up; his feet were heavy, his head light, and he rose like a bubble coming to the surface.

Then thunder like a stone loosened and rolled down the bank.

They all stood unwilling on the sandbar, holding to the net. In the eastern sky were the familiar castles and the round towers to which they were used, gray, pink, and blue, growing darker and filling with thunder. Lightning flickered in the sun along their thick walls. But in the west the sun shone with such a violence that in an illumination like a long-prolonged glare of lightning the heavens looked black and white; all color left the world, the goldenness of everything was like a memory, and only heat, a kind of glamor and oppression, lay on their heads. The thick heavy trees on the other side of the river were brushed with mile-long streaks of silver, and a wind touched each man on the forehead. At the same time there was a long roll of thunder that began behind them, came up and down mountains and valleys of air, passed over their heads, and left them listening still. With a small, near noise a mockingbird followed it, the little white bars of its body flashing over the willow trees.

"We are here for a storm now," Virgil said. "We will have to stay till it's over."

They retreated a little, and hard drops fell in the leathery leaves at their shoulders and about their heads.

"Magnolia's the loudest tree there is in a storm," said Doc.

Then the light changed the water, until all about them the woods in the rising wind seemed to grow taller and blow inward together and suddenly turn dark. The rain struck heavily. A huge tail seemed to lash through the air and the river broke in a wound of silver. In silence the party crouched and stooped beside the trunk of the great tree, which in the push of the storm rose full of a fragrance and unyielding weight. Where they all stared, past their tree, was another tree, and beyond that another and another, all the way down the bank of the river, all towering and darkened in the storm.

"The outside world is full of endurance," said Doc. "Full of endurance."

Robbie Bell and Sam squatted down low and embraced each other from the start.

"Runs in our family to get struck by lightnin'," said Robbie Bell. "Lightnin' drawed a pitchfork right on our grandpappy's cheek, stayed till he died. Pappy got struck by some bolts of lightnin' and was dead three days, dead as that-there axe."

There was a succession of glares and crashes.

"This'n's goin' to be either me or you," said Sam. "Here come a little bug. If he go to the left, be me, and to the right, be you."

But at the next flare a big tree on the hill seemed to turn into fire before their eyes, every branch, twig, and leaf, and a purple cloud hung over it.

"Did you hear that crack?" asked Robbie Bell. "That were its bones."

"Why do you little niggers talk so much!" said Doc. "Nobody's profiting by this information."

"We always talks this much," said Sam, "but now everybody so quiet, they hears us."

The great tree, split and on fire, fell roaring to earth. Just at its moment of falling, a tree like it on the opposite bank split wide open and fell in two parts.

"Hope they ain't goin' to be no balls of fire come rollin' over the water and fry all the fishes with they scales on," said Robbie Bell.

The water in the river had turned purple and was filled with sudden currents and whirlpools. The little willow trees bent almost to its surface, bowing one after another down the bank and almost breaking under the storm. A great curtain of wet leaves was borne along before a blast of wind, and every human being was covered.

"Now us got scales," wailed Sam. "Us is the fishes."

"Hush up, little-old colored children," said Virgil. "This isn't the way to act when somebody takes you out to drag a river."

"Poor lady's-ghost, I bet it is scareder than us," said Sam.

"All I hoping is, us don't find her!" screamed Robbie Bell.

William Wallace bent down and knocked their heads together. After that they clung silently in each other's arms, the two black heads resting, with wind-filled cheeks and tight-closed eyes, one upon the other until the storm was over.

"Right over yonder is Dover," said Virgil. "We've come all the way. William Wallace, you have walked on a sharp rock and cut your foot open."

3

In Dover it had rained, and the town looked somehow like new. The wavy heat of late afternoon came down from the watertank and fell over everything like shiny mosquito-netting. At the wide place where the road was paved and patched with tar, it seemed newly embedded with Coca-Cola tops. The old circus posters on the store were nearly gone, only bits, the snowflakes of white horses, clinging to its side. Morning-glory vines started almost visibly to grow over the roofs and cling round the ties of the railroad track, where bluejays lighted on the rails, and umbrella chinaberry trees hung heavily over the whole town, dripping intermittently upon the tin roofs.

Each with his counted fish on a string the members of the river-dragging party walked through the town. They went toward the town well, and there was Hazel's mother's house, but no sign of her yet coming out. They all drank a dipper of the water, and still there was not a soul on the street. Even the bench in front of the store was empty, except for a little corn-shuck doll.

But something told them somebody had come, for after one moment people began to look out of the store and out of the postoffice. All the bird dogs woke up to see the Doyle dogs and such a large number of men and boys materialize suddenly with such a big catch of fish, and they ran out barking. The Doyle dogs joyously barked back. The bluejays flashed up and screeched above the town, whipping through their tunnels in the chinaberry trees. In the café a nickel clattered inside a music box and a love song began to play. The whole town of Dover began to throb in its wood and tin, like an old tired heart, when the men walked through once more, coming around again and going down the street carrying the fish, so drenched, exhausted, and muddy that no one could help but admire them.

William Wallace walked through the town as though he did not see anybody or hear anything. Yet he carried his great string of fish held high where it could be seen by all. Virgil came next, imitating William Wallace exactly, then the modest Doyles crowded by the Malones, who were holding up their alligator, tossing it in the air, even, like a father tossing his child. Following behind and pointing authoritatively at the ones in front strolled Doc, with Sam and Robbie Bell still chanting in his wake. In and out of the whole little line Grady and Brucie jerked about. Grady, with his head ducked, and stiff as a rod, walked with a springy limp; it made him look forever angry and unapproachable. Under his breath he was whispering, "Sty, sty, git out of my eye, and git on somebody passin' by." He traveled on with narrowed shoulders, and kept his eye unerringly upon his little brother, wary and at the same time proud, as though he held a flying June-bug on a string. Brucie, making a twanging noise with his lips, had shot forth again, and he was darting rapidly everywhere at once, delighted and tantalized, running in circles around William Wallace, pointing to his fish. A frown of pleasure like the print of a bird's foot was stamped between his faint brows, and he trotted in some unknown realm of delight.

"Did you ever see so many fish?" said the people in Dover.

"How much are your fish, mister?"

"Would you sell your fish?"

"Is that all the fish in Pearl River?"

"How much you sell them all for? Everybody's?"

"Three dollars," said William Wallace suddenly, and loud.

The Malones were upon him and shouting, but it was too late.

And just as William Wallace was taking the money in his hand, Hazel's mother walked solidly out of her front door and saw it.

"You can't head her mother off," said Virgil. "Here she comes in full bloom."

But William Wallace turned his back on her, that was all, and on everybody, for that matter, and that was the breaking-up of the party.

Just as the sun went down, Doc climbed his back steps, sat in his chair on the back porch where he sat in the evenings, and lighted his pipe. William Wallace hung out the net and came back and Virgil was waiting for him, so they could say good evening to Doc.

"All in all," said Doc, when they came up, "I've never been on a better river-dragging, or seen better behavior. If it took catching catfish to move the Rock of Gibraltar, I believe this outfit could move it."

"Well, we didn't catch Hazel," said Virgil.

"What did you say?" asked Doc.

"He don't really pay attention," said Virgil. "I said, 'We didn't catch Hazel.'"

"Who says Hazel was to be caught?" asked Doc. "She wasn't in there. Girls don't like the water—remember that. Girls don't just haul off and go jumping in the river to get back at their husbands. They got other ways."

"Didn't you ever think she was in there?" asked William Wallace. "The whole time?"

"Nary once," said Doc.

"He's just smart," said Virgil, putting his hand on William Wallace's arm. "It's only because we didn't find her that he wasn't looking for her."

"I'm beholden to you for the net, anyway," said William Wallace.

"You're welcome to borry it again," said Doc.

On the way home Virgil kept saying, "Calm down, calm down, William Wallace."

"If he wasn't such an old skinny man I'd have wrung his neck for him," said William Wallace. "He had no business coming."

"He's too big for his britches," said Virgil. "Don't nobody know everything. And just because it's his net. Why does it have to be his net?"

"If it wasn't for being polite to old men, I'd have skinned him alive," said William Wallace.

"I guess he don't really know nothing about wives at all, his wife's so deaf," said Virgil.

"He don't know Hazel," said William Wallace. "I'm the only man alive knows Hazel: would she jump in the river or not, and I say she would. She jumped in because I was sitting on the back of my neck in a ditch singing, and that's just what she ought to done. Doc ain't got no right to say one word about it."

"Calm down, calm down, William Wallace," said Virgil.

"If it had been you that talked like that, I'd have broke every bone in your body," said William Wallace. "Just let you talk like that. You're my age and size."

"But I ain't going to talk like that," said Virgil. "What have I done the whole time but keep this river-dragging going straight and running even, without no hitches? You couldn't have drug the river a foot without me."

"What are you talking about! Without who!" cried William Wallace. "This wasn't your river-dragging! It wasn't your wife!" He jumped on Virgil and they began to fight.

"Let me up." Virgil was breathing heavily.

"Say it was my wife. Say it was my river-dragging."

"Yours!" Virgil was on the ground with William Wallace's hand putting dirt in his mouth.

"Say it was my net."

"Your net!"

"Get up then."

They walked along getting their breath, and smelling the honeysuckle in the evening. On a hill William Wallace looked down, and at the same time there went drifting by the sweet sounds of music outdoors. They were having the Sacred Harp Sing on the grounds of an old white church glimmering there at the crossroads, far below. He stared away as if he saw it minutely, as if he could see a lady in white take a flowered cover off the organ, which was set on a little slant in the shade, dust the keys, and start to pump and play. . . . He smiled faintly, as he would at his mother, and at Hazel, and at the singing women in his life, now all one young girl standing up to sing under the trees the oldest and longest ballads there were.

Virgil told him good night and went into his own house and the door shut on him.

When he got to his own house, William Wallace saw to his surprise that it had not rained at all. But there, curved over the roof, was something he had never seen before as long as he could remember, a rainbow at night. In the light of the moon, which had risen again, it looked small and of gauzy material, like a lady's summer dress, a faint veil through which the stars showed.

He went up on the porch and in at the door, and all exhausted he had walked through the front room and through the kitchen when he heard his name called. After a moment, he smiled, as if no matter what he might have hoped for in his wildest heart, it was better than that to hear his name called out in the house. The voice came out of the bedroom.

"What do you want?" he yelled, standing stock-still.

Then she opened the bedroom door with the old complaining creak, and there she stood. She was not changed a bit.

"How do you feel?" he said.

"I feel pretty good. Not too good," Hazel said, looking mysterious.

"I cut my foot," said William Wallace, taking his shoe off so she could see the blood.

"How in the world did you do that?" she cried, with a step back.

"Dragging the river. But it don't hurt any longer."

"You ought to have been more careful," she said. "Supper's ready and I wondered if you would ever come home, or if it would be last night all over again. Go and make yourself fit to be seen," she said, and ran away from him.

After supper they sat on the front steps a while.

"Where were you this morning when I came in?" asked William Wallace when they were ready to go in the house.

"I was hiding," she said. "I was still writing on the letter. And then you tore it up."

"Did you watch me when I was reading it?"

"Yes, and you could have put out your hand and touched me, I was so close."

But he bit his lip, and gave her a little tap and slap, and then turned her up and spanked her.

"Do you think you will do it again?" he asked.

"I'll tell my mother on you for this!"

"Will you do it again?"

"No!" she cried.

"Then pick yourself up off my knee."

It was just as if he had chased her and captured her again. She lay smiling in the crook of his arm. It was the same as any other chase in the end.

"I will do it again if I get ready," she said. "Next time will be different, too."

Then she was ready to go in, and rose up and looked out from the top step, out across their yard where the China tree was and beyond, into the dark fields where the lightning-bugs flickered away. He climbed to his feet too and stood beside her, with the frown on his face, trying to look where she looked. And after a few minutes she took him by the hand and led him into the house, smiling as if she were smiling down on him.

Flannery O'Connor (1925–1964)
The Artificial Nigger

Mr. Head awakened to discover that the room was full of moonlight. He sat up and stared at the floor boards—the color of silver—and then at the ticking on his pillow, which might have been brocade, and after a second, he saw half of the moon five feet away in his shaving mirror, paused as if it were waiting for his permission to enter. It rolled forward and cast a dignifying light on everything. The straight chair against the wall looked stiff and attentive as if it were awaiting an order and Mr. Head's trousers, hanging to the back of it, had an almost noble air, like the garment some great man had just flung to his servant; but the face on the moon was a grave one. It gazed across the room and out the window where it floated over the horse stall and appeared to contemplate itself with the look of a young man who sees his old age before him.

Mr. Head could have said to it that age was a choice blessing and that only with years does a man enter into that calm understanding of life that makes him a suitable guide for the young. This, at least, had been his own experience.

He sat up and grasped the iron posts at the foot of his bed and raised himself until he could see the face on the alarm clock which sat on an overturned bucket beside the chair. The hour was two in the morning. The alarm on the clock did not work but he was not dependent on any mechanical means to awaken him. Sixty years had not dulled his responses; his physical reactions, like his moral ones, were guided by his will and strong character, and these could be seen plainly in his features. He had a long tube-like face with a long rounded open jaw and a long depressed nose. His eyes were alert but quiet, and in the miraculous moonlight they had a look of composure and of ancient wisdom as if they belonged to one of the great guides of men. He might have been Vergil summoned in the middle of the night to go to Dante, or better, Raphael, awakened by a blast of God's light to fly to the side of Tobias. The only dark spot in the room was Nelson's pallet, underneath the shadow of the window.

Nelson was hunched over on his side, his knees under his chin and his heels under his bottom. His new suit and hat were in the boxes that they had been sent in and these were on the floor at the foot of the pallet where he could get his hands on them as soon as he woke up. The slop jar, out of the shadow and made snow-white in the moonlight, appeared to stand guard over him like a small personal angel. Mr. Head lay back down, feeling entirely confident that he could carry out the moral mission of the coming day. He meant to be up before Nelson and to have the breakfast cooking by the time he awakened. The boy was always irked when Mr. Head was the first up. They would have to leave the house at four to get to the railroad junction by five-thirty. The train was to stop for them at five forty-five and they had to be there on time for this train was stopping merely to accommodate them.

This would be the boy's first trip to the city though he claimed it would be his second because he had been born there. Mr. Head had tried to point out to him that when he was born he didn't have the intelligence to determine his whereabouts but this had made no impression on the child at all and he continued to insist that this was to be his second trip. It would be Mr. Head's third trip. Nelson had said, "I will've already been there twict and I ain't but ten."

Mr. Head had contradicted him.

"If you ain't been there in fifteen years, how you know you'll be able to find your way about?" Nelson had asked. "How you know it hasn't changed some?"

"Have you ever," Mr. Head had asked, "seen me lost?"

Nelson certainly had not but he was a child who was never satisfied until he had given an impudent answer and he replied, "It's nowhere around here to get lost at."

"The day is going to come," Mr. Head prophesied, "when you'll find you ain't as smart as you think you are." He had been thinking about this trip for several months but it was for the most part in moral terms that he conceived it. It was to be a lesson that the boy would never forget. He was to find out from it that he had no cause for pride merely because he had been born in a city. He was to find out that the city is not a great place. Mr. Head meant him to see everything there is to see in a city so that he would be content to stay at home for the rest of his life. He fell asleep thinking how the boy would at last find out that he was not as smart as he thought he was.

He was awakened at three-thirty by the smell of fatback frying and he leaped off his cot. The pallet was empty and the clothes boxes had been thrown open. He put on his trousers and ran into the other room. The boy had a corn pone on cooking and had fried the meat. He was sitting in the half-dark at the table, drinking cold coffee out of a can. He had on his new suit and his new gray hat pulled low over his eyes. It was too big for him but they had ordered it a size large because they expected his head to grow. He didn't say anything but his entire figure suggested satisfaction at having arisen before Mr. Head.

Mr. Head went to the stove and brought the meat to the table in the skillet. "It's no hurry," he said. "You'll get there soon enough and it's no guarantee you'll like it when you do neither," and he sat down across from the boy whose hat teetered back slowly to reveal a fiercely expressionless face, very much the same shape as the old man's. They were grandfather and grandson but they looked enough alike to be brothers and brothers not too far apart in age, for Mr. Head had a youthful expression by daylight, while the boy's look was ancient, as if he knew everything already and would be pleased to forget it.

Mr. Head had once had a wife and daughter and when the wife died, the daughter ran away and returned after an interval with Nelson. Then one morning, without getting out of bed, she died and left Mr. Head with sole care of the year-old child. He had made the mistake of telling Nelson that he had been born in Atlanta. If he hadn't told him that, Nelson couldn't have insisted that this was going to be his second trip.

"You may not like it a bit," Mr. Head continued. "It'll be full of niggers."

The boy made a face as if he could handle a nigger.

"All right," Mr. Head said. "You ain't ever seen a nigger."

"You wasn't up very early," Nelson said.

"You ain't ever seen a nigger," Mr. Head repeated. "There hasn't been a nigger in this county since we run that one out twelve years ago and that was before you were born." He looked at the boy as if he were daring him to say he had ever seen a Negro.

"How you know I never saw a nigger when I lived there before?" Nelson asked. "I probably saw a lot of niggers."

"If you seen one you didn't know what he was," Mr. Head said, completely exasperated. "A six-month-old child don't know a nigger from anybody else."

"I reckon I'll know a nigger if I see one," the boy said and got up and straightened his slick sharply creased gray hat and went outside to the privy.

They reached the junction some time before the train was due to arrive and stood about two feet from the first set of tracks. Mr. Head carried a paper sack with some biscuits and a can of sardines in it for their lunch. A coarse-looking orange-colored sun coming up behind the east range of mountains was making the sky a dull red behind them, but in front of them it was still gray and they faced a gray transparent moon, hardly stronger than a thumbprint and completely without light. A small tin switch box and a black fuel tank were all there was to mark the place as a junction; the tracks were double and did not converge again until they were hidden behind the bends at either end of the clearing. Trains passing appeared to emerge from a tunnel of trees and, hit for a second by the cold sky, vanish terrified into the woods again. Mr. Head had had to make special arrangements with the ticket agent to have this train stop and he was secretly afraid it would not, in which case, he knew Nelson would say, "I never thought no train was going to stop for you." Under the useless morning moon the tracks looked white and fragile. Both the old man and the child stared ahead as if they were awaiting an apparition.

Then suddenly, before Mr. Head could make up his mind to turn back, there was a deep warning bleat and the train appeared, gliding very slowly, almost silently around the bend of trees about two hundred yards down the track, with one yellow front light shining. Mr. Head was still not certain it would stop and he felt it would make an even bigger idiot of him if it went by slowly. Both he and Nelson, however, were prepared to ignore the train if it passed them.

The engine charged by, filling their noses with the smell of hot metal and then the second coach came to a stop exactly where they were standing. A conductor with the face of an ancient bloated bulldog was on the step as if he expected them, though he did not look as if it mattered one way or the other to him if they got on or not. "To the right," he said.

Their entry took only a fraction of a second and the train was already speeding on as they entered the quiet car. Most of the travelers were still sleeping, some with their heads hanging off the chair arms, some stretched across two seats, and some sprawled out with their feet in the aisle. Mr. Head saw two unoccupied seats and pushed Nelson toward them. "Get in there by the winder," he said in his normal voice which was very loud at this hour of the morning. "Nobody cares if you sit there because it's nobody in it. Sit right there."

"I heard you," the boy muttered. "It's no use in you yelling," and he sat down and turned his head to the glass. There he saw a pale ghost-like face scowling at him beneath the brim of a pale ghost-like hat. His grandfather, looking quickly too, saw a different ghost, pale but grinning, under a black hat.

Mr. Head sat down and settled himself and took out his ticket and started reading aloud everything that was printed on it. People began to stir. Several woke up and stared at him. "Take off your hat," he said to Nelson and took off his own and put it on his knee. He had a small amount of white hair that had turned tobacco-colored over the years and this lay flat across the back of his head. The front of his head was bald and creased. Nelson took off his hat and put it on his knee and they waited for the conductor to come ask for their tickets.

The man across the aisle from them was spread out over two seats, his feet propped on the window and his head jutting into the aisle. He had on a light blue suit and a yellow shirt unbuttoned at the neck. His eyes had just opened and Mr. Head was ready to introduce himself when the conductor came up from behind and growled, "Tickets."

When the conductor had gone, Mr. Head gave Nelson the return half of his ticket and said, "Now put that in your pocket and don't lose it or you'll have to stay in the city."

"Maybe I will," Nelson said as if this were a reasonable suggestion.

Mr. Head ignored him. "First time this boy has ever been on a train," he explained to the man across the aisle, who was sitting up now on the edge of his seat with both feet on the floor.

Nelson jerked his hat on again and turned angrily to the window.

"He's never seen anything before," Mr. Head continued. "Ignorant as the day he was born, but I mean for him to get his fill once and for all."

The boy leaned forward, across his grandfather and toward the stranger. "I was born in the city," he said. "I was born there. This is my second trip." He said it in a high positive voice but the man across the aisle didn't look as if he understood. There were heavy purple circles under his eyes.

Mr. Head reached across the aisle and tapped him on the arm. "The thing to do with a boy," he said sagely, "is to show him all it is to show. Don't hold nothing back."

"Yeah," the man said. He gazed down at his swollen feet and lifted the left one about ten inches from the floor. After a minute he put it down and lifted the other. All through the car people began to get up and move about and yawn and stretch. Separate voices could be heard here and there and then a general hum. Suddenly Mr. Head's serene expression changed. His mouth almost closed and a light, fierce and cautious both, came into his eyes. He was looking down the length of the car. Without turning, he caught Nelson by the arm and pulled him forward. "Look," he said.

A huge coffee-colored man was coming slowly forward. He had on a light suit and a yellow satin tie with a ruby pin in it. One of his hands rested on his stomach which rode majestically under his buttoned coat, and in the other he held the head of a black walking stick that he picked up and set down with a deliberate outward motion each time he took a step. He was proceeding very slowly, his large brown eyes gazing over the heads of the passengers. He had a small white mustache and white crinkly hair. Behind him there were two young women, both coffee-colored, one in a yellow dress and one in a green.

Their progress was kept at the rate of his and they chatted in low throaty voices as they followed him.

Mr. Head's grip was tightening insistently on Nelson's arm. As the procession passed them, the light from a sapphire ring on the brown hand that picked up the cane reflected in Mr. Head's eye, but he did not look up nor did the tremendous man look at him. The group proceeded up the rest of the aisle and out of the car. Mr. Head's grip on Nelson's arm loosened. "What was that?" he asked.

"A man," the boy said and gave him an indignant look as if he were tired of having his intelligence insulted.

"What kind of a man?" Mr. Head persisted, his voice expressionless.

"A fat man," Nelson said. He was beginning to feel that he had better be cautious.

"You don't know what kind?" Mr. Head said in a final tone.

"An old man," the boy said and had a sudden foreboding that he was not going to enjoy the day.

"That was a nigger," Mr. Head said and sat back.

Nelson jumped up on the seat and stood looking backward to the end of the car but the Negro had gone.

"I'd of thought you'd know a nigger since you seen so many when you was in the city on your first visit," Mr. Head continued. "That's his first nigger," he said to the man across the aisle.

The boy slid down into the seat. "You said they were black," he said in an angry voice. "You never said they were tan. How do you expect me to know anything when you don't tell me right?"

"You're just ignorant is all," Mr. Head said and he got up and moved over in the vacant seat by the man across the aisle.

Nelson turned backward again and looked where the Negro had disappeared. He felt that the Negro had deliberately walked down the aisle in order to make a fool of him and he hated him with a fierce raw fresh hate; and also, he understood now why his grandfather disliked them. He looked toward the window and the face there seemed to suggest that he might be inadequate to the day's exactions. He wondered if he would even recognize the city when they came to it.

After he had told several stories, Mr. Head realized that the man he was talking to was asleep and he got up and suggested to Nelson that they walk over the train and see the parts of it. He particularly wanted the boy to see the toilet so they went first to the men's room and examined the plumbing. Mr. Head demonstrated the ice-water cooler as if he had invented it and showed Nelson the bowl with the single spigot where the travelers brushed their teeth. They went through several cars and came to the diner.

This was the most elegant car in the train. It was painted a rich egg-yellow and had a wine-colored carpet on the floor. There were wide windows over the tables and great spaces of the rolling view were caught in miniature in the sides of the coffee pots and in the glasses. Three very black Negroes in white suits and aprons were running up and down the aisle, swinging trays and bowing and bending over the travelers eating breakfast. One of them rushed up to Mr. Head and Nelson and said, holding up two fingers, "Space for two!" but Mr. Head replied in a loud voice. "We eaten before we left!"

The waiter wore large brown spectacles that increased the size of his eye whites. "Stan' aside then please," he said with an airy wave of the arm as if he were brushing aside flies.

Neither Nelson nor Mr. Head moved a fraction of an inch. "Look," Mr. Head said.

The near corner of the diner, containing two tables, was set off from the rest by a saffron-colored curtain. One table was set but empty but at the other, facing them, his back to the drape, sat the tremendous Negro. He was speaking in a soft voice to the two women while he buttered a muffin. He had a heavy sad face and his neck bulged over his white collar on either side. "They rope them off," Mr. Head explained. Then he said, "Let's go see the kitchen," and they walked the length of the diner but the black waiter was coming fast behind them.

"Passengers are not allowed in the kitchen!" he said in a haughty voice. "Passengers are NOT allowed in the kitchen!"

Mr. Head stopped where he was and turned. "And there's good reason for that," he shouted into the Negro's chest, "because the cockroaches would run the passengers out!"

All the travelers laughed and Mr. Head and Nelson walked out, grinning. Mr. Head was known at home for his quick wit and Nelson felt a sudden keen pride in him. He realized the old man would be his only support in the strange place they were approaching. He would be entirely alone in the world if he were ever lost from his grandfather. A terrible excitement shook him and he wanted to take hold of Mr. Head's coat and hold on like a child.

As they went back to their seats they could see through the passing windows that the countryside was becoming speckled with small houses and shacks and that a highway ran alongside the train. Cars sped by on it, very small and fast. Nelson felt that there was less breath in the air than there had been thirty minutes ago. The man across the aisle had left and there was no one near for Mr. Head to hold a conversation with so he looked out the window, through his own reflection, and read aloud the names of the buildings they were passing. "The Dixie Chemical Corp!" he announced. "Southern Maid Flour! Dixie Doors! Southern Belle Cotton Products! Patty's Peanut Butter! Southern Mammy Cane Syrup!"

"Hush up!" Nelson hissed.

All over the car people were beginning to get up and take their luggage off the overhead racks. Women were putting on their coats and hats. The conductor stuck his head in the car and snarled, "Firstopppppmry," and Nelson lunged out of his sitting position, trembling. Mr. Head pushed him down by the shoulder.

"Keep your seat," he said in dignified tones. "The first stop is on the edge of town. The second stop is at the main railroad station." He had come by this knowledge on his first trip when he had got off at the first stop and had had to pay a man fifteen cents to take him into the heart of town. Nelson sat back down, very pale. For the first time in his life, he understood that his grand-father was indispensable to him.

The train stopped and let off a few passengers and glided on as if it had never ceased moving. Outside, behind rows of brown rickety houses, a line of blue buildings stood up, and beyond them a pale rose-gray sky faded away to nothing. The train moved into the railroad yard. Looking down, Nelson saw lines and lines of silver tracks multiplying and criss-crossing. Then before he could start counting them, the face in the window started out at him, gray but distinct, and he looked the other way. The train was in the station. Both he and Mr. Head jumped up and ran to the door. Neither noticed that they had left the paper sack with the lunch in it on the seat.

They walked stiffly through the small station and came out of a heavy door into the squall of traffic. Crowds were hurrying to work. Nelson didn't know where to look. Mr. Head leaned against the side of the building and glared in front of him.

Finally Nelson said, "Well, how do you see what all it is to see?"

Mr. Head didn't answer. Then as if the sight of people passing had given him the clue, he said, "You walk," and started off down the street. Nelson followed, steadying his hat. So many sights and sounds were flooding in on him that for the first block he hardly knew what he was seeing. At the second corner, Mr. Head turned and looked behind him at the station they had left, a putty-colored terminal with a concrete dome on top. He thought that if he could keep the dome always in sight, he would be able to get back in the afternoon to catch the train again.

As they walked along, Nelson began to distinguish details and take note of the store windows, jammed with every kind of equipment—hardware, dry-goods, chicken feed, liquor. They passed one that Mr. Head called his particular attention to where you walked in and sat on a chair with your feet upon two rests and let a Negro polish your shoes. They walked slowly and stopped and stood at the entrances so he could see what went on in each place but they did not go into any of them. Mr. Head was determined not to go into any city store because on his first trip here, he had got lost in a large one and had found his way out only after many people had insulted him.

They came in the middle of the next block to a store that had a weighing machine in front of it and they both in turn stepped up on it and put in a penny and received a ticket. Mr. Head's ticket said, "You weigh 120 pounds. You are upright and brave and all your friends admire you." He put the ticket in his pocket, surprised that the machine should have got his character correct but his weight wrong, for he had weighed on a grain scale not long before and knew he weighed 110. Nelson's ticket said, "You weigh 98 pounds. You have a great destiny ahead of you but beware of dark women." Nelson did not know any women and he weighed only 68 pounds but Mr. Head pointed out that the machine had probably printed the number upsidedown, meaning the 9 for a 6.

They walked on and at the end of five blocks the dome of the terminal sank out of sight and Mr. Head turned to the left. Nelson could have stood in front of every store window for an hour if there had not been another more interesting one next to it. Suddenly he said, "I was born here!" Mr. Head turned and looked at him with horror. There was a sweaty brightness about his face. "This is where I come from!" he said.

Mr. Head was appalled. He saw the moment had come for drastic action. "Lemme show you one thing you ain't seen yet," he said and took him to the corner where there was a sewer entrance. "Squat down," he said, "and stick you head in there," and he held the back of the boy's coat while he got down and put his head in the sewer. He drew it back quickly, hearing a gurgling in the depths under the sidewalk. Then Mr. Head explained the sewer system, how the entire city was underlined with it, how it contained all the drainage and was full of rats and how a man could slide into it and be sucked along down endless pitchblack tunnels. At any minute any man in the city might be sucked into the sewer and never heard from again. He described it so well that Nelson was for some seconds shaken. He connected the sewer passages with the entrance to hell and understood for the first time how the world was put together in its lower parts. He drew away from the curb.

Then he said, "Yes, but you can stay away from the holes," and his face took on that stubborn look that was so exasperating to his grandfather. "This is where I come from!" he said.

Mr. Head was dismayed but he only muttered, "You'll get your fill," and they walked on. At the end of two more blocks he turned to the left, feeling that he was circling the dome; and he was correct for in a half-hour they passed in front of the railroad station again. At first Nelson did not notice that he was seeing the same stores twice but when they passed the one where you put your feet on the rests while the Negro polished your shoes, he perceived that they were walking in a circle.

"We done been here!" he shouted. "I don't believe you know where you're at!"

"The direction just slipped my mind for a minute," Mr. Head said and they turned down a different street. He still did not intend to let the dome get too far away and after two blocks in their new direction, he turned to the left. This street contained two- and three-story wooden dwellings. Anyone passing on the sidewalk could see into the rooms and Mr. Head, glancing through one window, saw a woman lying on an iron bed, looking out, with a sheet pulled over her. Her knowing expression shook him. A fierce-looking boy on a bicycle came driving down out of nowhere and he had to jump to the side to keep from being hit. "It's nothing to them if they knock you down," he said. "You better keep closer to me."

They walked on for some time on streets like this before he remembered to turn again. The houses they were passing now were all unpainted and the wood in them looked rotten; the street between was narrower. Nelson saw a colored man. Then another. Then another. "Niggers live in these houses," he observed.

"Well come on and we'll go somewheres else," Mr. Head said. "We didn't come to look at niggers," and they turned down another street but they continued to see Negroes everywhere. Nelson's skin began to prickle and they stepped along at a faster pace in order to leave the neighborhood as soon as possible. There were colored men in their undershirts standing in the doors and colored women rocking on the sagging porches. Colored children played in the gutters and stopped what they were doing to look at them. Before long they began to pass rows of stores with colored customers in them but they didn't pause at the entrances of these. Black eyes in black faces were watching them from every direction. "Yes," Mr. Head said, "this is where you were born—right here with all these niggers."

Nelson scowled. "I think you done got us lost," he said.

Mr. Head swung around sharply and looked for the dome. It was nowhere in sight. "I ain't got us lost either," he said. "You're just tired of walking."

"I ain't tired, I'm hungry," Nelson said. "Give me a biscuit."

They discovered then that they had lost the lunch.

"You were the one holding the sack," Nelson said. "I would have kepaholt of it."

"If you want to direct this trip, I'll go on by myself and leave you right here," Mr. Head said and was pleased to see the boy turn white. However, he realized they were lost and drifting farther every minute from the station. He was hungry himself and beginning to be thirsty and since they had been in the colored neighborhood, they had both begun to sweat. Nelson had on his shoes and he was unaccustomed to them. The concrete sidewalks were very hard. They both wanted to find a place to sit down but this was impossible and they kept on walking, the boy muttering under his breath, "First you lost the sack and then you lost the way," and Mr. Head growling from time to time, "Anybody wants to be from this nigger heaven can be from it!"

By now the sun was well forward in the sky. The odor of dinners cooking drifted out to them. The Negroes were all at their doors to see them pass. "Whyn't you ast one of these niggers the way?" Nelson said. "You got us lost."

"This is where you were born," Mr. Head said. "You can ast one yourself if you want to."

Nelson was afraid of the colored men and he didn't want to be laughed at by the colored children. Up ahead he saw a large colored woman leaning in a doorway that opened onto the sidewalk. Her hair stood straight out from her head for about four inches all around and she was resting on bare brown feet that turned pink at the sides. She had on a pink dress that showed her exact shape. As they came abreast of her, she lazily lifted one hand to her head and her fingers disappeared into her hair.

Nelson stopped. He felt his breath drawn up by the woman's dark eyes. "How do you get back to town?" he said in a voice that did not sound like his own.

After a minute she said, "You in town now," in a rich low tone that made Nelson feel as if a cool spray had been turned on him.

"How do you get back to the train?" he said in the same reed-like voice.

"You can catch you a car," she said.

He understood she was making fun of him but he was too paralyzed even to scowl. He stood drinking in every detail of her. His eyes traveled up from her great knees to her forehead and then made a triangular path from the glistening sweat on her neck down and across her tremendous bosom and over her bare arm back to where her fingers lay hidden in her hair. He suddenly wanted her to reach down and pick him up and draw him against her and then he wanted to feel her breath on his face. He wanted to look down and down into her eyes while she held him tighter and tighter. He had never had such a feeling before. He felt as if he were reeling down through a pitchblack tunnel.

"You can go a block down yonder and catch you a car takᵥ you to the railroad station, Sugarpie," she said.

Nelson would have collapsed at her feet if Mr. Head had not pulled him roughly away. "You act like you don't have any sense!" the old man growled.

They hurried down the street and Nelson did not look back at the woman. He pushed his hat sharply forward over his face which was already burning with shame. The sneering ghost he had seen in the train window and all the foreboding feelings he had on the way returned to him and he remembered that his ticket from the scale had said to beware of dark women and that his grandfather's had said he was upright and brave. He took hold of the old man's hand, a sign of dependence that he seldom showed.

They headed down the street toward the car tracks where a long yellow rattling trolley was coming. Mr. Head had never boarded a streetcar and he let that one pass. Nelson was silent. From time to time his mouth trembled slightly but his grandfather, occupied with his own problems, paid him no attention. They stood on the corner and neither looked at the Negroes who were passing, going about their business just as if they had been white, except that most of them stopped and eyed Mr. Head and Nelson. It occurred to Mr. Head that since the streetcar ran on tracks, they could simply follow the tracks. He gave Nelson a slight push and explained that they would follow the tracks on into the railroad station, walking, and they set off.

Presently to their great relief they began to see white people again and Nelson sat down on the sidewalk against the wall of a building. "I got to rest myself some," he said. "You lost the sack and the direction. You can just wait on me to rest myself."

"There's the tracks in front of us," Mr. Head said. "All we got to do is keep them in sight and you could have remembered the sack as good as me. This is where you were born. This is your old home town. This is your second trip. You ought to know how to do," and he squatted down and continued in this vein but the boy, easing his burning feet out of his shoes, did not answer.

"And standing there grinning like a chim-pan-zee while a nigger woman gives you directions. Great Gawd!" Mr. Head said.

"I never said I was nothing but born here," the boy said in a shaky voice. "I never said I would or wouldn't like it. I never said I wanted to come. I only said I was born here and I never had nothing to do with that. I want to go home. I never wanted to come in the first place. It was all your big idea. How you know you ain't following the tracks in the wrong direction?"

This last had occurred to Mr. Head too. "All these people are white," he said.

"We ain't passed here before," Nelson said. This was a neighborhood of brick buildings that might have been lived in or might not. A few empty automobiles were parked along the curb and there was an occasional passerby. The heat of the pavement came up through Nelson's thin suit. His eyelids began to droop, and after a few minutes his head tilted forward. His shoulders twitched once or twice and then he fell over on his side and lay sprawled in an exhausted fit of sleep.

Mr. Head watched him silently. He was very tired himself but they could not both sleep at the same time and he could not have slept anyway because he did not know where he was. In a few minutes Nelson would wake up, refreshed by his sleep and very cocky, and would begin complaining that he had lost the sack and the way. You'd have a mighty sorry time if I wasn't here, Mr. Head thought; and then another idea occurred to him. He looked at the sprawled figure for several minutes; presently he stood up. He justified what he was going to do on the grounds that it is sometimes necessary to teach a child a lesson he won't forget, particularly when the child is always reasserting his position with some new impudence. He walked without a sound to the corner about twenty feet away and sat down on a covered garbage can in the alley where he could look out and watch Nelson wake up alone.

The boy was dozing fitfully, half conscious of vague noises and black forms moving up from some dark part of him into the light. His face worked in his sleep and he had pulled his knees up under his chin. The sun shed a dull dry light on the narrow street; everything looked like exactly what it was. After a while Mr. Head, hunched like an old monkey on the garbage can lid, decided that if Nelson didn't wake up soon, he would make a loud noise by bamming his foot against the can. He looked at his watch and discovered that it was two o'clock. Their train left at six and the possibility of missing it was too awful for him to think of. He kicked his foot backwards on the can and a hollow boom reverberated in the alley.

Nelson shot up onto his feet with a shout. He looked where his grandfather should have been and stared. He seemed to whirl several times and then, picking up his feet and throwing his head back, he dashed down the street like a wild maddened pony. Mr. Head jumped off the can and galloped after but the child was almost out of sight. He saw a streak of gray disappearing diagonally a block ahead. He ran as fast as he could, looking both ways down every intersection, but without sight of him again. Then as he passed the third intersection, completely winded, he saw about half a block down the street a scene that stopped him altogether. He crouched behind a trash box to watch and get his bearings.

Nelson was sitting with both legs spread out and by his side lay an elderly woman, screaming. Groceries were scattered about the sidewalk. A crowd of women had already gathered to see justice done and Mr. Head distinctly heard the old woman on the pavement shout, "You've broken my ankle and your daddy'll pay for it! Every nickel! Police! Police!" Several of the women were plucking at Nelson's shoulder but the boy seemed too dazed to get up.

Something forced Mr. Head from behind the trash box and forward, but only at a creeping pace. He had never in his life been accosted by a policeman. The women were milling around Nelson as if they might suddenly all dive on him at once and tear him to pieces, and the old woman continued to scream that her ankle was broken and to call for an officer. Mr. Head came on so slowly that he could have been taking a backward step after each forward one, but when he was about ten feet away, Nelson saw him and sprang. The child caught him around the hips and clung panting against him.

The women all turned on Mr. Head. The injured one sat up and shouted, "You sir! You'll pay every penny of my doctor's bill that your boy has caused. He's a juve-nile delinquent! Where is an officer? Somebody take this man's name and address!"

Mr. Head was trying to detach Nelson's fingers from the flesh in the back of his legs. The old man's head had lowered itself into his collar like a turtle's; his eyes were glazed with fear and caution.

"Your boy has broken my ankle!" the old woman shouted. "Police!"

Mr. Head sensed the approach of the policeman from behind. He stared straight ahead at the women who were massed in their fury like a solid wall to block his escape. "This is not my boy," he said. "I never seen him before."

He felt Nelson's fingers fall out of his flesh.

The women dropped back, staring at him with horror, as if they were so repulsed by a man who would deny his own image and likeness that they could not bear to lay hands on him. Mr. Head walked on, through a space they silently cleared, and left Nelson behind. Ahead of him he saw nothing but a hollow tunnel that had once been the street.

The boy remained standing where he was, his neck craned forward and his hands hanging by his sides. His hat was jammed on his head so that there were no longer any creases in it. The injured woman got up and shook her fist at him and the others gave him pitying looks, but he didn't notice any of them. There was no policeman in sight.

In a minute he began to move mechanically, making no effort to catch up with his grandfather but merely following at about twenty paces. They walked on for five blocks this way. Mr. Head's shoulders were sagging and his neck hung forward at such an angle that it was not visible from behind. He was afraid to turn his head. Finally he cut a short hopeful glance over his shoulder. Twenty feet behind him, he saw two small eyes piercing into his back like pitchfork prongs.

The boy was not of a forgiving nature but this was the first time he had ever had anything to forgive. Mr. Head had never disgraced himself before. After two more blocks, he turned and called over his shoulder in a high desperately gay voice, "Let's us go get us a Co' Cola somewheres!"

Nelson, with a dignity he had never shown before, turned and stood with his back to his grandfather.

Mr. Head began to feel the depth of his denial. His face as they walked on became all hollows and bare ridges. He saw nothing they were passing but he perceived that they had lost the car tracks. There was no dome to be seen anywhere and the afternoon was advancing. He knew that if dark overtook them in the city, they would be beaten and robbed. The speed of God's justice was only what he expected for himself, but he could not stand to think that his sins would be visited upon Nelson and that even now, he was leading the boy to his doom.

They continued to walk on block after block through an endless section of small brick houses until Mr. Head almost fell over a water spigot sticking up about six inches off the edge of a grass plot. He had not had a drink of water since early morning but he felt he did not deserve it now. Then he thought that Nelson would be thirsty and they would both drink and be brought together. He squatted down and put his mouth to the nozzle and turned a cold stream of water into his throat. Then he called out in the high desperate voice, "Come on and getcher some water!"

This time the child stared through him for nearly sixty seconds. Mr. Head got up and walked on as if he had drunk poison. Nelson, though he had not had water since some he had drunk out of a paper cup on the train, passed by the spigot, disdaining to drink where his grandfather had. When Mr. Head realized this, he lost all hope. His face in the waning afternoon light looked ravaged and abandoned. He could feel the boy's steady hate, traveling at an even pace behind him and he knew that (if by some miracle they escaped being murdered in the city) it would continue just that way for the rest of his life. He knew that now he was wandering into a black strange place where nothing was like it had ever been before, a long old age without respect and an end that would be welcome because it would be the end.

As for Nelson, his mind had frozen around his grandfather's treachery as if he were trying to preserve it intact to present at the final judgment. He walked without looking to one side or the other, but every now and then his mouth would twitch and this was when he felt, from some remote place inside himself, a black mysterious form reach up as if it would melt his frozen vision in one hot grasp.

The sun dropped down behind a row of houses and hardly noticing, they passed into an elegant suburban section where mansions were set back from the road by lawns with birdbaths on them. Here everything was entirely deserted. For blocks they didn't pass even a dog. The big white houses were like partially submerged icebergs in the distance. There were no sidewalks, only drives, and these wound around and around in endless ridiculous circles. Nelson made no move to come nearer to Mr. Head. The old man felt that if he saw a sewer entrance he would drop down into it and let himself be carried away; and he could imagine the boy standing by, watching with only a slight interest, while he disappeared.

A loud bark jarred him to attention and he looked up to see a fat man approaching with two bulldogs. He waved both arms like someone ship-wrecked on a desert island. "I'm lost!" he called. "I'm lost and can't find my way and me and this boy have got to catch this train and I can't find the station. Oh Gawd I'm lost! Oh hep me Gawd I'm lost!"

The man, who was bald-headed and had on golf knickers, asked him what train he was trying to catch and Mr. Head began to get out his tickets, trembling so violently he could hardly hold them. Nelson had come up to within fifteen feet and stood watching.

"Well," the fat man said, giving him back the tickets, "you won't have time to get back to town to make this but you can catch it at the suburb stop. That's three blocks from here," and he began explaining how to get there.

Mr. Head stared as if he were slowly returning from the dead and when the man had finished and gone off with the dogs jumping at his heels, he turned to Nelson and said breathlessly, "We're going to get home!"

The child was standing about ten feet away, his face bloodless under the gray hat. His eyes were triumphantly cold. There was no light in them, no feeling, no interest. He was merely there, a small figure, waiting. Home was nothing to him.

Mr. Head turned slowly. He felt he knew now what time would be like without seasons and what heat would be like without light and what man would be like without salvation. He didn't care if he never made the train and if it had not been for what suddenly caught his attention, like a cry out of the gathering dusk, he might have forgotten there was a station to go to.

He had not walked five hundred yards down the road when he saw, within reach of him, the plaster figure of a Negro sitting bent over on a low yellow brick fence that curved around a wide lawn. The Negro was about Nelson's size and he was pitched forward at an unsteady angle because the putty that held him to the wall had cracked. One of his eyes was entirely white and he held a piece of brown watermelon.

Mr. Head stood looking at him silently until Nelson stopped at a little distance. Then as the two of them stood there, Mr. Head breathed, "An artificial nigger!"

It was not possible to tell if the artificial Negro were meant to be young or old; he looked too miserable to be either. He was meant to look happy because his mouth was stretched up at the corners but the chipped eye and the angle he was cocked at gave him a wild look of misery instead.

"An artificial nigger!" Nelson repeated in Mr. Head's exact tone.

The two of them stood there with their necks forward at almost the same angle and their shoulders curved in almost exactly the same way and their hands trembling identically in their pockets. Mr. Head looked like an ancient child and Nelson like a miniature old man. They stood gazing at the artificial Negro as if they were faced with some great mystery, some monument to another's victory that brought them together in their common defeat. They could both feel it dissolving their differences like an action of mercy. Mr. Head had never known before what mercy felt like because he had been too good to deserve any, but he felt he knew now. He looked at Nelson and understood that he must say something to the child to show that he was still wise and in the look the boy returned he saw a hungry need for that assurance. Nelson's eyes seemed to implore him to explain once and for all the mystery of existence.

Mr. Head opened his lips to made a lofty statement and heard himself say, "They ain't got enough real ones here. They got to have an artificial one."

After a second, the boy nodded with a strange shivering about his mouth, and said, "Let's go home before we get ourselves lost again."

Their train glided into the suburb stop just as they reached the station and they boarded it together, and ten minutes before it was due to arrive at the junction, they went to the door and stood ready to jump off if it did not stop; but it did, just as the moon, restored to its full splendor, sprang from a cloud and flooded the clearing with light. As they stepped off, the sage grass was shivering gently in shades of silver and the clinkers under their feet glittered with a fresh black light. The treetops, fencing the junction like the protecting walls of a garden, were darker than the sky which was hung with gigantic white clouds illuminated like lanterns.

Mr. Head stood very still and felt the action of mercy touch him again but this time he knew that there were no words in the world that could name it. He understood that it grew out of agony, which is not denied to any man and which is given in strange ways to children. He understood it was all a man could carry into death to give his Maker and he suddenly burned with shame that he had so little of it to take with him. He stood appalled, judging himself with the thoroughness of God, while the action of mercy covered his pride like a flame and consumed it. He had never thought himself a great sinner before but he saw now that his true depravity had been hidden from him lest it cause him despair. He realized that he was forgiven for sins from the beginning of time, when he had conceived in his own heart the sin of Adam, until the present, when he had denied poor Nelson. He saw that no sin was too monstrous for him to claim as his own, and since God loved in proportion as He forgave, he felt ready at that instant to enter Paradise.

Nelson, composing his expression under the shadow of his hat brim, watched him with a mixture of fatigue and suspicion, but as the train glided past them and disappeared like a frightened serpent into the woods, even his face lightened and he muttered, "I'm glad I've went once, but I'll never go back again!"

Barry Hannah (b. 1942)
Testimony of Pilot

When I was ten, eleven and twelve, I did a good bit of my play in the backyard of a three-story wooden house my father had bought and rented out, his first venture into real estate. We lived right across the street from it, but over here was the place to do your real play. Here there was a harrowed but overgrown garden, a vine-swallowed fence at the back end, and beyond the fence a cornfield which belonged to someone else. This was not the country. This was the town, Clinton, Mississippi, between Jackson on the east and Vicksburg on the west. On this lot stood a few water oaks, a few plum bushes, and much overgrowth of honeysuckle vine. At the very back end, at the fence, stood three strong nude chinaberry trees.

In Mississippi it is difficult to achieve a vista. But my friends and I had one here at the back corner of the garden. We could see across the cornfield, see the one lone tin-roofed house this side of the railroad tracks, then on across the tracks many other bleaker houses with rustier tin roofs, smoke coming out of the chimneys in the late fall. This was niggertown. We had binoculars and could see the colored children hustling about and perhaps a hopeless sow or two with her brood enclosed in a tiny boarded-up area. Through the binoculars one afternoon in October we watched some men corner and beat a large hog on the brain. They used an ax and the thing kept running around, head leaning toward the ground, for several minutes before it lay down. I thought I saw the men laughing when it finally did. One of them was staggering, plainly drunk to my sight from three hundred yards away. He had the long knife. Because of that scene I considered Negroes savage cowards for a good five more years of my life. Our maid brought some sausage to my mother and when it was put in the pan to fry, I made a point of running out of the house.

I went directly across the street and to the back end of the garden behind the apartment house we owned, without my breakfast. That was Saturday. Eventually, Radcleve saw me. His parents had him mowing the yard that ran alongside my dad's property. He clicked off the power mower and I went over to his fence, which was storm wire. His mother maintained handsome flowery grounds at all costs; she had a leafmold bin and St. Augustine grass as solid as a rug.

Radcleve himself was a violent experimental chemist. When Radcleve was eight, he threw a whole package of .22 shells against the sidewalk in front of his house until one of them went off, driving lead fragments into his calf, most of them still deep in there where the surgeons never dared tamper. Radcleve knew about the sulfur, potassium nitrate and charcoal mixture for gunpowder when he was ten. He bought things through the mail when he ran out of ingredients in his chemistry sets. When he was an infant, his father, a quiet man who owned the Chevrolet agency in town, bought an entire bankrupt sporting-goods store, and in the middle of their backyard he built a house, plain-painted and neat, one room and a heater, where Radcleve's redundant toys forevermore were kept—all the possible toys he would need for boyhood. There were things in there that Radcleve and I were not mature enough for and did not know the real use of. When we were eleven, we uncrated the new Dunlop golf balls and went on up a shelf for the tennis rackets, went out in the middle of his yard, and served new golf ball after new golf ball with blasts of the rackets over into the cornfield, out of sight. When the strings busted we just went in and got another racket. We were absorbed by how a good smack would set the heavy little pills on an endless flight. Then Radcleve's father came down. He simply dismissed me. He took Radcleve into the house and covered his whole body with a belt. But within the week Radcleve had invented the mortar. It was a steel pipe into which a flashlight battery fit perfectly, like a bullet into a muzzle. He had drilled a hole for the fuse of an M-80 firecracker at the base, for the charge. It was a grand cannon, set up on a stack of bricks at the back of my dad's property, which was the free place to play. When it shot, it would back up violently with thick smoke and you could hear the flashlight battery whistling off. So that morning when I ran out of the house protesting the hog sausage, I told Radcleve to bring over the mortar. His ma and dad were in Jackson for the day, and he came right over with the pipe, the batteries and the M-80 explosives. He had two gross of them.

Before, we'd shot off toward the woods to the right of niggertown. I turned the bricks to the left; I made us a very fine cannon carriage pointing toward niggertown. When Radcleve appeared, he had two pairs of binoculars around his neck, one pair a newly plundered German unit as big as a brace of whiskey bottles. I told him I wanted to shoot for that house where we saw them killing the pig. Radcleve loved the idea. We singled out the house with heavy use of the binoculars.

There were children in the yard. Then they all went in. Two men came out of the back door. I thought I recognized the drunkard from the other afternoon. I helped Radcleve fix the direction of the cannon. We estimated the altitude we needed to get down there. Radcleve put the M-80 in the breech with its fuse standing out of the hole. I dropped the flashlight battery in. I lit the fuse. We backed off. The M-80 blasted off deafeningly, smoke rose, but my concentration was on that particular house over there. I brought the binoculars up. We waited six or seven seconds. I heard a great joyful wallop on tin. "We've hit him on the first try, the first try!" I yelled. Radcleve was ecstatic. "Right on his roof!" We bolstered up the brick carriage. Radcleve remembered the correct height of the cannon exactly. So we fixed it, loaded it, lit it and backed off. The battery landed on the roof, blat, again, louder. I looked to see if there wasn't a great dent or hole in the roof. I could not understand why niggers weren't pouring out distraught from that house. We shot the mortar again and again, and always our battery hit the tin roof. Sometimes there was only a dull thud, but other times there was a wild distress of tin. I was still looking through the binoculars, amazed that the niggers wouldn't even come out of their house to see what was hitting their roof. Radcleve was on to it better than me. I looked over at him and he had the huge German binocs much lower than I did. He was looking straight through the cornfield, which was all bare and open, with nothing left but rotten stalks. "What we've been hitting is the roof of that house just this side of the tracks. White people live in there," he said.

I took up my binoculars again. I looked around the yard of that white wooden house on this side of the tracks, almost next to the railroad. When I found the tin roof, I saw four significant dents in it. I saw one of our batteries lying in the middle of a sort of crater. I took the binoculars down into the yard and saw a blond middle-aged woman looking our way.

"Somebody's coming up toward us. He's from that house and he's got, I think, some sort of fancy gun with him. It might be an automatic weapon."

I ran my binoculars all over the cornfield. Then, in a line with the house, I saw him. He was coming our way but having some trouble with the rows and dead stalks of the cornfield.

"That is just a boy like us. All he's got is a saxophone with him," I told Radcleve. I had recently got in the school band, playing drums, and had seen all the weird horns that made up a band.

I watched this boy with the saxophone through the binoculars until he was ten feet from us. This was Quadberry. His name was Ard, short for Arden. His shoes were foot-square wads of mud from the cornfield. When he saw us across the fence and above him, he stuck out his arm in my direction.

"My dad says stop it!"

"We weren't doing anything," says Radcleve.

"Mother saw the smoke puff up from here. Dad has a hangover."

"A what?"

"It's a headache from indiscretion. You're lucky he does. He's picked up the poker to rap on you, but he can't move further the way his head is."

"What's your name? You're not in the band," I said, focusing on the saxophone.

"It's Ard Quadberry. Why do you keep looking at me through the binoculars?"

It was because he was odd, with his hair and its white ends, and his Arab nose, and now his name. Add to that the saxophone.

"My dad's a doctor at the college. Mother's a musician. You better quit what you're doing. . . . I was out practicing in the garage. I saw one of those flashlight batteries roll off the roof. Could I see what you shoot 'em with?"

"No," said Radcleve. Then he said: "If you'll play that horn."

Quadberry stood out there ten feet below us in the field, skinny, feet and pants booted with black mud, and at his chest the slung-on, very complex, radiant horn.

Quadberry began sucking and licking the reed. I didn't care much for this act, and there was too much desperate oralness in his face when he began playing. That was why I chose the drums. One had to engage himself like suck's revenge with a horn. But what Quadberry was playing was pleasant and intricate. I was sure it was advanced, and there was no squawking, as from the other eleven-year-olds on sax in the band room. He made the end with a clean upward riff, holding the final note high, pure and unwavering.

"Good!" I called to him.

Quadberry was trying to move out of the sunken row toward us, but his heavy shoes were impeding him.

"Sounded like a duck. Sounded like a girl duck," said Radcleve, who was kneeling down and packing a mudball around one of the M-80s. I saw and I was an accomplice, because I did nothing. Radcleve lit the fuse and heaved the mudball over the fence. An M-80 is a very serious firecracker; it is like the charge they use to shoot up those sprays six hundred feet on July Fourth at country clubs. It went off, this one, even bigger than most M-80s.

When we looked over the fence, we saw Quadberry all muck specks and fragments of stalks. He was covering the mouthpiece of his horn with both hands. Then I saw there was blood pouring out of, it seemed, his right eye. I thought he was bleeding directly out of his eye.

"Quadberry?" I called.

He turned around and never said a word to me until I was eighteen. He walked back holding his eye and staggering through the cornstalks. Radcleve had him in the binoculars. Radcleve was trembling . . . but intrigued.

"His mother just screamed. She's running out in the field to get him."

I thought we'd blinded him, but we hadn't. I thought the Quadberrys would get the police or call my father, but they didn't. The upshot of this is that Quadberry had a permanent white space next to his right eye, a spot that looked like a tiny upset crown.

I went from sixth through half of twelfth grade ignoring him and that wound. I was coming on as a drummer and a lover, but if Quadberry happened to appear within fifty feet of me and my most tender, intimate sweetheart, I would duck out. Quadberry grew up just like the rest of us. His father was still a doctor—professor of history—at the town college; his mother was still blond, and a musician. She was organist at an Episcopalian church in Jackson, the big capital city ten miles east of us.

As for Radcleve, he still had no ear for music, but he was there, my buddy. He was repentant about Quadberry, although not so much as I. He'd thrown the mud grenade over the fence only to see what would happen. He had not really wanted to maim. Quadberry had played his tune on the sax, Radcleve had played his tune on the mud grenade. It was just a shame they happened to cross talents.

Radcleve went into a long period of nearly nothing after he gave up violent explosives. Then he trained himself to copy the comic strips, *Steve Canyon* to *Major Hoople*, until he became quite a versatile cartoonist with some very provocative new faces and bodies that were gesturing intriguingly. He could never fill in the speech balloons with the smart words they needed. Sometimes he would pencil in "Err" or "What?" in the empty speech places. I saw him a great deal. Radcleve was not spooked by Quadberry. He even once asked Quadberry what his opinion was of his future as a cartoonist. Quadberry told Radcleve that if he took all his cartoons and stuffed himself with them, he would make an interesting dead man. After that, Radcleve was shy of him too.

When I was a senior we had an extraordinary band. Word was we had outplayed all the big A.A.A. division bands last April in the state contest. Then came news that a new blazing saxophone player was coming into the band as first chair. This person had spent summers in Vermont in music camps, and he was coming in with us for the concert season. Our director, a lovable aesthete named Richard Prender, announced to us in a proud silent moment that the boy was joining us tomorrow night. The effect was that everybody should push over a seat or two and make room for this boy and his talent. I was annoyed. Here I'd been with the band and had kept hold of the taste among the whole percussion section. I could play rock and jazz drum and didn't even really need to be here. I could be in Vermont too, give me a piano and a bass. I looked at the kid on first sax, who was going to be supplanted tomorrow. For two years he had thought he was the star, then suddenly enters this boy who's three times better.

The new boy was Quadberry. He came in, but he was meek, and when he tuned up he put his head almost on the floor, bending over trying to be inconspicuous. The girls in the band had wanted him to be handsome, but Quadberry refused and kept himself in such hiding among the sax section that he was neither handsome, ugly, cute or anything. What he was was pretty near invisible, except for the bell of his horn, the all-but-closed eyes, the Arabian nose, the brown hair with its halo of white ends, the desperate oralness, the giant reed punched into his face, and hazy Quadberry, loving the wound in a private dignified ecstasy.

I say dignified because of what came out of the end of his horn. He was more than what Prender had told us he would be. Because of Quadberry, we could take the band arrangement of Ravel's *Bolero* with us to the state contest. Quadberry would do the saxophone solo. He would switch to alto sax, he would do the sly Moorish ride. When he played, I heard the sweetness, I heard the horn which finally brought human *talk* into the realm of music. It could sound like the mutterings of a field nigger, and then it could get up into inhumanly careless beauty, it could get among mutinous helium bursts around Saturn. I already loved *Bolero* for the constant drum part. The percussion was always there, driving along with the subtly increasing triplets, insistent, insistent, at last outraged and trying to steal the whole show from the horns and the others. I knew a large boy with dirty blond hair, name of Wyatt, who played viola in the Jackson Symphony and sousaphone in our band— one of the rare closet transmutations of my time—who was forever claiming to have discovered the central *Bolero* one Sunday afternoon over FM radio as he had seven distinct sexual moments with a certain B., girl flutist with black bangs and skin like mayonnaise, while the drums of Ravel carried them on and on in a ceremony of Spanish sex. It was agreed by all the canny in the band that *Bolero* was exactly the piece to make the band soar—now especially as we had Quadberry, who made his walk into the piece like an actual lean Spanish bandit. This boy could blow his horn. He was, as I had suspected, a genius. His solo was not quite the same as the New York Phil's saxophonist's, but it was better. It came in and was with us. It entered my spine and, I am sure, went up the skirts of the girls. I had almost deafened myself playing drums in the most famous rock and jazz band in the state, but I could hear the voice that went through and out that horn. It sounded like a very troubled forty-year-old man, a man who had had his brow in his hands a long time.

The next time I saw Quadberry up close, in fact the first time I had seen him up close since we were eleven and he was bleeding in the cornfield, was in late February. I had only three classes this last semester, and went up to the band room often, to loaf and complain and keep up my touch on the drums. Prender let me keep my set in one of the instrument rooms, with a tarpaulin thrown over it, and I would drag it out to the practice room and whale away. Sometimes a group of sophomores would come up and I would make them marvel, whaling away as if not only deaf but blind to them, although I wasn't at all. If I saw a sophomore girl with exceptional bod or face, I would do miracles of technique I never knew were in me. I would amaze myself. I would be threatening Buddy Rich and Sam Morello. But this time when I went into the instrument room, there was Quadberry on one side, and, back in a dark corner, a small ninth-grade euphonium player whose face was all red. The little boy was weeping and grinning at the same time.

"Queerberry," the boy said softly.

Quadberry flew upon him like a demon. He grabbed the boy's collar, slapped his face, and yanked his arm behind him in a merciless wrestler's grip, the one that made them bawl on TV. Then the boy broke it and slugged Quadberry in the lips and ran across to my side of the room. He said "Queerberry" softly again and jumped for the door. Quadberry plunged across the room and tackled him on the threshold. Now that the boy was under him, Quadberry pounded the top of his head with his fist made like a mallet. The boy kept calling him "Queerberry" throughout this. He had not learned his lesson. The boy seemed to be going into concussion, so I stepped over and touched Quadberry, telling him to quit. Quadberry obeyed and stood up off the boy, who crawled on out into the band room. But once more the boy looked back with a bruised grin, saying "Queerberry." Quadberry made a move toward him, but I blocked it.

"Why are you beating up on this little guy?" I said. Quadberry was sweating and his eyes were wild with hate; he was a big fellow now, though lean. He was, at six feet tall, bigger than me.

"He kept calling me Queerberry."

"What do you care?" I asked.

"I care," Quadberry said, and left me standing there.

We were to play at Millsaps College Auditorium for the concert. It was April. We got on the buses, a few took their cars, and were a big tense crowd getting over there. To Jackson was only a twenty-minute trip. The director, Prender, followed the bus in his Volkswagen. There was a thick fog. A flashing ambulance, snaking the lanes, piled into him head on. Prender, who I would imagine was thinking of *Bolero* and hearing the young horn voices in his band—perhaps he was dwelling on Quadberry's spectacular gypsy entrance, or perhaps he was meditating on the percussion section, of which I was the king—passed into the airs of band-director heaven. We were told by the student director as we set up on the stage. The student director was a senior from the town college, very much afflicted, almost to the point of drooling, by a love and respect for Dick Prender, and now afflicted by a heartbreaking esteem for his ghost. As were we all.

I loved the tough and tender director awesomely and never knew it until I found myself bawling along with all the rest of the boys of the percussion. I told them to keep setting up, keep tuning, keep screwing the stands together, keep hauling in the kettledrums. To just quit and bawl seemed a betrayal to Prender. I caught some girl clarinetists trying to flee the stage and go have their cry. I told them to get the hell back to their section. They obeyed me. Then I found the student director. I had to have my say.

"Look. I say we just play *Bolero* and junk the rest. That's our horse. We can't play *Brighton Beach* and *Neptune's Daughter*. We'll never make it through them. And they're too happy."

"We aren't going to play anything," he said. "Man, to play is filthy. Did you ever hear Prender play piano? Do you know what a cool man he was in all things?"

"We play. He got us ready, and we play."

"Man, you can't play any more than I can direct. You're bawling your face off. Look out there at the rest of them. Man, it's a herd, it's a weeping herd."

"What's wrong? Why aren't you pulling this crowd together?" This was Quadberry, who had come up urgently. "I got those little brats in my section sitting down, but we've got people abandoning the stage, tearful little finks throwing their horns on the floor."

"I'm not directing," said the mustached college man.

"Then get out of here. You're weak, weak!"

"Man, we've got teen-agers in ruin here, we got sorrowville. Nobody can—"

"Go ahead. Do your number. Weak out on us."

"Man, I—"

Quadberry was already up on the podium, shaking his arms.

"We're right here! The band is right here! Tell your friends to get back in their seats. We're doing *Bolero.* Just put *Bolero* up and start tuning. *I'm* directing. I'll be right here in front of you. You look at *me!* Don't you dare quit on Prender. Don't you dare quit on me. You've got to be heard. *I've* got to be heard. Prender wanted me to be heard. I am the star, and I say we sit down and blow."

And so we did. We all tuned and were burning low for the advent into *Bolero,* though we couldn't believe that Quadberry was going to remain with his saxophone strapped to him and conduct us as well as play his solo. The judges, who apparently hadn't heard about Prender's death, walked down to their balcony desks.

One of them called out "Ready" and Quadberry's hand was instantly up in the air, his fingers hard as if around the stem of something like a torch. This was not Prender's way, but it had to do. We went into the number cleanly and Quadberry one-armed it in the conducting. He kept his face, this look of hostility, at the reeds and the trumpets. I was glad he did not look toward me and the percussion boys like that. But he must have known we would be constant and tasteful because I was the king there. As for the others, the soloists especially, he was scaring them into excellence. Prender had never got quite this from them. Boys became men and girls became women as Quadberry directed us through *Bolero.* I even became a bit better of a man myself, though Quadberry did not look my way. When he turned around toward the people in the auditorium to enter on his solo, I knew it was my baby. I and the drums were the metronome. That was no trouble. It was talent to keep the metronome ticking amidst any given chaos of sound.

But this keeps one's mind occupied and I have no idea what Quadberry sounded like on his sax ride. All I know is that he looked grief-stricken and pale, and small. Sweat had popped out on his forehead. He bent over extremely. He was wearing the red brass-button jacket and black pants, black bow tie at the throat, just like the rest of us. In this outfit he bent over his horn almost out of sight. For a moment, before I caught the glint of his horn through the music stands, I thought he had pitched forward off the stage. He went down so far to do his deep oral thing, his conducting arm had disappeared so quickly, I didn't know but what he was having a seizure.

When *Bolero* was over, the audience stood up and made meat out of their hands applauding. The judges themselves applauded. The band stood up, bawling again, for Prender and because we had done so well. The student director rushed out crying to embrace Quadberry, who eluded him with his dipping shoulders. The crowd was still clapping insanely. I wanted to see Quadberry myself. I waded through the red backs, through the bow ties, over the white bucks. Here was the first-chair clarinetist, who had done his bit like an angel; he sat close to the podium and could hear Quadberry.

"Was Quadberry good?" I asked him.

"Are you kidding? These tears in my eyes, they're for how good he was. He was too good. I'll never touch my clarinet again." The clarinetist slung the pieces of his horn into their case like underwear and a toothbrush.

I found Quadberry fitting the sections of his alto in the velvet holds of his case.

"Hooray," I said. "Hip damn hooray for you."

Arden was smiling too, showing a lot of teeth I had never seen. His smile was sly. He knew he had pulled off a monster unlikelihood.

"Hip hip hooray for me," he said. "Look at her. I had the bell of the horn almost smack in her face."

There was a woman of about thirty sitting in the front row of the auditorium. She wore a sundress with a drastic cleavage up front; looked like something that hung around New Orleans and kneaded your heart to death with her feet. She was still mesmerized by Quadberry. She bore on him with a stare and there was moisture in her cleavage.

"You played well."

"Well? Play well? Yes."

He was trying not to look at her directly. Look at *me*, I beckoned to her with full face: I was the *drums*. She arose and left.

"I was walking downhill in a valley, is all I was doing," said Quadberry. "Another man, a wizard, was playing my horn." He locked his sax case. "I feel nasty for not being able to cry like the rest of them. Look at them. Look at them crying."

True, the children of the band were still weeping, standing around the stage. Several moms and dads had come up among them, and they were misty-eyed too. The mixture of grief and superb music had been unbearable.

A girl in tears appeared next to Quadberry. She was a majorette in football season and played third-chair sax during the concert season. Not even her violent sorrow could take the beauty out of the face of this girl. I had watched her for a number of years—her alertness to her own beauty, the pride of her legs in the majorette outfit—and had taken out her younger sister, a second-rate version of her and a wayward overcompensating nymphomaniac whom several of us made a hobby out of pitying. Well, here was Lilian herself crying in Quadberry's face. She told him that she'd run off the stage when she heard about Prender, dropped her horn and everything, and had thrown herself into a tavern across the street and drunk two beers quickly for some kind of relief. But she had come back through the front doors of the auditorium and sat down, dizzy with beer, and seen Quadberry, the miraculous way he had gone on with *Bolero*. And now she was eaten up by feelings of guilt, weakness, cowardice.

"We didn't miss you," said Quadberry.

"Please forgive me. Tell me to do something to make up for it."

"Don't breathe my way, then. You've got beer all over your breath."

"I want to talk to you."

"Take my horn case and go out, get in my car, and wait for me. It's the ugly Plymouth in front of the school bus."

"I know," she said.

Lilian Field, this lovely teary thing, with the rather pious grace of her carriage, with the voice full of imminent swoon, picked up Quadberry's horn case and her own and walked off the stage.

I told the percussion boys to wrap up the packing. Into my suitcase I put my own gear and also managed to steal drum keys, two pairs of brushes, a twenty-inch Turkish cymbal, a Gretsch snare drum that I desired for my collection, a wood block, kettledrum mallets, a tuning harp and a score sheet of *Bolero* full of marginal notes I'd written down straight from the mouth of Dick Prender, thinking I might want to look at the score sheet sometime in the future when I was having a fit of nostalgia such as I am having right now as I write this. I had never done any serious stealing before, and I was stealing for my art. Prender was dead, the band had done its last thing of the year, I was a senior. Things were finished at the high school. I was just looting a sinking ship. I could hardly lift the suitcase. As I was pushing it across the stage, Quadberry was there again.

"You can ride back with me if you want to."

"But you've got Lilian."

"Please ride back with me . . . us. Please."

"Why?"

"To help me get rid of her. Her breath is full of beer. My father always had that breath. Every time he was friendly, he had that breath. And she looks a great deal like my mother." We were interrupted by the Tupelo band director. He put his baton against Quadberry's arm.

"You were big with *Bolero*, son, but that doesn't mean you own the stage."

Quadberry caught the end of the suitcase and helped me with it out to the steps behind the auditorium. The buses were gone. There sat his ugly ocher Plymouth; it was a failed, gay, experimental shade from the Chrysler people. Lilian was sitting in the front seat wearing her shirt and bow tie, her coat off.

"Are you going to ride back with me?" Quadberry said to me.

"I think I would spoil something. You never saw her when she was a majorette. She's not stupid, either. She likes to show off a little, but she's not stupid. She's in the History Club."

"My father has a doctorate in history. She smells of beer."

I said, "She drank two cans of beer when she heard about Prender."

"There are a lot of other things to do when you hear about death. What I did, for example. She ran away. She fell to pieces."

"She's waiting for us," I said.

"One damned thing I am never going to do is drink."

"I've never seen your mother up close, but Lilian doesn't look like your mother. She doesn't look like anybody's mother."

I rode with them silently to Clinton. Lilian made no bones about being disappointed I was in the car, though she said nothing. I knew it would be like this and I hated it. Other girls in town would not be so unhappy that I was in the car with them. I looked for flaws in Lilian's face and neck and hair, but there weren't any. Couldn't there be a mole, an enlarged pore, too much gum on a tooth, a single awkward hair around the ear? No. Memory, the whole lying opera of it, is killing me now. Lilian was faultless beauty, even sweating, even and especially in the white man's shirt and the bow tie clamping together her collar, when one knew her uncomfortable bosoms, her poor nipples. . . .

"Don't take me back to the band room. Turn off here and let me off at my house," I said to Quadberry. He didn't turn off.

"Don't tell Arden what to do. He can do what he wants to," said Lilian, ignoring me and speaking to me at the same time. I couldn't bear her hatred. I asked Quadberry to please just stop the car and let me out here, wherever he was: this front yard of the mobile home would do. I was so earnest that he stopped the car. He handed back the keys and I dragged my suitcase out of the trunk, then flung the keys back at him and kicked the car to get it going again.

My band came together in the summer. We were the Bop Fiends . . . that was our name. Two of them were from Ole Miss, our bass player was from Memphis State, but when we got together this time, I didn't call the tenor sax, who went to Mississippi Southern, because Quadberry wanted to play with us. During the school year the college boys and I fell into minor groups to pick up twenty dollars on a weekend, playing dances for the Moose Lodge, medical-student fraternities in Jackson, teen-age recreation centers in Greenwood, and such as that. But come summer we were the Bop Fiends again, and the price for us went up to $1,200 a gig. Where they wanted the best rock and bop and they had some bread, we were called. The summer after I was a senior, we played in Alabama, Louisiana and Arkansas. Our fame was getting out there on the interstate route.

This was the summer that I made myself deaf.

Years ago Prender had invited down an old friend from a high school in Michigan. He asked me over to meet the friend, who had been a drummer with Stan Kenton at one time and was now a band director just like Prender. This fellow was almost totally deaf and he warned me very sincerely about deafing myself. He said there would come a point when you had to lean over and concentrate all your hearing on what the band was doing and that was the time to quit for a while, because if you didn't you would be irrevocably deaf like him in a month or two. I listened to him but could not take him seriously. Here was an oldish man who had his problems. My ears had ages of hearing left. Not so. I played the drums so loud the summer after I graduated from high school that I made myself, eventually, stone deaf.

We were at, say, the National Guard Armory in Lake Village, Arkansas, Quadberry out in front of us on the stage they'd built. Down on the floor were hundreds of sweaty teen-agers. Four girls in sundresses, showing what they could, were leaning on the stage with broad ignorant lust on their minds. I'd play so loud for one particular chick, I'd get absolutely out of control. The guitar boys would have to turn the volume up full blast to compensate. Thus I went deaf. Anyhow, the dramatic idea was to release Quadberry on a very soft sweet ballad right in the middle of a long ear-piercing run of rock-and-roll tunes. I'd get out the brushes and we would astonish the crowd with our tenderness. By August, I was so deaf I had to watch Quadberry's fingers changing notes on the saxophone, had to use my eyes to keep time. The other members of the Bop Fiends told me I was hitting out of time. I pretended I was trying to do experimental things with rhythm when the truth was I simply could no longer hear. I was no longer a tasteful drummer, either. I had become deaf through lack of taste.

Which was—taste—exactly the quality that made Quadberry wicked on the saxophone. During the howling, during the churning, Quadberry had taste. The noise did not affect his personality; he was solid as a brick. He could blend. Oh, he could hoot through his horn when the right time came, but he could do supporting roles for an hour. Then, when we brought him out front for his solo on something like "Take Five," he would play with such light blissful technique that he even eclipsed Paul Desmond. The girls around the stage did not cause him to enter into excessive loudness or vibrato.

Quadberry had his own girl friend now, Lilian back at Clinton, who put all the sundressed things around the stage in the shade. In my mind I had congratulated him for getting up next to this beauty, but in June and July, when I was still hearing things a little, he never said a word about her. It was one night in August, when I could hear nothing and was driving him to his house, that he asked me to turn on the inside light and spoke in a retarded deliberate way. He knew I was deaf and counted on my being able to read lips.

"Don't . . . make . . . fun . . . of her . . . or me . . . . We . . . think . . . she . . . is . . . in trouble."

I wagged my head. Never would I make fun of him or her. She detested me because I had taken out her helpless little sister for a few weeks, but I would never think there was anything funny about Lilian, for all her haughtiness. I only thought of this event as monumentally curious.

"No one except you knows," he said.

"Why did you tell me?"

"Because I'm going away and you have to take care of her. I wouldn't trust her with anybody but you."

"She hates the sight of my face. Where are you going?"

"Annapolis."

"You aren't going to any damned Annapolis."

"That was the only school that wanted me."

"You're going to play your saxophone on a boat?"

"I don't know what I'm going to do."

"How . . . how can you just leave her?"

"She wants me to. She's very excited about me at Annapolis. William [this is my name], there is no girl I could imagine who has more inner sweetness than Lilian."

I entered the town college, as did Lilian. She was in the same chemistry class I was. But she was rows away. It was difficult to learn anything, being deaf. The professor wasn't a pantomimer—but finally he went to the blackboard with the formulas and the algebra of problems, to my happiness. I hung in and made a B. At the end of the semester I was swaggering around the grade sheet he'd posted. I happened to see Lilian's grade. She'd only made a C. Beautiful Lilian got only a C while I, with my handicap, had made a B.

It had been a very difficult chemistry class. I had watched Lilian's stomach the whole way through. It was not growing. I wanted to see her look like a watermelon, make herself an amazing mother shape.

When I made the B and Lilian made the C, I got up my courage and finally went by to see her. She answered the door. Her parents weren't home. I'd never wanted this office of watching over her as Quadberry wanted me to, and this is what I told her. She asked me into the house. The rooms smelled of nail polish and pipe smoke. I was hoping her little sister wasn't in the house, and my wish came true. We were alone.

"You can quit watching over me."

"Are you pregnant?"

"No." Then she started crying. "I wanted to be. But I'm not."

"What do you hear from Quadberry?"

She said something, but she had her back to me. She looked to me for an answer, but I had nothing to say. I knew she'd said something, but I hadn't heard it.

"He doesn't play the saxophone anymore," she said.

This made me angry.

"Why not?"

"Too much math and science and navigation. He wants to fly. That's what his dream is now. He wants to get into an F-something jet."

I asked her to say this over and she did. Lilian really was full of inner sweetness, as Quadberry had said. She understood that I was deaf. Perhaps Quadberry had told her.

The rest of the time in her house I simply witnessed her beauty and her mouth moving.

I went through college. To me it is interesting that I kept a B average and did it all deaf, though I know this isn't interesting to people who aren't deaf. I loved music, and never heard it. I loved poetry, and never heard a word that came out of the mouths of the visiting poets who read at the campus. I loved my mother and dad, but never heard a sound they made. One Christmas Eve, Radcleve was back from Ole Miss and threw an M-80 out in the street for old times' sake. I saw it explode, but there was only a pressure in my ears. I was at parties when lusts were raging and I went home with two girls (I am medium handsome) who lived in apartments of the old two-story 1920 vintage, and I took my shirt off and made love to them. But I have no real idea what their reaction was. They were stunned and all smiles when I got up, but I have no idea whether I gave them the last pleasure or not. I hope I did. I've always been partial to women and have always wanted to see them satisfied till their eyes popped out.

Through Lilian I got the word that Quadberry was out of Annapolis and now flying jets off the *Bonhomme Richard*, an aircraft carrier headed for Vietnam. He telegrammed her that he would set down at the Jackson airport at ten o'clock one night. So Lilian and I were out there waiting. It was a familiar place to her. She was a stewardess and her loops were mainly in the South. She wore a beige raincoat, had red sandals on her feet; I was in a black turtleneck and corduroy jacket, feeling significant, so significant I could barely stand it. I'd already made myself the lead writer at Gordon-Marx Advertising in Jackson. I hadn't seen Lilian in a year. Her eyes were strained, no longer the bright blue things they were when she was a pious beauty. We drank coffee together. I loved her. As far as I knew, she'd been faithful to Quadberry.

He came down in an F-something Navy jet right on the dot of ten. She ran out on the airport pavement to meet him. I saw her crawl up the ladder. Quadberry never got out of the plane. I could see him in his blue helmet. Lilian backed down the ladder. Then Quadberry had the cockpit cover him again. He turned the plane around so its flaming red end was at us. He took it down the runway. We saw him leap out into the night at the middle of the runway going west, toward San Diego and the *Bonhomme Richard*. Lilian was crying.

"What did he say?" I asked.

"He said, 'I am a dragon. America the beautiful, like you will never know.' He wanted to give you a message. He was glad you were here."

"What was the message?"

"The same thing. 'I am a dragon. America the beautiful, like you will never know.'"

"Did he say anything else?"

"Not a thing."

"Did he express any love toward you?"

"He wasn't Ard. He was somebody with a sneer in a helmet."

"He's going to war, Lilian."

"I asked him to kiss me and he told me to get off the plane, he was firing up and it was dangerous."

"Arden is going to war. He's just on his way to Vietnam and he wanted us to know that. It wasn't just him he wanted us to see. It was him in the jet he wanted us to see. He *is* that black jet. You can't kiss an airplane."

"And what are we supposed to do?" cried sweet Lilian.

"We've just got to hang around. He didn't have to lift off and disappear straight up like that. That was to tell us how he isn't with us anymore."

Lilian asked me what she was supposed to do now. I told her she was supposed to come with me to my apartment in the old 1920 Clinton place where I was. I was supposed to take care of her. Quadberry had said so. His six-year-old directive was still working.

She slept on the fold-out bed of the sofa for a while. This was the only bed in my place. I stood in the dark in the kitchen and drank a quarter bottle of gin on ice. I would not turn on the light and spoil her sleep. The prospect of Lilian asleep in my apartment made me feel like a chaplain on a visit to the Holy Land; I stood there getting drunk, biting my tongue when dreams of lust burst on me. That black jet Quadberry wanted us to see him in, its flaming rear end, his blasting straight up into the night at mid-runway—what precisely was he wanting to say in this stunt? Was he saying remember him forever or forget him forever? But I had my own life and was neither going to mother-hen it over his memory nor his old sweetheart. What did he mean, *America the beautiful, like you will never know?* I, William Howly, knew a goddamn good bit about America the beautiful, even as a deaf man. Being deaf had brought me up closer to people. There were only about five I knew, but I knew their mouth movements, the perspiration under their noses, their tongues moving over the crowns of their teeth, their fingers on their lips. Quadberry, I said, you don't have to get up next to the stars in your black jet to see America the beautiful.

I was deciding to lie down on the kitchen floor and sleep the night, when Lilian turned on the light and appeared in her panties and bra. Her body was perfect except for a tiny bit of fat on her upper thighs. She'd sunbathed herself so her limbs were brown, and her stomach, and the instinct was to rip off the white underwear and lick, suck, say something terrific into the flesh that you discovered.

She was moving her mouth.

"Say it again slowly."

"I'm lonely. When he took off in his jet, I think it meant he wasn't ever going to see me again. I think it meant he was laughing at both of us. He's an astronaut and he spits on us."

"You want me on the bed with you?" I asked.

"I know you're an intellectual. We could keep on the lights so you'd know what I said."

"You want to say things? This isn't going to be just sex?"

"It could never be just sex."

"I agree. Go to sleep. Let me make up my mind whether to come in there. Turn out the lights."

Again the dark, and I thought I would cheat not only Quadberry but the entire Quadberry family if I did what was natural.

I fell asleep.

Quadberry escorted B-52s on bombing missions into North Vietnam. He was catapulted off the *Bonhomme Richard* in his suit at 100 degrees temperature, often at night, and put the F-8 on all it could get—the tiny cockpit, the immense long two-million-dollar fuselage, wings, tail and jet engine, Quadberry, the genius master of his dragon, going up to twenty thousand feet to be cool. He'd meet with the big B-52 turtle of the air and get in a position, his cockpit glowing with green and orange lights, and turn on his transistor radio. There was only one really good band, never mind the old American rock-and-roll from Cambodia, and that was Red Chinese opera. Quadberry loved it. He loved the nasal horde in the finale, when the peasants won over the old fat dilettante mayor. Then he'd turn the jet around when he saw the squatty abrupt little fires way down there after the B-52s had dropped their diet. It was a seven-hour trip. Sometimes he slept, but his body knew when to wake up. Another thirty minutes and there was his ship waiting for him out in the waves.

All his trips weren't this easy. He'd have to blast out in daytime and get with the B-52s, and a SAM missile would come up among them. Two of his mates were taken down by these missiles. But Quadberry, as on saxophone, had endless learned technique. He'd put his jet perpendicular in the air and make the SAMs look silly. He even shot down two of them. Then, one day in daylight, a MIG came floating up level with him and his squadron. Quadberry couldn't believe it. Others in the squadron were shy, but Quadberry knew where and how the MIG could shoot. He flew below the cannons and then came in behind it. He knew the MIG wanted one of the B-52s and not mainly him. The MIG was so concentrated on the fat B-52 that he forgot about Quadberry. It was really an amateur suicide pilot in the MIG. Quadberry got on top of him and let down a missile, rising out of the way of it. The missile blew off the tail of the MIG. But then Quadberry wanted to see if the man got safely out of the cockpit. He thought it would be pleasant if the fellow got out with his parachute working. Then Quadberry saw that the fellow wanted to collide his wreckage with the B-52, so Quadberry turned himself over and cannoned, evaporated the pilot and cockpit. It was the first man he'd killed.

The next trip out, Quadberry was hit by a ground missile. But his jet kept flying. He flew it a hundred miles and got to the sea. There was the *Bonhomme Richard*, so he ejected. His back was snapped but, by God, he landed right on the deck. His mates caught him in their arms and cut the parachute off him. His back hurt for weeks, but he was all right. He rested and recuperated in Hawaii for a month.

Then he went off the front of the ship. Just like that, his F-6 plopped in the ocean and sank like a rock. Quadberry saw the ship go over him. He knew he shouldn't eject just yet. If he ejected now he'd knock his head on the bottom and get chewed up in the motor blades. So Quadberry waited. His plane was sinking in the green and he could see the hull of the aircraft carrier getting smaller, but he had oxygen through his mask and it didn't seem that urgent a decision. Just let the big ship get over. Down what later proved to be sixty feet, he pushed the ejection button. It fired him away, bless it, and he woke up ten feet under the surface swimming against an almost overwhelming body of underwater parachute. But two of his mates were in a helicopter, one of them on the ladder to lift him out.

Now Quadberry's back was really hurt. He was out of this war and all wars for good.

Lilian, the stewardess, was killed in a crash. Her jet exploded with a hijacker's bomb, an inept bomb which wasn't supposed to go off, fifteen miles out of Havana; the poor pilot, the poor passengers, the poor stewardesses were all splattered like flesh sparklers over the water just out of Cuba. A fisherman found one seat of the airplane. Castro expressed regrets.

Quadberry came back to Clinton two weeks after Lilian and the others bound for Tampa were dead. He hadn't heard about her. So I told him Lilian was dead when I met him at the airport. Quadberry was thin and rather meek in his civvies—a gray suit and an out-of-style tie. The white ends of his hair were not there—the halo had disappeared—because his hair was cut short. The Arab nose seemed a pitiable defect in an ash-whiskered face that was beyond anemic now. He looked shorter, stooped. The truth was he was sick, his back was killing him. His breath was heavy-laden with airplane martinis and in his limp right hand he held a wet cigar. I told him about Lilian. He mumbled something sideways that I could not possibly make out.

"You've got to speak right at me, remember? Remember me, Quadberry?"

"Mom and Dad of course aren't here."

"No. Why aren't they?"

"He wrote me a letter after we bombed Hué. Said he hadn't sent me to Annapolis to bomb the architecture of Hué. He had been there once and had some important experience—French-kissed the queen of Hué or the like. Anyway, he said I'd have to do a hell of a lot of repentance for that. But he and Mom are separate people. Why isn't *she* here?"

"I don't know."

"I'm not asking you the question. The question is to God."

He shook his head. Then he sat down on the floor of the terminal. People had to walk around. I asked him to get up.

"No. How is old Clinton?"

"Horrible. Aluminum subdivisions, cigar boxes with four thin columns in front, thick as a hive. We got a turquoise water tank; got a shopping center, a monster Jitney Jungle, fifth-rate teenyboppers covering the place like ants." Why was I being so frank just now, as Quadberry sat on the floor downcast, drooped over like a long weak candle? "It's not our town anymore, Ard. It's going to hurt to drive back into it. Hurts me every day. Please get up."

"And Lilian's not even over there now."

"No. She's a cloud over the Gulf of Mexico. You flew out of Pensacola once. You know what beauty those pink and blue clouds are. That's how I think of her."

"Was there a funeral?"

"Oh, yes. Her Methodist preacher and a big crowd over at Wright Ferguson funeral home. Your mother and father were there. Your father shouldn't have come. He could barely walk. Please get up."

"Why? What am I going to do, where am I going?"

"You've got your saxophone."

"Was there a coffin? Did you all go by and see the pink or blue cloud in it?" He was sneering now as he had done when he was eleven and fourteen and seventeen.

"Yes, they had a very ornate coffin."

"Lilian was the Unknown Stewardess. I'm not getting up."

"I said you still have your saxophone."

"No, I don't. I tried to play it on the ship after the last time I hurt my back. No go. I can't bend my neck or spine to play it. The pain kills me."

"Well, *don't* get up, then. Why am I asking you to get up? I'm just a deaf drummer, too vain to buy a hearing aid. Can't stand to write the ad copy I do. Wasn't I a good drummer?"

"Superb."

"But we can't be in this condition forever. The police are going to come and make you get up if we do it much longer."

The police didn't come. It was Quadberry's mother who came. She looked me in the face and grabbed my shoulders before she saw Ard on the floor. When she saw him she yanked him off the floor, hugging him passionately. She was shaking with sobs. Quadberry was gathered to her as if he were a rope she was trying to wrap around herself. Her mouth was all over him. Quadberry's mother was a good-looking woman of fifty. I simply held her purse. He cried out that his back was hurting. At last she let him go.

"So now we walk," I said.

"Dad's in the car trying to quit crying," said his mother.

"This is nice," Quadberry said. "I thought everything and everybody was dead around here." He put his arms around his mother. "Let's all go off and kill some time together." His mother's hair was on his lips. "You?" he asked me.

"Murder the devil out of it," I said.

I pretended to follow their car back to their house in Clinton. But when we were going through Jackson, I took the North 55 exit and disappeared from them, exhibiting a great amount of taste, I thought. I would get in their way in this reunion. I had an unimprovable apartment on Old Canton Road in a huge plaster house, Spanish style, with a terrace and ferns and yucca plants, and a green door where I went in. When I woke up I didn't have to make my coffee or fry my egg. The girl who slept in my bed did that. She was Lilian's little sister, Esther Field. Esther was pretty in a minor way and I was proud how I had tamed her to clean and cook around the place. The Field family would appreciate how I lived with her. I showed her the broom and the skillet, and she loved them. She also learned to speak very slowly when she had to say something.

Esther answered the phone when Quadberry called me seven months later. She gave me his message. He wanted to know my opinion on a decision he had to make. There was this Dr. Gordon, a surgeon at Emory Hospital in Atlanta, who said he could cure Quadberry's back problem. Quadberry's back was killing him. He was in torture even holding up the phone to say this. The surgeon said there was a seventy-five/twenty-five chance. Seventy-five that it would be successful, twenty-five that it would be fatal. Esther waited for my opinion. I told her to tell Quadberry to go over to Emory. He'd got through with luck in Vietnam, and now he should ride it out in this petty back operation.

Esther delivered the message and hung up.

"He said the surgeon's just his age; he's some genius from Johns Hopkins Hospital. He said this Gordon guy has published a lot of articles on spinal operations," said Esther.

"Fine and good. All is happy. Come to bed."

I felt her mouth and her voice on my ears, but I could hear only a sort of loud pulse from the girl. All I could do was move toward moisture and nipples and hair.

Quadberry lost his gamble at Emory Hospital in Atlanta. The brilliant surgeon his age lost him. Quadberry died. He died with his Arabian nose up in the air.

That is why I told this story and will never tell another.

QUESTIONS

1. In "A Rose for Emily," what steps does William Faulkner take to make it difficult for readers to dismiss the story as simply being about a crazy old woman?
2. How do you understand the last sentence of Robert Penn Warren's "Blackberry Winter"? What meaning does the narrator seem to give to the word *follow?* If the story were stripped of its last two sentences, what would be lost?
3. Is it possible to imagine other responses than the one Big Boy Morrison, in Richard Wright's story, makes to his terrible situation? As a reader, were you imagining other ways out of the trap that Big Boy faces after the death of the white man? For what reason does the story suggest that no other solutions exist?
4. Toward the end of "The Wide Net," a rainbow improbably appears at night. Many other unlikely phenomena fill Eudora Welty's story. What do they contribute to it, and to the picture of the South created by the author?
5. Why does such fierce tension exist between Mr. Head and Nelson in "The Artificial Nigger"? What different sets of beliefs and expectations do they each represent and try to defend? What might be some reasons that Flannery O'Connor has *two* such characters (rather than one) travel from the country to the city?
6. Can you find appropriate terms to describe the attitude the narrator in Barry Hannah's "Testimony of Pilot" takes toward the deaths of Lilian and of Quadberry? How do you explain this attitude? Does it make sense with respect to the attitude he takes toward other, happier, events in the story?

4

STORIES FOR FURTHER READING

Honoré de Balzac (1799–1850)
A Passion in the Desert

"The whole show is dreadful," she cried, coming out of the menagerie of M. Martin. She had just been looking at that daring speculator "working with his hyena,"—to speak in the style of the programme.

"By what means," she continued, "can he have tamed these animals to such a point as to be certain of their affection for——"

"What seems to you a problem," said I, interrupting, "is really quite natural."

"Oh!" she cried, letting an incredulous smile wander over her lips.

"You think that beasts are wholly without passions?" I asked her. "Quite the reverse; we can communicate to them all the vices arising in our own state of civilization."

She looked at me with an air of astonishment.

"But," I continued, "the first time I saw M. Martin, I admit, like you, I did give vent to an exclamation of surprise. I found myself next to an old soldier with the right leg amputated, who had come in with me. His face had struck me. He had one of those heroic heads, stamped with the seal of warfare, and on which the battles of Napoleon are written. Besides, he had that frank, good-humored expression which always impresses me favorably. He was without doubt one of those troopers who are surprised at nothing, who find matter for laughter in the contortions of a dying comrade, who bury or plunder him quite light-heartedly, who stand intrepidly in the way of bullets;—in fact, one of those men who waste no time in deliberation, and would not hesitate to make friends with the devil himself. After looking very attentively at the proprietor of the menagerie getting out of his box, my companion pursed up his lips with an air of mockery and contempt, with that peculiar and expressive twist which superior people assume to show they are not taken in. Then, when I was expatiating on the courage of M. Martin, he smiled, shook his head knowingly, and said, 'Well known.'"

"'How "well known"?' I said. 'If you would only explain me the mystery, I should be vastly obliged.'

"After a few minutes, during which we made acquaintance, we went to dine at the first *restaurateur's* whose shop caught our eye. At dessert a bottle of

226

champagne completely refreshed and brightened up the memories of this odd old soldier. He told me his story, and I saw that he was right when he exclaimed, 'Well known.'"

When she got home, she teased me to that extent, was so charming, and made so many promises, that I consented to communicate to her the confidences of the old soldier. Next day she received the following episode of an epic which one might call "The French in Egypt."

During the expedition in Upper Egypt under General Desaix, a Provençal soldier fell into the hands of the Maugrabins, and was taken by these Arabs into the deserts beyond the falls of the Nile.

In order to place a sufficient distance between themselves and the French army, the Maugrabins made forced marches, and only halted when night was upon them. They camped round a well overshadowed by palm trees under which they had previously concealed a store of provisions. Not surmising that the notion of flight would occur to their prisoner, they contented themselves with binding his hands, and after eating a few dates, and giving provender to their horses, went to sleep.

When the brave Provençal saw that his enemies were no longer watching him, he made use of his teeth to steal a scimiter, fixed the blade between his knees, and cut the cords which prevented him using his hands; in a moment he was free. He at once seized a rifle and a dagger, then taking the precaution to provide himself with a sack of dried dates, oats, and powder and shot, and to fasten a scimiter to his waist, he leaped on to a horse, and spurred on vigorously in the direction where he thought to find the French army. So impatient was he to see a bivouac again that he pressed on the already tired courser at such speed, that its flanks were lacerated with his spurs, and at last the poor animal died, leaving the Frenchman alone in the desert. After walking some time in the sand with all the courage of an escaped convict, the soldier was obliged to stop, as the day had already ended. In spite of the beauty of an Oriental sky at night, he felt he had not strength enough to go on. Fortunately he had been able to find a small hill, on the summit of which a few palm trees shot up into the air; it was their verdure seen from afar which had brought hope and consolation to his heart. His fatigue was so great that he lay down upon a rock of granite, capriciously cut out like a camp-bed; there he fell asleep without taking any precaution to defend himself while he slept. He had made the sacrifice of his life. His last thought was one of regret. He repented having left the Maugrabins, whose nomadic life seemed to smile upon him now that he was far from them and without help. He was awakened by the sun, whose pitiless rays fell with all their force on the granite and produced an intolerable heat—for he had had the stupidity to place himself inversely to the shadow thrown by the verdant majestic heads of the palm trees. He looked at the solitary trees and shuddered—they reminded him of the graceful shafts crowned with foliage which characterize the Saracen columns in the cathedral of Arles.

But when, after counting the palm tree, he cast his eyes around him, the most horrible despair was infused into his soul. Before him stretched an ocean without limit. The dark sand of the desert spread further than eye could reach in every direction, and glittered like steel struck with bright light. It might have been a sea of looking-glass, or lakes melted together in a mirror. A fiery vapor carried up in surging waves made a perpetual whirlwind over the quivering land. The sky was lit with an Oriental splendor of insupportable purity, leaving naught for the imagination to desire. Heaven and earth were on fire.

The silence was awful in its wild and terrible majesty. Infinity, immensity, closed in upon the soul from every side. Not a cloud in the sky, not a breath in the air, not a flaw on the bosom of the sand, ever moving in diminutive waves; the horizon ended as at sea on a clear day, with one line of light, definite as the cut of a sword.

The Provençal threw his arms round the trunk of one of the palm trees, as though it were the body of a friend, and then, in the shelter of the thin, straight shadow that the palm cast upon the granite, he wept. Then sitting down he remained as he was, contemplating with profound sadness the implacable scene, which was all he had to look upon. He cried aloud, to measure the solitude. His voice, lost in the hollows of the hill, sounded faintly, and aroused no echo—the echo was in his own heart. The Provençal was twenty-two years old:—he loaded his carbine.

"There'll be time enough," he said to himself, laying on the ground the weapon which alone could bring him deliverance.

Viewing alternately the dark expanse of the desert and the blue expanse of the sky, the soldier dreamed of France—he smelled with delight the gutters of Paris—he remembered the towns through which he had passed, the faces of his comrades, the most minute details of his life. His Southern fancy soon showed him the stones of his beloved Provence, in the play of the heat which undulated above the wide expanse of the desert. Realizing the danger of this cruel mirage, he went down the opposite side of the hill to that by which he had come up the day before. The remains of a rug showed that this place of refuge had at one time been inhabited; at a short distance he saw some palm trees full of dates. Then the instinct which binds us to life awoke again in his heart. He hoped to live long enough to await the passing of some Maugrabins, or perhaps he might hear the sound of cannon; for at this time Bonaparte was traversing Egypt.

This thought gave him new life. The palm tree seemed to bend with the weight of the ripe fruit. He shook some of it down. When he tasted this unhoped-for manna, he felt sure that the palms had been cultivated by a former inhabitant—the savory, fresh meat of the dates were proof of the care of his predecessor. He passed suddenly from dark despair to an almost insane joy. He went up again to the top of the hill, and spent the rest of the day in cutting down one of the sterile palm trees, which the night before had served him for shelter. A vague memory made him think of the animals of the desert; and in case they might come to drink at the spring, visible from the base of the rocks but lost further down, he resolved to guard himself from their visits by placing a barrier at the entrance of his hermitage.

In spite of his diligence, and the strength which the fear of being devoured asleep gave him, he was unable to cut the palm in pieces, though he succeeded in cutting it down. At eventide the king of the desert fell; the sound of its fall resounded far and wide, like a sigh in the solitude; the soldier shuddered as though he had heard some voice predicting woe.

But like an heir who does not long bewail a deceased relative, he tore off from this beautiful tree the tall broad green leaves which are its poetic adornment, and used them to mend the mat on which he was to sleep.

Fatigued by the heat and his work, he fell asleep under the red curtains of his wet cave.

In the middle of the night his sleep was troubled by an extraordinary noise; he sat up, and the deep silence around allowed him to distinguish the alternative accents of a respiration whose savage energy could not belong to a human creature.

A profound terror, increased still further by the darkness, the silence, and his waking images, froze his heart within him. He almost felt his hair stand on end, when by straining his eyes to their utmost he perceived through the shadow two faint yellow lights. At first he attributed these lights to the reflection of his own pupils, but soon the vivid brilliance of the night aided him gradually to distinguish the objects around him in the cave, and he beheld a huge animal lying but two steps from him. Was it a lion, a tiger, or a crocodile?

The Provençal was not sufficiently educated to know under what species his enemy ought to be classed; but his fright was all the greater, as his ignorance led him to imagine all terrors at once; he endured a cruel torture, noting every variation of the breathing close to him without daring to make the slightest movement. An odor, pungent like that of a fox, but more penetrating, more profound,—so to speak,—filled the cave, and when the Provençal became sensible of this, his terror reached its height, for he could no longer doubt the proximity of a terrible companion, whose royal dwelling served him for a shelter.

Presently the reflection of the moon descending on the horizon lit up the den, rendering gradually visible and resplendent the spotted skin of a panther.

This lion of Egypt slept, curled up like a big dog, the peaceful possessor of a sumptuous niche at the gate of an *hôtel*; its eyes opened for a moment and closed again; its face was turned towards the man. A thousand confused thoughts passed through the Frenchman's mind; first he thought of killing it with a bullet from his gun, but he saw there was not enough distance between them for him to take proper aim—the shot would miss the mark. And if it were to wake!—the thought made his limbs rigid. He listened to his own heart beating in the midst of the silence, and cursed the too violent pulsations which the flow of blood brought on, fearing to disturb that sleep which allowed him time to think of some means of escape.

Twice he placed his hand on his scimiter, intending to cut off the head of his enemy; but the difficulty of cutting the stiff short hair compelled him to abandon this daring project. To miss would be to die for *certain*, he thought;

he preferred the chances of fair fight, and made up his mind to wait till morning; the morning did not leave him long to wait.

He could now examine the panther at ease; its muzzle was smeared with blood.

"She's had a good dinner," he thought, without troubling himself as to whether her feast might have been on human flesh. "She won't be hungry when she gets up."

It was a female. The fur on her belly and flanks was glistening white; many small marks like velvet formed beautiful bracelets round her feet; her sinuous tail was also white, ending with black rings; the overpart of her dress, yellow like burnished gold, very lissome and soft, had the characteristic blotches in the form of rosettes, which distinguished the panther from every other feline species.

This tranquil and formidable hostess snored in an atittude as graceful as that of a cat lying on a cushion. Her blood-stained paws, nervous and well armed, were stretched out before her face, which rested upon them, and from which radiated her straight slender whiskers, like threads of silver.

If she had been like that in a cage, the Provençal would doubtless have admired the grace of the animal, and the vigorous contrasts of vivid color which gave her robe an imperial splendor; but just then his sight was troubled by her sinister appearance.

The presence of the panther, even asleep, could not fail to produce the effect which the magnetic eyes of the serpent are said to have on the nightingale.

For a moment the courage of the soldier began to fail before this danger, though no doubt it would have risen at the mouth of a cannon charged with shell. Nevertheless, a bold thought brought daylight to his soul and sealed up the source of the cold sweat which sprang forth on his brow. Like men driven to bay, who defy death and offer their body to the smiter, so he, seeing in this merely a tragic episode, resolved to play his part with honor to the last.

"The day before yesterday the Arabs would have killed me, perhaps," he said; so considering himself as good as dead already, he waited bravely, with excited curiosity, the awakening of his enemy.

When the sun appeared, the panther suddenly opened her eyes; then she put out her paws with energy, as if to stretch them and get rid of cramp. At last she yawned, showing the formidable apparatus of her teeth and pointed tongue, rough as a file.

"A regular *petite maîtresse*," thought the Frenchman, seeing her roll herself about so softly and coquettishly. She licked off the blood which stained her paws and muzzle, and scratched her head with reiterated gestures full of prettiness. "All right, make a little toilet," the Frenchman said to himself, beginning to recover his gaiety with his courage; "we'll say good-morning to each other presently;" and he seized the small, short dagger which he had taken from the Maugrabins.

At this moment the panther turned her head towards the man and looked at him fixedly without moving. The rigidity of her metallic eyes and their insupportable lustre made him shudder, especially when the animal walked towards him. But he looked at her caressingly, staring into her eyes in order to magnetize her, and let her come quite close to him; then with a movement both gentle and amorous, as though he were caressing the most beautiful of women, he passed his hand over her whole body, from the head to the tail, scratching the flexible vertebræ which divided the panther's yellow back. The animal waved her tail voluptuously, and her eyes grew gentle; and when for the third time the Frenchman accomplished this interesting flattery, she gave forth one of those purrings by which cats express their pleasure; but this murmur issued from a throat so powerful and so deep, that it resounded through the cave like the vast vibrations of an organ in a church. The man, understanding the importance of his caresses, redoubled them in such a way as to surprise and stupefy his imperious courtesan. When he felt sure of having extinguished the ferocity of his capricious companion, whose hunger had so fortunately been satisfied the day before, he got up to go out of the cave; the panther let him go out, but when he had reached the summit of the hill she sprang with the lightness of a sparrow hopping from twig to twig, and rubbed herself against his legs, putting up her back after the manner of all the race of cats. Then regarding her guest with eyes whose glare had softened a little, she gave vent to that wild cry which naturalists compare to the grating of a saw.

"She is exacting," said the Frenchman, smiling.

He was bold enough to play with her ears; he caressed her belly and scratched her head as hard as he could. When he saw he was successful he tickled her skull with the point of his dagger, watching for the moment to kill her, but the hardness of her bones made him tremble for his success.

The sultana of the desert showed herself gracious to her slave; she lifted her head, stretched out her neck, and manifested her delight by the tranquillity of her attitude. It suddenly occurred to the soldier that to kill this savage princess with one blow he must poniard her in the throat.

He raised the blade, when the panther, satisfied, no doubt, laid herself gracefully at his feet, and cast up at him glances in which, in spite of their natural fierceness, was mingled confusedly a kind of good-will. The poor Provençal ate his dates, leaning against one of the palm tress, and casting his eyes alternately on the desert in quest of some liberator and on his terrible companion to watch her uncertain clemency.

The panther looked at the place where the date stones fell, and every time that he threw one down her eyes expressed an incredible mistrust.

She examined the man with an almost commercial prudence. However, this examination was favorable to him, for when he had finished his meagre meal she licked his boots with her powerful rough tongue, brushing off with marvelous skill the dust gathered in the creases.

"Ah, but when she's really hungry!" thought the Frenchman. In spite of the shudder this thought caused him, the soldier began to measure curiously the proportions of the panther, certainly one of the most splendid specimens of its race. She was three feet high and four feet long without counting her tail; this powerful weapon, rounded like a cudgel, was nearly three feet long. The head, large as that of a lioness, was distinguished by a rare expression of refinement. The cold cruelty of a tiger was dominant, it was true, but there was also a vague resemblance to the face of a sensual woman. Indeed, the face of this solitary queen had something of the gaiety of a drunken Nero: she had satiated herself with blood, and she wanted to play.

The soldier tried if he might walk up and down, and the panther left him free, contenting herself with following him with her eyes, less like a faithful dog than a big Angora cat, observing everything, and every movement of her master.

When he looked round, he saw, by the spring, the remains of his horse; the panther had dragged the carcase all that way; about two-thirds of it had been devoured already. The sight reassured him.

It was easy to explain the panther's absence, and the respect she had had for him while he slept. The first piece of good luck emboldened him to tempt the future, and he conceived the wild hope of continuing on good terms with the panther during the entire day, neglecting no means of taming her and remaining in her good graces.

He returned to her, and had the unspeakable joy of seeing her wag her tail with an almost imperceptible movement at his approach. He sat down, then, without fear, by her side, and they began to play together; he took her paws and muzzle, pulled her ears, rolled her over on her back, stroked her warm, delicate flanks. She let him do whatever he liked, and when he began to stroke the hair on her feet she drew her claws in carefully.

The man, keeping the dagger in one hand, thought to plunge it into the belly of the too confiding panther, but he was afraid that he would be immediately strangled in her last convulsive struggle; besides, he felt in his heart a sort of remorse which bade him respect a creature that had done him no harm. He seemed to have found a friend, in a boundless desert; half unconsciously he thought of his first sweetheart, whom he had nicknamed "Mignonne" by way of contrast, because she was so atrociously jealous that all the time of their love he was in fear of the knife with which she had always threatened him.

This memory of his early days suggested to him the idea of making the young panther answer to this name, now that he began to admire with less terror her swiftness, suppleness, and softness. Towards the end of the day he had familiarized himself with his perilous position; he now almost liked the painfulness of it. At last his companion had got into the habit of looking up at him whenever he cried in a falsetto voice, "Mignonne."

At the setting of the sun Mignonne gave, several times running, a profound melancholy cry. "She's been well brought up," said the light-hearted soldier; "she says her prayers." But this mental joke only occurred to him when he noticed what a pacific attitude his companion remained in. "Come, *ma petite blonde*, I'll let you go to bed first," he said to her, counting on the activity of his own legs to run away as quickly as possible, directly she was asleep, and seek another shelter for the night.

The soldier awaited with impatience the hour of his flight, and when it had arrived he walked vigorously in the direction of the Nile; but hardly had he made a quarter of a league in the sand when he heard the panther bounding after him, crying with that saw-like cry, more dreadful even than the sound of her leaping.

"Ah!" he said, "then she's taken a fancy to me; she has never met any one before, and it is really quite flattering to have her first love." That instant the man fell into one of those movable quicksands so terrible to travelers and from which it is impossible to save oneself. Feeling himself caught he gave a shriek of alarm; the panther seized him with her teeth by the collar, and, springing vigorously backwards, drew him as if by magic out of the whirling sand.

"Ah, Mignonne!" cried the soldier, caressing her enthusiastically, "we're bound together for life and death—but no jokes, mind!" and he retraced his steps.

From that time the desert seemed inhabited. It contained a being to whom the man could talk, and whose ferocity was rendered gentle by him, though he could not explain to himself the reason for their strange friendship. Great as was the soldier's desire to stay up on guard, he slept.

On awakening he could not find Mignonne; he mounted the hill, and in the distance saw her springing towards him after the habit of these animals, who cannot run on account of the extreme flexibility of the vertebral column. Mignonne arrived, her jaws covered with blood; she received the wonted caress of her companion, showing with much purring how happy it made her. Her eyes, full of languor, turned still more gently than the day before towards the Provençal, who talked to her as one would to a tame animal.

"Ah! mademoiselle, you are a nice girl, aren't you? Just look at that! so we like to be made much of, don't we? Aren't you ashamed of yourself? So you have been eating some Arab or other, have you? That doesn't matter. They're animals just the same as you are; but don't you take to eating Frenchmen, or I shan't like you any longer."

She played like a dog with its master, letting herself be rolled over, knocked about, and stroked, alternately; sometimes she herself would provoke the soldier, putting up her paw with a soliciting gesture.

Some days passed in this manner. This companionship permitted the Provençal to appreciate the sublime beauty of the desert; now that he had a living thing to think about, alternations of fear and quiet, and plenty to eat, his mind became filled with contrasts and his life began to be diversified.

Solitude revealed to him all her secrets, and enveloped him in her delights. He discovered in the rising and setting of the sun sights unknown to the world. He knew what it was to tremble when he heard over his head the hiss of a bird's wings, so rarely did they pass, or when he saw the clouds, changing and many colored travelers, melt one into another. He studied in the night-time the effect of the moon upon the ocean of sand, where the simoom made waves swift of movement and rapid in their change. He lived the life of the Eastern day, marveling at its wonderful pomp; then, after having reveled in the sight of a hurricane over the plain where the whirling sands made red, dry mists and death-bearing clouds, he would welcome the night with joy, for then fell the healthful freshness of the stars, and he listened to imaginary music in the skies. Then solitude taught him to unroll the treasures of dreams. He passed whole hours in remembering mere nothings, and comparing his present life with his past.

At last he grew passionately fond of the panther; for some sort of affection was a necessity.

Whether it was that his will powerfully projected had modified the character of his companion, or whether, because she found abundant food in her predatory excursions in the deserts, she respected the man's life, he began to fear for it no longer, seeing her so well tamed.

He devoted the greater part of his time to sleep, but he was obliged to watch like a spider in its web that the moment of his deliverance might not escape him, if any one should pass the line marked by the horizon. He had sacrificed his shirt to make a flag with, which he hung at the top of a palm tree, whose foliage he had torn off. Taught by necessity, he found the means of keeping it spread out, by fastening it with little sticks; for the wind might not be blowing at the moment when the passing traveler was looking through the desert.

It was during the long hours, when he had abandoned hope, that he amused himself with the panther. He had come to learn the different inflections of her voice, the expressions of her eyes; he had studied the capricious patterns of all the rosettes which marked the gold of her robe. Mignonne was not angry even when he took hold of the tuft at the end of her tail to count the rings, those graceful ornaments which glittered in the sun like jewelry. It gave him pleasure to contemplate the supple, fine outlines of her form, the whiteness of her belly, the graceful pose of her head. But it was especially when she was playing that he felt most pleasure in looking at her; the agility and youthful lightness of her movements were a continual surprise to him; he wondered at the supple way which she jumped and climbed, washed herself and arranged her fur, crouched down and prepared to spring. However rapid her spring might be, however slippery the stone she was on, she would always stop short at the word "Mignonne."

One day, in a bright mid-day sun, an enormous bird coursed through the air. The man left his panther to look at his new guest; but after waiting a moment the deserted sultana growled deeply.

"My goodness! I do believe she's jealous," he cried, seeing her eyes become hard again; "the soul of Virginie has passed into her body, that's certain."

The eagle disappeared into the air, whilst the soldier admired the curved contour of the panther.

But there was such youth and grace in her form! she was beautiful as a woman! the blond fur of her robe mingled well with the delicate tints of faint white which marked her flanks.

The profuse light cast down by the sun made this living gold, these russet markings, to burn in a way to give them an indefinable attraction.

The man and the panther looked at one another with a look full of meaning; the coquette quivered when she felt her friend stroke her head; her eyes flashed like lightning—then she shut them tightly.

"She has a soul," he said, looking at the stillness of this queen of the sands, golden like them, white like them, solitary and burning like them.

"Well," she said, "I have read your plea in favor of beasts; but how did two so well adapted to understand each other end?"

"Ah, well! you see, they ended as all great passions do end—by a mis-understanding. From some reason *one* suspects the other of treason; they don't come to an explanation through pride, and quarrel and part from sheer obstinacy."

"Yet sometimes at the best moments a single word or a look is enough—but anyhow go on with your story."

"It's horribly difficult, but you will understand, after what the old villain told me over his champagne. He said—'I don't know if I hurt her, but she turned round, as if enraged, and with her sharp teeth caught hold of my leg—gently, I dare say; but I, thinking she would devour me, plunged my dagger into her throat. She rolled over, giving a cry that froze my heart; and I saw her dying, still looking at me without anger. I would have given all the world—my cross even, which I had not got then—to have brought her to life again. It was as though I had murdered a real person; and the soldiers who had seen my flag, and were come to my assistance, found me in tears.

" 'Well, sir," he said, after a moment of silence, 'since then I have been in war in Germany, in Spain, in Russia, in France; I've certainly carried my carcase about a good deal, but never have I seen anything like the desert. Ah! yes, it is very beautiful!'

" 'What did you feel there?' I asked him.

" 'Oh! that can't be described, young man! Besides, I am not always regretting my palm trees and my panther. I should have to be very mel-ancholy for that. In the desert, you see, there is anything, and nothing.'

" 'Yes, but explain—'

" 'Well,' he said, with an impatient gesture, 'it is God without mankind.' "

QUESTIONS

1. At one point, the soldier says of the leopard: "it is really quite flattering to have her first love." In what sense might this story be considered a "love story"?

2. What do you make of the last line of the story? What does it add to the story? And must the story, in order to succeed, include that last line?

3. This is a "story within a story." An unnamed narrator introduces us to the old soldier who then becomes the narrator of his own tale of adventure. For what reason is this device of a double narrator employed?

4. Given that the story is essentially implausible as a real-life event, what measures are invoked as the story proceeds to provide credibility to the account?

5. Most fictions are made of a beginning, middle, and end. The middle of this story is relatively long, and is told with a luxuriant slowness. The ending comes with sharp suddenness, and is quickly over. Why? What effect is produced by such an abrupt conclusion?

Leo Tolstoy (1828–1910)
How Much Land Does a Man Need?

An elder sister came to visit her younger sister in the country. The elder was married to a tradesman in town, the younger to a peasant in the village. As the sisters sat over their tea talking, the elder began to boast of the advantages of town life: saying how comfortably they lived there, how well they dressed, what fine clothes her children wore, what good things they ate and drank, and how she went to the theatre, promenades, and entertainments.

The younger sister was piqued, and in turn disparaged the life of a tradesman, and stood up for that of a peasant.

"I would not change my way of life for yours," said she. "We may live roughly, but at least we are free from anxiety. You live in better style than we do, but though you often earn more than you need, you are very likely to lose all you have. You know the proverb, 'Loss and gain are brothers twain.' It often happens that people who are wealthy one day are begging their bread the next. Our way is safer. Though a peasant's life is not a fat one, it is a long one. We shall never grow rich, but we shall always have enough to eat."

The elder sister said sneeringly:

"Enough? Yes, if you like to share with the pigs and the calves! What do you know of elegance or manners! However much your goodman may slave, you will die as you are living—on a dung heap—and your children the same."

"Well, what of that?" replied the younger. "Of course our work is rough and coarse. But, on the other hand, it is sure, and we need not bow down to anyone. But you, in your towns, are surrounded by temptations; to-day all may be right, but to-morrow the Evil One may tempt your husband with cards, wine, or women, and all will go to ruin. Don't such things happen often enough?"

Pahóm, the master of the house, was lying on the top of the stove and he listened to the women's chatter.

"It is perfectly true," thought he. "Busy as we are from childhood tilling mother earth, we peasants have no time to let any nonsense settle in our heads. Our only trouble is that we haven't land enough. If I had plenty of land, I shouldn't fear the Devil himself!"

The women finished their tea, chatted a while about dress, and then cleared away the tea-things and lay down to sleep.

But the Devil had been sitting behind the stove, and had heard all that was said. He was pleased that the peasant's wife had led her husband into boasting, and that he had said that if he had plenty of land he would not fear the Devil himself.

"All right," thought the Devil. "We will have a tussle. I'll give you land enough; and by means of that land I will get you into my power."

2

Close to the village there lived a lady, a small landowner who had an

estate of about three hundred acres.* She had always lived on good terms with
the peasants until she engaged as her steward an old soldier, who took to
burdening the people with fines. However careful Pahóm tried to be, it
happened again and again that now a horse of his got among the lady's oats,
now a cow strayed into her garden, now his calves found their way into her
meadows—and he always had to pay a fine.

Pahóm paid up, but grumbled and, going home in a temper, was rough
with his family. All through that summer, Pahóm had much trouble because
of this steward, and he was even glad when winter came and the cattle had to
be stabled. Though he grudged the fodder when they could no longer graze
on the pasture-land, at least he was free from anxiety about them.

In the winter the news got about that the lady was going to sell her land
and that the keeper of the inn on the high road was bargaining for it. When
the peasants heard this they were very much alarmed.

"Well," thought they, "if the innkeeper gets the land, he will worry us
with fines worse than the lady's steward. We all depend on that estate."

So the peasants went on behalf of their Commune, and asked the lady not
to sell the land to the innkeeper, offering her a better price for it themselves.
The lady agreed to let them have it. Then the peasants tried to arrange for the
Commune to buy the whole estate, so that it might be held by them all in
common. They met twice to discuss it, but could not settle the matter; the
Evil One sowed discord among them and they could not agree. So they
decided to buy the land individually, each according to his means; and the
lady agreed to this plan as she had to the other.

Presently Pahóm heard that a neighbor of his was buying fifty acres, and
that the lady had consented to accept one half in cash and to wait a year for
the other half. Pahóm felt envious.

"Look at that," thought he, "the land is all being sold, and I shall get none
of it. So he spoke to his wife.

"Other people are buying," said he, "and we must also buy twenty acres or
so. Life is becoming impossible. That steward is simply crushing us with his
fines."

So they put their heads together and considered how they could manage
to buy it. They had one hundred rúbles laid by. They sold a colt and one half
of their bees, hired out one of their sons as a laborer and took his wages in
advance; borrowed the rest from a brother-in-law, and so scraped together half
the purchase money.

Having done this, Pahóm chose out a farm of forty acres, some of it
wooded, and went to the lady to bargain for it. They came to an agreement,
and he shook hands with her upon it and paid her a deposit in advance. Then
they went to town and signed the deeds; he paying half the price down, and
undertaking to pay the remainder within two years.

So now Pahóm had land of his own. He borrowed seed, and sowed it on
the land he had bought. The harvest was a good one, and within a year he had
managed to pay off his debts both to the lady and to his brother-in-law. So he
became a landowner, ploughing and sowing his own land, making hay on his

*120 desyatíns. The desyatína is properly 2.7 acres; but in this story round numbers are used.

own land, cutting his own trees, and feeding his cattle on his own pasture. When he went out to plough his fields, or to look at his growing corn, or at his grass-meadows, his heart would fill with joy. The grass that grew and the flowers that bloomed there seemed to him unlike any that grew elsewhere. Formerly, when he had passed by that land, it had appeared the same as any other land, but now it seemed quite different.

3

So Pahóm was well-contented, and everything would have been right if the neighboring peasants would only not have trespassed on his corn-fields and meadows. He appealed to them most civilly, but they still went on: now the Communal herdsmen would let the village cows stray into his meadows, then horses from the night pasture would get among his corn. Pahóm turned them out again and again, and forgave their owners, and for a long time he forbore to prosecute any one. But at last he lost patience and complained to the District Court. He knew it was the peasants' want of land, and no evil intent on their part, that caused the trouble, but he thought:

"I cannot go on overlooking it or they will destroy all I have. They must be taught a lesson."

So he had them up, gave them one lesson, and then another, and two or three of the peasants were fined. After a time Pahóm's neighbors began to bear him a grudge for this, and would now and then let their cattle on to his land on purpose. One peasant even got into Pahóm's wood at night and cut down five young lime trees for their bark. Pahóm passing through the wood one day noticed something white. He came nearer and saw the stripped trunks lying on the ground, and close by stood the stumps where the trees had been. Pahóm was furious.

"If he had only cut one here and there it would have been bad enough," thought Pahóm, "but the rascal has actually cut down a whole clump. If I could only find out who did this, I would pay him out."

He racked his brain as to who it could be. Finally he decided: "It must be Simon—no one else could have done it." So he went to Simon's homestead to have a look round, but he found nothing, and only had an angry scene. However, he now felt more certain than ever that Simon had done it, and he lodged a complaint. Simon was summoned. The case was tried, and retried, and at the end of it all Simon was acquitted, there being no evidence against him. Pahóm felt still more aggrieved, and let his anger loose upon the Elder and the Judges.

"You let thieves grease your palms," said he. "If you were honest folk yourselves you would not let a thief go free."

So Pahóm quarrelled with the Judges and with his neighbors. Threats to burn his building began to be uttered. So though Pahóm had more land, his place in the Commune was much worse than before.

About this time a rumor got about that many people were moving to new parts.

"There's no need for me to leave my land," thought Pahóm. "But some of the others might leave our village and then there would be more room for us.

I would take over their land myse~~~
then live more at ease. As it is, I am ~~~

One day Pahóm was sitting at home ~~~
village, happened to call in. He was allow~~~
given him. Pahóm had a talk with this peas~~~
from. The stranger answered that he came fro~~~
had been working. One word led to another, an~~~
many people were settling in those parts. He told ~~~
village had settled there. They had joined the C~~~
twenty-five acres per man granted them. The land was ~~~
the rye sown on it grew as high as a horse, and so thick tha~~~
made a sheaf. One peasant, he said, had brought nothing ~~~
bare hands, and now he had six horses and two cows of his ~~~

Pahóm's heart kindled with desire. He thought:

"Why should I suffer in this narrow hole, if one can liv~~~
elsewhere? I will sell my land and my homestead here, and with the ~~~
will start afresh over there and get everything new. In this crowded plac~~~
is always having trouble. But I must first go and find out all about it myse~~~

Towards summer he got ready and started. He went down the Vólga on ~~~
steamer to Samára, then walked another three hundred miles on foot, and at
last reached the place. It was just as the stranger had said. The peasants had
plenty of land: every man had twenty-five acres of Communal land given him
for his use, and any one who had money could buy, besides, at a rúble an acre
as much good freehold land as he wanted.

Having found out all he wished to know, Pahóm returned home as
autumn came on, and began selling off his belongings. He sold his land at a
profit, sold his homestead and all his cattle, and withdrew from membership
in the Commune. He only waited till the spring, and then started with his
family for the new settlement.

4

As soon as Pahóm and his family reached their new abode, he applied for
admission into the Commune of a large village. He stood treat to the Elders
and obtained the necessary documents. Five shares of Communal land were
given him for his own and his sons' use: that is to say—125 acres (not all
together, but in different fields) besides the use of the Communal pasture.
Pahóm put up the buildings he needed, and bought cattle. Of the Communal
land alone he had three times as much as at his former home, and the land
was good corn-land. He was ten times better off than he had been. He had
plenty of arable land and pasturage, and could keep as many head of cattle as
he liked.

At first, in the bustle of building and settling down, Pahóm was pleased
with it all, but when he got used to it he began to think that even here he had
not enough land. The first year, he sowed wheat on his share of the Communal land and had a good crop. He wanted to go on sowing wheat, but had not
enough Communal land for the purpose, and what he had already used was
not available; for in those parts wheat is only sown on virgin soil or on fallow
land. It is sown for one or two years, and then the land lies fallow till it is

grass. There were many who wanted such land
Ho͝ ͝r all; so that people quarreled about it. Those who
ͺor growing wheat, and those who were poor wanted
again ͺ ͝at they might raise money to pay their taxes. Pahóm
and ͙ ᵗ wheat, so he rented land from a dealer for a year. He
werͺ and had a fine crop, but the land was too far from the
it ͝at had to be carted more than ten miles. After a time Pahóm
ͺme peasant-dealers were living on separate farms and were
͝hy; and he thought:

ͺe to buy some freehold land and have a homestead on it, it would
ͺent thing altogether. Then it would all be nice and compact."

ͺ question of buying freehold land recurred to him again and again.
ͺe went on in the same way for three years, renting land and sowing
ͺat. The seasons turned out well and the crops were good, so that he began
ͺlay money by. He might have gone on living contentedly, but he grew tired
of having to rent other people's land every year, and having to scramble for it.
Wherever there was good land to be had, the peasants would rush for it and it
was taken up at once, so that unless you were sharp about it you got none. It
happened in the third year that he and a dealer together rented a piece of
pasture-land from some peasants; and they had already ploughed it up, when
there was some dispute and the peasants went to law about it, and things fell
out so that the labor was all lost.

"If it were my own land," thought Pahóm, "I should be independent, and
there would not be all this unpleasantness."

So Pahóm began looking out for land which he could buy; and he came
across a peasant who had bought thirteen hundred acres, but having got into
difficulties was willing to sell again cheap. Pahóm bargained and haggled with
him, and at last they settled the price at 1,500 rúbles, part in cash and part to
be paid later. They had all but clinched the matter when a passing dealer
happened to stop at Pahóm's one day to get a feed for his horses. He drank tea
with Pahóm and they had a talk. The dealer said that he was just returning
from the land of the Bashkírs, far away, where he had bought thirteen
thousand acres of land, all for 1,000 rúbles. Pahóm questioned him further,
and the tradesman said:

"All one need do is to make friends with the chiefs. I gave away about one
hundred rúbles' worth of silk robes and carpets, besides a case of tea, and I
gave wine to those who would drink it; and I got the land for less than a penny
an acre." * And he showed Pahóm the title-deeds, saying:

"The land lies near a river, and the whole prairie is virgin soil."

Pahóm plied him with questions, and the tradesman said:

"There is more land there than you could cover if you walked a year, and
it all belongs to the Bashkírs. They are as simple as sheep, and land can be got
almost for nothing."

"There now," thought Pahóm, "with my one thousand rúbles, why
should I get only thirteen hundred acres, and saddle myself with a debt

---

*Five kopéks for a desyatína.

besides? If I take it out there, I can get more than ten times as much for the money."

5

Pahóm inquired how to get to the place, and as soon as the tradesman had left him, he prepared to go there himself. He left his wife to look after the homestead, and started on his journey taking his man with him. They stopped at a town on their way and bought a case of tea, some wine, and other presents, as the tradesman had advised. On and on they went until they had gone more than three hundred miles, and on the seventh day they came to a place where the Bashkírs had pitched their tents. It was all just as the trades-man had said. The people lived on the steppes, by a river, in felt-covered tents.* They neither tilled the ground, nor ate bread. Their cattle and horses grazed in herds on the steppe. The colts were tethered behind the tents, and the mares were driven to them twice a day. The mares were milked, and from the milk kumiss was made. It was the women who prepared kumiss, and they also made cheese. As far as the men were concerned, drinking kumiss and tea, eating mutton, and playing on their pipes, was all they cared about. They were all stout and merry, and all the summer long they never thought of doing any work. They were quite ignorant, and knew no Russian, but were good-natured enough.

As soon as they saw Pahóm, they came out of their tents and gathered round their visitor. An interpreter was found, and Pahóm told them he had come about some land. The Bashkírs seemed very glad; they took Pahóm and led him into one of the best tents, where they made him sit on some down cushions placed on a carpet, while they sat round him. They gave him some tea and kumiss, and had a sheep killed, and gave him mutton to eat. Pahóm took presents out of his cart and distributed them among the Bashkírs, and divided the tea amongst them. The Bashkírs were delighted. They talked a great deal among themselves, and then told the interpreter to translate.

"They wish to tell you," said the interpreter, "that they like you, and that it is our custom to do all we can to please a guest and to repay him for his gifts. You have given us presents, now tell us which of the things we possess please you best, that we may present them to you."

"What pleases me best here," answered Pahóm, "is your land. Our land is crowded and the soil is exhausted; but you have plenty of land and it is good land. I never saw the like of it."

The interpreter translated. The Bashkírs talked among themselves for a while. Pahóm could not understand what they were saying, but saw that they were much amused and that they shouted and laughed. Then they were silent and looked at Pahóm while the interpreter said:

"They wish me to tell you that in return for your presents they will gladly give you as much land as you want. You have only to point it out with your hand and it is yours."

---

*A kibítka is a movable dwelling, made up of detachable wooden frames, forming a round, and covered over with felt.

The Bashkírs talked again for a while and began to dispute. Pahóm asked what they were disputing about, and the interpreter told him that some of them thought they ought to ask their Chief about the land and not act in his absence, while others thought there was no need to wait for his return.

6

While the Bashkírs were disputing, a man in a large fox-fur cap appeared on the scene. They all became silent and rose to their feet. The interpreter said, "This is our Chief himself."

Pahóm immediately fetched the best dressing-gown and five pounds of tea, and offered these to the Chief. The Chief accepted them, and seated himself in the place of honor. The Bashkírs at once began telling him something. The Chief listened for a while, then made a sign with his head for them to be silent, and addressing himself to Pahóm, said in Russian:

"Well, let it be so. Choose whatever piece of land you like; we have plenty of it."

"How can I take as much as I like?" thought Pahóm. "I must get a deed to make it secure, or else they may say, 'It is yours,' and afterwards may take it away again."

"Thank you for your kind words," he said aloud. "You have much land, and I only want a little. But I should like to be sure which bit is mine. Could it not be measured and made over to me? Life and death are in God's hands. You good people give it to me, but your children might wish to take it away again."

"You are quite right," said the Chief. "We will make it over to you."

"I heard that a dealer had been here," continued Pahóm, "and that you gave him a little land, too, and signed title-deeds to that effect. I should like to have it done in the same way."

The Chief understood.

"Yes," replied he, "that can be done quite easily. We have a scribe, and we will go to town with you and have the deed properly sealed."

"And what will be the price?" asked Pahóm.

"Our price is always the same: one thousand rúbles a day."

Pahóm did not understand.

"A day? What measure is that? How many acres would that be?"

"We do not know how to reckon it out," said the Chief. "We sell it by the day. As much as you can go round on your feet in a day is yours, and the price is one thousand rúbles a day."

Pahóm was surprised.

"But in a day you can get round a large tract of land," he said.

The Chief laughed.

"It will all be yours!" said he. "But there is one condition: If you don't return on the same day to the spot whence you started, your money is lost."

"But how am I to mark the way that I have gone?"

"Why, we shall go to any spot you like, and stay there. You must start from that spot and make your round, taking a spade with you. Wherever you think necessary, make a mark. At every turning, dig a hole and pile up the turf; then afterwards we will go round with a plough from hole to hole. You may make as large a circuit as you please, but before the sun sets you must return to the place you started from. All the land you cover will be yours."

Pahóm was delighted. It was decided to start early next morning. They talked a while, and after drinking some more kumiss and eating some more mutton, they had tea again, and then the night came on. They gave Pahóm a feather-bed to sleep on, and the Bashkírs dispersed for the night, promising to assemble the next morning at daybreak and ride out before sunrise to the appointed spot.

7

Pahóm lay on the feather-bed, but could not sleep. He kept thinking about the land.

"What a large tract I will mark off!" thought he. "I can easily do thirty-five miles in a day. The days are long now, and within a circuit of thirty-five miles what a lot of land there will be! I will sell the poorer land, or let it to peasants, but I'll pick out the best and farm it. I will buy two oxteams, and hire two more laborers. About a hundred and fifty acres shall be plough-land, and I will pasture cattle on the rest."

Pahóm lay awake all night, and dozed off only just before dawn. Hardly were his eyes closed when he had a dream. He thought he was lying in that same tent and heard somebody chuckling outside. He wondered who it could be, and rose and went out, and he saw the Bashkír Chief sitting in front of the tent holding his sides and rolling about with laughter. Going nearer to the Chief, Pahóm asked: "What are you laughing at?" But he saw that it was no longer the Chief, but the dealer who had recently stopped at his house and had told him about the land. Just as Pahóm was going to ask, "Have you been here long?" he saw that it was not the dealer, but the peasant who had come up from the Vólga, long ago, to Pahóm's old home. Then he saw that it was not the peasant either, but the Devil himself with hoofs and horns, sitting there and chuckling, and before him lay a man barefoot, prostrate on the ground, with only trousers and a shirt on. And Pahóm dreamt that he looked more attentively to see what sort of a man it was that was lying there, and he saw that the man was dead, and that it was himself! He awoke horror-struck.

"What things one does dream," thought he.

Looking round he saw through the open door that the dawn was breaking. "It's time to wake them up," thought he. "We ought to be starting."

He got up, roused his man (who was sleeping in his cart), bade him harness; and went to call the Bashkírs.

"It's time to go to the steppe to measure the land," he said.

The Bashkírs rose and assembled, and the Chief came too. Then they began drinking kumiss again, and offered Pahóm some tea, but he would not wait.

"If we are to go, let us go. It is high time," said he.

8

The Bashkírs got ready and they all started: some mounted on horses, and some in carts. Pahóm drove in his own small cart with his servant and took a

spade with him. When they reached the steppe, the morning red was beginning to kindle. They ascended a hillock (called by the Bashkírs a *shikhan*) and
dismounting from their carts and their horses, gathered in one spot. The
Chief came up to Pahóm and stretching out his arm towards the plain:

"See," said he, "all this, as far as your eye can reach, is ours. You may
have any part of it you like."

Pahóm's eyes glistened: it was all virgin soil, as flat as the palm of your
hand, as black as the seed of a poppy, and in the hollows different kinds of
grasses grew breast high.

The Chief took off his fox-fur cap, placed it on the ground and said:

"This will be the mark. Start from here, and return here again. All the
land you go round shall be yours."

Pahóm took out his money and put it on the cap. Then he took off his
outer coat, remaining in his sleeveless under-coat. He unfastened his girdle
and tied it tight below his stomach, put a little bag of bread into the breast of
his coat, and tying a flask of water to his girdle, he drew up the tops of his
boots, took the spade from his man, and stood ready to start. He considered
for some moments which way he had better go—it was tempting everywhere.

"No matter," he concluded, "I will go towards the rising sun."

He turned his face to the east, stretched himself, and waited for the sun to
appear above the rim.

"I must lose no time," he thought, "and it is easier walking while it is still
cool."

The sun's rays had hardly flashed above the horizon, before Pahóm,
carrying the spade over his shoulder, went down into the steppe.

Pahóm started walking neither slowly nor quickly. After having gone a
thousand yards he stopped, dug a hole, and placed pieces of turf one on
another to make it more visible. Then he went on; and now that he had
walked off his stiffness he quickened his pace. After a while he dug another
hole.

Pahóm looked back. The hillock could be distinctly seen in the sunlight,
with the people on it, and the glittering tires of the cart-wheels. At a rough
guess Pahóm concluded that he had walked three miles. It was growing
warmer; he took off his under-coat, flung it across his shoulder, and went on
again. It had grown quite warm now; he looked at the sun, it was time to think
of breakfast.

"The first shift is done, but there are four in a day, and it is too soon yet to
turn. But I will just take off my boots," said he to himself.

He sat down, took off his boots, stuck them into his girdle, and went on. It
was easy walking now.

"I will go on for another three miles," thought he, "and then turn to the
left. This spot is so fine, that it would be a pity to lose it. The further one goes,
the better the land seems."

He went straight on for a while, and when he looked round, the hillock
was scarcely visible and the people on it looked like black ants, and he could
just see something glistening there in the sun.

"Ah," thought Pahóm, "I have gone far enough in this direction, it is time to turn. Besides I am in a regular sweat, and very thirsty."

He stopped, dug a large hole, and heaped up pieces of turf. Next he untied his flask, had a drink, and then turned sharply to the left. He went on and on; the grass was high, and it was very hot.

Pahóm began to grow tired: he looked at the sun and saw that it was noon.

"Well," he thought, "I must have a rest."

He sat down, and ate some bread and drank some water; but he did not lie down, thinking that if he did he might fall asleep. After sitting a little while, he went on again. At first he walked easily: the food had strengthened him; but it had become terribly hot and he felt sleepy, still he went on, thinking: "An hour to suffer, a life-time to live."

He went a long way in this direction also, and was about to turn to the left again, when he perceived a damp hollow: "It would be a pity to leave that out," he thought. "Flax would do well there." So he went on past the hollow, and dug a hole on the other side of it before he turned the corner. Pahóm looked towards the hillock. The heat made the air hazy: it seemed to be quivering, and through the haze the people on the hillock could scarcely be seen.

"Ah!" thought Pahóm, "I have made the sides too long; I must make this one shorter." And he went along the third side, stepping faster. He looked at the sun: it was nearly half-way to the horizon, and he had not yet done two miles of the third side of the square. He was still ten miles from the goal.

"No," he thought, "though it will make my land lop-sided, I must hurry back in a straight line now. I might go too far, and as it is I have a great deal of land."

So Pahóm hurriedly dug a hole, and turned straight towards the hillock.

9

Pahóm went straight towards the hillock, but he now walked with difficulty. He was done up with the heat, his bare feet were cut and bruised, and his legs began to fail. He longed to rest, but it was impossible if he meant to get back before sunset. The sun waits for no man, and it was sinking lower and lower.

"Oh dear," he thought, "if only I have not blundered trying for too much! What if I am too late?"

He looked towards the hillock and at the sun. He was still far from his goal, and the sun was already near the rim.

Pahóm walked on and on; it was very hard walking but he went quicker and quicker. He pressed on, but was still far from the place. He began running, threw away his coat, his boots, his flask, and his cap, and kept only the spade which he used as a support.

"What shall I do," he thought again. "I have grasped too much and ruined the whole affair. I can't get there before the sun sets."

And this fear made him still more breathless. Pahóm went on running, his soaking shirt and trousers stuck to him and his mouth was parched. His breast was working like a blacksmith's bellows, his heart was beating like a hammer, and his legs were giving way as if they did not belong to him. Pahóm was seized with terror lest he should die of the strain.

Though afraid of death, he could not stop. "After having run all that way they will call me a fool if I stop now," thought he. And he ran on and on, and drew near and heard the Bashkírs yelling and shouting to him, and their cries inflamed his heart still more. He gathered his last strength and ran on.

The sun was close to the rim, and cloaked in mist looked large, and red as blood. Now, yes now, it was about to set! The sun was quite low, but he was also quite near his aim. Pahóm could already see the people on the hillock waving their arms to hurry him up. He could see the fox-fur cap on the ground and the money on it, and the Chief sitting on the ground holding his sides. And Pahóm remembered his dream.

"There is plenty of land," thought he, "but will God let me live on it? I have lost my life, I have lost my life! I shall never reach that spot!"

Pahóm looked at the sun, which had reached the earth: one side of it had already disappeared. With all his remaining strength he rushed on, bending his body forward so that his legs could hardly follow fast enough to keep him from falling. Just as he reached the hillock it suddenly grew dark. He looked up—the sun had already set! He gave a cry: "All my labor has been in vain," thought he, and was about to stop, but he heard the Bashkírs still shouting, and remembered that though to him, from below, the sun seemed to have set, they on the hillock could still see it. He took a long breath and ran up the hillock. It was still light there. He reached the top and saw the cap. Before it sat the Chief laughing and holding his sides. Again Pahóm remembered his dream, and he uttered a cry: his legs gave way beneath him, he fell forward and reached the cap with his hands.

"Ah, that's a fine fellow!" exclaimed the Chief. "He has gained much land!"

Pahóm's servant came running up and tried to raise him, but he saw that blood was flowing from his mouth. Pahóm was dead!

The Bashkírs clicked their tongues to show their pity.

His servant picked up the spade and dug a grave long enough for Pahóm to lie in, and buried him in it. Six feet from his head to his heels was all he needed.

1886

Questions

1. How do you interpret the presence of the Devil, or "the unclean one," in this story? How real is he? Is *he* the cause of Pahóm's downfall? How would the story be changed if he were absent from it?

2. What do you make of the Bashkírs? Are they an innocent, or a cynical people? Do they trick Pahóm and take advantage of him, or do they merely take childish pleasure in watching his foolish downfall?

3. Why does the Chief laugh at the end of the story? What does your intuition tell you is the tone and spirit of that laughter?

4. If you were to consider this story a *parable*, how would you phrase the moral? Is there more than one moral to be drawn from it?

5. Is there anything to be said on behalf of Pahóm? Is he a virtuous or admirable man in any sense? Can you develop a defense of his various actions?

Ambrose Bierce (1842–1914)
An Occurrence at Owl Creek Bridge

1

A man stood upon a railroad bridge in northern Alabama, looking down into the swift water twenty feet below. The man's hands were behind his back, the wrists bound with a cord. A rope closely encircled his neck. It was attached to a stout cross-timber above his head and the slack fell to the level of his knees. Some loose boards laid upon the sleepers supporting the metals of the railway supplied a footing for him and his executioners—two private soldiers of the Federal army, directed by a sergeant who in civil life may have been a deputy sheriff. At a short remove upon the same temporary platform was an officer in the uniform of his rank, armed. He was a captain. A sentinel at each end of the bridge stood with his rifle in the position known as "support," that is to say, vertical in front of the left shoulder, the hammer resting on the forearm thrown straight across the chest—a formal and unnatural position, enforcing an erect carriage of the body. It did not appear to be the duty of these two men to know what was occurring at the centre of the bridge; they merely blockaded the two ends of the foot planking that traversed it.

Beyond one of the sentinels nobody was in sight; the railroad ran straight away into a forest for a hundred yards, then, curving, was lost to view. Doubtless there was an outpost farther long. The other bank of the stream was open ground—a gentle acclivity topped with a stockade of vertical tree trunks, loop-holed for rifles, with a single embrasure through which protruded the muzzle of a brass cannon commanding the bridge. Midway of the slope between bridge and fort were the spectators—a single company of infantry in line, at "parade rest," the butts of the rifles on the ground, the barrels inclining slightly backward against the right shoulder, the hands crossed upon the stock. A lieutenant stood at the right of the line, the point of his sword upon the ground, his left hand resting upon his right. Excepting the group of four at the centre of the bridge, not a man moved. The company faced the bridge, staring stonily, motionless. The sentinels, facing the banks of the stream, might have been statues to adorn the bridge. The captain stood with folded arms, silent, observing the work of his subordinates, but making no sign. Death is a dignitary who when he comes announced is to be received with formal manifestations of respect, even by those most familiar with him. In the code of military etiquette silence and fixity are forms of deference.

The man who was engaged in being hanged was apparently about thirty-five years of age. He was a civilian, if one might judge from his habit, which was that of a planter. His features were good—a straight nose, firm mouth, broad forehead, from which his long, dark hair was combed straight back, falling behind his ears to the collar of his well-fitting frock-coat. He wore a mustache and pointed beard, but no whiskers; his eyes were large and dark gray, and had a kindly expression which one would hardly have expected in one whose neck was in the hemp. Evidently this was no vulgar assassin. The liberal military code makes provision for hanging many kinds of persons, and gentlemen are not excluded.

The preparations being complete, the two private soldiers stepped aside and each drew away the plank upon which he had been standing. The sergeant turned to the captain, saluted and placed himself immediately behind that officer, who in turn moved apart one pace. These movements left the condemned man and the sergeant standing on the two ends of the same plank, which spanned three of the cross-ties of the bridge. The end upon which the civilian stood almost, but not quite, reached a fourth. This plank had been held in place by the weight of the captain; it was now held by that of the sergeant. At a signal from the former the latter would step aside, the plank would tilt and the condemned man go down between two ties. The arrangement commended itself to his judgment as simple and effective. His face had not been covered nor his eyes bandaged. He looked a moment at his "unsteadfast footing," then let his gaze wander to the swirling water of the stream racing madly beneath his feet. A piece of dancing driftwood caught his attention and his eyes followed it down the current. How slowly it appeared to move! What a sluggish stream!

He closed his eyes in order to fix his last thoughts upon his wife and children. The water, touched to gold by the early sun, the brooding mists under the banks at some distance down the stream, the fort, the soldiers, the piece of drift—all had distracted him. And now he became conscious of a new disturbance. Striking through the thought of his dear ones was a sound which he could neither ignore nor understand, a sharp, distinct, metallic percussion like the stroke of a blacksmith's hammer upon the anvil; it had the same ringing quality. He wondered what it was, and whether immeasurably distant or near by—it seemed both. Its recurrence was regular, but as slow as the tolling of a death knell. He awaited each stroke with impatience and—he knew not why—apprehension. The intervals of silence grew progressively longer; the delays became maddening. With their greater infrequency the sounds increased in strength and sharpness. They hurt his ear like the thrust of a knife; he feared he would shriek. What he heard was the ticking of his watch.

He unclosed his eyes and saw again the water below him. "If I could free my hands," he thought, "I might throw off the noose and spring into the stream. By diving I could evade the bullets and, swimming vigorously, reach the bank, take to the woods and get away home. My home, thank God, is as yet outside their lines; my wife and little ones are still beyond the invader's farthest advance."

As these thoughts, which have here to be set down in words, were flashed into the doomed man's brain rather than evolved from it the captain nodded to the sergeant. The sergeant stepped aside.

2

Peyton Farquhar was a well-to-do planter, of an old and highly respected Alabama family. Being a slave owner and like other slave owners a politician he was naturally an original secessionist and ardently devoted to the Southern cause. Circumstances of an imperious nature, which it is unnecessary to relate here, had prevented him from taking service with the gallant army that had fought the disastrous campaigns ending with the fall of Corinth, and he chafed under the inglorious restraint, longing for the release of his energies, the larger life of the soldier, the opportunity for distinction. That opportunity, he felt, would come, as it comes to all in war time. Meanwhile he did what he could. No service was too humble for him to perform in aid of the South, no adventure too perilous for him to undertake if consistent with the character of a civilian who was at heart a soldier, and who in good faith and without too much qualification assented to at least a part of the frankly villainous dictum that all is fair in love and war.

One evening while Farquhar and his wife were sitting on a rustic bench near the entrance to his grounds, a gray-clad soldier rode up to the gate and asked for a drink of water. Mrs. Farquhar was only too happy to serve him with her own white hands. While she was fetching the water her husband approached the dusty horseman and inquired eagerly for news from the front.

"The Yanks are repairing the railroads," said the man, "and are getting ready for another advance. They have reached the Owl Creek bridge, put it in order and built a stockade on the north bank. The commandant has issued an order, which is posted everywhere, declaring that any civilian caught interfering with the railroad, its bridges, tunnels or trains will be summarily hanged. I saw the order."

"How far is it to the Owl Creek bridge?" Farquhar asked.

"About thirty miles."

"Is there no force on this side the creek?"

"Only a picket post half a mile out, on the railroad, and a single sentinel at this end of the bridge."

"Suppose a man—a civilian and student of hanging—should elude the picket post and perhaps get the better of the sentinel," said Farquhar, smiling, "what could he accomplish?"

The soldier reflected. "I was there a month ago," he replied. "I observed that the flood of last winter had lodged a great quantity of driftwood against the wooden pier at this end of the bridge. It is now dry and would burn like tow."

The lady had now brought the water, which the soldier drank. He thanked her ceremoniously, bowed to her husband and rode away. An hour later, after nightfall, he repassed the plantation, going northward in the direction from which he had come. He was a Federal scout.

3

As Peyton Farquhar fell straight downward through the bridge he lost consciousness and was as one already dead. From this state he was awakened—ages later, it seemed to him—by the pain of a sharp pressure upon his throat, followed by a sense of suffocation. Keen, poignant agonies seemed to shoot from his neck downward through every fibre of his body and limbs. These pains appeared to flash along well-defined lines of ramification and to beat with an inconceivably rapid periodicity. They seemed like streams of pulsating fire heating him to an intolerable temperature. As to his head, he was conscious of nothing but a feeling of fulness—of congestion. These sensations were unaccompanied by thought. The intellectual part of his nature was already effaced; he had power only to feel, and feeling was torment. He was conscious of motion. Encompassed in a luminous cloud, of which he was now merely the fiery heart, without material substance, he swung through unthinkable arcs of oscillation, like a vast pendulum. Then all at once, with terrible suddenness, the light about him shot upward with the noise of a loud plash; a frightful roaring was in his ears, and all was cold and dark. The power of thought was restored; he knew that the rope had broken and he had fallen into the stream. There was no additional strangulation; the noose about his neck was already suffocating him and kept the water from his lungs. To die of hanging at the bottom of a river!—the idea seemed to him ludicrous. He opened his eyes in the darkness and saw above him a gleam of light, but how distant, how inaccessible! He was still sinking, for the light became fainter and fainter until it was a mere glimmer. Then it began to grow and brighten, and he knew that he was rising toward the surface—knew it with reluctance, for he was now very comfortable. "To be hanged and drowned," he thought, "that is not so bad; but I do not wish to be shot. No; I will not be shot; that is not fair."

He was not conscious of an effort, but a sharp pain in his wrist apprised him that he was trying to free his hands. He gave the struggle his attention, as an idler might observe the feat of a juggler, without interest in the outcome. What splendid effort!—what magnificent, what superhuman strength! Ah, that was a fine endeavor! Bravo! The cord fell away; his arms parted and floated upward, the hands dimly seen on each side in the growing light. He watched them with a new interest as first one and then the other pounced upon the noose at his neck. They tore it away and thrust it fiercely aside, its undulations resembling those of a water-snake. "Put it back, put it back!" He thought he shouted these words to his hands, for the undoing of the noose had been succeeded by the direst pang that he had yet experienced. His neck ached horribly; his brain was on fire; his heart, which had been fluttering faintly, gave a great leap, trying to force itself out at this mouth. His whole body was racked and wrenched with an insupportable anguish! But his disobedient hands gave no heed to the command. They beat the water vigorously with quick, downward strokes, forcing him to the surface. He felt his head emerge; his eyes were blinded by the sunlight; his chest expanded convulsively, and with a supreme and crowning agony his lungs engulfed a great draught of air, which instantly he expelled in a shriek!

He was now in full possession of his physical senses. They were, indeed, preternaturally keen and alert. Something in the awful disturbance of his organic system had so exalted and refined them that they made record of things never before perceived. He felt the ripples upon his face and heard their separate sounds as they struck. He looked at the forest on the bank of the stream, saw the individual trees, the leaves and the veining of each leaf—saw the very insects upon them: the locusts, the brilliant-bodied flies, the gray spiders stretching their webs from twig to twig. He noted the prismatic colors in all the dewdrops upon a million blades of grass. The humming of the gnats that danced above the eddies of the stream, the beating of the dragon-flies' wings, the strokes of the water-spiders' legs, like oars which had lifted their boat—all these made audible music. A fish slid along beneath his eyes and he heard the rush of its body parting the water.

He had come to the surface facing down the stream; in a moment the visible world seemed to wheel slowly round, himself the pivotal point, and he saw the bridge, the fort, the soldiers upon the bridge, the captain, the sergeant, the two privates, his executioners. They were in silhouette against the blue sky. They shouted and gesticulated, pointing at him. The captain had drawn his pistol, but did not fire; the others were unarmed. Their movements were grotesque and horrible, their forms gigantic.

Suddenly he heard a sharp report and something struck the water smartly within a few inches of his head, spattering his face with spray. He heard a second report, and saw one of the sentinels with his rifle at his shoulder, a light cloud of blue smoke rising from the muzzle. The man in the water saw the eye of the man on the bridge gazing into his own through the sights of the rifle. He observed that it was a gray eye and remembered having read that gray eyes were keenest, and that all famous markmen had them. Nevertheless, this one had missed.

A counter-swirl had caught Farquhar and turned him half round; he was again looking into the forest on the bank opposite the fort. The sound of a clear, high voice in a monotonous singsong now rang out behind him and came across the water with a distinctness that pierced and subdued all other sounds, even the beating of the ripples in his ears. Although no soldier, he had frequented camps enough to know the dread significance of that deliberate, drawling, aspirated chant; the lieutenant on shore was taking a part in the morning's work. How coldly and pitilessly—with what an even, calm intonation, presaging, and enforcing tranquillity in the men—with what accurately measured intervals fell those cruel words:

"Attention, company! . . . Shoulder arms! . . . Ready! . . . Aim! . . . Fire!"

Farquhar dived—dived as deeply as he could. The water roared in his ears like the voice of Niagara, yet he heard the dulled thunder of the volley and, rising again toward the surface, met shining bits of metal, singularly flattened, oscillating slowly downward. Some of them touched him on the face and hands, then fell away, continuing their descent. One lodged between his collar and neck; it was uncomfortably warm and he snatched it out.

As he rose to the surface, gasping for breath, he saw that he had been a long time under water; he was perceptibly farther down stream—nearer to safety. The soldiers had almost finished reloading; the metal ramrods flashed all at once in the sunshine as they were drawn from the barrels, turned in the air, and thrust into their sockets. The two sentinels fired again, independently and ineffectually.

The hunted man saw all this over his shoulder; he was now swimming vigorously with the current. His brain was as energetic as his arms and legs; he thought with the rapidity of lightning.

"The officer," he reasoned, "will not make that martinet's error a second time. It is as easy to dodge a volley as a single shot. He has probably already given the command to fire at will. God help me, I cannot dodge them all!"

An appalling plash within two yards of him was followed by a loud, rushing sound, *diminuendo*, which seemed to travel back through the air to the fort and died in an explosion which stirred the very river to its deeps! A rising sheet of water curved over him, fell down upon him, blinded him, strangled him! The cannon had taken a hand in the game. As he shook his head free from the commotion of the smitten water he heard the deflected shot humming through the air ahead, and in an instant it was cracking and smashing the branches in the forest beyond.

"They will not do that again," he thought; "the next time they will use a charge of grape. I must keep my eye upon the gun; the smoke will apprise me—the report arrives too late; it lags behind the missile. That is a good gun."

Suddenly he felt himself whirled round and round—spinning like a top. The water, the banks, the forests, the now distant bridge, fort and men—all were commingled and blurred. Objects were represented by their colors only; circular horizontal streaks of color—that was all he saw. He had been caught in a vortex and was being whirled on with a velocity of advance and gyration that made him giddy and sick. In a few moments he was flung upon the gravel at the foot of the left bank of the stream—the southern bank—and behind a projecting point which concealed him from his enemies. The sudden arrest of his motion, the abrasion of one of his hands on the gravel, restored him, and he wept with delight. He dug his fingers into the sand, threw it over himself in handfuls and audibly blessed it. It looked like diamonds, rubies, emeralds; he could think of nothing beautiful which it did not resemble. The trees upon the bank were giant garden plants; he noted a definite order in their arrangement, inhaled the fragrance of their blooms. A strange, roseate light shown through the spaces among their trunks and the wind made in their branches the music of æolian harps. He had no wish to perfect his escape—was content to remain in that enchanting spot until retaken.

A whiz and rattle of grapeshot among the branches high above his head roused him from his dream. The baffled cannoneer had fired him a random farewell. He sprang to his feet, rushed up the sloping bank, and plunged into the forest.

All that day he traveled, laying his course by the rounding sun. The forest seemed interminable; nowhere did he discover a break in it, not even a woodman's road. He had not known that he lived in so wild a region. There was something uncanny in the revelation.

By nightfall he was fatigued, footsore, famishing. The thought of his wife and children urged him on. At last he found a road which led him in what he knew to be the right direction. It was as wide and straight as a city street, yet it seemed untraveled. No fields bordered it; no dwelling anywhere. Not so much as the barking of a dog suggested human habitation. The black bodies of the trees formed a straight wall on both sides, terminating on the horizon in a point, like a diagram in a lesson in perspective. Overhead, as he looked up through this rift in the wood, shone great golden stars looking unfamiliar and grouped in strange constellations. He was sure they were arranged in some order which had a secret and malign significance. The wood on either side was full of singular noises, among which—once, twice, and again—he distinctly heard whispers in an unknown tongue.

His neck was in pain and lifting his hand to it he found it horribly swollen. He knew that it had a circle of black where the rope had bruised it. His eyes felt congested; he could no longer close them. His tongue was swollen with thirst; he relieved its fever by thrusting it forward from between his teeth into the cold air. How softly the turf had carpeted the untraveled avenue—he could no longer feel the roadway beneath his feet!

Doubtless, despite his suffering, he had fallen asleep while walking, for now he sees another scene—perhaps he has merely recovered from a delirium. He stands at the gate of his own home. All is as he left it, and all bright and beautiful in the morning sunshine. He must have traveled the entire night. As he pushes open the gate and passes up the wide white walk, he sees a flutter of female garments; his wife, looking fresh and cool and sweet, steps down from the veranda to meet him. At the bottom of the steps she stands waiting, with a smile of ineffable joy, an attitude of matchless grace and dignity. Ah, how beautiful she is! He springs forward with extended arms. As he is about to clasp her he feels a stunning blow upon the back of the neck; a blinding white light blazes all about him with a sound like the shock of a cannon—then all is darkness and silence!

Peyton Farquhar was dead; his body, with a broken neck, swung gently from side to side beneath the timbers of the Owl Creek bridge.

Questions

1. At one point early in the story the narrator says: "Death is a dignitary who when he comes announced is to be received with formal manifestations of respect, even by those most familiar with him." In the next paragraph he says: "The liberal military code makes provision for hanging many kinds of people, and gentlemen are not excluded." Neither of these comments is necessary in terms of advancing the action. What role, then, do they play?

2. How would you characterize the point of view in this story? The voice? What is the function of the narrator's rather florid, extravagant style?

3. A flashback occurs in the middle of the hanging in which the narrator tells a little about Farquhar and about the Federal Scout who comes onto his property. What is

the purpose of this episode? Do you feel that the flashback is abrupt and intrusive or artistically accomplished?

4. Once he has escaped, Farquhar finds himself almost mystically alive to his surroundings. Why is this? What is your reaction to his deepened sensibility?

5. Is the ending of this story a surprise? Are there hints along the way that the escape is an illusion? Find the point in the story when you begin to wonder and the places where your doubts about the success of the escape are confirmed.

Joseph Conrad (1857–1924)
The Secret Sharer

On my right hand there were lines of fishing stakes resembling a mysterious system of half-submerged bamboo fences, incomprehensible in its division of the domain of tropical fishes, and crazy of aspect as if abandoned forever by some nomad tribe of fishermen now gone to the other end of the ocean; for there was no sign of human habitation as far as the eye could reach. To the left a group of barren islets, suggesting ruins of stone walls, towers, and blockhouses, had its foundations set in a blue sea that itself looked solid, so still and stable did it lie below my feet; even the track of light from the westering sun shone smoothly, without that animated glitter which tells of an imperceptible ripple. And when I turned my head to take a parting glance at the tug which had just left us anchored outside the bar, I saw the straight line of the flat shore joined to the stable sea, edge to edge, with a perfect and unmarked closeness, in one leveled floor half brown, half blue under the enormous dome of the sky. Corresponding in their insignificance to the islets of the sea, two small clumps of trees, one on each side of the only fault in the impeccable joint, marked the mouth of the river Meinam we had just left on the first preparatory stage of our homeward journey; and, far back on the inland level, a larger and loftier mass, the grove surrounding the great Paknam pagoda, was the only thing on which the eye could rest from the vain task of exploring the monotonous sweep of the horizon. Here and there gleams as of a few scattered pieces of silver marked the windings of the great river; and on the nearest of them, just within the bar, the tug steaming right into the land became lost to my sight, hull and funnel and masts, as though the impassive earth had swallowed her up without an effort, without a tremor. My eye followed the light cloud of her smoke, now here, now there, above the plain, according to the devious curves of the stream, but always fainter and farther away, till I lost it at last behind the miter-shaped hill of the great pagoda. And then I was left alone with my ship, anchored at the head of the Gulf of Siam.

She floated at the starting point of a long journey, very still in an immense stillness, the shadows of her spars flung far to the eastward by the setting sun.

At that moment I was alone on her decks. There was not a sound in her—and around us nothing moved, nothing lived, not a canoe on the water, not a bird in the air, not a cloud in the sky. In this breathless pause at the threshold of a long passage we seemed to be measuring our fitness for a long and arduous enterprise, the appointed task of both our existences to be carried out, far from all human eyes, with only sky and sea for spectators and for judges.

There must have been some glare in the air to interfere with one's sight, because it was only just before the sun left us that my roaming eyes made out beyond the highest ridge of the principal islet of the group something which did away with the solemnity of perfect solitude. The tide of darkness flowed on swiftly; and with tropical suddenness a swarm of stars came out above the shadowy earth, while I lingered yet, my hand resting lightly on my ship's rail as if on the shoulder of a trusted friend. But, with all that multitude of celestial bodies staring down at one, the comfort of quiet communion with her was gone for good. And there were also disturbing sounds by this time— voices, footsteps forward; the steward flitted along the main deck, a busily ministering spirit; a hand bell tinkled urgently under the poop deck. . . .

I found my two officers waiting for me near the supper table, in the lighted cuddy. We sat down at once, and as I helped the chief mate, I said:

"Are you aware that there is a ship anchored inside the islands? I saw her mastheads above the ridge as the sun went down."

He raised sharply his simple face, overcharged by a terrible growth of whisker, and emitted his usual ejaculations: "Bless my soul, sir! You don't say so!"

My second mate was a round-cheeked, silent young man, grave beyond his years, I thought; but as our eyes happened to meet I detected a slight quiver on his lips. I looked down at once. It was not my part to encourage sneering on board my ship. It must be said, too, that I knew very little of my officers. In consequence of certain events of no particular significance, except to myself, I had been appointed to the command only a fortnight before. Neither did I know much of the hands forward. All these people had been together for eighteen months or so, and my position was that of the only stranger on board. I mention this because it has some bearing on what is to follow. But what I felt most was my being a stranger to the ship; and if all the truth must be told, I was somewhat of a stranger to myself. The youngest man on board (barring the second mate), and untried as yet by a position of the fullest responsibility, I was willing to take the adequacy of the others for granted. They had simply to be equal to their tasks; but I wondered how far I should turn out faithful to that ideal conception of one's own personality every man sets up for himself secretly.

Meantime the chief mate, with an almost visible effect of collaboration on the part of his round eyes and frightful whiskers, was trying to evolve a theory of the anchored ship. His dominant trait was to take all things into earnest consideration. He was of a painstaking turn of mind. As he used to say, he "liked to account to himself" for practically everything that came in his way, down to a miserable scorpion he had found in his cabin a week before. The why and the wherefore of that scorpion—how it got on board and came to select his room rather than the pantry (which was a dark place and more what a scorpion would be partial to), and how on earth it managed to drown itself in the inkwell of his writing desk—had exercised him infinitely. The ship within the islands was much more easily accounted for; and just as we were about to rise from the table he made his pronouncement. She was, he doubted not, a ship from home lately arrived. Probably she drew too much water to cross the bar except at the top of spring tides. Therefore she went into that natural harbor to wait for a few days in preference to remaining in an open roadstead.

"That's so," confirmed the second mate, suddenly, in his slightly hoarse voice. "She draws over twenty feet. She's the Liverpool ship *Sephora* with a cargo of coal. Hundred and twenty-three days from Cardiff."

We looked at him in surprise.

"The tugboat skipper told me when he came on board for your letters, sir," explained the young man. "He expects to take her up the river the day after tomorrow."

After thus overwhelming us with the extent of his information he slipped out of the cabin. The mate observed regretfully that he "could not account for that young fellow's whims." What prevented him telling us all about it at once, he wanted to know.

I detained him as he was making a move. For the last two days the crew had had plenty of hard work, and the night before they had very little sleep. I felt painfully that I—a stranger—was doing something unusual when I directed him to let all hands turn in without setting an anchor watch. I proposed to keep on deck myself till one o'clock or thereabouts. I would get the second mate to relieve me at that hour.

"He will turn out the cook and the steward at four," I concluded, "and then give you a call. Of course at the slightest sign of any sort of wind we'll have the hands up and make a start at once."

He concealed his astonishment. "Very well, sir." Outside the cuddy he put his head in the second mate's door to inform him of my unheard-of caprice to take a five hours' anchor watch on myself. I heard the other raise his voice incredulously: "What? The captain himself?" Then a few more murmurs, a door closed, then another. A few moments later I went on deck.

My strangeness, which had made me sleepless, had prompted that unconventional arrangement, as if I had expected in those solitary hours of the night to get on terms with the ship of which I knew nothing, manned by men of whom I knew very little more. Fast alongside a wharf, littered like any ship in port with a tangle of unrelated things, invaded by unrelated shore people, I had hardly seen her yet properly. Now, as she lay cleared for sea, the stretch of her main deck seemed to me very fine under the stars. Very fine, very roomy for her size, and very inviting. I descended the poop and paced the waist, my mind picturing to myself the coming passage through the Malay Archipelago, down the Indian Ocean, and up the Atlantic. All its phases were familiar enough to me, every characteristic, all the alternatives which were likely to face me on the high seas—everything! . . . except the novel responsibility of command. But I took heart from the reasonable thought that the ship was like other ships, the men like other men, and that the sea was not likely to keep any special surprises expressly for my discomfiture.

Arriving at that comforting conclusion, I bethought myself of a cigar and went below to get it. All was still down there. Everybody at the after end of the ship was sleeping profoundly. I came out again on the quarterdeck, agreeably at ease in my sleeping suit on that warm breathless night, barefooted, a glowing cigar in my teeth, and, going forward, I was met by the profound silence of the fore end of the ship. Only as I passed the door of the forecastle I heard a deep, quiet, trustful sigh of some sleeper inside. And suddenly I rejoiced in the great security of the sea as compared with the unrest of the land, in my choice of that untempted life presenting no disquieting problems, invested with an elementary moral beauty by the absolute straightforwardness of its appeal and by the singleness of its purpose.

The riding light in the fore-rigging burned with a clear, untroubled, as if symbolic, flame, confident and bright in the mysterious shades of the night. Passing on my way aft along the other side of the ship, I observed that the rope side ladder, put over, no doubt, for the master of the tug when he came to fetch away our letters, had not been hauled in as it should haved been. I became annoyed at this, for exactitude in small matters is the very soul of discipline. Then I reflected that I had myself peremptorily dismissed my officers from duty, and by my own act had prevented the anchor watch being formally set and things properly attended to. I asked myself whether it was wise ever to interfere with the established routine of duties even from the kindest of motives. My action might have made me appear eccentric. Goodnesss only knew how that absurdly whiskered mate would "account" for my conduct, and what the whole ship thought of that informality of their new captain. I was vexed with myself.

Not from compunction certainly, but, as it were mechanically, I proceeded to get the ladder in myself. Now a side-ladder of that sort is a light affair and comes in easily, yet my vigorous tug, which should have brought it flying on board, merely recoiled upon my body in a totally unexpected jerk. What the devil! . . . I was so astounded by the immovableness of that ladder that I remained stockstill, trying to account for it to myself like that imbecile mate of mine. In the end, of course, I put my head over the rail.

The side of the ship made an opaque belt of shadow on the darkling glassy shimmer of the sea. But I saw at once something elongated and pale floating very close to the ladder. Before I could form a guess a faint flash of phosphorescent light, which seemed to issue suddenly from the naked body of a man, flickered in the sleeping water with the elusive, silent play of summer lightning in a night sky. With a gasp I saw revealed to my stare a pair of feet, the long legs, a broad livid back immersed right up to the neck in a greenish cadaverous glow. One hand, awash, clutched the bottom rung of the ladder. He was complete but for the head. A headless corpse! The cigar dropped out of my gaping mouth with a tiny plop and a short hiss quite audible in the absolute stillness of all things under heaven. At that I suppose he raised up his face, a dimly pale oval in the shadow of the ship's side. But even then I could only barely make out down there the shape of his black-haired head. However, it was enough for the horrid, frost-bound sensation which had gripped me about the chest to pass off. The moment of vain exclamations was past, too. I only climbed on the spare spar and leaned over the rail as far as I could, to bring my eyes nearer to that mystery floating alongside.

As he hung by the ladder, like a resting swimmer, the sea lightning played about his limbs at every stir; and he appeared in it ghastly, silvery, fishlike. He remained as mute as a fish, too. He made no motion to get out of the water, either. It was inconceivable that he should not attempt to come on board, and strangely troubling to suspect that perhaps he did not want to. And my first words were prompted by just that troubled incertitude.

"What's the matter?" I asked in my ordinary tone, speaking down to the face upturned exactly under mine.

"Cramp," it answered, no louder. Then slightly anxious, "I say, no need to call anyone."

"I was not going to," I said.

"Are you alone on deck?"

"Yes."

I had somehow the impression that he was on the point of letting go the ladder to swim away beyond my ken—mysterious as he came. But, for the moment, this being appearing as if he had risen from the bottom of the sea (it was certainly the nearest land to the ship) wanted only to know the time. I told him. And he, down there, tentatively:

"I suppose your captain's turned in?"

"I am sure he isn't", I said.

He seemed to struggle with himself, for I heard something like the low, bitter murmur of doubt. "What's the good?" His next words came out with a hesitating effort.

"Look here, my man. Could you call him out quietly?"

I thought the time had come to declare myself.

"*I* am the captain."

I heard a "By Jove!" whispered at the level of the water. The phosphorescence flashed in the swirl of the water all about his limbs, his other hand seized the ladder.

"My name's Leggatt."

The voice was calm and resolute. A good voice. The self-possession of that man had somehow induced a corresponding state in myself. It was very quietly that I remarked:

"You must be a good swimmer."

"Yes. I've been in the water practically since nine o'clock. The question for me now is whether I am to let go this ladder and go on swimming till I sink from exhaustion, or—to come on board here."

I felt this was no mere formula of desperate speech, but a real alternative in the view of a strong soul. I should have gathered from this that he was young; indeed, it is only the young who are ever confronted by such clear issues. But at the time it was pure intuition on my part. A mysterious communication was established already between us two—in the face of that silent, darkened tropical sea. I was young, too; young enough to make no comment. The man in the water began suddenly to climb up the ladder, and I hastened away from the rail to fetch some clothes.

Before entering the cabin I stood still, listening in the lobby at the foot of the stairs. A faint snore came through the closed door of the chief mate's room. The second mate's door was on the hook, but the darkness in there was absolutely soundless. He, too, was young and could sleep like a stone. Remained the steward, but he was not likely to wake up before he was called. I got a sleeping suit out of my room and, coming back on deck, saw the naked man from the sea sitting on the main hatch, glimmering white in the darkness, his elbows on his knees and his head in his hands. In a moment he had concealed his damp body in a sleeping suit of the same gray-stripe pattern as the one I was wearing and followed me like my double on the poop. Together we moved right aft, barefooted, silent.

"What is it?" I asked in a deadened voice, taking the lighted lamp out of the binnacle, and raising it to his face.

"An ugly business."

He had rather regular features; a good mouth; light eyes under somewhat heavy, dark eyebrows; a smooth, square forehead, no growth on his cheeks; a small, brown mustache, and a well-shaped, round chin. His expression was concentrated, meditative, under the inspecting light of the lamp I held up to his face; such as a man thinking hard in solitude might wear. My sleeping suit was just right for his size. A well-knit young fellow of twenty-five at most. He caught his lower lip with the edge of white, even teeth.

"Yes," I said, replacing the lamp in the binnacle. The warm, heavy tropical night closed upon his head again.

"There's a ship over there," he murmured.

"Yes, I know. The *Sephora*. Did you know of us?"

"Hadn't the slightest idea. I am the mate of her—" He paused and corrected himself. "I should say I *was*."

"Aha! Something wrong?"

"Yes. Very wrong indeed. I've killed a man."

"What do you mean? Just now?"

"No, on the passage. Weeks ago. Thirty-nine south. When I say a man—"

"Fit of temper," I suggested, confidently.

The shadowy, dark head, like mine, seemed to nod imperceptibly above the ghostly gray of my sleeping suit. It was, in the night, as though I had been faced by my own reflection in the depths of a somber and immense mirror.

"A pretty thing to have to own up to for a Conway boy," murmured my double, distinctly.

"You're a Conway boy?"

"I am," he said, as if startled. Then, slowly . . . "Perhaps you too—"

It was so; but being a couple of years older I had left before he joined. After a quick interchange of dates a silence fell; and I thought suddenly of my absurd mate with his terrific whiskers and the "Bless my soul—you don't say so" type of intellect. My double gave me an inkling of his thoughts by saying:

"My father's a parson in Norfolk. Do you see me before a judge and jury on that charge? For myself I can't see the necessity. There are fellows that an angel from heaven— And I am not that. He was one of those creatures that are just simmering all the time with a silly sort of wickedness. Miserable devils that have no business to live at all. He wouldn't do his duty and wouldn't let anybody else do theirs. But what's the good of talking! You know well enough the sort of ill-conditioned snarling cur—"

He appealed to me as if our experiences had been as identical as our clothes. And I knew well enough the pestiferous danger of such a character where there are no means of legal repression. And I knew well enough also that my double there was no homicidal ruffian. I did not think of asking him for details, and he told me the story roughly in brusque, disconnected sentences. I needed no more. I saw it all going on as though I were myself inside that other sleeping suit.

"It happened while we were setting a reefed foresail, at dusk. Reefed foresail! You understand the sort of weather. The only sail we had left to keep the ship running; so you may guess what it had been like for days. Anxious sort of job, that. He gave me some of his cursed insolence at the sheet. I tell you I was overdone with this terrific weather that seemed to have no end to it. Terrific, I tell you—and a deep ship. I believe the fellow himself was half crazed with funk. It was no time for gentlemanly reproof, so I turned round and felled him like an ox. He up and at me. We closed just as an awful sea made for the ship. All hands saw it coming and took to the rigging, but I had him by the throat, and went on shaking him like a rat, the men above us yelling, 'Look out! look out!' Then a crash as if the sky had fallen on my head. They say that for over ten minutes hardly anything was to be seen of the ship—just the three masts and a bit of the forecastle head and of the poop all awash driving along in a smother of foam. It was a miracle that they found us, jammed together behind the forebitts. It's clear that I meant business, because I was holding him by the throat still when they picked us up. He was black in the face. It was too much for them. It seems they rushed us aft together, gripped as we were, screaming 'Murder!' like a lot of lunatics, and broke into the cuddy. And the ship running for her life, touch and go all the time, any minute her last in a sea fit to turn your hair gray only a-looking at it. I understand that the skipper, too, started raving like the rest of them. The man had been deprived of sleep for more than a week, and to have this sprung on him at the height of a furious gale nearly drove him out of his mind. I wonder they didn't fling me overboard after getting the carcass of their precious shipmate out of my fingers. They had rather a job to separate us, I've been told. A sufficiently fierce story to make an old judge and a respectable jury sit up a bit. The first thing I heard when I came to myself was the maddening howling of that endless gale, and on that the voice of the old man. He was hanging on to my bunk, staring into my face out of his sou'wester.

" 'Mr. Leggatt, you have killed a man. You can act no longer as chief mate of this ship.' "

His care to subdue his voice made it sound monotonous. He rested a hand on the end of the skylight to steady himself with, and all that time did not stir a limb, so far as I could see. "Nice little tale for a quiet tea party," he concluded in the same tone.

One of my hands, too, rested on the end of the skylight; neither did I stir a limb, so far as I knew. We stood less than a foot from each other. It occurred to me that if old "Bless my soul—you don't say so" were to put his head up the companion and catch sight of us, he would think he was seing double, or imagine himself come upon a scene of weird witchcraft; the strange captain having a quiet confabulation by the wheel with his own gray ghost. I became very much concerned to prevent anything of the sort. I heard the other's soothing undertone.

"My father's a parson in Norfolk," it said. Evidently he had forgotten he had told me this important fact before. Truly a nice little tale.

"You had better slip down into my stateroom now," I said, moving off stealthily. My double followed my movements; our bare feet made no sound; I let him in, closed the door with care, and, after giving a call to the second mate, returned on deck for my relief.

"Not much sign of any wind yet," I remarked when he approached.

"No, sir. Not much," he assented, sleepily, in his hoarse voice, with just enough deference, no more, and barely suppressing a yawn.

"Well, that's all you have to look out for. You have got your orders."

"Yes, sir."

I paced a turn or two on the poop and saw him take up his position face forward with his elbow in the ratlines of the mizzen-rigging before I went below. The mate's faint snoring was still going on peacefully. The cuddy lamp was burning over the table on which stood a vase with flowers, a polite attention from the ships' provision merchant—the last flowers we should see for the next three months at the very least. Two bunches of bananas hung from the beam symmetrically, one on each side of the rudder casing. Everything was as before in the ship—except that two of her captain's sleeping suits were simultaneously in use, one motionless in the cuddy, the other keeping very still in the captain's stateroom.

It must be explained here that my cabin had the form of the capital letter L, the door being within the angle and opening into the short part of the letter. A couch was to the left, the bed-place to the right; my writing desk and the chronometers' table faced the door. But anyone opening it, unless he stepped right inside, had no view of what I call the long (or vertical) part of the letter. It contained some lockers surmounted by a bookcase; and a few clothes, a thick jacket or two, caps, oilskin coat, and such like, hung on hooks. There was at the bottom of that part a door opening into my bathroom, which could be entered also directly from the saloon. But that way was never used.

The mysterious arrival had discovered the advantage of this particular shape. Entering my room, lighted strongly by a big bulkhead lamp swung on gimbals above my writing desk, I did not see him anywhere till he stepped out quietly from behind the coats hung in the recessed part.

"I heard somebody moving about, and went in there at once," he whispered.

I, too, spoke under my breath.

"Nobody is likely to come in here without knocking and getting permission."

He nodded. His face was thin and the sunburn faded, as though he had been ill. And no wonder. He had been, I heard presently, kept under arrest in his cabin for nearly seven weeks. But there was nothing sickly in his eyes or in his expression. He was not a bit like me, really; yet, as we stood leaning over my bed-place, whispering side by side, with our dark heads together and our backs to the door, anybody bold enough to open it stealthily would have been treated to the uncanny sight of a double captain busy talking in whispers with his other self.

"But all this doesn't tell me how you came to hang on to our side ladder," I inquired, in the hardly audible murmurs we used, after he had told me something more of the proceedings on board the *Sephora* once the bad weather was over.

"When we sighted Java Head I had had time to think all those matters out several times over. I had six weeks of doing nothing else, and with only an hour or so every evening for a tramp on the quarter-deck."

He whispered, his arms folded on the side of my bed-place, staring through the open port. And I could imagine perfectly the manner of this thinking out—a stubborn if not a steadfast operation; something of which I should have been perfectly incapable.

"I reckoned it would be dark before we closed with the land," he continued, so low that I had to strain my hearing, near as we were to each other, shoulder touching shoulder almost. "So I asked to speak to the old man. He always seemed very sick when he came to see me—as if he could not look me in the face. You know, that foresail saved the ship. She was too deep to have run long under bare poles. And it was I that managed to set it for him. Anyway, he came. When I had him in my cabin—he stood by the door looking at me as if I had the halter around my neck already—I asked him right away to leave my cabin door unlocked at night while the ship was going through Sunda Straits. There would be the Java coast within two or three miles, off Angier Point. I wanted nothing more. I've had a prize for swimming my second year in the Conway."

"I can believe it," I breathed out.

"God only knows why they locked me in every night. To see some of their faces you'd have thought they were afraid I'd go about at night strangling people. Am I a murdering brute? Do I look it? By Jove! if I had been he wouldn't have trusted himself like that into my room. You'll say I might have chucked him aside and bolted out, there and then—it was dark already. Well, no. And for the same reason I wouldn't think of trying to smash the door. There would have been a rush to stop me at the noise, and I did not mean to get into a confounded scrimmage. Somebody else might have got killed—for I would not have broken out only to get chucked back, and I did not want any more of that work. He refused, looking more sick than ever. He was afraid of the men, and also of that old second mate of his who had been sailing with him for years—a gray-headed old humbug; and his steward, too, had been with him devil knows how long—seventeen years or more—a dogmatic sort of loafer who hated me like poison, just because I was the chief mate. No chief mate ever made more than one voyage in the *Sephora*, you know. Those two old chaps ran the ship. Devil only knows what the skipper wasn't afraid of (all his nerve went to pieces altogether in that hellish spell of bad weather we had)—of what the law would do to him—of his wife, perhaps. Oh, yes! she's on board. Though I don't think she would have meddled. She would have been only too glad to have me out of the ship in any way. The 'brand of Cain' business, don't you see. That's all right. I was ready enough to go off wandering on the face of the earth—and that was price enough to pay for an Abel of that sort. Anyhow, he wouldn't listen to me. 'This thing must take its course. I represent the law here.' He was shaking like a leaf. 'So you won't?' 'No!' 'Then I hope you will be able to sleep on that,' I said, and turned my back on him. 'I wonder that *you* can,' cries he, and locks the door.

"Well, after that, I couldn't. Not very well. That was three weeks ago. We have had a slow passage through the Java Sea; drifted about Carimata for ten days. When we anchored here they thought, I suppose, it was all right. The nearest land (and that's five miles) is the ship's destination; the consul would soon set about catching me; and there would have been no object in bolting to these islets there. I don't suppose there's a drop of water on them. I don't know how it was, but tonight that steward, after bringing me my supper, went out to let me eat it, and left the door unlocked. And I ate it—all there was, too. After I had finished I strolled out on the quarter-deck. I don't know that I meant to do anything. A breath of fresh air was all I wanted, I believe. Then a sudden temptation came over me. I kicked off my slippers and was in the water before I had made up my mind fairly. Somebody heard the splash and they raised an awful hullabaloo. 'He's gone! Lower the boats! He's committed suicide! No, he's swimming.' Certainly I was swimming. It's not so easy for a swimmer like me to commit suicide by drowning. I landed on the nearest islet before the boat left the ship's side. I heard them pulling about in the dark, hailing, and so on, but after a bit they gave up. Everything quieted down and the anchorage became as still as death. I sat down on a stone and began to think. I felt certain they would start searching for me at daylight. There was no place to hide on those stony things—and if there had been, what would have been the good? But now I was clear of that ship, I was not going back. So after a while I took off all my clothes, tied them up in a bundle with a stone inside, and dropped them in the deep water on the outer side of that islet. That was suicide enough for me. Let them think what they liked, but I didn't mean to drown myself. I meant to swim till I sank—but that's not the same thing. I struck out for another of these little islands, and it was from that one that I first saw your riding light. Something to swim for. I went on easily, and on the way I came upon a flat rock a foot or two above water. In the daytime, I dare say, you might make it out with a glass from your poop. I scrambled up on it and rested myself for a bit. Then I made another start. That last spell must have been over a mile."

His whisper was getting fainter and fainter, and all the time he stared straight out through the porthole, in which there was not even a star to be seen. I had not interrupted him. There was something that made comment impossible in his narrative, or perhaps in himself; a sort of feeling, a quality, which I can't find a name for. And when he ceased, all I found was a futile whisper: "So you swam for our light?"

"Yes—straight for it. It was something to swim for. I couldn't see any stars low down because the coast was in the way, and I couldn't see the land, either. The water was like glass. One might have been swimming in a confounded thousand-feet deep cistern with no place for scrambling out anywhere; but what I didn't like was the notion of swimming round and round like a crazed bullock before I gave out; and as I didn't mean to go back . . . No. Do you see me being hauled back, stark naked, off one of these little islands by the scruff of the neck and fighting like a wild beast? Somebody would have got killed for certain, and I did not want any of that. So I went on. Then your ladder—"

"Why didn't you hail the ship?" I asked, a little louder.

He touched my shoulder lightly. Lazy footsteps came right over our heads and stopped. The second mate had crossed from the other side of the poop and might have been hanging over the rail, for all we knew.

"He couldn't hear us talking—could he?" My double breathed into my very ear, anxiously.

His anxiety was an answer, a sufficient answer, to the question I had put to him. An answer containing all the difficulty of that situation. I closed the porthole quietly, to make sure. A louder word might have been overheard.

"Who's that?" he whispered then.

"My second mate. But I don't know much more of the fellow than you do."

And I told him a little about myself. I had been appointed to take charge while I least expected anything of the sort, not quite a fortnight ago. I didn't know either the ship or the people. Hadn't had the time in port to look about me or size anybody up. And as to the crew, all they knew was that I was appointed to take the ship home. For the rest, I was almost as much of a stranger on board as himself, I said. And at the moment I felt it most acutely. I felt that it would take very little to make me a suspect person in the eyes of the ship's company.

He had turned about meantime; and we, the two strangers in the ship, faced each other in identical attitudes.

"Your ladder—" he murmured, after a silence. "Who'd have thought of finding a ladder hanging over at night in a ship anchored out here! I felt just then a very unpleasant faintness. After the life I've been leading for nine weeks, anybody would have got out of condition. I wasn't capable of swimming round as far as your rudder chains. And, lo and behold! there was a ladder to get hold of. After I gripped it I said to myself, 'What's the good?' When I saw a man's head looking over I thought I would swim away presently and leave him shouting—in whatever language it was. I didn't mind being looked at. I—I liked it. And then you speaking to me so quietly—as if you had expected me—made me hold on a little longer. It had been a confounded lonely time—I don't mean while swimming. I was glad to talk a little to somebody that didn't belong to the *Sephora*. As to asking for the captain, that was a mere impulse. It could have been no use, with all the ship knowing about me and the other people pretty certain to be round here in the morning. I don't know—I wanted to be seen, to talk with somebody, before I went on. I don't know what I would have said. . . . 'Fine night, isn't it?' or something of the sort."

"Do you think they will be round here presently?" I asked with some incredulity.

"Quite likely," he said, faintly.

He looked extremely haggard all of a sudden. His head rolled on his shoulders.

"H'm. We shall see then. Meantime get into that bed," I whispered. "Want help? There."

It was a rather high bed-place with a set of drawers underneath. This amazing swimmer really needed the lift I gave him by seizing his leg. He tumbled in, rolled over on his back, and flung one arm across his eyes. And then, with his face nearly hidden, he must have looked exactly as I used to look in that bed. I gazed upon my other self for a while before drawing across carefully the two green serge curtains which ran on a brass rod. I thought for a moment of pinning them together for greater safety, but I sat down on the couch, and once there I felt unwilling to rise and hunt for a pin. I would do it in a moment. I was extremely tired, in a peculiarly intimate way, by the strain of stealthiness, by the effort of whispering and the general secrecy of this excitement. It was three o'clock by now and I had been on my feet since nine, but I was not sleepy; I could not have gone to sleep. I sat there, fagged out, looking at the curtains, trying to clear my mind of the confused sensation of being in two places at once, and greatly bothered by an exasperating knocking in my head. It was a relief to discover suddenly that it was not in my head at all, but on the outside of the door. Before I could collect myself the words "Come in" were out of my mouth, and the steward entered with a tray, bringing in my morning coffee. I had slept, after all, and I was so frightened that I shouted, "This way! I am here, steward," as though he had been miles away. He put down the tray on the table next the couch and only then said, very quietly, "I can see you are here, sir." I felt him give me a keen look, but I dared not meet his eyes just then. He must have wondered why I had drawn the curtains of my bed before going to sleep on the couch. He went out, hooking the door open as usual.

I heard the crew washing decks above me. I knew I would have been told at once if there had been any wind. Calm, I thought, and I was doubly vexed. Indeed, I felt dual more than ever. The steward reappeared suddenly in the doorway. I jumped up from the couch so quickly that he gave a start.

"What do you want here?"

"Close your port, sir—they are washing decks."

"It is closed," I said, reddening.

"Very well, sir." But he did not move from the doorway and returned my stare in an extraordinary, equivocal manner for a time. Then his eyes wavered, all his expression changed, and in a voice unusually gentle, almost coaxingly:

"May I come in to take the empty cup away, sir?"

"Of course!" I turned my back on him while he popped in and out. Then I unhooked and closed the door and even pushed the bolt. This sort of thing could not go on very long. The cabin was as hot as an oven, too. I took a peep at my double, and discovered that he had not moved, his arm was still over his eyes; but his chest heaved; his hair was wet; his chin glistened with perspiration. I reached over him and opened the port.

"I must show myself on deck," I reflected.

Of course, theoretically, I could do what I liked, with no one to say nay to me within the whole circle of the horizon; but to lock my cabin door and take the key away I did not dare. Directly I put my head out of the companion I saw the group of my two officers, the second mate barefooted, the chief mate in long india-rubber boots, near the break of the poop, and the steward halfway down the poop ladder talking to them eagerly. He happened to catch sight of me and dived, the second ran down on the main deck shouting some order or other, and the chief mate came to meet me, touching his cap.

There was a sort of curiosity in his eye that I did not like. I don't know whether the steward had told them that I was "queer" only, or downright drunk, but I know the man meant to have a good look at me. I watched him coming with a smile which, as he got into point-blank range, took effect and froze his very whiskers. I did not give him time to open his lips.

"Square the yards by lifts and braces before the hands go to breakfast."

It was the first particular order I had given on board that ship; and I stayed on deck to see it executed, too. I had felt the need of asserting myself without loss of time. That sneering young cub got taken down a peg or two on that occasion, and I also seized the opportunity of having a good look at the face of every foremast man as they filed past me to go to the after braces. At breakfast time, eating nothing myself, I presided with such frigid dignity that the two mates were only too glad to escape from the cabin as soon as decency permitted; and all the time the dual working of my mind distracted me almost to the point of insanity. I was constantly watching myself, my secret self, as dependent on my actions as my own personality, sleeping in that bed, behind that door which faced me as I sat at the head of the table. It was very much like being mad, only it was worse because one was aware of it.

I had to shake him for a solid minute, but when at last he opened his eyes it was in the full possession of his senses, with an inquiring look.

"All's well so far," I whispered. "Now you must vanish into the bathroom."

He did so, as noiseless as a ghost, and I then rang for the steward, and facing him boldly, directed him to tidy up my stateroom while I was having my bath—"and be quick about it." As my tone admitted of no excuses, he said, "Yes, sir," and ran off to fetch his dustpan and brushes. I took a bath and did most of my dressing, splashing, and whistling softly for the steward's edification, while the secret sharer of my life stood drawn up bolt upright in that little space, his face looking very sunken in daylight, his eyelids lowered under the stern, dark line of his eyebrows drawn together by a slight frown.

When I left him there to go back to my room the steward was finishing dusting. I sent for the mate and engaged him in some insignificant con-versation. It was, as it were, trifling with the terrific character of his whiskers; but my object was to give him an opportunity for a good look at my cabin. And then I could at last shut, with a clear conscience, the door of my stateroom and get my double back into the recessed part. There was nothing else for it. He had to sit still on a small folding stool, half smothered by the heavy coats hanging there. We listened to the steward going into the bath-room out of the saloon, filling the water bottles there, scrubbing the bath, setting things to rights, whisk, bang, clatter—out again into the saloon—turn the key—click. Such was my scheme for keeping my second self invisible. Nothing better could be contrived under the circumstances. And there we sat; I at my writing desk ready to appear busy with some papers, he behind me, out of sight of the door. It would not have been prudent to talk in daytime; and I could not have stood the excitement of that queer sense of whispering to myself. Now and then, glancing over my shoulder, I saw him far back there, sitting rigidly on the low stool, his bare feet close together, his arms folded, his head hanging on his breast—and perfectly still. Anybody would have taken him for me.

I was fascinated by it myself. Every moment I had to glance over my shoulder. I was looking at him when a voice outside the door said:

"Beg pardon, sir."

"Well!" . . . I kept my eyes on him, and so, when the voice outside the door announced, "There's a ship's boat coming our way, sir," I saw him give a start—the first movement he had made for hours. But he did not raise his bowed head.

"All right. Get the ladder over."

I hesitated. Should I whisper something to him? But what? His im-mobility seemed to have been never disturbed. What could I tell him he did not know already? . . . Finally I went on deck.

2

The skipper of the *Sephora* had a thin red whisker all round his face, and the sort of complexion that goes with hair of that color; also the particular, rather smeary shade of blue in the eyes. He was not exactly a showy figure; his shoulders were high, his stature but middling—one leg slightly more bandy than the other. He shook hands, looking vaguely around. A spiritless tenacity was his main characteristic, I judged. I behaved with a politeness which seemed to disconcert him. Perhaps he was shy. He mumbled to me as if he were ashamed of what he was saying; gave his name (it was something like Archbold—but at this distance of years I hardly am sure), his ship's name, and a few other particulars of that sort, in the manner of a criminal making a reluctant and doleful confession. He had had terrible weather on the passage out—terrible—terrible—wife aboard, too.

By this time we were seated in the cabin and the steward brought in a tray with a bottle and glasses. "Thanks! No." Never took liquor. Would have some water, though. He drank two tumblerfuls. Terrible thirsty work. Ever since daylight had been exploring the islands round his ship.

"What was that for—fun?" I asked, with an appearance of polite interest.
"No!" He sighed. "Painful duty."

As he persisted in his mumbling and I wanted my double to hear every word, I hit upon the notion of informing him that I regretted to say I was hard of hearing.

"Such a young man, too!" he nodded, keeping his smeary blue, unintelligent eyes fastened upon me. What was the cause of it—some disease? he inquired, without the least sympathy and as if he thought that, if so, I'd got no more than I deserved.

"Yes; disease," I admitted in a cheerful tone which seemed to shock him. But my point was gained, because he had to raise his voice to give me his tale. It is not worth while to record that version. It was just over two months since all this had happened, and he had thought so much about it that he seemed completely muddled as to its bearings, but still immensely impressed.

"What would you think of such a thing happening on board your own ship? I've had the *Sephora* for these fifteen years. I am a well-known shipmaster."

He was densely distressed—and perhaps I should have sympathized with him if I had been able to detach my mental vision from the unsuspected sharer of my cabin as though he were my second self. There he was on the other side of the bulkhead, four or five feet from us, no more, as we sat in the saloon. I looked politely at Captain Archbold (if that was his name), but it was the other I saw, in a gray sleeping suit, seated on a low stool, his bare feet close together, his arms folded, and every word said between us falling into the ears of his dark head bowed on his chest.

"I've been at sea now, man and boy, for seven-and-thirty years, and I've never heard of such a thing happening in an English ship. And that it should be my ship. Wife on board, too."

I was hardly listening to him.

"Don't you think," I said, "that the heavy sea which, you told me, came aboard just then might have killed the man? I have seen the sheer weight of a sea kill a man very neatly, by simply breaking his neck."

"Good God!" he uttered, impressively, fixing his smeary blue eyes on me. "The sea! No man killed by the sea ever looked like that." He seemed positively scandalized at my suggestion. And as I gazed at him, certainly not prepared for anything original on his part, he advanced his head close to mine and thrust his tongue out at me so suddenly that I couldn't help starting back.

After scoring over my calmness in this graphic way he nodded wisely. If I had seen the sight, he assured me, I would never forget it as long as I lived. The weather was too bad to give the corpse a proper sea burial. So next day at dawn they took it up on the poop, covering its face with a bit of bunting; he read a short prayer, and then, just as it was, in its oilskins and long boots, they launched it amongst those mountainous seas that seemed ready every moment to swallow up the ship herself and the terrified lives on board of her.

"That reefed foresail saved you," I threw in.

"Under God—it did," he exclaimed fervently. "It was by a special mercy, I firmly believe, that it stood some of those hurricane squalls."

"It was the setting of that sail which—" I began.

"God's own hand in it," he interrupted me. "Nothing less could have done it. I don't mind telling you that I hardly dared give the order. It seemed impossible that we could touch anything without losing it, and then our last hope would have been gone."

The terror of that gale was on him yet. I let him go on for a bit, then said, casually—as if returning to a minor subject:

"You were very anxious to give up your mate to the shore people, I believe?"

He was. To the law. His obscure tenacity on that point had in it something incomprehensible and a little awful; something, as it were, mystical, quite apart from his anxiety that he should not be suspected of "countenancing any doings of that sort." Seven-and-thirty virtuous years at sea, of which over twenty of immaculate command, and the last fifteen in the *Sephora*, seemed to have laid him under some pitiless obligation.

"And you know," he went on, groping shamefacedly amongst his feelings, "I did not engage that young fellow. His people had some interest with my owners. I was in a way forced to take him on. He looked very smart, very gentlemanly, and all that. But do you know—I never liked him, somehow. I am a plain man. You see, he wasn't exactly the sort for the chief mate of a ship like the *Sephora*."

I had become so connected in thoughts and impressions with the secret sharer of my cabin that I felt as if I, personally, were being given to understand that I, too, was not the sort that would have done for the chief mate of a ship like the *Sephora*. I had no doubt of it in my mind.

"Not at all the style of man. You understand," he insisted, superfluously, looking hard at me.

I smiled urbanely. He seemed at a loss for a while.

"I suppose I must report a suicide."

"Beg pardon?"

"Sui-cide! That's what I'll have to write to my owners directly I get in."

"Unless you manage to recover him before tomorrow," I assented, dispassionately. . . . "I mean, alive."

He mumbled something which I really did not catch, and I turned my ear to him in a puzzled manner. He fairly bawled:

"The land—I say, the mainland is at least seven miles off my anchorage."

"About that."

My lack of excitement, of curiosity, of surprise, of any sort of pronounced interest, began to arouse his distrust. But except for the felicitous pretense of deafness I had not tried to pretend anything. I had felt utterly incapable of playing the part of ignorance properly, and therefore was afraid to try. It is also certain that he had brought some ready-made suspicions with him, and that he viewed my politeness as a strange and unnatural phenomenon. And yet how else could I have received him? Not heartily! That was impossible for psychological reasons, which I need not state here. My only object was to keep off his inquiries. Surlily? Yes, but surliness might have provoked a point-blank question. From its novelty to him and from its nature, punctilious courtesy was the manner best calculated to restrain the man. But there was the danger of his breaking through my defense bluntly. I could not, I think, have met him by a direct lie, also for psychological (not moral) reasons. If he had only known how afraid I was of his putting my feeling of identity with the other to the test! But, strangely enough—(I thought of it only afterward)—I believe that he was not a little disconcerted by the reverse side of that weird situation, by something in me that reminded him of the man he was seeking—suggested a mysterious similitude to the young fellow he had distrusted and disliked from the first.

However that might have been, the silence was not very prolonged. He took another oblique step.

"I reckon I had no more than a two-mile pull to your ship. Not a bit more."

"And quite enough, too, in this awful heat," I said.

Another pause full of mistrust followed. Necessity, they say, is mother of invention, but fear, too, is not barren of ingenious suggestions. And I was afraid he would ask me point-blank for news of my other self.

"Nice little saloon, isn't it?" I remarked, as if noticing for the first time the way his eyes roamed from one closed door to the other. "And very well fitted out, too. Here, for instance," I continued, reaching over the back of my seat negligently and flinging the door open, "is my bathroom."

He made an eager movement, but hardly gave it a glance. I got up, shut the door of the bathroom, and invited him to have a look round, as if I were very proud of my accommodation. He had to rise and be shown round, but he went through the business without any raptures whatever.

"And now we'll have a look at my stateroom," I declared, in a voice as loud as I dared to make it, crossing the cabin to the starboard side with purposely heavy steps.

He followed me in and gazed around. My intelligent double had vanished. I played my part.

"Very convenient—isn't it?"

"Very nice. Very comf . . ." He didn't finish, and went out brusquely as if to escape from some unrighteous wiles of mine. But it was not to be. I had been too frightened not to feel vengeful; I felt I had him on the run, and I meant to keep him on the run. My polite insistence must have had something menacing in it, because he gave in suddenly. And I did not let him off a single item; mate's room, pantry, storerooms, the very sail locker which was also under the poop—he had to look into them all. When at last I showed him out on the quarter-deck he drew a long, spiritless sigh, and mumbled dismally that he must really be going back to his ship now. I desired my mate, who had joined us, to see to the captain's boat.

The man of whiskers gave a blast on the whistle which he used to wear hanging round his neck, and yelled, "*Sephora's* away!" My double down there in my cabin must have heard, and certainly could not feel more relieved than I. Four fellows came running out from somewhere forward and went over the side, while my own men, appearing on deck too, lined the rail. I escorted my

visitor to the gangway ceremoniously, and nearly overdid it. He was a tenacious beast. On the very ladder he lingered, and in that unique, guiltily
conscientious manner of sticking to the point:

"I say . . . you . . . you don't think that—"

I covered his voice loudly:

"Certainly not. . . . I am delighted. Good-by."

I had an idea of what he meant to say, and just saved myself by the
privilege of defective hearing. He was too shaken generally to insist, but my
mate, close witness of that parting, looked mystified and his face took on a
thoughtful cast. As I did not want to appear as if I wished to avoid all
communication with my officers, he had the opportunity to address me.

"Seems a very nice man. His boat's crew told our chaps a very extraordinary story, if what I am told by the steward is true. I suppose you had it
from the captain, sir?"

"Yes. I had a story from the captain."

"A very horrible affair—isn't it, sir?"

"It is."

"Beats all these tales we hear about murders in Yankee ships."

"I don't think it beats them. I don't think it resembles them in the least."

"Bless my soul—you don't say so! But of course I've no acquaintance
whatever with American ships, not I, so I couldn't go against your knowledge.
It's horrible enough for me. . . . But the queerest part is that those fellows
seemed to have some idea the man was hidden aboard here. They had really.
Did you ever hear of such a thing?"

"Preposterous—isn't it?"

We were walking to and fro athwart the quarter-deck. No one of the crew
forward could be seen (the day was Sunday), and the mate pursued:

"There was some little dispute about it. Our chaps took offense. 'As if we
would harbor a thing like that,' they said. 'Wouldn't you like to look for him
in our coal hole?' Quite a tiff. But they made it up in the end. I suppose he did
drown himself. Don't you, sir?"

"I don't suppose anything."

"You have no doubt in the matter, sir?"

"None whatever."

I left him suddenly. I felt I was producing a bad impression, but with my
double down there it was most trying to be on deck. And it was almost as
trying to be below. Altogether a nerve-trying situation. But on the whole I felt
less torn in two when I was with him. There was no one in the whole ship
whom I dared take into my confidence. Since the hands had got to know his
story, it would have been impossible to pass him off for anyone else, and an
accidental discovery was to be dreaded now more than ever. . . .

The steward being engaged in laying the table for dinner, we could talk
only with our eyes when I first went down. Later in the afternoon we had a
cautious try at whispering. The Sunday quietness of the ship was against us;
the stillness of air and water around her was against us; the elements, the men
were against us—everything was against us in our secret partnership; time

itself—for this could not go on forever. The very trust in Providence was, I suppose, denied to his guilt. Shall I confess that this thought cast me down very much? And as to the chapter of accidents which counts for so much in the book of success, I could only hope that it was closed. For what favorable accident could be expected?

"Did you hear everything?" were my first words as soon as we took up our position side by side, leaning over my bed-place.

He had. And the proof of it was his earnest whisper, "The man told you he hardly dared to give the order."

I understood the reference to be to that saving foresail.

"Yes. He was afraid of it being lost in the setting."

"I assure you he never gave the order. He may think he did, but he never gave it. He stood there with me on the break of the poop after the maintopsail blew away, and whimpered about our last hope—positively whimpered about it and nothing else—and the night coming on! To hear one's skipper go on like that in such weather was enough to drive any fellow out of his mind. It worked me up into a sort of desperation. I just took it into my own hands and went away from him, boiling, and—. But what's the use telling you? *You* know! . . . Do you think that if I had not been pretty fierce with them I should have got the men to do anything? Not it! The bosun perhaps? Perhaps! It wasn't a heavy sea—it was a sea gone mad! I suppose the end of the world will be something like that; and a man may have the heart to see it coming once and be done with it—but to have to face it day after day—I don't blame anybody. I was precious little better than the rest. Only—I was an officer of that old coal-wagon, anyhow—"

"I quite understand," I conveyed that sincere assurance into his ear. He was out of breath with whispering; I could hear him pant slightly. It was all very simple. The same strung-up force which had given twenty-four men a chance, at least, for their lives, had, in a sort of recoil, crushed an unworthy mutinous existence.

But I had no leisure to weigh the merits of the matter—footsteps in the saloon, a heavy knock. "There's enough wind to get under way with, sir." Here was the call of a new claim upon my thoughts and even upon my feelings.

"Turn the hands up," I cried through the door. "I'll be on deck directly."

I was going out to make the acquaintance of my ship. Before I left the cabin our eyes met—the eyes of the only two strangers on board. I pointed to the recessed part where the little campstool awaited him and laid my finger on my lips. He made a gesture—somewhat vague—a little mysterious, accompanied by a faint smile, as if of regret.

This is not the place to enlarge upon the sensations of a man who feels for the first time a ship move under his feet to his own independent word. In my case they were not unalloyed. I was not wholly alone with my command; for there was that stranger in my cabin. Or rather, I was not completely and wholly with her. Part of me was absent. That mental feeling of being in two places at once affected me physically as if the mood of secrecy had penetrated my very soul. Before an hour had elapsed since the ship had begun to move, having occasion to ask the mate (he stood by my side) to take a compass bearing of the Pagoda, I caught myself reaching up to his ear in whispers. I say I caught myself, but enough had escaped to startle the man. I can't describe it otherwise than by saying that he shied. A grave, preoccupied manner, as though he were in possession of some perplexing intelligence, did not leave him henceforth. A little later I moved away from the rail to look at the compass with such a stealthy gait that the helmsman noticed it—and I could not help noticing the unusual roundness of his eyes. These are trifling instances, though it's to no commander's advantage to be suspected of ludicrous eccentricities. But I was also more seriously affected. There are to a seaman certain words, gestures, that should in given conditions come as naturally, as instinctively as the winking of a menaced eye. A certain order should spring on to his lips without thinking; a certain sign should get itself made, so to speak, without reflection. But all unconscious alertness had abandoned me. I had to make an effort of will to recall myself back (from the cabin) to the conditions of the moment. I felt that I was appearing an irresolute commander to those people who were watching me more or less critically.

And, besides, there were the scares. On the second day out, for instance, coming off the deck in the afternoon (I had straw slippers on my bare feet) I stopped at the open pantry door and spoke to the steward. He was doing something there with his back to me. At the sound of my voice he nearly jumped out of his skin, as the saying is, and incidentally broke a cup.

"What on earth's the matter with you?" I asked, astonished.

He was extremely confused. "Beg your pardon, sir. I made sure you were in your cabin."

"You see I wasn't."

"No, sir. I could have sworn I had heard you moving in there not a moment ago. It's most extraordinary . . . very sorry, sir."

I passed on with an inward shudder. I was so identified with my secret double that I did not even mention the fact in those scanty, fearful whispers we exchanged. I suppose he had made some slight noise of some kind or other. It would have been miraculous if he hadn't at one time or another. And yet, haggard as he appeared, he looked always perfectly self-controlled, more than calm—almost invulnerable. On my suggestion he remained almost entirely in the bathroom, which, upon the whole, was the safest place. There could be really no shadow of an excuse for anyone ever wanting to go in there, once the steward had done with it. It was a very tiny place. Sometimes he reclined on the floor, his legs bent, his head sustained on one elbow. At others I would find him on the campstool, sitting in his gray sleeping suit and with his cropped dark hair like a patient, unmoved convict. At night I would smuggle him into my bed-place, and we would whisper together, with the regular footfalls of the officer of the watch passing and repassing over our heads. It was an infinitely miserable time. It was lucky that some tins of fine preserves were stowed in a locker in my stateroom; hard bread I could always get hold of; and so he lived on stewed chicken, paté de foie gras, asparagus, cooked oysters, sardines—on all sorts of abominable sham delicacies out of tins. My early morning coffee he always drank; and it was all I dared do for him in that respect.

Every day there was the horrible maneuvering to go through so that my room and then the bathroom should be done in the usual way. I came to hate the sight of the steward, to abhor the voice of that harmless man. I felt that it was he who would bring on the disaster of discovery. It hung like a sword over our heads.

The fourth day out, I think (we were then working down the east side of the Gulf of Siam, tack for tack, in light winds and smooth water)—the fourth day, I say, of this miserable juggling with the unavoidable, as we sat at our evening meal, that man, whose slightest movement I dreaded, after putting down the dishes ran up on deck busily. This could not be dangerous. Presently he came down again; and then it appeared that he had remembered a coat of mine which I had thrown over a rail to dry after having been wetted in a shower which had passed over the ship in the afternoon. Sitting stolidly at the head of the table I became terrified at the sight of the garment on his arm. Of course he made for my door. There was no time to lose.

"Steward," I thundered. My nerves were so shaken that I could not govern my voice and conceal my agitation. This was the sort of thing that made my terrifically whiskered mate tap his forehead with his forefinger. I had detected him using that gesture while talking on deck with a confidential air to the carpenter. It was too far to hear a word, but I had no doubt that this pantomime could only refer to the strange new captain.

"Yes, sir," the pale-faced steward turned resignedly to me. It was this maddening course of being shouted at, checked without rhyme or reason, arbitrarily chased out of my cabin, suddenly called into it, sent flying out of his pantry on incomprehensible errands, that accounted for the growing wretchedness of his expression.

"Where are you going with that coat?"

"To your room, sir."

"Is there another shower coming?"

"I'm sure I don't know, sir. Shall I go up again and see, sir?"

"No! never mind."

My object was attained, as of course my other self in there would have heard everything that passed. During this interlude my two officers never raised their eyes off their respective plates; but the lip of that confounded cub, the second mate, quivered visibly.

I expected the steward to hook my coat on and come out at once. He was very slow about it; but I dominated my nervousness sufficiently not to shout after him. Suddenly I became aware (it could be heard plainly enough) that the fellow for some reason or other was opening the door of the bathroom. It was the end. The place was literally not big enough to swing a cat in. My voice died in my throat and I went stony all over. I expected to hear a yell of surprise and terror, and made a movement, but had not the strength to get on my legs. Everything remained still. Had my second self taken the poor wretch by the throat? I don't know what I would have done next moment if I had not seen the steward come out of my room, close the door, and then stand quietly by the sideboard.

Saved, I thought. But, no! Lost! Gone! He was gone!

I laid my knife and fork down and leaned back in my chair. My head swam. After a while, when sufficiently recovered to speak in a steady voice, I instructed my mate to put the ship round at eight o'clock himself.

"I won't come on deck," I went on. "I think I'll turn in, and unless the wind shifts I don't want to be disturbed before midnight. I feel a bit seedy."

"You did look middling bad a little while ago," the chief mate remarked without showing any great concern.

They both went out, and I stared at the steward clearing the table. There was nothing to be read on that wretched man's face. But why did he avoid my eyes I asked myself. Then I thought I should like to hear the sound of his voice.

"Steward!"

"Sir!" Startled as usual.

"Where did you hang up that coat?"

"In the bathroom, sir." The usual anxious tone. "It's not quite dry yet, sir."

For some time longer I sat in the cuddy. Had my double vanished as he had come? But of his coming there was an explanation, whereas his disappearance would be inexplicable. . . . I went slowly into my dark room, shut the door, lighted the lamp, and for a time dared not turn round. When at last I did I saw him standing bolt upright in the narrow recessed part. It would not be true to say I had a shock, but an irresistible doubt of his bodily existence flitted through my mind. Can it be, I asked myself, that he is not visible to other eyes than mine? It was like being haunted. Motionless, with a grave face, he raised his hands slightly at me in a gesture which meant clearly, "Heavens! what a narrow escape!" Narrow indeed. I think I had come creeping quietly as near insanity as any man who has not actually gone over the border. That gesture restrained me, so to speak.

The mate with the terrific whiskers was now putting the ship on the other tack. In the moment of profound silence which follows upon the hands going to their stations I heard on the poop his raised voice: "Hard alee!" and the distant shout of the order repeated on the maindeck. The sails, in that light breeze, made but a faint fluttering noise. It ceased. The ship was coming round slowly; I held my breath in the renewed stillness of expectation; one wouldn't have thought that there was a single living soul on her decks. A sudden brisk shout, "Mainsail haul!" broke the spell, and in the noisy cries and rush overhead of the men running away with the main brace we two, down in my cabin, came together in our usual position by the bed-place.

He did not wait for my question. "I heard him fumbling here and just managed to squat myself down in the bath," he whispered to me. "The fellow only opened the door and put his arm in to hang the coat up. All the same—"

"I never thought of that," I whispered back, even more appalled than before at the closeness of the shave, and marveling at that something unyielding in his character which was carrying him through so finely. There was no agitation in his whisper. Whoever was being driven distracted, it was not he. He was sane. And the proof of his sanity was continued when he took up the whispering again.

"It would never do for me to come to life again."

It was something that a ghost might have said. But what he was alluding to was his old captain's reluctant admission of the theory of suicide. It would obviously serve his turn—if I had understood at all the view which seemed to govern the unalterable purpose of his action.

"You must maroon me as soon as ever you can get amongst these islands off the Cambodje shore," he went on.

"Maroon you! We are not living in a boy's adventure tale," I protested. His scornful whispering took me up.

"We aren't indeed! There's nothing of a boy's tale in this. But there's nothing else for it. I want no more. You don't suppose I am afraid of what can be done to me? Prison or gallows or whatever they may please. But you don't see me coming back to explain such things to an old fellow in a wig and twelve respectable tradesmen, do you? What can they know whether I am guilty or not—or of *what* I am guilty, either? That's my affair. What does the Bible say? 'Driven off the face of the earth.' Very well. I am off the face of the earth now. As I came at night so I shall go."

"Impossible!" I murmured. "You can't"

"Can't? . . . Not naked like a soul on the Day of Judgment. I shall freeze on to this sleeping suit. The Last Day is not yet—and . . . you have understood thoroughly. Didn't you?"

I felt suddenly ashamed of myself. I may say truly that I understood—and my hesitation in letting that man swim away from my ship's side had been a mere sham sentiment, a sort of cowardice.

"It can't be done now till next night," I breathed out. "The ship is on the offshore tack and the wind may fail us."

"As long as I know that you understand," he whispered. "But of course you do. It's a great satisfaction to have got somebody to understand. You seem to have been there on purpose." And in the same whisper, as if we two whenever we talked had to say things to each other which were not fit for the world to hear, he added, "It's very wonderful."

We remained side by side talking in our secret way—but sometimes silent or just exchanging a whispered word or two at long intervals. And as usual he stared through the port. A breath of wind came now and again into our faces. The ship might have been moored in dock, so gently and on an even keel she slipped through the water, that did not murmur even at our passage, shadowy and silent like a phantom sea.

At midnight I went on deck, and to my mate's great surprise put the ship round on the other tack. His terrible whiskers flitted round me in silent criticism. I certainly should not have done it if it had been only a question of getting out of that sleepy gulf as quickly as possible. I believe he told the second mate, who relieved him, that it was a great want of judgment. The other only yawned. That intolerable cub shuffled about so sleepily and lolled against the rails in such a slack, improper fashion that I came down on him sharply.

"Aren't you properly awake yet?"

"Yes, sir! I am awake."

"Well, then, be good enough to hold yourself as if you were. And keep a lookout. If there's any current we'll be closing with some islands before daylight."

The east side of the gulf is fringed with islands, some solitary, others in groups. On the blue background of the high coast they seem to float on silvery patches of calm water, arid and gray, or dark green and rounded like clumps of evergreen bushes, with the larger ones, a mile or two long, showing the outlines of ridges, ribs of gray rock under the dark mantle of matted leafage. Unknown to trade, to travel, almost to geography, the manner of life they harbor is an unsolved secret. There must be villages—settlements of fishermen at least—on the largest of them, and some communication with the world is probably kept up by native craft. But all that forenoon, as we headed for them, fanned along by the faintest of breezes, I saw no sign of man or canoe in the field of the telescope I kept on pointing at the scattered group.

At noon I gave no orders for a change of course, and the mate's whiskers became much concerned and seemed to be offering themselves unduly to my notice. At last I said:

"I am going to stand right in. Quite in—as far as I can take her."

The stare of extreme surprise imparted an air of ferocity also to his eyes, and he looked truly terrific for a moment.

"We're not doing well in the middle of the gulf," I continued, casually. "I am going to look for the land breezes tonight."

"Bless my soul! Do you mean, sir, in the dark amongst the lot of all them islands and reefs and shoals?"

"Well—if there are any regular land breezes at all on this coast one must get close inshore to find them, mustn't one?"

"Bless my soul!" he exclaimed again under his breath. All that afternoon he wore a dreamy, contemplative appearance which in him was a mark of perplexity. After dinner I went into my stateroom as if I meant to take some rest. There we two bent our dark heads over a half-unrolled chart lying on my bed.

"There," I said. "It's got to be Koh-ring. I've been looking at it ever since sunrise. It has got two hills and a low point. It must be inhabited. And on the coast opposite there is what looks like the mouth of a biggish river—with some town, no doubt, not far up. It's the best chance for you that I can see."

"Anything. Koh-ring let it be."

He looked thoughtfully at the chart as if surveying chances and distances from a lofty height—and following with his eyes his own figure wandering on the blank land of Cochin-China, and then passing off that piece of paper clean out of sight into uncharted regions. And it was as if the ship had two captains to plan her course for her. I had been so worried and restless running up and down that I had not had the patience to dress that day. I had remained in my sleeping suit, with straw slippers and a soft floppy hat. The closeness of the heat in the gulf had been most oppressive, and the crew were used to see me wandering in that airy attire.

"She will clear the south point as she heads now," I whispered into his ear. "Goodness only knows when, though, but certainly after dark. I'll edge her in to half a mile, as far as I may be able to judge in the dark—"

"Be careful," he murmured, warningly—and I realized suddenly that all my future, the only future for which I was fit, would perhaps go irretrievably to pieces in any mishap to my first command.

I could not stop a moment longer in the room. I motioned him to get out of sight and made my way on the poop. That unplayful cub had the watch. I walked up and down for a while thinking things out, then beckoned him over.

"Send a couple of hands to open the two quarter-deck ports," I said, mildly.

He actually had the impudence, or else so forgot himself in his wonder at such an incomprehensible order, as to repeat:

"Open the quarter-deck ports! What for, sir?"

"The only reason you need concern yourself about is because I tell you to do so. Have them open wide and fastened properly."

He reddened and went off, but I believe made some jeering remark to the carpenter as to the sensible practice of ventilating a ship's quarter-deck. I know he popped into the mate's cabin to impart the fact to him because the whiskers came on deck, as it were by chance, and stole glances at me from below—for signs of lunacy or drunkenness, I suppose.

A little before supper, feeling more restless than ever, I rejoined, for a moment, my second self. And to find him sitting so quietly was surprising, like something against nature, inhuman.

I developed my plan in a hurried whisper.

"I shall stand in as close as I dare and then put her round. I shall presently find means to smuggle you out of here into the sail locker, which communicates with the lobby. But there is an opening, a sort of square for hauling the sails out, which gives straight on the quarter-deck and which is never closed in fine weather, so as to give air to the sails. When the ship's way is deadened in stays and all the hands are aft at the main braces you shall have a clear road to slip out and get overboard through the open quarter-deck port. I've had them both fastened up. Use a rope's end to lower yourself into the water so as to avoid a splash—you know. It could be heard and cause some beastly complication."

He kept silent for a while, then whispered, "I understand."

"I won't be there to see you go," I began with an effort. "The rest . . . I only hope I have understood, too."

"You have. From first to last," and for the first time there seemed to be a faltering, something strained in his whisper. He caught hold of my arm, but the ringing of the supper bell made me start. He didn't, though; he only released his grip.

After supper I didn't come below again till well past eight o'clock. The faint, steady breeze was loaded with dew; and the wet, darkened sails held all there was of propelling power in it. The night, clear and starry, sparkled darkly, and the opaque, lightless patches shifting slowly against the low stars were the drifting islets. On the port bow there was a big one more distant and shadowily imposing by the great space of sky it eclipsed.

On opening the door I had a back view of my very own self looking at a chart. He had come out of the recess and was standing near the table.

"Quite dark enough," I whispered.

He stepped back and leaned against my bed with a level, quiet glance. I sat on the couch. We had nothing to say to each other. Over our heads the officer of the watch moved here and there. Then I heard him move quickly. I knew what that meant. He was making for the companion; and presently his voice was outside my door.

"We are drawing in pretty fast, sir. Land looks rather close."

"Very well," I answered. "I am coming on deck directly."

I waited till he was gone out of the cuddy, then rose. My double moved too. The time had come to exchange our last whispers, for neither of us was ever to hear each other's natural voice.

"Look here!" I opened a drawer and took out three sovereigns. "Take this, anyhow. I've got six and I'd give you the lot, only I must keep a little money to buy some fruit and vegetables for the crew from native boats as we go through Sunda Straits."

He shook his head.

"Take it," I urged him, whispering desperately. "No one can tell what—"

He smiled and slapped meaningly the only pocket of the sleeping jacket. It was not safe, certainly. But I produced a large old silk handkerchief of mine, and tying the three pieces of gold in a corner, pressed it on him. He was touched, I suppose, because he took it at last and tied it quickly round his waist under the jacket, on his bare skin.

Our eyes met; several seconds elapsed, till, our glances still mingled, I extended my hand and turned the lamp out. Then I passed through the cuddy, leaving the door of my room wide open. . . . "Steward!"

He was still lingering in the pantry in the greatness of his zeal, giving a rub-up to a plated cruet stand the last thing before going to bed. Being careful not to wake up the mate, whose room was opposite, I spoke in an undertone.

He looked round anxiously. "Sir!"

"Can you get me a little hot water from the galley?"

"I am afraid, sir, the galley fire's been out for some time now."

"Go and see."

He fled up the stairs.

"Now," I whispered, loudly, into the saloon—too loudly, perhaps, but I was afraid I couldn't make a sound. He was by my side in an instant—the double captain slipped past the stairs—through the tiny dark passage . . . a sliding door. We were in the sail locker, scrambling on our knees over the sails. A sudden thought struck me. I saw myself wandering barefooted, bare-headed, the sun beating on my dark poll. I snatched off my floppy hat and tried hurriedly in the dark to ram it on my other self. He dodged and fended off silently. I wonder what he thought had come to me before he understood and suddenly desisted. Our hands met gropingly, lingered united in a steady, motionless clasp for a second. . . . No word was breathed by either of us when they separated.

I was standing quietly by the pantry door when the steward returned.

"Sorry, sir. Kettle barely warm. Shall I light the spirit lamp?"

"Never mind."

I came out on deck slowly. It was now a matter of conscience to shave the land as close as possible—for now he must go overboard whenever the ship was put in stays. Must! There could be no going back for him. After a moment I walked over to leeward and my heart flew into my mouth at the nearness of the land on the bow. Under any other circumstances I would not have held on a minute longer. The second mate had followed me anxiously.

I looked on till I felt I could command my voice.

"She will weather," I said then in a quiet tone.

"Are you going to try that, sir?" he stammered out incredulously.

I took no notice of him and raised my tone just enough to be heard by the helmsman.

"Keep her good full."

"Good full, sir."

The wind fanned my cheek, the sails slept, the world was silent. The strain of watching the dark loom of the land grow bigger and denser was too much for me. I had shut my eyes—because the ship must go closer. She must! The stillness was intolerable. Were we standing still?

When I opened my eyes the second view started my heart with a thump. The black southern hill of Koh-ring seemed to hang right over the ship like a towering fragment of the everlasting night. On that enormous mass of blackness there was not a gleam to be seen, not a sound to be heard. It was gliding irresistibly toward us and yet seemed already within reach of the hand. I saw the vague figures of the watch grouped in the waist, gazing in awed silence.

"Are you going on, sir?" inquired an unsteady voice at my elbow.

I ignored it. I had to go on.

"Keep her full. Don't check her way. That won't do now," I said warningly.

"I can't see the sails very well," the helmsman answered me, in strange, quavering tones.

Was she close enough? Already she was, I won't say in the shadow of the land, but in the very blackness of it, already swallowed up as it were, gone too close to be recalled, gone from me altogether.

"Give the mate a call," I said to the young man who stood at my elbow as still as death. "And turn all hands up."

My tone had a borrowed loudness reverberated from the height of the land. Several voices cried out together: "We are all on deck, sir."

Then stillness again, with the great shadow gliding closer, towering higher, without a light, without a sound. Such a hush had fallen on the ship that she might have been a bark of the dead floating in slowly under the very gate of Erebus.

"My God! Where are we?"

It was the mate moaning at my elbow. He was thunderstruck, and as it were deprived of the moral support of his whiskers. He clapped his hands and absolutely cried out, "Lost!"

"Be quiet," I said sternly.

He lowered his tone, but I saw the shadowy gesture of his despair. "What are we doing here?"

"Looking for the land wind."

He made as if to tear his hair, and addressed me recklessly.

"She will never get out. You have done it, sir. I knew it'd end in something like this. She will never weather, and you are too close now to stay. She'll drift ashore before she's round. O my God!"

I caught his arm as he was raising it to batter his poor devoted head, and shook it violently.

"She's ashore already," he wailed, trying to tear himself away.

"Is she? . . . Keep good full there!"

"Good full, sir," cried the helmsman in a frightened, thin, childlike voice.

I hadn't let go the mate's arm and went on shaking it. "Ready about, do you hear? You go forward"—shake—"and stop there"—shake—"and hold your noise"—shake—"and see these head sheets properly overhauled"—shake, shake—shake.

And all the time I dared not look toward the land lest my heart should fail me. I released my grip at last and he ran forward as if fleeing for dear life.

I wondered what my double there in the sail locker thought of this commotion. He was able to hear everything—and perhaps he was able to understand why, on my conscience, it had to be thus close—no less. My first order "Hard alee!" re-echoed ominously under the towering shadow of Koh-ring as if I had shouted in a mountain gorge. And then I watched the land intently. In that smooth water and light wind it was impossible to feel the ship coming-to. No! I could not feel her. And my second self was making now ready to slip out and lower himself overboard. Perhaps he was gone already . . . ?

The great black mass brooding over our very mastheads began to pivot away from the ship's side silently. And now I forgot the secret stranger ready to depart, and remembered only that I was a total stranger to the ship. I did not know her. Would she do it? How was she to be handled?

I swung the mainyard and waited helplessly. She was perhaps stopped, and her very fate hung in the balance, with the black mass of Koh-ring like the gate of the everlasting night towering over her taffrail. What would she do now? Had she way on her yet? I stepped to the side swiftly, and on the shadowy water I could see nothing except a faint phosphorescent flash revealing the glassy smoothness of the sleeping surface. It was impossible to tell—and I had not learned yet the feel of my ship. Was she moving? What I needed was something easily seen, a piece of paper, which I could throw overboard and watch. I had nothing on me. To run down for it I didn't dare. There was no time. All at once my strained, yearning stare distinguished a white object floating within a yard of the ship's side. White on the black water. A phosphorescent flash passed under it. What was that thing? . . . I recognized my own floppy hat. It must have fallen off his head . . . and he didn't bother. Now I had what I wanted—the saving mark for my eyes. But I hardly thought of my other self, now gone from the ship, to be hidden forever from all friendly faces, to be a fugitive and a vagabond on the earth, with no brand of the curse on his sane forehead to stay a slaying hand . . . too proud to explain.

And I watched the hat—the expression of my sudden pity for his mere flesh. It had been meant to save his homeless head from the dangers of the sun. And now—behold—it was saving the ship, by serving me for a mark to help out the ignorance of my strangeness. Ha! It was drifting forward, warning me just in time that the ship had gathered sternway.

"Shift the helm," I said in a low voice to the seaman standing still like a statue.

The man's eyes glistened wildly in the binnacle light as he jumped round to the other side and spun round the wheel.

I walked to the break of the poop. On the overshadowed deck all hands stood by the forebraces waiting for my order. The stars ahead seemed to be gliding from right to left. And all was so still in the world that I heard the quiet remark "She's round," passed in a tone of intense relief between two seamen.

"Let go and haul."

The foreyards ran round with a great noise amidst cheery cries. And now the frightful whiskers made themselves heard giving various orders. Already the ship was drawing ahead. And I was alone with her. Nothing! no one in the world should stand now between us, throwing a shadow on the way of silent knowledge and mute affection, the perfect communion of a seaman with his first command.

Walking to the taffrail, I was in time to make out, on the very edge of a darkness thrown by a towering black mass like the very gateway of Erebus— yes, I was in time to catch an evanescent glimpse of my white hat left behind to mark the spot where the secret sharer of my cabin and of my thoughts, as though he were my second self, had lowered himself into the water to take his punishment: a free man, a proud swimmer striking out for a new destiny.

QUESTIONS

1. Early on in their hidden relationship, the young captain brings to Leggatt a "sleeping suit." What might be the psychological significance of such a garment? What might it tell you about the relationship?

2. What do you make of the character of the captain of the *Sephora*? Is he meant to be compared to the captain who befriends Leggatt? How so?

3. How would you go about opposing the notion that Leggatt is unreal, that is, only a figment of the captain's imagination? How would you establish the reality of Leggatt's presence on the ship?

4. How does the story benefit from taking place at sea? A similar tale could be given the locale of an office, a home, or an army camp. What force does shipboard life give to the story?

5. Do you believe the narrator is correct when, at the story's end, he declares that Leggatt leaves the ship "a free man, a proud swimmer striking out for a new destiny"? Is the narrator's opinion at this moment to be trusted? How can you be sure?

Anton Chekhov (1860–1904)
The Lady With the Pet Dog

A new person, it was said, had appeared on the esplanade: a lady with a pet dog. Dmitry Dmitrich Gurov, who had spent a fortnight at Yalta and had got used to the place, had also begun to take an interest in new arrivals. As he sat in Vernet's confectionery shop, he saw, walking on the esplanade, a fair-haired young woman of medium height, wearing a beret; a white Pomeranian was trotting behind her.

And afterwards he met her in the public garden and in the square several times a day. She walked alone, always wearing the same beret and always with the white dog; no one knew who she was and everyone called her simply "the lady with the pet dog."

"If she is here alone without husband or friends," Gurov reflected, "it wouldn't be a bad thing to make her acquaintance."

He was under forty, but he already had a daughter twelve years old, and two sons at school. They had found a wife for him when he was very young, a student in his second year, and by now she seemed half as old again as he. She was a tall, erect woman with dark eyebrows, stately and dignified and, as she said of herself, intellectual. She read a great deal, used simplified spelling in her letters, called her husband, not Dmitry, but Dimitry, while he privately considered her of limited intelligence, narrow-minded, dowdy, was afraid of her, and did not like to be at home. He had begun being unfaithful to her long ago—had been unfaithful to her often and, probably for that reason, almost always spoke ill of women, and when they were talked of in his presence used to call them "the inferior race."

It seemed to him that he had been sufficiently tutored by bitter experience to call them what he pleased, and yet he could not have lived without "the inferior race" for two days together. In the company of men he was bored and ill at ease, he was chilly and uncommunicative with them; but when he was among women he felt free, and knew what to speak to them about and how to comport himself; and even to be silent with them was no strain on him. In his appearance, in his character, in his whole make-up there was something attractive and elusive that disposed women in his favor and allured them. He knew that, and some force seemed to draw him to them, too.

Oft-repeated and really bitter experience had taught him long ago that with decent people—particularly Moscow people—who are irresolute and slow to move, every affair which at first seems a light and charming adventure inevitably grows into a whole problem of extreme complexity, and in the end a painful situation is created. But at every new meeting with an interesting woman this lesson of experience seemed to slip from his memory, and he was eager for life, and everything seemed so simple and diverting.

One evening while he was dining in the public garden the lady in the beret walked up without haste to take the next table. Her expression, her gait, her dress, and the way she did her hair told him that she belonged to the upper class, that she was married, that she was in Yalta for the first time and alone, and that she was bored there. The stories told of the immorality in Yalta are to a great extent untrue; he despised them, and knew that such stories were made up for the most part by persons who would have been glad to sin themselves if they had had the chance; but when the lady sat down at the next table three paces from him, he recalled these stories of easy conquests, of trips to the mountains, and the tempting thought of a swift, fleeting liaison, a romance with an unknown woman of whose very name he was ignorant suddenly took hold of him.

He beckoned invitingly to the Pomeranian, and when the dog approached him, shook his finger at it. The Pomeranian growled; Gurov threatened it again.

The lady glanced at him and at once dropped her eyes.

"He doesn't bite," she said and blushed.

"May I give him a bone?" he asked; and when she nodded he inquired affably, "Have you been in Yalta long?"

"About five days."

"And I am dragging out the second week here."

There was a short silence.

"Time passes quickly, and yet it is so dull here!" she said, not looking at him.

"It's only the fashion to say it's dull here. A provincial will live in Belyov or Zhizdra and not be bored, but when he comes here it's 'Oh, the dullness! Oh, the dust!' One would think he came from Granada."

She laughed. Then both continued eating in silence, like strangers, but after dinner they walked together and there sprang up between them the light banter of people who are free and contented, to whom it does not matter where they go or what they talk about. They walked and talked of the strange light on the sea: the water was a soft, warm, lilac color, and there was a golden band of moonlight upon it. They talked of how sultry it was after a hot day. Gurov told her that he was a native of Moscow, that he had studied languages and literature at the university, but had a post in a bank; that at one time he had trained to become an opera singer but had given it up, that he owned two houses in Moscow. And he learned from her that she had grown up in

Petersburg, but had lived in S—— since her marriage two years previously, that she was going to stay in Yalta for about another month, and that her husband, who needed a rest, too, might perhaps come to fetch her. She was not certain whether her husband was a member of a Government Board or served on a Zemstvo Council, and this amused her. And Gurov learned too that her name was Anna Sergeyevna.

Afterwards in his room at the hotel he thought about her—and was certain that he would meet her the next day. It was bound to happen. Getting into bed he recalled that she had been a schoolgirl only recently, doing lessons like his own daughter; he thought how much timidity and angularity there was still in her laugh and her manner of talking with a stranger. It must have been the first time in her life that she was alone in a setting in which she was followed, looked at, and spoken to for one secret purpose alone, which she could hardly fail to guess. He thought of her slim, delicate throat, her lovely gray eyes.

"There's something pathetic about her, though," he thought, and dropped off.

2

A week had passed since they had struck up an acquaintance. It was a holiday. It was close indoors, while in the street the wind whirled the dust about and blew people's hats off. One was thirsty all day, and Gurov often went into the restaurant and offered Anna Sergeyevna a soft drink or ice cream. One did not know what to do with oneself.

In the evening when the wind had abated they went out on the pier to watch the steamer come in. There were a great many people walking about the dock; they had come to welcome someone and they were carrying bunches of flowers. And two peculiarities of a festive Yalta crowd stood out: the elderly ladies were dressed like young ones and there were many generals.

Owing to the choppy sea, the steamer arrived late, after sunset, and it was a long time tacking about before it put in at the pier. Anna Sergeyevna peered at the steamer and the passengers through her lorgnette as though looking for acquaintances, and whenever she turned to Gurov her eyes were shining. She talked a great deal and asked questions jerkily, forgetting the next moment what she had asked; then she lost her lorgnette in the crush.

The festive crowd began to disperse; it was now too dark to see people's faces; there was no wind any more, but Gurov and Anna Sergeyevna still stood as though waiting to see someone else come off the steamer. Anna Sergeyevna was silent now, and sniffed her flowers without looking at Gurov.

"The weather has improved this evening," he said. "Where shall we go now? Shall we drive somewhere?"

She did not reply.

Then he looked at her intently, and suddenly embraced her and kissed her on the lips, and the moist fragrance of her flowers enveloped him; and at once he looked round him anxiously, wondering if anyone had seen them.

"Let us go to your place," he said softly. And they walked off together rapidly.

The air in her room was close and there was the smell of the perfume she had bought at the Japanese shop. Looking at her, Gurov thought: "What encounters life offers!" From the past he preserved the memory of carefree, good-natured women whom love made gay and who were grateful to him for the happiness he gave them, however brief it might be; and of women like his wife who loved without sincerity, with too many words, affectedly, hysterically, with an expression that it was not love or passion that engaged them but something more significant; and of two or three others, very beautiful, frigid women, across whose faces would suddenly flit a rapacious expression—an obstinate desire to take from life more than it could give, and these were women no longer young, capricious, unreflecting, domineering, unintelligent, and when Gurov grew cold to them their beauty aroused his hatred, and the lace on their lingerie seemed to him to resemble scales.

But here there was the timidity, the angularity of inexperienced youth, a feeling of awkwardness; and there was a sense of embarrassment, as though someone had suddenly knocked at the door. Anna Sergeyevna, "the lady with the pet dog," treated what had happened in a peculiar way, very seriously, as though it were her fall—so it seemed, and this was odd and inappropriate. Her features drooped and faded, and her long hair hung down sadly on either side of her face; she grew pensive and her dejected pose was that of a Magdalene in a picture by an old master.

"It's not right," she said. "You don't respect me now, you first of all."

There was a watermelon on the table. Gurov cut himself a slice and began eating it without haste. They were silent for at least half an hour.

There was something touching about Anna Sergeyevna; she had the purity of a well-bred, naive woman who has seen little of life. The single candle burning on the table barely illumined her face, yet it was clear that she was unhappy.

"Why should I stop respecting you, darling?" asked Gurov. "You don't know what you're saying."

"God forgive me," she said, and her eyes filled with tears. "It's terrible."

"It's as though you were trying to exonerate yourself."

"How can I exonerate myself? No. I am a bad, low woman; I despise myself and I have no thought of exonerating myself. It's not my husband but myself I have deceived. And not only just now; I have been deceiving myself for a long time. My husband may be a good, honest man, but he is a flunkey! I don't know what he does, what his work is, but I know he is a flunkey! I was twenty when I married him. I was tormented by curiosity; I wanted something better. 'There must be a different sort of life,' I said to myself. I wanted to live! To live, to live! Curiosity kept eating at me—you don't understand it, but I swear to God I could no longer control myself; something was going on in me: I could not be held back. I told my husband I was ill, and came here. And here I have been walking about as though in a daze, as though I were mad; and now I have become a vulgar, vile woman whom anyone may despise."

Gurov was already bored with her; he was irritated by her naive tone, by her repentance, so unexpected and so out of place; but for the tears in her eyes he might have thought she was joking or play-acting.

"I don't understand, my dear," he said softly. "What do you want?"

She hid her face on his breast and pressed close to him.

"Believe me, believe me, I beg you," she said, "I love honesty and purity, and sin is loathsome to me; I don't know what I'm doing. Simple people say, 'The Evil One has led me astray.' And I may say of myself now that the Evil One has led me astray."

"Quiet, quiet," he murmured.

He looked into her fixed, frightened eyes, kissed her, spoke to her softly and affectionately, and by degrees she calmed down, and her gaiety returned; both began laughing.

Afterwards when they went out there was not a soul on the esplanade. The town with its cypresses looked quite dead, but the sea was still sounding as it broke upon the beach; a single launch was rocking on the waves and on it a lantern was blinking sleepily.

They found a cab and drove to Oreanda.

"I found out your surname in the hall just now: it was written on the board—von Dideritz," said Gurov. "Is your husband German?"

"No; I believe his grandfather was German, but he is Greek Orthodox himself."

At Oreanda they sat on a bench not far from the church, looked down at the sea, and were silent. Yalta was barely visible through the morning mist; white clouds rested motionlessly on the mountaintops. The leaves did not stir on the trees, cicadas twanged, and the monotonous muffled sound of the sea that rose from below spoke of the peace, the eternal sleep awaiting us. So it rumbled below when there was no Yalta, no Oreanda here; so it rumbles now, and it will rumble as indifferently and as hollowly when we are no more. And in this constancy, in this complete indifference to the life and death of each of us, there lies, perhaps, a pledge of our eternal salvation, of the unceasing advance of life upon earth, of unceasing movement towards perfection. Sitting beside a young woman who in the dawn seemed so lovely, Gurov, soothed and spellbound by these magical surroundings—the sea, the mountains, the clouds, the wide sky—thought how everything is really beautiful in this world when one reflects: everything except what we think or do ourselves when we forget the higher aims of life and our own human dignity.

A man strolled up to them—probably a guard—looked at them and walked away. And this detail, too, seemed so mysterious and beautiful. They saw a steamer arrive from Feodosia, its lights extinguished in the glow of dawn.

"There is dew on the grass," said Anna Sergeyevna, after a silence.

"Yes, it's time to go home."

They returned to the city.

Then they met every day at twelve o'clock on the esplanade, lunched and dined together, took walks, admired the sea. She complained that she slept badly, that she had palpitations, asked the same questions, troubled now by jealousy and now by the fear that he did not respect her sufficiently. And often in the square or the public garden, when there was no one near them, he suddenly drew her to him and kissed her passionately. Complete idleness, these kisses in broad daylight exchanged furtively in dread of someone's seeing them, the heat, the smell of the sea, and the continual flitting before his eyes of idle, well-dressed, well-fed people, worked a complete change in him; he kept telling Anna Sergeyevna how beautiful she was, how seductive, was urgently passionate; he would not move a step away from her, while she was often pensive and continually pressed him to confess that he did not respect her, did not love her in the least, and saw in her nothing but a common woman. Almost every evening rather late they drove somewhere out of town, to Oreanda or to the waterfall; and the excursion was always a success, the scenery invariably impressed them as beautiful and magnificent.

They were expecting her husband, but a letter came from him saying that he had eye-trouble, and begging his wife to return home as soon as possible. Anna Sergeyevna made haste to go.

"It's a good thing I am leaving," she said to Gurov. "It's the hand of Fate!"

She took a carriage to the railway station, and he went with her. They were driving the whole day. When she had taken her place in the express, and when the second bell had rung, she said, "Let me look at you once more—let me look at you again. Like this."

She was not crying but was so sad that she seemed ill, and her face was quivering.

"I shall be thinking of you—remembering you," she said. "God bless you; be happy. Don't remember evil against me. We are parting forever—it has to be, for we ought never to have met. Well, God bless you."

The train moved off rapidly, its lights soon vanished, and a minute later there was no sound of it, as though everything had conspired to end as quickly as possible that sweet trance, that madness. Left alone on the platform, and gazing into the dark distance, Gurov listened to the twang of the grasshoppers and the hum of the telegraph wires, feeling as though he had just waked up. And he reflected, musing, that there had now been another episode or adventure in his life, and it, too, was at an end, and nothing was left of it but a memory. He was moved, sad, and slightly remorseful: this young woman whom he would never meet again had not been happy with him; he had been warm and affectionate with her, but yet in his manner, his tone, and his caresses there had been a shade of light irony, the slightly coarse arrogance of a happy male who was, besides, almost twice her age. She had constantly called him kind, exceptional, high-minded; obviously he had seemed to her different from what he really was, so he had involuntarily deceived her.

Here at the station there was already a scent of autumn in the air; it was a chilly evening.

"It is time for me to go north, too," thought Gurov as he left the platform. "High time!"

3

At home in Moscow the winter routine was already established: the stoves were heated, and in the morning it was still dark when the children were having breakfast and getting ready for school, and the nurse would light the lamp for a short time. There were frosts already. When the first snow falls, on the first day the sleighs are out, it is pleasant to see the white earth, the white roofs; one draws easy, delicious breaths, and the season brings back the days of one's youth. The old limes and birches, white with hoar-frost, have a good-natured look; they are closer to one's heart than cypresses and palms, and near them one no longer wants to think of mountains and the sea.

Gurov, a native of Moscow, arrived there on a fine frosty day, and when he put on his fur coat and warm gloves and took a walk along Petrovka, and when on Saturday night he heard the bells ringing, his recent trip and the places he had visited lost all charm for him. Little by little he became immersed in Moscow life, greedily read three newspapers a day, and declared that he did not read the Moscow papers on principle. He already felt a longing for restaurants, clubs, formal dinners, anniversary celebrations, and it flattered him to entertain distinguished lawyers and actors, and to play cards with a professor at the physicians' club. He could eat a whole portion of meat stewed with pickled cabbage and served in a pan, Moscow style.

A month or so would pass and the image of Anna Sergeyevna, it seemed to him, would become misty in his memory, and only from time to time he would dream of her with her touching smile as he dreamed of others. But more than a month went by, winter came into its own, and everthing was still clear in his memory as though he had parted from Anna Sergeyevna only yesterday. And his memories glowed more and more vividly. When in the evening stillness the voices of his children preparing their lessons reached his study, or when he listened to a song or to an organ playing in a restaurant, or when the storm howled in the chimney, suddenly everything would rise up in his memory: what had happened on the pier and the early morning with the mist on the mountains, and the steamer coming from Feodosia, and the kisses. He would pace about his room a long time, remembering and smiling; then his memories passed into reveries, and in his imagination the past would mingle with what was to come. He did not dream of Anna Sergeyevna, but she followed him about everywhere and watched him. When he shut his eyes he saw her before him as though she were there in the flesh, and she seemed to him lovelier, younger, tenderer than she had been, and he imagined himself a finer man than he had been in Yalta. Of evenings she peered out at him from the bookcase, from the fireplace, from the corner—he heard her breathing, the caressing rustle of her clothes. In the street he followed the women with his eyes, looking for someone who resembled her.

Already he was tormented by a strong desire to share his memories with someone. But in his home it was impossible to talk of his love, and he had no one to talk to outside; certainly he could not confide in his tenants or in anyone at the bank. And what was there to talk about? He hadn't loved her then, had he? Had there been anything beautiful, poetical, edifying, or simply interesting in his relations with Anna Sergeyevna? And he was forced to talk vaguely of love, of women, and no one guessed what he meant; only his wife would twitch her black eyebrows and say, "The part of a philanderer does not suit you at all, Dimitry."

One evening, coming out of the physicians' club with an official with whom he had been playing cards, he could not resist saying:

"If you only knew what a fascinating woman I became acquainted with at Yalta!"

The official got into his sledge and was driving away, but turned suddenly and shouted:

"Dmitry Dmitrich!"

"What is it?"

"You were right this evening: the sturgeon was a bit high."

These words, so commonplace, for some reason moved Gurov to indignation, and struck him as degrading and unclean. What savage manners, what mugs! What stupid nights, what dull, humdrum days! Frenzied gambling, gluttony, drunkenness, continual talk always about the same things! Futile pursuits and conversations always about the same topics take up the better part of one's time, the better part of one's strength, and in the end there is left a life clipped and wingless, an absurd mess, and there is no escaping or getting away from it—just as though one were in a madhouse or a prison.

Gurov, boiling with indignation, did not sleep all night. And he had a headache all the next day. And the following nights too he slept badly; he sat up in bed, thinking, or paced up and down his room. He was fed up with his children, fed up with the bank; he had no desire to go anywhere or to talk of anything.

In December during the holidays he prepared to take a trip and told his wife he was going to Petersburg to do what he could for a young friend—and he set off for S——. What for? He did not know, himself. He wanted to see Anna Sergeyevna and talk with her, to arrange a rendezvous if possible.

He arrived at S—— in the morning, and at the hotel took the best room, in which the floor was covered with gray army cloth, and on the table there was an inkstand, gray with dust and topped by a figure on horseback, its hat in its raised hand and its head broken off. The porter gave him the necessary information: von Dideritz lived in a house of his own on Staro-Goncharnaya Street, not far from the hotel: he was rich and lived well and kept his own horses; everyone in the town knew him. The porter pronounced the name: "Dridiritz."

Without haste Gurov made his way to Staro-Goncharnaya Street and found the house. Directly opposite the house stretched a long gray fence studded with nails.

"A fence like that would make one run away," thought Gurov, looking now at the fence, now at the windows of the house.

He reflected: this was a holiday, and the husband was apt to be at home. And in any case, it would be tactless to go into the house and disturb her. If he were to send her a note, it might fall into her husband's hands, and that might spoil everything. The best thing was to rely on chance. And he kept walking up and down the street and along the fence, waiting for the chance. He saw a beggar go in at the gate and heard the dogs attack him; then an hour later he heard a piano, and the sound came to him faintly and indistinctly. Probably it was Anna Sergeyevna playing. The front door opened suddenly, and an old woman came out, followed by the familiar white Pomeranian. Gurov was on the point of calling to the dog, but his heart began beating violently, and in his excitement he could not remember the Pomeranian's name.

He kept walking up and down, and hated the gray fence more and more, and by now he thought irritably that Anna Sergeyevna had forgotten him, and was perhaps already diverting herself with another man, and that that was very natural in a young woman who from morning till night had to look at that damn fence. He went back to his hotel room and sat on the couch for a long while, not knowing what to do, then he had dinner and a long nap.

"How stupid and annoying all this is!" he thought when he woke and looked at the dark windows: it was already evening. "Here I've had a good sleep for some reason. What am I going to do at night?"

He sat on the bed, which was covered with a cheap gray blanket of the kind seen in hospitals, and he twitted himself in his vexation:

"So there's your lady with the pet dog. There's your adventure. A nice place to cool your heels in."

That morning at the station a playbill in large letters had caught his eye. *The Geisha* was to be given for the first time. He thought of this and drove to the theater.

"It's quite possible that she goes to first nights," he thought.

The theater was full. As in all provincial theaters, there was a haze above the chandelier, the gallery was noisy and restless; in the front row, before the beginning of the performance the local dandies were standing with their hands clasped behind their backs; in the Governor's box the Governor's daughter, wearing a boa, occupied the front seat, while the Governor himself hid modestly behind the portiere and only his hands were visible; the curtain swayed; the orchestra was a long time tuning up. While the audience were coming in and taking their seats, Gurov scanned the faces eagerly.

Anna Sergeyevna, too, came in. She sat down in the third row, and when Gurov looked at her his heart contracted, and he understood clearly that in the whole world there was no human being so near, so precious, and so important to him; she, this little, undistinguished woman, lost in a provincial crowd, with a vulgar lorgnette in her hand, filled his whole life now, was his sorrow and his joy, the only happiness that he now desired for himself, and to the sounds of the bad orchestra, of the miserable local violins, he thought how lovely she was. He thought and dreamed.

A young man with small side-whiskers, very tall and stooped, came in with Anna Sergeyevna and sat down beside her; he nodded his head at every step and seemed to be bowing continually. Probably this was the husband whom at Yalta, in an access of bitter feeling, she had called a flunkey. And there really was in his lanky figure, his side-whiskers, his small bald patch, something of a flunkey's retiring manner; his smile was mawkish, and in his buttonhole there was an academic badge like a waiter's number.

During the first intermission the husband went out to have a smoke; she remained in her seat. Gurov, who was also sitting in the orchestra, went up to her and said in a shaky voice, with a forced smile:

"Good evening!"

She glanced at him and turned pale, then looked at him again in horror, unable to believe her eyes, and gripped the fan and the lorgnette tightly together in her hands, evidently trying to keep herself from fainting. Both were silent. She was sitting, he was standing, frightened by her distress and not daring to take a seat beside her. The violins and the flute that were being tuned up sang out. He suddenly felt frightened: it seemed as if all the people in the boxes were looking at them. She got up and went hurriedly to the exit; he followed her, and both of them walked blindly along the corridors and up and down stairs, and figures in the uniforms prescribed for magistrates, teachers, and officials of the Department of Crown Lands, all wearing badges, flitted before their eyes, as did also ladies, and fur coats on hangers; they were conscious of drafts and the smell of stale tobacco. And Gurov, whose heart was beating violently, thought:

"Oh, Lord! Why are these people here and this orchestra!"

And at that instant he suddenly recalled how when he had seen Anna Sergeyevna off at the station he had said to himself that all was over between them and that they would never meet again. But how distant the end still was!

On the narrow, gloomy staircase over which it said "To the Amphitheatre," she stopped.

"How you frightened me!" she said, breathing hard, still pale and stunned. "Oh, how you frightened me. I am barely alive. Why did you come? Why?"

"But do understand, Anna, do understand—" he said hurriedly, under his breath. "I implore you, do understand—"

She looked at him with fear, with entreaty, with love; she looked at him intently, to keep his features more distinctly in her memory.

"I suffer so," she went on, not listening to him. "All this time I have been thinking of nothing but you; I live only by the thought of you. And I wanted to forget, to forget; but why, oh, why have you come?"

On the landing above them two high school boys were looking down and smoking, but it was all the same to Gurov; he drew Anna Sergeyevna to him and began kissing her face and her hands.

"What are you doing, what are you doing!" she was saying in horror, pushing him away. "We have lost our senses. Go away today; go away at once— I conjure you by all that is sacred, I implore you— People are coming this way!"

Someone was walking up the stairs.

"You must leave," Anna Sergeyevna went on in a whisper. "Do you hear, Dmitry Dmitrich? I will come and see you in Moscow. I have never been happy; I am unhappy now, and I never, never shall be happy, never! So don't make me suffer still more! I swear I'll come to Moscow. But now let us part. My dear, good, precious one, let us part!"

She pressed his hand and walked rapidly downstairs, turning to look round at him, and from her eyes he could see that she really was unhappy. Gurov stood for a while, listening, then when all grew quiet, he found his coat and left the theater.

4

And Anna Sergeyevna began coming to see him in Moscow. Once every two or three months she left S——, telling her husband that she was going to consult a doctor about a woman's ailment from which she was suffering—and her husband did and did not believe her. When she arrived in Moscow she would stop at the Slavyansky Bazar Hotel, and at once send a man in a red cap to Gurov. Gurov came to see her, and no one in Moscow knew of it.

Once he was going to see her in this way on a winter morning (the messenger had come the evening before and not found him in). With him walked his daughter, whom he wanted to take to school: it was on the way. Snow was coming down in big wet flakes.

"It's three degrees above zero, and yet it's snowing," Gurov was saying to his daughter. "But this temperature prevails only on the surface of the earth; in the upper layers of the atmosphere there is quite a different temperature."

"And why doesn't it thunder in winter, papa?"

He explained that, too. He talked, thinking all the while that he was on his way to a rendezvous, and no living soul knew of it, and probably no one would ever know. He had two lives: an open one, seen and known by all who needed to know it, full of conventional truth and conventional falsehood, exactly like the lives of his friends and acquaintances; and another life that went on in secret. And through some strange, perhaps accidental, combination of circumstances, everything that was of interest and importance to him, everything that was essential to him, everything about which he felt sincerely and did not deceive himself, everything that constituted the core of his life, was going on concealed from others; while all that was false, the shell in which he hid to cover the truth—his work at the bank, for instance, his discussions at the club, his references to the "inferior race," his appearances at anniversary celebrations with his wife—all that went on in the open. Judging others by himself, he did not believe what he saw, and always fancied that every man led his real, most interesting life under cover of secrecy as under cover of night. The personal life of every individual is based on secrecy, and perhaps it is partly for that reason that civilized man is so nervously anxious that personal privacy should be respected.

Having taken his daughter to school, Gurov went on to the Slavyansky Bazar Hotel. He took off his fur coat in the lobby, went upstairs, and knocked gently at the door. Anna Sergeyevna, wearing his favorite gray dress, exhausted by the journey and by waiting, had been expecting him since the previous evening. She was pale, and looked at him without a smile, and he had hardly entered when she flung herself on his breast. Their kiss was a long, lingering one, as though they had not seen one another for two years.

"Well, darling, how are you getting on there?" he asked. "What news?"

"Wait; I'll tell you in a moment— I can't speak."

She could not speak; she was crying. She turned away from him, and pressed her handkerchief to her eyes.

"Let her have her cry; meanwhile I'll sit down," he thought, and he seated himself in an armchair.

Then he rang and ordered tea, and while he was having his tea she remained standing at the window with her back to him. She was crying out of sheer agitation, in the sorrowful consciousness that their life was so sad; that they could only see each other in secret and had to hide from people like thieves! Was it not a broken life?

"Come, stop now, dear!" he said.

It was plain to him that this love of theirs would not be over soon, that the end of it was not in sight. Anna Sergeyevna was growing more and more attached to him. She adored him, and it was unthinkable to tell her that their love was bound to come to an end some day; besides, she would not have believed it!

He went up to her and took her by the shoulders, to fondle her and say something diverting, and at that moment he caught sight of himself in the mirror.

His hair was already beginning to turn gray. And it seemed odd to him that he had grown so much older in the last few years, and lost his looks. The shoulders on which his hands rested were warm and heaving. He felt compassion for this life, still so warm and lovely, but probably already about to begin to fade and wither like his own. Why did she love him so much? He always seemed to women different from what he was, and they loved in him not himself, but the man whom their imagination created and whom they had been eagerly seeking all their lives; and afterwards, when they saw their mistake, they loved him nevertheless. And not one of them had been happy with him. In the past he had met women, come together with them, parted from them, but he had never once loved; it was anything you please, but not love. And only now when his head was gray he had fallen in love, really, truly—for the first time in his life.

Anna Sergeyevna and he loved each other as people do who are very close and intimate, like man and wife, like tender friends; it seemed to them that Fate itself had meant them for one another, and they could not understand why he had a wife and she a husband; and it was as though they were a pair of migratory birds, male and female, caught and forced to live in different cages. They forgave each other what they were ashamed of in their past, they forgave everything in the present, and felt that this love of theirs had altered them both.

Formerly in moments of sadness he had soothed himself with whatever logical arguments came into his head, but now he no longer cared for logic; he felt profound compassion, he wanted to be sincere and tender.

"Give it up now, my darling," he said. "You've had your cry; that's enough. Let us have a talk now, we'll think up something."

Then they spent a long time taking counsel together, they talked of how to avoid the necessity for secrecy, for deception, for living in different cities, and not seeing one another for long stretches of time. How could they free themselves from these intolerable fetters?

"How? How?" he asked, clutching his head. "How?"

And it seemed as though in a little while the solution would be found, and then a new and glorious life would begin; and it was clear to both of them that the end was still far off, and that what was to be most complicated and difficult for them was only just beginning.

QUESTIONS

1. As the first part of the story ends, Dmitry Gurov says of his new woman friend: "There's something pathetic about her, though." Is this perception proven true as the story proceeds to its end? Is she pathetic?

2. As the new lovers look at the sea near Oreanda, the narrator speaks of the sound coming from the sea: "So it rumbled below when there was no Yalta, no Oreanda here; so it rumbles now, and it will rumble as indifferently and as hollowly when we are no more." Why are such reflections in the story? What effect do they add? Would the story be stronger if such an effect were removed?

3. How does the story end? Indeed, does it end? Do you experience a sense of conclusion with the last lines? What, in general, is necessary to "end" a story?

4. Can you establish any sense of the author's attitude towards the events in the story? The author's voice seems quite detached and remote. Is it?

5. How do you, as a reader, bring together two of the apparent themes of the story—that of love in a difficult and awkward situation, and that of the aging of an individual? Are the two themes related?

Edith Wharton (1862–1937)
Roman Fever

1

From the table at which they had been lunching two American ladies of ripe but well-cared-for middle age moved across the lofty terrace of the Roman restaurant and, leaning on its parapet, looked first at each other, and then down on the outspread glories of the Palatine and the Forum, with the same expression of vague but benevolent approval.

As they leaned there a girlish voice echoed up gaily from the stairs leading to the court below. "Well, come along, then," it cried, not to them but to an invisible companion, "and let's leave the young things to their knitting"; and a voice as fresh laughed back: "Oh, look here, Babs, not actually *knitting*—" "Well, I mean figuratively," rejoined the first. "After all, we haven't left our poor parents much else to do. . ." and at that point the turn of the stairs engulfed the dialogue.

The two ladies looked at each other again, this time with a tinge of smiling embarrassment, and the smaller and paler one shook her head and coloured slightly.

"Barbara!" she murmured, sending an unheard rebuke after the mocking voice in the stairway.

The other lady, who was fuller, and higher in colour, with a small determined nose supported by vigorous black eyebrows, gave a good-humoured laugh. "That's what our daughters think of us!"

Her companion replied by a deprecating gesture. "Not of us individually. We must remember that. It's just the collective modern idea of Mothers. And you see—" Half guiltily she drew from her handsomely mounted black hand-bag a twist of crimson silk run through by two fine knitting needles. "One never knows," she murmured. "The new system has certainly given us a

good deal of time to kill; and sometimes I get tired just looking—even at this."
Her gesture was now addressed to the stupendous scene at their feet.

The dark lady laughed again, and they both relapsed upon the view,
contemplating it in silence, with a sort of diffused serenity which might have
been borrowed from the spring effulgence of the Roman skies. The luncheon-
hour was long past, and the two had their end of the vast terrace to themselves. At its opposite extremity a few groups, detained by a lingering look at
the outspread city, were gathering up guide-books and fumbling for tips. The
last of them scattered, and the two ladies were alone on the air-washed height.

"Well, I don't see why we shouldn't just stay here," said Mrs. Slade, the
lady of the high colour and energetic brows. Two derelict basket-chairs stood
near, and she pushed them into the angle of the parapet, and settled herself in
one, her gaze upon the Palatine. "After all, it's still the most beautiful view in
the world."

"It always will be, to me," assented her friend Mrs. Ansley, with so slight a
stress on the "me" that Mrs. Slade, though she noticed it, wondered if it were
not merely accidental, like the random underlinings of old-fashioned letter-
writers.

"Grace Ansley was always old-fashioned," she thought; and added aloud,
with a retrospective smile: "It's a view we've both been familiar with for a good
many years. When we first met here we were younger than our girls are now.
You remember?"

"Oh, yes, I remember," murmured Mrs. Ansley, with the same unde-
finable stress.— "There's that head-waiter wondering," she interpolated. She
was evidently far less sure than her companion of herself and of her rights in
the world.

"I'll cure him of wondering," said Mrs. Slade, stretching her hand toward
a bag as discreetly opulent-looking as Mrs. Ansley's. Signing to the head-
waiter, she explained that she and her friend were old lovers of Rome, and
would like to spend the end of the afternoon looking down on the view—that
is, if it did not disturb the service? The head-waiter, bowing over her gratuity,
assured her that the ladies were most welcome, and would be still more so if
they would condescend to remain for dinner. A full moon night, they would
remember. . .

Mrs. Slade's black brows drew together, as though references to the moon
were out-of-place and even unwelcome. But she smiled away her frown as the
head-waiter retreated. "Well, why not? We might do worse. There's no
knowing, I suppose, when the girls will be back. Do you even know back from
where? I don't!"

Mrs. Ansley again coloured slightly. "I think those young Italian aviators
we met at the Embassy invited them to fly to Tarquinia for tea. I suppose
they'll want to wait and fly back by moonlight."

"Moonlight—moonlight! What a part it still plays. Do you suppose
they're as sentimental as we were?"

"I've come to the conclusion that I don't in the least know what they are,"
said Mrs. Ansley. "And perhaps we didn't know much more about each
other."

Edith Wharton 297

"No; perhaps we didn't."

Her friend gave her a shy glance. "I never should have supposed you were sentimental, Alida."

"Well, perhaps I wasn't." Mrs. Slade drew her lids together in retrospect; and for a few moments the two ladies, who had been intimate since childhood, reflected how little they knew each other. Each one, of course, had a label ready to attach to the other's name; Mrs. Delphin Slade, for instance, would have told herself, or any one who asked her, that Mrs. Horace Ansley, twenty-five years ago, had been exquisitely lovely—no, you wouldn't believe it, would you? . . . though, of course, still charming, distinguished. . . Well, as a girl she had been exquisite; far more beautiful than her daughter Barbara, though certainly Babs, according to the new standards at any rate, was more effective—had more *edge*, as they say. Funny where she got it, with those two nullities as parents. Yes; Horace Ansley was—well, just the duplicate of his wife. Museum specimens of old New York. Good-looking, irreproachable, exemplary. Mrs. Slade and Mrs. Ansley had lived opposite each other— actually as well as figuratively—for years. When the drawing-room curtains in No. 20 East 73rd Street were renewed, No. 23, across the way, was always aware of it. And of all the movings, buyings, travels, anniversaries, illnesses—the tame chronicle of an estimable pair. Little of it escaped Mrs. Slade. But she had grown bored with it by the time her husband made his big *coup* in Wall Street, and when they bought in upper Park Avenue had already begun to think: "I'd rather live opposite a speak-easy for a change; at least one might see it raided." The idea of seeing Grace raided was so amusing that (before the move) she launched it at a woman's lunch. It made a hit, and went the rounds—she sometimes wondered if it had crossed the street, and reached Mrs. Ansley. She hoped not, but didn't much mind. Those were the days when respectability was at a discount, and it did the irreproachable no harm to laugh at them a little.

A few years later, and not many months apart, both ladies lost their husbands. There was an appropriate exchange of wreaths and condolences, and a brief renewal of intimacy in the half-shadow of their mourning; and now, after another interval, they had run across each other in Rome, at the same hotel, each of them the modest appendage of a salient daughter. The similarity of their lot had again drawn them together, lending itself to mild jokes, and the mutual confession that, if in old days it must have been tiring to "keep up" with daughters, it was now, at times, a little dull not to.

No doubt, Mrs. Slade reflected, she felt her unemployment more than poor Grace ever would. It was a big drop from being the wife of Delphin Slade to being his widow. She had always regarded herself (with a certain conjugal pride) as his equal in social gifts, as contributing her full share to the making of the exceptional couple they were: but the difference after his death was irremediable. As the wife of the famous corporation lawyer, always with an international case or two on hand, every day brought its exciting and unexpected obligation: the impromptu entertaining of eminent colleagues from abroad, the hurried dashes on legal business to London, Paris or Rome, where the entertaining was so handsomely reciprocated; the amusement of hearing in her wake: "What, that handsome woman with the good clothes and the eyes is Mrs. Slade—*the* Slade's wife? Really? Generally the wives of celebrities are such frumps."

Yes; being *the* Slade's widow was a dullish business after that. In living up to such a husband all her faculties had been engaged; now she had only her daughter to live up to, for the son who seemed to have inherited his father's gifts had died suddenly in boyhood. She had fought through that agony because her husband was there, to be helped and to help; now, after the father's death, the thought of the boy had become unbearable. There was nothing left but to mother her daughter; and dear Jenny was such a perfect daughter that she needed no excessive mothering. "Now with Babs Ansley I don't know that I *should* be so quiet," Mrs. Slade sometimes half-enviously reflected; but Jenny, who was younger than her brilliant friend, was that rare accident, an extremely pretty girl who somehow made youth and prettiness seem as safe as their absence. It was all perplexing—and to Mrs. Slade a little boring. She wished that Jenny would fall in love—with the wrong man, even; that she might have to be watched, out-manoeuvred, rescued. And instead, it was Jenny who watched her mother, kept her out of draughts, made sure that she had taken her tonic. . .

Mrs. Ansley was much less articulate than her friend, and her mental portrait of Mrs. Slade was slighter, and drawn with fainter touches. "Alida Slade's awfully brilliant; but not as brilliant as she thinks," would have summed it up; though she would have added, for the enlightenment of strangers, that Mrs. Slade had been an extremely dashing girl; much more so than her daughter, who was pretty, of course, and clever in a way, but had none of her mother's—well, "vividness", some one had once called it. Mrs. Ansley would take up current words like this, and cite them in quotation marks, as unheard-of audacities. No; Jenny was not like her mother. Sometimes Mrs. Ansley thought Alida Slade was disappointed; on the whole she had had a sad life. Full of failures and mistakes; Mrs. Ansley had always been rather sorry for her. . .

So these two ladies visualized each other, each through the wrong end of her little telescope.

2

For a long time they continued to sit side by side without speaking. It seemed as though, to both, there was a relief in laying down their somewhat futile activities in the presence of the vast Memento Mori which faced them. Mrs. Slade sat quite still, her eyes fixed on the golden slope of the Palace of the Cæsars, and after a while Mrs. Ansley ceased to fidget with her bag, and she too sank into meditation. Like many intimate friends, the two ladies had never before had occasion to be silent together, and Mrs. Ansley was slightly embarrassed by what seemed, after so many years, a new stage in their intimacy, and one with which she did not yet know how to deal.

Suddenly the air was full of the deep clangour of bells which periodically covers Rome with a roof of silver. Mrs. Slade glanced at her wrist-watch. "Five o'clock already," she said, as though surprised.

Mrs. Ansley suggested interrogatively: "There's bridge at the Embassy at five." For a long time Mrs. Slade did not answer. She appeared to be lost in contemplation, and Mrs. Ansley thought the remark had escaped her. But after a while she said, as if speaking out of a dream: "Bridge, did you say? Not unless you want to. . . But I don't think I will, you know."

"Oh, no," Mrs. Ansley hastened to assure her. "I don't care to at all. It's so lovely here; and so full of old memories, as you say." She settled herself in her chair, and almost furtively drew forth her knitting. Mrs. Slade took sideway note of this activity, but her own beautifully cared-for hands remained motionless on her knee.

"I was just thinking," she said slowly, "what different things Rome stands for to each generation of travellers. To our grandmothers, Roman fever; to our mothers, sentimental dangers—how we used to be guarded!—to our daughters, no more dangers than the middle of Main Street. They don't know it—but how much they're missing!"

The long golden light was beginning to pale, and Mrs. Ansley lifted her knitting a little closer to her eyes. "Yes; how we were guarded!"

"I always used to think," Mrs. Slade continued, "that our mothers had a much more difficult job than our grandmothers. When Roman fever stalked the streets it must have been comparatively easy to gather in the girls at the danger hour; but when you and I were young, with such beauty calling us, and the spice of disobedience thrown in, and no worse risk than catching cold during the cool hour after sunset, the mothers used to be put to it to keep us in—didn't they?"

She turned again toward Mrs. Ansley, but the latter had reached a delicate point in her knitting. "One, two, three—slip two; yes, they must have been," she assented, without looking up.

Mrs. Slade's eyes rested on her with a deepened attention. "She can knit—in the face of *this!* How like her. . ."

Mrs. Slade leaned back, brooding, her eyes ranging from the ruins which faced her to the long green hollow of the Forum, the fading glow of the church fronts beyond it, and the outlying immensity of the Colosseum. Suddenly she thought: "It's all very well to say that our girls have done away with sentiment and moonlight. But if Babs Ansley isn't out to catch that young aviator—the one who's a Marchese—then I don't know anything. And Jenny has no chance beside her. I know that too. I wonder if that's why Grace Ansley likes the two girls to go everywhere together? My poor Jenny as a foil—!" Mrs. Slade gave a hardly audible laugh, and at the sound Mrs. Ansley dropped her knitting.

"Yes—?"

"I—oh, nothing. I was only thinking how your Babs carries everything before her. That Campolieri boy is one of the best matches in Rome. Don't look so innocent, my dear—you know he is. And I was wondering, ever so respectfully, you understand . . . wondering how two such exemplary characters as you and Horace had managed to produce anything quite so dynamic." Mrs. Slade laughed again, with a touch of asperity.

Mrs. Ansley's hands lay inert across her needles. She looked straight out at the great accumulated wreckage of passion and splendour at her feet. But her small profile was almost expressionless. At length she said: "I think you overrate Babs, my dear."

Mrs. Slade's tone grew easier. "No; I don't. I appreciate her. And perhaps envy you. Oh, my girl's perfect; if I were a chronic invalid I'd—well, I think I'd rather be in Jenny's hands. There must be times . . . but there! I always wanted a brilliant daughter . . . and never quite understood why I got an angel instead."

Mrs. Ansley echoed her laugh in a faint murmur. "Babs is an angel too."

"Of course—of course! But she's got rainbow wings. Well, they're wandering by the sea with their young men; and here we sit . . . and it all brings back the past a little too acutely."

Mrs. Ansley had resumed her knitting. One might almost have imagined (if one had known here less well, Mrs. Slade reflected) that, for her also, too many memories rose from the lengthening shadows of those august ruins. But no; she was simply absorbed in her work. What was there for her to worry about? She knew that Babs would almost certainly come back engaged to the extremely eligible Campolieri. "And she'll sell the New York house, and settle down near them in Rome, and never be in their way . . . she's much too tactful. But she'll have an excellent cook, and just the right people in for bridge and cocktails . . . and a perfectly peaceful old age among her grandchildren."

Mrs. Slade broke off this prophetic flight with a recoil of self-disgust. There was no one of whom she had less right to think undkindly than of Grace Ansley. Would she never cure herself of envying her? Perhaps she had begun too long ago.

She stood up and leaned against the parapet, filling her troubled eyes with the tranquillizing magic of the hour. But instead of tranquillizing her the sight seemed to increase her exasperation. Her gaze turned toward the Colosseum. Already its golden flank was drowned in purple shadow, and above it the sky curved crystal clear, without light or colour. It was the moment when afternoon and evening hang balanced in mid-heaven.

Mrs. Slade turned back and laid her hand on her friend's arm. The gesture was so abrupt that Mrs. Ansley looked up, startled.

"The sun's set. You're not afraid, my dear?"

"Afraid—?"

"Of Roman fever or pneumonia? I remember how ill you were that winter. As a girl you had a very delicate throat, hadn't you?"

"Oh, we're all right up here. Down below, in the Forum, it does get deathly cold, all of a sudden . . . but not here."

"Ah, of course you know because you had to be so careful." Mrs. Slade turned back to the parapet. She thought: "I must make one more effort not to hate her." Aloud she said: "Whenever I look at the Forum from up here, I remember that story about a great-aunt of yours, wasn't she? A dreadfully wicked great-aunt?"

"Oh, yes; Great-aunt Harriet. The one who was supposed to have sent her young sister out to the Forum after sunset to gather a night-blooming flower for her album. All our great-aunts and grandmothers used to have albums of dried flowers."

Mrs. Slade nodded. "But she really sent her because they were in love with the same man—"

"Well, that was the family tradition. They said Aunt Harriet confessed it years afterward. At any rate, the poor little sister caught the fever and died. Mother used to frighten us with the story when we were children."

"And you frightened *me* with it, that winter when you and I were here as girls. The winter I was engaged to Delphin."

Mrs. Ansley gave a faint laugh. "Oh, did I? Really frightened you? I don't believe you're easily frightened."

"Not often; but I was then. I was easily frightened because I was too happy. I wonder if you know what that means?"

"I—yes . . ." Mrs. Ansley faltered.

"Well, I suppose that was why the story of your wicked aunt made such an impression on me. And I thought: 'There's no more Roman fever, but the Forum is deathly cold after sunset—especially after a hot day. And the Colosseum's even colder and damper'."

"The Colosseum—?"

"Yes. It wasn't easy to get in, after the gates were locked for the night. Far from easy. Still, in those days it could be managed; it *was* managed, often. Lovers met there who couldn't meet elsewhere. You knew that?"

"I—I daresay. I don't remember."

"You don't remember? You don't remember going to visit some ruins or other one evening, just after dark, and catching a bad chill? You were supposed to have gone to see the moon rise. People always said that expedition was what caused your illness."

There was a moment's silence; then Mrs. Ansley rejoined: "Did they? It was all so long ago."

"Yes. And you got well again—so it didn't matter. But I suppose it struck your friends—the reason given for your illness, I mean—because everybody knew you were so prudent on account of your throat, and your mother took such care of you. . . You *had* been out late sight-seeing, hadn't you, that night?"

"Perhaps I had. The most prudent girls aren't always prudent. What made you think of it now?"

Mrs. Slade seemed to have no answer ready. But after a moment she broke out: "Because I simply can't bear it any longer—!"

Mrs. Ansley lifted her head quickly. Her eyes were wide and very pale. "Can't bear what?"

"Why—your not knowing that I've always known why you went."

"Why I went—?"

"Yes. You think I'm bluffing, don't you? Well, you went to meet the man I was engaged to—and I can repeat every word of the letter that took you there."

While Mrs. Slade spoke Mrs. Ansley had risen unsteadily to her feet. Her bag, her knitting and gloves, slid in a panic-stricken heap to the ground. She looked at Mrs. Slade as though she were looking at a ghost.

"No, no—don't," she faltered out.

"Why not? Listen, if you don't believe me. 'My one darling, things can't go on like this. I must see you alone. Come to the Colosseum immediately after dark tomorrow. There will be somebody to let you in. No one whom you need fear will suspect'—but perhaps you've forgotten what the letter said?"

Mrs. Ansley met the challenge with an unexpected composure. Steadying herself against the chair she looked at her friend, and replied: "No; I know it by heart too."

"And the signature? 'Only *your* D.S.' Was that it? I'm right, am I? That was the letter that took you out that evening after dark?"

Mrs. Ansley was still looking at her. It seemed to Mrs. Slade that a slow struggle was going on behind the voluntarily controlled mask of her small quiet face. "I shouldn't have thought she had herself so well in hand," Mrs. Slade reflected, almost resentfully. But at this moment Mrs. Ansley spoke. "I don't know how you knew. I burnt that letter at once."

"Yes; you would, naturally—you're so prudent!" The sneer was open now. "And if you burnt the letter you're wondering how on earth I know what was in it. That's it, isn't it?"

Mrs. Slade waited, but Mrs. Ansley did not speak.

"Well, my dear, I know what was in that letter because I wrote it!"

"You wrote it?"

"Yes."

The two women stood for a minute staring at each other in the last golden light. Then Mrs. Ansley dropped back into her chair. "Oh," she murmured, and covered her face with her hands.

Mrs. Slade waited nervously for another word or movement. None came, and at length she broke out: "I horrify you."

Mrs. Ansley's hands dropped to her knee. The face they uncovered was streaked with tears. "I wasn't thinking of you. I was thinking—it was the only letter I ever had from him!"

"And I wrote it. Yes; I wrote it! But I was the girl he was engaged to. Did you happen to remember that?"

Mrs. Ansley's head drooped again. "I'm not trying to excuse myself. . . I remembered. . ."

"And still you went?"

"Still I went."

Mrs. Slade stood looking down on the small bowed figure at her side. The flame of her wrath had already sunk, and she wondered why she had ever thought there would be any satisfaction in inflicting so purposeless a wound on her friend. But she had to justify herself.

"You do understand? I'd found out—and I hated you, hated you. I knew you were in love with Delphin—and I was afraid; afraid of you, of your quiet ways, your sweetness . . . your . . . well, I wanted you out of the way, that's all. Just for a few weeks; just till I was sure of him. So in a blind fury I wrote that letter. . . I don't know why I'm telling you now."

"I suppose," said Mrs. Ansley slowly, "it's because you've always gone on hating me."

"Perhaps. Or because I wanted to get the whole thing off my mind." She paused. "I'm glad you destroyed the letter. Of course I never thought you'd die."

Mrs. Ansley relapsed into silence, and Mrs. Slade, leaning above her, was conscious of a strange sense of isolation, of being cut off from the warm current of human communion. "You think me a monster!"

"I don't know. . . It was the only letter I had, and you say he didn't write it?"

"Ah, how you care for him still!"

"I cared for that memory," said Mrs. Ansley.

Mrs. Slade continued to look down on her. She seemed physically reduced by the blow—as if, when she got up, the wind might scatter her like a puff of dust. Mrs. Slade's jealousy suddenly leapt up again at the sight. All these years the woman had been living on that letter. How she must have loved him, to treasure the mere memory of its ashes! The letter of the man her friend was engaged to. Wasn't it she who was the monster?

"You tried your best to get him away from me, didn't you? But you failed; and I kept him. That's all."

"Yes. That's all."

"I wish now I hadn't told you. I'd no idea you'd feel about it as you do; I thought you'd be amused. It all happened so long ago, as you say; and you must do me the justice to remember that I had no reason to think you'd ever taken it seriously. How could I, when you were married to Horace Ansley two months afterward? As soon as you could get out of bed your mother rushed you off to Florence and married you. People were rather surprised—they wondered at its being done so quickly; but I thought I knew. I had an idea you did it out of *pique*—to be able to say you'd got ahead of Delphin and me. Girls have such silly reasons for doing the most serious things. And your marrying so soon convinced me that you'd never really cared."

"Yes. I suppose it would," Mrs. Ansley assented.

The clear heaven overhead was emptied of all its gold. Dusk spread over it, abruptly darkening the Seven Hills. Here and there lights began to twinkle through the foliage at their feet. Steps were coming and going on the deserted terrace—waiters looking out of the doorway at the head of the stairs, then reappearing with trays and napkins and flasks of wine. Tables were moved, chairs straightened. A feeble string of electric lights flickered out. Some vases of faded flowers were carried away, and brought back replenished. A stout lady in a dust-coat suddenly appeared, asking in broken Italian if any one had seen the elastic band which held together her tattered Baedeker. She poked with her stick under the table at which she had lunched, the waiters assisting.

The corner where Mrs. Slade and Mrs. Ansley sat was still shadowy and deserted. For a long time neither of them spoke. At length Mrs. Slade began again: "I suppose I did it as a sort of joke—"

"A joke?"

"Well, girls are ferocious sometimes, you know. Girls in love especially. And I remember laughing to myself all that evening at the idea that you were waiting around there in the dark, dodging out of sight, listening for every sound, trying to get in—. Of course I was upset when I heard you were so ill afterward."

Mrs. Ansley had not moved for a long time. But now she turned slowly toward her companion. "But I didn't wait. He'd arranged everything. He was there. We were let in at once," she said.

Mrs. Slade sprang up from her leaning position. "Delphin there? They let you in?— Ah, now you're lying!" she burst out with violence.

Mrs. Ansley's voice grew clearer, and full of surprise. "But of course he was there. Naturally he came—"

"Came? How did he know he'd find you there? You must be raving!"

Mrs. Ansley hesitated, as though reflecting. "But I answered the letter. I told him I'd be there. So he came."

Mrs. Slade flung her hands up to her face. "Oh, God—you answered! I never thought of your answering. . ."

"It's odd you never thought of it, if you wrote the letter."

"Yes. I was blind with rage."

Mrs. Ansley rose, and drew her fur scarf about her. "It is cold here. We'd better go. . . I'm sorry for you," she said, as she clasped the fur about her throat.

The unexpected words sent a pang through Mrs. Slade. "Yes; we'd better go." She gathered up her bag and cloak. "I don't know why you should be sorry for me," she muttered.

Mrs. Ansley stood looking away from her toward the dusky secret mass of the Colosseum. "Well—because I didn't have to wait that night."

Mrs. Slade gave an unquiet laugh. "Yes; I was beaten there. But I oughtn't to begrudge it to you, I suppose. At the end of all these years. After all, I had everything; I had him for twenty-five years. And you had nothing but that one letter that he didn't write."

Mrs. Ansley was again silent. At length she turned toward the door of the terrace. She took a step, and turned back, facing her companion.

"I had Barbara," she said, and began to move ahead of Mrs. Slade toward the stairway.

QUESTIONS

1. You will note that a great deal of this story consists of conversation. Why? What advantages as an author does Edith Wharton derive from placing so much emphasis on dialogue?

2. When the narrator says, at the end of the first section, that "Mrs. Ansley had always been rather sorry" for Alida Slade, the phrase is not an accurate and full description of Mrs. Ansley's attitude towards her companion. What does the narrator leave out, or seem ignorant about? Why doesn't the narrator seem in command of the whole truth of the relationship?

3. What is the importance to the story of the two unseen daughters of the two traveling companions? What importance do the respective mothers give them?

4. Which of the two women has gained the position of emotional superiority as the story suddenly comes to an end? What does her superiority amount to?

5. Does the story gain any force or depth by being given the Roman locale? Or is its geographical place merely incidental?

James Joyce (1882–1941)
Counterparts

The bell rang furiously and, when Miss Parker went to the tube, a furious voice called out in a piercing North of Ireland accent:

—Send Farrington here!

Miss Parker returned to her machine, saying to a man who was writing at a desk:

—Mr Alleyne wants you upstairs.

The man muttered *Blast him!* under his breath and pushed back his chair to stand up. When he stood up he was tall and of great bulk. He had a hanging face, dark wine-coloured, with fair eyebrows and moustache: his eyes bulged forward slightly and the whites of them were dirty. He lifted up the counter and, passing by the clients, went out of the office with a heavy step.

He went heavily upstairs until he came to the second landing, where a door bore a brass plate with the inscription *Mr Alleyne.* Here he halted, puffing with labour and vexation, and knocked. The shrill voice cried:

—Come in!

The man entered Mr Alleyne's room. Simultaneously Mr Alleyne, a little man wearing gold-rimmed glasses on a clean-shaven face, shot his head up over a pile of documents. The head itself was so pink and hairless that it seemed like a large egg reposing on the papers. Mr Alleyne did not lose a moment:

—Farrington? What is the meaning of this? Why have I always to complain of you? May I ask you why you haven't made a copy of that contract between Bodley and Kirwan? I told you it must be ready by four o'clock.

—But Mr Shelley said, sir—

—*Mr Shelley said, sir.* . . . Kindly attend to what I say and not to what *Mr Shelley says,* sir. You have always some excuse or another for shirking work. Let me tell you that if the contract is not copied before this evening I'll lay the matter before Mr Crosbie. . . . Do you hear me now?

—Yes, sir.

—Do you hear me now? . . . Ay and another little matter! I might as well be talking to the wall as talking to you. Understand once for all that you get a half an hour for your lunch and not an hour and a half. How many courses do you want, I'd like to know. . . . Do you mind me, now?

—Yes, sir.

Mr Alleyne bent his head again upon his pile of papers. The man stared fixedly at the polished skull which directed the affairs of Crosbie & Alleyne, gauging its fragility. A spasm of rage gripped his throat for a few moments and then passed, leaving after it a sharp sensation of thirst. The man recognized the sensation and felt that he must have a good night's drinking. The middle of the month was passed and, if he could get the copy done in time, Mr Alleyne might give him an order on the cashier. He stood still, gazing fixedly at the head upon the pile of papers. Suddenly Mr Alleyne began to upset all the papers, searching for something. Then, as if he had been unaware of the man's presence till that moment, he shot up his head again, saying:

—Eh? Are you going to stand there all day? Upon my word, Farrington, you take things easy!

—I was waiting to see . . .

—Very good, you needn't wait to see. Go downstairs and do your work.

The man walked heavily towards the door and, as he went out of the room, he heard Mr Alleyne cry after him that if the contract was not copied by evening Mr Crosbie would hear of the matter.

He returned to his desk in the lower office and counted the sheets which remained to be copied. He took up his pen and dipped it in the ink but he continued to stare stupidly at the last words he had written: *In no case shall the said Bernard Bodley be* . . . The evening was falling and in a few minutes they would be lighting the gas: then he could write. He felt that he must slake the thirst in his throat. He stood up from his desk and, lifting the counter as before, passed out of the office. As he was passing out the chief clerk looked at him inquiringly.

—It's all right, Mr Shelley, said the man, pointing with his finger to indicate the objective of his journey.

The chief clerk glanced at the hat-rack but, seeing the row complete, offered no remark. As soon as he was on the landing the man pulled a shepherd's plaid cap out of his pocket, put it on his head and ran quickly down the rickety stairs. From the street door he walked on furtively on the inner side of the path towards the corner and all at once dived into a doorway. He was now safe in the dark snug of O'Neill's shop, and, filling up the little window that looked into the bar with his inflamed face, the colour of dark wine or dark meat, he called out:

—Here, Pat, give us a g.p., like a good fellow.

The curate brought him a glass of plain porter. The man drank it at a gulp and asked for a caraway seed. He put his penny on the counter and, leaving the curate to grope for it in the gloom, retreated out of the snug as furtively as he had entered it.

Darkness, accompanied by a thick fog, was gaining upon the dusk of February and the lamps in Eustace Street had been lit. The man went up by the houses until he reached the door of the office, wondering whether he could finish his copy in time. On the stairs a moist pungent odour of perfumes saluted his nose: evidently Miss Delacour had come while he was out in O'Neill's. He crammed his cap back again into his pocket and re-entered the office, assuming an air of absent-mindedness.

—Mr Alleyne has been calling for you, said the chief clerk severely. Where were you?

The man glanced at the two clients who were standing at the counter as if to intimate that their presence prevented him from answering. As the clients were both male the chief clerk allowed himself a laugh.

—I know that game, he said. Five times in one day is a little bit. . . . Well, you better look sharp and get a copy of our correspondence in the Delacour case for Mr Alleyne.

This address in the presence of the public, his run upstairs and the porter he had gulped down so hastily confused the man and, as he sat down at his desk to get what was required, he realized how hopeless was the task of finishing his copy of the contract before half past five. The dark damp night was coming and he longed to spend it in the bars, drinking with his friends amid the glare of gas and the clatter of glasses. He got out the Delacour correspondence and passed out of the office. He hoped Mr Alleyne would not discover that the last two letters were missing.

The moist pungent perfume lay all the way up to Mr Alleyne's room. Miss Delacour was a middle-aged woman of Jewish appearance. Mr Alleyne was said to be sweet on her or on her money. She came to the office often and stayed a long time when she came. She was sitting beside his desk now in an aroma of perfumes, smoothing the handle of her umbrella and nodding the great black feather in her hat. Mr Alleyne had swivelled his chair round to face her and thrown his right foot jauntily upon his left knee. The man put the correspondence on the desk and bowed respectfully but neither Mr Alleyne nor Miss Delacour took any notice of his bow. Mr Alleyne tapped a finger on the correspondence and then flicked it towards him as if to say: *That's all right: you can go.*

The man returned to the lower office and sat down again at his desk. He stared intently at the incomplete phrase: *In no case shall the said Bernard Bodley be* . . . and thought how strange it was that the last three words began with the same letter. The chief clerk began to hurry Miss Parker, saying she would never have the letters typed in time for post. The man listened to the clicking of the machine for a few minutes and then set to work to finish his copy. But his head was not clear and his mind wandered away to the glare and rattle of the public-house. It was a night for hot punches. He struggled on with his copy, but when the clock struck five he had still fourteen pages to write. Blast it! He couldn't finish it in time. He longed to execrate aloud, to bring his fist down on something violently. He was so enraged that he wrote *Bernard Bernard* instead of *Bernard Bodley* and had to begin again on a clean sheet.

He felt strong enough to clear out the whole office single-handed. His body ached to do something, to rush out and revel in violence. All the indignities of his life enraged him. . . . Could he ask the cashier privately for an advance? No, the cashier was no good, no damn good: he wouldn't give an advance. . . . He knew where he would meet the boys: Leonard and O'Halloran and Nosey Flynn. The barometer of his emotional nature was set for a spell of riot.

His imagination had so abstracted him that his name was called twice before he answered. Mr Alleyne and Miss Delacour were standing outside the counter and all the clerks had turned round in anticipation of something. The man got up from his desk. Mr Alleyne began a tirade of abuse, saying that two letters were missing. The man answered that he knew nothing about them, that he had made a faithful copy. The tirade continued: it was so bitter and violent that the man could hardly restrain his fist from descending upon the head of the manikin before him.

—I know nothing about any other two letters, he said stupidly.

—*You—know—nothing.* Of course you know nothing, said Mr Alleyne. Tell me, he added, glancing first for approval to the lady beside him, do you take me for a fool? Do you think me an utter fool?

The man glanced from the lady's face to the little egg-shaped head and back again; and, almost before he was aware of it, his tongue had found a felicitous moment:

—I don't think, sir, he said, that that's a fair question to put to me.

There was a pause in the very breathing of the clerks. Everyone was astounded (the author of the witticism no less than his neighbours) and Miss Delacour, who was a stout amiable person, began to smile broadly. Mr Alleyne flushed to the hue of a wild rose and his mouth twitched with a dwarf's passion. He shook his fist in the man's face till it seemed to vibrate like the knob of some electric machine:

—You impertinent ruffian! You impertinent ruffian! I'll make short work of you! Wait till you see! You'll apologize to me for your impertinence or you'll quit the office instanter! You'll quit this, I'm telling you, or you'll apologize to me!

He stood in a doorway opposite the office watching to see if the cashier would come out alone. All the clerks passed out and finally the cashier came out with the chief clerk. It was no use trying to say a word to him when he was with the chief clerk. The man felt that his position was bad enough. He had been obliged to offer an abject apology to Mr Alleyne for his impertinence but he knew what a hornet's nest the office would be for him. He could remember the way in which Mr Alleyne had hounded little Peake out of the office in order to make room for his own nephew. He felt savage and thirsty and revengeful, annoyed with himself and with everyone else. Mr Alleyne would never give him an hour's rest; his life would be a hell to him. He had made a proper fool of himself this time. Could he not keep his tongue in his cheek? But they had never pulled together from the first, he and Mr Alleyne, ever since the day Mr Alleyne had overheard him mimicking his North of Ireland accent to amuse Higgins and Miss Parker: that had been the beginning of it. He might have tried Higgins for the money, but sure Higgins never had anything for himself. A man with two establishments to keep up, of course he couldn't . . . .

He felt his great body again aching for the comfort of the public-house. The fog had begun to chill him and he wondered could he touch Pat in O'Neill's. He could not touch him for more than a bob—and a bob was no use. Yet he must get money somewhere or other: he had spent his last penny for the g.p. and soon it would be too late for getting money anywhere. Suddenly, as he was fingering his watch-chain, he thought of Terry Kelly's pawn-office in Fleet Street. That was the dart! Why didn't he think of it sooner?

He went through the narrow alley of Temple Bar quickly, muttering to himself that they could all go to hell because he was going to have a good night of it. The clerk in Terry Kelly's said *A crown!* but the consignor held out for six shillings; and in the end the six shillings was allowed him literally. He came out of the pawn-office joyfully, making a little cylinder of the coins between his thumb and fingers. In Westmoreland Street the footpaths were crowded with young men and women returning from business and ragged urchins ran here and there yelling out the names of the evening editions. The man passed through the crowd, looking on the spectacle generally with proud satisfaction and staring masterfully at the office-girls. His head was full of the noises of tram-gongs and swishing trolleys and his nose already sniffed the curling fumes of punch. As he walked on he preconsidered the terms in which he would narrate the incident to the boys:

—So, I just looked at him—coolly, you know, and looked at her. Then I looked back at him again—taking my time, you know. *I don't think that that's a fair question to put to me,* says I.

Nosey Flynn was sitting up in his usual corner of Davy Bryne's and, when he heard the story, he stood Farrington a half-one, saying it was as smart a thing as ever he heard. Farrington stood a drink in his turn. After a while O'Halloran and Paddy Leonard came in and the story was repeated to them. O'Halloran stood tailors of malt, hot, all round and told the story of the retort he had made to the chief clerk when he was in Callan's of Fownes's Street; but, as the retort was after the manner of the liberal shepherds in the eclogues, he had to admit that it was not so clever as Farrington's retort. At this Farrington told the boys to polish off that and have another.

Just as they were naming their poisons who should come in but Higgins! Of course he had to join in with the others. The men asked him to give his version of it, and he did so with great vivacity for the sight of five small hot whiskies was very exhilarating. Everyone roared laughing when he showed the way in which Mr Alleyne shook his fist in Farrington's face. Then he imitated Farrington, saying, *And here was my nabs, as cool as you please,* while Farrington looked at the company out of his heavy dirty eyes, smiling and at times drawing forth stray drops of liquor from his moustache with the aid of his lower lip.

When that round was over there was a pause. O'Halloran had money but neither of the other two seemed to have any; so the whole party left the shop somewhat regretfully. At the corner of Duke Street Higgins and Nosey Flynn bevelled off to the left while the other three turned back towards the city. Rain was drizzling down on the cold streets and, when they reached the Ballast Office, Farrington suggested the Scotch House. The bar was full of men and loud with the noise of tongues and glasses. The three men pushed past the whining match-sellers at the door and formed a little party at the corner of the counter. They began to exchange stories. Leonard introduced them to a young fellow named Weathers who was performing at the Tivoli as an acrobat and knock-about *artiste*. Farrington stood a drink all round. Weathers said he would take a small Irish and Apollinaris. Farrington, who had definite notions of what was what, asked the boys would they have an Apollinaris too; but the boys told Tim to make theirs hot. The talk became theatrical. O'Halloran stood a round and then Farrington stood another round, Weathers protesting that the hospitality was too Irish. He promised to get them in behind the scenes and introduce them to some nice girls. O'Halloran said that he and Leonard would go but that Farrington wouldn't go because he was a married man; and Farrington's heavy dirty eyes leered at the company in token that he understood he was being chaffed. Weathers made them all have just one little tincture at his expense and promised to meet them later on at Mulligan's in Poolbeg Street.

When the Scotch House closed they went round to Mulligan's. They went into the parlour at the back and O'Halloran ordered small hot specials all round. They were all beginning to feel mellow. Farrington was just standing another round when Weathers came back. Much to Farrington's relief he drank a glass of bitter this time. Funds were running low but they had enough to keep them going. Presently two young women with big hats and a young man in a check suit came in and sat at a table close by. Weathers saluted them and told the company that they were out of the Tivoli. Farrington's eyes wandered at every moment in the direction of one of the young women. There was something striking in her appearance. An immense scarf of peacock-blue muslin was wound round her hat and knotted in a great bow under her chin; and she wore bright yellow gloves, reaching to the elbow. Farrington gazed admiringly at the plump arm which she moved very often and with much grace; and when, after a little time, she answered his gaze he admired still more her large dark brown eyes. The oblique staring expression in them fascinated him. She glanced at him once or twice and, when the party was leaving the room, she brushed against his chair and said *O, pardon!* in a London accent. He watched her leave the room in the hope that she would look back at him, but he was disappointed. He cursed his want of money and cursed all the rounds he had stood, particularly all the whiskies and Apollinaris which he had stood to Weathers. If there was one thing that he hated it was a sponge. He was so angry that he lost count of the conversation of his friends.

When Paddy Leonard called him he found that they were talking about feats of strength. Weathers was showing his biceps muscle to the company and boasting so much that the other two had called on Farrington to uphold the national honour. Farrington pulled up his sleeve accordingly and showed his biceps muscle to the company. The two arms were examined and compared and finally it was agreed to have a trial of strength. The table was cleared and the two men rested their elbows on it, clasping hands. When Paddy Leonard said *Go!* each was to try to bring down the other's hand on to the table. Farrington looked very serious and determined.

The trial began. After about thirty seconds Weathers brought his opponent's hand slowly down on to the table. Farrington's dark wine-coloured face flushed darker still with anger and humiliation at having been defeated by such a stripling.

—You're not to put the weight of your body behind it. Play fair, he said.

—Who's not playing fair? said the other.

—Come on again. The two best out of three.

The trial began again. The veins stood out on Farrington's forehead, and the pallor of Weathers' complexion changed to peony. Their hands and arms trembled under the stress. After a long struggle Weathers again brought his opponent's hand slowly on to the table. There was a murmur of applause from the spectators. The curate, who was standing beside the table, nodded his red head toward the victor and said with loutish familiarity:

—Ah! that's the knack!

—What the hell do you know about it? said Farrington fiercely, turning on the man. What do you put in your gab for?

—Sh, sh! said O'Halloran, observing the violent expression of Farrington's face. Pony up, boys. We'll have just one little smahan more and then we'll be off.

A very sullen-faced man stood at the corner of O'Connell Bridge waiting for the little Sandymount tram to take him home. He was full of smouldering anger and revengefulness. He felt humiliated and discontented; he did not even feel drunk; and he had only twopence in his pocket. He cursed everything. He had done for himself in the office, pawned his watch, spent all his money; and he had not even got drunk. He began to feel thirsty again and he longed to be back again in the hot reeking public-house. He had lost his reputation as a strong man, having been defeated twice by a mere boy. His heart swelled with fury and, when he thought of the woman in the big hat who had brushed against him and said *Pardon!* his fury nearly choked him.

His tram let him down at Shelbourne Road and he steered his great body along in the shadow of the wall of the barracks. He loathed returning to his home. When he went in by the side-door he found the kitchen empty and the kitchen fire nearly out. He bawled upstairs:

—Ada! Ada!

His wife was a little sharp-faced woman who bullied her husband when he was sober and was bullied by him when he was drunk. They had five children. A little boy came running down the stairs.

—Who is that? said the man, peering through the darkness.

—Me, pa.

—Who are you? Charlie?

—No, pa. Tom.

—Where's your mother?

—She's out at the chapel.

—That's right . . . . Did she think of leaving any dinner for me?

—Yes, pa. I—

—Light the lamp. What do you mean by having the place in darkness? Are the other children in bed?

The man sat down heavily on one of the chairs while the little boy lit the lamp. He began to mimic his son's flat accent, saying half to himself: *At the chapel. At the chapel, if you please!* When the lamp was lit he banged his fist on the table and shouted:

—What's for my dinner?

—I'm going . . . to cook it, pa, said the little boy.

The man jumped up furiously and pointed to the fire.

—On that fire! You let the fire out! By God, I'll teach you to do that again!

He took a step to the door and seized the walking-stick which was standing behind it.

—I'll teach you to let the fire out! he said, rolling up his sleeve in order to give his arm free play.

The little boy cried *O, pa!* and ran whimpering round the table, but the man followed him and caught him by the coat. The little boy looked about him wildly but, seeing no way of escape, fell upon his knees.

—Now, you'll let the fire out the next time! said the man, striking at him viciously with the stick. Take that, you little whelp!

The boy uttered a squeal of pain as the stick cut his thigh. He clasped his hands together in the air and his voice shook with fright.

—O, pa! he cried. Don't beat me, pa! And I'll . . . I'll say a *Hail Mary* for you . . . . I'll say a *Hail Mary* for you, pa, if you don't beat me . . . . I'll say a *Hail Mary.* . . .

QUESTIONS

1. Farrington looks forward to "drinking with his friends amid the glare of gas and the clatter of glasses." What is your judgment of these friends? And, as the story develops, does Farrington's judgment of them change?

2. The first voice in the story calls out in "a piercing North of Ireland accent." The young woman in the pub says "O, *pardon!*" in a London accent. Why is such attention paid by the narrator to varieties of accent? Why might Farrington be sensitive to such differences?

3. Before his evening of drinking, Farrington's body "ached to do something, to rush out and revel in violence." After drinking, "he was full of smouldering anger and revengefulness." The story then ends with the beating of a child. How is violence employed in the story? What is its function in the narrative structure?

4. We are told, late in the story, that Farrington's wife "was a little sharp-faced woman who bullied her husband when he was sober and was bullied by him when he was drunk." Does your opinion of Farrington change in any way when you are given this information? Why do you think it is held until such a late moment in the narrative?

5. What do you make of the narrator in this story? Does he give any clues as to his own attitude towards the events surrounding Farrington? How would you characterize his involvement in the narrative?

Franz Kafka (1883–1924)
A Hunger Artist

A Fasting Showman

During these last decades the interest in professional fasting has markedly diminished. It used to pay very well to stage such great performances under one's own management, but to-day that is quite impossible. We live in a different world now. At one time the whole town took a lively interest in the fasting showman; from day to day of his fast the excitement mounted; everybody wanted to see him at least once a day; there were people who bought season tickets for the last few days and sat from morning till night in front of his small barred cage; even in the night-time there were visiting hours, when the whole effect was heightened by torch flares; on fine days the cage was set out in the open air, and then it was the children's special treat to see the fasting showman; for their elders he was often just a joke that happened to be in fashion, but the children stood open-mouthed, holding each other's hands for greater security, marvelling at him as he sat there pallid in black tights, with his ribs sticking out so prominently, not even on a seat but down among straw on the ground, sometimes giving a courteous nod, answering questions with a constrained smile, or perhaps stretching an arm through the bars so that one might feel how thin it was, and then again withdrawing deep into himself, paying no attention to anyone or anything, not even to the striking of the clock that was the only piece of furniture in his cage, but merely staring into vacancy with half-shut eyes, now and then taking a sip from a tiny glass of water to moisten his lips.

Besides casual onlookers there were also relays of permanent watchers selected by the public, usually butchers, strangely enough, and it was their task to watch the fasting showman day and night, three of them at a time, in case he should have some secret recourse to nourishment. This was nothing but a formality, instituted to reassure the masses, for the initiates knew well enough that during his fast the artiste would never in any circumstances, not even under forcible compulsion, swallow the smallest morsel of food; the honour of his profession forbade it. Not every watcher, of course, was capable of understanding this, there were often groups of night watchers who were very lax in carrying out their duties and deliberately huddled together in a retired corner to play cards with great absorption, obviously intending to give the fasting showman the chance of a little refreshment, which they supposed he could draw from some private hoard. Nothing annoyed the artiste more than such watchers; they made him miserable; they made his fast seem unendurable; sometimes he mastered his feebleness sufficiently to sing during their watch for as long as he could keep going, to show them how unjust their suspicions were. But that was of little use; they only wondered at his cleverness in being able to fill his mouth even while singing. Much more to his taste were the watchers who sat close up to the bars, who were not content with the dim night lighting of the hall but focussed him in the full glare of the electric pocket-torch given them by the impresario. The harsh light did not trouble him at all, in any case he could never sleep properly, and he could always drowse a little, whatever the light, at any hour, even when the hall was thronged with noisy onlookers. He was quite happy at the prospect of spending a sleepness night with such watchers; he was ready to exchange jokes with them, to tell them stories out of his nomadic life, anything at all to keep them awake and demonstrate to them again that he had no eatables in his cage and that he was fasting as not one of them could fast. But his happiest moment was when the morning came and an enormous breakfast was brought them, at his expense, on which they flung themselves with the keen appetites of healthy men after a weary night of wakefulness. Of course there were people who argued that this breakfast was an unfair attempt to bribe the watchers, but that was going rather too far, and when they were invited to take on a night's vigil without a breakfast, merely for the sake of the cause, they made themselves scarce, although they stuck stubbornly to their suspicions.

Such suspicions, anyhow, were a necessary accompaniment to the profession of fasting. No one could possibly watch the fasting showman continuously, day and night, and so no one could produce first hand evidence that the fast had really been rigorous and continuous; only the artiste himself could know that, he was, therefore, bound to be the sole completely satisfied spectator of his own fast. Yet for other reasons he was never satisfied; it was not perhaps mere fasting that had brought him to such skeleton thinness that many people had regretfully to keep away from his exhibitions because the sight of him was too much for them, perhaps it was dissatisfaction with himself that had worn him down. For he alone knew, what no other initiate knew, how easy it was to fast. It was the easiest thing in the world. He made no secret of this, yet people did not believe him, at the best they set him down as modest, most of them however thought he was out for publicity or else was some kind of cheat who found it easy to fast because he had discovered a way of getting round it, and then had the impudence to admit the fact, more or less. He had to put up with all that, and in the course of time had got used to it, but his inner dissatisfaction always rankled, and never yet, after any term of fasting—this must be granted to his credit—had he left the cage of his own free will. The longest time he could fast was fixed by his impresario at forty days, beyond that term he was not allowed to go—not even in great cities, and there was good reason for it, too. Experience had proved that for about forty days the interest of the public could be stimulated by steady pressure of advertisement, but after that the town began to lose interest, sympathetic support began notably to fall off; there were, of course, local variations as between one town and another or one country and another, but as a general rule forty days marked the limit. So on the fortieth day the flower-bedecked cage was opened, enthusiastic spectators filled the hall, a military band played, two doctors entered the cage to measure the results of the fast, which were announced through a megaphone, and finally two young ladies appeared, blissful at having been selected for the honour, to help the fasting showman down the few steps leading to a small table on which was spread a carefully chosen invalid repast. And at this very moment the artiste always turned stubborn. True, he would entrust his bony arms to the outstretched helping hands of the ladies bending over him, but stand up he would not. Why stop fasting at this particular moment, after forty days of it? He had held out for a long time, an illimitably long time; why stop now, when he was in his best fasting form, or rather, not yet quite in his best fasting form? Why should he be cheated of the fame he would get for fasting longer, for being not only the record fasting showman of all time—which presumably he was already—but for beating his own record by a performance beyond human imagination, since he felt that there were no limits to his capacity for fasting. His public pretended to admire him so much, why should it have so little patience with him; if he could endure fasting longer, why shouldn't the public endure it? Besides, he was tired, he was comfortable sitting in the straw, and now he was supposed to lift himself to his full height and go down to a meal the very thought of which gave him a nausea that only the presence of the ladies kept him from betraying, and even that with an effort. And he looked up into the eyes of the ladies who were apparently so friendly and in reality so cruel, and shook his head, which felt too heavy on its strengthless neck. But then there happened yet again what always happened. The impresario came forward, without a word—for the band made speech impossible—lifted his arms in the air above the artiste, as if inviting Heaven to look down upon its creature here in the straw, this suffering martyr, which indeed he was, although in quite another sense; grasped him around the emaciated waist, with exaggerated caution, so that the frail condition he was in might be appreciated; and committed him to the care of the blenching ladies, not without secretly giving him a shaking so that his legs and body tottered and swayed. The artiste now submitted completely; his head lolled on his breast as if it had landed there by chance, his body was hollowed out, his legs in a spasm of self-preservation clung close to each other at the knees, yet scraped on the ground as if it were not really solid ground, as if they were only trying to find solid ground; and the whole weight of his body, a featherweight after all, relapsed on to one of the ladies, who, looking round for help and panting a little—this post of honour was not at all what she had expected it to be—first stretched her neck as far as she could to keep her face at least free from contact with the artiste, then finding this impossible, and her more fortunate companion not coming to her aid but merely holding extended on her own trembling hand the little bunch of knuckle bones that was the artiste's, to the great delight of the spectators burst into tears and had to be replaced by an attendant who had long been stationed in readiness. Then came the food, a little of which the impresario managed to get between the artiste's lips, while he sat in a kind of half-fainting trance, to the accompaniment of cheerful patter designed to distract the public's attention from the artiste's condition; after that, a toast was drunk to the public, supposedly prompted by a whisper from the artiste in the impresario's ear; the band confirmed it with a mighty flourish, the spectators melted away, and no one had any cause to be dissatisfied with the proceedings, no one except the fasting showman himself, he only, as always.

So he lived for many years, with small regular intervals of recuperation, in visible glory, honoured by the world, yet in spite of that troubled in spirit, and all the more troubled because no one would take his trouble seriously. What comfort could he possibly need? What more could he possibly wish for? And if some good-natured person, feeling sorry for him, tried to console him by pointing out that his melancholy was probably caused by fasting, it could happen, especially when he had been fasting for some time, that he reacted with an outburst of fury and to the general alarm began to shake the bars of his cage like a wild animal. Yet the impresario had a way of punishing these outbreaks which he rather enjoyed putting into operation. He would apologise publicly for the artiste's behaviour, which was only to be excused, he admitted, because of the irritability caused by fasting; a condition hardly to be understood by well-fed people; then by natural transition he went on to mention the artiste's equally incomprehensible boast that he could fast for much longer than he was doing; he praised the high ambition, the goodwill, the great self-denial undoubtedly implicit in such a statement; and then quite simply countered it by bringing out photographs, which were also on sale to the public, showing the artiste on the fortieth day of a fast lying in bed almost dead from exhaustion. This perversion of the truth, familiar to the artiste though it was, always unnerved him afresh and proved too much for him. What was a consequence of the premature ending of his fast was here presented as the cause of it! To fight against this lack of understanding, against a whole world of non-understanding, was impossible. Time and again in good faith he stood by the bars listening to the impresario, but as soon as the photographs appeared he always let go and sank with a groan back on to his straw, and the reassured public could once more come close and gaze at him.

A few years later when the witnesses of such scenes called them to mind, they often failed to understand themselves at all. For meanwhile the aforementioned change in public interest had set in; it seemed to happen almost overnight; there may have been profound causes for it, but who was going to bother about that? At any rate the pampered fasting showman suddenly found himself deserted one fine day by the amusement seekers, who went streaming past him to other more favoured attractions. For the last time the impresario hurried him over half Europe to discover whether the old interest might still survive here and there; all in vain; everywhere, as if by secret agreement, a positive revulsion from professional fasting was in evidence. Of course it could not really have sprung up so suddenly as all that, and many premonitory symptoms which had not been sufficiently remarked or suppressed during the rush and glitter of success now came retrospectively to mind, but it was now too late to take any counter-measures. Fasting would surely come into fashion again at some future date, yet that was no comfort for those living in the present. What, then, was the fasting showman to do? He had been applauded by thousands in his time and could hardly come down to showing himself in a street booth at village fairs, and as for adopting another profession, he was not only too old for that but too fanatically devoted to fasting. So he took leave of the impresario, his partner in an unparalleled career, and hired himself to a large circus; in order to spare his own feelings he avoided reading the conditions of his contract.

A large circus with its enormous traffic in replacing and recruiting men, animals and apparatus, can always find a use for people at any time, even for a fasting showman, provided, of course, that he does not ask too much, and in this particular case anyhow it was not only the artiste who was taken on but his famous and long-known name as well, indeed, considering the peculiar nature of his performance, which was not impaired by advancing age, it could not be objected that here was an artiste past his prime, no longer at the height of his professional skill, seeking a refuge in some quiet corner of a circus; on the contrary, the fasting showman averred that he could fast as well as ever, which was entirely credible, he even alleged that if he were allowed to fast as he liked, and this was at once promised him without more ado, he could astound the world by establishing a record never yet achieved, a statement which certainly provoked a smile among the other professionals, since it left out of account the change in public opinion, which the fasting showman in his zeal conveniently forgot.

He had not, however, actually lost his sense of the real situation and took it as a matter of course that he and his cage should be stationed, not in the middle of the ring as a main attraction, but outside, near the animal cages, on a site that was after all casily accessible. Large and gaily painted placards made a frame for the cage and announced what was to be scen inside it. When the public came thronging out in the intervals to see the animals, they could hardly avoid passing the fasting showman's cage and stopping there for a moment, perhaps they might even have stayed longer had not those pressing behind them in the narrow gangway, who did not understand why they should be held up on their way towards the excitements of the menagerie, made it impossible for anyone to stand gazing quietly for any length of time. And that was the reason why the fasting showman, who had of course been looking forward to these visiting hours as the main achievement of his life, began instead to shrink from them. At first he could hardly wait for the intervals; it was exhilarating to watch the crowds come streaming his way, until only too soon—not even the most obstinate self-deception, clung to almost consciously, could hold out against the fact—the conviction was borne in upon him that these people, most of them, to judge from their actions, again and again, without exception, were all on their way to the menagerie. And the first sight of them from the distance remained the best. For when they reached his cage he was at once deafened by the storm of shouting and abuse that arose from the two contending factions, which renewed themselves continuously, of those who wanted to stop and stare at him—he soon began to hate them more than the others—not out of real interest but only out of obstinate self-assertiveness, and those who wanted to go straight on to the animals. When the first great rush was past, the stragglers came along, and these, whom nothing could have prevented from stopping to look at him as long as they had breath, raced past with long strides, hardly even glancing at him, in their haste to get to the menagerie in time. And all too rarely did it happen that he had a stroke of luck, when some father of a family fetched up before him with his children, pointed a finger at the fasting showman and explained at length what the phenomenon meant, telling stories of earlier years when he himself had watched similar but much more thrilling performances, and the children, still rather incomprehending, since neither inside nor outside school had they been sufficiently prepared for this lesson—fasting was a commonplace to them—yet showed by the brightness of their intent eyes that new and better times might be coming. Perhaps, said the fasting showman to himself many a time, things would be a little better if his cage were set not quite so near the menagerie. That made it too easy for people to make their choice—to say nothing of what he suffered from the stench of the menagerie, the animals' restlessness by night, the carrying past of raw lumps of flesh for the beasts of prey, the roaring at feeding times, which depressed him continually. But he did not dare to present himself in person to the management; after all, he had the animals to thank for the troops of people who passed his cage, among whom there might always be one here and there to take an interest in him, and who could tell where they might seclude him if he called attention to his existence and thereby to the fact that, strictly speaking, he was only an impediment on the way to the menagerie?

A small impediment, to be sure, one that grew steadily less. People grew familiar with the strange idea that they could be expected, in times like these, to take an interest in a fasting showman, and with this familiarity the verdict went out against him. He might fast as much as he could, and he did so; but nothing could save him now, people passed him by. Just try to explain to anyone the art of fasting! Anyone who has no feeling for it cannot be made to understand it. The fine placards grew dirty and illegible, they were torn down; the little notice-board telling the number of fast-days achieved, which at first was changed carefully every day, had long stayed at the same figure, for after the first few weeks even this small task seemed pointless to the staff; and so the artiste simply fasted on and on, as he had once dreamed of doing, and it was no trouble to him, just as he had always foretold, but no one counted the days, no one, not even the artiste himself, knew what records he was already breaking, and his heart grew heavy. And when once in a time some leisurely passer-by stopped, made merry over the old figure on the board and spoke of swindling, that was in its way the stupidest lie ever invented by indifference and inborn malice, since it was not the fasting showman who was cheating, he was working honestly, but the world was cheating him of his reward.

More days went by, however, and that too came to an end. An overseer's eye fell on the cage one day and he asked the attendants why this perfectly good cage should be left standing there unused with dirty straw inside it; nobody knew, until one man, helped out by the notice-board, remembered about the fasting showman. They poked into the straw with sticks and found him in it. "Are you still fasting?" asked the overseer. "When on earth do you mean to stop?" "Forgive me, everybody," whispered the fasting showman; only the overseer, who had his ear to the bars, understood him. "Of course," said the overseer and tapped his forehead with a finger to let the attendants know what state the man was in, "we forgive you." "I always wanted you to admire my fasting," said the fasting showman. "We do admire it," said the overseer, affably. "But you shouldn't admire it," said the fasting showman. "Well then we don't admire it," said the overseer, "but why shouldn't we admire it?" "Because I have to fast, I can't do anything else," said the fasting showman. "What a fellow you are," said the overseer, "and why can't you do anything else?" "Because," said the fasting showman, lifting his head a little and speaking with his lips pursed, as if for a kiss, right into the overseer's ear, so that no syllable might be lost, "because I couldn't find any food I liked. If I had found any, believe me, I should have made no bones about it and stuffed myself like you or anyone else." These were his last words, but in his dimming eyes remained the firm though no longer proud persuasion that he was still continuing to fast.

"Well, clear this out now!" said the overseer, and they buried the fasting showman, straw and all. Into the cage they put a young panther. Even the most insensitive felt it refreshing to see this wild creature leaping around the cage that had so long been dreary. The panther was all right. The food he liked was brought him without hesitation by the attendants; he seemed not even to miss his freedom; his noble body, furnished almost to bursting point with all that it needed, seemed to carry freedom around with it too; somewhere in his jaws it seemed to lurk; and the joy of life streamed with such ardent passion from his throat that for the onlookers it was not easy to stand the shock of it. But they braced themselves, crowded round the cage, and did not want ever to move away.

QUESTIONS

1 Kafka's voice, as we pointed out in the discussion of point of view, is so distinctive that an adjective, *Kafkaesque*, has sprung up to define it. What is "Kafkaesque" about this story?
2. What is the hunger artist's "art"?
3. How and why do the hunger artist and impresario differ in their interpretations of the importance of his art?
4. What is the function of the panther in the story? To what extent does the animal help define what is bizarrely human in the hunger artist?
5. Why do you suppose that Kafka leaves out any reference to a specific era in this story? How would grounding "The Hunger Artist" in a certain time and place have changed our perception of its meaning?

D. H. Lawrence (1885–1930)
The Rocking-Horse Winner

There was a woman who was beautiful, who started with all the advantages, yet she had no luck. She married for love, and the love turned to dust. She had bonny children, yet she felt they had been thrust upon her, and she could not love them. They looked at her coldly, as if they were finding fault with her. And hurriedly she felt she must cover up some fault in herself. Yet what it was that she must cover up she never knew. Nevertheless, when her children were present, she always felt the centre of her heart go hard. This troubled her, and in her manner she was all the more gentle and anxious for her children, as if she loved them very much. Only she herself knew that at the centre of her heart was a hard little place that could not feel love, no, not for anybody. Everybody else said of her: "She is such a good mother. She adores her children." Only she herself, and her children themselves, knew it was not so. They read it in each other's eyes.

There were a boy and two little girls. They lived in a pleasant house, with a garden, and they had discreet servants, and felt themselves superior to anyone in the neighbourhood.

Although they lived in style, they felt always an anxiety in the house. There was never enough money. The mother had a small income, and the father had a small income, but not nearly enough for the social position which they had to keep up. The father went into town to some office. But though he had good prospects, these prospects never materialised. There was always the grinding sense of the shortage of money, though the style was always kept up.

At last the mother said: "I will see if *I* can't make something." But she did not know where to begin. She racked her brains, and tried this thing and the other, but could not find anything successful. The failure made deep lines come into her face. Her children were growing up, they would have to go to school. There must be more money, there must be more money. The father, who was always very handsome and expensive in his tastes, seemed as if he never *would* be able to do anything worth doing. And the mother, who had a great belief in herself, did not succeed any better, and her tastes were just as expensive.

And so the house came to be haunted by the unspoken phrase: *There must be more money! There must be more money!* The children could hear it all the time, though nobody said it aloud. They heard it at Christmas, when the expensive and splendid toys filled the nursery. Behind the shining modern rocking-horse, behind the smart doll's house, a voice would start whispering: "There *must* be more money! There *must* be more money!" And the children would stop playing, to listen for a moment. They would look into each other's eyes, to see if they had all heard. And each one saw in the eyes of the other two that they too had heard. "There *must* be more money! There *must* be more money!"

It came whispering from the springs of the still-swaying rocking-horse, and even the horse, bending his wooden, champing head, heard it. The big doll, sitting so pink and smirking in her new pram, could hear it quite plainly, and seemed to be smirking all the more self-consciously because of it. The foolish puppy, too, that took the place of the teddy-bear, he was looking so extraordinarily foolish for no other reason but that he heard the secret whisper all over the house: "There *must* be more money!"

Yet nobody ever said it aloud. The whisper was everywhere, and therefore no one spoke it. Just as no one ever says: "We are breathing!" in spite of the fact that breath is coming and going all the time.

"Mother," said the boy Paul one day, "why don't we keep a car of our own? Why do we always use uncle's, or else a taxi?"

"Because we're the poor members of the family," said the mother.

"But why *are* we, mother?"

"Well—I suppose," she said slowly and bitterly, "it's because your father has no luck."

The boy was silent for some time.

"Is luck money, mother?" he asked, rather timidly.

"No, Paul. Not quite. It's what causes you to have money."

"Oh!" said Paul vaguely. "I thought when Uncle Oscar said *filthy lucker,* it meant money."

"*Filthy lucre* does mean money," said the mother. "But it's lucre, not luck."

"Oh!" said the boy. "Then what *is* luck, mother?"

"It's what causes you to have money. If you're lucky you have money. That's why it's better to be born lucky than rich. If you're rich, you may lose your money. But if you're lucky, you will always get more money."

"Oh! Will you? And is father not lucky?"

"Very unlucky, I should say," she said bitterly.

The boy watched her with unsure eyes.

"Why?" he asked.

"I don't know. Nobody ever knows why one person is lucky and another unlucky."

"Don't they? Nobody at all? Does *nobody* know?"

"Perhaps God. But He never tells."

"He ought to, then. And aren't you lucky either, mother?"

"I can't be, if I married an unlucky husband."

"But by yourself, aren't you?"

"I used to think I was, before I married. Now I think I am very unlucky indeed."

"Why?"

"Well—never mind! Perhaps I'm not really," she said.

The child looked at her to see if she meant it. But he saw, by the lines of her mouth, that she was only trying to hide something from him.

"Well, anyhow," he said stoutly, "I'm a lucky person."

"Why?" said his mother, with a sudden laugh.

He stared at her. He didn't even know why he had said it.

"God told me," he asserted, brazening it out.

"I hope He did, dear!" she said, again with a laugh, but rather bitter.

"He did, mother!"

"Excellent!" said the mother, using one of her husband's exclamations.

The boy saw she did not believe him; or rather, that she paid no attention to his assertion. This angered him somewhat, and made him want to compel her attention.

He went off by himself, vaguely, in a childish way, seeking for the clue to 'luck'. Absorbed, taking no heed of other people, he went about with a sort of stealth, seeking inwardly for luck. He wanted luck, he wanted it, he wanted it.

When the two girls were playing dolls in the nursery, he would sit on his big rocking-horse, charging madly into space, with a frenzy that made the little girls peer at him uneasily. Wildly the horse careered, the waving dark hair of the boy tossed, his eyes had a strange glare in them. The little girls dared not speak to him.

When he had ridden to the end of his mad little journey, he climbed down and stood in front of his rocking-horse, staring fixedly into its lowered face. Its red mouth was slightly open, its big eye was wide and glassy-bright.

"Now!" he would silently command the snorting steed. "Now, take me to where there is luck! Now take me!"

And he would slash the horse on the neck with the little whip he had asked Uncle Oscar for. He *knew* the horse could take him to where there was luck, if only he forced it. So he would mount again and start on his furious ride, hoping at last to get there. He knew he could get there.

"You'll break your horse, Paul!" said the nurse.

"He's always riding like that! I wish he'd leave off!" said his elder sister Joan.

But he only glared down on them in silence. Nurse gave him up. She could make nothing of him. Anyhow, he was growing beyond her.

One day his mother and his Uncle Oscar came in when he was on one of his furious rides. He did not speak to them.

"Hallo, you young jockey! Riding a winner?" said his uncle.

"Aren't you growing too big for a rocking-horse? You're not a very little boy any longer, you know," said his mother.

But Paul only gave a blue glare from his big, rather close-set eyes. He would speak to nobody when he was in full tilt. His mother watched him with an anxious expression on her face.

At last he suddenly stopped forcing his horse into the mechanical gallop and slid down.

"Well, I got there!" he announced fiercely, his blue eyes still flaring, and his sturdy long legs straddling apart.

"Where did you get to?" asked his mother.

"Where I wanted to go," he flared back at her.

"That's right, son!" said Uncle Oscar. "Don't you stop till you get there. What's the horse's name?"

"He doesn't have a name," said the boy.

"Gets on without all right?" asked the uncle.

"Well, he has different names. He was called Sansovino last week."

"Sansovino, eh? Won the Ascot. How did you know his name?"

"He always talks about horse-races with Bassett," said Joan.

The uncle was delighted to find that his small nephew was posted with all the racing news. Bassett, the young gardener, who had been wounded in the left foot in the war and had got his present job through Oscar Cresswell, whose batman he had been, was a perfect blade of the 'turf'. He lived in the racing events, and the small boy lived with him.

Oscar Cresswell got it all from Bassett.

"Master Paul comes and asks me, so I can't do more than tell him, sir," said Bassett, his face terribly serious, as if he were speaking of religious matters.

"And does he ever put anything on a horse he fancies?"

"Well—I don't want to give him away—he's a young sport, a fine sport, sir. Would you mind asking him yourself? He sort of takes a pleasure in it, and perhaps he'd feel I was giving him away, sir, if you don't mind."

Bassett was serious as a church.

The uncle went back to his nephew and took him off for a ride in the car.

"Say, Paul, old man, do you ever put anything on a horse?" the uncle asked.

The boy watched the handsome man closely.

"Why, do you think I oughtn't to?" he parried.

"Not a bit of it! I thought perhaps you might give me a tip for the Lincoln."

The car sped on into the country, going down to Uncle Oscar's place in Hampshire.

"Honour bright?" said the nephew.

"Honour bright, son!" said the uncle.

"Well, then, Daffodil."

"Daffodil! I doubt it, sonny. What about Mirza?"

"I only know the winner," said the boy. "That's Daffodil."

"Daffodil, eh?"

There was a pause. Daffodil was an obscure horse comparatively.

"Uncle!"

"Yes, son?"

"You won't let it go any further, will you? I promised Bassett."

"Bassett be damned, old man! What's he got to do with it?"

"We're partners. We've been partners from the first. Uncle, he lent me my first five shillings, which I lost. I promised him, honour bright, it was only between me and him; only you gave me that ten-shilling note I started winning with, so I thought you were lucky. You won't let it go any further, will you?"

The boy gazed at his uncle from those big, hot, blue eyes, set rather close together. The uncle stirred and laughed uneasily.

"Right you are, son! I'll keep your tip private. Daffodil, eh? How much are you putting on him?"

"All except twenty pounds," said the boy. "I keep that in reserve."

The uncle thought it a good joke.

"You keep twenty pounds in reserve, do you, you young romancer? What are you betting, then?"

"I'm betting three hundred," said the boy gravely. "But it's between you and me, Uncle Oscar! Honour bright?"

The uncle burst into a roar of laughter.

"It's between you and me all right, you young Nat Gould," he said, laughing. "But where's your three hundred?"

"Bassett keeps it for me. We're partners."

"You are, are you! And what is Bassett putting on Daffodil?"

"He won't go quite as high as I do, I expect. Perhaps he'll go a hundred and fifty."

"What, pennies?" laughed the uncle.

"Pounds," said the child, with a surprised look at his uncle. "Bassett keeps a bigger reserve than I do."

Between wonder and amusement Uncle Oscar was silent. He pursued the matter no further, but he determined to take his nephew with him to the Lincoln races.

"Now, son," he said, "I'm putting twenty on Mirza, and I'll put five on for you on any horse you fancy. What's your pick?"

"Daffodil, uncle."

"No, not the fiver on Daffodil!"

"I should if it was my own fiver," said the child.

"Good! Good! Right you are! A fiver for me and a fiver for you on Daffodil."

The child had never been to a race-meeting before, and his eyes were blue fire. He pursed his mouth tight and watched. A Frenchman just in front had put his money on Lancelot. Wild with excitement, he flayed his arms up and down, yelling *"Lancelot! Lancelot!"* in his French accent.

Daffodil came in first, Lancelot second, Mirza third. The child, flushed and with eyes blazing, was curiously serene. His uncle brought him four five-pound notes, four to one.

"What am I to do with these?" he cried, waving them before the boy's eyes.

"I suppose we'll talk to Bassett," said the boy. "I expect I have fifteen hundred now; and twenty in reserve; and this twenty."

His uncle studied him for some moments.

"Look here, son!" he said. "You're not serious about Bassett and that fifteen hundred, are you?"

"Yes, I am. But it's between you and me, uncle. Honour bright?"

"Honour bright all right, son! But I must talk to Bassett."

"If you'd like to be a partner, uncle, with Bassett and me, we could all be partners. Only, you'd have to promise, honour bright, uncle, not to let it go beyond us three. Bassett and I are lucky, and you must be lucky, because it was your ten shillings I started winning with. . . ."

Uncle Oscar took both Bassett and Paul into Richmond Park for an afternoon, and there they talked.

"It's like this, you see, sir," Bassett said. "Master Paul would get me talking about racing events, spinning yarns, you know, sir. And he was always keen on knowing if I'd made or if I'd lost. It's about a year since, now, that I put five shillings on Blush of Dawn for him: and we lost. Then the luck turned, with that ten shillings he had from you: that we put on Singhalese. And since that time, it's been pretty steady, all things considering. What do you say, Master Paul?"

"We're all right when we're sure," said Paul. "It's when we're not quite sure that we go down."

"Oh, but we're careful then," said Bassett.

"But when are you *sure?*" smiled Uncle Oscar.

"It's Master Paul, sir," said Bassett in a secret, religious voice. "It's as if he had it from heaven. Like Daffodil, now, for the Lincoln. That was as sure as eggs."

"Did you put anything on Daffodil?" asked Oscar Cresswell.

"Yes, sir. I made my bit."

"And my nephew?"

Bassett was obstinately silent, looking at Paul.

"I made twelve hundred, didn't I, Bassett? I told uncle I was putting three hundred on Daffodil."

"That's right," said Bassett, nodding.

"But where's the money?" asked the uncle.

"I keep it safe locked up, sir. Master Paul he can have it any minute he likes to ask for it."

"What, fifteen hundred pounds?"

"And twenty! And *forty*, that is, with the twenty he made on the course."

"It's amazing!" said the uncle.

"If Master Paul offers you to be partners, sir, I would, if I were you: if you'll excuse me," said Bassett.

Oscar Cresswell thought about it.

"I'll see the money," he said.

They drove home again, and, sure enough, Bassett came round to the garden-house with fifteen hundred pounds in notes. The twenty pounds reserve was left with Joe Glee, in the Turf Commission deposit.

"You see, it's all right, uncle, when I'm *sure!* Then we go strong, for all we're worth. Don't we, Bassett?"

"We do that, Master Paul."

"And when are you sure?" said the uncle, laughing.

"Oh, well, sometimes I'm *absolutely* sure, like about Daffodil," said the boy; "and sometimes I have an idea; and sometimes I haven't even an idea, have I, Bassett? Then we're careful, because we mostly go down."

"You do, do you! And when you're sure, like about Daffodil, what makes you sure, sonny?"

"Oh, well, I don't know," said the boy uneasily. "I'm sure, you know, uncle; that's all."

"It's as if he had it from heaven, sir," Bassett reiterated.

"I should say so!" said the uncle.

But he became a partner. And when the Leger was coming on Paul was 'sure' about Lively Spark, which was a quite inconsiderable horse. The boy insisted on putting a thousand on the horse, Bassett went for five hundred, and Oscar Cresswell two hundred. Lively Spark came in first, and the betting had been ten to one against him. Paul had made ten thousand.

"You see," he said, "I was absolutely sure of him."

Even Oscar Cresswell had cleared two thousand.

"Look here, son," he said, "this sort of thing makes me nervous."

"It needn't, uncle! Perhaps I shan't be sure again for a long time."

"But what are you going to do with your money?" asked the uncle.

"Of course," said the boy, "I started it for mother. She said she had no luck, because father is unlucky, so I thought if *I* was lucky, it might stop whispering."

"What might stop whispering?"

"Our house. I *hate* our house for whispering."

"What does it whisper?"

"Why—why"—the boy fidgeted—"why, I don't know. But it's always short of money, you know, uncle."

"I know it, son, I know it."

"You know people send mother writs, don't you, uncle?"

"I'm afraid I do," said the uncle.

"And then the house whispers, like people laughing at you behind your back. It's awful, that is! I thought if I was lucky——"

"You might stop it," added the uncle.

The boy watched him with big blue eyes, that had an uncanny cold fire in them, and he said never a word.

"Well, then!" said the uncle. "What are we doing?"

"I shouldn't like mother to know I was lucky," said the boy.

"Why not, son?"

"She'd stop me."

"I don't think she would."

"Oh!"—and the boy writhed in an odd way—"I *don't* want her to know, uncle."

"All right, son! We'll manage it without her knowing."

They managed it very easily. Paul, at the other's suggestion, handed over five thousand pounds to his uncle, who deposited it with the family lawyer, who was then to inform Paul's mother that a relative had put five thousand pounds into his hands, which sum was to be paid out a thousand pounds at a time, on the mother's birthday, for the next five years.

"So she'll have a birthday present of a thousand pounds for five successive years," said Uncle Oscar. "I hope it won't make it all the harder for her later."

Paul's mother had her birthday in November. The house had been 'whispering' worse than ever lately, and, even in spite of his luck, Paul could not bear up against it. He was very anxious to see the effect of the birthday letter, telling his mother about the thousand pounds.

When there were no visitors, Paul now took his meals with his parents, as he was beyond the nursery control. His mother went into town nearly every day. She had discovered that she had an odd knack of sketching furs and dress materials, so she worked secretly in the studio of a friend who was the chief 'artist' for the leading drapers. She drew the figures of ladies in furs and ladies in silk and sequins for the newspaper advertisements. This young woman artist earned several thousand pounds a year, but Paul's mother only made several hundreds, and she was again dissatisfied. She so wanted to be first in something, and she did not succeed, even in making sketches for drapery advertisements.

She was down to breakfast on the morning of her birthday. Paul watched her face as she read her letters. He knew the lawyer's letter. As his mother read it, her face hardened and became more expressionless. Then a cold, determined look came on her mouth. She hid the letter under the pile of others, and said not a word about it.

"Didn't you have anything nice in the post for your birthday, mother?" said Paul.

"Quite moderately nice," she said, her voice cold and absent.

She went away to town without saying more.

But in the afternoon Uncle Oscar appeared. He said Paul's mother had had a long interview with the lawyer, asking if the whole five thousand could not be advanced at once, as she was in debt.

"What do you think, uncle?" said the boy.

"I leave it to you, son."

"Oh, let her have it, then! We can get some more with the other," said the boy.

"A bird in the hand is worth two in the bush, laddie!" said Uncle Oscar.

"But I'm sure to *know* for the Grand National; or the Lincolnshire; or else the Derby. I'm sure to know for *one* of them," said Paul.

So Uncle Oscar signed the agreement, and Paul's mother touched the whole five thousand. Then something very curious happened. The voices in the house suddenly went mad, like a chorus of frogs on a spring evening. There were certain new furnishings, and Paul had a tutor. He was *really* going to Eton, his father's school, in the following autumn. There were flowers in the winter, and a blossoming of the luxury Paul's mother had been used to. And yet the voices in the house, behind the sprays of mimosa and almond-blossom, and from under the piles of iridescent cushions, simply trilled and screamed in a sort of ecstasy: "There *must* be more money! Oh-h-h; there *must* be more money. Oh, now now-w! Now-w-w—there *must* be more money!—more than ever! More than ever!"

It frightened Paul terribly. He studied away at his Latin and Greek with his tutor. But his intense hours were spent with Bassett. The Grand National had gone by: he had not 'known', and had lost a hundred pounds. Summer was at hand. He was in agony for the Lincoln. But even for the Lincoln he didn't 'know', and he lost fifty pounds. He became wild-eyed and strange, as if something were going to explode in him.

"Let it alone, son! Don't you bother about it!" urged Uncle Oscar. But it was as if the boy couldn't really hear what his uncle was saying.

"I've got to know for the Derby! I've got to know for the Derby!" the child reiterated, his big blue eyes blazing with a sort of madness.

His mother noticed how overwrought he was.

"You'd better go to the seaside. Wouldn't you like to go now to the seaside, instead of waiting? I think you'd better," she said, looking down at him anxiously, her heart curiously heavy because of him.

But the child lifted his uncanny blue eyes.

"I couldn't possibly go before the Derby, mother!" he said. "I couldn't possibly!"

"Why not?" she said, her voice becoming heavy when she was opposed. "Why not? You can still go from the seaside to see the Derby with your Uncle Oscar, if that's what you wish. No need for you to wait here. Besides, I think you care too much about these races. It's a bad sign. My family has been a gambling family, and you won't know till you grow up how much damage it has done. But it has done damage. I shall have to send Bassett away, and ask Uncle Oscar not to talk racing to you, unless you promise to be reasonable about it: go away to the seaside and forget it. You're all nerves!"

"I'll do what you like, mother, so long as you don't send me away till after the Derby," the boy said.

"Send you away from where? Just from this house?"

"Yes," he said, gazing at her.

"Why, you curious child, what makes you care about this house so much, suddenly? I never knew you loved it."

He gazed at her without speaking. He had a secret within a secret, something he had not divulged, even to Bassett or to his Uncle Oscar.

But his mother, after standing undecided and a little bit sullen for some moments, said:

"Very well, then! Don't go to the seaside till after the Derby, if you don't wish it. But promise me you won't let your nerves go to pieces. Promise you won't think so much about horse-racing and *events*, as you call them!"

"Oh no," said the boy casually. "I won't think much about them, mother. You needn't worry. I wouldn't worry, mother, if I were you."

"If you were me and I were you," said his mother, "I wonder what we *should* do!"

"But you know you needn't worry, mother, don't you?" the boy repeated.

"I should be awfully glad to know it," she said wearily.

"Oh, well, you *can*, you know. I mean, you *ought* to know you needn't worry," he insisted.

"Ought I? Then I'll see about it," she said.

Paul's secret of secrets was his wooden horse, that which had no name. Since he was emancipated from a nurse and a nursery-governess, he had had his rocking-horse removed to his own bedroom at the top of the house.

"Surely you're too big for a rocking-horse!" his mother had remonstrated.

"Well, you see, mother, till I can have a *real* horse, I like to have *some* sort of animal about," had been his quaint answer.

"Do you feel he keeps you company?" she laughed.

"Oh yes! He's very good, he always keeps me company, when I'm there," said Paul.

So the horse, rather shabby, stood in an arrested prance in the boy's bedroom.

The Derby was drawing near, and the boy grew more and more tense. He hardly heard what was spoken to him, he was very frail, and his eyes were really uncanny. His mother had sudden strange seizures of uneasiness about him. Sometimes, for half an hour, she would feel a sudden anxiety about him that was almost anguish. She wanted to rush to him at once, and know he was safe.

Two nights before the Derby, she was at a big party in town, when one of her rushes of anxiety about her boy, her first-born, gripped her heart till she could hardly speak. She fought with the feeling, might and main, for she believed in common sense. But it was too strong. She had to leave the dance and go downstairs to telephone to the country. The children's nursery-governess was terribly surprised and startled at being rung up in the night.

"Are the children all right, Miss Wilmot?"

"Oh yes, they are quite all right."

"Master Paul? Is he all right?"

"He went to bed as right as a trivet. Shall I run up and look at him?"

"No," said Paul's mother reluctantly. "No! Don't trouble. It's all right. Don't sit up. We shall be home fairly soon." She did not want her son's privacy intruded upon.

"Very good," said the governess.

It was about one o'clock when Paul's mother and father drove up to their house. All was still. Paul's mother went to her room and slipped off her white fur cloak. She had told her maid not to wait up for her. She heard her husband downstairs, mixing a whisky and soda.

And then, because of the strange anxiety at her heart, she stole upstairs to her son's room. Noiselessly she went along the upper corridor. Was there a faint noise? What was it?

She stood, with arrested muscles, outside his door, listening. There was a strange, heavy, and yet not loud noise. Her heart stood still. It was a soundless noise, yet rushing and powerful. Something huge, in violent, hushed motion. What was it? What in God's name was it? She ought to know. She felt that she knew the noise. She knew what it was.

Yet she could not place it. She couldn't say what it was. And on and on it went, like a madness.

Softly, frozen with anxiety and fear, she turned the doorhandle.

The room was dark. Yet in the space near the window, she heard and saw something plunging to and fro. She gazed in fear and amazement.

Then suddenly she switched on the light, and saw her son, in his green pyjamas, madly surging on the rocking-horse. The blaze of light suddenly lit him up, as he urged the wooden horse, and lit her up, as she stood, blonde, in her dress of pale green and crystal, in the doorway.

"Paul!" she cried. "Whatever are you doing?"

"It's Malabar!" he screamed in a powerful, strange voice. "It's Malabar!"

His eyes blazed at her for one strange and senseless second, as he ceased urging his wooden horse. Then he fell with a crash to the ground, and she, all her tormented motherhood flooding upon her, rushed to gather him up.

But he was unconscious, and unconscious he remained, with some brain-fever. He talked and tossed, and his mother sat stonily by his side.

"Malabar! It's Malabar! Bassett, Bassett, I *know!* It's Malabar!"

So the child cried, trying to get up and urge the rocking-horse that gave him his inspiration.

"What does he mean by Malabar?" asked the heart-frozen mother.

"I don't know," said the father stonily.

"What does he mean by Malabar?" she asked her brother Oscar.

"It's one of the horses running for the Derby," was the answer.

And, in spite of himself, Oscar Cresswell spoke to Bassett, and himself put a thousand on Malabar: at fourteen to one.

The third day of the illness was critical: they were waiting for a change. The boy, with his rather long, curly hair, was tossing ceaselessly on the pillow. He neither slept nor regained consciousness, and his eyes were like blue stones. His mother sat, feeling her heart had gone, turned actually into a stone.

In the evening, Oscar Cresswell did not come, but Bassett sent a message, saying could he come up for one moment, just one moment? Paul's mother was very angry at the intrusion, but on second thoughts she agreed. The boy was the same. Perhaps Bassett might bring him to consciousness.

The gardener, a shortish fellow with a little brown moustache and sharp little brown eyes, tiptoed into the room, touched his imaginary cap to Paul's mother, and stole to the bedside, staring with glittering, smallish eyes at the tossing, dying child.

"Master Paul!" he whispered. "Master Paul! Malabar came in first all right, a clean win. I did as you told me. You've made over seventy thousand pounds, you have; you've got over eighty thousand. Malabar came in all right, Master Paul."

"Malabar! Malabar! Did I say Malabar, mother? Did I say Malabar? Do you think I'm lucky, mother? I knew Malabar, didn't I? Over eighty thousand pounds! I call that lucky, don't you, mother? Over eighty thousand pounds! I knew, didn't I know I knew? Malabar came in all right. If I ride my horse till I'm sure, then I tell you, Bassett, you can go as high as you like. Did you go for all you were worth, Bassett?"

"I went a thousand on it, Master Paul."

"I never told you, mother, that if I can ride my horse, and *get there*, then I'm absolutely sure—oh, absolutely! Mother, did I ever tell you? I *am* lucky!"

"No, you never did," said his mother.

But the boy died in the night.

And even as he lay dead, his mother heard her brother's voice saying to her: "My God, Hester, you're eighty-odd thousand to the good, and a poor devil of a son to the bad. But, poor devil, poor devil, he's best gone out of a life where he rides his rocking-horse to find a winner."

QUESTIONS

1. It has been noted that the tone of the opening paragraphs of this story resembles that of a fairy tale. How does this tone affect your reaction to the events that follow?

2. *Luck* is a word recurring throughout this story. How do the various characters use the notion of luck in the decisions they make about their lives?
3. Some critics have said that the revelation of what Paul does on the rocking-horse comes too late in the story. Do you agree? Would it be better if we knew about his states of mind aboard the wooden horse when we first find out he is winning large sums of money on the races?
4. Do you have any premonition that Paul will die in this story? What do you expect to happen and why?
5. This story is like "The Blue Hotel" in that one of the characters steps up at the conclusion and delivers what seems to be the moral. How would you paraphrase the moral of "The Rocking- Horse Winner"? Compare the effectiveness of this story with that of Stephen Crane's story.

James Thurber (1894–1961)
You Could Look It Up

It all begun when we dropped down to C'lumbus, Ohio, from Pittsburgh to play a exhibition game on our way out to St. Louis. It was gettin' on into September, and though we'd been leadin' the league by six, seven games most of the season, we was now in first place by a margin you could 'a' got it into the eye of a thimble, bein' only a half a game ahead of St. Louis. Our slump had given the boys the leapin' jumps, and they was like a bunch a old ladies at a lawn fete with a thunderstorm comin' up, runnin' around snarlin' at each other, eatin' bad and sleepin' worse, and battin' for a team average of maybe .186. Half the time nobody'd speak to nobody else, without it was to bawl 'em out.

Squawks Magrew was managin' the boys at the time, and he was darn near crazy. They called him "Squawks" 'cause when things was goin' bad he lost his voice, or perty near lost it, and squealed at you like a little girl you stepped on her doll or somethin'. He yelled at everybody and wouldn't listen to nobody, without maybe it was me. I'd been trainin' the boys for ten year, and he'd take more lip from me than from anybody else. He knowed I was smarter'n him, anyways, like you're goin' to hear.

This was thirty, thirty-one year ago; you could look it up, 'cause it was the same year C'lumbus decided to call itself the Arch City, on account of a lot of iron arches with electric-light bulbs into 'em which stretched acrost High Street. Thomas Albert Edison sent 'em a telegram, and they was speeches and maybe even President Taft opened the celebration by pushin' a button. It was a great week for the Buckeye capital, which was why they got us out there for this exhibition game.

Well, we just lose a double-header to Pittsburgh, 11 to 5 and 7 to 3, so we snarled all the way to C'lumbus, where we put up at the Chittaden Hotel, still snarlin'. Everybody was tetchy, and when Billy Klinger took a sock at Whitey Cott at breakfast, Whitey threw marmalade all over his face.

"Blind each other, whatta I care?" says Magrew. "You can't see nothin' anyways."

C'lumbus win the exhibition game, 3 to 2, whilst Magrew set in the dugout, mutterin' and cursin' like a fourteen-year-old Scotty. He bad-mouthed everybody on the ball club and he bad-mouthed everybody offa the ball club, includin' the Wright brothers, who, he claimed, had yet to build a airship big enough for any of our boys to hit it with a ball bat.

"I wisht I was dead," he says to me. "I wisht I was in heaven with the angels."

I told him to pull hisself together, 'cause he was drivin' the boys crazy, the way he was goin' on, sulkin' and bad-mouthin' and whinin'. I was older'n he was and smarter'n he was, and he knowed it. I was ten times smarter'n he was about this Pearl du Monville, first time I ever laid eyes on the little guy, which was one of the saddest days of my life.

Now, most people name of Pearl is girls, but this Pearl du Monville was a man, if you could call a fella a man who was only thirty-four, thirty-five inches high. Pearl du Monville was a midget. He was part French and part Hungarian, and maybe even part Bulgarian or somethin'. I can see him now, a sneer on his little pushed-in pan, swingin' a bamboo cane and smokin' a big cigar. He had a gray suit with a big black check into it, and he had a gray felt hat with one of them rainbow-colored hatbands onto it, like the young fellas wore in them days. He talked like he was talkin' into a tin can, but he didn't have no foreign accent. He might a been fifteen or he might a been a hundred, you couldn't tell. Pearl du Monville.

After the game with C'lumbus, Magrew headed straight for the Chittaden bar—the train for St. Louis wasn't goin' for three, four hours—and there he set, drinkin' rye and talkin' to this bartender.

"How I pity me, brother," Magrew was tellin' this bartender. "How I pity me." That was alwuz his favorite tune. So he was settin' there, tellin' this bartender how heartbreakin' it was to be manager of a bunch a blindfolded circus clowns, when up pops this Pearl du Monville outa nowheres.

It give Magrew the leapin' jumps. He thought at first maybe the D.T.'s had come back on him; he claimed he'd had 'em once, and little guys had popped up all around him, wearin' red, white and blue hats.

"Go on, now!" Magrew yells. "Get away from me!"

But the midget clumb up on a chair acrost the table from Magrew and says, "I seen that game today, Junior, and you ain't got no ball club. What you got there, Junior," he says, "is a side show."

"Whatta ya mean, 'Junior'?" says Magrew, touchin' the little guy to satisfy hisself he was real.

"Don't pay him no attention, mister," says the bartender. "Pearl calls everybody 'Junior,' 'cause it alwuz turns out he's a year older'n anybody else."

"Yeh?" says Magrew. "How old is he?"

"How old are you, Junior?" says the midget.

"Who, me? I'm fifty-three," says Magrew.

"Well, I'm fifty-four," says the midget.

Magrew grins and asts him what he'll have, and that was the beginnin' of their beautiful friendship, if you don't care what you say.

Pearl du Monville stood up on his chair and waved his cane around and pretended like he was ballyhooin' for a circus. "Right this way, folks!" he yells. "Come on in and see the greatest collection of freaks in the world! See the armless pitchers, see the eyeless batters, see the infielders with five thumbs!" and on and on like that, feedin' Magrew gall and handin' him a laugh at the same time, you might say.

You could hear him and Pearl du Monville hootin' and hollerin' and singin' way up to the fourth floor of the Chittaden, where the boys was packin' up. When it come time to go to the station, you can imagine how disgusted we was when we crowded into the doorway of that bar and seen them two singin' and goin' on.

"Well, well, well," says Magrew, lookin' up and spottin' us. "Look who's here. . . . Clowns, this is Pearl du Monville, a monseer of the old, old school. . . . Don't shake hands with 'em, Pearl, 'cause their fingers is made of chalk and would bust right off in your paws," he says, and he starts guffawin' and Pearl starts titterin' and we stand there givin' 'em the iron eye, it bein' the lowest ebb a ball-club manager'd got hisself down to since the national pastime was started.

Then the midget begun givin' us the ballyhoo. "Come on in!" he says, wavin' his cane. "See the legless base runners, see the outfielders with the butter fingers, see the southpaw with the arm of a little chee-ild!"

Then him and Magrew begun to hoop and holler and nudge each other till you'd of thought this little guy was the funniest guy than even Charlie Chaplin. The fellas filed outa the bar without a word and went on up to the Union Depot, leavin' me to handle Magrew and his new-found crony.

Well, I got 'em outa there finely. I had to take the little guy along, 'cause Magrew had a holt onto him like a vise and I couldn't pry him loose.

"He's comin' along as masket," says Magrew, holdin' the midget in the crouch of his arm like a football. And come along he did, hollerin' and protestin' and beatin' at Magrew with his little fists.

"Cut it out, will ya, Junior?" the little guy kept whinin'. "Come on, leave a man loose, will ya, Junior?"

But Junior kept a holt onto him and begun yellin', "See the guys with the glass arm, see the guys with the cast-iron brains, see the fielders with the feet on their wrists!"

So it goes, right through the whole Union Depot, with people starin' and catcallin', and he don't put the midget down till he gets him through the gates.

"How'm I goin' to go along without no toothbrush?" the midget asts. "What'm I goin' to do without no other suit?" he says.

"Doc here," says Magrew, meanin' me—"doc here will look after you like you was his own son, won't you, doc?"

I give him the iron eye, and he finely got on the train and prob'ly went to sleep with his clothes on.

This left me alone with the midget. "Lookit," I says to him. "Why don't you go on home now? Come mornin', Magrew'll forget all about you. He'll prob'ly think you was somethin' he seen in a nightmare maybe. And he ain't goin' to laugh so easy in the mornin', neither," I says. "So why don't you go on home?"

"Nix," he says to me. "Skiddoo," he says, "twenty-three for you," and he tosses his cane up into the vestibule of the coach and clam'ers on up after it like a cat. So that's the way Pearl du Monville come to go to St. Louis with the ball club.

I seen 'em first at breakfast the next day, settin' opposite each other, the midget playin' "Turkey in the Straw" on a harmonium and Magrew starin' at his eggs and bacon like they was a uncooked bird with its feathers still on.

"Remember where you found this?" I says, jerkin' my thumb at the midget. "Or maybe you think they come with breakfast on these trains," I says, bein' a good hand at turnin' a sharp remark in them days.

The midget puts down the harmonium and turns on me. "Sneeze," he says; "your brains is dusty." Then he snaps a couple drops of water at me from a tumbler. "Drown," he says, tryin' to make his voice deep.

Now, both them cracks is Civil War cracks, but you'd of thought they was brand new and the funniest than any crack Magrew'd ever heard in his whole life. He started hoopin' and hollerin', and the midget started hoopin' and hollerin', so I walked on away and set down with Bugs Courtney and Hank Metters, payin' no attention to this weak-minded Damon and Phidias acrost the aisle.

Well, sir, the first game with St. Louis was rained out, and there we was facin' a double-header next day. Like maybe I told you, we lose the last three double-headers we play, makin' maybe twenty-five errors in the six games, which is all right for the intimates of a school for the blind, but is disgraceful for the world's champions. It was too wet to go to the zoo, and Magrew wouldn't let us go to the movies, 'cause they flickered so bad in them days. So we just set around, stewin' and frettin'.

One of the newspaper boys come over to take a pitture of Billy Klinger and Whitey Cott shakin' hands—this reporter'd heard about the fight—and whilst they was standin' there, toe to toe, shakin' hands, Billy give a back lunge and a jerk, and throwed Whitey over his shoulder into a corner of the room, like a sack a salt. Whitey come back at him with a chair, and Bethlehem broke loose in that there room. The camera was tromped to pieces like a berry basket. When we finely got 'em pulled apart, I heard a laugh, and there was Magrew and the midget standin' in the door and givin' us the iron eye.

"Wrasslers," says Magrew, cold-like, "that's what I got for a ball club, Mr. Du Monville, wrasslers—and not very good wrasslers at that, you ast me."

"A man can't be good at everythin'," says Pearl, "but he oughta be good at somethin'."

This sets Magrew guffawin' again, and away they go, the midget taggin' along by his side like a hound dog and handin' him a fast line of so-called comic cracks.

When we went out to face that battlin' St. Louis club in a double-header the next afternoon, the boys was jumpy as tin toys with keys in their back. We lose the first game, 7 to 2, and are trailin', 4 to 0, when the second game ain't but ten minutes old. Magrew set there like a stone statue, speakin' to nobody.

Then, in their half a the fourth, somebody singled to center and knocked in two more runs for St. Louis.

That made Magrew squawk. "I wisht one thing," he says. "I wisht I was manager of a old ladies' sewin' circus 'stead of a ball club."

"You are, Junior, you are," says a familyer and disagreeable voice.

It was that Pearl du Monville again, poppin' up outa nowheres, swingin' his bamboo cane and smokin' a cigar that's three sizes too big for his face. By this time we'd finely got the other side out, and Hank Metters slithered a bat acrost the ground, and the midget had to jump to keep both his ankles from bein' broke.

I thought Magrew'd bust a blood vessel. "You hurt Pearl and I'll break your neck!" he yelled.

Hank muttered somethin' and went on up to the plate and struck out.

We managed to get a couple runs acrost in our half a the sixth, but they come back with three more in their half a the seventh, and this was too much for Magrew.

"Come on, Pearl," he says. "We're gettin' outa here."

"Where you think you're goin'?" I ast him.

"To the lawyer's again," he says cryptly.

"I didn't know you'd been to the lawyer's once, yet," I says.

"Which that goes to show how much you don't know," he says.

With that, they was gone, and I didn't see 'em the rest of the day, nor know what they was up to, which was a God's blessin'. We lose the nightcap, 9 to 3, and that puts us into second place plenty, and as low in our mind as a ball club can get.

The next day was a horrible day, like anybody that lived through it can tell you. Practice was just over and the St. Louis club was takin' the field, when I hears this strange sound from the stands. It sounds like the nervous whickerin' a horse gives when he smells somethin' funny on the wind. It was the fans ketchin' sight of Pearl du Monville, like you have prob'ly guessed. The midget had popped up onto the field all dressed up in a minacher club uniform, sox, cap, little letters sewed onto his chest, and all. He was swingin' a kid's bat and the only thing kept him from lookin' like a real ballplayer seen through the wrong end of a microscope was this cigar he was smokin'.

Bugs Courtney reached over and jerked it outa his mouth and throwed it away. "You're wearin' that suit on the playin' field," he says to him, severe as a judge. "You go insultin' it and I'll take you out to the zoo and feed you to the bears."

Pearl just blowed some smoke at him which he still has in his mouth.

Whilst Whitey was foulin' off four or five prior to strikin' out, I went on over to Magrew. "If I was as comic as you," I says, "I'd laugh myself to death," I says. "Is that any way to treat the uniform, makin' a mockery out of it?"

"It might surprise you to know I ain't makin' no mockery outa the uniform," says Magrew. "Pearl du Monville here has been made a bone-of-fida member of this so-called ball club. I fixed it up with the front office by long-distance phone."

"Yeh?" I says. "I can just hear Mr. Dillworth or Bart Jenkins agreein' to hire a midget for the ball club. I can just hear 'em." Mr. Dillworth was the owner of the club and Bart Jenkins was the secretary, and they never stood for no monkey business. "May I be so bold as to inquire," I says, "just what you told 'em?"

"I told 'em," he says, "I wanted to sign up a guy they ain't no pitcher in the league can strike him out."

"Uh-huh," I says, "and did you tell 'em what size of a man he is?"

"Never mind about that," he says. "I got papers on me, made out legal and proper, constitutin' one Pearl du Monville a bone-of-fida member of this former ball club. Maybe that'll shame them big babies into gettin' in there and swingin', knowin' I can replace any one of 'em with a midget, if I have a mind to. A St. Louis lawyer I seen twice tells me it's all legal and proper."

"A St. Louis lawyer would," I says, "seein' nothin' could make him happier than havin' you makin' a mockery outa this one-time baseball outfit," I says.

Well, sir, it'll all be there in the papers of thirty, thirty-one year ago, and you could look it up. The game went along without no scorin' for seven innings, and since they ain't nothin' much to watch but guys poppin' up or strikin' out, the fans pay most of their attention to the goin's-on of Pearl du Monville. He's out there in front a the dugout, turnin' handsprings, balancin' his bat on his chin, walkin' a imaginary line, and so on. The fans clapped and laughed at him, and he ate it up.

So it went up to the last a the eighth, nothin' to nothin', not more'n seven, eight hits all told, and no errors on neither side. Our pitcher gets the first two men out easy in the eighth. Then up come a fella name of Porter or Billings, or some such name, and he lammed one up against the tobacco sign for three bases. The next guy up slapped the first ball out into left for a base hit, and in come the fella from third for the only run of the ball game so far. The crowd yelled, the look a death come onto Magrew's face again, and even the midget quit his tom-foolin'. Their next man fouled out back a third, and we come up for our last bats like a bunch a schoolgirls steppin' into a pool of cold water. I was lower in my mind than I'd been since the day in Nineteen-four when Chesbro throwed the wild pitch in the ninth inning with a man on third and lost the pennant for the Highlanders. I knowed something just as bad was goin' to happen, which shows I'm a clairvoyun, or was then.

When Gordy Mills hit out to second, I just closed my eyes. I opened 'em up again to see Dutch Muller standin' on second, dustin' off his pants, him havin' got his first hit in maybe twenty times to the plate. Next up was Harry Loesing, battin' for our pitcher, and he got a base on balls, walkin' on a fourth one you could a combed your hair with.

Then up come Whitey Cott, our lead-off man. He crotches down in what was prob'ly the most fearsome stanch in organized ball, but all he can do is pop out to short. That brung up Billy Klinger, with two down and a man on first and second. Billy took a cut at one you could a knocked a plug hat offa this here Carnera with it, but then he gets sense enough to wait 'em out, and finely he walks, too, fillin' the bases.

Yes, sir, there you are; the tyin' run on third and the winnin' run on second, first a the ninth, two men down, and Hank Metters comin' to the bat. Hank was built like a Pope-Hartford and he couldn't run no faster'n President

Taft, but he had five home runs to his credit for the season, and that wasn't bad in them days. Hank was still hittin' better'n anybody else on the ball club, and it was mighty heartenin', seein' him stridin' up towards the plate. But he never got there.

"Wait a minute!" yells Magrew, jumpin' to his feet. "I'm sendin' in a pinch hitter!" he yells.

You could a heard a bomb drop. When a ballclub manager says he's sendin' in a pinch hitter for the best batter on the club, you know and I know and everybody knows he's lost his holt.

"They're goin' to be sendin' the funny wagon for you, if you don't watch out," I says, grabbin' a holt of his arm.

But he pulled away and run out towards the plate, yellin', "Du Monville battin' for Metters!"

All the fellas begun squawlin' at once, except Hank, and he just stood there starin' at Magrew like he'd gone crazy and was claimin' to be Ty Cobb's grandma or somethin'. Their pitcher stood out there with his hands on his hips and a disagreeable look on his face, and the plate umpire told Magrew to go on and get a batter up. Magrew told him again Du Monville was battin' for Metters, and the St. Louis manager finely got the idea. It brung him outa his dugout, howlin' and bawlin' like he'd lost a female dog and her seven pups.

Magrew pushed the midget towards the plate and he says to him, he says, "Just stand up there and hold that bat on your shoulder. They ain't a man in the world can throw three strikes in there 'fore he throws four balls!" he says.

"I get it, Junior!" says the midget. "He'll walk me and force in the tyin' run!" And he starts on up to the plate as cocky as if he was Willie Keeler.

I don't need to tell you Bethlehem broke loose on that there ball field. The fans got onto their hind legs, yellin' and whistlin', and everybody on the field begun wavin' their arms and hollerin' and shovin'. The plate umpire stalked over to Magrew like a traffic cop, waggin' his jaw and pointin' his finger, and the St. Louis manager kept yellin' like his house was on fire. When Pearl got up to the plate and stood there, the pitcher slammed his glove down onto the ground and started stompin' on it, and they ain't nobody can blame him. He's just walked two normal-sized human bein's, and now here's a guy up to the plate they ain't more'n twenty inches between his knees and his shoulders.

The plate umpire called in the field umpire, and they talked a while, like a couple doctors seein' the bucolic plague or somethin' for the first time. Then the plate umpire come over to Magrew with his arms folded acrost his chest, and he told him to go on and get a batter up, or he'd forfeit the game to St. Louis. He pulled out his watch, but somebody batted it outa his hand in the scufflin', and I thought there'd be a free-for-all, with everybody yellin' and shovin' except Pearl du Monville, who stood up at the plate with his little bat on his shoulder, not movin' a muscle.

Then Magrew played his ace. I seen him pull some papers outa his pocket and show 'em to the plate umpire. The umpire begun lookin' at 'em like they was bills for somethin' he not only never bought it, he never even heard of it. The other umpire studied 'em like they was a death warren, and all this time the St. Louis manager and the fans and the players is yellin' and hollerin'.

Well, sir, they fought about him bein' a midget, and they fought about him usin' a kid's bat, and they fought about where'd he been all season. They was eight or nine rule books brung out and everybody was thumbin' through 'em, tryin' to find out what it says about midgets, but it don't say nothin' about midgets, 'cause this was somethin' never'd come up in the history of the game before, and nobody'd ever dreamed about it, even when they has nightmares. Maybe you can't send no midgets in to bat nowadays, 'cause the old game's changed a lot, mostly for the worst, but you could then, it turned out.

The plate umpire finely decided the contrack papers was all legal and proper, like Magrew said, so he waved the St. Louis players back to their places and he pointed his finger at their manager and told him to quit hollerin' and get on back in the dugout. The manager says the game is percedin' under protest, and the umpire bawls, "Play ball!" over 'n' above the yellin' and booin', him havin' a voice like a hog-caller.

The St. Louis pitcher picked up his glove and beat at it with his fist six or eight times, and then got set on the mound and studied the situation. The fans realized he was really goin' to pitch to the midget, and they went crazy, hoopin' and hollerin' louder'n ever, and throwin' pop bottles and hats and cushions down onto the field. It took five, ten minutes to get the fans quieted down again, whilst our fellas that was on base set down on the bags and waited. And Pearl du Monville kept standin' up there with the bat on his shoulder, like he'd been told to.

So the pitcher starts studyin' the setup again, and you got to admit it was the strangest setup in a ball game since the players cut off their beards and begun wearin' gloves. I wisht I could call the pitcher's name—it wasn't old Barney Pelty nor Nig Jack Powell nor Harry Howell. He was a big right-hander, but I can't call his name. You could look it up. Even in a crotchin' position, the ketcher towers over the midget like the Washington Monument.

The plate umpire tries standin' on his tiptoes, then he tries crotchin' down, and he finely gets hisself into a stanch nobody'd ever seen on a ball field before, kinda squattin' down on his hanches.

Well, the pitcher is sore as a old buggy horse in fly time. He slams in the first pitch, hard and wild, and maybe two foot higher'n the midget's head.

"Ball one!" hollers the umpire over 'n' above the racket, 'cause everybody is yellin' worsten ever.

The ketcher goes on out towards the mound and talks to the pitcher and hands him the ball. This time the big right-hander tried a undershoot, and it comes in a little closer, maybe no higher'n a foot, foot and a half above Pearl's head. It would a been a strike with a human bein' in there, but the umpire's got to call it, and he does.

"Ball two!" he bellers.

The ketcher walks on out to the mound again, and the whole infield comes over and gives advice to the pitcher about what they'd do in a case like this, with two balls and no strikes on a batter that oughta be in a bottle of alcohol 'stead of up there at the plate in a big-league game between the teams that is fightin' for first place.

For the third pitch, the pitcher stands there flatfooted and tosses up the ball like he's playin' ketch with a little girl.

Pearl stands there motionless as a hitchin' post, and the ball comes in big and slow and high—high for Pearl, that is, it bein' about on a level with his eyes, or a little higher'n a grown man's knees.

They ain't nothin' else for the umpire to do, so he calls, "Ball three!"

Everybody is onto their feet, hoopin' and hollerin', as the pitcher sets to throw ball four. The St. Louis manager is makin' signs and faces like he was a contorturer, and the infield is givin' the pitcher some more advice about what to do this time. Our boys who was on base stick right onto the bag, runnin' no risk of bein' nipped for the last out.

Well, the pitcher decides to give him a toss again, seein' he come closer with that than with a fast ball. They ain't nobody ever seen a slower ball throwed. It come in big as a balloon and slower'n any ball ever throwed before in the major leagues. It come right in over the plate in front of Pearl's chest, lookin' prob'ly big as a full moon to Pearl. They ain't never been a minute like the minute that followed since the United States was founded by the Pilgrim grandfathers.

Pearl du Monville took a cut at that ball, and he hit it! Magrew give a groan like a poleaxed steer as the ball rolls out in front a the plate into fair territory.

"Fair ball!" yells the umpire, and the midget starts runnin' for first, still carryin' that little bat, and makin' maybe ninety foot an hour. Bethlehem breaks loose on that ball field and in them stands. They ain't never been nothin' like it since creation was begun.

The ball's rollin' slow, on down towards third, goin' maybe eight, ten foot. The infield comes in fast and our boys break from their bases like hares in a brush fire. Everybody is standin' up, yellin' and hollerin', and Magrew is tearin' his hair outa his head, and the midget is scamperin' for first with all the speed of one of them little dashhounds carryin' a satchel in his mouth.

The ketcher gets to the ball first, but he boots it on out past the pitcher's box, the pitcher fallin' on his face tryin' to stop it, the shortstop sprawlin' after it full length and zaggin' it on over towards the second baseman, whilst Muller is scorin' with the tyin' run and Loesing is roundin' third with the winnin' run. Ty Cobb could a made a three-bagger outa that bunt, with everybody fallin' over theirself tryin' to pick the ball up. But Pearl is still maybe fifteen, twenty feet from the bag, toddlin' like a baby and yeepin' like a trapped rabbit, when the second baseman finely gets a holt of that ball and slams it over to first. The first baseman ketches it and stomps on the bag, the base umpire waves Pearl out, and there goes your old ball game, the craziest ball game ever played in the history of the organized world.

Their players start runnin' in, and then I see Magrew. He starts after Pearl, runnin' faster'n any man ever run before. Pearl sees him comin' and runs behind the base umpire's legs and gets a holt onto 'em. Magrew comes up, pantin' and roarin', and him and the midget plays ring-around-a-rosy with the umpire, who keeps shovin' at Magrew with one hand and tryin' to slap the midget loose from his legs with the other.

Finely Magrew ketches the midget, who is still yeepin' like a stuck sheep. He gets holt of that little guy by both his ankles and starts whirlin' him round and round his head like Magrew was a hammer thrower and Pearl was the hammer. Nobody can stop him without gettin' their head knocked off, so everybody just stands there and yells. Then Magrew lets the midget fly. He flies on out towards second, high and fast, like a human home run, headed for the soap sign in center field.

Their shortstop tries to get to him, but he can't make it, and I knowed the little fella was goin' to bust to pieces like a dollar watch on a asphalt street when he hit the ground. But it so happens their center fielder is just crossin' second, and he starts runnin' back, tryin' to get under the midget, who had took to spiralin' like a football 'stead of turnin' head over foot, which give him more speed and more distance.

I know you never seen a midget ketched, and you prob'ly never even seen one throwed. To ketch a midget that's been throwed by a heavy-muscled man and is flyin' through the air, you got to run under him and with him and pull your hands and arms back and down when you ketch him, to break the compact of his body, or you'll bust him in two like a matchstick. I seen Bill Lange and Willie Keeler and Tris Speaker make some wonderful ketches in my day, but I never seen nothin' like that center fielder. He goes back and back and still further back and he pulls that midget down outa the air like he was liftin' a sleepin' baby from a cradle. They wasn't a bruise onto him, only his face was the color of cat's meat and he ain't got no air in his chest. In his excitement, the base umpire, who was runnin' back with the center fielder when he ketched Pearl, yells, "Out!" and that give hysteries to the Bethlehem which was ragin' like Niagry on that ball field.

Everybody was hoopin' and hollerin' and yellin' and runnin', with the fans swarmin' onto the field, and the cops tryin' to keep order, and some guys laughin' and some of the women fans cryin', and six or eight of us holdin' onto Magrew to keep him from gettin' at that midget and finishin' him off. Some of the fans picks up the St. Louis pitcher and the center fielder, and starts carryin' 'em around on their shoulders, and they was the craziest goin's-on knowed to the history of organized ball on this side of the 'Lantic Ocean.

I seen Pearl du Monville strugglin' in the arms of a lady fan with a ample bosom, who was laughin' and cryin' at the same time, and him beatin' at her with his little fists and bawlin' and yellin'. He clawed his way loose finely and disappeared in the forest of legs which made that ball field look like it was Coney Island on a hot summer's day.

That was the last I ever seen of Pearl du Monville. I never seen hide nor hair of him from that day to this, and neither did nobody else. He just vanished into the thin of the air, as the fella says. He was ketched for the final out of the ball game and that was the end of him, just like it was the end of the ball game, you might say, and also the end of our losin' streak, like I'm goin' to tell you.

That night we piled onto a train for Chicago, but we wasn't snarlin' and snappin' any more. No, sir, the ice was finely broke and a new spirit come into that ball club. The old zip come back with the disappearance of Pearl du Monville out back a second base. We got to laughin' and talkin' and kiddin' together, and 'fore long Magrew was laughin' with us. He got a human look onto his pan again, and he quit whinin' and complainin' and wishtin' he was in heaven with the angels.

Well, sir, we wiped up that Chicago series, winnin' all four games, and makin' seventeen hits in one of 'em. Funny thing was, St. Louis was so shook up by that last game with us, they never did hit their stride again. Their center fielder took to misjudgin' everything that come his way, and the rest a the fellas followed suit, the way a club'll do when one guy blows up.

'Fore we left Chicago, I and some of the fellas went out and bought a pair of them little baby shoes, which we had 'em golded over and give 'em to Magrew for a souvenir, and he took it all in good spirit. Whitey Cott and Billy Klinger made up and was fast friends again, and we hit our home lot like a ton of dynamite and they was nothin' could stop us from then on.

I don't recollect things as clear as I did thirty, forty year ago. I can't read no fine print no more, and the only person I got to check with on the golden days of the national pastime, as the fella says, is my friend, old Milt Kline, over in Springfield, and his mind ain't as strong as it once was.

He gets Rube Waddell mixed up with Rube Marquard, for one thing, and anybody does that oughta be put away where he won't bother nobody. So I can't tell you the exact margin we win the pennant by. Maybe it was two and a half games, or maybe it was three and a half. But it'll all be there in the newspapers and record books of thirty, thirty-one year ago and, like I was sayin', you could look it up.

QUESTIONS

1. To whom is the narrator telling his story? Does he seem to be talking or writing? Are there moments in his account when he seems to be artfully designing the tale?

2. For what reason is the manager Squawks Magrew drawn to Pearl du Monville? Almost everyone else is suspicious of him. Why isn't Magrew?

3. Why is the title phrase, "you could look it up," repeatedly echoed in the story? Almost from the start, we know we couldn't "look it up." What, then, is the purpose of the repetition?

4. Why does Pearl du Monville swing his bat at the fourth pitch? Does he want to spoil Magrew's strategy? Does athletic ambition suddenly take control of his mind?

5. After Pearl du Monville vanishes, the team dramatically improves, going on to win the pennant. How do you understand the apparent cause-and-effect relationship between the midget's momentary presence on the team and its later victorious history?

Joyce Carol Oates (b. 1938)
Unmailed, Unwritten Letters

Dear Mother and Father,
    The weather is lovely here. It rained yesterday. Today the sky is blue. The trees are changing colors, it is October 20, I have got to buy some new clothes

sometime soon, we've changed dentists, doctors, everything is lovely here and I hope the same with you. Greg is working hard as usual. The doctor we took Father to see, that time he hurt his back visiting here, has died and so we must change doctors. Dentists also. I want to change dentists because I can't stand to go back to the same dentist any more. He is too much of a fixed point, a reference point. It is such a chore, changing doctors and dentists.

Why are you so far away in the Southwest? Is there something about the Southwest that lures old people? Do they see images there, shapes in the desert? Holy shapes? Why are you not closer to me, or farther away? In an emergency it would take hours or days for you to get to me. I think of the two of you in the Southwest, I see the highways going off into space and wonder at your courage, so late in life, to take on space. Father had all he could do to manage that big house of yours, and the lawn. Even with workers to help him it was terrifying, all that space, because he owned it. Maybe that was why it terrified him, because he owned it. Out in the Southwest I assume no one owns anything. Do people even live there? Some people live there, I know. But I think of the Southwest as an optical illusion, sunshine and sand and a mountainous (mountainous?) horizon, with highways perfectly divided by their white center lines, leading off to Mars or the moon, unhurried. And there are animals, the designs of animals, mashed into the highways! The shape of a dog, a dog's pelty shadow, mashed into the hot, hot road—in mid-flight, so to speak, mid-leap, run over again and again by big trucks and retired people seeing America. That vastness would terrify me. I think of you and I think of protoplasm being drawn off into space, out there, out in the West, with no human limits to keep it safe.

Dear Marsha Katz,

Thank you for the flowers, white flowers, but why that delicate hint of death, all that fragrance wasted on someone like myself who is certain to go on living? Why are you pursuing me? Why in secrecy? (I see all the letters you write to your father, don't forget; and you never mention me in them.) Even if your father were my lover, which is not true and cannot be verified, why should you pursue me? Why did you sign the card with the flowers *Trixie*? I don't know anyone named Trixie! How could I know anyone named Trixie? It is a dog's name, a high school cheerleader's name, an aunt's name . . . why do you play these games, why do you pursue me?

Only ten years old, and too young for evil thoughts—do you look in your precocious heart and see only grit, the remains of things, a crippled shadow of a child? Do you see in all this the defeat of your Daughterliness? Do you understand that a Daughter, like a Mistress, must be feminine or all is lost, must keep up the struggle with the demonic touch of matter-of-fact irony that loses us all our men . . . ? I think you have lost, yes. A ten-year-old cannot compete with a thirty-year-old. Send me all the flowers you want. I pick them apart one by one, getting bits of petals under my fingernails, I throw them out before my husband gets home.

Nor did I eat that box of candies you sent. Signed "Uncle Bumble"!

Are you beginning to feel terror at having lost? Your father and I are not lovers, we hardly see each other any more, since last Wednesday and today is

Monday, still you've lost because I gather he plans on continuing the divorce proceedings, long distance, and what exactly can a child do about that . . . ? I see all the letters you write him. No secrets. Your Cape Cod sequence was especially charming. I like what you did with that kitten, the kitten that is found dead on the beach! Ah, you clever little girl, even with your I.Q. of uncharted heights, you couldn't quite conceal from your father and me your attempt to make him think 1) the kitten suggests a little girl, namely you 2) its death suggests your pending, possible death, if Father does not return. Ah, how we laughed over that! . . . Well, no, we didn't laugh, he did not laugh, perhaps he did not even understand the trick you were playing . . . your father can be a careless, abrupt man, but things stick in his mind, you know that and so you write of a little white kitten, alive one day and dead the next, so you send me flowers for a funeral parlor, you keep me in your thoughts constantly so that I can feel a tug all the way here in Detroit, all the way from Boston, and I hate it, I hate that invisible pulling, tugging, that witch's touch of yours. . . .

Dear Greg,

We met about this time years ago. It makes me dizzy, it frightens me to think of that meeting. Did so much happen, and yet nothing? Miscarriages, three or four, one loses count, and eight or nine sweet bumbling years—why do I use the word *bumbling*, it isn't a word I would ever use—and yet there is nothing there, if I go to your closet and open the door your clothes tell me as much as you do. You are a good man. A faithful husband. A subdued and excellent husband. The way you handled my parents alone would show how good you are, how excellent. . . . My friend X, the one with the daughter said to be a genius and the wife no one has ever seen, X couldn't handle my parents, couldn't put up with my father's talk about principles, the Principles of an Orderly Universe, which he sincerely believes in though he is an intelligent man. . . . X couldn't handle anything, anyone. He loses patience. He is vulgar. He watches himself swerve out of control but can't stop. Once, returning to his car, we found a ticket on the windshield. He snatched it and tore it up, very angry, and then when he saw my surprise he thought to make a joke of it—pretending to be tearing it with his teeth, a joke. And he is weak, angry men are weak. He lets me close doors on him. His face seems to crack with sorrow, but he lets me walk away, why is he so careless and weak . . . ?

But I am thinking of us, our first meeting. An overheated apartment, graduate school . . . a girl in dark stockings, myself, frightened and eager, trying to be charming in a voice that didn't carry, a man in a baggy sweater, gentle, intelligent, a little perplexed, the two of us gravitating together, fearful of love and fearful of not loving, of not being loved. . . . So we met. The evening falls away, years fall away. I count only three miscarriages, really. The fourth a sentimental miscalculation.

My darling,

I am out somewhere, I see a telephone booth on a corner, the air is windy and too balmy for October. I won't go in the phone booth. Crushed papers, a beer bottle, a close violent stench. . . . I walk past it, not thinking of you. I am out of the house so that you can't call me and so that I need not think of you. Do you talk to your wife every night, still? Does she weep into your ear? How many nights have you lain together, you and that woman now halfway across the country, in Boston, weeping into a telephone? Have you forgotten all those nights?

Last night I dreamed about you mashed into a highway. More than dead. I had to wake Greg up, I couldn't stop trembling, I wanted to tell him of the waste, the waste of joy and love, your being mashed soundlessly into a road and pounded into a shape no one would recognize as yours. . . . Your face was gone. What will happen to me when your face is gone from this world?

I parked the car down here so that I could go shopping at Saks but I've been walking, I'm almost lost. The streets are dirty. A tin can lies on the sidewalk, near a vacant lot. Campbell's Tomato Soup. I am dressed in the suit you like, though it is a little baggy on me, it would be a surprise for someone driving past to see a lady in such a suit bend to pick up a tin can. . . . I pick the can up. The edge is jagged and rusty. No insects inside. Why would insects be inside, why bother with an empty can? Idly I press the edge of the lid against my wrist; it isn't sharp, it makes only a fine white line on my skin, not sharp enough to penetrate the skin.

Dear Greg,

I hear you walking downstairs. You are going outside, out into the back yard. I am tempted, heart pounding, to run to the window and spy on you. But everything is tepid, the universe is dense with molecules, I can't get up. My legs won't move. You said last night, "The Mayor told me to shut up in front of Arthur Grant. He told me to shut up." You were amused and hurt at the same time, while I was furious, wishing you were . . . were someone else, someone who wouldn't be amused and hurt, a good man, a subdued man, but someone else who would tell that bastard to go to hell. I am a wife, jealous for her husband.

Three years you've spent working for the Mayor, His Honor, dodging reporters downtown. Luncheons, sudden trips, press conferences, conferences with committees from angry parts of Detroit, all of Detroit angry, white and black, bustling, ominous. Three years. Now he tells you to shut up. All the lies you told for him, not knowing how to lie with dignity, he tells you to shut up, my body suffers as if on the brink of some terrible final expulsion of our love, some blood-smear of a baby. When a marriage ends, who is left to understand it? No witnesses. No young girl in black stockings, no young man, all those witnesses gone, grown up, moved on, lost.

Too many people know you now, your private life is dwindling. You are dragged back again and again to hearings, commission meetings, secret meetings, desperate meetings, television interviews, interviews with kids from college newspapers. Everyone has a right to know everything! *What Detroit Has Done to Combat Slums. What Detroit Has Done To Prevent Riots,* updated to *What Detroit Has Done to Prevent a Recurrence of the 1967 Riot.* You people are rewriting history as fast as history happens. I love you, I suffer for you, I lie here in a paralysis of love, sorrow, density, idleness, lost in my love for you, my shame for having betrayed you. . . . Why should slums be combatted? Once I wept to see photographs of kids playing in garbage heaps, now I weep at crazy sudden visions of my lover's body become only a body, I have no tears left for anyone else, for anything else. Driving in the city I have a sudden vision of my lover dragged along by a stranger's car, his body somehow caught up under the bumper or the fender and dragged along, bleeding wildly in the street. . . .

My dear husband, betraying you was the most serious act of my life. Far more serious than marrying you. I knew my lover better when he finally became my lover than I knew you when you became my husband. I know him better now than I know you. You and I have lived together for eight years. Smooth coins, coins worn smooth by constant handling. . . . I am a woman trapped in love, in the terror of love. Paralysis of love. Like a great tortoise, trapped in a heavy deathlike shell, a mask of the body pressing the body down to earth. . . . I went for a week without seeing him, an experiment. The experiment failed. No husband can keep his wife's love. So you walk out in the back yard, admiring the leaves, the sky, the flagstone terrace, you are a man whom betrayal would destroy and yet your wife betrayed you, deliberately.

To The Editor:

Anonymously and shyly I want to ask—why are white men so weak, so feeble? The other day I left a friend at his hotel and walked quickly, alone, to my car, and the eyes of black men around me moved onto me with a strange hot perception, seeing everything. They knew, seeing me, what I was. Tension rose through the cracks in the sidewalk. Where are white men who are strong, who see women in this way? The molecules in the air of Detroit are humming. I wish I could take a knife and cut out an important piece of my body, my insides, and hold it up . . . on a street corner, an offering. Then will they let me alone? The black men jostle one another on street corners, out of work and not wanting work, content to stare at me, knowing everything in me, not surprised. My lover, a white man, remains back in the hotel, his head in his hands because I have walked out, but he won't run after me, he won't follow me. *They* follow me. One of them bumped into me, pretending it was an accident. I want to cut up my body, I can't live in this body.

Next door to us a boy is out in his driveway, sitting down, playing a drum. Beating on a drum. Is he crazy? A white boy of about sixteen pounding on a drum. He wants to bring the city down with that drum and I don't blame him. I understand that vicious throbbing.

Dear Marsha Katz,

Thank you for the baby clothes. Keep sending me things, test your imagination. I feel that you are drowning. I sense a tightness in your chest, your throat. Are your eyes leaden with defeat, you ten-year-old wonder? How many lives do children relive at the moment of death?

Dear Mother and Father,

The temperature today is ———. Yesterday at this time, ———. Greg has been very busy as usual with ————, ————, ————. This weekend we must see the ————'s, whom you have met. How is the weather there? How is your vacation? Thank you for the postcard from ————. I had not thought lawns would be green there.

. . . The Mayor will ask all his aides for resignations, signed. Some he will accept and others reject. A kingly man, plump and alcoholic. Divorced. Why can't I tell you about my husband's job, about my life, about anything real? Scandals fall on the head of my husband's boss, reading the paper is torture, yet my husband comes home and talks seriously about the future, about improvements, as if no chaos is waiting. No picketing ADC mothers, no stampede to buy guns, no strangled black babies found in public parks. In the midst of this my husband is clean and untouched, innocent, good. He has dedicated his life to helping others. I love him but cannot stop betraying him, again and again, having reclaimed my life as my own to throw away, to destroy, to lose. My life is my own. I keep on living.

My darling,

It is one-thirty and if you don't call by two, maybe you won't call; I know that you have a seminar from two to four, maybe you won't call; I know that you have a seminar from two to four, maybe you won't call today and everything will end. My heart pounds bitterly, in fear, in anticipation? Your daughter sent me some baby clothes, postmarked Boston. I understand her hatred, but one thing: how much did you tell your wife about me? About my wanting children? You told her you no longer loved her and couldn't live with her, that you loved another woman who could not marry you, but . . . did you tell her this other woman had no children? And what else?

I will get my revenge on you.

I walk through the house in a dream, in a daze. I am sinking slowly through the floor of this expensive house, a married woman in a body grown light as a shell, empty as a shell. My body has no other life in it, only its own. What you discharge in me is not life but despair. I can remember my body having life, holding it. It seemed a trick, a feat that couldn't possibly work: like trying to retain liquid up a reed, turning the reed upside down. The doctor said, "Babies are no trouble. Nothing." But the liquid ran out. All liquid runs out of me. That first week, meeting with you at the Statler, everything ran out of me like blood. I alarmed you, you with your nervous sense of fate, your fear of getting cancer, of having a nervous breakdown. I caused you to say stammering *But what if you get pregnant?* I am not pregnant but I feel a strange tingling of life, a tickling, life at a distance, as if the spirit of your daughter is somehow in me, lodged in me. She sucks at my insides with her pinched jealous lips, wanting blood. My body seeks to discharge her magically.

My dear husband,

I wanted to test being alone. I went downtown to the library, the old library. I walked past the hotel where he and I have met, my lover and I, but we were not meeting today and I was alone, testing myself as a woman alone, a human being alone. The library was filled with old men. Over seventy, dressed in black, with white shirts. Black and white: a reading room of old men, dressed in black and white.

I sat alone at a table. Some of the old men glanced at me. In a dream I began to leaf through a magazine, thinking, *Now I am leafing through a magazine: this is expected.* Why can't I be transformed to something else—to a mask, a shell, a statue? I glance around shyly, trying to gauge the nature of the story I am in. Is it tragic or only sad? The actors in this play all seem to be wearing masks, even I am wearing a mask, I am never naked. My nakedness, with my lover, is a kind of mask—something he sees, something I can't quite believe in. Women who are loved are in perpetual motion, dancing. We dance and men follow to the brink of madness and death, but what of us, the dancers?—when the dancing ends we stand back upon our heels, back upon our heels, dazed and hurt. Beneath the golden cloth on our thighs is flesh, and flesh hurts. Men are not interested in the body, which feels pain, but in the rhythm of the body as it goes about its dance, the body of a woman who cannot stop dancing.

A confession. In Ann Arbor last April, at the symposium, I fell in love with a man. The visiting professor from Boston University—a man with black-rimmed glasses, Jewish, dark-eyed, dark-haired, nervous and arrogant and restless. Drumming his fingers. Smoking too much. (And you, my husband, were sane enough to give up smoking five years ago.) A student stood up in the first row and shouted out something and it was he, my lover, the man who would become my lover, who stood up in turn and shouted something back . . . it all happened so fast, astounding everyone, even the kid who reported for the campus newspaper didn't catch the exchange. How many men could handle a situation like that, being wilder and more profane than a heckler? . . . He was in the group at the party afterward, your friend Bryan's house. All of you talked at once, excited and angry over the outcome of the symposium, nervous at the sense of agitation in the air, the danger, and he and I wandered to the hostess's table, where food was set out. We made pigs of ourselves, eating. He picked out the shrimp and I demurely picked out tiny flakes of dough with miniature asparagus in them. Didn't you notice us? Didn't you notice this dark-browed man with the glasses that kept slipping down his nose, with the untidy black har? We talked. We ate. I could see in his bony knuckles a hunger that would never be satisfied. And I, though I think I am starving slowly to death now, I leaped upon the food as if it were a way of getting at him, of drawing him into me. We talked. We wandered around the house. He looked out a window, drawing a curtain aside, at the early spring snowfall, falling gently outside, and he said that he didn't know why he had come to this part of the country, he was frightened of traveling, of strangers. He said that he was very tired. He seduced me with the slump of his shoulders. And when he turned back to me we entered another stage of the evening, having grown nervous and brittle with each other, the two of us suddenly conscious of being together. My eyes grew hot and searing. I said carelessly that he must come over to Detroit sometime, we could have lunch, and he said at once, "I'd like that very much. . . ." and then paused. Silence.

Later, in the hotel, in the cheap room he rented, he confessed to me that seeing my face had been an experience for him—did he believe in love at first sight, after all? Something so childish? It had been some kind of love, anyway. We talked about our lives, about his wife, about my husband, and then he swung onto another subject, talking about his daughter for forty-five minutes . . . a genius, a ten-year-old prodigy. I am brought low, astounded. I want to cry out to him, *But what about me! Don't stop thinking about me!* At the age of six his daughter was writing poems, tidy little poems, like Blake's. *Like Blake's? Yes.* At the age of eight she was publishing those poems.

No, I don't want to marry him. I'm not going to marry him. What we do to each other is too violent, I don't want it brought into marriage and domesticated, nor do I want him to see me at unflattering times of the day . . . getting up at three in the morning to be sick, a habit of mine. He drinks too much. He reads about the connection between smoking and death, and turns the page of the newspaper quickly. Superstitious, stubborn. In April he had a sore throat, that was why he spoke so hoarsely on the program . . . but a month later he was no better: "I'm afraid of doctors," he said. This is a brilliant man, the father of a brilliant child? We meet nowhere, at an unimaginative point X, in a hotel room, in the anonymous drafts of air from blowers that never stop blowing, the two of us yearning to be one, in this foreign dimension where anything is possible. Only later, hurrying to my car, do I feel resentment and fury at him . . . why doesn't he buy me anything, why doesn't he get a room for us, something permanent? And hatred for him rises in me in long shuddering surges, overwhelming me. I don't want to marry him. Let me admit the worst—anxious not to fall in love with him, I think of not loving him at the very moment he enters me, I think of him already boarding a plane and disappearing from my life, with relief, I think with pity of human beings and this sickness of theirs, this desire for unity. Why this desire for unity, why? We walk out afterward, into the sunshine or into the smog. Obviously we are lovers. Once I saw O'Leary, from the Highway Commission, he nodded and said a brisk hello to me, ignored my friend; obviously we are lovers, anyone could tell. We walked out in the daylight, looking for you. That day, feverish and aching, we were going to tell you everything. He was going to tell his wife everything. But nothing happened . . . we ended up in a cocktail lounge, we calmed down. The air conditioning calmed us. On the street we passed a Negro holding out pamphlets to other Negroes but drawing them back when whites passed. I saw the headline— *Muslim Killed in Miami Beach by Fascist Police.* A well-dressed Negro woman turned down a pamphlet with a toothy, amused smile—none of that junk for her! My lover didn't even notice.

Because he is not my husband I don't worry about him. I worry about my own husband, whom I own. I don't own this man. I am thirty and he is forty-one; to him I am young—what a laugh. I don't worry about his coughing, his drinking (sometimes over the telephone I can hear ice cubes tinkling in a glass—he drinks to get the courage to call me), his loss of weight, his professional standing. He didn't return to his job in Boston, but stayed on here. A strange move. The department at Michigan considered it a coup to get him, this disintegrating, arrogant man, they were willing to pay him well, a man who has already made enemies there. No, I don't worry about him.

On a television program he was moody and verbose, moody and silent by turns. Smokes too much. Someone asked him about the effect of something on something—Vietnam on the presidential election, I think—and he missed subtleties, he sounded distant, vague. Has lost passion for the truth. He has lost his passion for politics, discovering in himself a passion for me. It isn't my fault. On the street he doesn't notice things, he smiles slowly at me, complimenting me, someone brushes against him and he doesn't notice, what am I doing to this man? Lying in his arms I am inspired to hurt him. I say that we will have to give this up, these meetings; too much risk, shame. What about my husband, what about his wife? (A deliberate insult—I know he doesn't love his wife.) I can see at once that I've hurt him, his face shows everything, and as soon as this registers in both of us I am stunned with the injustice of what I've done to him, I must erase it, cancel it out, undo it; I caress his body in desperation. . . . Again and again. A pattern. What do I know about caressing the bodies of men? I've known only two men in my life. My husband and his successor. I have never wanted to love anyone, the strain and risk are too great, yet I have fallen in love for the second time in my life and this time the sensation is terrifying, bitter, violent. It ends the first cycle, supplants all that love, erases all that affection—destroys everything. I stand back dazed, flat on my heels, the dance being over. I will not move on into another marriage. I will die slowly in this marriage rather than come to life in another.

Dear Mrs. Katz,

I received your letter of October 25 and I can only say
I don't know how to begin this letter except to tell you
Your letter is here on my desk. I've read it over again and again all morning. It is true, yes, that I have made the acquaintance of a man who is evidently your husband, though he has not spoken of you. We met through mutual friends in Ann Arbor and Detroit. Your informant at the University is obviously trying to upset you, for her own reasons. I assume it is a woman— who else would write you such a letter? I know nothing of your personal affairs. Your husband and I have only met a few times, socially. What do you want from me?

And your daughter, tell your daughter to let me alone!

Thank you both for thinking of me. I wish I could be equal to your hatred. But the other day an old associate of my husband's, a bitch of a man, ran into me in the Fisher lobby and said, "What's happened to you—you look terrible! You've lost weight!" He pinched the waist of my dress, drawing it out to show how it hung loose on me, he kept marveling over how thin I am, not releasing me. A balding, pink-faced son of a bitch who has made himself rich by being on the board of supervisors for a country north of here, stuffing himself at the trough. I know all about him. A subpolitician, never elected. But I trust the eyes of these submen, their hot keen perception. Nothing escapes them. "One month ago," he said, "you were a beautiful woman." Nothing in my life has hurt me as much as that remark, *One month ago you were a beautiful woman.* . . .

Were you ever beautiful? He says not. So he used you, he used you up. That isn't my fault. You say in your letter—thank you for typing it, by the way—that I could never understand your husband, his background of mental instability, his weaknesses, his penchant (your word) for blaming other people for his own faults. Why tell me this? He isn't going to be my husband. I have a husband. Why should I betray my husband for yours, your nervous, guilty, hypochrondriac husband? The first evening we met, believe it or not, he told me about his *hurts*—people who've hurt him deeply! "The higher you go in a career, the more people take after you, wanting to bring you down," he told me. And listen: "The worst hurt of my life was when my first book came out, and an old professor of mine, a man I had idolized at Columbia, reviewed it. He began by saying, *Bombarded as we are by prophecies in the guise of serious historical research . . .* and my heart was broken." We were at a party but apart from the other people, we ate, he drank, we played a game with each other that made my pulse leap, and certainly my pulse leaped to hear a man, a stranger, speak of his heart being broken—where I come from men don't talk like that! I told him a *hurt* of my own, which I've never told anyone before: "The first time my mother saw my husband, she took me aside and said, *Can't you tell him to stand up straighter?* and my heart was broken. . . ."

And so, with those words, I had already committed adultery, betraying my husband to a stranger.

Does he call you every night? I am jealous of those telephone calls. What if he changes his mind and returns to you, what then? When he went to the Chicago convention I'm sure he telephoned you constantly (he telephoned me only three times, the bastard) and joked to you about his fear of going out into the street. "Jesus, what if somebody smashes in my head, there goes my next book!" he said over the phone, but he wasn't kidding me. I began to cry, imagining him beaten up, bloody, far away from me. Why does he joke like that? Does he joke like that with you?

Dear Mother and Father,

My husband Greg is busy with ————. Doing well. Not fired. Pressure on, pressure off. Played golf with ————. I went to a new doctor yesterday, a woman. I had made an appointment to go to a man but lost my courage, didn't show up. Better a woman. She examined me, she looked at me critically and said, "Why are you trying to starve yourself?" *To keep myself from feeling love, from feeling lust, from feeling anything at all.* I told her I didn't know I was starving myself. I had no appetite. Food sickened me . . . how could I eat? She gave me a vitamin shot that burned me, like fire. Things good for you burn like fire, shot up into you, no escape. You would not like my lover, you would take me aside and say, *Jews are very brilliant and talented, yes, but. . . .*

I am surviving at half-tempo. A crippled waltz tempo. It is only my faith in the flimsiness of love that keeps me going—I know this will end. I've been waiting for it to end since April, having faith. Love can't last. Even lust can't last. I loved my husband and now I do not love him, we never sleep together, that's through. Since he isn't likely to tell you that, I will.

Lloyd Burt came to see my husband the other day, downtown. Eleven in the morning and already drunk. His kid had been stopped in Grosse Pointe, speeding. The girl with him knocked out on pills. *He* had no pills on him, luckily. Do you remember Lloyd? Do you remember any of us? I am your daughter. Do you regret having had a daughter? I do not regret having no children, not now. Children, more children, children upon children, protoplasm upon protoplasm. . . . Once I thought I couldn't bear to live without having children, now I can't bear to live at all. I must be the wife of a man I can't have, I don't even want children from him. I sit here in my room with my head and body aching with a lust that has become metaphysical and skeptical and bitter, living on month after month, cells dividing and heating endlessly. I don't regret having no children. I don't thank you for having me. No gratitude in me, nothing. No, I feel no gratitude. I can't feel gratitude.

My dear husband,
 I want to tell you everything. I am in a motel room, I've just taken a bath. How can I keep a straight face telling you this? Sat in the bathtub for an hour, not awake, not asleep, the water was very hot. . . .
 I seem to want to tell you something else, about Sally Rodgers. I am lightheaded, don't be impatient. I met Sally at the airport this afternoon, she was going to New York, and she saw me with a man, a stranger to her, the man who is the topic of this letter, the crucial reason for this letter. . . . Sally came right up to me and started talking, exclaiming about her bad fortune, her car had been stolen last week! Then, when she and a friend took her boat out of the yacht club and docked it at a restaurant on the Detroit River, she forgot to take the keys out and someone stole her boat! Twenty thousand dollars' worth of boat, a parting gift from her ex-husband, pirated away down-river. She wore silver eyelids, silver stockings, attracting attention not from men but from small children, who stared. My friend, my lover, did not approve of her—her clanking jewelry made his eye twitch.
 I am thirty miles from Detroit. In Detroit the multiplication of things is too brutal, I think it broke me down. Weak, thin, selfish, a wreck, I have become oblivious to the deaths of other people. (Robert Kennedy was murdered since I became this man's mistress, but I had no time to think of him—I put the thought of his death aside, to think of later. No time now.) Leaving him and walking in Detroit, downtown, on those days we met to make love, I began to understand what love is. Holding a man between my thighs, my knees, in my arms, one single man out of all this multiplication of men, this confusion, this din of human beings. So it is we choose someone. Someone chooses us. I admit that if he did not love me so much I couldn't love him. It would pass. But a woman has no choice, let a man love her and she must love him, if the man is strong enough. I stopped loving you, I am a criminal. . . . I see myself sinking again and again beneath his body, those heavy shoulders with tufts of dark hair on them, again and again pressing my mouth against his, wanting something from him, betraying you, giving myself up to that throbbing that arises out of my heartbeat and builds to madness and then subsides again, slowly, to become my ordinary heartbeat again, the heartbeat of an ordinary body from which divinity has fled.
 Flesh with an insatiable soul. . . .
 You would hear in a few weeks, through your innumerable far-flung cronies, that my lover's daughter almost died of aspirin poison, a ten-year-old girl with an I.Q. of about 200. But she didn't die. She took aspirin because her father was leaving her, divorcing her mother. The only gratitude I can feel

is for her not having died. . . . My lover, whom you hardly know (he's the man of whom you said that evening, "He certainly can talk!") telephoned me to give me this news, weeping over the phone. A man weeping. A man weeping turns a woman's heart to stone. I told him I would drive out at once, I'd take him to the airport. He had to catch the first plane home and would be on stand-by at the airport. So I drove to Ann Arbor to get him. I felt that we were already married and that passion had raced through us and left us years ago, as soon as I saw him lumbering to the car, a man who has lost weight in the last few months but who carries himself a little clumsily, out of absent-mindedness. He wore a dark suit, rumpled. His necktie pulled away from his throat. A father distraught over his daughter belongs to mythology. . . .

Like married people, like conspirators, like characters in a difficult scene hurrying their lines, uncertain of the meaning of lines . . . "It's very thought-ful of you to do this," he said, and I said, "What else can I do for you? Make telephone calls? Anything?" *Should I go along with you?* So I drive him to the airport. I let him out at the curb, he hesitates, not wanting to go without me. He says, "But aren't you coming in . . . ?" and I see fear in his face. I tell him yes, yes, but I must park the car. This man, so abrupt and insulting in his profession, a master of whining rhetoric, stares at me in bewilderment as if he cannot remember why I have brought him here to let him out at the United Air Lines terminal, why I am eager to drive away. "I can't park here," I tell him sanely, "I'll get a ticket." He respects all minor law; he nods and backs away. It takes me ten minutes to find a parking place. All this time I am sweating in the late October heat, thinking that his daughter is going to win after all, has already won. Shouldn't I just drive home and leave him, put an end to it? A bottle of aspirin was all it took. The tears I might almost shed are not tears of shame or regret but tears of anger—that child has taken my lover from me. That child! I don't cry, I don't allow myself to cry, I drive all the way through a parking lot without finding a place and say to the girl at the booth, who puts her hand out expecting a dime, "But I couldn't find a place! I've driven right through! This isn't fair!" Seeing my hysteria, she relents, opens the gate, lets me through. *Once a beautiful woman,* she is thinking. I try another parking lot.

Inside the terminal, a moment of panic—what if he has already left? Then he hurries to me. I take his arm. He squeezes my hand. Both of us very nervous, agitated. "They told me I can probably make the two-fifteen, can you wait with me?" he says. His face, now so pale, is a handsome man's face gone out of control; a pity to look upon it. In a rush I feel my old love for him, hopeless. I begin to cry. Silently, almost without tears. A girl in a very short skirt passes us with a smile—lovers, at their age! "You're not to blame," he says, very nervous, "she's just a child and didn't know what she was doing— please don't blame yourself! It's my fault—" But a child tried to commit suicide, shouldn't someone cry? I am to blame. She is hurting me across the country. I have tried to expel her from life and she, the baby, the embryo, stirs with a will of her own and chooses death calmly. . . . "But she's going to recover," I say to him for the twentieth time, "isn't she? You're sure of that?" He reassures me. We walk.

The airport is a small city. Outside the plate glass, airplanes rise and sink without effort. Great sucking vacuums of power, enormous wings, windows brilliant with sunlight. We look on unamazed. To us these airplanes are unspectacular. We walk around the little city, walking fast and then slowing down, wandering, holding hands. It is during one of those strange lucky moments that lovers have—he lighting a cigarette—that Sally comes up to us. We are not holding hands at that moment. She talks, bright with attention for my friend, she herself being divorced and not equipped to live without a man. He smiles nervously, ignoring her, watching people hurry by with their luggage. She leaves. We glance at each other, understanding each other. Nothing to say. *My darling!* . . .

Time does not move quickly. I am sweating again, I hope he won't notice, he is staring at me in that way . . . the way that frightens me. I am not equal to your love, I want to tell him. Not equal, not strong enough. I am ashamed. Better for us to say good-by. A child's corpse between us? A few hundred miles away, in Boston, are a woman and a child I have wronged, quite intentionally; aren't these people real? But he stares at me, the magazine covers on a newsstand blur and wink, I feel that everything is becoming a dream and I must get out of here, must escape from him, before it is too late. . . . "I should leave," I tell him. He seems not to hear. He is sick. Not sick; frightened. He shows too much. He takes my hand, caresses it, pleading in silence. A terrible sensation of desire rises in me, surprising me. I don't want to feel desire for him! I don't want to feel it for anyone, I don't want to feel anything at all! I don't want to be drawn to an act of love, or even to think about it; I want freedom, I want the smooth sterility of coins worn out from friendly handling, rubbing together, I want to say good-by to love at the age of thirty, not being strong enough for it. A woman in the act of love feels no joy but only terror, a parody of labor, giving birth. Torture. Heartbeat racing at 160, 180 beats a minute, where is joy in this, what is this deception, this joke. Isn't the body itself a joke?

He leads me somewhere, along a corridor. Doesn't know where he is going. people head toward us with suitcases. A soldier on leave from Vietnam, we don't notice, a Negro woman weeping over another soldier, obviously her son, my lover does not see. A man brushes against me and with exaggerated fear I jump to my lover's side . . . but the man keeps on walking, it is nothing. My lover strokes my damp hand. "You won't. . . . You're not thinking of. . . . What are you thinking of?" he whispers. Everything is open in him, everything. He is not ashamed of the words he says, of his fear, his pleading. No irony in him, this ironic man. And I can hear myself saying that we must put an end to this, it's driving us both crazy and there is no future, nothing ahead of us, but I don't say these words or anything like them. We walk along. I am stunned. I feel a heavy, ugly desire for him, for his body. I want him as I've wanted him many times before, when our lives seemed simpler, when we were both deluded about what we were doing . . . both of us thought, in the beginning, that no one would care if we fell in love . . . not my husband, not his family. I don't know why. Now I want to say good-by to him but nothing comes out, nothing. I am still crying a little. It is not a weapon of mine—it is an admission of defeat. I am not a woman who cries well. Crying is a confession of failure, a giving in. I tell him no, I am not thinking of anything, only of him. I love him. I am not thinking of anything else.

We find ourselves by Gate 10. What meaning has Gate 10 to us? People are lingering by it, obviously a plane has just taken off, a stewardess is shuffling papers together, everything is normal. I sense normality and am drawn to it. We wander on. We come to a doorway, a door held open by a large block of wood. Where does that lead to? A stairway. The stairway is evidently not open. We can see that it leads up to another level, a kind of runway, and though it is not open he takes my hand and leads me to the stairs. In a delirium I follow him, why not? The airport is so crowded that we are alone and anonymous. He kicks the block of wood away, wisely. We are alone. On this stairway—which smells of disinfectant and yet is not very clean—my lover embraces me eagerly, wildly, he kisses me, kisses my damp cheeks, rubs his face against mine. I half-fall, half-sit on the stairs. He begins to groan, or to weep. He presses his face against me, against my breasts, my body. It is like wartime—a battle is going on outside, in the corridor. Hundreds of people! A world of people jostling one another! Here, in a dim stairway, clutching each other, we are oblivious to their deaths. But I want to be good! What have I wanted in my life except to be good? To lead a simple, good, intelligent life? He kisses my knees, my thighs, my stomach. I embrace him against me. Everything has gone wild, I am seared with the desire to be unfaithful to a husband who no longer exists, nothing else matters except this act of unfaithfulness. I feel that I am a character in a story, a plot, who has not understood until now exactly what is going to happen to her. Selfish, eager, we come together and do not breathe, we are good friends and anxious to help each other, I am particularly anxious to help him, my soul is sweated out of me in those two or three minutes that we cling together in love. Then, moving from me, so quickly exhausted, he puts his hands to his face and seems to weep without tears, while I feel my eyelids closing slowly upon the mangled length of my body. . . .

This is a confession but part of it is blacked out. Minutes pass in silence, mysteriously. It is those few minutes that pass after we make love that are most mysterious to me, uncanny. And then we cling to each other again, like people too weak to stand by ourselves; we are sick in our limbs but warm with affection, very good friends, the kind of friends who tell each other only good news. He helps me to my feet. We laugh. Laughter weakens me, he has to hold me, I put my arms firmly around his neck and we kiss, I am ready to give up all my life for him, just to hold him like this. My body is all flesh. There is nothing empty about us, only a close space, what appears to be a stairway in some public place. . . . He draws my hair back from my face, he stares at me. It is obvious that he loves me.

When we return to the public corridor no one has missed us. It is strangely late, after three. This is a surprise, I am really surprised, but my lover is more businesslike and simply asks at the desk—the next plane? to Boston? what chance of his getting on? His skin is almost ruddy with pleasure.

I can see what pleasure does to a man. But now I must say good-by, I must leave. He holds my hand. I linger. We talk seriously and quietly in the middle of the great crowded floor about his plans—he will stay in Boston as long as he must, until things are settled; he will see his lawyer; he will talk it over, *talk it over*, with his wife and his daughter, he will not leave until they understand why he has to leave. . . . I want to cry out at him, *Should you come back?* but I can't say anything. Everything in me is a curving to submission, in spite of what you, my husband, have always thought.

Finally . . . he boards a plane at four. I watch him leave. He looks back at me, I wave, the plane taxis out onto the runway and rises . . . no accident, no violent ending. There is nothing violent about us, everything is natural and gentle. Walking along the long corridor I bump into someone, a woman my own age. I am suddenly dizzy. She says, "Are you all right?" I turn away, ashamed. I am on fire! My body is on fire! I feel his semen stirring in my loins, that rush of heat that always makes me pause, staring into the sky or at a wall, at something blank to mirror the blankness in my mind . . . stunned, I feel myself so heavily a body, so lethargic with the aftermath of passion. How did I hope to turn myself into a statue, into the constancy of a soul? No hope. The throbbing in my loins has not yet resolved itself into the throbbing of my heart. A woman does not forget so quickly, nothing lets her forget. I am transparent with heat. I walk on, feeling my heart pound weakly, feeling the moisture between my legs, wondering if I will ever get home. My vision seems blotched. The air—air conditioning—is humming, unreal. It is not alien to me but a part of my own confusion, a long expulsion of my own breath. What do I look like making love? Is my face distorted, am I ugly? Does he see me? Does he judge? Or does he see nothing but beauty, transported in love as I am, helpless?

I can't find the car. Which parking lot? The sun is burning. A man watches me, studies me. I walk fast to show that I know what I'm doing. And if the car is missing, stolen . . . ? I search through my purse, noting how the lining is soiled, ripped. Fifty thousand dollars in the bank and no children and I can't get around to buying a new purse; everything is soiled, ripped, worn out . . . the keys are missing . . . only wadded tissue, a sweetish smell, liquid stiffening on the tissue . . . everything hypnotizes me. . . . I find the keys, my vision swims, I will never get home.

My knees are trembling. There is an ocean of cars here at Metropolitan Airport. Families stride happily to cars, get in, drive away. I wander around, staring. I must find my husband's car in order to get home. . . . I check in my purse again, panicked. No, I haven't lost the keys. I take the keys out of my purse to look at them. The key to the ignition, to the trunk, to the front door of the house. All there. I look around slyly and see, or think I see, a man watching me. He moves behind a car. He is walking away. My body still throbs from the love of another man, I can't concentrate on a stranger, I lose interest and forget what I am afraid of. . . .

The heat gets worse. Thirty, forty, forty-five minutes pass . . . I have given up looking for the car . . . I am not lost, I am still heading home in my imagination, but I have given up looking for the car. I turn terror into logic. I ascend the stairway to the wire-guarded overpass that leads back to the terminal, walking sensibly, and keep on walking until I come to one of the airport motels. I ask them for a room. A single. Why not? Before I can go home I must bathe, I must get the odor of this man out of me, I must clean myself. I take a room, I close the door to the room behind me; alone, I go to the bathroom and run a tubful of water. . . .

And if he doesn't call me from Boston then all is finished, at an end. What good luck, to be free again and alone, the way I am alone in this marvelous empty motel room! the way I am alone in this bathtub, cleansing myself of him, of every cell of him!

My darling,
You have made me so happy. . . .

QUESTIONS

1. What is the true chronology of events in this story? What happens? Would the events seem melodramatic if narrated more directly?

2. Since the letters that comprise this narrative are not only unmailed but unwritten, the story is essentially the heroine's stream of consciousness. How reliable a narrator is she? At which points do you doubt her version of events? How do you see the truth?

3. Who is "in the right" in this story? Whom do you identify with and why? How does Oates determine where your sympathies finally lie?

4. How would you describe the narrator of this story? How does Oates give her characterization and complexity?

5. This story was written in the late 1960s, during a time of profound social unrest. What do you make of the references to the death of Robert Kennedy and other aspects of this troubled era? How important a role do they play in the story?

John Gardner (1933–1982)
Nimram

Ich bin von Gott und will wieder zu Gott.

Seated by the window in the last row of the first-class no-smoking section, his large attaché case edged under the seat in front of him, his seatbelt snug and buckled, Benjamin Nimram drew off his dark glasses, tucked them into his inside coat-pocket, and in the same motion turned to look out at the rain on the gleaming tarmac. The dark glasses were his wife's idea, an idea he'd accepted in the way he accepted nearly all her ideas, with affection and a tuck at the corner of his mouth that signified, though his wife did not know it—or so he imagined—private amusement tinged with that faint trace of fatalistic melancholy one might catch, if one were watchful, at the periphery of all he did. Not that Nimram was a gloomy man. When he'd put behind him, at least for public appearances, that famous "Beethoven frown"—once a private joke between his wife and himself but now a thing as public as the mileage of his Rolls, since his wife had mentioned both, in an unguarded moment, to an interviewer—he'd discovered that smiling like a birthday child as he strode, tails flying, toward the light-drenched podium came as naturally to him as breathing, or at any rate as naturally as the second-nature breathing of an oboist. He had mentioned to her—more in the way of trying it out than as sober communication of a determined fact—that it made him uneasy, being recognized everywhere he went these days.

"You poor dear!" she'd said, eyes slightly widening, and he had smiled privately, realizing that now he was in for it. "We'll get a pair of those Polaroid prescription dark glasses," she'd said.

"Good idea," he'd agreed, seeing himself in them the instant he said it—the dark, heavy face, thick eyebrows, large nose, the somewhat embarrassingly expensive suit. "And a shoulder-holster, maybe," he'd thought, but had carefully shown nothing but the tuck at the corner of his mouth.

"Is something wrong?" she'd asked. She stood in the doorway, half in, half out, trowel in hand, a paper bag of some kind of chemical clamped under her arm. He'd caught her on her way out to her gardening. She was smiling brightly, head tipped and thrown toward him, back into the room. It was the look she sometimes got on the tennis court, extravagantly polite, aggressive.

"What could be wrong?" he said, tossing his arms out. "I'll pick up a pair this afternoon."

"Jerry can get them," she said. "I'll phone in ahead." Jerry was their outside man, a grinning young half-Japanese. What he did around the place—besides stand with his arms folded, or ride around the lawn on the huge green mower—had never been clear to Nimram.

"Fine," he said, "fine."

She blew him a kiss and ran out.

Poor Arline, he thought, shaking his head, slightly grinning. "I believe I was destined for this marriage," she had once told an interviewer. Though she was sometimes embarrassed almost to tears by what she read in the interviews she'd given to newspapers and magazines, she continued to give them. She saw it as part of her duty as his wife, keeping his name out there. And though she tried to be more careful, knowing how "different" things could sound in print, to say nothing of how reporters could distort if they were, as she said, "that kind"—turning trifles to tragedies, missing jokes, even suddenly attacking her for no reason (one had once called her "a musical ignoramus")—she continued to forget and speak her mind. Nimram praised her, needless to say, no matter what she said. Certainly there was never any harm in her words.

Even her cunning, when she schemed about his "image" or the I.R.S., had the innocent openness of the Michigan fields around her father's little place in the country, as he called it—a house sometimes visited, long before her father had bought it, by the elder Henry Ford.

There wasn't a great deal Arline could do for him in the world, or anyway not a great deal he could make her feel he needed and appreciated—aside, of course, from her elegant company at social gatherings, for instance fundraisers. She was "a good Michigan girl," as she said; Republican, a member (lapsed) of the D.A.R. Subtly—or no, not subtly, but openly, flagrantly—she had been trained from birth for the sacred and substantial position of Good Wife. She was a quick learner—even brilliant, he might have said in an unguarded moment, if Nimram ever had such moments—and she had snapped up the requisite skills of her position the way a streetdog snaps up meat. She was not a great reader (books were one of Nimram's passions), and music was not really her first interest in life, except, of course, when Nimram conducted it; but she could keep a household like an old-time Viennese aristocrat; she could "present" her husband, choosing the right restaurants, wines, and charities, buying him not only the exactly right clothes, as it seemed to her (and for all he knew she had unerring taste, though sometimes her choices raised his eyebrows at first), but also finding him the exactly right house, or, rather, Brentwood mansion—formerly the home of a reclusive movie star—the suitable cars—first the Porsche, then on second thought, of course, the Rolls—the suitably lovable fox terrier, which Arline had named Trixie. She had every skill known to the well-to-do Midwestern wife, including certain bedroom skills that Nimram waited with a smile of dread for her to reveal, in her open-hearted, Michigan way, to some yenta fom *People* magazine or the L.A. *Times*. But for all that, she had moments, he knew, when she seemed to herself inadequate, obscurely unprepared.

"Do you like the house?" she had asked him once, with a bright smile and an uneasiness around the eyes that made his heart go out to her. It was only his heart that got up from the chair, the rest of him sat solid as a rock, with a marked-up score on his knees.

"Of course I like it," he'd answered. "I love it!" When they were alone or among intimate friends his voice had, at times, a hearty bellow that could make Arline jump.

"Good!" she'd said, and had smiled more brightly, then had added, her expression unsure again, "It does seem a solid investment."

Nimram might have said, if he were someone else, "What's the difference? What's a house? I'm the greatest conductor in the world! Civilization is my house!" That, however, was the kind of thing Nimram never said to anyone, even in one of his rare but notorious rages.

Her look of uncertainty was almost anguish now, though she labored to conceal it, and so he'd laid down the score he was fiddling with, had renounced the brief flash of doubt over whether he should leave it there—defenseless on the carpet, where the dog could come in and, say, drool on it—and had swung up out of his chair and strode over to seize her in his arms and press his cheek to hers, saying, "What's this craziness? It's a beautiful house and I love it!"

There had been, apparently, an edge of uncontrol in his heartiness, or perhaps it was simply the age-old weight of the world distracting her, time and the beauty of things falling away, nothing sure, nothing strong enough to bear her up—not yet, anyway, not as quickly as that—not even the strength in her famous conductor's arms. "I'm sorry," she'd said, blinking away tears, giving her embarrassed Midwesterner laugh. "Aren't I a fool?"—biting her lips now, taking on the sins of the world.

"Come," he'd said, "we eat out." It was his standard response to all sorrows no energy of the baton could transmute; a brief arrogation of the power of God—no offense, since God had no interest in it, it seemed.

"But dinner's been—" she'd begun, drawing back from him, already of two minds.

"No no," he'd said, tyrannical. "Go get dressed. We eat out." Candlelight burning through the wine bottle, silverware shining like her dream of eternity, people across the room showing one by one and four by four their covert signs of having recognized the famous conductor, a thing they could speak of tomorrow and next week, next year, perhaps, buoy themselves up on in dreary times, the memory of that dinner miraculously blessed, as if God Himself had come to sit with them. The tuck of private amusement and sadness touched the corner of Nimram's mouth.

He was not a man who had ever given thought to whether or not his opinions of himself and his effect on the world were inflated. He was a musician simply, or not so simply; an interpreter of Mahler and Bruckner, Sibelius and Nielsen—much as his wife Arline, buying him clothes, transforming his Beethoven frown to his now just as famous bright smile, brushing her lips across his cheek as he plunged (always hurrying) toward sleep, was the dutiful and faithful interpreter of Benjamin Nimram. His life was sufficient, a joy to him, in fact. One might have thought of it—and so Nimram himself thought of it, in certain rare moods—as one resounding success after another. He had conducted every major symphony in the world, had been granted by Toscanini's daughters the privilege of studying their father's scores, treasure-horde of the old man's secrets; he could count among his closest friends some of the greatest musicians of his time. He had so often been called a genius by critics everywhere that he had come to take it for granted that he was indeed just that—"just that" in both senses, exactly that and merely that: a fortunate accident, a man supremely lucky. Had he been born with an ear just a little less exact, a personality more easily ruffled, dexterity less precise, or some physical weakness—a heart too feeble for the demands he made of it, or arthritis, the plague of so many conductors—he would still, no doubt, have been a symphony man, but his ambition would have been checked a little, his ideas of self-fulfillment scaled down. Whatever fate had dealt him he would have learned, no doubt, to put up with, guarding his chips. But Nimram had been dealt all high cards, and he knew it. He revelled in his fortune, sprawling when he sat, his big-boned fingers splayed wide on his belly like a man who's just had dinner, his spirit as playful as a child's for all the gray at his temples, all his middle-aged bulk and weight—packed muscle, all of it—a man too much enjoying himself to have time for scorn or for fretting over whether or not he was getting his due, which, anyway, he was. He was one of the elect. He sailed through the world like a white yacht jubilant with flags.

The rain fell steadily, figures and dark square tractors hurrying toward the belly of the plane and then away again, occasionally glowing under blooms of silent lightning, in the aisle behind him passengers still moving with the infinite patience of Tolstoy peasants toward their second-class seats. With a part of his mind he watched their reflections in the window and wondered idly how many of them, if any, had seen him conduct, seen anyone conduct, cared at all for the shimmering ghost he had staked his life on. None of them, so far as he could tell, had even noticed the Muzak leaking cheerfully, mindlessly, from the plane's invisible speakers. It would be turned off when the plane was safely airborne, for which he was grateful, needless to say. Yet it was touching, in a way, that the airline should offer this feeble little gesture of reassurance—*All will be well! Listen to the Muzak! All will be well!* They scarcely heard it, these children of accident, old and young, setting out across the country in the middle of the night; yet perhaps it was true that they were comforted, lulled.

Now a voice said behind him, professionally kind, "There you are. There! Shall I take these? All right?"

When he turned, the stewardess was taking the metal crutches from the young woman—girl, rather—newly planted in the seat beside him.

"Thank you," the girl was saying, reaching down to each side of her for the straps of her seatbelt.

"They'll be right up in front," the stewardess said, drawing the crutches toward her shoulder to clamp them in one arm. "If you need anything, you just sing. All right?"

"Thank you," the girl said again, nodding, drawing up the straps now, studying the buckle. She nodded one more time, smiling suddenly, seeing how the buckle worked, and closed it. She glanced briefly at Nimram, then away again. She was perhaps sixteen.

He too looked away and, with his heart jumping, considered the image of her fixed in his mind. She was so much like his wife Arline—though of course much younger—that he was ready to believe her a lost sister. It was impossible, he knew; Arline's people were not the kind who lost things, much less the kind who had secrets, except on Christmas morning. Yet for all his certainty, some stubborn, infantile part of his brain seized on the idea with both fists and refused to let go. Her hair, like Arline's, was reddish brown, with an outer layer of yellow; hair so soft and fine it was like a brush of light. Their foreheads, noses, mouths, and chins were identical too, or so he'd thought at first. As he turned now, furtively checking, he saw that the girl's nose was straighter than Arline's—prettier, if anything—and more lightly freckled. For all that, the likeness grew stronger as he studied it.

She looked up, caught him watching her, smiled, and looked away. The blue of her eyes was much paler than the blue of Arline's, and the difference so startled him that for a moment—shifting in his seat, clearing his throat, turning to look out at the rain again—he could hardly believe he'd thought the two faces similar. He watched the girl's reflection, in the window eight inches from his face, as she reached toward the pocket on the back of the seat in front of her and drew out a magazine, or perhaps the plasticized safety card.

"I hope they know what they're doing," she said.

Her face, when he half turned to look, showed no sign of joking. Ordinarily, Nimram would have smiled and said nothing. For some reason he spoke. "This your first trip on an airplane?"

She nodded, smiling back, a smile so full of panic he almost laughed.

"Don't worry," he said, "the pilot's in front. Anything happens, he gets it first. He's very concerned about that." Nimram winked.

The girl studied him as if lost in thought, the smile on her face still there but forgotten, and it seemed to him he knew what she was thinking. She was in no condition to pick up ironies. When he'd told her the pilot was "very concerned," did he mean that the pilot was nervous? neurotic? beginning to slip? Did this big, expensive-looking man in the seat beside her *know* the pilot?

"Do you know the pilot?" she asked innocently, brightening up her smile.

"A joke," he said. "Among people who fly airplanes it's the oldest joke in the world. It means don't worry."

She turned away and looked down at the plasticized card. "It's just, with the rain and everything," she said softly, "what happens if a plane gets hit by lightning?"

"I doubt that it would do any harm," he said, knowing it wasn't true. The Vienna Quartet had been killed just a year ago when their plane had been knocked down by lightning. "Anyway, we won't be going anywhere near where the lightning is. They have sophisticated weather charts, radar . . . anyway, most of the time we'll be high above it all. You live here in Los Angeles?"

The girl glanced at him, smiling vaguely. She hadn't heard. The Captain had broken in on the Muzak to tell them his name and the usual trivia, their projected altitude, flight time, weather, the airline's friendly advice about seatbelts. Nimram examined the girl's arm and hand on the armrest, then looked at his own and frowned. She had something wrong with her. He remembered that she'd come on with crutches, and glanced again at her face. Like her hand, it was slightly off-color, slightly puffy. Some blood disease, perhaps.

Now the stewardess was leaning down toward them, talking to both of them as if she thought they were together. Nimram studied the sharp, dark red sheen of her hair, metallic ox-blood. Her face, in comparison with the girl's, was shockingly healthy. She addressed them by their names, "Mr. Nimram, Miss Curtis," a trifle that brought the melancholy tuck to Nimram's mouth, he could hardly have told you why himself—something about civility and human vulnerability, a commercially tainted civility, no doubt (he could see her quickly scanning the first-class passenger list, as per instruction, memorizing names), but civility nonetheless, the familiar old defiance of night and thunder: when they plunged into the Pacific, on the way out for the turn, or snapped off a wing on the horn of some mountain, or exploded in the air or burst into shrapnel and flame on the Mojave, they would die by name: "Mr. Nimram. Miss Curtis." Or anyway so it would be for the people in first class. "When we're airborne," the stewardess was saying, "we'll be serving complimentary drinks. . . ." As she named them off, Miss Curtis sat frowning with concentration, as panicky as ever. She ordered a Coke; Nimram ordered wine. The stewardess smiled as if delighted and moved away.

Neither of them noticed when the plane began to move. The girl had asked him if he flew on airplanes often, and he'd launched a full and elaborate answer—New York, Paris, Rome, Tokyo. . . . He beamed, gesturing as he spoke, as if flying were the greatest of his pleasures. Nothing could be farther from the truth, in fact; flying bored and annoyed him, not that he was afraid—Nimram was afraid of almost nothing, at any rate nothing he'd experienced so far, and he'd be forty-nine in June. Or rather, to be precise, he was afraid of nothing that could happen to himself, only of things that threatened others. Once he'd been hit on the Los Angeles expressway, when Arline was with him. Her head had been thrown against the dashboard and she'd been knocked unconscious. Nimram, dragging her from the car, cursing the police, who were nowhere to be seen, and shouting at the idiot by-standers, had found himself shaking like a leaf. Sometimes, lying in bed with his arm around her as she slept, Nimram, listening to the silence of the house, the very faint whine of trucks on the highway two miles away, would feel almost crushed by the weight of his fear for her, heaven bearing down on their roof like the base of a graveyard monument—though nothing was wrong, she was well, ten years younger than he was and strong as a horse from all the tennis and swimming.

In his hundreds of flights—maybe it was thousands—he'd never had once what he could honestly describe as a close call, and he'd come to believe that he probably never would have one; but he knew, as surely as a human being can know anything, that if he ever did, he probably wouldn't be afraid. Like most people, he'd heard friends speak, from time to time, about their fear of dying, and the feeling was not one he scorned or despised; but the fact remained, he was not the kind of man who had it. "Well, you're lucky," Arline had said, refusing to believe him, getting for an instant the hard look that came when she believed she was somehow being criticized. "Yes, lucky," he'd said thoughtfully. It was the single most notable fact about his life.

Abruptly, the girl, Miss Curtis, broke in on his expansive praise of airlines. "We're moving!" she exclaimed, darting her head past his shoulder in the direction of the window, no less surprised, it seemed, than she'd have been if they were sitting in a building.

Nimram joined her in looking out, watching yellow lights pass, the taxiway scored by rain-wet blue-and-white beams thrown by lights farther out.

Now on the loudspeaker an invisible stewardess began explaining the use of oxygen masks and the positions of the doors, while their own stewardess, with slightly parted lips and her eyes a little widened, pointed and gestured without a sound, like an Asian dancer. The girl beside him listened as if in despair, glum as a student who's fallen hopelessly behind. Her hand on the armrest was more yellow than before.

"Don't worry," Nimram said, "you'll like it."

She was apparently too frightened to speak or turn her head.

Now the engines wound up to full power, a sound that for no real reason reminded Nimram of the opening of Brahms' First, and lights came on, surprisingly powerful, like a searchlight or the headlight of a railroad engine, smashing through the rain as if by violent will, flooding the runway below and ahead of the wing just behind him, and the plane began its quickly accelerating, furious run down the field for take-off. Like a grandfather, Nimram put his hand on the girl's. "Look," he said, showing his smile, tilting his head in the direction of the window, but she shook her head just perceptibly and shut her eyes tight. Again for an instant he was struck by the likeness, as remarkable now as it had been when he'd first seen her, and he tried to remember when Arline had squeezed her eyes shut in exactly that way. He could see her face vividly—they were outdoors somewhere, in summer, perhaps in England—but the background refused to fill in for him, remained just a sunlit, ferny green, and the memory tingling in the cellar of his mind dimmed out. The Brahms was still playing itself inside him, solemn and magnificent, aglow, like the lights of the city now fallen far beneath them, lurid in the rain. Now the plane was banking, yawing like a ship as it founders and slips over, the headlights rushing into churning spray, the unbelievably large black wing upended, suddenly white in a blast of clouded lightning, then black again, darker than before. As the plane righted itself, the pilot began speaking to the passengers again. Nimram, frowning his Beethoven frown, hardly noticed. The plane began to bounce, creaking like a carriage, still climbing to get above the weather.

"Dear God," the girl whispered.

"It's all right, it's all all right," Nimram said, and pressed her hand.

Her name was Anne. She was, as he'd guessed, sixteen; from Chicago; and though she did not tell him what her disease was or directly mention that she was dying, she made her situation clear enough. "It's incredible," she said. "One of my grandmothers is ninety-two, the other one's eighty-six. But I guess it doesn't matter. If you're chosen, you're chosen." A quick, embarrassed smile. "Are you in business or something?"

"More or less," he said. "You're in school?"

"High school," she said.

"You have boyfriends?"

"No."

Nimram shook his head as if in wonderment and looked quickly toward the front of the plane for some distraction. "Ah," he said, "here's the stewardess with our drinks."

The girl smiled and nodded, though the stewardess was still two seats away. "We don't seem to have gotten above the storm, do we." She was looking past him, out the window at the towers of cloud lighting up, darkening, then lighting again. The plane was still jouncing, as if bumping things more solid than any possible air or cloud, maybe Plato's airy beasts.

"Things'll settle down in a minute," Nimram said.

Innocently, the girl asked, "Are you religious or anything?"

"Well, no—" He caught himself. "More or less," he said.

"You're more or less in business and you're more or less religious," the girl said, and smiled as if she'd caught him. "Are you a gambler, then?"

He laughed. "Is that what I look like?"

She continued to smile, but studied him, looking mainly at his black-and-gray unruly hair. "Actually, I never saw one, that I know of. Execpt in movies."

Nimram mused. "I guess we're pretty much all of us gamblers," he said, and at once felt embarrassment at having come on like a philosopher or, worse, a poet.

"I know," she said without distress. "Winners and losers."

He shot her a look. If she was going to go on like this she was going to be trouble. Was she speaking so freely because they were strangers?—travellers who'd never meet again? He folded and unfolded his hands slowly, in a way that would have seemed to an observer not nervous but judicious; and, frowning more severely than he knew, his graying eyebrows low, Nimram thought about bringing out the work in his attaché case.

Before he reached his decision, their stewardess was bending down toward them, helping the girl drop her tray into position. Nimram lowered his, then took the wineglass and bottle the stewardess held out. No sooner had he set down the glass than the plane hit what might have been a slanted stone wall in the middle of the sky and veered crazily upward, then laboriously steadied.

"Oh my God, dear God, my God!" the girl whispered.

"You *are* religious," Nimram said, and smiled.

She said nothing, but sat rigid, slightly cross at him, perhaps, steadying the glass on the napkin now soaked in Coke.

The pilot came on again, casual, as if amused by their predicament. "Sorry we can't give you a smoother ride, folks, but looks like Mother Nature's in a real tizzy tonight. We're taking the ship up to thirty-seven thousand, see if we can't just outfox her."

"Is that safe?" the girl asked softly.

He nodded and shrugged. "Safe as a ride in a rockingchair," he said.

They could feel the plane nosing up, climbing so sharply that for a moment even Nimram felt a touch of dismay. The bumping and creaking became less noticeable. Nimram took a deep breath and poured his wine.

Slowly, carefully, the girl raised the Coke to her lips and took a small sip, then set it down again. "I hope it's not like this in Chicago," she said.

"I'm sure it won't be." He toasted her with the wineglass—she seemed not to notice—then drew it to his mouth and drank.

He couldn't tell how long he'd slept or what, if anything, he'd dreamed. The girl slept beside him, fallen toward his shoulder, the cabin around them droning quietly, as if singing to itself, below them what might have been miles of darkness, as if the planet had silently fallen out from under them, tumbling toward God knew what. Here in the dimly lit cabin, Nimram felt serene. They'd be landing at O'Hare shortly—less than two hours. Arline would be waiting in the lounge, smiling eagerly, even more pleased than usual to see him, after three long days with her parents. He'd be no less glad to see her, of course; yet just now, though he knew that that moment was rushing toward him, he felt aloof from it, suspended above time's wild drive like the note of a single flute above a poised and silent orchestra. For all he could tell, the plane itself might have been hanging motionless, as still as the pinprick stars overhead.

The cabin had grown chilly, and, carefully, making sure he didn't wake her, Nimram raised the girl's blanket toward her throat. She stirred, a muscle along her jaw twitching, but continued to sleep, her breathing deep and even. Across the aisle from them, an old woman opened her eyes and stared straight ahead, listening like someone who imagines she's heard a burglar in the kitchen, then closed them again, indifferent.

Thoughtfully, Nimram gazed at the sleeping girl. On her forehead, despite the cold, there were tiny beads of sweat. He considered brushing the hair back from her face—it looked as if it tickled—but with his hand already in the air he checked himself, then lowered the hand. She was young enough to be his daughter, he mused, pursing his lips. Thank God she wasn't. Instantly, he hated it that he'd thought such a thing. She was *some* poor devil's daughter. Then it dawned on Nimram that she was young enough, too, to be Arline's daughter, from the time before Arline and he had met. Arline was thirty-nine, the girl sixteen. The faintest trace of a prickling came to his scalp, and he felt now a different kind of chill in the cabin, as if a cloud had passed between his soul and some invisible sun. "Don't ask!" Arline would say when he drew her toward the subject of her life—that is, her love-life—before they knew each other. "I was wild," she would say, laughing, "God!" and would touch his cheek with the back of her hand. The dark, infantile part of Nimram's mind seized on that now with the same blind obstinance as it had earlier seized on the idea that the girl was Arline's sister. Consciously, or with his brain's left lobe, perhaps, he knew the idea was nonsense. Arline's laugh had no abandoned child in it, only coy hints of old escapades—love-making on beaches or in the back seats of cars, drunken parties in the houses of friends when the parents were far away in Cleveland or Detroit, and then when she was older, affairs more serious and miserable. She had been married, briefly, to a man who had something to do with oil-rigs. About that he knew a fair amount, though with her Anglo-Saxon ideas of what was proper she hated to speak of it. In any case, the idea that the girl might be her daughter was groundless and absurd; if it remained, roaming in the dark of his mind, it remained against his will, like a rat in the basement, too canny to be poisoned or trapped. Even so, even after he'd rejected it utterly, he found that the groundless suspicion had subtly transmuted the way he saw the girl. He felt in his chest and at the pit of his stomach an echo of the anguish her parents must be feeling, a shadowy sorrow that, for all his notorious good fortune, made him feel helpless.

Strange images began to molest Nimram's thoughts, memories of no real significance, yet intense, like charged images in a dream. Memories, ideas . . . It was hard to say what they were. It was as if he had indeed, by a careless misstep, slipped out of time, as if the past and present had collapsed into one unbroken instant, so that he was both himself and himself at sixteen, the age of the girl asleep beside him.

He was riding on a train, late at night, through Indiana, alone. The seats were once-red plush, old and stiff, discolored almost to black. There was a round black handle, like the handle on a gearshift, that one pulled to make the back recline. Toward the rear of the car an old man in black clothes was coughing horribly, hacking as if to throw up his lungs. The conductor, sitting in the car's only light, his black cap pulled forward to the rim of his glasses, was laboriously writing something, muttering, from time to time—never looking up from his writing toward the cougher—"God damn you, die!" It was so vivid it made his scalp prickle, the musical thrumming of wheels on rails as distinct in Nimram's mind as the drone of the airplane he sat in. The wheels and railjoints picked up the muttered words, transforming them to music, a witless, everlastingly repetitive jingle: *God damn you, die!* (click) *God damn you, die!* (click) . . .

Sometimes he'd awakened in terror, he remembered, riding on the train, convinced that the train had fallen off the tracks and was hurtling through space; but when he looked out the window at the blur of dark trees and shrubs rushing by, the ragged fields gray as bones in the moonlight, he would be reassured—the train was going lickety-split, but all was well. Though it seemed only an instant ago, if not happening right now, it also seemed ages ago: he'd lived, since then, through innumerable train rides, bus rides, plane rides—lived through two marriages and into a third, lived through God knew how many playing jobs, conducting jobs, fund-raising benefits, deaths of friends. He'd lived through warplane formations over Brooklyn; explosions in the harbor, no comment in the papers; lived through the birth and rise of Israel, had conducted the Israel Philharmonic; lived through . . . but that was not the point. She was sixteen, her head hanging loose, free of the pillow, like a flower on a weak, bent stem. All that time, the time he'd already consumed too fast to notice he was losing it—it might have been centuries, so it felt to him now—was time the girl would never get.

It wasn't pity he felt, or even anger at the general injustice of things; it was bewilderment, a kind of shock that stilled the wits. If he were religious—he was, of course, but not in the common sense—he might have been furious at God's mishandling of the universe, or at very least puzzled by the disparity between real and ideal. But none of that was what he felt. God had nothing to do with it, and the whole question of real and ideal was academic. Nimram felt only, looking at the girl—her skin off-color, her head unsupported yet untroubled by the awkwardness, tolerant as a corpse—Nimram felt only a profound embarrassment and helplessness: helplessly fortunate and therefore unfit, unworthy, his whole life light and unprofitable as a puff-ball, needless as ascending smoke. He hardly knew her, yet he felt now—knowing it was a lie but knowing also that if the girl were really his daughter it would be true—that if Nature allowed it, Mother of tizzies and silences, he would change lives with the girl beside him in an instant.

Suddenly the girl cried out sharply and opened her eyes.

"Here now! It's okay!" he said, and touched her shoulder.

She shook her head, not quite awake, disoriented. "Oh!" she said, and blushed—a kind of thickening of the yellow-gray skin. "Oh, I'm sorry!" She flashed her panicky smile. "I was having a dream."

"Everything's all right," he said, "don't worry now, everything's fine."

"It's really funny," she said, shaking her head again, so hard the soft hair flew. She drew back from him and raised her hands to her eyes. "It was the strangest dream!" she said, and lowered her hands to look out the window, squinting a little, trying to recapture what she'd seen. He saw that his first impression had been mistaken; it had not, after all, been a nightmare. "I dreamed I was in a room, a kind of moldy old cellar where there were animals of some kind, and when I tried to open the door—" She broke off and glanced around to see if anyone was listening. No one was awake. She slid her eyes toward him, wanting to go on but unsure of herself. He bent his head, waiting with interest. Hesitantly, she said, "When I tried to open the door, the doorknob came off in my hands. I started scraping at the door with my fingers and, somehow—" She scowled, trying to remember. "I don't know, somehow the door broke away and I discovered that behind the door, where the world outside should be, there was . . . there was this huge, like, parlor. Inside it there was every toy or doll I ever had that had been broken or lost, all in perfect condition."

"Interesting dream," he said, looking at her forehead, not her eyes; then, feeling that something more was expected, "Dreams are strange things."

"I know." She nodded, then quickly asked, "What time is it, do you know? How long before we get to Chicago?"

"They're two hours ahead of us. According to my watch—"

Before he could finish, she broke in, "Yes, that's right. I forgot." A shudder went through her, and she asked, "Is it cold in here?"

"Freezing," he said.

"Thank God!" She looked past him, out the window, and abruptly brightened. "It's gotten nice out—anyway, I don't see any lightning." She gave her head a jerk, tossing back the hair.

"It's behind us," he said. "I see you're not afraid anymore."

"You're wrong," she said, and smiled. "But it's true, it's not as bad as it was. All the same, I'm still praying."

"Good idea," he said.

She shot a quick look at him, then smiled uncertainly, staring straight ahead. "A lot of people don't believe in praying and things," she said. "They try to make you feel stupid for doing it, like when a boy wants to play the violin instead of trumpet or drums. In our orchestra at school the whole string section's made up of girls except for one poor guy that plays viola." She paused and glanced at him, then smiled. "It's really funny how I never make sense when I talk to you."

"Sure you do."

She shrugged. "Anyway, some say there's a God and some say there isn't, and they're both so positive you wouldn't believe it. Personally, I'm not sure one way or the other, but when I'm scared I pray."

"It's like the old joke," he began.

"Do you like music?" she asked. "Classical, I mean?"

Nimram frowned. "Oh, sometimes."

"Who's your favorite composer?"

It struck him for the first time that perhaps his favorite composer was Machaut. "Beethoven?" he said.

It was apparently the right answer. "Who's your favorite conductor?"

He pretended to think about it.

"Mine's Seiji Ozawa," she said.

Nimram nodded, lips pursed. "I hear he's good."

She shook her head again to get the hair out of her eyes. "Oh well," she said. Some thought had possessed her, making her face formal, pulling the lines all downward. She folded her hands and looked at them, then abruptly, with an effort, lifted her eyes to meet his. "I guess I told you a kind of lie," she said.

He raised his eyebrows.

"I do have a boyfriend, actually." Quickly, as if for fear that he might ask the young man's name, she said, "You know how when you meet someone you want to sound more interesting than you are? Well—" She looked back at her folded hands, and he could see her forcing herself up to it. "I do this tragic act."

He sat very still, nervously prepared to grin, waiting.

She mumbled something, and when he leaned toward her she raised her voice, still without looking at him, her voice barely audible even now, and said, "I'm what they call 'terminal,' but, well, I mean, it doesn't *mean* anything, you know? It's sort of . . . The only time it makes me scared, or makes me cry, things like that, is when I say to myself in words, 'I'm going to . . .'" He saw that it was true; if she finished the sentence she would cry. She breathed very shallowly and continued, "If the airplane crashed, it wouldn't make much difference as far as I'm concerned, just make it a little sooner, but just the same when we were taking off, with the lightning and everything . . ." Now she did, for an instant, look up at him. "I never make any sense." Her eyes were full of tears.

"No," he said, "you make sense enough."

She was wringing her hands, smiling as if in chagrin, but smiling with pleasure too, the happiness lifting off as if defiantly above the deadweight of discomfort. "Anyway, I do have a boyfriend. He's the one that plays viola, actually. He's nice. I mean, he's wonderful. His name's Stephen." She raised both hands to wipe the tears away. "I mean, it's really funny. My life's really wonderful." She gave a laugh, then covered her face with both hands, her shoulders shaking.

He patted the side of her arm, saying nothing.

"The reason I wanted to tell you," she said when she was able to speak, "is, you've really been nice. I didn't want to—"

"That's all right," he said. "Look, that's how we all are."

"I know," she said, and suddenly laughed, crying. "That really is true, isn't it! It's just like my uncle Charley says. He lives with us. He's my mother's older brother. He says the most interesting thing about Noah's Ark is that all the animals on it were scared and stupid."

Nimram laughed.

"He really is wonderful," she said, "except that he coughs all the time. He's dying of emphysema, but mention that he ought to stop smoking his pipe, or mention that maybe he should go see a doctor, Uncle Charley goes right through the ceiling. It's really that spending money terrifies him, but he pretends it's doctors he hates. Just mention the word and he starts yelling 'False prophets! Profiteers! Pill-pushers! Snake-handlers!' He can really get loud. My father says we should tie him out front for a watchdog." She laughed again.

Nimram's ears popped. They were beginning the long descent. After a moment he said, "Actually, I haven't been strictly honest with you either. I'm not really in business."

She looked at him, waiting with what seemed to him a curiously childish eagerness.

"I'm a symphony conductor."

"Are you really?" she asked, lowering her eyebrows, studying him to see if he was lying. "What's your name?"

"Benjamin Nimram," he said.

Her eyes narrowed, and the embarrassment was back. He could see her searching her memory. "I think I've heard of you," she said.

"*Sic transit gloria mundi*," he said, mock-morose.

She smiled and pushed her hair back. "I know what that means," she said.

The no-smoking sign came on. In the distance the earth was adazzle with lights.

In the lounge at O'Hare he spotted his wife at once, motionless and smiling in the milling crowd—she hadn't yet seen him—her beret and coat dark red, almost black. He hurried toward her. Now she saw him and, breaking that stillness like the stillness of an old, old painting, raised her arm to wave, threw herself back into time, and came striding to meet him. He drew off and folded the dark glasses.

"Ben!" she exclaimed, and they embaced. "Honey, you look terrible!" She pulled back to look at him, then hugged him again. "On TV it said there was a thunderstorm in L.A., one of the worst ever. I was worried sick!"

"Now now," he said, holding her a moment longer. "So how were Poppa and Momma?"

"How was the flight?" she asked. "I bet it was awful! Did the man from the kennel come for Trixie?"

He took her hand and they started, moving with long, matched strides, toward the terminal.

"Trixie's fine, the flight was fine, everything's fine," he said.

She tipped her head, mocking. "Are you drunk, Benjamin?"

They veered out, passing an old couple inching along on canes, arguing.

"I met a girl," he said.

She checked his eyes. "Pretty?" she asked—laughingly, teasingly; but part of her was watching like a hawk. And why not, of course. He'd been married twice before, and they were as different, she and himself, as day and night. Why should she have faith? He thought again of the conviction he'd momentarily felt that the girl was her daughter. Sooner or later, he knew, he would find himself asking her about it; but not now. *Scared and stupid*, he thought, remembering, and the tuck at the corner of his mouth came back. He got an image of Noah's Ark as a great, blind, dumb thing nosing carefully, full of fear, toward the smell of Ararat

"Too young," he said. "Practically not yet of this world."

They were walking very fast, as they always did, gliding smoothly past all the others. Now and then he glanced past his shoulder, hoping to spot Anne Curtis; but it was absurd, he knew. She'd be the last of the last, chattering, he hoped, or doing her tragic act. Arline's coat flared out behind her and her face was flushed.

Almost as soon as she stepped off the plane, Anne Curtis found out from her father who it was that had befriended her. The following night, when Nimram conducted the Chicago Symphony in Mahler's Fifth, she was in the audience, in the second balcony, with her parents. They arrived late, after the Water Music, with which he had opened the program. Her father had gotten tickets only at the last minute, and it was a long drive in from La Grange. They edged into their seats while the orchestra was being rearranged, new instruments being added, the people who'd played the Handel scrunching forward and closer together.

She had never before seen a Mahler orchestra—nine French horns, wave on wave of violins and cellos, a whole long row of gleaming trumpets, brighter than welders' lights, another of trombones, two rows of basses, four harps. It was awesome, almost frightening. It filled the vast stage from wingtip to wingtip like some monstrous black creature too enormous to fly, guarding the ground with its head thrust forward—the light-drenched, empty podium. When the last of the enlarged orchestra was assembled and the newcomers had tuned, the houselights dimmed, and as if at some signal invisible to commoners, the people below her began to clap, then the people all around her. Now she too was clapping, her mother and father clapping loudly beside her, the roar of applause growing louder and deeper, drawing the conductor toward the light. He came like a panther, dignified yet jubilant, flashing his teeth in a smile, waving at the orchestra with both long arms. He shook hands with the concertmaster, bounded to the podium—light shot off his hair— turned to the audience and bowed with his arms stretched wide, then straightened, chin high, as if revelling in their pleasure and miraculous faith in him. Then he turned, threw open the score—the applause sank away—and for a moment studied it like a man reading dials and gauges of infinite complexity.

He picked up his baton; they lifted their instruments. He threw back his shoulders and raised both hands till they were level with his shoulders, where he held them still, as if casting a spell on his army of musicians, all motionless as a crowd in suspended animation, the breathless dead of the whole world's history, awaiting the impossible. And then his right hand moved—nothing much, almost playful—and the trumpet call began, a kind of warning both to the auditorium, tier on tier of shadowy white faces rising in the dark, and to the still orchestra bathed in light. Now his left hand moved and the orchestra stirred, tentative at first, but presaging such an awakening as she'd never before dreamed of. Then something new began, all that wide valley of orchestra playing, calm, serene, a vast sweep of music as smooth and sharp-edged as an enormous scythe—she had never in her life heard a sound so broad, as if all of humanity, living and dead, had come together for one grand onslaught. The sound ran, gathering its strength, along the ground, building in intensity, full of doubt, even terror, but also fury, and then—amazingly, quite easily—lifted. She pressed her father's hand as Benjamin Nimram, last night, had pressed hers.

Her mother leaned toward her, tilting like a tree in high wind. "Are you sure that's him?" she asked.

"Of course it is," she said.

Sternly, the man behind them cleared his throat.

QUESTIONS

1. Early in the story Gardner writes of Benjamin Nimram: "His life was sufficient, a joy to him, in fact." To what degree is the "sufficiency" of his existence part of the thematic material of the story? How does the dying girl change his perception of his life?

2. Nimram thinks a good deal about his wife, Arline, before and during his flight. What is her function in his life and in the story?

3. What do you make of the dying girl's repeated use of the phrase "Oh my God, dear God, my God" during the flight? Are there symbolic implications in this story?

4. If you were to analyze the plot structure of "Nimram," where would you place the complication, climax, and resolution of the action?

5. Most of this story is told from Nimram's point of view. However, the last portion is told from the point of view of the dying girl, Anne Curtis. Do you find the transition jarring? Why do you think Gardner felt he had to end the story from her perspective?

Raymond Carver (b. 1939)
The Third Thing That Killed My Father Off

I'll tell you what did my father in. The third thing was Dummy, that Dummy died. The first thing was Pearl Harbor. And the second thing was moving to my grandfather's farm near Wenatchee. That's where my father finished out his days, except they were probably finished before that.

My father blamed Dummy's death on Dummy's wife. Then he blamed it on the fish. And finally he blamed himself—because he was the one that showed Dummy the ad in the back of *Field and Stream* for live black bass shipped anywhere in the U.S.

It was after he got the fish that Dummy started acting peculiar. The fish changed Dummy's whole personality. That's what my father said.

I never knew Dummy's real name. If anyone did, I never heard it. Dummy it was then, and it's Dummy I remember him by now. He was a little wrinkled man, bald-headed, short but very powerful in the arms and legs. If he grinned, which was seldom, his lips folded back over brown, broken teeth. It gave him a crafty expression. His watery eyes stayed fastened on your mouth when you were talking—and if you weren't, they'd go to someplace queer on your body.

I don't think he was really deaf. At least not as deaf as he made out. But he sure couldn't talk. That was for certain.

Deaf or no, Dummy'd been on as a common laborer out at the sawmill since the 1920s. This was the Cascade Lumber Company in Yakima, Washington. The years I knew him, Dummy was working as a cleanup man. And all those years I never saw him with anything different on. Meaning a felt hat, a khaki workshirt, a denim jacket over a pair of coveralls. In his top pockets he carried rolls of toilet paper, as one of his jobs was to clean and supply the toilets. It kept him busy, seeing as how the men on nights used to walk off after their tours with a roll or two in their lunchboxes.

Dummy carried a flashlight, even though he worked days. He also carried wrenches, pliers, screwdrivers, friction tape, all the same things the millwrights carried. Well, it made them kid Dummy, the way he was, always carrying everything. Carl Lowe, Ted Slade, Johnny Wait, they were the worst kidders of the ones that kidded Dummy. But Dummy took it all in stride. I think he'd gotten used to it.

My father never kidded Dummy. Not to my knowledge, anyway. Dad was a big, heavy-shouldered man with a crew-haircut, double chin, and a belly of real size. Dummy was always staring at that belly. He'd come to the filing room where my father worked, and he'd sit on a stool and watch my dad's belly while he used the big emery wheels on the saws.

Dummy had a house as good as anyone's.

It was a tarpaper-covered affair near the river, five or six miles from town. Half a mile behind the house, at the end of a pasture, there lay a big gravel pit that the state had dug when they were paving the roads around there. Three good-sized holes had been scooped out, and over the years they'd filled with water. By and by, the three ponds came together to make one.

It was deep. It had a darkish look to it.

Dummy had a wife as well as a house. She was a woman years younger and said to go around with Mexicans. Father said it was busybodies that said that, men like Lowe and Wait and Slade.

She was a small stout woman with glittery little eyes. The first time I saw her, I saw those eyes. It was when I was with Pete Jensen and we were on our bicycles and we stopped at Dummy's to get a glass of water.

When she opened the door, I told her I was Del Fraser's son. I said, "He works with—" And then I realized. "You know, your husband. We were on our bicycles and thought we could get a drink."

"Wait here," she said.

She came back with a little tin cup of water in each hand. I downed mine in a single gulp.

But she didn't offer us more. She watched us without saying anything. When we started to get on our bicycles, she came over to the edge of the porch.

"You little fellas had a car now, I might catch a ride with you."

She grinned. Her teeth looked too big for her mouth.

"Let's go," Pete said, and we went.

There weren't many places you could fish for bass in our part of the state. There was rainbow mostly, a few brook and Dolly Varden in some of the high mountain streams, and silvers in Blue Lake and Lake Rimrock. That was mostly it, except for the runs of steelhead and salmon in some of the fresh-water rivers in late fall. But if you were a fisherman, it was enough to keep you busy. No one fished for bass. A lot of people I knew had never seen a bass except for pictures. But my father had seen plenty of them when he was growing up in Arkansas and Georgia, and he had high hopes to do with Dummy's bass, Dummy being a friend.

The day the fish arrived, I'd gone swimming at the city pool. I remember coming home and going out again to get them since Dad was going to give Dummy a hand—three tanks Parcel Post from Baton Rouge, Louisiana.

We went in Dummy's pickup, Dad and Dummy and me.

These tanks turned out to be barrels, really, the three of them crated in pine lath. They were standing in the shade out back of the train depot, and it took my dad and Dummy both to lift each crate into the truck.

Dummy drove very carefully through town and just as carefully all the way to his house. He went right through his yard without stopping. He went on down to within feet of the pond. By that time it was nearly dark, so he kept his headlights on and took out a hammer and a tire iron from under the seat, and then the two of them lugged the crates up close to the water and started tearing open the first one.

The barrel inside was wrapped in burlap, and there were these nickel-sized holes in the lid. They raised it off and Dummy aimed his flashlight in.

It looked like a million bass fingerlings were finning inside. It was the strangest sight, all those live things busy in there, like a little ocean that had come on the train.

Dummy scooted the barrel to the edge of the water and poured it out. He took his flashlight and shined it into the pond. But there was nothing to be seen anymore. You could hear the frogs going, but you could hear them going anytime it newly got dark.

"Let me get the other crates," my father said, and he reached over as if to take the hammer from Dummy's coveralls. But Dummy pulled back and shook his head.

He undid the other two crates himself, leaving dark drops of blood on the lath where he ripped his hand doing it.

From that night on, Dummy was different.

Dummy wouldn't let anyone come around now anymore. He put up fencing all around the pasture, and then he fenced off the pond with electrical barbed wire. They said it cost him all his savings for that fence.

Of course, my father wouldn't have anything to do with Dummy after that. Not since Dummy ran him off. Not from fishing, mind you, because the bass were just babies still. But even from trying to get a look.

One evening two years after, when Dad was working late and I took him his food and a jar of iced tea, I found him standing talking with Syd Glover, the millwright. Just as I came in, I heard Dad saying, "You'd reckon the fool was married to them fish, the way he acts."

"From what I hear," Syd said, "he'd do better to put that fence round his house."

My father saw me then, and I saw him signal Syd Glover with his eyes.

But a month later my dad finally made Dummy do it. What he did was, he told Dummy how you had to thin out the weak ones on account of keeping things fit for the rest of them. Dummy stood there pulling at his ear and staring at the floor. Dad said, Yeah, he'd be down to do it tomorrow because it had to be done. Dummy never said yes, actually. He just never said no, is all. All he did was pull on his ear some more.

When Dad got home that day, I was ready and waiting. I had his old bass plugs out and was testing the treble hooks with my finger.

"You set?" he called to me, jumping out of the car. "I'll go to the toilet, you put the stuff in. You can drive us out there if you want."

I'd stowed everything in the back seat and was trying out the wheel when he came back out wearing his fishing hat and eating a wedge of cake with both hands.

Mother was standing in the door watching. She was a fair-skinned woman, her blonde hair pulled back in a tight bun and fastened down with a rhinestone clip. I wonder if she ever went around back in those happy days, or what she ever really did.

I let out the handbrake. Mother watched until I'd shifted gears, and then, still unsmiling, she went back inside.

It was a fine afternoon. We had all the windows down to let the air in. We crossed the Moxee Bridge and swung west onto Slater Road. Alfalfa fields stood off to either side, and farther on it was cornfields.

Dad had his hand out the window. He was letting the wind carry it back. He was restless, I could see.

It wasn't long before we pulled up at Dummy's. He came out of the house wearing his hat. His wife was looking out the window.

"You got your frying pan ready?" Dad hollered out to Dummy, but Dummy just stood there eyeing the car. "Hey, Dummy!" Dad yelled. "Hey, Dummy, where's your pole, Dummy?"

Dummy jerked his head back and forth. He moved his weight from one leg to the other and looked at the ground and then at us. His tongue rested on his lower lip, and he began working his foot into the dirt.

I shouldered the creel. I handed Dad his pole and picked up my own.

"We set to go?" Dad said. "Hey, Dummy, we set to go?"

Dummy took off his hat and, with the same hand, he wiped his wrist over his head. He turned abruptly, and we followed him across the spongy pasture. Every twenty feet or so a snipe sprang up from the clumps of grass at the edge of the old furrows.

At the end of the pasture, the ground sloped gently and became dry and rocky, nettle bushes and scrub oaks scattered here and there. We cut to the right, following an old set of car tracks, going through a field of milkweed that came up to our waists, the dry pods at the tops of the stalks rattling angrily as we pushed through. Presently, I saw the sheen of water over Dummy's shoulder, and I heard Dad shout, "Oh, Lord, look at that!"

But Dummy slowed down and kept bringing his hand up and moving his hat back and forth over his head, and then he just stopped flat.

Dad said, "Well, what do you think, Dummy? One place good as another? Where do you say we should come onto it?"

Dummy wet his lower lip.

"What's the matter with you, Dummy?" Dad said. "This your pond, ain't it?"

Dummy looked down and picked an ant off his coveralls.

"Well, hell," Dad said, letting out his breath. He took out his watch. "If it's still all right with you, we'll get to it before it gets too dark."

Dummy stuck his hands in his pockets and turned back to the pond. He started walking again. We trailed along behind. We could see the whole pond now, the water dimpled with rising fish. Every so often a bass would leap clear and come down in a splash.

"Great God," I heard my father say.

We came up to the pond at an open place, a gravel beach kind of.

Dad motioned to me and dropped into a crouch. I dropped too. He was peering into the water in front of us, and when I looked, I saw what had taken him so.

"Honest to God," he whispered.

A school of bass was cruising, twenty, thirty, not one of them under two pounds. They veered off, and then they shifted and came back, so densely spaced they looked like they were bumping up against each other. I could see their big, heavy-lidded eyes watching us as they went by. They flashed away again, and again they came back.

They were asking for it. It didn't make any difference if we stayed squatted or stood up. The fish just didn't think a thing about us. I tell you, it was a sight to behold.

We sat there for quite a while, watching that school of bass go so innocently about their business, Dummy the whole time pulling at his fingers and looking around as if he expected someone to show up. All over the pond the bass were coming up to nuzzle the water, or jumping clear and falling back, or coming up to the surface to swim along with their dorsals sticking out.

Dad signaled, and we got up to cast. I tell you, I was shaky with excitement. I could hardly get the plug loose from the cork handle of my pole. It was while I was trying to get the hooks out that I felt Dummy seize my shoulder with his big fingers. I looked, and in answer Dummy worked his chin in Dad's direction. What he wanted was clear enough, no more than one pole.

Dad took off his hat and then put it back on and then he moved over to where I stood.

"You go on, Jack," he said. "That's all right, son—you do it now."

I looked at Dummy just before I laid out my cast. His face had gone rigid, and there was a thin line of drool on his chin.

"Come back stout on the sucker when he strikes," Dad said. "Sons of bitches got mouths hard as doorknobs."

I flipped off the drag lever and threw back my arm. I sent her out a good forty feet. The water was boiling even before I had time to take up the slack.

"Hit him!" Dad yelled. "Hit the son of a bitch! Hit him good!"

I came back hard, twice. I had him, all right. The rod bowed over and jerked back and forth. Dad kept yelling what to do.

"Let him go, let him go! Let him run! Give him more line! Now wind in! Wind in! No, let him run! Woo-ee! Will you look at that!"

The bass danced around the pond. Every time it came up out of the water, it shook its head so hard you could hear the plug rattle. And then he'd take off again. But by and by I wore him out and had him in up close. He looked enormous, six or seven pounds maybe. He lay on his side, whipped, mouth open, gills working. My knees felt so weak I could hardly stand. But I held the rod up, the line tight.

Dad waded out over his shoes. But when he reached for the fish, Dummy started sputtering, shaking his head, waving his arms.

"Now what the hell's the matter with you, Dummy? The boy's got hold of the biggest bass I ever seen, and he ain't going to throw him back, by God!"

Dummy kept carrying on and gesturing toward the pond.

"I ain't about to let this boy's fish go. You hear me, Dummy? You got another think coming if you think I'm going to do that."

Dummy reached for my line. Meanwhile, the bass had gained some strength back. He turned himself over and started swimming again. I yelled and then I lost my head and slammed down the brake on the reel and started winding. The bass made a last, furious run.

That was that. The line broke. I almost fell over on my back.

"Come on, Jack," Dad said, and I saw him grabbing up his pole. "Come on, goddamn the fool, before I knock the man down."

That February the river flooded.

It had snowed pretty heavy the first weeks of December, and turned real cold before Christmas. The ground froze. The snow stayed where it was. But toward the end of January, the Chinook wind struck. I woke up one morning to hear the house getting buffeted and the steady drizzle of water running off the roof.

It blew for five days, and on the third day the river began to rise.

"She's up to fifteen feet," my father said one evening, looking over his newspaper. "Which is three feet over what you need to flood. Old Dummy going to lose his darlings."

I wanted to go down to the Moxee Bridge to see how high the water was running. But my dad wouldn't let me. He said a flood was nothing to see.

Two days later the river crested, and after that the water began to subside.

Orin Marshall and Danny Owens and I bicycled out to Dummy's one morning a week after. We parked our bicycles and walked across the pasture that bordered Dummy's property.

It was a wet, blustery day, the clouds dark and broken, moving fast across the sky. The ground was soppy wet and we kept coming to puddles in the thick grass. Danny was just learning how to cuss, and he filled the air with the best he had every time he stepped in over his shoes. We could see the swollen river at the end of the pasture. The water was still high and out of its channel, surging around the trunks of trees and eating away at the edge of the land. Out toward the middle, the current moved heavy and swift, and now and then a bush floated by, or a tree with its branches sticking up.

We came to Dummy's fence and found a cow wedged in up against the wire. She was bloated and her skin was shiny-looking and gray. It was the first dead thing of any size I'd ever seen. I remember Orin took a stick and touched the open eyes.

We moved on down the fence, toward the river. We were afraid to go near the wire because we thought it might still have electricity in it. But at the edge of what looked like a deep canal, the fence came to an end. The ground had simply dropped into the water here, and the fence along with it.

We crossed over and followed the new channel that cut directly into Dummy's land and headed straight for his pond, going into it lengthwise and forcing an outlet for itself at the other end, then twisting off until it joined up with the river farther on.

You didn't doubt that most of Dummy's fish had been carried off. But those that hadn't been were free to come and go.

Then I caught sight of Dummy. It scared me, seeing him. I motioned to the other fellows, and we all got down.

Dummy was standing at the far side of the pond near where the water was rushing out. He was just standing there, the saddest man I ever saw.

"I sure do feel sorry for old Dummy, though," my father said at supper a few weeks after. "Mind, the poor devil brought it on himself. But you can't help but be troubled for him."

Dad went on to say George Laycock saw Dummy's wife sitting in the Sportsman's Club with a big Mexican fellow.

"And that ain't the half of it—"

Mother looked up at him sharply and then at me. But I just went on eating like I hadn't heard a thing.

Dad said, "Damn it to hell, Bea, the boy's old enough!"

He'd changed a lot, Dummy had. He was never around any of the men anymore, not if he could help it. No one felt like joking with him either, not since he'd chased Carl Lowe with a two-by-four stud after Carl tipped Dummy's hat off. But the worst of it was that Dummy was missing from work a day or two a week on the average now, and there was some talk of his being laid off.

"The man's going off the deep end," Dad said. "Clear crazy if he don't watch out."

Then on a Sunday afternoon just before my birthday, Dad and I were cleaning the garage. It was a warm, drifty day. You could see the dust hanging in the air. Mother came to the back door and said, "Del, it's for you. I think it's Vern."

I followed Dad in to wash up. When he was through talking, he put the phone down and turned to us.

"It's Dummy," he said. "Did in his wife with a hammer and drowned himself. Vern just heard it in town."

When we got out there, cars were parked all around. The gate to the pasture stood open, and I could see tire marks that led on to the pond.

The screen door was propped ajar with a box, and there was this lean, pock-faced man in slacks and sports shirt and wearing a shoulder holster. He watched Dad and me get out of the car.

"I was his friend," Dad said to the man.

The man shook his head. "Don't care who you are. Clear off unless you got business here."

"Did they find him?" Dad said.

"They're dragging," the man said, and adjusted the fit of his gun.

"All right if we walk down? I knew him pretty well."

The man said, "Take your chances. They chase you off, don't say you wasn't warned."

We went on across the pasture, taking pretty much the same route we had the day we tried fishing. There were motorboats going on the pond, dirty fluffs of exhaust hanging over it. You could see where the high water had cut away the ground and carried off trees and rocks. The two boats had uniformed men in them, and they were going back and forth, one man steering and the other man handling the rope and hooks.

An ambulance waited on the gravel beach where we'd set ourselves to cast for Dummy's bass. Two men in white lounged against the back, smoking cigarettes.

One of the motorboats cut off. We all looked up. The man in back stood up and started heaving on his rope. After a time, an arm came out of the water. It looked like the hooks had gotten Dummy in the side. The arm went back down and then it came out again, along with a bundle of something.

It's not him, I thought. It's something else that has been in there for years.

The man in the front of the boat moved to the back, and together the two men hauled the dripping thing over the side.

I looked at Dad. His face was funny the way it was set.

"Women," he said. He said, "That's what the wrong kind of woman can do to you, Jack."

But I don't think Dad really believed it. I think he just didn't know who to blame or what to say.

It seemed to me everything took a bad turn for my father after that. Just like Dummy, he wasn't the same man anymore. That arm coming up and going back down in the water, it was like so long to good times and hello to bad. Because it was nothing but that all the years after Dummy drowned himself in that dark water.

Is that what happens when a friend dies? Bad luck for the pals he left behind?

But as I said, Pearl Harbor and having to move back to his dad's place didn't do my dad one bit of good, either.

QUESTIONS

1. What is it about the events in this story that help "kill off" the narrator's father?
2. The narrator is somewhat naive about the implications of the story he is telling. At what points do you begin to feel that you may understand Dummy and the crises in his life better than the narrator does? How would you compare this narrator's level of awareness with that of Bonaparte in "Guests of the Nation"?
3. Determine where the climax of this story occurs. How do the fish Dummy plants in the pond function in the complication and resolution of the action?
4. What makes this story seem authentic? What is there in its point of view that keeps it from being written off as just another "fish story"?

Ann Beattie (b.1947)
Waiting

"It's beautiful," the woman says. "How did you come by this?"

She wiggles her finger in the mousehole. It's a genuine mousehole: sometime in the eighteenth century a mouse gnawed its way into the cupboard, through the two inside shelves, and out the bottom.

"We bought it from an antique dealer in Virginia," I say.

"Where in Virginia?"

"Ruckersville. Outside of Charlottesville."

"That's beautiful country," she says. "I know where Ruckersville is. I had an uncle who lived in Keswick."

"Keswick was nice," I say. "The farms."

"Oh," she says. "The tax writeoffs, you mean? Those mansions with one sheep grazing out front?"

She is touching the wood, stroking lightly in case there might be a splinter. Even after so much time, everything might not have been worn down to smoothness. She lowers her eyes. "Would you take eight hundred?" she says.

"I'd like to sell it for a thousand," I say. "I paid thirteen hundred, ten years ago."

"It's beautiful," she says. "I suppose I should try to tell you it has some faults, but I've never seen one like it. Very nice. My husband wouldn't like my spending more than six hundred to begin with, but I can see that it's worth eight." She is resting her index finger on the latch. "Could I bring my husband to see it tonight?"

"All right."

"You're moving?" she says.

"Eventually," I say.

"That would be something to load around." She shakes her head. "Are you going back South?"

"I doubt it," I say.

"You probably think I'm kidding about coming back with my husband," she says suddenly. She lowers her eyes again. "Are other people interested?"

"There's just been one other call. Somebody who wanted to come out Saturday." I smile. "I guess I should pretend there's great interest."

"I'll take it," the woman says. "For a thousand. You probably could sell it for more and I could probably resell it for more. I'll tell my husband that."

She picks up her embroidered shoulder bag from the floor by the corner cabinet. She sits at the oak table by the octagonal window and rummages for her checkbook.

"I was thinking, What if I left it home? But I didn't." She takes out a checkbook in a red plastic cover. "My uncle in Keswick was one of those gentleman farmers," she says. "He lived until he was eighty-six, and enjoyed his life. He did everything in moderation, but the key was that he did *everything*." She looks appraisingly at her signature. "Some movie actress just bought a farm across from the Cobham store," she says. "A girl. I never saw her in the movies. Do you know who I'm talking about?"

"Well, Art Garfunkel used to have a place out there," I say.

"Maybe she bought his place." The woman pushes the check to the center of the table, tilts the vase full of phlox, and puts the corner of the check underneath. "Well," she says. "Thank you. We'll come with my brother's truck to get it on the weekend. What about Saturday?"

"That's fine," I say.

"You're going to have some move," she says, looking around at the other furniture. "I haven't moved in thirty years, and I wouldn't want to."

The dog walks through the room.

"What a well-mannered dog," she says.

"That's Hugo. Hugo's moved quite a few times in thirteen years. Virginia. D.C. Boston. Here."

"Poor old Hugo," she says.

Hugo, in the living room now, thumps down and sighs.

"Thank you," she says, putting out her hand. I reach out to shake it, but our hands don't meet and she clasps her hand around my wrist. "Saturday afternoon. Maybe Saturday evening. Should I be specific?"

"Any time is all right."

"Can I turn around on your grass or no?"

"Sure. Did you see the tire marks? I do it all the time."

"Well," she says. "People who back into traffic. I don't know. I honk at them all the time."

I go to the screen door and wave. She is driving a yellow Mercedes, an old one that's been repainted, with a license that says "RAVE-1." The car stalls. She re-starts it and waves. I wave again.

When she's gone, I go out the back door and walk down the driveway. A single daisy is growing out of the foot-wide crack in the concrete. Somebody has thrown a beer can into the driveway. I pick it up and marvel at how light it is. I get the mail from the box across the street and look at it as cars pass by. One of the stream of cars honks a warning at me, although I am not moving, except for flipping through the mail. There is a C.L.&P. bill, a couple of pieces of junk mail, a postcard from Henry in Los Angeles, and a letter from my husband in—he's made it to California. Berkeley, California, mailed four days ago. Years ago, when I visited a friend in Berkeley we went to a little park and some people wandered in walking two dogs and a goat. An African pygmy goat. The woman said it was housebroken to urinate outside and as for the other she just picked up the pellets.

I go inside and watch the moving red hand on the digital clock in the kitchen. Behind the clock is an old coffee tin decorated with a picture of a woman and a man in a romantic embrace; his arms are nearly rusted away, her hair is chipped, but a perfectly painted wreath of coffee beans rises in an arc above them. Probably I should have advertised the coffee tin, too, but I like to hear the metal top creak when I lift it in the morning to take the jar of coffee out. But if not the coffee tin, I should probably have put the tin breadbox up for sale.

John and I liked looking for antiques. He liked the ones almost beyond repair—the kind that you would have to buy twenty dollars' worth of books to understand how to restore. When we used to go looking, antiques were much less expensive than they are now. We bought them at a time when we had the patience to sit all day on folding chairs under a canopy at an auction. We were organized; we would come and inspect the things the day before. Then we would get there early the next day and wait. Most of the auctioneers in that part of Virginia were very good. One, named Wicked Richard, used to lace his fingers together and crack his knuckles as he called the lots. His real name was Wisted. When he did classier auctions and there was a pamphlet, his name was listed as Wisted. At most of the regular auctions, though, he introduced himself as Wicked Richard.

I cut a section of cheese and take some crackers out of a container. I put them on a plate and carry them into the dining room, feeling a little sad about parting with the big corner cupboard. Suddenly it seems older and bigger—a very large thing to be giving up.

The phone rings. A woman wants to know the size of the refrigerator that I have advertised. I tell her.

"Is it white?" she says.

The ad said it was white.

"Yes," I tell her.

"This is your refrigerator?" she says.

"One of them," I say. "I'm moving."

"Oh," she says. "You shouldn't tell people that. People read these ads to figure out who's moving and might not be around, so they can rob them. There were a lot of robberies in your neighborhood last summer."

The refrigerator is too small for her. We hang up.

The phone rings again, and I let it ring. I sit down and look at the corner cupboard. I put a piece of cheese on top of a cracker and eat it. I get up and go into the living room and offer a piece of cheese to Hugo. He sniffs and takes it lightly from my fingers. Earlier today, in the morning, I ran him in Putnam Park. I could hardly keep up with him, as usual. Thirteen isn't so old, for a dog. He scared the ducks and sent them running into the water. He growled at a beagle a man was walking, and tugged on his leash until he choked. He pulled almost as hard as he could a few summers ago. The air made his fur fluffy. Now he is happy, slowly licking his mouth, getting ready to take his afternoon nap.

John wanted to take Hugo across country, but in the end we decided that, as much as Hugo would enjoy terrorizing so many dogs along the way, it was going to be a hot July and it was better if he stayed home. We discussed this reasonably. No frenzy—nothing like the way we had been swept in at some auctions to bid on things that we didn't want, just because so many other people were mad for them. A reasonable discussion about Hugo, even if it was at the last minute: Hugo, in the car, already sticking his head out the window to bark goodbye. "It's too hot for him," I said. I was standing outside in my nightgown. "It's almost July. He'll be a hassle for you if campgrounds won't take him or if you have to park in the sun." So Hugo stood beside me, barking his highpitched goodbye, as John backed out of the driveway. He forgot: his big battery lantern and his can opener. He remembered: his tent, the cooler filled with ice (he couldn't decide when he left whether he was going to stock up on beer or Coke), a camera, a suitcase, a fiddle, and a banjo. He forgot his driver's license, too. I never understood why he didn't keep it in his wallet, but it always seemed to get taken out for some reason and then be lost. Yesterday I found it leaning up against the Excedrin in the medicine cabinet.

Bobby calls. He fools me with his imitation of a man with an English accent who wants to know if I also have an avocado-colored refrigerator for sale. When I say I don't, he asks if I know somebody who paints refrigerators.

"Of course not," I tell him.

"That's the most decisive thing I've heard you say in five years," Bobby says in his real voice. "How's it going, Sally?"

"Jesus," I say. "If you'd answered this phone all morning, you wouldn't think that was funny. Where are you?"

"New York. Where do you think I am? It's my lunch hour. Going to Le Relais to get tanked up. A little *le pain et le beurre*, put down a few Scotches."

"Le Relais," I say. "Hmm."

"Don't make a bad eye on me," he says, going into his Muhammad Ali imitation. "Step on my foot and I kick you to the moon. Glad-hand me and I shake you like a loon." Bobby clears his throat. "I got the company twenty big ones today," he says. "Twenty Gs."

"Congratulations. Have a good lunch. Come out for dinner, if you feel like the drive."

"I don't have any gas and I can't face the train." He coughs again. "I gave up cigarettes," he says. "Why am I coughing?" He moves away from the phone to cough loudly.

"Are you smoking grass in the office?" I say.

"Not this time," he gasps. "I'm goddam dying of something." A pause. "What did you do yesterday?"

"I was in town. You'd laugh at what I did."

"You went to the fireworks."

"Yeah, that's right. I wouldn't hesitate to tell you that part."

"What'd you do?" he says.

"I met Andy and Tom at the Plaza and drank champagne. They didn't. I did. Then we went to the fireworks."

"Sally at the *Plaza*?" He laughs. "What were they doing in town?"

"Tom was there on business. Andy came to see the fireworks."

"It rained, didn't it?"

"Only a little. It was O.K. They were pretty."

"The fireworks," Bobby says. "I didn't make the fireworks."

"You're going to miss lunch, Bobby," I say.

"God," he says. "I am. Bye."

I pull a record out from under the big library table, where they're kept on the wide mahogany board that connects the legs. By coincidence, the record I pull out is the Miles Davis Sextet's "Jazz at the Plaza." At the Palm Court on the Fourth of July, a violinist played "Play Gypsies, Dance Gypsies" and "Oklahoma!" I try to remember what else and can't.

"What do you say, Hugo?" I say to the dog. "Another piece of cheese, or would you rather go on with your siesta?"

He knows the word "cheese." He knows it as well as his name. I love the way his eyes light up and he perks his ears for certain words. Bobby tells me that you can speak gibberish to people, ninety per cent of the people, as long as you throw in a little catchword now and then, and it's the same when I talk to Hugo: "Cheese." "Tag." "Out."

No reaction. Hugo is lying where he always does, on his right side, near the stereo. His nose is only a fraction of an inch away from a plant in a basket beneath the window. The branches of the plant sweep the floor. He seems very still.

"Cheese?" I whisper. "Hugo?" It is as loud as I can speak.

No reaction. I start to take a step closer, but stop myself. I put down the record and stare at him. Nothing changes. I walk out into the back yard. The sun is shinging directly down from overhead, striking the dark-blue doors of the garage, washing out the color to the palest tint of blue. The peach tree by the garage, with one dead branch. The wind chimes tinkling in the peach tree. A bird hopping by the iris underneath the tree. Mosquitoes or gnats, a puff of them in the air, clustered in front of me. I sink down into the grass. I pick a blade, split it slowly with my fingernail. I count the times I breathe in and out. When I open my eyes, the sun is shining hard on the blue doors.

After a while—maybe ten minutes, maybe twenty—a truck pulls into the driveway. The man who usually delivers packages to the house hops out of the United Parcel truck. He is a nice man, about twenty-five, with long hair tucked behind his ears, and kind eyes.

Hugo did not bark when the truck pulled into the drive.

"Hi," he says. "What a beautiful day. Here you go."

He holds out a clipboard and a pen.

"Forty-two," he says, pointing to the tiny numbered block in which I am to sign my name. A mailing envelope is under his arm.

"Another book," he says. He hands me the package.

I reach up for it. there is a blue label with my name and address typed on it.

He locks his hands behind his back and raises his arms, bowing. "Did you notice that?" he says, straightening out of the yoga stretch, pointing to the envelope. "What's the joke?" he says.

The return address says "John F. Kennedy."

"Oh," I say. "A friend in publishing." I look up at him. I realize that that hasn't explained it. "We were talking on the phone last week. He was— People are still talking about where they were when he was shot, and I've known my friend for almost ten years and we'd never talked about it before."

The U.P.S. man is wiping sweat off his forehead with a handkerchief. He stuffs the handkerchief into his pocket.

"He wasn't making fun," I say. "He admired Kennedy."

The U.P.S. man crouches, runs his fingers across the grass. He looks in the direction of the garage. He looks at me. "Are you all right?" he says.

"Well—" I say.

He is still watching me.

"Well," I say, trying to catch my breath. "Let's see what this is."

I pull up the flap, being careful not to get cut by the staples. A large paperback called "If Mountains Die." Color photographs. The sky above the Pueblo River gorge in the book is very blue. I show the U.P.S. man.

"Were you all right when I pulled in?" he says. "You were sitting sort of funny."

I still am. I realize that my arms are crossed over my chest and I am leaning forward. I uncross my arms and lean back on my elbows. "Fine," I say. "Thank you."

Another car pulls into the driveway, comes around the truck, and stops on the lawn. Ray's car. Ray gets out, smiles, leans back in through the open window to turn off the tape that's still playing. Ray is my best friend. Also my husband's best friend.

"What are you doing here?" I say to Ray.

"Hi," the U.P.S. man says to Ray. "I've got to get going. Well." He looks at me. "See you," he says.

"See you," I say. "Thanks."

"What am I doing here?" Ray says. He taps his watch. "Lunchtime. I'm on a business lunch. Big deal. Important negotiations. Want to drive down to the Redding Market and buy a couple of sandwiches, or have you already eaten?"

"You drove all the way out here for lunch?"

"Big business lunch. Difficult client. Takes time to bring some clients around. Coaxing. Takes hours." Ray shrugs.

"Don't they care?"

Ray sticks out his tongue and makes a noise, sits beside me and puts his arm around my shoulder and shakes me lightly toward him and away from him a couple of times. "Look at that sunshine," he says. "Finally. I thought the rain would never stop." He hugs my shoulder and takes his arm away. "It depresses me, too," he says. "I don't like what I sound like when I keep saying that nobody cares." Ray sighs. He reaches for a cigarette. "Nobody cares," he says. "Two-hour lunch. Four. Five."

We sit silently. He picks up the book, leafs through. "Pretty," he says. "You eat already?"

I look behind me at the screen door. Hugo is not there. No sound, either, when the car came up the driveway and the truck left.

"Yes," I say. "But there's some cheese in the house. All the usual things. Or you could go to the market."

"Maybe I will," he says. "Want anything?"

"Ray," I say, reaching my hand up. "Don't go to the market."

"What?" he says. He sits on his heels and takes my hand. He looks into my face.

"Why don't you— There's cheese in the house," I say.

He looks puzzled. Then he sees the stack of mail on the grass underneath our hands. "Oh," he says. "Letter from John." He picks it up, sees that it hasn't been opened. "O.K.," he says. "Then I'm perplexed again. Just that he wrote you? That he's already in Berkeley? Well, he had a bad winter. We all had a bad winter. It's going to be all right. He hasn't called? You don't know if he hooked up with that band?"

I shake my head no.

"I tried to call you yesterday," he says. "You weren't home."

"I went into New York."

"And?"

"I went out for drinks with some friends. We went to the fireworks."

"So did I," Ray says. "Where were you?"

"Seventy-sixth Street."

"I was at Ninety-eighth. I knew it was crazy to think I might run into you at the fireworks."

A cardinal flies into the peach tree.

"I did run into Bobby last week," he says. "Of course, it's not really running into him at one o'clock at Le Relais."

"How was Bobby?"

"You haven't heard from him, either?"

"He called today, but he didn't say how he was. I guess I didn't ask."

"He was O.K. He looked good. You can hardly see the scar above his eyebrow where they took the stitches. I imagine in a few weeks when it fades you won't notice it at all."

"You think he's done with dining in Harlem?"

"Doubt it. It could have happened anywhere, you know. People get mugged all over the place."

I hear the phone ringing and don't get up. Ray squeezes my shoulder again. "Well," he says. "I'm going to bring some food out here."

"If there's anything in there that isn't the way it ought to be, just take care of it, will you?"

"What?" he says.

"I mean— If there's anything wrong, just fix it."

He smiles. "Don't tell me. You painted a room what you thought was a nice pastel color and it came out electric pink. Or the chairs—you didn't have them reupholstered again, did you?" Ray comes back to where I'm sitting. "Oh, God," he says. "I was thinking the other night about how you'd had that horrible chintz you bought on Madison Avenue put onto the chairs and when John and I got back here you were afraid to let him into the house. God—that awful striped material. Remember John standing in back of the chair and putting his chin over the back and screaming, 'I'm innocent!' Remember him doing that?" Ray's eyes are about to water, the way they watered because he laughed so hard the day John did that. "That was about a year ago this month," he says.

I nod yes.

"Well," Ray says. "Everything's going to be all right, and I don't say that just because I want to believe in one nice thing. Bobby thinks the same thing. We agree about this. I keep talking about this, don't I? I keep coming out to the house, like you've cracked up or something. You don't want to keep hearing my sermons." Ray opens the screen door. "Anybody can take a trip," he says.

I stare over at him.

"I'm getting lunch," he says. He is holding the door open with his foot. He moves his foot and goes into the house. The door slams behind him.

"Hey!" he calls out. "Want iced tea or something?"

The phone begins to ring.

"Want me to get it?" he says.

"No. Let it ring."

"Let it ring?" he hollers.

The cardinal flies out of the peach tree and onto the sweeping branch of a tall fir tree that borders the lawn—so many trees so close together that you can't see the house on the other side. The bird becomes a speck of red and disappears.

"Hey, pretty lady!" Ray calls. "Where's your mutt?"

Over the noise of the telephone, I can hear him knocking around in the kitchen. The stuck drawer opening.

"You *honestly* want me not to answer the phone?" he calls.

I look back at the house. Ray, balancing a tray, opens the door with one hand, and Hugo is beside him—not rushing out, the way he usually does to get through the door, but padding slowly, shaking himself out of sleep. He comes over and lies down next to me, blinking because his eyes are not yet accustomed to the sunlight.

Ray sits down with his plate of crackers and cheese and a beer. He looks at the tears streaming down my cheeks and shoves over close to me. He takes a big drink and puts the beer on the grass. He pushes the tray next to the beer can.

"Hey," Ray says. "Everything's cool, O.K.? No right and no wrong. People do what they do. A neutral observer, and friend to all. Same easy advice from Ray all around. Our discretion assured." He pushes my hair gently off my wet cheeks. "It's O.K.," he says softly, turning and cupping his hands over my forehead. "Just tell me what you've done."

QUESTIONS

1. What exactly is the narrator waiting for?
2. What is the function of the episode at the beginning of the story in which the woman comes looking for antiques? An impatient reader might say that this episode merely slows down the pace of the story. How would you respond to such criticism?
3. What role does the narrator's dog Hugo play in the story? How does the dog help Beattie establish and resolve the conflict of "Waiting"?
4. What sort of person is the narrator? What has happened to her life and why?
5. One critic has said that Beattie is like a "social anthropologist" and predicted that readers would one day refer to her work "as if looking into a time capsule to discover the fads and fashions—of material goods and lifestyles—in the 1970s and 80s." On the basis of this story can you see why he would have said such things?

POETRY

1
APPRECIATING POETRY

I, too, dislike it: there are things that are important beyond all this fiddle
  Reading it, however, with a perfect contempt for it, one discovers in
  it after all, a place for the genuine.
    Hands that can grasp, eyes
    that can dilate, hair that can rise
      if it must, these things are important not because a

high-sounding interpretation can be put upon them but because they are
  useful.

—from "Poetry" by Marianne Moore (1887–1972)

These lines are worth considering. Some people do indeed "fiddle" over poems too much, forgetting about more important things. It is at times hard not to be put off by all their "high-sounding interpretations." But even if we come to poetry, because of such people, with feelings of "contempt," we still must admit that it is a form of literature capable of making us feel deep sentiment and profound wonder. Even the skeptical reader can find something "genuine" in poetry, the kinds of emotions that will be truly "useful" throughout life.

If early burial sites contained primitive poems that could be analyzed with the same precision as splinters of bone and fragments of jaw, we would no doubt find that poetry is almost as old as language itself. We think of words as a practical means of communication between human beings; they have also provided a way of addressing the mysterious forces of nature. Primitive hunters no doubt spoke poetic chants over their prey in hopes of placating the dead animal's spirit. Certainly by the time humankind made the transition from a nomadic existence into stable agricultural societies, poetry had become a *useful* cultural tool, spoken in the form of incantation over crops to make them grow and repeated at harvest to make sure the ground remained fertile for the next cycle.

Poetry has been a major artifact of every civilization that has left a history. In fact, poetry has sometimes been the form in which that history was preserved. The Children of Israel may have received the Ten Commandments in prose, but many of the most dramatic incidents in the Old Testament are told in poetry. In the culture of ancient Greece, narrative, lyric, and drama were all *poetic* forms, as was some history and science. Poetry was a communal celebration, a link forged between generations. We attribute *The Iliad* and *The Odyssey* to Homer, but these great epics were actually created over hundreds of years through the interplay between the "singers" who recited the episodes from memory and the audiences who called for additions to or subtractions from what they had heard. As late as the Middle Ages, folk poems like *Beowulf* and *The Song of Roland* were composed and reworked by being passed from generation to generation; they were part of the spoken (and listened to) life of the community—entertainment to be sure, but also a *useful* way for people to understand their origins, affirm their values, and assert a place for themselves in what at times seemed an incomprehensible and hostile world.

With the development of the printing press and the spread of literacy during the Renaissance, poetry became individualized, both in the way it was composed and the way it was experienced: there were writers and readers instead of "singers" and audience. Poetry was still the dominant form of literature; prose, a practical way of keeping the records and accounts of daily life, did not become as important or as widespread an "art" until the sixteenth century. And it was another two hundred years before novels began to compete successfully with poetry for readers' attention.

Why has poetry survived? In part, because it is so diverse, ranging from brief lyrics to long narratives such as Milton's *Paradise Lost*, from two-line epigrams to Dante's epic progress through Hell and Heaven in the *Divine Comedy*. It has survived also because it is adaptable, constantly developing new forms while preserving the old. Thus, while a contemporary poet might decide to write in free verse, a dominant form of this century, he can also write sonnets, a form developed five hundred years ago, or a ballad, a form that goes back to the medieval period.

Most of all, poetry has survived because it continues to be useful. It is often noted that we live in an age dominated by science and mass communications—an "age of prose." But it is also true that our century, like the Renaissance and other eras of transition, has witnessed a great surge in the composition and publication of poetry. It is as if writers and readers alike recognize that a poem is a way of asserting permanence in the face of random change. Poetry is especially useful for an age assaulted by words—the words of military planners, the words of advertising writers and the words of official forms and official spokesmen. In a time when language can be trivial or dangerous, poetry remains one place we can go to look for words that are genuine, words that count.

WHAT POETRY IS

Poem

> The rose fades
> and is renewed again
> by its seed, naturally
> but where
>
> save in the poem   5
> shall it go
> to suffer no diminution
> of its splendor

William Carlos Williams (1887–1963)

Samuel Taylor Coleridge defined good prose as "words in the best order" and good poetry as "the *best* words in the best order." The French poet Paul Valéry said that "prose is walking and poetry is dancing." How we define poetry is dependent in part on how we see its relationship with prose, a form commonly regarded as its opposite. The question becomes especially significant when we read a poem like this one by William Carlos Williams, where rhyme and meter are absent and the diction is purposefully simple, devoid of the embellishments and ornamentation commonly thought to accompany what is "poetic."

We can begin by saying that the basic unit of composition in poetry is the *line*, while in prose it is the sentence or paragraph. In other words, we perceive a piece of writing as a poem at least in part because of the way it is arranged on the page. Rearrange Williams's poem so that it looks like prose:

> The rose fades and is renewed again by its seed, naturally. But where, save in the poem, shall it go to suffer no diminution of its splendor?

Lacking the author's subtle cues about phrasing and about the shifts and balances between the words and ideas, we tend to flatten the diction of the poem, reading it the way we might an owner's manual or magazine article. But if the poetry goes out of our voices, it doesn't go out of the words themselves. Although diminished somewhat by having been arbitrarily rearranged, the language remains poetic. Williams's poem captures our imaginations in a web of meaning that similar sentiments in prose could never do.

What makes a poem special—whatever the typography—are the words. In poetry, language is dense and concentrated, supercharged with meanings. Greeting-card verse may look and even *sound* like poetry, but its excessively sentimental language is usually very prosaic indeed. Yet it must also be said that in many works of prose—fiction such as *Moby Dick* or *Ulysses* and nonfiction such as Bacon's *Essays* and Thoreau's *Walden*—there are passages in which the words are almost pure poetry. Prose and poetry are as different as rain and snow, but sometimes we have to admit that we are experiencing a weather that is neither one nor the other.

What is distinctive about poetry is the sheer number of elements— musical devices (rhyme, meter, etc.), theme, tone, figurative language, dramatic setting, purpose—working on the reader all at once to produce an overall effect far greater than any one of them separately could generate. Poems have *external form*—what we hear when we read them aloud or to ourselves, and what we see when we look at the printed page. They also have *internal form*—the logical relationships between the words and concepts. We can clearly see how this second kind of form functions in Williams's poem. The first three lines state an obvious fact of botany: roses, like other plants, *do* fade and renew themselves through the distribution of seeds. The next five lines, however, transform this botanical fact into a poetic truth: the very life cycle that insures survival of the rose as a species dooms the individual flower whose *particular* splendor can be preserved only by poetic language, which is outside of nature and never fades.

Teachers of literature often recommend that a student trying to understand a poem begin by paraphrasing it. This can be a valuable exercise, demonstrating to the reader that a poem is not just an imprecise sentiment that can be interpreted in any number of ways, but a specific and concrete statement with a single meaning. Paraphrasing is useful in another way as well, showing not only what a poem is saying but how special its use of language is. Consider this formulation:

> Roses bloom and then drop their petals, exposing seeds that eventually renew the plant. The splendor of an individual rose, however, will diminish unless preserved in the words of a poem.

Two things are immediately clear. First, the sentiment that in Williams's poem seemed somehow profound has become commonplace in this paraphrase. Second, there are many more words, but in this case more is less, for the essence of the poem has been lost. In poetry *what* is said is inseparable from *how* it is said. When Robert Frost said "poetry is what evaporates from all translations," he was not simply referring to the difficulty of making poems written in English available in other languages but to the difficulty of summarizing the sentiment of a poem in prose.

If we want to know how to grow roses, we would go to the ornamental horticulture section of the library. If we want to know how to preserve them we would get a plant press and a jar of silica gel. We do not often read poems for information, and if we do it is to inform our imaginations rather than the data-gathering part of our minds. To quote Robert Frost again: "Poetry is never to tell [readers] something they don't know, but something they know and hadn't thought of saying." The sense of *discovery* is a central part of reading poetry. Critics have used phrases like "the process of recognition" to describe this sensation. Whatever we call it, we experience this sensation as the moment when we say to ourselves, "Yes, that's true!" In the William Carlos Williams poem this discovery comes when the poet forces us to make a transition from roses to *the* rose, from the impermanent world of nature to the eternal world of poetry.

What is poetry then? Let us say that it is *the interpretive dramatization of experience in patterned language.* Such a definition contains most of the important concepts that we will deal with in the pages ahead: drama, experience, pattern, language, and, of course, interpretation. But it is also true, to paraphrase Frost, that poetry is what evaporates in all definitions. It would not be flippant to cite Louis Armstrong's response when someone asked him what jazz was: "If you got to ask the question, you ain't gonna understand the answer." No formal analysis can describe exactly the way Williams keeps a rose from diminishing when he puts it into a poem. More than other kinds of literature, we know poetry best when we are experiencing it.

WHAT POETRY IS NOT

Hawk Roosting

I sit in the top of the wood, my eyes closed.
Inaction, no falsifying dream
Between my hooked head and hooked feet:
Or in sleep rehearse perfect kills and eat.

The convenience of the high trees!   5
The air's buoyancy and the sun's ray
Are of advantage to me;
And the earth's face upward for my inspection.

My feet are locked upon the rough bark.
It took the whole of Creation   10
To produce my foot, my each feather:
Now I hold Creation in my foot

Or fly up, and revolve it all slowly—
I kill where I please because it is all mine.
There is no sophistry in my body: 15
My manners are tearing off heads—

The allotment of death.
For the one path of my flight is direct
Through the bones of the living.
No arguments assert my right: 20

The sun is behind me.
Nothing has changed since I began.
My eye has permitted no change.
I am going to keep things like this.

Ted Hughes (b. 1930)

As recently as the Victorian period, poetry had a broad audience—not just teachers and students of literature, but people from all walks of life who considered verse an indispensable part of their lives. Poetry provided them with entertainment and instruction. It was also a way for them to participate in their culture and to feel part of their social world. New volumes of poems by favorite authors were awaited as eagerly as some fiction best sellers are today.

A similar situation exists in some Eastern European countries today, where collections of suppressed poems involving pressing political problems circulate from hand to hand in manuscript form. In America, however, poetry, like other forms of modern art, has been affected by theories of relativity and loss of religious faith, and as a consequence has become more subjective, interior, and difficult to penetrate. Much of modern poetry is part of the general retreat of twentieth-century art into the intricacies of the self as the only thing which can be "known" with certainty. Many readers therefore find fiction easier and more approachable than poetry because it deals with a real, commonly experienced world. We will confront the issue of the difficulty of modern poetry later on in this section when we deal with the work of the great Irish poet William Butler Yeats. For now we will simply suggest that if poetry has come to seem forbidding, it is probably less because poems are difficult than because of certain misconceptions that block a reader's approach to the poem.

Poets are remote from everyday life. One popular image of the "poet" is of a pale and fragile individual sitting on some lonely moor cultivating melancholy and hiding from the hurly-burly of real life. Poets of the nineteenth century are sometimes presumed to have been tubercular; poets of today are sometimes presumed to be madly self-destructive. Such stereotypes are meaningless. Poets are also teachers, critics, editors: William Carlos Williams was a doctor, Wallace Stevens was an insurance executive, Walt Whitman, a newspaperman. We would all probably be surprised at the number of people who are not "poets" according to the popular stereotype but nonetheless write poetry. Rather than being frail and effete, the poet is actually a subtle subversive. It is instructive that Plato worried that poets would disturb the peace in his ideal Republic and that he wanted to banish them from it. It is also instructive that poets behind the Iron Curtain face jail as well as censorship because they do pose a threat to the established order.

Poetry is about "beauty." Poems have been written about everything from marine biology and mathematics to fleas and farm life. It is hard, in fact, to imagine a subject that hasn't been touched upon in some poem. There are, of course, certain classic themes of poetry—love and death, the individual's relationship to God and nature, and, to be sure, beauty and art. A significant number of poems have been written about roses, but poetry is not "about" roses.

Ted Hughes's "Hawk Roosting," for instance, gives us a deadly animal clinging to a treetop, dreaming about prey of the past, savoring the act of killing, and ruminating about its place in the order of things. This is a poem about "tearing off heads" and "the allotment of death." It is beautiful in its own way, but only because it contains a beautifully realized vision of one of nature's killers. It might be argued, in fact, that the only thing that makes the poem beautiful is the unique opportunity it offers to listen to a hawk talk about its "hawkness."

Poetry has a "message." Some poetry does undertake large intellectual tasks. We have already cited the example of *Paradise Lost,* an epic poem tens of thousands of words long in which the poet tells of the fall from grace of Adam and Eve and attempts to "justify God's ways to man." The fact is, however, that many tracts containing far more learned theology than is in Milton's work have fallen into oblivion while *Paradise Lost* continues to be read and regarded as a masterpiece. Generally speaking, we do not go to poems for ideas or information, as we might a treatise or a text; we go to them to be excited, amused, moved.

Look at "Hawk Roosting." What is its message? That "nature is red in tooth and claw," as the English poet Tennyson once wrote? That hawks are justified in what they do, or, for that matter, not justified? That Creation made a mistake when it contrived the hawk? It would be hard to claim that these ideas *as such* play much of a role in our reaction to the poem. To the degree that the poem has ideas, they are those of the hawk itself, a tyrant whose power is so supreme that it is self-justifying ("No arguments assert my right," line 20). Part of the enjoyment in the poem comes from the hawk's imperiousness ("the earth's face upward for my inspection," line 8) and the brazenness of its claims ("I kill where I please because it is all mine," line 14). We also take pleasure from our perception that while the hawk may be right that there is no sophistry in its body, there is considerable sophistry in its manner. There is more argument here than the hawk admits. In a sense, the reader is the hawk's prey, victim of its rhetoric. The pleasure we take in this poem comes from listening to this creature expound on its "hawkness."

Poetry must have rhyme and meter. Musical devices, as we've called them, are an important aspect of poetry. We can sense exactly how pleasurable they can be by listening to the way children react to heavily accented, rhyming poems they learn by heart. Some poets feel that rhyme and meter are part of the "ground rules" of poetry. Others feel that these devices make a poem too artificial; that poetry should have the cadences of normal speech, and that every poem creates its own ground rules.

Much of the impact of "Hawk Roosting," for instance, comes from the way that the patterns of the poem help fill in the character of the hawk. Parallelisms suggest the lethal narrowness of its view of the universe, a universe which it assumes to revolve around its own ability to kill ("It took the whole of Creation / To produce my foot, my each feather: / Now I hold Creation in my foot," lines 10–12). The short, staccato sentences suggest that what we are hearing is not discourse per se, but a series of primal assertions admitting of no counterargument. It is possible that a poem like "Hawk Roosting" could be written in rhyme and meter; it is unlikely that we would react to it as we do to this one.

Poetry must be analyzed. Analyzed is a most unpoetic word, calling up an image of some anxiety-ridden cryptographer sweating to break an enemy code. The first requirement of poetry is enjoyment, letting the poem strike the ear and the heart as well as the mind, perhaps reading it aloud to make sure one *hears* it. Rather than analyzing the poem as if it were something apart from us, we should try to understand its effect on us, asking questions that will intensify and deepen its impact.

We can ask ourselves about form. Why does the poet use unconventional syntax in "Hawk Roosting," for instance? Take even a small example, the hawk's use of the phrase "my each feather" (line 11). Does this tell you something about the animal's self-absorption?

We should also ask ourselves about the context in which a poem is created. We will deal with this issue in more detail in Chapter 6 when we consider how the poets Robert Lowell and Sylvia Plath have responded to their world, but for now it should be noted that while good poetry is timeless, it usually mirrors, even if only indirectly, the values of the age in which it was written. A poem must therefore be approached on its own terms, as an artifact of a particular time and place. When we read sixteenth-century poets, for example, we should try to understand their vocabulary as well as their view of the world. We should do the same with poets of our own time. We might ask, for instance, how "Hawk Roosting" is *contemporary*. In what sense does it embody the thoughts of our own time? Could it have been written before the political and philosophical developments—especially those involving totalitarian regimes—of the last fifty years?

Finally, we should ask ourselves questions that make a poem's meaning clear. Do our interpretations square with the poet's basic intent? What are the cues the poet gives us about the meaning of his work? Why, in "Hawk Roosting," is the matter of Creation brought up? Why Creation, say, and not God or Nature?

THE DRAMATIC CONTEXT

Song

Go and catch a falling star,
    Get with child a mandrake root,°
Tell me where all past years are,
    Or who cleft the Devil's foot,
Teach me to hear mermaids singing,   5
Or to keep off envy's stinging,
        And find
        What wind
Serves to advance an honest mind.

2. **mandrake root** a root thought to resemble the lower part of the human torso and thus to have magical properties

If thou beest born to strange sights,   10
   Things invisible to see,
Ride ten thousand days and nights,
   Till age snow white hairs on thee.
Thou, when thou return'st, wilt tell me
All strange wonders that befell thee,   15
     And swear
     Nowhere
Lives a woman true, and fair.

If thou find'st one, let me know,
   Such a pilgrimage were sweet;   20
Yet do not, I would not go,
   Though at next door we might meet;
Though she were true when you met her,
And last till you write your letter,
     Yet she   25
     Will be
False, ere I come, to two, or three.

John Donne (1572–1631)

    In some poems—"Hawk Roosting" happens to be a good example—we seem to have come into the middle of a play. We overhear a character thinking (or speaking) aloud—almost as if in a soliloquy—sometimes revealing quite a different dimension of self from the one that he or she (or *it*, in the case of Hughes's hawk) intends. Such a disparity occurs most significantly in the *dramatic monologue,* a form we will consider in Chapter 3. But all poems, even those which at first glance do not seem so, are dramatic, in that they present or imply human situations, desires, conflicts, or hopes. All poems are, moreover, "fictions"; they try to persuade the reader, however subtly, about something—a thought, an emotion, the nature of a dilemma, the revelation of a character.

    It is tempting to assume that the voice we hear in the poem is that of the author, especially in lyric poems where the drama is perhaps less obvious than in a work like "Hawk Roosting." To return for a moment to the William Carlos Williams poem, it may be true that the poet actually believed that poetry immortalizes beauty better than nature does. Even so, we should not make the mistake of assuming that it is *Williams* the man speaking in "Poem." It is a voice created for the occasion, and this voice is an aspect of the calculated effect the poet wants to produce. In all poems, however close the sentiment is to what we assume to be the poet's own view, we should try to see the *dramatic context* of the work, the interaction between *speaker*, and *situation,* and the ultimate objective this interaction helps achieve.

    The speaker. What do we know about the speaker? How do we infer our "characterization"? What is the speaker's attitude toward the matter at hand? Is the speaker's version of things trustworthy? These are some of the questions we should ask of all poems.

400 *Appreciating Poetry*

In John Donne's "Song," we are struck first by the sheer lyricism of the voice as it offers a list of impossible demands. As we consider the specifics of what is being said, we begin to form a tentative impression of the speaker. According to folklore of the sixteenth century, mandrake root was thought to possess magical properties; even more important, however, is the fact that it is shaped like the lower torso of a human being. "Get with child a mandrake root" (line 2), therefore, is a somewhat lewd demand. The allusion to mermaids, fabulous half-women and half-fish thought to be able to charm a man out of his senses, further helps to establish the speaker as someone concerned about the beguilements of love.

By the sixth and seventh lines of the poem—when the speaker begins to talk about how envy stings and how an honest mind does not achieve advancement—we start to hear a hint of bitterness. And by the second stanza, we begin to understand that, among his other attributes, the speaker is also a sly rhetorician who has used the lyricism of the poem's opening to draw us into an argument about woman's lack of constancy.

The situation. What is the speaker of a poem reacting to? Is he or she merely "thinking aloud"? Or is someone particular being addressed? If so, what is this other person's attitude toward what is being said and how does that affect our view? Is the setting of the poem important in determining meaning? These are some of the questions it is important to ask about a poem's situation.

In "Song," we assume that the speaker's interest in and cynicism about women comes from his having been jilted. The "thou" he is speaking to could be a particular person. But it is also the reader, who is naturally resistant to the argument. Listener or reader, whoever becomes involved with the speaker of this poem, is intellectually pressed, dared to refute what is being said.

The objective. As we have said, poetry communicates in several ways at once. Many things act on us as we read a poem, reinforcing, qualifying, even contradicting the impressions with which we begin. In "Song," the lyrical grace of the poem—its rhymes and rhythms—seems at first to be at odds with what is being said about women. But we later realize that the external form helps make what might otherwise seem a form of misogyny (unreasoning mistrust of women) into an amorous ambivalence. The speaker may not be able to do with women, but we sense that he cannot do without them either.

The speaker's argument is phrased in the most extreme terms. Even someone capable of seeing the invisible and willing to undertake a pilgrimage "of ten thousand days and nights" (line 12) that will yield many wonders will never find a woman who is "true, and fair" (line 18). By the third stanza the speaker has become comically irrational, suggesting that even if the impossible demands he has listed were met he would still refuse to change his mind about woman's lack of constancy. By undercutting his own strenuous arguments, he indicates that what is on his mind is really not a life and death matter; his view of woman is a personal fancy rather than a serious proposition. The final effect, therefore, is of a love poem about inconstancy; a complaint about woman with the properties of an aphrodisiac.

POEMS FOR FURTHER DISCUSSION

Ars Poetica°

A poem should be palpable and mute
As a globed fruit,

Dumb
As old medallions to the thumb,

Silent as the sleeve-worn stone   5
Of casement ledges where the moss has grown—

A poem should be wordless
As the flight of birds.

A poem should be motionless in time
As the moon climbs,   10

Leaving, as the moon releases
Twig by twig the night-entangled trees,

Leaving, as the moon behind the winter leaves,
Memory by memory the mind—

A poem should be motionless in time   15
As the moon climbs.

A poem should be equal to:
Not true.

For all the history of grief
An empty doorway and a maple leaf.   20

For love
The leaning grasses and two lights above the sea—

A poem should not mean
But be.

1926

Archibald MacLeish (1892–1982)

QUESTIONS

1. Compare "Ars Poetica" to "Poem" (p. 393). What exactly is each poet saying about
   the nature of poetry? Which "argument" do you find more persuasive?

Ars Poetica "The Art of Poetry"; also the title of a treatise on poetry by the Roman poet Horace
(65–8 BC)

2. Note how MacLeish constructs "Ars Poetica" as a series of epigrammatic prop-
   ositions about the nature of a poem. But then, on lines 19–21, he abandons this
   pattern. Why? To what extent do these three lines prepare the reader for the poem's
   conclusion?

3. The rhymes in this poem involve a basic pattern that is occasionally violated. Why
   do you think the poet has chosen an inconsistent pattern?

4. What do the final lines of the poem "mean"? In what sense are they an appropriate
   conclusion to what has gone before?

Hurt Hawks

1

The broken pillar of the wing jags from the clotted shoulder,
The wing trails like a banner in defeat,
No more to use the sky forever but live with famine
And pain a few days: cat nor coyote
Will shorten the week of waiting for death, there is game without
    talons.   5
He stands under the oak-bush and waits
The lame feet of salvation; at night he remembers freedom
And flies in a dream, the dawns ruin it.
He is strong and pain is worse to the strong, incapacity is worse.
The curs of the day come and torment him   10
At distance, no one but death the redeemer will humble that head,
The intrepid readiness, the terrible eyes.
The wild God of the world is sometimes merciful to those
That ask mercy, not often to the arrogant.
You do not know him, you communal people, or you have forgotten
    him;   15
Intemperate and savage, the hawk remembers him;
Beautiful and wild, the hawks, and men that are dying, remember him.

2

I'd sooner, except the penalties, kill a man than a hawk; but the great
    redtail
Had nothing left but unable misery
From the bone too shattered for mending, the wing that trailed under his
    talons when he moved.   20
We had fed him six weeks, I gave him freedom,
He wandered over the foreland hill and returned in the evening, asking for
    death,
Not like a beggar, still eyed with the old
Implacable arrogance, I gave him the lead gift in the twilight. What fell
    was relaxed,

Owl-downy, soft feminine feathers; but what   25
Soared: the fierce rush: the night-herons by the flooded river cried fear at
    its rising
Before it was quite unsheathed from reality.

1928

Robinson Jeffers (1887–1962)

QUESTIONS

1. Compare the hawk in this poem to the hawk in "Hawk Roosting." What qualities
    do the animals share? Are there qualities which are admirable in one but less so in
    the other? What is the role of God in each poem? In "Hurt Hawks" why does
    salvation have "lame feet" (line 7)?

2. How would you characterize the speaker in "Hurt Hawks"? What factors in the
    poem lead you to this characterization? How do you respond, for instance, to line
    18: "I'd sooner, except the penalties, kill a man than a hawk"? How does what you
    infer to be the speaker's character help determine your interpretation of the work?

3. In addition to discussing "the nature of nature," this poem also tells a story. After
    paraphrasing the poem to make sure you understand it, discuss both aspects of
    "Hurt Hawks": the philosophy of the speaker and the narrative he describes.

4. Explain the last line of the poem. In what sense has the hawk, before the speaker
    kills it, been "sheathed" in reality? What are the implications of the word
    "unsheathed"?

My Mistress' Eyes Are Nothing Like the Sun

My mistress' eyes are nothing like the sun;
Coral is far more red than her lips' red;
If snow be white, why then her breasts are dun;°   *brownish*
If hairs be wires, black wires grow on her head.
I have seen roses damasked,° red and white,   *varied in color*   5
But no such roses see I in her cheeks;
And in some perfumes is there more delight
Than in the breath that from my mistress reeks.
I love to hear her speak, yet well I know
That music hath a far more pleasing sound;   10
I grant I never saw a goddess go;°   *walk*
My mistress, when she walks, treads on the ground.
And yet, by heaven, I think my love as rare
As any she belied with false compare.

William Shakespeare (1564–1616)

Appreciating Poetry

QUESTIONS

1. How would you describe the speaker in this poem? Compare him to the speaker in Donne's "Song."

2. How do you see the speaker's mistress? Do you imagine her to be as homely as he paints her? Why might the poet have exaggerated her physical appearance to abet his argument?

3. In what sense would it be correct to see this sonnet as a poem about poetry?

Out upon It!

Out upon it! I have loved
  Three whole days together;
And am like to love three more,
  If it prove fair weather.

Time shall molt° away his wings,   *shed feathers*   5
  Ere he shall discover
In the whole wide world again
  Such a constant lover.

But the spite on 't is, no praise
  Is due at all to me: 10
Love with me had made no stays
  Had it any been but she.

Had it any been but she,
  And that very face,
There had been at least ere this   15
  A dozen dozen in her place.

Sir John Suckling (1609–1642)

QUESTIONS

1. Analyze the argument in this poem. What is the speaker saying about his emotions?

2. Compare the tone of this poem to that of Donne's "Song." How does each speaker regard the possibility of constant love?

3. In what way is the speaker in this poem paying a tribute to his beloved? Compare his sentiments with those of the speaker in Shakespeare's sonnet. Which of the women addressed in these two poems should feel more appreciated?

2
THE WORDS IN A POEM

The uniqueness of poetry comes from its compactness and intensity —its ability to say a great deal in a short space; its ability to make words mean more than they do in ordinary communication. The poet faces the same problem that all other writers do—finding the perfect word—but in his case the problem is more critical because there is less margin for error. The novelist has tens of thousands of words in his work and if a handful are stale or flat, they can easily take refuge in the sheer size of the book. For the most part the poet has hundreds of words—and in some cases only dozens—and if one of them is wrong it can destroy the effect of the whole work.

Learning to appreciate the words of a poem requires a sensitivity to language in general. In reading poems from other eras we should bear in mind that language is constantly changing, renewing and streamlining itself. Some words are falling out of favor as others are coming into vogue; the words that persist may well have meanings that are dramatically altered over the years. When reading poems written some time ago, we should make special allowances for what may seem an archaic poetic diction, realizing that it might well have been closer to colloquial speech in the poet's own day. But whether we are reading a poem written yesterday or five hundred years ago, we should ask ourselves certain basic questions. Why did the poet choose this one particular word rather than another with a similar meaning? How does this word subtly alter the context in which it appears? Are there patterns of words in the poem that we should be aware of, meaningful contrasts or contradictions?

WORD MEANINGS AND WORD ORDER

My Papa's Waltz

The whiskey on your breath
Could make a small boy dizzy;
But I hung on like death:
Such waltzing was not easy.

405

We romped until the pans   5
Slid from the kitchen shelf;
My mother's countenance
Could not unfrown itself.

The hand that held my wrist
Was battered on one knuckle;   10
At every step you missed
My right ear scraped a buckle.

You beat time on my head
With a palm caked hard by dirt,
Then waltzed me off to bed   15
Still clinging to your shirt.

Theodore Roethke (1908–1963)

The question of what a given word in a poem means is not as simple as it may seem. Words have a *denotation*, a lexical meaning. (*Lexical*, for example, has the denotative meaning of "pertaining to a dictionary and its definitions.") They also have a *connotation*, a suggestive meaning. (In this sense *lexical* might have the connotative meaning of "pedantic" or "overly precise.") What a word suggests, as opposed to what it literally means, affects our response to the context in which it appears.

Many people associate denotation with prose, which generally attempts to communicate data and information and thus relies on being literal, and connotation with poetry, which generally attempts to communicate emotion. This is an oversimplification. "My Papa's Waltz," for instance, shows how a poem can draw on both types of meaning.

The poem begins simply with denotative words that build a picture of a particular kind of family. It is not scotch or bourbon or rum that the father drinks, but ordinary and presumably cheap "whiskey." The knuckle is "battered" (line 10) and the buckle is "scraped" (line 12) not because more elegant words are not available, but because Roethke wants to communicate the elementary and unsophisticated nature of the life the people of the poem lead. When the father's palm is described as "caked" by dirt (line 14), the word is not used as casually as it may seem on first glance. The dictionary definition reveals the care with which "caked" was chosen: "to be formed into a compact mass." This caked palm is heavy, made that way by a lifetime of hard work.

There is also connotative language in this poem. In the third line, for example, the speaker says that he hung onto his father "like death." He is not only talking about death as an inevitability, the termination of organic life, but using the term to characterize the frightened tenacity of the boy's grasp as he was whirled about the room. "Romped" (line 5) suggests the childlike exuberance of the waltz as well as its lack of artistry. When the speaker says that his mother's face could not "unfrown" itself (line 8), we are invited to go beyond the literal meaning (she was frowning) and understand that she would perhaps have liked to have smiled at this romp, but it was simply too threatening for her to relax. When the speaker says that his father "beat time" (line 13) on his head, the violence just below the surface of this odd ritual is once again suggested. This phrase is also an example of the word play poetry is supremely capable of, for as we probe it we see that, in addition to meaning that he was keeping time to the tempo of the music, it also suggests that the father was also marking the time that will lead to his son's coming of age and his own decline and trying to "beat down" that process. In the last two lines when the speaker says that he was waltzed off to bed still "clinging" to his father's shirt, we are reminded of the tenacity of his grip and think back to the third line of the poem and understand that this has been a dance of death as well as a dance of love. In addition to waltzing with his son the father has been trying to shake the boy off him because of what their relationship suggests about his own mortality.

It is not only dictionaries and the natural suggestiveness of language that determine word meanings, but also sentence structure and syntax. Consider the second line of "My Papa's Waltz." Why does Roethke write that whiskey "could make a small boy dizzy" instead of saying more directly "made me dizzy"? The seeming obliqueness of the syntax is actually a way of creating meaning. It not only informs us that we are hearing about an event that occurred when the speaker was a small boy, but also suggests that the smell of the liquor on the man's breath was so strong that it would have many *any* small boy dizzy. Or, in the third stanza, why does the poet say "the hand that held my wrist," instead of simply "your hand"? Again, the phrasing itself contains meaning. It forces us to see the father's battered hand from the perspective of a small boy for whom it would be at eye-level; we consider it (as he does) as disembodied, a sort of artifact created by the hard work the father does for a living.

We can now begin to see how language works in a poem—through an interplay of denotation and connotation and through syntax, all of these elements collaborating to guide and shape our responses. What is amazing about Roethke's brief poem, of course, is how much it tells in such a short compass. After reading a few lines we have formed a picture of a sparse working-class life in which emotions are not easily expressed; in which love and violence and joy and death are not clearly segregated from each other; and in which triumphs over the difficulties of daily life come only after the hard effort embodied in an awkward waltz whose ritual nature is fully realized only many years after the fact.

IMAGERY

Poetry is distinct from other forms of literature in the degree to which it appeals to our senses. There are times when we can almost taste the apple in the poem, hear the roar of the sea, smell the rose, feel the soft skin of the loved one. The sense that the poem most often appeals to, of course, is sight. "My Papa's Waltz" is not unique: most poems allow us to *see* the scene portrayed in a few brief words, see it so acutely, in fact, that we feel that we are there. The *images* of a poem are the vivid impressions the poet gives us, almost like snapshots that develop in our mind.

October

Certain branches cut
certain leaves fallen
the grapes
        cooked and put up
for winter   5

mountains without one
shrug of cloud
no feint of blurred
wind-willow leaf-light

their chins up   10
in blue of the eastern sky
their red cloaks
wrapped tight to the bone

Denise Levertov (b. 1923)

There is no complex argument being made in "October," no drama being enacted. The poem is communicated through a series of extremely brief images. Branches cut and grapes cooked, mountains with "chins up in blue" (lines 10–11) and "red cloaks wrapped tight to the bone" (lines 12–13)—this imagery takes us directly into the heart of the fall season. We *sense* autumn rather than thinking about it—we feel this one last moment of clarity nature allows before insulating itself against the coming harshness of winter.

In this relatively simple and unassuming poem, as with others more complex and demanding, the effectiveness of the imagery rests on its vividness and the degree of detail. "Red cloak" provides a contrast to the blue sky and indicates the color of the mountains by comparing them to a familiar article of clothing. "Wrapped tight to the bone" not only completes the comparison to a person snuggled into a wrap, but also makes us see the mountains as they lose all their spring and summer foliage and are reduced to an elemental state to face the coming chill.

FIGURATIVE LANGUAGE

Someone with a literal turn of mind might object that mountains don't shrug, wear cloaks, or have bones that can be chilled. This is true, but irrelevant. The ability to make what might seem far-fetched comparisons—what is sometimes called "poetic license"—and make us believe in them is the essence of the poet's art.

We use figurative language all the time in our daily conversation. Someone is "growing like a weed," we say, or is "sick as a dog." Because they have been so overused, they fail to call up a visual comparison (we don't actually see that weed shooting up or that dog retching); such figures of speech are *clichés*, although perhaps serviceable as an economical or shorthand way of describing a complicated phenomenon. (We don't have to specify exactly how many inches the person has grown over what period of time; we don't have to be medically exact in diagnosing the sick person's malady nor do we have to provide a gruesome list of his symptoms.)

Poetry is the undying enemy of the cliché. The poem creates figurative language that is always fresh and new, suggesting ways of seeing things and understanding their essence that might not previously have occurred to us. Thus some of the hidden meanings in human experience are uncovered. Once we open our minds to the language of Denise Levertov's poem, for instance, we can see that there is indeed something like a person drawing a cloak around himself in the mountains' autumnal changes, something in their seasonal change akin to a person bracing for winter. The comparison is not explicit, but within the context of "October" it succeeds quite well. The comparison shows what a poet achieves through figures of speech: compression and emotion. An exact botanical and topographical description of what happens to a mountain as it makes the transition into late fall would take tens of thousands of words. Even after reading such a description, we would not feel, as we do after reading this poem, that seasonal changes affect all nature down to the bone.

A Narrow Fellow in the Grass

A narrow Fellow in the Grass
Occasionally rides—
You may have met Him—did you not
His notice sudden is—

The Grass divides as with a Comb—   5
A spotted shaft is seen—
And then it closes at your feet
And opens further on—

He likes a Boggy Acre
A Floor too cool for Corn—   10
Yet when a Boy, and Barefoot—
I more than once at Noon

Have passed, I thought, a Whip lash
Unbraiding in the Sun
When stooping to secure it   15
It wrinkled, and was gone—

Several of Nature's People
I know, and they know me—
I feel for them a transport
Of cordiality—   20

But never met this Fellow
Attended, or alone
Without a tighter breathing
And Zero at the Bone—

Emily Dickinson (1830–1886)

Students of rhetoric have identified some two hundred and fifty different figures of speech. Since a good poet is often also a master rhetorician, many of these figures are found in poetry. There are only a few of them, however, that are centrally important to poetic composition, and of these, three— *personification, simile,* and *metaphor*—are worth discussing in detail.

Personification, the attribution of human characteristics to something that is not human, is an important element in "A narrow Fellow in the Grass." The key to Dickinson's poem is ambivalence to the snake and all it represents. When it is referred to as a "narrow Fellow" in the first stanza, the snake seems familiar, even rather charming. In the second stanza, however, the snake is compared not to a person but to a "spotted shaft," a phrase that is vaguely menacing because of its connotations involving arrows and weaponry. In the third stanza the snake is once again "he," a fellow who has endearingly eccentric preferences for one environment over another. In the fourth stanza it is "Whip lash," another term with negative connotations. In the last two stanzas of the poem the snake is once again personified as one of "Nature's People" and "this Fellow," but there is no longer charm and familiarity, only ambivalence and fear.

In this poem personification makes the snake seem harmless at the same time that it makes its latent danger more apparent. And, in the background of Dickinson's treatment of this narrow fellow is the personification of a snake at the core of Christian mythology: the snake as the form Satan took when he wanted to tempt Adam and Eve and cause the fall of mankind. It is this reference, more than any natural repulsiveness in the snake, that causes the freezing sensation with which the poem concludes.

The Truth the Dead Know

FOR MY MOTHER, BORN MARCH 1902, DIED MARCH 1959
AND MY FATHER, BORN FEBRUARY 1900, DIED JUNE 1959

Gone, I say and walk from church,
refusing the stiff procession to the grave,
letting the dead ride alone in the hearse.
It is June. I am tired of being brave.

We drive to the Cape.° I cultivate   5
myself where the sun gutters from the sky,
where the sea swings in like an iron gate
and we touch. In another country people die.

My darling, the wind falls in like stones
from the whitehearted water and when we touch   10
we enter touch entirely. No one's alone.
Men kill for this, or for as much.

And what of the dead? They lie without shoes
in their stone boats. They are more like stone
than the sea would be if it stopped. They refuse   15
to be blessed, throat, eye and knucklebone.

Anne Sexton (1928–1974)

The most essential figures of speech in poetry, the figures most closely identified with the very essence of poetry, are *simile* and *metaphor*. Both involve comparisons between things which are, on the surface, unalike. These comparisons give us a new way of seeing and understanding the object, person, or emotion being described.

Simile is an explicit comparison using *like* or *as*. One of the most famous similes in English poetry is Robert Burns's "My love is like a red, red rose." (Partly because of the success of this line, roses and loved ones are now so firmly associated in the popular mind that it is perhaps difficult to see the power this figure of speech once had.) Many similes are more complex, drawing us into the heart of the poet's view of things and the heart of the poem as well. In "My Papa's Waltz" we saw the effect of the speaker's assertion that he clung to his father "like death." We can also see the power of simile in Anne Sexton's "The Truth the Dead Know."

In the poem's seventh line, after the funeral and the trip to Cape Cod are described, the speaker compares the movement of the sea to the closing of an "iron gate." The simile not only characterizes the heavy movement of the waves, but also suggests the extent of the speaker's desire to close herself off from the experience of death, to keep its horror at arm's length by shutting herself within the renewing warmth and water of the seashore. In the ninth line, however, when the speaker says that the wind is "like stones" as she and her companion come together on the beach, the simile suggests the literal pelting sensation of the wind at oceanside, and also that the emotional barricade she has erected is incapable of keeping her isolated and invulnerable.

In the last stanza of the poem, the deaths the speaker hoped to evade intrude once again on her consciousness, and affect the world of the living and loving. The dead parents are more "like stone" than life would be if it

5. **the Cape** Cape Cod, Massachusetts

stopped. Not only are they dead, but they are far beyond the speaker's ability to deal with them through grief. They cannot be blessed as the lovers can when they caress each other's throats and eyelids.

Let Me Not to the Marriage of True Minds

Let me not to the marriage of true minds
Admit impediments. Love is not love
Which alters when it alteration finds,
Or bends with the remover to remove:
Oh, no! it is an ever-fixèd mark,   5
That looks on tempests and is never shaken;
It is the star to every wandering bark,°   *ship*
Whose worth's unknown, although his height be taken.
Love's not Time's fool, though rosy lips and cheeks
Within his bending sickle's compass come;°   *reach* 10
Love alters not with his brief hours and weeks,
But bears it out even to the edge of doom.
If this be error and upon me proved,
I never writ, nor no man ever loved.

William Shakespeare (1564–1616)

Metaphor is like simile in that it proposes a comparison between two unlike things. It is different in that it is a direct assertion (without the mediation of *like* or *as*) of the identity of things which, on the literal level, do not appear close. (If he had chosen to begin his poem with a metaphor, Robert Burns would have written, "My love *is* a red, red rose . . .") *Metaphor* means transfer, and this is what a metaphor does: transfer experience from one realm of life to another. In "The Truth the Dead Know," for example, when the speaker uses the metaphor of "stone boats" in the final stanza, she does not choose to say that this is what the caskets resemble or are "like," but declares that this is what they *are*, thus suggesting that death so permeates her imagination that it affects her most basic perceptions by changing an object from one thing to another. The metaphor is doubly effective because it grows out of the speaker's immediate surroundings. She sees (as we do) the dead parents as resembling the other shoeless sunbathers lolling in boats along the beach except that their boats are heavier than life and are sinking into the deep forever.

In his sonnet, Shakespeare uses a series of metaphors to define and redefine true love. First he says that love that changes when it finds change is not truly love. Then he says that love is a landmark that can be buffeted by storms without being moved; and that it is a star whose certainty can always be relied on. Finally, he says that Love is not a victim of Time and its ravages but persists even to death.

It can be argued that love and stars share a few important properties, among them constancy, but we have to admit that their differences out-number those shared properties. Through the strength of his metaphor, however, Shakespeare suppresses our everyday awareness of the differences and makes the similarities seem paramount. We finish the poem aware that love is still love and stars are still stars. But we also know that this new thing—love equals stars—has been created. The effect is to alter, however subtly, our perception of love and stars from then onward.

Dover Beach°

The sea is calm tonight.
The tide is full, the moon lies fair
Upon the straits; on the French coast the light
Gleams and is gone; the cliffs of England stand,
Glimmering and vast, out in the tranquil bay.   5
Come to the window, sweet is the night-air!
Only, from the long line of spray
Where the sea meets the moon-blanched land,
Listen! you hear the grating roar
Of pebbles which the waves draw back, and fling,   10
At their return, up the high strand,
Begin, and cease, and then again begin,
With tremulous cadence slow, and bring
The eternal note of sadness in.

Sophocles° long ago   15
Heard it on the Aegean, and it brought
Into his mind the turbid ebb and flow
Of human misery; we
Find also in the sound a thought,
Hearing it by this distant northern sea.   20

The Sea of Faith
Was once, too, at the full, and round earth's shore
Lay like the folds of a bright girdle° furled.   *encircling band*
But now I only hear
Its melancholy, long, withdrawing roar,   25
Retreating, to the breath
Of the night-wind, down the vast edges drear
And naked shingles° of the world.   *gravel beaches*

Dover Beach a point on the English coast from which the lights of France, about twenty miles distant, are sometimes visible   **15. Sophocles** Greek dramatist (ca. 496–405 BC) who wrote classic tragedies

Ah, love, let us be true
To one another! for the world, which seems   30
To lie before us like a land of dreams,
So various, so beautiful, so new,
Hath really neither joy, nor love, nor light,
Nor certitude, nor peace, nor help for pain;
And we are here as on a darkling plain   35
Swept with confused alarms of struggle and flight,
Where ignorant armies clash by night.

Matthew Arnold (1822–1888)

We should not assume that imagery, simile, and metaphor exist independently of each other in neat compartments. The images of a poem are often similes and metaphors, comparisons which make us see something in a new and vivid way. In good poetry, moreover, imagery and figures of speech collaborate to produce an overall effect, as "Dover Beach," one of the classic poetic arguments in English literature, shows very well.

The first fourteen lines of the poem are filled with images that make us see, hear, and feel the setting. First we see a calm sea, the gleaming lights of France across the Channel, and Dover's famous white cliffs glimmering in the moonlight. Then the speaker summons his beloved to the window. We smell, with them, the sweetness of the night air; we hear the monotony of the tidal flow.

The imagery makes us feel that a real place is being described, a real setting that the speaker is actually looking at and out of which his reflections on the meaning of life (beginning with "the eternal note of sadness," line 14) grow. Sophocles, the greatest of Greek tragic-dramatists, probably saw such a scene ages ago, the speaker says, while looking out onto a different body of water, and it brought into his mind the metaphor linking the eternal motion of the sea with the eternal presence of human misery. It brings into the speaker's mind a similar metaphor: faith (in God, in belief itself) is a sea that was once as "full" as the sea he is looking at. In a bygone time this sea of faith was *like* (a simile within the metaphor) a bright girdle with all its folds stretched tight as it covered a great expanse. But now this sea of faith is retreating in the same way that the waves of the sea the speaker is watching are.

In the last nine lines of the poem the speaker returns to the scene he set at the beginning of the poem. But now, as a result of the associations it has brought to mind, his attitude toward Dover Beach has changed. It is no longer charming and beautiful, *like* a "land of dreams" (line 31). A truer comparison, he says, would be with a dark battleground where war is waged by armies without purpose.

We don't have to feel the Victorian melancholy over the way science and secularity had undermined belief in religion to sense the power of this poem. The emotion of the poem is largely the result of the way that imagery and figurative language work together to draw us into the scene and from it into areas of thought that lead the speaker to such distressing conclusions. We too feel that the world, which at the beginning of the poem seemed so calm and promising, is actually an illusion masking a reality that offers no comfort at all.

SYMBOLS

No subject is more controversial than symbolism. Students sometimes get the impression—not unjustifiably—that people who read poetry spend most of their time stalking symbols and finally managing to uncover them in the least probable places. There are probably far fewer symbols intended than are actually located. The fact remains, however, that some poets do consciously use symbolism, which is among the richest of all the elements of figurative language.

A *symbol* is an object, action, or even a situation which stands for something so complex that it would be difficult to deal with it directly. (For instance, by the end of "Dover Beach," the formerly pleasing scene that the speaker sees outside his window has taken on an ominous symbolic significance.) Symbols are like metaphors in that they fuse the meanings of things from different zones of experience. They are unlike metaphors, however, in that what they stand for is often not specified with the clarity, for example, of Shakespeare's equation of love and stars.

A symbol is not just a means of comparison; it also usually evokes the feelings of the thing it symbolizes. A swastika, for instance, calls up the genocidal terror of the Third Reich; and a cross calls up Christ's suffering and Christianity itself. Often symbols are shorthand. Two dots above a semicircular line enclosed within a circle admonishes us to have a good day. And when we see a bumper sticker that says, "I ♡ New York" we know that it doesn't mean "I heart New York."

How do we know when we are in the presence of a symbol in a poem? There is no infallible guide. We do know that there are certain *traditional symbols* that recur in poetry. The rose often stands for love, the snake for sin, the dove for peace. The circle, as the "perfect" geometric form, has always called up completion, unity, infinity, and so on. The seasons suggest stages in human life. (T. S. Eliot turned the familiar symbolism in spring as a time of rebirth and regeneration back upon itself when he began one of his poems, "April is the cruelest month.")

Generally speaking, symbolism is *contextual* in that the meaning of symbols derives from the specific role they play in a given poem. Consider William Blake's "The Tiger."

The Tiger

Tiger, tiger, burning bright
In the forests of the night,
What immortal hand or eye
Could frame they fearful symmetry?

In what distant deeps or skies   5
Burnt the fire of thine eyes?
On what wings dare he aspire?
What the hand dare seize the fire?

And what shoulder and what art
Could twist the sinews of thy heart?   10
And, when thy heart began to beat,
What dread hand and what dread feet?

What the hammer? What the chain?
In what furnace was thy brain?
What the anvil? What dread grasp   15
Dare its deadly terrors clasp?

When the stars threw down their spears,
And water'd heaven with their tears,
Did He smile His work to see?
Did He who made the lamb make thee?   20

Tiger, tiger, burning bright
In the forests of the night,
What immortal hand or eye
Dare frame thy fearful symmetry?

William Blake (1757–1827)

The tiger here is more than just the animal of the jungle, although that creature's legendary ferocity is an aspect of the meaning of the symbol. Repetition is the first indication that Blake gives us that we are in the presence of a symbol. We are being told, in effect, to weigh the word "tiger" more carefully than we would an unrepeated word. Furthermore, in the very first stanza of the poem, we are asked to consider the tiger as something more than a species of animal with the question about the origins of its "fearful symmetry." And if we still don't know what the tiger stands for by the end of the poem, we are given an important clue when the speaker asks, "Did He who made the lamb make thee?" (line 20). The lamb, of course, is a traditional symbol for goodness and purity. As its opposite, the tiger symbolizes motiveless evil and rapacity.

The Oven Bird

There is a singer everyone has heard,
Loud, a mid-summer and a mid-wood bird,
Who makes the solid tree trunks sound again.
He says that leaves are old and that for flowers
Mid-summer is to spring as one to ten.   5

He says the early petal-fall is past,
When pear and cherry bloom went down in showers
On sunny days a moment overcast;
And comes that other fall we name the fall.
He says the highway dust is over all.   10
The bird would cease and be as other birds
But that he knows in singing not to sing.
The question that he frames in all but words
Is what to make of a diminished thing.

Robert Frost (1874–1963)

    We should be wary of being too ingenious in our identification of symbols. Reading a poem should not be the literary equivalent of an Easter-egg hunt. But in our desire to feel we are on solid ground, we should not *under*interpret a poem. On one level, for instance, Robert Frost's "The Oven Bird" is about a thrushlike North American ground warbler, *Seiurus aurocapillus*. But if we read the poem only on its most literal level—as a report on the behavior of this species of bird at different seasons of the year—we deprive ourselves of the full meaning of the poem. For Frost's oven bird does more than make tree trunks reverberate with its songs. It prompts thoughts not only about fall as a time of the year, but *the* fall of man—and about how all life around us, the natural setting and moral environment—has been somehow "diminished" as a result of this fall from grace. It may at first be difficult to specify what exactly the bird symbolizes, but the fact that there is symbolism in its song should be unmistakable.

POEMS FOR FURTHER DISCUSSION

Mystic

They call all experience of the senses *mystic*, when the experience is
    considered.
So an apple becomes *mystic* when I taste in it
the summer and the snows, the wild welter° of earth   *confusion*
and the insistence of the sun.
All of which things I can surely taste in a good apple.   5
Though some apples taste preponderantly of water, wet and sour
and some of too much sun, brackish sweet
like lagoon-water, that has been too much sunned.

If I say I taste these things in an apple, I am called *mystic*, which means a liar.
The only way to eat an apple is to hog it down like a pig   10
and taste nothing
that is *real*.

But if I eat an apple, I like to eat it with all my senses awake.
Hogging it down like a pig I call the feeding of corpses.

D. H. Lawrence (1885–1930)

QUESTIONS

1. How do the images here help establish the argument of the poem?
2. To some degree the success of this poem depends on our sharing the speaker's view of the word *mystic*. Discuss the speaker's definition and redefinition of that word and the role it plays in the poem's meaning.
3. The speaker in this poem has a distinctive tone of voice. How would you characterize it? Compare it to the speaker's voice in "My Papa's Waltz."

Word

The word bites like a fish.
Shall I throw it back free
Arrowing to that sea
Where thoughts lash tail and fin?
Or shall I pull it in
To rhyme upon a dish?

Stephen Spender (b. 1909)

QUESTIONS

1. In what sense might it be said that this poem is dependent upon the initial simile? How does this simile become an extended metaphor?
2. What are the connotations of "sea" (line 3) and "dish" (line 6)?
3. What is the poem about? What is the speaker's dilemma?

The Lamb

Dost thou know who made thee?
Little Lamb, who made thee?
Gave thee life, and bid thee feed
By the stream and o'er the mead;
Gave thee clothing of delight,   5
Softest clothing, woolly, bright;
Gave thee such a tender voice,
Making all the vales rejoice?
    Little Lamb, who made thee?
    Dost thou know who made thee?   10

Little Lamb, I'll tell thee,
Little Lamb, I'll tell thee:
He is callèd by thy name,
For he calls himself a Lamb.
He is meek, and he is mild; 15
He became a little child.
I a child, and thou a lamb,
We are callèd by his name.
Little Lamb, God bless thee!
Little Lamb, God bless thee! 20

William Blake (1757–1827)

QUESTIONS

1. Explain the symbolism in lines 13–17. How do the preceding lines of the poem prepare you to accept this symbolism? Is the lamb what we have called a "traditional symbol"? How so?

2. Compare this poem to "The Tiger" on pages 415–16. The two works are companion pieces, although "The Tiger" was composed three years after "The Lamb." Compare the speaker in each poem. What aspects of God do they emphasize? Are their views in any way compatible?

The Heavy Bear Who Goes with Me

"the withness of the body"°

The heavy bear who goes with me,
A manifold honey to smear his face,
Clumsy and lumbering here and there,
The central ton of every place,
The hungry beating brutish one 5
In love with candy, anger, and sleep,
Crazy factotum°, dishevelling all,
Climbs the building, kicks the football,
Boxes his brother in the hate-ridden city.

Breathing at my side, that heavy animal, 10
That heavy bear who sleeps with me,
Howls in his sleep for a world of sugar,
A sweetness intimate as the water's clasp,

"**the withness of the body**" This phrase was attributed in earlier editions of the poem to Harvard professor Alfred North Whitehead; later the attribution was removed.   7. **factotum** a nonentity at someone's beck and call

Howls in his sleep because the tight-rope
Trembles and shows the darkness beneath.   15
—The strutting show-off is terrified,
Dressed in his dress-suit, bulging his pants,
Trembles to think that his quivering meat
Must finally wince to nothing at all.

That inescapable animal walks with me,   20
Has followed me since the black womb held,
Moves where I move, distorting my gesture,
A caricature, a swollen shadow,
A stupid clown of the spirit's motive,
Perplexes and affronts with his own darkness,   25
The secret life of belly and bone,
Opaque, too near, my private, yet unknown,
Stretches to embrace the very dear
With whom I would walk without him near,
Touches her grossly, although a word   30
Would bare my heart and make me clear,
Stumbles, flounders, and strives to be fed
Dragging me with him in his mouthing care,
Amid the hundred million of his kind,
The scrimmage of appetite everywhere.   35

Delmore Schwartz (1913–1966)

QUESTIONS

1. Schwartz's bear might be compared to the snake in Emily Dickinson's "A narrow
   Fellow in the Grass." How do each of these animals function to define the
   meaning of the respective poems?
2. What are some of the natural attributes of the bear that make it an appropriate
   symbol for the speaker's baser self? Is this bear wild or domestic?
3. Discuss the connotative language in this poem. How does Schwartz make us "see"
   the bear?

3

THE RHETORIC OF A POEM

W e have seen that words are the building blocks of poems—highly charged units that can conjure up strong images and force us to make connections between areas of experience customarily segregated from each other. In addition to creating images and figures of speech that make us see and think in certain ways, the poet also uses language *rhetorically* to establish the *tone* of the poem and thus to give the reader an emotional key to meaning. In other words, poetry, like every other form of writing, involves *argument*. Sometimes the argument is almost invisible, asking only that we assent to the reality, or authenticity, of a fragile lyric emotion. But in other cases (as we have seen in our discussion of Matthew Arnold's "Dover Beach") the argument is quite complex, involving weighty intellectual issues. In either case, we should be aware of some of the intellectual strategies and the special linguistic resources that a poet can employ to get the reader to feel one way rather than another.

PARADOX

My Heart Leaps Up When I Behold

My heart leaps up when I behold
  A rainbow in the sky:
So was it when my life began;
So is it now I am a man;
So be it when I shall grow old,
  Or let me die!
The Child is father of the Man;
And I could wish my days to be
Bound each to each by natural piety.

William Wordsworth (1770–1850)

Paradox, a statement that seems false or at odds with common experience, can be an important part of a poet's repertory. The statement in Wordsworth's

421

well-known line—"The Child is father of the Man"—is, of course, absolutely contrary to the facts of human biology. Below the literal contradiction, however, there is a deeper truth: we are indeed formed by our childhood experiences, and what we are as adults is, in large part, defined by what we are as children. The poet's purpose in announcing this paradox, however, is less to propose a general truth about human development than to make us ponder our "natural piety." The paradox is a way of drawing our attention to the speaker's contention that he (like us) must continue to be part of the natural world if his own life is to have meaning. If he is not to die a spiritual death, nature must go on—in the cycles that make the child "father" to the man.

Batter My Heart, Three-Personed God

Batter my heart, three-personed God;° for You   *the Trinity*
As yet but knock, breathe, shine, and seek to mend;
That I may rise and stand, o'erthrow me, and bend
Your force to break, blow, burn, and make me new.
I, like an usurped° town, to another due,   *betrayed*   5
Labor to admit You, but O, to no end;
Reason, Your viceroy in me, me should defend,
But is captived, and proves weak or untrue.
Yet dearly I love You, and would be loved fain,°   *gladly*
But am betrothed unto Your enemy.   10
Divorce me, untie or break that knot again;
Take me to You, imprison me, for I,
Except You enthrall me, never shall be free,
Nor ever chaste, except You ravish me.

John Donne (1572–1631)

The subject of Donne's poem is paradox itself, the central paradox of Christianity: that true freedom exists only in absolute submission to God. In a series of interlocked metaphors, the speaker explores this contradiction, first asking the "three-personed God" (the Trinity) to "o'erthrow" him so that he will be "new" (lines 3–4). He then says that "Reason," which should be a viceroy working for his master (God), is actually a captive (lines 7–8). He compares himself to a lover betrothed to God's enemy, the Devil, but one who wants to be divorced. Finally, in a most remarkable instance of paradox, the speaker announces that the only way he can be free is to be "enthralled," and the only way he can be "chaste" is to be ravished by God.

As these two poems suggest, paradox carries shock value. Wordsworth's assertion that the child fathers the man forces us to focus on the truth that a love of nature has given coherence to the poet's life. And when Donne proposes a series of paradoxes—each one more extreme than the last, culminating in the request for enslavement and assault—we recognize some of the contradictions involved in trying to be faithful to God while living in a world of traps and snares. In both cases, paradox takes us directly and forcefully into the heart of the poem's meaning.

ALLUSION

The Parable of the Old Man and the Young

So Abram° rose, and clave the wood, and went,
And took the fire with him, and a knife.
And as they sojourned both of them together,
Isaac the first-born spake and said, My Father,
Behold the preparations, fire and iron,   5
But where the lamb for this burnt offering?
Then Abram bound the youth with belts and straps,
And builded parapets and trenches there,
And stretchèd forth the knife to slay his son.
When lo! an angel called him out of heaven,   10
Saying, Lay not thy hand upon the lad,
Neither do anything to him. Behold,
A ram,° caught in a thicket by its horns;
Offer the Ram of Pride instead of him.
But the old man would not so, but slew his son,   15
And half the seed of Europe, one by one.

Wilfred Owen (1893–1918)

Allusion is a way for a poet to broaden the implications of his work by reference to events, situations, or characters in myth, history, or even other poems. Owen's bitter antiwar poem carries allusions from the biblical story of Abraham and Isaac to the bloody waste of the First World War (in which Owen himself died). The archaic diction of the poem—"clave," "spake," "both of them together"—helps make the allusion work. The reader begins to suspect that the biblical story is being put to other ends when Isaac is bound with "belts and straps" (line 7)—clearly parts of an infantry soldier's gear— and when Abram builds "parapets and trenches" (line 8)—part of the devastated landscape in which World War I was fought. In the poem, an angel introduces the ram as a substitute victim, just as an angel does in the biblical version of the story. But in the poem, it is a "Ram of Pride" (line 14) and instead of sacrificing it in place of his son, as he does in the Bible, this Abram,

1. **Abram** Abraham, Old Testament patriarch, whose faith God tested by commanding him to sacrifice his son Isaac 13. **a ram** God substituted a ram at the last moment for Isaac.

now representing the leaders of the warring countries, kills Isaac, who now represents all the young casualties of World War I. Thus what in the Bible was a parable of divine justice here becomes a parable of political murder.

The World Is Too Much with Us

The world is too much with us; late and soon,
Getting and spending, we lay waste our powers;
Little we see in Nature that is ours;
We have given our hearts away, a sordid boon!
This Sea that bares her bosom to the moon,   5
The winds that will be howling at all hours,
And are up-gathered now like sleeping flowers,
For this, for everthing, we are out of tune;
It moves us not.—Great God! I'd rather be
A Pagan suckled in a creed outworn;   10
So might I, standing on this pleasant lea,°   *meadow*
Have glimpses that would make me less forlorn;
Have sight of Proteus rising from the sea;
Or hear old Triton blow his wreathèd horn.

William Wordsworth (1770–1850)

This poem employs allusion somewhat differently. The speaker laments the spread of materialism ("getting and spending," line 2) and the consequent alienation from Nature, an alienation exemplified by our inability to be moved by a beautiful seascape or by winds that can vary from sweet docility to howling grandeur. He tells us that he would rather have been a "pagan" Greek than a modern man, for then at least he would have been in touch with the natural world, a world represented by Proteus, a sea god, and by Triton, son of Poseidon, ruler of the seas.

The allusion to these mythical figures reinforces the argument about the way the modern world and the Industrial Revolution of the nineteenth century have degraded man's sensibilities. The allusion directs the reader to a time when humankind was intimately involved with nature, seeing all its moods as a reflection of the gods who used it as their habitat. By mentioning Triton and Proteus, once thought to be gods of the sea at which the poet is gazing, he puts us imaginatively in touch with the world whose disappearance is his poem's very subject.

EXAGGERATION AND UNDERSTATEMENT

When, in conversation, we say "I'm freezing" or "I'm starving," we are saying more than we really mean. Likewise, when we say, "It's getting somewhat chilly" or "I guess I could eat," we probably mean more than we say. In these cases, we are using, respectively, exaggeration and understatement. These figures of speech are especially useful to poets, who employ them for a variety of effects.

The Negro Speaks of Rivers

(TO W. E. B. DUBOIS)°

I've known rivers:
I've known rivers ancient as the world and older than the
  flow of human blood in human veins.

My soul has grown deep like the rivers.

I bathed in the Euphrates° when dawns were young.   5
I built my hut near the Congo and it lulled me to sleep.
I looked upon the Nile and raised the pyramids above it.
I heard the singing of the Mississippi when Abe Lincoln
  went down to New Orleans, and I've seen its muddy
  bosom turn all golden in the sunset.   10

I've known rivers:
Ancient, dusky rivers.

My soul has grown deep like the rivers.

Langston Hughes (1902–1967)

A completely rational and sober response to the above lines would be to say that such things are simply not so, and simply cannot be so. No person could reasonably claim to have done all these things; such experiences and such identifications are beyond human capability. But the reader of the poem knows that while they are literally false these statements are imaginatively true. *Exaggeration* (or *hyperbole*) allows the poet to move to a high place where *all* of the experience of being black is his own, and he speaks for every black person who ever lived. Exaggeration works to allow the poet, and then us, to think about leaving the smallness of our own beings and entering the vastness of all humanity.

If exaggeration in Hughes's poem works to elevate the significance of the subject matter, in another context it can be used to deflate or undercut a situation. In Alexander Pope's "The Rape of the Lock," for instance, the solemn conventions of the Homeric epic are employed to tell the wholly mundane story of the snipping of a lock of hair from a highborn but frivolous lady. When we first come to the poem, we are prepared to think that it might

W. E. B. DuBois black scholar, educator, and reformer (1868–1963)   5. Euphrates a river of Southwestern Asia

pose some serious questions about a serious crime. We find, in short order, that this is not so, and, as a result of the use of grossly inflated assertions, we are led instead to see the superficiality of "polite" society. A good example of Pope's use of overstatement comes in the fourth canto of his poem, just after the moment when the hair is snipped.

From The Rape of the Lock

But anxious cares the pensive nymph oppressed,
And secret passions labored in her breast.
Not youthful kings in battle seized alive,
Not scornful virgins who their charms survive,
Not ardent lovers robbed of all their bliss,   5
Not ancient ladies when refused a kiss,
Not tyrants fierce that unrepenting die,
Not Cynthia when her manteau's° pinned awry,   *loose cloak*
E'er felt such rage, resentment, and despair,
As thou, sad virgin! for thy ravished hair.   10

Alexander Pope (1688–1744)

To compare, on the same level, tyrants and kings with maidens whose hair has been clipped is to use exaggeration to make a social comment. We are made to see the triviality of the concerns of society. The exaggeration here diminishes rather than magnifies the situation.

Understatement (the technical term is *meiosis*) can be thought of as another kind of purposeful misstatement, and our reaction to understatement is comparable to that we experience when confronted with overstatement. With understatement we compensate or add; with overstatement we subtract. In either case, what we are doing is providing a correction for situations in which the poet has purposefully left an imbalance.

Understatement, exemplified here in a masterful elegy, can be particularly effective when intense emotions are involved.

Bells for John Whiteside's Daughter

There was such speed in her little body,
And such lightness in her footfall,
It is no wonder her brown study
Astonishes us all.

Her wars were bruited in our high window.   5
We looked among orchard trees and beyond
Where she took arms against her shadow,
Or harried unto the pond

The lazy geese, like a snow cloud
Dripping their snow on the green grass,   10
Tricking and stopping, sleepy and proud,
Who cried in goose, Alas,

For the tireless heart within the little
Lady with rod that made them rise
From their noon apple-dreams and scuttle   15
Goose-fashion under the skies!

But now go the bells, and we are ready,
In one house we are sternly stopped
To say we are vexed at her brown study,
Lying so primly propped.   20

John Crowe Ransom (1888–1974)

In this poem, no direct grappling with the death of the little girl occurs. In fact, the death seems almost concealed. We see her in life, with her speed, her lightness, and her playfulness in fighting her own shadow and chasing her flock of geese. Not until the last stanza do we recognize that the understatement "brown study" (a term customarily meaning a look of concentration) of the first stanza is, in fact, the perplexed look on the face of the little girl's propped-up corpse. But there is no flood of tears in this poem, no anguished lament. We are made to focus on the girl's provocation of the geese rather than on her tragic death. Yet, by the end of the poem, we can feel a deep sense of loss because we have been made to see, through the understated emotions, that her death is like most deaths, perhaps our own death to come. In this poem, death becomes familiar, natural, ordinary. The fate of John Whiteside's daughter becomes in our minds an archetypal event standing for the caprice and the inevitability of death's power in the world. If the emotions were not subdued and controlled, kept at arm's length, we would not be so powerfully moved.

IRONY

In daily conversation, we use irony when we say one thing while meaning another. For example, when we see someone wearing a particularly grotesque or ugly article of clothing and remark, "My, what an attractive hat," or "I don't believe I've ever seen a tie quite as stunning as that one," we are using irony. Although it is not necessary that the person against whom this casual irony is directed "gets it," it is necessary, for irony to work, that *someone* does. Irony is a source of pleasure, that is, for at least two people: its creator and some onlooker, a listener, or a reader who shares with the creator a quiet understanding that there is something different in the words from what they literally say.

Poets use irony in many different ways. In the following poem by Siegfried Sassoon, the tone of voice is one that reveals a powerful ironic truth about the realities of the First World War.

Does It Matter?

Does it matter—losing your legs? . . .
For people will always be kind,
And you need not show that you mind
When the others come in after hunting
To gobble their muffins and eggs.   5

Does it matter—losing your sight? . . .
There's such splendid work for the blind;
And people will always be kind,
As you sit on the terrace remembering
And turning your face to the light.   10

Do they matter—those dreams from the pit? . . .
You can drink and forget and be glad,
And people won't say that you're mad;
For they'll know that you've fought for your country,
And no one will worry a bit.   15

Siegfried Sassoon (1886–1967)

The speaker here poses his questions as if wholly unaware that they immediately answer themselves. *Of course* it matters that one loses a leg, or one's sight; *of course* it matters that one has terrible nightmares. And a word such as "gobble" (line 5) betrays, with ironic force, the speaker's profound bitterness about the unwounded and insensitive people surrounding him. Phrases such as "people will always be kind" (line 2) are saturated with irony; they give the poem its distinctive mocking tone.

Richard Cory

Whenever Richard Cory went down town,
We people on the pavement looked at him:
He was a gentleman from sole to crown,
Clean favored, and imperially slim.

And he was always quietly arrayed,
And he was always human when he talked;   5
But still he fluttered pulses when he said,
"Good-morning," and he glittered when he walked.

And he was rich—yes, richer than a king—
And admirably schooled in every grace: 10
In fine, we thought that he was everything
To make us wish that we were in his place.

So on we worked, and waited for the light,
And went without the meat, and cursed the bread;
And Richard Cory, one calm summer night,   15
Went home and put a bullet through his head.

Edwin Arlington Robinson (1869–1935)

While the Sassoon poem depends on *tonal irony*, Robinson's "Richard Cory" depends on *situational irony*; situational irony occurs when there is a gap between what we expect to result from a situation and what actually happens. In "Richard Cory" the speaker devotes considerable attention to the details that revealed the superiority of one individual to all that surrounded him. Consistently associated with images of royalty—"from sole to *crown*" (line 3), "*imperially* slim" (line 4), "richer than a *king*" (line 9)—such a man nevertheless puts a bullet through his head, and his own sense of total worthlessness is revealed. Perhaps this is no tragedy, but the difference between the public estimation of his situation and Richard Cory's own could hardly be stronger. The speaker of the poem holds both evaluations in mind; he sees both the outward splendor and the inward desperation. And he knows that it was envy that prevented the public estimation of Cory from being any more perceptive than it was.

My Last Duchess

FERRARA°

That's my last duchess painted on the wall,
Looking as if she were alive. I call
That piece a wonder, now: Frà Pandolf's° hands
Worked busily a day, and there she stands.
Will 't please you sit and look at her? I said   5
"Frà Pandolf" by design, for never read
Strangers like you that pictured countenance,
The depth and passion of its earnest glance,
But to myself they turned (since none puts by
The curtain I have drawn for you, but I)   10
And seemed as they would ask me, if they durst,
How such a glance came there; so, not the first
Are you to turn and ask thus. Sir, 'twas not
Her husband's presence only, called that spot
Of joy into the Duchess' cheek: perhaps   15

Ferrara The poem is based loosely on a story Browning heard about Alfonso II, a sixteenth-century Italian duke whose first wife died under suspicious circumstances. Not long after her death, the duke began negotiating for her successor.   **3. Frà Pandolf** name of a fictitious painter

Frà Pandolf chanced to say "Her mantle laps
"Over my lady's wrist too much," or "Paint
"Must never hope to reproduce the faint
"Half-flush that dies along her throat": such stuff
Was courtesy, she thought, and cause enough   20
For calling up that spot of joy. She had
A heart—how shall I say?—too soon made glad,
Too easily impressed; she liked whate'er
She looked on, and her looks went everywhere.
Sir, 'twas all one! My favor at her breast,   25
The dropping of the daylight in the West,
The bough of cherries some officious fool
Broke in the orchard for her, the white mule
She rode with round the terrace—all and each
Would draw from her alike the approving speech,   30
Or blush, at least. She thanked men—good! but thanked
Somehow—I know not how—as if she ranked
My gift of a nine-hundred-years-old name
With anybody's gift. Who'd stoop to blame
This sort of trifling? Even had you skill   35
In speech—which I have not—to make your will
Quite clear to such an one, and say, "Just this
"Or that in you disgusts me; here you miss,
"Or there exceed the mark"—and if she let
Herself be lessoned so, nor plainly set   40
Her wits to yours, forsooth, and made excuse,
—E'en then would be some stooping; and I choose
Never to stoop. Oh sir, she smiled, no doubt,
Whene'er I passed her; but who passed without
Much the same smile? This grew; I gave commands;   45
Then all smiles stopped together. There she stands
As if alive. Will 't please you rise? We'll meet
The company below, then. I repeat,
The Count your master's known munificence
Is ample warrant that no just pretense   50
Of mine for dowry will be disallowed;
Though his fair daughter's self, as I avowed
At starting, is my object. Nay, we'll go
Together down, sir. Notice Neptune,° though,
Taming a sea-horse, thought a rarity,   55
Which Claus of Innsbruck° cast in bronze for me!

Robert Browning (1812–1889)

---

54. **Neptune** Roman god of the sea   56. **Claus of Innsbruck** name of a fictitious metalsmith

Dramatic irony is the term describing those situations in poems where we are allowed to perceive a reality at odds with the facts as they are literally presented to us. In the poem above, for instance, the speaker tells us one story, about a painting, a foolish woman, and the consequent disintegration of a marriage. Listening between the lines, however, we hear another story, and this one is about a cruel and oppressive husband, a sweetly generous wife, and what looks suspiciously like murder. That the Duchess had a heart "too soon made glad" (line 22) may have been a fault to her husband, but it is not to us. While he seems to think her open nature to have been seriously flawed, we sense that she was wholly responsive to everything that life had to offer her. When we come to lines 45–46, we recognize full well what must have occurred in the relationship: "I gave commands; / Then all smiles stopped together." This is, of course, a chilling understatement, meaning that the Duke *saw to it* that the smiles ceased. It dawns on us, moreover, that this tale of cruelty has only been a digression during negotiations for the dowry of yet another duchess.

Perhaps the Duke reveals more of himself than he intends to in this dramatic monologue, but perhaps he wants his listener to understand that the story of his *last* Duchess is a cautionary tale, one to be carried back to the father of his *next* Duchess. She will then make no mistakes, unless she wishes to suffer similar consequences. In either case, by the conclusion of the poem we can see the dramatic irony that has been present almost from the first lines of the poem: "That's my last Duchess painted on the wall, / Looking as if she were alive." We now know she is dead, having incurred her husband's wrath by her innocent generosity. We read this poem with a growing awareness that we are overhearing a story with sinister depths, seeing events in a way we are not meant to.

AMBIGUITY

Stopping by Woods on a Snowy Evening

Whose woods these are I think I know.
His house is in the village though;
He will not see me stopping here
To watch his woods fill up with snow.

My little horse must think it queer   5
To stop without a farmhouse near
Between the woods and frozen lake
The darkest evening of the year.

He gives his harness bells a shake
To ask if there is some mistake.   10
The only other sound's the sweep
Of easy wind and downy flake.

The woods are lovely, dark and deep,
But I have promises to keep,
And miles to go before I sleep,   15
And miles to go before I sleep.

Robert Frost (1874–1963)

Ambiguity, or what is ordinarily called "double meaning," generally makes for confusion when it occurs in our daily communication. In life, we want to make ourselves clearly and directly understood. In poetry, however, ambiguity can enrich and deepen meaning. It can remind us that the world is a place of complexity, that things both are and are not what they seem. We know that the traveler in Frost's poem is no more than a traveler, a person on a journey. But we sense that his journey is not only through woods and snow, but also through life itself. The woods might be "lovely," but they are also "dark" and "deep" (line 13). Is the journey a routine or a risky one? And how are we to explain the repeated note of urgency with which the poem closes?

Such questions arise from a poem whose surface is placid, but whose depths hide a great deal. Indeed, some readers have concluded that "Stopping by Woods" is really a poem about death and its attractions, and that what we are made to feel is the sensuous attractiveness of a perfect escape from the grinding conflicts of everyday existence. This reading, supported by the ambiguity of many of the poem's lines, says that the traveler is only with difficulty able to resist the temptations of perfect obliteration and to return to the world of responsibility represented by the word "promises" (line 14). His obligations draw him back to the workaday world, but we have been with him as he has pondered other possibilities.

Questioned about such a reading, Frost himself said, "I never intended that, but I did have the feeling it [the poem] was loaded with ulteriority." He thus put his finger on one element of ambiguity, namely its power to extend our concerns beyond the literal. He was, in addition, reminding us that even the poet is not always certain of the resonances his work might generate, and that there might be an "ulteriority" for the reader to uncover.

How "deeply" are we to read poems? Are we to look for every possible ambiguity in them? How do we make sure we are interpreting successfully, and how do we guard against the folly of just being overly clever and ingenious? The answer to these important questions is that just as there is an art to the writing of poetry, so is there an art to reading it. We should first read poems on their own literal terms for the sense they provide. Without that sense, they are probably not worth reading. But we should be modest about our first findings and proceed with a willingness to allow other possibilities to come into our minds. We should also proceed with the awareness that several interpretations can peacefully coexist. As we read and think, we should prepare ourselves for those delightful moments when the poem simply opens up and becomes richer and richer the more closely we inspect it. If it is a great poem, its meanings will seem inexhaustible and we will gladly take all the intellectual and emotional pleasure it can provide.

POEMS FOR FURTHER DISCUSSION

To His Coy Mistress

stop being coy!

Had we but world enough, and time,
This coyness,° lady, were no crime.   modesty
We would sit down, and think which way
To walk, and pass our long love's day.   *hyperbole*
Thou by the Indian Ganges'° side   5
Shouldst rubies find; I by the tide
Of Humber° would complain. I would

if things were dif.

Love you ten years before the flood,
And you should, if you please, refuse
Till the conversion of the Jews.°   10
My vegetable love should grow
Vaster than empires and more slow;
An hundred years should go to praise
Thine eyes, and on thy forehead gaze;
Two hundred to adore each breast,   15
But thirty thousand to the rest;
An age at least to every part,
And the last age should show your heart.
For, lady, you deserve this state,°   *dignified treatment*
Nor would I love at lower rate.   20
    But at my back I always hear
Time's wingèd chariot hurrying near;
And yonder all before us lie   *irony* —
Deserts of vast eternity.
Thy beauty shall no more be found;   *hmm vs*   25
Nor, in thy marble vault, shall sound   *blunt*
My echoing song; then worms shall try

exaggerated praise of lady

getting impatient

That long-preserved virginity,
And your quaint honor turn to dust,
And into ashes all my lust: 30
The grave's a fine and private place,
But none, I think, do there embrace.
    Now therefore, while the youthful hue
Sits on thy skin like morning glow,
And while thy willing soul transpires   35
At every pore with instant fires,
Now let us sport us while we may,   *asks her to have sex*

---

5. **Ganges** a river in northern India sacred to Hindus   7. **Humber** a small river flowing through the English town of Hull   10. **conversion of the Jews** According to popular myths of the Renaissance, this event would occur just before the Last Judgment.

> And now, like amorous birds of prey,
> Rather at once our time devour
> Than languish in his slow-chapped° power.   40
> Let us roll all our strength and all
> Our sweetness up into one ball,
> And tear our pleasures with rough strife
> Thorough° the iron gates of life: *through*
> Thus, though we cannot make our sun   45
> Stand still,° yet we will make him run.

Andrew Marvell (1621–1678)

QUESTIONS

1. Identify the exaggerations and allusions in the first twenty lines of the poem. Why does the speaker use these particular references? What is he trying to prove?
2. Discuss the understatement in lines 31 and 32. How do the lines immediately preceding justify this assertion? Why is understatement the correct rhetorical posture for this moment in the poem?
3. Are the last lines of the poem a paradox? Try to describe logically exactly what they mean.
4. In this poem what we have called the "argument" is a strong element (the speaker is, after all, trying to persuade his mistress to capitulate). Analyze the three movements of the poem. Compare it as a rhetorical exercise to "Dover Beach" on pages 413–14.

Ozymandias°

> I met a traveler from an antique land
> Who said: Two vast and trunkless legs of stone
> Stand in the desert . . . Near them, on the sand,
> Half sunk, a shattered visage lies, whose frown,
> And wrinkled lip, and sneer of cold command,   5
> Tell that its sculptor well those passions read
> Which yet survive, stamped on these lifeless things,
> The hand that mocked them, and the heart that fed:
> And on the pedestal these words appear:
> "My name is Ozymandias, king of kings: 10
> Look on my works, ye Mighty, and despair!"

---

40. slow-chapped slow-lipped; refers to the early Greek myth of Chronos (Time), god of the world, who ate all his children except Zeus   **46. stand still** Zeus made the sun stand still so that his night of love with Alcmene would be longer.   **Ozymandias** Greek name for Egyptian Pharaoh Rameses II whose statue was inscribed, "I am Ozymandias, king of kings; if anyone would know what I am and where I lie, let him surpass me in my exploits."

Nothing beside remains. Round the decay
Of that colossal wreck, boundless and bare
The lone and level sands stretch far away.

Percy Bysshe Shelley (1792–1822)

QUESTIONS

1. Describe Ozymandias. How much is your perception of him based on his physical characteristics and how much on his attitudes?
2. Look carefully at the construction of lines 7–8. What is the grammatical connection between "survive" and the phrases that follow?
3. There are two levels of irony in this poem, one having to do with the fact that Ozymandias did not "survive" through the sculptor's representation and the other having to do with the fact that he did. Discuss the differences between these levels of irony.
4. Compare the use of irony in this poem to that found in "Richard Cory" (pp. 428–29).

Saint Judas

When I went out to kill myself, I caught
A pack of hoodlums beating up a man.
Running to spare his suffering, I forgot
My name, my number, how my day began,
How soldiers milled around the garden stone   5
And sang amusing songs; how all that day
Their javelins measured crowds; how I alone
Bargained the proper coins, and slipped away.

Banished from heaven, I found this victim beaten,
Stripped, kneed, and left to cry. Dropping my rope   10
Aside, I ran, ignored the uniforms:
Then I remembered bread my flesh had eaten.
The kiss that ate my flesh. Flayed without hope,
I held the man for nothing in my arms.

James Wright (1927–1980)

QUESTIONS

1. This poem rests on well-known incidents in the biblical story of Judas, Jesus Christ's betrayer. How does the author extend that story? What are the "coins" on line 8 and the "rope" on line 10? What is the significance of the repetition of "flesh" on lines 12 and 13?

2. Compare the use of biblical materials in this poem with their use in "Parable of the Old Man and the Young" on page 423. How does the fact that this poem is narrated in the first person and Owen's poem is not affect your response? Does it make sense to think of one poem as about salvation denied and the other as about salvation achieved?

3. Is there a cause and effect relationship in line 9? What is the relevance of the final line to the poem as a whole?

4. Do you find ambiguities such as those noted in Frost's "Stopping by Woods on a Snowy Evening" in this poem?

Channel Firing

That night your great guns, unawares,
Shook all our coffins as we lay,
And broke the chancel window-squares,°   *glass panes near altar*
We thought it was the Judgment-day°

And sat upright. While drearisome   5
Arose the howl of wakened hounds:
The mouse let fall the altar-crumb,
The worms drew back into the mounds,

The glebe cow° drooled. Till God called, "No;
It's gunnery practice out at sea   10
Just as before you went below;
The world is as it used to be:

"All nations striving strong to make
Red war yet redder. Mad as hatters
They do no more for Christès sake   15
Than you who are helpless in such matters.

"That this is not the judgment-hour
For some of them's a blessed thing,
For if it were they'd have to scour
Hell's floor for so much threatening. . . .   20

"Ha, ha. It will be warmer when
I blow the trumpet (if indeed
I ever do; for you are men,
And rest eternal sorely need)."

So down we lay again. "I wonder,   25
Will the world ever saner be,"
Said one, "than when He sent us under
In our indifferent century!"

---

4. **Judgment-day** when all the dead would awaken   9. **glebe cow** parish cow pastured near the church

And many a skeleton shook his head.
"Instead of preaching forty year,"   30
My neighbour Parson Thirdly said,
"I wish I had stuck to pipes and beer."

Again the guns disturbed the hour,
Roaring their readiness to avenge,
As far inland as Stourton Tower,°   35
And Camelot,° and starlit Stonehenge.°

Thomas Hardy (1840–1928)

QUESTIONS

1. At what point in this poem do you understand who is discussing the gunfire from battleships? What event are the battleships preparing for? Why is that event relevant to the tone of the poem?

2. We have defined one facet of irony as the gap between expectation and occurrence. How is that definition relevant to this poem? In what sense is God Himself being ironic when He speaks to the dead?

3. Discuss the relevance of the allusions in the last stanza.

35. Stourton Tower eighteenth-century tower in the English town of Wiltshire
36. Camelot mythical seat of King Arthur's kingdom   **36. Stonehenge** stone arrangement on Salisbury Plain thought to be early experiment in astronomy

4

THE TECHNIQUE OF A POEM

F or the sake of argument, we sometimes pretend that we can separate
content (what a poem says) from technique (how it says it). In fact, this is
impossible. Think how differently we would react to Matthew Arnold's
"Dover Beach" (pp. 413–14) if its large and speculative ideas were crammed
into a series of short, rhymed lines. Or how the effect of John Donne's "Song"
(pp. 398–99) would be damaged if its witty and pointed lines were allowed to
float freely in the kind of verse paragraph that Arnold employs.

What we think and feel about a poem is, to a large degree, a reaction to
how the work is presented. Poems are not simply sequences of ideas and
sentiments that happened to have come prepackaged into a poet's mind. A
poem's very substance is almost wholly dependent on the form it is given, and
on the other technical decisions that the poet has made. A successful poem
thus represents a fusion of thought and form, content and technique.

RHYME

Rhyme, the repetition of sounds of importantly positioned words in a poem, is
not a necessary component of poetry, but it can be one of its greatest sources
of pleasure. We can begin to appreciate exactly how pleasurable the "music"
of poetry can be by noting children's responses to nursery rhymes. They take
enormous joy not only in the repetition of sounds and cadences, but also in
the expectation that a rhyming pattern can provide. Rhyme is a quality that
can order the experience of poetry—for adults as well as children.

Rhyme is associated with the origins of poetry—a spoken medium that
traditionally used memory devices to help the reciter of a poem keep lengthy
passages ordered in his mind. Long after the printing press had largely transformed poetry from an oral medium into a written one, rhyme remained a
part of the art of the poem—an aspect of technique that had to be mastered,
part of the form within whose well-defined boundaries creativity flourished.
During the last century or so, poets have tended to move away from rhyme
and other conventions of poetry in an attempt to find forms that correspond to
our less structured sense of experience and to modern ideas about the need for
spontaneity in the creative process. Most contemporary poets would probably
not agree with Robert Frost's declaration that writing poetry without rhyme is
like playing tennis without a net. But for many poets rhyme continues to be
important, because of the sensitivity of the human ear to its delicate per-

cussion, and also because rhyme can help amplify meanings and bind a poem into one coherent unit.

A poet will sometimes use *internal rhyme* within the line to create emphases as well as melodies, as Samuel Taylor Coleridge does in "Rime of the Ancient Mariner":

> The fair breeze *blew*, the white foam *flew*,
> The furrow followed free;
> We were the *first* that ever *burst*
> Into that silent sea.

But most rhymed poems use *end rhyme* at the conclusion of the lines.

The Bat

> By day the bat is cousin to the mouse.
> He likes the attic of an aging house.
>
> His fingers make a hat about his head.
> His pulse beat is so slow we think him dead.
>
> He loops in crazy figures half the night   5
> Among the trees that face the corner light.
>
> But when he brushes up against a screen,
> We are afraid of what our eyes have seen:
>
> For something is amiss or out of place
> When mice with wings can wear a human face.   10

Theodore Roethke (1908–1963)

We can see in this poem how each set of rhymes presents a further definition of the bat, refining our view of the animal until we finally come face to face with it in all its frightfulness. The rhymes in the poem help bring the bat out of the animal kingdom (as a cousin to the mouse) and into the human world where its hybrid form makes it a symbol of the supernatural (a mouse *with wings* and a *human face!*).

End-rhymed poems have what is called a *rhyme scheme*. In diagramming this we give each new rhyme a successive letter of the alphabet. Thus the four lines from "Rime of the Ancient Mariner" previously quoted would have the rhyme scheme *abab*. The rhyme scheme of "The Bat" would be *aa bb cc* and so on.

"The Bat" employs *exact rhyme*; that is, the vowels and consonants of the rhyming words match exactly. Some poets favor *approximate rhyme*, in which the sounds are similar but not identical. Modern poets find this sort of rhyme especially congenial (it is sometimes also referred to as *slant rhyme*) because it introduces a note of uncertainty into the poem, a slight dissonance which itself can underscore the theme of the work. Think back to the opening lines of Theodore Roethke's "My Papa's Waltz" (pp. 405–406):

> The whiskey on your breath
> Could make a small boy dizzy;
> But I held on like death:
> Such waltzing was not easy.

The rhymes of lines 1 and 3 are exact but those of lines 2 and 4 are approximate. Why does Roethke work this way? One reason might be that he wants the four-line stanzas of the poem to evoke the boxy rhythm of a workingman's waltz and that this slight asymmetry helps—almost subliminally—to suggest how halting and inexact the dance between father and son is.

OTHER SOUND EFFECTS

In addition to rhyme, there are a variety of other ways in which a poet can use the sounds of single words or patterns of words to impart meaning to his work. *Alliteration* is the repetition of initial consonant sounds at the beginning of words. Consider these opening lines of a sonnet by Shakespeare:

> When to the sessions of sweet silent thought
> I summon up remembrance of things past . . .

The repetition of "s" sounds is no accident. What Shakespeare has in mind is to "shush" the reader and to remind him of the subdued qualities of "silent thought."

The repetition of final consonant sounds is *consonance*. The repetition of vowel sounds is *assonance*. The well-known lines from Thomas Gray's "Elegy Written in a Country Churchyard" contain both:

> The curfew tolls the knell of parting day,
> The lowing herd winds slowly o'er the lea,
> The plowman homeward plods his weary way,
> And leaves the world to darkness and to me.

In the first line, we hear echoes of the sound of the tolling bells in the consonance of the repeated "l" sounds. In the second line, we hear the mooing cattle in the assonance of the repeated "o" vowels.

Onomatopoeia is the imitation of natural sounds or noises in the sound of words. Some words—*hum, moo, buzz,* and so on—are by their very nature onomatopoetic, having sounds that reflect their meanings. The famous lines by Alfred, Lord Tennyson give us the sounds of doves and bees:

> The moan of doves in immemorial elms,
> And murmuring of innumerable bees.

Velvet Shoes

> Let us walk in the white snow
> In a soundless space;
> With footsteps quiet and slow,
> At a tranquil pace,
> Under veils of white lace.

5

I shall go shod in silk,
  And you in wool,
White as a white cow's milk,
  More beautiful
  Than the breast of a gull.   10

We shall walk through the still town
  In a windless peace;
We shall step upon white down,
  Upon silver fleece,
  Upon softer than these.   15

We shall walk in velvet shoes:
  Wherever we go
Silence will fall like dews
  On white silence below.
  We shall walk in the snow.   20

Elinor Wylie (1885–1928)

This poem shows how some of the sound effects that we have been discussing help produce an impression of quiet and tranquility. The rhymes and the alternation of long and short lines suggest the syncopation of a walk in the snow, laborious and filled with high-stepping effort. Alliteration occurs in the poem, especially in the "s" sounds which suggest the distinctive silence that comes after snow has insulated the ground. The assonance of the vowel patterns sprinkled throughout the poem conveys peacefulness. There are, finally, the "wh" sounds that collaborate with the repetition of the images of white to produce whiteness itself in the reader's mind, an emotional landscape like the one described in the poem—soft, serene, and without contrast.

RHYTHM

The truth, of course, is that many poems lack the rhyme and other sound effects we have just discussed. But all poetry has *rhythm*—a pattern of stresses and pauses linking the words into a unit. Rhythm is central to poetry, and is its most natural and subtle strength. It is an attribute suggestive of the importance, in human life, of the larger rhythms of the natural world: seasonal alternation; tidal flow and lunar change; our breath and heartbeat.

The poet Ezra Pound once said that rhythm in poetry is "form cut into time." Thus it is similar to music. As children we love the rhythm of nursery rhymes even more than the words themselves; it is the reassuring regularity of the beat that captivates us. As we grow older, our ears become more sophisticated and more demanding; we recognize that, like good music, poetic rhythms are best when varied and diverse.

Understanding poetic rhythm involves an appreciation of *prosody*—the study of meter and versification. This subject may seem forbidding, but it is not. It is certainly not a science, although it has its own symbols and nomenclature. We study prosody because it is a good way of understanding exactly how the well-made poem is put together, a way of seeing how poetic technique becomes poetic meaning.

Meter is the regular pattern of stressed and unstressed sounds in a poem. To describe the kinds of meter, we have used certain well-known symbols:

/ for a strong or stressed syllable;

‿ for a weak or unstressed syllable.

The most common meters in English are the *iambic* (‿/), as in the word *enough*; the *trochaic* (/‿), as in *meter*; the *anapestic* (‿‿/), as in *interrupt*; and the *dactylic* (/‿‿), as in *nastily*.

The word *meter* comes from the Latin term for "measure," and the unit of measurement in a poetic line is the *foot*, consisting of two or three syllables, one or two of which are stressed according to one of the patterns above. Only one foot in a line makes that line a *monometer*, two feet a *dimeter*, three feet a *trimeter*, four feet a *tetrameter*, five feet a *pentameter*, and so on. Thus line 21 of Arnold's "Dover Beach" is *iambic dimeter* (two iambic feet): The Séa òf Fáith.

The iambic foot is the most common one in English poetry, and, some experts feel, the one from which all the others in our poetry are derived. Much of Shakespeare's drama is composed in unrhymed iambic pentameter or *blank verse*. Andrew Marvell's "To His Coy Mistress" is written in iambics, indeed *iambic tetrameter:*

> Had we but world enough and time
> This coyness, lady, were no crime.

An example of trochaic meter comes in the menacing chant of one of the witches in Act IV, Scene I of *Macbeth* as she prepares her ghastly potion:

> Scale of dragon, tooth of wolf,
> Witches' mummy, maw and gulf
> Of the ravin'd salt-sea shark,
> Root of hemlock digg'd i' th' dark. . . .

Trochaic rhythms can themselves lead to singsong patterns and childish repetition, and that fact might explain why the work of a poet like Henry Wadsworth Longfellow, which now and again employed trochaics, is not now as highly esteemed as it once was.

An example of anapestic lines are these from Percy Bysshe Shelley's "The Cloud":

> The volcanoes are dim, and the stars reel and swim,
> When the whirlwinds my banner unfurl.

The dactylic rhythm is, like the trochaic, an emphatic pattern ("hickory, dickory, dock") and demands careful use by a poet with a subtle ear if it is to be successful. Robert Browning's poem on William Wordsworth, "The Lost Leader," is written in dactylics:

Just for a handful of silver he left us
Just for a riband to stick in his coat
Found the one gift of which fortune bereft us.
Lost all the others she lets us devote. . . .

Two poetic feet, neither of which can ever be used exclusively in any poem, remain to be mentioned. One is the *spondee*. Neither rising nor falling, it consists of two stressed syllables, marked (*/ /*). Some hyphenated or compound words (*football, gym-class, wristwatch* or *noontide*) are natural spondees. When found in poems, they often replace, for a moment, an iambic or trochaic foot. In John Milton's *Paradise Lost*, for instance, the earth is described as Satan sees it from far away:

A globe far off
It seemed; now seems a boundless continent
Dark, waste, and wild, under the frown of night.

The essential rhythm here is, of course, iambic, but "Dark, waste" has two strong and unavoidable emphases: they constitute a spondee.

The other unusual foot is the *pyrrhic*; it consists of two unstressed syllables (‿ ‿) and can often be found at the beginning of poetic lines, at which point the controlling rhythm has not asserted itself. Robert Browning writes:

And after April, when May follows,
And the whitethroat builds, and all the swallows!

Noting the repeated weak stresses in the second line ("And the"), we find a pyrrhic foot.

In order to keep all these technical matters straight for his son, Samuel Taylor Coleridge (1772–1834) wrote a poem called "Metrical Feet," the first six lines of which are a convenient digest of what we have said here:

Trochee trips from long to short;
From long to long in solemn sort
Slow Spondee stalks; strong foot! yet ill able
Ever to come up with Dactyl trisyllable.
Iambics march from short to long—
With a leap and a bound the swift Anapests throng.

I Look into My Glass

I look into my glass,
And view my wasting skin,
And say, "Would God it came to pass
My heart had shrunk as thin!"

For then, I, undistressed   5
By hearts grown cold to me,
Could lonely wait my endless rest
With equanimity.

But Time, to make me grieve,
Part steals, lets part abide;   10
And shakes this fragile frame at eve
With throbbings of noontide.

Thomas Hardy (1840–1928)

Hardy's poem shows that poetry works best when it is not forced to obey the tyranny of the metronome. The iambic repetitions in Hardy's verse establish for us a feeling of order and expectation. But the rhythm is not oppressive to our senses because Hardy varies and delays the fall of the stresses. While lines like "And view my wasting skin" and "But Time to make me grieve" are unerringly true to the iambic pattern, other lines, such as "For then, I, undistressed" and "With throbbings of noontide," are not. The first of these slightly errant lines pauses exactly where the commas appear. While the six syllables generally characteristic of the poem are certainly present, the speaking voice (or the reading eye) hesitates twice, and thus softly disturbs the customary flow. The second of the errant lines cannot really be read in the iambic way, for that would be to give the word "of" a strong emphasis, although it deserves none, and to give the first syllable of "noontide" a weak emphasis, whereas both syllables of that word would seem to deserve equal, and strong, emphasis. We note, in addition, that the poet sees to it that another kind of variation is included in the poem: the third line of each of the three stanzas has eight, not six, syllables; this periodic alternation also serves to surprise our expectations, but not in an uncomfortable or disorienting way.

The line "For then, I, undistressed" contains two pauses where the punctuation appears. Such pauses, called *caesuras*, are sometimes left unidentified by punctuation, but the meter nonetheless stalls for a split second. The metrical feet remain in place, but the reader knows a slight rhythmic variation has been introduced. Another feature of the poem worth noting is that while some of the lines are *end-stopped* ("I look into my glass"), in others the thought runs over one line into the next ("For then, I, undistressed / By hearts grown cold to me"). This feature is called *enjambment*. In this poem, the enjambed lines give a suppleness and flexibility to the verse, allowing the poet to work against the apparent finality of the ordinary line of poetry.

The purpose of *scansion*, or the analysis of the metrical features of a poem, is not to force you to read poetry as if it were a computer program or an operating manual for a complicated machine. It is most unlikely that you will want to scan every poem you read; it is certainly true, moreover, that some readers can become quite proficient at scanning poems without being able to appreciate them. The one good reason to understand the technical side of poetry is that you will then be better equipped to grasp why certain poems have the effect on you that they do. A recognition of the subtleties and intricacies of rhythm allows you to hear and feel the advance and the retreat of the waves in line 12 of "Dover Beach" ("Begin and cease, and then again begin. . . ."). It allows you to hear the awkward capering of father and son in Roethke's "My Papa's Waltz" ("We romped until the pans / Slid from the kitchen shelf. . . ."). And it reminds you that poetry is sometimes beauty, sometimes morality, sometimes mystery and adventure. But it is always words linked to each other in a controlled way by sound as well as sense, technique as well as theme.

PATTERN

Reading poems on a printed page is obviously different from hearing poems recited or read aloud. The visual appearance of a poem makes us aware of features of writing otherwise quite elusive. We *see* the fourteen lines of a sonnet; we note the size of stanzas (a group of lines whose pattern is repeated throughout a poem). Thus the length and placement of lines and the arrangement of the printed words becomes an important aspect of the process of composition. *Look at* (as well as read) these two poems.

I Heard a Fly Buzz—When I Died

I heard a Fly buzz—when I died—
The Stillness in the Room
Was like the Stillness in the Air—
Between the Heaves of Storm—

The Eyes around—had wrung them dry— 5
And Breaths were gathering firm
For that last Onset—when the King
Be witnessed—in the Room—

I willed my Keepsakes—Signed away
What portion of me be 10
Assignable—and then it was
There interposed a Fly—

With Blue—uncertain stumbling Buzz—
Between the light—and me—
And then the Windows failed—and then 15
I could not see to see—

Emily Dickinson (1830–1886)

Buffalo Bill's

Buffalo Bill's
defunct

who used to
          ride a watersmooth-silver
                              stallion   5
and break onetwothreefourfive pigeonsjustlikethat
                                        Jesus
he was a handsome man
                    and what i want to know is
how do you like your blueeyed boy   10
Mister Death

e. e. cummings (1894–1962)

At different points in these two poems, the reading eye is asked to move quickly, then slowly, to pause and then to accelerate. Hyphens, line lengths, stanzas, and words alone, or words fused together, all work to create the dramatic poetic experience. In the poem by Emily Dickinson the hyphens impede an easy or loose reading and we are made to concentrate on the capitalized subjects that she presents. The capitalization, in turn, forces each of those subjects to appear more stark and isolated to the reading eye. The poem is about the way in which the inevitable process of dying is interrupted by trivial appearances, such as that of a fly, and the unconventional typography and punctuation reinforce the idea of interruption. In e. e. cummings's poem, on the other hand, a visual contrast is sharply drawn between what Buffalo Bill could so effortlessly do ("break onetwothreefourfive pigeonsjustlikethat") when alive and how he has now been rendered "defunct." The graceful fluidity of a life ("he was a handsome man") is answered by the simple phrase ("Mister Death"). Long poetic expressions are given short responses, and the look of the poem on the page bears this out.

These examples underscore the obvious: all poems have formal structure just as they have metaphorical language, rhetorical devices, and rhythms. Some poets create their own appropriate form, as the poem by cummings shows. (Nor is this solely a modern device: Matthew Arnold lets the same thing happen in "Dover Beach," where, as we have seen, the arrangement of the lines into verse paragraphs is dictated by the flow of the argument). Some poets, on the other hand, choose to work in *fixed forms*. There the arrangement of the poem is fixed by a traditional rhyme scheme or a pattern of stanzas.

Some poems are composed in two-line units or *couplets:*

> By day the bat is cousin to the mouse.
> He likes the attic of the aging house.

Some are composed in three-line units or *tercets:*

> Do not go gentle into that good night,
> Old age should burn and rave at close of day;
> Rage, rage against the dying of the light.

Some are composed in four-line units or *quatrains:*

> Whenever Richard Cory went down town,
> We people on the pavement looked at him:
> He was a gentleman from sole to crown,
> Clean favored, and imperially slim.

Among the other stanzaic forms available to poets, one, *terza rima,* was made famous by Dante in his *Divine Comedy.* The rhyme scheme is a chain-linked *aba, bcb, cdc, ded, efe,* and so forth, which works well in Italian, for the words of that language all end in vowels. But terza rima is not much used in English, a language many of whose words end in unrhyming consonants, although Shelley used it effectively in his "Ode to the West Wind," which concludes:

Drive my dead thoughts over the universe	a
Like withered leaves to quicken a new birth!	b
And, by the incantation of this verse,	a
Scatter, as from an unextinguished hearth	b
Ashes and sparks, my words among mankind!	c
Be through my lips to unawakened Earth	b
The trumpet of a prophecy! O Wind,	c
If Winter comes, can Spring be far behind?	c

As terza rima is composed of three-line stanzas, *ottava rima* is composed of eight. The rhyme scheme is *ababbabcc* and, in English, has been most effectively used by Lord Byron. In his poem *Don Juan,* for instance, this stanzaic pattern affords the means to tell a long and eventful comic story by providing the reader with discreet, episodic moments. Both the rollicking iambic pentameter of the individual lines of poetry, and the steady progression of the eight-line units on the page, compel the reader to acknowledge the immense intricacy of the adventures he is reading. The poet abruptly confesses at one point that the endless chain of stanzas is meant to be no more, minute by minute, than a source of pleasure:

Some have accused me of a strange design	a
Against the creed and morals of the land,	b
And trace it in this poem every line:	a
I don't pretend that I quite understand	b
My own meaning when I would be *very* fine;	a
But the fact is that I have nothing planned,	b
Unless it were to be a moment merry,	c
A novel word in my vocabulary.	c

Other poetic structures, such as *rime royal*, the *Spenserian stanza*, and the *villanelle*, each with its own historical interest, look different on the page. Each has a structure which, if properly employed, gives force to the poem using it.

THE SONNET

Of all the forms in which English poetry has been written, the sonnet has given life to the greatest number of stunning achievements. Shakespeare, Milton, Wordsworth, Keats, Dante Gabriel Rossetti, Edna St. Vincent Millay, W. H. Auden, and Robert Lowell, among others, have used it to great effect. It offers a strict challenge to poets to be at once concise and complete in their handling of a situation, usually one with strong personal meaning.

As a form created in Italy in the thirteenth century, it is known as an *Italianate* or *Petrarchan* sonnet (after Petrarch, the Italian Renaissance poet). The sonnet consists of two parts, an *octave* and a *sestet*, and it employs a regular rhyme scheme. To see the poem on the page is to recognize what might only be vaguely appreciated when hearing the poem: that the eight lines of the octave are usually rhymed *abba abba* and that the six lines of the sestet are usually rhymed *cde cde*. Often the octave sets up a problem or a question and the sestet solves or answers it. A nice balance is struck: something is first proposed and is then disposed. The look of the poem, as well as the change of the rhyme scheme, informs the reader about the balance. A good nineteenth-century example of the Italian or Petrarchan sonnet, ever so slightly modified, is by Elizabeth Barrett Browning:

When our two souls stand up erect and strong,	a
Face to face, silent, drawing nigh and nigher,	b
Until the lengthening wings break into fire	b
At either curvèd point—what bitter wrong	a
Be here contented? Think. In mounting higher,	b
The angels would press on us and aspire	b
To drop some golden orb of perfect song	a
Into our deep, dear silence. Let us stay	c
Rather on earth, Belovèd—where the unfit	d
Contrarious moods of men recoil away	c
And isolate pure spirits, and permit	d
A place to stand and love in for a day,	c
With darkness and the death-hour rounding it.	d

The octave asks if two loving souls can be contented on earth. The sestet answers that earth is the best place because other people, jealous of this love, will give the lovers the isolation they require.

The other major sonnet form is called the *Shakespearean* because the great Elizabethan dramatist brought it to perfection. Its rhyme scheme, *abab cdcd efef gg*, permits the poet using it to consider an event, or a problem, for three *quatrains* and then to bring everything to a succinct close (sometimes wittily epigrammatic, sometimes somber) in the concluding rhymed couplet. This sonnet by Shakespeare exemplifies the genre.

When to the Sessions of Sweet Silent Thought

> When to the sessions of sweet silent thought
> I summon up remembrance of things past,
> I sigh the lack of many a thing I sought
> And with old woes new wail my dear time's waste.
> Then can I drown an eye (unused to flow)   5
> For precious friends hid in death's dateless° night,   *endless*
> And weep afresh love's long since canceled woe,
> And moan th' expense° of many a vanished sight.   *loss*
> Then can I grieve at grievances foregone,
> And heavily from woe to woe tell o'er   10
> The sad account of fore-bemoanèd moan,
> Which I new pay as if not paid before.
>> But if the while I think on thee, dear friend,
>> All losses are restored and sorrows end.

William Shakespeare (1564–1616)

Again, just as in the preceding poem by Elizabeth Barrett Browning, the poet's art lies in meeting, within a tightly confined space, the challenge of expressing a telling sentiment. Shakespeare considers the time that seems to have been wasted and the loss of friends and of love; his sorrow in the face of such waste and loss never seems to leave him. In the end, however, he thinks of a continuing friendship whose longevity cancels out all else that his life lacks. Considerable emotion and thought are packed into these fourteen lines. But what is true of this sonnet is true of the sonnet in general: love, disgust, hope, surprise, and even political passion can be found in sonnets. Just remember that such things exist only by virtue of artistic discipline and intensity. By studying the two sonnets above and others, you can come to appreciate how much a fixed form, far from being a liability, can force the kind of discipline that leads to great writing.

FREE VERSE

Some poets choose to reject predetermined metric and stanzaic structures in favor of what might be called *organic form*, in which ideas themselves give the work its distinctive shape and unique pattern. We have already seen an example of such form in e. e. cummings's "Buffalo Bill's"; it lacks the orthodox arrangement of "regular" poetry but is far from being simply a piece of prose allowed to fall into an arbitrary pattern.

Certain poets in the nineteenth and twentieth centuries—notably Walt Whitman, Matthew Arnold, Stephen Crane, Carl Sandburg, and Ezra Pound—brought *free verse* to great prominence. But the technique has been present in poetry since the Bible (see, for instance, "The Song of Solomon"). What poets at the end of the last century and throughout our own welcomed was the means to be true to the cadences of speech, the rising and falling of the human voice. At its very best, as in Whitman's "The Dalliance of the Eagles," free verse, in its own naturalness, brings out that which is free and natural about the poem's subject.

The Dalliance of the Eagles

Skirting the river road, (my forenoon walk, my rest,)
Skyward in air a sudden muffled sound, the dalliance of the eagles,
The rushing amorous contact high in space together,
The clinching interlocking claws, a living, fierce, gyrating wheel,
Four beating wings, two beaks, a swirling mass tight grappling,   5
In tumbling turning clustering loops, straight downward falling,
Till o'er the river pois'd, the twain yet one, a moment's lull,
A motionless still balance in the air, then parting, talons loosing,
Upward again on slow-firm pinions slanting, their separate diverse flight,
She hers, he his, pursuing.   10

Walt Whitman (1819–1892)

A different kind of free verse, one that is insistent and uncompromising in its cadences, is found in Ezra Pound's "The Rest."

The Rest

O helpless few in my country,
O remnant enslaved!

Artists broken against her,
A-stray, lost in the villages,
Mistrusted, spoken-against,   5

Lovers of beauty, starved,
Thwarted with systems,
Helpless against the control;

You who can not wear yourselves out
By persisting to successes,   10
You who can only speak,
Who can not steel yourselves into reiteration;

You of the finer sense,
Broken against false knowledge,
You who can know at first hand,   15
Hated, shut in, mistrusted:

Take thought:
I have weathered the storm,
I have beaten out my exile.

Ezra Pound (1885–1972)

Studying these two poems, you will note that while systematic loyalty to a fixed metrical or rhyming scheme is absent, other patterns can be found. In Whitman's poem, the chief source of musicality and cadence comes from the many participles he employs, from the first word to the last. "Skirting" opens the poem and "pursuing" closes it, while words such as "rushing," "clinching," "loosing" and "slanting" are generously distributed throughout. Participles are "action" words; they give to language a sense of motion and activity, exactly what the poem is talking about, and they unify the thought of the poem through their parallelism. In the poem by Pound, free verse emphases are struck by the drum-beat repetition of the word "you," coupled as it is to a series of adjectives and descriptive phrases, by the imperative mood ("Take thought," line 17), and by the way the poem both opens and closes with words or phrases sounded twice ("O helpless few . . . O remnant enslaved") and ("I have weathered . . . I have beaten").

We learn, then, from the example of free verse that poetry has many ways of representing the force of rhythm. At times prose works to achieve such ends, but more often it has other duties in mind. In poetry, however, you will *always* be able to discover one kind of music or another, sometimes subtle and sometimes strong, but always there as an aspect of the pleasure we take in the reading—and listening—experience.

POEMS FOR FURTHER DISCUSSION

The Word *Plum*

The word *plum* is delicious

pout and push, luxury of
self-love, and savoring murmur

full in the mouth and falling
like fruit 5

taut skin
pierced, bitten, provoked into
juice, and tart flesh

question
and reply, lip and tongue 10
of pleasure.

Helen Chasin

QUESTIONS

1. In this poem we seem to taste the fruit by savoring not its flesh but the words that describe the act of taste. Discuss the significance of the sounds in the second stanza. Note that the first word in the stanza begins with a "p" sound and the last one begins with "m."
2. What is the significance of the sounds in the fourth stanza? What do the lips and teeth do with words like "pierced," "bitten," "provoked"?
3. Do you get a sense of the experience of tasting a fruit in the final stanza? How so?
4. Analyze the poem as a whole, from stanza to stanza, indicating what acts you feel the poet is trying to suggest by the manipulation of sounds.

His Being Was in Her Alone

His being was in her alone:
And he not being, she was none.

They joyed one joy, one grief they grieved;
One love they loved, one life they lived.
The hand was one, one was the sword,
That did his death, her death afford.

As all the rest, so now the stone
That tombs the two is justly one.

Sir Philip Sidney (1554–1586)

QUESTIONS

1. Using the information provided in the preceding pages, *scan* this poem, marking the stressed and unstressed syllables and separating the feet. Is there a consistent pattern? What would you call it?
2. How does rhyme serve to link the sentiments in this poem and provide for a logical progression of thought?

Bats

A bat is born
Naked and blind and pale.
His mother makes a pocket of her tail
And catches him. He clings to her long fur
By his thumbs and toes and teeth.   5
And then the mother dances through the night

Doubling and looping, soaring, somersaulting—
Her baby hangs on underneath.
All night, in happiness, she hunts and flies.
Her high sharp cries   10
Like shining needlepoints of sound
Go out into the night and, echoing back,
Tell her what they have touched.
She hears how far it is, how big it is,
Which way it's going: 15
She lives by hearing.
The mother eats the moths and gnats she catches
In full flight; in full flight
The mother drinks the water of the pond
She skims across. Her baby hangs on tight.   20
Her baby drinks the milk she makes him
In moonlight or starlight, in mid-air.
Their single shadow, printed on the moon
Or fluttering across the stars,
Whirls on all night; at daybreak   25
The tired mother flaps home to her rafter.
The others all are there.
They hang themselves up by their toes,
They wrap themselves in their brown wings.
Bunched upside-down, they sleep in air.   30
Their sharp ears, their sharp teeth, their quick sharp faces
Are dull and slow and mild.
All the bright day, as the mother sleeps,
She folds her wings about her sleeping child.

Randall Jarrell (1914–1965)

Questions

1. The rhymes in this poem are random, almost haphazard. What effect does this have on meaning?

2. There is a contrast in the poem between a sort of scientific curiosity about the habits of the bat and of the bat as a loving parent. Discuss each of these approaches in detail. What is the function of this contrast?

3. Compare this poem to Roethke's "The Bat" on page 439. Which details about the animal has each poet chosen to emphasize? How do the details illumine the themes of the respective poems? Discuss the contrasting moods of these poems and how they are achieved.

4. In this poem and in Roethke's there is an interest in the bat's similarity to a human being. Why?

Do Not Go Gentle into That Good Night

Do not go gentle into that good night,
Old age should burn and rave at close of day;
Rage, rage against the dying of the light.

Though wise men at their end know dark is right,
Because their words had forked no lightning they   5
Do not go gentle into that good night.

Good men, the last wave by, crying how bright
Their frail deeds might have danced in a green bay,
Rage, rage against the dying of the light.

Wild men who caught and sang the sun in flight,   10
And learn, too late, they grieved it on its way,
Do not go gentle into that good night.

Grave men, near death, who see with blinding sight
Blind eyes could blaze like meteors and be gay,
Rage, rage against the dying of the light.   15

And you, my father, there on the sad height,
Curse, bless, me now with your fierce tears, I pray.
Do not go gentle into that good night.
Rage, rage against the dying of the light.

Dylan Thomas (1914–1953)

QUESTIONS

1. Many of the words in this poem—"burn," "rave," "rage," etc.—contain potential violence, yet the overall effect of the work is almost placid. How do you account for this?
2. Diagram the rhyme scheme. (It happens to be a French form called a *villanelle*.) Discuss the way in which the rhyme "weaves" the stanzas of the poem together.
3. Discuss what the speaker is saying, respectively, about "wise men," "good men," "wild men," and "grave men." What do they have to do with what he says to his father at the end of the poem?

When I Have Fears

When I have fears that I may cease to be
  Before my pen has gleaned my teeming brain,
Before high-pilèd books, in charact'ry,°   *writing*
  Hold like rich garners the full-ripened grain;
When I behold, upon the night's starred face,   5

Huge cloudy symbols of a high romance,
And think that I may never live to trace
    Their shadows, with the magic hand of chance;
And when I feel, fair creature of an hour,
    That I shall never look upon thee more,   10
Never have relish in the faery° power   *bewitching*
    Of unreflecting love!—then on the shore
Of the wide world I stand alone, and think
Till Love and Fame to nothingness do sink.

                                        John Keats (1795–1821)

QUESTIONS

1. Analyze the rhyme scheme of this sonnet. How do the units of thought within it contribute to the overall meaning? Which kind of sonnet is it? Why did the author choose this form of the sonnet and not another?
2. In what sense is this a "death poem"?
3. Compare the sense you get of the speaker here to the speaker in the Shakespeare sonnet on page 403.

For the Children

The rising hills, the slopes,
of statistics
lie before us.
the steep climb
of everything, going up,   5
up, as we all
go down.
In the next century
or the one beyond that,
they say,   10
are valleys, pastures,
we can meet there in peace
if we make it.

To climb these coming crests   15
one word to you, to
you and your children:

stay together
learn the flowers
go light

                                        Gary Snyder (b. 1930)

QUESTIONS

1. Compare the use of free verse here to that in the poems by Whitman and Pound on pages 450 and 451. What are the means by which each of these three poets achieves a sense of order?

2. How would you characterize the speaker in this poem? What is the basis for your assumptions about him?

3. Certain images from nature are used in this poem—"the rising hills, the slopes," (line 1) "valleys, pastures" (line 11). Do you "see" a natural setting or a social one in the poem? Does the last stanza make this a poem about nature, or about something else?

5

THE THEMES IN A POEM

I n the last three chapters we have dealt with what might be called the elements of poetic composition. In poetry (as in the Bible) first comes the word—a special kind of language capable of producing vivid and lasting images and also of making profound connections between dissimilar realms of experience. Another aspect of poetic language, as we have seen, is its capacity for conveying meanings through extremely subtle networks of exaggeration and understatement, irony, ambiguity, and other tonal nuances that make us react in a certain way to the matter at hand. Finally there is technique—rhyme and other sound effects, and especially rhythm and visual patterns which help give a poem its distinctive shape and meaning.

Language, tone, and form—these three elements certainly play a central role in the making of a poem. Yet what most of us would probably consider the key element of poetry is missing from this list. It is what a poem is *about*. That is, most of us read poetry not because it is an unusual collection of linguistic, rhetorical, or stylistic devices, but because it provides a rich emotional and intellectual exploration of a theme that would not be possible in ordinary, rational discourse. We read poetry because it is about subjects we consider vitally important—love and death, for example, or our relationship to nature. Although we are ultimately interested in emotional rather than factual data, we read poetry for the same reason that we read other types of literature—to learn about the world we inhabit.

If theme is the most obvious aspect of a poem, however, it is also the one most encumbered with misconceptions. One misconception is that the importance of a theme corresponds to its magnitude. Poetry does indeed tend to explore the "grand" themes, yet it also has the ability to focus with the intensity of an electron microscope on the small and the mundane. It can extract meaning out of what may seem insignificant and even trivial, and often makes a thematic statement not by directly approaching a large philosophical issue, but by sidling up to it.

Another misconception is that theme is somehow separable from the rest of the poem, a sort of cream to be skimmed off the top. In fact, theme is part of the formal and stylistic decisions a poet makes. It is impossible to talk about the argument in behalf of seduction in "To His Coy Mistress," for instance, without referring to Marvell's organization of the poem, the shifting moods of its versification, the movement from solemn exaggeration to cutting under-statement. It is impossible to talk about Thomas's attitudes toward death in "Do Not Go Gentle Into That Good Night" without talking also about the pattern of rhyme, the way that sorrow and rage are interwoven through an elaborate, highly artificial stanzaic form. Something the contemporary Amer-ican poet Robert Lowell said on this subject is worth remembering: "A poet writes a lot of lines in his life. Four or five times in his life, if he's lucky, everything comes together and he strikes paydirt." Four or five times in a career, that is, theme meshes perfectly with the technical aspects of poetry, allowing the poet to create a work that has lasting value.

But even after the basic misconceptions have been cleared away a formi-dable obstacle to talking about poetic themes remains: their variety and profusion. Poetry is about everything under the sun, and exploring the ques-tion of theme thoroughly might well require an anthology including every poem ever written. Moreover, it must be remembered that poets do not agree to confine themselves to a single theme when they begin their poems; in fact, they often manage to strike many themes at once. Nor do all poems on a single theme fit into neat categories. A love poem might be filled with deeply sincere sentiment, or it might be satirical and mocking. A poem about death might be bitter and defiant or it might be awed and humble. A poem (as we saw in Anne Sexton's "The Truth the Dead Know" on page 410) might in fact be a love poem and a poem about death at the same time. Fully aware of these obstacles and ambiguities, we have nonetheless devoted the next few pages to two broad thematic areas that have interested poets for hundreds of years—the public world of people, places, and events; and the private world of the self.

THE PUBLIC WORLD

Poetry is often thought to be an art of purely personal expressiveness. Poets are frequently depicted as lonely, private or isolated, writing only about that which is close to them, and thus having little connection with the large and turbulent world of public affairs. In fact, the poet's world is often quite public in its concerns. Poets do enter, sometimes noisily and passionately, the arena of civic affairs, of national policy, of social conflict and even of war. Poets such as Dante and Shakespeare have grasped the political, civic, and cultural forces of their respective societies so well that they can rightly be said to have influenced, by what they wrote, the actual course of events, and the under-standing later generations have had of those events. Poets may not be, as Percy Bysshe Shelley declared, "the unacknowledged legislators of the world," but neither are they naive about what takes place in the real world.

London

I wander through each chartered street,
Near where the chartered Thames does flow,
And mark in every face I meet
Marks of weakness, marks of woe.

In every cry of every man,   5
In every infant's cry of fear,
In every voice, in every ban,
The mind-forged manacles I hear.

How the chimney-sweeper's cry
Every black'ning church appalls;   10
And the hapless soldier's sigh
Runs in blood down palace walls.

But most through midnight streets I hear
How the youthful harlot's curse
Blasts the new born infant's tear,   15
And blights with plagues the marriage hearse.

William Blake (1757–1827)

England in 1819

An old, mad, blind, despised, and dying king—
Princes, the dregs of their dull race, who flow
Through public scorn—mud from a muddy spring;
Rulers who neither see, nor feel, nor know,
But leechlike to their fainting country cling,   5
Till they drop, blind in blood, without a blow;
A people starved and stabbed in the untilled field—
An army, which liberticide and prey
Makes as a two-edged sword to all who wield;
Golden and sanguine laws which tempt and slay;   10
Religion Christless, Godless—a book sealed;
A Senate—Time's worst statute unrepealed—
Are graves, from which a glorious Phantom° may   *evolution*
Burst, to illumine our tempestuous day.

Percy Bysshe Shelley (1792–1822)

These two poems by Blake and Shelley are profound indictments of what each poet saw as the collapse of the culture in which he lived. For Blake, London as a city symbolizes general human sickness; for Shelley, the sickness is local and specific, caused by parasitic public officials. Blake and Shelley come as witnesses, even as judges of events and conditions not of their own making. Blake sees how disease, specifically venereal disease, scars generation after generation and then haunts the urban landscape in which countless people, hemmed in and circumscribed, desperately live. Shelley levels his wrath at particular people—the Hanoverian line of British royalty (including the senile and unpopular George III), and at particular events—an infamous massacre of British working people in 1819 and the Act of Union (1801) excluding Roman Catholics from full English citizenship.

Although these two poems are graphic and passionate, the poets themselves keep their distance. But some poets who write of public events and great
struggles keep external event and internal reaction in the same focus. They
see, at once, both the objective and subjective realities. An example of such a
dual vision is Robert Bly's "Driving Through Minnesota During the Hanoi
Bombings." We learn something of the poet as we learn about the war in
Vietnam.

Driving Through Minnesota During the Hanoi Bombings

We drive between lakes just turning green;
Late June. The white turkeys have been moved
To new grass.
How long the seconds are in great pain!
Terror just before death,   5
Shoulders torn, shot
From helicopters, the boy
Tortured with the telephone generator,
"I felt sorry for him,
And blew his head off with a shotgun."   10
These instants become crystals,
Particles
The grass cannot dissolve. Our own gaiety
Will end up
In Asia, and in your cup you will look down   15
And see
Black Starfighters,
We were the ones we intended to bomb!
Therefore we will have
To go far away   20
To atone
For the sufferings of the stringy-chested
And the small rice-fed ones, quivering
In the helicopter like wild animals,
Shot in the chest, taken to be questioned.   25

Robert Bly (b. 1926)

Written during the war in Vietnam, Bly's poem became in effect, an
aspect of the antiwar struggle, a part of a specific cause in American history.
In adopting a public posture, a poet can also choose to speak out on a more
general issue. The following work, for instance, turns the Biblical story of the
creation inside out in a vision of the end of life that seems particularly chilling
for the nuclear age.

Seven Days

Thunder moved in sleep,
Birds dropped from the sky, white-eyed,
Every animal died
The evening of the first day.
Fish curdled the sea   5
Whales panting on their side
Clogged the uneven tide
The evening of the second day.
On the third day the stars
Darkened, sun and moon   10
Ended their alternate reign.
The fourth day the last leaf
Perished, herb and seed
Shrivelled from the flayed
Earth. Water and land   15
Merged on the fifth day, on the sixth
Darkness and light. The seventh
Became a thousand aeons without word.

J. R. Rowland (b. 1925)

Not all poems concerned with the public world need be anguished or critical. Some very moving poems do not dwell exclusively on censure of the present age, but on the promise of a time yet to come. Such poems urge, indeed celebrate, a triumph of spirit. Margaret Walker's "For My People," for example, reviews in a powerful free-verse form the chapters of black American history so that she may see rising out of them a new chapter in which everything will be transformed. This kind of poetry is meant as an instrument for change. If history is altered, the poem has been involved in that alteration.

For My People

For my people everywhere singing their slave songs repeatedly: their
    dirges and their ditties and their blues and jubilees, praying their
    prayers nightly to an unknown god, bending their knees humbly to
    an unseen power;

For my people lending their strength to the years, to the gone years and   5
    the now years and the maybe years, washing ironing cooking scrub-
    bing sewing mending hoeing plowing digging planting pruning
    patching dragging along never gaining never reaping never knowing
    and never understanding;

For my playmates in the clay and dust and sand of Alabama backyards   10
  playing baptizing and preaching and doctor and jail and soldier and
  school and mama and cooking and playhouse and concert and store
  and hair and Miss Choomby and company;

For the cramped bewildered years we went to school to learn to know
  the reasons why and the answers to and the people who and the   15
  places where and the days when, in memory of the bitter hours
  when we discovered we were black and poor and small and different
  and nobody cared and nobody wondered and nobody understood;

For the boys and girls who grew in spite of these things to be man and
  woman, to laugh and dance and sing and play and drink their wine   20
  and religion and success, to marry their playmates and bear children
  and then die of consumption and anemia and lynching;

For my people thronging 47th Street in Chicago and Lenox Avenue in
  New York and Rampart Street in New Orleans, lost disinherited
  dispossessed and happy people filling the cabarets and taverns and   25
  other people's pockets needing bread and shoes and milk and land
  and money and something—something all our own;

For my people walking blindly spreading joy, losing time being lazy,
  sleeping when hungry, shouting when burdened, drinking when
  hopeless, tied and shackled and tangled among ourselves by the   30
  unseen creatures who tower over us omnisciently and laugh;

For my people blundering and groping and floundering in the dark of
  churches and schools and clubs and societies, associations and
  councils and committees and conventions, distressed and disturbed
  and deceived and devoured by money-hungry glory-craving leeches,   35
  preyed on by facile force of state and fad and novelty, by false
  prophet and holy believer;

For my people standing staring trying to fashion a better way from
  confusion, from hypocrisy and misunderstanding, trying to fashion
  a world that will hold all the people, all the faces, all the adams and   40
  eves and their countless generations;

Let a new earth rise. Let another world be born. Let a bloody peace be
  written in the sky. Let a second generation full of courage issue
  forth; let a people loving freedom come to growth. Let a beauty full
  of healing and a strength of final clenching be the pulsing in our   45
  spirits and our blood. Let the martial songs be written, let the dirges
  disappear. Let a race of men now rise and take control.

Margaret Walker (b. 1918)

THE PRIVATE EXPERIENCE

What does it feel like to be in love, to face death, to achieve a mystical
oneness with nature? For most of us, subjects like these are shunted off to the

edges of our conscious lives by the press of daily events. Even if there is time to discuss such matters, we often prefer not to do so because they are so daunting in their magnitude that they make us feel that we lack the words to deal with them. That is another reason we read poetry: to find the right words. The poet provides a vocabulary and a context for the subjects that render most of us mute. In effect, the poet dares to speak about the unspeakable.

We have just seen some of the ways in which the poet bears witness to the events in the public world—interpreting and trying to understand them, trying to find a point of personal balance within the turbulence of history, trying also to put a thumb print on history and politics. An even more characteristic task for the poet, however, is trying to make sense of the private moment; trying to transform the individual experience into a perception *all* readers will recognize as applicable to *all* experience. This is not to say that poetry resembles either the stream of consciousness that might take place in a psychiatrist's office, or the guilty admissions of the confessional booth. In writing about the intimacies of the inner life, the poet uses art—the devices and techniques that we have discussed—to transform raw and undigested feeling into general truth.

Sometimes this is a complex matter. Some of the poems we have already dealt with require considerable effort to appreciate fully. Yet some great poetry is also often simple and direct. Consider this anonymous lyric from the fifteenth century:

Western Wind

> Western wind, when wilt thou blow,
> The small rain down can rain?
> Christ, if my love were in my arms
> And I in my bed again!

We don't know what events had separated speaker and loved one; we don't know what will be required to get them together again. It really doesn't matter because the focus here is on the sense of longing, desire, loneliness, even frustration which are perfectly and economically expressed in this brief poem. "Western Wind" is an expression of heartfelt emotion, the sort of deep anxiety upon separation we have all felt at one time or another. But to see it as no more than this is to undervalue the accomplishment of the poet, whoever he or she was. Embedded in the four lines of this poem is an implied comparison between the perishable world of individual love and the enduring world of nature. The poem says, in effect, that just as the wind will come in its own time and bring with it the rain, so love also will have its seasons and regularity. This comparison provides a special combination of poignancy and confidence that is the foundation of the poem. As people living in nature, we learn to depend on the rain; as people who love, we can learn (even when aching with longing) to depend on an eventual reunion with those we deeply care about.

Mother of the Groom

What she remembers
Is his glistening back
In the bath, his small boots
In the ring of boots at her feet.

Hands in her voided lap,   5
She hears a daughter welcomed.
It's as if he kicked when lifted
And slipped her soapy hold.

Once soap would ease off
The wedding ring   10
That's bedded forever now
In her clapping hand.

Seamus Heaney (b. 1939)

Here a poet uses vivid and concrete details to try to suggest a mother's complex emotions on the marriage of her son. The images appear with a kind of psychological realism—a plausibility of association—throughout the poem, dramatizing the process by which a problem is grappled with and resolved. The first stanza gives us the evocative memories of the son's babyhood—notably his slick and slippery skin in his bath. In the second stanza, as the mother sits with "voided lap" (words which not only remind us that the lap no longer has a child sitting on it but also suggests a womb no longer fecund), her sudden and profound sense of loss is conveyed by the recurring thought of a baby in his bath—this time slipping dangerously from her hold. In the third stanza the thoughts of the infant son in his bath lead to a dispassionate consideration of her own state. The wedding ring, so easily slipped off with soap when she was younger, is now embedded in the flesh of her finger, a reminder of the permanence of her identity as wife and mother. Yet that finger is part of a hand that is now "clapping" for joy, amidst the trauma of loss, about a marriage which an instant earlier had seemed so threatening. By the conclusion of "Mother of the Groom," a miraculous thing has happened. A male poet has entered into the experience of a mother and not only managed to make it live, but also to make the brief sketch into a statement about the cycles and passages that make up life.

God's Grandeur

The world is charged with the grandeur of God.
    It will flame out, like shining from shook foil;°   *tinsel*
    It gathers to a greatness, like the ooze of oil
Crushed. Why do men then now not reck his rod?°   *acknowledge*
                                                                           his power

Generations have trod, have trod, have trod;   5
  And all is seared with trade; bleared, smeared with toil;
  And wears man's smudge and shares man's smell: the soil
Is bare now, nor can foot feel, being shod.

And for all this, nature is never spent;
  There lives the dearest freshness deep down things;   10
And though the last lights off the black West went
  Oh, morning, at the brown brink eastward, springs—
Because the Holy Ghost over the bent
  World broods with warm breast and with ah! bright wings.

Gerard Manley Hopkins (1844–1889)

    This poem also uses a private experience to reach for a larger truth. The speaker announces the subject at the outset—the grandeur of God. Such grandeur is not a passive or gentle quality, but something strong and kinetic, almost violent, capable of flaming out and shining like "shook foil." The fact that mankind does not "reck his rod"—that is, obey God—therefore fills the speaker with gloom. He himself is led into doubt, and enumerates the ways in which life has become degraded. The internal rhymes "seared," "bleared," and "smeared" (line 6), along with the alliterative words "smudge" and "smell" (line 7), convey something like repugnance. The earth is "bare" and man ("shod" like an animal) is so alienated from the natural scheme of things that he is no longer sensitive to its "feel" (line 8).

    In the second stanza, however, the speaker realizes that nature is "never spent," and he becomes newly aware of the "freshness" deep down in things. And we become aware that this is no abstract argument about man and nature, but a meditation that depends on the poem's specific setting. The speaker has been standing in the night, watching the lights go off "the black West" (line 11). Now morning—the flame and shining referred to at the poem's beginning—suddenly springs out of the east. Watching the first light begin to illumine the sky, the speaker sees the sun as the Holy Ghost, sitting like a brooding dove with the bright wings of the sun.

    The affirmation in this poem grows out of the specific experience of a night of doubt paralleling humanity's apparent alienation from God. But the coming sunrise shows a divinity so intense that it suffuses the world with grace and redemption. The moment when the sun finally appears—the moment when the speaker says "ah!"—reestablishes the grandeur of God and creates the world anew.

Woodchucks

Gassing the woodchucks didn't turn out right.
The knockout bomb from the Feed and Grain Exchange
was featured as merciful, quick at the bone
and the case we had against them was airtight,
both exits shoehorned shut with puddingstone,°   *rock in mortar* 5
but they had a sub-sub-basement out of range.

Next morning they turned up again, no worse
for the cyanide than we for our cigarettes
and state-store Scotch, all of us up to scratch.
They brought down the marigolds as a matter of course   10
and then took over the vegetable patch
nipping the broccoli shoots, beheading the carrots.

The food from our mouths, I said, righteously thrilling
to the feel of the .22, the bullets' neat noses.
I, a lapsed pacifist fallen from grace   15
puffed with Darwinian pieties for killing,
now drew a bead on the littlest woodchuck's face.
He died down in the everbearing roses.

Ten minutes later I dropped the mother. She
flipflopped in the air and fell, her needle teeth   20
still hooked in a leaf of early Swiss chard.
Another baby next. O one-two-three
the murderer inside me rose up hard,
the hawkeye killer came on stage forthwith.

There's one chuck left. Old wily fellow, he keeps   25
me cocked and ready day after day after day.
All night I hunt his humped-up form. I dream
I sight along the barrel in my sleep.
If only they'd all consented to die unseen
gassed underground the quiet Nazi way.   30

Maxine Kumin (b. 1925)

This poem uses great tonal variety to develop from an amused story about garden nuisances to a stark perception of the killer in us all. At the beginning, the speaker's tone is jaunty and flippant, certain of the propriety of the undertaking and even expressing a kind of embarrassment about going to such elaborate measures to get rid of woodchucks. The "knockout bomb" has the feel of a toy contrivance; it is, after all, "merciful." In the word "airtight" in the fourth line, the speaker is confident enough to indulge in a little pun: the case against the pests was "airtight" and so was the burrow that had been shoehorned shut.

The woodchucks themselves are almost foolish creatures, euphemistically nipping the broccoli and hyperbolically beheading the carrots. But by the third stanza of the poem they begin to get under the speaker's skin. The "Darwinian pieties for killing" (line 16) presumably involve absurd assertions about the survival of the fittest and competition for scarce resources. The seriousness that enters the poem at this point doesn't have anything to do with the nobility of the woodchucks themselves. Actually they die in almost comic pratfalls, flipflopping in the air still chewing Swiss chard. What is important is that the speaker is aware of how the killing takes hold, how the murderer within us all can rise in bloodlust.

In the final stanza, these themes reach a climax. Killing has become addictive, haunting the speaker's waking and sleeping hours. There is always one more woodchuck to hunt down; the merciful knockout bomb of the beginning of the poem has now become connected to a Nazi gas chamber. The speaker has seen—and we have too—the suppressed killer inside us all waiting for the thin restraints of civilization to fall and provide an excuse to pick up the gun. This fall from grace isolates us forever from the garden of innocence with which the poem begins.

W. B. YEATS: THE THEMES OF A "DIFFICULT" POET

No poet writing in English in this century was more ambitious in laying claim to a full range of personal emotions than William Butler Yeats (1865–1939). Nor was any poet of his era more concerned with the way the world of real events—politics, revolution, and nationalism—could be made the subject of poetry. In fact, Yeats's long career involved a strenuous effort to join the public and private realms we have been discussing into one comprehensive artistic vision.

It was Yeats's conviction that a poet must "hammer his thoughts into a unity." By this he meant that the poet must develop powerful central ideas in his work, themes that will give his poems a consistent identity. His use of the specific events of his life—ranging from participation in the bloody nationalistic politics of Ireland to the bittersweet experience of unrequited love—along with his knowledge of such arcane subjects as spiritualism and mysticism produced an artistic vision that is sometimes easy to grasp but is often deeply challenging for the reader. There is a Yeats whom we will understand almost immediately, but there is also a Yeats who might baffle us at first. His poetry can have a sweet lyrical beauty; it can also have troubling depths. Yet even when his work seems hard to penetrate, Yeats rewards our effort. It is worth discussing the themes of this "difficult" poet in some detail to show exactly how available they are.

Politics

'In our time the destiny of man presents its meaning in political terms.'—
THOMAS MANN°

> How can I, that girl standing there,
> My attention fix
> On Roman or on Russian
> Or on Spanish politics?
> Yet here's a travelled man that knows   5
> What he talks about,
> And there's a politician

Thomas Mann German author (1875–1955) of novels and criticism

That has read and thought,
And maybe what they say is true
Of war and war's alarms,   10
But O that I were young again
And held her in my arms!

Yeats was not a poet whose work had been appealingly simple in his youth
and became more difficult only as his career matured. From the very beginning, he was both easy and difficult in his writing. He wrote "Politics," a
poem of lyrical regret, a year before his death. Nearly fifty years earlier, in
1890, when he was a very young man, he had written a poem whose sentiments and references are almost identical.

The Lamentation of the Old Pensioner

Although I shelter from the rain
Under a broken tree
My chair was nearest to the fire
In every company
That talked of love or politics,   5
Ere Time transfigured me.

Though lads are making pikes again
For some conspiracy,
And crazy rascals rage their fill
At human tyranny,   10
My contemplations are of Time
That has transfigured me.

There's not a woman turns her face
Upon a broken tree,
And yet the beauties that I loved   15
Are in my memory;
I spit into the face of Time
That has transfigured me.

Thus, from 1890 to 1938, little had changed, and, looking at both poems,
we can see that Yeats achieved the "unity" of emotional life that he had
wanted. One lesson we may draw from this fact is that, even amid the poetic
difficulties we shall inspect shortly in his work, his artistic vision successfully
made its authority felt.

These two poems evoke a theme—the striking and dramatic tensions
between the world of youth and the world of old age—that can be found
everywhere in Yeats's poetry. The first world is one of passion and rapture; the
second world is one of reflection and passivity. Yeats was to return, again and
again, to both worlds and to consider their respective merits. As a man, he

recognized the strong attractions of each. And, as a poet, he found himself giving the theme involving their relationship greater and greater insight and subtlety. The world of youthful passion certainly had its glories, and he grew increasingly more eloquent in describing them. But the world of aged wisdom grew, at the same time, to be more attractive. A relatively early poem, one written in 1915, puts the conflict in simple terms.

The Scholars

Bald heads forgetful of their sins,
Old, learned, respectable bald heads
Edit and annotate the lines
That young men, tossing on their beds,
Rhymed out in loves's despair   5
To flatter beauty's ignorant ear.

All shuffle there; all cough in ink;
All wear the carpet with their shoes;
All think what other people think;
All know the man their neighbor knows.   10
Lord, what would they say
Did their Catullus walk that way?

In taking such a strong stand against the passionless, and in proclaiming the virtues of the passionate, Yeats here sides with all lovers, including the Roman poet of love, Catullus. But Yeats was quite often faithless to his own stand on issues such as this one, and we can find him in a few years taking the opposite position, and doing so with profound conviction. Four years later in phrases that would seem prophetic as totalitarian regimes began to take power in Germany and Italy, he was speaking of "the best" who "lack all conviction," and "the worst" who are "full of passionate intensity."

In 1928, he published a volume of poetry, *The Tower*, which represented a major reconsideration of many of the problems that for years had held his emotional attention. The first poem in that book, "Sailing to Byzantium," shows Yeats grappling with youth and age again. But the language and the references of that poem are a bit more formal and difficult than in his previous work. The poet appeals to us to meditate on the refined majesty of the ancient city of Byzantium, the seat of the Holy Roman Empire after 330 A.D., and the center, for some one thousand years, of the Eastern Empire. Yeats imagines that the artists of Byzantium crafted works of art that were to exist for all of eternity, not just for the here and now. The permanence of such works, and their transcendence over the superficial things of the world, have a powerful attraction for him. For Yeats, who was sixty-three when this poem was published, one's physical body is no longer a source of pleasure, but rather a casing in which the soul is forced to live.

Sailing to Byzantium

I

That is no country° for old men. The young
In one another's arms, birds in the trees
—Those dying generations—at their song,
The salmon-falls, the mackerel-crowded seas
Fish, flesh, or fowl, commend all summer long   5
Whatever is begotten, born, and dies.
Caught in that sensual music all neglect
Monuments of unaging intellect.

II

An aged man is but a paltry thing,
A tattered coat upon a stick, unless   10
Soul clap its hands and sing, and louder sing
For every tatter in its mortal dress,
Nor is there singing school but studying
Monuments of its own magnificence;
And therefore I have sailed the seas and come   15
To the holy city of Byzantium.

III

O sages standing in God's holy fire
As in the gold mosaic of a wall,
Come from the holy fire, perne in a gyre,
And be the singing-masters of my soul   20
Consume my heart away; sick with desire
And fastened to a dying animal
It knows not what it is; and gather me
Into the artifice of eternity.

IV

Once out of nature I shall never take   25
My bodily form from any natural thing,
But such a form as Grecian goldsmiths make
Of hammered gold and gold enameling
To keep a drowsy Emperor° awake;
Or set upon a golden bough to sing   30
To lords and ladies of Byzantium
Of what is past, or passing, or to come.

Most of the allusions in this poem can be understood with some effort.
But most readers might stumble when first coming upon line 19 of this poem:
"Come from the holy fire, perne in a gyre." In order to make sense of the

1. **That is no country** the ordinary world; Ireland   29. **a drowsy Emperor** Theophilus,
Emperor of Byzantium, had craftsmen make mechanical golden birds which sat on branches of
golden trees.

unfamiliar words, it is necessary to understand that Yeats at times used a special language of his own invention in his poetry. Many poets in our time have done likewise—contriving an idiosyncratic means of expression because the ordinary means of expression seems weak and inadequate. Here, for example, Yeats wished to urge the saints, or sages, to leave the eternal world of God's holy fire and descend to him, a mortal being living in the world of the everyday. "Perne" means a spool, the spool on which all of time is wound and is a word he first heard from his grandfather. The word "gyre" comes from the philosophical system Yeats had developed and represents his theory that all of history is a result of the conflicts arising from the intersection of two gyres, or cones, the one flat on its base and the other standing on its endpoint. According to Yeats, the power of anything in history is simultaneously increasing and decreasing, growing stronger in some respects and weaker in others, depending on where it is to be found in relation to the two gyres. Here, in this poem, Yeats beseeches the timeless sages to come to him and find him where he is in time. He knows his physical strength is ebbing and that his spiritual strength is growing. He wants now to be "gathered" into a parallel world—a world of the imagination, of art—that is not infected by physical decay.

We can trace Yeats's special language in scores of his poems, finding "perne" and "gyre" and many other terms repeated. But we should not think that these poems are just codes or word games. Yeats customarily gives us his meanings in ordinary language, surrounding that language with a few fragments of his special vocabulary. One of his best known poems, "The Second Coming," for instance, is clearly a prophetic warning about the confused civilization of Europe that seemed on the brink of collapse following the First World War. In this poem, profound personal emotions mix with equally profound public anxieties, and the notes of chaos and apocalyptic change are struck.

The Second Coming

Turning and turning in the widening gyre
The falcon cannot hear the falconer;
Things fall apart; the centre cannot hold;
Mere anarchy is loosed upon the world,
The blood-dimmed tide is loosed, and everywhere   5
The ceremony of innocence is drowned;
The best lack all conviction, while the worst
Are full of passionate intensity.

Surely some revelation is at hand;
Surely the Second Coming is at hand.   10
The Second Coming! Hardly are those words out
When a vast image out of *Spiritus Mundi*°   world spirit
Troubles my sight: somewhere in sands of the desert
A shape with lion body and the head of a man,
A gaze blank and pitiless as the sun,   15

Is moving its slow thighs, while all about it
Reel shadows of the indignant desert birds.
The darkness drops again; but now I know
That twenty centuries of stony sleep
Were vexed to nightmare by a rocking cradle,   20
And what rough beast, its hour come round at last,
Slouches towards Bethlehem to be born?

This is the anxious Yeats, a man and a poet who, when writing this poem
in 1919, had come to know the violence of partisan politics. He had recently
seen British auxiliary troops, the infamous "Black and Tans," put down Irish
Republicans struggling for national independence. He once summed all of
Irish history thus: "Great hatred, little room, / Maimed us from the start." The
First World War, an even greater instance of violence, had concluded a few
months before. The Russian Revolution of 1917 was fresh in the minds of
everyone. The bloodthirsty age itself seemed driven mad. This poem, with its
strong and surprising images, with its fascination riveted on extremes, and
with its exclamatory mood, reflects that international and personal urgency.

But Yeats characteristically has more than one face to show his readers.
The same poet, writing only a few years before, and with the same tumultuous Irish conflict on his mind, was a studious, detached, and wholly meditative writer. When, on Easter Sunday, April 24, 1916, Irish Republicans
with whose cause Yeats was at times deeply sympathetic, seized the General
Post Office in Dublin, they set loose a spasm of urban warfare that ended only
with their rapid capture, death, or execution at the hands of the British.
Ireland was then launched into a struggle that, even today, has not come to an
end. As Yeats saw the events take shape, it seemed that ordinary people were
suddenly being devoured by forces far more powerful than themselves. Those
people were swept into a destiny that swiftly redefined them. But the poet,
knowing all this, remains distant from it in his mind and verse. His poem
"Easter 1916," composed in that year, is a fine example of writing that
achieves a great calm, both in its steady rhythmic and stanzaic control, and in
its philosophical atmosphere.

Easter 1916

I have met them at close of day
Coming with vivid faces
From counter or desk among gray
Eighteenth-century houses.
I have passed with a nod of the head   5
Or polite meaningless words,
Or have lingered awhile and said
Polite meaningless words,
And thought before I had done
Of a mocking tale or a gibe   10
To please a companion

Around the fire at the club,
Being certain that they and I
But lived where motley° is worn:
All changed, changed utterly: 15
A terrible beauty is born.

That woman's days were spent
In ignorant good-will,
Her nights in argument
Until her voice grew shrill.   20
What voice more sweet than hers
When, young and beautiful,
She rode to harriers?
This man had kept a school
And rode our winged horse;   25
This other his helper and friend
Was coming into his force;
He might have won fame in the end,
So sensitive his nature seemed,
So daring and sweet his thought.   30
This other man I had dreamed
A drunken, vainglorious lout.
He had done most bitter wrong
To some who are near my heart,
Yet I number him in the song;   35
He, too, has resigned his part
In the casual comedy;
He, too, has been changed in his turn,
Transformed utterly:
A terrible beauty is born.   40

Hearts with one purpose alone
Through summer and winter seem
Enchanted to a stone
To trouble the living stream.
The horse that comes from the road,   45
The rider, the birds that range
From cloud to tumbling cloud,
Minute by minute they change;
A shadow of cloud on the stream
Changes minute by minute;   50
A horse-hoof slides on the brim,
And a horse plashes within it;
The long-legged moor-hens dive,
And hens to moor-cocks call;
Minute by minute they live: 55
The stone's in the midst of all.

14. motley   multicolored attire of a jester

> Too long a sacrifice
> Can make a stone of the heart.
> O when may it suffice?
> That is Heaven's part, our part   60
> To murmur name upon name,
> As a mother names her child
> When sleep at last has come
> On limbs that had run wild.
> What is it but nightfall?   65
> No, no, not night but death;
> Was it needless death after all?
> For England may keep faith
> For all that is done and said.
> We know their dream; enough   70
> To know they dreamed and are dead;
> And what if excess of love
> Bewildered them till they died?
> I write it out in a verse—
> MacDonagh and MacBride   75
> And Connolly and Pearse
> Now and in time to be,
> Wherever green is worn,
> Are changed, changed utterly:
> A terrible beauty is born.   80

It will help the reader to know that the woman of the poem's second stanza was Countess Markiewicz, a prominent participant in the uprising, and that the man who kept a school was Patrick Pearse. He led the revolution, and was helped by the poet and dramatist Thomas MacDonagh. The "lout" to whom Yeats refers was Major John MacBride; he had married Maud Gonne, the woman to whom Yeats was deeply attracted. But having these things annotated does not "explain" the poem. The poem is not really about them, after all, but about the savage transformations that can occur to people, rendering them different and strange. We lose sight of these individuals in the poem, just as history has lost sight of them. What replaces them is the "terrible beauty" of a new political order. Gazing at these extraordinary transformations, Yeats is indifferent, mild, godlike. His poem reminds us of the wise detachment of which he, and his art, are capable. It is, in short, a poem in which the artist succeeds in having his personal and emotional understanding gain the upper hand over the public circumstances with which it is confronted.

Another poem exemplifying this same detachment was written in 1918 when the son of one of Yeats's closest friends died in battle. In it the poet imagines the heroism of perfect calmness in the face of danger. The young airman "chooses" his death after having made a cool appraisal of his achievements and his future prospects in this world. As Yeats puts the young man's reasoning into poetic language, it is made to seem elegant, even noble.

An Irish Airman Foresees His Death

I know that I shall meet my fate
Somewhere among the clouds above;
Those that I fight I do not hate,
Those that I guard I do not love;
My country is Kiltartan Cross,   5
My countrymen Kiltartan's poor,
No likely end could bring them loss
Or leave them happier than before.
Nor law, nor duty bade me fight,
Nor public men, nor cheering crowds,   10
A lonely impulse of delight
Drove to this tumult in the clouds;
I balanced all, brought all to mind,
The years to come seemed waste of breath,
A waste of breath the years behind   15
In balance with this life, this death.

This poem should alert us to two essential forces in Yeats's career. One is his concern with a life well-lived, with a nobility of action in the face of everything that destiny forced him to confront. The other is his struggle to embrace, in his art, everything that he knew and experienced. He wanted himself and others, such as the young airman, to possess nobility, bravery, and grace. But at the same time he believed that art was superior to life, and that, as a poet, he must see to it that his poetry was able to assimilate everything that came its way. These two forces were always in conflict as his career developed, and Yeats once summed up the tension by saying that "the intellect of man is forced to choose / Perfection of the life, or of the work." He himself was never able to make a final choice, to prefer one form of perfection to another, and then to remain absolutely certain in his choice: at times he responded to the one; at times to the other.

We will conclude with two of Yeats's poems that reflect the preoccupations we have discussed. In the first, "The Wild Swans at Coole," Yeats deals with the passage of time and its effect on both nature and the beholder. The poem is a stunning example of his ability to *compose* the images, lines, and stanzas of his verse so that the result is a wholly finished and gracefully stable poetic object. We are meant to admire the calm beauty, the coherence, the rhythmic balance of that object.

The Wild Swans at Coole

The trees are in their autumn beauty,
The woodland paths are dry,
Under the October twilight the water
Mirrors a still sky;
Upon the brimming water among the stones   5
Are nine-and-fifty swans.

The nineteenth autumn has come upon me
Since I first made my count;
I saw, before I had well finished,
All suddenly mount   10
And scatter wheeling in great broken rings
Upon their clamorous wings.

I have looked upon those brilliant creatures,
And now my heart is sore.
All's changed since I, hearing at twilight,   15
The first time on this shore,
The bell-beat of their wings above my head,
Trod with a lighter tread.

Unwearied still, lover by lover,
They paddle in the cold   20
Companionable streams or climb the air;
Their hearts have not grown old;
Passion or conquest, wander where they will,
Attend upon them still.

But now they drift on the still water,   25
Mysterious, beautiful;
Among what rushes will they build,
By what lake's edge or pool
Delight men's eyes when I awake some day
To find they have flown away?   30

In vivid contrast to this poem, in which a beautiful ritual is, in the poet's mind, enacted again and again, and in which perfection seems complete, is a poem like "An Acre of Grass." "The Wild Swans of Coole," written sometime around 1916, casts a quiet spell on the reader's mind, prompting him to rest easily and securely amid a world of images all suggesting continuity and resolution. But "An Acre of Grass," written in 1936 and published in the last (1939) volume of Yeats's poetry, finds the poet trying to make himself anew, to repudiate the inevitability of old age, to find passion, and to defy what is "expected" of him. Yeats here is not concerned with the perfection of his work, but with the perfection of his life. He wants to know how he will find energy, how he will be more than merely wise and passive. Inner satisfaction and detachment are not enough.

An Acre of Grass

Picture and book remain,
An acre of green grass
For air and exercise,
Now strength of body goes;
Midnight, an old house   5
Where nothing stirs but a mouse.

My temptation is quiet.
Here at life's end.
Neither loose imagination,
Nor the mill of the mind   10
Consuming its rag and bone,
Can make the truth known.

Grant me an old man's frenzy,
Myself must I remake
Till I am Timon and Lear°   15
Or that William Blake
Who beat upon the wall
Till Truth obeyed his call;

A mind Michael Angelo knew
That can pierce the clouds,   20
Or inspired by frenzy
Shake the dead in their shrouds;
Forgotten else by mankind,
An old man's eagle mind.

In this poem, we are in the presence of a writer who, knowing he is old, nonetheless asks for exactly those energies that would prove embarrassing to the old. There is nothing in this poem that celebrates stability, or that asks for further rituals. The poet, seeking "frenzy," reaches out to those literary creations—Shakespeare's crazed Timon of Athens and his tormented King Lear—who experienced wildness and savage changes in the world around them. Yeats himself now seeks a sudden transformation, knowing that merely praising the recurring stabilities of life, without wanting to set loose the great energies of life, is insufficient. One must do more than fulfill one's reputation; one must throw oneself into the center of human confusions. One must enter life, the real life of the world, and one must ask, as Yeats repeatedly did as his career was coming to an end, what one's own imaginative strengths and weaknesses were. And then one must work, as he did, out of those weaknesses in order to confront reality.

The powerful contradictions at the heart of Yeats's work are also at the heart of any literary achievement. One such powerful contradiction, as we have noted here, is between the demands of the private and the public worlds. Yeats was deeply responsive to both. Another is between the demands of life—with all its vigorous activism—and art—with its requirement for philosophical and esthetic discipline. We encourage our poets to wrestle with such problems, problems that do not, by their very nature, have perfect solutions. In watching their magnificent struggles, we are onlookers who can be enriched and strengthened.

---

15. **Timon and Lear** aging tragic heroes of Shakespeare's *Timon of Athens* and *King Lear*

POEMS FOR FURTHER DISCUSSION

The Unknown Citizen

(To JS/07/M/378 This Marble Monument Is Erected by the State)

He was found by the Bureau of Statistics to be
One against whom there was no official complaint,
And all the reports on his conduct agree
That, in the modern sense of an old-fashioned word, he was a saint,
For in everything he did he served the Greater Community.   5
Except for the War till the day he retired
He worked in a factory and never got fired,
But satisfied his employers, Fudge Motors Inc.
Yet he wasn't a scab or odd in his views,
For his Union reports that he paid his dues,   10
(Our report on his Union shows it was sound)
And our Social Psychology workers found
That he was popular with his mates and liked a drink.
The Press are convinced that he bought a paper every day
And that his reactions to advertisements were normal in every way.   15
Policies taken out in his name prove that he was fully insured,
And his Health-card shows he was once in hospital but left it cured.
Both Producers Research and High-Grade Living declare
He was fully sensible to the advantages of the Installment Plan
And had everything necessary to the Modern Man,   20
A phonograph, a radio, a car and a frigidaire.
Our researchers into Public Opinion are content
That he held the proper opinions for the time of year;
When there was peace, he was for peace; when there was war, he went.
He was married and added five children to the population,   25
Which our Eugenist says was the right number for a parent of his
     generation,
And our teachers report that he never interfered with their education.
Was he free? Was he happy? The question is absurd:
Had anything been wrong, we should certainly have heard.

W. H. Auden (1907–1973)

Questions

1. The idea of a monument to the Unknown Citizen brings to mind the Tomb of the
   Unknown Soldier. That figure, however, stands for certain ideal qualities: selfless
   sacrifice, patriotism, and so on. What does the monument of the Unknown
   Citizen stand for?

2. Who is the speaker in this poem? Discuss the irony in the relationship between speaker, occasion, and subject matter.

3. From whose point of view would this Unknown Citizen have been a "saint" (line 4)? What constitutes his "sainthood"? Analyze the last two lines of the poem in relation to the whole.

4. In what sense is Auden grappling with what we have called "the public world" in this work?

What Were They Like?

   1) Did the people of Viet Nam
      use lanterns of stone?
   2) Did they hold ceremonies
      to reverence the opening of buds?
   3) Were they inclined to rippling laughter?   5
   4) Did they use bone and ivory,
      jade and silver, for ornament?
   5) Had they an epic poem?
   6) Did they distinguish between speech and singing?

   1) Sir, their light hearts turned to stone.   10
      It is not remembered whether in gardens
      stone lanterns illumined pleasant ways.
   2) Perhaps they gathered once to delight in blossom,
      but after the children were killed
      there were no more buds.   15
   3) Sir, laughter is bitter to the burned mouth.
   4) A dream ago, perhaps. Ornament is for joy.
      All the bones were charred.
   5) It is not remembered. Remember,
      most were peasants; their life   20
      was in rice and bamboo.
      When peaceful clouds were reflected in the paddies
      and the water buffalo stepped surely along terraces,
      maybe fathers told their sons old tales.
      When bombs smashed the mirrors   25
      there was time only to scream.
   6) There is an echo yet, it is said,
      of their speech which was like a song.
      It is reported their singing resembled
      the flight of moths in moonlight.   30
      Who can say? It is silent now.

Denise Levertov (b. 1923)

480   *The Themes in a Poem*

Questions

1. Discuss the poet's decision here to use a question and answer format. What is gained? How would a more direct approach to the subject matter have altered the emotional effect?
2. Why are the questions almost "anthropological"? Why are some of the answers prefaced with the word "Sir"? Do you begin to form an idea of the respective characters of questioner and answerer?
3. Compare this poem to "Driving Through Minnesota During the Hanoi Bombings" on page 460. Which is the more effective antiwar poem? Why?
4. Why do you think that a poet working during the height of the social upheaval and national debate caused by the United States' involvement in Vietnam would have felt it necessary to write poems such as the ones by Bly and Levertov? Compare their poems to those about London by Blake and about England by Shelley on pages 458 and 459.

The Collar

I struck the board° and cried, "No more;   *table*
    I will abroad!
What? shall I ever sigh and pine?
My lines and life are free, free as the road,
  Loose as the wind, as large as store.°   *abundance* 5
    Shall I be still in suit?
Have I no harvest but a thorn
To let me blood, and not restore
What I have lost with cordial° fruit?   *life enhancing*
    Sure there was wine   10
Before my sighs did dry it; there was corn
Before my tears did drown it.
Is the year only lost to me?
  Have I no bays° to crown it,
No flowers, no garlands gay? All blasted?   15
    All wasted?
Not so, my heart; but there is fruit,
    And thou hast hands.
Recover all thy sigh-blown age
On double pleasures: leave thy cold dispute   20
Of what is fit and not. Forsake thy cage,
    Thy rope of sands,
Which petty thoughts have made, and made to thee
  Good cable, to enforce and draw,
    And be thy law,   25
While thou didst wink and wouldst not see.

14. **bays** laurel; a laurel wreath is a symbol of victory

Away! take heed;
I will abroad.
Call in thy death's-head there; tie up thy fears.
He that forbears   30
To suit and serve his need,
Deserves his load."
But as I raved and grew more fierce and wild
At every word,
Methought I heard one calling, *Child!*   35
And I replied, *My Lord.*

George Herbert (1593–1633)

QUESTIONS

1. Characterize the speaker in this poem. Analyze the nature of his rebelliousness. What are his grievances in lines 3–16? How does he plan to find relief in lines 17–32?
2. How does delaying the introduction of God until the end of the poem alter and underscore its drama? How does it change your perception of the speaker and of his "dilemma"? What is the effect of the word "Methought" (line 35)?
3. How does this very private account of a person and his relationship with God achieve a general resonance? Compare this poem with John Donne's "Batter My Heart" on page 422.

What Lips My Lips Have Kissed

What lips my lips have kissed, and where, and why,
I have forgotten, and what arms have lain
Under my head till morning; but the rain
Is full of ghosts tonight, that tap and sigh
Upon the glass and listen for reply,   5
And in my heart there stirs a quiet pain
For unremembered lads that not again
Will turn to me at midnight with a cry.
Nor knows what birds have vanished one by one,
Thus in the winter stands the lonely tree,   10
Yet knows its boughs more silent than before:
I cannot say what loves have come and gone;
I only know that summer sang in me
A little while, that in me sings no more.

Edna St. Vincent Millay (1892–1950)

QUESTIONS

1. If this poem were a piece of music, one might say that it has three movements. Identify them. How do they establish a "logic" for the poem?

2. As a modern author, Millay used the sonnet form fully aware of the use that Shakespeare and other classic authors had made of it. Compare this poem to "My Mistress' Eyes Are Nothing Like the Sun" on page 403 or "When to the Sessions of Sweet Silent Thought" on page 449. What are the differences in rhyme scheme? In the respective poets' resolution of the issues raised in these works?

3. This poem has the "feel" of an intimate revelation, an autobiographical statement. Yet the poet attempts to universalize the experience so that we feel we are not just listening to a disappointed middle-aged woman but hearing something about human experience in general. How does this happen? How does the private statement yield a wider truth?

In Memory of W. B. Yeats

(d. Jan. 1939)

I

He disappeared in the dead of winter:
The brooks were frozen, the airports almost deserted,
And snow disfigured the public statues;
The mercury sank in the mouth of the dying day.
What instruments we have agree   5
The day of his death was a dark cold day.

Far from his illness
The wolves ran on through the evergreen forests,
The peasant river was untempted by the fashionable quays;
By mourning tongues   10
The death of the poet was kept from his poems.

But for him it was his last afternoon as himself,
An afternoon of nurses and rumours;
The provinces of his body revolted,
The squares of his mind were empty,   15
Silence invaded the suburbs,
The current of his feeling failed; he became his admirers.

Now he is scattered among a hundred cities
And wholly given over to unfamiliar affections,
To find his happiness in another kind of wood   20
And be punished under a foreign code of conscience.
The words of a dead man
Are modified in the guts of the living.

But in the importance and noise of to-morrow
When the brokers are roaring like beasts on the floor of the Bourse,   25

And the poor have the sufferings to which they are fairly accustomed,
And each in the cell of himself is almost convinced of his freedom,
A few thousand will think of this day
As one thinks of a day when one did something slightly unusual.
What instruments we have agree   30
The day of his death was a dark cold day.

II

You were silly like us; your gift survived it all:
The parish of rich women, physical decay,
Yourself. Mad Ireland hurt you into poetry.
Now Ireland has her madness and her weather still,   35
For poetry makes nothing happen: it survives
In the valley of its making where executives
Would never want to tamper, flows on south
From ranches of isolation and the busy griefs,
Raw towns that we believe and die in; it survives,   40
A way of happening, a mouth.

III

Earth, receive an honoured guest:
William Yeats is laid to rest.
Let the Irish vessel lie
Emptied of its poetry.   45

In the nightmare of the dark
All the dogs of Europe bark,
And the living nations wait,
Each sequestered in its hate;

Intellectual disgrace   50
Stares from every human face,
And the seas of pity lie
Locked and frozen in each eye.

Follow, poet, follow right
To the bottom of the night,   55
With your unconstraining voice
Still persuade us to rejoice;

With the farming of a verse
Make a vineyard of the curse,
Sing of human unsuccess   60
In a rapture of distress;

In the deserts of the heart
Let the healing fountain start,
In the prison of his days
Teach the free man how to praise.

W. H. Auden (1907–1973)

QUESTIONS

1. In line 36 of his tribute to Yeats, Auden notes that "poetry makes nothing happen." He also observes that many people are indifferent to it. Yet, as he says, "it survives" (line 40). What is the nature of its survival? How does the poem argue that poetry can live in surroundings hostile to it?

2. What qualities in Yeats prompted Auden to compose such an elegy? In the third section of the poem, Auden says: "In the nightmare of the dark / All the dogs of Europe bark, / And the living nations wait, / Each sequestered in its hate." In what ways is the poem about Yeats and his death *at a certain moment* in European history?

3. Note how the very look of the poem changes as it moves through its three sections. It begins with long stanzas and ends in short ones. At first its rhymes are only occasional and then, at the conclusion, its rhymes are steady and unmistakable. Why does Auden do this? How is this pattern related to the poem's themes? What other changes in the construction of the poem do you see, and how do you account for them?

4. To what extent is this poem about Yeats, and to what extent is it about poetry in general? Are the concluding lines of the poem directed to the occasion of Yeats's death, or do they seem to have something else in mind? Who is "the poet" mentioned in the fourth stanza of the third section of the poem?

5. The last line of the poem refers to "the free man." Who is he? Has he been seen before in the poem?

6

Two American Poets
in Perspective:
Robert Lowell and Sylvia Plath

W hen we look at how an individual poet stamps his or her identity on many poems during a lifetime, we should bear in mind that the poet draws on many strengths. First, there are the inexhaustible possibilities of language itself—metaphor, sound effects, versification, and all the other elements of poetic composition that we have surveyed in the preceding pages. Secondly, there are the themes that have always intrigued poets, and the rich and complex tradition of poetry as it actually has been written throughout the ages, a tradition illustrating the many possibilities of poetic craft. In sum, poets use two things: techniques and models. They look around to see the artistic means available to them and also examine what other poets have done. What a single poet makes of this inheritance is determined by his or her unique consciousness—by the distinctive angle of vision, the unexpected perception of an everyday event, the uncommon response to the common dilemmas of the self and the surrounding world.

We focus here on two contemporary American poets: Robert Lowell and Sylvia Plath. Their work has had an undeniable and significant effect on both readers and fellow writers. Owing to the fact that Lowell and Plath employed the most intimate details of their respective lives in their work, we can learn a great deal from their poetry about the impact of personal experience on art. We should remember, however, that while both Lowell and Plath wanted their poems to reflect, with power and authenticity, the crises of lives at times careening toward madness and self-destruction, they also wanted those poems to be much more than mere fragments of autobiography. As we will see, they both wanted to transcend their pain and transform their individual moments into larger truths.

ROBERT LOWELL (1917–1977)

Part of the glory, and part of the problem, of being Robert Lowell was the Lowell family itself. It is one of the most distinguished and remarkable families in the United States, including in its long history a Mayflower pilgrim, a governor of the Plymouth Colony, a Revolutionary War general, a president of Harvard University, an ambassador to Great Britain who wrote highly regarded poetry and literary criticism, and a woman poet of this century, Amy Lowell, who was at the center of some of the most dramatic and important transformations of technique and taste in modern writing.

The patrician reputation of the family, a reputation to which the young Robert Lowell was acutely sensitive, has been wryly treated in a few doggerel verses about Boston:

> Home of the bean and the cod
> Where the Lowells talk only to Cabots
> And the Cabots talk only to God.

Lowell's poetry is a response—richly complicated, often indirect, and sometimes quite agonized—to this familial and historical fate.

Lowell is above all a *responsive* poet. Noting the way in which fate seemed to have ordained him to provide a kind of historical continuity between the earliest moments of American life and its present condition as a world power, Lowell once commented that he was perhaps meant to be a kind of Virgil or Matthew Arnold for America. He felt the pressure of describing in his poetry the good and bad of being an American and to point out both the past the country had endured and the future it could expect.

Lowell's response to this burdensome privilege is the key to his work. He writes about himself, sometimes with excruciating honesty, revealing in absolute candor his innermost fears and weaknesses; he also writes about his country, etching with savage strokes his indictment of a national destiny that he believed had gone terribly wrong. The result is the work of a long career (his first volume of poetry appeared in 1944, the last in 1973, four years before his death) that can be summed up as a "lover's quarrel" with his culture and his century. The way in which the quarrel was managed over those years, the artistry and the inventive honesty that informed it, make Lowell arguably the most important American poet of his time.

Much of Lowell's early poetry comes out of his sense of man's relationship to God, a God whose power and wrathful authority derive from Puritan America's conceptions of the Almighty. Lowell's God is a stern, magisterial being, unappeasable and fierce. Even late in his life, Lowell seemed to carry in his mind this conception of God. Describing Lowell in 1967, the novelist Norman Mailer said:

> [He] has the expression on his face of a dues payer who is just about keeping up with the interest on some enormous debt. As he sits on the floor with his long arms clasped mournfully about his long Yankee legs, 'I am here,' says the expression, 'but I do not pretend I like what I see.' The hollows in his cheeks give a hint of the hanging judge. Lowell is of good weight, not too heavy, not too light, but the hollows speak of the great Puritan gloom in which the country was founded—man was simply not good enough for God.

The poem in which Lowell most brilliantly evokes this complex and difficult relationship of man to God, "Mr. Edwards and the Spider," is also a fine example of the poet's ability to talk with figures of the past in such a way that the present is also illuminated. Jonathan Edwards was an influential Calvinist

divine of the eighteenth century in this country and a spokesman for the
doctrine that we had much to fear, and little to hope, from God. In his most
famous sermon, he said that "the God that holds you over the pit of hell,
much as one holds a spider or some loathsome insect over the fire, abhors
you, and is dreadfully provoked. . . . You hang by a slender thread, with the
flames of divine wrath flashing about it. . . . " Utilizing some of the same
imagery, Lowell writes a poem about death and the possibilities of salvation in
both the eighteenth and the twentieth centuries. Josiah Hawley, Edwards'
uncle and a man who killed himself, is at once both himself and ourselves in
this century.

Mr. Edwards and the Spider

I saw the spiders marching through the air,
Swimming from tree to tree that mildewed day
  In latter August when the hay
  Came creaking to the barn. But where
    The wind is westerly.   5
Where gnarled November makes the spiders fly
Into the apparitions of the sky,
  They purpose nothing but their ease and die
Urgently beating east to sunrise and the sea;

  What are we in the hands of the great God?   10
It was in vain you set up thorn and briar
  In battle array against the fire
  And treason cracking in your blood;
    For the wild thorns grow tame
And will do nothing to oppose the flame;   15
Your lacerations tell the losing game
You play against a sickness past your cure.
How will the hands be strong? How will the heart endure?

  A very little thing, a little worm,
Or hourglass-blazoned spider, it is said,   20
  Can kill a tiger. Will the dead
  Hold up his mirror and affirm
    Against the four winds the smell
And flash of his authority? It's well
If God who holds you to the pit of hell,   25
  Much as one holds a spider, will destroy,
Baffle and dissipate your soul. As a small boy

  On Windsor Marsh, I saw the spider die
When thrown into the bowels of fierce fire:
    There's no long struggle, no desire   30
    To get up on its feet and fly—
    It stretches out its feet

And dies. This is the sinner's last retreat;
Yes, and no strength exerted on the heat
Then sinews the abolished will, when sick   35
And full of burning, it will whistle on a brick.

But who can plumb the sinking of that soul?
Josiah Hawley, picture yourself cast
Into a brick-kiln where the blast
Fans your quick vitals to a coal—   40
    If measured by a glass,
How long would it seem burning! Let there pass
A minute, ten, ten trillion; but the blaze
Is infinite, eternal: this is death,
To die and know it. This is the Black Widow, death.   45

    This early poem has the kind of knotted intensity and strong verbal "spikiness" that is characteristic of the poet at every moment in his career. (Note the way many s sounds are crowded together in lines 33–36: "This is the sinner's last retreat; / Yes, and no strength exerted on the heat / Then sinews the abolished will, when sick / And full of burning, it will whistle on a brick.") But the poem, for all its compressed power and tightly wound force, is uncharacteristic of perhaps the most notable feature of Robert Lowell as a poet, namely his willingness to expose his own life, in all of its terrors and embarrassments, to the light of public knowledge. His volume of 1959, *Life Studies*, revolutionized American (and later British) poetry because of the way it legitimized this kind of disclosure. Lowell was intuitively aware of the strangely powerful attractions of his new departure when he said that "it may be that some people have turned to my poems because of the very things that are wrong with me, I mean the difficulty I have with ordinary living, the impracticability, the myopia."

    The reader who comes to Lowell's "confessional" poems must never allow himself to think that they are the work of an undisciplined individual simply blurting out the raw facts of his private life. In such poems Lowell is the same Lowell who learned the rigorous craft of poetry from such teachers as Allen Tate and John Crowe Ransom in the 1940s; who turned again and again to the guiding mastery of such poets as Dante, T. S. Eliot, and Ezra Pound; and who never forgot his early training in Latin and Greek and in the verse of the seventeenth-century metaphysical poets. Part of the electric force of the poems in *Life Studies* stems from Lowell's twin desires: to speak of himself, and to speak poetry.

    Lowell let his readers know that he had for some years been afflicted with periodic mental collapses that required hospitalization. In such places as McLean's, a private hospital in Belmont, Massachusetts, Lowell met other well-born and Harvard-educated patients. In "Waking in the Blue" when he mentions "these victorious figures of bravado ossified young" (line 33), and then says, "We are all old-timers, / each of us holds a locked razor" (lines

49–50), we feel he is speaking not just for a few disturbed individuals, but for all those Americans who, in a country of rich traditions and great familial promise, have failed to live up to their expectations and to the expectations of others.

Waking in the Blue

The night attendant, a B.U.° sophomore,
rouses from the mare's-nest of his drowsy head
propped on *The Meaning of Meaning.*°
He catwalks down our corridor.
Azure day   5
makes my agonized blue window bleaker.
Crows maunder on the petrified fairway.
Absence! My heart grows tense
as though a harpoon were sparring for the kill.
(This is the house for the "mentally ill.")   10

What use is my sense of humour?
I grin at "Stanley," now sunk in his sixties,
once a Harvard all-American fullback,
(if such were possible!)
still hoarding the build of a boy in his twenties,   15
as he soaks, a ramrod
with the muscle of a seal
in his long tub,
vaguely urinous from the Victorian plumbing.
A kingly granite profile in a crimson golf-cap,   20
worn all day, all night,
he thinks only of his figure,
of slimming on sherbet and ginger ale—
more cut off from words than a seal.

This is the way day breaks in Bowditch Hall at McLean's;   25
the hooded night lights bring out "Bobbie,"
Porcellian° '29,
a replica of Louis XVI
without the wig—
redolent and roly-poly as a sperm whale,   30
as he swashbuckles about in his birthday suit
and horses at chairs.

These victorious figures of bravado ossified young.

---

1. **B.U.** Boston University   3. **The Meaning of Meaning** a book on language and philosophy by Charles Ogden and I. A. Richards published in 1959   27. **Porcellian** prestigious club at Harvard University

In between the limits of day,
hours and hours go by under the crew haircuts   35
and slightly too little nonsensical twinkle
of the Roman Catholic attendants.
(There are no Mayflower
screwballs in the Catholic Church.)

After a hearty New England breakfast,   40
I weight two hundred pounds
this morning. Cock of the walk,
I strut in my turtle-necked French sailor's jersey
before the metal shaving mirrors,
and see the shaky future grow familiar   45
in the pinched, indigenous faces
of these thoroughbred mental cases,
twice my age and half my weight.
We are all old-timers,
each of us holds a locked razor.   50

Another poem in *Life Studies,* "Memories of West Street and Lepke,"
describes the other form of incarceration that Lowell underwent, namely his
brief term in jail during the Second World War for having declared himself a
conscientious objector. There he met Jehovah's Witnesses, leaders of organized crime, pacifists and pimps. His memories of that experience are summoned up, however, in the nineteen-fifties, a decade in American social
history notable for its apathetic conformity. Lowell had good reason to think
that much that had been passionate in his life had now left him. Beneath the
surface of the poem, a surface that is placid and affably conversational, is a
depth of turbulent passion and desperate violence. That particular contrast—
one between elegant appearance and crazed depth—was never to disappear
from Lowell's poetry once it had been established in *Life Studies.*

Memories of West Street and Lepke

Only teaching on Tuesdays, book-worming
in pajamas fresh from the washer each morning,
I hog a whole house on Boston's
"hardly passionate Marlborough Street,"
where even the man   5
scavenging filth in the back alley trash cans,
has two children, a beach wagon, a helpmate,
and is "a young Republican."
I have a nine months' daughter,
young enough to be my granddaughter.   10
Like the sun she rises in her flame-flamingo infants' wear.

These are the tranquilized *Fifties*,
and I am forty. Ought I to regret my seedtime?
I was a fire-breathing Catholic C.O.,°   *conscientious objector*
and made my manic statement,   15
telling off the state and president, and then
sat waiting sentence in the bull pen
beside a negro boy with curlicues
of marijuana in his hair.

Given a year,   20
I walked on the roof of the West Street Jail, a short
enclosure like my school soccer court,
and saw the Hudson River once a day
through sooty clothesline entanglements
and bleaching khaki tenements.   25
Strolling, I yammered metaphysics with Abramowitz,
a jaundice-yellow ("it's really tan")
and fly-weight pacifist,
so vegetarian,
he wore rope shoes and preferred fallen fruit.   30
He tried to convert Bioff and Brown,
the Hollywood pimps, to his diet.
Hairy, muscular, suburban,
wearing chocolate double-breasted suits,
they blew their tops and beat him black and blue.   35

I was so out of things, I'd never heard
of the Jehovah's Witnesses.
"Are you a C.O.?" I asked a fellow jailbird.
"No," he answered, "I'm a J.W."
He taught me the hospital "tuck,"   40
and pointed out the T-shirted back
of *Murder Incorporated's* Czar Lepke,°
there piling towels on a rack,
or dawdling off to his little segregated cell full

of things forbidden the common man: 45
a portable radio, a dresser, two toy American
flags tied together with a ribbon of Easter palm.
Flabby, bald, lobotomized,
he drifted in a sheepish calm,
where no agonizing reappraisal   50
jarred his concentration on the electric chair—
hanging like an oasis in his air
of lost connections . . .

42. **Czar Lepke** a notorious organized crime figure

Lowell was to reveal more than just himself in the poems in *Life Studies*. His critically ironic and formally detached manner was also concentrated on his parents. His father, for instance, is portrayed in such poems as "Terminal Days at Beverly Farms" as an oddly foolish, even irrelevant man. He proceeds from one small and meaningless errand to another, armed only with his own collection of clichés and blessed only by his own kind of self-ignorance. The poet never lets us forget that the man was a Lowell, and hence the inheritor of a great tradition. That tradition, however, has come to nothing in his life.

The poem, as a piece of craft, employs a number of *oxymorons*, by which Lowell unites apparently incompatible concepts (line 12, "efficient" and "hairless"; line 28, "sensationally sober"; line 34, "inattentive and beaming"; line 42, "abrupt and unprotesting") to create a sense of dislocation and surprise beneath a surface of apparent calmness. This technique, by which the strangely disturbing makes its way into an environment of straightforward description, was never to be discarded as Lowell continued his career.

Terminal Days at Beverly Farms°

At Beverly Farms, a portly, uncomfortable boulder
bulked in the garden's centre—
an irregular Japanese touch.
After his Bourbon "old fashioned," Father,
bronzed, breezy, a shade too ruddy,   5
swayed as if on deck-duty
under his six-pointed star-lantern—
last July's birthday present.
He smiled his oval Lowell smile,
he wore his cream gabardine dinner-jacket,   10
and indigo cummerbund.
His head was efficient and hairless,
his newly dieted figure was vitally trim.

Father and Mother moved to Beverly Farms
to be a two minute walk from the station,   15
half an hour by train from the Boston doctors.
They had no sea-view,
but sky-blue tracks of the commuters' railroad shone
like a double-barrelled shotgun
through the scarlet late August sumac,   20
multiplying like cancer
at their garden's border.

Beverly Farms a town north of Boston on the Massachusetts coast

Father had had two coronaries.
He still treasured underhand economies,
but his best friend was his little black *Chevie*,   25
garaged like a sacrificial steer
with gilded hooves,
yet sensationally sober,
and with less side than an old dancing pump.
The local dealer, a "buccaneer,"   30
had been bribed a "king's ransom"
to quickly deliver a car without chrome.

Each morning at eight-thirty,
inattentive and beaming,
loaded with his "calc" and "trig" books,   35
his clipper ship statistics,
and his ivory slide-rule,
Father stole off with the *Chevie*
to loaf in the Maritime Museum at Salem.°
He called the curator   40
"the commander of the Swiss Navy"

Father's death was abrupt and unprotesting.
His vision was still twenty-twenty.
After a morning of anxious, repetitive smiling,
his last words to Mother were: 45
"I feel awful."

Lowell's autobiographical intensities are summed up in "Skunk Hour," a poem about his growing psychological imbalance, his deteriorating social environment, and the implacable power possessed by the world of bestial nature. His mind "not right," Lowell can nonetheless see that while he himself is "hell," the world of nature proceeds with a sane rapacity and directness that are admirable. Human confusion and disappointment are held in ironic contrast to the elemental energies deployed by the mother skunk and her brood. The poet almost seems to wish to join the swilling and unconfused animals. Note the way in which the poem grows by an accumulation of small details and physical description. Lowell once remarked that "a lot of poetry seems to me very good in the tradition but just doesn't move me very much because it doesn't have personal vibrance to it. I probably exaggerate the value of it, but it's precious to me. Some little image, some detail you've noticed— you're writing about a little country shop, just describing it, and your poem ends up with an existential account of your experience. But it's the shop that started it off."

39. **Salem** an historic port town north of Boston

Skunk Hour

(for Elizabeth Bishop)°

Nautilus Island's° hermit
heiress still lives through winter in her Spartan cottage;
her sheep still graze above the sea.
Her son's a bishop. Her farmer
is first selectman in our village,   5
she's in her dotage.

Thirsting for
the hierarchic privacy
of Queen Victoria's century,
she buys up all   10
the eyesores facing her shore,
and lets them fall.

The season's ill—
we've lost our summer millionaire,
who seemed to leap from an L. L. Bean°   15
catalogue. His nine-knot yawl
was auctioned off to lobstermen.
A red fox stain covers Blue Hill.°

And now our fairy
decorator brightens his shop for fall,   20
his fishnet's filled with orange cork,
orange, his cobbler's bench and awl,
there is no money in his work,
he'd rather marry.

One dark night,   25
my Tudor Ford climbed the hill's skull,
I watched for love-cars. Lights turned down,
they lay together, hull to hull,
where the graveyard shelves on the town. . . .
My mind's not right.   30

A car radio bleats,
"Love, O careless Love . . ." I hear
my ill-spirit sob in each blood cell,
as if my hand were at its throat . . .
I myself am hell,   35
nobody's here—

Elizabeth Bishop American poet (1911–1979) to whom Lowell was close   **1. Nautilus Island**
an island in Penobscot Bay, Maine   **15. L. L. Bean** a Maine catalogue sales firm for outdoor
clothing and paraphernalia   **18. Blue Hill** a town on the Maine coast

only skunks, that search
in the moonlight for a bite to eat.
They march on their soles up Main Street:
white stripes, moonstruck eyes' red fire   40
under the chalk-dry and spar spire
of the Trinitarian Church.

I stand on top
of our back steps and breathe the rich air—
a mother skunk with her column of kittens swills the garbage pail   45
She jabs her wedge head in a cup
of sour cream, drops her ostrich tail,
and will not scare.

The same desire, to relinquish that which is human, urban, historical,
"civilized," and despoiled, and to join that which is pure, elemental, and
unconscious, is evoked with great power in Lowell's stunning poem about
national duty and private integrity, "For the Union Dead." It is perhaps his
greatest achievement as a public poet. Its civic themes are two great subjects:
the American Civil War and the racial exploitation it was meant to end; and
the tradition of selfless responsibility to which Americans have on occasion
been called. One such American was the young Colonel Robert Gould Shaw,
the descendant (like Lowell) of a distinguished Boston family and a person of
such promise that he was later to be remembered as "the blue-eyed child of
fortune upon whose youth every divinity had smiled." Yet, leading a black
regiment against a Confederate stronghold, Shaw was killed. In his heroic
death, he was being responsive to the motto—"Reliquit Omnia Servare Rem
Publicam"—of the Society of the Cincinnati, an organization made up of the
descendants of American officers in the Revolutionary War. The poem's
epigraph, slightly modifying the Latin, means "They left everything behind to
serve the nation."

By means of unremitting irony, Lowell contrasts the heroism of the young
Shaw with the look and feel of contemporary Boston ("barbed and galvanized," "tons of mush and grass," "a savage servility / slides by on grease").
Where once the spirit of handsome generosity to a noble civic ideal
flourished, now all that is alive is urban renewal, racism, and the sad memories of better times in Massachusetts. Where once Shaw maintained "an
angry wrenlike vigilance" in the face of black slavery, now an equally oppressive racial standoff seems remote and disembodied ("the drained faces of
Negro school-children rise like balloons").

In the face of such large historical disappointments, Lowell's own response, as an individual human being, is hardly noble or grand. Instead, he
retreats within his own personal being, seeking there a security made up of
nostalgia ("I often sigh still / for the dark downward and vegetating kingdom /
of the fish and reptile"). He thus allies himself with one of the strongest
human desires—to subside into some earlier form of purely inarticulate and
organic existence.

The poem, then, unites civic themes with personal themes and becomes a political poem about a real person. Its art consists in the way it so adroitly moves between the two spheres of its existence. Unlike some public poems, it doesn't aim to persuade its readers with explicit arguments. And, unlike some personal poems, it doesn't pretend that the world "out there" is unworthy of our attention. The exterior world of history, sacrifice, slavery, and death is fused by Lowell with the interior world of memory.

For the Union Dead

"Relinquunt Omnia Servare Rem Publicam."

The old South Boston Aquarium stands
in a Sahara of snow now. Its broken windows are boarded.
The bronze weathervane cod has lost half its scales.
The airy tanks are dry.

Once my nose crawled like a snail on the glass;   5
my hand tingled
to burst the bubbles
drifting from the noses of the cowed, compliant fish.

My hand draws back. I often sigh still
for the dark downward and vegetating kingdom   10
of the fish and reptile. One morning last March,
I pressed against the new barbed and galvanized

fence on the Boston Common.° Behind their cage,
yellow dinosaur steamshovels were grunting
as they cropped up tons of mush and grass   15
to gouge their underworld garage.

Parking spaces luxuriate like civic
sandpiles in the heart of Boston.
A girdle of orange, Puritan-pumpkin colored girders
braces the tingling Statehouse,   20

shaking over the excavations, as it faces Colonel Shaw
and his bell-cheeked Negro infantry
on St. Gaudens'° shaking Civil War relief,
propped by a plank splint against the garage's earthquake.

Two months after marching through Boston,   25
half the regiment was dead;
at the dedication,
William James° could almost hear the bronze Negroes breathe.

13. **Boston Common** a park in the city   23. **St. Gaudens'** Augustus St. Gaudens (1848–1907), Irish-born sculptor who worked in America   28. **William James** pioneering American philosopher and psychologist (1842–1910)

Their monument sticks like a fishbone
in the city's throat   30
Its Colonel is as lean
as a compass-needle.

He has an angry wrenlike vigilance,
a greyhound's gentle tautness;
he seems to wince at pleasure,   35
and suffocate for privacy.

He is out of bounds now. He rejoices in man's lovely,
peculiar power to choose life and die—
when he leads his black soldiers to death,
he cannot bend his back.   40

On a thousand small town New England greens,
the old white churches hold their air
of sparse, sincere rebellion; frayed flags
quilt the graveyards of the Grand Army of the Republic.

The stone statues of the abstract Union Soldier   45
grow slimmer and younger each year—
wasp-waisted, they doze over muskets
and muse through their sideburns . . .

Shaw's father wanted no monument
except the ditch,   50
where his son's body was thrown
and lost with his "niggers."

The ditch is nearer.
There are no statues for the last war here;
on Boylston Street, a commercial photograph   55
shows Hiroshima boiling

over a Mosler Safe, the "Rock of Ages"
that survived the blast. Space is nearer.
When I crouch to my television set,
the drained faces of Negro school-children rise like balloons.   60

Colonel Shaw
is riding on his bubble,
he waits
for the blessèd break.

The Aquarium is gone. Everywhere,   65
giant finned cars nose forward like fish;
a savage servility
slides by on grease.

Much, but not all, of Lowell's poetic career after the great period of "For the Union Dead" was given over to writing a long series of sonnets about his life, the malaise of America during the years of the war in Vietnam, his changing marital circumstances, his literary friendships and memories, his children, and his new existence in England, where he moved in the 1970s and lived, off and on, until his death. Lowell had much to survey, and his eye lost none of its sharpness and his voice none of its acerbic tone. What some readers feel has been diminished in these later poems is the manic intensity that made the earlier Lowell poetry crackle with anger, candor, and devastating intelligence.

But in a poem like "Central Park," the characteristic tone is certainly in place. The New York park, at once green, welcoming, and violent, serves as the place from which a vigilant passerby can see the great wealth and the great poverty that defines America's most densely populated city. The proud lion, caged in the zoo, is now not unlike the poor and squeaking kitten whom Lowell finds starving while surrounded by plenty. Nature itself seems threatened and impoverished in the midst of so much urban power. That power, comparable to an Egyptian Pharoah's, presses down on every living thing and only a frail paper kite can graze Cleopatra's Needle and aspire to lift itself beyond the "drying crust" that is Earth.

Central Park

Scaling small rocks, exhaling smog,
gasping at game-scents like a dog,
now light as pollen, now as white
and winded as a grounded kite—
I watched the lovers occupy   5
every inch of earth and sky:
one figure of geometry,
multiplied to infinity,
straps down, and sunning openly . . .
each precious, public, pubic tangle   10
an equilateral triangle,
lost in the park, half covered by
the shade of some low stone or tree.
The stain of fear and poverty
spread through each trapped anatomy,   15
and darkened every mote of dust.
All wished to leave this drying crust,
borne on the delicate wings of lust
like bees, and cast their fertile drop
into the overwhelming cup.   20

Drugged and humbled by the smell
of zoo-straw mixed with animal,
the lion prowled his slummy cell,
serving his life-term in jail—
glaring, grinding, on his heel,   25
with tingling step and testicle . . .
Behind a dripping rock, I found

a one-day kitten on the ground—
deprived, weak, ignorant and blind,
squeaking, tubular, left behind—   30
dying with its deserter's rich
Welfare lying out of reach:
milk cartons, kidney heaped to spoil,
two plates sheathed with silver foil.

Shadows had stained the afternoon;   35
high in an elm, a snagged balloon
wooed the attraction of the moon.
Scurrying from the mouth of night,
a single, fluttery, paper kite
grazed Cleopatra's Needle,° and sailed   40
where the light of the sun had failed.
Then night, the night—the jungle hour,
the rich in his slit-windowed tower . . .
Old Pharoahs starving in your foxholes,
with painted banquets on the walls,   45
fists knotted in your captives' hair,
tyrants with little food to spare—
all your embalming left you mortal,
glazed, black, and hideously eternal,
all your plunder and gold leaf   50
only served to draw the thief . . .

We beg delinquents for our life.
Behind each bush, perhaps a knife;
each landscaped crag, each flowering shrub,
hides a policeman with a club.   55

Also characteristic of Lowell's late poetry is a sonnet made up entirely of the quoted words of someone else, an American soldier recounting his actions in the Vietnam war. The poem speaks for itself, reminding us that intense and informative verse can be constituted of the loose formality of conversation. The horror of war comes instantly through this quick "photograph" of a man trained to kill and conditioned not to care.

Women, Children, Babies, Cows, Cats

"It was at My Lai or Sonmy° or something,
it was this afternoon. . . . We had these orders,
we had all night to think about it—
we was to burn and kill, then there'd be nothing
standing, women, children, babies, cows, cats. . . .   5
As soon as we hopped the choppers, we started shooting.

40. Cleopatra's Needle an obelisk in the park   **l. My Lai or Sonmy** Vietnamese towns associated with the worst violence of the war in Vietnam

> I remember . . . as we was coming up upon one area
> in Pinkville, a man with a gun . . . running—this lady . . .
> Lieutenant LaGuerre said, 'Shoot her.' I said,
> 'You shoot her, I don't want to shoot no lady.'   10
> She had one foot in the door. . . . When I turned her,
> there was this little one-month-year-old baby
> I thought was her gun. It kind of cracked me up."

Finally, one way to gain perspective on the design and meaning of Robert Lowell's career as an American poet is to consider George Orwell's words about why writers write. With his customary unflinching honesty, Orwell said: "Writing a book is a horrible, exhausting struggle, like a long bout of some painful illness. One would never undertake such a thing if one were not driven on by some demon whom one can neither resist nor understand." But, as Lowell's career demonstrates, being driven by a demon does not necessarily mean that the demon must emerge as the victor. The artist can be the victor. That truth is the subject of one of Lowell's last poems, "Dolphin." Representing the possibility that beauty and truth can arise from the oceanic depths of pain and hurt, the dolphin is part woman, part fish, in other words, the beckoning mermaid that leads a man on to see and do things he otherwise thought impossible. As the seventeenth-century French playwright Jean Racine was drawn on by the imaginative figure of his Phèdre and into the controversy caused by the play of her name, so Lowell is drawn on by the compulsions and attractions of his art. That art has, in the last analysis, saved him. "Troubled in mind . . . not avoiding injury to others, / not avoiding injury to myself," the poet has nonetheless been given a craft, a technique by which he can cope with the mysteries of his life. He calls that craft "this book, half fiction / an eelnet made by man for the eel fighting," and it is the means by which he can bring order to his existence. That he was, as an artist, able to order his existence is perhaps what his fellow American poet Elizabeth Bishop had in mind when she said of him: "Somehow or other, by fair means or foul, and in the middle of our worst century so far, we have produced a magnificent poet."

Dolphin

> My Dolphin, you only guide me by surprise,
> a captive as Racine, the man of craft,
> drawn through his maze of iron composition°
> by the incomparable wandering voice of Phèdre.°

---

3. **iron composition** Racine wrote his verse in the strict classical form of the *alexandrine*, an iambic line having six feet (or twelve syllables).   4. **Phèdre** Racine based his tragedy *Phèdre* on a character from Greek mythology, the wife of Theseus, king of Athens. Phèdre fell madly in love with Hippolytus, Theseus' son by another marriage, who rejected her advances. Phèdre accused Hippolytus of violating her, and Theseus had the Gods send a monster to kill him. In remorse, Phèdre hanged herself.

When I was troubled in mind, you made for my body   5
caught in its hangman's-knot of sinking lines,
the glassy bowing and scraping of my will. . . .
I have sat and listened to too many
words of the collaborating muse,
and plotted perhaps too freely with my life,   10
not avoiding injury to others,
not avoiding injury to myself—
to ask compassion . . . this book, half fiction,
an eelnet made by man for the eel fighting—

my eyes have seen what my hand did.   15

SYLVIA PLATH (1932–1963)

If Robert Lowell is the most influential male American poet of our age, Sylvia Plath is quite likely the most influential female poet. They share an auto-biographical focus. For both of them, in fact, the life and the work are inseparable. And each at last became an almost legendary figure—Lowell because he assumed the role of America's poet laureate during the violent and chaotic 1960s; Plath because of the fevered sense of doom that haunts her work and her tragic life, a life that the emerging feminist movement of the 1970s made into a parable of the fate of a gifted woman in a male-dominated world.

As we have already noted, the central artistic and personal problem for Lowell was how to come to terms with his prominent New England family and its long involvement in American history. Sylvia Plath's sensibility, however, was formed in the claustrophobic atmosphere of a household whose roots in American life were shallow and incomplete. Her father, Otto Plath, was a Pole of German descent who, after emigrating to this country as a teenager, became a successful college teacher. His death when she was eight years old, and her mother's attempt to compensate for the loss by a suffocating and overly protective love, became the emotional timebomb that ticked ominously for the rest of Plath's life and formed the subject matter for her best work.

As an adult, Plath became obsessed with this family past, turning it into a bizarre and unbearably painful Freudian drama. But while she was growing up, this nightmare world seemed far away. She was blonde and attractive, the most exceptional individual at every school she attended, the lead in class plays and the outstanding writer in school magazines—an "American Dream Girl," in the words of one close friend. By the time she was a senior in high school, her verse was appearing in national publications. She went to Smith College on a scholarship where one of her classmates preserved this memory of her: "Writing poetry on a precise schedule, she sat with her back to whoever entered the room, as she circled words in the red letter thesaurus which had belonged to Otto Plath."

But there were also fits of incomprehensible depression on her part. And in 1953, during her junior year at Smith, Plath swallowed a handful of sleeping pills and crawled under the porch of the family home, where she was found barely alive two days later. Rushed to the hospital, she was revived and later spent several months at McLean's, the same New England institution for the emotionally disturbed to which Robert Lowell had been sent. She later wrote about this experience in the autobiographical novel *The Bell Jar*.

After graduating from Smith with high honors, Plath went to England on a Fulbright Fellowship. While studying literature at Cambridge University, she met and fell in love with Ted Hughes, then regarded as the most promising of England's younger generation of poets. (For an example of his work, see "Hawk Roosting," page 395.) Shortly before their marriage in 1956, she wrote a poem that conveys her awe of him and shows her own developing poetic gifts.

Ode for Ted

From under crunch of my man's boot
green oat-sprouts jut;
he names a lapwing, starts rabbits in a rout
legging it most nimble
to sprigged hedge of bramble,   5
stalks red fox, shrewd stoat.

Loam-humps, he says, moles shunt
up from delved worm-haunt;
blue fur, moles have; hefting chalk-hulled flint
he with rock splits open   10
knobbed quartz; flayed colors ripen
rich, brown, sudden in sunglint.

For his least look, scant acres yield:
each finger-furrowed field
heaves forth stalk, leaf, fruit-nubbed emerald;   15
bright grain sprung so rarely
he hauls to his will early;
at his hand's staunch hest, birds build.

Ringdoves roost well within his wood,
shirr songs to suit which mood   20
he saunters in; how but most glad
could be this adam's woman
when all earth his words do summon
leaps to laud such man's blood!

This poem is distinctive for the subtlety of its sounds and rhymes and the richness of its language, especially in the images of fecundity and power. The speaker mythologizes the beloved as the natural man *par excellence*, at one with nature and making nature yield to his touch. He is a sort of wood spirit; he is also an Adam naming the beasts of the field and forest.

"Sow," a poem written a year or so later, is perhaps a more characteristic piece of work. It has the tone of conversational matter-of-factness that became so important a part of Plath's poetry, especially when she adopted the scalding irony that became her distinctive poetic signature. This poem also has a linguistic playfulness throughout—in phrases like "feat-foot ninnies / Shrilling her hulk" (lines 21–22), and in the way Plath encrusts the huge animal with myth and legend and then lets all the additions drop away like the dried mud on its back. A fascination with and faint repugnance for the femaleness of this most female of animals is also evident.

 Sow

God knows how our neighbor managed to breed
His great sow:
Whatever his shrewd secret, he kept it hid

In the same way
He kept the sow—impounded from public stare,   5
Prize ribbon and pig show.

But one dusk our questions commended us to a tour
Through his lantern-lit
Maze of barns to the lintel of the sunk sty door

To gape at it: 10
This was no rose-and-larkspurred china suckling
With a penny slot

For thrifty children, nor dolt pig ripe for heckling,
About to be
Glorified for prime flesh and golden crackling   15

In a parsley halo;
Nor even one of the common barnyard sows,
Mire-smirched, blowzy,

Maunching thistle and knotweed on her snout-cruise—
Bloat tun of milk   20
On the move, hedged by a litter of feat-foot ninnies

Shrilling her hulk
To halt for a swig at the pink teats. No. This vast
Brobdingnag° bulk

Of a sow lounged belly-bedded on that black compost,   25
Fat-rutted eyes
Dream-filmed. What a vision of ancient hoghood must

Thus wholly engross
The great grandam!—our marvel blazoned a knight,
Helmed, in cuirass,°   30

24. Brobdingnag land where Swift's Gulliver finds everything disproportionately huge
30. cuirass piece of armor protecting chest

Unhorsed and shredded in the grove of combat
By a grisly-bristled
Boar, fabulous enough to straddle that sow's heat.

But our farmer whistled,
Then, with a jocular fist thwacked the barrel nape,   35
And the green-copse-castled

Pig hove, letting legend like dried mud drop,
Slowly, grunt
On grunt, up in the flickering light to shape

A monument   40
Prodigious in gluttonies as that hog whose want
Made lean Lent°

Of kitchen slops and, stomaching no constraint,
Proceeded to swill
The seven troughed seas and every earthquaking continent.   45

In 1958, Plath returned to the United States with Hughes to teach for a
year at Smith. She then decided to audit a poetry class taught by Robert
Lowell at Boston University. Lowell was about to publish *Life Studies*, the
collection that would establish him as the most important American poet of
his day. Like Anne Sexton, another student in the class who would also gain
recognition later on (and also end her life in suicide), Plath was deeply
influenced by Lowell's accomplishment—making the microscopic inspection
of intimate and often unflattering aspects of personal experience the subject
matter for his verse, while working skillfully with traditional forms as if better
to win a hearing for the excesses of his themes. She ultimately took Lowell's
"confessional" approach a step further, using her work to map the psychic
deathscape in which she came to travel.

By the time she was back in England in 1960, Plath's writing began to
exhibit the dissonant tonal effects and hallucinatory glow for which she later
became noted. What was most characteristic of her work, however, were
startling images and audacious metaphors.

Metaphors

I'm a riddle in nine syllables,
An elephant, a ponderous house,
A melon strolling on two tendrils.
O red fruit, ivory, fine timbers!
This loaf's big with its yeasty rising.
Money's new-minted in this fat purse.
I'm a means, a stage, a cow in calf.
I've eaten a bag of green apples,
Boarded the train there's no getting off.

42. **Lent** forty days before Easter regarded as season of penitence

This poem is, obviously enough, an exercise in metaphor. Plath uses several popular clichés about pregnancy and constructs the poem in nine lines to give the reader a hint about the meaning. Yet, there is an underlying autobiographical content even in this playful work. At the time it was written, early in 1959, Plath was seeing doctors about her own temporary inability to conceive, and so in some sense she, like the poem itself, was a "riddle" to be solved.

Mirror

I am silver and exact. I have no preconceptions.
Whatever I see I swallow immediately
Just as it is, unmisted by love or dislike.
I am not cruel, only truthful—
The eye of a little god, four-cornered.   5
Most of the time I meditate on the opposite wall.
It is pink, with speckles. I have looked at it so long
I think it is a part of my heart. But it flickers.
Faces and darkness separate us over and over.

Now I am a lake. A woman bends over me,   10
Searching my reaches for what she really is.
Then she turns to those liars, the candles or the moon.
I see her back, and reflect it faithfully.
She rewards me with tears and an agitation of hands.
I am important to her. She comes and goes.   15
Each morning it is her face that replaces the darkness.
In me she has drowned a young girl, and in me an old woman
Rises toward her day after day, like a terrible fish.

"Mirror" uses an extended metaphor that becomes increasingly ominous as the poem progresses. At the beginning the mirror "swallows" what it sees. Then it becomes a lake—not a body of water in which one drowns, as the mythological figure Narcissus did upon falling in love with his own image, but rather a menacing deep where predatory fishes of the self swim, ready to rise up and eat one's youth.

By 1961, Plath and Hughes were living in the English countryside. She had one child, a daughter, and was pregnant again. Outwardly her life involved the conventional roles of wife and mother. Yet the marriage was becoming unstable, and an angry and darkly surreal quality entered her work:

Zoo Keeper's Wife

I can stay awake all night, if need be—
Cold as an eel, without eyelids.
Like a dead lake the dark envelops me,
Blueblack, a spectacular plum fruit.

No airbubbles start from my heart, I am lungless   5
And ugly, my belly a silk stocking
Where the heads and tails of my sisters decompose.
Look, they are melting like coins in the powerful juices—

The spidery jaws, the spine bones bared for a moment
Like the white lines on a blueprint.   10
Should I stir, I think this pink and purple plastic
Guts bag would clack like a child's rattle,
Old grievances jostling each other, so many loose teeth.
But what do you know about that
My fat pork, my marrowy sweetheart, face-to-the-wall?   15
Some things of this world are indigestible.

You wooed me with the wolf-headed fruit bats
Hanging from their scorched hooks in the moist
Fug of the Small Mammal House.
The armadillo dozed in his sandbin   20
Obscene and bald as a pig, the white mice
Multiplied to infinity like angels on a pinhead
Out of sheer boredom. Tangled in the sweat-wet sheets
I remember the bloodied chicks and the quartered rabbits.

You checked the diet charts and took me to play   25
With the boa constrictor in the Fellows' Garden.
I pretended I was the Tree of Knowledge.
I entered your bible, I boarded your ark
With the sacred baboon in his wig and wax ears
And the bear-furred, bird-eating spider   30
Clambering round its glass box like an eight-fingered hand.
I can't get it out of my mind

How our courtship lit the tindery cages—
Your two-horned rhinoceros opened a mouth
Dirty as a bootsole and big as a hospital sink   35
For my cube of sugar: its bog breath
Gloved my arm to the elbow.
The snails blew kisses like black apples.
Nightly now I flog apes owls bears sheep
Over their iron stile. And still don't sleep.   40

In contrast to the robustness of an earlier work such as "Ode for Ted," this poem has a nasty reptilian coldness. Plath gives readers a nightmare world where nature is perverted and decadent, and where sex and procreation are seen as furtive and obscene. The allusion to the Garden and the Tree of Knowledge equates sexuality with original sin and with humanity's plunge into moral darkness. The male is corrupter. The exuberantly powerful Adam of "Ode for Ted" is now the devious seducer who causes the Fall, and the speaker's capitulation to his courtship imprisons her in a waking nightmare.

Plath's separation from her husband in 1962 increased her vulnerability to a menacing past that had never released its hold on her. She began to write almost frantically, as if poetry were the only salvation from the thoughts of suicide that increasingly obsessed her. The past and present came together in her strongest and most controversial poem, "Daddy."

Daddy

You do not do, you do not do
Any more, black shoe
In which I have lived like a foot
For thirty years, poor and white,
Barely daring to breathe or Achoo.   5

Daddy, I have had to kill you.
You died before I had time——
Marble-heavy, bag full of God,
Ghastly statue with one grey toe
Big as a Frisco seal   10

And a head in the freakish Atlantic
Where it pours bean green over blue
In the waters off beautiful Nauset.°
I used to pray to recover you.
Ach, du.°   15

In the German tongue, in the Polish town
Scraped flat by the roller
Of wars, wars, wars.
But the name of the town is common.
My Polack friend   20

Says there are a dozen or two:
So I never could tell where you
Put your foot, your root,
I never could talk to you.
The tongue stuck in my jaw.   25

It stuck in a barb wire snare.
Ich, ich, ich, ich,°
I could hardly speak.
I thought every German was you.
And the language obscene   30

13. **Nauset** a place on Cape Cod, Massachusetts   15. **Ach, du** German for "Oh, you"
27. **ich** German for "I"

An engine, an engine
Chuffing me off like a Jew.
A Jew to Dachau, Auschwitz, Belsen.°
I began to talk like a Jew.
I think I may well be a Jew.   35

The snows of the Tyrol, the clear beer of Vienna
Are not very pure or true.
With my gypsy ancestress and my weird luck
And my Taroc° pack and my Taroc pack
I may be a bit of a Jew.   40

I have always been scared of *you*,
With your Luftwaffe, your gobbledygoo.
And your neat moustache
And your Aryan eye, bright blue,
Panzer-man, panzer-man, O You—   45

Not God but a swastika
So black no sky could squeak through.
Every woman adores a Fascist,
The boot in the face, the brute
Brute heart of a brute like you.   50

You stand at the blackboard, daddy,
In the picture I have of you,
A cleft in your chin° instead of your foot
But no less a devil for that, no not
Any less the black man who   55

Bit my pretty red heart in two.
I was ten when they buried you.
At twenty I tried to die
And get back, back, back to you.
I thought even the bones would do.   60

But they pulled me out of the sack,
And they stuck me together with glue,
And then I knew what to do.
I made a model of you,
A man in black with a Meinkampf° look   65

And a love of the rack and the screw.
And I said I do, I do.
So daddy, I'm finally through.

---

33. **Dachau, Auschwitz, Belsen** sites of the most infamous of the Nazi concentration camps   39. **Taroc** fourteenth-century Italian card game   53. **cleft in chin** The Devil was said to have a cloven foot.   65. **Meinkampf** *Mein Kampf,* Hitler's autobiography and manifesto for the Nazi movement

The black telephone's off at the root,
The voices just can't worm through.   70

If I've killed one man, I've killed two—
The vampire who said he was you
And drank my blood for a year,
Seven years, if you want to know.
Daddy, you can lie back now.   75

There's a stake° in your fat black heart
And the villagers never liked you.
They are dancing and stamping on you.
They always *knew* it was you.
Daddy, daddy, you bastard, I'm through.   80

Later on, when this poem became something like an anthem for the women's liberation movement, critic Irving Howe wrote: "What we have here is a revenge fantasy, feeding upon filial love-hatred, and thereby mostly of clinical interest. But seemingly aware that the merely clinical can't provide the materials for a satisfying poem, Sylvia Plath tries to enlarge upon the personal plight, give meaning to the personal outcry, by fancying the girl as the victim of a Nazi father." What Howe and others objected to was Plath's appropriation of the Holocaust as a metaphor for the father-daughter-husband relationship. They felt that this trivialized the preeminent tragedy of modern history and gave a personal relationship a weight it was incapable of bearing. Yet it might also be said that this extreme metaphor makes the poem work. The allusion shows how the memory of the dead father persecutes the speaker, attempts to kill and obliterate her, as the Nazis did the Jews. The relationship Plath is discussing here is a war in which there are only tyrants and victims. The Nazi becomes a Dracula figure as well, not only killing his prey but, even worse, draining her essence and making her one of the walking dead.

On one level this poem is intensely private, requiring a knowledge of such facts as Otto Plath's German background and the wrecked marriage to Hughes, which had lasted seven years before coming apart. But Plath goes from the dark world of an individual child who has been betrayed to the common experience of *all* women: "Every woman adores a Fascist, / The boot in the face, the brute / Brute heart of a brute like you." (lines 48–50). The subject of the poem is thus not only the persecution of the speaker, but also the persecution of women by men in general. By its conclusion, "Daddy" has become an attempt to use language to exorcise the demons haunting all women.

The imagery of the Holocaust is also present in another poem written during the last few months of Plath's life:

---

76. **stake** According to myth, a vampire could be killed only by driving a stake through its heart.

Lady Lazarus

I have done it again.
One year in every ten
I manage it——

A sort of walking miracle, my skin
Bright as a Nazi lampshade,°   5
My right foot

A paperweight,
My face a featureless, fine
Jew linen.

Peel off the napkin   10
O my enemy.
Do I terrify?——

The nose, the eye pits, the full set of teeth?
The sour breath
Will vanish in a day.   15

Soon, soon the flesh
The grave cave ate will be
At home on me

And I a smiling woman.
I am only thirty.   20
And like the cat I have nine times to die.

This is Number Three.
What a trash
To annihilate each decade.

What a million filaments.   25
The peanut-crunching crowd
Shoves in to see

Them unwrap me hand and foot——
The big strip tease.
Gentlemen, ladies   30

These are my hands
My knees.
I may be skin and bone,

Nevertheless, I am the same, identical woman.
The first time it happened I was ten.   35
It was an accident.

---

5. **Nazi lampshade** In some cases the Nazis made shades from the skin of Jews they had killed.

The second time I meant
To last it out and not come back at all.
I rocked shut

As a seashell.   40
They had to call and call
And pick the worms off me like sticky pearls.

Dying
Is an art, like everything else.
I do it exceptionally well.   45

I do it so it feels like hell.
I do it so it feels real.
I guess you could say I've a call.

It's easy enough to do it in a cell.
It's easy enough to do it and stay put.   50
It's the theatrical

Comeback in broad day
To the same place, the same face, the same brute
Amused shout:

'A miracle!'   55
That knocks me out.
There is a charge

For the eyeing of my scars, there is a charge
For the hearing of my heart——
It really goes.   60

And there is a charge, a very large charge
For a word or a touch
Or a bit of blood

Or a piece of my hair or my clothes.
So, so, Herr Doktor.   65
So, Herr Enemy.

I am your opus,
I am your valuable,
The pure gold baby

That melts to a shriek.   70
I turn and burn.
Do not think I underestimate your great concern.

Ash, ash—
You poke and stir.
Flesh, bone, there is nothing there——   75

A cake of soap,
A wedding ring,
A gold filling.

Herr God, Herr Lucifer
Beware   80
Beware.

Out of the ash
I rise with my red hair
And I eat men like air.

The speaker is a Jew returned from the crematorium, Lazarus raised from
the dead, a woman revived from another suicide attempt. Yet none of these
rebirths is a relief. She goes from one death to the promise of another. She is a
cat who has exhausted three of her nine lives; instead of this being offered as a
breathing space, however, survival means that she has six more deaths to
endure.

The second suicide attempt to which Plath refers in lines 41–42 is the one
that occurred while she was at Smith College. ("They had to call and call /
And pick the worms off me like sticky pearls.") She discusses it with the same
clinical detachment that she gives to the other aspects of her death wish.
What distinguishes this poem is the tone of outrage that takes over half-way
through, beginning with lines 57 and 58: "There is a charge / For the eyeing
of my scars . . ." By the end of "Lady Lazarus," the speaker sees herself as a
Jew again, her physical being destroyed, her fat rendered into soap and her
jawbone prodded for a gold filling. But her spirit has been released and rises
phoenix-like to exact its revenge.

By late 1962, Plath had moved to London and was living alone with her
two small children in a house once occupied by the Irish poet W. B. Yeats. Ill
with fever and subject to blackouts, she felt that even the outer world was
conspiring against her as the city sank into paralysis caused by its worst
snowstorm in years. She and the children sat huddled around a heater,
isolated and alone. She felt that death was everywhere, forming an almost
palpable presence. She wrote about it in "Death & Co.," a poem in which she
sees Death as a duality—as a predator with the blank eyes of a figure in a
William Blake watercolor who regards her as red meat to be eaten and as a
long-haired and attractive man, narcissistically sexual, who craves woman's
love. There are wonderful touches in the poem, such as the vision of babies in
the hospital icebox with "flutings of their Ionian / Death-gowns" perfectly
Greek in repose. There is also the figure of the speaker, very still, preternaturally aware of Death in both its guises, trying to let each one of them
pass her by. A few weeks after the poem was written, Sylvia Plath attempted
suicide for the last time.

Death & Co.

Two, of course there are two.
It seems perfectly natural now——
The one who never looks up, whose eyes are lidded
And balled, like Blake's,
Who exhibits   5

The birthmarks that are his trademark——
The scald scar of water,
The nude
Verdigris of the condor.
I am red meat. His beak   10

Claps sidewise: I am not his yet.
He tells me how badly I photograph.
He tells me how sweet
The babies look in their hospital
Icebox, a simple   15

Frill at the neck,
Then the flutings of their Ionian
Death-gowns,
Then two little feet.
He does not smile or smoke.   20

The other does that,
His hair long and plausive.
Bastard
Masturbating a glitter,
He wants to be loved.   25

I do not stir.
The frost makes a flower,
The dew makes a star,
The dead bell,
The dead bell.   30

Somebody's done for.

In evaluating Plath's achievement, one critic has aptly termed it "a holy scream, a splendid agony." By the end of her life, death, as she had written, had become an art at which she was extremely accomplished. But the operant word in this poetic assertion is "art." Alongside the flamboyant victim in Plath was a determined artist using poetry to make her experience something more than pain, trying to force her particular circumstances to yield larger truths. This, far more than the sensationalism of her verse, is what assures Sylvia Plath an enduring relevance in modern American poetry.

7

POEMS FOR FURTHER READING

Lord Randal

"O where hae ye been, Lord Randal, my son?
O where hae ye been, my handsome young man?"
"I hae been to the wild wood; mother, make my bed soon,
For I'm weary wi' hunting, and fain wald° lie down."   *would gladly*

"Where gat° ye your dinner, Lord Randal, my son?   *where did you get*   5
Where gat ye your dinner, my handsome young man?"
"I dined wi' my true-love; mother, make my bed soon,
For I'm weary wi' hunting, and fain wald lie down."

"What gat ye to your dinner, Lord Randal, my son?
What gat ye to your dinner, my handsome young man?"   10
"I gat eels boiled in broo;° mother, make my bed soon,   *broth*
For I'm weary wi' hunting, and fain wald lie down."

"What became of your bloodhounds, Lord Randal, my son?
What became of your bloodhounds, my handsome young man?"
"O they swelled and they died; mother, make my bed soon,   15
For I'm weary wi' hunting, and fain wald lie down."

"O I fear ye are poisoned, Lord Randal, my son!
O I fear ye are poisoned, my handsome young man!"
"O yes! I am poisoned; mother, make my bed soon,
For I'm sick at the heart, and I fain wald lie down."   20

Anonymous

Get Up and Bar the Door

The wind it blew from east to west,
And it blew all over the floor;
Said old John Jones to Jane, his wife,
"Get up and shut the door."

"My hands are in the sausage meat,   5
So I cannot get them free;
And if you do not shut the door yourself,
It never will be shut by me."

Then they agreed between the two
And gave their hands on it,   10
That whoever spoke a word the first
Was to rise and shut the door.

There were two travelers journeying late,
A-journeying across the hill,
And they came to old John Jones's   15
By the light from the open door.

"Does this house to a rich man belong?
Or does it belong to a poor?"
But never a word would the stubborn two say
On account of shutting the door.   20

The travelers said good-evening to them,
And then they said good-day;
But never a word would the stubborn two say
On account of shutting the door.

And so they drank of the liquor strong,   25
And so they drank of the ale:
"For since we have got a house of our own,
I'm sure we can take of our fill."

And then they ate of the sausage meat
And sopped their bread in the fat;   30
And at every bite old Jane she thought,
"May the devil slip down with that."

Then says the one to the other,
"Here, man, take out my knife,
And while you shave the old man's chin,   35
I will be kissing the wife."

"You have eat my meat and drinked my ale,
And would you make of my old wife a whore?"
"John Jones, you have spoken the first word,
Now get up and shut the door."   40

Anonymous

Weep You No More, Sad Fountains

Weep you no more, sad fountains;
    What need you flow so fast?
Look how the snowy mountains
    Heaven's sun doth gently waste.
But my sun's heavenly eyes   5
    View not your weeping,
    That now lies sleeping
Softly, now softly lies
    Sleeping.

> Sleep is a reconciling,   10
>   A rest that peace begets.
> Doth not the sun rise smiling
>   When fair at even he sets?
> Rest you then, rest, sad eyes,
>   Melt not in weeping   15
>   While she lies sleeping
>   Softly, now softly lies
>   Sleeping.

Anonymous

They Flee from Me

> They flee from me, that sometime did me seek,
> With naked foot stalking in my chamber.
> I have seen them, gentle, tame, and meek,
> That now are wild, and do not remember
> That sometime they put themselves in danger   5
> To take bread at my hand; and now they range,
> Busily seeking with a continual change.
>
> Thankèd be Fortune it hath been otherwise,
> Twenty times better; but once in special.
> In thin array, after a pleasant guise,   10
> When her loose gown from her shoulders did fall,
> And she me caught in her arms long and small.
> And therewith all sweetly did me kiss
> And softly said, "Dear heart, how like you this?"
>
> It was no dream, I lay broad waking.   15
> But all is turned, thorough° my gentleness,   *through*
> Into a strange fashion of forsaking;
> And I have leave to go, of her goodness,
> And she also to use newfangleness.°   *desire for novelty*
> But since that I so kindly am servèd,   20
> I fain would know what she hath deservèd.

Sir Thomas Wyatt (1503?–1542)

On the Life of Man

> What is our life? a play of passion;
> Our mirth the music of division;°
> Our mothers' wombs the tiring-houses° be
> Where we are dressed for this short comedy.
> Heaven the judicious sharp spectator is,   5

2. **division** variation of a musical theme   3. **tiring-houses** dressing rooms in the Elizabethan theater

That sits and marks still who doth act amiss;
Our graves that hide us from the searching sun
Are like drawn curtains when the play is done.
Thus march we, playing, to our latest rest,
Only we die in earnest—that's no jest.   10

Sir Walter Raleigh (1552–1618)

Who Will in Fairest Book of Nature

Who will in fairest book of Nature know
How virtue may best lodged in beauty be,
Let him but learn of love to read in thee,
Stella, those fair lines which true goodness show.
There shall he find all vices' overthrow,   5
Not by rude force, but sweetest sovereignty
Of reason, from whose light those night-birds fly,
That inward sun in thine eyes shineth so.
And, not content to be perfection's heir
Thyself, dost strive all minds that way to move,   10
Who mark in thee what is in thee most fair.
So while thy beauty draws the heart to love,
  As fast thy virtue bends that love to good.
  But, ah, Desire still cries, 'Give me some food.'

Sir Philip Sidney (1554–1586)

Since There's No Help

Since there's no help, come let us kiss and part;
Nay, I have done, you get no more of me,
And I am glad, yea, glad with all my heart
That thus so cleanly I myself can free;
Shake hands forever, cancel all our vows,   5
And when we meet at any time again,
Be it not seen in either of our brows
That we one jot of former love retain.
Now at the last gasp of Love's latest breath,
When, his pulse failing, Passion speechless lies,   10
When Faith is kneeling by his bed of death,
And Innocence is closing up his eyes,
Now, if thou wouldst, when all have given him over,
From death to life thou mightst him yet recover.

Michael Drayton (1563–1631)

The Passionate Shepherd to His Love

Come live with me and be my love,
And we will all the pleasures prove°   *try*
That valleys, groves, hills, and fields,
Woods, or steepy mountain yields.

And we will sit upon the rocks,   5
Seeing the shepherds feed their flocks,
By shallow rivers to whose falls
Melodious birds sing madrigals.

And I will make thee beds of roses
And a thousand fragrant posies,   10
A cap of flowers, and a kirtle°   *tunic*
Embroidered all with leaves of myrtle;

A gown made of the finest wool
Which from our pretty lambs we pull;
Fair lined slippers for the cold,   15
With buckles of the purest gold;

A belt of straw and ivy buds,
With coral clasps and amber studs:
And if these pleasures may thee move,
Come live with me, and be my love.   20

The shepherd swains° shall dance and sing   *youths*
For thy delight each May morning:
If these delights thy mind may move,
Then live with me and be my love.

Christopher Marlowe (1564–1593)

That Time of Year

That time of year thou mayst in me behold
When yellow leaves, or none, or few, do hang
Upon those boughs which shake against the cold,
Bare ruined choirs where late the sweet birds sang.
In me thou see'st the twilight of such day   5
As after sunset fadeth in the west,
Which by and by black night doth take away,
Death's second self, that seals up all in rest.
In me thou see'st the glowing of such fire,
That on the ashes of his youth doth lie   10
As the deathbed whereon it must expire,
Consumed with that which it was nourished by.
  This thou perceivest, which makes thy love more strong,
  To love that well which thou must leave ere long.

William Shakespeare (1564–1616)

When in Disgrace with Fortune

When, in disgrace with Fortune and men's eyes,
I all alone beweep my outcast state,
And trouble deaf heaven with my bootless° cries,   *hopeless*
And look upon myself and curse my fate,
Wishing me like to one more rich in hope,   5
Featured like him, like him with friends possessed,
Desiring this man's art, and that man's scope,
With what I most enjoy contented least;
Yet in these thoughts myself almost despising,
Haply° I think on thee, and then my state,   *perhaps* 10
Like to the lark at break of day arising
From sullen earth, sings hymns at heaven's gate;
 For thy sweet love rememb'red such wealth brings,
 That then I scorn to change my state with kings.

William Shakespeare (1564–1616)

Elegy

Written with his own hand in the Tower before his execution.

My prime of youth is but a frost of cares;
 My feast of joy is but a dish of pain;
My crop of corn is but a field of tares;°   *weeds*
 And all my good is but vain hope of gain:
The day is past, and yet I saw no sun;   5
And now I live, and now my life is done.

My tale was heard, and yet it was not told;
 My fruit is fallen, and yet my leaves are green;
My youth is spent, and yet I am not old;
 I saw the world, and yet I was not seen: 10
My thread is cut, and yet it is not spun;
And now I live, and now my life is done.

I sought my death, and found it in my womb;
 I looked for life, and saw it was a shade;
I trod the earth, and knew it was my tomb;   15
 And now I die, and now I was but made:
My glass is full, and now my glass is run;
And now I live, and now my life is done.

Chidiock Tichborne (1568?–1586)

Death Be Not Proud

Death be not proud, though some have callèd thee
Mighty and dreadful, for thou art not so;
For those whom thou think'st thou dost overthrow
Die not, poor Death, nor yet canst thou kill me.
From rest and sleep, which but thy pictures° be,   *likenesses* 5
Much pleasure; then from thee much more must flow,
And soonest° our best men with thee do go,   *without complaint*
Rest of their bones, and soul's delivery.
Thou art slave to Fate, Chance, kings, and desperate men,
And dost with Poison, War, and Sickness dwell;   10
And poppy or charms can make us sleep as well,
And better than thy stroke; why swell'st° thou then?   *puff with pride*
One short sleep past, we wake eternally
And death shall be no more; Death, thou shalt die.

John Donne (1572–1631)

A Valediction: Forbidding Mourning

As virtuous men pass mildly away,
    And whisper to their souls to go,
While some of their sad friends do say,
    The breath goes now, and some say, no:

So let us melt, and make no noise,   5
    No tear-floods, nor sigh-tempests move;
'Twere profanation of our joys
    To tell the laity° our love.   *common people*

Moving of th' earth brings harms and fears,
    Men reckon what it did and meant,   10
But trepidation of the spheres,°
    Though greater far, is innocent.°

Dull sublunary° lovers' love
    (Whose soul is sense) cannot admit
Absence, because it doth remove   15
    Those things which elemented° it.   *comprised*

---

11. trepidation of the spheres a reference to the Renaissance theory that celestial bodies were
capable of unexpected and spasmodic movements within their orbits   **12. innocent** not
worrisome, as earthquakes are, because they are not experienced first hand   **13. sublunary**
below the moon and affected by its notorious changeability

But we by a love so much refined,
  That ourselves know not what it is,
Inter-assurèd of the mind,
  Care less, eyes, lips, and hands to miss.   20

Our two souls therefore, which are one,
  Though I must go, endure not yet
A breach, but an expansion,
  Like gold to airy thinness beat.

If they be two, they are two so   25
  As stiff twin compasses are two;
Thy soul the fixed foot, makes no show
  To move, but doth, if th' other do.

And though it in the center sit,
  Yet when the other far doth roam,   30
It leans, and hearkens after it,
  And grows erect, as that comes home.

Such wilt thou be to me, who must
  Like th' other foot, obliquely run;
Thy firmness makes my circle just,   35
  And makes me end, where I begun.

John Donne (1572–1631)

Come, My Celia

Come, my Celia, let us prove,°   *try*
While we can, the sports of love;
Time will not be ours forever:
He at length our good will sever.
Spend not, then, his gifts in vain;   5
Suns that set may rise again,
But if once we lose this light,
'Tis with us perpetual night.
Why should we defer our joys?
Fame and rumor are but toys.   10
Cannot we delude the eyes
Of a few poor household spies?
Or his easier ears beguile,
Thus removèd by our wile?
'Tis no sin love's fruits to steal,   15
But the sweet thefts to reveal;
To be taken, to be seen,
These have crimes accounted been.

Ben Jonson (1572–1637)

To the Virgins, to Make Much of Time

Gather ye rosebuds while ye may,
　Old Time is still a-flying;
And this same flower that smiles today
　Tomorrow will be dying.

The glorious lamp of heaven, the Sun,　　　　　5
　The higher he's a-getting,
The sooner will his race be run,
　And nearer he's to setting.

That age is best which is the first,
　When youth and blood are warmer;　　　　　10
But being spent, the worse, and worst
　Times still succeed the former.

Then be not coy, but use your time;
　And while ye may, go marry;
For having lost but once your prime,　　　　　15
　You may forever tarry.

Robert Herrick (1591–1674)

Go Lovely Rose

Go, lovely rose,
Tell her that wastes her time and me,
　That now she knows,
When I resemble° her to thee,　　　　　*compare*
　How sweet and fair she seems to be.　　　　　5

Tell her that's young,
And shuns to have her graces spied,
　That hadst thou sprung
In deserts where no men abide,
　Thou must have uncommended died.　　　　　10

Small is the worth
Of beauty from the light retired:
　Bid her come forth,
Suffer her self to be desired,
　And not blush so to be admired.　　　　　15

Then die, that she
The common fate of all things rare
　May read in thee,
How small a part of time they share,
　That are so wondrous sweet and fair.　　　　　20

Edmund Waller (1606–1687)

How Soon Hath Time

How soon hath Time, the subtle thief of youth,
   Stoln on his wing my three and twentieth year!
   My hasting days fly on with full career,
   But my late spring no bud or blossom show'th.
Perhaps my semblance might deceive the truth,   5
   That I to manhood am arrived so near,
   And inward ripeness doth much less appear,
   That some more timely-happy spirits endu'th.°   *endows*
Yet be it less or more, or soon or slow,
   It shall be still in strictest measure even°   10
   To that same lot, however mean or high,
Toward which Time leads me, and the will of Heaven;
   All is, if I have grace to use it so,
   As ever in my great Taskmaster's eye.

John Milton (1608–1674)

On His Blindness

When I consider how my light is spent
   Ere half my days, in this dark world and wide,
   And that one talent° which is death to hide
   Lodged with me useless, though my soul more bent
To serve therewith my Maker, and present   5
   My true account, lest he returning chide;
   "Doth God exact day-labor, light denied?"
   I fondly° ask; but Patience to prevent   *foolishly*
That murmur, soon replies, "God doth not need
   Either man's work or his own gifts; who best   10
   Bear his mild yoke, they serve him best. His state
Is kingly. Thousands at his bidding speed
   And post o'er land and ocean without rest:
   They also serve who only stand and wait."

John Milton (1608–1674)

To Lucasta, Going to the Wars

Tell me not, Sweet, I am unkind
That from the nunnery
Of thy chaste breast and quiet mind,
To war and arms I fly.

---

10. even adequate; whenever the inner growth appears and however great it is, Milton will find it adequate to the destiny God has prepared for him   **3. talent** In a pun, Milton compares his literary talent to the Parable of the Talents (Matthew 25: 14–30) in which a servant is rebuked for not putting his talent (a unit of money) to use.

True, a new mistress now I chase,   5
The first foe in the field;
And with a stronger faith embrace
A sword, a horse, a shield.

Yet this inconstancy is such
As you too shall adore;   10
I could not love thee, Dear, so much,
Loved I not honor more.

Richard Lovelace (1618–1658)

The Garden

How vainly men themselves amaze°   *become upset*
To win the palm, the oak, or bays,°
And their incessant labors see
Crowned from some single herb, or tree,
Whose short and narrow-vergèd shade   5
Does prudently their toils upbraid;
While all flowers and all trees do close
To weave the garlands of repose!

Fair Quiet, have I found thee here,
And Innocence, thy sister dear?   10
Mistaken long, I sought you then
In busy companies of men.
Your sacred plants, if here below,
Only among the plants will grow;
Society is all but rude°   *barbarous* 15
To° this delicious solitude.   *compared to*

No white nor red was ever seen
So am'rous as this lovely green.
Fond lovers, cruel as their flame,
Cut in these trees their mistress' name: 20
Little, alas, they know, or heed
How far these beauties hers exceed!
Fair trees, wheresoe'er your barks I wound,
No name shall but your own be found.

When we have run our passion's heat,   25
Love hither makes his best retreat.
The gods, that mortal beauty chase,
Still in a tree did end their race:
Apollo hunted Daphne so,
Only that she might laurel grow;   30
And Pan did after Syrinx speed,
Not as a nymph, but for a reed.°

2. palm, oak, or bays symbols, respectively, for athletic, political, and poetic achievement
32. but for a reed Charmed by her beauty, Apollo pursued Daphne, who, almost overtaken,
prayed for aid and was transformed by the gods into a laurel tree. Syrinx was similarly pursued by
Pan and, at her own prayer, turned into a reed that Pan later made into a flute.

What wondrous life is this I lead!
Ripe apples drop about my head;
The luscious clusters of the vine   35
Upon my mouth do crush their wine;
The nectarine and curious° peach   *exquisite*
Into my hands themselves do reach;
Stumbling on melons, as I pass,
Insnared with flowers, I fall on grass.   40

    Meanwhile the mind, from pleasure less,
Withdraws into its happiness;
The mind, that ocean where each kind
Does straight its own resemblance find;
Yet it creates, transcending these,   45
Far other worlds and other seas,
Annihilating all that's made
To a green thought in a green shade.

    Here at the fountain's sliding foot,
Or at some fruit tree's mossy root,   50
Casting the body's vest° aside,
My soul into the boughs does glide:
There, like a bird, it sits and sings,
Then whets° and combs its silver wings,   *grooms*
And, till prepared for longer flight,   55
Waves in its plumes the various° light.   *multicolored*

    Such was that happy garden-state,
While man there walked without a mate:
After a place so pure, and sweet,
What other help could yet be meet°!   *appropriate* 60
But 'twas beyond a mortal's share
To wander solitary there:
Two paradises 'twere in one
To live in paradise alone.

    How well the skillful gardener drew   65
Of flowers and herbs this dial° new,
Where, from above, the milder sun
Does through a fragrant zodiac run;
And as it works, th' industrious bee
Computes its time as well as we!   70
How could such sweet and wholesome hours
Be reckoned but with herbs and flowers?

Andrew Marvell (1621–1678)

---

51. vest vestment or clothings; in the Renaissance, the body was thought to be a vestment for the soul   **66. dial** The imagined garden is shaped like a sundial.

To the Memory of Mr. Oldham°

Farewell, too little, and too lately known,
Whom I began to think and call my own;
For sure our souls were near allied, and thine
Cast in the same poetic mold with mine.
One common note on either lyre did strike,   5
And knaves and fools we both abhorred alike.
To the same goal did both our studies drive;
The last set out the soonest did arrive.
Thus Nisus° fell upon the slippery place,
While his young friend performed and won the race.   10
O early ripe! to thy abundant store
What could advancing age have added more?
It might (what nature never gives the young)
Have taught the numbers° of thy native tongue.   *rhythms*
But satire needs not those, and wit will shine   15
Through the harsh cadence of a rugged line.
A noble error, and but seldom made,
When poets are by too much force betrayed.
Thy generous fruits, though gathered ere their prime,
Still showed a quickness; and maturing time   20
But mellows what we write to the dull sweets of rhyme.
Once more, hail and farewell; farewell, thou young,
But ah too short, Marcellus° of our tongue;
Thy brows with ivy, and with laurels bound;
But fate and gloomy night encompass thee around.   25

John Dryden (1631–1700)

A Satirical Elegy on the Death of a Late Famous General°

His Grace! impossible! what dead!
Of old age too, and in his bed!
And could that mighty warrior fall,
And so inglorious after all!
Well, since he's gone, no matter how,   5
The last loud trump° must wake him now;   *trumpet*
And, trust me, as the noise grows stronger,
He'll wish to sleep a little longer.

Mr. Oldham John Oldham (1653–1683), another poet who, like Dryden, wrote satirical verse   **9. Nisus** In an episode of Virgil's *Aeneid*, Nisus fell when leading a race but managed to trip his nearest competitor so that his friend Euryalus could win.   **23. Marcellus** a nephew of the Roman emperor Augustus who died at age 20   **Famous General** The object of this satire is John Churchill, first Duke of Marlborough (1650–1722), English soldier and statesman.

And could he be indeed so old
As by the news-papers we're told!   10
Threescore, I think, is pretty high,
'Twas time in conscience he should die:
This world he cumber'd° long enough,   *encumbered*
He burnt his candle to a snuff,
And that's the reason some folks think,   15
He left behind *so great a stink*.

Behold his funeral appears,
Nor widows sighs, nor orphans tears,
Wont at such time each heart to pierce,
Attend the progress of his herse.   20
But what of that, his friends may say,
He had those honours in his day;
True to his profit and his pride,
He made them weep before he dy'd.

   Come hither, all ye empty things   25
Ye bubbles rais'd by breath of kings,
Who float upon the tide of state,
Come hither, and behold your fate:
Let pride be taught by this rebuke,
How very mean a thing's a D—ke;   30
From all his ill-got honours flung,
Turn'd to that dirt, from whence he sprung.

Jonathan Swift (1667–1745)

An Epitaph

Interr'd beneath this marble stone,
Lie saunt'ring JACK, and idle JOAN.
While rolling threescore years and one
Did round this globe their courses run;
If human things went ill or well;   5
If changing empires rose or fell;
The morning past, the evening came,
And found this couple still the same.
They walk'd and eat, good folks: What then?
Why then they walk'd and eat again: 10
They soundly slept the night away:
They did just nothing all the day:
And having bury'd children four,
Wou'd not take pains to try for more.
Nor sister either had, nor brother: 15
They seem'd just tally'd° for each other.   *suited*

Their moral° and economy   *morality*
Most perfectly they made agree:
Each virtue kept it's proper bound,
Nor trespass'd on the other's ground.   20
For fame, nor censure they regarded:
They neither punish'd, nor rewarded.
He car'd not what the footmen did:
Her maids she neither prais'd, nor chid:
So ev'ry servant took his course;   25
And bad at first, they all grew worse.
Slothful disorder fill'd his stable;
And sluttish plenty deck'd her table.
Their beer was strong; their wine was *Port*;
Their meal was large; their grace was short.   30

They gave the poor the remnant-meat,
Just when it grew not fit to eat.

They paid the church and parish-rate;
And took, but read not the receit:
For which they claim'd their *Sunday's* due,   35
Of slumb'ring in an upper pew.

No man's defects sought they to know;
So never made themselves a foe.
No man's good deeds did they commend;
So never rais'd themselves a friend.   40
Nor cherish'd they relations poor:
That might decrease their present store:
Nor barn nor house did they repair:
That might oblige their future heir.

They neither added, nor confounded:°   *wasted* 45
They neither wanted, nor abounded.
Each *Christmas* they accompts did clear;
And wound their bottom° round the year.
Nor tear, nor smile did they imploy
At news of public grief, or joy.   50
When bells were rung, and bonfires made;
If ask'd, they ne'er deny'd their aid:
Their jugg was to the ringers carry'd;
Who ever either dy'd, or marry'd.
Their billet° at the fire was found;   *firewood* 55
Who ever was depos'd, or crown'd.

Nor good, nor bad, nor fools, nor wise;
They wou'd not learn, nor cou'd advise:
Without love, hatred, joy, or fear,

48. wound . . . bottom literally: wound their thread up; put things in order

They led—a kind of—as it were: 60
Nor wish'd, nor car'd, nor laugh'd, nor cry'd:
And so they liv'd; and so they dy'd.

Matthew Prior (1664–1721)

Ode on Solitude

Happy the man whose wish and care
    A few paternal acres bound,
Content to breathe his native air,
        In his own ground.

Whose herds with milk, whose fields with bread,   5
    Whose flocks supply him with attire,
Whose trees in summer yield him shade,
        In winter fire.

Blest, who can unconcernedly find
    Hours, days, and years slide soft away,   10
In health of body, peace of mind,
        Quiet by day,

Sound sleep by night; study and ease,
    Together mixed; sweet recreation;
And innocence, which most does please   15
        With meditation.

Thus let me live, unseen, unknown;
    Thus unlamented let me die;
Steal from the world, and not a stone
        Tell where I lie.   20

Alexander Pope (1688–1744)

On the Death of Dr. Robert Levet°

Condemn'd to hope's delusive mine,°   *undermine*
    As on we toil from day to day,
By sudden blasts, or slow decline,
    Our social comforts drop away.

Well tried through many a varying year,   5
    See LEVET to the grave descend;
Officious,° innocent, sincere,   *doing good deeds*
    Of ev'ry friendless name the friend.

Dr. Robert Levet Robert Levet (1705–1782) was an impoverished lay physician who lived in Samuel Johnson's home with other unfortunate people. He won a reputation for treating neighbors for nothing or for minimal fees when they were ill.

Yet still he fills affection's eye,
    Obscurely wise, and coursely kind;   10
Nor, letter'd arrogance, deny
    Thy praise to merit unrefin'd.

When fainting nature call'd for aid,
    And hov'ring death prepar'd the blow,
His vig'rous remedy display'd   15
    The power of art without the show.

In misery's darkest caverns known,
    His useful care was ever nigh,
Where hopeless anguish pour'd his groan,
    And lonely want retir'd to die.   20

No summons mock'd by chill delay,
    No petty gain disdain'd by pride,
The modest wants of ev'ry day
    The toil of ev'ry day supplied.

His virtues walk'd their narrow round,   25
    Nor made a pause, nor left a void;
And sure th' Eternal Master found
    The single talent well employ'd.

The busy day, the peaceful night,
    Unfelt, uncounted, glided by;   30
His frame was firm, his powers were bright,
    Tho' now his eightieth year was nigh.

Then with no throbbing fiery pain,
    No cold gradations of decay,
Death broke at once the vital chain,   35
    And free'd his soul the nearest way.

Samuel Johnson (1709–1784)

Elegy Written in a Country Churchyard

The curfew tolls the knell of parting day,
    The lowing herd wind slowly o'er the lea,°   *meadow*
The plowman homeward plods his weary way,
    And leaves the world to darkness and to me.

Now fades the glimmering landscape on the sight,   5
    And all the air a solemn stillness holds,
Save where the beetle wheels his droning flight,
    And drowsy tinklings lull the distant folds;

Save that from yonder ivy-mantled tower
    The moping owl does to the moon complain   10
Of such, as wandering near her secret bower,
    Molest her ancient solitary reign.

Beneath those rugged elms, that yew tree's shade,
  Where heaves the turf in many a moldering heap,
Each in his narrow cell forever laid,   15
  The rude° forefathers of the hamlet sleep.   *untutored*

The breezy call of incense-breathing morn,
  The swallow twittering from the straw-built shed,
The cock's shrill clarion, or the echoing horn,°   *of the hunting party*
  No more shall rouse them from their lowly bed.   20

For them no more the blazing hearth shall burn,
  Or busy housewife ply her evening care;
No children run to lisp their sire's return,
  Or climb his knees the envied kiss to share.

Oft did the harvest to their sickle yield,   25
  Their furrow oft the stubborn glebe° has broke;   *soil*
How jocund did they drive their team afield!
  How bowed the woods beneath their sturdy stroke!

Let not Ambition mock their useful toil,
  Their homely joys, and destiny obscure;   30
Nor Grandeur hear with a disdainful smile
  The short and simple annals of the poor.

The boast of heraldry° the pomp of power,   *high birth*
  And all that beauty, all that wealth e'er gave,
Awaits alike the inevitable hour.   35
  The paths of glory lead but to the grave.

Nor you, ye proud, impute to these the fault,
  If Memory o'er their tomb no trophies raise,
Where through the long-drawn aisle and fretted° vault *ornamented*
  The pealing anthem swells the note of praise.   40

Can storied urn or animated° bust   *lifelike*
  Back to its mansion call the fleeting breath?
Can Honor's voice provoke the silent dust,
  Or Flattery soothe the dull cold ear of Death?

Perhaps in this neglected spot is laid   45
  Some heart once pregnant with celestial fire;
Hands that the rod of empire might have swayed,
  Or waked to ecstasy the living lyre.

But Knowledge to their eyes her ample page
  Rich with the spoils of time did ne'er unroll;   50
Chill Penury repressed their noble rage,
  And froze the genial current of the soul.

Full many a gem of purest ray serene,
  The dark unfathomed caves of ocean bear:
Full many a flower is born to blush unseen,   55
  And waste its sweetness on the desert air.

Some village Hampden,° that with dauntless breast
    The little tyrant of his fields withstood;
Some mute inglorious Milton° here may rest,
    Some Cromwell° guiltless of his country's blood.   60

The applause of listening senates to command,
    The threats of pain and ruin to despise,
To scatter plenty o'er a smiling land,
    And read their history in a nation's eyes.

Their lot forbade: nor circumscribed alone   65
    Their growing virtues, but their crimes confined;
Forbade to wade through slaughter to a throne,
    And shut the gates of mercy on mankind,

The struggling pangs of conscious truth to hide,
    To quench the blushes of ingenuous shame,   70
Or heap the shrine of Luxury and Pride
    With incense kindled at the Muse's flame.

Far from the madding° crowd's ignoble strife,   *frenzied*
    Their sober wishes never learned to stray;
Along the cool sequestered vale of life   75
    They kept the noiseless tenor of their way.

Yet even these bones from insult to protect
    Some frail memorial still erected nigh,
With uncouth° rhymes and shapeless sculpture decked,   *unlettered*
    Implores the passing tribute of a sigh.   80

Their name, their years, spelt by the unlettered Muse,
    The place of fame and elegy supply:
And many a holy text around she strews,
    That teach the rustic moralist to die.

For who to dumb Forgetfulness a prey,   85
    This pleasing anxious being e'er resigned,
Left the warm precincts of the cheerful day,
    Nor cast one longing lingering look behind?

On some fond breast the parting soul relies,
    Some pious drops the closing eye requires;   90
Even from the tomb the voice of Nature cries,
    Even in our ashes live their wonted fires.

For thee, who mindful of the unhonored dead
    Dost in these lines their artless tale relate;
If chance, by lonely contemplation led,   95
    Some kindred spirit shall inquire thy fate,

---

57. Hampden John Hampden (1594–1643), member of Parliament who opposed the excesses of King Charles I   **59. Milton** John Milton (1608–1674), great poet and partisan of the Puritan cause against Charles I   **60. Cromwell** Oliver Cromwell (1599–1658), Puritan soldier and statesman who governed England after Charles I was overthrown and executed

Haply° some hoary-headed swain may say,   *perhaps*
  "Oft have we seen him at the peep of dawn
Brushing with hasty steps the dews away
  To meet the sun upon the upland lawn.   100

"There at the foot of yonder nodding beech
  That wreathes its old fantastic roots so high,
His listless length at noontide would he stretch,
  And pore upon the brook that babbles by.

"Hard by yon wood, now smiling as in scorn,   105
  Muttering his wayward fancies he would rove,
Now drooping, woeful wan, like one forlorn,
  Or crazed with care, or crossed in hopeless love.

"One morn I missed him on the customed hill,
  Along the heath and near his favorite tree;   110
Another came; nor yet beside the rill,
  Nor up the lawn, nor at the wood was he;

"The next with dirges due in sad array
  Slow through the churchway path we saw him borne.
Approach and read (for thou canst read) the lay,°   *story* 115
  Graved on the stone beneath yon aged thorn."

    The Epitaph
Here rests his head upon the lap of Earth
  A youth to Fortune and to Fame unkown.
Fair Science frowned not on his humble birth,
  And Melancholy marked him for her own.   120

Large was his bounty, and his soul sincere,
  Heaven did a recompense as largely send:
He gave to Misery all he had, a tear,
  He gained from Heaven ('twas all he wished) a friend.

No farther seek his merits to disclose,   125
  Or draw his frailties from their dread abode
(There they alike in trembling hope repose),
  The bosom of his Father and his God.

    Thomas Gray (1716–1771)

Ode on the Death of a Favorite Cat Drowned in a Tub of Gold-Fishes

    'Twas on a lofty vase's side,
    Where China's gayest art had dyed
      The azure flowers that blow;
    Demurest of the tabby kind,
    The pensive Selima, reclined,   5
      Gazed on the lake below.

Her conscious tail her joy declared;
The fair round face, the snowy beard,
    The velvet of her paws,
Her coat, that with the tortoise vies,   10
Her ears of jet, and emerald eyes,
    She saw; and purred applause.

Still had she gazed; but 'midst the tide
Two angel forms were seen to glide,
    The genii° of the stream: *guardian spirits* 15
Their scaly armor's Tyrian hue°   *reddish color*
Through richest purple to the view
    Betrayed a golden gleam.

The hapless nymph with wonder saw:
A whisker first and then a claw,   20
    With many an ardent wish,
She stretched in vain to reach the prize.
What female heart can gold despise?
    What cat's averse to fish?

Presumptuous maid! with looks intent   25
Again she stretched, again she bent,
    Nor knew the gulf between.
(Malignant Fate sat by and smiled)
The slippery verge her feet beguiled,
    She tumbled headlong in.   30

Eight times emerging from the flood
She mewed to every watery god,
    Some speedy aid to send.
No dolphin came, no Nereid° stirred;   *sea nymph*
Nor cruel Tom, nor Susan heard;   35
    A favorite has no friend!

From hence, ye beauties, undeceived,
Know, one false step is ne'er retrieved,
    And be with caution bold.
Not all that tempts your wandering eyes   40
And heedless hearts, is lawful prize;
    Nor all that glisters,° gold.   *glistens*

Thomas Gray (1716–1771)

The Poet's Cat°

For I will consider my Cat Jeoffry.
For he is the servant of the Living God duly and daily serving him.
For at the first glance of the glory of God in the East he worships in his way.

The Poet's Cat Smart wrote this experimental poem while confined in a madhouse; his only companion was a cat named Jeoffry.

For is this done by wreathing his body seven times round with elegant
    quickness.
For then he leaps up to catch the musk, which is the blessing of God upon his
    prayer.   5
For he rolls upon prank to work it in.
For having done duty and received blessing he begins to consider himself.
For this he performs in ten degrees.
For first he looks upon his fore-paws to see if they are clean.
For secondly he kicks up behind to clear away there.   10
For thirdly he works it upon stretch with the fore-paws extended.
For fourthly he sharpens his paws by wood.
For fifthly he washes himself.
For sixthly he rolls upon wash.
For seventhly he fleas himself, that he may not be interrupted
    upon the beat.°   *in his normal activity* 15
For eighthly he rubs himself against a post.
For ninthly he looks up for his instructions.
For tenthly he goes in quest of food.
For having considered God and himself he will consider his neighbour.
For if he meets another cat he will kiss her in kindness.   20
For when he takes his prey he plays with it to give it a chance.
For one mouse in seven escapes by his dallying.
For when his day's work is done his business more properly begins.
For he keeps the Lord's watch in the night against the adversary.
For he counteracts the powers of darkness by his electrical skin and glaring
    eyes.   25
For he counteracts the Devil, who is death, by brisking about the life.
For in his morning orisons he loves the sun and the sun loves him.
For he is of the tribe of Tiger.
For the Cherub Cat is a term of the Angel Tiger.
For he has the subtlety and hissing of a serpent, which in goodness he
    suppresses.   30
For he will not do destruction if he is well-fed, neither will he spit without
    provocation.
For he purrs in thankfulness, when God tells him he's a good Cat.
For he is an instrument for the children to learn benevolence upon.
For every house is incomplete without him and a blessing is lacking in the
    spirit.
For the Lord commanded Moses concerning the cats at the departure of the
    Children of Israel from Egypt.   35
For every family had one cat at least in the bag.
For the English Cats are the best in Europe.
For he is the cleanest in the use of his fore-paws of any quadruped.
For the dexterity of his defence is an instance of the love of God to him
    exceedingly.
For he is the quickest to his mark of any creature.   40
For he is tenacious of his point.
For he is a mixture of gravity and waggery.

For he knows that God is his Saviour.
For there is nothing sweeter than his peace when at rest.
For there is nothing brisker than his life when in motion.   45
For he is of the Lord's poor and so indeed is he called by benevolence
    perpetually—Poor Jeoffry! poor Jeoffry! the rat has bit thy throat.
For I bless the name of the Lord Jesus that Jeoffry is better.
For the divine spirit comes about his body to sustain it in complete cat.
For his tongue is exceeding pure so that it has in purity what it wants in
    music.
For he is docile and can learn certain things.   50
For he can set up with gravity which is patience upon approbation.
For he can fetch and carry, which is patience in employment.
For he can jump over a stick which is patience upon proof positive.
For he can spraggle upon waggle at the word of command.
For he can jump from an eminence into his master's bosom.   55
For he can catch the cork and toss it again.
For he is hated by the hypocrite and miser.
For the former is afraid of detection.
For the latter refuses the charge.
For he camels his back to bear the first notion of business.   60
For he is good to think on, if a man would express himself neatly.
For he made a great figure in Egypt for his signal services.
For he killed the Ichneumon-rat° very pernicious by land.   *type of weasel*
For his ears are so acute that they sting again.
For from this proceeds the passing quickness of his attention.   65
For by stroking of him I have found out electricity.
For I perceived God's light about him both wax and fire.
For the electrical fire is the spiritual substance, which God sends from heaven
    to sustain the bodies both of man and beast.
For God has blessed him in the variety of his movements.
For, though he cannot fly, he is an excellent clamberer.   70
For his motions upon the face of the earth are more than any other
    quadruped.
For he can tread to all the measures upon the music.
For he can swim for life.
For he can creep.

Christopher Smart (1722--1771)

I Was a Stricken Deer

I was a stricken deer, that left the herd
Long since; with many an arrow deep infixed
My panting side was charged, when I withdrew
To seek a tranquil death in distant shades.
There was I found by one who had himself   5
Been hurt by the archers. In his side he bore,
And in his hands and feet, the cruel scars.

With gentle force soliciting the darts,
He drew them forth, and healed, and bade me live.
Since then, with few associates, in remote   10
And silent woods I wander, far from those
My former partners of the peopled scene;
With few associates, and not wishing more.
Here much I ruminate, as much I may,
With other views of men and manners now   15
Than once, and others of a life to come.
I see that all are wanderers, gone astray
Each in his own delusions; they are lost
In chase of fancied happiness, still wooed
And never won. Dream after dream ensues;   20
And still they dream that they shall still succeed.
And still are disappointed. Rings the world
With the vain stir. I sum up half mankind
And add two-thirds of the remaining half,
And find the total of their hopes and fears   25
Dreams, empty dreams.

William Cowper (1731–1800)

Ah Sunflower

Ah Sunflower! weary of time,
Who countest the steps of the Sun,
Seeking after that sweet golden clime
Where the traveler's journey is done,

Where the Youth pined away with desire,
And the pale Virgin shrouded in snow,
Arise from their graves and aspire,
Where my Sunflower wishes to go.

William Blake (1757–1827)

A Slumber Did My Spirit Seal

A slumber did my spirit seal;
    I had no human fears:
She seemed a thing that could not feel
    The touch of earthly years.

No motion has she now, no force:
    She neither hears nor sees;
Rolled round in earth's diurnal° course,   daily
    With rocks, and stones, and trees.

William Wordsworth (1770–1850)

Composed upon Westminster Bridge

Earth has not anything to show more fair:
Dull would he be of soul who could pass by
A sight so touching in its majesty:
This City now doth, like a garment, wear
The beauty of the morning; silent, bare,   5
Ships, towers, domes, theatres, and temples lie
Open unto the fields, and to the sky;
All bright and glittering in the smokeless air.
Never did sun more beautifully steep
In his first splendor, valley, rock, or hill;   10
Ne'er saw I, never felt, a calm so deep!
The river glideth at his own sweet will:
Dear God! the very houses seem asleep;
And all that mighty heart is lying still!

William Wordsworth (1770–1850)

Kubla Khan°

In Xanadu did Kubla Khan
A stately pleasure-dome decree:
Where Alph, the sacred river, ran
Through caverns measureless to man
  Down to a sunless sea.   5
So twice five miles of fertile ground
With walls and towers were girdled round:
And here were gardens bright with sinuous rills,
Where blossomed many an incense-bearing tree;
And here were forests ancient as the hills,   10
Enfolding sunny spots of greenery.

But oh! that deep romantic chasm which slanted
Down the green hill athwart a cedarn cover!
A savage place! as holy and enchanted
As e'er beneath a waning moon was haunted   15
By woman wailing for her demon-lover!
And from this chasm, with ceaseless turmoil seething,
As if this earth in fast thick pants were breathing,
A mighty fountain momently was forced:
Amid whose swift half-intermitted burst   20

Kubla Khan Coleridge subtitled the poem "A Vision in a Dream," claiming that the fragment came to him during an opium dream but remained unfinished because he was interrupted during the composition by a caller.

Huge fragments vaulted like rebounding hail,
Or chaffy grain beneath the thresher's flail:
And 'mid these dancing rocks at once and ever
It flung up momently the sacred river.
Five miles meandering with a mazy motion   25
Through wood and dale the sacred river ran,
Then reached the caverns measureless to man,
And sank in tumult to a lifeless ocean:
And 'mid this tumult Kubla heard from far
Ancestral voices prophesying war!   30

   The shadow of the dome of pleasure
   Floated midway on the waves;
   Where was heard the mingled measure
   From the fountain and the caves.
It was a miracle of rare device,   35
A sunny pleasure-dome with caves of ice!

   A damsel with a dulcimer°   *stringed instrument*
   In a vision once I saw:
   It was an Abyssinian maid,
   And on her dulcimer she played,   40
   Singing of Mount Abora.
   Could I revive within me
   Her symphony and song,
To such a deep delight 'twould win me,
That with music loud and long,   45
I would build that dome in air,
That sunny dome! those caves of ice!
And all who heard should see them there,
And all should cry, Beware! Beware!
His flashing eyes, his floating hair!   50
Weave a circle round him thrice,
And close your eyes with holy dread,
For he on honey-dew hath fed,
And drunk the milk of Paradise.

Samuel Taylor Coleridge (1772–1834)

Dying Speech of an Old Philosopher

   I strove with none; for none was worth my strife:
     Nature I loved, and, next to Nature, Art:
   I warmed both hands before the fire of life;
     It sinks; and I am ready to depart.

Walter Savage Landor (1775–1864)

Past Ruined Ilion Helen Lives

Past ruined Ilion° Helen lives,   *Troy*
  Alcestis° rises from the shades;
Verse calls them forth; 'tis verse that gives
  Immortal youth to mortal maids.

Soon shall Oblivion's deepening veil   5
  Hide all the peopled hills you see,
The gay, the proud, while lovers hail
  In distant ages you and me.

The tear for fading beauty check,
  For passing glory cease to sigh;   10
One form shall rise above the wreck,
  One name, Ianthe, shall not die.

Walter Savage Landor (1775–1864)

When We Two Parted

When we two parted
  In silence and tears,
Half broken-hearted
  To sever for years,
Pale grew the cheek and cold,   5
  Colder thy kiss;
Truly that hour foretold
  Sorrow to this.

The dew of the morning
  Sunk chill on my brow—   10
It felt like the warning
  Of what I feel now.
Thy vows are all broken,
  And light is thy fame:
I hear thy name spoken,   15
  And share in its shame.

They name thee before me,
  A knell to mine ear;
A shudder comes o'er me—
  Why wert thou so dear?   20
They know not I knew thee,
  Who knew thee too well:—
Long, long shall I rue thee,
  Too deeply to tell.

---

2. **Alcestis** died to save her husband Admetus, and was allowed to return from Hades

In secret we met—   25
    In silence I grieve,
That thy heart could forget,
    Thy spirit deceive.
If I should meet thee
    After long years,   30
How should I greet thee?—
    With silence and tears.

George Gordon, Lord Byron (1788–1824)

Ode on a Grecian Urn

Thou still unravished bride of quietness,
    Thou foster-child of silence and slow time,
Sylvan° historian, who canst thus express
    A flowery tale more sweetly than our rhyme:
What leaf-fringed legend haunts about thy shape   5
    Of deities or mortals, or of both,
        In Tempe° or the dales of Arcady?°
    What men or gods are these? What maidens loth?
What mad pursuits? What struggle to escape?
        What pipes and timbrels? What wild ecstasy?   10

Heard melodies are sweet, but those unheard
    Are sweeter; therefore, ye soft pipes, play on;
Not to the sensual° ear, but, more endeared,
    Pipe to the spirit ditties of no tone:
Fair youth, beneath the trees, thou canst not leave   15
    Thy song, nor ever can those trees be bare;
        Bold Lover, never, never canst thou kiss,
    Though winning near the goal—yet, do not grieve;
        She cannot fade, though thou hast not thy bliss,
    For ever wilt thou love, and she be fair!   20

Ah, happy, happy boughs! that cannot shed
    Your leaves, nor ever bid the Spring adieu;
And, happy melodist, unwearièd,
    For ever piping songs for ever new;
More happy love! more happy, happy love!   25
    For ever warm and still to be enjoyed,
        For ever panting and for ever young;
All breathing human passion far above,
    That leaves a heart high-sorrowful and cloyed,
        A burning forehead, and a parching tongue.   30

---

3. Sylvan pastoral, as in the scene depicted on the urn   **7. Tempe** a tranquil valley near Mt.
Olympus in Greece   **7. Arcady** Arcadia, a lovely site in Greece that came to be associated
with the pastoral ideal   **13. sensual** sensory; the ear of the body as opposed to the "ear" of the
soul

Who are these coming to the sacrifice?
  To what green altar, O mysterious priest,
Lead'st thou that heifer lowing at the skies,
    And all her silken flanks with garlands drest?
What little town by river or sea shore,   35
  Or mountain-built with peaceful citadel,
    Is emptied of its folk, this pious morn?
And, little town, thy streets for evermore
  Will silent be; and not a soul to tell
    Why thou art desolate, can e'er return.   40

O Attic° shape! Fair attitude! with brede°   *ornamentation*
  Of marble men and maidens overwrought,
With forest branches and the trodden weed;
  Thou, silent form, dost tease us out of thought
As doth eternity: Cold Pastoral!   45
  When old age shall this generation waste,
    Thou shalt remain, in midst of other woe
Than ours, a friend to man, to whom thou say'st,
Beauty is truth, truth beauty,—that is all
  Ye know on earth, and all ye need to know.   50

John Keats (1795–1821)

Ode to a Nightingale

My heart aches, and a drowsy numbness pains
  My sense, as though of hemlock° I had drunk,   *poisoned drink*
Or emptied some dull opiate to the drains
  One minute past, and Lethe-wards° had sunk:
'Tis not through envy of thy happy lot,   5
  But being too happy in thine happiness,—
    That thou, light-wingèd Dryad° of the trees,   *wood spirit*
    In some melodious plot
Of beechen green, and shadows numberless,
  Singest of summer in full-throated ease.   10

O, for a draught of vintage! that hath been
  Cooled a long age in the deep-delvèd° earth,   *deeply dug*
Tasting of Flora° and the country green,   *goddess of flowers*
  Dance, and Provençal song, and sunburnt mirth!
O for a beaker full of the warm South,   15
  Full of the true, the blushful Hippocrene,°
    With beaded bubbles winking at the brim,
    And purple-stainèd mouth;
That I might drink, and leave the world unseen,
  And with thee fade away into the forest dim: 20

41. **Attic** Attica surrounded Athens in ancient Greece.   4. **Lethe-wards** toward Lethe, the river of forgetting   16. **Hippocrene** fountain of the Muses, whose waters brought poetic inspiration

Fade far away, dissolve, and quite forget
  What thou among the leaves hast never known,
The weariness, the fever, and the fret
  Here, where men sit and hear each other groan;
Where palsy shakes a few, sad, last gray hairs,   25
  Where youth grows pale, and specter-thin, and dies;
    Where but to think is to be full of sorrow
      And leaden-eyed despairs,
  Where Beauty cannot keep her lustrous eyes,
    Or new Love pine at them beyond to-morrow.   30

Away! away! for I will fly to thee,
  Not charioted by Bacchus and his pards,°
But on the viewless° wings of Poesy,°   *invisible; poetry*
  Though the dull brain perplexes and retards:
Already with thee! tender is the night,   35
  And haply the Queen-Moon is on her throne,
    Clustered around by all her starry Fays;°   *faeries*
      But here there is no light,
  Save what from heaven is with the breezes blown
    Through verdurous glooms and winding mossy ways. 40

I cannot see what flowers are at my feet,
  Nor what soft incense hangs upon the boughs,
But, in embalmèd° darkness, guess each sweet   *fragrant*
  Wherewith the seasonable month endows
The grass, the thicket, and the fruit-tree wild;   45
  White hawthorn, and the pastoral eglantine;
    Fast fading violets covered up in leaves;
      And mid-May's eldest child,
  The coming musk-rose, full of dewy wine,
    The murmurous haunt of flies on summer eves. 50

Darkling° I listen; and, for many a time   *in the dark*
  I have been half in love with easeful Death,
Called him soft names in many a musèd rhyme,
  To take into the air my quiet breath;
Now more than ever seems it rich to die,   55
  To cease upon the midnight with no pain,
    While thou art pouring forth thy soul abroad
      In such an ecstasy!
  Still wouldst thou sing, and I have ears in vain—
    To thy high requiem become a sod.   60

Thou wast not born for death, immortal Bird!
  No hungry generations tread thee down;
The voice I hear this passing night was heard

32. Bacchus and his pards Roman god of wine and the leopards which were sometimes depicted pulling his chariot

In ancient days by emperor and clown:
Perhaps the self-same song that found a path   65
  Through the sad heart of Ruth,° when, sick for home,
    She stood in tears amid the alien corn;
      The same that oft-times hath
  Charmed magic casements, opening on the foam
    Of perilous seas, in faery lands forlorn.   70

Forlorn! the very word is like a bell
  To toll me back from thee to my sole self!
Adieu! the fancy cannot cheat so well
  As she is famed to do, deceiving elf.
Adieu! adieu! thy plaintive anthem fades   75
  Past the near meadows, over the still stream,
    Up the hill-side; and now 'tis buried deep
      In the next valley-glades:
Was it a vision, or a waking dream?
  Fled is that music:—Do I wake or sleep?   80

John Keats (1795–1821)

To Helen

Helen, thy beauty is to me
  Like those Nicèan barks° of yore,
That gently, o'er a perfumed sea,
  The weary, way-worn wanderer bore
    To his own native shore.   5

On desperate seas long wont to roam,
  Thy hyacinth hair,° thy classic face,
Thy Naiad° airs have brought me home
  To the glory that was Greece
    And the grandeur that was Rome.   10

Lo! in yon brilliant window-niche
  How statue-like I see thee stand,
  The agate lamp within thy hand!
Ah, Psyche,° from the regions which
    Are Holy Land!   15

Edgar Allan Poe (1809–1849)

66. **Ruth** Old Testament widow who found a husband while tilling the wheat fields of Judah
2. **Nicèan barks** ships of Nicea, an ancient city of the Byzantine Empire   7. **hyacinth hair** hair curled to resemble a hyacinth flower   8. **Naiad** one of the nymphs presiding over waterways   14. **Psyche** the beloved of Cupid, whose identity she was forbidden to know and who vanished when she lit a lamp to see him

Ulysses

It little profits that an idle king,
By this still hearth, among these barren crags,
Matched with an agèd wife, I mete and dole
Unequal laws unto a savage race,
That hoard, and sleep, and feed, and know not me.   5
I cannot rest from travel; I will drink
Life to the lees.° All times I have enjoyed   *bottom of the glass*
Greatly, have suffered greatly, both with those
That loved me, and alone; on shore, and when
Through scudding drifts the rainy Hyades°   10
Vext the dim sea. I am become a name;
For always roaming with a hungry heart
Much have I seen and known,—cities of men
And manners, climates, councils, governments,
Myself not least, but honored of them all;   15
And drunk delight of battle with my peers,
Far on the ringing plains of windy Troy.
I am a part of all that I have met;
Yet all experience is an arch wherethrough
Gleams that untraveled world, whose margin fades   20
For ever and for ever when I move.
How dull it is to pause, to make an end,
To rust unburnished, not to shine in use!

As though to breathe were life! Life piled on life
Were all too little, and of one to me   25
Little remains; but every hour is saved
From that eternal silence, something more,
A bringer of new things; and vile it were
For some three suns to store and hoard myself,
And this grey spirit yearning in desire   30
To follow knowledge like a sinking star,
Beyond the utmost bound of human thought.

This is my son, mine own Telemachus,
To whom I leave the scepter and the isle—
Well-loved of me, discerning to fulfil   35
This labor, by slow prudence to make mild
A rugged people, and through soft degrees
Subdue them to the useful and the good.
Most blameless is he, centered in the sphere
Of common duties, decent not to fail   40
In offices of tenderness, and pay
Meet adoration to my household gods,
When I am gone. He works his work, I mine.

10. **Hyades** a group of stars supposedly able to foretell rain

There lies the port; the vessel puffs her sail:
There gloom the dark, broad seas. My mariners,   45
Souls that have toiled, and wrought, and thought with me—
That ever with a frolic welcome took
The thunder and the sunshine, and opposed
Free hearts, free foreheads—you and I are old;
Old age hath yet his honor and his toil.   50
Death closes all; but something ere the end,
Some work of noble note, may yet be done,
Not unbecoming men that strove with Gods.
The lights begin to twinkle from the rocks;
The long day wanes; the slow moon climbs; the deep   55
Moans round with many voices. Come, my friends,
'Tis not too late to seek a newer world.
Push off, and sitting well in order smite
The sounding furrows; for my purpose holds
To sail beyond the sunset, and the baths   60
Of all the western stars, until I die.
It may be that the gulfs will wash us down;
It may be we shall touch the Happy Isles,°
And see the great Achilles, whom we knew.
Though much is taken, much abides; and though   65
We are not now that strength which in old days
Moved earth and heaven, that which we are, we are:
One equal temper of heroic hearts,
Made weak by time and fate, but strong in will
To strive, to seek, to find, and not to yield.   70

Alfred, Lord Tennyson (1809–1892)

The Splendor Falls

The splendor falls on castle walls
    And snowy summits old in story;
The long light shakes across the lakes,
    And the wild cataract leaps in glory.
Blow, bugle, blow, set the wild echoes flying   5
Blow, bugle; answer, echoes, dying, dying, dying.

O, hark, O, hear! how thin and clear,
    And thinner, clearer, farther going!
O, sweet and far from cliff and scar°   *mountainside*
    The horns of Elfland faintly blowing!   10
Blow, let us hear the purple glens replying
Blow, bugle; answer, echoes, dying, dying, dying.

63. Happy Isles Elysium, where it was thought that Achilles and other heroes rested for eternity

O love, they die in yon rich sky,
   They faint on hill or field or river;
Our echoes roll from soul to soul,
   And grow forever and forever.   15
Blow, bugle, blow, set the wild echoes flying,
And answer, echoes, answer, dying, dying, dying.

Alfred, Lord Tennyson (1809–1892)

Animals

I think I could turn and live with animals, they are so placid and self-
   contained;
I stand and look at them long and long.
They do not sweat and whine about their condition;
They do not lie awake in the dark and weep for their sins;
They do not make me sick discussing their duty to God;
Not one is dissatisfied—not one is demented with the mania of owning
   things;
Not one kneels to another, nor to his kind that lived thousands of years ago;
Not one is respectable or industrious over the whole earth.

Walt Whitman (1819–1892)

Cavalry Crossing a Ford

A line in long array where they wind betwixt green islands,
They take a serpentine course, their arms flash in the sun—hark to the
   musical clank,
Behold the silvery river, in it the splashing horses loitering stop to drink,
Behold the brown-faced men, each group, each person a picture, the
   negligent rest on the saddles,
Some emerge on the opposite bank, others are just entering the ford—while,
Scarlet and blue and snowy white,
The guidon flags flutter gayly in the wind.

Walt Whitman (1819–1892)

Because I Could Not Stop for Death

      Because I could not stop for Death—
      He kindly stopped for me—
      The Carriage held but just Ourselves—
      And Immortality.

We slowly drove—He knew no haste   5
And I had put away
My labor and my leisure too,
For His Civility—

We passed the School, where Children strove
At Recess—in the Ring—   10
We passed the Fields of Gazing Grain—
We passed the Setting Sun—

Or rather—He passed Us—
The Dews drew quivering and chill—
For only Gossamer, my Gown—   15
My Tippet°—only Tulle°—   *overscarf; starched silk netting*

We paused before a House that seemed
A Swelling of the Ground—
The Roof was scarcely visible—
The Cornice—in the Ground—   20

Since then—'tis Centuries—and yet
Feels shorter than the Day
I first surmised the Horses Heads
Were toward Eternity—

Emily Dickinson (1830–1886)

Wild Nights, Wild Nights!

Wild nights, wild nights!
Were I with thee,
Wild nights should be
Our luxury.

Futile the winds   5
To a heart in port,
Done with the compass,
Done with the chart.

Rowing in Eden —
Ah, the sea!   10
Might I but moor
To-night in thee.

Emily Dickinson (1830–1886)

The Windhover°

To Christ Our Lord

I caught this morning morning's minion,° king-   *favorite*
    dom of daylight's dauphin,° dapple-dawn-drawn Falcon, in his
      riding   *heir to royalty*
    Of the rolling level underneath him steady air, and striding
High there, how he rung upon the rein of a wimpling° wing   *rippling*
In his ecstasy! then off, off forth on swing,   5
    As a skate's heel sweeps smooth on a bow-bend: the hurl and
      gliding
    Rebuffed the big wind. My heart in hiding
Stirred for a bird,—the achieve of, the mastery of the thing!

Brute beauty and valor and act, oh, air, pride, plume, here
    Buckle!° AND the fire that breaks from thee then, a billion   10
Times told lovelier, more dangerous, O my chevalier!°   *knight*

    No wonder of it: sheér plód makes plow down sillion°
Shine, and blue-bleak embers, ah my dear,
    Fall, gall themselves, and gash gold-vermilion.

Gerard Manley Hopkins (1844–1889)

To an Athlete Dying Young

    The time you won your town the race
    We chaired you through the market-place;
    Man and boy stood cheering by,
    And home we brought you shoulder-high.

    To-day, the road all runners come,   5
    Shoulder-high, we bring you home,
    And set you at your threshold down,
    Townsman of a stiller town.

    Smart lad, to slip betimes away
    From fields where glory does not stay   10
    And early though the laurel grows
    It withers quicker than the rose.

    Eyes the shady night has shut
    Cannot see the record cut,
    And silence sounds no worse than cheers   15
    After earth has stopped the ears:

windhover kestral hawk that typically hovers facing the wind   **10. buckle** collapse, as a hawk does when diving to the attack   **12. sillion** piece of ground between furrows in a cultivated field

Now you will not swell the rout
Of lads that wore their honors out,
Runners whom renown outran
And the name died before the man.   20

So set, before its echoes fade,
The fleet foot on the sill of shade,
And hold to the low lintel up
The still-defended challenge-cup.

And round that early-laureled head   25
Will flock to gaze the strengthless dead,
And find unwithered on its curls
The garland briefer than a girl's.

A. E. Housman (1859–1936)

Cynara

Last night, ah, yesternight, betwixt her lips and mine
There fell thy shadow, Cynara! thy breath was shed
Upon my soul between the kisses and the wine;
And I was desolate and sick of an old passion,
    Yea, I was desolate and bowed my head: 5
I have been faithful to thee, Cynara! in my fashion.

All night upon mine heart I felt her warm heart beat,
Night-long within mine arms in love and sleep she lay;
Surely the kisses of her bought red mouth were sweet;
But I was desolate and sick of an old passion,   10
    When I awoke and found the dawn was gray:
I have been faithful to thee, Cynara! in my fashion.

I have forgot much, Cynara! gone with the wind,
Flung roses, roses riotously with the throng,
Dancing, to put thy pale, lost lilies out of mind;   15
But I was desolate and sick of an old passion,
    Yea, all the time, because the dance was long:
I have been faithful to thee, Cynara! in my fashion.

I cried for madder music and for stronger wine,
But when the feast is finished and the lamps expire,   20
Then falls thy shadow, Cynara! the night is thine;
And I am desolate and sick of an old passion,
    Yea, hungry for the lips of my desire:
I have been faithful to thee, Cynara! in my fashion.

Ernest Dowson (1867–1900)

Lucinda Matlock

I went to the dances at Chandlerville,
And played snap-out at Winchester.
One time we changed partners,
Driving home in the moonlight of middle June,
And then I found Davis.   5
We were married and lived together for seventy years,
Enjoying, working, raising the twelve children,
Eight of whom we lost
Ere I had reached the age of sixty.
I spun, I wove, I kept the house, I nursed the sick,   10
I made the garden, and for holiday
Rambled over the fields where sang the larks,
And by Spoon River gathering many a shell,
And many a flower and medicinal weed—
Shouting to the wooded hills, singing to the green valleys.   15
At ninety-six I had lived enough, that is all,
And passed to a sweet repose.
What is this I hear of sorrow and weariness,
Anger, discontent and drooping hopes?
Degenerate sons and daughters,   20
Life is too strong for you—
It takes life to love Life.

Edgar Lee Masters (1868–1950)

Mr. Flood's Party

Old Eben Flood, climbing alone one night
Over the hill between the town below
And the forsaken upland hermitage
That held as much as he should ever know
On earth again of home, paused warily.   5
The road was his with not a native near;
And Eben, having leisure, said aloud,
For no man else in Tilbury Town to hear:

"Well, Mr. Flood, we have the harvest moon
Again, and we may not have many more;   10
The bird is on the wing, the poet says,°
And you and I have said it here before.
Drink to the bird." He raised up to the light
The jug that he had gone so far to fill,
And answered huskily: "Well, Mr. Flood,   15
Since you propose it, I believe I will."

11. **the poet says** *The Rubaiyat of Omar Khayyam* and the line, "The bird of Time . . . is on the wing"

Alone, as if enduring to the end
A valiant armor of scarred hopes outworn,
He stood there in the middle of the road
Like Roland's° ghost winding a silent horn.   20
Below him, in the town among the trees,
Where friends of other days had honored him,
A phantom salutation of the dead
Rang thinly till old Eben's eyes were dim.

Then, as a mother lays her sleeping child   25
Down tenderly, fearing it may awake,
He set the jug down slowly at his feet
With trembling care, knowing that most things break;
And only when assured that on firm earth
It stood, as the uncertain lives of men   30
Assuredly did not, he paced away,
And with his hand extended paused again:

"Well, Mr. Flood, we have not met like this
In a long time; and many a change has come
To both of us, I fear, since last it was   35
We had a drop together. Welcome home!"
Convivially returning with himself,
Again he raised the jug up to the light;
And with an acquiescent quaver said:
"Well, Mr. Flood, if you insist, I might.   40

"Only a very little, Mr. Flood—
For auld lang syne. No more, sir; that will do."
So, for the time, apparently it did,
And Eben evidently thought so too;
For soon amid the silver loneliness   45
Of night he lifted up his voice and sang,
Secure, with only two moons listening,
Until the whole harmonious landscape rang—

"For auld lang syne." The weary throat gave out,
The last word wavered, and the song was done.   50
He raised again the jug regretfully
And shook his head, and was again alone.
There was not much that was ahead of him,
And there was nothing in the town below—
Where strangers would have shut the many doors   55
That many friends had opened long ago.

Edwin Arlington Robinson (1869–1935)

---

20. Roland hero of the French epic poem *The Song of Roland* who sounded a call for help on his
famous horn as he was dying

Neither Out Far nor In Deep

The people along the sand
All turn and look one way.
They turn their back on the land.
They look at the sea all day.

As long as it takes to pass   5
A ship keeps raising its hull;
The wetter ground like glass
Reflects a standing gull.

The land may vary more;
But wherever the truth may be—   10
The water comes ashore,
And the people look at the sea.

They cannot look out far.
They cannot look in deep.
But when was that ever a bar   15
To any watch they keep?

Robert Frost (1874–1963)

Anecdote of the Jar

I placed a jar in Tennessee,
And round it was, upon a hill.
It made the slovenly wilderness
Surround that hill.

The wilderness rose up to it,   5
And sprawled around, no longer wild.
The jar was round upon the ground
And tall and of a port in air.

It took dominion everywhere.
The jar was gray and bare.   10
It did not give of bird or bush,
Like nothing else in Tennessee.

Wallace Stevens (1879–1955)

I Hear an Army Charging upon the Land

I hear an army charging upon the land,
  And the thunder of horses plunging, foam about their knees:
Arrogant, in black armour, behind them stand,
  Disdaining the reins, with fluttering whips, the charioteers.

They cry unto the night their battle-name: 5
  I moan in sleep when I hear afar their whirling laughter.
They cleave the gloom of dreams, a blinding flame,
  Clanging, clanging upon the heart as upon an anvil.

They come shaking in triumph their long, green hair:
  They come out of the sea and run shouting by the shore.   10
My heart, have you no wisdom thus to despair?
  My love, my love, my love, why have you left me alone?

James Joyce (1882–1941)

The Red Wheelbarrow

images

so much depends
upon

a red wheel
barrow

glazed with rain
water

beside the white
chickens.

William Carlos Williams (1883–1963)

The Dance

In Breughel's° great picture, The Kermess,
the dancers go round, they go round and
around, the squeal and the blare and the
tweedle of bagpipes, a bugle and fiddles
tipping their bellies (round as the thick-   5
sided glasses whose wash they impound)
their hips and their bellies off balance
to turn them. Kicking and rolling about
the Fair Grounds, swinging their butts, those
shanks must be sound to bear up under such   10
rollicking measures, prance as they dance
in Breughel's great picture, The Kermess.

William Carlos Williams (1883–1963)

1. **Breughel** Pieter Breughel (1525–1569), Flemish painter

The River-Merchant's Wife: A Letter

(after Rihaku°)

While my hair was still cut straight across my forehead
I played about the front gate, pulling flowers.
You came by on bamboo stilts, playing horse,
You walked about my seat, playing with blue plums.
And we went on living in the village of Chokan: 5
Two small people, without dislike or suspicion.

At fourteen I married My Lord you.
I never laughed, being bashful.
Lowering my head, I looked at the wall.
Called to, a thousand times, I never looked back.   10

At fifteen I stopped scowling,
I desired my dust to be mingled with yours
For ever and for ever and for ever.
Why should I climb the look out?

At sixteen you departed,   15
You went into far Ku-to-yen, by the river of swirling eddies,
And you have been gone five months.
The monkeys make sorrowful noise overhead.

You dragged your feet when you went out.
By the gate now, the moss is grown, the different mosses,   20
Too deep to clear them away!
The leaves fall early this autumn, in wind.
The paired butterflies are already yellow with August
Over the grass in the West garden;
They hurt me. I grow older.   25
If you are coming down through the narrows of the river Kiang,
Please let me know beforehand,
And I will come out to meet you
    As far as Cho-fu-Sa.

Ezra Pound (1885–1972)

The Love Song of J. Alfred Prufrock

S'io credesse che mia risposta fosse
A persona che mai tornasse al mondo,
Questa fiamma staria senza più scosse.

Rihaku Japanese name for eighth-century Chinese poet Li Po, whose poem Pound has loosely
paraphrased

Ma perciocche giammai di questo fondo
Non torno vivo alcun, s'i'odo il vero,
Senza tema d'infamia ti rispondo.°

Let us go then, you and I,
When the evening is spread out against the sky
Like a patient etherized upon a table;
Let us go, through certain half-deserted streets,
The muttering retreats   5
Of restless nights in one-night cheap hotels
And sawdust restaurants with oyster-shells:
Streets that follow like a tedious argument
Of insidious intent
To lead you to an overwhelming question . . .   10
Oh, do not ask, "What is it?"
Let us go and make our visit.

    In the room the women come and go
Talking of Michelangelo.°

    The yellow fog that rubs its back upon the window-panes,   15
The yellow smoke that rubs its muzzle on the window-panes
Licked its tongue into the corners of the evening,
Lingered upon the pools that stand in drains,
Let fall upon its back the soot that falls from chimneys,
Slipped by the terrace, made a sudden leap,   20
And seeing that it was a soft October night,
Curled once about the house, and fell asleep.

    And indeed there will be time
For the yellow smoke that slides along the street,
Rubbing its back upon the window-panes;   25
There will be time, there will be time
To prepare a face to meet the faces that you meet;
There will be time to murder and create,
And time for all the works and days of hands
That lift and drop a question on your plate;   30
Time for you and time for me,
And time yet for a hundred indecisions,
And for a hundred visions and revisions,
Before the taking of a toast and tea.

S'io credesse . . . ti rispondo This epigraph is from a scene in Dante's *Inferno* in which Dante and Virgil descend to the chasm of evil counselors and hear a spirit imprisoned in a flame admit his sinful, deceitful, and fraudulent behavior during his term on earth.   **14. Michelangelo** Michelangelo Buonarroti (1475–1564), great sculptor, painter, and architect of the Italian Renaissance

In the room the women come and go   35
Talking of Michelangelo.

And indeed there will be time
To wonder, "Do I dare?" and "Do I dare?"
Time to turn back and descend the stair,
With a bald spot in the middle of my hair—   40
(They will say: "How his hair is growing thin!")
My morning coat, my collar mounting firmly to the chin,
My necktie rich and modest, but asserted by a simple pin—
(They will say: "But how his arms and legs are thin!")
Do I dare   45
Disturb the universe?
In a minute there is time
For decisions and revisions which a minute will reverse.

For I have known them all already, known them all:—
Have known the evenings, mornings, afternoons,   50
I have measured out my life with coffee spoons;
I know the voices dying with a dying fall
Beneath the music from a farther room.
    So how should I presume?

And I have known the eyes already, known them all—   55
The eyes that fix you in a formulated phrase,
And when I am formulated, sprawling on a pin,
When I am pinned and wriggling on the wall,
Then how should I begin
To spit out all the butt-ends of my days and ways   60
    And how should I presume?

And I have known the arms already, known them all—
Arms that are braceleted and white and bare
(But in the lamplight, downed with light brown hair!)
Is it perfume from a dress   65
That makes me so digress?
Arms that lie along a table, or wrap about a shawl.
    And should I then presume?
    And how should I begin?

                    *   *   *

Shall I say, I have gone at dusk through narrow streets   70
And watched the smoke that rises from the pipes
Of lonely men in shirt-sleeves, leaning out of windows? . . .

    I should have been a pair of ragged claws
Scuttling across the floors of silent seas.

                    *   *   *

And the afternoon, the evening, sleeps so peacefully!   75
Smoothed by long fingers,
Asleep . . . tired . . . or it malingers,
Stretched on the floor, here beside you and me.
Should I, after tea and cakes and ices,
Have the strength to force the moment to its crisis?   80
But though I have wept and fasted, wept and prayed,
Though I have seen my head (grown slightly bald) brought in upon a platter,°
I am no prophet—and here's no great matter;
I have seen the moment of my greatness flicker,
And I have seen the eternal Footman hold my coat, and snicker,   85
And in short, I was afraid.

    And would it have been worth it, after all,
After the cups, the marmalade, the tea,
Among the porcelain, among some talk of you and me,
Would it have been worth while,   90
To have bitten off the matter with a smile,
To have squeezed the universe into a ball
To roll it toward some overwhelming question,
To say: "I am Lazarus,° come from the dead,
Come back to tell you all, I shall tell you all"—   95
If one, settling a pillow by her head,
    Should say: "That is not what I meant at all.
    That is not it, at all."

    And would it have been worth it, after all,
Would it have been worth while,   100
After the sunsets and the dooryards and the sprinkled streets,
After the novels, after the teacups, after the skirts that trail along the floor—
And this, and so much more?—
It is impossible to say just what I mean!
But as if a magic lantern threw the nerves in patterns on a screen: 105
Would it have been worth while
If one, settling a pillow or throwing off a shawl,
And turning toward the window, should say:
    "That is not it at all,
    That is not what I meant, at all."   110

                    *   *   *

No! I am not Prince Hamlet, nor was meant to be;
Am an attendant lord, one that will do
To swell a progress, start a scene or two,
Advise the prince; no doubt, an easy tool,

---

82. platter a reference to the beheading of John the Baptist   **94. Lazarus** Biblical figure who returned from the dead

Deferential, glad to be of use,   115
Politic, cautious, and meticulous:
Full of high sentence, but a bit obtuse;
At times, indeed, almost ridiculous—
Almost, at times, the Fool.

  I grow old . . . I grow old . . .   120
I shall wear the bottoms of my trousers rolled.

  Shall I part my hair behind? Do I dare to eat a peach?
I shall wear white flannel trousers, and walk upon the beach.
I have heard the mermaids singing, each to each.

  I do not think that they will sing to me.   125

  I have seen them riding seaward on the waves
Combing the white hair of the waves blown back
When the wind blows the water white and black.

  We have lingered in the chambers of the sea
By sea-girls wreathed with seaweed red and brown   130
Till human voices wake us, and we drown.

T. S. Eliot (1888–1965)

Dulce et Decorum Est°

Bent double, like old beggars under sacks,
Knock-kneed, coughing like hags, we cursed through sludge,
Till on the haunting flares we turned our backs,
And towards our distant rest began to trudge.
Men marched asleep. Many had lost their boots,   5
But limped on, blood-shod. All went lame, all blind;
Drunk with fatigue; deaf even to the hoots
Of gas-shells dropping softly behind.

Gas! GAS! Quick, boys!—An ecstasy of fumbling,
Fitting the clumsy helmets just in time,   10
But someone still was yelling out and stumbling
And flound'ring like a man in fire or lime.—
Dim through the misty panes and thick green light,
As under a green sea, I saw him drowning.

In all my dreams before my helpless sight   15
He plunges at me, guttering, choking, drowning.

Dulce et decorum est a phrase from the Roman poet Horace which is quoted in full in the
concluding lines of this poem: "It is sweet and proper to die for one's country"

If in some smothering dreams, you too could pace
Behind the wagon that we flung him in,
And watch the white eyes writhing in his face,
His hanging face, like a devil's sick of sin,   20
If you could hear, at every jolt, the blood
Come gargling from the froth-corrupted lungs
Bitter as the cud
Of vile, incurable sores on innocent tongues, —
My friend, you would not tell with such high zest   25
To children ardent for some desperate glory,
The old lie: *Dulce et decorum est*
Pro patria mori.

Wilfred Owen (1893–1918)

Not Waving But Drowning

Nobody heard him, the dead man,
But still he lay moaning:
I was much further out than you thought
And not waving but drowning.

Poor chap, he always loved larking   5
And now he's dead
It must have been too cold for him his heart gave way,
They said.

Oh, no no no, it was too cold always
(Still the dead one lay moaning)   10
I was much too far out all my life
And not waving but drowning.

Stevie Smith (1902–1971)

The Groundhog

In June, amid the golden fields,
I saw a groundhog lying dead.
Dead lay he; my senses shook,
And mind outshot our naked frailty.
There lowly in the vigorous summer   5
His form began its senseless change,
And made my senses waver dim
Seeing nature ferocious in him.
Inspecting close his maggots' might
And seething cauldron of his being,   10
Half with loathing, half with a strange love,
I poked him with an angry stick.
The fever arose, became a flame

And Vigour circumscribed the skies,
Immense energy in the sun,   15
And through my frame a sunless trembling.
My stick had done nor good nor harm.
Then stood I silent in the day
Watching the object, as before;
And kept my reverence for knowledge   20
Trying for control, to be still,
To quell the passion of the blood;
Until I had bent down on my knees
Praying for joy in the sight of decay.
And so I left; and I returned   25
In Autumn strict of eye, to see
The sap gone out of the groundhog,
But the bony sodden hulk remained.
But the year had lost its meaning,
And in intellectual chains   30
I lost both love and loathing,
Mured up in the wall of wisdom.
Another summer took the fields again
Massive and burning, full of life,
But when I chanced upon the spot   35
There was only a little hair left,
And bones bleaching in the sunlight
Beautiful as architecture;
I watched them like a geometer,
And cut a walking stick from a birch.   40
It has been three years, now.
There is no sign of the groundhog.
I stood there in the whirling summer,
My hand capped a withered heart,
And thought of China and of Greece,   45
Of Alexander° in his tent;
Of Montaigne° in his tower,
Of Saint Theresa° in her wild lament.

Richard Eberhart (b. 1904)

Musée des Beaux Arts°

About suffering they were never wrong,
The Old Masters: how well they understood
Its human position; how it takes place

---

46. Alexander Alexander the Great, who conquered the world   **47. Montaigne** French essayist who commented ironically on human foibles   **48. Saint Theresa** the mystic St. Theresa of Avila, founder of a religious order   **Musée des Beaux Arts** The Museum of Fine Arts

While someone else is eating or opening a window or just walking
    dully along;
How, when the aged are reverently, passionately waiting   5
For the miraculous birth, there always must be
Children who did not specially want it to happen, skating
On a pond at the edge of the wood:
They never forgot
That even the dreadful martyrdom must run its course   10
Anyhow in a corner, some untidy spot
Where the dogs go on with their doggy life and the torturer's horse
Scratches its innocent behind on a tree.

In Brueghel's *Icarus*,° for instance: how everything turns away
Quite leisurely from the disaster; the ploughman may   15
Have heard the splash, the forsaken cry,
But for him it was not an important failure; the sun shone
As it had to on the white legs disappearing into the green
Water; and the expensive delicate ship that must have seen
Something amazing, a boy falling out of the sky,   20
Had somewhere to get to and sailed calmly on.

W. H. Auden (1907–1973)

The Fish

I caught a tremendous fish
and held him beside the boat
half out of water, with my hook
fast in a corner of his mouth.
He didn't fight.   5
He hadn't fought at all.
He hung a grunting weight,
battered and venerable
and homely. Here and there
his brown skin hung in strips   10
like ancient wallpaper,
and its pattern of darker brown
was like wallpaper:
shapes like full-blown roses
stained and lost through age.   15
He was speckled with barnacles,

---

14. Brueghel's *Icarus* This is a reference to a canvas by the Flemish painter Pieter Brueghel (1525–1569) showing the mythic Greek figure Icarus, who, with his father Daedalus, had escaped from imprisonment by flying on wings of wax, but sailed too close to the sun and fell to earth when his wings melted. In Brueghel's painting Icarus is a relatively unimportant figure disappearing inconspicuously into the water as daily life goes on.

fine rosettes of lime,
and infested
with tiny white sea-lice,
and underneath two or three   20
rags of green weed hung down.
While his gills were breathing in
the terrible oxygen
—the frightening gills,
fresh and crisp with blood,   25
that can cut so badly—
I thought of the coarse white flesh
packed in like feathers,
the big bones and the little bones,
the dramatic reds and blacks   30
of his shiny entrails,
and the pink swim-bladder
like a big peony.
I looked into his eyes
which were far larger than mine   35
but shallower, and yellowed,
the irises backed and packed
with tarnished tinfoil
seen through the lenses
of old scratched isinglass.   40
They shifted a little, but not
to return my stare.
—It was more like the tipping
of an object toward the light.
I admired his sullen face,   45
the mechanism of his jaw,
and then I saw
that from his lower lip
—if you could call it a lip—
grim, wet, and weaponlike,   50
hung five old pieces of fish-line,
or four and a wire leader
with the swivel still attached,
with all their five big hooks
grown firmly in his mouth   55
A green line, frayed at the end
where he broke it, two heavier lines,
and a fine black thread
still crimped from the strain and snap
when it broke and he got away.   60
Like medals with their ribbons
frayed and wavering,
a five-haired beard of wisdom

trailing from his aching jaw.
I stared and stared   65
and victory filled up
the little rented boat,
from the pool of bilge
where oil had spread a rainbow
around the rusted engine   70
to the bailer rusted orange,
the sun-cracked thwarts,
the oarlocks on their strings,
the gunnels—until everything
was rainbow, rainbow, rainbow!   75
And I let the fish go.

Elizabeth Bishop (1911–1979)

Those Winter Sundays

Sundays too my father got up early
and put his clothes on in the blueblack cold,
then with cracked hands that ached
from labor in the weekday weather made
banked fires blaze. No one ever thanked him.   5

I'd wake and hear the cold splintering, breaking.
When the rooms were warm, he'd call,
and slowly I would rise and dress,
fearing the chronic angers of that house,

Speaking indifferently to him,   10
who had driven out the cold
and polished my good shoes as well.
What did I know, what did I know
of love's austere and lonely offices?

Robert Hayden (1913–1980)

Judging Distances°

Not only how far away, but the way that you say it
Is very important. Perhaps you may never get
The knack of judging a distance, but at least you know
How to report on a landscape: the central sector,
The right of arc and that, which we had last Tuesday,   5
    And at least you know

Judging Distances This poem, along with "Naming of Parts," was published as part of a series of three poems called "Lessons of War."

That maps are of time, not place, so far as the army
Happens to be concerned—the reason being,
Is one which need not delay us. Again, you know
There are three kinds of tree, three only, the fir and the poplar,   10
And those which have bushy tops to; and lastly
    That things only seem to be things.

A barn is not called a barn, to put it more plainly,
Or a field in the distance, where sheep may be safely grazing.
You must never be over-sure. You must say, when reporting: 15
At five o'clock in the central sector is a dozen
Of what appear to be animals; whatever you do,
    Don't call the bleeders sheep.

I am sure that's quite clear; and suppose, for the sake of example,
The one at the end, asleep, endeavors to tell us   20
What he sees over there to the west, and how far away,
After first having come to attention. There to the west,
On the fields of summer the sun and the shadows bestow
    Vestments of purple and gold.

The still white dwellings are like a mirage in the heat,   25
And under the swaying elms a man and a woman
Lie gently together. Which is, perhaps, only to say
That there is a row of houses to the left of arc,
And that under some poplars a pair of what appear to be humans
    Appear to be loving.   30

Well that, for an answer, is what we might rightly call
Moderately satisfactory only, the reason being,
Is that two things have been omitted, and those are important.
The human beings, now: in what direction are they,
And how far away, would you say? And do not forget   35
    There may be dead ground° in between.

There may be dead ground in between; and I may not have got
The knack of judging a distance; I will only venture
A guess that perhaps between me and the apparent lovers,
(Who, incidentally, appear by now to have finished,)   40
At seven o'clock from the houses, is roughly a distance
    Of about one year and a half.

Henry Reed (b. 1914)

Naming of Parts

Today we have naming of parts. Yesterday,
We had daily cleaning. And tomorrow morning,
We shall have what to do after firing. But today,

36. dead ground space that cannot be reached by friendly fire

Today we have naming of parts. Japonica°   *flowering shrub*
Glistens like coral in all of the neighboring gardens,   5
        And today we have naming of parts.

This is the lower sling swivel. And this
Is the upper sling swivel, whose use you will see,
When you are given your slings. And this is the piling swivel,
Which in your case you have not got. The branches   10
Hold in the gardens their silent, eloquent gestures,
        Which in our case we have not got.

This is the safety-catch, which is always released
With an easy flick of the thumb. And please do not let me
See anyone using his finger. You can do it quite easy   15
If you have any strength in your thumb. The blossoms
Are fragile and motionless, never letting anyone see
        Any of them using their finger.

And this you can see is the bolt. The purpose of this
Is to open the breech, as you see. We can slide it   20
Rapidly backwards and forwards: we call this
Easing the spring. And rapidly backwards and forwards
The early bees are assaulting and fumbling the flowers:
        They call it easing the Spring.

They call it easing the Spring: it is perfectly easy   25
If you have any strength in your thumb: like the bolt,
And the breech, and the cocking-piece, and the point of balance,
Which in our case we have not got; and the almond-blossom
Silent in all of the gardens and the bees going backwards and forwards,
        For today we have naming of parts.   30

Henry Reed (b. 1914)

We Real Cool
The Pool Players.
Seven At The Golden Shovel.

                        We real cool. We
                        Left school. We

                        Lurk late. We
                        Strike straight. We

                        Sing sin. We
                        Thin gin. We

                        Jazz June. We
                        Die soon.

Gwendolyn Brooks (b. 1917)

Life Cycle of Common Man

Roughly figured, this man of moderate habits,
This average consumer of the middle class,
Consumed in the course of his average life span
Just under half a million cigarettes,
Four thousand fifths of gin and about   5
A quarter as much vermouth; he drank
Maybe a hundred thousand cups of coffee,
And counting his parents' share it cost
Something like half a million dollars
To put him through life. How many beasts   10
Died to provide him with meat, belt and shoes
Cannot be certainly said.
                    But anyhow,
It is in this way that a man travels through time,
Leaving behind him a lengthening trail   15
Of empty bottles and bones, of broken shoes,
Frayed collars and worn out or outgrown
Diapers and dinnerjackets, silk ties and slickers.
Given the energy and security thus achieved,
He did . . . ? What? The usual things, of course,   20
The eating, dreaming, drinking and begetting,
And he worked for the money which was to pay
For the eating, et cetera, which were necessary
If he were to go on working for the money, et cetera,
But chiefly he talked. As the bottles and bones   25
Accumulated behind him, the words proceeded
Steadily from the front of his face as he
Advanced into the silence and made it verbal.
Who can tally the tale of his words? A lifetime
Would barely suffice for their repetition;   30
If you merely printed all his commas the result
Would be a very large volume, and the number of times
He said "thank you" or "very little sugar, please,"
Would stagger the imagination. There were also
Witticisms, platitudes, and statements beginning   35
"It seems to me" or "As I always say."

Consider the courage in all that, and behold the man
Walking into deep silence, with the ectoplastic
Cartoon's balloon of speech proceeding
Steadily out of the front of his face, the words   40
Borne along on the breath which is his spirit
Telling the numberless tale of his untold Word
Which makes the world his apple, and forces him to eat.

Howard Nemerov (b. 1920)

Poems for Further Reading

The Pardon

My dog lay dead five days without a grave
In the thick of summer, hid in a clump of pine
And a jungle of grass and honeysuckle-vine.
I who had loved him while he kept alive

Went only close enough to where he was   5
To sniff the heavy honeysuckle-smell
Twined with another odor heavier still
And hear the flies' intolerable buzz.

Well, I was ten and very much afraid.
In my kind world the dead were out of range   10
And I could not forgive the sad or strange
In beast or man. My father took the spade

And buried him. Last night I saw the grass
Slowly divide (it was the same scene
But now it glowed a fierce and mortal green)   15
And saw the dog emerging. I confess

I felt afraid again, but still he came
In the carnal sun, clothed in a hymn of flies,
And death was breeding in his lively eyes.
I started in to cry and call his name,   20

Asking forgiveness of his tongueless head.
. . . I dreamt the past was never past redeeming:
But whether this was false or honest dreaming
I beg death's pardon now. And mourn the dead.

Richard Wilbur (b. 1921)

The Performance

The last time I saw Donald Armstrong
He was staggering oddly off into the sun,
Going down, off the Philippine Islands.
I let my shovel fall, and put that hand
Above my eyes, and moved some way to one side   5
That his body might pass through the sun,

And I saw how well he was not
Standing there on his hands,
On his spindle-shanked forearms balanced,
Unbalanced, with his big feet looming and waving   10
In the great, untrustworthy air
He flew in each night, when it darkened.

Dust fanned in scraped puffs from the earth
Between his arms, and blood turned his face inside out,
To demonstrate its suppleness   15
Of veins, as he perfected his role.
Next day, he toppled his head off
On an island beach to the south,

And the enemy's two-handed sword
Did not fall from anyone's hands   20
At that miraculous sight,
As the head rolled over upon
Its wide-eyed face, and fell
Into the inadequate grave

He had dug for himself, under pressure.   25
Yet I put my flat hand to my eyebrows
Months later, to see him again
In the sun, when I learned how he died,
And imagined him, there,
Come, judged, before his small captors,   30

Doing all his lean tricks to amaze them—
The back somersault, the kip-up—
And at last, the stand on his hands,
Perfect, with his feet together,
His head down, evenly breathing   35
As the sun poured up from the sea

And the headsman broke down
In a blaze of tears, in that light
Of the thin, long human frame
Upside down in its own strange joy,   40
And, if some other one had not told him,
Would have cut off the feet

Instead of the head,
And if Armstrong had not presently risen
In kingly, round-shouldered attendance,   45
And then knelt down in himself
Beside his hacked, glittering grave, having done
All things in this life that he could.

James Dickey (b. 1923)

First Party at Ken Kesey's with Hell's Angels

Cool black night thru the redwoods
cars parked outside in shade
behind the gate, stars dim above

the ravine, a fire burning by the side
porch and a few tired souls hunched over   5
in black leather jackets. In the huge
wooden house, a yellow chandelier
at 3AM the blast of loudspeakers
hi-fi Rolling Stones Ray Charles Beatles
Jumping Joe Jackson and twenty youths   10
dancing to the vibration thru the floor,
a little weed in the bathroom, girls in scarlet
tights, one muscular smooth skinned man
sweating dancing for hours, beer cans
bent littering the yard, a hanged man   15
sculpture dangling from a high creek branch,
children sleeping softly in bedroom bunks,
And 4 police cars parked outside the painted
gate, red lights revolving in the leaves.

Allen Ginsberg (b. 1926)

April Inventory

The green catalpa tree has turned
All white; the cherry blooms once more.
In one whole year I haven't learned
A blessed thing they pay you for.
The blossoms snow down in my hair;   5
The trees and I will soon be bare.

The trees have more than I to spare.
The sleek, expensive girls I teach,
Younger and pinker every year,
Bloom gradually out of reach.   10
The pear tree lets its petals drop
Like dandruff on a tabletop.

The girls have grown so young by now
I have to nudge myself to stare.
This year they smile and mind me how   15
My teeth are falling with my hair.
In thirty years I may not get
Younger, shrewder, or out of debt.

The tenth time, just a year ago,
I made myself a little list   20
Of all the things I'd ought to know,
Then told my parents, analyst,
And everyone who's trusted me
I'd be substantial, presently.

I haven't read one book about   25
A book or memorized one plot.
Or found a mind I did not doubt.
I learned one date. And then forgot.
And one by one the solid scholars
Get the degrees, the jobs, the dollars.   30

And smile above their starchy collars.
I taught my classes Whitehead's° notions;
One lovely girl, a song of Mahler's.°
Lacking a source-book or promotions,
I showed one child the colors of   35
A luna moth and how to love.

I taught myself to name my name,
To bark back, loosen love and crying;
To ease my woman so she came,
To ease an old man who was dying.   40
I have not learned how often I
Can win, can love, but choose to die.

I have not learned there is a lie
Love shall be blonder, slimmer, younger;
That my equivocating eye   45
Loves only by my body's hunger;
That I have forces, true to feel,
Or that the lovely world is real.

While scholars speak authority
And wear their ulcers on their sleeves,   50
My eyes in spectacles shall see
These trees procure and spend their leaves.
There is a value underneath
The gold and silver in my teeth.

Though trees turn bare and girls turn wives,   55
We shall afford our costly seasons;
There is a gentleness survives
That will outspeak and has its reasons.
There is a loveliness exists,
Preserves us, not for specialists.   60

W. D. Snodgrass (b. 1926)

In the Tank

A man sat in the felon's tank, alone,
Fearful, ungrateful, in a cell for two.
And from his metal bunk, the lower one,
He studied where he was, as felons do.

---

32. Whitehead English philosopher Alfred North Whitehead (1861–1947)   **33. Mahler** Austrian composer Gustav Mahler (1860–1911)

The cell was clean and cornered, and contained   5
A bowl, grey gritty soap, and paper towels,
A mattress lumpy and not over-stained,
Also a toilet, for the felon's bowels.

He could see clearly all there was to see,
And later when the lights flicked off at nine   10
He saw as clearly all there was to see:
An order without colour, bulk, or line.

And then he knew exactly where he sat.
For though the total riches could not fail
—Red weathered brick, fountains, wisteria—yet   15
Still they contained the silence of a jail,

The jail contained a tank, the tank contained
A box, a mere suspension, at the centre,
Where there was nothing left to understand,
And where he must re-enter and re-enter.   20

Thom Gunn (b. 1929)

From a Survivor

The pact that we made was the ordinary pact
of men & women in those days

I don't know who we thought we were
that our personalities
could resist the failures of the race   5

Lucky or unlucky, we didn't know
the race had failures of that order
and that we were going to share them

Like everybody else, we thought of ourselves as special

Your body is as vivid to me   10
as it ever was: even more

since my feeling for it is clearer:
I know what it could do and could not do

it is no longer
the body of a god   15
or anything with power over my life

Next year it would have been 20 years
and you are wastefully dead
who might have made the leap

we talked, too late, of making   20
which I live now
not as a leap
but a succession of brief, amazing movements

each one making possible the next

Adrienne Rich (b. 1929)

The Photos

My sister in her well-tailored silk blouse hands me
the photo of my father
in naval uniform and white hat.
I say, "Oh, this is the one which Mama used to have on her dresser."

My sister controls her face and furtively looks at my mother,   5
a sad rag bag of a woman, lumpy and sagging everywhere,
like a mattress at the Salvation Army, though with no holes or tears,
and says, "No."

I look again,
and see that my father is wearing a wedding ring,   10
which he never did
when he lived with my mother. And that there is a legend on it,
"To my dearest wife,
         Love
         Chief"   15
And I realize the photo must have belonged to his second wife,
whom he left our mother to marry.

My mother says, with her face as still as the whole unpopulated part of the
state of North Dakota,
"May I see it too?"   20
She looks at it.

I look at my tailored sister
and my own blue-jeaned self. Have we wanted to hurt our mother,
sharing these pictures on this, one of the few days I ever visit or
spend with family? For her face is curiously haunted,   25
not now with her usual viperish bitterness,
but with something so deep it could not be spoken

I turn away and say I must go on, as I have a dinner engagement with friends.
But I drive all the way to Pasadena from Whittier,
thinking of my mother's face; how I could never love her;
      how my father   30
could not love her either. Yet knowing I have inherited
the rag-bag body,
stony face with bulldog jaws.

I drive, thinking of that face.
Jeffers' California Medea° who inspired me to poetry.   35
I killed my children,
but there as I am changing lanes on the freeway, necessarily glancing in the
rearview mirror, I see the face,
not even a ghost, but always with me, like a photo in a
    beloved's wallet.   40

How I hate my destiny.

Diane Wakoski (b. 1937)

Running on Empty

As a teenager I would drive Father's
Chevrolet cross-country, given me

reluctantly: "Always keep the tank
half full, boy, half full, ya hear?"

The fuel gauge dipping, dipping   5
toward Empty, hitting Empty, then

—thrilling!—'way below Empty,
myself driving cross-country

mile after mile, faster and faster,
all night long, this crazy kid driving   10

the earth's rolling surface,
against all laws, defying chemistry,

rules, and time, riding on nothing
but fumes, pushing luck harder

than anyone pushed before, the wind   15
screaming past like the Furies . . .

I stranded myself only once, a white
night with no gas station open, ninety miles

from nowhere. Panicked for a while,
at standstill, myself stalled.   20

At dawn the car and I both refilled. But,
Father, I am running on empty still.

Robert Phillips (b. 1938)

---

35. Jeffers' California Medea California poet Robinson Jeffers (1887–1962) wrote about the tragic
Greek figure Medea who revenged herself on her unfaithful husband Jason by murdering their
children.

DRAMA

1
INTRODUCTION TO DRAMA

In its remarkable differences from poetry and fiction, drama offers us its own pleasures and its own challenges. When we read the dialogue of a play and attempt to understand the playwright's hints about what is meant to happen on the stage, we might be able to see the various characters in our imaginations—men and women with distinctive voices, faces, and traits. We might find ourselves arranging their entrances and exits, choreographing their movements, timing their actions and speeches. We think of them coming together in conflict or in harmony. Yet, no matter how creatively we might direct a play in the theater of our minds, the play itself—that literary artifact we hold in our hands—remains only a set of mental possibilities until the moment it comes alive in an actual performance that we *see* rather than *read*.

Drama is unique in this regard. It is like fiction and poetry in that it attempts to portray and illuminate human experience. But, unlike fiction and poetry, which we experience in wholly private moments, drama is part of a *formal occasion*. Unlike works of fiction or of poetry, plays are spectacles, and they are public. They come to us from a tradition emphasizing the importance of artistic activity being visible to an audience, to a people, to a civic or religious gathering. A story or a poem can be read almost anywhere, and needs only the attention of a reader and the presence of a book. Indeed, one of the pleasures of reading is that, wherever we are, we feel we can leave the world behind for a while and can disappear into the total privacy of our imaginations. Not so with plays. They announce to us that they are part of an occasion, even a formal occasion. We *go* to a play, and when we arrive, the play, the players, the lighting, the props, and all the rest, are ready for us. In the theater, moreover, we are compelled to follow the pace of the play, not our own pace. We submit to the various contrivances and illusions that make plays work. Plays, then, are like musical scores in that they require interpretation to be themselves. Guided by that interpretation, we believe for a moment that the actors are the characters they play; that the stage on which they move is a real drawing room, public square, and so on; that what happens is unfolding spontaneously instead of according to a carefully crafted script. When we watch a play, we have no ability to skip acts (as we might leaf through the pages of a book) or to ask for instant replays of some crucial piece of dialogue (as we might simply review a favorite or difficult passage). We laugh, cry, applaud or even jeer—things we probably wouldn't do at home when we read a book. We are aware of how those sitting near us are taking to the experience, and hence we feel that the time spent in the presence of a play is one that can never completely be our own. It is shared.

The Backgrounds of Drama

As a literary form, plays are different now because they have always been different as a means of artistic expression and appreciation. In order to understand drama, then, it is necessary to look back at its origins, to a time when it was so powerful a literary form that it could satisfy both the need for lyrical beauty that is the province of poetry and the story-telling need that later would become the province of fiction. The beginning of drama as it is known in the Western world is usually attributed to the Greeks. In perhaps the sixth century B.C., in the city of Athens, playwrights began to compete at festivals that had long been a part of Greek culture. They would compose tragedies for one festival, comedies for another. Prizes were awarded for the best plays, but it was understood that the prizes, and even the plays themselves, were only parts of something much more important to Greek society: its hopes for continued health. The festivals were to remind everyone of the power of the god Dionysus who, with his annual death and subsequent rebirth, represented the great cycle of nature with its births and deaths. The plays were one element of an immensely important civic event, and to be in attendance at that event was to participate in something at once entertaining, religious, and communal. Attending a play like *Oedipus Rex*, people might see, in the tragic circumstances of the main character, the way the universe operated; they might feel closer to each other and to the state that protected and nourished them.

Historians of the theater tell us that the next great moment in the development of the drama came in the eleventh and twelfth centuries A.D., with the Christian church playing the role that the state had in Greek drama. Again, at important religious moments in the year, such as Christmas or Easter, short plays emphasizing the meaning of such things as Christ's birth or his resurrection were presented. They were intended to explain or to reinforce the doctrines of the medieval church, but they need not have taken place in a church or cathedral since religion was part of the ritual life permeating the entire community. As these plays developed and spread throughout Europe, they took on elements not strictly religious—elements of pure entertainment, of simple comedy or the development of certain character types. People gathered to watch the plays when they would appear in a village or city and, like the Greeks centuries before them, derived part of their pleasure from being together as spectators and seeing commonly accepted truths about the world reinforced.

With the establishment of the Elizabethan theater (so named after the reigning queen of the time, Elizabeth I) just outside London in the latter part of the sixteenth century, the transition was made from religious to secular drama. This theater gave the local population, and thereafter the world, the plays of Shakespeare, Ben Jonson, Christopher Marlowe, and many other great writers. The Elizabethan theater (the Globe Theater was the most memorable example) offered plays to upwards of three thousand people and was accessible to all classes and elements of the society. Thus it fulfilled the same function of binding people together which, in earlier periods, Greek and medieval drama had. For instance, the crowd coming to see one of Shakespeare's history plays would be made up of a cross section of the population, and for two or three hours this event would make them forget their differences by reminding them of what their past glories as Englishmen had been and what the future held in store for them.

Thus Elizabethan theater was much like earlier kinds of theater—civic, communal, and saturated with the values of the surrounding culture—but it was more. By instituting a small admission fee to witness this rich celebration, the Elizabethans made the theater a commercial reality as well as an artistic one. They were creating a structure in which highly skilled artists of many kinds—playwrights, actors, costumers, designers, builders—could join to present entertainments for which people would pay. The writing of plays, performing in them, and getting them staged became a profession. It gave fame to some playwrights and to some actors, thus inaugurating the pre-occupation with individual expression that characterizes the modern theater. While we know that Sophocles did something extraordinary in writing *Oedipus Rex*, we feel his skill lay in brilliantly exemplifying and articulating the values, and the fears, of his society. His own voice is thus drowned out by the collective voice of the Greek experience. Shakespeare's greatness, on the other hand, rests only partly in his ability to mirror the values of Elizabethan England. That genius is also found in his individuality as an artist: in his characters and plots, problems and solutions, the lines of poetry, and insights into the human predicament that we would simply not possess had he not lived. Shakespeare the individual is thus of crucial importance to us and to our sense of drama.

A great deal of modern drama, which constitutes the next important development in the history of the theater, is based on the pursuit of *realism*. During the Industrial Revolution of the nineteenth century, manufacturing cities took on immense importance to the cultural life of most European countries and the United States. More and more people were coming to live in cities and to experience problems that previously had been unknown or ignored. A large and prosperous middle class established itself as the chief consumer of culture and it wanted the drama to deal with the issues it thought important, issues already beginning to appear in novels of the day. Rather than creating works that would bind diverse social groups together, a playwright like Henrik Ibsen wrote plays mirroring the life actually lived by people in the world as he knew it, expressing the problems and the questions they had to grapple with. The great accomplishment of Ibsen and other playwrights of his time was to change the focus of drama. It moved from the lofty passions of kings and nobles to the more authentic—and frequently more explosive—dilemmas taking place in middle-class parlors and bedrooms. There the situations involved greed and hypocrisy, the oppressiveness of wealth and social power, and the compromises that men and women are asked to make with society. The *social realism* of playwrights like Ibsen took audiences more deeply into the world around them—a world of uncertainty, discontent, and animosity.

As a major force in twentieth-century theater, such realism meant that characters no longer spoke in measured verse and elegant language, as they had in Greek drama and in the plays of Shakespeare and Molière. Playwrights strove to capture the cadences of real speech and they produced scenes that would have the texture of real life. The stage itself took on the appearance of rooms as people knew them from their own homes, of offices like their own. As a theatrical medium, realism was strengthened, moreover, by the parallel rise of the movies as the mass art form of our time. With its remarkable ability to take the audience directly into life as it is lived in a wide variety of circumstances, both public and private, film helped the theater to expand its range of subjects and concerns.

The chief objective of many modern dramatists has been to give their work *psychological realism*, to incorporate the insights of Sigmund Freud and other theorists of human motivation and pathology. The interior problems caused by society's pressures are vividly present in a play like Arthur Miller's *Death of a Salesman:* we feel those pressures closing in on the main character Willy Loman, and we are made to witness his inward collapse. In much the same way, Tennessee Williams's *The Glass Menagerie* fastens its attention on the ways in which the interior life of the characters is forced to the surface of consciousness by social circumstances.

Thus, for the last hundred or so years, playwrights have been trying to narrow the distance between life as it is actually lived and life as it is presented on the stage. In the years after World War I, however, a number of dramatists recognized the limits of realism. They were no longer sure that the physical and social world operated according to rules and principles that everyone could rely on. Einstein's theory of relativity had called the notion of such fixed and universal laws into question. Anthropologists had declared that culture too was relative: some non-European societies with varying degrees of technological development had cultures that were different from but not inferior to the European. Later in the century the horrors of World War II—the Holocaust, the use of the atomic bomb on Hiroshima and Nagasaki— called into question many of the assumptions about the human enterprise on which the theater of social and psychological realism had been based. Finally, a new theological movement claimed that God was dead or irrelevant. All of these forces led to the revolution in dramatic practice known as the *theater of the absurd*. In absurdist plays, the playwright explores, directly or obliquely, the irrational or even hostile elements controlling human destiny. A play like Edward Albee's *The American Dream*, for instance, poses questions about the lack of moral structure in life and the triviality of human relations, using the stage not as a "real" scene but as a forum to raise disturbing philosophical issues. Rather than receiving an affirmation of universal order, contemporary audiences of absurdists plays witness symbolic confirmations of some of their own worst fears.

Change and Continuity

While we must bear in mind the traditions that have made drama unique as a literary form, we must also recognize that, like other forms, it has been the focus of great change and experimentation. While it is true that a playwright's use of *conventions*—what a particular historical era regards as *the* way to do things—is what gives his plays their power, it is also true that the great playwrights constantly challenge and push against limitations, and try to enlarge the boundaries available to their art.

As we have noted, conventions are transformed from one era to another. Concerning the appropriate subject matter for a play, the Greeks, for instance, felt that violence should not be seen on stage, and thus such horrific events as Oedipus' gouging out his eyes were not seen by the audience but only recounted to it. The Elizabethans, on the other hand, employed violence as an integral part of the dramatic environment; in *Hamlet* (by no means the most bloody play of its day), for example, there is poisoning, suicide, and stabbing; the play ends with the stage strewn with corpses. Ibsen was not reluctant to deal with venereal disease, marital infidelity, or mental illness. On the other hand, he introduced no obscene language into his plays. The modern stage is perfectly at home with obscenity and nudity, and sees the very existence of any taboos as alien to the theater.

Some dramatic conventions have been rendered obsolete. The Greeks, for example, felt that the *chorus* was indispensable to drama as a means to comment on the action and to point out the moral of the play. The chorus can be thought of as a kind of character, but also as part of the author's presence, and even as one's own mind interpreting the drama. But a chorus would destroy the aura of reality that Ibsen creates in *Hedda Gabler* or that Lillian Hellman creates in *The Little Foxes*. Yet some conventions endure through the many changes of generations. The *soliloquy* is an example. Developed by Shakespeare and other Elizabethan dramatists, this device provided a means to resolve the problem of conveying what is occurring inside a character. The soliloquy allows a character to let the audience know what he is thinking by simply speaking his mind. When Hamlet, for instance, delivers his soliloquies, no other character in the play hears him, and time and the dramatic rush of events seem to be suspended momentarily while this extraordinary event takes place before our eyes and ears. This device might seem dated, yet in *Death of A Salesman* Willy Loman now and again speaks to himself (and thus to us) about his memories, hopes, and disappointments. Even in a recent Broadway play, *A Chorus Line*, soliloquies are used as character after character comes before the audience to tell of dreams and ambitions. So the device itself has not vanished from the theater, but we are relaxed in the face of its modern instances, and so perhaps think it has.

Another convention that has greatly changed is *dramatic form*. What has been regarded as proper form in one age is considered improper in another. The *running time* of a play, for instance, has ranged from relatively brief one-act works to such mammoth productions as the Royal Shakespeare Company's production of an adaptation of Charles Dickens' *Nicholas Nickleby*, an eight-hour play complete with a dinner break. *Internal form* has also changed. At one time, the *ideal plot* was thought to require a series of prescribed moments: the *introduction* of the conflict; the *complication* in which the drama becomes more intense; a *climax* in which the fate of the character (or characters) is set; a *resolution* of the issues; and, finally, a *denouement* or unraveling of all the dramatic issues in the play. This sense of form, easily diagrammed as a pyramid or a triangle, is obviously present in a work like *Hamlet* and gives it great power. But it is less conspicuous, and even absent, in other plays. In comedy, which tends to be a much less perfectly organized theatrical form, the ideal plot can be submerged or sacrificed. And in *The American Dream*, such plot is out of the question, for that play argues that life is a series of irrational and unconnected happenings.

A final convention worth thinking about is that of the *stage* itself. While it is tempting to think of it as a given, it has undergone great changes. In the Greek theater, the audience sat on a raised semicircle around a circular area known as the *orchestra*, on which the chorus stood, danced, and spoke. At the rear of the orchestra was a broad area called the *skene*, representing the palace or temple before which the action took place. During the Elizabethan Age, the audience surrounded the stage on three sides, and the stage was a complex three-tiered affair capable of representing, say, a balcony, or a public square, or a graveyard such as the one in *Hamlet*.

Unlike the Greek or Elizabethan theater, the modern theater of Ibsen had regular evening performances. As the curtain rose and the lights dimmed, the audience was invited to imagine that it was looking through an invisible fourth wall directly into a realistic scene: the audience, in effect, became witnesses to some private drama. And today, the stage of absurdist drama is likely to be bare, devoid of scenery or props, reminding us that we are watching a contrivance, not life itself, and that we should pay attention to the ideas of the play and not to its lack of verisimilitude.

The Art of Drama

Shakespeare's *Hamlet* contains some of the greatest poetry in the English language; Molière's *Tartuffe* incisively probes hypocrisy, stubborn pride, and obsequiousness; Williams's *The Glass Menagerie* is one of the most powerful portraits we have of people trying to believe that their lives are something more than chronicles of petty failure. Great plays, as these examples show, are indeed great literature. But we must not ignore the fact that the pages of a play, held in a director's or an actor's hands, provide only the verbal basis of what, after much work and imagination, will at last become a performance. The actor is not customarily free to deviate from that text, nor is the director, but the words of a play leave countless questions unanswered, and those questions must be asked and must be answered before the play is ready for performance. The life of an actor or a director is one made up of choices. How, for instance, is Hamlet to speak his first lines: "A little more than kin and less than kind"? These nine words, spoken in an aside to the audience, introduce Hamlet the character; they are given as a response to some apparently warm welcoming remarks made by Claudius, King of Denmark and uncle to Hamlet. What should Hamlet show he knows about the king and about his rise to power? Should Hamlet be portrayed as sad, as resentful, as cynical? Scholars may disagree; the people performing in *Hamlet* cannot. Since these lines come very early in the play, they will serve to set a definition of Hamlet's character as he moves through the rest of the play. The actor playing Hamlet will have to remain true to the quality of those lines, but he will also have to retain the freedom to show other sides of Hamlet's character as Hamlet faces challenges and lives up to other duties. Is *Hamlet* a play about the proper way to maintain a kingdom, or is it a play about neurotic procrastination, or is it a play about a man too good for this squalid world? This question is basic to the play, and it can be answered in many ways. But answered it must be—by every actor in the play, and by the director and everyone reporting to him.

If these are among the thousands of questions deserving answers in any production of a play such as *Hamlet,* there are other considerations relevant to a play that, while they can be anticipated by the actors and the director, cannot be wholly controlled by them. One such consideration is the simple fact that a play can never be done the same way twice. The audience is always a bit different, bringing to a play varying expectations and hopes. If, for instance, *Death of a Salesman* is performed before an audience of businesspeople in New York City, their reaction might be one of self-examination and considerable empathy for the plight of Willy Loman as he looks around at his life of personal and commercial misfortune. But if the same play is performed before an audience in China (as it has been), then the reaction might well be bemused wonder at the difficulties of a people in a land of capitalism far away. It is the same play, but yet the effect is very different. Also the actors might be elated one night and flat the next. As actors inevitably bring to a play slightly changed understandings of their roles every time they adopt them, we know that such repetition can induce heightened awarenes of the character or it can induce fatigue. We know, in addition, that great plays place great responsibilities on actors. The character of Molière's Tartuffe demands that the actor playing him exercise superb control of his faculties of speech, intelligence, physical movement, and facial expression. Tartuffe must be brilliant, manipulative, suave, corrupt, and yet wholly plausible to his victims while being perfectly implausible to everyone else. Not to determine a way to manage such a difficult characterization is probably not to have a successful rendition of the play.

To read a play is to enjoy a great imaginative freedom and pleasure. One can be, simultaneously, actor and director. One can make the choices, all of them, that must be made to set the production in motion. One can visualize one's success and revise things to eliminate all the errors. But one is then not really at the theater, where human victory and error, community excitement, and anticipation rule the day. And because plays, when successful, represent the collective energies and skills of a great many people, it is difficult for a play to have the impact on a person reading it that a truly fine production of the play will have. At its best, drama can compress rich and complex human emotion into moments of exquisite intensity. In no other literary form can we hear the doors of fate slam shut with quite the same finality as character becomes destiny.

2
TRAGEDY

"A ll tragedy ends in death; all comedy ends in marriage." This saying is not altogether accurate, of course. There are tragedies in which the protagonists live on, and comedies ending in divorce. But it is true that these two genres approach life from wholly different perspectives, aptly symbolized by the Greeks' two masks, one smiling and one frowning. Comedy, as we will see in more detail in the next section, is a way of deflating human pretension. Tragedy, on the other hand, allows such pretension to run its fateful course. Comedy tells us to relax; tragedy tells us to take ourselves seriously. Comedy sees us as scheming mortals; tragedy assumes that we are only a little lower than the angels. Yet just as we sometimes leave a comedy not in laughter but with bittersweet insights into human complexity, so we often leave a tragedy feeling exalted and ennobled rather than merely sad.

In everyday conversation, we tend to use the term *tragic* to describe occurrences ranging from the mid-air collision of passenger planes to the late-season collapse of baseball teams. When we are discussing drama, however, we must be more technical and more precise, because tragedy involves much more than accidental catastrophe. Tragic drama explores the relation of men and women to the larger forces in their world, the way they challenge these forces, and, through suffering, reaffirm their validity.

The Theory of Tragedy

The Greeks were the first and perhaps the greatest practitioners of tragedy. They were also the first to theorize about what tragedy was and what made it "work." Much of what has been written and said about tragic drama returns in one way or another to Aristotle's famous definition in the *Poetics*: "A tragedy, then, is an imitation of an action that is serious, complete in itself, and of a certain magnitude . . . cast in the form of drama, not narrative; accomplishing through incidents that arouse pity and fear the purgation of these emotions."

In specifying that tragedy involved action "of a certain magnitude," Aristotle was saying that the subject matter must be elevated, removed from the everyday, going to the heart of human striving, and asking profound questions about the nature of human life. He saw the ideal *tragic hero* as someone of "high estate," a king or noble; this was not social snobbery on his part but rather a perception that the tragic hero must stand apart from the ordinary as someone who is consequential and has a great distance to fall— someone who stands for us all. But while this figure must possess extraordinary qualities, he or she cannot be infallible. In fact, all tragic heroes have a weakness embedded in their characters. Aristotle used the term *hamartia*, generally translated as "tragic flaw." One such weakness frequently portrayed in Greek drama was *hubris*, an overreaching pride causing the heroes to take upon themselves the power of the gods, an arrogance for which they ultimately had to suffer.

Aristotle talked about the importance of *unity* in tragedy. Some of his ideas about unity of time (a play should take place within a single day) and unity of place (the action should be completed in a single locale) no longer seem important to practicing playwrights. But *unity of action* is still a crucial aspect of most dramatic composition. The play should begin, Aristotle proposed, with an individual secure in his place and should trace his progressive descent into tragic depths. All the steps in this process—beginning, middle, and end—should be coordinated in such a way that they follow each other with an inescapable *internal logic*. What happens to tragic heroes should grow out of their characters. Centrally important is the *peripeteia* or "reversal," that moment when those heroes suddenly begin to see what they have done and what its consequences are likely to be. This recognition on their parts is what gives the play scope and resonance and keeps it from becoming simply a chronicle of unenlightened suffering.

Finally Aristotle speaks of *catharsis* or "purgation," as the ultimate object of tragedy. What he calls "pity and fear" are aroused in an audience by the situation in which the hero finds himself and then purged by how he handles his destiny. A tragedy should not send an audience away simply feeling drained, as after some violent or harrowing spectacle. Nor should spectators leave with a feeling of smugness about having witnessed arrogance punished, pride broken, or even justice done. The spectators' feeling is more complex, resulting from their having identified with the tragic hero's aspirations and his fate. If the limitations of humankind are reaffirmed, so is the audience's sense of the grandeur of human intelligence and courage.

Aristotle wrote thousands of years ago, and we cannot judge all tragedies composed since his *Poetics* strictly by the criteria he sets forth. (Nor should we read plays with an eye to defining what is and isn't tragedy. A play, like any other literary work, must ultimately be understood on its own merits.) Yet, as we read tragedies written since the great age of Greek drama, we will be surprised at the continuing relevance of Aristotlean theory. The tragic hero must indeed be extraordinary, if not by birth or station in life then in terms of his sensibility. And the situation in which the tragic figure finds himself must be relevant to our own lives. We may have abandoned the classical word *peripeteia*, but the moment of recognition continues to be central in tragedy if the protagonist is to be something more than a mere victim. Aristotle was correct also in discussing the integrity of plot. A tragedy is different from a *melodrama*, for instance, which may seem to be about life and death matters, but rarely has outcomes which grow out of character; moreover, melodrama usually relies on twists of plot that make sure that virtue is triumphant. Tragedy offers no such easy answers. In this it mirrors rather than simplifies the complexity of life.

Oedipus Rex

Oedipus was a familiar figure to Greek audiences. A figure of myth, he was mentioned by Homer and other writers. Scholars believe that several Greek tragedies were written about him, although Sophocles' is the only one that survives. A Greek audience would, therefore, have known the significant events of Oedipus' life, some of which are recapitulated in the play and some not. His story begins when Laïos, King of Thebes, hears the prophecy that his newborn son will grow up and kill him. He and his Queen Iokastê give the infant to a shepherd who is directed to leave him to die in the wilderness. The shepherd, as commanded, pins the child's ankles together, but then, in an act of impulsive humanity that becomes one key to the tragedy, gives it to another shepherd. He, in turn, gives the boy to the childless King and Queen of Corinth. In his adoptive household, Oedipus grows to manhood. In time, he is told by a drunken companion that he is not the real child of the royal couple and so he goes to the Delphic Oracle to unravel the mystery of his birth. There, the prophecy that he will kill his father is repeated to him. To avoid committing such a crime, he leaves Corinth, and in his travels, meets a chariot that forces him off the road. In a rage, he kills the occupants, not knowing that one of them happens to be King Laïos. He travels on to Thebes, which is being terrorized by the Sphinx. The Sphinx asks Oedipus the same riddle which others have died unable to answer: What goes on four legs in the morning, two legs at noon, and three legs in the evening? Oedipus correctly answers "Man." (A baby crawls, an adult walks erect, an old man uses a cane.) In chagrin, the Sphinx dives off its rocky perch and destroys itself. Oedipus is then welcomed to Thebes as a savior and made King. He marries the widowed queen and has four children by her. The city prospers until it is suddenly afflicted by another plague. The city elders consult the Delphic Oracle and are told that the plague will cease only when the murderer of Laïos is discovered. As the play opens, the elders have come to Oedipus, who had saved the city before, to ask him to solve this new mystery.

Since this much of the story would have been known to the Greek audience, Sophocles' artistry did not lie in his choice of events, even though he could have included other aspects of the Oedipus myth in his play. His originality rested instead in the way he made the story come alive through character and conflict, poetry, and structure. His Oedipus pushes restlessly against fate, secure in his sense of himself and his importance. He is, after all, the one who knew enough about mankind to have defeated the Sphinx. He is a hero and determined to act like one in confronting this new task. ("Once more I must bring what is dark to light," he says when confronted with the problem). We begin, however, to get a sense of his *hubris* early in the play when he chastises the others for their inaction: "You should have found the murderer: Your king / A noble king, has been destroyed!"

The structure of the play relies heavily on *dramatic irony*, a technique that allows us to see implications in Oedipus' words and deeds beyond what he sees in them. We know, for instance, that the problem he wants to solve, the plague ravaging Thebes, will lead inexorably to a deeper mystery he doesn't know about, a mystery in which he is centrally involved. We sense the possible consequences, as Oedipus himself cannot, when he impatiently ignores warnings not to proceed, and insists on relentlessly pursuing each and every clue. This pervasive sense of irony is also reinforced by verbal patterns involving light and darkness. At its most basic level, this play is about who *sees* the truth, and how long Oedipus himself will remain blind to it. In this respect, a key comment comes when the seer Teiresias, who in his blindness sees what Oedipus cannot, says: "You mock my blindness, do you? But I say that you, with both your eyes are blind!" Oedipus' reaction to this is to revert to his heroic conception of himself and his past achievements: "Tell us: Has your mystic mummery ever approached the truth? / When that hellcat Sphinx was performing here, / What help were you to these people? / Her magic was not for the first man who came along: / It demanded a real exorcist . . ." This pattern culminates in the final scenes when Oedipus blinds himself by plunging brooches from the dress of his dead wife and mother into his eyes; in his own blindness, he is at last able to "see" his dilemma.

Some part of the original *Oedipus* is lost to us. We can only imagine the music, the choreographed movement of the chorus standing in front of the main characters, the effect of the stylized masks each player wore. It may be difficult also to visualize how, in an authentic performance, the choral odes would have served both to separate the four scenes of the play and also to draw the audience into the philosophical heart of the action, or how the leader, Choragos, would have functioned both as part of the action and part of the chorus. But while we cannot see *Oedipus* with the eyes of an ancient Greek, we can certainly sense the power that the play must have had through our reading of it. We feel the force of the revelations that strike Oedipus' conception of himself almost like hammer strokes. We feel the way that a fate beyond his control takes over as he encounters the doom he thinks he has avoided. We feel his heroism as he attempts to maintain, even in the face of great danger, his own identity. In the end, although worlds away from ancient Greece, we see that *Oedipus Rex* has the essential attribute of great tragedy— *tragic knowledge* on the part of the hero, as this great solver of riddles finally unravels the riddle of his own being and of his relation to his world.

Hamlet

While Oedipus is a figure of myth, Hamlet is very much the individual, quirky and eccentric, one of the first characters in literature to have a fully developed interior dimension. He is witty, self-mocking, amusing, a punster and a metaphysician. He is, above all else, aware of himself and of his relation to his world. In his very first words—an aside after Claudius calls him cousin and son—he says: "A little more than kin and less than kind." Thus he lets the audience know that *he knows* the King, as his stepfather, is not blood kin, and, as the man who hurried his mother into a hasty remarriage, has been less than kind to him, the grieving son.

Hamlet is at once very human and quite extraordinary. Shakespeare has endowed him with magnificent gifts of self-awareness, making him introspective and analytical about his dilemma, and fully able to generalize from this dilemma to the universe itself. Like all tragic heroes, however, his virtues seem inextricably bound up with his weaknesses. The same qualities of mind and imagination that make him so attractive also keep him, in his own terms, from being effective. Every time he thinks about taking revenge, he begins to consider the implications of any vengeful act. Whenever he sees the possibility of acting, he pauses to consider the very meaning of action itself. If this is a flaw, it is not merely "inaction," as some critics have said. Hamlet is not merely a melancholy procrastinator: his problem is that he perceives things all too well. He sees exactly how rotten things are in Denmark (a city as much under a plague as Thebes is in *Oedipus*). Murder, gross ambition, and corruption of every kind stain the world. It is therefore difficult for Hamlet to see how any one action on his part will restore political and moral equilibrium. Moreover, his remarkable ability to project himself and his dilemma into a world of ideas makes him aware of consequences in a way that might elude a more limited thinker. Perhaps to temper any tendency we might have to judge Hamlet too harshly for his inaction (although it is unlikely that we could judge him more harshly than he judges himself), Shakespeare has given us the rash and shallow Laertes, a tool of someone else's evil, as an example of what happens to someone who acts without thinking.

Hamlet's flaw, not so much insufficient action as excessive thought, is, moreover, a source of immense gratification for us. Not only is he more eloquent than any other character in the theater, speaking some of the greatest lines Shakespeare or anyone else ever wrote; he is also simply a pleasure to watch. He is like a superb actor, trying on and discarding personalities as the play proceeds—jilted lover, madman, faithful son, social critic, avenging angel. The scene with the players (Act III, Scene II) is the climax of the action, that moment of recognition when Hamlet does catch the conscience of the king. It is also the moment when the actor becomes director—literally telling the players what to do at this particular moment, but also directing what is to happen in the rest of the play. He controls the dramatic action from that point on, manipulting the other characters, setting up one confrontation after another, making Polonius, Ophelia, Rosencrantz and Guildenstern, and all the others into supporting characters in his own personal drama.

By the end of the play, he becomes the man of action he never thought he could become at its beginning. What has changed are not only the external issues of the play—the certainty of Claudius' guilt, and so on—but also Hamlet's view of the world. At the beginning, he had generalized from the suspicious death of his father and the hasty marriage of his mother to the universe itself, seeing it as a place controlled by faithlessness, decadent sexuality, and political corruption. By the end of the play, however, he comes to see the universe as a place in which the bestial disorder of Denmark is only temporary. Behind this disorder lies a reality in which Providence notes the fall of a single sparrow, in which, as he says to Horatio, "There's a divinity that shapes our ends, / Rough-hew them how we will." The reversal occurs, oddly enough, when he is off stage, away with Rosencrantz and Guildenstern on what was to be his death trip to England. Returning, he is philosophically changed and now ready to do whatever must be done. (Many costume directors, it is worth noting, mark this change in Hamlet by dressing him in black for the first part of the play and in soothing pastels in the last part.) In the last scene of the play, Hamlet cleanses Denmark of its affliction even though he understands that as one who has also been contaminated by the sickness, one who has been forced to kill and to be cruel, he too must die. In the end, after Horatio has bid his sweet prince a final adieu, we have Fortinbras as a symbol of the political vigor and stability that Denmark lacked. He is far less appealing than Hamlet, but he is what is required for the tragedy finally to be over.

Shakespeare and Sophocles

Elizabethan tragedy, exemplified here by *Hamlet*, is much indebted to Greek practices, but it is hardly the same. Sophocles and other Greek dramatists kept a play free of elements not directly contributing to its central effect and meaning, and ruled that a great many important events, particularly violent ones, should not even occur on stage. Elizabethan dramatists, on the other hand, permitted the introduction of a wide variety of elements only tangentially related to that central effect, and they also brought directly onto the stage virtually every kind of event, violent and otherwise. Comic scenes, romantic tangles, swordplay, subsidiary characters, battles, and philosophical interludes fill the Shakespearean stage. Those "extra" things make it the high and glorious entertainment it remains today. What, for instance, do the figures of Rosencrantz and Guildenstern add to the major emphases of *Hamlet*? Why must Hamlet be so attracted to Ophelia, and yet so indifferent to her? Is sententious old Polonious absolutely necessary to the meaning of *Hamlet*? And why is Laertes even in the play? True, there are answers, good answers, to all these questions, but merely to raise them is to suggest that the purity of action that Aristotle in theory and Sophocles in practice thought necessary to tragedy was not appealing to Shakespeare. Elizabethan dramatic practice depended on a much looser structure, a readiness to admit humorous or grotesque elements (for instance, the graveyard scene in *Hamlet*).

While Sophocles and other Greek tragedians were interested in conflicts between man and the gods, Shakespeare and other Elizabethan dramatists concerned themselves with questions of morality. They asked after the rightness or wrongness of an action. They inquired into the justice of an individual's conduct. Claudius, for instance, is held up before the audience as a *bad* man who has killed his brother, hastily married his own sister-in-law, and is designing ways to get rid of Hamlet. Gertrude is seen as weak and confused, Rosencrantz and Guildenstern as amoral and insipid, and Polonious as morally vacuous. Indeed, one primary question of the play is whether Hamlet will respond to the imperatives of justice and morality that he knows full well are staring him in the face. Let us remember, however, that moral questions such as these are not a part of *Oedipus Rex* or of other Greek plays. In them, no question arises as to the moral *goodness* of the chief character or protagonist. Oedipus acts as he must to fulfill his destiny; he proceeds as his character prompts him to proceed. The sense of moral conflict, so prominent on the Shakespearean stage, is simply not a part of the Greek dramatic practice.

In conclusion, we must observe that tragedy, whether it is Greek or Shakespearean, issues from a particular view of life that must be acknowledged as underlying any definition of the term. That view of life sees great aspiration and great suffering at the heart of the human condition. It sees that men and women will always want to know, at any cost, what life, in all its mystery and terror and surprise, really is and what it really means. The ways in which the costs of tragic knowledge are totalled up is the stuff of tragic drama. The courage that human beings can demonstrate in seeking to determine their individual natures is the source of inspiration that we can find in tragedies. We should not leave the theater after watching a successful performance of a play like *Oedipus Rex* or *Hamlet* with gloom in our minds. Rather, we should be filled with the awareness of how extraordinary human beings can become when they confront so directly their own identities and destinies. A modern playwright, Arthur Miller, whose *Death of a Salesman* exemplifies modern tragedy, put it this way:

> There is a misconception of tragedy with which I have been struck in review after review, and in many conversations with writers and readers alike. It is the idea that tragedy is of necessity allied to pessimism. Even the dictionary says nothing more about the word than it means a story with a sad or unhappy ending. This impression is so firmly fixed that I almost hesitate to claim that in truth tragedy implies more optimism in its author than does comedy, and that its final result ought to be the reinforcement of the onlooker's brightest opinions of the human animal.
>
> For, if it is true to say that in essence the tragic hero is intent upon claiming his whole due as a personality, and if this struggle must be total and without reservation, then it automatically demonstrates the indestructible will of man to achieve his humanity.

Sophocles
Oedipus Rex

CHARACTERS

OEDIPUS, *King of Thebes, supposed son of Polybos and Meropê, King and Queen of Corinth*
IOKASTÊ, *wife of Oedipus and widow of the late King Laïos*
KREON, *brother of Iokastê, a prince of Thebes; son of Menoikens*
TEIRESIAS, *a blind seer who serves Apollo*
PRIEST
MESSENGER, *from Corinth*
SHEPHERD, *former servant of Laïos*
SECOND MESSENGER, *from the palace*
CHORUS OF THEBAN ELDERS
CHORAGOS, *leader of the Chorus*
ANTIGONE *and* ISMENE, *young daughters of Oedipus and Iokastê. They appear in the Exodus but do not speak.*
SUPPLIANTS, GUARDS, SERVANTS

THE SCENE. *Before the palace of* OEDIPUS, *King of Thebes. A central door and two lateral doors open onto a platform which runs the length of the façade. On the platform, right and left, are altars; and three steps lead down into the* orchêstra, *or chorus-ground. At the beginning of the action these steps are crowded by suppliants who have brought branches and chaplets of olive leaves and who sit in various attitudes of despair.* OEDIPUS *enters.*

PROLOGUE

OEDIPUS.   My children, generations of the living
In the line of Kadmos,° nursed at his ancient hearth:
Why have you strewn yourselves before these altars
In supplication, with your boughs and garlands?
The breath of incense rises from the city   5
With a sound of prayer and lamentation.
                                              Children,
I would not have you speak through messengers,
And therefore I have come myself to hear you—
I, Oedipus, who bear the famous name.
(To a PRIEST*)* You, there, since you are eldest in the company,   10
Speak for them all, tell me what preys upon you,
Whether you come in dread, or crave some blessing:
Tell me, and never doubt that I will help you
In every way I can; I should be heartless
Were I not moved to find you suppliant here.   15

2. **Kadmos:** the legendary founder of Thebes; son of Agenor, husband to Harmonia.

PRIEST.   Great Oedipus, O powerful king of Thebes!
You see how all the ages of our people
Cling to your altar steps: here are boys
Who can barely stand alone, and here are priests
By weight of age, as I am a priest of God,   20
And young men chosen from those yet unmarried;
As for the others, all that multitude,
They wait with olive chaplets in the squares,
At the two shrines of Pallas,° and where Apollo°
Speaks in the glowing embers.
                              Your own eyes   25
Must tell you: Thebes is tossed on a murdering sea
And can not lift her head from the death surge.
A rust consumes the buds and fruits of the earth;
The herds are sick; children die unborn,
And labor is vain. The god of plague and pyre   30
Raids like detestable lightning through the city,
And all the house of Kadmos is laid waste,
All emptied, and all darkened: Death alone
Battens upon the misery of Thebes.

You are not one of the immortal gods, we know;   35
Yet we have come to you to make our prayer
As to the man surest in mortal ways
And wisest in the ways of God. You saved us
From the Sphinx, that flinty singer, and the tribute
We paid to her so long; yet you were never   40
Better informed than we, nor could we teach you:
A god's touch, it seems, enabled you to help us.

Therefore, O mighty power, we turn to you:
Find us our safety, find us a remedy,
Whether by counsel of the gods or of men.   45
A king of wisdom tested in the past
Can act in a time of troubles, and act well.
Noblest of men, restore
Life to your city! Think how all men call you
Liberator for your boldness long ago;   50
Ah, when your years of kingship are remembered,
Let them not say *We rose, but later fell*—
Keep the State from going down in the storm!
Once, years ago, with happy augury,
You brought us fortune; be the same again!   55
No man questions your power to rule the land:
But rule over men, not over a dead.city!
Ships are only hulls, high walls are nothing,
When no life moves in the empty passageways.

24. Pallas: Pallas Athena, the goddess of wisdom, skills, and warfare; **Apollo:** the son of Zeus and
the god of light, moral law, philosophy, and the arts.

OEDIPUS.   Poor children! You may be sure I know   60
All that you longed for in your coming here.
I know that you are deathly sick; and yet,
Sick as you are, not one is as sick as I.
Each of you suffers in himself alone
His anguish, not another's; but my spirit   65
Groans for the city, for myself, for you.

I was not sleeping, you are not waking me.
No, I have been in tears for a long while
And in my restless thought walked many ways.
In all my search I found one remedy,   70
And I have adopted it: I have sent Kreon,
Son of Menoikeus, brother of the queen,
To Delphi,° Apollo's place of revelation,
To learn there, if he can,
What act or pledge of mine may save the city.   75
I have counted the days, and now, this very day,
I am troubled, for he has overstayed his time.
What is he doing? He has been gone too long.
Yet whenever he comes back, I should do ill
Not to take any action the god orders.   80
PRIEST.   It is a timely promise. At this instant
They tell me Kreon is here.
OEDIPUS.   O Lord Apollo!
May his news be fair as his face is radiant!
PRIEST.   Good news, I gather! he is crowned with bay,
The chaplet is thick with berries.
OEDIPUS.   We shall soon know;   85
He is near enough to hear us now.

(*Enter* KREON.)

                              O Prince:
Brother: son of Menoikeus:
What answer do you bring us from the god?
KREON.   A strong one. I can tell you, great afflictions
Will turn out well, if they are taken well.   90
OEDIPUS.   What was the oracle? These vague words
Leave me still hanging between hope and fear.
KREON.   Is it your pleasure to hear me with all these
Gathered around us? I am prepared to speak,
But should we not go in?
OEDIPUS.   Speak to them all,   95
It is for them I suffer, more than for myself.
KREON.   Then I will tell you what I heard at Delphi.
In plain words
The god commands us to expel from the land of Thebes

73. **Delphi:** seat of the most famous and powerful oracle of ancient Greece.

An old defilement we are sheltering.   100
It is a deathly thing, beyond cure;
We must not let it feed upon us longer.
OEDIPUS.   What defilement? How shall we rid ourselves of it?
KREON.   By exile or death, blood for blood. It was
Murder that brought the plague-wind on the city.   105
OEDIPUS.   Murder of whom? Surely the god has named him?
KREON.   My lord: Laïos once ruled this land,
Before you came to govern us.
OEDIPUS.   I know;
I learned of him from others; I never saw him.
KREON.   He was murdered; and Apollo commands us now   110
To take revenge upon whoever killed him.
OEDIPUS.   Upon whom? Where are they? Where shall we find a clue
To solve that crime, after so many years?
KREON.   Here in this land, he said. Search reveals
Things that escape an inattentive man.   115
OEDIPUS.   Tell me: Was Laïos murdered in his house,
Or in the fields, or in some foreign country?
KREON.   He said he planned to make a pilgrimage.
He did not come home again.
OEDIPUS.   And was there no one,
No witness, no companion, to tell what happened?   120
KREON.   They were all killed but one, and he got away
So frightened that he could remember one thing only.
OEDIPUS.   What was that one thing? One may be the key
To everything, if we resolve to use it.
KREON.   He said that a band of highwaymen attacked them,   125
Outnumbered them, and overwhelmed the king.
OEDIPUS.   Strange, that a highwayman should be so daring—
Unless some faction here bribed him to do it.
KREON.   We thought of that. But after Laïos' death
New troubles arose and we had no avenger.   130
OEDIPUS.   What troubles could prevent your hunting down the killers?
KREON.   The riddling Sphinx's° song
Made us deaf to all mysteries but her own.
OEDIPUS.   Then once more I must bring what is dark to light.
It is most fitting that Apollo shows,   135
As you do, this compunction for the dead.
You shall see how I stand by you, as I should,
Avenging this country and the god as well,
And not as though it were for some distant friend,
But for my own sake, to be rid of evil.   140
Whoever killed King Laïos might—who knows?—
Lay violent hands even on me—and soon.
I act for the murdered king in my own interest.

---

132. Sphinx: a winged monster with a lion's body and the head and breasts of a woman who
strangled passersby unable to solve its riddle.

Come, then, my children: leave the altar steps,
Lift up your olive boughs!
                    One of you go   145
And summon the people of Kadmos to gather here.
I will do all that I can; you may tell them that.

(*Exit a* PAGE.)

So, with the help of God,
We shall be saved—or else indeed we are lost.

PRIEST.   Let us rise, children. It was for this we came,   150
And now the king has promised it.
Phoibos° has sent us an oracle; may he descend
Himself to save us and drive out the plague.

(*Exeunt* OEDIPUS *and* KREON *into the palace by the central door. The*
PRIEST *and the* SUPPLIANTS *disperse right and left. After a short pause the*
CHORUS *enters the orchêstra.*)

PÁRODOS°

STROPHE 1

CHORUS.   What is God singing in his profound
Delphi of gold and shadow?   155
What oracle for Thebes, the sunwhipped city?
Fear unjoints me, the roots of my heart tremble.
Now I remember, O Healer, your power, and wonder:
Will you send doom like a sudden cloud, or weave it
Like nightfall of the past?   160
Speak to me, tell me, O
Child of golden Hope, immortal Voice.

ANTISTROPHE 1

Let me pray to Athenê,° the immortal daughter of Zeus,°
And to Artemis° her sister
Who keeps her famous throne in the market ring,   165
And to Apollo, archer from distant heaven—
O gods, descend! Like three streams leap against
The fires of our grief, the fires of darkness;
Be swift to bring us rest!
As in the old time from the brilliant house   170
Of air you stepped to save us, come again!

152. Phoibos: Apollo.   **Párados:** In order for the scenes of the play to be divided, and for a running commentary on the action to be provided, various choral odes and dances form part of the drama. As the chorus moves from one side of the stage to the other, its motions are known as *strophe* or *antistrophe.* In this play, the chorus represents the elder citizens of Thebes; remaining visible for the rest of the play, the chorus sings its commentary, performs its dances, and occasionally converses with characters in the drama through the choral leader, the Choragos.   **163. Athenê:** Pallas Athena, among whose important functions was to guard cities;   **Zeus:** supreme among gods, he represented power, rule, and law.   **164. Artemis:** goddess of earth, wildlife and patroness of hunters.

STROPHE 2

Now our afflictions have no end,
Now all our stricken host lies down
And no man fights off death with his mind;
The noble plowland bears no grain,   175
And groaning mothers can not bear—
See, how our lives like birds take wing,
Like sparks that fly when a fire soars,
To the shore of the god of evening.

ANTISTROPHE 2

The plague burns on, it is pitiless,   180
Though pallid children laden with death
Lie unwept in the stony ways,
And old gray women by every path
Flock to the strand about the altars
There to strike their breasts and cry   185
Worship of Phoibos in wailing prayers:
Be kind, God's golden child!

STROPHE 3

There are no swords in this attack by fire,
No shields, but we are ringed with cries.
Send the besieger plunging from our homes   190
Into the vast sea-room of the Atlantic
Or into the waves that foam eastward of Thrace—
For the day ravages what the night spares—
Destroy our enemy, lord of the thunder!
Let him be riven by lightning from heaven!   195

ANTISTROPHE 3

Phoibos Apollo, stretch the sun's bowstring,
That golden cord, until it sing for us,
Flashing arrows in heaven!
                              Artemis, Huntress,
Race with flaring lights upon our mountains!
O scarlet god,° O golden-banded brow,   200
O Theban Bacchos in a storm of Maenads,

(Enter OEDIPUS, *center.)*

Whirl upon Death, that all the Undying hate!
Come with blinding torches, come in joy!

---

200. **scarlet god:** Bacchos, god of wine, vegetation, and fertility. Worship of him as orgiastic. The
Maenads were his female devotees.

SCENE I

OEDIPUS. Is this your prayer? It may be answered. Come,
    Listen to me, act as the crisis demands,   205
    And you shall have relief from all these evils.

    Until now I was a stranger to this tale,
    As I had been a stranger to the crime.
    Could I track down the murderer without a clue?
    But now, friends,   210
    As one who became a citizen after the murder,
    I make this proclamation to all Thebans:
    If any man knows by whose hand Laïos, son of Labdakos,
    Met his death, I direct that man to tell me everything,
    No matter what he fears for having so long withheld it.   215
    Let it stand as promised that no further trouble
    Will come to him, but he may leave the land in safety.
    Moreover: If anyone knows the murderer to be foreign,
    Let him not keep silent: he shall have his reward from me.
    However, if he does conceal it; if any man   220
    Fearing for his friend or for himself disobeys this edict,
    Hear what I propose to do:

    I solemnly forbid the people of this country,
    Where power and throne are mine, ever to receive that man
    Or speak to him, no matter who he is, or let him   225
    Join in sacrifice, lustration, or in prayer.
    I decree that he be driven from every house,
    Being, as he is, corruption itself to us: the Delphic
    Voice of Apollo has pronounced this revelation.
    Thus I associate myself with the oracle   230
    And take the side of the murdered king.

    As for the criminal, I pray to God—
    Whether it be a lurking thief, or one of a number—
    I pray that that man's life be consumed in evil and wretchedness.
    And as for me, this curse applies no less   235
    If it should turn out that the culprit is my guest here,
    Sharing my hearth.
                You have heard the penalty.
    I lay it on you now to attend to this
    For my sake, for Apollo's, for the sick
    Sterile city that heaven has abandoned.   240
    Suppose the oracle had given you no command:
    Should this defilement go uncleansed for ever?
    You should have found the murderer: your king,
    A noble king, had been destroyed!
                Now I,
    Having the power that he held before me,   245

Having his bed, begetting children there
Upon his wife, as he would have, had he lived—
Their son would have been my children's brother,
If Laïos had had luck in fatherhood!
(And now his bad fortune has struck him down)—   250
I say I take the son's part, just as though
I were his son, to press the fight for him
And see it won! I'll find the hand that brought
Death to Labdakos' and Polydoros' child,
Heir of Kadmos' and Agenor's line.°   255
And as for those who fail me,
May the gods deny them the fruit of the earth,
Fruit of the womb, and may they rot utterly!
Let them be wretched as we are wretched, and worse!

For you, for loyal Thebans, and for all   260
Who find my actions right, I pray the favor
Of justice, and of all the immortal gods.
CHORAGOS.   Since I am under oath, my lord, I swear
I did not do the murder, I can not name
The murderer. Phoibos ordained the search;   265
Why did he not say who the culprit was?
OEDIPUS.   An honest question. But no man in the world
Can make the gods do more than the gods will.
CHORAGOS.   There is an alternative, I think—
OEDIPUS.   Tell me.
Any or all, you must not fail to tell me.   270
CHORAGOS.   A lord clairvoyant to the lord Apollo,
As we all know, is the skilled Teiresias.
One might learn much about this from him, Oedipus.
OEDIPUS.   I am not wasting time:
Kreon spoke of this, and I have sent for him—   275
Twice, in fact; it is strange that he is not here.
CHORAGOS.   The other matter—that old report—seems useless.
OEDIPUS.   What was that? I am interested in all reports.
CHORAGOS.   The king was said to have been killed by highwaymen.
OEDIPUS.   I know. But we have no witnesses to that.   280
CHORAGOS.   If the killer can feel a particle of dread,
Your curse will bring him out of hiding!
OEDIPUS.   No.
The man who dared that act will fear no curse.

(*Enter the blind seer* TEIRESIAS, *led by a* PAGE.)

CHORAGOS.   But there is one man who may detect the criminal.
This is Teiresias, this is the holy prophet   285
In whom, alone of all men, truth was born.

255. Labdakos, Polydoros, Kadmos, and Agenor: the ancestors, in order, of Laïos.

OEDIPUS.   Teiresias: seer: student of mysteries,
   Of all that's taught and all that no man tells,
   Secrets of Heaven and secrets of the earth:
   Blind though you are, you know the city lies   290
   Sick with plague; and from this plague, my lord,
   We find that you alone can guard or save us.

   Possibly you did not hear the messengers?
   Apollo, when we sent to him,
   Sent us back word that this great pestilence   295
   Would lift, but only if we established clearly
   The identity of those who murdered Laïos.
   They must be killed or exiled.
                              Can you use
   Birdflight or any art of divination
   To purify yourself, and Thebes, and me   300
   From this contagion? We are in your hands.
   There is no fairer duty
   Than that of helping others in distress.
TEIRESIAS.   How dreadful knowledge of the truth can be
   When there's no help in truth! I knew this well,   305
   But did not act on it: else I should not have come.
OEDIPUS.   What is troubling you? Why are your eyes so cold?
TEIRESIAS.   Let me go home. Bear your own fate, and I'll
   Bear mine. It is better so: trust what I say.
OEDIPUS.   What you say is ungracious and unhelpful   310
   To your native country. Do not refuse to speak.
TEIRESIAS.   When it comes to speech, your own is neither temperate
   Nor opportune. I wish to be more prudent.
OEDIPUS.   In God's name, we all beg you—
TEIRESIAS.   You are all ignorant.
   No; I will never tell you what I know.   315
   Now it is my misery; then, it would be yours.
OEDIPUS.   What! You do know something, and will not tell us?
   You would betray us all and wreck the State?
TEIRESIAS.   I do not intend to torture myself, or you.
   Why persist in asking? You will not persuade me.   320
OEDIPUS.   What a wicked old man you are! You'd try a stone's
   Patience! Out with it! Have you no feeling at all?
TEIRESIAS.   You call me unfeeling. If you could only see
   The nature of your own feelings . . .
OEDIPUS.   Why,
   Who would not feel as I do? Who could endure   325
   Your arrogance toward the city?
TEIRESIAS.   What does it matter?
   Whether I speak or not, it is bound to come.
OEDIPUS.   Then, if "it" is bound to come, you are bound to tell me.

TEIRESIAS.   No, I will not go on. Rage as you please.
OEDIPUS.   Rage? Why not!

                          And I'll tell you what I think: 330
You planned it, you had it done, you all but
Killed him with your own hands: if you had eyes,
I'd say the crime was yours, and yours alone.
TEIRESIAS.   So? I charge you, then,
Abide by the proclamation you have made: 335
From this day forth
Never speak again to these men or to me;
You yourself are the pollution of this country.
OEDIPUS.   You dare say that! Can you possibly think you have
Some way of going free, after such insolence?   340
TEIRESIAS.   I have gone free. It is the truth sustains me.
OEDIPUS.   Who taught you shamelessness? It was not your craft.
TEIRESIAS.   You did. You made me speak. I did not want to.
OEDIPUS.   Speak what? Let me hear it again more clearly.
TEIRESIAS.   Was it not clear before? Are you tempting me?   345
OEDIPUS.   I did not understand it. Say it again.
TEIRESIAS.   I say that you are the murderer whom you seek.
OEDIPUS.   Now twice you have spat out infamy. You'll pay for it!
TEIRESIAS.   Would you care for more? Do you wish to be really angry?
OEDIPUS.   Say what you will. Whatever you say is worthless.   350
TEIRESIAS.   I say you live in hideous shame with those
Most dear to you. You can not see the evil.
OEDIPUS.   Can you go on babbling like this for ever?
TEIRESIAS.   I can, if there is power in truth.
OEDIPUS.   There is:

But not for you, not for you,   355
You sightless, witless, senseless, mad old man!
TEIRESIAS.   You are the madman. There is no one here
Who will not curse you soon, as you curse me.
OEDIPUS.   You child of total night! I would not touch you;
Neither would any man who sees the sun.   360
TEIRESIAS.   True: it is not from you my fate will come.
That lies within Apollo's competence,
As it is his concern.
OEDIPUS.   Tell me, who made
These fine discoveries? Kreon? or someone else?
TEIRESIAS.   Kreon is no threat. You weave your own doom.   365
OEDIPUS.   Wealth, power, craft of statesmanship!
Kingly position, everywhere admired!
What savage envy is stored up against these,
If Kreon, whom I trusted, Kreon my friend,
For this great office which the city once   370
Put in my hands unsought—if for this power
Kreon desires in secret to destroy me!

He has bought this decrepit fortune-teller, this
Collector of dirty pennies, this prophet fraud—
Why, he is no more clairvoyant than I am!

                           Tell us: 375
Has your mystic mummery ever approached the truth?
When that hellcat the Sphinx was performing here,
What help were you to these people?
Her magic was not for the first man who came along:
It demanded a real exorcist. Your birds—   380
What good were they? or the gods, for the matter of that?
But I came by,
Oedipus, the simple man, who knows nothing—
I thought it out for myself, no birds helped me!
And this is the man you think you can destroy,   385
That you may be close to Kreon when he's king!
Well, you and your friend Kreon, it seems to me,
Will suffer most. If you were not an old man,
You would have paid already for your plot.

CHORAGOS.   We can not see that his words or yours   390
    Have been spoken except in anger, Oedipus,
    And of anger we have no need. How to accomplish
    The god's will best: that is what most concerns us.
TEIRESIAS.   You are a king. But where argument's concerned
    I am your man, as much a king as you.   395
    I am not your servant, but Apollo's.
    I have no need of Kreon or Kreon's name.

    Listen to me. You mock my blindness, do you?
    But I say that you, with both your eyes, are blind:
    You can not see the wretchedness of your life,   400
    Nor in whose house you live, no, nor with whom.
    Who are your father and mother? Can you tell me?
    You do not even know the blind wrongs
    That you have done them, on earth and in the world below.
    But the double lash of your parents' curse will whip you   405
    Out of this land some day, with only night
    Upon your precious eyes.
    Your cries then—where will they not be heard?
    What fastness of Kithairon° will not echo them?
    And that bridal-descant of yours—you'll know it then,   410
    The song they sang when you came here to Thebes
    And found your misguided berthing.
    All this, and more, that you can not guess at now,
    Will bring you to yourself among your children.

    Be angry, then. Curse Kreon. Curse my words.   415
    I tell you, no man that walks upon the earth
    Shall be rooted out more horribly than you.

409. **Kithairon:** the mountain on which the child Oedipus was left to die.

OEDIPUS.   Am I to bear this from him?—Damnation
Take you! Out of this place! Out of my sight!
TEIRESIAS.   I would not have come at all if you had not asked me.   420
OEDIPUS.   Could I have told that you'd talk nonsense, that
You'd come here to make a fool of yourself, and of me?
TEIRESIAS.   A fool? Your parents thought me sane enough.
OEDIPUS.   My parents again!—Wait: who were my parents?
TEIRESIAS.   This day will give you a father, and break your heart.   425
OEDIPUS.   Your infantile riddles! Your damned abracadabra!
TEIRESIAS.   You were a great man once at solving riddles.
OEDIPUS.   Mock me with that if you like; you will find it true.
TEIRESIAS.   It was true enough. It brought about your ruin.
OEDIPUS.   But if it saved this town?
TEIRESIAS (*to the* PAGE).   Boy, give me your hand.   430
OEDIPUS.   Yes, boy; lead him away.
                            —While you are here
We can do nothing. Go; leave us in peace.
TEIRESIAS.   I will go when I have said what I have to say.
How can you hurt me? And I tell you again:
The man you have been looking for all this time,   435
The damned man, the murderer of Laïos,
That man is in Thebes. To your mind he is foreign-born,
But it will soon be shown that he is a Theban,
A revelation that will fail to please.
                            A blind man,
Who has his eyes now; a penniless man, who is rich now;   440
And he will go tapping the strange earth with his staff.
To the children with whom he lives now he will be
Brother and father—the very same; to her
Who bore him, son and husband—the very same
Who came to his father's bed, wet with his father's blood.   445

Enough. Go think that over.
If later you find error in what I have said,
You may say that I have no skill in prophecy.

(*Exit* TEIRESIAS, *led by his* PAGE. OEDIPUS *goes into the palace.*)

ODE I

STROPHE 1

CHORUS.   The Delphic stone of prophecies
    Remembers ancient regicide   450
    And a still bloody hand.
    That killer's hour of flight has come.
    He must be stronger than riderless
    Coursers of untiring wind,

For the son of Zeus armed with his father's thunder   455
Leaps in lightning after him;
And the Furies hold his track, the sad Furies.

ANTISTROPHE 1

Holy Parnassos'° peak of snow
Flashes and blinds that secret man,
That all shall hunt him down: 460
Though he may roam the forest shade
Like a bull gone wild from pasture
To rage through glooms of stone.
Doom comes down on him; flight will not avail him;
For the world's heart calls him desolate,   465
And the immortal voices follow, for ever follow.

STROPHE 2

But now a wilder thing is heard
From the old man skilled at hearing Fate in the wing-beat of a bird.
Bewildered as a blown bird, my soul hovers and can not find
Foothold in this debate, or any reason or rest of mind.   470
But no man ever brought—none can bring
Proof of strife between Thebes' royal house,
Labdakos' line, and the son of Polybos;
And never until now has any man brought word
Of Laïos' dark death staining Oedipus the King.   475

ANTISTROPHE 2

Divine Zeus and Apollo hold
Perfect intelligence alone of all tales ever told;
And well though this diviner works, he works in his own night;
No man can judge that rough unknown or trust in second sight,
For wisdom changes hands among the wise.   480
Shall I believe my great lord criminal
At a raging word that a blind old man let fall?
I saw him, when the carrion woman° faced him of old,
Prove his heroic mind. These evil words are lies.

SCENE II

KREON.   Men of Thebes: 485
I am told that heavy accusations
Have been brought against me by King Oedipus.

I am not the kind of man to bear this tamely.

---

458. Parnassos: a mountain sacred to Apollo, Dionysus, and the Muses.   **483. woman:** the
Sphinx.

If in these present difficulties
He holds me accountable for any harm to him   490
Through anything I have said or done—why, then,
I do not value life in this dishonor.
It is not as though this rumor touched upon
Some private indiscretion. The matter is grave.
The fact is that I am being called disloyal   495
To the State, to my fellow citizens, to my friends.
CHORAGOS.   He may have spoken in anger, not from his mind.
KREON.   But did you not hear him say I was the one
   Who seduced the old prophet into lying?
CHORAGOS.   The thing was said; I do not know how seriously.   500
KREON.   But you were watching him! Were his eyes steady?
   Did he look like a man in his right mind?
CHORAGOS.   I do not know.
   I can not judge the behavior of great men.
   But here is the king himself.

   (*Enter* OEDIPUS.)

OEDIPUS.   So you dared come back.
   Why? How brazen of you to come to my house,   505
   You murderer!
                        Do you think I do not know
   That you plotted to kill me, plotted to steal my throne?
   Tell me, in God's name: am I coward, a fool,
   That you should dream you could accomplish this?
   A fool who could not see your slippery game?   510
   A coward, not to fight back when I saw it?
   You are the fool, Kreon, are you not? hoping
   Without support or friends to get a throne?
   Thrones may be won or bought: you could do neither.
KREON.   Now listen to me. You have talked; let me talk, too.   515
   You can not judge unless you know the facts.
OEDIPUS.   You speak well: there is one fact; but I find it hard
   To learn from the deadliest enemy I have.
KREON.   That above all I must dispute with you.
OEDIPUS.   That above all I will not hear you deny.   520
KREON.   If you think there is anything good in being stubborn
   Against all reason, then I say you are wrong.
OEDIPUS.   If you think a man can sin against his own kind
   And not be punished for it, I say you are mad.
KREON.   I agree. But tell me: what have I done to you?   525
OEDIPUS.   You advised me to send for that wizard, did you not?
KREON.   I did. I should do it again.
OEDIPUS.   Very well. Now tell me:
   How long has it been since Laïos—
KREON.   What of Laïos?

OEDIPUS.   Since he vanished in that onset by the road?
KREON.   It was long ago, a long time.
OEDIPUS.   And this prophet,   530
    Was he practicing here then?
KREON.   He was; and with honor, as now.
OEDIPUS.   Did he speak of me at that time?
KREON.   He never did,
    At least, not when I was present.
OEDIPUS.   But . . . the enquiry?
    I suppose you held one?
KREON.   We did, but we learned nothing.
OEDIPUS.   Why did the prophet not speak against me then?   535
KREON.   I do not know; and I am the kind of man
    Who holds his tongue when he has no facts to go on.
OEDIPUS.   There's one fact that you know, and you could tell it.
KREON.   What fact is that? If I know it, you shall have it.
OEDIPUS.   If he were not involved with you, he could not say   540
    that it was I who murdered Laïos.
KREON.   If he says that, you are the one that knows it!—
    But now it is my turn to question you.
OEDIPUS.   Put your questions. I am no murderer.
KREON.   First, then: You married my sister?
OEDIPUS.   I married your sister.   545
KREON.   And you rule the kingdom equally with her?
OEDIPUS.   Everything that she wants she has from me.
KREON.   And I am the third, equal to both of you?
OEDIPUS.   That is why I call you a bad friend.
KREON.   No. Reason it out, as I have done.   550
    Think of this first: Would any sane man prefer
    Power, with all a king's anxieties,
    To that same power and the grace of sleep?
    Certainly not I.
    I have never longed for the king's power—only his rights.   555
    Would any wise man differ from me in this?
    As matters stand, I have my way in everything
    With your consent, and no responsibilities.
    If I were king, I should be a slave to policy.
    How could I desire a scepter more   560
    Than what is now mine—untroubled influence?
    No, I have not gone mad; I need no honors,
    Except those with the perquisites I have now.
    I am welcome everywhere; every man salutes me,
    And those who want your favor seek my ear,   565
    Since I know how to manage what they ask.
    Should I exchange this ease for that anxiety?
    Besides, no sober mind is treasonable.
    I hate anarchy
    And never would deal with any man who likes it.   570

Test what I have said. Go to the priestess
At Delphi, ask if I quoted her correctly.
And as for this other thing: if I am found
Guilty of treason with Teiresias,
Then sentence me to death. You have my word   575
It is a sentence I should cast my vote for—
But not without evidence!
                              You do wrong
When you take good men for bad, bad men for good.
A true friend thrown aside—why, life itself
Is not more precious!
                              In time you will know this well: 580
For time, and time alone, will show the just man,
Though scoundrels are discovered in a day.
CHORAGOS.   This is well said, and a prudent man would ponder it.
Judgments too quickly formed are dangerous.
OEDIPUS.   But is he not quick in his duplicity?   585
And shall I not be quick to parry him?
Would you have me stand still, hold my peace, and let
This man win everything, through my inaction?
KREON.   And you want—what is it, then? To banish me?
OEDIPUS.   No, not exile. It is your death I want,   590
So that all the world may see what treason means.
KREON.   You will persist, then? You will not believe me?
OEDIPUS.   How can I believe you?
KREON.   Then you are a fool.
OEDIPUS.   To save myself?
KREON.   In justice, think of me.
OEDIPUS.   You are evil incarnate.
KREON.   But suppose that you are wrong?   595
OEDIPUS.   Still I must rule.
KREON.   But not if you rule badly.
OEDIPUS.   O city, city!
KREON.   It is my city, too!
CHORAGOS.   Now, my lords, be still. I see the queen,
Iokastê, coming from her palace chambers;
And it is time she came, for the sake of you both.   600
This dreadful quarrel can be resolved through her.

(*Enter* IOKASTÊ.)

IOKASTÊ.   Poor foolish men, what wicked din is this?
With Thebes sick to death, is it not shameful
That you should rake some private quarrel up?
(*To* OEDIPUS.) Come into the house.
                              —And you, Kreon, go now: 605
Let us have no more of this tumult over nothing.

KREON.   Nothing? No, sister: what your husband plans for me
Is one of two great evils: exile or death.
OEDIPUS.   He is right.
                                  Why, woman I have caught him squarely
Plotting against my life.
KREON.   No! Let me die   610
Accurst if ever I have wished you harm!
IOKASTÊ.   Ah, believe it, Oedipus!
In the name of the gods, respect this oath of his
For my sake, for the sake of these people here!

STROPHE 1

CHORAGOS.   Open your mind to her, my lord. Be ruled by her, I
    beg you!   615
OEDIPUS.   What would you have me do?
CHORAGOS.   Respect Kreon's word. He has never spoken like a fool,
And now he has sworn an oath.
OEDIPUS.   You know what you ask?
CHORAGOS.   I do.
OEDIPUS.   Speak on, then.
CHORAGOS.   A friend so sworn should not be baited so,
In blind malice, and without final proof.   620
OEDIPUS.   You are aware, I hope, that what you say
Means death for me, or exile at the least.

STROPHE 2

CHORAGOS.   No, I swear by Helios, first in heaven!
                May I die friendless and accurst,
                The worst of deaths, if ever I meant that!   625
                It is the withering fields
                    That hurt my sick heart:
                Must we bear all these ills,
                    And now your bad blood as well?
OEDIPUS.   Then let him go. And let me die, if I must,   630
Or be driven by him in shame from the land of Thebes.
It is your unhappiness, and not his talk,
That touches me.
                    As for him—
Wherever he goes, hatred will follow him.
KREON.   Ugly in yielding, as you were ugly in rage!   635
Natures like yours chiefly torment themselves.
OEDIPUS.   Can you not go? Can you not leave me?
KREON.   I can.
You do not know me; but the city knows me,
And in its eyes I am just, if not in yours. (*Exit* KREON.)

ANTISTROPHE 1

CHORAGOS.   Lady Iokastê, did you not ask the King to go to his
chambers?   640
IOKASTÊ.   First tell me what has happened.
CHORAGOS.   There was suspicion without evidence; yet it rankled
As even false charges will.
IOKASTÊ.   On both sides?
CHORAGOS.   On both.
IOKASTÊ.   But what was said?
CHORAGOS.   Oh let it rest, let it be done with!
Have we not suffered enough?   645
OEDIPUS.   You see to what your decency has brought you:
You have made difficulties where my heart saw none.

ANTISTROPHE 2

CHORAGOS.   Oedipus, it is not once only I have told you—
You must know I should count myself unwise
To the point of madness, should I now forsake you—   650
You, under whose hand,
In the storm of another time,
Our dear land sailed out free.
But now stand fast at the helm!
IOKASTÊ.   In God's name, Oedipus, inform your wife as well: 655
Why are you so set in this hard anger?
OEDIPUS.   I will tell you, for none of these men deserves
My confidence as you do. It is Kreon's work,
His treachery, his plotting against me.
IOKASTÊ.   Go on, if you can make this clear to me.   660
OEDIPUS.   He charges me with the murder of Laïos.
IOKASTÊ.   Has he some knowledge? Or does he speak from hearsay?
OEDIPUS.   He would not commit himself to such a charge,
But he has brought in that damnable soothsayer
To tell his story.
IOKASTÊ.   Set your mind at rest.   665
If it is a question of soothsayers, I tell you
That you will find no man whose craft gives knowledge
Of the unknowable.
Here is my proof:
An oracle was reported to Laïos once
(I will not say from Phoibos himself, but from   670
His appointed ministers, at any rate)
That his doom would be death at the hands of his own son—
His son, born of his flesh and of mine!

Now, you remember the story: Laïos was killed
By marauding strangers where three highways meet;   675

But his child had not been three days in this world
Before the king had pierced the baby's ankles
And left him to die on a lonely mountainside.

Thus, Apollo never caused that child
To kill his father, and it was not Laïos' fate   680
To die at the hands of his son, as he had feared.
This is what prophets and prophecies are worth!
Have no dread of them.
                              It is God himself
Who can show us what he wills, in his own way.
OEDIPUS.   How strange a shadowy memory crossed my mind,   685
  Just now while you were speaking; it chilled my heart.
IOKASTÊ.   What do you mean? What memory do you speak of?
OEDIPUS.   If I understand you, Laïos was killed
  At a place where three roads meet.
IOKASTÊ.   So it was said;
  We have no later story.
OEDIPUS.   Where did it happen?   690
IOKASTÊ.   Phokis, it is called: at a place where the Theban Way
  Divides into the roads toward Delphi and Daulia.
OEDIPUS.   When?
IOKASTÊ.   We had the news not long before you came
  And proved the right to your succession here.
OEDIPUS.   Ah, what net has God been weaving for me?   695
IOKASTÊ.   Oedipus! Why does this trouble you?
OEDIPUS.   Do not ask me yet.
  First, tell me how Laïos looked, and tell me
  How old he was.
IOKASTÊ.   He was tall, his hair just touched
  With white; his form was not unlike your own.
OEDIPUS.   I think that I myself may be accurst   700
  By my own ignorant edict.
IOKASTÊ.   You speak strangely.
  It makes me tremble to look at you, my king.
OEDIPUS.   I am not sure that the blind man can not see.
  But I should know better if you were to tell me—
IOKASTÊ.   Anything—though I dread to hear you ask it.   705
OEDIPUS.   Was the king lightly escorted, or did he ride
  With a large company, as a ruler should?
IOKASTÊ.   There were five men with him in all: one was a herald;
  And a single chariot, which he was driving.
OEDIPUS.   Alas, that makes it plain enough!
                              But who—   710
  Who told you how it happened?
IOKASTÊ.   A household servant,
  The only one to escape.

OEDIPUS.   And is he still
   A servant of ours?
IOKASTÊ.   No; for when he came back at last
   And found you enthroned in the place of the dead king,
   He came to me, touched my hand with his, and begged   715
   That I would send him away to the frontier district
   Where only the shepherds go—
   As far away from the city as I could send him.
   I granted his prayer; for although the man was a slave,
   He had earned more than this favor at my hands.   720
OEDIPUS.   Can he be called back quickly?
IOKASTÊ.   Easily.
   But why?
OEDIPUS.   I have taken too much upon myself
   Without enquiry; therefore I wish to consult him.
IOKASTÊ.   Then he shall come.
                              But am I not one also
   To whom you might confide these fears of yours?   725
OEDIPUS.   That is your right; it will not be denied you,
   Now least of all; for I have reached a pitch
   Of wild foreboding. Is there anyone
   To whom I should sooner speak?

   Polybos of Corinth is my father.   730
   My mother is a Dorian: Meropê.
   I grew up chief among the men of Corinth
   Until a strange thing happened—
   Not worth my passion, it may be, but strange.
   At a feast, a drunken man maundering in his cups   735
   Cries out that I am not my father's son!

   I contained myself that night, though I felt anger
   And a sinking heart. The next day I visited
   My father and mother, and questioned them. They stormed,
   Calling it all the slanderous rant of a fool;   740
   And this relieved me. Yet the suspicion
   Remained always aching in my mind;
   I knew there was talk; I could not rest;
   And finally, saying nothing to my parents,
   I went to the shrine at Delphi.   745

   The god dismissed my question without reply;
   He spoke of other things.
                              Some were clear,
   Full of wretchedness, dreadful, unbearable:
   As, that I should lie with my own mother, breed
   Children from whom all men would turn their eyes;   750
   And that I should be my father's murderer.

I heard all this, and fled. And from that day
Corinth to me was only in the stars
Descending in that quarter of the sky,
As I wandered farther and farther on my way   755
To a land where I should never see the evil
Sung by the oracle. And I came to this country
Where, so you say, King Laïos was killed.

I will tell you all that happened there, my lady.

There were three highways   760
Coming together at a place I passed;
And there a herald came towards me, and a chariot
Drawn by horses, with a man such as you describe
Seated in it. The groom leading the horses
Forced me off the road at his lord's command;   765
But as this charioteer lurched over towards me
I struck him in my rage. The old man saw me
And brought his double goad down upon my head
As I came abreast.
        He was paid back, and more!
Swinging my club in this right hand I knocked him   770
Out of his car, and he rolled on the ground.
                  I killed him.

I killed them all.
Now if that stranger and Laïos were—kin,
Where is a man more miserable than I?
More hated by the gods? Citizen and alien alike   775
Must never shelter me or speak to me—
I must be shunned by all.
        And I myself
Pronounced this malediction upon myself!

Think of it: I have touched you with these hands,
These hands that killed your husband. What defilement!   780

Am I all evil, then? It must be so,
Since I must flee from Thebes, yet never again
See my own countrymen, my own country,
For fear of joining my mother in marriage
And killing Polybos, my father.
           Ah,   785
If I was created so, born to this fate,
Who could deny the savagery of God?

O holy majesty of heavenly powers!
May I never see that day! Never!
Rather let me vanish from the race of men   790
Than know the abomination destined me!

CHORAGOS.   We too, my lord, have felt dismay at this.
But there is hope: you have yet to hear the shepherd.
OEDIPUS.   Indeed, I fear no other hope is left me.
IOKASTÊ.   What do you hope from him when he comes?
OEDIPUS.   This much: 795
If his account of the murder tallies with yours,
Then I am cleared.
IOKASTÊ.   What was it that I said
Of such importance?
OEDIPUS.   Why, "marauders," you said,
Killed the king, according to this man's story.
If he maintains that still, if there were several,   800
Clearly the guilt is not mine: I was alone.
But if he says one man, singlehanded, did it,
Then the evidence all points to me.
IOKASTÊ.   You may be sure that he said there were several;
And can he call back that story now? He can not.   805
The whole city heard it as plainly as I.
But suppose he alters some detail of it:
He can not ever show that Laïos' death
Fulfilled the oracle: for Apollo said
My child was doomed to kill him; and my child—   810
Poor baby!—it was my child that died first.

No. From now on, where oracles are concerned,
I would not waste a second thought on any.
OEDIPUS.   You may be right.
                            But come: let someone go
For the shepherd at once. This matter must be settled.   815
IOKASTÊ.   I will send for him.
I would not wish to cross you in anything,
And surely not in this.—Let us go in.

(Exeunt into the palace.)

ODE II

STROPHE 1

CHORUS.   Let me be reverent in the ways of right,
    Lowly the paths I journey on;   820
    Let all my words and actions keep
    The laws of the pure universe
    From highest Heaven handed down.
    For Heaven is their bright nurse,
    Those generations of the realms of light;   825
    Ah, never of mortal kind were they begot,
    Nor are they slaves of memory, lost in sleep:
    Their Father is greater than Time, and ages not.

ANTISTROPHE 1

The tyrant is a child of Pride
Who drinks from his great sickening cup   830
Recklessness and vanity,
Until from his high crest headlong
He plummets to the dust of hope.
That strong man is not strong.
But let no fair ambition be denied;   835
May God protect the wrestler for the State
In government, in comely policy,
Who will fear God, and on His ordinance wait.

STROPHE 2

Haughtiness and the high hand of disdain
Tempt and outrage God's holy law;   840
And any mortal who dares hold
No immortal Power in awe
Will be caught up in a net of pain:
The price for which his levity is sold.
Let each man take due earnings, then,   845
And keep his hands from holy things,
And from blasphemy stand apart—
Else the crackling blast of heaven
Blows on his head, and on his desperate heart.
Though fools will honor impious men,   850
In their cities no tragic poet sings.

ANTISTROPHE 2

Shall we lose faith in Delphi's obscurities,
We who have heard the world's core
Discredited, and the sacred wood
Of Zeus at Elis praised no more?   855
The deeds and the strange prophecies
Must make a pattern yet to be understood.
Zeus, if indeed you are lord of all,
Throned in light over night and day,
Mirror this in your endless mind: 860
Our masters call the oracle
Words on the wind, and the Delphic vision blind!
Their hearts no longer know Apollo,
And reverence for the gods has died away.

SCENE III

(*Enter* IOKASTÊ.)

IOKASTÊ.   Princes of Thebes, it has occurred to me   865
To visit the altars of the gods, bearing
These branches as a suppliant, and this incense.

Our king is not himself: his noble soul
Is overwrought with fantasies of dread,
Else he would consider   870
The new prophecies in the light of the old.
He will listen to any voice that speaks disaster,
And my advice goes for nothing.

(She approaches the altar, right.)

                              To you, then, Apollo,
Lycéan lord, since you are nearest, I turn in prayer.
Receive these offerings, and grant us deliverance   875
From defilement. Our hearts are heavy with fear
When we see our leader distracted, as helpless sailors
Are terrified by the confusion of their helmsman.

(Enter MESSENGER.*)*

MESSENGER.   Friends, no doubt you can direct me:
Where shall I find the house of Oedipus,   880
Or, better still, where is the king himself?
CHORAGOS.   It is this very place, stranger; he is inside.
This is his wife and mother of his children.
MESSENGER.   I wish her happiness in a happy house,
Blest in all the fulfillment of her marriage.   885
IOKASTÊ.   I wish as much for you: your courtesy
Deserves a like good fortune. But now, tell me:
Why have you come? What have you to say to us?
MESSENGER.   Good news, my lady, for your house and your husband.
IOKASTÊ.   What news? Who sent you here?
MESSENGER.   I am from Corinth.   890
The news I bring ought to mean joy for you,
Though it may be you will find some grief in it.
IOKASTÊ.   What is it? How can it touch us in both ways?
MESSENGER.   The word is that the people of the Isthmus
Intend to call Oedipus to be their king.   895
IOKASTÊ.   But old King Polybos—is he not reigning still?
MESSENGER.   No. Death holds him in his sepulchre.
IOKASTÊ.   What are you saying? Polybos is dead?
MESSENGER.   If I am not telling the truth, may I die myself.
IOKASTÊ *(to a* MAIDSERVANT*)*.   Go in, go quickly; tell this to your
    master.   900
O riddlers of God's will, where are you now!
This was the man whom Oedipus, long ago,
Feared so, fled so, in dread of destroying him—
But it was another fate by which he died.

(Enter OEDIPUS, *center.)*

OEDIPUS.   Dearest Iokastê, why have you sent for me?   905
IOKASTÊ.   Listen to what this man says, and then tell me
What has become of the solemn prophecies.

OEDIPUS.	Who is this man? What is his news for me?	
IOKASTÊ.	He has come from Corinth to announce your father's death!	
OEDIPUS.	Is it true, stranger? Tell me in your own words.	910
MESSENGER.	I can not say it more clearly: the king is dead.	
OEDIPUS.	Was it by treason? Or by an attack of illness?	
MESSENGER.	A little thing brings old men to their rest.	
OEDIPUS.	It was sickness, then?	
MESSENGER.	Yes, and his many years.	
OEDIPUS.	Ah!	915

Why should a man respect the Pythian hearth,° or
Give heed to the birds that jangle above his head?
They prophesied that I should kill Polybos,
Kill my own father; but he is dead and buried,
And I am here—I never touched him, never,   920
Unless he died of grief for my departure,
And thus, in a sense, through me. No. Polybos
Has packed the oracles off with him underground.
They are empty words.

IOKASTÊ.	Had I not told you so?	
OEDIPUS.	You had; it was my faint heart that betrayed me.	925
IOKASTÊ.	From now on never think of those things again.	
OEDIPUS.	And yet—must I not fear my mother's bed?	
IOKASTÊ.	Why should anyone in this world be afraid,	

Since Fate rules us and nothing can be foreseen?
A man should live only for the present day.   930

Have no more fear of sleeping with your mother:
How many men, in dreams, have lain with their mothers!
No reasonable man is troubled by such things.

OEDIPUS.	That is true; only—	

If only my mother were not still alive!   935
But she is alive. I can not help my dread.

IOKASTÊ.	Yet this news of your father's death is wonderful.	
OEDIPUS.	Wonderful. But I fear the living woman.	
MESSENGER.	Tell me, who is this woman that you fear?	
OEDIPUS.	It is Meropê, man; the wife of King Polybos.	940
MESSENGER.	Meropê? Why should you be afraid of her?	
OEDIPUS.	An oracle of the gods, a dreadful saying.	
MESSENGER.	Can you tell me about it or are you sworn to silence?	
OEDIPUS.	I can tell you, and I will.	

Apollo said through his prophet that I was the man   945
Who should marry his own mother, shed his father's blood
With his own hands. And so, for all these years
I have kept clear of Corinth, and no harm has come—
Though it would have been sweet to see my parents again.

MESSENGER.	And is this the fear that drove you out of Corinth?	950

916. **Pythian hearth:** another name for Delphi was Pythia.

OEDIPUS.   Would you have me kill my father?

MESSENGER.   As for that
You must be reassured by the news I gave you.

OEDIPUS.   If you could reassure me, I would reward you.

MESSENGER.   I had that in mind, I will confess: I thought
I could count on you when you returned to Corinth.   955

OEDIPUS.   No: I will never go near my parents again.

MESSENGER.   Ah, son, you still do not know what you are doing—

OEDIPUS.   What do you mean? In the name of God tell me!

MESSENGER.   —If these are your reasons for not going home.

OEDIPUS.   I tell you, I fear the oracle may come true.   960

MESSENGER.   And guilt may come upon you through your parents?

OEDIPUS.   That is the dread that is always in my heart.

MESSENGER.   Can you not see that all your fears are groundless?

OEDIPUS.   Groundless? Am I not my parents' son?

MESSENGER.   Polybos was not your father.

OEDIPUS.   Not my father?   965

MESSENGER.   No more your father than the man speaking to you.

OEDIPUS.   But you are nothing to me!

MESSENGER.   Neither was he.

OEDIPUS.   Then why did he call me son?

MESSENGER.   I will tell you:
Long ago he had you from my hands, as a gift.

OEDIPUS.   Then how could he love me so, if I was not his?   970

MESSENGER.   He had no children, and his heart turned to you.

OEDIPUS.   What of you? Did you buy me? Did you find me by chance?

MESSENGER.   I came upon you in the woody vales of Kithairon.

OEDIPUS.   And what were you doing there?

MESSENGER.   Tending my flocks.

OEDIPUS.   A wandering shepherd?

MESSENGER.   But your savior, son, that day.   975

OEDIPUS.   From what did you save me?

MESSENGER.   Your ankles should tell you that.

OEDIPUS.   Ah, stranger, why do you speak of that childhood pain?

MESSENGER.   I pulled the skewer that pinned your feet together.

OEDIPUS.   I have had the mark as long as I can remember.

MESSENGER.   That was why you were given the name you bear.   980

OEDIPUS.   God! Was it my father or my mother who did it?
Tell me!

MESSENGER.   I do not know. The man who gave you to me
Can tell you better than I.

OEDIPUS.   It was not you that found me, but another?

MESSENGER.   It was another shepherd gave you to me.   985

OEDIPUS.   Who was he? Can you tell me who he was?

MESSENGER.   I think he was said to be one of Laïos' people.

OEDIPUS.   You mean the Laïos who was king here years ago?

MESSENGER.   Yes; King Laïos; and the man was one of his herdsmen.

OEDIPUS.   Is he still alive? Can I see him?
MESSENGER.   These men here   990
Know best about such things.
OEDIPUS.   Does anyone here
Know this shepherd that he is talking about?
Have you seen him in the fields, or in the town?
If you have, tell me. It is time things were made plain.
CHORAGOS.   I think the man he means is that same shepherd   995
You have already asked to see. Iokastê perhaps
Could tell you something.
OEDIPUS.   Do you know anything
About him, Lady? Is he the man we have summoned?
Is that the man this shepherd means?
IOKASTÊ.   Why think of him?
Forget this herdsman. Forget it all.   1000
This talk is a waste of time.
OEDIPUS.   How can you say that,
When the clues to my true birth are in my hands?
IOKASTÊ.   For God's love, let us have no more questioning!
Is your life nothing to you?
My own is pain enough for me to bear.   1005
OEDIPUS.   You need not worry. Suppose my mother a slave,
And born of slaves: no baseness can touch you.
IOKASTÊ.   Listen to me, I beg you: do not do this thing!
OEDIPUS.   I will not listen; the truth must be made known.
IOKASTÊ.   Everything that I say is for your own good!
OEDIPUS.   My own good   1010
Snaps my patience, then; I want none of it.
IOKASTÊ.   You are fatally wrong! May you never learn who you are!
OEDIPUS.   Go, one of you, and bring the shepherd here.
Let us leave this woman to brag of her royal name.
IOKASTÊ.   Ah, miserable!   1015
That is the only word I have for you now.
That is the only word I can ever have. (*Exit into the palace.*)
CHORAGOS.   Why has she left us, Oedipus? Why has she gone
In such a passion of sorrow? I fear this silence:
Something dreadful may come of it.
OEDIPUS.   Let it come!   1020
However base my birth, I must know about it.
The Queen, like a woman, is perhaps ashamed
To think of my low origin. But I
Am a child of Luck; I can not be dishonored.
Luck is my mother; the passing months, my brothers,   1025
Have seen me rich and poor.
                          If this is so,
How could I wish that I were someone else?
How could I not be glad to know my birth?

ODE III

STROPHE

CHORUS.   If ever the coming time were known
    To my heart's pondering,   1030
    Kithairon, now by Heaven I see the torches
    At the festival of the next full moon,
    And see the dance, and hear the choir sing
    A grace to your gentle shade:
    Mountain where Oedipus was found,   1035
    O mountain guard of a noble race!
    May the god who heals us lend his aid,
    And let that glory come to pass
    For our king's cradling-ground.

ANTISTROPHE

    Of the nymphs that flower beyond the years,   1040
    Who bore you, royal child,
    To Pan of the hills or the timberline Apollo,
    Cold in delight where the upland clears,
    Or Hermês for whom Kyllenê's heights are piled?
    Or flushed as evening cloud,   1045
    Great Dionysos, roamer of mountains,
    He—was it he who found you there,
    And caught you up in his own proud
    Arms from the sweet god-ravisher
    Who laughed by the Muses' fountains?   1050

SCENE IV

OEDIPUS.   Sirs: though I do not know the man,
    I think I see him coming, this shepherd we want:
    He is old, like our friend here, and the men
    Bringing him seem to be servants of my house.
    But you can tell, if you have ever seen him.   1055

    (*Enter* SHEPHERD *escorted by* SERVANTS.)

CHORAGOS.   I know him, he was Laïos' man. You can trust him.
OEDIPUS.   Tell me first, you from Corinth: is this the shepherd
    We were discussing?
MESSENGER.   This is the very man.
OEDIPUS (*to* SHEPHERD).   Come here. No, look at me. You must answer
    Everything I ask.—You belonged to Laïos?   1060
SHEPHERD.   Yes: born his slave, brought up in his house.
OEDIPUS.   Tell me: what kind of work did you do for him?
SHEPHERD.   I was a shepherd of his, most of my life.

OEDIPUS.   Where mainly did you go for pasturage?
SHEPHERD.   Sometimes Kithairon, sometimes the hills near-by.   1065
OEDIPUS.   Do you remember ever seeing this man out there?
SHEPHERD.   What would he be doing there? This man?
OEDIPUS.   This man standing here. Have you ever seen him before?
SHEPHERD.   No. At least, not to my recollection.
MESSENGER.   And that is not strange, my lord. But I'll refresh   1070
His memory: he must remember when we two
Spent three whole seasons together, March to September,
On Kithairon or thereabouts. He had two flocks;
I had one. Each autumn I'd drive mine home
And he would go back with his to Laïos' sheepfold.—   1075
Is this not true, just as I have described it?
SHEPHERD.   True, yes; but it was all so long ago.
MESSENGER.   Well, then: do you remember, back in those days,
That you gave me a baby boy to bring up as my own?
SHEPHERD.   What if I did? What are you trying to say?   1080
MESSENGER.   King Oedipus was once that little child.
SHEPHERD.   Damn you, hold your tongue!
OEDIPUS.   No more of that!
It is your tongue needs watching, not this man's.
SHEPHERD.   My king, my master, what is it I have done wrong?
OEDIPUS.   You have not answered his question about the boy.   1085
SHEPHERD.   He does not know . . . He is only making trouble . . .
OEDIPUS.   Come, speak plainly, or it will go hard with you.
SHEPHERD.   In God's name, do not torture an old man!
OEDIPUS.   Come here, one of you; bind his arms behind him.
SHEPHERD.   Unhappy king! What more do you wish to learn?   1090
OEDIPUS.   Did you give this man the child he speaks of?
SHEPHERD.   I did.
And I would to God I had died that very day.
OEDIPUS.   You will die now unless you speak the truth.
SHEPHERD.   Yet if I speak the truth, I am worse than dead.
OEDIPUS (*to* ATTENDANT). He intends to draw it out, apparently—   1095
SHEPHERD.   No! I have told you already that I gave him the boy.
OEDIPUS.   Where did you get him? From your house? From somewhere
else?
SHEPHERD.   Not from mine, no. A man gave him to me.
OEDIPUS.   Is that man here? Whose house did he belong to?
SHEPHERD.   For God's love, my king, do not ask me any more!   1100
OEDIPUS.   You are a dead man if I have to ask you again.
SHEPHERD.   Then . . . Then the child was from the palace of Laïos.
OEDIPUS.   A slave child? or a child of his own line?
SHEPHERD.   Ah, I am on the brink of dreadful speech!
OEDIPUS.   And I of dreadful hearing. Yet I must hear.   1105
SHEPHERD.   If you must be told, then . . .
                                          They said it was Laïos' child;
But it is your wife who can tell you about that.

OEDIPUS.   My wife!—Did she give it to you?
SHEPHERD.   My lord, she did.
OEDIPUS.   Do you know why?
SHEPHERD.   I was told to get rid of it.
OEDIPUS.   Oh heartless mother!
SHEPHERD.   But in dread of prophecies . . .   1110
OEDIPUS.   Tell me.
SHEPHERD.   It was said that the boy would kill his own father.
OEDIPUS.   Then why did you give him over to this old man?
SHEPHERD.   I pitied the baby, my king,
    And I thought that this man would take him far away
    To his own country.
                        He saved him—but for what a fate!   1115
    For if you are what this man says you are,
    No man living is more wretched than Oedipus.
OEDIPUS.   Ah God!
    It was true!
            All the prophecies!
                        —Now,
    O Light, may I look on you for the last time!   1120
    I, Oedipus,
    Oedipus, damned in his birth, in his marriage damned,
    Damned in the blood he shed with his own hand! *(He rushes into the
    palace.)*

ODE IV

STROPHE 1

CHORUS.   Alas for the seed of men.
    What measure shall I give these generations   1125
    That breathe on the void and are void
    And exist and do not exist?
    Who bears more weight of joy
    Than mass of sunlight shifting in images,
    Or who shall make his thought stay on   1130
    That down time drifts away?
    Your splendor is all fallen.
    O naked brow of wrath and tears,
    O change of Oedipus!
    I who saw your days call no man blest—   1135
    Your great days like ghósts góne.

ANTISTROPHE 1

    That mind was a strong bow.
    Deep, how deep you drew it then, hard archer,
    At a dim fearful range,
    And brought dear glory down!   1140
    You overcame the stranger°—

1141. **stranger:** the Sphinx.

The virgin with her hooking lion claws—
And though death sang, stood like a tower
To make pale Thebes take heart.
Fortress against our sorrow!   1145
True king, giver of laws,
Majestic Oedipus!
No prince in Thebes had ever such renown,
No prince won such grace of power.

STROPHE 2

And now of all men ever known   1150
Most pitiful is this man's story:
His fortunes are most changed, his state
Fallen to a low slave's
Ground under bitter fate.
O Oedipus, most royal one!   1155
The great door that expelled you to the light
Gave at night—ah, gave night to your glory:
As to the father, to the fathering son.
All understood too late.
How could that queen whom Laïos won,   1160
The garden that he harrowed at his height,
Be silent when that act was done?

ANTISTROPHE 2

But all eyes fail before time's eye,
All actions come to justice there.
Though never willed, though far down the deep past,   1165
Your bed, your dread sirings,
Are brought to book at last.
Child by Laïos doomed to die,
Then doomed to lose that fortunate little death,
Would God you never took breath in this air   1170
That with my wailing lips I take to cry:
For I weep the world's outcast.
I was blind, and now I can tell why:
Asleep, for you had given ease of breath
To Thebes, while the false years went by.   1175

EXODOS°

(*Enter, from the palace,* SECOND MESSENGER.)

SECOND MESSENGER.   Elders of Thebes, most honored in this land,
    What horrors are yours to see and hear, what weight
    Of sorrow to be endured, if, true to your birth,
    You venerate the line of Labdakos!

Exodos: the concluding scene.

I think neither Istros nor Phasis, those great rivers,   1180
Could purify this place of all the evil
It shelters now, or soon must bring to light—
Evil not done unconsciously, but willed.

The greatest griefs are those we cause ourselves.
CHORAGOS.   Surely, friend, we have grief enough already;   1185
What new sorrow do you mean?
SECOND MESSENGER.   The queen is dead.
CHORAGOS.   O miserable queen! But at whose hand?
SECOND MESSENGER.   Her own.
The full horror of what happened you can not know,
For you did not see it; but I, who did, will tell you
As clearly as I can how she met her death.   1190

When she had left us,
In passionate silence, passing through the court,
She ran to her apartment in the house,
Her hair clutched by the fingers of both hands.
She closed the doors behind her; then, by that bed   1195
Where long ago the fatal son was conceived—
That son who should bring about his father's death—
We heard her call upon Laïos, dead so many years,
And heard her wail for the double fruit of her marriage,
A husband by her husband, children by her child.   1200

Exactly how she died I do not know:
For Oedipus burst in moaning and would not let us
Keep vigil to the end: it was by him
As he stormed about the room that our eyes were caught.
From one to another of us he went, begging a sword,   1205
Hunting the wife who was not his wife, the mother
Whose womb had carried his own children and himself.
I do not know: it was none of us aided him,
But surely one of the gods was in control!
For with a dreadful cry   1210
He hurled his weight, as though wrenched out of himself,
At the twin doors: the bolts gave, and he rushed in.
And there we saw her hanging, her body swaying
From the cruel cord she had noosed about her neck.
A great sob broke from him, heartbreaking to hear,   1215
As he loosed the rope and lowered her to the ground.

I would blot out from my mind what happened next!
For the king ripped from her gown the golden brooches
That were her ornament, and raised them, and plunged them down
Straight into his own eyeballs, crying, "No more,   1220
No more shall you look on the misery about me,
The horrors of my own doing! Too long you have known
The faces of those whom I should never have seen,

Too long been blind to those for whom I was searching!
From this hour, go in darkness!" And as he spoke, 1225
He struck at his eyes—not once, but many times;
And the blood spattered his beard,
Bursting from his ruined sockets like red hail.

So from the unhappiness of two this evil has sprung,
A curse on the man and woman alike. The old 1230
Happiness of the house of Labdakos
Was happiness enough: where is it today?
It is all wailing and ruin, disgrace, death—all
The misery of mankind that has a name—
And it is wholly and for ever theirs. 1235

CHORAGOS.   Is he in agony still? Is there no rest for him?

SECOND MESSENGER.   He is calling for someone to open the doors wide
So that all the children of Kadmos may look upon
His father's murderer, his mother's—no,
I can not say it!
                             And then he will leave Thebes, 1240
Self-exiled, in order that the curse
Which he himself pronounced may depart from the house.
He is weak, and there is none to lead him,
So terrible is his suffering.
                             But you will see:
Look, the doors are opening; in a moment 1245
You will see a thing that would crush a heart of stone.

(The central door is opened; OEDIPUS, *blinded, is led in.)*

CHORAGOS.   Dreadful indeed for men to see.
Never have my own eyes
Looked on a sight so full of fear.

Oedipus! 1250
What madness came upon you, what daemon
Leaped on your life with heavier
Punishment than a mortal man can bear?
No: I can not even
Look at you, poor ruined one. 1255
And I would speak, question, ponder,
If I were able. No.
You make me shudder.

OEDIPUS.   God. God.
Is there a sorrow greater? 1260
Where shall I find harbor in this world?
My voice is hurled far on a dark wind.
What has God done to me?

CHORAGOS.   Too terrible to think of, or to see.

1251. **daemon:** a powerful, supernatural being who lacks the dignity of a god but who can bring either good or bad to mankind.

STROPHE 1

OEDIPUS.   O cloud of night,   1265
    Never to be turned away: night coming on,
    I can not tell how: night like a shroud!
    My fair winds brought me here.
                      O God. Again
    The pain of the spikes where I had sight,
    The flooding pain   1270
    Of memory, never to be gouged out.
CHORAGOS.   This is not strange.
    You suffer it all twice over, remorse in pain,
    Pain in remorse.
OEDIPUS.   Ah dear friend   1275
    Are you faithful even yet, you alone?
    Are you still standing near me, will you stay here,
    Patient, to care for the blind?
                    The blind man!
    Yet even blind I know who it is attends me,
    By the voice's tone—   1280
    Though my new darkness hide the comforter.
CHORAGOS.   Oh fearful act!
    What god was it drove you to rake black
    Night across your eyes?

STROPHE 2

OEDIPUS.   Apollo. Apollo. Dear   1285
    Children, the god was Apollo.
    He brought my sick, sick fate upon me.
    But the blinding hand was my own!
    How could I bear to see
    When all my sight was horror everywhere?   1290
CHORAGOS.   Everywhere; that is true.
OEDIPUS.   And now what is left?
    Images? Love? A greeting even,
    Sweet to the senses? Is there anything?
    Ah, no, friends: lead me away.   1295
    Lead me away from Thebes.
                    Lead the great wreck
    And hell of Oedipus, whom the gods hate.
CHORAGOS.   Your misery, you are not blind to that.
    Would God you had never found it out!

ANTISTROPHE 2

OEDIPUS.   Death take the man who unbound   1300
    My feet on that hillside
    And delivered me from death to life! What life?
    If only I had died,

This weight of monstrous doom
Could not have dragged me and my darlings down.   1305
CHORAGOS.   I would have wished the same.
OEDIPUS.   Oh never to have come here
With my father's blood upon me! Never
To have been the man they call his mother's husband!
Oh accurst! Oh child of evil,   1310
To have entered that wretched bed—
                         The selfsame one!
More primal than sin itself, this fell to me.
CHORAGOS.   I do not know what words to offer you.
You were better dead than alive and blind.
OEDIPUS.   Do not counsel me any more. This punishment   1315
That I have laid upon myself is just.
If I had eyes,
I do not know how I could bear the sight
Of my father, when I came to the house of Death,
Or my mother: for I have sinned against them both   1320
So vilely that I could not make my peace
By strangling my own life.
                     Or do you think my children,
Born as they were born, would be sweet to my eyes?
Ah never, never! Nor this town with its high walls,
Nor the holy images of the gods.
                For I,   1325
Thrice miserable!—Oedipus, noblest of all the line
Of Kadmos, have condemned myself to enjoy
These things no more, by my own malediction
Expelling that man whom the gods declared
To be a defilement in the house of Laïos.   1330
After exposing the rankness of my own guilt,
How could I look men frankly in the eyes?
No, I swear it,
If I could have stifled my hearing at its source,
I would have done it and made all this body   1335
A tight cell of misery, blank to light and sound:
So I should have been safe in my dark mind
Beyond external evil.
              Ah Kithairon!
Why did you shelter me? When I was cast upon you,
Why did I not die? Then I should never   1340
Have shown the world my execrable birth.

Ah Polybos! Corinth, city that I believed
The ancient seat of my ancestors: how fair
I seemed, your child! And all the while this evil
Was cancerous within me!
              For I am sick   1345
In my own being, sick in my origin.

O three roads, dark ravine, woodland and way
Where three roads met: you, drinking my father's blood,
My own blood, spilled by my own hand: can you remember
The unspeakable things I did there, and the things   1350
I went on from there to do?
                              O marriage, marriage!
The act that engendered me, and again the act
Performed by the son in the same bed—
                              Ah, the net
Of incest, mingling fathers, brothers, sons,
With brides, wives, mothers: the last evil   1355
That can be known by men: no tongue can say
How evil!
              No. For the love of God, conceal me
Somewhere far from Thebes; or kill me; or hurl me
Into the sea, away from men's eyes for ever.

Come, lead me. You need not fear to touch me.   1360
Of all men, I alone can bear this guilt.

(*Enter* KREON.)

CHORAGOS.   Kreon is here now. As to what you ask,
    He may decide the course to take. He only
    Is left to protect the city in your place.
OEDIPUS.   Alas, how can I speak to him? What right have I   1365
    To beg his courtesy whom I have deeply wronged?
KREON.   I have not come to mock you, Oedipus,
    Or to reproach you, either.
              (*To* ATTENDANTS)—You, standing there:
    If you have lost all respect for man's dignity,
    At least respect the flame of Lord Helios: 1370
    Do not allow this pollution to show itself
    Openly here, an affront to the earth
    And Heaven's rain and the light of day. No, take him
    Into the house as quickly as you can.
    For it is proper   1375
    That only the close kindred see his grief.
OEDIPUS.   I pray you in God's name, since your courtesy
    Ignores my dark expectation, visiting
    With mercy this man of all men most execrable:
    Give me what I ask—for your good, not for mine.   1380
KREON.   And what is it that you turn to me begging for?
OEDIPUS.   Drive me out of this country as quickly as may be
    To a place where no human voice can ever greet me.
KREON.   I should have done that before now—only,
    God's will had not been wholly revealed to me.   1385
OEDIPUS.   But his command is plain: the parricide
    Must be destroyed. I am that evil man.

KREON.   That is the sense of it, yes; but as things are,
We had best discover clearly what is to be done.
OEDIPUS.   You would learn more about a man like me?   1390
KREON.   You are ready now to listen to the god.
OEDIPUS.   I will listen. But it is to you
That I must turn for help. I beg you, hear me.

The woman in there—
Give her whatever funeral you think proper: 1395
She is your sister.
                    —But let me go, Kreon!
Let me purge my father's Thebes of the pollution
Of my living here, and go out to the wild hills,
To Kithairon, that has won such fame with me,
The tomb my mother and father appointed for me,   1400
And let me die there, as they willed I should.
And yet I know
Death will not ever come to me through sickness
Or in any natural way: I have been preserved
For some unthinkable fate. But let that be.   1405

As for my sons, you need not care for them.
They are men, they will find some way to live.
But my poor daughters, who have shared my table,
Who never before have been parted from their father—
Take care of them, Kreon; do this for me.   1410

And will you let me touch them with my hands
A last time, and let us weep together?
Be kind, my lord,
Great prince, be kind!
                    Could I but touch them,
They would be mine again, as when I had my eyes.   1415

(Enter ANTIGONE *and* ISMENE, *attended.)*

Ah, God!
Is it my dearest children I hear weeping?
Has Kreon pitied me and sent my daughters?
KREON.   Yes, Oedipus: I knew that they were dear to you
In the old days, and know you must love them still.   1420
OEDIPUS.   May God bless you for this—and be a friendlier
Guardian to you than he has been to me!

Children, where are you?
Come quickly to my hands: they are your brother's—
Hands that have brought your father's once clear eyes   1425
To this way of seeing—
                    Ah dearest ones,
I had neither sight nor knowledge then, your father

By the woman who was the source of his own life!
And I weep for you—having no strength to see you—,
I weep for you when I think of the bitterness   1430
That men will visit upon you all your lives.
What homes, what festivals can you attend
Without being forced to depart again in tears?
And when you come to marriageable age,
Where is the man, my daughters, who would dare   1435
Risk the bane that lies on all my children?
Is there any evil wanting? Your father killed
His father; sowed the womb of her who bore him;
Engendered you at the fount of his own existence!
That is what they will say of you.
                                        Then, whom   1440
Can you ever marry? There are no bridegrooms for you,
And your lives must wither away in sterile dreaming.

O Kreon, son of Menoikeus!
You are the only father my daughters have,
Since we, their parents, are both of us gone for ever.   1445
They are your own blood: you will not let them
Fall into beggary and loneliness;
You will keep them from the miseries that are mine!
Take pity on them; see, they are only children,
Friendless except for you. Promise me this,   1450
Great prince, and give me your hand in token of it.

(KREON *clasps his right hand.*)

Children:
I could say much, if you could understand me,
But as it is, I have only this prayer for you:
Live where you can, be as happy as you can—   1455
Happier, please God, than God has made your father.

KREON.   Enough. You have wept enough. Now go within.
OEDIPUS.   I must; but it is hard.
KREON.   Time eases all things.
OEDIPUS.   You know my mind, then?
KREON.   Say what you desire.
OEDIPUS.   Send me from Thebes!
KREON.   God grant that I may!   1460
OEDIPUS.   But since God hates me . . .
KREON.   No, he will grant your wish.
OEDIPUS.   You promise?
KREON.   I can not speak beyond my knowledge.
OEDIPUS.   Then lead me in.
KREON.   Come now, and leave your children.

OEDIPUS.   No! Do not take them from me!
KREON.   Think no longer
That you are in command here, but rather think   1465
How, when you were, you served your own destruction.

(*Exeunt into the house all but the* CHORUS; *the* CHORAGOS *chants directly to the audience.*)

CHORAGOS.   Men of Thebes: look upon Oedipus.

This is the king who solved the famous riddle
And towered up, most powerful of men.
No mortal eyes but looked on him with envy,   1470
Yet in the end ruin swept over him.

Let every man in mankind's frailty
Consider his last day; and let none
Presume on his good fortune until he find
Life, at his death, a memory without pain.   1475

QUESTIONS

1. The Greeks saw the tragic figure as a person of high estate who falls as a result of a serious character flaw. How well does this definition fit Oedipus? In what sense does he occupy a high estate? What is the tragic flaw in his character? How does it cause his downfall?

2. Discuss the role of fate in *Oedipus Rex*. Does Oedipus create his own fate, or is he a victim of forces wholly beyond his control? To what extent is free will necessary to tragedy?

3. Iokastê takes her own life. Why doesn't Oedipus? Why does he blind himself only? Is blindness an especially appropriate fate for Oedipus? Analyze the various ways in which his fate is foreshadowed in the early parts of the play.

4. Consider lines 1023–29 of the play:

> But I
> Am a child of Luck; I can not be dishonored.
> Luck is my mother; the passing months, my brothers,
> Have seen me rich and poor.
>   If this is so,
> How could I wish that I were someone else?
> How could I not be glad to know my birth?

On the edge of disaster, Oedipus nonetheless presses on toward the revelation of the circumstances of his birth. Is this foolish? Is it heroic?

5. *Oedipus Rex* has been admired for centuries because of the formulations in the play about human destiny and man's place in the scheme of things. What, in your opinion, is Sophocles' attitude with respect to these important subjects?

6. Specify your feelings at the end of the play. Are you exhilarated? Depressed? In what sense do you experience Aristotle's "pity and fear"?

William Shakespeare (1564–1616)
Hamlet

CHARACTERS

CLAUDIUS, *King of Denmark*
HAMLET, *son to the late, and nephew to the present King*
POLONIUS, *Lord Chamberlain*
HORATIO, *friend to Hamlet*
LAERTES, *son to Polonius*

VOLTIMAND
CORNELIUS
ROSENCRANTZ   } *courtiers*
GUILDENSTERN
OSRIC
A GENTLEMAN

A PRIEST

MARCELLUS   } *officers*
BERNARDO

FRANCISCO, *a soldier*
REYNALDO, *servant to Polonius*
PLAYERS
TWO CLOWNS, *gravediggers*
FORTINBRAS, *Prince of Norway*
A CAPTAIN
ENGLISH AMBASSADORS
GERTRUDE, *Queen of Denmark, and mother to Hamlet*
OPHELIA, *daughter to Polonius*
LORDS, LADIES, OFFICERS, SOLDIERS, SAILORS, MESSENGERS, *and other*
    ATTENDANTS
GHOST *of Hamlet's father*

SCENE. *Denmark.*

ACT I

SCENE I. Elsinore. A platform° before the castle.

(FRANCISCO *at his post. Enter to him* BERNARDO.)

BERNARDO.   Who's there?
FRANCISCO.   Nay, answer me. Stand, and unfold yourself.°

Act I, Sc. i: s.d., **platform:** the level place on the ramparts where the cannon were
mounted.   2. **unfold yourself:** reveal who you are.

BERNARDO.   Long live the King!°
FRANCISCO.   Bernardo?
BERNARDO.   He.   5
FRANCISCO.   You come most carefully upon your hour.
BERNARDO.   'Tis now struck twelve. Get thee to bed, Francisco.
FRANCISCO.   For this relief much thanks. 'Tis bitter cold,
And I am sick at heart.
BERNARDO.   Have you had quiet guard?
FRANCISCO.   Not a mouse stirring.   10
BERNARDO.   Well, good night.
If you do meet Horatio and Marcellus,
The rivals° of my watch, bid them make haste.
FRANCISCO.   I think I hear them. Stand, ho! Who is there?

(Enter HORATIO *and* MARCELLUS.*)*

HORATIO.   Friends to this ground.
MARCELLUS.   And liegemen° to the Dane.   15
FRANCISCO.   Give you good night.
MARCELLUS.   Oh, farewell, honest soldier.
Who hath relieved you?
FRANCISCO.   Bernardo hath my place.
Give you good night.   *(Exit.)*
MARCELLUS.   Holloa! Bernardo!
BERNARDO.   Say,
What, is Horatio there?
HORATIO.   A piece of him.
BERNARDO.   Welcome, Horatio. Welcome, good Marcellus.   20
MARCELLUS.   What, has this thing appeared again tonight?
BERNARDO.   I have seen nothing.
MARCELLUS.   Horatio says 'tis but our fantasy,°
And will not let belief take hold of him
Touching this dreaded sight twice seen of us.   25
Therefore I have entreated him along
With us to watch the minutes of this night,
That if again this apparition come,
He may approve our eyes° and speak to it.
HORATIO.   Tush tush, 'twill not appear.
BERNARDO.   Sit down awhile,   30
And let us once again assail your ears,
That are so fortified against our story,
What we have two nights seen.
HORATIO.   Well, sit we down,
And let us hear Bernardo speak of this.

---

3. **Long . . . King:** probably the password for the night.   13. **rivals:** partners.   15. **liegemen:**
loyal subjects.   23. **fantasy:** imagination.   29. **approve our eyes:** verify what we have seen.

BERNARDO.   Last night of all,   35
    When yond same star that's westward from the pole°
    Had made his course to illume° that part of heaven
    Where now it burns, Marcellus and myself,
    The bell then beating one—
    (Enter GHOST.*)*
MARCELLUS.   Peace, break thee off. Look where it comes again!   40
BERNARDO.   In the same figure, like the King that's dead.
MARCELLUS.   Thou art a scholar.° Speak to it, Horatio.
BERNARDO.   Looks it not like the King? Mark it, Horatio.
HORATIO.   Most like. It harrows° me with fear and wonder.
BERNARDO.   It would be spoke to.
MARCELLUS.   Question it, Horatio.   45
HORATIO.   What art thou that usurp'st this time of night,
    Together with° that fair and warlike form
    In which the majesty of buried Denmark°
    Did sometimes march? By Heaven I charge thee, speak!
MARCELLUS.   It is offended.
BERNARDO.   See, it stalks away!   50
HORATIO.   Stay! Speak, speak! I charge thee, speak!
    (Exit GHOST.*)*
MARCELLUS.   'Tis gone, and will not answer.
BERNARDO.   How now, Horatio! You tremble and look pale.
    Is not this something more than fantasy?
    What think you on 't?   55
HORATIO.   Before my God, I might not this believe
    Without the sensible and true avouch
    Of mine own eyes.°
MARCELLUS.   Is it not like the King?
HORATIO.   As thou art to thyself.
    Such was the very armor he had on   60
    When he the ambitious Norway combated.
    So frowned he once when, in an angry parle,°
    He smote the sledded Polacks on the ice.
    'Tis strange.
MARCELLUS.   Thus twice before, and jump at this dead hour,°   65
    With martial stalk hath he gone by our watch.
HORATIO.   In what particular thought to work I know not,
    But in the gross and scope° of my opinion
    This bodes some strange eruption° to our state.
MARCELLUS.   Good now, sit down and tell me, he that knows,   70
    Why this same strict and most observant watch

---

36. pole: Polestar.   **37. illume**: light.   **42. scholar**: As Latin was the proper language in which
to address and exorcise evil spirits, a scholar was necessary.   **44. harrows**: distresses; lit., plows
up.   **47. Together with**: i.e., appearing in.   **48. majesty . . . Denmark**: the dead
King.   **57–58. Without . . . eyes**: unless my own eyes had vouched for it.   **sensible**: perceived
by my senses.   **62. parle**: parley.   **65. jump . . . hour**: just at deep midnight.   **68. gross . . .
scope**: general conclusion.   **69. eruption**: violent disturbance.

So nightly toils° the subject° of the land;
And why such daily cast of brazen cannon
And foreign mart° for implements of war;
Why° such impress° of shipwrights, whose sore task   75
Does not divide the Sunday from the week;
What might be toward,° that this sweaty haste
Doth make the night joint laborer with the day.
Who is 't that can inform me?
HORATIO.   That can I,
At least the whisper goes so. Our last king,   80
Whose image even but now appeared to us,
Was, as you know, by Fortinbras of Norway,
Thereto pricked° on by a most emulate° pride,
Dared to the combat, in which our valiant Hamlet—
For so this side of our known world esteemed him—   85
Did slay this Fortinbras. Who° by a sealed compact,°
Well ratified by law and heraldry,°
Did forfeit, with his life, all those his lands
Which he stood seized of° to the conqueror.
Against the which, a moiety competent°   90
Was gaged° by our King, which had returned
To the inheritance of Fortinbras
Had he been vanquisher, as by the same covenant
And carriage of the article designed°
His fell to Hamlet. Now, sir, young Fortinbras,   95
Of unimproved mettle° hot and full,
Hath in the skirts° of Norway here and there
Sharked° up a list of lawless resolutes,°
For food and diet,° to some enterprise
That hath a stomach° in 't. Which is no other—   100
As it doth well appear unto our state—
But to recover of us, by strong hand
And terms compulsatory,° those foresaid lands
So by his father lost. And this, I take it,
Is the main motive of our preparations,   105
The source of this our watch and the chief head°
Of this posthaste and romage° in the land.

BERNARDO.   I think it be no other but e'en so.
Well may it sort° that this portentous figure
Comes armèd through our watch, so like the King   110
That was and is the question of these wars.
HORATIO.   A mote° it is to trouble the mind's eye.
In the most high and palmy° state of Rome,
A little ere the mightiest Julius fell,
The graves stood tenantless, and the sheeted° dead   115
Did squeak and gibber° in the Roman streets.
As stars° with trains of fire and dews of blood,
Disasters° in the sun, and the moist star°
Upon whose influence Neptune's empire stands
Was sick almost to doomsday with eclipse.   120
And even the like precurse° of fierce events,
As harbingers° preceding still the fates
And prologue to the omen° coming on,
Have Heaven and earth together demonstrated
Unto our climatures° and countrymen.   125
(*Re-enter* GHOST.) But soft, behold! Lo where it comes again!
I'll cross it,° though it blast me. Stay, illusion!
If thou hast any sound, or use of voice,
Speak to me.
If° there be any good thing to be done   130
That may to thee do ease and grace to me,°
Speak to me.
If thou art privy to° thy country's fate,
Which, happily,° foreknowing may avoid,
Oh, speak!   135
Or if thou hast uphoarded in thy life
Extorted° treasure in the womb of earth,
For which, they say, you spirits oft walk in death,
Speak of it. Stay, and speak! (*The cock crows.*°) Stop it, Marcellus.
MARCELLUS.   Shall I strike at it with my partisan?   140
HORATIO.   Do, if it will not stand.
BERNARDO.   'Tis here!
HORATIO.   'Tis here!

---

109. **Well . . . sort:** it would be a natural reason.   112. **mote:** speck of dust.   113. **palmy:** flourishing.   115. **sheeted:** in their shrouds.   116. **gibber:** utter strange sounds.   117. **As stars:** The sense of the passage is here broken; possibly a line has been omitted after l. 116.   118. **Disasters:** unlucky signs.   **moist star:** the moon, which influences the tides.   121. **precurse:** forewarning.   122. **harbingers:** forerunners. The harbinger was an officer of the Court who was sent ahead to make the arrangements when the Court went on progress.   123. **omen:** disaster.   125. **climatures:** regions.   127. **cross it:** stand in its way.   130-39. **If . . . speak:** In popular belief there were four reasons why the spirit of a dead man should *walk:* (a) to reveal a secret, (b) to utter a warning, (c) to reveal concealed treasure, (d) to reveal the manner of its death. Horatio thus adjures the ghost by three potent reasons, but before he can utter the fourth the cock crows.   131. **grace to me:** bring me into a state of spiritual grace.   133. **privy to:** have secret knowledge of.   134. **happily:** by good luck.   137. **Extorted:** evilly acquired.   139. **s.d., cock crows:** i.e., a sign that dawn is at hand.

MARCELLUS.   'Tis gone!   (*Exit* GHOST.)
  We do it wrong, being so majestical,
  To offer it the show of violence,
  For it is as the air invulnerable,   145
  And our vain blows malicious mockery.
BERNARDO.   It was about to speak when the cock crew.
HORATIO.   And then it started like a guilty thing
  Upon a fearful° summons. I have heard
  The cock, that is the trumpet to the morn,   150
  Doth with his lofty and shrill-sounding throat
  Awake the god of day, and at his warning,
  Whether in sea or fire, in earth or air,
  The extravagant and erring° spirit hies
  To his confine.° And of the truth herein   155
  This present object made probation.°
MARCELLUS.   It faded on the crowing of the cock.
  Some say that ever 'gainst° that season comes
  Wherein Our Savior's birth is celebrated,
  The bird of dawning singeth all night long.   160
  And then, they say, no spirit dare stir abroad,
  The nights are wholesome, then no planets° strike,
  No fairy takes° nor witch hath power to charm,
  So hallowed and so gracious is the time.
HORATIO.   So have I heard and do in part believe it.   165
  But look, the morn, in russet mantle clad,
  Walks o'er the dew of yon high eastward hill.
  Break we our watch up, and by my advice
  Let us impart what we have seen tonight
  Unto young Hamlet, for upon my life,   170
  This spirit, dumb to us, will speak to him.
  Do you consent we shall acquaint him with it,
  As needful in our loves, fitting our duty?
MARCELLUS.   Let's do 't, I pray. And I this morning know
  Where we shall find him most conveniently.   175
                                                        (*Exeunt.*)

SCENE II. *A room of state in the castle.*

(*Flourish.° Enter the* KING, QUEEN, HAMLET, POLONIUS, LAERTES, VOLTIMAND, CORNELIUS, LORDS, *and* ATTENDANTS.)

KING.   Though yet of Hamlet our dear brother's death
  The memory be green,° and that it us befitted
  To bear our hearts in grief and our whole kingdom

149. **fearful:** causing fear.   154. **extravagant . . . erring:** both words mean "wandering."
155. **confine:** place of confinement.   156. **probation:** proof.   158. **'gainst:** in anticipation of.
162. **planets:** Planets were supposed to bring disaster.   163. **takes:** bewitches.
  Sc. ii: **s.d., Flourish:** fanfare of trumpets.   2. **green:** fresh.

To be contracted in one brow of woe,°
Yet so far hath discretion° fought with nature°   5
That we with wisest sorrow think on him,
Together with remembrance of ourselves.
Therefore our sometime sister,° now our Queen,
The imperial jointress° to this warlike state,
Have we, as 'twere with a defeated joy—   10
With an auspicious and a dropping eye,°
With mirth in funeral and with dirge in marriage,
In equal scale weighing delight and dole°—
Taken to wife. Nor have we herein barred
Your better wisdoms,° which have freely gone   15
With this affair along. For all, our thanks.
Now follows that you know. Young Fortinbras,
Holding a weak supposal° of our worth,
Or thinking by our late dear brother's death
Our state to be disjoint and out of frame,   20
Colleagued with the dream of his advantage,°
He hath not failed to pester us with message
Importing the surrender of those lands
Lost by his father, with all bonds of law,°
To our most valiant brother. So much for him.   25
Now for ourself, and for this time of meeting.
Thus much the business is: We have here writ
To Norway, uncle of young Fortinbras—
Who, impotent and bedrid, scarcely hears
Of this his nephew's purpose—to suppress   30
His further gait° herein, in that the levies,
The lists° and full proportions,° are all made
Out of his subject.° And we here dispatch
You, good Cornelius, and you, Voltimand,
For bearers of this greeting to old Norway,   35
Giving to you no further personal power
To business with the King more than the scope°
Of these delated articles° allow.
Farewell, and let your haste commend° your duty.

---

4. **contracted . . . woe:** i.e., every subject's forehead should be puckered with grief.   5. **discretion:** common sense.   **nature:** natural sorrow.   8. **sister:** sister-in-law.   9. **jointress:** partner by marriage.   11. **auspicious . . . eye:** an eye at the same time full of joy and of tears.   13. **dole:** grief.   14–15. **barred . . . wisdoms:** i.e., in taking this step we have not shut out your advice. As is obvious throughout the play, the Danes chose their King by election and not by right of birth. See V.ii. 65, 323.   18. **weak supposal:** poor opinion.   21. **Colleagued . . . advantage:** uniting himself with this dream that here was a good opportunity.   24. **with . . . law:** legally binding.   31. **gait:** progress.   32. **lists:** rosters.   **proportions:** military-establishments.   33. **subject:** subjects.   37. **scope:** limit.   38. **delated articles:** detailed instructions. Claudius is following usual diplomatic procedure. Ambassadors sent on a special mission carried with them a letter of introduction and greeting to the King of the foreign Court and detailed instructions to guide them in the negotiations.   39. **commend:** display; lit., recommend.

CORNELIUS & VOLTIMAND.   In that and all things will we show our
    duty.   40
KING.   We doubt it nothing. Heartily farewell.

    (Exeunt VOLTIMAND *and* CORNELIUS.*)*

    And now, Laertes, what's the news with you?
    You told us of some suit°—what is 't, Laertes?
    You cannot speak of reason to the Dane
    And lose your voice. What wouldst thou beg, Laertes,   45
    That shall not be my offer, not thy asking?
    The head is not more native° to the heart,
    The hand more instrumental° to the mouth,
    Than is the throne of Denmark to thy father.
    What wouldst thou have, Laertes?
LAERTES.   My dread° lord,   50
    Your leave and favor to return to France,
    From whence though willingly I came to Denmark
    To show my duty in your coronation,
    Yet now, I must confess, that duty done,
    My thoughts and wishes bend again toward France   55
    And bow them to your gracious leave and pardon.
KING.   Have you your father's leave? What says Polonius?
POLONIUS.   He hath, my lord, wrung from me my slow leave
    By laborsome petition, and at last
    Upon his will° I sealed my hard consent.°   60
    I do beseech you give him leave to go.
KING.   Take thy fair hour, Laertes, time be thine,
    And thy best graces spend° it at thy will!
    But now, my cousin° Hamlet, and my son—
HAMLET *(Aside).*   A little more than kin and less than kind.°   65
KING.   How is it that the clouds still hang on you?
HAMLET.   Not so, my lord. I am too much i' the sun.
QUEEN.   Good Hamlet, cast thy nighted color° off,
    And let thine eye look like a friend on Denmark.
    Do not forever with thy vailèd lids°   70
    Seek for thy noble father in the dust.
    Thou know'st 'tis common—all that lives must die,
    Passing through nature to eternity.
HAMLET.   Aye, madam, it is common.
QUEEN.   If it be,
    Why seems it so particular with thee?   75

---

43. **suit:** petition.   47. **native:** closely related.   48. **instrumental:** serviceable.   50. **dread:**
dreaded, much respected.   60. **will:** desire.   **sealed . . . consent:** agreed to, but with great
reluctance.   63. **best . . . spend:** i.e., use your time well.   64. **cousin:** kinsman. The word was
used for any near relation.   65. **A . . . kind:** too near a relation (uncle-father) and too little
natural affection.   **kind:** affectionate.   68. **nighted color:** black. Hamlet alone is in deep
mourning; the rest of the Court wear gay clothes.   70. **vailed lids:** lowered eyelids.

HAMLET.   Seems, madam! Nay, it is. I know not "seems."
   'Tis not alone my inky cloak, good Mother,
   Nor customary suits of solemn black,
   Nor windy suspiration of forced breath—
   No, nor the fruitful river° in the eye,   80
   Nor the dejected havior of the visage,°
   Together with all forms, moods, shapes of grief—
   That can denote me truly. These indeed seem,
   For they are actions that a man might play.°
   But I have that within which passeth show,   85
   These but the trappings° and the suits of woe.
KING.   'Tis sweet and commendable in your nature, Hamlet,
   To give these mourning duties to your father.
   But you must know your father lost a father,
   That father lost, lost his, and the survivor bound   90
   In filial obligation for some term
   To do obsequious sorrow.° But to perséver
   In obstinate condolement° is a course
   Of impious stubbornness, 'tis unmanly grief.
   It shows a will most incorrect to Heaven,   95
   A heart unfortified,° a mind impatient,
   An understanding simple and unschooled.
   For what we know must be and is as common
   As any the most vulgar° thing to sense,
   Why should we in our peevish opposition   100
   Take it to heart? Fie! 'Tis a fault to Heaven,
   A fault against the dead, a fault to nature,
   To reason most absurd, whose common theme
   Is death of fathers, and who still hath cried,
   From the first corse° till he that died today,   105
   "This must be so." We pray you throw to earth
   This unprevailing° woe, and think of us
   As of a father. For let the world take note,
   You are the most immediate° to our throne,
   And with no less nobilty of love   110
   Than that which dearest father bears his son
   Do I impart toward you. For your intent
   In going back to school° in Wittenberg,
   It is most retrograde° to our desire.
   And we beseech you bend you° to remain   115
   Here in the cheer and comfort of our eye,
   Our chiefest courtier, cousin, and our son.

---

80. **fruitful river:** stream of tears.   81. **dejected . . . visage:** downcast countenance.   84. **play:** act, as in a play.   86. **trappings:** ornaments.   92. **obsequious sorrow:** the sorrow usual at funerals.   93. **obstinate condolement:** lamentation disregarding the will of God.   96. **unfortified:** not strengthened with the consolation of religion.   99. **vulgar:** common.   105. **corse:** corpse. There is unconscious irony in this remark, for the first corpse was that of Abel, also slain by his brother.   107. **unprevailing:** futile.   109. **most immediate:** next heir.   113. **school:** university.   114. **retrograde:** contrary.   115. **bend you:** incline.

QUEEN.   Let not thy mother lose her prayers, Hamlet.
I pray thee, stay with us, go not to Wittenberg.
HAMLET.   I shall in all my best obey you, madam.   120
KING.   Why, 'tis a loving and a fair reply.
Be as ourself in Denmark. Madam, come,
This gentle and unforced accord of Hamlet
Sits smiling to my heart. In grace whereof,
No jocund health that Denmark drinks today   125
But the great cannon° to the clouds shall tell,
And the King's rouse° the Heaven shall bruit° again,
Respeaking earthly thunder. Come away.

(Flourish. Exeunt all but HAMLET.*)*

HAMLET.   Oh, that this too too solid flesh would melt,
Thaw, and resolve itself into a dew!   130
Or that the Everlasting had not fixed
His canon° 'gainst self-slaughter! Oh, God! God!
How weary, stale, flat, and unprofitable
Seem to me all the uses° of this world!
Fie on 't, ah, fie! 'Tis an unweeded garden,   135
That grows to seed, things rank° and gross in nature
Possess it merely.° That it should come to this!
But two months dead! Nay, not so much, not two.
So excellent a King, that was, to this,
Hyperion° to a satyr.° So loving to my mother   140
That he might not beteem° the winds of heaven
Visit her face too roughly. Heaven and earth!
Must I remember? Why, she would hang on him
As if increase of appetite had grown
By what it fed on. And yet within a month——   145
Let me not think on 't.—Frailty, thy name is woman!—
A little month, or ere those shoes were old
With which she followed my poor father's body,
Like Niobe° all tears.—Why she, even she—
Oh, God! A beast that wants discourse of reason°   150
Would have mourned longer—married with my uncle,
My father's brother, but no more like my father
Than I to Hercules. Within a month,
Ere yet the salt of most unrighteous tears
Had left the flushing in her gallèd° eyes,   155

---

126. great cannon: This Danish custom of discharging cannon when the King proposed a toast
was much noted by Englishmen.   **127. rouse:** deep drink.   **bruit:** sound loudly, echo.
132. canon: rule, law.   **134. uses:** ways.   **136. rank:** coarse.   **137. merely:** entirely.
140. Hyperion: the sun god.   **satyr:** a creature half man, half goat—ugly and lecherous.
141. beteem: allow.   **149. Niobe:** She boasted of her children, to the annoyance of the goddess
Artemis, who slew them all. Thereafter Niobe became so sorrowful that she changed into a rock
everlastingly dripping water.   **150. wants . . . reason:** is without ability to reason.   **155. gallèd·**
sore.

She married. Oh, most wicked speed, to post°
With such dexterity° to incestuous sheets!
It is not, nor it cannot, come to good.
But break, my heart, for I must hold my tongue!

(Enter HORATIO, MARCELLUS, *and* BERNARDO.*)*

HORATIO.   Hail to your lordship!
HAMLET.   I am glad to see you well.   160
  Horatio—or I do forget myself.
HORATIO.   The same, my lord, and your poor servant ever.
HAMLET.   Sir, my good friend—I'll change that name° with you.
  And what make you from Wittenberg, Horatio?
  Marcellus?   165
MARCELLUS.   My good lord?
HAMLET.   I am very glad to see you. *(To* BERNARDO*)* Good even, sir.
  But what, in faith, make you from Wittenberg?
HORATIO.   A truant disposition, good my lord.
HAMLET.   I would not hear your enemy say so,   170
  Nor shall you do my ear that violence.
  To make it truster of your own report
  Against yourself. I know you are no truant.
  But what is your affair in Elsinore?
  We'll teach you to drink deep ere you depart.   175
HORATIO.   My lord, I came to see your father's funeral.
HAMLET.   I pray thee do not mock me, fellow student.
  I think it was to see my mother's wedding.
HORATIO.   Indeed, my lord, it followed hard upon.
HAMLET.   Thrift, thrift, Horatio! The funeral baked meats   180
  Did coldly furnish forth the marriage tables.°
  Would I had met my dearest° foe in Heaven
  Or ever I had seen that day, Horatio!
  My father!—Methinks I see my father.
HORATIO.   Oh, where, my lord?
HAMLET.   In my mind's eye, Horatio.   185
HORATIO.   I saw him once. He was a goodly King.
HAMLET.   He was a man, take him for all in all.
  I shall not look upon his like again.
HORATIO.   My lord, I think I saw him yesternight.
HAMLET.   Saw? Who?   190
HORATIO.   My lord, the King your father.
HAMLET.   The King my father!
HORATIO.   Season your admiration° for a while
  With an attent° ear till I may deliver,

---

156. **post:** hasten.   157. **dexterity:** nimbleness.   163. **that name:** i.e., friend.   180–81. **Thrift
. . . tables:** they hurried on the wedding for economy's sake, so that the remains of food served at
the funeral might be used cold for the wedding.   **baked meats:** feast.   182. **dearest:** best-
hated.   192. **Season . . . admiration:** moderate your wonder.   193. **attent:** attentive.

Upon the witness of these gentlemen,
This marvel to you.
HAMLET.   For God's love, let me hear.   195
HORATIO.   Two nights together had these gentlemen,
Marcellus and Bernardo, on their watch
In the dead vast and middle of the night,°
Been thus encountered. A figure like your father,
Armed at point exactly, cap-a-pie,°   200
Appears before them and with solemn march
Goes slow and stately by them. Thrice he walked
By their oppressed and fear-surprised eyes
Within his truncheon's° length, whilst they, distilled°
Almost to jelly with the act of fear,   205
Stand dumb, and speak not to him. This to me
In dreadful secrecy impart they did,
And I with them the third night kept the watch.
Where, as they had delivered, both in time,
Form of the thing, each word made true and good,   210
The apparition comes. I knew your father.
These hands are not more like.
HAMLET.   But where was this?
MARCELLUS.   My lord, upon the platform where we watched.
HAMLET.   Did you not speak to it?
HORATIO.   My lord, I did,
But answer made it none. Yet once methought   215
It lifted up it° head and did address
Itself to motion, like as it would speak.
But even then the morning cock crew loud,
And at the sound it shrunk in haste away
And vanished from our sight.
HAMLET.   'Tis very strange.   220
HORATIO.   As I do live, my honored lord, 'tis true,
And we did think it writ down in our duty
To let you know of it.
HAMLET.   Indeed, indeed, sirs, but this troubles me.
Hold you the watch tonight?
MARCELLUS & BERNARDO.   We do, my lord.   225
HAMLET.   Armed, say you?
MARCELLUS & BERNARDO.   Armed, my lord.
HAMLET.   From top to toe?
MARCELLUS & BERNARDO.   My lord, from head to foot.
HAMLET.   Then saw you not his face?
HORATIO.   Oh yes, my lord, he wore his beaver° up.
HAMLET.   What, looked he frowningly?   230
HORATIO.   A countenance more in sorrow than in anger.

198. **dead . . . night:** deep, silent midnight.   200. **at . . . cap-a-pie:** complete in every detail, head to foot.   204. **truncheon:** a general's staff.   **distilled:** melted.   216. **it:** its.   229. **beaver:** front part of the helmet, which could be raised.

HAMLET.   Pale, or red?
HORATIO.   Nay, very pale.
HAMLET.   And fixed his eyes upon you?
HORATIO.   Most constantly.
HAMLET.   I would I had been there.   235
HORATIO.   It would have much amazed you.
HAMLET.   Very like, very like. Stayed it long?
HORATIO.   While one with moderate haste might tell° a hundred.
MARCELLUS & BERNARDO.   Longer, longer.
HORATIO.   Not when I saw 't.
HAMLET.   His beard was grizzled?° No?   240
HORATIO.   It was as I have seen it in his life,
  A sable silvered.°
HAMLET.   I will watch tonight.
  Perchance 'twill walk again.
HORATIO.   I warrant it will.
HAMLET.   If it assume my noble father's person,
  I'll speak to it though Hell itself should gape   245
  And bid me hold my peace. I pray you all,
  If you have hitherto concealed this sight,
  Let it be tenable° in your silence still,
  And whatsoever else shall hap tonight,
  Give it an understanding, but no tongue.   250
  I will requite° your loves. So fare you well.
  Upon the platform, 'twixt eleven and twelve,
  I'll visit you.
ALL.   Our duty to your Honor.
HAMLET.   Your loves, as mine to you. Farewell.

  (Exeunt all but HAMLET.*)*
  My father's spirit in arms! All is not well.   255
  I doubt° some foul play. Would the night were come!
  Till then sit still, my soul. Foul deeds will rise,
  Though all the earth o'erwhelm them, to men's eyes.   *(Exit.)*

SCENE III. *A room in* POLONIUS'S *house.*

  (Enter LAERTES *and* OPHELIA.*)*
LAERTES.   My necessaries° are embarked. Farewell.
  And, Sister, as the winds give benefit
  And convoy is assistant,° do not sleep,
  But let me hear from you.
OPHELIA.   Do you doubt that?
LAERTES.   For Hamlet, and the trifling of his favor,°   5
  Hold it a fashion and a toy in blood,°

---

238. tell: count. **240. grizzled:** gray. **242. sable silvered:** black mingled with white.
248. tenable: held fast. **251. requite:** repay. **256. doubt:** suspect.
  Sc. iii: **1. necessaries:** baggage. **3. convoy . . . assistant:** means of conveyance is available. **5. favor:** i.e., toward you. **6. toy in blood:** trifling impulse.

A violet in the youth of primy° nature,
Forward, not permanent, sweet, not lasting,
The perfume and supplance of a minute°—
No more.
OPHELIA.   No more but so?
LAERTES.   Think it no more.   10
For Nature crescent does not grow alone
In thews and bulk,° but as this temple° waxes
The inward service of the mind and soul
Grows wide withal. Perhaps he loves you now,
And now no soil nor cautel° doth besmirch   15
The virtue of his will.° But you must fear,
His greatness weighed,° his will is not his own,
For he himself is subject to his birth.
He may not, as unvalued persons do,
Carve° for himself, for on his choice depends   20
The safety and health of this whole state,
And therefore must his choice be circumscribed°
Unto the voice and yielding of that body
Whereof he is the head. Then if he says he loves you,
It fits your wisdom so far to believe it   25
As he in his particular act and place
May give his saying deed, which is no further
Than the main voice of Denmark goes withal.
Then weigh what loss your honor may sustain
If with too credent° ear you list his songs,   30
Or lose your heart, or your chaste treasure° open
To his unmastered importunity.
Fear it, Ophelia, fear it, my dear sister,
And keep you in the rear° of your affection,
Out of the shot and danger of desire.   35
The chariest maid is prodigal enough
If she unmask her beauty to the moon.
Virtue itself 'scapes not calumnious strokes.
The canker galls the infants° of the spring
Too oft before their buttons° be disclosed,   40
And in the morn and liquid dew of youth
Contagious blastments° are most imminent.
Be wary, then, best safety lies in fear.
Youth to itself rebels, though none else near.°

---

7. **primy:** springtime; i.e., youthful.   8. **perfume . . . minute:** perfume which lasts only for a minute.   11–12. **For . . . bulk:** for natural growth is not only in bodily bulk.   12. **temple:** i.e., the body.   15. **cautel:** deceit.   16. **will:** desire.   17. **His . . . weighed:** when you consider his high position.   20. **Carve:** choose.   22. **circumscribed:** restricted.   30. **credent:** credulous.   31. **chaste treasure:** the treasure of your chastity.   34. **in . . . rear:** i.e., farthest from danger.   39. **canker . . . infants:** maggot harms the unopened buds.   40. **buttons:** buds.   42. **Contagious blastments:** infectious blasts.   44. **though . . . near:** without anyone else to encourage it.

OPHELIA.   I shall the effect of this good lesson keep   45
    As watchman to my heart. But, good my brother,
    Do not, as some ungracious pastors do,
    Show me the steep and thorny way to Heaven
    Whilst, like a puffed° and reckless libertine,
    Himself the primrose path of dalliance° treads   50
    And recks not his own rede.°
LAERTES.   Oh, fear me not.
    I stay too long. But here my father comes.
    (*Enter* POLONIUS.) A double blessing is a double grace,
    Occasion smiles° upon a second leave.
POLONIUS.   Yet here, Laertes! Aboard, aboard, for shame!   55
    The wind sits in the shoulder of your sail
    And you are stayed° for. There, my blessing with thee!
    And these few precepts in thy memory
    Look thou charácter.° Give thy thoughts no tongue,
    Nor any unproportioned° thought his act.   60
    Be thou familiar, but by no means vulgar.
    Those friends thou hast, and their adoption tried,°
    Grapple them to thy soul with hoops of steel,
    But do not dull thy palm with entertainment°
    Of each new-hatched unfledged° comrade. Beware   65
    Of entrance to a quarrel, but being in,
    Bear 't that the opposèd may beware of thee.
    Give every man thy ear, but few thy voice.°
    Take each man's censure,° but reserve thy judgment.
    Costly thy habit° as thy purse can buy,   70
    But not expressed in fancy°—rich, not gaudy.
    For the apparel oft proclaims the man,
    And they in France of the best rank and station
    Are of a most select and generous° chief in that.
    Neither a borrower nor a lender be,   75
    For loan oft loses both itself and friend
    And borrowing dulls the edge of husbandry.°
    This above all: To thine own self be true,
    And it must follow, as the night the day,
    Thou canst not then be false to any man.   80
    Farewell. My blessing season° this in thee!
LAERTES.   Most humbly do I take my leave, my lord.
POLONIUS.   The time invites you. Go, your servants tend.°

---

49. **puffed:** panting.   50. **primrose . . . dalliance:** i.e., the pleasant way of love-making.
51. **recks . . . rede:** takes no heed of his own advice.   54. **Occasion smiles:** i.e., here is a happy
chance.   57. **stayed:** waited.   59. **character:** inscribe.   60. **unproportioned:** unsuitable.
62. **adoption tried:** friendship tested by experience.   64. **dull . . . entertainment:** let your hand
grow callous with welcome.   65. **unfledged:** lit., newly out of the egg, immature.   68. **Give . . .
voice:** listen to everyone but commit yourself to few.   69. **censure:** opinion.   70. **habit:**
dress.   71. **expressed in fancy:** fantastic.   74. **generous:** of gentle birth.   77. **husbandry:** economy.   81. **season:** bring to fruit.   83. **tend:** attend.

LAERTES.   Farewell, Ophelia, and remember well
    What I have said to you.
OPHELIA.   'Tis in my memory locked,   85
    And you yourself shall keep the key of it.
LAERTES.   Farewell.   (*Exit.*)
POLONIUS.   What is 't, Ophelia, he hath said to you?
OPHELIA.   So please you, something touching the Lord Hamlet.
POLONIUS.   Marry,° well bethought.°   90
    'Tis told me he hath very oft of late
    Given private time to you, and you yourself
    Have of your audience been most free and bounteous.
    If it be so—as so 'tis put on me,
    And that in way of caution—I must tell you   95
    You do not understand yourself so clearly
    As it behooves° my daughter and your honor.
    What is between you? Give me up the truth.
OPHELIA.   He hath, my lord, of late made many tenders°
    Of his affection to me.   100
POLONIUS.   Affection! Pooh! You speak like a green girl,
    Unsifted° in such perilous circumstance.
    Do you believe his tenders, as you call them?
OPHELIA.   I do not know, my lord, what I should think.
POLONIUS.   Marry, I'll teach you. Think yourself a baby   105
    That you have ta'en these tenders° for true pay,
    Which are not sterling.° Tender yourself more dearly,
    Or—not to crack the wind of° the poor phrase,
    Running it thus—you'll tender me a fool.
OPHELIA.   My lord, he hath importuned me with love   110
    In honorable fashion.
POLONIUS.   Aye, fashion° you may call it. Go to, go to.
OPHELIA.   And hath given countenance to his speech,° my lord,
    With almost all the holy vows of Heaven.
POLONIUS.   Aye, springes° to catch woodcocks.° I do know,   115
    When the blood burns, how prodigal° the soul
    Lends the tongue vows. These blazes,° daughter,
    Giving more light than heat, extinct in both,
    Even in their promise as it is a-making,
    You must not take for fire. From this time   120
    Be something scanter of your maiden presence,
    Set your entreatments at a higher rate
    Than a command to parley.° For Lord Hamlet,

90. Marry: Mary, by the Virgin Mary. **well bethought:** well remembered. **97. behooves:** is the duty of. **99. tenders:** offers. **102. Unsifted:** untried. **106–09. tenders . . . tender:** Polonius puns on "tenders," counters (used for money in games); "tender," value; "tender," show. **107. sterling:** true currency. **108. crack . . . of:** i.e., ride to death. **112. fashion:** mere show. **113. given . . . speech:** confirmed his words. **115. springes:** snares. **woodcocks:** foolish birds. **116. prodigal:** extravagantly. **117. blazes:** flashes, quickly extinguished (*extinct*). **122–23. Set . . . parley:** when you are asked to see him do not regard it as a command to negotiate. **parley:** meeting to discuss terms.

Believe so much in him, that he is young,
And with a larger tether° may he walk   125
Than may be given you. In few,° Ophelia,
Do not believe his vows, for they are brokers,°
Not of that dye which their investments° show,
But mere implorators° of unholy suits,
Breathing like sanctified and pious bawds   130
The better to beguile. This is for all.
I would not, in plain terms, from this time forth
Have you so slander any moment leisure°
As to give words or talk with the Lord Hamlet.
Look to 't, I charge you. Come your ways.   135
OPHELIA.   I shall obey, my lord.   (*Exeunt.*)

SCENE IV. *The platform.*

(*Enter* HAMLET, HORATIO, *and* MARCELLUS.)

HAMLET.   The air bites shrewdly.° It is very cold.
HORATIO.   It is a nipping and an eager° air.
HAMLET.   What hour now?
HORATIO.   I think it lacks of twelve.
MARCELLUS.   No, it is struck.
HORATIO.   Indeed? I heard it not. It then draws near the season   5
Wherein the spirit held his wont to walk.

(*A flourish of trumpets, and ordnance shot off within.°*)

What doth this mean, my lord?
HAMLET.   The King doth wake° tonight and takes his rouse,°
Keeps wassail,° and the swaggering upspring reels.°
And as he drains his draughts of Rhenish° down,   10
The kettledrum and trumpet thus bray out
The triumph of his pledge.
HORATIO.   Is it a custom?
HAMLET.   Aye, marry, is 't.
But to my mind, though I am native here
And to the manner born, it is a custom   15
More honored in the breach than the observance.
This heavy-headed revel° east and west
Makes us traduced and taxed of° other nations.

125. **tether:** rope by which a grazing animal is fastened to its peg. 126. **In few:** in short.
127. **brokers:** traveling salesmen. 128. **investments:** garments. 129. **implorators:** men who
solicit. 133. **slander . . . leisure:** misuse any moment of leisure.
   Sc. iv: 1. **shrewdly:** bitterly. 2. **eager:** sharp. 6. **s.d., within:** off stage. 8. **wake:** "makes
a night of it." **rouse:** See I.ii.127,n. 9. **wassail:** revelry. **swaggering . . . reels:** reel in a riotous
dance. 10. **Rhenish:** Rhine wine. 17. **heavy-headed revel:** drinking which produces a thick
head. 18. **traduced . . . of:** disgraced and censured by.

They clepe° us drunkards, and with swinish phrase
Soil our addition,° and indeed it takes   20
From our achievements, though performed at height,°
The pith and marrow of our attribute.°
So oft it chances in particular men,
That for some vicious mole° of nature in them,
As in their birth—wherein they are not guilty,   25
Since nature cannot choose his origin—
By the o'ergrowth of some complexion,°
Oft breaking down the pales° and forts of reason,
Or by some habit that too much o'erleavens°
The form of plausive° manners, that these men—   30
Carrying, I say, the stamp of one defect,
Being Nature's livery,° or Fortune's star°—
Their virtues else—be they as pure as grace,
As infinite as man may undergo—
Shall in the general censure take corruption   35
From that particular fault. The dram of eale
Doth all the noble substance of a doubt
To his own scandal.

(Enter GHOST.*)*

HORATIO.   Look, my lord, it comes!
HAMLET.   Angels and ministers of grace defend us!
Be thou a spirit of health or goblin damned,°   40
Bring with thee airs from Heaven or blasts from Hell,
Be thy intents wicked or charitable,
Thou comest in such a questionable° shape
That I will speak to thee. I'll call thee Hamlet,
King, Father, royal Dane. Oh, answer me!   45
Let me not burst in ignorance, but tell
Why thy canónized° bones, hearsèd° in death,
Have burst their cerements,° why the sepulcher
Wherein we saw thee quietly inurned°
Hath oped his ponderous and marble jaws   50
To cast thee up again. What may this mean,

19. **clepe:** call. 20. **soil . . . addition:** smirch our honor. **addition:** lit., title of honor added to a man's name. 21. **though . . . height:** though of the highest merit. 22. **pith . . . attribute:** essential part of our honor; i.e., we lose the honor due to our achievements because of our reputation for drunkenness. 24. **mole:** blemish. 27. **o'ergrowth . . . complexion:** some quality allowed to overbalance the rest. 28. **pales:** defenses. 29. **o'erleavens:** mixes with. 30. **plausive:** agreeable. 32. **Nature's livery:** i.e., inborn. **Fortune's star:** the result of ill luck. 40. **spirit . . . damned:** a holy spirit or damned fiend. Hamlet, until convinced at the end of the play scene (III.ii.262–263), is perpetually in doubt whether the ghost which he sees is a good spirit sent to warn him, a devil sent to tempt him into some damnable action, or a hallucination created by his own diseased imagination. See II.ii.550–55. 43. **questionable:** inviting question. 47. **canonized:** buried with full rites according to the canon of the Church. **hearsed:** buried. 48. **cerements:** waxen shroud, used to wrap the bodies of the illustrious dead. 49. **inurned:** buried.

That thou, dead corse, again, in complete steel,°
Revisit'st thus the glimpses of the moon,
Making night hideous, and we fools° of nature
So horridly to shake our disposition°   55
With thoughts beyond the reaches of our souls?
Say, why is this? Wherefore? What should we do?

(GHOST *beckons* HAMLET.)

HORATIO.   It beckons you to go away with it,
As if it some impartment° did desire
To you alone.
MARCELLUS.   Look with what courteous action   60
It waves you to a more removèd ground.
But do not go with it.
HORATIO.   No, by no means.
HAMLET.   It will not speak. Then I will follow it.
HORATIO.   Do not, my lord.
HAMLET.   Why, what should be the fear?
I do not set my life at a pin's fee,°   65
And for my soul, what can it do to that,
Being a thing immortal as itself?
It waves me forth again. I'll follow it.
HORATIO.   What if it tempt you toward the flood, my lord,
Or to the dreadful summit of the cliff   70
That beetles o'er° his base into the sea,
And there assume some other horrible form
Which might deprive your sovereignty of reason°
And draw you into madness? Think of it.
The very place puts toys of desperation,°   75
Without more motive, into every brain
That looks so many fathoms to the sea
And hears it roar beneath.
HAMLET.   It waves me still.
Go on. I'll follow thee.
MARCELLUS.   You shall not go, my lord.
                        Hold off your hands.   80
HORATIO.   Be ruled. You shall not go.
HAMLET.   My fate cries out,
And makes each petty artery in this body
As hardy as the Nemean lion's nerve.°
Still am I called. Unhand me, gentlemen.
By Heaven, I'll make a ghost of him that lets° me!   85
I say, away! Go on. I'll follow thee.

52. complete steel: full armor. 54. fools: dupes. 55. disposition: nature. 59. impartment:
communication. 65. fee: value. 71. beetles o'er: juts out over. 73. sovereignty of reason:
control of your reason over your actions. 75. toys of desperation: desperate fancies.
83. Nemean . . . nerve: sinew of a fierce beast slain by Hercules. 85. lets: hinders.

(Exeunt GHOST *and* HAMLET.*)*

HORATIO.   He waxes desperate with imagination.
MARCELLUS.   Let's follow. 'Tis not fit thus to obey him.
HORATIO.   Have after. To what issue will this come?
MARCELLUS.   Something is rotten in the state of Denmark.   90
HORATIO.   Heaven will direct it.
MARCELLUS.   Nay, let's follow him.   *(Exeunt.)*

SCENE V. Another part of the platform.

(Enter GHOST *and* HAMLET.*)*

HAMLET.   Whither wilt thou lead me? Speak. I'll go no further.
GHOST.   Mark me.
HAMLET.   I will.
GHOST.   My hour is almost come
When I to sulphurous and tormenting flames
Must render up myself.
HAMLET.   Alas, poor ghost!
GHOST.   Pity me not, but lend thy serious hearing   5
To what I shall unfold.
HAMLET.   Speak. I am bound to hear.
GHOST.   So art thou to revenge, when thou shalt hear.
HAMLET.   What?
GHOST.   I am thy father's spirit,
Doomed for a certain term to walk the night   10
And for the day confined to fast in fires
Till the foul crimes done in my days of nature
Are burnt and purged away. But that I am forbid
To tell the secrets of my prison house,
I could a tale unfold whose lightest word   15
Would harrow up thy soul, freeze thy young blood,
Make thy two eyes, like stars, start from their spheres,
Thy knotted and combinèd° locks to part
And each particular° hair to stand an° end
Like quills upon the fretful porpentine.°   20
But this eternal blazon° must not be
To ears of flesh and blood. List, list, oh, list!
If thou didst ever thy dear father love—
HAMLET.   Oh, God!
GHOST.   Revenge his foul and most unnatural murder.   25
HAMLET.   Murder!
GHOST.   Murder most foul, as in the best° it is,
But this most foul, strange, and unnatural.

Sc. v: 18. knotted . . . combined: the hair that lies together in a mass.   **19. particular:** individual. **an:** on.   **20. porpentine:** porcupine.   **21. eternal blazon:** description of eternity.   **27. in . . . best:** i.e., murder is foul even when there is a good excuse.

HAMLET.　Haste me to know 't, that I, with wings as swift
　As meditation or the thoughts of love,　　　　　　　　　　30
　May sweep to my revenge.
GHOST.　　　　　　　　　　　I find thee apt,
　And duller shouldst thou be than the fat° weed
　That roots itself in ease° on Lethe wharf°
　Wouldst thou not stir in this. Now, Hamlet, hear.
　'Tis given out that, sleeping in my orchard,　　　　　　　35
　A serpent stung me—so the whole ear of Denmark
　Is by a forgèd process° of my death
　Rankly abused. But know, thou noble youth,
　The serpent that did sting thy father's life
　Now wears his crown.
HAMLET.　　　　　　　　Oh, my prophetic soul!　　　　　40
　My uncle!
GHOST.　Aye, that incestuous, that adulterate beast,
　With witchcraft of his wit, with traitorous gifts—
　O wicked wit and gifts, that have the power
　So to seduce!—won to his shameful lust　　　　　　　45
　The will of my most seeming-virtuous Queen.
　O Hamlet, what a falling-off was there!
　From me, whose love was of that dignity
　That it went hand in hand even with the vow
　I made to her in marriage, and to decline　　　　　　　50
　Upon a wretch whose natural gifts were poor
　To those of mine!
　But virtue, as it never will be moved
　Though lewdness court it in a shape of Heaven,°
　So Lust, though to a radiant angel linked,　　　　　　　55
　Will sate itself° in a celestial bed
　And prey on garbage.
　But soft! Methinks I scent the morning air.
　Brief let me be. Sleeping within my orchard,
　My custom always of the afternoon,　　　　　　　　　60
　Upon my secure hour° thy uncle stole
　With juice of cursèd hebenon° in a vial,
　And in the porches° of my ears did pour
　The leperous distillment,° whose effect
　Holds such an enmity with blood of man　　　　　　　65
　That swift as quicksilver it courses through
　The natural gates and alleys of the body,
　And with a sudden vigor it doth posset°

---

32. **fat:** thick, slimy, motionless.　33. **in ease:** undisturbed.　**Lethe wharf:** the bank of Lethe, the river of forgetfulness in the underworld.　37. **forged process:** false account.　54. **lewdness . . . Heaven:** though wooed by Lust disguised as an angel.　56. **sate itself:** gorge.　61. **secure hour:** time of relaxation.　62. **hebenon:** probably henbane, a poisonous plant.　63. **porches:** entrances.　64. **leperous distillment:** distillation causing leprosy.　68. **posset:** curdle.

And curd, like eager° droppings into milk,
The thin and wholesome blood. So did it mine, 70
And a most instant tetter barked° about,
Most lazarlike,° with vile and loathsome crust,
All my smooth body.
Thus was I, sleeping, by a brother's hand
Of life, of crown, of Queen, at once dispatched— 75
Cut off even in the blossoms of my sin,°
Unhouseled, disappointed, unaneled,°
No reckoning made, but sent to my account
With all my imperfections on my head.
Oh, horrible! Oh, horrible, most horrible! 80
If thou hast nature° in thee, bear it not.
Let not the royal bed of Denmark be
A couch for luxury° and damned incest.
But, howsoever thou pursuest this act,
Taint not thy mind, nor let thy soul contrive 85
Against thy mother aught. Leave her to Heaven
And to those thorns that in her bosom lodge
To prick and sting her. Fare thee well at once!
The glowworm shows the matin° to be near,
And 'gins to pale his uneffectual° fire. 90
Adieu, adieu, adieu! Remember me. (*Exit.*)
HAMLET.   O all you host of Heaven! O earth! What else?
And shall I couple Hell? Oh, fie! Hold, hold, my heart,
And you, my sinews, grow not instant old
But bear me stiffly up. Remember thee! 95
Aye, thou poor ghost, while memory holds a seat
In this distracted globe.° Remember thee!
Yea, from the table° of my memory
I'll wipe away all trivial fond° recórds,
All saws° of books, all forms,° all pressures° past, 100
That youth and observation copied there,
And thy commandment all alone shall live
Within the book and volume of my brain,
Unmixed with baser matter. Yes, by Heaven!
O most pernicious woman! 105
O villain, villain, smiling, damnèd villain!
My tables—meet it is I set it down
(*Writing*) That one may smile, and smile, and be a villain.

69. **eager:** acid. 71. **tetter barked:** eruption formed a bark. 72. **lazarlike:** like leprosy.
76. **Cut . . . sin:** cut off in a state of sin and so in danger of damnation. See III.iii.80–86.
77. **Unhouseled . . . unaneled:** without receiving the sacrament, not properly prepared, unanointed—without extreme unction. 81. **nature:** natural feelings. 83. **luxury:** lust.
89. **matin:** morning. 90. **uneffectual:** made ineffectual by daylight. 97. **globe:** i.e., head. 98. **table:** notebook. Intellectual young men carried notebooks in which they recorded good sayings and notable observations. 99. **fond:** trifling. 100. **saws:** wise sayings. **forms:** images in the mind. **pressures:** impressions.

At least I'm sure it may be so in Denmark.
So, Uncle, there you are. Now to my word.°   110
It is "Adieu, adieu! Remember me."
I have sworn 't
HORATIO & MARCELLUS *(Within).*   My lord, my lord!

(Enter HORATIO *and* MARCELLUS.*)*

MARCELLUS.   Lord Hamlet!
HORATIO.   Heaven secure him!
HAMLET.   So be it!
MARCELLUS.   Illo, ho, ho,° my lord!   115
HAMLET.   Hillo, ho, ho, boy! Come, bird, come.
MARCELLUS.   How is 't, my noble lord?
HORATIO.   What news, my lord?
HAMLET.   Oh, wonderful!
HORATIO.   Good my lord, tell it.
HAMLET.   No, you will reveal it.
HORATIO.   Not I, my lord, by Heaven.
MARCELLUS.   Nor I, my lord.   120
HAMLET.   How say you, then, would heart of man once think it?
    But you'll be secret?
HORATIO & MARCELLUS.   Aye, by Heaven, my lord.
HAMLET.   There's ne'er a villain dwelling in all Denmark
    But he's an arrant° knave.
HORATIO.   There needs no ghost, my lord, come from the grave   125
    To tell us this.
HAMLET.   Why, right, you are i' the right.
    And so, without more circumstance° at all,
    I hold it fit that we shake hands and part—
    You as your business and desire shall point you,
    For every man hath business and desire,   130
    Such as it is. And for my own poor part,
    Look you, I'll go pray.
HORATIO.   These are but wild and whirling° words, my lord.
HAMLET.   I'm sorry they offend you, heartily,
    Yes, faith, heartily.
HORATIO.   There's no offense, my lord.   135
HAMLET.   Yes, by Saint Patrick, but there is, Horatio,
    And much offense too. Touching this vision here,
    It is an honest° ghost, that let me tell you.
    For your desire to know what is between us,
    O'ermaster 't as you may. And now, good friends,   140
    As you are friends, scholars, and soldiers,
    Give me one poor request.

110. **word:** cue.   115. **Illo . . . ho:** the falconer's cry to recall the hawk.   124. **arrant:** out-and-out.   127. **circumstance:** ceremony.   133. **whirling:** violent.   138. **honest:** true. See I.iv.40,n.

HORATIO.   What is 't, my lord? We will.
HAMLET.   Never make known what you have seen tonight.
HORATIO & MARCELLUS.   My lord, we will not.
HAMLET.   Nay, but swear 't.
HORATIO.   In faith,   145
  My lord, not I.
MARCELLUS.   Nor I, my lord, in faith.
HAMLET.   Upon my sword.
MARCELLUS.   We have sworn, my lord, already.
HAMLET.   Indeed, upon my sword,° indeed.
GHOST *(Beneath)*.   Swear.
HAMLET.   Ah, ha, boy! Say'st thou so? Art thou there, truepenny?°   150
  Come on. You hear this fellow in the cellarage.
  Consent to swear.
HORATIO.   Propose the oath, my lord.
HAMLET.   Never to speak of this that you have seen,
  Swear by my sword.
GHOST *(Beneath)*.   Swear.   155
HAMLET.   *Hic et ubique?*° Then we'll shift our ground.
  Come hither, gentlemen,
  And lay your hands again upon my sword.
  Never to speak of this that you have heard,
  Swear by my sword.   160
GHOST *(Beneath)*.   Swear.
HAMLET.   Well said, old mole! Canst work i' the earth so fast?
  A worthy pioner!° Once more remove,° good friends.
HORATIO.   Oh, day and night, but this is wondrous strange!
HAMLET.   And therefore as a stranger give it welcome.   165
  There are more things in Heaven and earth, Horatio,
  Than are dreamt of in your philosophy.
  But come,
  Here, as before, never, so help you mercy,
  How strange or odd soe'er I bear myself,   170
  As I perchance hereafter shall think meet
  To put an antic disposition° on,
  That you, at such times seeing me, never shall,
  With arms encumbered° thus, or this headshake,
  Or by pronouncing of some doubtful phrase,   175
  As "Well, well, we know," or "We could an if we would,"
  Or "If we list to speak," or "There be, an if they might,"
  Or such ambiguous giving out, to note
  That you know aught of me. This not to do,
  So grace and mercy at your most need help you,   180
  Swear.

---

148. upon . . . sword: on the cross made by the hilt of the sword; but for soldiers the sword itself was a sacred object. **150. truepenny:** old boy. **156. Hic et ubique:** here and everywhere. **163. pioner:** miner. **remove:** move. **172. antic disposition:** mad behavior. **174. encumbered:** folded.

GHOST (*Beneath*).   Swear.
HAMLET.   Rest, rest, perturbèd spirit! (*They swear.*) So, gentlemen,
With all my love I do commend me to you.
And what so poor a man as Hamlet is   185
May do to express his love and friending° to you,
God willing, shall not lack. Let us go in together.
And still your fingers on your lips, I pray.
The time is out of joint. Oh, cursèd spite
That ever I was born to set it right!   190
Nay, come, let's go together.   (*Exeunt.*)

ACT II

SCENE I. A room in POLONIUS'S *house.*

(*Enter* POLONIUS *and* REYNALDO.)

POLONIUS.   Give him this money and these notes, Reynaldo.
REYNALDO.   I will, my lord.
POLONIUS.   You shall do marvelous wisely, good Reynaldo,
Before you visit him, to make inquire
Of his behavior.
REYNALDO.   My lord, I did intend it.   5
POLONIUS.   Marry, well said, very well said. Look you, sir,
Inquire me first what Danskers° are in Paris,
And how, and who, what means,° and where they keep,°
What company, at what expense, and finding
By this encompassment and drift of question°   10
That they do know my son, come you more nearer
Than your particular demands will touch it.°
Take you, as 'twere, some distant knowledge of him,
As thus, "I know his father and his friends,
And in part him." Do you mark this, Reynaldo?   15
REYNALDO.   Aye, very well, my lord.
POLONIUS.   "And in part him, but," you may say, "not well.
But if 't be he I mean, he's very wild,
Addicted so and so"—and there put on him
What forgeries° you please. Marry, none so rank°   20
As may dishonor him, take heed of that,
But, sir, such wanton, wild, and usual slips
As are companions noted and most known
To youth and liberty.

186. **friending:** friendship.
      Act II, Sc. i: 7. **Danskers:** Danes. 8. **what means:** what their income is. **keep:** live. 10. **encompassment . . . question:** roundabout method of questioning. 12. **your . . . it:** i.e., you won't get at the truth by straight questions. 20. **forgeries:** inventions. **rank:** gross.

REYNALDO.   As gaming, my lord.
POLONIUS.   Aye, or drinking, fencing,° swearing, quarreling,   25
     Drabbing.° You may go so far.
REYNALDO.   My lord, that would dishonor him.
POLONIUS.   Faith, no, as you may season° it in the charge.
     You must not put another scandal on him,
     That he is open to incontinency.°   30
     That's not my meaning. But breathe his faults so quaintly°
     That they may seem the taints of liberty,
     The flash and outbreak of a fiery mind,
     A savageness in unreclaimèd° blood,
     Of general assault.°
REYNALDO.   But, my good lord——   35
POLONIUS.   Wherefore should you do this?
REYNALDO.   Aye, my lord,
     I would know that.
POLONIUS.   Marry, sir, here's my drift,°
     And I believe it is a fetch of warrant.°
     You laying these slight sullies° on my son,
     As 'twere a thing a little soiled i' the working,   40
     Mark you,
     Your party in converse, him you would sound,
     Having ever seen° in the prenominate° crimes
     The youth you breathe of guilty, be assured
     He closes with you in this consequence°—   45
     "Good sir," or so, or "friend," or "gentleman,"
     According to the phrase or the addition°
     Of man and country.
REYNALDO.   Very good, my lord.   49
POLONIUS.   And then, sir, does he this—he does——What was I about to
     say? By the mass, I was about to say something. Where did I leave?
REYNALDO.   At "closes in the consequence," at "friend or so," and
     "gentleman."
POLONIUS.   At "closes in the consequence," aye, marry,
     He closes with you thus: "I know the gentleman.   55
     I saw him yesterday, or t'other day,
     Or then, or then, with such, or such, and, as you say,
     There was a' gaming, there o'ertook in 's rouse,
     There falling out at tennis."° Or perchance,

---

25. fencing: A young man who haunted fencing schools would be regarded as quarrelsome and
likely to belong to the sporting set. **26. Drabbing:** whoring. **28. season:** qualify. **30. open . . .
incontinency:** So long as Laertes does his drabbing inconspicuously Polonius would not be
disturbed. **31. quaintly:** skillfully. **34. unreclaimed:** naturally wild. **35. of . . . assault:**
common to all men. **37. drift:** intention. **38. fetch . . . warrant:** trick warranted to work.
39. sullies: blemishes. **43. Having . . . seen:** if ever he has seen. **prenominate:** aforementioned. **45. closes . . . consequence:** follows up with this reply. **47. addition:** title. See
I.iv.20. **59. tennis:** Visitors to France were much impressed by the enthusiasm of all classes of
Frenchmen for tennis, which in England was mainly a courtier's game.

"I saw him enter such a house of sale,"   60
Videlicet,° a brothel, or so forth.
See you now,
Your bait of falsehood takes this carp of truth.
And thus do we of wisdom and of reach,°
With windlasses° and with assays of bias,°   65
By indirections find directions out.°
So, by my former lecture and advice,
Shall you my son. You have me, have you not?
REYNALDO.   My lord, I have.
POLONIUS.   God be wi' ye, fare ye well.
REYNALDO.   Good my lord!   70
POLONIUS.   Observe his inclination in° yourself.
REYNALDO.   I shall, my lord.
POLONIUS.   And let him ply his music.
REYNALDO.   Well, my lord.
POLONIUS.   Farewell!   (*Exit* REYNALDO.)
(*Enter* OPHELIA.) How now, Ophelia! What's the matter?
OPHELIA.   Oh, my lord, my lord, I have been so affrighted!   75
POLONIUS.   With what, i' the name of God?
OPHELIA.   My lord, as I was sewing in my closet,°
Lord Hamlet, with his doublet° all unbraced,
No hat upon his head, his stockings fouled,
Ungartered and down-gyved° to his ankle,   80
Pale as his shirt, his knees knocking each other,
And with a look so piteous in purport
As if he had been loosèd out of Hell
To speak of horrors, he comes before me.
POLONIUS.   Mad for thy love?
OPHELIA.   My lord, I do not know,   85
But truly I do fear it.
POLONIUS.   What said he?
OPHELIA.   He took me by the wrist and held me hard.
Then goes he to the length of all his arm,
And with his other hand thus o'er his brow,
He falls to such perusal of my face   90
As he would draw it. Long stayed he so.
At last, a little shaking of mine arm,
And thrice his head thus waving up and down,
He raised a sigh so piteous and profound
As it did seem to shatter all his bulk   95
And end his being. That done, he lets me go.

---

61. Videlicet: namely, "viz."   **64. wisdom . . . reach:** of far-reaching wisdom.   **65. windlasses:** roundabout methods.   **assays of bias:** making our bowl take a curved course.   **66. indirections . . . out:** by indirect means come at the direct truth.   **71. in:** for.   **77. closet:** private room.   **78. doublet:** the short close-fitting coat which was braced to the hose by laces. When a man was relaxing or careless of appearance, he *unbraced,* as a modern man takes off his coat or unbuttons his waistcoat.   **80. down-gyved:** hanging around his ankles like fetters.

And with his head over his shoulder turned,
He seemed to find his way without his eyes;
For out o' doors he went without their helps,
And to the last bended their light on me.   100
POLONIUS.   Come, go with me. I will go seek the King.
This is the very ecstasy° of love,
Whose violent property fordoes° itself
And leads the will to desperate undertakings
As oft as any passion under heaven   105
That does afflict our natures. I am sorry.
What, have you given him any hard words of late?
OPHELIA.   No, my good lord, but, as you did command,
I did repel his letters and denied
His access to me.
POLONIUS.   That hath made him mad.   110
I am sorry that with better heed and judgment
I had not quoted° him. I feared he did but trifle
And meant to wreck thee, but beshrew° my jealousy!
By Heaven, it is as proper° to our age
To cast beyond ourselves° in our opinions   115
As it is common for the younger sort
To lack discretion. Come, go we to the King.
This must be known, which, being kept close, might move
More grief to hide than hate to utter love.°   119
Come.   (*Exeunt.*)

SCENE II. *A room in the castle.*

(*Flourish. Enter* KING, QUEEN, ROSENCRANTZ, GUILDENSTERN, *and*
ATTENDANTS.)

KING.   Welcome, dear Rosencrantz and Guildenstern!
Moreover° that we much did long to see you,
The need we have to use you did provoke
Our hasty sending. Something have you heard
Of Hamlet's transformation—so call it,   5
Sith° nor the exterior nor the inward man
Resembles that it was. What it should be,
More than his father's death, that thus hath put him
So much from the understanding of himself
I cannot dream of. I entreat you both   10
That, being of so young days brought up with him
And sith so neighbored to his youth and havior°

102. **ecstasy:** frenzy.   103. **property fordoes:** natural quality destroys.   112. **quoted:** observed carefully.   113. **beshrew:** a plague on.   114. **proper:** natural.   115. **cast . . . ourselves:** be too clever.   118–19. **which . . . love:** by being kept secret it may cause more sorrow than it will cause anger by being revealed; i.e., the King and Queen may be angry at the thought of the Prince's marrying beneath his proper rank.
  Sc. ii: 2. **Moreover:** in addition to the fact that.   6. **Sith:** since.   12. **neighbored . . . havior:** so near to his youthful manner of living.

That you vouchsafe your rest° here in our Court
Some little time, so by your companies
To draw him on to pleasures, and to gather   15
So much as from occasion you may glean,
Whether aught to us unkown afflicts him thus
That opened lies within our remedy.°
QUEEN.   Good gentlemen, he hath much talked of you,
And sure I am two men there art not living   20
To whom he more adheres.° If it will please you
To show us so much gentry° and goodwill
As to expend your time with us a while
For the supply and profit of our hope,°
Your visitation shall receive such thanks   25
As fits a king's remembrance.
ROSENCRANTZ.   Both your Majesties
Might, by the sovereign power you have of us,
Put your dread pleasures more into command
Than to entreaty.
GUILDENSTERN.   But we both obey,
And here give up ourselves, in the full bent°   30
To lay our service freely at your feet,
To be commanded.
KING.   Thanks, Rosencrantz and gentle Guildenstern.
QUEEN.   Thanks Guildenstern and gentle Rosencrantz.
And I beseech you instantly to visit   35
My too-much-changèd son. Go, some of you,
And bring these gentlemen where Hamlet is.
GUILDENSTERN.   Heavens make our presence and our practices
Pleasant and helpful to him!
QUEEN.   Aye, amen!

(*Exeunt* ROSENCRANTZ, GUILDENSTERN, *and some* ATTENDANTS.)

(*Enter* POLONIUS.)

POLONIUS.   The ambassadors from Norway, my good lord,   40
Are joyfully returned.
KING.   Thou still° hast been the father of good news.
POLONIUS.   Have I, my lord? I assure my good liege
I hold my duty as I hold my soul,
Both to my God and to my gracious King.   45
And I do think, or else this brain of mine
Hunts not the trail of policy so sure
As it hath used to do,° that I have found
The very cause of Hamlet's lunacy.

---

13. vouchsafe . . . rest: consent to stay.   18. opened . . . remedy: if revealed, might be put right
by us.   21. To . . . adheres: whom he regards more highly.   22. gentry: courtesy.
24. supply . . . hope: to bring a profitable conclusion to our hope.   30. in . . . bent: stretched to
our uttermost.   42. still: always.   47–48. Hunts . . . do: is not so good at following the scent of
political events as it used to be.

KING.   Oh, speak of that. That do I long to hear.   50
POLONIUS.   Give first admittance to the ambassadors.
    My news shall be the fruit° to that great feast.
KING.   Thyself do grace° to them and bring them in.

    (Exit POLONIUS.*)*

    He tells me, my dear Gertrude, he hath found
    The head and source of all your son's distemper.°   55
QUEEN.   I doubt it is no other but the main,°
    His father's death and our o'erhasty marriage.
KING.   Well, we shall sift him.

    (Re-enter POLONIUS, *with* VOLTIMAND *and* CORNELIUS.*)*
                              Welcome, my good friends!
    Say, Voltimand, what from our brother Norway?
VOLTIMAND.   Most fair return of greetings and desires.   60
    Upon our first,° he sent out to suppress
    His nephew's levies, which to him appeared
    To be a preparation 'gainst the Polack,
    But better looked into, he truly found
    It was against your Highness, whereat, grieved   65
    That so his sickness, age, and impotence
    Was falsely borne in hand,° sends out arrests
    On Fortinbras; which he, in brief, obeys,
    Receives rebuke from Norway, and in fine°
    Makes vow before his uncle never more   70
    To give the assay of arms° against your Majesty.
    Whereon old Norway, overcome with joy,
    Gives him three thousand crowns in annual fee
    And his commission to employ those soldiers,
    So levied as before, against the Polack.   75
    With an entreaty, herein further shown,

    (Giving a paper)

    That it might please you to give quiet pass°
    Through your dominions for this enterprise,
    On such regards of safety and allowance°
    As therein are set down.
KING.   It likes° us well,   80
    And at our more considered time we'll read,
    Answer, and think upon this business.
    Meantime we thank you for your well-took labor.
    Go to your rest. At night we'll feast together.
    Most welcome home!

---

52. **fruit:** the dessert, which comes at the end of the feast.   53. **do grace:** honor; i.e., by escorting them into the royal presence.   55. **distemper:** mental disturbance.   56. **main:** principal cause.   61. **first:** i.e., audience.   67. **borne in hand:** imposed upon.   69. **in fine:** in the end.   71. **give . . . arms:** make an attack.   77. **quiet pass:** unmolested passage.   79. **regards . . . allowance:** safeguard and conditions.   80. **likes:** pleases.

(Exeunt VOLTIMAND *and* CORNELIUS.*)*

POLONIUS.	This business is well ended.	85

My liege, and madam, to expostulate°
What majesty should be, what duty is,
Why day is day, night night, and time is time,
Were nothing but to waste night, day, and time.
Therefore, since brevity is the soul of wit   90
And tediousness the limbs and outward flourishes,°
I will be brief. Your noble son is mad.
Mad call I it, for to define true madness,
What is 't but to be nothing else but mad?
But let that go.
QUEEN.   More matter, with less art.°   95
POLONIUS.   Madam, I swear I use no art at all.
That he is mad, 'tis true. 'Tis true 'tis pity,
And pity 'tis 'tis true—a foolish figure,°
But farewell it, for I will use no art.
Mad let us grant him, then. And now remains   100
That we find out the cause of this effect,
Or rather say the cause of this defect,
For this effect defective comes by cause.
Thus it remains and the remainder thus.
Perpend.°   105
I have a daughter—have while she is mine—
Who in her duty and obedience, mark,
Hath given me this. Now gather and surmise.° *(Reads.)*
"To the celestial, and my soul's idol, the most beautified° Ophelia—"
That's an ill phrase, a vile phrase, "beautified" is a vile phrase. But you
shall hear. Thus: *(Reads.)* "In her excellent white bosom, these," and so
forth.
QUEEN.   Came this from Hamlet to her?
POLONIUS.   Good madam, stay awhile, I will be faithful. *(Reads.)*

          "Doubt thou the stars are fire,
               Doubt that the sun doth move,   115
          Doubt truth to be a liar,
               But never doubt I love.

     "O dear Ophelia, I am ill at these numbers,° I have not art to reckon my
groans, but that I love thee best, O most best, believe it. Adieu.
     "Thine evermore, most dear lady, whilst this machine° is to him,
HAMLET."   121
This in obedience hath my daughter shown me,
And more above, hath his solicitings,

---

86. **expostulate:** indulge in an academic discussion. 91. **flourishes:** ornaments. 95. **art:**
ornament. 98. **figure:** i.e., a figure of speech. 105. **Perpend:** note carefully. 108. **surmise:**
guess the meaning. 109. **beautified:** beautiful. 118. **numbers:** verses. 120. **machine:** i.e.,
body, an affected phrase.

As they fell out by time, by means and place,
All given to mine ear.
KING.   But how hath she   125
Received his love?
POLONIUS.   What do you think of me?
KING.   As of a man faithful and honorable.
POLONIUS.   I would fain prove so. But what might you think,
When I had seen this hot love on the wing—
As I perceived it, I must tell you that,   130
Before my daughter told me—what might you
Or my dear Majesty your Queen here think
If I had played the desk or table book,°
Or given my heart awinking, mute and dumb,
Or looked upon this love with idle sight—   135
What might you think? No, I went round° to work,
And my young mistress thus I did bespeak:°
"Lord Hamlet is a Prince, out of thy star.°
This must not be." And then I prescripts° gave her
That she should lock herself from his resort,   140
Admit no messengers, receive no tokens.
Which done, she took the fruits of my advice.
And he, repulsèd, a short tale to make,
Fell into a sadness, then into a fast,
Thence to a watch, thence into a weakness,   145
Thence to a lightness,° and by this declension°
Into the madness wherein now he raves
And all we mourn for.
KING.   Do you think this?
QUEEN.   It may be, very like.
POLONIUS.   Hath there been such a time, I'd fain know that,   150
That I have positively said " 'Tis so"
When it proved otherwise?
KING.   Not that I know.
POLONIUS (*Pointing to his head and shoulder*).   Take this from this, if this be
otherwise.
If circumstances lead me, I will find   155
Where truth is hid, though it were hid indeed
Within the center.°
KING.   How may we try it further?
POLONIUS.   You know sometimes he walks four hours together
Here in the lobby.

---

133. desk . . . book: i.e., acted as silent go-between (desks and books being natural post offices for
a love letter), or been a recipient of secrets but took no action (as desks and notebooks are the
natural but inanimate places for keeping secrets).   **136. round:** straight.   **137. bespeak:** address.   **138. out . . . star:** above your destiny.   **139. prescripts:** instructions.   **144–46. Fell . . .
lightness:** Hamlet's case history, according to Polonius, develops by stages—melancholy, loss of
appetite, sleeplessness, physical weakness, mental instability, and finally madness.   **146. de-
clension:** decline.   **157. center:** the very center of the earth.

QUEEN.   So he does indeed.
POLONIUS.   At such a time I'll loose° my daughter to him.   160
   Be you and I behind an arras° then.
   Mark the encounter. If he love her not,
   And be not from his reason fall'n thereon,
   Let me be no assistant for a state,
   But keep a farm and carters.°
KING.   We will try it.   165
QUEEN.   But look where sadly the poor wretch comes reading.
POLONIUS.   Away, I do beseech you, both away.
   I'll board° him presently.

   (*Exeunt* KING, QUEEN, *and* ATTENDANTS.)

   (*Enter* HAMLET, *reading*.) Oh, give me leave. How does my good Lord
   Hamlet?   170
HAMLET.   Well, God-a-mercy.
POLONIUS.   Do you know me, my lord?
HAMLET.   Excellent well. You are a fishmonger.°
POLONIUS.   Not I, my lord.
HAMLET.   Then I would you were so honest a man.   175
POLONIUS.   Honest, my lord!
HAMLET.   Aye, sir, to be honest, as this world goes, is to be one man picked
   out of ten thousand.
POLONIUS.   That's very true, my lord.
HAMLET.   For if the sun breed maggots° in a dead dog, being a god kissing
   carrion°——Have you a daughter?
POLONIUS.   I have, my lord.
HAMLET.   Let her not walk i' the sun. Conception is a blessing, but not as
   your daughter may conceive—friend, look to 't.   184
POLONIUS (*Aside*).   How say you by that? Still harping on my daughter. Yet
   he knew me not at first, he said I was a fishmonger. He is far gone, far
   gone. And truly in my youth I suffered much extremity for love, very near
   this. I'll speak to him again.—What do you read, my lord?
HAMLET.   Words, words, words.
POLONIUS.   What is the matter, my lord?   190
HAMLET.   Between who?
POLONIUS.   I mean the matter that you read, my lord.
HAMLET.   Slanders, sir. For the satirical rogue says here that old men have
   gray beards, that their faces are wrinkled, their eyes purging thick amber
   and plum-tree gum, and that they have a plentiful lack of wit, together
   with most weak hams.° All which, sir, though I most powerfully and
   potently believe, yet I hold it not honesty to have it thus set down; for
   yourself, sir, should be old as I am if like a crab you could go backward.

---

160. **loose:** turn loose.   161. **arras:** tapestry hanging.   165. **keep . . . carters:** i.e., turn country
squire.   168. **board:** accost.   173. **fishmonger:** Hamlet is now in his "antic disposition," enjoying himself by fooling Polonius.   180. **sun . . . maggots:** a general belief.   181. **carrion:**
flesh.   196. **hams:** knee joints.

POLONIUS *(Aside).*   Though this be madness, yet there is method° in
't.—Will you walk out of the air, my lord?   200
HAMLET.   Into my grave.
POLONIUS.   Indeed, that's out of the air. *(Aside)* How pregnant° sometimes
his replies are! A happiness° that often madness hits on, which reason and
sanity could not so prosperously be delivered of. I will leave him, and
suddenly contrive the means of meeting between him and my daughter.—My honorable lord, I will most humbly take my leave of
you.
HAMLET.   You cannot, sir, take from me anything that I will more willingly
part withal—except my life, except my life, except my life.
POLONIUS.   Fare you well, my lord.   210
HAMLET.   These tedious old fools!

(Enter ROSENCRANTZ *and* GUILDENSTERN.*)*

POLONIUS.   You go to seek the Lord Hamlet. There he is.
ROSENCRANTZ *(To* POLONIUS*).*   God save you, sir!

(Exit POLONIUS.*)*

GUILDENSTERN.   My honored lord!
ROSENCRANTZ.   My most dear lord!   215
HAMLET.   My excellent good friends!° How dost thou, Guildenstern? Ah,
Rosencrantz! Good lads, how do you both?
ROSENCRANTZ.   As the indifferent° children of the earth.
GUILDENSTERN.   Happy in that we are not overhappy.
On Fortune's cap we are not the very button.°   220
HAMLET.   Nor the soles of her shoe?
ROSENCRANTZ.   Neither, my lord.
HAMLET.   Then you live about her waist, or in the middle of her favors?
GUILDENSTERN.   Faith, her privates° we.
HAMLET.   In the secret parts of Fortune? Oh, most true, she is a strumpet.
What's the news?
ROSENCRANTZ.   None, my lord, but that the world's grown honest.
HAMLET.   Then is Doomsday near. But your news is not true. Let me
question more in particular. What have you, my good friends, deserved at
the hands of Fortune, that she sends you to prison hither?   230
GUILDENSTERN.   Prison, my lord!
HAMLET.   Denmark's a prison.
ROSENCRANTZ.   Then is the world one.
HAMLET.   A goodly one, in which there are many confines,° wards,° and
dungeons, Denmark being one o' the worst.   235
ROSENCRANTZ.   We think not so, my lord.

199. **method:** order, sense.   202. **pregnant:** apt, meaningful.   203. **happiness:** good turn of
phrase.   216. **My . . . friends:** As soon as Polonius has gone, Hamlet drops his assumed madness
and greets Rosencrantz and Guildenstern naturally.   218. **indifferent:** neither too great nor too
little.   220. **button:** i.e., at the top.   224. **privates:** with a pun on "private parts" and "private,"
not concerned with politics.   234. **confines:** places of confinement.   **wards:** cells.

HAMLET.   Why, then 'tis none to you, for there is nothing either good or bad but thinking makes it so. To me it is a prison.

ROSENCRANTZ.   Why, then your ambition° makes it one. 'Tis too narrow for your mind.   240

HAMLET.   Oh, God, I could be bounded in a nutshell and count myself a king of infinite space were it not that I have bad dreams.

GUILDENSTERN.   Which dreams indeed are ambition, for the very substance of the ambitious° is merely the shadow of a dream.

HAMLET.   A dream itself is but a shadow.   245

ROSENCRANTZ.   Truly, and I hold ambition of so airy and light a quality that it is but a shadow's shadow.

HAMLET.   Then are our beggars bodies, and our monarchs and outstretched heroes the beggars' shadows.° Shall we to the Court? For, by my fay,° I cannot reason.°   250

ROSENCRANTZ & GUILDENSTERN.   We'll wait upon you.°

HAMLET.   No such matter. I will not sort° you with the rest of my servants, for, to speak to you like an honest man, I am most dreadfully attended.° But in the beaten way of friendship, what make you at Elsinore?

ROSENCRANTZ.   To visit you, my lord, no other occasion.   255

HAMLET.   Beggar that I am, I am even poor in thanks, but I thank you. And sure, dear friends, my thanks are too dear a halfpenny.° Were you not sent for? Is it your own inclining? Is it a free visitation?° Come, deal justly with me. Come, come. Nay, speak.

GUILDENSTERN.   What should we say, my lord?   260

HAMLET.   Why, anything, but to the purpose.° You were sent for, and there is a kind of confession in your looks which your modesties have not craft enough to color.° I know the good King and Queen have sent for you.

ROSENCRANTZ.   To what end, my lord?   264

HAMLET.   That you must teach me. But let me conjure° you, by the rights of our fellowship,° by the consonancy° of our youth, by the obligation of our ever preserved love, and by what more dear a better proposer could charge you withal, be even° and direct with me, whether you were sent for, or no.

ROSENCRANTZ (*Aside to* GUILDENSTERN).   What say you?   270

HAMLET (*Aside*).   Nay, then, I have an eye of you.—If you love me, hold not off.

---

239. **your ambition:** Rosencrantz is feeling after one possible cause of Hamlet's melancholy—thwarted ambition.   244. **substance . . . ambitious:** that on which an ambitious man feeds his fancies.   248–49. **Then . . . shadows:** i.e., by your reasoning beggars are the only men of substance, for kings and heroes are by nature ambitious and therefore "the shadows of a dream."   **outstretched:** of exaggerated reputation.   249. **fay:** faith.   250. **reason:** argue.   251. **wait . . . you:** be your servants.   252. **sort:** class.   253. **dreadfully attended:** my attendants are a poor crowd.   257. **too . . . halfpenny:** not worth a halfpenny.   258. **free visitation:** voluntary visit.   261. **anything . . . purpose:** anything so long as it is not true.   263. **color:** conceal.   265. **conjure:** make solemn appeal to.   266. **fellowship:** comradeship.   **consonancy:** concord.   268. **even:** straight.

GUILDENSTERN.   My lord, we were sent for.

HAMLET.   I will tell you why. So shall my anticipation prevent your discovery, and your secrecy to the King and Queen molt no feather.° I have of late—but wherefore I know not—lost all my mirth, forgone all custom of exercises, and indeed it goes so heavily with my disposition that this goodly frame the earth seems to me a sterile promontory.   278
This most excellent canopy,° the air, look you, this brave o'erhanging firmament,° this majestical roof fretted° with golden fire—why, it appears no other thing to me than a foul and pestilent congregation of vapors. What a piece of work is a man!   282
How noble in reason! How infinite in faculty!° In form and moving° how express° and admirable! In action how like an angel! In apprehension how like a god! The beauty of the world! The paragon of animals! And yet, to me, what is this quintessence° of dust? Man delights not me—no, nor woman neither, though by your smiling you seem to say so.   287

ROSENCRANTZ.   My lord, there was no such stuff in my thoughts.

HAMLET.   Why did you laugh, then, when I said "Man delights not me"?

ROSENCRANTZ.   To think, my lord, if you delight not in man, what lenten entertainment° the players shall receive from you. We coted° them on the way, and hither are they coming to offer you service.   292

HAMLET.   He that plays the King shall be welcome, His Majesty shall have tribute of me. The adventureous knight shall use his foil and target,° the lover shall not sigh gratis, the humorous man° shall end his part in peace, the clown shall make those laugh whose lungs are tickle o' the sere,° and the lady shall say her mind freely or the blank verse shall halt° for 't. What players are they?   298

ROSENCRANTZ.   Even those you were wont to take such delight in, the tragedians of the city.

HAMLET.   How chances it they travel? Their residence, both in reputation and profit, was better both ways.°

ROSENCRANTZ.   I think their inhibition° comes by the means of the late innovation.°   304

HAMLET.   Do they hold the same estimation they did when I was in the city? Are they so followed?

ROSENCRANTZ.   No, indeed are they not.

HAMLET.   How comes it? Do they grow rusty?   308

274–75. So . . . feather: i.e., so by my telling you first you will not be obliged to betray the secrets of the King. **prevent:** forestall. **molt no feather:** be undisturbed. **279. canopy:** covering. **280. firmament:** sky. **fretted:** ornamented. **283. faculty:** power of the mind. **moving:** movement. **284. express:** exact. **286. quintessence:** perfection; the fifth essence, which would be left if the four elements were taken away. **290–91. lenten entertainment:** meager welcome. **coted:** overtook. **294. foil . . . target:** rapier and small shield. **295. humorous man:** the man who specializes in character parts. **296. are . . . sere:** explode at a touch. The *sere* is part of the trigger mechanism of a gun which if "ticklish" will go off at a touch. **297. halt:** limp. **301–02. Their . . . ways:** i.e., if they stayed in the city, it would bring them more profit and fame. **303. inhibition:** formal prohibition. **304. innovation:** riot.

ROSENCRANTZ.   Nay, their endeavor keeps in the wonted pace.° But there
is, sir, an eyrie° of children, little eyases,° that cry out on the top of
question° and are most tyrannically° clapped for 't. These are now the
fashion, and so berattle° the common stages°—so they call them—that
many wearing rapiers are afraid of goose quills° and dare scarce come
thither.   314
HAMLET.   What, are they children? Who maintains 'em? How are they
escoted?° Will they pursue the quality° no longer than they can sing? Will
they not say afterward, if they should grow themselves to common
players—as it is most like if their means are no better—their writers
do them wrong to make them exclaim against their own
succession?°   320
ROSENCRANTZ.   Faith, there has been much to-do on both sides, and the
nation holds it no sin to tarre° them to controversy. There was for a while
no money bid for argument° unless the poet and the player went to cuffs°
in the question.   324
HAMLET.   Is 't possible?
GUILDENSTERN.   Oh, there has been much throwing-about of brains.
HAMLET.   Do the boys carry it away?
ROSENCRANTZ.   Aye, that they do, my lord, Hercules and his load°
too.   329
HAMLET.   It is not very strange, for my uncle is King of Denmark, and those
that would make mows° at him while my father lived give twenty, forty,
fifty, a hundred ducats apiece for his picture in little. 'Sblood,° there is
something in this more than natural, if philosophy could find it
out.   334

(Flourish of trumpets within.)

GUILDENSTERN.   There are the players.
HAMLET.   Gentlemen, you are welcome to Elsinore. Your hands. Come
then. The appurtenance of welcome is fashion and ceremony.° Let me
comply° with you in this garb,° lest my extent° to the players—which, I
tell you, must show fairly outward—should more appear like entertain-
ment° than yours. You are welcome. But my uncle-father and aunt-
mother are deceived.
GUILDENSTERN.   In what, my dear lord?

309. endeavor . . . pace: they try as hard as ever.   310. eyrie: nest. eyases: young
hawks.   310–11. cry . . . question: either "cry in a shrill voice" or perhaps "cry out the latest
detail of the dispute."   311. tyrannically: outrageously.   312. berattle: abuse. common
stages: the professional players. The boys acted in "private" playhouses.   313. goose quills: pens.
316. escoted: paid. quality: acting profession.   319–20. exclaim . . . succession: abuse the
profession to which they will afterward belong.   322. tarre: urge on to fight; generally used of
encouraging a dog.   323. argument: plot of a play. See III.ii.214. went to cuffs: boxed each
other's ears.   328. Hercules . . . load: Hercules carrying the globe on his shoulders was the sign
of the Globe Playhouse.   331. mows: grimaces.   332. 'Sblood: by God's blood.   337. appurtenance . . . ceremony: that which pertains to welcome is formal ceremony.   338. comply:
use the formality of welcome; i.e., shake hands with you. garb: fashion. extent: outward
behavior.   339. entertainment: welcome.

HAMLET.   I am but mad north-northwest.° When the wind is southerly,° I know a hawk from a handsaw.° 344

(Re-enter POLONIUS.*)*

POLONIUS.   Well be with you, gentlemen!
HAMLET.   Hark you, Guildenstern, and you too—at each ear a hearer. That great baby you see there is not yet out of his swaddling clouts.°
ROSENCRANTZ.   Happily he's the second time come to them, for they say an old man is twice a child. 350
HAMLET.   I will prophesy he comes to tell me of the players, mark it. You say right, sir. O' Monday morning, 'twas so indeed.
POLONIUS.   My lord, I have news to tell you.
HAMLET.   My lord, I have news to tell you. When Roscius° was an actor in Rome—— 355
POLONIUS.   The actors are come hither, my lord.
HAMLET.   Buzz, buzz!°
POLONIUS.   Upon my honor——
HAMLET.   Then came each actor on his ass—— 359
POLONIUS.   The° best actors in the world, either for tragedy, comedy, history, pastoral, pastoral-comical, historical-pastoral, tragical-historical, tragical-comical-historical-pastoral, scene individable° or poem unlimited.° Seneca cannot be too heavy, nor Plautus° too light. For the law of writ° and the liberty,° these are the only men. 364
HAMLET.   O Jephthah,° judge of Israel, what a treasure hadst thou!
POLONIUS.   What a treasure had he, my lord?
HAMLET.   Why,
"One° fair daughter, and no more,
The which he lovèd passing well." 369
POLONIUS *(Aside).*   Still° on my daughter.
HAMLET.   Am I not i' the right, old Jephthah?
POLONIUS.   If you call me Jephthah, my lord, I have a daughter that I love passing well.
HAMLET.   Nay, that follows not. 374
POLONIUS.   What follows, then, my lord?

---

343. north-northwest: i.e., 327° (out of 360°) of the compass.   **wind is southerly:** The south wind was considered unhealthy.   **344. hawk . . . handsaw:** Either "handsaw" is a corruption of "heronshaw," heron, or a hawk is a tool like a pickax. The phrase means "I'm not so mad as you think."   **348. clouts:** clothes.   **354. Roscius:** the most famous of Roman actors.   **357. Buzz, buzz:** slang for "stale news."   **360–64. The . . . men:** Polonius reads out the accomplishments of the actors from the license which they have presented him.   **362. scene individable:** i.e., a play preserving the unities.   **362–63. poem unlimited:** i.e., a play which disregards the rules.   **363. Seneca . . . Plautus:** the Roman writers of tragedy and comedy with whose plays every educated man was familiar.   **363–64. law of writ:** the critical rules; i.e., classical plays.   **364. liberty:** plays freely written; i.e., "modern" drama.   **365. Jephthah:** The story of Jephthah is told in Judges, Chapter II. He vowed that if successful against the Ammonites he would sacrifice the first creature to meet him on his return, which was his daughter.   **368–79. One . . . was:** Quotations from a ballad of Jephthah.   **370. Still:** always.

HAMLET.   Why,
                           "As by lot, God wot,"°
and then you know,
                           "It came to pass, as most like it was—"   379
the first row° of the pious chanson° will show you more, for look where
my abridgement° comes. (*Enter four or five* PLAYERS.) You are welcome,
masters, welcome all. I am glad to see thee well. Welcome, good friends.
Oh, my old friend!° Why, thy face is valanced° since I saw thee last.
Comest thou to beard° me in Denmark? What, my young lady° and
mistress! By 'r Lady, your ladyship is nearer to Heaven than when I saw
you last, by the altitude of a chopine.° Pray God your voice, like a piece of
uncurrent gold, be not cracked within the ring.° Masters, you are all
welcome. We'll e'en to 't like French falconers,° fly at anything we see.
We'll have a speech straight. Come, give us a taste of your qual-
ity°—come, a passionate speech.   390
FIRST PLAYER.   What speech, my good lord?
HAMLET.   I heard thee speak me a speech once, but it was never acted, or if
it was, not above once; for the play, I remember, pleased not the million,
'twas caviar° to the general.° But it was—as I received it, and others,
whose judgments in such matters cried in the top of mine°—an excellent
play, well digested° in the scenes, set down with as much modesty° as
cunning. I remember one said there were no sallets° in the lines to make
the matter savory, nor no matter in the phrase that might indict the author
of affection,° but called it an honest method, as wholesome as sweet, and
by very much more handsome than fine.° One speech in it I chiefly loved.
'Twas Aeneas' tale to Dido,° and thereabout of it especially where he
speaks of Priam's° slaughter. If it live in your memory, begin at this
line—let me see, let me see—
                           "The rugged Pyrrhus,° like th' Hyrcanian beast,°—"   404
It is not so. It begins with "Pyrrhus."

"The° rugged Pyrrhus, he whose sable° arms,

---

377. **wot**: knows.   380. **row**: line.   **pious chanson**: godly poem.   381. **abridgement**: entertainment.   383. **old friend**: i.e., the leading player.   **valanced**: bearded. A valance is a fringe
hung round the sides and bottom of a bed.   384. **beard**: dare, with a pun on "valanced."   **young lady**: i.e., the boy who takes the woman's parts.   386. **chopine**: lady's shoe
with thick cork sole.   387. **cracked . . . ring**: Before coins were milled on the rim they were
liable to crack. When the crack reached the ring surrounding the device, the coin was no longer
valid.   388. **French falconers**: They were famous for their skill in hawking.   390. **quality**: skill
as an actor.   394. **caviar**: sturgeon's roe, a Russian delicacy not then appreciated (or known)
by any but gourmets.   **general**: common herd.   395. **cried . . . mine**: surpassed mine.
396. **digested**: composed.   **modesty**: moderation.   397. **sallets**: tasty bits.   398–99. **phrase . . .
affection**: nothing in the language which could charge the author with affectation.   400. **fine**:
subtle.   401. **Aeneas' . . . Dido**: the story of the sack of Troy as told by Aeneas to Dido, Queen
of Carthage. The original is in Virgil's *Aeneid*. A similar speech occurs in Marlowe's play *Dido,
Queen of Carthage*.   402. **Priam**: the old King of Troy.   404. **Phyrrhus**: the son of Achilles,
one of the Greeks concealed in the Wooden Horse.   **Hyrcanian beast**: the tiger.
406–71. **The . . . gods**: The speech may be from some lost play of *Dido and Aeneas*, but more
likely it is Shakespeare's own invention. It is written in the heavy elaborate style still popular in
the dramas of the Admiral's Men. The first player delivers it with excessive gesture and emotion.   406. **sable**: black.

Black as his purpose, did the night resemble
When he lay couchèd in the ominous° horse,°
Hath now this dread and black complexion smeared   409
With heraldry° more dismal. Head to foot
Now is he total gules, horridly tricked
With blood of fathers, mothers, daughters, sons,
Baked and impasted° with the parching streets
That lend a tyrannous and damnèd light   414
To their lord's murder. Roasted in wrath and fire,
And thus o'ersized with coagulate gore,°
With eyes like carbuncles, the hellish Pyrrhus
Old grandsire Priam seeks."

So, proceed you.   419
POLONIUS.   'Fore God, my lord, well spoken, with good accent and good
    discretion.
FIRST PLAYER.   "Anon he finds him
    Striking too short at Greeks. His antique sword,
    Rebellious to his arm, lies where it falls,
    Repugnant to command.° Unequal matched,   425
    Pyrrhus at Priam drives, in rage strikes wide,
    But with the whiff and wind of his fell sword
    The unnerved father falls. Then senseless Ilium,°
    Seeming to feel this blow, with flaming top
    Stoops to his base,° and with a hideous crash   430
    Takes prisoner Pyrrhus' ear. For, lo! his sword,
    Which was declining° on the milky° head
    Of reverend Priam, seemed i' the air to stick.
    So as a painted tyrant° Pyrrhus stood,
    And like a neutral to his will and matter,°   435
    Did nothing.
    But as we often see, against° some storm
    A silence in the heavens, the rack° stand still,
    The bold winds speechless and the orb° below
    As hush as death, anon the dreadful thunder   440
    Doth rend the region°—so after Pyrrhus' pause
    Arousèd vengeance sets him new awork.
    And never did the Cyclops'° hammers fall

---

408. **ominous:** fateful.   **horse:** the Wooden Horse by which a small Greek force was enabled to
make a secret entry into Troy.   410. **heraldry:** painting. The image of heraldic painting is kept
up in *gules* (the heraldic term for red) and *tricked* (painted).   413. **impasted:** turned into a crust
by the heat of the burning city.   416. **o'ersized . . . gore:** covered over with congealed
blood.   425. **Repugnant to command:** refusing to be used.   428. **Ilium:** the citadel of
Troy.   430. **stoops . . . base:** collapses.   432. **declining:** bending toward.   **milky:** milk-
white.   434. **painted tyrant:** as in the painting of a tyrant.   435. **neutral . . . matter:** one
midway (*neutral*) between his desire (*will*) and action (*matter*).   437. **against:** just before.
438. **rack:** the clouds in the upper air.   439. **orb:** world.   441. **region:** the country
round.   443. **Cyclops':** of Titans, giants who aided Vulcan, the blacksmith god, to make armor
for Mars, the war god.

On Mars's armor, forged for proof eterne,°
With less remorse° than Pyrrhus' bleeding sword   445
Now falls on Priam.
Out, out, thou strumpet, Fortune! All you gods,
In general synod° take away her power,
Break all the spokes and fellies° from her wheel,
And bowl the round nave° down the hill of Heaven   450
As low as to the fiends!"

POLONIUS.   This is too long.

HAMLET.   It shall to the barber's, with your beard.
Prithee, say on. He's for a jig° or a tale of bawdry,
or he sleeps. Say on. Come to Hecuba.   455

FIRST PLAYER.   "But who, oh, who had seen the mobled° Queen—"

HAMLET.   "The mobled Queen"?

POLONIUS.   That's good, "mobled Queen" is good.

FIRST PLAYER.   "Run barefoot up and down, threatening the flames
With bisson rheum,° a clout° upon that head
Where late the diadem stood, and for a robe,   460
About her lank and all o'erteemèd° loins
A blanket, in the alarm of fear caught up.
Who this had seen, with tongue in venom steeped
'Gainst Fortune's state would treason have pronounced.°
But if the gods themselves did see her then,   465
When she saw Pyrrhus make malicious sport
In mincing with his sword her husband's limbs,
The instant burst of clamor that she made,
Unless things mortal move them not at all,
Would have made milch° the burning eyes of Heaven   470
And passion in the gods."

POLONIUS.   Look whether he has not turned his color and has tears in 's
eyes. Prithee, no more.

HAMLET.   'Tis well; I'll have thee speak out the rest of this soon. Good my
lord, will you see the players well bestowed?° Do you hear, let them be
well used, for they are the abstract and brief chronicles of the time.° After
your death you were better have a bad epitaph than their ill report while
you live.   478

POLONIUS.   My lord, I will use them according to their desert.°

---

444. proof eterne: everlasting protection.   **445. remorse:** pity.   **448. synod:** council.
449. fellies: the pieces forming the circumference of a wooden wheel.   **450. nave:** center of the
wheel.   **454. jig:** bawdy dance.   **456. mobled:** muffled.   **459. bisson rheum:** blinding
moisture.   **clout:** rag.   **461. o'erteemed:** exhausted by bearing children; she had borne fifty-
two.   **463–64. Who . . . pronounced:** anyone who had seen this sight would with bitter words
have uttered treason against the tyranny of Fortune.   **470. milch:** milky, i.e., dripping moisture.   **475. bestowed:** housed.   **476. abstract . . . time:** they summarize and record the events
of our time. Elizabethan players were often in trouble for too saucily commenting on their betters
in plays dealing with history or contemporary events and persons.   **479. desert:** rank.

HAMLET. God's bodykins,° man, much better. Use every man after his desert and who shall 'scape whipping? Use them after your own honor and dignity. The less they deserve, the more merit is in your bounty. Take them in.

POLONIUS. Come, sirs. 484

HAMLET. Follow him, friends. We'll hear a play tomorrow. (*Exit* POLONIUS *with all the* PLAYERS *but the* FIRST.) Dost thou hear me, old friend? Can you play *The Murder of Gonzago?*

FIRST PLAYER. Aye, my lord.

HAMLET. We'll ha 't tomorrow night. You could, for a need, study a speech of some dozen or sixteen lines which I would set down and insert in 't, could you not? 491

FIRST PLAYER. Aye, my lord.

HAMLET. Very well. Follow that lord, and look you mock him not. (*Exit* FIRST PLAYER.) My good friends, I'll leave you till night. You are welcome to Elsinore. 495

ROSENCRANTZ. Good my lord!

HAMLET. Aye, so, God be wi' ye! (*Exeunt* ROSENCRANTZ *and* GUILD-ENSTERN.) Now I am alone.
Oh, what a rogue and peasant slave am I!
Is it not monstrous that this player here, 500
But in a fiction, in a dream of passion,°
Could force his soul so to his own conceit°
That from her working° all his visage wanned,°
Tears in his eyes, distraction° in 's aspect,°
A broken voice, and his whole function° suiting 505
With forms to his conceit? And all for nothing!
For Hecuba!
What's Hecuba to him or he to Hecuba,
That he should weep for her? What would he do
Had he the motive and the cue for passion 510
That I have? He would drown the stage with tears
And cleave the general ear° with horrid speech,
Make mad the guilty and appal the free,°
Confound the ignorant, and amaze indeed
The very faculties of eyes and ears. 515
Yet I,
A dull and muddy-mettled° rascal, peak,°
Like John-a-dreams,° unpregnant of my cause,°
And can say nothing—no, not for a King
Upon whose property° and most dear life 520

480. God's bodykins: by God's little body. 501. dream of passion: imaginary emotion. 502. conceit: imagination. 503. her working: i.e., the effect of imagination. wanned: went pale. 504. distraction: frenzy. aspect: countenance. 505. function: behavior. 512. general ear: ears of the audience. 513. free: innocent. 517. muddy-mettled: made of mud, not iron. peak: mope. 518. John-a-dreams: "Sleepy Sam." unpregnant . . . cause: barren of plans for vengeance. 520. property: personality, life.

A damned defeat° was made. Am I a coward?
Who° calls me villain? Breaks my pate across?
Plucks off my beard and blows it in my face?
Tweaks me by the nose? Gives me the lie i' the throat
As deep as to the lungs? Who does me this?   525
Ha!
'Swounds,° I should take it. For it cannot be
But I am pigeon-livered° and lack gall°
To make oppression bitter, or ere this
I should have fatted all the region kites   530
With this slave's offal.° Bloody, bawdy villain!
Remorseless, treacherous, lecherous, kindless° villain!
Oh, vengeance!
Why, what an ass am I! This is most brave,
That I, the son of a dear father murdered,   535
Prompted to my revenge by Heaven and Hell,
Must, like a whore, unpack my heart with words
And fall a-cursing like a very drab,°
A scullion!°
Fie upon 't! Foh! About, my brain! Hum, I have heard   540
That guilty creatures sitting at a play
Have by the very cunning of the scene
Been struck so to the soul that presently°
They have proclaimed their malefactions;°
For murder, though it have no tongue, will speak   545
With most miraculous organ. I'll have these players
Play something like the murder of my father
Before mine uncle. I'll observe his looks,
I'll tent° him to the quick. If he but blench,°
I know my course. The spirit that I have seen   550
May be the Devil, and the Devil hath power
To assume a pleasing shape. Yea, and perhaps
Out of my weakness and my melancholy,
As he is very potent with such spirits,
Abuses me to damn me.° I'll have grounds°   555
More relative than this.° The play's the thing
Wherein I'll catch the conscience of the King.   (*Exit.*)

---

521. **defeat:** ruin.   522–25. **Who . . . this:** Hamlet runs through all the insults which provoked
a resolute man to mortal combat.   **pate:** head.   **lie . . . throat:** the bitterest of insults.
527. **'Swounds:** by God's wounds.   528. **pigeon-livered:** "as gentle as a dove."   **gall:**
spirit.   530–31. **I . . . offal:** before this I would have fed this slave's (i.e., the King's) guts to the
kites.   **fatted:** made fat.   532. **kindless:** unnatural.   538. **drab:** "moll."   539. **scullion:** the
lowest of the kitchen servants.   543. **presently:** immediately.   544. **proclaimed . . . malefactions:** shouted out their crimes.   549. **tent:** probe.   **blench:** flinch.   555. **Abuses . . . me:** i.e.,
deceives me so that I may commit the sin of murder which will bring me to dam-
nation.   **grounds:** reasons for action.   556. **relative . . . this:** i.e., more convincing than the
appearance of a ghost.

ACT III

SCENE I. A room in the castle.

(*Enter* KING, QUEEN, POLONIUS, OPHELIA, ROSENCRANTZ, *and* GUILDENSTERN.)

KING.   And can you, by no drift of circumstance,°
Get from him why he puts on this confusion,
Grating° so harshly all his days of quiet
With turbulent and dangerous lunacy?
ROSENCRANTZ.   He does confess he feels himself distracted,   5
But from what cause he will by no means speak.
GUILDENSTERN.   Nor do we find him forward to be sounded,°
But, with a crafty madness, keeps aloof
When we would bring him on to some confession
Of his true state.
QUEEN.   Did he receive you well?   10
ROSENCRANTZ.   Most like a gentleman.
GUILDENSTERN.   But with much forcing of his disposition.°
ROSENCRANTZ.   Niggard of question,° but of our demands
Most free in his reply.
QUEEN.   Did you assay him
To any pastime?°   15
ROSENCRANTZ.   Madam, it so fell out that certain players
We o'erraught° on the way. Of these we told him,
And there did seem in him a kind of joy
To hear of it. They are about the Court,
And, as I think, they have already order   20
This night to play before him.
POLONIUS.   'Tis most true.
And he beseeched me to entreat your Majesties
To hear and see the matter.
KING.   With all my heart, and it doth much content me
To hear him so inclined.   25
Good gentlemen, give him a further edge,°
And drive his purpose on to these delights.
ROSENCRANTZ.   We shall, my lord.

(*Exeunt* ROSENCRANTZ *and* GUILDENSTERN.)

KING.   Sweet Gertrude, leave us too,
For we have closely° sent for Hamlet hither,
That he, as 'twere by accident, may here   30
Affront° Ophelia.

Act III, Sc. i: 1. **drift of circumstance:** circumstantial evidence, hint.   3. **grating:** disturbing.   7. **forward . . . sounded:** eager to be questioned.   12. **much . . . disposition:** making a great effort to be civil to us.   13. **Niggard of question:** not asking many questions.   14–15. **Did . . . pastime:** did you try to interest him in any amusement.   17. **o'erraught:** overtook.   26. **edge:** encouragement.   29. **closely:** secretly.   31. **Affront:** encounter.

Her father and myself, lawful espials,°
Will so bestow ourselves that, seeing unseen,
We may of their encounter frankly judge
And gather by him, as he is behaved,°   35
If 't be the affliction of his love or no
That thus he suffers for.
QUEEN.   I shall obey you.
And for your part, Ophelia, I do wish
That your good beauties be the happy cause
Of Hamlet's wildness. So shall I hope your virtues   40
Will bring him to his wonted way° again,
To both your honors.
OPHELIA.   Madam, I wish it may.

(*Exit* QUEEN.)

POLONIUS.   Ophelia, walk you here, Gracious,° so please you,
We will bestow ourselves. (*To* OPHELIA) Read on this book,°
That show of such an exercise may color   45
Your loneliness. We are oft to blame in this—
'Tis too much proved—that with devotion's visage°
And pious action we do sugar o'er
The Devil himself.
KING (*Aside*).   Oh, 'tis too true!
How smart a lash that speech doth give my conscience!   50
The harlot's cheek, beautied with plastering art,
Is not more ugly to the thing that helps it°
Than is my deed to my most painted° word.
Oh, heavy burden!
POLONIUS.   I hear him coming. Let's withdraw, my lord.   55

(*Exeunt* KING *and* POLONIUS.)

(*Enter* HAMLET.)

HAMLET.   To be, or not to be—that is the question.
Whether 'tis nobler in the mind to suffer
The slings and arrows of outrageous° fortune,
Or to take arms against a sea° of troubles
And by opposing end them. To die, to sleep—   60
No more, and by a sleep to say we end
The heartache and the thousand natural shocks
That flesh is heir to. 'Tis a consummation°
Devoutly to be wished. To die, to sleep,
To sleep—perchance to dream. Aye, there's the rub,°   65

32. **lawful espials:** who are justified in spying on him.   35. **by . . . behaved:** from him, from his behavior.   41. **wonted way:** normal state.   43. **Gracious:** your Majesty—addressed to the King.   44. **book:** i.e., of devotions.   47. **devotion's visage:** an outward appearance of religion.   52. **ugly . . . it:** i.e., lust, which is the cause of its artificial beauty.   53. **painted:** i.e., false.   58. **outrageous:** cruel.   59. **sea:** i.e., an endless turmoil.   63. **consummation:** completion.   65. **rub:** impediment.

For in that sleep of death what dreams may come
When we have shuffled off this mortal coil°
Must give us pause. There's the respect°
That makes calamity of so long life.°
For who would bear the whips and scorns of time,   70
The oppressor's wrong, the proud man's contumely°
The pangs of dèspised love, the law's delay,
The insolence of office° and the spurns
That patient merit of the unworthy takes,°
When he himself might his quietus° make   75
With a bare bodkin?° Who would fardels° bear,
To grunt and sweat under a weary life,
But that the dread of something after death,
The undiscovered country from whose bourn°
No traveler returns, puzzles the will,°   80
And makes us rather bear those ills we have
Than fly to others that we know not of?
Thus° conscience does make cowards of us all,
And thus the native hue° of resolution
Is sicklied o'er with the pale cast° of thought,   85
And enterprises of great pitch° and moment
With this regard their currents turn awry
And lose the name of action.°—Soft you now!
The fair Ophelia! Nymph, in thy orisons°
Be all my sins remembered.
OPHELIA.   Good my lord,   90
How does your Honor for this many a day?
HAMLET.   I humbly thank you—well, well, well.
OPHELIA.   My lord, I have remembrances of yours
That I have longed long to redeliver.
I pray you now receive them.
HAMLET.   No, not I.   95
I never gave you aught.
OPHELIA.   My honored lord, you know right well you did,
And with them words of so sweet breath composed
As made the things more rich. Their perfume lost,
Take these again, for to the noble mind   100
Rich gifts wax poor when givers prove unkind.
There, my lord.

---

67. shuffled . . . coil: cast off this fuss of life. **68. respect:** reason. **69. makes . . . life:** makes it a calamity to have to live so long. **71. contumely:** insulting behavior. **73. insolence of office:** insolent behavior of government officials. **73–74. spurns . . . takes:** insults which men of merit have patiently to endure from the unworthy. **75. quietus:** discharge. **76. bodkin:** dagger. **fardels:** burdens, the coolie's pack. **79. bourn:** boundary. **80. will:** resolution, ability to act. **83–88. Thus . . . action:** the religious fear that death may not be the end makes men shrink from heroic actions. **84. native hue:** natural color. **85. cast:** color. **86. pitch:** height; used of the soaring flight of a hawk. **87–88. With . . . action:** by brooding on this thought great enterprises are diverted from their course and fade away. **89. orisons:** prayers.

HAMLET.   Ha, ha! Are you honest?°
OPHELIA.   My lord?
HAMLET.   Are you fair?   105
OPHELIA.   What means your lordship?
HAMLET.   That if you be honest and fair, your honesty should admit no
discourse to your beauty.°
OPHELIA.   Could beauty, my lord, have better commerce than with
honesty?   110
HAMLET.   Aye, truly, for the power of beauty will sooner transform honesty
from what it is to a bawd° than the force of honesty can translate beauty
into his likeness. This was sometime a paradox,° but now the time gives it
proof. I did love you once.
OPHELIA.   Indeed, my lord, you made me believe so.   115
HAMLET.   You should not have believed me, for virtue cannot so inoculate
our old stock but we shall relish° of it. I loved you not.
OPHELIA.   I was the more deceived.   118
HAMLET.   Get thee to a nunnery. Why wouldst thou be a breeder of
sinners? I am myself indifferent honest,° but yet I could accuse me of such
things that it were better my mother had not borne me. I am very proud,
revengeful, ambitious, with more offenses at my beck° than I have
thoughts to put them in, imagination to give them shape, or time to act
them in. What should such fellows as I do crawling between heaven and
earth? We are arrant knaves all. Believe none of us. Go thy ways to
nunnery.° Where's your father?   126
OPHELIA.   At home, my lord.
HAMLET.   Let the doors be shut upon him, that he may play the fool
nowhere but in 's own house. Farewell.
OPHELIA.   Oh, help him, you sweet Heavens!   130
HAMLET.   If thou dost marry, I'll give thee this plague for thy dowry: Be
thou as chaste as ice, as pure as snow—thou shalt not escape calumny.°
Get thee to a nunnery, go. Farewell. Or if thou wilt needs marry, marry a
fool, for wise men know well enough what monsters° you make of them.
To a nunnery, go, and quickly too. Farewell.   135
OPHELIA.   O heavenly powers, restore him!
HAMLET.   I have heard of your paintings° too, well enough. God hath given
you one face and you make yourselves another. You jig,° you amble,° and
you lisp,° and nickname God's creatures, and make your wantonness your
ignorance.° Go to, I'll no more on 't—it hath made me mad. I say we will

---

103. **honest:** chaste.   107–08. **That . . . beauty:** if you are chaste and beautiful your chastity
should have nothing to do with your beauty—because (so Hamlet thinks in his bitterness)
beautiful women are seldom chaste.   112. **bawd:** brothel-keeper.   113. **paradox:** statement
contrary to accepted opinion.   117. **relish:** have some trace.   120. **indifferent honest:** moderately honorable.   122. **at . . . beck:** waiting to come when I beckon.   126. **nunnery:** i.e., a
place where she will be removed from temptation.   132. **calumny:** slander.   134. **monsters:**
horned beasts, cuckolds.   137. **paintings:** using make-up.   138. **jig:** dance lecherously.
amble: walk artificially.   139. **lisp:** talk affectedly.   139–40. **nickname . . . ignorance:** give
things indecent names and pretend to be too simple to understand their meanings.

have no more marriages. Those that are married already, all but one, shall
live; the rest shall keep as they are. To a nunnery, go.   (*Exit.*)
OPHELIA.   Oh, what a noble mind is here o'erthown!
The courtier's, soldier's, scholar's, eye, tongue, sword—
The expectancy and rose° of the fair state,   145
The glass° of fashion and the mold of form,°
The observed of all observers—quite, quite down!
And I, of ladies most deject and wretched,
That sucked the honey of his music vows,
Now see that noble and most sovereign reason,   150
Like sweet bells jangled, out of tune and harsh,
That unmatched° form and feature of blown° youth
Blasted with ecstasy.° Oh, woe is me,
To have seen what I have seen, see what I see!

(*Re-enter* KING *and* POLONIUS.)

KING.   Love! His affections° do not that way tend,   155
Nor what he spake, though it lacked form a little,
Was not like madness. There's something in his soul
O'er which his melancholy sits on brood,°
And I do doubt the hatch and the disclose°
Will be some danger. Which for to prevent,   160
I have in quick determination
Thus set it down: He shall with speed to England,
For the demand of our neglected tribute.
Haply° the seas and countries different
With variable objects° shall expel   165
This something-settled° matter in his heart
Whereon his brains still beating puts him thus
From fashion of himself.° What think you on 't?
POLONIUS.   It shall do well. But yet do I believe
The origin and commencement of his grief   170
Sprung from neglected love. How now, Ophelia!
You need not tell us what Lord Hamlet said,
We heard it all. My lord, do as you please,
But, if you hold it fit, after the play
Let his Queen mother all alone entreat him   175
To show his grief. Let her be round° with him,
And I'll be placed, so please you, in the ear
Of all their conference. If she find him not,

---

145. expectancy . . . rose: bright hope. The rose is used as a symbol for beauty and
perfection. **146. glass:** mirror. **mold of form:** perfect pattern of manly beauty. **152. un-
matched:** unmatchable. **blown:** perfect, like an open flower at its best. **153. Blasted . . .
ecstasy:** ruined by madness. **155. affections:** state of mind. **158. sits . . . brood:** sits hatch-
ing. **159. doubt . . . disclose:** suspect the brood which will result. **164. Haply:** perhaps. **165. variable objects:** novel sights. **166. something-settled:** somewhat settled; i.e., not
yet incurable. **167–68. puts . . . himself:** i.e., separates him from his normal self.
176. round: direct.

To England send him, or confine him where
Your wisdom best shall think.

KING.   It shall be so.   180
Madness in great ones must not unwatched go.

(Exeunt.)

SCENE II. *A hall in the castle.*

(Enter HAMLET *and* PLAYERS.*)*

HAMLET.   Speak the speech,° I pray you, as I pronounced it to you, trip-
pingly° on the tongue. But if you mouth° it, as many of your players do, I
had as lief° the town crier spoke my lines. Nor do not saw the air too
much with your hand, thus, but use all gently. For in the very torrent,
tempest, and, as I may say, whirlwind of passion, you must acquire and
beget a temperance that may give it smoothness. Oh, it offends me to the
soul to hear a robustious° periwig-pated° fellow tear a passion to tatters, to
very rags, to split the ears of the groundlings,° who for the most part are
capable of nothing but inexplicable dumb shows° and noise. I would have
such a fellow whipped for o'erdoing Termagant°—it out-Herods Herod.
Pray you, avoid it.   11

FIRST PLAYER.   I warrant your Honor.

HAMLET.   Be not too tame neither, but let your own discretion be your
tutor. Suit the action to the word, the word to the action, with this special
observance, that you o'erstep not the modesty of nature. For anything so
overdone is from° the purpose of playing, whose end, both at the first and
now, was and is to hold as 'twere the mirror up to Nature—to show Virtue
her own feature, scorn her own image, and the very age and body of the
time his form and pressure.° Now this overdone or come tardy off, though
it make the unskillful laugh, cannot but make the judicious grieve, the
censure of the which one° must in your allowance o'erweigh a whole
theater of others. Oh, there be players° that I have seen play, and heard
others praise—and that highly, not to speak it profanely—that neither
having the accent of Christians nor the gait of Christian, pagan, nor man,
have so strutted and bellowed that I have thought some of Nature's
journeymen° had made men, and not made them well, they imitated
humanity so abominably.   27

Sc. ii: 1. the speech: which he has written. The whole passage which follows is Shakespeare's own comment on the actor's art and states the creed and practice of his company as
contrasted with the more violent methods of Edward Alleyn and his fellows.
2. trippingly: smoothly, easily.   mouth: "ham" it.   3. lief: soon.   7. robustious: ranting.   periwig-pated: wearing a wig.   8. groundlings: the poorer spectators, who stood in the
yard of the playhouse.   9. dumb shows: an old-fashioned dramatic device; before a tragedy, and
sometimes before each act, the characters mimed the action which was to follow. See later, l.
120.   10. Termagant: God of the Saracens, who, like Herod, was presented in early stage plays
as a roaring tyrant.   16. from: contrary to.   18–19. very . . . pressure: an exact reproduction of
the age.   form: shape.   pressure: imprint (of a seal).   21. the . . . one: i.e., the judicious
spectator.   22. there . . . players: An attack on Edward Alleyn, a famous actor of Shakespeare's
time.   26. journeymen: hired workmen, not masters of the trade.

FIRST PLAYER.   I hope we have reformed that indifferently° with us, sir.

HAMLET.   Oh, reform it altogether. And let those that play your clowns° speak no more than is set down for them. For there be of them that will themselves laugh, to set on some quantity of barren spectators to laugh too, though in the meantime some necessary question of the play be then to be considered. That's villainous, and shows a most pitiful° ambition in the fool that uses it. Go, make you ready. (*Exeunt* PLAYERS. *Enter* POLONIUS, ROSENCRANTZ, *and* GUILDENSTERN.) How now, my lord! Will the King hear this piece of work?

POLONIUS.   And the Queen too, and that presently.

HAMLET.   Bid the players make haste. (*Exit* POLONIUS.) Will you two help to hasten them?   40

ROSENCRANTZ & GUILDENSTERN.   We will, my lord.

(*Exeunt* ROSENCRANTZ *and* GUILDENSTERN.)

HAMLET.   What ho! Horatio!

(*Enter* HORATIO.)

HORATIO.   Here, sweet lord, at your service.

HAMLET.   Horatio, thou art e'en as just a man
As e'er my conversation coped° withal.   45

HORATIO.   Oh, my dear lord——

HAMLET.   Nay, do not think I flatter,
For what advancement° may I hope from thee,
That no revénue hast but thy good spirits
To feed and clothe thee? Why should the poor be flattered?
No, let the candied° tongue lick absurd pomp   50
And crook the pregnant hinges of the knee
Where thrift may follow fawning.° Dost thou hear?
Since my dear soul was mistress of her choice
And could of men distinguish, her election
Hath sealed° thee for herself. For thou hast been   55
As one in suffering all that suffers nothing,
A man that fortune's buffets and rewards
Hast ta'en with equal thanks. And blest are those
Whose blood and judgment are so well commingled
That they are not a pipe° for fortune's finger   60
To sound what stop she please. Give me that man
That is not passion's slave, and I will wear him
In my heart's core—ay, in my heart of heart,
As I do thee. Something too much of this.
There is a play tonight before the King.   65

---

28. indifferently: moderately. **30. those . . . clowns:** A hit at Will Kempe, the former clown of Shakespeare's company. **34. pitiful:** contemptible. **45. coped:** met. **47. advancement:** promotion. **50. candied:** sugared over with hypocrisy. **51–52. crook . . . fawning:** bend the ready knees whenever gain will follow flattery. **55. sealed:** set a mark on. **60. pipe:** an instrument that varies its notes.

One scene of it comes near the circumstance
Which I have told thee of my father's death.
I prithee when thou seest that act afoot,
Even with the very comment° of thy soul
Observe my uncle. If his occulted° guilt   70
Do not itself unkennel° in one speech
It is a damnèd ghost° that we have seen
And my imaginations are as foul
As Vulcan's stithy.° Give him heedful note,°
For I mine eyes will rivet to his face,   75
And after we will both our judgments join
In censure of his seeming.°
HORATIO.   Well, my lord.
If he steal aught the whilst this play is playing,
And 'scape detecting, I will pay the theft.
HAMLET.   They are coming to the play. I must be idle°   80
Get you a place.

(*Danish march. A flourish. Enter* KING, QUEEN, POLONIUS, OPHELIA,
ROSENCRANTZ, GUILDENSTERN, *and other* LORDS *attendant, with the* GUARD
carrying torches.)

KING.   How fares our cousin Hamlet?
HAMLET.   Excellent, i' faith, of the chameleon's dish. I eat the air,
promise-crammed. You cannot feed capons so.°
KING.   I have nothing with this answer,° Hamlet. These words are not
mine.
HAMLET.   No, nor mine now.° (*To* POLONIUS) My lord, you played once i'
the university, you say?
POLONIUS.   That did I, my lord, and was accounted a good actor.
HAMLET.   What did you enact?   90
POLONIUS.   I did enact Julius Caesar. I was killed i' the Capitol. Brutus
killed me.
HAMLET.   It was a brute part of him to kill so capital a calf there. Be the
players ready?
ROSENCRANTZ.   Aye, my lord, they stay upon your patience.°   95
QUEEN.   Come hither, my dear Hamlet, sit by me.
HAMLET.   No, good Mother, here's metal more attractive.
POLONIUS (*To the* KING).   Oh ho! Do you mark that?
HAMLET.   Lady, shall I lie in your lap?

---

69. comment: close observation.   **70. occulted:** concealed.   **71. unkennel:** come to light; lit.,
force a fox from his hole.   **72. damned ghost:** See II.ii.550.   **74. Vulcan:** the blacksmith god.
stithy: smithy.   **heedful note:** careful observation.   **77. censure . . . seeming:** judgment on his
looks.   **80. be idle:** seem crazy.   **83–84. Excellent . . . so:** Hamlet takes "fare" literally as "what
food are you eating." The chameleon was supposed to feed on air.   **promise-crammed:** stuffed,
like a fattened chicken (*capon*)—but with empty promises.   **85. I . . . answer:** I cannot make any
sense of your answer.   **87. nor . . . now:** i.e., once words have left the lips they cease to belong to
the speaker.   **95. stay . . . patience:** wait for you to be ready.

(Lying down at OPHELIA'S *feet)*

OPHELIA. No, my lord. 100
HAMLET. I mean, my head upon your lap?
OPHELIA. Aye, my lord.
HAMLET. Do you think I meant country matters?°
OPHELIA. I think nothing, my lord.
HAMLET. That's a fair thought to lie between maids' legs. 105
OPHELIA. What is, my lord?
HAMLET. Nothing.
OPHELIA. You are merry, my lord.
HAMLET. Who, I?
OPHELIA. Aye, my lord. 110
HAMLET. Oh God, your only jig-maker.° What should a man do but be merry? For look you how cheerfully my mother looks, and my father died within 's two hours.
OPHELIA. Nay, 'tis twice two months, my lord. 114
HAMLET. So long? Nay, then, let the Devil wear black, for I'll have a suit of sables.° Oh heavens! Die two months ago, and not forgotten yet? Then there's hope a great man's memory may outlive his life half a year. But, by 'r Lady, he must build churches then, or else shall he suffer not thinking on, with the hobbyhorse,° whose epitaph is "For, oh, for oh, the hobbyhorse is forgot." 120

(Hautboys° play. The dumb show enters.° Enter a KING *and a* QUEEN *very lovingly, the* QUEEN *embracing him and he her. She kneels, and makes show of protestation unto him. He takes her up, and declines his head upon her neck, lays him down upon a bank of flowers. She, seeing him asleep, leaves him. Anon comes in a fellow, takes off his crown, kisses it, and pours poison in the* KING'S *ears, and exit. The* QUEEN *returns, finds the* KING *dead, and makes passionate action. The Poisoner, with some two or three Mutes, comes in again, seeming to lament with her. The dead body is carried away. The Poisoner woos the* QUEEN *with gifts. She seems loath and unwilling awhile, but in the end accepts his love. Exeunt.)*

OPHELIA. What means this, my lord?
HAMLET. Marry, this is miching mallecho.° It means mischief.
OPHELIA. Belike this show imports the argument° of the play.

(Enter PROLOGUE.*)*

---

103. **country matters:** something indecent. 111. **jig-maker:** composer of jigs. 115–16. **suit of sables:** a quibble on "sable," black, and "sable," gown trimmmed with sable fur, worn by wealthy gentlemen. 119. **hobbyhorse:** imitation horse worn by performers in a morris dance, an amusement much disapproved of by the godly. 120. **s. d., Hautboys:** oboes. **The dumb show enters:** Critics have been disturbed because this dumb show cannot be exactly paralleled in any other Elizabethan play, and because the King is apparently not disturbed by it. Shakespeare's intention, however, in presenting a play within a play is to produce something stagy and artificial compared with the play proper. Moreover, as Hamlet has already complained, dumb shows were often inexplicable. 122. **miching mallecho:** slinking mischief. 123. **argument:** plot. She too is puzzled by the dumb show.

HAMLET.   We shall know by this fellow. The players cannot keep counsel,
they'll tell all.   125
OPHELIA.   Will he tell us what this show meant?
HAMLET.   Aye, or any show that you'll show him. Be not you ashamed to
show, he'll not shame to tell you what it means.
OPHELIA.   You are naught,° you are naught. I'll mark the play.
PROLOGUE.   For us, and for our tragedy,   130
                              Here stooping to your clemency,
                              We beg your hearing patiently.
HAMLET.   Is this a prologue, or the posy of a ring?°
OPHELIA.   'Tis brief, my lord.
HAMLET.   As woman's love.   135

(Enter two PLAYERS, KING *and* QUEEN.*)*

PLAYER KING.   Full° thirty times hath Phoebus' cart° gone round
Neptune's'° salt wash and Tellus'° orbèd ground,
And thirty dozen moons with borrowed sheen°
About the world have times twelve thirties been,
Since love our hearts and Hymen° did our hands   140
Unite commutual° in most sacred bands.
PLAYER QUEEN.   So many journeys may the sun and moon
Make us again count o'er ere love be done!
But, woe is me, you are so sick of late,
So far from cheer and from your former state,   145
That I distrust° you. Yet, though I distrust,
Discomfort you, my lord, it nothing must.
For women's fear and love holds quantity°
In neither aught or in extremity.°
Now what my love is, proof hath made you know,   150
And as my love is sized, my fear is so.
Where love is great, the littlest doubts are fear,
Where little fears grow great, great love grows there.
PLAYER KING.   Faith, I must leave thee,° love, and shortly too,
My operant powers° their functions leave to do.   155
And thou shalt live in this fair world behind,
Honored, beloved, and haply one as kind
For husband shalt thou——
PLAYER QUEEN.   Oh, confound the rest!
Such love must needs be treason in my breast.   160
In second husband let me be accurst!
None wed the second but who killed the first.

---

129. **naught:** i.e., disgusting.   133. **posy . . . ring:** It was a pretty custom to inscribe rings with
little mottoes or messages, which were necessarily brief.   136–210. **Full . . . twain:** The play is
deliberately written in crude rhyming verse, full of ridiculous and bombastic phrases.
136. **Phoebus' cart:** the chariot of the sun.   137. **Neptune:** the sea god.   **Tellus:** the earth
goddess.   138. **borrowed sheen:** light borrowed from the sun.   140. **Hymen:** god of marriage   141. **commutual:** mutually.   146. **distrust:** am anxious about.   148. **quantity:**
proportion.   149. **In . . . extremity:** either nothing or too much.   154. **leave thee:** i.e., die.
155. **operant powers:** bodily strength.

HAMLET (*Aside*).   Wormwood,° wormwood.

PLAYER QUEEN.   The instances° that second marriage move
Are base respects of thrift,° but none of love.   165
A second time I kill my husband dead
When second husband kisses me in bed.

PLAYER KING.   I do believe you think what now you speak,
But what we do determine oft we break.
Purpose is but the slave to memory.   170
Of violent birth but poor validity,
Which now, like fruit unripe, sticks on the tree
But fall unshaken when they mellow be.
Most necessary 'tis that we forget
To pay ourselves what to ourselves is debt.   175
What to ourselves in passion we propose,
The passion ending, doth the purpose lose.
The violence of either grief or joy
Their own enactures° with themselves destroy.
Where joy most revels, grief doth most lament,   180
Grief joys, joy grieves, on slender accident.
This world is not for aye,° nor 'tis not strangé
That even our loves should with our fortunes change,
For 'tis a question left us yet to prove
Whether love lead fortune or else fortune love.   185
The great man down, you mark his favorite flies,
The poor advanced makes friends of enemies.
And hitherto doth love on fortune tend,
For who not needs shall never lack a friend,
And who in want a hollow friend doth try   190
Directly seasons° him his enemy.
But, orderly to end where I begun,
Our wills and fates do so contráry run
That our devices still are overthrown,
Our thoughts are ours, their ends none of our own.   195
So think thou wilt no second husband wed,
But die thy thoughts when thy first lord is dead.

PLAYER QUEEN.   Nor earth to me give food nor Heaven light!
Sport and repose lock from me day and night!
To desperation turn my trust and hope!   200
An anchor's° cheer in prison be my scope!
Each opposite that blanks° the face of joy
Meet what I would have well and it destroy!
Both here and hence pursue me lasting strife
If, once a widow, ever I be wife!   205

HAMLET.   If she should break it now!

---

163. **Wormwood:** bitterness.   164. **instances:** arguments.   165. **respects of thrift:** considerations of gain.   179. **enactures:** performances.   182. **aye:** ever.   191. **seasons:** ripens into.   201. **anchor:** anchorite, hermit.   202. **blanks:** makes pale.

PLAYER KING.   'Tis deeply sworn. Sweet, leave me here a while.
My spirits grow dull, and fain I would beguile
The tedious day with sleep.   (*Sleeps.*)
PLAYER QUEEN.   Sleep rock thy brain,
And never come mischance between us twain   210
(*Exit.*)
HAMLET.   Madam, how like you this play?
QUEEN.   The lady doth protest too much, methinks.
HAMLET.   Oh, but she'll keep her word.
KING.   Have you heard the argument?° Is there no offense in 't?
HAMLET.   No, no, they do but jest, poison in jest—no offense i' the
world.
KING.   What do you call the play?   217
HAMLET.   *The Mousetrap.*° Marry, how? Tropically.° This play is the image
of a murder done in Vienna. Gonzago is the Duke's name, his wife,
Baptista. You shall see anon. 'Tis a knavish piece of work, but what o'
that? Your Majesty, and we that have free° souls, it touches us not. Let the
galled jade wince, our withers are unwrung.° (*Enter* LUCIANUS.) This is
one Lucianus, nephew to the King.
OPHELIA.   You are as good as a chorus,° my lord.   224
HAMLET.   I could interpret between you and your love, if I could see the
puppets dallying.°
OPHELIA.   You are keen, my lord, you are keen.
HAMLET.   It would cost you a groaning to take off my edge.
OPHELIA.   Still better, and worse.   229
HAMLET.   So you must take your husbands.° Begin, murderer. Pox, leave
thy damnable faces and begin. Come, the croaking raven doth bellow for
revenge.
LUCIANUS.   Thoughts black, hands apt, drugs fit, and time agreeing,
Confederate season, else no creature° seeing,
Thou mixture rank of midnight weeds collected,   235
With Hecate's ban° thrice blasted, thrice infected,
Thy natural magic and dire property°
On wholesome life usurp immediately.

(*Pours the poison into the sleeper's ear.*)

HAMLET.   He poisons him i' the garden for his estate.° His name's

214. **argument:** plot. When performances were given at Court it was sometimes customary to provide a written or printed synopsis of the story for the distinguished spectators.   218. **Mousetrap:** The phrase was used of a device to entice a person to his own destruction (OED). **Tropically:** figuratively, with a pun on "trap."   221. **free:** innocent.   222. **galled . . . unwrung:** let a nag with a sore back flinch when the saddle is put on; our shoulders (being ungalled) feel no pain.   224. **chorus:** the chorus sometimes introduced the characters and commented on what was to follow.   226. **puppets dallying:** Elizabethan puppets were crude marionettes, popular at fairs. While the figures were put through their motions, the puppet master explained what was happening.   230. **So . . . husbands:** i.e., as the marriage service expresses it, "for better, for worse."   234. **confederate . . . creature:** the opportunity conspiring with me, no other creature.   236. **Hecate's ban:** the curse of Hecate, goddess of witchcraft.   237. **property:** nature.   239. **estate:** kingdom.

Gonzago. The story is extant, and written in very choice Italian. You shall
see anon how the murderer gets the love of Gonzago's wife.

OPHELIA. The King rises. 242
HAMLET. What, frighted with false fire!°
QUEEN. How fares my lord?
POLONIUS. Give o'er the play. 245
KING. Give me some light. Away!
POLONIUS. Lights, lights, lights!

(Exeunt all but HAMLET *and* HORATIO.*)*

HAMLET. "Why, let the stricken deer go weep,
   The hart ungallèd play,
For some must watch while some must sleep. 250
   Thus runs the world away."
Would not this, sir, and a forest of feathers°—if the rest of my fortunes
turn Turk° with me—with two Provincial roses° on my razed° shoes, get
me a fellowship° in a cry° of players, sir?
HORATIO. Half a share. 255
HAMLET. A whole one, I.
"For thou dost know, O Damon° dear,
   This realm dismantled° was
Of Jove himself, and now reigns here
   A very, very—pajock."° 260
HORATIO. You might have rhymed.
HAMLET. O good Horatio, I'll take the ghost's word for a thousand pound.
Didst perceive?
HORATIO. Very well, my lord.
HAMLET. Upon the talk of the poisoning? 265
HORATIO. I did very well note him.
HAMLET. Ah, ha! Come, some music! Come, the recorders!°
"For if the King like not the comedy,
Why then, belike, he likes it not, perdy."°
Come, some music! 270

(Re-enter ROSENCRANTZ *and* GUILDENSTERN.*)*

GUILDENSTERN. Good my lord, vouchsafe me a word with you.
HAMLET. Sir, a whole history.
GUILDENSTERN. The King, sir——
HAMLET. Aye, sir, what of him?
GUILDENSTERN. Is in his retirement marvelous distempered.° 275
HAMLET. With drink, sir?

---

243. **false fire:** a mere show. 252. **forest of feathers:** set of plumes, much worn by play-ers. 253. **turn Turk:** turn heathen, and treat me cruelly. **Provincial roses:** rosettes, worn on the shoes. **razed:** slashed, ornamented with cuts. 254. **fellowship:** partnership. **cry:** pack. 257. **Damon:** Damon and Pythias were types of perfect friends. 258. **dismantled:** robbed. 260. **pajock:** peacock, a strutting, lecherous bird. These verses, and the lines above, may have come from some ballad, otherwise lost. 267. **recorders:** wooden pipes. 269. **perdy:** by God. 275. **distempered:** disturbed; but Hamlet takes the word in its other sense of "drunk."

GUILDENSTERN.   No, my lord, rather with choler.°

HAMLET.   Your wisdom should show itself more richer to signify this to the doctor, for for me to put him to his purgation° would perhaps plunge him into far more choler.   280

GUILDENSTERN.   Good my lord, put your discourse into some frame,° and start not so wildly from my affair.

HAMLET.   I am tame, sir. Pronounce.

GUILDENSTERN.   The Queen your mother, in most great affliction of spirit, hath sent me to you.   285

HAMLET.   You are welcome.

GUILDENSTERN.   Nay, good my lord, this courtesy is not of the right breed. If it shall please you to make me a wholesome answer, I will do your mother's commandment. If not, your pardon and my return shall be the end of my business.   290

HAMLET.   Sir, I cannot.

GUILDENSTERN.   What, my lord?

HAMLET.   Make you a wholesome answer, my wit's diseased. But, sir, such answer as I can make you shall command, or rather, as you say, my mother. Therefore no more, but to the matter. My mother, you say——   296

ROSENCRANTZ.   Then thus she says. Your behavior hath struck her into amazement and admiration.°

HAMLET.   Oh, wonderful son that can so astonish a mother! But is there no sequel at the heels of this mother's admiration? Impart.   300

ROSENCRANTZ.   She desires to speak with you in her closet ere you go to bed.

HAMLET.   We shall obey, were she ten times our mother. Have you any further trade with us?

ROSENCRANTZ.   My lord, you once did love me.   305

HAMLET.   So I do still, by these pickers and stealers.°

ROSENCRANTZ.   Good my lord, what is your cause of distemper? You do surely bar the door upon your own liberty if you deny your griefs° to your friend.

HAMLET.   Sir, I lack advancement.°   310

ROSENCRANTZ.   How can that be when you have the voice of the King himself for your succession in Denmark?

HAMLET.   Aye, sir, but "While the grass grows"°—the proverb is something musty. (*Re-enter* PLAYERS *with recorders.*) Oh, the recorders! Let me see one. To withdraw° with you——why do you go about to recover the wind° of me, as if you would drive me into a toil?°   316

---

277. **choler:** anger, which Hamlet again pretends to understand as meaning "biliousness." 279. **put . . . purgation:** "give him a dose of salts." 281. **frame:** shape; i.e., "please talk sense." 298. **admiration:** wonder. 306. **pickers . . . stealers:** i.e., hands—an echo from the Christian's duty in the catechism to keep his hands "from picking and stealing." 308. **deny . . . griefs:** refuse to tell your troubles. 310. **advancement:** promotion. Hamlet harks back to his previous interview with Rosencrantz and Guildenstern. See II.ii.239. 313. **While . . . grows:** the proverb ends "the steed starves." 315. **withdraw:** go aside. Hamlet leads Guildenstern to one side of the stage. 315–16. **recover . . . wind:** a hunting metaphor; approach me with the wind against you. **toil:** net.

GUILDENSTERN.   O my lord, if my duty be too bold, my love is too un-
mannerly.°
HAMLET.   I do not well understand that. Will you play upon this pipe?
GUILDENSTERN.   My lord, I cannot.   320
HAMLET.   I pray you.
GUILDENSTERN.   Believe me, I cannot.
HAMLET.   I do beseech you.
GUILDENSTERN.   I know no touch of it, my lord.
HAMLET.   It is as easy as lying. Govern these ventages° with your fingers and
thumb, give it breath with your mouth, and it will discourse most elo-
quent music. Look you, these are the stops.   327
GUILDENSTERN.   But these cannot I command to any utterance of harmony, I have not the skill.
HAMLET.   Why, look you now, how unworthy a thing you make of me!
You would play upon me, you would seem to know my stops, you would
pluck out the heart of my mystery, you would sound me from my lowest
note to the top of my compass—and there is much music, excellent
voice, in this little organ—yet cannot you make it speak. 'Sblood, do you
think I am easier to be played on than a pipe? Call me what instrument
you will, though you can fret° me, you cannot play upon me. (*Re-enter*
POLONIUS.) God bless you, sir!   337
POLONIUS.   My lord, the Queen would speak with you, and presently.
HAMLET.   Do you see yonder cloud that's almost in shape of a camel?
POLONIUS.   By the mass, and 'tis like a camel indeed.
HAMLET.   Methinks it is like a weasel.
POLONIUS.   It is backed like a weasel.
HAMLET.   Or like a whale?
POLONIUS.   Very like a whale.
HAMLET.   Then I will come to my mother by and by. They fool me to the
top of my bent.° I will come by and by.   346
POLONIUS.   I will say so.   (*Exit* POLONIUS.)
HAMLET.   "By and by" is easily said. Leave me, friends.

(*Exeunt all but* HAMLET.)

'Tis now the very witching time° of night,
When churchyards yawn and Hell itself breathes out   350
Contagion° to this world. Now could I drink hot blood,
And do such bitter business as the day
Would quake to look on. Soft! Now to my mother.
O heart, lose not thy nature, let not ever
The soul of Nero° enter this firm bosom.   355

317–18. if . . . unmannerly: if I exceed my duty by asking these questions, then my affection for
you shows lack of manners; i.e., forgive me if I have been impertinent.   **325. ventages:** holes,
stops.   **336. fret:** annoy, with a pun on the frets or bars on stringed instruments by which the
fingering is regulated.   **346. top . . . bent:** see II.ii.30,n.   **349. witching time:** when witches
perform their foul rites.   **351. Contagion:** infection.   **355. Nero:** Nero killed his own mother.
Hamlet is afraid that in the interview to come he will lose all self-control.

Let me be cruel, not unnatural.
I will speak daggers to her, but use none.
My tongue and soul in this be hypocrites,
How in my words soever she be shent,°
To give them seals° never, my soul, consent!   360

(Exit.)

SCENE III. *A room in the castle.*

(Enter KING, ROSENCRANTZ, *and* GUILDENSTERN.*)*

KING.   I like him not, nor stands it safe with us
To let his madness range.° Therefore prepare you.
I your commission will forthwith dispatch,
And he to England shall along with you.
The terms of our estate° may not endure   5
Hazard so near us as doth hourly grow
Out of his lunacies.
GUILDENSTERN.   We will ourselves provide.°
Most holy and religious fear° it is
To keep those many many bodies safe
That live and feed upon your Majesty.   10
ROSENCRANTZ.   The single and peculiar° life is bound
With all the strength and armor of the mind
To keep itself from noyance,° but much more
That spirit upon whose weal° depends and rests
The lives of many. The cease of majesty°   15
Dies not alone, but like a gulf° doth draw
What's near it with it. It is a massy° wheel
Fixed on the summit of the highest mount,
To whose huge spokes ten thousand lesser things
Are mortised° and adjoined; which, when it falls,   20
Each small annexment, petty consequence,°
Attends° the boisterous ruin. Never alone
Did the King sigh but with a general groan.
KING.   Arm you, I pray you, to this speedy voyage,
For we will fetters put upon this fear,   25
Which now goes too free-footed.
ROSENCRANTZ & GUILDENSTERN.   We will haste us.

(Exeunt ROSENCRANTZ *and* GUILDENSTERN.*)*

(Enter POLONIUS.*)*

---

359. **shent:** rebuked.   360. **give . . . seals:** ratify words by actions.
  Sc. iii: 2. **range:** roam freely.   5. **terms . . . estate:** i.e., one in my position.   7. **ourselves provide:** make our preparations.   8. **fear:** anxiety.   11. **peculiar:** individual.   13. **noyance:** injury.   14. **weal:** welfare.   15. **cease of majesty:** death of a king.   16. **gulf:** whirlpool.   17. **massy:** massive.   20. **mortised:** firmly fastened.   21. **annexment . . . consequence:** attachment, smallest thing connected with it.   22. **Attends:** waits on, is involved in.

POLONIUS.   My lord, he's going to his mother's closet.
 Behind the arras I'll convey myself
 To hear the process.° I'll warrant she'll tax° him home.
 And, as you said,° and wisely was it said,   30
 'Tis meet that some more audience than a mother,
 Since nature makes them partial, should o'erhear
 The speech, of vantage.° Fare you well, my liege.
 I'll call upon you ere you go to bed
 And tell you what I know.
KING. Thanks, dear my lord.   (*Exit* POLONIUS.) 35
 Oh, my offense is rank,° it smells to Heaven.
 It hath the primal eldest curse° upon 't,
 A brother's murder. Pray can I not,
 Though inclination be as sharp as will.°
 My stronger guilt defeats my strong intent,   40
 And like a man to double business bound,
 I stand in pause where I shall first begin,
 And both neglect. What if this cursèd hand
 Were thicker than itself with brother's blood,
 Is there not rain enough in the sweet heavens   45
 To wash it white as snow? Whereto serves mercy
 But to confront the visage of offense?°
 And what's in prayer but this twofold force,
 To be forestalled° ere we come to fall
 Or pardoned being down? Then I'll look up,   50
 My fault is past. But oh, what form of prayer
 Can serve my turn? "Forgive me my foul murder"?
 That cannot be, since I am still possessed
 Of those effects° for which I did the murder—
 My crown, mine own ambition, and my Queen.   55
 May one be pardoned and retain the offense?°
 In the corrupted currents° of this world
 Offense's gilded hand may shove by justice,
 And oft 'tis seen the wicked prize° itself
 Buys out the law. But 'tis not so above.   60
 There is no shuffling, there the action lies
 In his true nature,° and we ourselves compelled
 Even to the teeth and forehead° of our faults
 To give in evidence. What then? What rests?
 Try what repentance can. What can it not?   65
 Yet what can it when one cannot repent?

---

29. process: proceeding. **tax:** censure. **30. as . . . said:** Actually Polonius himself had said it
(III.i.174–78). **33. of vantage:** from a place of vantage: i.e., concealment. **36. rank:**
foul. **37. primal . . . curse:** the curse laid upon Cain, the first murderer, who also slew his
brother. **39. will:** desire. **47. confront . . . offense:** look crime in the face. **49. forestalled:**
prevented. **54. effects:** advantages. **56. offense:** i.e., that for which he has offended.
57. currents: courses, ways. **59. wicked prize:** the proceeds of the crime. **61–62. there . . .
nature:** in Heaven the case is tried on its own merits. **63. teeth . . . forehead:** i.e., face to face.

Oh, wretched state! Oh, bosom black as death!
Oh, limèd° soul, that struggling to be free
Art more engaged!° Help, angels! Make assay!°
Bow, stubborn knees, and heart with strings of steel,   70
Be soft as sinews of the newborn babe!
All may be well.   (*Retires and kneels.*)

(*Enter* HAMLET.)

HAMLET.   Now might I do it pat, now he is praying,
And now I'll do 't. And so he goes to Heaven,
And so am I revenged. That would be scanned: 75
A villain kills my father, and for that
I, his sole son, do this same villain send
To Heaven.
Oh, this is hire and salary,° not revenge.
He took my father grossly,° full of bread,   80
With all his crimes broad blown, as flush° as May,
And how his audit° stands who knows save Heaven?
But in our circumstance and course of thought,°
'Tis heavy with him. And am I then revenged,
To take him in the purging of his soul,   85
When he is fit and seasoned,° for his passage?
No.
Up, sword, and know thou a more horrid hent.°
When he is drunk asleep, or in his rage,
Or in the incestuous pleasure of his bed—   90
At gaming, swearing, or about some act
That has no relish of salvation in 't—
Then trip him, that his heels may kick at Heaven
And that his soul may be as damned and black
As Hell, whereto it goes. My mother stays.   95
This physic but prolongs thy sickly days.   (*Exit.*)
KING (*Rising*).   My words fly up, my thoughts remain below.
Words without thoughts never to Heaven go.   (*Exit.*)

SCENE IV. *The* QUEEN'S *closet.*

(*Enter* QUEEN *and* POLONIUS.)

POLONIUS.   He will come straight. Look you lay home to° him.
Tell him his pranks have been too broad° to bear with,
And that your grace hath screened and stood between

---

68. limed: caught as in birdlime.   **69. engaged:** stuck fast.   **assay:** attempt.   **79. hire . . .
salary:** i.e., a kind action deserving pay.   **80. grossly:** i.e., when he was in a state of sin. See
I.v.74–80.   **81. broad . . . flush:** in full blossom, as luxuriant.   **82. audit:** account.
83. circumstance . . . thought: as it appears to my mind.   **86. seasoned:** ripe.   **88. hent:**
opportunity.
    Sc. iv: **1. lay . . . to:** be strict with.   **2. broad:** unrestrained. Polonius is thinking of the
obvious insolence of the remarks about second marriage in the play scene.

Much heat and him. I'll sconce me° even here.
Pray you, be round with him.   5
HAMLET (*Within*).   Mother, Mother, Mother!
QUEEN.   I'll warrant you,
Fear me not. Withdraw, I hear him coming.
(POLONIUS *hides behind the arras.*)
(*Enter* HAMLET.)
HAMLET.   Now, Mother, what's the matter?
QUEEN.   Hamlet, thou hast thy father much offended.
HAMLET.   Mother, you have my father much offended.   10
QUEEN.   Come, come, you answer with an idle° tongue.
HAMLET.   Go, go, you question with a wicked tongue.
QUEEN.   Why, how now, Hamlet!
HAMLET.   What's the matter now?
QUEEN.   Have you forgot me?
HAMLET.   No, by the rood,° not so.
You are the Queen, your husband's brother's wife,   15
And—would it were not so!—you are my mother.
QUEEN.   Nay, then, I'll set those to you that can speak.
HAMLET.   Come, come, and sit you down. You shall not budge,
You go not till I set you up a glass°
Where you may see the inmost part of you.   20
QUEEN.   What wilt thou do? Thou wilt not murder me?
Help, help, ho!
POLONIUS (*Behind*).   What ho! Help, help, help!
HAMLET (*Drawing*).   How now! A rat? Dead, for a ducat, dead! (*Makes a
pass through the arras.*)
POLONIOUS (*Behind*).   Oh, I am slain!   (*Falls and dies.*)
QUEEN.   Oh me, what hast thou done?   25
HAMLET.   Nay, I know not. Is it the King?
QUEEN.   Oh, what a rash and bloody deed is this!
HAMLET.   A bloody deed! Almost as bad, good Mother,
As kill a king and marry with his brother.
QUEEN.   As kill a king!
HAMLET.   Aye, lady, 'twas my word.   30
(*Lifts up the arras and discovers* POLONIUS.)
Thou wretched, rash, intruding fool, farewell!
I took thee for thy better. Take thy fortune.
Thou find'st to be too busy is some danger.
Leave wringing of your hands. Peace! Sit you down,
And let me wring your heart. For so I shall   35
If it be made of penetrable stuff,
If damnèd custom have not brassed° it so
That it be proof and bulwark against sense.

4. sconce me: hide myself.   **11. idle**: foolish.   **14. rood**: crucifix.   **19. glass**: looking-glass.
37. brassed: made brazen; i.e., impenetrable.

QUEEN.   What have I done that thou darest wag thy tongue
 In noise so rude against me?
HAMLET.   Such an act   40
 That blurs the grace and blush of modesty,
 Calls virtue hypocrite, takes off the rose
 From the fair forehead of an innocent love,
 And sets a blister° there—makes marriage vows
 As false as dicers' oaths. Oh, such a deed   45
 As from the body of contraction° plucks
 The very soul, and sweet religion makes
 A rhapsody of words.° Heaven's face doth glow,
 Yea, this solidity and compound mass,°
 With tristful visage, as against the doom,°   50
 Is thought-sick at the act
QUEEN.   Aye me, what act
 That roars so loud and thunders in the index?°
HAMLET.   Look here upon this picture,° and on this,
 The counterfeit presentment° of two brothers.
 See what a grace was seated on this brow—   55
 Hyperion's curls, the front° of Jove himself,
 An eye like Mars, to threaten and command,
 A station° like the herald Mercury°
 New-lighted° on a heaven-kissing hill,
 A combination° and a form indeed   60
 Where every god did seem to set his seal°
 To give the world assurance of a man.
 This was your husband. Look you now what follows.
 Here is your husband, like a mildewed ear,
 Blasting his wholesome brother. Have you eyes?   65
 Could you on this fair mountain leave to feed
 And batten° on this moor? Ha! Have you eyes?
 You cannot call it love, for at your age
 The heyday° in the blood is tame, it's humble,
 And waits upon the judgment. And what judgment   70
 Would step from this to this? Sense° sure you have,
 Else could you not have motion.° But sure that sense
 Is apoplexed;° for madness would not err,

44. **sets a blister:** brands as a harlot.   46. **contraction:** the marriage contract.   48. **rhapsody of words:** string of meaningless words.   49. **solidity . . . mass:** i.e., solid earth.   50. **tristful . . . doom:** sorrowful face, as in anticipation of Doomsday.   52. **in . . . index:** i.e., if the beginning (*index*, i.e., table of contents) is so noisy, what will follow?   53. **picture:** Modern producers usually interpret the pictures as miniatures, Hamlet wearing one of his father, Gertrude one of Claudius. In the eighteenth century, wall portraits were used.   54. **counterfeit presentment:** portrait.   56. **front:** forehead.   58. **station:** figure; lit., standing. **Mercury:** messenger of the gods, and one of the most beautiful.   59. **New-lighted:** newly alighted.   60. **combination:** i.e., of physical qualities.   61. **set . . . seal:** guarantee as a perfect man.   67. **batten:** glut yourself.   69. **heyday:** excitement.   71. **Sense:** feeling.   72. **motion:** desire.   73. **apoplexed:** paralyzed.

Nor sense to ecstasy° was ne'er so thralled°
But it reserved some quantity of choice   75
To serve in such a difference.° What devil was 't
That thus hath cozened° you at hoodman-blind?°
Eyes without feeling, feeling without sight,
Ears without hands or eyes, smelling sans° all,
Or but a sickly part of one true sense   80
Could not so mope.°
Oh, shame! Where is thy blush? Rebellious° Hell.
If thou canst mutine° in a matron's bones,
To flaming youth let virtue be as wax
And melt in her own fire. Proclaim no shame   85
When the compulsive ardor° gives the charge,
Since frost itself as actively doth burn,
And reason panders° will.
QUEEN.   O Hamlet, speak no more.
Thou turn'st mine eyes into my very soul,
And there I see such black and grainèd° spots   90
As will not leave their tinct.°
HAMLET.   Nay, but to live
In the rank sweat of an enseamèd° bed,
Stewed in corruption, honeying and making love
Over the nasty sty——
QUEEN.   Oh, speak to me no more,
These words like daggers enter in my ears.   95
No more, sweet Hamlet!
HAMLET.   A murderer and a villain,
A slave that is not twentieth part the tithe°
Of your precedent° lord, a vice of kings,°
A cutpurse° of the empire and the rule,
That from a shelf the precious diadem stole   100
And put it in his pocket!
QUEEN.   No more!
HAMLET.   A king of shreds and patches——
(*Enter* GHOST.) Save me, and hover o'er me with your wings,
You heavenly guards! What would your gracious figure?
QUEEN.   Alas, he's mad!

---

74. ecstasy: excitement, passion. See II.i.102. **thralled:** enslaved. **76. serve . . . difference:** to enable you to see the difference between your former and your present husband. **77. cozened:** cheated. **hoodman-blind:** blind-man's-buff. **79. sans:** without. **81. mope:** be dull. **82–88. Rebellious . . . will:** i.e., if the passion (*Hell*) of a woman of your age is uncontrollable (*rebellious*), youth can have no restraints; there is no shame in a young man's lust when the elderly are just as eager and their reason (which should control desire) encourages them. **83. mutine:** mutiny. **86. compulsive ardor:** compelling lust. **88. panders:** acts as go-between. **90. grained:** dyed in the grain. **91. tinct:** color. **92. enseamed:** greasy. **97. tithe:** tenth part. **98. precedent:** former. **vice of kings:** caricature of a king. **99. cutpurse:** thief.

HAMLET.   Do you not come your tardy son to chide
That, lapsed in time and passion, lets go by
The important acting of your dread command?°
Oh, say!
GHOST.   Do not forget. This visitation   110
Is but to whet thy almost blunted purpose.
But look, amazement on thy mother sits.
Oh, step between her and her fighting soul.
Conceit° in weakest bodies strongest works.
Speak to her, Hamlet.
HAMLET.   How is it with you, Lady?   115
QUEEN.   Alas, how is 't with you
That you do bend your eye on vacancy°
And with the incorporal° air do hold discourse?
Forth at your eyes your spirits wildly peep,
And as the sleeping soldiers in the alarm,   120
Your bedded° hairs, like life in excrements,°
Start up and stand an° end. O gentle son,
Upon the heat and flame of thy distemper°
Sprinkle cool patience. Whereon do you look?
HAMLET.   On him, on him! Look you how pale he glares   125
His form and cause conjoined,° preaching to stones,
Would make them capable.° Do not look upon me,
Lest with this piteous action you convert
My stern effects.° Then what I have to do
Will want true color—tears perchance for blood.   130
QUEEN.   To whom do you speak this?
HAMLET.   Do you see nothing there?
QUEEN.   Nothing at all, yet all that is I see.
HAMLET.   Nor did you nothing hear?
QUEEN.   No, nothing but ourselves
HAMLET.   Why, look you there! Look how it steals away!
My father, in his habit as he lived!   135
Look where he goes, even now, out at the portal!   (*Exit* GHOST.)
QUEEN.   This is the very coinage of your brain.
This bodiless creation ecstasy°
Is very cunning in.
HAMLET.   Ecstasy!
My pulse, as yours, doth temperately keep time,   140
And makes as healthful music. It is not madness

107–08. **That . . . command:** who has allowed time to pass and passion to cool, and neglects the
urgent duty of obeying your dread command.   114. **Conceit:** imagination.   117. **vacancy:**
empty space.   118. **incorporal:** bodiless.   121. **bedded:** evenly laid.   **excrements:** anything
that grows out of the body, such as hair or fingernails; here hair.   122. **an:** on.   123. **distemper:**
mental disturbance.   126. **form . . . conjoined:** his appearance and the reason for his appearance joined.   127. **capable:** i.e., of feeling.   128–29. **convert . . . effects:** change the stern
action which should follow.   138. **ecstasy:** madness.

That I have uttered. Bring me to the test
And I the matter will reword, which madness
Would gambol° from. Mother, for love of grace,
Lay not that flattering unction° to your soul,   145
That not your trespass but my madness speaks.
It will but skin and film the ulcerous place,
While rank corruption, mining° all within,
Infects unseen. Confess yourself to Heaven,
Repent what's past, avoid what is to come,   150
And do not spread the compost° on the weeds
To make them ranker. Forgive me this my virtue,
For in the fatness° of these pursy° times
Virtue itself of vice must pardon beg—
Yea, curb° and woo for leave to do him good,   155
QUEEN.   O Hamlet, thou hast cleft my heart in twain.
HAMLET.   Oh, throw away the worser part of it,
And live the purer with the other half.
Good night. But go not to my uncle's bed.
Assume a virtue if you have it not.   160
That° monster, custom, who all sense doth eat,
Of habits devil, is angel yet in this,
That to the use° of actions fair and good
He likewise gives a frock or livery
That aptly° is put on. Refrain tonight,   165
And that shall lend a kind of easiness
To the next abstinence, the next more easy.
For use almost can change the stamp° of nature,
And either the Devil,° or throw him out
With wondrous potency. Once more, good night.   170
And when you are desirous to be blest,
I'll blessing beg of you. For this same lord,
(Pointing to POLONIUS)
I do repent; but Heaven hath pleased it so,
To punish me with this, and this with me,
That I must be their scourge and minister.   175
I will bestow° him, and will answer well
The death I gave him. So again good night.
I must be cruel only to be kind.
Thus bad begins, and worse remains behind.
One word more, good lady.

---

144. gambol: start away. **145. unction:** healing ointment. **148. mining:** undermining. **151. compost:** manure. **153. fatness:** grossness. **pursy:** bloated. **155. curb:** bow low. **161–65. That . . . on:** i.e., custom (bad habits) like an evil monster destroys all sense of good and evil, but yet can become an angel (good habits) when it makes us perform good actions as mechanically as we put on our clothes. **163. use:** practice. **165. aptly:** readily. **168. stamp:** impression. **176. bestow:** get rid of.

QUEEN.   What shall I do?   180
HAMLET.   Not this, by no means, that I bid you do.
    Let the bloat° king tempt you again to bed,
    Pinch wanton° on your cheek, call you his mouse,
    And let him, for a pair of reechy° kisses
    Or paddling in your neck with his damned fingers,   185
    Make you to ravel° all this matter out,
    That I essentially am not in madness,
    But mad in craft. 'Twere good you let him know.
    For who that's but a Queen, fair, sober, wise,
    Would from a paddock,° from a bat, a gib,°   190
    Such dear concernings° hide? Who would do so?
    No, in despite° of sense and secrecy,
    Unpeg the basket on the house's top,
    Let the birds fly, and like the famous ape,°
    To try conclusions,° in the basket creep   195
    And break your own neck down.
QUEEN.   Be thou assured if words be made of breath
    And breath of life, I have no life to breathe
    What thou hast said to me.
HAMLET.   I must to England. You know that?
QUEEN.   Alack,   200
    I had forgot. 'Tis so concluded on.
HAMLET.   There's letters sealed, and my two schoolfellows,
    Whom I will trust as I will adders fanged,
    They bear the mandate.° They must sweep my way,
    And marshal me to knavery. Let it work,   205
    For 'tis the sport to have the enginer°
    Hoist with his own petar.° And 't shall go hard
    But I will delve one yard below their mines
    And blow them at the moon: Oh, 'tis most sweet
    When in one line two crafts° directly meet.   210
    This man shall set me packing.
    I'll lug the guts into the neighbor room.
    Mother, good night. Indeed this counselor
    Is now most still, most secret, and most grave
    Who was in life a foolish prating knave.   215
    Come, sir, to draw toward an end with you.
    Good night, Mother.
    (Exeunt severally,° HAMLET dragging in POLONIUS.)

182. **bloat:** bloated.   183. **wanton:** lewdly.   184. **reechy:** foul.   186. **ravel:** unravel, reveal.   190. **paddock:** toad.   **gib:** tomcat.   191. **dear concernings:** important matters. 192. **despite:** spite.   194. **famous ape:** The story is not known, but evidently told of an ape that let the birds out of their cage and, seeing them fly, crept into the cage himself and jumped out, breaking his own neck.   195. **try conclusions:** repeat the experiment.   204. **mandate:** command.   206. **enginer:** engineer.   207. **petar:** petard, land mine.   210. **crafts:** devices. 217. **s.d., Exeunt severally:** i.e., by separate exits.

ACT IV

SCENE I. A room in the castle.

(*Enter* KING, QUEEN, ROSENCRANTZ, *and* GUILDENSTERN.)

KING.　There's matter° in these sighs, these profound heaves,
You must translate. 'Tis fit we understand them.
Where is your son?
QUEEN.　Bestow this place° on us a little while.

(*Exeunt* ROSENCRANTZ *and* GUILDENSTERN.)

Ah, mine own lord, what have I seen tonight!　　　　　　　5
KING.　What, Gertrude? How does Hamlet?
QUEEN.　Mad as the sea and wind when both contend
Which is the mightier. In his lawless fit,
Behind the arras hearing something stir,
Whips out his rapier, cries "A rat, a rat!"　　　　　　　10
And in this brainish apprehension° kills
The unseen good old man.
KING.　　　　　　　　Oh, heavy deed!
It had been so with us had we been there.
His liberty is full of threats to all,
To you yourself, to us, to everyone.　　　　　　　15
Alas, how shall this bloody deed be answered?
It will be laid to us, whose providence°
Should have kept short,° restrained and out of haunt,°
This mad young man. But so much was our love
We would not understand what was most fit,　　　　　　　20
But, like the owner of a foul disease,
To keep it from divulging° let it feed
Even on the pith° of life. Where is he gone?
QUEEN.　To draw apart the body he hath killed,
O'er whom his very madness, like some ore　　　　　　　25
Among a mineral of metals base,
Shows itself pure. He weeps for what is done.
KING.　O Gertrude, come away!
The sun no sooner shall the mountains touch
But we will ship him hence. And this vile deed　　　　　　　30
We must, with all our majesty and skill,
Both countenance° and excuse. Ho, Guildenstern!

(*Re-enter* ROSENCRANTZ *and* GUILDENSTERN.)

Act IV. Sc. i: 1. matter: something serious. **4. Bestow . . . place:** give place, leave us. **11. brainish apprehension:** mad imagination. **17. providence:** foresight. **18. short:** confined. **out of haunt:** away from others. **22. divulging:** becoming known. **23. pith:** marrow. **32. countenance:** take responsibility for.

Friends both, go join you with some further aid.
Hamlet in madness hath Polonius slain,
And from his mother's closet hath he dragged him.   35
Go seek him out, speak fair, and bring the body
Into the chapel. I pray you, haste in this.

(Exeunt ROSENCRANTZ *and* GUILDENSTERN.*)*

Come, Gertrude, we'll call up our wisest friends,
And let them know both what we mean to do
And what's untimely done,°   40
Whose whisper o'er the world's diameter
As level as the cannon to his blank°
Transports his poisoned shot, may miss our name
And hit the woundless air. Oh, come away!
My soul is full of discord and dismay.   *(Exeunt.)*

SCENE II. Another room in the castle.

(Enter HAMLET.*)*

HAMLET.   Safely stowed.
ROSENCRANTZ & GUILDENSTERN *(Within)*.   Hamlet! Lord Hamlet!
HAMLET.   But soft, what noise? Who calls on Hamlet?
Oh, here they come.

(Enter ROSENCRANTZ *and* GUILDENSTERN.*)*

ROSENCRANTZ.   What have you done, my lord, with the dead body?   5
HAMLET.   Compounded it with dust, whereto 'tis kin.
ROSENCRANTZ.   Tell us where 'tis, that we may take it thence
And bear it to the chapel.
HAMLET.   Do not believe it.
ROSENCRANTZ.   Believe what?   10
HAMLET.   That I can keep your counsel and not mine own. Besides, to be
demanded of a sponge! What replication° should be made by the son of a
king?
ROSENCRANTZ.   Take you me for a sponge, my lord?   14
HAMLET.   Aye, sir, that soaks up the King's countenance,° his rewards, his
authorities. But such officers do the King best service in the end. He keeps
them, like an ape, in the corner of his jaw, first mouthed, to be last
swallowed. When he needs what you have gleaned, it is but squeezing
you and, sponge, you shall be dry again.
ROSENCRANTZ.   I understand you not, my lord.   20
HAMLET.   I am glad of it. A knavish speech sleeps in a foolish ear.°

---

40. done: A half-line has been omitted. Some editors fill the gap with "So, haply slander."
42. blank: target.
    Sc. ii: 12. replication: answer.   **15. countenance:** favor.   **21. A . . . ear:** a fool never
understands the point of a sinister speech.

ROSENCRANTZ.   My lord, you must tell us where the body is, and go with
    us to the King.
HAMLET.   The body is with the King, but the King is not with the body.°
    The King is a thing——   25
GUILDENSTERN.   A thing, my lord?
HAMLET.   Of nothing. Bring me to him. Hide fox, and all after.°

(Exeunt.)

SCENE III. *Another room in the castle.*

(Enter KING, *attended.)*

KING.   I have sent to seek him, and to find the body.
    How dangerous is it that this man goes loose!
    Yet must not we put the strong law on him.
    He's loved of the distracted° multitude,
    Who like not in their judgment but their eyes;°   5
    And where 'tis so, the offender's scourge° is weighed,
    But never the offense. To bear° all smooth and even,
    This sudden sending him away must seem
    Deliberate pause.° Diseases desperate grown
    By desperate appliance are relieved,   10
    Or not at all.
    (Enter ROSENCRANTZ.*)* How now! What hath befall'n?
ROSENCRANTZ.   Where the dead body is bestowed, my lord,
    We cannot get from him.
KING.   But where is he?
ROSENCRANTZ.   Without, my lord, guarded, to know your pleasure.
KING.   Bring him before us.   15
ROSENCRANTZ.   Ho, Guildenstern! Bring in my lord.

(Enter HAMLET *and* GUILDENSTERN.*)*

KING.   Now, Hamlet, where's Polonius?
HAMLET.   At supper.
KING.   At supper! Where?   19
HAMLET.   Not where he eats, but where he is eaten. A certain convocation
    of politic worms° are e'en at him. Your worm is your only emperor for
    diet. We fat all creatures else to fat us, and we fat ourselves for maggots.
    Your fat king and your lean beggar is but variable service,° two dishes, but
    to one table. That's the end.
KING.   Alas, alas!   25

---

24. The . . . body: Hamlet deliberately bewilders his companions.   **27. Hide . . . after:** a form of
the game of hide-and-seek. With these words Hamlet runs away from them.
    Sc. iii: 4. distracted: bewildered.   **5. like . . . eyes:** whose likings are swayed not by
judgment but by looks.   **6. scourge:** punishment.   **7. bear:** make.   **9. Deliberate pause:** the
result of careful planning.   **20–21. convocation . . . worms:** an assembly of political-minded
worms.   **23. variable service:** choice of alternatives.

HAMLET.   A man may fish with the worm that hath eat of a king, and eat of
the fish that hath fed of that worm.
KING.   What dost thou mean by this?
HAMLET.   Nothing but to show you how a king may go a progress° through
the guts of a beggar.
KING.   Where is Polonius?   30
HAMLET.   In Heaven—send thither to see. If your messenger find him not
there, seek him i' the other place yourself. But indeed if you find him not
within this month, you shall nose him as you go up the stairs into the
lobby.
KING *(To some* ATTENDANTS).   Go seek him there.   35
HAMLET.   He will stay till you come.

(*Exeunt* ATTENDANTS.)

KING.   Hamlet, this deed, for thine especial safety,
Which we do tender,° as we dearly grieve
For that which thou hast done, must send thee hence
With fiery quickness. Therefore prepare thyself.   40
The bark is ready and the wind at help,°
The associates tend,° and every thing is bent°
For England.
HAMLET.   For England?
KING.   Aye, Hamlet.
HAMLET.   Good.
KING.   So is it if thou knew'st our purposes.
HAMLET.   I see a cherub that sees them. But, come, for England! Farewell,
dear Mother.   46
KING.   Thy loving father, Hamlet.
HAMLET.   My mother. Father and mother is man and wife, man and wife is
one flesh, and so, my mother. Come, for England!   (*Exit.*)
KING.   Follow him at foot,° tempt° him with speed aboard.   50
Delay it not, I'll have him hence tonight.
Away! For everything is sealed and done
That else leans on the affair. Pray you make haste.

(*Exeunt* ROSENCRANTZ *and* GUILDENSTERN.)

And, England, if my love thou hold'st at aught—
As my great power thereof may give thee sense,   55
Since yet thy cicatrice° looks raw and red
After the Danish sword, and thy free awe°
Pays homage to us—thou mayst not coldly set
Our sovereign process,° which imports at full,

---

29. **go a progress**: make a state journey.   38. **tender**: regard highly.   41. **at help**: favorable.   42. **associates tend**: your companions are waiting.   **bent**: ready.   50. **at foot**: at his
heels.   **tempt**: entice.   56. **cicatrice**: scar. There is nothing in the play to explain this incident.   57. **free awe**: voluntary submission.   58–59. **coldly . . . process**: hesitate to carry out our
royal command.

By letters congruing° to that effect,   60
The present° death of Hamlet. Do it, England,
For like the hectic° in my blood he rages,
And thou must cure me. Till I know 'tis done,
Howe'er my haps,° my joys were ne'er begun.   (*Exit.*)

SCENE IV. *A plain in Denmark.*

(*Enter* FORTINBRAS, *a* CAPTAIN *and* SOLDIERS, *marching.*)

FORTINBRAS.   Go, Captain, from me greet the Danish King.
Tell him that by his license Fortinbras
Craves the conveyance of a promised march°
Over his kingdom. You know the rendezvous.
If that His Majesty would aught with us,   5
We shall express our duty in his eye,°
And let him know so.
CAPTAIN.   I will do 't, my lord.
FORTINBRAS.   Go softly on.

(*Exeunt* FORTINBRAS *and* SOLDIERS.)

(*Enter* HAMLET, ROSENCRANTZ, GUILDENSTERN, *and others.*)

HAMLET.   Good sir, whose powers° are these?
CAPTAIN.   They are of Norway, sir.   10
HAMLET.   How purposed, sir, I pray you?
CAPTAIN.   Against some part of Poland.
HAMLET.   Who commands them, sir?
CAPTAIN.   The nephew to old Norway, Fortinbras.
HAMLET.   Goes it against the main° of Poland, sir,   15
Or for some frontier?
CAPTAIN.   Truly to speak, and with no addition,°
We go to gain a little patch of ground
That hath in it no profit but the name.
To pay five ducats, five, I would not farm it,   20
Nor will it yield to Norway or the Pole
A ranker° rate should it be sold in fee.°
HAMLET.   Why, then the Polack never will defend it.
CAPTAIN.   Yes, it is already garrisoned.
HAMLET.   Two thousand souls and twenty thousand ducats   25
Will not debate the question of this straw.
This is the imposthume of° much wealth and peace,
That inward breaks, and shows no cause without
Why the man dies. I humbly thank you, sir.

60. **congruing:** agreeing. 61. **present:** immediate. 62. **hectic:** fever. 64. **Howe'er my haps:** whatever may happen to me.
Sc. iv: 3. **Craves . . . march:** asks for permission to transport his army as had already been promised. See II.ii.76–82. 6. **in . . . eye:** before his eyes; i.e., in person. 9. **powers:** forces. 15. **main:** mainland. 17. **addition:** exaggeration. 22. **ranker:** richer. **in fee:** with possession as freehold. 27. **imposthume of:** inward swelling caused by.

CAPTAIN.　God be wi' you, sir.		*(Exit.)*
ROSENCRANTZ.　　　　　Will 't please you go, my lord?		30
HAMLET.　I'll be with you straight. Go a little before.		

(Exeunt all but HAMLET.*)*

How all occasions do inform against° me
And spur my dull revenge! What is a man
If his chief good and market° of his time
Be but to sleep and feed? A beast, no more.　　　　　　35
Sure, He that made us with such large discourse,
Looking before and after,° gave us not
That capability and godlike reason
To fust° in us unused. Now whether it be
Bestial oblivion, or some craven scruple　　　　　　40
Of thinking too precisely on the event—
A thought which, quartered, hath but one part wisdom
And ever three parts coward—I do not know
Why yet I live to say "This thing's to do,"
Sith I have cause, and will, and strength, and means　　45
To do 't. Examples gross° as earth exhort me.
Witness this army, of such mass and charge,°
Led by a delicate and tender Prince
Whose spirit with divine ambition puffed
Makes mouths at the invisible event,°　　　　　　50
Exposing what is mortal and unsure
To all that fortune, death, and danger dare,
Even for an eggshell.° Rightly to be great
Is not to stir without great argument,
But greatly to find quarrel in a straw　　　　　　55
When honor's at the stake.° How stand I then,
That have a father killed, a mother stained,
Excitements of my reason and my blood,
And let all sleep while to my shame I see
The imminent death of twenty thousand men　　　　60
That for a fantasy and trick° of fame
Go to their graves like beds, fight for a plot
Whereon the numbers cannot try the cause,°
Which is not tomb enough and continent°
To hide the slain? Oh, from this time forth,　　　　65
My thoughts be bloody or be nothing worth!
(Exit.)

---

32. inform against: accuse.　**34. market:** profit.　**36–37. such . . . after:** intelligence that enables us to consider the future and the past.　**39. fust:** grow musty.　**46. gross:** large.　**47. charge:** expense.　**50. Makes . . . event:** mocks at the unseen risk.　**53. eggshell:** i.e., worthless trifle.　**53–56. Rightly . . . stake:** true greatness is a matter of fighting not for a mighty cause but for the merest trifle when honor is concerned.　**61. fantasy . . . trick:** illusion and whim.　**63. Whereon . . . cause:** a piece of ground so small that it would not hold the combatants.　**64. continent:** large enough to contain.

SCENE V. *Elsinore. A room in the castle.*

(Enter QUEEN, HORATIO, *and a* GENTLEMAN.*)*

QUEEN. I will not speak with her.
GENTLEMAN. She is importunate, indeed distract.°
Her mood will needs be pitied.
QUEEN. What would she have?
GENTLEMAN. She speaks much of her father, says she hears
There's tricks° i' the world, and hems° and beats her heart, 5
Spurns enviously° at straws, speaks things in doubt
That carry but half-sense. Her speech is nothing,
Yet the unshaped use° of it doth move
The hearers to collection.° They aim° at it,
And botch° the words up fit to their own thoughts, 10
Which, as her winks and nods and gestures yield them,
Indeed would make one think there might be thought,
Though nothing sure, yet much unhappily.
HORATIO. 'Twere good she were spoken with, for she may strew
Dangerous conjectures in ill-breeding minds. 15
QUEEN. Let her come in.

(Exit GENTLEMAN.*)*

(Aside) To my sick soul, as sin's true nature is,
Each toy° seems prologue to some great amiss.°
So full of artless jealousy° is guilt,
It spills itself in fearing to be spilt.° 20

(Re-enter GENTLEMAN, *with* OPHELIA.*)*

OPHELIA. Where is the beauteous Majesty of Denmark?
QUEEN. How now, Ophelia!
OPHELIA *(Sings)*.
"How should I your truelove know
From another one?
By his cockle hat° and staff 25
And his sandal shoon."°
QUEEN. Alas, sweet lady, what imports this song?
OPHELIA. Say you? nay, pray you, mark. *(Sings.)*
"He is dead and gone, lady,
He is dead and gone, 30
At his head a grass-green turf,
At his heels a stone."
Oh, oh!

Sc. v: **2. distract:** out of her mind. **5. tricks:** trickery. **hems:** makes significant noises. **6. Spurns enviously:** kicks spitefully. **8. unshaped use:** disorder. **9. collection:** i.e., attempts to find a sinister meaning. **aim:** guess. **10. botch:** patch. **18. toy:** trifle. **amiss:** calamity. **19. artless jealousy:** clumsy suspicion. **20. It . . . spilt:** guilt reveals itself by its efforts at concealment. **25. cockle hat:** a hat adorned with a cockleshell worn by pilgrims. **26. sandal shoon:** sandals, the proper footwear of pilgrims.

QUEEN.   Nay, but, Ophelia——

OPHELIA.   Pray you, mark. (*Sings.*)
              "White his shroud as the mountain snow——"   35

(*Enter* KING.)

QUEEN.   Alas, look here, my lord.

OPHELIA (*Sings*).
                        "Larded° with sweet flowers,
                        Which bewept to the grave did go
                        With truelove showers."°

KING.   How do you, pretty lady?   40

OPHELIA.   Well, God 'ild° you! They say the owl was a baker's daughter.°
    Lord, we know what we are but know not what we may be. God be at
    your table!

KING.   Conceit upon her father.

OPHELIA.   Pray you let's have no words of this, but when they ask you   45
    what it means, say you this (*Sings*):
                        "Tomorrow is Saint Valentine's day,°
                        All in the morning betime,
                        And I a maid at your window,
                        To be your Valentine.   50

                        "Then up he rose, and donned his clothes,
                        And dupped° the chamber door,
                        Let in the maid, that out a maid
                        Never departed more."

KING.   Pretty Ophelia!   55

OPHELIA.   Indeed, la, without an oath, I'll make an end on 't. (*Sings.*)
                        "By Gis°· and by Saint Charity,
                        Alack, and fie for shame!
                        Young men will do 't, if they come to 't,
                        By cock, they are to blame.   60
                        Quoth she, before you tumbled me,
                        You promised me to wed."

He answers:
                        "So would I ha' done, by yonder sun,
                        An thou hadst not come to my bed."   65

KING.   How long hath she been thus?

OPHELIA.   I hope all will be well. We must be patient. But I cannot
    choose but weep to think they should lay him i' the cold ground. My
    brother shall know of it. And so I thank you for your good counsel.

---

37. Larded: garnished.   **39. truelove showers:** the tears of his faithful love.   **41. 'ild (yield):**
reward.   **owl . . . daughter:** An allusion to a legend that Christ once went into a baker's shop and
asked for bread. The baker's wife gave him a piece but was rebuked by her daughter for giving him
too much. Thereupon the daughter was turned into an owl.   **47. Saint . . . day:** February 14,
the day when birds are supposed to mate. According to the old belief the first single man then
seen by a maid is destined to be her husband.   **52. dupped:** opened.   **57–60. Gis . . . cock:** for
"Jesus" and "God," both words being used instead of the sacred names, like the modern "Jeez"
and "Gee."

Come, my coach! Good night, ladies, good night, sweet ladies, good
night, good night. *(Exit.)*
KING.   Follow her close,° give her good watch, I pray you.   72

(Exit HORATIO.*)*
Oh, this is the poison of deep grief. It springs
All from her father's death. O Gertrude, Gertrude,
When sorrows come, they come not single spies,°   75
But in battalions! First, her father slain.
Next, your son gone, and he most violent author°
Of his own just remove. The people muddied,
Thick and unwholesome in their thoughts and whispers,
For good Polonius' death. And we have done but greenly°   80
In huggermugger° to inter him. Poor Ophelia
Divided from herself and her fair judgment,°
Without the which we are pictures,° or mere beasts.
Last, and as much containing as all these,
Her brother is in secret come from France,   85
Feeds on his wonder, keeps himself in clouds,
And wants not buzzers° to infect his ear
With pestilent speeches of his father's death,
Wherein necessity, of matter beggared,
Will nothing stick our person to arraign°   90
In ear and ear. O my dear Gertrude, this,
Like to a murdering piece,° in many places
Gives me superfluous death.   *(A noise within)*
QUEEN.   Alack, what noise is this?
KING.   Where are my Switzers?° Let them guard the door.

(Enter another GENTLEMAN.*)*
What is the matter?
GENTLEMAN.   Save yourself, my lord.   95
The ocean, overpeering of his list,°
Eats not the flats° with more impetuous haste
Than young Laertes, in a riotous head,°
O'erbears your officers. The rabble call him lord,
And as the world were now but to begin,   100
Antiquity forgot, custom not known,
The ratifiers and props of every word,°
They cry "Choose we—Laertes shall be King!"

---

72. close: closely. **75. spies:** scouts. **77. author:** cause. **80. done . . . greenly:** shown
immature judgment. **81. huggermugger:** secret haste, "any which way." **82. Divided . . .
judgment:** no longer able to use her judgment. **83. pictures:** lifeless imitations. **87. buzzers:**
scandalmongers. **89–90. Wherein . . . arraign:** in which, knowing nothing of the true facts, he
must necessarily accuse us. **92. murdering piece:** cannon loaded with grapeshot. **94. Switzers:** Swiss bodyguard. **96. overpeering . . . list:** looking over its boundary; i.e., flooding the
mainland. **97. Eats . . . flats:** floods not the flat country. **98. in . . . head:** with a force of
rioters. **101–02. Antiquity . . . word:** forgetting ancient rule and ignoring old custom, by
which all promises must be maintained.

Caps, hands, and tongues applaud it to the clouds—
"Laertes shall be King, Laertes King!"   105
QUEEN.   How cheerfully on the false trail they cry!
Oh, this is counter,° you false Danish dogs!   (*Noise within*)
KING.   The doors are broke.

(*Enter* LAERTES, *armed,* DANES *following.*)

LAERTES.   Where is this King? Sirs, stand you all without.
DANES.   No, let's come in.
LAERTES.   I pray you, give me leave.   110
DANES.   We will, we will.

(*They retire without the door.*)

LAERTES.   I thank you. Keep the door. O thou vile King,
Give me my father!
QUEEN.   Calmly, good Laertes.
LAERTES.   That drop of blood that's calm proclaims me bastard,
Cries cuckold° to my father, brands the harlot°   115
Even here, between the chaste unsmirchèd brows
Of my true mother.
KING.   What is the cause, Laertes,
That thy rebellion looks so giantlike?
Let him go, Gertrude. Do not fear° our person.
There's such divinity doth hedge a king°   120
That treason can but peep° to what it would,
Acts little of his will. Tell me, Laertes,
Why thou art thus incensed. Let him go, Gertrude.
Speak, man.
LAERTES.   Where is my father?
KING.   Dead.
QUEEN.   But not by him.
KING.   Let him demand his fill.   125
LAERTES.   How came he dead? I'll not be juggled with.
To Hell, allegiance! Vows, to the blackest devil!
Conscience and grace, to the profoundest pit!
I dare damnation. To this point I stand,
That both the worlds I give to negligence.°   130
Let come what comes, only I'll be revenged
Most throughly° for my father.
KING.   Who shall stay you?
LAERTES.   My will, not all the world.
And for my means, I'll husband° them so well
They shall go far with little.

---

107. **counter:** in the wrong direction of the scent.   115. **cuckold:** a husband deceived by his
wife.   **brands . . . harlot:** Convicted harlots were branded with a hot iron. Cf. III.iv.44.
119. **fear:** fear for.   120. **divinity . . . king:** divine protection surrounds a king as with a
hedge.   121. **peep:** look over, not break through.   130. **That . . . negligence:** I do not care
what happens to me in this world or the next.   132. **throughly:** thoroughly.   134. **husband:** use
economically.

KING.   Good Laertes,   135
  If you desire to know the certainty
  Of your dear father's death, is't writ in your revenge
  That, swoopstake,° you will draw both friend and foe,
  Winner and loser?
LAERTES.   None but his enemies.
KING.   Will you know them, then?   140
LAERTES.   To his good friends thus wide I'll ope my arms,
  And like the kind life-rendering pelican,°
  Repast° them with my blood.
KING.   Why, now you speak
  Like a good child and a true gentleman.
  That I am guiltless of your father's death,   145
  And am most sensibly° in grief for it,
  It shall as level° to your judgment pierce
  As day does to your eye.
DANES (*Within*).   Let her come in.
LAERTES.   How now! What noise is that?   150
  (*Re-enter* OPHELIA.)
  O heat, dry up my brains! Tears seven times salt
  Burn out the sense and virtue of mine eye!
  By Heaven, thy madness shall be paid with weight
  Till our scale turn the beam.° O rose of May!°
  Dear maid, kind sister, sweet Ophelia!   155
  Oh heavens! Is 't possible a young maid's wits
  Should be as mortal as an old man's life?
  Nature is fine in love, and where 'tis fine
  It sends some precious instance of itself
  After the thing it loves.°   160
OPHELIA (*Sings*).
      "They bore him barefaced on the bier,
      Hey non nonny, nonny, hey nonny,
      And in his grave rained many a tear——"
  Fare you well, my dove!
LAERTES.   Hadst thou thy wits and didst persuade revenge,   165
  It could not move thus.
OPHELIA (*Sings*).
      "You must sing down a-down
      An you call him a-down-a."
  Oh, how the wheel° becomes it! It is the false steward, that stole his
  master's daughter.   170

---

138. swoopstake: "sweeping the board." **142. life-rendering pelican:** The mother pelican was supposed to feed her young with blood from her own breast. **143. Repast:** feed. **146. sensibly:** feelingly. **147. level:** clearly. **154. turn . . . beam:** weigh down the beam of the scale. **rose of May:** perfection of young beauty. See III.i.145. **158-60. Nature . . . loves:** i.e., her love for her father was so exquisite that she has sent her sanity after him. Laertes, especially in moments of emotion, is prone to use highly exaggerated speech. **169. wheel:** explained variously as the spinning wheel, Fortune's wheel, or the refrain. The likeliest explanation is that she breaks into a little dance at the words "You must sing," and that the *wheel* is the turn as she circles round.

LAERTES.   This nothing's more than matter.°

OPHELIA.   There's° rosemary, that's for remembrance—pray you, love, remember. And there is pansies, that's for thoughts.

LAERTES.   A document° in madness, thoughts and remembrance fitted.   175

OPHELIA.   There's fennel for you, and columbines. There's rue for you, and here's some for me—we may call it herb of grace o' Sundays. Oh, you must wear your rue with a difference. There's a daisy. I would give you some violets, but they withered all when my father died. They say a' made a good end. (*Sings.*)   180

"For bonny sweet Robin is all my joy."

LAERTES.   Thought and affliction, passion, Hell itself, She turns to favor° and to prettiness.

OPHELIA (*Sings*).

> "And will a' not come again?
> And will a' not come again?   185
>   No, no, he is dead,
>   Go to thy deathbed,
> He never will come again.
>
> "His beard was as white as snow,
> All flaxen was his poll.°   190
>   He is gone, he is gone,
>   And we cast away moan.
> God ha' mercy on his soul!"

And of all Christian souls, I pray God. God be wi' you.   (*Exit.*)

LAERTES.   Do you see this, O God?   195

KING.   Laertes, I must commune with your grief,
Or you deny me right. Go but apart,
Make choice of whom your wisest friends you will,
And they shall hear and judge 'twixt you and me.
If by direct or by collateral° hand   200
They find us touched,° we will our kingdom give,
Our crown, our life, and all that we call ours,
To you in satisfaction. But if not,
Be you content to lend your patience to us
And we shall jointly labor with your soul   205
To give it due content.

LAERTES.   Let this be so.
His means of death, his obscure funeral,°

---

171. **This . . . matter:** this nonsense means more than sense.   172–79. **There's . . . died:** In the language of flowers, each has its peculiar meaning, and Ophelia distributes them appropriately: for her brother rosemary (remembrance) and pansies (thoughts); for the King fennel (flattery) and columbine (thanklessness); for the Queen rue, called also herb o' grace (sorrow), and daisy (light of love). Neither is worthy of violets (faithfulness).   174. **document:** instruction.   182. **favor:** charm.   190. **flaxen . . . poll:** white as flax was his head.   200. **collateral:** i.e., as an accessory.   201. **touched:** implicated.   207. **obscure funeral:** Men of rank were buried with much ostentation. To bury Polonius "huggermugger" was thus an insult to his memory and to his family.

No trophy, sword, nor hatchment° o'er his bones,
No noble rite nor formal ostentation,°
Cry to be heard, as 'twere from Heaven to earth,   210
That I must call 't in question.
KING.   So you shall,
And where the offense is let the great ax fall.
I pray you, go with me.   (*Exeunt.*)

SCENE VI. *Another room in the castle.*

(*Enter* HORATIO *and a* SERVANT.)

HORATIO. What are they that would speak with me?
SERVANT. Seafaring men, sir. They say they have letters for you.
HORATIO. Let them come in.   (*Exit* SERVANT.)
I do not know from what part of the world
I should be greeted, if not from Lord Hamlet.   5

(*Enter* SAILORS.)

FIRST SAILOR. God bless you, sir.
HORATIO. Let Him bless thee, too.
FIRST SAILOR. He shall, sir, an 't please Him. There's a letter for you, sir. It
comes from the ambassador that was bound for England—if your name
be Horatio, as I am let to know it is.   10
HORATIO (*Reads*). "Horatio, when thou shalt have overlooked° this, give
these fellows some means° to the King. They have letters for him. Ere we
were two days old at sea, a pirate of very warlike appointment° gave us
chase. Finding ourselves too slow of sail, we put on a compelled valor,
and in the grapple I boarded them. On the instant they got clear of our
ship, so I alone became their prisoner. They have dealt with me like
thieves of mercy; but they knew what they did—I am to do a good turn for
them. Let the King have the letters I have sent, and repair thou to me with
as much speed as thou wouldest fly death. I have words to speak in thine
ear will make thee dumb, yet are they much too light for the bore of the
matter.° These good fellows will bring thee where I am. Rosencrantz and
Guildenstern hold their course for England. Of them I have much to tell
thee. Farewell.   23
                              "He that thou knowest thine,
                                              "HAMLET"

Come, I will make you way for these your letters,
And do 't the speedier that you may direct me
To him from whom you brought them.   (*Exeunt.*)

---

208. **hatchment:** device of the coat of arms carried in a funeral and hung up over the
tomb.   209. **formal ostentation:** ceremony properly ordered.
  Sc. vi: 11. **overlooked:** read. 12. **means:** access. 13. **appointment:** equipment.
20–21. **too . . . matter:** i.e., words fall short, like a small shot fired from a cannon with too wide
a bore.

SCENE VII. *Another room in the castle.*

(*Enter* KING *and* LAERTES.)

KING.   Now must your conscience my acquittance seal,°
And you must put me in your heart for friend,
Sith you have heard, and with a knowing ear,
That he which hath your noble father slain
Pursued my life.
LAERTES.   It well appears. But tell me   5
Why you proceeded not against these feats,°
So crimeful and so capital° in nature,
As by your safety, wisdom, all things else,
You mainly were stirred up.
KING.   Oh, for two special reasons,
Which may to you perhaps seem much unsinewed,°   10
But yet to me they're strong. The Queen his mother
Lives almost by his looks, and for myself—
My virtue or my plague, be it either which—
She's so conjunctive° to my life and soul
That as the star moves not but° in his sphere,   15
I could not but by her. The other motive
Why to a public count° I might not go
Is the great love the general gender° bear him,
Who, dipping all his faults in their affection,°
Would, like the spring that turneth wood to stone,°   20
Convert his gyves to graces.° So that my arrows,
Too slightly timbered° for so loud a wind,
Would have reverted to my bow again
And not where I had aimed them.
LAERTES.   And so have I a noble father lost,   25
A sister driven into desperate terms,°
Whose worth, if praises may go back again,°
Stood challenger on mount of all the age
For her perfections.° But my revenge will come.
KING.   Break not your sleeps for that. You must not think   30
That we are made of stuff so flat and dull
That we can let our beard be shook with danger
And think it pastime. You shortly shall hear more.°

Sc. vii: 1. my . . . seal: acquit me.   6. feats: acts.   7. capital: deserving death.   10. unsinewed: weak, flabby.   14. conjunctive: joined inseparably.   15. moves . . . but: moves only
in.   17. count: trial.   18. general gender: common people.   19. dipping . . . affection: gilding
his faults with their love.   20. like . . . stone: In several places in England there are springs of
water so strongly impregnated with lime that they will quickly cover with stone anything placed
under them.   21. Convert . . . graces: regard his fetters as honorable ornaments.   22. tim-
bered: shafted. A light arrow is caught by the wind and blown back.   26. terms: condition.
27. if . . . again: if one may praise her for what she used to be.   28–29. Stood . . . perfections:
i.e., her worth challenged the whole world to find one as perfect.   33. hear more: i.e., when
news comes from England that Hamlet is dead.

I loved your father, and we love ourself,
And that, I hope, will teach you to imagine——   35

(Enter a MESSENGER, *with letters.)*

How now! What news?
MESSENGER.   Letters, my lord, from Hamlet.
This to your Majesty, this to the Queen.
KING.   From Hamlet! Who brought them?
MESSENGER.   Sailors, my lord, they say—I saw them not.
They were given me by Claudio, he received them   40
Of him that brought them.
KING.   Laertes, you shall hear them.
Leave us.

(Exit MESSENGER.*)*

(Reads) "High and Mighty, you shall know I am set naked° on your
kingdom. Tomorrow shall I beg leave to see your kingly eyes, when I
shall, first asking your pardon thereunto, recount the occasion of my
sudden and more strange return.
                                                        "HAMLET"

What should this mean? Are all the rest come back?
Or is it some abuse,° and no such thing?   50
LAERTES.   Know you the hand?
KING.   'Tis Hamlet's character.° "Naked!"
And in a postscript here, he says "alone."
Can you advise me?
LAERTES.   I'm lost in it, my lord. But let him come.   55
It warms the very sickness in my heart
That I shall live and tell him to his teeth
"Thus didest thou."
KING.   If it be so, Laertes—
As how should it be so, how otherwise?—
Will you be ruled by me?
LAERTES.   Aye, my lord,   60
So you will not o'errule° me to a peace.
KING.   To thine own peace. If he be now returned,
As checking at° his voyage, and that he means
No more to undertake it, I will work him
To an exploit now ripe in my device,   65
Under the which he shall not choose but fall.
And for his death no wind of blame shall breathe,
But even his mother shall uncharge the practice°
And call it accident.

---

45. naked: destitute.   **50. abuse:** attempt to deceive.   **52. character:** handwriting.   **61. o'errule:** command.   **63. checking at:** swerving aside from, like a hawk that leaves the pursuit of his prey.   **68. uncharge . . . practice:** not suspect that his death was the result of the plot.

LAERTES.   My lord, I will be ruled,
  The rather if you could devise it so   70
  That I might be the organ.°
KING.   It falls right.
  You have been talked of since your travel much,
  And that in Hamlet's hearing, for a quality
  Wherein they say you shine. Your sum of parts°
  Did not together pluck such envy from him   75
  As did that one, and that in my regard
  Of the unworthiest siege.°
LAERTES.   What part is that, my lord?
KING.   A very ribbon in the cap of youth,
  Yet needful too; for youth no less becomes
  The light and careless livery that it wears   80
  Than settled age his sables and his weeds,°
  Importing health and graveness. Two months since,
  Here was a gentleman of Normandy.
  I've seen myself, and served against, the French,
  And they can well° on horseback; but this gallant   85
  Had witchcraft in 't, he grew unto his seat,
  And to such wondrous doing brought his horse
  As had he been incorpsed and deminatured°
  With the brave beast. So far he topped my thought°
  That I, in forgery of shapes and tricks,°   90
  Come short of what he did.
LAERTES.   A Norman was 't?
KING.   A Norman.
LAERTES.   Upon my life, Lamond.
KING.   The very same.
LAERTES.   I know him well. He is the brooch° indeed
  And gem of all the nation.   95
KING.   He made confession° of you,
  And gave you such a masterly report
  For art and exercise in your defense,
  And for your rapier most especial,
  That he cried out 'twould be a sight indeed   100
  If one could match you. The scrimers° of their nation,
  He swore, had neither motion, guard, nor eye
  If you opposed them. Sir, this report of his
  Did Hamlet so envenom° with his envy
  That he could nothing do but wish and beg   105

---

71. **organ:** instrument.   74. **sum of parts:** accomplishments as a whole.   77. **siege:** seat, place.   81. **sables . . . weeds:** dignified robes. See III.ii.116.   85. **can well:** can do well. 88. **incorpsed . . . deminatured:** of one body.   89. **topped my thought:** surpassed what I could imagine.   90. **forgery . . . tricks:** imagination of all kinds of fancy tricks.   **shapes:** fancies. 94. **brooch:** ornament.   96. **confession:** report.   101. **scrimers:** fencers.   104. **envenom:** poison.

Your sudden coming o'er, to play with him.
Now, out of this——
LAERTES.   What out of this, my lord?
KING.   Laertes, was your father dear to you?
Or are you like the painting° of a sorrow,
A face without a heart?
LAERTES.   Why ask you this?   110
KING.   Not that I think you did not love your father,
But that I know love is begun by time,
And that I see, in passages of proof,°
Time qualifies° the spark and fire of it.
There lives within the very flame of love   115
A kind of wick or snuff° that will abate it.
And nothing is at a like goodness still,°
For goodness, growing to a pleurisy,°
Dies in his own too much. That we would do
We should do when we would; for this "would" changes   120
And hath abatements and delays as many
As there are tongues, are hands, are accidents,
And then this "should" is like a spendthrift° sigh
That hurts by easing. But to the quick o' the ulcer.°
Hamlet comes back. What would you undertake   125
To show yourself your father's son in deed
More than in words?
LAERTES.   To cut his throat i' the church.°
KING.   No place indeed should murder sanctuarize,°
Revenge should have no bounds. But, good Laertes,
Will you do this, keep close within your chamber.   130
Hamlet returned shall know you are come home.
We'll put on those° shall praise your excellence
And set a double varnish on the fame
The Frenchman gave you, bring you in fine° together
And wager on your heads. He, being remiss,°   135
Most generous° and free from all contriving,°
Will not peruse the foils, so that with ease,
Or with a little shuffling, you may choose
A sword unbated,° and in a pass of practice°
Requite him for your father.

---

109. **painting:** i.e., imitation.   113. **passages of proof:** experiences which prove.   114. **qual-
ifies:** diminishes.   116. **snuff:** Before the invention of self-consuming wicks for candles, the wick
smoldered and formed a ball of soot which dimmed the light and gave out a foul smoke.
117. **still:** always.   118. **pleurisy:** fullness.   123. **spendthrift:** wasteful, because sighing was
supposed to be bad for the blood.   124. **quick . . . ulcer:** i.e., to come to the real issue.   **quick:**
flesh, sensitive part.   127. **cut . . . church:** i.e., to commit murder in a holy place, which would
bring Laertes in danger of everlasting damnation; no crime could be worse.   128. **sanctuarize:**
give sanctuary to.   132. **put . . . those:** set on some.   134. **fine:** short.   135. **remiss:** careless.   136. **generous:** noble.   **contriving:** plotting.   139. **unbated:** not blunted, with a sharp
point.   **pass of practice:** treacherous thrust.

LAERTES.   I will do't,   140
  And for that purpose I'll anoint my sword.
  I bought an unction° of a mountebank°
  So mortal that but dip a knife in it,
  Where it draws blood no cataplasm° so rare,
  Collected from all simples° that have virtue   145
  Under the moon,° can save the thing from death
  That is but scratched withal. I'll touch my point
  With this contagion, that if I gall° him slightly,
  It may be death.
KING.   Let's further think of this,
  Weigh what convenience both of time and means   150
  May fit us to our shape.° If this should fail,
  And that our drift look through our bad performance,°
  'Twere better not assayed. Therefore this project
  Should have a back or second, that might hold
  If this did blast in proof.° Soft! Let me see—   155
  We'll make a solemn wager on your cunnings.
  I ha 't.
  When in your motion you are hot and dry—
  As make your bouts° more violent to that end—
  And that he calls for drink, I'll have prepared him   160
  A chalice° for the nonce,° whereon but sipping,
  If he by chance escape your venomed stuck,°
  Our purpose may hold there. But stay, what noise?
  (*Enter* QUEEN.) How now, sweet Queen!
QUEEN.   One woe doth tread upon another's heel,
  So fast they follow. Your sister's drowned, Laertes.   165
LAERTES.   Drowned! Oh, where?
QUEEN.   There is a willow grows aslant a brook
  That shows his hoar° leaves in the glassy stream.
  There with fantastic garlands did she come
  Of crowflowers, nettles, daisies, and long purples   170
  That liberal° shepherds give a grosser name,
  But our cold maids do dead-men's-fingers call them.
  There on the pendent° boughs her coronet weeds°
  Clambering to hang, an envious sliver° broke,
  When down her weedy trophies and herself   175

---

142. **unction:** poison.   **mountebank:** quack doctor.   144. **cataplasm:** poultice.   145. **simples:** herbs.   146. **Under . . . moon:** herbs collected by moonlight were regarded as particularly potent.   148. **gall:** break the skin.   150–51. **Weigh . . . shape:** consider the best time and method of carrying out our plan.   152. **drift . . . performance:** intention be revealed through bungling.   155. **blast in proof:** break in trial, like a cannon which bursts when being tested.   159. **bouts:** attacks, in the fencing match.   161. **chalice:** cup.   **nonce:** occasion.   162. **stuck:** thrust.   168. **hoar:** gray. The underside of the leaves of the willow are silver-gray.   171. **liberal:** coarse-mouthed.   173. **pendent:** hanging over the water.   **coronet weeds:** wild flowers woven into a crown.   174. **envious sliver:** malicious branch.

Fell in the weeping brook. Her clothes spread wide,
And mermaidlike awhile they bore her up—
Which time she chanted snatches of old tunes,
As one incapable° of her own distress,
Or like a creature native and indued°   180
Unto that element. But long it could not be
Till that her garments, heavy with their drink,
Pulled the poor wretch from her melodious lay°
To muddy death.

LAERTES.   Alas, then, she is drowned!
QUEEN.   Drowned, drowned.   185
LAERTES.   Too much of water hast thou, poor Ophelia,
And therefore I forbid my tears. But yet
It is our trick°—Nature her custom holds,
Let shame say what it will. When these° are gone,
The woman will be out.° Adieu, my lord.   190
I have a speech of fire that fain° would blaze
But that this folly douts° it.   (*Exit.*)

KING.   Let's follow, Gertrude.
How much I had to do to calm his rage!
Now fear I this will give it start again,
Therefore let's follow.   (*Exeunt.*)

ACT V

SCENE I. A churchyard.

(*Enter two* CLOWNS,° *with spades, etc.*)

FIRST CLOWN.   Is she to be buried in Christian burial° that willfully seeks
her own salvation?

SECOND CLOWN.   I tell thee she is, and therefore make her grave straight.°
The crowner° hath sat on her, and finds it Christian burial.   4

FIRST CLOWN.   How can that be, unless she drowned herself in her own
defense?

SECOND CLOWN.   Why, 'tis found so.

FIRST CLOWN.   It must be "se offendendo,"° it cannot be else. For here lies
the point. If I drown myself wittingly,° it argues an act, and an act hath
three branches—it is to act, to do, and to perform. Argal,° she drowned
herself wittingly.

---

179. **incapable:** not realizing.   180. **indued:** endowed: i.e., a creature whose natural home is
the water (*element*).   183. **lay:** song.   187–88. **But . . . trick:** it is our habit; i.e., to break into
tears at great sorrow.   189. **these:** i.e., my tears.   190. **woman . . . out:** I shall be a man
again.   191. **fain:** willingly.   192. **douts:** puts out.
   Act V, Sc. i: s.d., **Clowns:** countrymen.   1. **Christian burial:** Suicides were not allowed
burial in consecrated ground, but were buried at crossroads. The gravediggers and the priest are
professionally scandalized that Ophelia should be allowed Christian burial solely because she is a
lady of the Court.   3. **straight:** straightway.   4. **crowner:** coroner.   8. **se offendendo:** for
defendendo, in self-defense.   9. **wittingly:** with full knowledge.   10. **Argal:** for the Latin *ergo*,
therefore.

SECOND CLOWN.   Nay, but hear you, goodman delver.°   12
FIRST CLOWN.   Give me leave. Here lies the water, good. Here stands the man, good. If the man go to this water and drown himself, it is will he, nill he° he goes, mark you that; but if the water come to him and drown him, he drowns not himself. Argal, he that is not guilty of his own death shortens not his own life.   17
SECOND CLOWN.   But is this law?
FIRST CLOWN.   Ay, marry, is 't, crowner's quest° law.
SECOND CLOWN.   Will you ha' the truth on 't? If this had not been a gentlewoman, she should have been buried out o' Christian burial.
FIRST CLOWN.   Why, there thou say'st. And the more pity that great folks should have countenance° in this world to drown or hang themselves more than their even° Christian. Come, my spade. There is no ancient gentlemen but gardeners, ditchers, and gravemakers. They hold up° Adam's profession.   26
SECOND CLOWN.   Was he a gentleman?
FIRST CLOWN.   A' was the first that ever bore arms.°
SECOND CLOWN.   Why, he had none.   29
FIRST CLOWN.   What, art a heathen? How dost thou understand the Scripture? The Scripture says Adam digged. Could he dig without arms? I'll put another question to thee. If thou answerest me not to the purpose, confess thyself——
SECOND CLOWN.   Go to.   34
FIRST CLOWN.   What is he that builds stronger than either the mason, the shipwright, or the carpenter?
SECOND CLOWN.   The gallows-maker, for that frame outlives a thousand tenants.   38
FIRST CLOWN.   I like thy wit well, in good faith. The gallows does well, but how does it well? It does well to those that do ill. Now thou dost ill to say the gallows is built stronger than the church; argal, the gallows may do well to thee. To 't again, come.
SECOND CLOWN.   Who builds stronger than a mason, a shipwright, or a carpenter?
FIRST CLOWN.   Aye, tell me that, and unyoke.°
SECOND CLOWN.   Marry, now I can tell.   45
FIRST CLOWN.   To 't.
SECOND CLOWN.   Mass,° I cannot tell.

(*Enter* HAMLET *and* HORATIO, *afar off.*)

FIRST CLOWN.   Cudgel thy brains no more about it, for your dull ass will not mend his pace with beating, and when you are asked this question next, say "A gravemaker." The houses that he makes last till Doomsday. Go, get thee to Yaughan,° fetch me a stoup° of liquor.   51

---

12. **delver**: digger.   14–15. **will he, nill he**: willy-nilly, whether he wishes or not.   19. **quest**: inquest.   23. **countenance**: favor.   24. **even**: fellow.   25. **hold up**: support.   28. **bore arms**: had a coat of arms—the outward sign of a gentleman.   44. **unyoke**: finish the job, unyoking the plow oxen being the end of the day's work.   47. **Mass**: by the mass.   51. **Yaughan**: apparently an innkeeper near the Globe Theatre.   **stoup**: large pot.

(*Exit* SECOND CLOWN.)

(FIRST CLOWN *digs, and sings.*)

> "In youth,° when I did love, did love,
>   Methought it was very sweet,
> To contract; oh, the time, for-a my behoove,°
>   Oh, methought, there-a was nothing-a meet."   55

HAMLET.   Has this fellow no feeling of his business, that he sings at grave-making?

HORATIO.   Custom hath made it in him a property of easiness.°

HAMLET.   'Tis e'en so. The hand of little employment hath the daintier sense.°   60

FIRST CLOWN (*Sings*).

> "But age, with his stealing steps,
>   Hath clawed me in his clutch,
> And hath shipped me intil the land°
>   As if I had never been such."   64

(*Throws up a skull.*)

HAMLET.   That skull had a tongue in it, and could sing once. How the knave jowls° it to the ground, as if it were Cain's jawbone, that did the first murder! It might be the pate of a politician which this ass now o'erreaches°—one that would circumvent° God, might it not?

HORATIO.   It might, my lord.   69

HAMLET.   Or of a courtier, which could say "Good morrow, sweet lord! How dost thou, good lord?" This might be my lord Such-a-one that praised my lord Such-a-one's horse when he meant to beg it, might it not?

HORATIO.   Aye, my lord.   73

HAMLET.   Why, e'en so. And now my Lady Worm's chapless,° and knocked about the mazzard° with a sexton's spade. Here's fine revolution, an we had the trick to see 't. Did these bones cost no more the breeding but to play at loggats° with 'em? Mine ache to think on 't.   77

FIRST CLOWN (*Sings*).

> "A pickax and a spade, a spade,
>   For and a shrouding sheet—
> Oh, a pit of clay for to be made   80
>   For such a guest is meet."

(*Throws up another skull.*)

52–81. **In youth . . . meet:** The song which the gravedigger sings without much care for accuracy or sense was first printed in *Tottel's Miscellany*, 1558.   54. **behoove:** benefit.   58. **property of easiness:** careless habit.   59–60. **hand . . . sense:** those who have little to do are the most sensitive.   63. **shipped . . . land:** shoved me into the ground.   66. **jowls:** dashes.   68. **o'erreaches:** gets the better of.   **circumvent:** get around.   74. **chapless:** without jaws. 75. **mazzard:** head, a slang word; lit., drinking-bowl.   77. **loggats:** a game in which billets of wood or bones were stuck in the ground and knocked over by throwing at them.

HAMLET.   There's another. Why may not that be the skull of a lawyer?°
Where be his quiddities now, his quillets, his cases, his tenures, and his
tricks? Why does he suffer this rude knave now to knock him about the
sconce° with a dirty shovel, and will not tell him of his action of battery?
Hum! This fellow might be in 's time a great buyer of land, with his
statues, his recognizances, his fines, his double vouchers, his recoveries.
Is this the fine° of his fines and the recovery of his recoveries, to have his
fine pate full of fine dirt? Will his vouchers vouch him no more of his
purchases, and double ones too, than the length and breadth of a pair of
indentures? The very conveyances of his lands will hardly lie in this box,°
and must the inheritor himself have no more, ha?   92
HORATIO.   Not a jot more, my lord.
HAMLET.   Is not parchment made of sheepskins?
HORATIO.   Aye, my lord, and of calfskins too.   95
HAMLET.   They are sheep and calves which seek out assurance in that. I
will speak to this fellow. Whose grave's this, sirrah?
FIRST CLOWN.   Mine, sir. (*Sings.*)
            "Oh, a pit of clay for to be made
            For such a guest is meet."   100
HAMLET.   I think it be thine indeed, for thou liest in 't.
FIRST CLOWN.   You lie out on 't, sir, and therefore 'tis not yours. For my
part, I do not lie in 't, and yet it is mine.
HAMLET.   Thou doest lie in 't, to be in 't and say it is thine. 'Tis for the
dead, not for the quick, therefore thou liest.   105
FIRST CLOWN.   'Tis a quick lie, sir, 'twill away again, from me to you.
HAMLET.   What man dost thou dig it for?
FIRST CLOWN.   For no man, sir.
HAMLET.   What woman, then?   110
FIRST CLOWN.   For none, neither.
HAMLET.   Who is to be buried in 't?
FIRST CLOWN.   One that was a woman, sir, but, rest her soul, she's dead.
HAMLET.   How absolute° the knave is! We must speak by the card,° or
equivocation° will undo us. By the Lord, Horatio, this three years I have
taken note of it—the age is grown so picked° that the toe of the peasant
comes so near the heel of the courtier, he galls his kibe.° How long hast
thou been a grave-maker?   118
FIRST CLOWN.   Of all the days i' the year, I came to 't that day that our last
King Hamlet o'ercame Fortinbras.   120

82–91. lawyer . . . indentures: Hamlet strings out a number of the legal phrases loved by lawyers:
quiddities: subtle arguments; *quillets:* quibbles; *tenures:* titles to property; *tricks:* knavery; *stat-
utes:* bonds; *recognizances:* obligations; *fines:* conveyances; *vouchers:* guarantors; *recoveries:* trans-
fers; *indentures:* agreements.   85. sconce: head; lit., blockhouse.   88. fine: ending.   91. box:
coffin.   114. absolute: exact.   by . . . card: exactly. The card is the mariner's compass.
115. equivocation: speaking with a double sense. The word was much discussed when *Hamlet*
was written.   116. picked: refined.   116–17. toe . . . kibe: i.e., the peasant follows the courtier
so closely that he rubs the courtier's heel into a blister. From about 1598 onward, writers,
especially dramatists, often satirized the practice of yeomen farmers grown rich from war profits
in sending their awkward sons to London to learn gentlemanly manners. Ben Jonson portrays one
specimen as Stephen in *Every Man in His Humour.*

HAMLET. How long is that since?

FIRST CLOWN. Cannot you tell that? Every fool can tell that. It was that very day that young Hamlet was born, he that is mad, and sent into England.

HAMLET. Aye, marry, why was he sent into England? 125

FIRST CLOWN. Why, because a' was mad. A' shall recover his wits there, or, if a' do not, 'tis no great matter there.

HAMLET. Why?

FIRST CLOWN. 'Twill not be seen in him there—there the men are as mad as he. 130

HAMLET. How came he mad?

FIRST CLOWN. Very strangely, they say.

HAMLET. How "strangely"?

FIRST CLOWN. Faith, e'en with losing his wits.

HAMLET. Upon what ground? 135

FIRST CLOWN. Why, here in Denmark. I have been sexton here, man and boy, thirty years.°

HAMLET. How long will a man lie i' the earth ere he rot?

FIRST CLOWN. I' faith, if a' be not rotten before a' die—as we have many pocky° corses nowadays that will scarce hold the laying in—a' will last you some eight or nine year. A tanner will last you nine year.

HAMLET. Why he more than another? 142

FIRST CLOWN. Why, sir, his hide is so tanned with his trade that a' will keep out water a great while, and your water is a sore decayer of your whoreson° dead body. Here's a skull now. This skull has lain in the earth three and twenty years. 146

HAMLET. Whose was it?

FIRST CLOWN. A whoreson mad fellow's it was. Whose do you think it was?

HAMLET. Nay, I know not. 149

FIRST CLOWN. A pestilence on him for a mad rogue! A' poured a flagon of Rhenish on my head once. This same skull, was Yorick's skull, the King's jester.

HAMLET. This?

FIRST CLOWN. E'en that.

HAMLET. Let me see. (*Takes the skull.*) Alas, poor Yorick! I knew him, Horatio—a fellow of infinite jest, of most excellent fancy. He hath borne me on his back a thousand times, and now how abhorred in my imagination it is! My gorge rises° at it. Here hung those lips that I have kissed I know not how oft. Where be your gibes now? Your gambols? Your songs? Your flashes of merriment that were wont to set the table on a roar? Not one now, to mock your own grinning? Quite chopfallen?° Now get you to my lady's chamber and tell her, let her paint an inch thick, to this favor° she must come—make her laugh at that. Prithee, Horatio, tell me one thing.

137. **thirty years:** The Clown's chronology has puzzled critics, for the general impression is that Hamlet was much younger. 140. **pocky:** suffering from the pox (venereal disease). 145. **whoreson:** bastard, "son of a bitch." 155. **My . . . rises:** I feel sick. **gorge:** throat. 158. **chopfallen:** downcast, with a pun on "chapless," (see 1. 74). 160. **favor:** appearance, especially in the face.

HORATIO.   What's that, my lord?   162
HAMLET.   Dost thou think Alexander looked o' this fashion i' the earth?
HORATIO.   E'en so.
HAMLET.   And smelt so? Pah!   165

(Puts down the skull.)

HORATIO.   E'en so, my lord.
HAMLET.   To what base uses we may return, Horatio! Why may not imagination trace the noble dust of Alexander till he find it stopping a bunghole?°
HORATIO.   'Twere to consider too curiously° to consider so.   170
HAMLET.   No, faith, not a jot, but to follow him thither with modesty°
enough and likelihood to lead it. As thus: Alexander died, Alexander was
buried, Alexander returneth into dust; the dust is earth; of earth we make
loam;° and why of that loam, whereto he was converted, might they not
stop a beer barrel?   175
    "Imperious Caesar, dead and turned to clay,
    Might stop a hole to keep the wind away.
    Oh, that that earth which kept the world in awe
    Should patch a wall to expel the winter's flaw!"°
But soft! But soft! Aside—here comes the King.   180

(Enter PRIESTS, *etc., in procession; the corpse of* Ophelia, LAERTES *and*
MOURNERS *following;* KING, QUEEN, *their trains, etc.)*

    The Queen, the courtiers—who is this they follow?
    And with such maimèd° rites? This doth betoken°
    The corse they follow did with desperate hand
    Fordo° its own life. 'Twas of some estate.°
    Couch° we awhile, and mark.   185

(Retiring with HORATIO.*)*

LAERTES.   What ceremony else?
HAMLET.   That is Laertes, a very noble youth. Mark.
LAERTES.   What ceremony else?
FIRST PRIEST.   Her obsequies have been as far enlarged
    As we have warranty.° Her death was doubtful,   190
    And but that great command o'ersways the order,°
    She should in ground unsanctified have lodged
    Till the last trumpet; for° charitable prayers,
    Shards,° flints, and pebbles should be thrown on her.
    Yet here she is allowed her virgin crants,°   195
    Her maiden strewments° and the bringing home
    Of bell and burial.

169. **bunghole:** the hole in a beer barrel. 170. **curiously:** precisely. 171. **with modesty:**
without exaggeration. 174. **loam:** mixture of clay and sand, used in plastering walls.
179. **flaw:** blast. 182. **maimed:** curtailed. **betoken:** indicate. 184. **Fordo:** destroy. **estate:**
high rank. 185. **Couch:** lie down. 189–90. **Her . . . warranty:** the funeral rites have been as
complete as may be allowed. 191. **but . . . order:** if the King's command had not overruled the
proper procedure. 193. **for:** instead of. 194. **Shards:** pieces of broken crockery. 195. **crants:**
wreaths of flowers—a sign that she had died unwed. 196. **maiden strewments:** the flowers
strewn on the corpse of a maiden.

LAERTES.   Must there no more be done?
FIRST PRIEST.   No more be done.
We should profane the service of the dead
To sing a requiem and such rest to her   200
As to peace-parted souls.°
LAERTES.   Lay her i' the earth.
And from her fair and unpolluted flesh
May violets spring! I tell thee, churlish priest,
A ministering angel shall my sister be
When thou liest howling.
HAMLET.   What, the fair Ophelia!   205
QUEEN (*Scattering flowers*).   Sweets to the sweet. Farewell!
I hoped thou shouldst have been my Hamlet's wife.
I thought thy bride bed to have decked, sweet maid,
And not have strewed thy grave.
LAERTES.   Oh, treble woe
Fall ten times treble on that cursèd head   210
Whose wicked deed thy most ingenious sense°
Deprived thee of! Hold off the earth a while
Till I have caught her once more in mine arms.
(Leaps into the grave.)
Now pile your dust upon the quick° and dead
Till of this flat a mountain you have made   215
To o'ertop old Pelion° or the skyish° head
Of blue Olympus.
HAMLET (*Advancing*).   What is he whose grief
Bears such an emphasis? Whose phrase of sorrow
Conjures the wandering stars and makes them stand°
Like wonder-wounded hearers? This is I,   220
Hamlet the Dane.
(Leaps into the grave.)
LAERTES.   The Devil take thy soul!
(Grappling with him)
HAMLET.   Thou pray'st not well.
I prithee, take thy fingers from my throat,
For though I am not splenitive° and rash,
Yet have I in me something dangerous,   225
Which let thy wisdom fear. Hold off thy hand.
KING.   Pluck them asunder.
QUEEN.   Hamlet, Hamlet!
ALL.   Gentlemen——
HORATIO.   Good my lord, be quiet.

---

201. peace-parted souls: souls which departed in peace, fortified with the rites of the Church.   **211. most . . . sense:** lively intelligence.   **214. quick:** living.   **216. Pelion:** When the giants fought against the gods in order to reach Heaven, they tried to pile Mount Pelion and Mount Ossa on Mount Olympus, the highest mountain in Greece.   **skyish:** reaching the sky.   **219. stand:** stand still.   **224. splenitive:** hot-tempered.

(The ATTENDANTS *part them, and they come out of the grave.)*

HAMLET.   Why, I will fight with him upon this theme
 Until my eyelids will no longer wag.   230
QUEEN.   O my son, what theme?
HAMLET.   I loved Ophelia. Forty thousand brothers
 Could not, with all their quantity of love,
 Make up my sum. What wilt thou do for her?
KING.   Oh, he is mad, Laertes.   235
QUEEN.   For love of God, forbear him.°
HAMLET.   'Swounds,° show me what thou'lt do.
 Woo 't weep? Woo 't fight? Woo 't fast? Woo 't tear thyself?
 Woo 't drink up eisel?° Eat a crocodile?
 I'll do 't. Dost thou come here to whine?   240
 To outface° me with leaping in her grave?
 Be buried quick with her, and so will I.
 And if thou prate of mountains, let them throw
 Millions of acres on us, till our ground,
 Singeing his pate against the burning zone,   245
 Make Ossa° like a wart! Nay, an thou 'lt mouth,
 I'll rant as well as thou.
QUEEN.   This is mere madness.
 And thus awhile the fit will work on him.
 Anon, as patient as the female dove
 When that her golden couplets° are disclosed,° 250
 His silence will sit drooping.
HAMLET.   Hear you, sir.
 What is the reason that you use me thus?
 I loved you ever. But it is no matter,
 Let Hercules himself do what he may,   254
 The cat will mew and dog will have his day.° *(Exit.)*
KING.   I pray thee, good Horatio, wait upon him.

(Exit HORATIO.*)*

(To LAERTES*)* Strengthen your patience in our last night's speech.
We'll put the matter to the present push.°
Good Gertrude, set some watch over your son.
This grave shall have a living monument.°   260
An hour of quiet shortly shall we see,
Till then, in patience our proceeding be.

(Exeunt.)

---

236. forbear him: leave him alone. **237–47. 'Swounds . . . thou:** Hamlet in his excitement
cries out that if Laertes wishes to make extravagant boasts of what he will do to show his sorrow,
he will be even more extravagant. **239. eisel:** vinegar. **241. outface:** browbeat. **246. Ossa:**
See V.i.216,n. **250. couplets:** eggs, of which the dove lays two only. **disclosed:** hatched.
254–55. Let . . . day: i.e., let this ranting hero have his turn; mine will come sometime.
258. push: test; lit., thrust of a pike. **260. living monument:** with the double meaning of "lifelike
memorial" and "the death of Hamlet."

SCENE II. A hall in the castle.

(Enter HAMLET *and* HORATIO.)

HAMLET.   So much for this, sir. Now shall you see the other.
      You do remember all the circumstance?
HORATIO.   Remember it, my lord!
HAMLET.   Sir, in my heart there was a kind of fighting
      That would not let me sleep. Methought I lay   5
      Worse than the mutines in the bilboes.° Rashly,
      And praised be rashness for it, let us know,
      Our indiscretion sometime serves us well
      When our deep plots do pall.° And that should learn° us
      There's a divinity that shapes our ends,   10
      Roughhew them how we will.°
HORATIO.   That is most certain.
HAMLET.   Up from my cabin,
      My sea gown° scarfed° about me, in the dark
      Groped I to find out them,° had my desire,
      Fingered their packet, and in fine withdrew   15
      To mine own room again, making so bold,
      My fears forgetting manners, to unseal
      Their grand commission where I found, Horatio—
      Oh royal knavery!—an exact command,
      Larded° with many several sorts of reasons,   20
      Importing Denmark's health and England's too,
      With, ho! such bugs° and goblins in my life°
      That, on the supervise,° no leisure bated,°
      No, not to stay the grinding of the ax,
      My head should be struck off.
HORATIO.   Is 't possible?   25
HAMLET.   Here's the commission. Read it at more leisure
      But wilt thou hear me how I did proceed?
HORATIO.   I beseech you.
HAMLET.   Being thus benetted round with villainies—
      Ere I could make a prologue to my brains,   30
      They had begun the play—I sat me down,
      Devised a new commission, wrote it fair.
      I once did hold it, as our statists° do,

Sc. ii: 6. **mutines . . . bilboes:** mutineers in the shackles used on board ship.   9. **pall:**
fail.   **learn:** teach.   10-11. **There's . . . will:** though we may make the rough beginning, God
finishes our designs.   13. **sea gown:** a thick coat with a high collar worn by seamen.   **scarfed:**
wrapped.   14. **them:** i.e., Rosencrantz and Guildenstern.   20. **Larded:** garnished.   22. **bugs:**
bugbears.   **in my life:** so long as I was alive.   23. **supervise:** reading.   **bated:** allowed.
33. **statists:** statesmen. As scholars who have had to read Elizabethan documents know, the more
exalted the writer, the worse his handwriting. As a girl Queen Elizabeth wrote a beautiful script;
as Queen her letters are as illegible as any. All but the most confidential documents were copied
out in a fair hand by a secretary.

A baseness to write fair, and labored much
How to forget that learning, but, sir, now   35
It did me yeoman's service.° Wilt thou know
The effect of what I wrote?
HORATIO.   Aye, good my lord.
HAMLET.   An earnest conjuration from the King,
As England was his faithful tributary,
As love between them like the palm might flourish,   40
As peace should still her wheaten garland wear
And stand a comma 'tween their amities,°
And many suchlike "Ases"° of great charge,°
That, on the view and knowing of these contents,
Without debatement° further, more or less,   45
He should the bearers put to sudden death,
Not shriving time allowed.°
HORATIO.   How was this sealed?
HAMLET.   Why, even in that was Heaven ordinant.°
I had my father's signet in my purse,
Which was the model° of that Danish seal—   50
Folded the writ° up in the form of the other,
Subscribed° it, gave 't the impression,° placed it safely,
The changeling° never known. Now the next day
Was our sea fight, and what to this was sequent°
Thou know'st already.   55
HORATIO.   So Guildenstern and Rosencrantz go to 't.
HAMLET.   Why, man, they did make love to this employment.
They are not near my conscience, their defeat°
Does by their own insinuation° grow.
'Tis dangerous when the baser nature comes   60
Between the pass and fell incensèd points
Of mighty opposites.°
HORATIO.   Why, what a King is this!
HAMLET.   Does it not, think'st thee, stand me now upon—
He that hath killed my King and whored my mother,
Popped in between the election and my hopes,°   65
Thrown out his angle° for my proper° life,

<hr/>

36. **yeoman's service:** faithful service. The most reliable English soldiers were yeomen—farmers and their men.   42. **stand . . . amities:** be a connecting link of their friendship.   43. **"Ases":** Official documents were written in flowery language full of metaphorical clauses beginning with "As." Hamlet puns on "asses."   **great charge:** "great weight" and "heavy burden."   45. **debatement:** argument.   47. **Not . . . allowed:** without giving them time even to confess their sins.   48. **ordinant:** directing, in control.   50. **model:** copy.   51. **writ:** writing.   52. **Subscribed:** signed.   **impression:** of the seal.   53. **changeling:** lit., an ugly child exchanged by the fairies for a fair one.   54. **sequent:** following.   58. **defeat:** destruction.   59. **by . . . insinuation:** because they insinuated themselves into this business.   60–62. **'Tis . . . opposites:** it is dangerous for inferior men to interfere in a duel between mighty enemies.   **pass:** thrust.   **fell:** fierce.   65. **Popped . . . hopes:** As is from time to time shown in the play, the Danes chose their King by election.   66. **angle:** fishing rod and line.   **proper:** own.

And with such cozenage°— is 't not perfect conscience,
To quit° him with this arm? And is 't not to be damned,
To let this canker° of our nature come
In further evil?   70
HORATIO.   It must be shortly known to him from England
What is the issue of the business there.
HAMLET.   It will be short. The interim° is mine,
And a man's life's no more than to say "One."
But I am very sorry, good Horatio,   75
That to Laertes I forgot myself,
For by the image of my cause I see
The portraiture of his. I'll court his favors.
But, sure, the bravery° of his grief did put me
Into a towering passion.
HORATIO.   Peace! Who comes here?   80

(Enter OSRIC.°*)*

OSRIC.   Your lordship is right welcome back to Denmark.
HAMLET.   I humbly thank you, sir. Dost know this water fly?°
HORATIO.   No, my good lord.   83
HAMLET.   Thy state is the more gracious,° for 'tis a vice to know him. He
hath much land, and fertile. Let a beast be lord of beasts and his crib shall
stand at the King's mess.° 'Tis a chough,° but, as I say, spacious° in the
possession of dirt.   87
OSRIC.   Sweet lord, if your lordship were at leisure, I should import a thing
to you from His Majesty.
HAMLET.   I will receive it, sir, with all diligence of spirit. Put your bonnet
to his right use,° 'tis for the head.
OSRIC.   I thank your lordship, it is very hot.   92
HAMLET.   No, believe me, 'tis very cold. The wind is northerly.
OSRIC.   It is indifferent° cold, my lord, indeed.   94
HAMLET.   But yet methinks it is very sultry and hot, for my complexion—
OSRIC.   Exceedingly, my lord. It is very sultry, as 'twere—I cannot tell
how. But, my lord, His Majesty bade me signify to you that he has laid a
great wager on your head. Sir, this is the matter——
HAMLET.   I beseech you, remember——   99

*(*HAMLET *moves him to put on his hat.)*

---

67. **cozenage:** cheating.   68. **quit:** pay back.   69. **canker:** maggot. See I.iii.39.   73. **interim:** interval; between now and the news from England.   79. **bravery:** excessive show.   80. **s.d., Osric:** Osric is a specimen of the fashionable, effeminate courtier. He dresses prettily and talks the jargon of his class, which at this time affected elaborate and allusive metaphors and at all costs avoided saying plain things plainly.   82. **water fly:** a useless little creature that flits about.   84. **Thy . . . gracious:** you are in the better state.   85–86. **Let . . . mess:** i.e., any man, however low, who has wealth enough will find a good place at Court.   **crib:** manger.   **mess:** table.   86. **chough:** jackdaw.   **spacious:** wealthy.   90–91. **Put . . . use:** i.e., put your hat on your head. Osric is so nice-mannered that he cannot bring himself to wear his hat in the presence of the Prince.   94. **indifferent:** moderately.

OSRIC.   Nay, good my lord, for mine ease, in good faith. Sir, here is newly
come to Court Laertes—believe me, an absolute° gentleman, full of most
excellent differences,° of very soft society° and great showing.° Indeed, to
speak feelingly° of him, he is the card or calendar of gentry,° for you shall
find in him the continent of what part a gentleman would see.°   104

HAMLET.   Sir,° his definement suffers no perdition in you, though I know
to devide him inventorially would dizzy the arithmetic of memory, and
yet but yaw neither, in respect of his quick sail. But in the verity of
extolment, I take him to be a soul of great article, and his infusion of such
dearth and rareness as, to make true diction of him, his semblable is his
mirror, and who else would trace him, his umbrage—nothing
more.   111

OSRIC.   Your lordship speaks most infallibly of him.

HAMLET.   The concernancy,° sir? Why do we wrap the gentleman in our
more rawer breath?°

OSRIC.   Sir?°   115

HORATIO.   Is 't not possible to understand in another tongue? You will do 't,
sir, really.

HAMLET.   What imports the nomination° of this gentleman?

OSRIC.   Of Laertes?

HORATIO.   His purse is empty already, all's golden words are spent.   120

HAMLET.   Of him, sir.

OSRIC.   I know you are not ignorant——

HAMLET.   I would you did, sir. Yet, in faith, if you did, it would not much
approve° me. Well, sir?

OSRIC.   You are not ignorant of what excellence Laertes is——   125

HAMLET.   I dare not confess that, lest I should compare with him in
excellence, but to know a man well were to know himself.

OSRIC.   I mean, sir, for his weapon,° but in the imputation° laid on him by
them, in his meed° he's unfellowed.°

HAMLET.   What's his weapon?   130

OSRIC.   Rapier and dagger.

---

101. **absolute:** perfect.   102. **differences:** qualities peculiar to himself.   **soft society:** gentle
breeding.   **great showing:** distinguished appearance.   103. **feelingly:** with proper appreciation.   **card . . . gentry:** the very fashion plate of what a gentleman should be.
104. **continent . . . see:** all the parts that should be in a perfect gentleman.   105-11. **Sir . . .
more:** Hamlet retorts in similar but even more extravagant language. This is too much for Osric
(and for most modern readers). Hamlet's words may be paraphrased: "Sir, the description of this
perfect gentleman loses nothing in your account of him; though I realize that if one were to try to
enumerate his excellences, it would exhaust our arithmetic, and yet"—here he changes the
image to one of sailing—"we should still lag behind him as he outsails us. But in the true
vocabulary of praise, I take him to be a soul of the greatest worth, and his perfume"—i.e., his
personal essence—"so scarce and rare that to speak truly of him, the only thing like him is
his own reflection in his mirror, and everyone else who tries to follow him merely his
shadow."   **yaw:** fall off from the course laid.   **verity . . . extolment:** in true praise.   **infusion:**
essence.   **semblable:** resemblance.   **trace:** follow.   **umbrage:** shadow.   113. **concernancy:**
i.e., what is all this talk about?   113-14. **Why . . . breath:** why do we discuss the gentleman
with our inadequate voices?   115. **Sir:** Osric is completely baffled.   118. **nomination:** naming.   124. **approve:** commend.   128. **his weapon:** i.e., skill with his weapon.   **imputation:**
reputation.   129. **meed:** merit.   **unfellowed:** without an equal.

HAMLET.   That's two of his weapons, but, well.

OSRIC.   The King, sir, hath wagered with him six Barbary horses, against
the which he has imponed,° as I take it, six French rapiers and poniards,
with their assigns,° as girdle, hanger,° and so—three of the carriages, in
faith, are very dear to fancy,° very responsive to° the hilts, most delicate
carriages, and of very liberal conceit.°

HAMLET.   What call you the carriages?

HORATIO.   I knew you must be edified by the margent° ere you had done.

OSRIC.   The carriages, sir, are the hangers.   140

HAMLET.   The phrase would be more germane° to the matter if we could
carry a cannon by our sides. I would it might be hangers till then. But,
on—six Barbary horses against six French swords, their assigns, and three
liberal-conceited carriages. That's the French bet against the Danish.
Why is this "imponed," as you call it?   145

OSRIC.   The King, sir, hath laid, sir, that in a dozen passes between yourself
and him, he shall not exceed you three hits. He hath laid on twelve for
nine, and it would come to immediate trial if your lordship would
vouchsafe the answer.

HAMLET.   How if I answer no?   150

OSRIC.   I mean, my lord, the opposition of your person in trial.

HAMLET.   Sir, I will walk here in the hall. If it please His Majesty, it is the
breathing-time of day with me.° Let the foils be brought, the gentleman
willing, and the King hold his purpose, I will win for him an I can. If not,
I will gain nothing but my shame and the odd hits.   155

OSRIC.   Shall I redeliver you e'en so?

HAMLET.   To this effect, sir, after what flourish° your nature will.

OSRIC.   I commend my duty to your lordship.

HAMLET.   Yours, yours. (*Exit* OSRIC.) He does well to commend it himself,
there are no tongues else for 's turn.   160

HORATIO.   This lapwing° runs away with the shell on his head.

HAMLET.   He did comply with his dug° before he sucked it. Thus has
he—and many more of the same breed that I know the drossy° age dotes
on—only got the tune of the time and outward habit of encounter,° a kind
of yesty collection° which carries them through and through the most
fond° and winnowed° opinions—and do but blow them to their trial, the
bubbles are out.°   167

---

134. imponed: laid down as a stake.   **135. assigns:** that which goes with them.   **hanger:** straps
by which the scabbard was hung from the belt; for specimens.   **136. dear to fancy:** of beautiful
design.   **responsive to:** matching.   **137. liberal conceit:** elaborately artistic.   **139. edified . . .
margent:** informed by the notes. In Shakespeare's time the notes were often printed in the
margin.   **141. germane:** related.   **153. breathing-time . . . me:** time when I take exercise.   **157. flourish:** fanfare, elaborate phrasing.   **161. lapwing:** a pretty, lively little bird. It is so
lively that it can run about the moment it is hatched.   **162. did . . . dug:** was ceremonious with
the nipple; i.e., behaved in this fantastic way from his infancy. See II.ii.337.   **163. drossy:**
scummy, frivolous.   **164. tune . . . encounter:** i.e., they sing the same tune as everyone else and
have the same society manners.   **165. yesty collection:** frothy catchwords.   **166. fond:** foolish.   **winnowed:** light as chaff. Winnowing is the process of fanning the chaff from the
grain.   **166–67. do . . . out:** force them to make sense of their words and they are deflated, as
Hamlet has just deflated Osric.

(Enter a LORD.*)*

LORD. My lord, His Majesty commended him to you by young Osric, who brings back to him that you attend him in the hall. He sends to know if your pleasure hold to play with Laertes, or that you will take longer time. 171

HAMLET. I am constant to my purposes, they follow the King's pleasure. If his fitness speaks, mine is ready, now or whensoever, provided I be so able as now.

LORD. The King and Queen and all are coming down. 175

HAMLET. In happy time.°

LORD. The Queen desires you to use some gentle entertainment° to Laertes before you fall to play.

HAMLET. She well instructs me. *(Exit* LORD.*)*

HORATIO. You will lose this wager, my lord. 180

HAMLET. I do not think so. Since he went into France I have been in continual practice, I shall win at the odds. But thou wouldst not think how ill all's here about my heart—but it is no matter.

HORATIO. Nay, good my lord——

HAMLET. It is but foolery, but it is such a kind of gaingiving° as would perhaps trouble a woman. 186

HORATIO. If your mind dislike anything, obey it. I will forestall their repair hither and say you are not fit.

HAMLET. Not a whit, we defy augury.° There's special providence in the fall of a sparrow.° If it be now, 'tis not to come; if it be not to come, it will be now; if it be not now, yet it will come. The readiness is all. Since no man has aught of what he leaves, what is 't to leave betimes? Let be.

(Enter KING, QUEEN, LAERTES, *and* LORDS, OSRIC *and other* ATTENDANTS *with foils; a table and flagons of wine on it.)*

KING. Come, Hamlet, come, and take this hand from me.

(The KING *puts* LAERTES' *hand into* HAMLET'S.*)*

HAMLET. Give me your pardon, sir. I've done you wrong, 195
But pardon 't, as you are a gentleman.
This presence° knows,
And you must needs have heard, how I am punished
With sore distraction. What I have done
That might your nature, honor, and exception° 200
Roughly awake, I here proclaim was madness.
Was 't Hamlet wronged Laertes? Never Hamlet.

---

176. In . . . time: at a good moment. 177. gentle entertainment: kindly treatment; i.e., be reconciled after the brawl in the churchyard. 185. gaingiving: misgiving. 189. augury: omens. 189–90. special . . . sparrow: The idea comes from Matthew 10:29. "Are not two sparrows sold for a farthing? and one of them shall not fall to the ground without your Father." 197. presence: the whole Court. 200. exception: resentment.

If Hamlet from himself be ta'en away,°
And when he's not himself does wrong Laertes,
Then Hamlet does it not, Hamlet denies it. 205
Who does it, then? His madness. If 't be so,
Hamlet is of the faction that is wronged,
His madness is poor Hamlet's enemy.
Sir, in this audience
Let my disclaiming from a purposed evil° 210
Free me so far in your most generous thoughts
That I have shot mine arrow o'er the house,
And hurt my brother.
LAERTES.   I am satisfied in nature,
Whose motive, in this case, should stir me most
To my revenge. But in my terms of honor 215
I stand aloof, and will no reconcilement
Till by some elder masters of known honor
I have a voice and precedent of peace
To keep my name ungored.° But till that time
I do receive your offered love like love 220
And will not wrong it.
HAMLET: I embrace it freely,
And will this brother's wager frankly play.
Give us the foils. Come on.
LAERTES.   Come, one for me.
HAMLET.   I'll be your foil,° Laertes. In mine ignorance
Your skill shall, like a star i' the darkest night, 225
Stick° fiery off indeed.
LAERTES.   You mock me, sir.
HAMLET.   No, by this hand.
KING.   Give them the foils, young Osric. Cousin Hamlet,
You know the wager?
HAMLET.   Very well, my lord.
Your Grace has laid the odds o' the weaker side. 230
KING.   I do not fear it, I have seen you both.
But since he is bettered,° we have therefore odds.
LAERTES.   This is too heavy, let me see another.
HAMLET.   This likes° me well. These foils have all a length?°

(They prepare to play.)

203. If . . . away: i.e., Hamlet mad is not Hamlet.   **210. Let . . . evil:** let my declaration that I did not intend any harm.   **213–19. I . . . ungored:** I bear you no grudge so far as concerns my personal feelings, which would most readily move me to vengeance; but as this matter touches my honor, I cannot accept your apology until I have been assured by those expert in matters of honor that I may so do without loss of reputation.   **224. foil:** Hamlet puns on the other meaning of foil—tin foil set behind a gem to give it luster.   **226. Stick . . . off:** Shine out.   **232. bettered:** considered your superior.   **234. likes:** pleases.   **have . . . length:** are all of equal length.

OSRIC.   Aye, my good lord.   235
KING.   Set me the stoups° of wine upon that table.
   If Hamlet give the first or second hit,
   Or quit° in answer of the third exchange,
   Let all the battlements their ordnance fire.
   The King shall drink to Hamlet's better breath,   240
   And in the cup a union° shall he throw
   Richer than that which four successive kings
   In Denmark's crown have worn. Give me the cups,
   And let the kettle° to the trumpet speak,
   The trumpet to the cannoneer without,   245
   The cannon to the Heavens, the Heaven to earth,
   "Now the King drinks to Hamlet." Come, begin,
   And you, the judges, bear a wary eye.
HAMLET.   Come on, sir.
LAERTES.   Come, my lord.   (*They play.*)
HAMLET.   One.
LAERTES.   No.
HAMLET.   Judgment.
OSRIC.   A hit, a very palpable° hit.
LAERTES.   Well, again.   250
KING.   Stay, give me drink. Hamlet, this pearl is thine°—
   Here's to thy health.

(Trumpets sound, and cannon shot off within.)

                              Give him the cup.
HAMLET.   I'll play this bout first. Set it by a while.
   Come. (*They play.*) Another hit, what say you?
LAERTES.   A touch, a touch, I do confess.
KING.   Our son shall win.
QUEEN.   He's fat° and scant of breath.   255
   Here, Hamlet, take my napkin, rub thy brows.
   The Queen carouses to thy fortune, Hamlet.
HAMLET.   Good madam!
KING.   Gertrude, do not drink.
QUEEN.   I will, my lord, I pray you pardon me.

(She drinks.)

KING (*Aside*).   It is the poisoned cup, it is too late.   260
HAMLET.   I dare not drink yet, madam—by and by.
QUEEN.   Come, let me wipe thy face.
LAERTES.   My lord, I'll hit him now.
KING.   I do not think 't.
LAERTES (*Aside*).   And yet 'tis almost against my conscience.

---

236. **stoups:** drinking-vessels.   238. **quit:** strike back.   241. **union:** a large pearl.   244. **kettle:** kettledrum.   250. **palpable:** clear.   251. **this . . . thine:** With these words the King drops the poisoned pearl into the cup intended for Hamlet.   255. **fat:** out of condition.

HAMLET.   Come, for the third, Laertes. You but dally.°   265
I pray you pass with your best violence,
I am afeard you make a wanton of me.°
LAERTES.   Say you so? Come on.

(They play.)

OSRIC.   Nothing, neither way.
LAERTES.   Have at you now!

*(*LAERTES *wounds* HAMLET; *then, in scuffling, they change rapiers, and* HAMLET *wounds* LAERTES.)*

KING.   Part them, they are incensed.   270
HAMLET.   Nay, come, again.

(The QUEEN *falls.)*

OSRIC.   Look to the Queen there, ho!
HORATIO.   They bleed on both sides. How is it, my lord?
OSRIC.   How is 't, Laertes?
LAERTES.   Why, as a woodcock to mine own springe,° Osric,
I am justly killed with mine own treachery.   275
HAMLET.   How does the Queen?
KING.   She swounds to see them bleed.
QUEEN.   No, no, the drink, the drink!—O my dear Hamlet—
The drink, the drink! I am poisoned.   *(Dies.)*
HAMLET.   Oh, villainy! Ho! Let the door be locked.
Treachery! Seek it out.   *(*LAERTES *falls.)*
LAERTES.   It is here, Hamlet. Hamlet, thou art slain.   281
No medicine in the world can do thee good,
In thee there is not half an hour of life.
The treacherous instrument is in thy hand,
Unbated and envenomed. The foul practice   285
Hath turned itself on me. Lo, here I lie
Never to rise again. Thy mother's poisoned.
I can no more. The King, the King's to blame.
HAMLET.   The point envenomed too!
Then, venom, to thy work.   *(Stabs the* KING.)*
ALL.   Treason! Treason!   291
KING.   Oh, yet defend me, friends, I am but hurt.
HAMLET.   Here, thou incestuous, murderous, damnèd Dane,
Drink off this potion. Is thy union° here?
Follow my mother.   *(*KING *dies.)*
LAERTES.   He is justly served.   295
It is a poison tempered° by himself.
Exchange forgiveness with me, noble Hamlet.
Mine and my father's death come not upon thee,°
Nor thine on me!   *(Dies.)*

---

265. **dally:** play.   267. **make . . . me:** treat me like a child by letting me win.   274. **springe:** snare.   294. **union:** pearl, as in l. 241.   296. **tempered:** mixed.   298. **come . . . thee:** are not on your head.

HAMLET.   Heaven make thee free of it!° I follow thee.   300
   I am dead, Horatio. Wretched Queen, adieu!
   You that look pale and tremble at this chance,
   That are but mutes or audience to this act,
   Had I but time—as this fell° sergeant,° Death,
   Is strict in his arrest—oh, I could tell you——   305
   But let it be. Horatio, I am dead,
   Thou livest. Report me and my cause aright
   To the unsatisfied.°
HORATIO.   Never believe it.
   I am more an antique Roman° than a Dane.
   Here's yet some liquor left.
HAMLET.   As thou 'rt a man,   310
   Give me the cup. Let go—by Heaven, I'll have 't.
   O good Horatio, what a wounded name,
   Things standing thus unknown, shall live behind me!
   If thou didst ever hold me in thy heart,
   Absent thee from felicity a while,   315
   And in this harsh world draw thy breath in pain
   To tell my story.

   (March afar off, and shot within.)

               What warlike noise is this?
OSRIC.   Young Fortinbras, with conquest come from Poland,
   To the ambassadors of England gives
   This warlike volley.
HAMLET.   Oh, I die, Horatio,   320
   The potent poison quite o'ercrows° my spirit.
   I cannot live to hear the news from England,
   But I do prophesy the election° lights
   On Fortinbras. He has my dying voice.°
   So tell him, with the occurrents, more and less,   325
   Which have solicited.° The rest is silence.   *(Dies.)*
HORATIO.   Now cracks a noble heart. Good night, sweet Prince,
   And flights of angels sing thee to thy rest!

   (March within.)

   Why does the drum come hither?

   (Enter FORTINBRAS, *and the* ENGLISH AMBASSADORS, *with drum, colors,*
and ATTENDANTS.*)*

---

300. Heaven . . . it: God forgive you.   **304. fell:** dread.   **sergeant:** the officer of the Court who
made arrests.   **308. unsatisfied:** who do not know the truth.   **309. antique Roman:** like Cato
and Brutus, who killed themselves rather than survive in a world which was unpleasing to
them.   **321. o'ercrows:** overpowers.   **323. election:** as King of Denmark. See l. 65
above.   **324. voice:** support.   **325–26. occurrents . . . solicited:** events great and small which
have caused me to act.

FORTINBRAS.   Where is this sight?

HORATIO.   What is it you would see?   330
   If aught of woe or wonder, cease your search.

FORTINBRAS.   This quarry cries on havoc.° O proud Death,
   What feast is toward° in thine eternal cell
   That thou so many princes at a shot
   So bloodily hast struck?

FIRST AMBASSADOR.   The sight is dismal,   335
   And our affairs from England come too late.
   The ears are senseless that should give us hearing.
   To tell him his commandment is fulfilled,
   That Rosencrantz and Guildenstern are dead.
   Where should we have our thanks?

HORATIO.   Not from his mouth   340
   Had it the ability of life to thank you.
   He never gave commandment for their death.
   But since, so jump° upon this bloody question,°
   You from the Polack wars, and you from England,
   Are here arrived, give order that these bodies   345
   High on a stage be placèd to the view,
   And let me speak to the yet unknowing world
   How these things came about. So shall you hear
   Of carnal, bloody, and unnatural acts,
   Of accidental judgments, casual slaughters,   350
   Of deaths put on by cunning and forced cause,
   And, in this upshot, purposes mistook
   Fall'n on the inventors' heads.° All this can I
   Truly deliver.

FORTINBRAS.   Let us haste to hear it,
   And call the noblest to the audience.   355
   For me, with sorrow I embrace my fortune.
   I have some rights of memory° in this kingdom,
   Which now to claim my vantage° doth invite me.

HORATIO.   Of that I shall have also cause to speak,
   And from his mouth whose voice will draw on more.°   360
   But let this same be presently performed,
   Even while men's minds are wild, lest more mischance
   On plots and errors happen.

---

332. quarry . . . havoc: heap of slain denotes a pitiless slaughter.   **333. toward:** being prepared.   **343. jump:** exactly. See I.i.65.   **question:** matter.   **349–53. carnal . . . heads:** These lines sum up the whole tragedy: Claudius' adultery with Gertrude, his murder of his brother, the death of Ophelia due to an accident, that of Polonius by casual chance, Hamlet's device which caused the deaths of Rosencrantz and Guildenstern, the plan which went awry and caused the deaths of Claudius and Laertes.   **357. rights of memory:** rights which will be remembered; i.e., with the disappearance of all the family of the original King Hamlet the situation reverts to what it was before the death of Fortinbras' father. See I.i.80–95.   **358. vantage:** i.e., my advantage, there being none to dispute my claim.   **360. voice . . . more:** i.e., Hamlet's dying voice will strengthen your claim.

FORTINBRAS.   Let four captains
　Bear Hamlet, like a soldier, to the stage.
　For he was likely, had he been put on,°   365
　To have proved most royally. And for his passage
　The soldiers' music and the rites of war
　Speak loudly for him.
　Take up the bodies. Such a sight as this
　Becomes the field, but here shows much amiss.
　Go, bid the soldiers shoot.

(A dead march. Exeunt, bearing off the bodies; after which a peal of ordnance is shot off.)

QUESTIONS

1. The first insight we get into Hamlet's mind comes with his initial soliloquy (I, ii, 129–59). This key moment in the play begins to take us into his dilemma. What is Hamlet's problem? Is it simply grief over his father's death? In order to respond, you might consider how Hamlet sees the world in which he lives, the cosmos outside this world, his own relation to these forces?

2. Polonius's much-quoted speech to Laertes (I, iii, 59–80) is often seen as a piece of good advice ("to thine own self be true"). Do you think it is? In the larger thematic emphasis of the play, is it also possible to see the speech as part of the "rotten state" of Denmark? How is the confidence Polonius exhibits affected by what we have already seen of Hamlet and of his self doubts?

3. Act II, Scene ii opens with Claudius and Gertrude talking to Rosencrantz and Guildenstern and ends with Hamlet's soliloquy ("O, what a rogue and peasant slave am I!"). What happens in this scene? How does it refine our respective attitudes toward all the figures who play a role in it: the King, the Queen, Rosencrantz and Guildenstern, and Hamlet? In what sense does this scene add complexity to the action? How does this soliloquy differ in tone and content from the soliloquy in I, ii, 129–59?

4. In Act II, Scene iii Hamlet has an opportunity to kill Claudius. At this point, he has no uncertainty about Claudius' guilt. The reasons he might have given at the opening of the play for inaction no longer hold true. Should he have completed his revenge at this point? How does his inability to do so condition our view of him and his internal state?

5. What is the function of the gravedigger scene (Act V, Scene i)? Discuss the subject matter of this scene—what the characters actually say—in relation to the themes of the play as a whole. Discuss comic relief as it occurs in this and other episodes in the play. Sometimes such scenes are regarded as being outside the tragic action of the play. Is this one outside *Hamlet's* tragic action?

365. had . . . on: had he become King.

6. As the play is drawing to a conclusion (V, ii, 10–11), Hamlet speaks about a "divinity that shapes our ends." What would be lost if this speech and the one about finding Providence in the fall of a sparrow (V, ii, 189–90) were omitted from the play? Refer back to Hamlet's first soliloquy in the play and analyze what has changed in his outlook. Why has his view of the universe altered? To what extent has the change been caused by external events? How does such a change allow Hamlet's death to stand for something positive about human existence?

3
COMEDY

A s we saw in the preceding section, tragedy fastens upon individuals, concentrating its focus on the single man or woman who suffers alone in a world from which he or she, owing to fate or flaw, is separated. Oedipus, for instance, shoulders, with no help, the terrifying burden of being king; he is the single cause of the plague visited upon Thebes and the single cause of the city's eventual release. And Hamlet alone grasps the true nature of the corruption that has afflicted Denmark; in the solitary confinement of his imagination, he faces the necessity of acting, self-destructively, to annihilate the source of that affliction. In contrast to the world of tragedy represented by these two figures, the world of comedy concentrates its attention on individuals who are *in* and *of* society. The comic individual cannot escape the presence and the judgment of those surrounding him. He is customarily seen with them, and they serve to illuminate his foibles and foolishness. In Molière's *Tartuffe*, for instance, we know how to understand the foolish Orgon, the victim of Tartuffe's scheming, by seeing him through the eyes of members of his family and by those dismayed by his folly.

Another striking difference between tragedy and comedy resides in the fact that we use terms such as *foibles* and *foolishness* in describing the plight of the comic hero. Such terms would be ludicrously out of place in describing either Oedipus or Hamlet. Such terms are perfectly appropriate to the world of comedy because no real or irremediable disasters occur in comedy. Comic heroes might be embarrassed, and they might be the objects of scorn or ridicule. They might suffer. They are endowed, however, with perfect powers of recovery, just like cartoon figures who are dynamited or flattened by steamrollers but who, in the next scene, are whole once again and ready for yet another escapade. Thus Molière's Orgon, gulled, disgraced, and soon to go to debtor's prison, is suddenly saved and is put into a position to begin his life again, perhaps even to make further misjudgments.

Comparing the chief characters of a comedy with those of a tragedy is immediately to see another difference between the two genres. There is little real complexity in the construction of a comic figure. He is made up of a few stock elements, such as foppishness, pride, avarice, naïveté, or boastfulness. His vices, the equivalent of a "comic flaw," ultimately prove the cause of his ridiculous downfall or embarrassment, but have no further consequence in terms of change, insight, or development. Orgon, for instance, is no more and no less than the very obstinate and imperceptive man he seems.

If the characters in a comedy come out of a stockpile of familiar elements and hence are easily recognizable stereotypes, so also are the plots of comedy usually based on wholly familiar situations. A vain man wishes to have his daughter marry someone wholly inappropriate to her, and yet she is in love with someone else and ultimately marries him; or a miser hoards everything and ruins himself through blind greed; or a family that thinks all of its members lost and separated from each other suddenly finds itself reunited. Writers of comedy customarily use for their plots whatever comes easily to hand. In contrast, consider the uniqueness of the situations that make up *Oedipus Rex* or *Hamlet*; those situations are extreme, challenging their respective protagonists to answer desperate problems with desperate means.

Comic plots, moreover, find their end in happiness, in the triumph of the good. Human joy and security ultimately emerge from even the most unlikely places in comedy and we are meant to celebrate their arrival. The good marriage that was always meant to be, the reconciliation that brings peace, the lost child who is found: these are the typical conclusions of comedy. Death is not oppressive, nor is pain long-lasting. The land of comedy, then, is a beneficent one, providing abundant charity and prosperity for its inhabitants. Entering its realm is to find oneself in a golden land, where the innocent, the young, and the life-giving reign supreme.

When this happiness arrives, it can do so even at considerable cost to the plausibility of the comic plot. Since comic plots sometimes tend to be casual, even improbable, we tend not to object to the outlandish means by which the good triumphs, and the silly or cruel is bested. A well-known convention in comic drama, the *deus ex machina*, literally the "god from a machine," refers to a device employed in some ancient plays by which, in order to bring a happy outcome to the plot, the god who had the power to do so was lowered onto the stage and saw to it that everything came out right. This providential convention is not lost in Molière's *Tartuffe:* all is at last made well by the power of the king reigning at the time the play was written and produced, the Sun King, Louis XIV, in whom Molière invested the healing power that is an integral element in all comedy.

Another element of comedy that distinguishes it from tragedy is its corrective aim. We feel in a comic drama that we are being instructed, amid all the amusement and hilarity, as to a way to behave, a way that is sensible, moderate, and wise. We are being asked to respect generosity and amiability. In tragedy, however, there is no moral lesson easily to be drawn from the catastrophe we witness. We cannot say of Hamlet or of Oedipus that there was a "better" way for them to have acted. We recognize that they did, at last, everything they could have done. In being as brave and true to themselves as they were, they fastened themselves to their own doom. We cannot criticize their actions but can only be moved by their inevitability. About Orgon, however, we can say that he acted as a silly man acts, and that he should have known better. Comedy, then, promotes the faculty of criticism; it allows us to say that people act absurdly and should not.

In short, tragedy can fill us with a sense of awe, for we are put in the presence of human greatness. The imagination and the power of sympathy (Aristotle's "pity and terror") are expanded as we see figures larger than life confronting overwhelming circumstances. The world of comedy, on the other hand, has smaller dimensions. It brings into focus the frailty and the handicaps of humankind. It sees that people are weak. It examines the fundamental disparity between the ridiculous way we behave and the justifications and the rationales we supply for that behavior. Orgon believes in his own piety, his high standards of judgment, and in his ability to distinguish his friends from his enemies. He couldn't be more wrong in each and every instance. We are amused by the contrast between his perceptions of reality and that reality itself.

In being amused, we find ourselves looking down on the figures occupying the world of comedy. In recognizing their absurdity and limitations, we derive pleasure from the superior stance we are given by the comic dramatist. This is in obvious contrast with our position *vis-à-vis* the tragic world. There, we are made to look up, to feel dwarfed by a greatness not our own. In tragedy, moreover, we are meant to respect the worth of ideals. Those who possess them might perish because of them, but that doesn't imply that the ideals themselves are faulty. We do not feel that Oedipus' desire to probe the truth of his life is wrong, but we acknowledge that the fulfillment of such a desire will lead to his downfall. In comedy, however, even ideals themselves can seem absurd. Orgon's seriousness and high-mindedness, his implacable religiosity, are simply ludicrous given all the mistakes he makes at their behest. Where Oedipus' tenacity is admirable, Orgon's is laughable.

This last distinction should remind us of the most important attribute of comedy: it is funny. It should bring laughter or a knowing smile to the audience. If it does not, it fails. That is because it is an art whose primary aim has always been to provide pleasure, relief, and a detachment from the world as it is. From the privileged position offered to us by the comic dramatist, we are, for a moment, spectators of an activity that is busy, ultimately painless, and yet true to what it means to be human.

In turning to some of the specific characteristics of *Tartuffe*, we note that Molière himself made a sharp distinction between his own work, all of it written in the comic vein, and the work of tragic dramatists. He said that comedy deals in an amiable fashion with people as they are and rivets its attention on what is ridiculous and weak about them. The writer of comedy must, he declared, produce lifelike depictions of "the people of our own age," doing so in order to provide a "public mirror" whose function is "to make respectable people laugh." It must also amuse its audience, Molière said, while at the same time "improving its morals."

These several aims are fused in *Tartuffe* and help to make it the rich, complex, and fascinating creation that it has remained for centuries. Part of its power comes from the fact that Molière compressed so much understanding of human nature into such narrow confines. French dramatists of the seventeenth century, responsive to Aristotelean principles, obeyed the rule of the three *unities*. Plays, they believed, should have but one main action, should begin and end in the course of one day, and should have all their action limited to one place. Thus the play takes place entirely in Orgon's house in Paris, is seemingly completed in one day, and is focused entirely on the victimization of Orgon by the brilliant and hypocritical Tartuffe. As with the action of *Oedipus Rex*, every character in the play, and all its events, contribute to the transformation of the central character. In addition, Molière observed another rule of the time, namely that drama should have a three-part structure: an *exposition* of the situation, a *complication* of that situation, and a *denouement* that resolves it. We are thus given Orgon infatuated by Tartuffe's brilliant hypocrisy and religious charlatanry, then Orgon brought to his senses but threatened with eviction from his house and on his way to prison, and at last Orgon saved by the Prince of the realm who, as it turns out, had been waiting to nab the cruel Tartuffe.

One other technical strategem, called by the French term *liaison des scènes*, contributes to the effect of speed in the play: each scene is made to interlock with the one succeeding it. This is accomplished by never permitting the stage to be empty; at least one character from the earlier scene must remain to be a part of the next. Thus the action is continuous, and the attention of the audience is never allowed to break its connection with the line of action. There is also the verse itself. Like other French dramatists of his time, Molière wrote in verse, and this English version reproduces the lightness and playfulness of the original. The verse is pleasurable in and of itself, but it also establishes a tone for the play—the neatly rhyming lines following so nimbly upon each other help reassure us that nothing too serious is likely to happen on the stage, in much the same way that the blank verse of *Hamlet* forces us to take the sentiments of that play very seriously.

Tartuffe also illustrates another general truth about drama. While it is helpful to see the many differences between tragedy and comedy, it is also important to recognize their ultimate kinship. From their earliest origins in ancient Greece and medieval Europe, they are linked as ceremonial portrayals of the rhythm and changes of life. The one genre, tragedy, looks at decline, collapse, and death. The other, comedy, celebrates birth and unification. And we all know that laughter and tears, our own reactions to the comic and the tragic, are closely related as psychological responses to the realities of life.

The way in which Molière wrote *Tartuffe* resulted in a play that fuses elements of the tragic with essentially comic material. The first version of the play was the target of much protest and controversy in seventeenth-century France. Some people were indignant about what they saw as Molière's attacks on the church and religiosity. So fierce were such criticisms of the play that even the king himself, long a protector of the playwright, was forced to withdraw his support. Molière was hurt by these reactions and sensed that a powerful adversary, namely a combination of religious hypocrisy and state power, was working against him. The figure of Tartuffe in the revised version of the play (the one included here) is meant to represent that adversary.

Hence the play, for all its comic force, introduces something quite disturbing: Tartuffe is not only a hypocrite but is also fundamentally evil. He will do anything, not just to fool Orgon and cuckold him, but also to destroy him. Thus what begins as a play of a household in disarray owing to the obsession of the father with a man everyone else can see as an impostor almost ends as serious drama. Tartuffe nearly succeeds in dispossessing the family of everything they own. But, at last, the comic life of the play overwhelms even such malignancy, the king's officer comes to the rescue, and all is made well.

The introduction of evil into such a comedy meant that Molière was playing with fire as a playwright. But the darker elements of the drama only serve to strengthen its more important comic elements. The result is a play that, lasting on the stage as long as it has, reminds us that great comedy need not be simple froth and boisterous excitement. It can also be another powerful way of looking into the nature of life.

Molière (1622–1673)
Tartuffe

CHARACTERS

MME PERNELLE, *Orgon's mother*
ORGON, *Elmire's husband*
ELMIRE, *Orgon's wife*
DAMIS, *Orgon's son, Elmire's stepson*
MARIANE, *Orgon's daughter, Elmire's stepdaughter, in love with Valère*
VALÈRE, *in love with Mariane*
CLÉANTE, *Orgon's brother-in-law*
TARTUFFE, *a hypocrite*
DORINE, *Mariane's lady's-maid*
M. LOYAL, *a bailiff*
A POLICE OFFICER
FLIPOTE, *Mme Pernelle's maid*

The scene throughout: Orgon's house in Paris.

ACT I

SCENE I

MADAME PERNELLE *and* FLIPOTE, *her maid,* ELMIRE, MARIANE, DORINE, DAMIS, CLÉANTE.

MADAME PERNELLE.   Come, come, Flipote; it's time I left this place.
ELMIRE.   I can't keep up, you walk at such a pace.
MADAME PERNELLE.   Don't trouble, child; no need to show me out.
    It's not your manners I'm concerned about.
ELMIRE.   We merely pay you the respect we owe.
    But, Mother, why this hurry? Must you go?
MADAME PERNELLE.   I must. This house appalls me. No one in it
    Will pay attention for a single minute.
    Children, I take my leave much vexed in spirit.
    I offer good advice, but you won't hear it.
    You all break in and chatter on and on.
    It's like a madhouse with the keeper gone.
DORINE.   If . . .
MADAME PERNELLE.   Girl, you talk too much, and I'm afraid
    You're far too saucy for a lady's-maid.
    You push in everywhere and have your say.
DAMIS.   But . . .
MADAME PERNELLE.   You, boy, grow more foolish every day.
    To think my grandson should be such a dunce!
    I've said a hundred times, if I've said it once,
    That if you keep the course on which you've started,
    You'll leave your worthy father broken-hearted.

MARIANE.   I think . . .
MADAME PERNELLE.   And you, his sister, seem so pure,
   So shy, so innocent, and so demure.
   But you know what they say about still waters.
   I pity parents with secretive daughters.
ELMIRE.   Now, Mother . . .
MADAME PERNELLE.   And as for you, child, let me add
   That your behavior is extremely bad,
   And a poor example for these children, too.
   Their dear, dead mother did far better than you.
   You're much too free with money, and I'm distressed
   To see you so elaborately dressed.
   When it's one's husband that one aims to please,
   One has no need of costly fripperies.
CLÉANTE.   Oh, Madam, really . . .
MADAME PERNELLE.   You are her brother, Sir,
   And I respect and love you; yet if I were
   My son, this lady's good and pious spouse,
   I wouldn't make you welcome in my house.
   You're full of worldly counsels which, I fear,
   Aren't suitable for decent folk to hear.
   I've spoken bluntly, Sir; but it behooves us
   Not to mince words when righteous fervor moves us.
DAMIS.   Your man Tartuffe is full of holy speeches . . .
MADAME PERNELLE.   And practises precisely what he preaches.
   He's a fine man, and should be listened to.
   I will not hear him mocked by fools like you.
DAMIS.   Good God! Do you expect me to submit
   To the tyranny of that carping hypocrite?
   Must we forgo all joys and satisfactions
   Because that bigot censures all our actions?
DORINE.   To hear him talk—and he talks all the time—
   There's nothing one can do that's not a crime.
   He rails at everything, your dear Tartuffe.
MADAME PERNELLE.   Whatever he reproves deserves reproof.
   He's out to save your souls, and all of you
   Must love him, as my son would have you do.
DAMIS.   Ah no, Grandmother, I could never take
   To such a rascal, even for my father's sake.
   That's how I feel, and I shall not dissemble.
   His every action makes me seethe and tremble
   With helpless anger, and I have no doubt
   That he and I will shortly have it out.
DORINE.   Surely it is a shame and a disgrace
   To see this man usurp the master's place—
   To see this beggar who, when first he came,
   Had not a shoe or shoestring to his name

So far forget himself that he behaves
As if the house were his, and we his slaves.
MADAME PERNELLE.   Well, mark my words, your souls would fare far better
If you obeyed his precepts to the letter.
DORINE.   You see him as a saint. I'm far less awed;
In fact, I see right through him. He's a fraud.
MADAME PERNELLE.   Nonsense!
DORINE.   His man Laurent's the same, or worse;
I'd not trust either with a penny purse.
MADAME PERNELLE.   I can't say what his servant's morals may be;
His own great goodness I can guarantee.
You all regard him with distaste and fear
Because he tells you what you're loath to hear,
Condemns your sins, points out your moral flaws,
And humbly strives to further Heaven's cause.
DORINE.   If sin is all that bothers him, why is it
He's so upset when folk drop in to visit?
Is Heaven so outraged by a social call
That he must prophesy against us all?
I'll tell you what I think: if you ask me,
He's jealous of my mistress' company.
MADAME PERNELLE.
Rubbish! (*To* ELMIRE.) He's not alone, child, in complaining
Of all your promiscuous entertaining.
Why, the whole neighborhood's upset, I know,
By all these carriages that come and go,
With crowds of guests parading in and out
And noisy servants loitering about.
In all of this, I'm sure there's nothing vicious;
But why give people cause to be suspicious?
CLÉANTE.   They need no cause; they'll talk in any case.
Madam, this world would be a joyless place
If, fearing what malicious tongues might say,
We locked our doors and turned our friends away.
And even if one did so dreary a thing,
D'you think those tongues would cease their chattering?
One can't fight slander; it's a losing battle;
Let us instead ignore their tittle-tattle.
Let's strive to live by conscience' clear decrees,
And let the gossips gossip as they please.
DORINE.   If there is talk against us, I know the source:
It's Daphne and her little husband, of course.
Those who have greatest cause for guilt and shame
Are quickest to besmirch a neighbor's name.
When there's a chance for libel, they never miss it;
When something can be made to seem illicit

They're off at once to spread the joyous news,
Adding to fact what fantasies they choose.
By talking up their neighbor's indiscretions
They seek to camouflage their own transgressions,
Hoping that others' innocent affairs
Will lend a hue of innocence to theirs,
Or that their own black guilt will come to seem
Part of a general shady color-scheme.

MADAME PERNELLE.   All that is quite irrelevant. I doubt
That anyone's more virtuous and devout
Than dear Orante; and I'm informed that she
Condemns your mode of life most vehemently.

DORINE.   Oh, yes, she's strict, devout, and has no taint
Of worldliness; in short, she seems a saint.
But it was time which taught her that disguise;
She's thus because she can't be otherwise.
So long as her attractions could enthrall,
She flounced and flirted and enjoyed it all,
But now that they're no longer what they were
She quits a world which fast is quitting her,
And wears a veil of virtue to conceal
Her bankrupt beauty and her lost appeal.
That's what becomes of old coquettes today:
Distressed when all their lovers fall away,
They see no recourse but to play the prude,
And so confer a style on solitude.
Thereafter, they're severe with everyone,
Condemning all our actions, pardoning none,
And claiming to be pure, austere, and zealous
When, if the truth were known, they're merely jealous,
And cannot bear to see another know
The pleasures time has forced them to forego.

MADAME PERNELLE (*Initially to* ELMIRE).
That sort of talk is what you like to hear;
Therefore you'd have us all keep still, my dear,
While Madam rattles on the livelong day.
Nevertheless, I mean to have my say.
I tell you that you're blest to have Tartuffe
Dwelling, as my son's guest, beneath this roof;
That Heaven has sent him to forestall its wrath
By leading you, once more, to the true path;
That all he reprehends its reprehensible,
And that you'd better heed him, and be sensible.
These visits, balls, and parties in which you revel
Are nothing but inventions of the Devil.
One never hears a word that's edifying:
Nothing but chaff and foolishness and lying,

As well as vicious gossip in which one's neighbor
Is cut to bits with epee, foil, and saber.
People of sense are driven half-insane
At such affairs, where noise and folly reign
And reputations perish thick and fast.
As a wise preacher said on Sunday last,
Parties are Towers of Babylon, because
The guests all babble on with never a pause;
And then he told a story which, I think . . .

(To CLÉANTE.*)*

I heard that laugh, Sir, and I saw that wink!
Go find your silly friends and laugh some more!
Enough; I'm going; don't show me to the door.
I leave this household much dismayed and vexed;
I cannot say when I shall see you next.

(Slapping FLIPOTE.*)*

Wake up, don't stand there gaping into space!
I'll slap some sense into that stupid face.
Move, move, you slut.

SCENE II.

CLÉANTE, DORINE.

CLÉANTE.   I think I'll stay behind:
  I want no further pieces of her mind.
  How that old lady . . .
DORINE.   Oh, what wouldn't she say
  If she could hear you speak of her that way!
  She'd thank you for the *lady*, but I'm sure
  She'd find the *old* a little premature.
CLÉANTE.   My, what a scene she made, and what a din!
  And how this man Tartuffe has taken her in!
DORINE.   Yes, but her son is even worse deceived;
  His folly must be seen to be believed.
  In the late troubles,° he played an able part
  And served his king° with wise and loyal heart,
  But he's quite lost his senses since he fell
  Beneath Tartuffe's infatuating spell.
  He calls him brother, and loves him as his life,
  Preferring him to mother, child, or wife.
  In him and him alone will he confide;
  He's made him his confessor and his guide;

late troubles: an allusion to the Fronde, a political party that opposed Cardinal Mazarin, tutor to the young Louis XIV ("his king") and his first chief minister.

He pets and pampers him with love more tender
Than any pretty mistress could engender,
Gives him the place of honor when they dine,
Delights to see him gorging like a swine,
Stuffs him with dainties till his guts distend,
And when he belches, cries "God bless you, friend!"
In short, he's mad; he worships him; he dotes;
His deeds he marvels at, his words he quotes,
Thinking each act a miracle, each word
Oracular as those that Moses heard.
Tartuffe, much pleased to find so easy a victim,
Has in a hundred ways beguiled and tricked him,
Milked him of money, and with his permission
Established here a sort of Inquisition.°
Even Laurent, his lackey, dares to give
Us arrogant advice on how to live;
He sermonizes us in thundering tones
And confiscates our ribbons and colognes.
Last week he tore a kerchief into pieces
Because he found it pressed in a *Life of Jesus:*°
He said it was a sin to juxtapose
Unholy vanities and holy prose.

SCENE III

ELMIRE, MARIANE, DAMIS, CLÉANTE, DORINE.

ELMIRE (*To* CLÉANTE).
    You did well not to follow; she stood in the door
    And said *verbatim* all she'd said before.
    I saw my husband coming. I think I'd best
    Go upstairs now, and take a little rest.
CLÉANTE.   I'll wait and greet him here; then I must go.
    I've really only time to say hello.
DAMIS.   Sound him about my sister's wedding, please.
    I think Tartuffe's against it, and that he's
    Been urging Father to withdraw his blessing.
    As you well know, I'd find that most distressing.
    Unless my sister and Valère can marry,
    My hopes to wed *his* sister will miscarry,
    And I'm determined . . .
DORINE.   He's coming.

Inquisition: an allusion to a tribunal of the Roman Catholic Church charged with the suppression of heresy.   **Life of Jesus:** an allusion to any such work glorifying the life and deeds of extraordinary Christians.

SCENE IV

ORGON, CLÉANTE, DORINE.

ORGON.   Ah, Brother, good-day.
CLÉANTE.   Well, welcome back. I'm sorry I can't stay.
    How was the country? Blooming, I trust, and green?
ORGON.   Excuse me, Brother; just one moment.

(To DORINE.*)*   Dorine . . .

(To CLÉANTE.*)*

    To put my mind at rest, I always learn
    The household news the moment I return.

(To DORINE.*)*

    Has all been well, these two days I've been gone?
    How are the family? What's been going on?
DORINE.   Your wife, two days ago, had a bad fever,
    And a fierce headache which refused to leave her.
ORGON.   Ah. And Tartuffe?
DORINE.   Tartuffe? Why, he's round and red,
    Bursting with health, and excellently fed.
ORGON.   Poor fellow!
DORINE.   That night, the mistress was unable
    To take a single bite at the dinner-table.
    Her headache-pains, she said, were simply hellish.
ORGON.   Ah. And Tartuffe?
DORINE.   He ate his meal with relish,
    And zealously devoured in her presence
    A leg of mutton and a brace of pheasants.
ORGON.   Poor fellow!
DORINE.   Well, the pains continued strong,
    And so she tossed and tossed the whole night long,
    Now icy-cold, now burning like a flame.
    We sat beside her bed till morning came.
ORGON.   Ah. And Tartuffe?
DORINE.   Why, having eaten, he rose
    And sought his room, already in a doze,
    Got into his warm bed, and snored away
    In perfect peace until the break of day.
ORGON.   Poor fellow!
DORINE.   After much ado, we talked her
    Into dispatching someone for the doctor.
    He bled her, and the fever quickly fell.

ORGON.   Ah. And Tartuffe?
DORINE.   He bore it very well.
  To keep his cheerfulness at any cost,
  And make up for the blood *Madame* had lost,
  He drank, at lunch, four beakers full of port.
ORGON.   Poor fellow!
DORINE.   Both are doing well, in short.
  I'll go and tell *Madame* that you've expressed
  Keen sympathy and anxious interest.

SCENE V

ORGON, CLÉANTE.

CLÉANTE.   That girl was laughing in your face, and though
  I've no wish to offend you, even so
  I'm bound to say that she had some excuse.
  How can you possibly be such a goose?
  Are you so dazed by this man's hocus-pocus
  That all the world, save him, is out of focus?
  You've given him clothing, shelter, food, and care;
  Why must you also . . .
ORGON.   Brother, stop right there.
  You do not know the man of whom you speak.
CLÉANTE.   I grant you that. But my judgment's not so weak
  That I can't tell, by his effect on others . . .
ORGON.   Ah, when you meet him, you two will be like brothers!
  There's been no loftier soul since time began.
  He is a man who . . . a man who . . . an excellent man.
  To keep his precepts is to be reborn,
  And view this dunghill of a world with scorn.
  Yes, thanks to him I'm a changed man indeed.
  Under his tutelage my soul's been freed
  From earthly loves, and every human tie:
  My mother, children, brother, and wife could die,
  And I'd not feel a single moment's pain.
CLÉANTE.   That's a fine sentiment, Brother; most humane.
ORGON.   Oh, had you seen Tartuffe as I first knew him,
  Your heart, like mine, would have surrendered to him.
  He used to come into our church each day
  And humbly kneel nearby, and start to pray.
  He'd draw the eyes of everybody there
  By the deep fervor of his heartfelt prayer;
  He'd sigh and weep, and sometimes with a sound
  Of rapture he would bend and kiss the ground;
  And when I rose to go, he'd run before
  To offer me holy-water at the door.
  His serving-man, no less devout than he,

Informed me of his master's poverty;
I gave him gifts, but in his humbleness
He'd beg me every time to give him less.
"Oh, that's too much," he'd cry, "too much by twice!
I don't deserve it. The half, Sir, would suffice."
And when I wouldn't take it back, he'd share
Half of it with the poor, right then and there.
At length, Heaven prompted me to take him in
To dwell with us, and free our souls from sin.
He guides our lives, and to protect my honor
Stays by my wife, and keeps an eye upon her;
He tells me whom she sees, and all she does,
And seems more jealous than I ever was!
And how austere he is! Why, he can detect
A mortal sin where you would least suspect;
In smallest trifles, he's extremely strict.
Last week, his conscience was severely pricked
Because, while praying, he had caught a flea
And killed it, so he felt, too wrathfully.

CLÉANTE.   Good God, man! Have you lost your common sense—
    Or is this all some joke at my expense?
    How can you stand there and in all sobriety . . .

ORGON.   Brother, your language savors of impiety.
    Too much free-thinking's made your faith unsteady,
    And as I've warned you many times already,
    'Twill get you into trouble before you're through.

CLÉANTE.   So I've been told before by dupes like you:
    Being blind, you'd have all others blind as well;
    The clear-eyed man you call an infidel,
    And he who sees through humbug and pretense
    Is charged, by you, with want of reverence.
    Spare me your warnings, Brother; I have no fear
    Of speaking out, for you and Heaven to hear,
    Against affected zeal and pious knavery.
    There's true and false in piety, as in bravery,
    And just as those whose courage shines the most
    In battle, are the least inclined to boast,
    So those whose hearts are truly pure and lowly
    Don't make a flashy show of being holy.
    There's a vast difference, so it seems to me,
    Between true piety and hypocrisy:
    How do you fail to see it, may I ask?
    Is not a face quite different from a mask?
    Cannot sincerity and cunning art,
    Reality and semblance, be told apart?
    Are scarecrows just like men, and do you hold
    That a false coin is just as good as gold?

Ah, Brother, man's a strangely fashioned creature
Who seldom is content to follow Nature,
But recklessly pursues his inclination
Beyond the narrow bounds of moderation,
And often, by transgressing Reason's laws,
Perverts a lofty aim or noble cause.
A passing observation, but it applies.
ORGON.   I see, dear Brother, that you're profoundly wise;
You harbor all the insight of the age.
You are our one clear mind, our only sage,
The era's oracle, its Cato too,
And all mankind are fools compared to you.
CLÉANTE.   Brother, I don't pretend to be a sage,
Nor have I all the wisdom of the age.
There's just one insight I would dare to claim:
I know that true and false are not the same;
And just as there is nothing I more revere
Than a soul whose faith is steadfast and sincere,
Nothing that I more cherish and admire
Than honest zeal and true religious fire,
So there is nothing that I find more base
Than specious piety's dishonest face—
Than these bold mountebanks, these histrios°
Whose impious mummeries and hollow shows
Exploit our love of Heaven, and make a jest
Of all that men think holiest and best;
These calculating souls who offer prayers
Not to their Maker, but as public wares,
And seek to buy respect and reputation
With lifted eyes and sighs of exaltation;
These charlatans, I say, whose pilgrim souls
Proceed, by way of Heaven, toward earthly goals,
Who weep and pray and swindle and extort,
Who preach the monkish life, but haunt the court,
Who make their zeal the partner of their vice—
Such men are vengeful, sly, and cold as ice,
And when there is an enemy to defame
They cloak their spite in fair religion's name,
Their private spleen and malice being made
To seem a high and virtuous crusade,
Until, to mankind's reverent applause,
They crucify their foe in Heaven's cause.
Such knaves are all too common; yet, for the wise,
True piety isn't hard to recognize,
And, happily, these present times provide us
With bright examples to instruct and guide us.

histrio: an actor, one who deliberately displays emotion for effect.

Consider Ariston and Périandre;
Look at Oronte, Alcidamas, Clitandre;°
Their virtue is acknowledged; who could doubt it?
But you won't hear them beat the drum about it.
They're never ostentatious, never vain,
And their religion's moderate and humane;
It's not their way to criticize and chide:
They think censoriousness a mark of pride,
And therefore, letting others preach and rave,
They show, by deeds, how Christians should behave.
They think no evil of their fellow man,
But judge of him as kindly as they can.
They don't intrigue and wangle and conspire;
To lead a good life is their one desire;
The sinner wakes no rancorous hate in them;
It is the sin alone which they condemn;
Nor do they try to show a fiercer zeal
For Heaven's cause than Heaven itself could feel.
These men I honor, these men I advocate
As models for us all to emulate.
Your man is not their sort at all, I fear:
And, while your praise of him is quite sincere,
I think that you've been dreadfully deluded.

ORGON.   Now then, dear Brother, is your speech concluded?
CLÉANTE.   Why, yes.
ORGON.   Your servant, Sir. (*He turns to go.*)
CLÉANTE.   No, Brother; wait.
There's one more matter. You agreed of late
That young Valère might have your daughter's hand.
ORGON.   I did.
CLÉANTE.   And set the date, I understand.
ORGON.   Quite so.
CLÉANTE.   You've now postponed it; is that true?
ORGON.   No doubt.
CLÉANTE.   The match no longer pleases you?
ORGON.   Who knows?
CLÉANTE.   D'you mean to go back on your word?
ORGON.   I won't say that.
CLÉANTE.   Has anything occurred
Which might entitle you to break your pledge?
ORGON.   Perhaps.
CLÉANTE.   Why must you hem, and haw, and hedge?
The boy asked me to sound you in this affair . . .
ORGON.   It's been a pleasure.
CLÉANTE.   But what shall I tell Valère?
ORGON.   Whatever you like.

Ariston . . . Clitandre: characteristic names of virtuous men of the time.

CLÉANTE.   But what have you decided?
   What are your plans?
ORGON.   I plan, Sir, to be guided
   By Heaven's will.
CLÉANTE.   Come, Brother, don't talk rot.
   You've given Valère your word; will you keep it, or not?
ORGON.   Good day.
CLÉANTE.   This looks like poor Valère's undoing;
   I'll go and warn him that there's trouble brewing.

ACT II

SCENE I

ORGON, MARIANE.

ORGON.   Mariane.
MARIANE.   Yes, Father?
ORGON.   A word with you; come here.
MARIANE.   What are you looking for?
ORGON (*Peering into a small closet*).   Eavesdroppers, dear.
   I'm making sure we shan't be overheard.
   Someone in there could catch our every word.
   Ah, good, we're safe. Now, Mariane, my child,
   You're a sweet girl who's tractable and mild,
   Whom I hold dear, and think most highly of.
MARIANE.   I'm deeply grateful, Father, for your love.
ORGON.   That's well said, Daughter; and you can repay me
   If, in all things, you'll cheerfully obey me.
MARIANE.   To please you, Sir, is what delights me best.
ORGON.   Good, good. Now, what d'you think of Tartuffe, our guest?
MARIANE.   I, Sir?
ORGON.   Yes. Weigh your answer; think it through.
MARIANE.   Oh, dear. I'll say whatever you wish me to.
ORGON.   That's wisely said, my Daughter. Say of him, then,
   That he's the very worthiest of men,
   And that you're fond of him, and would rejoice
   In being his wife, if that should be my choice.
   Well?
MARIANE.   What?
ORGON.   What's that?
MARIANE.   I . . .
ORGON.   Well?
MARIANE.   Forgive me, pray.
ORGON.   Did you not hear me?
MARIANE.   Of *whom*, Sir, must I say
   That I am fond of him, and would rejoice
   In being his wife, if that should be your choice?

ORGON.   Why, of Tartuffe.
MARIANE.   But, Father, that's false, you know.
Why would you have me say what isn't so?
ORGON.   Because I am resolved it shall be true.
That it's my wish should be enough for you.
MARIANE.   You can't mean, Father . . .
ORGON.   Yes, Tartuffe shall be
Allied by marriage to this family,
And he's to be your husband, is that clear?
It's a father's privilege . . .

SCENE II

DORINE, ORGON, MARIANE.

ORGON (*To* DORINE).   What are you doing in here?
Is curiosity so fierce a passion
With you, that you must eavesdrop in this fashion?
DORINE.   There's lately been a rumor going about—
Based on some hunch or chance remark, no doubt—
That you mean Mariane to wed Tartuffe.
I've laughed it off, of course, as just a spoof.
ORGON.   You find it so incredible?
DORINE.   Yes, I do.
I won't accept that story, even from you.
ORGON.   Well, you'll believe it when the thing is done.
DORINE.   Yes, yes, of course. Go on and have your fun.
ORGON.   I've never been more serious in my life.
DORINE.   Ha!
ORGON.   Daughter, I mean it; you're to be his wife.
DORINE.   No, don't believe your father; it's all a hoax.
ORGON.   See here, young woman . . .
DORINE.   Come, Sir, no more jokes;
You can't fool us.
ORGON.   How dare you talk that way?
DORINE.   All right, then: we believe you, sad to say.
But how a man like you, who looks so wise
And wears a moustache of such splendid size,
Can be so foolish as to . . .
ORGON.   Silence, please!
My girl, you take too many liberties.
I'm master here, as you must not forget.
DORINE.   Do let's discuss this calmly; don't be upset.
You can't be serious, Sir, about this plan.
What should that bigot want with Mariane?
Praying and fasting ought to keep him busy.
And then, in terms of wealth and rank, what is he?
Why should a man of property like you
Pick out a beggar son-in-law?

ORGON.   That will do.
  Speak of his poverty with reverence.
  His is a pure and saintly indigence
  Which far transcends all worldly pride and pelf.°
  He lost his fortune, as he says himself,
  Because he cared for Heaven alone, and so
  Was careless of his interests here below.
  I mean to get him out of his present straits
  And help him to recover his estates—
  Which, in his part of the world, have no small fame.
  Poor though he is, he's a gentleman just the same.
DORINE.   Yes, so he tells us; and, Sir, it seems to me
  Such pride goes very ill with piety.
  A man whose spirit spurns this dungy earth
  Ought not to brag of lands and noble birth;
  Such worldly arrogance will hardly square
  With meek devotion and the life of prayer.
  . . . But this approach, I see, has drawn a blank;
  Let's speak, then, of his person, not his rank.
  Doesn't it seem to you a trifle grim
  To give a girl like her to a man like him?
  When two are so ill-suited, can't you see
  What the sad consequence is bound to be?
  A young girl's virtue is imperilled, Sir,
  When such a marriage is imposed on her;
  For if one's bridegroom isn't to one's taste,
  It's hardly an inducement to be chaste,
  And many a man with horns upon his brow
  Has made his wife the thing that she is now.
  It's hard to be a faithful wife, in short,
  To certain husbands of a certain sort,
  And he who gives his daughter to a man she hates
  Must answer for her sins at Heaven's gates.
  Think, Sir, before you play so risky a role.
ORGON.   This servant-girl presumes to save my soul!
DORINE.   You would do well to ponder what I've said.
ORGON.   Daughter, we'll disregard this dunderhead.
  Just trust your father's judgment. Oh, I'm aware
  That I once promised you to young Valère;
  But now I hear he gambles, which greatly shocks me;
  What's more, I've doubts about his orthodoxy.
  His visits to church, I note, are very few.
DORINE.   Would you have him go at the same hours as you,
  And kneel nearby, to be sure of being seen?
ORGON.   I can dispense with such remarks, Dorine.

pelf: money, riches.

(To MARIANE.*)*

Tartuffe, however, is sure of Heaven's blessing,
And that's the only treasure worth possessing.
This match will bring you joys beyond all measure;
Your cup will overflow with every pleasure;
You two will interchange your faithful loves
Like two sweet cherubs, or two turtle-doves.
No harsh word shall be heard, no frown be seen,
And he shall make you happy as a queen.

DORINE.   And she'll make him a cuckold, just wait and see.

ORGON.   What language!

DORINE.   Oh, he's a man of destiny;
He's *made* for horns, and what the stars demand
Your daughter's virtue surely can't withstand.

ORGON.   Don't interrupt me further. Why can't you learn
That certain things are none of your concern?

DORINE.   It's for your own sake that I interfere.

(She repeatedly interrupts ORGON *just as he is turning to speak to his daughter.)*

ORGON.   Most kind of you. Now, hold your tongue, d'you hear?

DORINE.   If I didn't love you . . .

ORGON.   Spare me your affection.

DORINE.   I'll love you, Sir, in spite of your objection.

ORGON.   Blast!

DORINE.   I can't bear, Sir, for your honor's sake,
To let you make this ludicrous mistake.

ORGON.   You mean to go on talking?

DORINE.   If I didn't protest
This sinful marriage, my conscience couldn't rest.

ORGON.   If you don't hold your tongue, you little shrew . . .

DORINE.   What, lost your temper? A pious man like you?

ORGON.   Yes! Yes! You talk and talk. I'm maddened by it.
Once and for all, I tell you to be quiet.

DORINE.   Well, I'll be quiet. But I'll be thinking hard.

ORGON.   Think all you like, but you had better guard
That saucy tongue of yours, or I'll . . .

(Turning back to MARIANE.*)*

                              Now, child,
I've weighed this matter fully.

DORINE *(Aside).*   It drives me wild
That I can't speak.

*(*ORGON *turns his head, and she is silent.)*

                              Tartuffe is no young dandy,
But, still, his person . . .

DORINE *(Aside).*   Is as sweet as candy.

ORGON.   Is such that, even if you shouldn't care
For his other merits . . .

(He turns and stands facing DORINE, *arms crossed.)*

DORINE *(Aside).*
They'll make a lovely pair.
If I were she, no man would marry me
Against my inclination, and go scot-free
He'd learn, before the wedding-day was over,
How readily a wife can find a lover.
ORGON *(To* DORINE).   It seems you treat my orders as a joke.
DORINE.   Why, what's the matter? 'Twas not to you I spoke.
ORGON.   What *were* you doing?
DORINE.   Talking to myself, that's all.
ORGON.   Ah! *(Aside.)* One more bit of impudence and gall,
And I shall give her a good slap in the face.

(He puts himself in position to slap her; DORINE, *whenever he glances at her, stands immobile and silent.)*

Daughter, you shall accept, and with good grace,
The husband I've selected . . . Your wedding-day . . .

(To DORINE.)

Why don't you talk to yourself?
DORINE.   I've nothing to say.
ORGON.   Come, just one word.
DORINE.   No thank you, Sir. I pass.
ORGON.   Come, speak; I'm waiting.
DORINE.   I'd not be such an ass.
ORGON *(Turning to* MARIANE).
In short, dear Daughter, I mean to be obeyed,
And you must bow to the sound choice I've made.
DORINE *(Moving away).*   I'd not wed such a monster, even in jest.

*(*ORGON *attempts to slap her, but misses.)*

ORGON.   Daughter, that maid of yours is a thorough pest;
She makes me sinfully annoyed and nettled.
I can't speak further; my nerves are too unsettled.
She's so upset me by her insolent talk,
I'll calm myself by going for a walk.

SCENE III

DORINE, MARIANE.

DORINE *(Returning).*   Well, have you lost your tongue, girl? Must I play
Your part, and say the lines you ought to say?
Faced with a fate so hideous and absurd,
Can you not utter one dissenting word?

MARIANE.   What good would it do? A father's power is great.
DORINE.   Resist him now, or it will be too late.
MARIANE.   But . . .
DORINE.   Tell him one cannot love at a father's whim;
That you shall marry for yourself, not him;
That since it's you who are to be the bride,
It's you, not he, who must be satisfied;
And that if his Tartuffe is so sublime,
He's free to marry him at any time.
MARIANE.   I've bowed so long to Father's strict control,
I couldn't oppose him now, to save my soul.
DORINE.   Come, come, Mariane. Do listen to reason, won't you?
Valère has asked your hand. Do you love him, or don't you?
MARIANE.   Oh, how unjust of you! What can you mean
By asking such a question, dear Dorine?
You know the depth of my affection for him;
I've told you a hundred times how I adore him.
DORINE.   I don't believe in everything I hear;
Who knows if your professions were sincere?
MARIANE.   They were, Dorine, and you do me wrong to doubt it;
Heaven knows that I've been all too frank about it.
DORINE.   You love him, then?
MARIANE.   Oh, more than I can express.
DORINE.   And he, I take it, cares for you no less?
MARIANE.   I think so.
DORINE.   And you both, with equal fire,
Burn to be married?
MARIANE.   That is our one desire.
DORINE.   What of Tartuffe, then? What of your father's plan?
MARIANE.   I'll kill myself, if I'm forced to wed that man.
DORINE.   I hadn't thought of that recourse. How splendid!
Just die, and all your troubles will be ended!
A fine solution. Oh, it maddens me
To hear you talk in that self-pitying key.
MARIANE.   Dorine, how harsh you are! It's most unfair.
You have no sympathy for my despair.
DORINE.   I've none at all for people who talk drivel
And, faced with difficulties, whine and snivel.
MARIANE.   No doubt I'm timid, but it would be wrong . . .
DORINE.   True love requires a heart that's firm and strong.
MARIANE.   I'm strong in my affection for Valère,
But coping with my father is his affair.
DORINE.   But if your father's brain has grown so cracked
Over his dear Tartuffe that he can retract
His blessing, though your wedding-day was named,
It's surely not Valère who's to be blamed.
MARIANE.   If I defied my father, as you suggest,
Would it not seem unmaidenly, at best?

Shall I defend my love at the expense
Of brazenness and disobedience?
Shall I parade my heart's desires, and flaunt . . .

DORINE.   No, I ask nothing of you. Clearly you want
To be Madame Tartuffe, and I feel bound
Not to oppose a wish so very sound.
What right have I to criticize the match?
Indeed, my dear, the man's a brilliant catch.
Monsieur Tartuffe! Now, there's a man of weight!
Yes, yes, Monsieur Tartuffe, I'm bound to state,
Is quite a person; that's not to be denied;
'Twill be no little thing to be his bride.
The world already rings with his renown;
He's a great noble—in his native town;
His ears are red, he has a pink complexion,
And all in all, he'll suit you to perfection.

MARIANE.   Dear God!

DORINE.   Oh, how triumphant you will feel
At having caught a husband so ideal!

MARIANE.   Oh, do stop teasing, and use your cleverness
To get me out of this appalling mess.
Advise me, and I'll do whatever you say.

DORINE.   Ah no, a dutiful daughter must obey
Her father, even if he weds her to an ape.
You've a bright future; why struggle to escape?
Tartuffe will take you back where his family lives,
To a small town aswarm with relatives—
Uncles and cousins whom you'll be charmed to meet.
You'll be received at once by the elite,
Calling upon the bailiff's° wife, no less—
Even, perhaps, upon the mayoress,
Who'll sit you down in the *best* kitchen chair.
Then, once a year, you'll dance at the village fair
To the drone of bagpipes—two of them, in fact—
And see a puppet-show, or an animal act.
Your husband . . .

MARIANE.   Oh, you turn my blood to ice!
Stop torturing me, and give me your advice.

DORINE (*Threatening to go*).
Your servant, Madam.

MARIANE.   Dorine, I beg of you . . .

DORINE.   No, you deserve it; this marriage must go through.

MARIANE.   Dorine!

DORINE.   No.

MARIANE.   Not Tartuffe! You know I think him . . .

---

bailiff: a court attendant; a sheriff's assistant.

DORINE. Tartuffe's your cup of tea, and you shall drink him.
MARIANE. I've always told you everything, and relied . . .
DORINE. No. You deserve to be tartuffified.
MARIANE. Well, since you mock me and refuse to care,
I'll henceforth seek my solace in despair:
Despair shall be my counsellor and friend,
And help me bring my sorrows to an end.

(She starts to leave.)

DORINE. There now, come back; my anger has subsided.
You do deserve some pity, I've decided.
MARIANE. Dorine, if Father makes me undergo
This dreadful martyrdom, I'll die, I know.
DORINE. Don't fret; it won't be difficult to discover
Some plan of action . . . But here's Valère, your lover.

SCENE IV

VALÈRE, MARIANE, DORINE.

VALÈRE. Madam, I've just received some wondrous news
Regarding which I'd like to hear your views.
MARIANE. What news?
VALÈRE. You're marrying Tartuffe.
MARIANE. I find
That Father does have such a match in mind.
VALÈRE. Your father, Madam . . .
MARIANE. . . . has just this minute said
That it's Tartuffe he wishes me to wed.
VALÈRE. Can he be serious?
MARIANE. Oh, indeed he can;
He's clearly set his heart upon the plan.
VALÈRE. And what position do you propose to take,
Madam?
MARIANE. Why—I don't know.
VALÈRE. For heaven's sake—
You don't know?
MARIANE. No.
VALÈRE. Well, well!
MARIANE. Advise me, do.
VALÈRE. Marry the man. That's my advice to you.
MARIANE. That's your advice?
VALÈRE. Yes.
MARIANE. Truly?
VALÈRE. Oh, absolutely.
You couldn't choose more wisely, more astutely.
MARIANE. Thanks for this counsel; I'll follow it, of course.
VALÈRE. Do, do; I'm sure 'twill cost you no remorse.

MARIANE.　To give it didn't cause your heart to break.

VALÈRE.　I gave it, Madam, only for your sake.

MARIANE.　And it's for your sake that I take it, Sir.

DORINE (*Withdrawing to the rear of the stage*).

Let's see which fool will prove the stubborner.

VALÈRE.　So! I am nothing to you, and it was flat

Deception when you . . .

MARIANE.　　　　　　　　Please, enough of that.

You've told me plainly that I should agree

To wed the man my father's chosen for me,

And since you've deigned to counsel me so wisely,

I promise, Sir, to do as you advise me.

VALÈRE.　Ah, no, 'twas not by me that you were swayed.

No, your decision was already made;

Though now, to save appearances, you protest

That you're betraying me at my behest.

MARIANE.　Just as you say.

VALÈRE.　　　　　　　Quite so. And I now see

That you were never truly in love with me.

MARIANE.　Alas, you're free to think so if you choose.

VALÈRE.　I choose to think so, and here's a bit of news:

You've spurned my hand, but I know where to turn

For kinder treatment, as you shall quickly learn

MARIANE.　I'm sure you do. Your noble qualities

Inspire affection . . .

VALÈRE.　　　　　　　Forget my qualities, please.

They don't inspire you overmuch, I find.

But there's another lady I have in mind

Whose sweet and generous nature will not scorn

To compensate me for the loss I've borne.

MARIANE.　I'm no great loss, and I'm sure that you'll transfer

Your heart quite painlessly from me to her.

VALÈRE.　I'll do my best to take it in my stride.

The pain I feel at being cast aside

Time and forgetfulness may put an end to.

Or if I can't forget, I shall pretend to.

No self-respecting person is expected

To go on loving once he's been rejected.

MARIANE.　Now, that's a fine, high-minded sentiment.

VALÈRE.　One to which any sane man would assent.

Would you prefer it if I pined away

In hopeless passion till my dying day?

Am I to yield you to a rival's arms

And not console myself with other charms?

MARIANE.　Go then: console yourself; don't hesitate.

I wish you to; indeed, I cannot wait.

VALÈRE.　You wish me to?

MARIANE. Yes.
VALÈRE. That's the final straw.
Madam, farewell. Your wish shall be my law.

(*He starts to leave, and then returns: this repeatedly.*)

MARIANE. Splendid.
VALÈRE (*Coming back again*). This breach, remember, is of your making;
It's you who've driven me to the step I'm taking.
MARIANE. Of course.
VALÈRE (*Coming back again*). Remember, too, that I am merely
Following your example.
MARIANE. I see that clearly.
VALÈRE. Enough. I'll go and do your bidding, then.
MARIANE. Good.
VALÈRE (*Coming back again*). You shall never see my face again.
MARIANE. Excellent.
VALÈRE. (*Walking to the door, then turning about*).
Yes?
MARIANE. What?
VALÈRE. What's that? What did you say?
MARIANE. Nothing. You're dreaming.
VALÈRE. Ah. Well, I'm on my way.
Farewell, *Madame.*

(*He moves slowly away.*)

MARIANE. Farewell.
DORINE (*To* MARIANE). If you ask me,
Both of you are as mad as mad can be.
Do stop this nonsense, now. I've only let you
Squabble so long to see where it would get you.
Whoa there, Monsieure Valère!

(*She goes and seizes* VALÈRE *by the arm; he makes a great show of resistance.*)

VALÈRE. What's this, Dorine?
DORINE. Come here.
VALÈRE. No, no, my heart's too full of spleen.
Don't hold me back; her wish must be obeyed.
DORINE. Stop!
VALÈRE. It's too late now; my decision's made.
DORINE. Oh, pooh!
MARIANE (*Aside*). He hates the sight of me, that's plain.
I'll go, and so deliver him from pain.
DORINE (*Leaving* VALÈRE, *running after* MARIANE).
And now *you* run away! Come back.
MARIANE. No, no.
Nothing you say will keep me here. Let go!

VALÈRE (*Aside*).   She cannot bear my presence, I perceive.
  To spare her further torment, I shall leave.
DORINE (*Leaving* MARIANE, *running after* VALÈRE).
  Again! You'll not escape, Sir; don't you try it.
  Come here, you two. Stop fussing, and be quiet.

  (*She takes* VALÈRE *by the hand, then* MARIANE, *and draws them together.*)

VALÈRE (*To* DORINE).   What do you want of me?
MARIANE (*To* DORINE).   What is the point of this?
DORINE.   We're going to have a little armistice.

  (*To* VALÈRE.)

  Now, weren't you silly to get so overheated?
VALÈRE.   Didn't you see how badly I was treated?
DORINE (*To* MARIANE).   Aren't you a simpleton, to have lost your head?
MARIANE.   Didn't you hear the hateful things he said?
DORINE (*To* VALÈRE).   You're both great fools. Her sole desire, Valère,
  Is to be yours in marriage. To that I'll swear.

  (*To* MARIANE.)

  He loves you only, and he wants no wife
  But you, Mariane. On that I'll stake my life.
MARIANE (*To* VALÈRE).   Then why you advised me so, I cannot see.
VALÈRE (*To* MARIANE).   On such a question, why ask advice of *me*?
DORINE.   Oh, you're impossible. Give me your hands, you two.

  (*To* VALÈRE.)

  Yours first.
VALÈRE (*Giving* DORINE *his hand*).   But why?
DORINE (*To* MARIANE).   And now a hand from you.
MARIANE (*Also giving* DORINE *her hand*).
  What are you doing?
DORINE.   There: a perfect fit.
  You suit each other better than you'll admit.

  (VALÈRE *and* MARIANE *hold hands for some time without looking at each other.*)

VALÈRE (*Turning toward* MARIANE).
  Ah, come, don't be so haughty. Give a man
  A look of kindness, won't you, Mariane?

  (MARIANE *turns toward* VALÈRE *and smiles.*)

DORINE.   I tell you, lovers are completely mad!
VALÈRE (*To* MARIANE).   Now come, confess that you were very bad
  To hurt my feelings as you did just now.
  I have a just complaint, you must allow.
MARIANE.   *You* must allow that you were most unpleasant . . .
DORINE.   Let's table that discussion for the present;
  Your father has a plan which must be stopped.
MARIANE.   Advise us, then; what means must we adopt?

DORINE.   We'll use all manner of means, and all at once.

(To MARIANE.)

Your father's addled; he's acting like a dunce.
Therefore you'd better humor the old fossil.
Pretend to yield to him, be sweet and docile,
And then postpone, as often as necessary,
The day on which you have agreed to marry.
You'll thus gain time, and time will turn the trick.
Sometimes, for instance, you'll be taken sick,
And that will seem good reason for delay;
Or some bad omen will make you change the day—
You'll dream of muddy water, or you'll pass
A dead man's hearse, or break a looking-glass.
If all else fails, no man can marry you
Unless you take his ring and say "I do."
But now, let's separate. If they should find
Us talking here, our plot might be divined.

(To VALÈRE.)

Go to your friends, and tell them what's occurred,
And have them urge her father to keep his word.
Meanwhile, we'll stir her brother into action,
And get Elmire, as well, to join our faction.
Good-bye.
VALÈRE *(To* MARIANE).   Though each of us will do his best,
    It's your true heart on which my hopes shall rest.
MARIANE *(To* VALÈRE).   Regardless of what Father may decide,
    None but Valère shall claim me as his bride.
VALÈRE.   Oh, how those words content me! Come what will . . .
DORINE.   Oh, lovers, lovers! Their tongues are never still.
    Be off, now.
VALÈRE *(Turning to go, then turning back).*
                        One last word . . .
DORINE.   No time to chat:
    You leave by this door; and *you* leave by that.

*(*DORINE *pushes them, by the shoulders, toward opposing doors.)*

ACT III

SCENE I

DAMIS, DORINE.

DAMIS.   May lightning strike me even as I speak,
    May all men call me cowardly and weak,
    If any fear or scruple holds me back
    From settling things, at once, with that great quack!

DORINE.   Now, don't give way to violent emotion.
Your father's merely talked about this notion,
And words and deeds are far from being one.
Much that is talked about is left undone.
DAMIS.   No, I must stop that scoundrel's machinations;
I'll go and tell him off; I'm out of patience.
DORINE.   Do calm down and be practical. I had rather
My mistress dealt with him—and with your father.
She has some influence with Tartuffe, I've noted.
He hangs upon her words, seems most devoted,
And may, indeed, be smitten by her charm.
Pray Heaven it's true! 'Twould do our cause no harm.
She sent for him, just now, to sound him out
On this affair you're so incensed about;
She'll find out where he stands, and tell him, too,
What dreadful strife and trouble will ensue
If he lends countenance to your father's plan.
I couldn't get in to see him, but his man
Says that he's almost finished with his prayers.
Go, now. I'll catch him when he comes downstairs.
DAMIS.   I want to hear this conference, and I will.
DORINE.   No, they must be alone.
DAMIS.   Oh, I'll keep still.
DORINE.   Not you. I know your temper. You'd start a brawl,
And shout and stamp your foot and spoil it all.
Go on.
DAMIS.   I won't; I have a perfect right . . .
DORINE.   Lord, you're a nuisance! He's coming; get out of sight.

(DAMIS *conceals himself in a closet at the rear of the stage.*)

SCENE II

TARTUFFE, DORINE.

TARTUFFE (*Observing* DORINE, *and calling to his manservant offstage*).
Hang up my hair-shirt, put my scourge in place,
And pray, Laurent, for Heaven's perpetual grace.
I'm going to the prison now, to share
My last few coins with the poor wretches there.
DORINE (*Aside*).   Dear God, what affectation! What a fake!
TARTUFFE.   You wished to see me?
DORINE.   Yes . . .
TARTUFFE (*Taking a handkerchief from his pocket*).
                                For mercy's sake,
Please take this handkerchief, before you speak.
DORINE.   What?
TARTUFFE.   Cover that bosom, girl. The flesh is weak,
And unclean thoughts are difficult to control.
Such sights as that can undermine the soul.

DORINE.   Your soul, it seems, has very poor defenses,
And flesh makes quite an impact on your senses.
It's strange that you're so easily excited;
My own desires are not so soon ignited,
And if I saw you naked as a beast,
Not all your hide would tempt me in the least.
TARTUFFE.   Girl, speak more modestly; unless you do,
I shall be forced to take my leave of you.
DORINE.   Oh, no, it's I who must be on my way;
I've just one little message to convey.
Madame is coming down, and begs you, Sir,
To wait and have a word or two with her.
TARTUFFE.   Gladly.
DORINE (*Aside*).   *That* had a softening effect!
I think my guess about him was correct.
TARTUFFE.   Will she be long?
DORINE.   No: that's her step I hear.
Ah, here she is, and I shall disappear.

SCENE III

ELMIRE, TARTUFFE.

TARTUFFE.   May Heaven, whose infinite goodness we adore,
Preserve your body and soul forevermore,
And bless your days, and answer thus the plea
Of one who is its humblest votary.
ELMIRE.   I thank you for that pious wish. But please,
Do take a chair and let's be more at ease.

(They sit down.)

TARTUFFE.   I trust that you are once more well and strong?
ELMIRE.   Oh, yes: the fever didn't last for long.
TARTUFFE.   My prayers are too unworthy, I am sure,
To have gained from Heaven this most gracious cure;
But lately, Madam, my every supplication
Has had for object your recuperation.
ELMIRE.   You shouldn't have troubled so. I don't deserve it.
TARTUFFE.   Your health is priceless, Madam, and to preserve it
I'd gladly give my own, in all sincerity.
ELMIRE.   Sir, you outdo us all in Christian charity.
You've been most kind. I count myself your debtor.
TARTUFFE.   'Twas nothing, Madam. I long to serve you better.
ELMIRE.   There's a private matter I'm anxious to discuss.
I'm glad there's no one here to hinder us.
TARTUFFE.   I too am glad; it floods my heart with bliss
To find myself alone with you like this.
For just this chance I've prayed with all my power—
But prayed in vain, until this happy hour.

ELMIRE.   This won't take long, Sir, and I hope you'll be
   Entirely frank and unconstrained with me.
TARTUFFE.   Indeed, there's nothing I had rather do
   Than bare my inmost heart and soul to you.
   First, let me say what remarks I've made
   About the constant visits you are paid
   Were prompted not by any mean emotion,
   But rather by a pure and deep devotion,
   A fervent zeal . . .
ELMIRE.   No need for explanation.
   Your sole concern, I'm sure, was my salvation.
TARTUFFE (*Taking* ELMIRE'S *hand and pressing her fingertips*).
   Quite so; and such great fervor do I feel . . .
ELMIRE.   Ooh! Please! You're pinching!
TARTUFFE.   'Twas from excess of zeal.
   I never meant to cause you pain, I swear.
   I'd rather . . .

   (*He places his hand on* ELMIRE'S *knee.*)

ELMIRE.   What can your hand be doing there?
TARTUFFE.   Feeling your gown; what soft, fine-woven stuff!
ELMIRE.   Please, I'm extremely ticklish. That's enough.

   (*She draws her chair away;* TARTUFFE *pulls his after her.*)

TARTUFFE (*Fondling the lace collar of her gown*).
   My, my, what lovely lacework on your dress!
   The workmanship's miraculous, no less.
   I've not seen anything to equal it.
ELMIRE.   Yes, quite. But let's talk business for a bit.
   They say my husband means to break his word
   And give his daughter to you, Sir. Had you heard?
TARTUFFE.   He did once mention it. But I confess
   I dream of quite a different happiness.
   It's elsewhere, Madam, that my eyes discern
   The promise of that bliss for which I yearn.
ELMIRE.   I see: you care for nothing here below.
TARTUFFE.   Ah, well—my heart's not made of stone, you know.
ELMIRE.   All your desires mount heavenward, I'm sure,
   In scorn of all that's earthly and impure.
TARTUFFE.   A love of heavenly beauty does not preclude
   A proper love for earthly pulchritude;
   Our senses are quite rightly captivated
   By perfect works our Maker has created.
   Some glory clings to all that Heaven has made;
   In you, all Heaven's marvels are displayed.
   On that fair face, such beauties have been lavished,
   The eyes are dazzled and the heart is ravished;
   How could I look on you, O flawless creature,

And not adore the Author of all Nature,
Feeling a love both passionate and pure
For you, his triumph of self-portraiture?
At first, I trembled lest that love should be
A subtle snare that Hell had laid for me;
I vowed to flee the sight of you, eschewing
A rapture that might prove my soul's undoing;
But soon, fair being, I became aware
That my deep passion could be made to square
With rectitude, and with my bounden duty.
I thereupon surrendered to your beauty.
It is, I know, presumptuous on my part
To bring you this poor offering of my heart,
And it is not my merit, Heaven knows,
But your compassion on which my hopes repose.
You are my peace, my solace, my salvation;
On you depends my bliss—or desolation;
I bide your judgment and, as you think best,
I shall be either miserable or blest.

ELMIRE.   Your declaration is most gallant, Sir,
But don't you think it's out of character?
You'd have done better to restrain your passion
And think before you spoke in such a fashion.
It ill becomes a pious man like you . . .

TARTUFFE.   I may be pious, but I'm human too:
With your celestial charms before his eyes,
A man has not the power to be wise.
I know such words sound strangely, coming from me,
But I'm no angel, nor was meant to be,
And if you blame my passion, you must needs
Reproach as well the charms on which it feeds.
Your loveliness I had no sooner seen
Than you became my soul's unrivalled queen;
Before your seraph glance, divinely sweet,
My heart's defenses crumbled in defeat,
And nothing fasting, prayer, or tears might do
Could stay my spirit from adoring you.
My eyes, my sighs have told you in the past
What now my lips make bold to say at last,
And if, in your great goodness, you will deign
To look upon your slave, and ease his pain,—
If, in compassion for my soul's distress,
You'll stoop to comfort my unworthiness,
I'll raise to you, in thanks for that sweet manna,°
An endless hymn, an infinite hosanna.°

---

manna: unexpected gift of nourishment.   **hosanna:** fervent praise.

With me, of course, there need be no anxiety,
No fear of scandal or of notoriety.
These young court gallants, whom all the ladies fancy,
Are vain in speech, in action rash and chancy;
When they succeed in love, the world soon knows it;
No favor's granted them but they disclose it
And by the looseness of their tongues profane
The very altar where their hearts have lain.
Men of my sort, however, love discreetly,
And one may trust our reticence completely.
My keen concern for my good name insures
The absolute security of yours;
In short, I offer you, my dear Elmire,
Love without scandal, pleasure without fear.

ELMIRE.   I've heard your well-turned speeches to the end,
And what you urge I clearly apprehend.
Aren't you afraid that I may take a notion
To tell my husband of your warm devotion,
And that, supposing he were duly told,
His feelings toward you might grow rather cold?

TARTUFFE.   I know, dear lady, that your exceeding charity
Will lead your heart to pardon my temerity;
That you'll excuse my violent affection
As human weakness, human imperfection;
And that—O fairest!—you will bear in mind
That I'm but flesh and blood, and am not blind.

ELMIRE.   Some women might do otherwise, perhaps,
But I shall be discreet about your lapse;
I'll tell my husband nothing of what's occurred
If, in return, you'll give your solemn word
To advocate as forcefully as you can
The marriage of Valère and Mariane,
Renouncing all desire to dispossess
Another of his rightful happiness,
And . . .

SCENE IV

DAMIS, ELMIRE, TARTUFFE.

DAMIS (*Emerging from the closet where he has been hiding*).
          No! We'll not hush up this vile affair;
I heard it all inside that closet there,
Where Heaven, in order to confound the pride
Of this great rascal, prompted me to hide.
Ah, now I have my long-awaited chance
To punish his deceit and arrogance,
And give my father clear and shocking proof
Of the black character of his dear Tartuffe.

ELMIRE.   Ah no, Damis; I'll be content if he
Will study to deserve my leniency.
I've promised silence—don't make me break my word;
To make a scandal would be too absurd.
Good wives laugh off such trifles, and forget them;
Why should they tell their husbands, and upset them?
DAMIS.   You have your reasons for taking such a course,
And I have reasons, too, of equal force.
To spare him now would be insanely wrong.
I've swallowed my just wrath for far too long
And watched this insolent bigot bringing strife
And bitterness into our family life.
Too long he's meddled in my father's affairs,
Thwarting my marriage-hopes, and poor Valère's.
It's high time that my father was undeceived,
And now I've proof that can't be disbelieved—
Proof that was furnished me by Heaven above.
It's too good not to take advantage of.
This is my chance, and I deserve to lose it
If, for one moment, I hesitate to use it.
ELMIRE.   Damis . . .
DAMIS.   No, I must do what I think right.
Madam, my heart is bursting with delight,
And, say whatever you will, I'll not consent
To lose the sweet revenge on which I'm bent.
I'll settle matters without more ado;
And here, most opportunely, is my cue.

SCENE V

ORGON, DAMIS, TARTUFFE, ELMIRE.

DAMIS.   Father, I'm glad you've joined us. Let us advise you
Of some fresh news which doubtless will surprise you.
You've just now been repaid with interest
For all your loving-kindness to our guest.
He's proved his warm and grateful feelings toward you;
It's with a pair of horns° he would reward you.
Yes, I surprised him with your wife, and heard
His whole adulterous offer, every word.
She, with her all too gentle disposition,
Would not have told you of his proposition;
But I shall not make terms with brazen lechery,
And feel that not to tell you would be treachery.
ELMIRE.   And I hold that one's husband's peace of mind
Should not be spoilt by tattle of this kind.
One's honor doesn't require it: to be proficient

pair of horns: figurative expression for the evidence of having been cuckolded.

In keeping men at bay is quite sufficient.
These are my sentiments, and I wish, Damis,
That you had heeded me and held your peace.

SCENE VI

ORGON, DAMIS, TARTUFFE.

ORGON.   Can it be true, this dreadful thing I hear?
TARTUFFE.   Yes, Brother, I'm a wicked man, I fear:
  A wretched sinner, all depraved and twisted,
  The greatest villain that has ever existed.
  My life's one heap of crimes, which grows each minute;
  There's naught but foulness and corruption in it;
  And I perceive that Heaven, outraged by me,
  Has chosen this occasion to mortify me.
  Charge me with any deed you wish to name;
  I'll not defend myself, but take the blame.
  Believe what you are told, and drive Tartuffe
  Like some base criminal from beneath your roof;
  Yes, drive me hence, and with a parting curse:
  I shan't protest, for I deserve far worse.
ORGON (*To* DAMIS).   Ah, you deceitful boy, how dare you try
  To stain his purity with so foul a lie?
DAMIS.   What! Are you taken in by such a bluff?
  Did you not hear . . . ?
ORGON.   Enough, you rogue, enough!
TARTUFFE.   Ah, Brother, let him speak: you're being unjust.
  Believe his story; the boy deserves your trust.
  Why, after all, should you have faith in me?
  How can you know what I might do, or be?
  Is it on my good actions that you base
  Your favor? Do you trust my pious face?
  Ah, no, don't be deceived by hollow shows;
  I'm far, alas, from being what men suppose;
  Though the world takes me for a man of worth,
  I'm truly the most worthless man on earth.

  (*To* DAMIS.)

  Yes, my dear son, speak out now: call me the chief
  Of sinners, a wretch, a murderer, a thief;
  Load me with all the names men most abhor;
  I'll not complain; I've earned them all, and more;
  I'll kneel here while you pour them on my head
  As a just punishment for the life I've led.

ORGON (*To* TARTUFFE).
   This is too much, dear Brother.

   (To DAMIS.)

                       Have you no heart?
DAMIS.   Are you so hoodwinked by this rascal's art . . . ?
ORGON.   Be still, you monster.

   (To TARTUFFE.)

                      Brother, I pray you, rise.

   (To DAMIS.)

   Villain!
DAMIS.   But . . .
ORGON.   Silence!
DAMIS.   Can't you realize . . . ?
ORGON.   Just one word more, and I'll tear you limb from limb.
TARTUFFE.   In God's name, Brother, don't be harsh with him.
   I'd rather far be tortured at the stake
   Than see him bear one scratch for my poor sake.
ORGON (*To* DAMIS).   Ingrate!
TARTUFFE.   If I must beg you, on bended knee,
   To pardon him . . .
ORGON (*Falling to his knees, addressing* TARTUFFE).
                  Such goodness cannot be!

   (To DAMIS.)

   Now, *there's* true charity!
DAMIS.   What, you . . . ?
ORGON.   Villain, be still!
   I know your motives; I know you wish him ill:
   Yes, all of you—wife, children, servants, all—
   Conspire against him and desire his fall,
   Employing every shameful trick you can
   To alienate me from this saintly man.
   Ah, but the more you seek to drive him away,
   The more I'll do to keep him. Without delay,
   I'll spite this household and confound its pride
   By giving him my daughter as his bride.
DAMIS.   You're going to force her to accept his hand?
ORGON.   Yes, and this very night, d'you understand?
   I shall defy you all, and make it clear
   That I'm the one who gives the orders here.
   Come, wretch, kneel down and clasp his blessed feet,
   And ask his pardon for your black deceit.
DAMIS.   I ask that swindler's pardon? Why, I'd rather . . .

ORGON.   So! You insult him, and defy your father!
A stick! A stick! (*To* TARTUFFE.) No, no—release me, do.

(*To* DAMIS.)

Out of my house this minute! Be off with you,
And never dare set foot in it again.
DAMIS.   Well, I shall go, but . . .
ORGON.   Well, go quickly, then.
I disinherit you; an empty purse
Is all you'll get from me—except my curse!

SCENE VII

ORGON, TARTUFFE.

ORGON.   How he blasphemed your goodness! What a son!
TARTUFFE.   Forgive him, Lord, as I've already done.

(*To* ORGON.)

You can't know how it hurts when someone tries
To blacken me in my dear Brother's eyes.
ORGON.   Ahh!
TARTUFFE.   The mere thought of such ingratitude
Plunges my soul into so dark a mood . . .
Such horror grips my heart . . . I gasp for breath,
And cannot speak, and feel myself near death.
ORGON.

(*He runs, in tears, to the door through which he has just driven his son.*)

You blackguard! Why did I spare you? Why did I not
Break you in little pieces on the spot?
Compose yourself, and don't be hurt, dear friend.
TARTUFFE.   These scenes, these dreadful quarrels, have got to end.
I've much upset your household, and I perceive
That the best thing will be for me to leave.
ORGON.   What are you saying!
TARTUFFE.   They're all against me here;
They'd have you think me false and insincere.
ORGON.   Ah, what of that? Have I ceased believing in you?
TARTUFFE.   Their adverse talk will certainly continue,
And charges which you now repudiate
You may find credible at a later date.
ORGON.   No, Brother, never.
TARTUFFE.   Brother, a wife can sway
Her husband's mind in many a subtle way.
ORGON.   No, no.
TARTUFFE.   To leave at once is the solution;
Thus only can I end their persecution.

ORGON.   No, no, I'll not allow it; you shall remain.
TARTUFFE.   Ah, well; 'twill mean much martyrdom and pain,
But if you wish it . . .
ORGON.   Ah!
TARTUFFE.   Enough; so be it.
But one thing must be settled, as I see it.
For your dear honor, and for our friendship's sake,
There's one precaution I feel bound to take.
I shall avoid your wife, and keep away . . .
ORGON.   No, you shall not, whatever they may say.
It pleases me to vex them, and for spite
I'd have them see you with her day and night.
What's more, I'm going to drive them to despair
By making you my only son and heir;
This very day, I'll give to you alone
Clear deed and title to everything I own.
A dear, good friend and son-in-law-to-be
Is more than wife, or child, or kin to me.
Will you accept my offer, dearest son?
TARTUFFE.   In all things, let the will of Heaven be done.
ORGON.   Poor fellow! Come, we'll go draw up the deed.
Then let them burst with disappointed greed!

ACT IV

SCENE I

CLÉANTE, TARTUFFE.

CLÉANTE.   Yes, all the town's discussing it, and truly,
Their comments do not flatter you unduly.
I'm glad we've met, Sir, and I'll give my view
Of this sad matter in a word or two.
As for who's guilty, that I shan't discuss;
Let's say it was Damis who caused the fuss;
Assuming, then, that you have been ill-used
By young Damis, and groundlessly accused,
Ought not a Christian to forgive, and ought
He not to stifle every vengeful thought?
Should you stand by and watch a father make
His only son an exile for your sake?
Again I tell you frankly, be advised:
The whole town, high and low, is scandalized;
This quarrel must be mended, and my advice is
Not to push matters to a further crisis.
No, sacrifice your wrath to God above,
And help Damis regain his father's love.

TARTUFFE.   Alas, for my part I should take great joy
  In doing so. I've nothing against the boy.
  I pardon all, I harbor no resentment;
  To serve him would afford me much contentment.
  But Heaven's interest will not have it so:
  If he comes back, then I shall have to go.
  After his conduct—so extreme, so vicious—
  Our further intercourse would look suspicious.
  God knows what people would think! Why, they'd describe
  My goodness to him as a sort of bribe;
  They'd say that out of guilt I made pretense
  Of loving-kindness and benevolence—
  That, fearing my accuser's tongue, I strove
  To buy his silence with a show of love.
CLÉANTE.   Your reasoning is badly warped and stretched,
  And these excuses, Sir, are most far-fetched.
  Why put yourself in charge of Heaven's cause?
  Does Heaven need our help to enforce its laws?
  Leave vengeance to the Lord, Sir; while we live,
  Our duty's not to punish, but forgive;
  And what the Lord commands, we should obey
  Without regard to what the world may say.
  What! Shall the fear of being misunderstood
  Prevent our doing what is right and good?
  No, no; let's simply do what Heaven ordains,
  And let no other thoughts perplex our brains.
TARTUFFE.   Again, Sir, let me say that I've forgiven
  Damis, and thus obeyed the laws of Heaven;
  But I am not commanded by the Bible
  To live with one who smears my name with libel.
CLÉANTE.   Were you commanded, Sir, to indulge the whim
  Of poor Orgon, and to encourage him
  In suddenly transferring to your name
  A large estate to which you have no claim?
TARTUFFE.   'Twould never occur to those who know me best
  To think I acted from self-interest.
  The treasures of this world I quite despise;
  Their specious glitter does not charm my eyes;
  And if I have resigned myself to taking
  The gift which my dear Brother insists on making,
  I do so only, as he well understands,
  Lest so much wealth fall into wicked hands,
  Lest those to whom it might descend in time
  Turn it to purposes of sin and crime,
  And not, as I shall do, make use of it
  For Heaven's glory and mankind's benefit.

CLÉANTE.   Forget these trumped-up fears. Your argument
Is one the rightful heir might well resent;
It *is* a moral burden to inherit
Such wealth, but give Damis a chance to bear it.
And would it not be worse to be accused
Of swindling, than to see that wealth misused?
I'm shocked that you allowed Orgon to broach
This matter, and that you feel no self-reproach;
Does true religion teach that lawful heirs
May freely be deprived of what is theirs?
And if the Lord has told you in your heart
That you and young Damis must dwell apart,
Would it not be the decent thing to beat
A generous and honorable retreat,
Rather than let the son of the house be sent,
For your convenience, into banishment?
Sir, if you wish to prove the honesty
Of your intentions . . .
TARTUFFE.   Sir, it is half-past three.
I've certain pious duties to attend to,
And hope my prompt departure won't offend you.
CLÉANTE (*Alone*). Damn.

SCENE II

ELMIRE, MARIANE, CLÉANTE, DORINE.

DORINE.   Stay, Sir, and help Mariane, for Heaven's sake!
She's suffering so, I fear her heart will break.
Her father's plan to marry her off tonight
Has put the poor child in a desperate plight.
I hear him coming. Let's stand together, now,
And see if we can't change his mind, somehow,
About this match we all deplore and fear.

SCENE III

ORGON, ELMIRE, MARIANE, CLÉANTE, DORINE.

ORGON.   Hah! Glad to find you all assembled here.

(*To* MARIANE).

This contract, child, contains your happiness,
And what it says I think your heart can guess.
MARIANE (*Falling to her knees*).
Sir, by that Heaven which sees me here distressed,
And by whatever else can move your breast,
Do not employ a father's power, I pray you,

To crush my heart and force it to obey you,
Nor by your harsh commands oppress me so
That I'll begrudge the duty which I owe—
And do not so embitter and enslave me
That I shall hate the very life you gave me.
If my sweet hopes must perish, if you refuse
To give me to the one I've dared to choose,
Spare me at least—I beg you, I implore—
The pain of wedding one whom I abhor;
And do not, by a heartless use of force,
Drive me to contemplate some desperate course.

ORGON (*Feeling himself touched by her*).
　　Be firm, my soul. No human weakness, now.

MARIANE.　　I don't resent your love for him. Allow
　　Your heart free rein, Sir; give him your property,
　　And if that's not enough, take mine from me;
　　He's welcome to my money; take it, do,
　　But don't, I pray, include my person too.
　　Spare me, I beg you; and let me end the tale
　　Of my sad days behind a convent veil.

ORGON.　　A convent! Hah! When crossed in their amours,
　　All lovesick girls have the same thought as yours.
　　Get up! The more you loathe the man, and dread him,
　　The more ennobling it will be to wed him.
　　Marry Tartuffe, and mortify your flesh!
　　Enough; don't start that whimpering afresh.

DORINE.　　But why . . . ?

ORGON.　　　　　　　　Be still, there. Speak when you're spoken to.
　　Not one more bit of impudence out of you.

CLÉANTE.　　If I may offer a word of counsel here . . .

ORGON.　　Brother, in counseling you have no peer;
　　All your advice is forceful, sound, and clever;
　　I don't propose to follow it, however.

ELMIRE (*To* ORGON).　　I am amazed, and don't know what to say;
　　Your blindness simply takes my breath away.
　　You are indeed bewitched, to take no warning
　　From our account of what occurred this morning.

ORGON.　　Madam, I know a few plain facts, and one
　　Is that you're partial to my rascal son;
　　Hence, when he sought to make Tartuffe the victim
　　Of a base lie, you dared not contradict him.
　　Ah, but you underplayed your part, my pet;
　　You should have looked more angry, more upset.

ELMIRE.　　When men make overtures, must we reply
　　With righteous anger and a battle-cry?
　　Must we turn back their amorous advances
　　With sharp reproaches and with fiery glances?

Myself, I find such offers merely amusing,
And make no scenes and fusses in refusing;
My taste is for good-natured rectitude,
And I dislike the savage sort of prude
Who guards her virtue with her teeth and claws,
And tears men's eyes out for the slightest cause:
The Lord preserve me from such honor as that,
Which bites and scratches like an alley-cat!
I've found that a polite and cool rebuff
Discourages a lover quite enough.

ORGON.   I know the facts, and I shall not be shaken.

ELMIRE.   I marvel at your power to be mistaken.
Would it, I wonder, carry weight with you
If I could *show* you that our tale was true?

ORGON.   Show me?

ELMIRE.   Yes.

ORGON.   Rot.

ELMIRE.   Come, what if I found a way
To make you see the facts as plain as day?

ORGON.   Nonsense.

ELMIRE.   Do answer me; don't be absurd.
I'm not now asking you to trust our word.
Suppose that from some hiding-place in here
You learned the whole sad truth by eye and ear—
What would you say of your good friend, after that?

ORGON.   Why, I'd say . . . nothing, by Jehoshaphat!
It can't be true.

ELMIRE.   You've been too long deceived,
And I'm quite tired of being disbelieved.
Come now: let's put my statements to the test,
And you shall see the truth made manifest.

ORGON.   I'll take that challenge. Now do your uttermost.
We'll see how you make good your empty boast.

ELMIRE (*To* DORINE).   Send him to me.

DORINE.   He's crafty; it may be hard
To catch the cunning scoundrel off his guard.

ELMIRE.   No, amorous men are gullible. Their conceit
So blinds them that they're never hard to cheat.
Have him come down. (*To* CLÉANTE *and* MARIANE.) Please leave us, for a
bit.

SCENE IV

ELMIRE, ORGON.

ELMIRE.   Pull up this table, and get under it.

ORGON.   What?

ELMIRE.   It's essential that you be well-hidden.

ORGON.   Why there?
ELMIRE.   Oh, Heavens! Just do as you are bidden.
I have my plans; we'll soon see how they fare.
Under the table, now; and once you're there,
Take care that you are neither seen nor heard.
ORGON.   Well, I'll indulge you, since I gave my word
To see you through this infantile charade.
ELMIRE.   Once it is over, you'll be glad we played.

(To her husband, who is now under the table.)

I'm going to act quite strangely, now, and you
Must not be shocked at anything I do.
Whatever I may say, you must excuse
As part of that deceit I'm forced to use.
I shall employ sweet speeches in the task
Of making that imposter drop his mask;
I'll give encouragement to his bold desires,
And furnish fuel to his amorous fires.
Since it's for your sake, and for his destruction,
That I shall seem to yield to his seduction,
I'll gladly stop whenever you decide
That all your doubts are fully satisfied.
I'll count on you, as soon as you have seen
What sort of man he is, to intervene,
And not expose me to his odious lust
One moment longer than you feel you must.
Remember: you're to save me from my plight
Whenever . . . . He's coming! Hush! Keep out of sight!

SCENE V

TARTUFFE, ELMIRE, ORGON.

TARTUFFE.   You wish to have a word with me, I'm told.
ELMIRE.   Yes. I've a little secret to unfold.
Before I speak, however, it would be wise
To close that door, and look about for spies.

(TARTUFFE goes to the door, closes it, and returns.)

The very last thing that must happen now
Is a repetition of this morning's row.
I've never been so badly caught off guard.
Oh, how I feared for you! You saw how hard
I tried to make that troublesome Damis
Control his dreadful temper, and hold his peace.
In my confusion, I didn't have the sense
Simply to contradict his evidence;
But as it happened, that was for the best,

And all has worked out in our interest.
This storm has only bettered your position;
My husband doesn't have the least suspicion,
And now, in mockery of those who do,
He bids me be continually with you.
And that is why, quite fearless of reproof,
I now can be alone with my Tartuffe,
And why my heart—perhaps too quick to yield—
Feels free to let its passion be revealed.
TARTUFFE.   Madam, your words confuse me. Not long ago,
You spoke in quite a different style, you know.
ELMIRE.   Ah, sir, if that refusal made you smart,
It's little that you know of woman's heart,
Or what that heart is trying to convey
When it resists in such a feeble way!
Always, at first, our modesty prevents
The frank avowal of tender sentiments;
However high the passion which inflames us,
Still, to confess its power somehow shames us.
Thus we reluct, at first, yet in a tone
Which tells you that our heart is overthrown,
That what our lips deny, our pulse confesses,
And that, in time, all noes will turn to yesses.
I fear my words are all too frank and free,
And a poor proof of woman's modesty;
But since I'm started, tell me, if you will—
Would I have tried to make Damis be still,
Would I have listened, calm and unoffended,
Until your lengthy offer of love was ended,
And been so very mild in my reaction,
Had your sweet words not given me satisfaction?
And when I tried to force you to undo
The marriage-plans my husband has in view,
What did my urgent pleading signify
If not that I admired you, and that I
Deplored the thought that someone else might own
Part of a heart I wished for mine alone?
TARTUFFE.   Madam, no happiness is so complete
As when, from lips we love, come words so sweet;
Their nectar floods my every sense, and drains
In honeyed rivulets through all my veins.
To please you is my joy, my only goal;
Your love is the restorer of my soul;
And yet I must beg leave, now, to confess
Some lingering doubts as to my happiness.
Might this not be a trick? Might not the catch
Be that you wish me to break off the match

With Mariane, and so have feigned to love me?
I shan't quite trust your fond opinion of me
Until the feelings you've expressed so sweetly
Are demonstrated somewhat more concretely,
And you have shown, by certain kind concessions,
That I may put my faith in your professions.

ELMIRE (*She coughs, to warn her husband*).
Why be in such a hurry? Must my heart
Exhaust its bounty at the very start?
To make that sweet admission cost me dear,
But you'll not be content, it would appear,
Unless my store of favors is disbursed
To the last farthing, and at the very first.

TARTUFFE.   The less we merit, the less we dare to hope,
And with our doubts, mere words can never cope.
We trust no promised bliss till we receive it;
Not till a joy is ours can we believe it.
I, who so little merit your esteem,
Can't credit this fulfillment of my dream,
And shan't believe it, Madam, until I savor
Some palpable assurance of your favor.

ELMIRE.   My, how tyrannical your love can be,
And how it flusters and perplexes me!
How furiously you take one's heart in hand,
And make your every wish a fierce command!
Come, must you hound and harry me to death?
Will you not give me time to catch my breath?
Can it be right to press me with such force,
Give me no quarter, show me no remorse,
And take advantage, by your stern insistence,
Of the fond feelings which weaken my resistance?

TARTUFFE.   Well, if you look with favor upon my love,
Why, then, begrudge me some clear proof thereof?

ELMIRE.   But how can I consent without offense
To Heaven, toward which you feel such reverence?

TARTUFFE.   If Heaven is all that holds you back, don't worry.
I can remove that hindrance in a hurry.
Nothing of that sort need obstruct our path.

ELMIRE.   Must one not be afraid of Heaven's wrath?

TARTUFFE.   Madam, forget such fears, and be my pupil,
And I shall teach you how to conquer scruple.
Some joys, it's true, are wrong in Heaven's eyes;
Yet Heaven is not averse to compromise;
There is a science, lately formulated,
Whereby one's conscience may be liberated,
And any wrongful act you care to mention
May be redeemed by purity of intention.
I'll teach you, Madam, the secrets of that science;

Meanwhile, just place on me your full reliance.
Assuage my keen desires, and feel no dread:
The sin, if any, shall be on my head.

(ELMIRE *coughs, this time more loudly.*)

You've a bad cough.
ELMIRE.   Yes, yes. It's bad indeed.
TARTUFFE (*Producing a little paper bag*).
A bit of licorice may be what you need.
ELMIRE.   No, I've a stubborn cold, it seems. I'm sure it
Will take much more than licorice to cure it.
TARTUFFE.   How aggravating.
ELMIRE.   Oh, more than I can say.
TARTUFFE.   If you're still troubled, think of things this way:
No one shall know our joys, save us alone,
And there's no evil till the act is known;
It's scandal, Madam, which makes it an offense,
And it's no sin to sin in confidence.
ELMIRE (*Having coughed once more*).
Well, clearly I must do as you require,
And yield to your importunate desire.
It is apparent, now, that nothing less
Will satisfy you, and so I acquiesce.
To go so far is much against my will;
I'm vexed that it should come to this; but still,
Since you are so determined on it, since you
Will not allow mere language to convince you,
And since you ask for concrete evidence, I
See nothing for it, now, but to comply.
If this is sinful, if I'm wrong to do it,
So much the worse for him who drove me to it.
The fault can surely not be charged to me.
TARTUFFE.   Madam, the fault is mine, if fault there be,
And . . .
ELMIRE.   Open the door a little, and peek out;
I wouldn't want my husband poking about.
TARTUFFE.   Why worry about the man? Each day he grows
More gullible; one can lead him by the nose.
To find us here would fill him with delight,
And if he saw the worst, he'd doubt his sight.
ELMIRE.   Nevertheless, do step out for a minute
Into the hall, and see that no one's in it.

SCENE VI

ORGON, ELMIRE.

ORGON (*Coming out from under the table*).
That man's a perfect monster, I must admit!
I'm simply stunned. I can't get over it.

ELMIRE.   What, coming out so soon? How premature!
Get back in hiding, and wait until you're sure.
Stay till the end, and be convinced completely;
We mustn't stop till things are proved concretely.
ORGON.   Hell never harbored anything so vicious!
ELMIRE.   Tut, don't be hasty. Try to be judicious.
Wait, and be certain that there's no mistake.
No jumping to conclusions, for Heaven's sake!

(She places ORGON *behind her, as* TARTUFFE *re-enters.)*

SCENE VII

TARTUFFE, ELMIRE, ORGON.

TARTUFFE (*Not seeing* ORGON).
Madam, all things have worked out to perfection;
I've given the neighboring rooms a full inspection;
No one's about; and now I may at last . . .
ORGON (*Intercepting him*).   Hold on, my passionate fellow, not so fast!
I should advise a little more restraint.
Well, so you thought you'd fool me, my dear saint!
How soon you wearied of the saintly life—
Wedding my daughter, and coveting my wife!
I've long suspected you, and had a feeling
That soon I'd catch you at your double-dealing.
Just now, you've given me evidence galore;
It's quite enough; I have no wish for more.
ELMIRE (*To* TARTUFFE).   I'm sorry to have treated you so slyly,
But circumstances forced me to be wily.
TARTUFFE.   Brother, you can't think . . .
ORGON.   No more talk from you;
Just leave this household, without more ado.
TARTUFFE.   What I intended . . .
ORGON.   That seems fairly clear.
Spare me your falsehoods and get out of here.
TARTUFFE.   No, I'm the master, and you're the one to go!
This house belongs to me, I'll have you know,
And I shall show you that you can't hurt *me*
By this contemptible conspiracy,
That those who cross me know not what they do,
And that I've means to expose and punish you,
Avenge offended Heaven, and make you grieve
That ever you dared order me to leave.

SCENE VIII

ELMIRE, ORGON.

ELMIRE.   What was the point of all that angry chatter?
ORGON.   Dear God, I'm worried. This is no laughing matter.

ELMIRE.   How so?
ORGON.   I fear I understood his drift.
    I'm much disturbed about that deed of gift.
ELMIRE.   You gave him . . . ?
ORGON.   Yes, it's all been drawn and signed.
    But one thing more is weighing on my mind.
ELMIRE.   What's that?
ORGON.   I'll tell you; but first let's see if there's
    A certain strong-box in his room upstairs.

ACT V

SCENE I

ORGON, CLÉANTE.

CLÉANTE.   Where are you going so fast?
ORGON.   God knows!
CLÉANTE.   Then wait;
    Let's have a conference, and deliberate
    On how this situation's to be met.
ORGON.   That strong-box has me utterly upset;
    This is the worst of many, many shocks.
CLÉANTE.   Is there some fearful mystery in that box?
ORGON.   My poor friend Argas brought that box to me
    With his own hands, in utmost secrecy;
    'Twas on the very morning of his flight.
    It's full of papers which, if they came to light,
    Would ruin him—or such is my impression.
CLÉANTE.   They why did you let it out of your possession?
ORGON.   Those papers vexed my conscience, and it seemed best
    To ask the counsel of my pious guest.
    The cunning scoundrel got me to agree
    To leave the strong-box in his custody,
    So that, in case of an investigation,
    I could employ a slight equivocation
    And swear I didn't have it, and thereby,
    At no expense of conscience, tell a lie.
CLÉANTE.   It looks to me as if you're out on a limb.
    Trusting him with that box, and offering him
    That deed of gift, were actions of a kind
    Which scarcely indicate a prudent mind.
    With two such weapons, he has the upper hand,
    And since you're vulnerable, as matters stand,
    You erred once more in bringing him to bay.
    You should have acted in some subtler way.
ORGON.   Just think of it: behind that fervent face,
    A heart so wicked, and a soul so base!
    I took him in, a hungry beggar, and then . . .

Enough, by God! I'm through with pious men:
Henceforth I'll hate the whole false brotherhood,
And persecute them worse than Satan could.
CLÉANTE.   Ah, there you go—extravagant as ever!
Why can you not be rational? You never
Manage to take the middle course, it seems,
But jump, instead, between absurd extremes.
You've recognized your recent grave mistake
In falling victim to a pious fake;
Now, to correct that error, must you embrace
An even greater error in its place,
And judge our worthy neighbors as a whole
By what you've learned of one corrupted soul?
Come, just because one rascal made you swallow
A show of zeal which turned out to be hollow,
Shall you conclude that all men are deceivers,
And that, today, there are no true believers?
Let atheists make that foolish inference;
Learn to distinguish virtue from pretense,
Be cautious in bestowing admiration,
And cultivate a sober moderation.
Don't humor fraud, but also don't asperse
True piety; the latter fault is worse,
And it is best to err, if err one must,
As you have done, upon the side of trust.

SCENE II

DAMIS, ORGON, CLÉANTE.

DAMIS.   Father, I hear that scoundrel's uttered threats
Against you; that he pridefully forgets
How, in his need, he was befriended by you,
And means to use your gifts to crucify you.
ORGON.   It's true, my boy. I'm too distressed for tears.
DAMIS.   Leave it to me, Sir; let me trim his ears.
Faced with such insolence, we must not waver.
I shall rejoice in doing you the favor
Of cutting short his life, and your distress.
CLÉANTE.   What a display of young hotheadedness!
Do learn to moderate your fits of rage,
In this just kingdom,° this enlightened age,
One does not settle things by violence.

---

kingdom: that of Louis XIV, who reigned 1643–1715.

SCENE III

MADAME PERNELLE, MARIANE, ELMIRE, DORINE, DAMIS, ORGON, CLÉANTE.

MADAME PERNELLE.   I hear strange tales of very strange events.
ORGON.   Yes, strange events which these two eyes beheld.
The man's ingratitude is unparalleled.
I save a wretched pauper from starvation,
House him, and treat him like a blood relation,
Shower him every day with my largesse,
Give him my daughter, and all that I possess;
And meanwhile the unconscionable knave
Tries to induce my wife to misbehave;
And not content with such extreme rascality,
Now threatens me with my own liberality,
And aims, by taking base advantage of
The gifts I gave him out of Christian love,
To drive me from my house, a ruined man,
And make me end a pauper, as he began.
DORINE.   Poor fellow!
MADAME PERNELLE.   No, my son, I'll never bring
Myself to think him guilty of such a thing.
ORGON.   How's that?
MADAME PERNELLE.   The righteous always were maligned.
ORGON.   Speak clearly, Mother. Say what's on your mind.
MADAME PERNELLE.   I mean that I can smell a rat, my dear.
You know how everybody hates him, here.
ORGON.   That has no bearing on the case at all.
MADAME PERNELLE.   I told you a hundred times, when you were small,
That virtue in this world is hated ever;
Malicious men may die, but malice never.
ORGON.   No doubt that's true, but how does it apply?
MADAME PERNELLE.   They've turned you against him by a clever lie.
ORGON.   I've told you, I was there and saw it done.
MADAME PERNELLE.   Ah, slanderers will stop at nothing, Son.
ORGON.   Mother, I'll lose my temper . . . For the last time,
I tell you I was witness to the crime.
MADAME PERNELLE.   The tongues of spite are busy night and noon,
And to their venom no man is immune.
ORGON.   You're talking nonsense. Can't you realize
I saw it; saw it; saw it with my eyes?
Saw, do you understand me? Must I shout it
Into your ears before you'll cease to doubt it?
MADAME PERNELLE.   Appearances can deceive, my son. Dear me,
We cannot always judge by what we see.
ORGON.   Drat! Drat!
MADAME PERNELLE.   One often interprets things awry;
Good can seem evil to a suspicious eye.

ORGON.   Was I to see his pawing at Elmire
As an act of charity?
MADAME PERNELLE.   Till his guilt is clear,
A man deserves the benefit of the doubt.
You should have waited, to see how things turned out.
ORGON.   Great God in Heaven, what more proof did I need?
Was I to sit there, watching, until he'd . . .
You drive me to the brink of impropriety.
MADAME PERNELLE.   No, no, a man of such surpassing piety
Could not do such a thing. You cannot shake me.
I don't believe it, and you shall not make me.
ORGON.   You vex me so that, if you weren't my mother,
I'd say to you . . . some dreadful thing or other.
DORINE.   It's your turn now, Sir, not to be listened to;
You'd not trust us, and now she won't trust you.
CLÉANTE.   My friends, we're wasting time which should be spent
In facing up to our predicament.
I fear that scoundrel's threats weren't made in sport.
DAMIS.   Do you think he'd have the nerve to go to court?
ELMIRE.   I'm sure he won't: they'd find it all too crude
A case of swindling and ingratitude.
CLÉANTE.   Don't be too sure. He won't be at a loss
To give his claims a high and righteous gloss;
And clever rogues with far less valid cause
Have trapped their victims in a web of laws.
I say again that to antagonize
A man so strongly armed was most unwise.
ORGON.   I know it; but the man's appalling cheek
Outraged me so, I couldn't control my pique.
CLÉANTE.   I wish to Heaven that we could devise
Some truce between you, or some compromise.
ELMIRE.   If I had known what cards he held, I'd not
Have roused his anger by my little plot.
ORGON (*To* DORINE, *as* M. LOYAL *enters*).
What is that fellow looking for? Who is he?
Go talk to him—and tell him that I'm busy.

SCENE IV

MONSIEUR LOYAL, MADAME PERNELLE, ORGON, DAMIS, MARIANE, DORINE, ELMIRE, CLÉANTE.

MONSIEUR LOYAL.   Good day, dear sister. Kindly let me see
Your master.
DORINE.   He's involved with company,
And cannot be disturbed just now, I fear.

MONSIEUR LOYAL.   I hate to intrude; but what has brought me here
   Will not disturb your master, in any event.
   Indeed, my news will make him most content.
DORINE.   Your name?
MONSIEUR LOYAL.   Just say that I bring greetings from
   Monsieur Tartuffe, on whose behalf I've come.
DORINE (*To* ORGON).   Sir, he's a very gracious man, and bears
   A message from Tartuffe, which, he declares,
   Will make you most content.
CLÉANTE.   Upon my word,
   I think this man had best be seen, and heard.
ORGON.   Perhaps he has some settlement to suggest.
   How shall I treat him? What manner would be best?
CLÉANTE.   Control your anger, and if he should mention
   Some fair adjustment, give him your full attention.
MONSIEUR LOYAL.   Good health to you, good Sir. May Heaven confound
   Your enemies, and may your joys abound.
ORGON (*Aside, to* CLÉANTE).   A gentle salutation: it confirms
   My guess that he is here to offer terms.
MONSIEUR LOYAL.   I've always held your family most dear;
   I served your father, Sir, for many a year.
ORGON.   Sir, I must ask your pardon; to my shame,
   I cannot now recall your face or name.
MONSIEUR LOYAL.   Loyal's my name; I come from Normandy,
   And I'm a bailiff, in all modesty.
   For forty years, praise God, it's been my boast
   To serve with honor in that vital post,
   And I am here, Sir, if you will permit
   The liberty, to serve you with this writ . . .
ORGON.   To—*what?*
MONSIEUR LOYAL.   Now, please, Sir, let us have no friction:
   It's nothing but an order of eviction.
   You are to move your goods and family out
   And make way for new occupants, without
   Deferment or delay, and give the keys . . .
ORGON.   I? Leave this house?
MONSIEUR LOYAL.   Why yes, Sir, if you please.
   This house, Sir, from the cellar to the roof,
   Belongs now to the good Monsieur Tartuffe,
   And he is lord and master of your estate
   By virtue of a deed of present date,
   Drawn in due form, with clearest legal phrasing . . .
DAMIS.   Your insolence is utterly amazing!
MONSIEUR LOYAL.   Young man, my business here is not with you,
   But with your wise and temperate father, who,
   Like every worthy citizen, stands in awe
   Of justice, and would never obstruct the law.

ORGON.   But . . .

MONSIEUR LOYAL.   Not for a million, Sir, would you rebel
    Against authority; I know that well.
    You'll not make trouble, Sir, or interfere
    With the execution of my duties here.

DAMIS.   Someone may execute a smart tattoo
    On that black jacket of yours, before you're through.

MONSIEUR LOYAL.   Sir, bid your son be silent. I'd much regret
    Having to mention such a nasty threat
    Of violence, in writing my report.

DORINE (*Aside*).   This man Loyal's a most disloyal sort!

MONSIEUR LOYAL.   I love all men of upright character,
    And when I agreed to serve these papers, Sir,
    It was your feelings that I had in mind.
    I couldn't bear to see the case assigned
    To someone else, who might esteem you less
    And so subject you to unpleasantness.

ORGON.   What's more unpleasant than telling a man to leave
    His house and home?

MONSIEUR LOYAL.   You'd like a short reprieve?
    If you desire it, Sir, I shall not press you,
    But wait until tomorrow to dispossess you.
    Splendid. I'll come and spend the night here, then,
    Most quietly, with half a score of men.
    For form's sake, you might bring me, just before
    You go to bed, the keys to the front door.
    My men, I promise, will be on their best
    Behavior, and will not disturb your rest.
    But bright and early, Sir, you must be quick
    And move out all your furniture, every stick:
    The men I've chosen are both young and strong,
    And with their help it shouldn't take you long.
    In short, I'll make things pleasant and convenient,
    And since I'm being so extremely lenient,
    Please show me, Sir, a like consideration,
    And give me your entire cooperation.

ORGON (*Aside*).   I may be all but bankrupt, but I vow
    I'd give a hundred louis, here and now,
    Just for the pleasure of landing one good clout
    Right on the end of that complacent snout.

CLÉANTE.   Careful; don't make things worse.

DAMIS.   My bootsole itches
    To give that beggar a good kick in the breeches.

DORINE.   Monsieur Loyal, I'd love to hear the whack
    Of a stout stick across your fine broad back.

MONSIEUR LOYAL.   Take care: a woman too may go to jail if
    She uses threatening language to a bailiff.

CLÉANTE.   Enough, enough, Sir. This must not go on.
  Give me that paper, please, and then begone.
MONSIEUR LOYAL.   Well, *au revoir.* God give you all good cheer!
ORGON.   May God confound you, and him who sent you here!

SCENE V

  ORGON, CLÉANTE, MARIANE, ELMIRE, MADAME PERNELLE, DORINE, DAMIS.

ORGON.   Now, Mother, was I right or not? This writ
  Should change your notion of Tartuffe a bit.
  Do you perceive his villainy at last?
MADAME PERNELLE.   I'm thunderstruck. I'm utterly aghast.
DORINE.   Oh, come, be fair. You mustn't take offense
  At this new proof of his benevolence.
  He's acting out of selfless love, I know.
  Material things enslave the soul, and so
  He kindly has arranged your liberation
  From all that might endanger your salvation.
ORGON.   Will you not ever hold your tongue, you dunce?
CLÉANTE.   Come, you must take some action, and at once.
ELMIRE.   Go tell the world of the low trick he's tried.
  The deed of gift is surely nullified
  By such behavior, and public rage will not
  Permit the wretch to carry out his plot.

SCENE VI

  VALÈRE, ORGON, CLÉANTE, ELMIRE, MARIANE, MADAME PERNELLE, DAMIS, DORINE.

VALÈRE.   Sir, though I hate to bring you more bad news,
  Such is the danger that I cannot choose.
  A friend who is extremely close to me
  And knows my interest in your family
  Has, for my sake, presumed to violate
  The secrecy that's due to things of state,
  And sends me word that you are in a plight
  From which your one salvation lies in flight.
  That scoundrel who's imposed upon you so
  Denounced you to the King an hour ago
  And, as supporting evidence, displayed
  The strong-box of a certain renegade
  Whose secret papers, so he testified,
  You had disloyally agreed to hide.
  I don't know just what charges may be pressed,
  But there's a warrant out for your arrest;
  Tartuffe has been instructed, furthermore,
  To guide the arresting officer to your door.

CLÉANTE.   He's clearly done this to facilitate
　His seizure of your house and your estate.
ORGON.   That man, I must say, is a vicious beast!
VALÈRE.   Quick, Sir; you mustn't tarry in the least.
　My carriage is outside, to take you hence;
　This thousand louis should cover all expense.
　Let's lose no time, or you shall be undone;
　The sole defense, in this case, is to run.
　I shall go with you all the way, and place you
　In a safe refuge to which they'll never trace you.
ORGON.   Alas, dear boy, I wish that I could show you
　My gratitude for everything I owe you.
　But now is not the time; I pray the Lord
　That I may live to give you your reward.
　Farewell, my dears; be careful . . .
CLÉANTE.   Brother, hurry.
　We shall take care of things, you needn't worry.

SCENE VII

THE OFFICER, TARTUFFE, VALÈRE, ORGON, ELMIRE, MARIANE, MADAME
PERNELLE, DORINE, CLÉANTE, DAMIS.

TARTUFFE.   Gently, Sir, gently; stay right where you are.
　No need for haste; your lodging isn't far.
　You're off to prison, by order of the Prince.
ORGON.   This is the crowning blow, you wretch; and since
　It means my total ruin and defeat,
　Your villainy is now at last complete.
TARTUFFE.   You needn't try to provoke me; it's no use.
　Those who serve Heaven must expect abuse.
CLÉANTE.   You are indeed most patient, sweet, and blameless.
DAMIS.   How he exploits the name of Heaven! It's shameless.
TARTUFFE.   Your taunts and mockeries are all for naught;
　To do my duty is my only thought.
MARIANE.   Your love of duty is most meritorious,
　And what you've done is little short of glorious.
TARTUFFE.   All deeds are glorious, Madam, which obey
　The sovereign prince who sent me here today.
ORGON.   I rescued you when you were destitute;
　Have you forgotten that, you thankless brute?
TARTUFFE.   No, no, I well remember everything;
　But my first duty is to serve my King.
　That obligation is so paramount
　That other claims, beside it, do not count;
　And for it I would sacrifice my wife,
　My family, my friend, or my own life.
ELMIRE.   Hypocrite!

DORINE.   All that we most revere, he uses
   To cloak his plots and camouflage his ruses.
CLÉANTE.   If it is true that you are animated
   By pure and loyal zeal, as you have stated,
   Why was this zeal not roused until you'd sought
   To make Orgon a cuckold, and been caught?
   Why weren't you moved to give your evidence
   Until your outraged host had driven you hence?
   I shan't say that the gift of all his treasure
   Ought to have damped your zeal in any measure;
   But if he is a traitor, as you declare,
   How could you condescend to be his heir?
TARTUFFE (*To the* OFFICER).
   Sir, spare me all this clamor; it's growing shrill.
   Please carry out your orders, if you will.
OFFICER.   Yes, I've delayed too long, Sir. Thank you kindly.
   You're just the proper person to remind me.
   Come, you are off to join the other boarders
   In the King's prison, according to his orders.
TARTUFFE.   Who? I, Sir?
OFFICER.   Yes.
TARTUFFE.   To prison? This can't be true!
OFFICER.   I owe an explanation, but not to you.

   (*To* ORGON.)

   Sir, all is well; rest easy, and be grateful.
   We serve a Prince° to whom all sham is hateful,
   A Prince who sees into our inmost hearts,
   And can't be fooled by any trickster's arts.
   His royal soul, though generous and human,
   Views all things with discernment and acumen;
   His sovereign reason is not lightly swayed,
   And all his judgments are discreetly weighed.
   He honors righteous men of every kind,
   And yet his zeal for virtue is not blind,
   Nor does his love of piety numb his wits
   And make him tolerant of hypocrites.
   'Twas hardly likely that this man could cozen
   A King who's foiled such liars by the dozen.
   With one keen glance, the King perceived the whole
   Perverseness and corruption of his soul,
   And thus high Heaven's injustice was displayed:
   Betraying you, the rogue stood self-betrayed.
   The King soon recognized Tartuffe as one
   Notorious by another name, who'd done

Prince: King Louis XIV

So many vicious crimes that one could fill
Ten volumes with them, and be writing still.
But to be brief: our sovereign was appalled
By this man's treachery toward you, which he called
The last, worst villainy of a vile career,
And bade me follow the imposter here
To see how gross his impudence could be,
And force him to restore your property.
Your private papers, by the King's command,
I hereby seize and give into your hand.
The King, by royal order, invalidates
The deed which gave this rascal your estates,
And pardons, furthermore, your grave offense
In harboring an exile's documents.
By these decrees, our Prince rewards you for
Your loyal deeds in the late civil war,
And shows how heartfelt is his satisfaction
In recompensing any worthy action,
How much he prizes merit, and how he makes
More of men's virtues than of their mistakes.

DORINE.   Heaven be praised!

MADAME PERNELLE.   I breathe again, at last.

ELMIRE.   We're safe.

MARIANE.   I can't believe the danger's past.

ORGON *(To* TARTUFFE*)*.
    Well, traitor, now you see . . .

CLÉANTE.   Ah, Brother, please,
    Let's not descend to such indignities.
    Leave the poor wretch to his unhappy fate,
    And don't say anything to aggravate
    His present woes; but rather hope that he
    Will soon embrace an honest piety,
    And mend his ways, and by a true repentance
    Move our just King to moderate his sentence.
    Meanwhile, go kneel before your sovereign's throne
    And thank him for the mercies he has shown.

ORGON.   Well said: let's go at once and, gladly kneeling,
    Express the gratitude which all are feeling.
    Then, when that first great duty has been done,
    We'll turn with pleasure to a second one,
    And give Valère, whose love has proven so true,
    The wedded happiness which is his due.

QUESTIONS

1. In Act I, Scene V, Cléante gives a rather long speech in which, after referring to
   certain hypocrites and charlatans as people "Who weep and pray and swindle and
   extort,/ Who preach the monkish life, but haunt the court,/ Who make their zeal

the partner of their vice," he declares that "True piety isn't hard to recognize." Yet, in the case of Orgon, it is very hard indeed to recognize. Why? What prevents Orgon from seeing those truths about Tartuffe that others in the play can so clearly see?

2. In the same scene, Orgon praises and defends Tartuffe ("There's been no loftier soul since time began") but adds, as something of an aside, that to follow Tartuffe is to "view this dunghill of a world with scorn." What evidence does the play offer that this cynical vision of the world is correct? Are Orgon's words here to be taken with true seriousness? If so, how is his bleak wisdom about the world to be reconciled with his abject foolishness about Tartuffe?

3. As you follow the words of advice offered by Dorine to her mistress Mariane about the planned marriage to Tartuffe, and as you observe the way in which she constructs the plot to make that marriage impossible, what perceptions of her character do you form? What values does she represent? Why are those values held by a person of her social standing, that of a lady's maid? Are her values shared by others in the play? Who?

4. In Act V, Scene II, Orgon's son Damis pledges violent revenge upon Tartuffe for his having tricked and humiliated his father. Yet Cléante, disagreeing, urges a moderate course of action, one in which violence will play no part. In so doing, what moral principles and attitudes about the world does Cléante represent? What *would* be so wrong about violently ruining a man who has cruelly manipulated the lives of others?

5. Many modern readers have felt uncomfortable with the conclusion of the play and with the moment (Act V, Scene VII) at which the will of the Prince is enacted by his representative Officer. They have felt that the dramatic action has unfairly been taken out of the hands of the characters and has, at the last moment, been put into the hands of a distant and unseen authority. Is there a counter-argument to be made that the values of that authority have actually been present in the play throughout its development? Where might you find expression of those values earlier in *Tartuffe?*

4

DRAMA OF SOCIAL REALISM

T hus far we have been dealing with genres of drama: tragedy and comedy. In considering the impact of realism on the theater, however, we come to a wholly different matter. Realistic drama may be comic, as in the work of George Bernard Shaw, or it may have tragic overtones, as we shall shortly see in our discussion of Henrik Ibsen's *Hedda Gabler*. *Realism* is an artistic point of view rather than a genre. It is concerned with how life itself is portrayed on stage. Avoiding the elements of ritual, fantasy, and farce important to drama of earlier eras, realism attempts to open a window onto life as it is actually lived and to deal with themes arising from the real social world.

The term *real*, it should be understood, is not used here in an evaluative way. In employing it to describe the work of Ibsen (or Anton Chekhov, August Strindberg, or any of Ibsen's other late nineteenth-century contemporaries) we are not thereby claiming that his plays are more "real" (and therefore better) than the work of Sophocles, Shakespeare, Molière, and other great playwrights preceding him. All plays are "real" in the sense that they take us into self-contained worlds (like those, for instance, of Hamlet and Tartuffe), each with a coherence and plausibility all its own.

Realism, then, does not imply a value judgment, but refers to an artistic movement that swept through Europe in the late nineteenth century and came to exercise a powerful hold on the theater as well as on the novel. The emphasis of realism is on everyday experience. Instead of kings and heroes, the protagonists are middle-class people not unlike the members of the audiences watching the plays. Instead of speaking in blank verse or in rhymed couplets, the characters speak in the prose of daily conversation. Realistic drama attempts, moreover, to reproduce the feeling of ordinary life (in some plays the set designers originally went to such lengths that they made water actually come out of faucets) in order to establish a context of plausibility that will highlight the inner crises of the characters, their conflicts with each other and with the larger social world.

For the Greek drama the focus of concern is the city-state. For the Elizabethan drama it is the realm, the royal world—of Denmark or of England itself. For Ibsen and other social realists, however, the focus of concern is society—the cold and impersonal "out there" that is more likely to crush individuals than to nourish or provide them with opportunities for

794

glory. Hence the audience imagines that it can sense, just beyond the three walls of the realistic play's set, the presence of a public world, a world enforcing values that are often corrupt, a world where greed and hypocrisy flourish and where the individual's fate is wholly determined by norms and sanctions over which he is powerless to act. If most of the things that are rotten in the state of Denmark at the beginning of *Hamlet* are set right by the hero's actions in the course of the play and by his eventual decision to revenge his father's murder, a realistic play, in contrast, offers no such corrective resolution, no such cleansing. The characters in an Ibsen play may declare a separate peace from the world in which they live, or, like Hedda Gabler herself, may take arms against that world. After their struggle for understanding and freedom is over, however, society continues onward, unaltered, and uncaring.

Henrik Ibsen (1828–1906), an expatriate who lived for long periods in Italy, Germany, and Austria, nonetheless remained trapped, in his imagination, by the constraints of his Norwegian homeland. While the winds of liberation prevailed over the rest of the continent, no ventilation entered the smug pieties of bourgeois life in his country. Ibsen's characters try again and again to break through the suffocating crush of social conventions to achieve their self-realization. Some, but not all, make it. Perhaps the most famous of his characters in this regard is Nora in *A Doll's House*, a woman stifled by the role of mindless mother and wife into which she has been thrust. She finally gathers up the courage to walk out of her doll's house of unreality, but other of Ibsen's characters have a harder time than she. Hedda Gabler, for instance, must pay a tragic price for her own declaration of independence.

Ibsen once said: "A dramatist's business is not to answer questions, but merely to ask them." His plays always have at least one character who questions and doubts, who insists on trying to bring light to the dark spots in his or her past and present life. These characters are determined to uncover what is genuine in themselves, in the people around them, and in the larger world surrounding them. Yet, if Ibsen is a realist in his portrayal of well-defined social worlds, his plays are also artfully constructed works and not just mere "slices of life." Consider, for instance, the characterization put forward in the first scene of *Hedda Gabler*: we see the obtuse and self-absorbed George Tesman with his infantile dependence on his aunt; the maid Berta with her small duties and small worries; Aunt Julie with her concern for correct titles, money, and the proper wearing of hats; and Hedda herself immersed in an icy withdrawal behind closed curtains. Or consider the way that the character of Eilert Løvborg advances the action—on the literal level by being a possible competitor for the job Tesman so desperately needs, and on the thematic level by demonstrating what happens to someone who tries to live outside the rules. Consider also the way Ibsen deals with Hedda's pregnancy, first handling it through hints that she impatiently ignores and then by the symbolic scene in which she feeds the pages of Løvborg's book—another kind of "child"—into the flames of the fire.

Ibsen once said of *Hedda Gabler*: "It was not my desire to deal in this play with so-called problems. What I wanted to do was depict human beings, human emotions and human destinies upon a groundwork of certain of the social conditions and principles of the modern day." Some of those principles are clear: the stifling sense of propriety, represented by Tesman, his old aunts, and the faithful servant Berta, that wafts like toxic fumes over the movement of the play; the sense that Hedda has that the world is made for man's exploration and excitement, but that for women biology alone is destiny; the unyielding nature of a society that demands strict adherence to its moral codes and condemns a transgressor to shame or even to banishment.

All of this provides the background of the play. In the foreground is Hedda herself. At the very beginning, it might not be immediately clear what the play is about. An insensitive husband and a neurotic wife? A possible love triangle? A case of academic fraud and plagiarism? Nor is it instantly clear how we are to regard the heroine herself. As a shrewish nag uncommonly rude to her husband and her in-laws? As a cynic who manipulates people for her devious pleasure? As a potential adultress? Part of the great subtlety of *Hedda Gabler* consists in its offering such complex possibilities. But just when we think we *know* exactly what Hedda is, she reveals yet another aspect of her character, and we are again forced to revise our profile. George Bernard Shaw, fascinated by the play, once described Hedda: "Though she has imagination and an intense appetite for beauty, she has no conscience, no conviction: with plenty of cleverness, energy and personal fascination, she remains mean, envious, insolent, cruel in protest against others' happiness, fiendish in her dislike of inartistic people and things; a bully in reaction to her own cowardice." Like all descriptions of her character, however, Shaw's leaves out something while saying a great deal.

As Ibsen begins to fill in more and more details of the oppressive world of *Hedda Gabler*, we see that the play is fundamentally about the heroine's struggle to gain control of her inner life, and that Hedda, for all her sharpness of tongue, is infinitely superior as a human creation to the people surrounding her—the weak and shallow Tesman, the repulsive Judge Brack, and all the others. Hedda is sympathetic not because she is generous, charming, or sweet, but because she understands herself so well and because she is so desperate to transcend her circumstances. She sees that the masculine world of achievement is closed to her, and she knows that no other will open up. As she tells Judge Brack when he makes his lewd proposition to her, she married Tesman beause she'd reached that point in life at which women—even women as well-born and high-spirited as herself—have no choice but to become wives. ("I'd danced myself tired. . . . I felt my time was up.") Now she is married and has become an expectant mother with the world closing in all around her. The only possibility of escape lies in arranging an affair, but that would not alter the basic circumstances of her life. She recognizes, with courage, that the great enemy of life is boredom, and she admits, with that stubborn honesty which is her trademark, that in a marriage such as her own, love is "a sickly stupid word."

No one but Hedda Gabler, not even Løvborg, is able to see the appeal of doing "something really brave." At the end of the play, when Brack threatens sexual blackmail over Løvborg's death, Hedda recognizes her dilemma: "Not free! Still not free!" She decides to do something brave.

Henrik Ibsen (1828–1906)
Hedda Gabler

CHARACTERS

GEORGE TESMAN, *research fellow in cultural history*
HEDDA TESMAN, *his wife*
MISS JULIANA TESMAN, *his aunt*
MRS. ELVSTED
JUDGE BRACK
EILERT LØVBORG
BERTA, *the* TESMAN'S *maid*

The action takes place in TESMAN'S *residence in the fashionable part of town.*

ACT I

A large, attractively furnished drawing room, decorated in dark colors. In the rear wall, a wide doorway with curtains drawn back. The doorway opens into a smaller room in the same style as the drawing room. In the right wall of the front room, a folding door that leads to the hall. In the left wall opposite, a glass door, with curtains similarly drawn back. Through the panes one can see part of an overhanging veranda and trees in autumn colors. In the foreground is an oval table with tablecloth and chairs around it. By the right wall, a wide, dark porcelain stove, a high-backed armchair, a cushioned footstool, and two taborets. In the right-hand corner, a settee with a small round table in front. Nearer, on the left and slightly out from the wall, a piano. On either side of the doorway in back, étagères with terra-cotta and majolica ornaments. Against the back wall of the inner room, a sofa, a table, and a couple of chairs can be seen. Above this sofa hangs a portrait of a handsome, elderly man in a general's uniform. Over the table, a hanging lamp with an opalescent glass shade. A number of bouquets of flowers are placed about the drawing room in vases and glasses. Others lie on the tables. The floors in both rooms are covered with thick carpets. Morning light. The sun shines in through the glass door.

MISS JULIANA TESMAN, *wearing a hat and carrying a parasol, comes in from the hall, followed by* BERTA, *who holds a bouquet wrapped in paper.* MISS TESMAN *is a lady around sixty-five with a kind and good-natured look, nicely but simply dressed in a gray tailored suit.* BERTA *is a maid somewhat past middle age, with a plain and rather provincial appearance.*

MISS TESMAN (*stops close by the door, listens, and says softly*).   Goodness, I don't think they're even up yet!
BERTA (*also softly*).   That's just what I said, Miss Juliana. Remember how late the steamer got in last night. Yes, and afterward! My gracious, how much the young bride had to unpack before she could get to bed.

MISS TESMAN.   Well, then—let them enjoy a good rest. But they must have some of this fresh morning air when they do come down. *(She goes to the glass door and opens it wide.)*

BERTA *(by the table, perplexed, with the bouquet in her hand).*   I swear there isn't a bit of space left. I think I'll have to put it here, miss. *(Places the bouquet on the piano.)*

MISS TESMAN.   So now you have a new mistress, Berta dear. Lord knows it was misery for me to give you up.

BERTA *(on the verge of tears).*   And for me, miss! What can I say? All those many blessed years I've been in your service, you and Miss Rina.

MISS TESMAN.   We must take it calmly, Berta. There's really nothing else to do. George needs you here in this house, you know that. You've looked after him since he was a little boy.

BERTA.   Yes, but miss, I'm all the time thinking of her, lying at home. Poor thing—completely helpless. And with that new maid! She'll never take proper care of an invalid, that one.

MISS TESMAN.   Oh, I'll manage to teach her. And most of it, you know, I'll do myself. So you mustn't be worrying over my poor sister.

BERTA.   Well, but there's something else too, miss. I'm really so afraid I won't please the young mistress.

MISS TESMAN.   Oh, well—there might be something or other at first—

BERTA.   Because she's so very particular.

MISS TESMAN.   Well, of course. General Gabler's daughter. What a life she had in the general's day! Remember seeing her out with her father—how she'd go galloping past in that long black riding outfit, with a feather in her hat?

BERTA.   Oh yes—I remember! But I never would have dreamed then that she and George Tesman would make a match of it.

MISS TESMAN.   Nor I either. But now, Berta—before I forget: from now on, you mustn't say George Tesman. You must call him Doctor Tesman.

BERTA.   Yes, the young mistress said the same thing—last night, right after they came in the door. Is that true then, miss?

MISS TESMAN.   Yes, absolutely. Think of it, Berta—they gave him his doctor's degree. Abroad, that is—on this trip, you know. I hadn't heard one word about it, till he told me down on the pier.

BERTA.   Well, he's clever enough to be anything. But I never thought he'd go in for curing people.

MISS TESMAN.   No, he wasn't made that kind of doctor. *(Nods significantly.)* But as a matter of fact, you may soon now have something still greater to call him.

BERTA.   Oh, really! What's that, miss?

MISS TESMAN *(smiling).*   Hm, wouldn't you like to know! *(Moved.)* Ah, dear God—if only my poor brother could look up from his grave and see what his little boy has become! *(Glancing about.)* But what's this, Berta? Why, you've taken all the slipcovers off the furniture—?

BERTA.   Madam told me to. She doesn't like covers on chairs, she said.

MISS TESMAN.   Are they going to make this their regular living room, then?

BERTA.   It seems so—with her. For his part—the doctor—he said nothing.

(GEORGE TESMAN *enters the inner room from the right, singing to himself and carrying an empty, unstrapped suitcase. He is a youngish-looking man of thirty-three, medium sized, with an open, round, cheerful face, blond hair and beard. He is somewhat carelessly dressed in comfortable lounging clothes.*)

MISS TESMAN.   Good morning, good morning, George!

TESMAN *(in the doorway)*.   Aunt Julie! Dear Aunt Julie! *(Goes over and warmly shakes her hand.)* Way out here—so early in the day—uh?

MISS TESMAN.   Yes, you know I simply had to look in on you a moment.

TESMAN.   And that without a decent night's sleep.

MISS TESMAN.   Oh, that's nothing at all to me.

TESMAN.   Well, then you did get home all right from the pier? Uh?

MISS TESMAN.   Why, of course I did—thank goodness. Judge Brack was good enough to see me right to my door.

TESMAN.   We were sorry we couldn't drive you up. But you saw for yourself—Hedda had all those boxes to bring along.

MISS TESMAN.   Yes, that was quite something, the number of boxes she had.

BERTA *(to TESMAN)*.   Should I go in and ask Mrs. Tesman if there's anything I can help her with?

TESMAN.   No, thanks, Berta—don't bother. She said she'd ring if she needed anything.

BERTA *(going off toward the right)*.   All right.

TESMAN.   But wait now—you can take this suitcase with you.

BERTA *(taking it)*.   I'll put it away in the attic. *(She goes out by the hall door.)*

TESMAN.   Just think, Aunt Julie—I had that whole suitcase stuffed full of notes. You just can't imagine all I've managed to find, rummaging through archives. Marvelous old documents that nobody knew existed—

MISS TESMAN.   Yes, you've really not wasted any time on your wedding trip, George.

TESMAN.   I certainly haven't. But do take your hat off, Auntie. Here—let me help you—uh?

MISS TESMAN *(as he does so)*.   Goodness—this is exactly as if you were still back at home with us.

TESMAN *(turning the hat in his hand and studying it from all sides)*.   My—what elegant hats you go in for!

MISS TESMAN.   I bought that for Hedda's sake.

TESMAN.   For Hedda's sake? Uh?

MISS TESMAN.   Yes, so Hedda wouldn't feel ashamed of me if we walked down the street together.

TESMAN *(patting her cheek)*.   You think of everything, Aunt Julie! *(Laying the hat on a chair by the table.)* So—look, suppose we sit down on the sofa and have a little chat till Hedda comes. *(They settle themselves. She puts her parasol on the corner of the sofa.)*

MISS TESMAN *(takes both of his hands and gazes at him).* How wonderful it is having you here, right before my eyes again, George! You—dear Jochum's own boy!

TESMAN.   And for me too, to see you again, Aunt Julie! You, who've been father and mother to me both.

MISS TESMAN.   Yes, I'm sure you'll always keep a place in your heart for your old aunts.

TESMAN.   But Auntie Rina—hm? Isn't she any better?

MISS TESMAN.   Oh no—we can hardly expect that she'll ever be better, poor thing. She lies there, just as she has all these years. May God let me keep her a little while longer! Because otherwise, George, I don't know what I'd do with my life. The more so now, when I don't have you to look after.

TESMAN *(patting her on the back).*   There, there, there—

MISS TESMAN *(suddenly changing her tone).*   No, but to think of it, that now you're a married man! And that it was *you* who carried off Hedda Gabler. The beautiful Hedda Gabler! Imagine! She, who always had so many admirers!

TESMAN *(hums a little and smiles complacently).*   Yes, I rather suspect I have several friends who'd like to trade places with me.

MISS TESMAN.   And then to have such a wedding trip! Five—almost six months—

TESMAN.   Well, remember, I used it for research, too. All those libraries I had to check—and so many books to read!

MISS TESMAN.   Yes, no doubt. *(More confidentially; lowering her voice.)* But now listen, George—isn't there something—something special you have to tell me?

TESMAN.   From the trip?

MISS TESMAN.   Yes.

TESMAN.   No, I can't think of anything beyond what I wrote in my letters. I got my doctor's degree down there—but I told you that yesterday.

MISS TESMAN.   Yes, of course. But I mean—whether you have any kind of—expectations—?

TESMAN.   Expectations?

MISS TESMAN.   My goodness, George—I'm your old aunt!

TESMAN.   Why, naturally I have expectations.

MISS TESMAN.   Ah!

TESMAN.   I have every expectation in the world of becoming a professor shortly.

MISS TESMAN.   Oh, a professor, yes—

TESMAN.   Or I might as well say, I'm sure of it. But, Aunt Julie—you know that perfectly well yourself.

MISS TESMAN *(with a little laugh).*   That's right, so I do. *(Changing the subject.)* But we were talking about your trip. It must have cost a terrible amount of money.

TESMAN.   Well, that big fellowship, you know—it took us a good part of the way.

MISS TESMAN.   But I don't see how you could stretch it enough for two.

TESMAN.   No, that's not so easy to see—uh?

MISS TESMAN.   And especially traveling with a lady. For I hear tell that's much more expensive.

TESMAN.   Yes, of course—it's a bit more expensive. But Hedda just had to have that trip. She *had* to. There was nothing else to be done.

MISS TESMAN.   No, no, I guess not. A honeymoon abroad seems to be the thing nowadays. But tell me—have you had a good look around your house?

TESMAN.   You can bet I have! I've been up since daybreak.

MISS TESMAN.   And how does it strike you, all in all?

TESMAN.   First-rate! Absolutely first-rate! Only I don't know what we'll do with the two empty rooms between the back parlor and Hedda's bedroom.

MISS TESMAN *(laughing again)*.   Oh, my dear George, I think you can use them—as time goes on.

TESMAN.   Yes, you're quite right about that, Aunt Julie! In time, as I build up my library—uh?

MISS TESMAN.   Of course, my dear boy. It was your library I meant.

TESMAN.   I'm happiest now for Hedda's sake. Before we were engaged, she used to say so many times there was no place she'd rather live than here, in Secretary Falk's town house.

MISS TESMAN.   Yes, and then to have it come on the market just after you'd sailed.

TESMAN.   We really have had luck, haven't we?

MISS TESMAN.   But expensive, George dear! You'll find it expensive, all this here.

TESMAN *(looks at her, somewhat crestfallen)*.   Yes, I suppose I will.

MISS TESMAN.   Oh, Lord, yes!

TESMAN.   How much do you think? Approximately? Hm?

MISS TESMAN.   It's impossible to say till the bills are all in.

TESMAN.   Well, fortunately Judge Brack has gotten me quite easy terms. That's what he wrote Hedda.

MISS TESMAN.   Don't worry yourself about that, dear. I've also put up security to cover the carpets and furniture.

TESMAN.   Security? Aunt Julie, dear—you? What kind of security could *you* give?

MISS TESMAN.   I took out a mortgage on our pension.

TESMAN *(jumping up)*.   What! On your—and Auntie Rina's pension!

MISS TESMAN.   I saw nothing else to do.

TESMAN *(standing in front of her)*.   But you're out of your mind, Aunt Julie! That pension—it's all Aunt Rina and you have to live on.

MISS TESMAN.   Now, now—don't make so much of it. It's only a formality; Judge Brack said so. He was good enough to arrange the whole thing for me. Just a formality, he said.

TESMAN.   That's all well enough. But still—

MISS TESMAN.   You'll be drawing your own salary now. And, good gracious, if we have to lay out a bit, just now at the start—why, it's no more than a pleasure for us.

TESMAN.　Oh, Aunt Julie—you never get tired of making sacrifices for me!

MISS TESMAN *(rises and places her hands on his shoulders)*.　What other joy do I have in this world than smoothing the path for you, my dear boy? You, without father or mother to turn to. And now we've come to the goal, George! Things may have looked black at times; but now, thank heaven, you've made it.

TESMAN.　Yes, it's remarkable, really, how everything's turned out for the best.

MISS TESMAN.　Yes—and those who stood against you—who wanted to bar your way—they've gone down. They've fallen, George. The one most dangerous to you—he fell farthest. And he's lying there now, in the bed he made—poor, misguided creature.

TESMAN.　Have you heard any news of Eilert? I mean, since I went away.

MISS TESMAN.　Only that he's supposed to have brought out a new book.

TESMAN.　What's that? Eilert Løvborg? Just recently, uh?

MISS TESMAN.　So they say. But considering everything, it can hardly amount to much. Ah, but when *your* new book comes out—it'll be a different story, George! What will it be about?

TESMAN.　It's going to treat the domestic handicrafts of Brabant in the Middle Ages.

MISS TESMAN.　Just imagine—that you can write about things like that!

TESMAN.　Actually, the book may take quite a while yet. I have this tremendous collection of material to put in order, you know.

MISS TESMAN.　Yes, collecting and ordering—you do that so well. You're not my brother's son for nothing.

TESMAN.　I look forward so much to getting started. Especially now, with a comfortable home of my own to work in.

MISS TESMAN.　And most of all, dear, now that you've won her, the wife of your heart.

TESMAN *(embracing her)*.　Yes, yes, Aunt Julie! Hedda—that's the most beautiful part of it all! *(Glancing toward the doorway.)* But I think she's coming—uh?

(HEDDA enters from the left through the inner room. She is a woman of twenty-nine. Her face and figure show breeding and distinction; her complexion is pallid and opaque. Her steel gray eyes express a cool, unruffled calm. Her hair is an attractive medium brown, but not particularly abundant. She wears a tasteful, rather loose-fitting gown.)

MISS TESMAN *(going to meet HEDDA)*.　Good morning, Hedda dear— how good to see you!

HEDDA *(holding out her hand)*.　Good morning, my dear Miss Tesman! Calling so early? This *is* kind of you.

MISS TESMAN *(slightly embarrassed)*.　Well—did the bride sleep well in her new home?

HEDDA.　Oh yes, thanks. Quite adequately.

TESMAN.　Adequately! Oh, I like that, Hedda! You were sleeping like a stone when I got up.

HEDDA. Fortunately. But of course one has to grow accustomed to anything new, Miss Tesman—little by little. (*Looking toward the left.*) Oh! That maid has left the door open—and the sunlight's just flooding in.

MISS TESMAN (*going toward the door*). Well, we can close it.

HEDDA. No, no—don't! (*To* TESMAN.) There, dear, draw the curtains. It gives a softer light.

TESMAN (*by the glass door*). All right—all right. Look, Hedda—now you have shade and fresh air both.

HEDDA. Yes, we really need some fresh air here, with all these piles of flowers— But—won't you sit down, Miss Tesman?

MISS TESMAN. Oh no, thank you. Now that I know that everything's fine—thank goodness—I will have to run along home. My sister's lying there waiting, poor thing.

TESMAN. Give her my very, very best, won't you? And say I'll be looking in on her later today.

MISS TESMAN. Oh, you can be sure I will. But what do you know, George—(*Searching in her bag.*)—I nearly forgot. I have something here for you.

TESMAN. What's that, Aunt Julie? Hm?

MISS TESMAN (*brings out a flat package wrapped in newspaper and hands it to him*). There, dear. Look.

TESMAN (*opening it*). Oh, my—you kept them for me, Aunt Julie! Hedda! That's really touching! Uh!

HEDDA (*by the* étagère *on the right*). Yes, dear, what is it?

TESMAN. My old bedroom slippers! My slippers!

HEDDA. Oh yes, I remember how often you spoke of them during the trip.

TESMAN. Yes, I missed them terribly. (*Going over to her.*) Now you can see them, Hedda!

HEDDA (*moves toward the stove*). Thanks, but I really don't care to.

TESMAN (*following her*). Imagine—Auntie Rina lay and embroidered them, sick as she was. Oh, you couldn't believe how many memories are bound up in them.

HEDDA (*at the table*). But not for me.

MISS TESMAN. I think Hedda is right, George.

TESMAN. Yes, but I only thought, now that she's part of the family—

HEDDA (*interrupting*). We're never going to manage with this maid, Tesman.

MISS TESMAN. Not manage with Berta?

TESMAN. But dear—why do you say that? Uh?

HEDDA (*pointing*). See there! She's left her old hat lying out on a chair.

TESMAN (*shocked; dropping the slippers*). But Hedda—!

HEDDA. Suppose someone came in and saw it.

TESMAN. Hedda—that's Aunt Julie's hat!

HEDDA. Really?

MISS TESMAN (*picking it up*). That's right, it's mine. And what's more, it certainly is not old—Mrs. Tesman.

HEDDA. I really hadn't looked closely at it, Miss Tesman.

MISS TESMAN *(putting on the hat).*   It's actually the first time I've had it on. The very first time.

TESMAN.   And it's lovely, too. Most attractive!

MISS TESMAN.   Oh, it's hardly all that, George. *(Looks about.)* My parasol—? Ah, here. *(Takes it.)* For that's mine too. *(Murmurs.)* Not Berta's.

TESMAN.   New hat and new parasol! Just imagine, Hedda!

HEDDA.   Quite charming, really.

TESMAN.   Yes, aren't they, uh? But Auntie, take a good look at Hedda before you leave. See how charming *she* is!

MISS TESMAN.   But George dear, there's nothing new in that. Hedda's been lovely all her life. *(She nods and starts out, right.)*

TESMAN *(following her).*   But have you noticed how plump and buxom she's grown? How much she's filled out on the trip?

HEDDA *(crossing the room).*   Oh, do be quiet—!

MISS TESMAN *(who has stopped and turned).*   Filled out?

TESMAN.   Of course, you can't see it so well when she has that dressing gown on. But I, who have the opportunity to—

HEDDA *(by the glass door, impatiently).*   Oh, you have no opportunity for anything!

TESMAN.   It must have been the mountain air, down in the Tyrol—

HEDDA *(brusquely interrupting).*   I'm exactly as I was when I left.

TESMAN.   Yes, that's your claim. But you certainly are not. Auntie, don't you agree?

MISS TESMAN *(gazing at her with folded hands).*   Hedda is lovely—lovely—lovely. *(Goes up to her, takes her head in both hands, bends it down and kisses her hair.)* God bless and keep Hedda Tesman—for George's sake.

HEDDA *(gently freeing herself).*   Oh—! Let me go.

MISS TESMAN *(with quiet feeling).*   I won't let a day go by without looking in on you two.

TESMAN.   Yes, please do that, Aunt Julie! Uh?

MISS TESMAN.   Good-bye—good-bye!

(She goes out by the hall door. TESMAN *accompanies her, leaving the door half open. He can be heard reiterating his greetings to Aunt Rina and his thanks for the slippers. At the same time,* HEDDA *moves about the room, raising her arms and clenching her fists as if in a frenzy. Then she flings back the curtains from the glass door and stands there, looking out. A moment later* TESMAN *comes back, closing the door after him.)*

TESMAN *(retrieving the slippers from the floor).*   What are you standing and looking at, Hedda?

HEDDA *(again calm and controlled).*   I'm just looking at the leaves—they're so yellow—and so withered.

TESMAN *(wraps up the slippers and puts them on the table).*   Yes, well, we're into September now.

HEDDA *(once more restless).*   Yes, to think—that already we're in—in September.

TESMAN.   Didn't Aunt Julie seem a bit strange? A little—almost formal? What do you suppose was bothering her? Hm?

HEDDA.   I hardly know her at all. Isn't that how she usually is?

TESMAN.   No, not like this, today.

HEDDA *(leaving the glass door)*.   Do you think this thing with the hat upset her?

TESMAN.   Oh, not very much. A little, just at the moment, perhaps—

HEDDA.   But really, what kind of manners has she—to go throwing her hat about in a drawing room! It's just not proper.

TESMAN.   Well, you can be sure Aunt Julie won't do it again.

HEDDA.   Anyhow, I'll manage to smooth it over with her.

TESMAN.   Yes, Hedda dear, I wish you would!

HEDDA.   When you go in to see them later on, you might ask her out for the evening.

TESMAN.   Yes, I'll do that. And there's something else you could do that would make her terribly happy.

HEDDA.   Oh?

TESMAN.   If only you could bring yourself to speak to her warmly, by her first name. For my sake, Hedda? Uh?

HEDDA.   No, no—don't ask me to do that. I told you this once before. I'll try to call her "Aunt." That should be enough.

TESMAN.   Oh, all right. I was only thinking, now that you belong to the family—

HEDDA.   Hm—I really don't know—*(She crosses the room to the doorway.)*

TESMAN *(after a pause)*.   Is something the matter, Hedda? Uh?

HEDDA.   I'm just looking at my old piano. It doesn't really fit in with all these other things.

TESMAN.   With the first salary I draw, we can see about trading it in on a new one.

HEDDA.   No, not traded in. I don't want to part with it. We can put it there, in the inner room, and get another here in its place. When there's a chance, I mean.

TESMAN *(slightly cast down)*.   Yes, we could do that, of course.

HEDDA *(picks up the bouquet from the piano)*.   These flowers weren't here when we got in last night.

TESMAN.   Aunt Julie must have brought them for you.

HEDDA *(examining the bouquet)*.   A visiting card. *(Takes it out and reads it.)* "Will stop back later today." Can you guess who this is from?

TESMAN.   No. Who? Hm?

HEDDA.   It says "Mrs. Elvsted."

TESMAN.   No, really? Sheriff Elvsted's wife. Miss Rysing, she used to be.

HEDDA.   Exactly. The one with the irritating hair that she was always showing off. An old flame of yours, I've heard.

TESMAN *(laughing)*.   Oh, that wasn't for long. And it was before I knew you, Hedda. But imagine—that she's here in town.

HEDDA.   It's odd that she calls on us. I've hardly seen her since we were in school.

TESMAN.   Yes, I haven't seen her either—since God knows when. I wonder how she can stand living in such an out-of-the-way place. Hm?

HEDDA *(thinks a moment, then bursts out).*   But wait—isn't it some-where up in those parts that he—that Eilert Løvborg lives?

TESMAN.   Yes, it's someplace right around there. (BERTA *enters by the hall door.)*

BERTA.   She's back again, ma'am—that lady who stopped by and left the flowers an hour ago. *(Pointing.)* The ones you have in your hand, ma'am.

HEDDA.   Oh, is she? Good. Would you ask her to come in.

(BERTA *opens the door for* MRS. ELVSTED *and goes out.* MRS. ELVSTED *is a slender woman with soft, pretty features. Her eyes are light blue, large, round, and somewhat prominent, with a startled, questioning look. Her hair is re-markably light, almost a white-gold, and unusually abundant and wavy. She is a couple of years younger than* HEDDA. *She wears a dark visiting dress, tasteful, but not quite in the latest fashion.)*

HEDDA *(going to greet her warmly).*   Good morning, my dear Mrs. Elvsted. How delightful to see you again!

MRS. ELVSTED *(nervously; struggling to control herself).*   Yes, it's a very long time since we last met.

TESMAN *(gives her his hand).*   Or since *we* met, uh?

HEDDA.   Thank you for your beautiful flowers—

MRS. ELVSTED.   Oh, that's nothing—I would have come straight out here yesterday afternoon, but then I heard you weren't at home—

TESMAN.   Have you just now come to town? Uh?

MRS. ELVSTED.   I got in yesterday toward noon. Oh, I was in desperation when I heard that you weren't at home.

HEDDA.   Desperation! Why?

TESMAN.   But my dear Mrs. Rysing—Mrs. Elvsted, I mean—

HEDDA.   You're not in some kind of trouble?

MRS. ELVSTED.   Yes, I am. And I don't know another living soul down here I can turn to.

HEDDA *(putting the bouquet down on the table).*   Come, then—let's sit here on the sofa—

MRS. ELVSTED.   Oh, I can't sit down. I'm really too much on edge!

HEDDA.   Why, of course you can. Come here.

(She draws MRS. ELVSTED *down on the sofa and sits beside her.)*

TESMAN.   Well? What is it, Mrs. Elvsted?

HEDDA.   Has anything particular happened at home?

MRS. ELVSTED.   Yes, that's both it—and not it. Oh, I do want so much that you don't misunderstand me—

HEDDA.   But then the best thing, Mrs. Elvsted, is simply to speak your mind.

TESMAN.   Because I suppose that's why you've come. Hm?

MRS. ELVSTED.   Oh yes, that's why. Well, then, I have to tell you—if you don't already know—that Eilert Løvborg's also in town.

HEDDA.   Løvberg—!

TESMAN.   What! Is Eilert Løvborg back! Just think, Hedda!

HEDDA.   Good Lord, I can hear.

MRS. ELVSTED.   He's been back all of a week's time now. A whole week—in this dangerous town! Alone! With all the bad company that's around.

HEDDA.   But my dear Mrs. Elvsted, what does *he* have to do with you?

MRS. ELVSTED *(glances anxiously at her and says quickly)*.   He was the children's tutor.

HEDDA.   Your children's?

MRS. ELVSTED.   My husband's. I have none.

HEDDA.   Your stepchildren's, then.

MRS. ELVSTED.   Yes.

TESMAN *(somewhat hesitantly)*.   But was he—I don't know quite how to put it—was he sufficiently—responsible in his habits for such a job? Uh?

MRS. ELVSTED.   In these last two years, there wasn't a word to be said against him.

TESMAN.   Not a word? Just think of that, Hedda!

HEDDA.   I heard it.

MRS. ELVSTED.   Not even a murmur, I can assure you! Nothing. But anyway—now that I know he's here—in this big city—and with so much money in his hands—then I'm just frightened to death for him.

TESMAN.   But why didn't he stay up there where he was? With you and your husband? Uh?

MRS. ELVSTED.   After the book came out, he just couldn't rest content with us.

TESMAN.   Yes, that's right—Aunt Julie was saying he'd published a new book.

MRS. ELVSTED.   Yes, a great new book, on the course of civilization—in all its stages. It's been out two weeks. And now it's been bought and read so much—and it's made a tremendous stir—

TESMAN.   Has it really? It must be something he's had lying around from his better days.

MRS. ELVSTED.   Years back, you mean?

TESMAN.   I suppose.

MRS. ELVSTED.   No, he's written it all up there with us. Now—in this last year.

TESMAN.   That's marvelous to hear. Hedda! Just imagine!

MRS. ELVSTED.   Yes, if only it can go on like this!

HEDDA.   Have you seen him here in town?

MRS. ELVSTED.   No, not yet. I had such trouble finding out his address. But this morning I got it at last.

HEDDA *(looks searchingly at her)*.   I must say it seems rather odd of your husband—

MRS. ELVSTED *(with a nervous start)*.   Of my husband—! What?

HEDDA.   To send you to town on this sort of errand. Not to come and look after his friend himself.

MRS. ELVSTED.   No, no, my husband hasn't the time for that. And then I had—some shopping to do.

HEDDA *(with a slight smile).*   Oh, that's different.

MRS. ELVSTED *(getting up quickly and uneasily).*   I beg you, please, Mr. Tesman—be good to Eilert Løvborg if he comes to you. And he will, I'm sure. You know—you were such good friends in the old days. And you're both doing the same kind of work. The same type of research—from what I can gather.

TESMAN.   We were once, at any rate.

MRS. ELVSTED.   Yes, and that's why I'm asking you, please—you too—to keep an eye on him. Oh, you will do that, Mr. Tesman—promise me that?

TESMAN.   I'll be only too glad to, Mrs. Rysing—

HEDDA.   Elvsted.

TESMAN.   I'll certainly do everything in my power for Eilert. You can depend on that.

MRS. ELVSTED.   Oh, how terribly kind of you! *(Pressing his hands.)* Many, many thanks! *(Frightened.)* He means so much to my husband, you know.

HEDDA *(rising).*   You ought to write him, dear. He might not come by on his own.

TESMAN.   Yes, that probably would be the best, Hedda? Hm?

HEDDA.   And the sooner the better. Right now, I'd say.

MRS. ELVSTED *(imploringly).*   Oh yes, if you could!

TESMAN.   I'll write him this very moment. Have you got his address, Mrs.—Mrs. Elvsted?

MRS. ELVSTED.   Yes. *(Takes a slip of paper from her pocket and hands it to him.)* Here it is.

TESMAN.   Good, good. Then I'll go in—*(Looking about.)* But wait—my slippers? Ah! Here. *(Takes the package and starts to leave.)*

HEDDA.   Write him a really warm, friendly letter. Nice and long, too.

TESMAN.   Don't worry, I will.

MRS. ELVSTED.   But please, not a word that I asked you to!

TESMAN.   No, that goes without saying. Uh? *(Leaves by the inner room, to the right.)*

HEDDA *(goes over to* MRS. ELVSTED, *smiles, and speaks softly).*   How's that! Now we've killed two birds with one stone.

MRS. ELVSTED.   What do you mean?

HEDDA.   Didn't you see that I wanted him out of the room?

MRS. ELVSTED.   Yes, to write the letter—

HEDDA.   But also to talk with you alone.

MRS. ELVSTED *(confused).*   About this same thing?

HEDDA.   Precisely.

MRS. ELVSTED *(upset).*   But Mrs. Tesman, there's nothing more to say! Nothing!

HEDDA.   Oh yes, but there is. There's a great deal more—I can see that. Come, sit here—and let's speak openly now, the two of us. *(She forces* MRS. ELVSTED *down into the armchair by the stove and sits on one of the taborets.)*

MRS. ELVSTED *(anxiously glancing at her watch).*   But Mrs. Tesman, dear—I was just planning to leave.

HEDDA.   Oh, you can't be in such a rush— Now! Tell me a little about how things are going at home.

MRS. ELVSTED.   Oh, that's the last thing I'd ever want to discuss.

HEDDA.   But with me, dear—? After all, we were in school together.

MRS. ELVSTED.   Yes, but you were a class ahead of me. Oh, I was terribly afraid of you then!

HEDDA.   Afraid of me?

MRS. ELVSTED.   Yes, terribly. Because whenever we met on the stairs, you'd always pull my hair.

HEDDA.   Did I really?

MRS. ELVSTED.   Yes, and once you said you would burn it off.

HEDDA.   Oh, that was just foolish talk, you know.

MRS. ELVSTED.   Yes, but I was so stupid then. And, anyway, since then—we've drifted so far—far apart from each other. We've moved in such different circles.

HEDDA.   Well, let's try now to come closer again. Listen, at school we were quite good friends, and we called each other by our first names—

MRS. ELVSTED.   No, I'm sure you're mistaken.

HEDDA.   Oh, I couldn't be! I remember it clearly. And that's why we have to be perfectly open, just as we were. (*Moves the stool nearer* MRS. ELVSTED.) There now! (*Kissing her cheek.*) You have to call me Hedda.

MRS. ELVSTED (*pressing and patting her hands*).   Oh, you're so good and kind—! It's not at all what I'm used to.

HEDDA.   There, there! And I'm going to call you my own dear Thora.

MRS. ELVSTED.   My name is Thea.

HEDDA.   Oh yes, of course. I meant Thea. (*Looks at her compassionately.*) So you're not much used to goodness or kindness, Thea? In your own home?

MRS. ELVSTED.   If only I had a home! But I don't. I never have.

HEDDA (*glances quickly at her*).   I thought it had to be something like that.

MRS. ELVSTED (*gazing helplessly into space*).   Yes—yes—yes.

HEDDA.   I can't quite remember now—but wasn't it as a housekeeper that you first came up to the Elvsteds?

MRS. ELVSTED.   Actually as a governess. But his wife—his first wife— she was an invalid and mostly kept to her bed. So I had to take care of the house too.

HEDDA.   But finally you became mistress of the house yourself.

MRS. ELVSTED (*heavily*).   Yes, I did.

HEDDA.   Let me see—about how long ago was that?

MRS. ELVSTED.   That I was married?

HEDDA.   Yes.

MRS. ELVSTED.   It's five years now.

HEDDA.   That's right. It must be.

MRS. ELVSTED.   Oh, these five years—! Or the last two or three, anyway. Oh, if you only knew, Mrs. Tesman—

HEDDA (*gives her hand a little slap*).   Mrs. Tesman! Now, Thea!

MRS. ELVSTED.   I'm sorry; I'll try— Yes, if you could only understand— Hedda—

HEDDA *(casually)*.   Eilert Løvborg has lived up there about three years too, hasn't he?

MRS. ELVSTED *(looks at her doubtfully)*.   Eilert Løvborg? Yes—he has.

HEDDA.   Had you already known him here in town?

MRS. ELVSTED.   Hardly at all. Well, I mean—by name, of course.

HEDDA.   But up there—I suppose he'd visit you both?

MRS. ELVSTED.   Yes, he came to see us every day. He was tutoring the children, you know. Because, in the long run, I couldn't do it all myself.

HEDDA.   No, that's obvious. And your husband—? I suppose he often has to be away?

MRS. ELVSTED.   Yes, you can imagine, as sheriff, how much traveling he does around in the district.

HEDDA *(leaning against the chair arm)*.   Thea—my poor, sweet Thea—now you must tell me everything—just as it is.

MRS. ELVSTED.   Well, then you have to ask the questions.

HEDDA.   What sort of man is your husband, Thea? I mean—you know—to be with. Is he good to you?

MRS. ELVSTED *(evasively)*.   He believes he does everything for the best.

HEDDA.   I only think he must be much too old for you. More than twenty years older, isn't he?

MRS. ELVSTED *(irritated)*.   That's true. Along with everything else. I just can't stand him! We haven't a single thought in common. Nothing at all—he and I.

HEDDA.   But doesn't he care for you all the same—in his own way?

MRS. ELVSTED.   Oh, I don't know what he feels. I'm no more than useful to him. And then it doesn't cost much to keep me. I'm inexpensive.

HEDDA.   That's stupid of you.

MRS. ELVSTED *(shaking her head)*.   It can't be otherwise. Not with him. He really doesn't care for anyone but himself—and maybe a little for the children.

HEDDA.   And for Eilert Løvborg, Thea.

MRS. ELVSTED *(looking at her)*.   Eilert Løvborg! Why do you think so?

HEDDA.   But my dear—it seems to me, when he sends you all the way into town to look after him— *(Smiles almost imperceptibly.)* Besides, it's what you told my husband.

MRS. ELVSTED *(with a little nervous shudder)*.   Really? Yes, I suppose I did. *(In a quiet outburst.)* No—I might as well tell you here and now! It's bound to come out in time.

HEDDA.   But my dear Thea—?

MRS. ELVSTED.   All right, then! My husband never knew I was coming here.

HEDDA.   What! Your husband never knew—

MRS. ELVSTED.   Of course not. Anyway, he wasn't at home. Off traveling somewhere. Oh, I couldn't bear it any longer, Hedda. It was impossible! I would have been so alone up there now.

HEDDA.   Well? What then?

MRS. ELVSTED.   So I packed a few of my things together—the barest necessities—without saying a word. And I slipped away from the house.

HEDDA.   Right then and there?

MRS. ELVSTED.   Yes, and took the train straight into town.

HEDDA.   But my dearest girl—that you could dare to do such a thing!

MRS. ELVSTED *(rising and walking about the room)*.   What else could I possibly do!

HEDDA.   But what do you think your husband will say when you go back home?

MRS. EVLSTED *(by the table, looking at her)*.   Back to *him?*

HEDDA.   Yes, of course.

MRS. ELVSTED.   I'll never go back to him.

HEDDA *(rising and approaching her)*.   You mean you've left, in dead earnest, for good?

MRS. ELVSTED.   Yes. There didn't seem anything else to do.

HEDDA.   But—to go away so openly.

MRS. ELVSTED.   Oh, you can't keep a thing like that secret.

HEDDA.   But what do you think people will say about you, Thea?

MRS. ELVSTED.   God knows they'll say what they please. *(Sitting wearily and sadly on the sofa.)* I only did what I had to do.

HEDDA *(after a short silence)*.   What do you plan on now? What kind of work?

MRS. ELVSTED.   I don't know yet. I only know I have to live here, where Eilert Løvborg is—if I'm going to live at all.

HEDDA *(moves a chair over from the table, sits beside her, and strokes her hands)*.   Thea dear—how did this—this friendship—between you and Eilert Løvborg come about?

MRS. ELVSTED.   Oh, it happened little by little. I got some kind of power, almost, over him.

HEDDA.   Really?

MRS. ELVSTED.   He gave up his old habits. Not because I'd asked him to. I never dared do that. But he could tell they upset me, and so he dropped them.

HEDDA *(hiding an involuntary, scornful smile)*.   My dear little Thea—just as they say—you rehabilitated him.

MRS. ELVSTED.   Well, he says so, at any rate. And he—on his part—he's made a real human being out of me. Taught me to think—and understand so many things.

HEDDA.   You mean he tutored you also?

MRS. ELVSTED.   No, not exactly. But he'd talk to me—talk endlessly on about one thing after another. And then came the wonderful, happy time when I could share in his work! When I could help him!

HEDDA.   Could you really?

MRS. ELVSTED.   Yes! Whenever he wrote anything, we'd always work on it together.

HEDDA.   Like two true companions.

MRS. ELVSTED *(eagerly)*.   Companions! You know, Hedda—that's what he said too! Oh, I ought to feel so happy—but I can't. I just don't know if it's going to last.

HEDDA.   You're no more sure of him than that?

MRS. ELVSTED *(despondently)*.   There's a woman's shadow between Eilert Løvborg and me.

HEDDA *(looks at her intently)*.   Who could that be?

MRS. ELVSTED.   I don't know. Someone out of his—his past. Someone he's really never forgotten.

HEDDA.   What has he said—about this!

MRS. ELVSTED.   It's only once—and just vaguely—that he touched on it.

HEDDA.   Well! And what did he say!

MRS. ELVSTED.   He said that when they broke off she was going to shoot him with a pistol.

HEDDA *(with cold constraint)*.   That's nonsense! Nobody behaves that way around here.

MRS. ELVSTED.   No. And that's why I think it must have been that redheaded singer that at one time he—

HEDDA.   Yes, quite likely.

MRS. ELVSTED.   I remember they used to say about her that she carried loaded weapons.

HEDDA.   Ah—then of course it must have been her.

MRS. ELVSTED *(wringing her hands)*.   But you know what, Hedda—I've heard that this singer—that she's in town again! Oh, it has me out of my mind—

HEDDA *(glancing toward the inner room)*.   Shh! Tesman's coming. *(Gets up and whispers.)* Thea—keep all this just between us.

MRS. ELVSTED *(jumping up)*.   Oh yes! In heaven's name—!

(GEORGE TESMAN, with a letter in his hand, enters from the right through the inner room.)

TESMAN.   There, now—the letter's signed and sealed.

HEDDA.   That's fine. I think Mrs. Elvsted was just leaving. Wait a minute. I'll go with you to the garden gate.

TESMAN.   Hedda, dear—could Berta maybe look after this?

HEDDA *(taking the letter)*.   I'll tell her to.

(BERTA enters from the hall.)

BERTA.   Judge Brack is here and says he'd like to greet you and the Doctor, ma'am.

HEDDA.   Yes, ask Judge Brack to come in. And, here—put this letter in the mail.

BERTA *(takes the letter)*.   Yes, ma'am.

(She opens the door for JUDGE BRACK and goes out. BRACK is a man of forty-five, thickset, yet well-built, with supple movements. His face is roundish, with a distinguished profile. His hair is short, still mostly black, and carefully groomed. His eyes are bright and lively. Thick eyebrows; a moustache

to match, with neatly clipped ends. He wears as trimly tailored walking suit, a bit too youthful for his age. Uses a monocle, which he now and then lets fall.)

JUDGE BRACK *(hat in hand, bowing).*   May one dare to call so early?

HEDDA.   Of course one may.

TESMAN *(shakes his hand).*   You're always welcome here. *(Introducing him.)* Judge Brack—Miss Rysing—

HEDDA.   Ah—!

BRACK *(bowing).*   I'm delighted.

HEDDA *(looks at him and laughs).*   It's really a treat to see you by daylight Judge!

BRACK.   You find me—changed?

HEDDA.   Yes. A bit younger, I think.

BRACK.   Thank you, most kindly.

TESMAN.   But what do you say for Hedda, uh? Doesn't she look flourishing? She's actually—

HEDDA.   Oh, leave me out of it! You might thank Judge Brack for all the trouble he's gone to—

BRACK.   Nonsense—it was a pleasure—

HEDDA.   Yes, you're a true friend. But here's Thea, standing here, aching to get away. Excuse me, Judge; I'll be right back.

(Mutual good-byes. MRS. ELVSTED *and* HEDDA *go out by the hall door.)*

BRACK.   So—is your wife fairly well satisfied, then—?

TESMAN.   Yes, we can't thank you enough. Of course—I gather there's some rearrangement called for here and there. And one or two things are lacking. We still have to buy a few minor items.

BRACK.   Really?

TESMAN.   But that's nothing for you to worry about. Hedda said she'd pick up those things herself. Why don't we sit down, hm?

BRACK.   Thanks. Just for a moment. *(Sits by the table.)* There's something I'd like to discuss with you, Tesman.

TESMAN.   What? Oh, I understand! *(Sitting.)* It's the serious part of the banquet we're coming to, uh?

BRACK.   Oh, as far as money matters go, there's no great rush—though I must say I wish we'd managed things a bit more economically.

TESMAN.   But that was completely impossible! Think about Hedda, Judge! You, who know her so well— I simply couldn't have her live like a grocer's wife.

BRACK.   No, no—that's the trouble, exactly.

TESMAN.   And then—fortunately—it can't be long before I get my appointment.

BRACK.   Well, you know—these things can often hang fire.

TESMAN.   Have you heard something further? Hm?

BRACK.   Nothing really definite—*(Changing the subject.)* But incidentally—I do have one piece of news for you.

TESMAN.   Well?

BRACK.   Your old friend Eilert Løvborg is back in town.

TESMAN.   I already know.

BRACK.   Oh? How did you hear?

TESMAN.   She told me. The lady that left with Hedda.

BRACK.   I see. What was her name again? I didn't quite catch it—

TESMAN.   Mrs. Elvsted.

BRACK.   Aha—Sheriff Elvsted's wife. Yes—it's up near them he's been staying.

TESMAN.   And, just think—what a pleasure to hear that he's completely stable again!

BRACK.   Yes, that's what they claim.

TESMAN.   And that he's published a new book, uh?

BRACK.   Oh yes!

TESMAN.   And it's created quite a sensation.

BRACK.   An extraordinary sensation.

TESMAN.   Just imagine—isn't that marvelous? He, with his remarkable talents—I was so very afraid that he'd really gone down for good.

BRACK.   That's what everyone thought.

TESMAN.   But I've no idea what he'll find to do now. How on earth can he ever make a living? Hm?

(During the last words, HEDDA *comes in by the hall door.)*

HEDDA *(to* BRACK, *laughing, with a touch of scorn).*   Tesman always goes around worrying about how people are going to make a living.

TESMAN.   My Lord—its' poor Eilert Løvborg we're talking of, dear.

HEDDA *(glancing quickly at him).*   Oh, really? *(Sits in the armchair by the stove and asks casually.)* What's the matter with him?

TESMAN.   Well—he must have run through his inheritance long ago. And he can't write a new book every year. Uh? So I was asking, really, what's going to become of him.

BRACK.   Perhaps I can shed some light on that.

TESMAN.   Oh?

BRACK.   You must remember that he does have relatives with a great deal of influence.

TESMAN.   Yes, but they've washed their hands of him altogether.

BRACK.   They used to call him the family's white hope.

TESMAN.   They used to, yes! But he spoiled all that himself.

HEDDA.   Who knows? *(With a slight smile.)* He's been rehabilitated up at the Elvsteds—

BRACK.   And then this book that he's published—

TESMAN.   Oh, well, let's hope they really help him some way or other. I just now wrote to him. Hedda dear, I asked him out here this evening.

BRACK.   But my dear fellow, you're coming to my stag party this evening. You promised down on the pier last night.

HEDDA.   Had you forgotten, Tesman?

TESMAN.   Yes, I absolutely had.

BRACK.   For that matter, you can rest assured that he'd never come.

TESMAN. What makes you say that, hm?

BRACK *(hesitating, rising and leaning on the back of the chair)*. My dear Tesman—and you too, Mrs. Tesman—I can't, in all conscience, let you go on without knowing something that—that—

TESMAN. Something involving Eilert—?

BRACK. Both you and him.

BRACK. You must be prepared that your appointment may not come through as quickly as you've wished or expected.

TESMAN *(jumping up nervously)*. Has something gone wrong? Uh?

BRACK. It may turn out that there'll have to be a competition for the post—

TESMAN. A competition! Imagine, Hedda!

HEDDA *(leaning further back in the chair)*. Ah, there—you see!

TESMAN. But with whom! You can't mean—?

BRACK. Yes, exactly. With Eilert Løvborg.

TESMAN *(striking his hands together)*. No, no—that's completely unthinkable! It's impossible! Uh?

BRACK. Hm—but it may come about, all the same.

TESMAN. No, but, Judge Brack—that would just be incredibly inconsiderate toward me! *(Waving his arms.)* Yes, because—you know—I'm a married man! We married on my prospects, Hedda and I. We went into debt. And even borrowed money from Aunt Julie. Because that job—my Lord, it was as good as promised to me, uh?

BRACK. Easy now—I'm sure you'll get the appointment. But you will have to compete for it.

HEDDA *(motionless in the armchair)*. Just think, Tesman—it will be like a kind of championship match.

TESMAN. But Hedda dearest, how can you take it so calmly!

HEDDA *(as before)*. I'm not the least bit calm. I can't wait to see how it turns out.

BRACK. In any case, Mrs. Tesman, it's well that you know now how things stand. I mean—with respect to those little purchases I hear you've been threatening to make.

HEDDA. This business can't change anything.

BRACK. I see! Well, that's another matter. Good-bye. *(To* TESMAN.*)* When I take my afternoon walk, I'll stop by and fetch you.

TESMAN. Oh yes, please do—I don't know where I'm at.

HEDDA *(leaning back and reaching out her hand)*. Goodbye, Judge. And come again soon.

BRACK. Many thanks. Good-bye now.

TESMAN *(accompanying him to the door)*. Good-bye, Judge! You really must excuse me—

*(*BRACK *goes out by the hall door.)*

TESMAN *(pacing about the room)*. Oh, Hedda—one should never go off and lose oneself in dreams, uh?

HEDDA *(looks at him and smiles)*. Do *you* do that?

TESMAN.   No use denying it. It was living in dreams to go and get married and set up house on nothing but expectations.

HEDDA.   Perhaps you're right about that.

TESMAN.   Well, at least we have our comfortable home, Hedda! The home that we always wanted. That we both fell in love with, I could almost say. Hm?

HEDDA *(rising slowly and wearily)*.   It was part of our bargain that we'd live in society—that we'd keep a great house—

TESMAN.   Yes, of course—how I'd looked forward to that! Imagine— seeing you as a hostess—in our own select circle of friends! Yes, yes—well, for a while, we two will just have to get on by ourselves, Hedda. Perhaps have Aunt Julie here now and then. Oh, you—for you I wanted to have things so—so utterly different—!

HEDDA.   Naturally this means I can't have a butler now.

TESMAN.   Oh no—I'm sorry, a butler—we can't even talk about that, you know.

HEDDA.   And the riding horse I was going to have—

TESMAN *(appalled)*.   Riding horse!

HEDDA.   I suppose I can't think of that anymore.

TESMAN.   Good Lord, no—that's obvious!

HEDDA *(crossing the room)*.   Well, at least I have one thing left to amuse myself with.

TESMAN *(beaming)*.   Ah, thank heaven for that! What is it, Hedda? Uh?

HEDDA *(in the center doorway, looking at him with veiled scorn)*.   My pistols, George.

TESMAN *(in fright)*.   Your pistols!

HEDDA *(her eyes cold)*.   General Gabler's pistols. *(She goes through the inner room and out to the left.)*

TESMAN *(runs to the center doorway and calls after her)*.   No, for heaven's sake, Hedda darling—don't touch those dangerous things! For my sake, Hedda! Uh?

ACT II

The rooms at the TESMANS', *same as in the first act, except that the piano has been moved out, and an elegant little writing table with a bookcase put in its place. A smaller table stands by the sofa to the left. Most of the flowers have been removed.* MRS. ELVSTED'S *bouquet stands on the large table in the foreground. It is afternoon.*

HEDDA, *dressed to receive callers, is alone in the room. She stands by the open glass door, loading a revolver. The match to it lies in an open pistol case on the writing table.*

HEDDA *(looking down into the garden and calling)*.   Good to see you again, Judge!

BRACK *(heard from below, at a distance)*.   Likewise, Mrs. Tesman!

HEDDA *(raises the pistol and aims).*   And now, Judge, I'm going to shoot you!

BRACK *(shouting from below).*   No-no-no! Don't point that thing at me!

HEDDA.   That's what comes of sneaking in the back way. *(She fires.)*

BRACK *(nearer).*   Are you out of your mind—!

HEDDA.   Oh, dear—I didn't hit you, did I?

BRACK *(still outside).*   Just stop this nonsense!

HEDDA.   All right, you can come in, Judge.

(JUDGE BRACK, dressed for a stag party, enters through the glass door. He carries a light overcoat on his arm.)

BRACK.   Good God! Are you still playing such games? What are you shooting at?

HEDDA.   Oh, I was just shooting into the sky.

BRACK *(gently taking the pistol out of her hand).*   Permit me. *(Looks at it.)* Ah, this one—I know it well. *(Glancing around.)* Where's the case? Ah, here. *(Puts the pistol away and shuts the case.)* We'll have no more of that kind of fun today.

HEDDA.   Well, what in heaven's name do you want me to do with myself?

BRACK.   You haven't had any visitors?

HEDDA *(closing the glass door).*   Not a single one. All of our set are still in the country, I guess.

BRACK.   And Tesman isn't home either?

HEDDA *(at the writing table, putting the pistol case away in a drawer).*   No. Right after lunch he ran over to his aunts'. He didn't expect you so soon.

BRACK.   Hm— I should have realized. That was stupid of me.

HEDDA *(turning her head and looking at him).*   Why stupid?

BRACK.   Because in that case I would have stopped by a little bit—earlier.

HEDDA *(crossing the room).*   Well, you'd have found no one here then at all. I've been up in my room dressing since lunch.

BRACK.   And there's not the least little crack in the door we could have conferred through.

HEDDA.   You forgot to arrange it.

BRACK.   Also stupid of me.

HEDDA.   Well, we'll just have to settle down here—and wait. Tesman won't be back for a while.

BRACK.   Don't worry, I can be patient.

(HEDDA sits in the corner of the sofa. BRACK lays his coat over the back of the nearest chair and sits down, keeping his hat in his hand. A short pause. They look at each other.)

HEDDA.   Well?

BRACK *(in the same tone).*   Well?

HEDDA.   I spoke first.

BRACK *(leaning slightly forward).*   Then let's have a nice little cozy chat, Mrs. Hedda.

HEDDA *(leaning further back on the sofa).*   Doesn't it seem like a whole eternity since the last time we talked together? Oh, a few words last night and this morning—but they don't count.

BRACK.   You mean, like this—between ourselves? Just the two of us?

HEDDA.   Well, more or less.

BRACK.   There wasn't a day that I didn't wish you were home again.

HEDDA.   And I was wishing exactly the same.

BRACK.   You? Really, Mrs. Hedda? And I thought you were having such a marvelous time on this trip.

HEDDA.   Oh, you can imagine!

BRACK.   But that's what Tesman always wrote.

HEDDA.   Oh, him! There's nothing he likes better than grubbing around in libraries and copying out old parchments, or whatever you call them.

BRACK *(with a touch of malice).*   But after all, it's his calling in life. In good part, anyway.

HEDDA.   Yes, that's true. So there's nothing wrong with it— But what about *me*! Oh, Judge, you don't know—I've been so dreadfully bored.

BRACK *(sympathetically).*   You really mean that? In all seriousness?

HEDDA.   Well, you can understand—! To go for a whole six months without meeting a soul who knew the least bit about our circle. No one that one could talk to about our kind of things.

BRACK.   Ah, yes— I think that would bother me too.

HEDDA.   But then the most unbearable thing of all—

BRACK.   What?

HEDDA.   To be everlastingly together with—with one and the same person—

BRACK *(nodding in agreement).*   Morning, noon, and night—yes. At every conceivable hour.

HEDDA.   I said "everlastingly."

BRACK.   All right. But with our good friend Tesman, I really should have thought—

HEDDA.   My dear Judge, Tesman is—a specialist.

BRACK.   Undeniably.

HEDDA.   And specialists aren't at all amusing to travel with. Not in the long run, anyway.

BRACK.   Not even—the specialist that one *loves.*

HEDDA.   Ugh—don't use that syrupy word!

BRACK *(startled).*   What's that, Mrs. Hedda!

HEDDA *(half laughing, half annoyed).*   Well, just try it yourself! Try listening to the history of civilization morning, noon, and—

BRACK.   Everlastingly.

HEDDA.   Yes! Yes! And then all this business about domestic crafts in the Middle Ages—! That really is just too revolting!

BRACK *(looks searchingly at her).*   But tell me—I can't see how it ever came about that—? Hm—

HEDDA.   That George Tesman and I could make a match?

BRACK.   All right, let's put it that way.

HEDDA.   Good Lord, does it seem so remarkable?

BRACK.   Well, yes—and no, Mrs. Hedda.

HEDDA.   I really had danced myself out, Judge. My time was up. *(With a slight shudder.)* Ugh! No, I don't want to say that. Or think it, either.

BRACK.   You certainly have no reason to.

HEDDA.   Oh—reasons—   *(Watching him carefully.)* And George Tesman—he is, after all, a thoroughly acceptable choice.

BRACK.   Acceptable and dependable, beyond a doubt.

HEDDA.   And I don't find anything especially ridiculous about him. Do you?

BRACK.   Ridiculous? No-o-o, I wouldn't say that.

HEDDA.   Hm. Anyway, he works incredibly hard on his research! There's every chance that, in time, he could still make a name for himself.

BRACK *(looking at her with some uncertainty)*.   I thought you believed, like everyone else, that he was going to be quite famous some day.

HEDDA *(wearily)*.   Yes, so I did. And then when he kept pressing and pleading to be allowed to take care of me—I didn't see why I ought to resist.

BRACK.   No. From that point of view, of course not—

HEDDA.   It was certainly more than my other admirers were willing to do for me, Judge.

BRACK *(laughing)*.   Well, I can't exactly answer for all the others. But as far as I'm concerned, you know that I've always cherished a—a certain respect for the marriage bond. Generally speaking, that is.

HEDDA *(bantering)*.   Oh, I never really held out any hopes for *you*.

BRACK.   All I want is to have a warm circle of intimate friends, where I can be of use one way or another, with the freedom to come and go as—as a trusted friend—

HEDDA.   Of the man of the house, you mean?

BRACK *(with a bow)*.   Frankly—I prefer the lady. But the man, too, of course, in his place. That kind of—let's say, triangular arrangement—you can't imagine how satisfying it can be all around.

HEDDA.   Yes, I must say I longed for some third person so many times on that trip. Oh—those endless tête-à-têtes in railway compartments—!

BRACK.   Fortunately the wedding trip's over now.

HEDDA *(shaking her head)*.   The trip will go on—and on. I've only come to one stop on the line.

BRACK.   Well, then what you do is jump out—and stretch yourself a little, Mrs. Hedda.

HEDDA.   I'll never jump out.

BRACK.   Never?

HEDDA.   No. Because there's always someone on the platform who—

BRACK *(with a laugh)*.   Who looks at your legs, is that it?

HEDDA.   Precisely.

BRACK.   Yes, but after all—

HEDDA *(with a disdainful gesture)*.   I'm not interested. I'd rather keep my seat—right here, where I am. Tête-à-tête.

BRACK.   Well, but suppose a third person came on board and joined the couple.

HEDDA.   Ah! That's entirely different.

BRACK.   A trusted friend, who understands—

HEDDA.   And can talk about all kinds of lively things—

BRACK.   Who's not in the least a specialist.

HEDDA *(with an audible sigh)*.   Yes, that would be a relief.

BRACK *(hearing the front door open and glancing toward it)*.   The triangle is complete.

HEDDA *(lowering her voice)*.   And the train goes on.

(GEORGE TESMAN, *in a gray walking suit and a soft felt hat, enters from the hall. He has a good number of unbound books under his arm and in his pockets.*)

TESMAN *(going up to the table by the corner settee)*.   Phew! Let me tell you, that's hot work—carrying all these. *(Setting the books down.)* I'm actually sweating, Hedda. And what's this—you're already here, Judge? Hm? Berta didn't tell me.

BRACK *(rising)*.   I came in through the garden.

HEDDA.   What are all these books you've gotten?

TESMAN *(stands leafing through them)*.   They're new publications in my special field. I absolutely need them.

HEDDA.   Your special field?

BRACK.   Of course. Books in his special field, Mrs. Tesman.

(BRACK *and* HEDDA *exchange a knowing smile.*)

HEDDA.   You need still more books in your special field?

TESMAN.   Hedda, my dear, it's impossible ever to have too many. You have to keep up with what's written and published.

HEDDA.   Oh, I suppose so.

TESMAN *(searching among the books)*.   And look—I picked up Eilert Løvborg's new book too. *(Offering it to her.)* Maybe you'd like to have a look at it? Uh?

HEDDA.   No, thank you. Or—well, perhaps later.

TESMAN.   I skimmed through some of it on the way home.

HEDDA.   Well, what do you think of it—as a specialist?

TESMAN.   I think it's amazing how well it holds up. He's never written like this before. *(Gathers up the books.)* But I'll take these into the study now. I can't wait to cut the pages—! And then I better dress up a bit. *(To* BRACK.*)* We don't have to rush right off, do we? Hm?

BRACK.   No, not at all. There's ample time.

TESMAN.   Ah, then I'll be at my leisure. *(Starts out with the books, but pauses and turns in the doorway.)* Oh, incidentally, Hedda—Aunt Julie won't be by to see you this evening.

HEDDA.   She won't? I suppose it's that business with the hat?

TESMAN.   Don't be silly. How can you think that of Aunt Julie? Imagine—! No, it's Auntie Rina—she's very ill.

HEDDA.   She always is.

TESMAN.   Yes, but today she really took a turn for the worse.

HEDDA.   Well, then it's only right for her sister to stay with her. I'll have to bear with it.

TESMAN.   But you can't imagine how delighted Aunt Julie was all the same—because you'd filled out so nicely on the trip!

HEDDA *(under her breath; rising)*.   Oh, these eternal aunts!

TESMAN.   What?

HEDDA *(going over to the glass door)*.   Nothing.

TESMAN.   All right, then. *(He goes through the inner room and out, right.)*

BRACK.   What were you saying about a hat?

HEDDA.   Oh, it's something that happened with Miss Tesman this morning. She'd put her hat down over there on the chair. *(Looks at him and smiles.)* And I pretended I thought it was the maid's.

BRACK *(shaking his head)*.   But my dear Mrs. Hedda, how could you do that! Hurt that fine old lady!

HEDDA *(nervously, pacing the room)*.ᐧ   Well, it's—these things come over me, just like that, suddenly. And I can't hold back. *(Throws herself down in the armchair by the stove.)* Oh, I don't know myself how to explain it.

BRACK *(behind the armchair)*.   You're not really happy—that's the heart of it.

HEDDA *(gazing straight ahead)*.   And I don't know why I ought to be— happy. Or maybe you can tell me why?

BRACK.   Yes—among other things, because you've gotten just the home you've always wanted.

HEDDA *(looks up at him and laughs)*.   You believe that story too?

BRACK.   You mean there's nothing to it?

HEDDA.   Oh yes—there's something to it.

BRACK.   Well?

HEDDA.   There's this much to it, that I used Tesman as my escort home from parties last summer—

BRACK.   Unfortunately—I was going in another direction then.

HEDDA.   How true. Yes, you had other directions to go last summer.

BRACK *(laughing)*.   For shame, Mrs. Hedda! Well—so you and Tesman—?

HEDDA.   Yes, so one evening we walked by this place. And Tesman, poor thing, was writhing in torment, because he couldn't find anything to say. And I felt sorry for a man of such learning—

BRACK *(smiling skeptically)*.   Did you? Hm—

HEDDA.   No, I honestly did. And so—just to help him off the hook—I came out with some rash remark about this lovely house being where I'd always wanted to live.

BRACK.   No more than that?

HEDDA.   No more that evening.

BRACK.   But afterward?

HEDDA.   Yes, my rashness had its consequences, Judge.

BRACK.   I'm afraid our rashness all too often does, Mrs. Hedda.

HEDDA.   Thanks! But don't you see, it was this passion for the old Falk mansion that drew George Tesman and me together! It was nothing more than that, that brought on our engagement and the marriage and the wedding trip and everything else. Oh yes, Judge—I was going to say, you make your bed and then you lie in it.

BRACK.   But that's priceless! So actually you couldn't care less about all this?

HEDDA.   God knows, not in the least.

BRACK.   But even now? Now that we've made it somewhat comfortable for you here?

HEDDA.   Ugh—all the rooms seem to smell of lavender and dried roses. But maybe that scent was brought in by Aunt Julie.

BRACK *(laughing)*.   No, I think it's a bequest from the late Mrs. Falk.

HEDDA.   Yes, there's something in it of the odor of death. It's like a corsage—the day after the dance. *(Folds her hands behind her neck, leans back in her chair, and looks at him.)* Oh, my dear Judge—you can't imagine how horribly I'm going to bore myself here.

BRACK.   But couldn't you find some goal in life to work toward? Others do, Mrs. Hedda.

HEDDA.   A goal—that would really absorb me?

BRACK.   Yes, preferably.

HEDDA.   God only knows what that could be. I often wonder if— *(Breaks off.)* But that's impossible too.

BRACK.   Who knows? Tell me.

HEDDA.   I was thinking—if I could get Tesman to go into politics.

BRACK *(laughing)*.   Tesman! No, I can promise you—politics is absolutely out of his line.

HEDDA.   No, I can believe you. But even so, I wonder if I could get him into it?

BRACK.   Well, what satisfaction would you have in that, if he can't succeed? Why push him in that direction?

HEDDA.   Because, I've told you, I'm bored! *(After a pause.)* Then you think it's really out of the question that he could ever be a cabinet minister?

BRACK.   Hm—you see, Mrs. Hedda—to be anything like that, he'd have to be fairly wealthy to start with.

HEDDA *(rising impatiently)*.   Yes, there it is! It's this tight little world I've stumbled into— *(Crossing the room.)* That's what makes life so miserable! So utterly ludicrous! Because that's what it *is*.

BRACK.   I'd say the fault lies elsewhere.

HEDDA.   Where?

BRACK.   You've never experienced anything that's really stirred you.

HEDDA.   Anything serious, you mean.

BRACK.   Well, you can call it that, if you like. But now perhaps it's on the way.

HEDDA *(tossing her head)*.   Oh, you mean all the fuss over that wretched professorship! But that's Tesman's problem. I'm not going to give it a single thought.

BRACK.   No, that isn't—ah, never mind. But suppose you were to be confronted now by what—in rather elegant language—is called your most solemn responsibility. *(Smiling.)* A new responsibility, Mrs. Hedda.

HEDDA *(angrily)*.   Be quiet! You'll never see me like that!

BRACK *(delicately)*.   We'll discuss it again in a year's time—at the latest.

HEDDA *(curtly)*.   I have no talent for such things, Judge. I won't have responsibilities!

BRACK.   Don't you think you've a talent for what almost every woman finds the most meaningful—

HEDDA *(over by the glass door)*.   Oh, I told you, be quiet! I often think I have talent for only one thing in life.

BRACK *(moving closer)*.   And what, may I ask, is that?

HEDDA *(stands looking out)*.   Boring myself to death. And that's the truth. *(Turns, looks toward the inner room, and laughs.)* See what I mean! Here comes the professor.

BRACK *(in a low tone of warning)*.   Ah-ah-ah, Mrs. Hedda!

(GEORGE TESMAN, *dressed for the party, with hat and gloves in hand, enters from the right through the inner room.*)

TESMAN.   Hedda—there's been no word from Eilert Løvborg, has there? Hm?

HEDDA.   No.

TESMAN.   Well, he's bound to be here soon then. You'll see.

BRACK.   You really believe he'll come?

TESMAN.   Yes, I'm almost positive of it. Because I'm sure they're nothing but rumors, what you told us this morning.

BRACK.   Oh?

TESMAN.   Yes. At least Aunt Julie said she couldn't for the world believe that he'd stand in my way again. Can you imagine that!

BRACK.   So, then everything's well and good.

TESMAN *(putting his hat with the gloves inside on a chair to the right)*.   Yes, but I really would like to wait for him as long as possible.

BRACK.   We have plenty of time for that. There's no one due at my place till seven or half past.

TESMAN.   Why, then we can keep Hedda company for a while. And see what turns up. Uh?

HEDDA *(taking BRACK's hat and coat over to the settee)*.   And if worst comes to worst, Mr. Løvborg can sit and talk with me.

BRACK *(trying to take his things himself)*.   Ah, please, Mrs. Tesman—! What do you mean by "worst," in this case?

HEDDA.   If he won't go with you and Tesman.

TESMAN *(looks doubtfully at her)*.   But Hedda dear—is it quite right that he stays with you here? Uh? Remember that Aunt Julie isn't coming.

HEDDA.   No, but Mrs. Elvsted is. The three of us can have tea together.

TESMAN.   Oh, well, that's all right.

BRACK *(smiling)*.   And that might be the soundest plan for him too.

HEDDA.   Why?

BRACK.   Well, really, Mrs. Tesman, you've made enough pointed remarks about my little bachelor parties. You've always said they're only fit for men of the strictest principles.

HEDDA.   But Mr. Løvborg is surely a man of principle now. After all, a reformed sinner—

(BERTA *appears at the hall door.*)

BERTA.   Ma'am, there's a gentleman here who'd like to see you—
HEDDA.   Yes, show him in.
TESMAN *(softly)*.   I'm sure it's him! Just think!

(EILERT LØVBORG *enters from the hall. He is lean and gaunt, the same age as* TESMAN, *but looks older and rather exhausted. His hair and beard are dark brown, his face long and pale, but with reddish patches over the cheekbones. He is dressed in a trim black suit, quite new, and holds dark gloves and a top hat in his hand. He hesitates by the door and bows abruptly. He seems somewhat embarrassed.*)

TESMAN *(crosses over and shakes his hand)*.   Ah, my dear Eilert—so at last we meet again!
EILERT LØVBORG *(speaking in a hushed voice)*.   Thanks for your letter, George! *(Approaching* HEDDA.*)* May I shake hands with you too, Mrs. Tesman?
HEDDA *(taking his hand)*.   So glad to see you, Mr. Løvborg. *(Gesturing with her hand.)* I don't know if you two gentlemen—?
LØVBORG *(bowing slightly)*.   Judge Brack, I believe.
BRACK *(reciprocating)*.   Of course. It's been some years—
TESMAN *(to* LØVBORG, *with his hands on his shoulders)*.   And now, Eilert, make yourself at home, completely! Right, Hedda? I hear you'll be settling down here in town again? Uh?
LØVBORG.   I plan to.
TESMAN.   Well, that makes sense. Listen—I just got hold of your new book. But I really haven't had time to read it yet.
LØVBORG.   You can save yourself the bother.
TESMAN.   Why? What do you mean?
LØVBORG.   There's very little to it.
TESMAN.   Imagine—you can say that!
BRACK.   But it's won such high praise, I hear.
LØVBORG.   That's exactly what I wanted. So I wrote a book that everyone could agree with.
BRACK.   Very sound.
TESMAN.   Yes, but my dear Eilert—!
LØVBORG.   Because now I want to build up my position again—and try to make a fresh start.
TESMAN *(somewhat distressed)*.   Yes, that is what you want, I suppose. Uh?
LØVBORG *(smiling, puts down his hat and takes a thick manila envelope out of his pocket)*.   But when this comes out—George Tesman—you'll have to read it. Because this is the real book—the one that speaks for my true self.
TESMAN.   Oh, really? What sort of book is that?
LØVBORG.   It's the sequel.
TESMAN.   Sequel? To what?

LØVBORG.　To the book.

TESMAN.　The one just out?

LØVBORG.　Of course.

TESMAN.　Yes, but my dear Eilert—that comes right down to our own time!

LØVBORG.　Yes, it does. And this one deals with the future.

TESMAN.　The future! But good Lord, there's nothing we know about that!

LØVBORG.　True. But there are one or two things worth saying about it all the same. *(Opens the envelope.)* Here, take a look—

TESMAN.　But that's not your handwriting.

LØVBORG.　I dictated it. *(Paging through the manuscript.)* It's divided into two sections. The first is about the forces shaping the civilization of the future. And the second part, here—*(Paging further on.)* suggests what lines of development it's likely to take.

TESMAN.　How extraordinary! It never would have occurred to me to write about anything like that.

HEDDA *(at the glass door, drumming on the pane).*　Hm—no, of course not.

LØVBORG *(puts the manuscript back in the envelope and lays it on the table).*　I brought it along because I thought I might read you a bit of it this evening.

TESMAN.　Ah, that's very good of you, Eilert; but this evening— *(Glancing at BRACK.)* I'm really not sure that it's possible—

LØVBORG.　Well, some other time, then. There's no hurry.

BRACK.　I should explain, Mr. Løvborg—there's a little party at my place tonight. Mostly for Tesman, you understand.

LØVBORG *(looking for his hat).*　Ah—then I won't stay—

BRACK.　No, listen—won't you give me the pleasure of having you join us?

LØVBORG *(sharply and decisively).*　No, I can't. Thanks very much.

BRACK.　Oh, nonsense! Do that. We'll be a small, select group. And you can bet we'll have it "lively," as Mrs. Hed—Mrs. Tesman says.

LØVBORG.　I don't doubt it. But nevertheless—

BRACK.　You could bring your manuscript with you and read it to Tesman there, at my place. I have a spare room you could use.

TESMAN.　Why, of course, Eilert—you could do that, couldn't you? Uh?

HEDDA *(intervening).*　But dear, if Mr. Løvborg simply doesn't want to! I'm sure Mr. Løvborg would much prefer to settle down here and have supper with me.

LØVBORG *(looking at her).*　With you, Mrs. Tesman!

HEDDA.　And with Mrs. Elvsted.

LØVBORG.　Ah. *(Casually.)* I saw her a moment this afternoon.

HEDDA.　Oh, did you? Well, she'll be here soon. So it's almost essential for you to stay, Mr. Løvborg. Otherwise, she'll have no one to see her home.

LØVBORG.　That's true. Yes, thank you, Mrs. Tesman—I'll be staying, then.

HEDDA.　Then let me just tell the maid—

(She goes to the hall door and rings. BERTA *enters.* HEDDA *talks to her quietly and points toward the inner room.* BERTA *nods and goes out again.)*

TESMAN *(at the same time, to* LØVBORG*).*   Tell me, Eilert—is it this new material—about the future—that you're going to be lecturing on?

LØVBORG.   Yes.

TESMAN.   Because I heard at the bookstore that you'll be giving a lecture series here this autumn.

LØVBORG.   I intend to. I hope you won't be offended, Tesman.

TESMAN.   Why, of course not! But—?

LØVBORG.   I can easily understand that it makes things rather difficult for you.

TESMAN *(dispiritedly).*   Oh, I could hardly expect that for my sake you'd—

LØVBORG.   But I'm going to wait till you have your appointment.

TESMAN.   You'll wait! Yes, but—but—you're not competing for it, then? Uh?

LØVBORG.   No. I only want to win in the eyes of the world.

TESMAN.   But, my Lord—then Aunt Julie was right after all! Oh yes—I knew it all along! Hedda! Can you imagine—Eilert Løvborg won't stand in our way!

HEDDA *(brusquely).*   Our way? Leave me out of it.

(She goes up toward the inner room where BERTA *is putting a tray with decanters and glasses on the table.* HEDDA *nods her approval and comes back again.* BERTA *goes out.)*

TESMAN *(at the same time).*   But you, Judge—what do you say to all this? Uh?

BRACK.   Well, I'd say that victory and honor—hm—after all, they're very sweet—

TESMAN.   Yes, of course. But still—

HEDDA *(regarding* TESMAN *with a cold smile).*   You look as if you'd been struck by lightning.

TESMAN.   Yes—something like it—I guess—

BRACK.   That's because a thunderstorm just passed over us, Mrs. Tesman.

HEDDA *(pointing toward the inner room).*   Won't you gentlemen please help yourselves to a glass of cold punch?

BRACK *(looking at his watch).*   A parting cup? That's not such a bad idea.

TESMAN.   Marvelous, Hedda! Simply marvelous! The way I feel now, with this weight off my mind—

HEDDA.   Please, Mr. Løvborg, you too,

LØVBORG *(with a gesture of refusal).*   No, thank you. Not for me.

BRACK.   Good Lord, cold punch—it isn't poison, you know.

LØVBORG.   Perhaps not for everyone.

HEDDA.   I'll keep Mr. Løvborg company a while.

TESMAN.   All right, Hedda dear, you do that.

(He and BRACK *go into the inner room, sit down, drink punch, smoke cigarettes, and talk animatedly during the following.* LØVBORG *remains standing by the stove.* HEDDA *goes to the writing table.)*

HEDDA *(slightly raising her voice).*   I can show you some photographs, if you like. Tesman and I traveled through the Tyrol on our way home.

(She brings over an album and lays it on the table by the sofa, seating herself in the farthest corner. EILERT LØVBORG *comes closer, stops and looks at her. Then he takes a chair and sits down on her left, his back toward the inner room.)*

HEDDA *(opening the album).*   You see this view of the mountains, Mr. Løvborg. That's the Ortler group. Tesman's labeled them underneath. Here it is: "The Ortler group, near Meran."

LØVBORG *(whose eyes have never left her, speaking in a low, soft voice).*   Hedda—Gabler!

HEDDA *(with a quick glance at him).*   Ah! Shh!

LØVBORG *(repeating softly).*   Hedda Gabler!

HEDDA *(looks at the album).*   Yes, I used to be called that. In those days—when we two knew each other.

LØVBORG.   And from now on—for the rest of my life—I have to teach myself not to say Hedda Gabler.

HEDDA *(turning the pages).*   Yes, you have to. And I think you ought to start practicing it. The sooner the better, I'd say.

LØVBORG *(resentment in his voice).*   Hedda Gabler married? And to George Tesman!

HEDDA.   Yes—that's how it goes.

LØVBORG.   Oh, Hedda, Hedda—how could you throw yourself away like that!

HEDDA *(looks at him sharply).*   All right—no more of that!

LØVBORG.   What do you mean?

(TESMAN comes in and over to the sofa.)

HEDDA *(hears him coming and says casually).*   And this one, Mr. Løvborg, was taken from the Val d'Ampezzo. Just look at the peaks of those mountains. *(Looks warmly up at* TESMAN.*)* Now what were those marvelous mountains called, dear?

TESMAN.   Let me see. Oh, those are the Dolomites.

HEDDA.   Why, of course! Those are the Dolomites, Mr. Løvborg.

TESMAN.   Hedda dear—I only wanted to ask if we shouldn't bring in some punch anyway. At least for you, hm?

HEDDA.   Yes, thank you. And a couple of *petits fours*, please.

TESMAN.   No cigarettes?

HEDDA.   No.

TESMAN.   Right.

(He goes through the inner room and out to the right. BRACK *remains sitting inside, keeping his eye from time to time on* HEDDA *and* LØVBORG.*)*

LØVBORG (*softly, as before*).   Answer me, Hedda—how could you go and do such a thing?

HEDDA (*apparently immersed in the album*).   If you keep on saying Hedda like that to me, I won't talk to you.

LØVBORG.   Can't I say Hedda even when we're alone?

HEDDA.   No. You can think it, but you mustn't say it like that.

LØVBORG.   Ah, I understand. It offends your—love for George Tesman.

HEDDA (*glances at him and smiles*).   Love? You *are* absurd!

LØVBORG.   Then you don't love him!

HEDDA.   I don't expect to be unfaithful, either. I'm not having any of that!

LØVBORG.   Hedda, just answer me one thing—

HEDDA.   Shh!

(TESMAN, *carrying a tray, enters from the inner room.*)

TESMAN.   Look out! Here come the goodies. (*He sets the tray on the table.*)

HEDDA.   Why do you do the serving?

TESMAN (*filling the glasses*).   Because I think it's such fun to wait on you, Hedda.

HEDDA.   But now you've poured out two glasses. And you know Mr. Løvborg doesn't want—

TESMAN.   Well, but Mrs. Elvsted will be along soon.

HEDDA.   Yes, that's right—Mrs. Elvsted—

TESMAN.   Had you forgotten her? Uh?

HEDDA.   We've been so caught up in these. (*Showing him a picture.*) Do you remember this little village?

TESMAN.   Oh, that's the one just below the Brenner Pass! It was there that we stayed overnight—

HEDDA.   And met all those lively summer people.

TESMAN.   Yes, that's the place. Just think—if we could have had *you* with us, Eilert! My! (*He goes back and sits beside* BRACK.)

LØVBORG.   Answer me just one thing, Hedda—

HEDDA.   Yes?

LØVBORG.   Was there no love with respect to me, either? Not a spark—not one glimmer of love at all?

HEDDA.   I wonder, really, was there? To me it was as if we were two true companions—two very close friends. (*Smiling.*) You, especially, were so open with me.

LØVBORG.   You wanted it that way.

HEDDA.   When I look back on it now, there was really something beautiful and fascinating—and daring, it seems to me, about—about our secret closeness—our companionship that no one, not a soul, suspected.

LØVBORG.   Yes, Hedda, that's true! Wasn't there? When I'd come over to your father's in the afternoon—and the general sat by the window reading his papers—with his back to us—

HEDDA.   And we'd sit on the corner sofa—

LØVBORG.   Always with the same illustrated magazine in front of us—

HEDDA.   Yes, for the lack of an album.

LØVBORG.   Yes, Hedda—and the confessions I used to make—telling you things about myself that no one else knew of then. About the way I'd go out, the drinking, the madness that went on day and night, for days at a time. Ah, what power was it in you, Hedda, that made me tell you such things?

HEDDA.   You think it was some kind of power in me?

LØVBORG.   How else can I explain it? And all those—those devious questions you asked me—

HEDDA.   That you understood so remarkably well—

LØVBORG.   To think you could sit there and ask such questions! So boldly.

HEDDA.   Deviously, please.

LØVBORG.   Yes, but boldly, all the same. Interrogating me about—all that kind of thing!

HEDDA.   And to think you could answer, Mr. Løvborg.

LØVBORG.   Yes, that's exactly what I don't understand—now, looking back. But tell me, Hedda—the root of that bond between us, wasn't it love? Didn't you feel, on your part, as if you wanted to cleanse and absolve me—when I brought those confessions to you? Wasn't that it?

HEDDA.   No, not quite.

LØVBORG.   What was your power, then?

HEDDA.   Do you find it so very surprising that a young girl—if there's no chance of anyone knowing—

LØVBORG.   Yes?

HEDDA.   That she'd like some glimpse of a world that—

LØVBORG.   That—?

HEDDA.   That she's forbidden to know anything about.

LØVBORG.   So that was it?

HEDDA.   Partly. Partly that, I guess.

LØVBORG.   Companionship in a thirst for life. But why, then, couldn't it have gone on?

HEDDA.   But that was your fault.

LØVBORG.   You broke it off.

HEDDA.   Yes, when that closeness of ours threatened to grow more serious. Shame on you, Eilert Løvborg! How could you violate my trust when I'd been so—so bold with my friendship?

LØVBORG *(clenching his fists)*.   Oh, why didn't you do what you said! Why didn't you shoot me down!

HEDDA.   I'm—much too afraid of scandal.

LØVBORG.   Yes, Hedda, you're a coward at heart.

HEDDA.   A terrible coward. *(Changing her tone.)* But that was lucky for you. And now you're so nicely consoled at the Elvsteds'.

LØVBORG.   I know what Thea's been telling you.

HEDDA.   And perhaps you've been telling her all about us?

LØVBORG.   Not a word. She's too stupid for that sort of thing.

HEDDA.   Stupid?

LØVBORG.   When it comes to those things, she's stupid.

HEDDA.   And I'm a coward. *(Leans closer, without looking him in the eyes, and speaks softly.)* But there *is* something now that I can tell you.

LØVBORG *(intently)*.   What?

HEDDA.   When I didn't dare shoot you—

LØVBORG.   Yes?

HEDDA.   That wasn't my worst cowardice—that night.

LØVBORG *(looks at her a moment, understands, and whispers passionately)*.   Oh, Hedda! Hedda Gabler! Now I begin to see it, the hidden reason why we've been so close! You and I—! It was the hunger for *life* in you—

HEDDA *(quietly, with a sharp glance)*.   Careful! That's no way to think!

(It has begun to grow dark. The hall door is opened from without by BERTA.*)*

HEDDA *(clapping the album shut and calling out with a smile)*.   Well, at last! Thea dear—please come in!

*(*MRS. ELVSTED *enters from the hall. She is in evening dress. The door is closed behind her.)*

HEDDA *(on the sofa, stretching her arms out toward her)*.   Thea, my sweet—I thought you were never coming!

(In passing, MRS. ELVSTED *exchanges light greetings with the gentlemen in the inner room, then comes over to the table and extends her hand to* HEDDA. LØVBORG *has gotten up. He and* MRS. ELVSTED *greet each other with a silent nod.)*

MRS. ELVSTED.   Perhaps I ought to go in and talk a bit with your husband?

HEDDA.   Oh, nonsense. Let them be. They're leaving soon.

MRS. ELVSTED.   They're leaving?

HEDDA.   Yes, for a drinking party.

MRS. ELVSTED *(quickly, to* LØVBORG*)*.   But you're not?

LØVBORG.   No.

HEDDA.   Mr. Løvborg—is staying with us.

MRS. ELVSTED *(taking a chair, about to sit down beside him)*.   Oh, it's so good to be here!

HEDDA.   No, no, Thea dear! Not there! You have to come over here by me. I want to be in the middle.

MRS. ELVSTED.   Any way you please.

(She goes around the table and sits on the sofa to HEDDA's *right.* LØVBORG *resumes his seat.)*

LØVBORG *(after a brief pause, to* HEDDA*)*.   Isn't she lovely to look at?

HEDDA *(lightly stroking her hair)*.   Only to look at?

LØVBORG.   Yes. Because we two—she and I—we really *are* true companions. We trust each other completely. We can talk things out together without any reservations—

HEDDA. Never anything devious, Mr. Løvborg?

LØVBORG. Well—

MRS. ELVSTED *(quietly, leaning close to* HEDDA*)*. Oh, Hedda, you don't know how happy I am! Just think—he says that I've inspired him.

HEDDA *(regarding her with a smile)*. Really, dear; did he say that?

LØVBORG. And then the courage she has, Mrs. Tesman, when it's put to the test.

MRS. ELVSTED. Good heavens, me! Courage!

LØVBORG. Enormous courage—where I'm concerned.

HEDDA. Yes, courage—yes! If one only had that.

LØVBORG. Then what?

HEDDA. Then life might still be bearable. *(Suddenly changing her tone.)* But now, Thea dearest—you really must have a nice cold glass of punch.

MRS. ELVSTED. No, thank you. I never drink that sort of thing.

HEDDA. Well, then you, Mr. Løvborg.

LØVBORG. Thanks, not for me either.

MRS. ELVSTED. No, not for him either!

HEDDA *(looking intently at him)*. But if I insist?

LØVBORG. Makes no difference.

HEDDA *(with a laugh)*. Poor me, than I have no power over you at all?

LØVBORG. Not in that area.

HEDDA. But seriously, I think you ought to, all the same. For your own sake.

MRS. ELVSTED. But Hedda—!

LØVBORG. Why do you think so?

HEDDA. Or, to be more exact, for others' sakes.

LØVBORG. Oh?

HEDDA. Otherwise, people might get the idea that you're not very bold at heart. That you're not really sure of yourself at all.

MRS. ELVSTED *(softly)*. Oh, Hedda, don't—!

LØVBORG. People can think whatever they like, for all I care.

MRS. ELVSTED *(happily)*. Yes, that's right!

HEDDA. I saw it so clearly in Judge Brack a moment ago.

LØVBORG. What did you see?

HEDDA. The contempt in his smile when you didn't dare join them for a drink.

LØVBORG. Didn't dare! Obviously I'd rather stay here and talk with you.

MRS. ELVSTED. That's only reasonable, Hedda.

HEDDA. But how could the judge know that? And besides, I noticed him smile and glance at Tesman when you couldn't bring yourself to go to their wretched little party.

LØVBORG. Couldn't! Are you saying I couldn't?

HEDDA. *I'm* not. But that's the way Judge Brack sees it.

LØVBORG. All right, let him.

HEDDA. Then you won't go along?

LØVBORG. I'm staying here with you and Thea.

MRS. ELVSTED. Yes, Hedda—you can be sure he is!

HEDDA *(smiles and nods approvingly at* LØVBORG). I see. Firm as a rock. True to principle, to the end of time. There, that's what a man ought to be! *(Turning to* MRS. ELVSTED *and patting her.)* Well, now, didn't I tell you that, when you came here so distraught this morning—

LØVBORG *(surprised).* Distraught?

MRS. ELVSTED *(terrified).* Hedda—! But Hedda—!

HEDDA. Can't you see for yourself? There's no need at all for your going around so deathly afraid that— *(Changing her tone.)* There! Now we can all enjoy ourselves!

LØVBORG *(shaken).* What is all this, Mrs. Tesman?

MRS. ELVSTED. Oh, God, oh, God, Hedda! What are you saying! What are you doing!

HEDDA. Not so loud. That digusting judge is watching you.

LØVBORG. So deathly afraid? For my sake?

MRS. ELVSTED *(in a low moan).* Oh, Hedda, you've made me so miserable!

LØVBORG *(looks intently at her a moment, his face drawn).* So that's how completely you trusted me.

MRS. ELVSTED *(imploringly).* Oh, my dearest—if you'll only listen—!

LØVBORG *(takes one of the glasses of punch, raises it, and says in a low, hoarse voice).* Your health, Thea! *(He empties the glass, puts it down, and takes the other.)*

MRS. ELVSTED *(softly).* Oh, Hedda, Hedda—how could you want such a thing!

HEDDA. Want it? I? Are you crazy?

LØVBORG. And your health too, Mrs. Tesman. Thanks for the truth. Long live truth! *(Drains the glass and starts to refill it.)*

HEDDA *(laying her hand on his arm).* All right—no more for now. Remember, you're going to a party.

MRS. ELVSTED. No, no, no!

HEDDA. Shh! They're watching you.

LØVBORG *(putting down his glass).* Now, Thea—tell me honestly—

MRS. ELVSTED. Yes!

LØVBORG. Did your husband know that you followed me?

MRS. ELVSTED *(wringing her hands).* Oh, Hedda—listen to him!

LØVBORG. Did you have it arranged, you and he, that you should come down into town and spy on me? Or maybe he got you to do it himself? Ah, yes—I'm sure he needed me back in the office! Or maybe he missed my hand at cards?

MRS. ELVSTED *(softly, in anguish).* Oh, Eilert, Eilert—!

LØVBORG *(seizing his glass to fill it).* Skoal to the old sheriff, too!

HEDDA *(stopping him).* That's enough. Don't forget, you're giving a reading for Tesman.

LØVBORG *(calmly, setting down his glass).* That was stupid of me, Thea. I mean, taking it like this. Don't be angry at me, my dearest. You'll see—you and all the others—that if I stumbled and fell—I'm back on my feet again now! With your help, Thea.

MRS. ELVSTED *(radiant with joy).* Oh, thank God—!

*(*BRACK, *in the meantime, has looked at his watch. He and* TESMAN *stand up and enter the drawing room.)*

BRACK *(takes his hat and overcoat).* Well, Mrs. Tesman, our time is up.

HEDDA. I suppose it is.

LØVBORG *(rising).* Mine too, Judge.

MRS. ELVSTED *(softly pleading).* Oh, Eilert—don't!

HEDDA *(pinching her arm).* They can hear you!

MRS. ELVSTED *(with a small cry).* Ow!

LØVBORG *(to* BRACK). You were kind enough to ask me along.

BRACK. Oh, then you *are* coming, after all?

LØVBORG. Yes, thank you.

BRACK. I'm delighted—

LØVBORG *(putting the manila envelope in his pocket, to* TESMAN). I'd like to show you one or two things before I turn this in.

TESMAN. Just think—how exciting! But Hedda dear, how will Mrs. Elvsted get home? Uh?

HEDDA. Oh, we'll hit on something.

LØVBORG *(glancing toward the ladies).* Mrs. Elvsted? Don't worry, I'll stop back and fetch her. *(Coming nearer.)* Say about ten o'clock, Mrs. Tesman? Will that do?

HEDDA. Yes. That will do very nicely.

TESMAN. Well, then everything's all set. But you mustn't expect *me* that early, Hedda.

HEDDA. Dear, you stay as long—just as long as you like.

MRS. ELVSTED *(with suppressed anxiety).* Mr. Løvborg—I'll be waiting here till you come.

LØVBORG *(his hat in his hand).* Yes, I understand.

BRACK. So, gentlemen—the excursion train is leaving! I hope it's going to be lively, as a certain fair lady puts it.

HEDDA. Ah, if only that fair lady could be there, invisible—!

BRACK. Why invisible?

HEDDA. To hear a little of your unadulterated liveliness, Judge.

BRACK *(laughs).* I wouldn't advise the fair lady to try.

TESMAN *(also laughing).* Hedda, you are the limit! What an idea!

BRACK. Well, good night. Good night, ladies.

LØVBORG *(bowing).* About ten o'clock then.

*(*BRACK, LØVBORG, *and* TESMAN *go out the hall door. At the same time,* BERTA *enters from the inner room with a lighted lamp, which she sets on the drawing room table, then goes out the same way.)*

MRS. ELVSTED *(having risen, moving restlessly about the room).* Hedda—Hedda—what's going to come of all this?

HEDDA. At ten o'clock—he'll be here. I can see him now—with vine leaves in his hair—fiery and bold—

MRS. ELVSTED.   Oh, how good that would be!

HEDDA.   And then, you'll see—he'll be back in control of himself. He'll be a free man, then, for the rest of his days.

MRS. ELVSTED.   Oh, God—if only he comes as you see him now!

HEDDA.   He'll come back like that, and no other way! *(Gets up and goes closer.)* Go on and doubt him as much as you like. *I* believe in him. And now we'll find out—

MRS. ELVSTED.   There's something behind what you're doing, Hedda.

HEDDA.   Yes, there is. For once in my life, I want to have power over a human being.

MRS. ELVSTED.   But don't you have that?

HEDDA.   I don't have it. I've never had it.

MRS. ELVSTED.   Not with your husband?

HEDDA.   Yes, what a bargain *that* was! Oh, if you only could understand how poor I am. And you're allowed to be so rich! *(Passionately throws her arms about her.)* I think I'll burn your hair off, after all!

MRS. ELVSTED.   Let go! Let me go! I'm afraid of you, Hedda!

BERTA *(in the doorway to the inner room).*   Supper's waiting in the dining room, ma'am.

HEDDA.   All right, we're coming.

MRS. ELVSTED.   No, no, no! I'd rather go home alone! Right away—now!

HEDDA.   Nonsense! First you're going to have tea, you little fool. And then—ten o'clock—Eilert Løvborg comes—with vine leaves in his hair.

(She drags MRS. ELVSTED, *almost by force, toward the doorway.)*

ACT III

The same rooms at the TESMANS'. *The curtains are down across the doorway to the inner room, and also across the glass door. The lamp, shaded and turned down low, is burning on the table. The door to the stove stands open; the fire has nearly gone out.*

MRS. ELVSTED, *wrapped in a large shawl, with her feet up on a footstool, lies back in the armchair close by the stove.* HEDDA, *fully dressed, is asleep on the sofa, with a blanket over her. After a pause,* MRS. ELVSTED *suddenly sits straight up in the chair, listening tensely. Then she sinks wearily back again.*

MRS. ELVSTED *(in a low moan).*   Not yet—oh, God—oh, God—not yet!

*(*BERTA *slips in cautiously by the hall door. She holds a letter in her hand.)*

MRS. ELVSTED *(turns and whispers anxiously).*   Yes? Has anyone come?

BERTA *(softly).*   Yes, a girl just now stopped by with this letter.

MRS. ELVSTED *(quickly, reaching out her hand).*   A letter! Give it to me!

BERTA.   No, it's for the Doctor, ma'am.

MRS. ELVSTED.   Oh.

BERTA.   It was Miss Tesman's maid that brought it. I'll leave it here on the table.

MRS. ELVSTED.   Yes, do.

BERTA *(putting the letter down).*   I think I'd best put out the lamp. It's smoking.

MRS. ELVSTED.   Yes, put it out. It'll be daylight soon.

BERTA *(does so).*   It's broad daylight already, ma'am.

MRS. ELVSTED.   It's daylight! And still no one's come—!

BERTA.   Oh, mercy—I knew it would go like this.

MRS. ELVSTED.   You knew?

BERTA.   Yes, when I saw that a certain gentleman was back here in town—and that he went off with them. We've heard plenty about that gentleman over the years.

MRS. ELVSTED.   Don't talk so loud. You'll wake Mrs. Tesman.

BERTA *(looks toward the sofa and sighs).*   Goodness me—yes, let her sleep, poor thing. Should I put a bit more on the fire?

MRS. ELVSTED.   Thanks, not for me.

BERTA.   All right. *(She goes quietly out the hall door.)*

HEDDA *(wakes as the door shuts and looks up).*   What's that?

MRS. ELVSTED.   It was just the maid—

HEDDA *(glancing about).*   In here—? Oh yes, I remember now. *(Sits up on the sofa, stretches, and rubs her eyes.)* What time is it, Thea?

MRS. ELVSTED *(looking at her watch).*   It's after seven.

HEDDA.   When did Tesman get in?

MRS. ELVSTED.   He isn't back.

HEDDA.   Not back yet?

MRS. ELVSTED *(getting up).*   No one's come in.

HEDDA.   And we sat here and waited up for them till four o'clock—

MRS. ELVSTED *(wringing her hands).*   And *how* I've waited for him!

HEDDA *(yawns, and speaks with her hand in front of her mouth).*   Oh, dear—we could have saved ourselves the trouble.

MRS. ELVSTED.   Did you get any sleep?

HEDDA.   Oh yes. I slept quite well, I think. Didn't you?

MRS. ELVSTED.   No, not at all. I couldn't, Hedda! It was just impossible.

HEDDA *(rising and going toward her).*   There, there, now! There's nothing to worry about. It's not hard to guess what happened.

MRS. ELVSTED.   Oh, what? Tell me!

HEDDA.   Well, it's clear that the party must have gone on till all hours—

MRS. ELVSTED.   Oh, Lord, yes—it must have. But even so—

HEDDA.   And then, of course, Tesman didn't want to come home and make a commotion in the middle of the night. *(Laughs.)* Probably didn't care to show himself, either—so full of his party spirits.

MRS. ELVSTED.   But where else could he have gone?

HEDDA.   He must have gone up to his aunts' to sleep. They keep his old room ready.

MRS. ELVSTED.   No, he can't be with them. Because he just now got a letter from Miss Tesman. It's over there.

HEDDA.   Oh? *(Looking at the address.)* Yes, that's Aunt Julie's handwriting, all right. Well, then he must have stayed over at Judge Brack's. And Eilert Løvborg—he's sitting with vine leaves in his hair, reading away.

MRS. ELVSTED.   Oh, Hedda, you say these things, and you really don't believe them at all.

HEDDA.   You're such a little fool, Thea.

MRS. ELVSTED.   That's true; I guess I am.

HEDDA.   And you really look dead tired.

MRS. ELVSTED.   Yes, I feel dead tired.

HEDDA.   Well, you just do as I say, then. Go in my room and stretch out on the bed for a while.

MRS. ELVSTED.   No, no—I still wouldn't get any sleep.

HEDDA.   Why, of course you would.

MRS. ELVSTED.   Well, but your husband's sure to be home now soon. And I've got to know right away—

HEDDA.   I'll call you the moment he comes.

MRS. ELVSTED.   Yes? Promise me, Hedda?

HEDDA.   You can count on it. Just go and get some sleep.

MRS. ELVSTED.   Thanks, I'll try. *(She goes out through the inner room.)*

(HEDDA goes over to the glass door and draws the curtains back. Bright daylight streams into the room. She goes over to the writing table, takes out a small hand mirror, regards herself and arranges her hair. She then goes to the hall door and presses the bell. After a moment, BERTA enters.)

BERTA.   Did you want something, ma'am?

HEDDA.   Yes, you can build up the fire. I'm freezing in here.

BERTA.   Why, my goodness—we'll have it warm in no time. *(She rakes the embers together and puts some wood on, then stops and listens.)* There's the front doorbell, ma'am.

HEDDA.   Go see who it is. I'll take care of the stove.

BERTA.   It'll be burning soon. *(She goes out the hall door.)*

(HEDDA kneels on the footstool and lays more wood on the fire. After a moment GEORGE TESMAN comes in from the hall. He looks tired and rather serious. He tiptoes toward the doorway to the inner room and is about to slip through the curtains.)

HEDDA *(at the stove, without looking up).*   Good morning.

TESMAN *(turns).*   Hedda! *(Approaching her.)* But what on earth—! You're up so early? Uh?

HEDDA.   Yes, I'm up quite early today.

TESMAN.   And I was so sure you were still in bed sleeping. Isn't that something, Hedda!

HEDDA.   Not so loud. Mrs. Elvsted's resting in my room.

TESMAN.   Was Mrs. Elvsted here all night?

HEDDA.   Well, no one returned to take her home.

TESMAN.   No, I guess that's right.

HEDDA *(shuts the door to the stove and gets up).*   So—did you enjoy your party?

TESMAN.   Were you worried about me? Hm?

HEDDA.   No, that never occurred to me. I just asked if you'd had a good time.

TESMAN.   Oh yes, I really did, for once. But more at the beginning, I'd say—when Eilert read to me out of his book. We got there more than an hour too soon—imagine! And Brack had so much to get ready. But then Eilert read to me.

HEDDA *(sitting at the right-hand side of the table).*   Well? Tell me about it—

TESMAN *(sitting on a footstool by the stove).*   Really, Hedda—you can't imagine what a book that's going to be! I do believe it's one of the most remarkable things ever written. Just think!

HEDDA.   Yes, I don't mean the book—

TESMAN.   But I have to make a confession, Hedda. When he'd finished reading—I had such a nasty feeling—

HEDDA.   Nasty?

TESMAN.   I found myself envying Eilert, that he was able to write such a book. Can you imagine, Hedda!

HEDDA.   Oh yes, I can imagine!

TESMAN.   And then how sad to see—that with all his gifts—he's still quite irreclaimable.

HEDDA.   Don't you mean that he has more courage to live than the others?

TESMAN.   Good Lord, no—I mean, he simply can't take his pleasures in moderation.

HEDDA.   Well, what happened then—at the end?

TESMAN.   I suppose I'd have to say it turned into an orgy, Hedda.

HEDDA.   Were there vine leaves in his hair?

TESMAN.   Vine leaves? Not that I noticed. But he gave a long, muddled speech in honor of the woman who'd inspired his work. Yes, that was his phrase for it.

HEDDA.   Did he give her name?

TESMAN.   No, he didn't. But it seems to me it has to be Mrs. Elvsted. Wait and see!

HEDDA.   Oh? Where did you leave him?

TESMAN.   On the way here. We broke up—the last of us—all together. And Brack came along with us too, to get a little fresh air. And then we did want to make sure that Eilert got home safe. Because he really had a load on, you know.

HEDDA.   He must have.

TESMAN.   But here's the curious part of it, Hedda. Or perhaps I should say, the distressing part. Oh, I'm almost ashamed to speak of it—for Eilert's sake—

HEDDA.   Yes, go on—

TESMAN.   Well, as we were walking toward town, you see, I happened to drop back a little behind the others. Only for a minute or two—you follow me?

HEDDA.   Yes, yes, so—?

TESMAN.   And then when I was catching up with the rest of them, what do you think I found on the sidewalk? Uh?

HEDDA.   Oh, how should I know!

TESMAN.   You mustn't breathe a word to anyone, Hedda—you hear me? Promise me that, for Eilert's sake. *(Takes a manila envelope out of his coat pocket.)* Just think—I found this.

HEDDA.   Isn't that what he had with him yesterday?

TESMAN.   That's right. It's the whole of his precious, irreplaceable manuscript. And he went and lost it—without even noticing. Can you imagine, Hedda! How distressing—

HEDDA.   But why didn't you give it right back to him?

TESMAN.   No, I didn't dare do that—in the state he was in—

HEDDA.   And you didn't tell any of the others you'd found it?

TESMAN.   Of course not. I'd never do that, you know—for Eilert's sake.

HEDDA.   Then there's no one who knows you have Eilert Løvborg's manuscript?

TESMAN.   No. And no one must ever know, either.

HEDDA.   What did you say to him afterwards?

TESMAN.   I had no chance at all to speak with him. As soon as we reached the edge of town, he and a couple of others got away from us and disappeared. Imagine!

HEDDA.   Oh? I expect they saw him home.

TESMAN.   Yes, they probably did, I suppose. And also Brack went home.

HEDDA.   And where've you been carrying on since then?

TESMAN.   Well, I and some of the others—we were invited up by one of the fellows and had morning coffee at his place. Or a post-midnight snack, maybe—uh? But as soon as I've had a little rest—and given poor Eilert time to sleep it off, then I've got to take this back to him.

HEDDA *(reaching out for the envelope)*.   No—don't give it back! Not yet, I mean. Let me read it first.

TESMAN.   Hedda dearest, no. My Lord, I can't do that.

HEDDA.   You can't?

TESMAN.   No. Why, you can just imagine the anguish he'll feel when he wakes up and misses the manuscript. He hasn't any copy of it, you know. He told me that himself.

HEDDA *(looks searchingly at him)*.   Can't such a work be rewritten? I mean, over again?

TESMAN.   Oh, I don't see how it could. Because the inspiration, you know—

HEDDA.   Yes, yes—that's the thing, I suppose. *(Casually.)* Oh, by the way—there's a letter for you.

TESMAN.   No, really—?

HEDDA *(handing it to him)*.   It came early this morning.

TESMAN.   Dear, from Aunt Julie! What could that be? *(Sets the envelope on the other taboret, opens the letter, skims through it, and springs to his feet.)* Oh, Hedda—she says poor Auntie Rina's dying!

HEDDA.   It's no more than we've been expecting.

TESMAN.   And if I want to see her one last time, I've got to hurry. I'll have to hop right over.

HEDDA *(suppressing a smile)*.   Hop?

TESMAN.   Oh, Hedda dearest, if you could only bring yourself to come with me! Think of it!

HEDDA *(rises and dismisses the thought wearily).*   No, no, don't ask me to do such things. I don't want to look on sickness and death. I want to be free of everything ugly.

TESMAN.   Yes, all right, then—*(Dashing about.)* My hat—? My overcoat—? Oh, in the hall— I do hope I'm not there too late, Hedda! Hm?

HEDDA.   Oh, if you hurry—

(BERTA appears at the hall door.)

BERTA.   Judge Brack's outside, asking if he might stop in.

TESMAN.   At a time like this! No, I can't possibly see him now.

HEDDA.   But I can. *(To BERTA.)* Ask the judge to come in.

(BERTA goes out.)

HEDDA *(quickly, in a whisper).*   Tesman, the manuscript! *(She snatches it from the taboret.)*

TESMAN.   Yes, give it here!

HEDDA.   No, no, I'll keep it till you're back.

(She moves over to the writing table and slips it in the bookcase. TESMAN stands flustered, unable to get his gloves on. BRACK enters from the hall.)

HEDDA.   Well, aren't you the early bird.

BRACK.   Yes, wouldn't you say so? *(To TESMAN.)* Are you off and away too?

TESMAN.   Yes, I absolutely have to get over to my aunts'. Just think—the invalid one, she's dying.

BRACK.   Good Lord, she is? But then you mustn't let me detain you. Not at a moment like this—

TESMAN.   Yes, I really must run— Good-bye! Good-bye! *(He goes hurriedly out the hall door.)*

HEDDA.   It would seem you had quite a time of it last night, Judge.

BRACK.   I've not been out of my clothes yet, Mrs. Hedda.

HEDDA.   Not you, either?

BRACK.   No, as you can see. But what's Tesman been telling you about our night's adventures?

HEDDA.   Oh, some tedious tale. Something about stopping up somewhere for coffee.

BRACK.   Yes, I know all about the coffee party. Eilert Løvborg wasn't with them, I expect?

HEDDA.   No, they'd already taken him home.

BRACK.   Tesman, as well.

HEDDA.   No, but he said some others had.

BRACK *(smiles).*   George Tesman is really a simple soul, Mrs. Hedda.

HEDDA.   God knows he's that. But was there something else that went on?

BRACK.   Oh, you might say so.

HEDDA.   Well, now! Let's sit down, Judge; you'll talk more easily then.

(*She sits at the left-hand side of the table, with* BRACK *at the long side, near her.*)

HEDDA.   So?

BRACK.   I had particular reasons for keeping track of my guests—or, I should say, certain of my guests, last night.

HEDDA.   And among them Eilert Løvborg, perhaps?

BRACK.   To be frank—yes.

HEDDA.   Now you really have me curious—

BRACK.   You know where he and a couple of the others spent the rest of the night, Mrs. Hedda?

HEDDA.   Tell me—if it's fit to be told.

BRACK.   Oh, it's very much fit to be told. Well, it seems they showed up at a quite animated soiree.

HEDDA.   Of the lively sort.

BRACK.   Of the liveliest.

HEDDA.   Do go on, Judge—

BRACK.   Løvborg, and the others also, had advance invitations. I knew all about it. But Løvborg had begged off, because now, of course, he was supposed to have become a new man, as you know.

HEDDA.   Up at the Elvsteds', yes. But he went anyway?

BRACK.   Well, you see, Mrs. Hedda—unfortunately the spirit moved him up at my place last evening—

HEDDA.   Yes, I hear that he *was* inspired there.

BRACK.   To a very powerful degree, I'd say. Well, so his mind turned to other things, that's clear. We males, sad to say—we're not always so true to principle as we ought to be.

HEDDA.   Oh, I'm sure you're an exception, Judge. But what about Løvborg—?

BRACK.   Well, to cut it short—the result was that he wound up in Mademoiselle Diana's parlors.

HEDDA.   Mademoiselle Diana's?

BRACK.   It was Mademoiselle Diana who was holding the soiree. For a select circle of lady friends and admirers.

HEDDA.   Is she a redhaired woman?

BRACK.   Precisely.

HEDDA.   Sort of a—singer?

BRACK.   Oh yes—she's that too. And also a mighty huntress—of men, Mrs. Hedda. You've undoubtedly heard about her. Løvborg was one of her ruling favorites—back there in his palmy days.

HEDDA.   And how did all this end?

BRACK.   Less amicably, it seems. She gave him a most tender welcoming, with open arms, but before long she'd taken to fists.

HEDDA.   Against Løvborg?

BRACK.   That's right. He accused her or her friends of having robbed him. He claimed that his wallet was missing—along with some other things. In short, he must have made a frightful scene.

HEDDA. And what did it come to?

BRACK. It came to a regular free-for-all, the men and the women both. Luckily the police finally got there.

HEDDA. The police too?

BRACK. Yes. But it's likely to prove an expensive little romp for Eilert Løvborg. That crazy fool.

HEDDA. So?

BRACK. He apparently made violent resistance. Struck one of the officers on the side of the head and ripped his coat. So they took him along to the station house.

HEDDA. Where did you hear all this?

BRACK. From the police themselves.

HEDDA (*gazing straight ahead*). So that's how it went. Then he had no vine leaves in his hair.

BRACK. Vine leaves, Mrs. Hedda?

HEDDA (*changing her tone*). But tell me, Judge—just why do you go around like this, spying on Eilert Løvborg?

BRACK. In the first place, it's hardly a matter of no concern to me, if it's brought out during the investigation that he'd come direct from my house.

HEDDA. There'll be an investigation—?

BRACK. Naturally. Anyway, that takes care of itself. But I felt that as a friend of the family I owed you and Tesman a full account of his nocturnal exploits.

HEDDA. Why, exactly?

BRACK. Well, because I have a strong suspicion that he'll try to use you as a kind of screen.

HEDDA. Oh, how could you ever think such a thing!

BRACK. Good Lord—we're really not blind, Mrs. Hedda. You'll see! This Mrs. Elvsted, she won't be going home now so quickly.

HEDDA. Well, even supposing there were something between them, there are plenty of other places where they could meet.

BRACK. Not one single home. From now on, every decent house will be closed to Eilert Løvborg.

HEDDA. So mine ought to be too, is that what you mean?

BRACK. Yes, I'll admit I'd find it more than annoying if that gentleman were to have free access here. If he came like an intruder, an irrelevancy, forcing his way into—

HEDDA. Into the triangle?

BRACK. Precisely. It would almost be like turning me out of my home.

HEDDA (*looks at him with a smile*). I see. The one cock of the walk— that's what you want to be.

BRACK (*nodding slowly and lowering his voice*). Yes, that's what I want to be. And that's what I'll fight for—with every means at my disposal.

HEDDA (*her smile vanishing*). You can be a dangerous person, can't you—in a tight corner.

BRACK. Do you think so?

HEDDA. Yes, now I'm beginning to think so. And I'm thoroughly grateful—that you have no kind of hold over me.

BRACK (*with an ambiguous laugh*).   Ah, yes, Mrs. Hedda—perhaps you're right about that. If I had, then who knows just what I might do?

HEDDA.   Now you listen here, Judge! That sounds too much like a threat.

BRACK (*rising*).   Oh, nothing of the kind! A triangle, after all—is best fortified and defended by volunteers.

HEDDA.   There we're agreed.

BRACK.   Well, now that I've said all I have to say, I'd better get back to town. Good-bye, Mrs. Hedda. (*He goes toward the glass door.*)

HEDDA (*rising*).   Are you going through the garden?

BRACK.   Yes, I find it's shorter.

HEDDA.   Yes, and then it's the back way, too.

BRACK.   How true. I have nothing against back ways. At certain times they can be rather piquant.

HEDDA.   You mean, when somebody's sharpshooting?

BRACK (*in the doorway, laughing*).   Oh, people don't shoot their tame roosters!

HEDDA (*also laughing*).   I guess not. Not when there's only one—

(*Still laughing, they nod good-bye to each other. He goes. She shuts the door after him, then stands for a moment, quite serious, looking out. She then goes over and glances through the curtains to the inner room. Moves to the writing table, takes* LØVBORG'S *envelope from the bookcase, and is about to page through it, when* BERTA'S *voice is heard loudly in the hall.* HEDDA *turns and listens. She hurriedly locks the envelope in the drawer and lays the key on the inkstand.* EILERT LØVBORG, *with his overcoat on and his hat in his hand, throws open the hall door. He looks confused and excited.*)

LØVBORG (*turned toward the hall*).   And I'm telling you, I have to go in! I will, you hear me! (*He shuts the door, turns, sees* HEDDA, *immediately gains control of himself and bows.*)

HEDDA (*at the writing table*).   Well, Mr. Løvborg, it's late to call for Thea.

LØVBORG.   Or rather early to call on you. You must forgive me.

HEDDA.   How did you know she was still with me?

LØVBORG.   They said at her lodgings that she'd been out all night.

HEDDA (*goes to the center table*).   Did you notice anything in their faces when they said that?

LØVBORG (*looking at her inquiringly*).   Notice anything?

HEDDA.   I mean, did it look like they had their own thoughts on the matter?

LØVBORG (*suddenly understanding*).   Oh yes, that's true! I'm dragging her down with me! Actually, I didn't notice anything. Tesman—I don't suppose he's up yet?

HEDDA.   No, I don't think so.

LØVBORG.   When did he get in?

HEDDA.   Very late.

LØVBORG.   Did he tell you anything?

HEDDA.   Well, I heard you'd had a high time of it out at Judge Brack's.
LØVBORG.   Anything else?
HEDDA.   No, I don't think so. As a matter of fact, I was terribly sleepy—

(MRS. ELVSTED *comes in through the curtains to the inner room.*)

MRS. ELVSTED *(running toward him).*   Oh, Eilert! At last—!
LØVBORG.   Yes, at last. And too late.
MRS. ELVSTED *(looking anxiously at him).*   What's too late?
LØVBORG.   Everything's too late now. It's over with me.
MRS. ELVSTED.   Oh no, no—don't say that!
LØVBORG.   You'll say the same thing when you've heard—
MRS. ELVSTED.   I won't hear anything!
HEDDA.   Maybe you'd prefer to talk with her alone. I can leave.
LØVBORG.   No, stay—you too. Please.
MRS. ELVSTED.   But I tell you, I don't want to hear anything!
LØVBORG.   It's nothing about last night.
MRS. ELVSTED.   What is it, then—?
LØVBORG.   It's simply this, that from now on, we separate.
MRS. ELVSTED.   Separate!
HEDDA *(involuntarily).*   I knew it!
LØVBORG.   Because I have no more use for you, Thea.
MRS. ELVSTED.   And you can stand there and say that! No more use for me! Then I'm not going to help you now, as I have? We're not going to go on working together?
LØVBORG.   I have no plans for any more work.
MRS. ELVSTED *(in desperation).*   Then what will I do with my life?
LØVBORG.   You must try to go on living as if you'd never known me.
MRS. ELVSTED.   But I can't do that!
LØVBORG.   You must try to, Thea. You'll have to go home again—
MRS. ELVSTED *(in a fury of protest).*   Never! No! Where you are, that's where I want to be! I won't be driven away like this! I'm going to stay right here—and be together with you when the book comes out.
HEDDA *(in a tense whisper).*   Ah, yes—the book!
LØVBORG *(looks at her).*   My book and Thea's—for that's what it is.
MRS. ELVSTED.   Yes, that's what I feel it is. And that's why I have the right, as well, to be with you when it comes out. I want to see you covered with honor and respect again. And the joy—I want to share the joy of it with you too.
LØVBORG.   Thea—our book's never coming out.
MRS. ELVSTED.   Never coming out!
LØVBORG.   *Can* never come out.
MRS. ELVSTED *(with anguished foreboding).*   Eilert—what have you done with the manuscript?
HEDDA *(watching him intently).*   Yes, the manuscript—?
MRS. ELVSTED.   Where is it!
LØVBORG.   Oh, Thea—don't ask me that.
MRS. ELVSTED.   Yes, yes, I have to know. I've got a right to know, this minute!

LØVBORG.   The manuscript—well, you see—I tore the manuscript into a thousand pieces.

MRS. ELVSTED *(screams)*.   Oh no, no—!

HEDDA *(involuntarily)*.   But that just isn't—!

LØVBORG *(looks at her)*.   Isn't so, you think?

HEDDA *(composing herself)*.   All right. Of course; if you say it yourself. But it sounds so incredible—

LØVBORG.   It's true, all the same.

MRS. ELVSTED *(wringing her hands)*.   Oh, God—oh, God, Hedda—to tear his own work to bits!

LØVBORG.   I've torn my own life to bits. So why not tear up my life's work as well—

MRS. ELVSTED.   And you did this thing last night!

LØVBORG.   Yes, you heard me. In a thousand pieces. And scattered them into the fjord. Far out. At least there, there's clean salt water. Let them drift out to sea—drift with the tide and the wind. And after a while, they'll sink. Deeper and deeper. As I will, Thea.

MRS. ELVSTED.   Do you know, Eilert, this thing you've done with the book—for the rest of my life it will seem to me as if you'd killed a little child.

LØVBORG.   You're right. It was like murdering a child.

MRS. ELVSTED.   But how could you do it—! It was my child too.

HEDDA *(almost inaudible)*.   Ah, the child—

MRS. ELVSTED *(breathes heavily)*.   Then it *is* all over. Yes, yes, I'm going now, Hedda.

HEDDA.   But you're not leaving town, are you?

MRS. ELVSTED.   Oh, I don't know myself what I'll do. Everything's dark for me now. *(She goes out the hall door.)*

HEDDA *(stands waiting a moment)*.   You're not going to take her home, then, Mr. Løvborg?

LØVBORG.   I? Through the streets? So people could see that she'd been with me?

HEDDA.   I don't know what else may have happened last night. But is it so completely irredeemable?

LØVBORG.   It won't just end with last night—I know that well enough. But the thing is, I've lost all desire for that kind of life. I don't want to start it again, not now. It's the courage and daring for life—that's what she's broken in me.

HEDDA *(staring straight ahead)*.   To think that pretty little fool could have a man's fate in her hands. *(Looks at him.)* But still, how could you treat her so heartlessly?

LØVBORG.   Oh, don't say it was heartless!

HEDDA.   To go ahead and destroy what's filled her whole being for months and years! That's not heartless?

LØVBORG.   To you, Hedda—I can tell the truth.

HEDDA.   The truth?

LØVBORG.   Promise me first—give me your word that what I tell you now, you'll never let Thea know.

HEDDA. You have my word.

LØVBORG. Good. I can tell you, then, that what I said here just now isn't true.

HEDDA. About the manuscript?

LØVBORG. Yes. I didn't tear it up—or throw it in the fjord.

HEDDA. No, but—where is it, then?

LØVBORG. I've destroyed it all the same, Hedda. Utterly destroyed it.

HEDDA. I don't understand.

LØVBORG. Thea said that what I've done, for her was like killing a child.

HEDDA. Yes—that's what she said.

LØVBORG. But killing his child—that's not the worst thing a father can do.

HEDDA. *That's* not the worst?

LØVBORG. No. I wanted to spare Thea the worst.

HEDDA. And what's that—the worst?

LØVBORG. Suppose now, Hedda, that a man—in the early morning hours, say—after a wild, drunken night, comes home to his child's mother and says: "Listen—I've been out to this place and that—here and there. And I had our child with me. In this place and that. And I lost the child. Just lost it. God only knows what hands it's come into. Or who's got hold of it."

HEDDA. Well—but when all's said and done—it was only a book—

LØVBORG. Thea's pure soul was in that book.

HEDDA. Yes, I understand.

LØVBORG. Well, then you can understand that for her and me there's no future possible any more.

HEDDA. What do you intend to do?

LØVBORG. Nothing. Just put an end to it all. The sooner the better.

HEDDA *(coming a step closer)*. Eilert Løvborg—listen to me. Couldn't you arrange that—that it's done beautifully?

LØVBORG. Beautifully? *(Smiles.)* With vine leaves in my hair, as you used to dream in the old days—

HEDDA. No. I don't believe in vine leaves any more. But beautifully, all the same. For this once—! Good-bye! You must go now—and never come here again.

LØVBORG. Good-bye, then. And give my best to George Tesman. *(He turns to leave.)*

HEDDA. No, wait. I want you to have a souvenir from me.

(She goes to the writing desk and opens the drawer and the pistol case, then comes back to LØVBORG with one of the pistols.)

LØVBORG *(looks at her)*. That? Is that the souvenir?

HEDDA *(nods slowly)*. Do you recognize it? It was aimed at you once.

LØVBORG. You should have used it then.

HEDDA. Here! Use it now.

LØVBORG *(puts the pistol in his breast pocket)*. Thanks.

HEDDA. And beautifully, Eilert Løvborg. Promise me that!

LØVBORG. Good-bye, Hedda Gabler.

(He goes out the hall door. HEDDA *listens a moment at the door. Then she goes over to the writing table, takes out the envelope with the manuscript, glances inside, pulls some of the sheets half out and looks at them. She then goes over to the armchair by the stove and sits, with the envelope in her lap. After a moment, she opens the stove door, then brings out the manuscript.)*

HEDDA *(throwing some of the sheets into the fire and whispering to herself).*   Now I'm burning your child, Thea! You, with your curly hair! *(Throwing another sheaf in the stove.)* Your child and Eilert Løvborg's. *(Throwing in the rest.)* Now I'm burning—I'm burning the child.

ACT IV

The same rooms at the TESMANS'. *It is evening. The drawing room is in darkness. The inner room is lit by the hanging lamp over the table. The curtains are drawn across the glass door.* HEDDA, *dressed in black, is pacing back and forth in the dark room. She then enters the inner room, moving out of sight toward the left. Several chords are heard on the piano. She comes in view again, returning into the drawing room.* BERTA *enters from the right through the inner room with a lighted lamp, which she puts on the table in front of the settee in the drawing room. Her eyes are red from crying, and she has black ribbons on her cap. She goes quietly and discreetly out to the right.* HEDDA *moves to the glass door, lifts the curtains aside slightly, and gazes out into the darkness.*
Shortly after, MISS TESMAN, *in mourning, with a hat and veil, comes in from the hall.* HEDDA *goes toward her, extending her hand.*

MISS TESMAN.   Well, Hedda, here I am, all dressed in mourning. My poor sister's ordeal is finally over.

HEDDA.   As you see, I've already heard. Tesman sent me a note.

MISS TESMAN.   Yes he promised he would. But all the same I thought that, to Hedda—here in the house of life—I ought to bear the news of death myself.

HEDDA.   That was very kind of you.

MISS TESMAN.   Ah, Rina ought not to have passed on just now. This is no time for grief in Hedda's house.

HEDDA *(changing the subject).*   She had a peaceful death, then, Miss Tesman?

MISS TESMAN.   Oh, she went so calmly, so beautifully. And so inexpressibly happy that she could see George once again. And say good-bye to him properly. Is it possible that he's still not home?

HEDDA.   No, he wrote that I shouldn't expect him too early. But won't you sit down?

MISS TESMAN.   No, thank you, my dear—blessed Hedda. I'd love to, but I have so little time. I want to see her dressed and made ready as best as I can. She should go to her grave looking her finest.

HEDDA.   Can't I help you with something?

MISS TESMAN.   Oh, you mustn't think of it. This is nothing for Hedda Tesman to put her hands to. Or let her thoughts dwell on, either. Not at a time like this, no.

HEDDA.   Ah, thoughts—they're not so easy to control—

MISS TESMAN *(continuing)*.   Well, there's life for you. At my house now we'll be sewing a shroud for Rina. And here, too, there'll be sewing soon, I imagine. But a far different kind, praise God!

(GEORGE TESMAN *enters from the hall.*)

HEDDA.   Well, at last! It's about time.

TESMAN.   Are you here, Aunt Julie? With Hedda? Think of that!

MISS TESMAN.   I was just this minute leaving, dear boy. Well, did you get done all you promised you would?

TESMAN.   No, I'm really afraid I've forgotten half. I'll have to run over and see you tomorrow. My brain's completely in a whirl today. I can't keep my thoughts together.

MISS TESMAN.   But George dear, you mustn't take it that way.

TESMAN.   Oh? Well, how should I, then?

MISS TESMAN.   You should rejoice in your grief. Rejoice in everything that's happened, as I do.

TESMAN.   Oh yes, of course. You're thinking of Auntie Rina.

HEDDA.   It's going to be lonely for you, Miss Tesman.

MISS TESMAN.   For the first few days, yes. But it won't be for long, I hope. I won't let dear Rina's little room stand empty.

TESMAN.   No? Who would you want to have in it? Hm?

MISS TESMAN.   Oh, there's always some poor invalid in need of care and attention.

HEDDA.   Would you really take another burden like that on yourself?

MISS TESMAN.   Burden! Mercy on you, child—it's been no burden for me.

HEDDA.   But now, with a stranger—

MISS TESMAN.   Oh, you soon make friends with an invalid. And I do so much need someone to live for—I, too. Well, thank God, in this house as well, there soon ought to be work that an old aunt can turn her hand to.

HEDDA.   Oh, forget about us—

TESMAN.   Yes, think how pleasant it could be for the three of us if—

HEDDA.   If—?

TESMAN *(uneasily)*.   Oh, nothing. It'll all take care of itself. Let's hope so. Uh?

MISS TESMAN.   Ah, yes. Well, I expect you two have things to talk about. *(Smiles.)* And perhaps Hedda has something to tell you, George. Good-bye. I'll have to get home now to Rina. *(Turning at the door.)* Goodness me, how strange! Now Rina's both with me and with poor dear Jochum as well.

TESMAN.   Yes, imagine that, Aunt Julie! Hm?

(MISS TESMAN *goes out the hall door.*)

HEDDA *(follows* TESMAN *with a cold, probing look).*   I almost think you feel this death more than she.

TESMAN.   Oh, it's not just Auntie Rina's death. It's Eilert who has me worried.

HEDDA *(quickly).*   Any news about him?

TESMAN.   I stopped up at his place this afternoon, thinking to tell him that the manuscript was safe.

HEDDA.   Well? Didn't you see him then?

TESMAN.   No, he wasn't home. But afterward I met Mrs. Elvsted, and she said he'd been here early this morning.

HEDDA.   Yes, right after you left.

TESMAN.   And apparently he said he'd torn his manuscript up. Uh?

HEDDA.   Yes, he claimed that he had.

TESMAN.   But good Lord, then he must have been completely demented! Well, then I guess you didn't dare give it back to him, Hedda, did you?

HEDDA.   No, he didn't get it.

TESMAN.   But you did tell him we had it, I suppose?

HEDDA.   No. *(Quickly.)* Did you tell Mrs. Elvsted anything?

TESMAN.   No, I thought I'd better not. But you should have said something to him. Just think, if he goes off in desperation and does himself some harm! Give me the manuscript, Hedda! I'm taking it back to him right away. Where do you have it?

HEDDA *(cold and impassive, leaning against the armchair).*   I don't have it anymore.

TESMAN.   You don't have it! What on earth do you mean by that?

HEDDA.   I burned it—the whole thing.

TESMAN *(with a start of terror).*   Burned it! Burned Eilert Løvborg's manuscript!

HEDDA.   Stop shouting. The maid could hear you.

TESMAN.   Burned it! But my God in heaven—! No, no, no—that's impossible!

HEDDA.   Yes, but it's true, all the same.

TESMAN.   But do you realize what you've done, Hedda! It's illegal disposition of lost property. Just think! Yes, you can ask Judge Brack; he'll tell you.

HEDDA.   It would be wiser not mentioning this—either to the judge or to anyone else.

TESMAN.   But how could you go and do such an incredible thing! Whatever put it into your head? What got into you, anyway? Answer me! Well?

HEDDA *(suppressing an almost imperceptible smile).*   I did it for your sake, George.

TESMAN.   For my sake!

HEDDA.   When you came home this morning and told about how he'd read to you—

TESMAN.   Yes, yes, then what?

HEDDA.   Then you confessed that you envied him this book.

TESMAN.   Good Lord, I didn't mean it literally.

HEDDA.   Never mind. I still couldn't bear the thought that anyone should eclipse you.

TESMAN *(in an outburst of mingled doubt and joy).*   Hedda—is this true, what you say! Yes, but—but—I never dreamed you could show your love like this. Imagine!

HEDDA.   Well, then it's best you know that—that I'm going to— *(Impatiently, breaking off.)* No, no—you ask your Aunt Julie. She's the one who can tell you.

TESMAN.   Oh, I'm beginning to understand you, Hedda! *(Claps his hands together.)* Good heavens, no! Is it actually *that*! Can it be? Uh?

HEDDA.   Don't shout so. The maid can hear you.

TESMAN.   The maid! Oh, Hedda, you're priceless, really! The maid— but that's Berta! Why, I'll go out and tell her myself.

HEDDA *(clenching her fists in despair).*   Oh, I'll die—I'll die of all this!

TESMAN.   Of what, Hedda? Uh?

HEDDA.   Of all these—absurdities—George.

TESMAN.   Absurdities? What's absurd about my being so happy? Well, all right—I guess there's no point in my saying anything to Berta.

HEDDA.   Oh, go ahead—why not that, too?

TESMAN.   No, no, not yet. But Aunt Julie will have to hear. And then, that you've started to call me George, too. Imagine! Oh, Aunt Julie will be so glad—so glad!

HEDDA.   When she hears that I burned Eilert Løvborg's book—for your sake?

TESMAN.   Well, as far as that goes—this thing with the book—of course, no one's to know about that. But that you have a love that burns for me, Hedda—Aunt Julie can certainly share in that! You know, I wonder, really, if things such as this are common among young wives? Hm?

HEDDA.   I think you should ask Aunt Julie about that, too.

TESMAN.   Yes, I definitely will, when I have the chance.

(MRS. ELVSTED, dressed as on her first visit, with hat and coat, comes in the hall door.)

MRS. ELVSTED *(greets them hurriedly and speaks in agitation).*   Oh, Hedda dear, don't be annoyed that I'm back again.

HEDDA.   Has something happened, Thea?

TESMAN.   Something with Eilert Løvborg? Uh?

MRS. ELVSTED.   Yes, I'm so terribly afraid he's met with an accident.

HEDDA *(seizing her arm).*   Ah—you think so!

TESMAN.   But, Mrs. Elvsted, where did you get that idea?

MRS. ELVSTED.   Well, because I heard them speaking of him at the boardinghouse, just as I came in. Oh, there are the most incredible rumors about him in town today.

TESMAN.   Yes, you know, I heard them too! And yet I could swear that he went right home to bed last night. Imagine!

HEDDA.   Well—what did they say at the boardinghouse?

MRS. ELVSTED.   Oh, I couldn't get anything clearly. They either didn't know much themselves, or else— They stopped talking when they saw me. And I didn't dare to ask.

TESMAN *(restlessly moving about)*.   Let's hope—let's hope you misunderstood them, Mrs. Elvsted!

MRS. ELVSTED.   No, no, I'm sure they were talking of him. And then I heard them say something or other about the hospital, or—

TESMAN.   The hospital!

HEDDA.   No—but that's impossible!

MRS. ELVSTED.   Oh, I'm so deathly afraid for him now. And later I went up to his lodging to ask about him.

HEDDA.   But was that very wise to do, Thea?

MRS. ELVSTED.   What else could I do? I couldn't bear the uncertainty any longer.

TESMAN.   But didn't you find him there either? Hm?

MRS. ELVSTED.   No. And no one had any word of him. He hadn't been in since yesterday afternoon, they said.

TESMAN.   Yesterday! Imagine them saying that!

MRS. ELVSTED.   I think there can only be one reason—something terrible must have happened to him!

TESMAN.   Hedda dear—suppose I went over and made a few inquiries?

HEDDA.   No, no—don't you get mixed up in this business.

(JUDGE BRACK, with hat in hand, enters from the hall, BERTA *letting him in and shutting the door after him. He looks grave and bows silently.)*

TESMAN.   Oh, is that you, Judge? Uh?

BRACK.   Yes, it's imperative that I see you this evening.

TESMAN.   I can see that you've heard the news from Aunt Julie.

BRACK.   Among other things, yes.

TESMAN.   It's sad, isn't it? Uh?

BRACK.   Well, my dear Tesman, that depends on how you look at it.

TESMAN *(eyes him doubtfully)*.   Has anything else happened?

BRACK.   Yes, as a matter of fact.

HEDDA *(intently)*.   Something distressing, Judge?

BRACK.   Again, that depends on how you look at it, Mrs. Tesman.

MRS. ELVSTED *(in an uncontrollable outburst)*.   Oh, it's something about Eilert Løvborg!

BRACK *(glancing at her)*.   Now how did you hit upon that, Mrs. Elvsted? Have you, perhaps, heard something already—?

MRS. ELVSTED *(in confusion)*.   No, no, nothing like that—but—

TESMAN.   Oh, for heaven's sake, tell us!

BRACK *(with a shrug)*.   Well—I'm sorry, but—Eilert Løvborg's been taken to the hospital. He's dying!

MRS. ELVSTED *(crying out)*.   Oh, God, oh, God—!

TESMAN.   To the hospital! And dying!

HEDDA *(involuntarily)*.   All so soon—!

MRS. ELVSTED *(wailing)*.   And we parted in anger, Hedda!

HEDDA *(in a whisper)*.   Thea—be careful, Thea!

MRS. ELVSTED *(ignoring her)*.   I have to see him! I have to see him alive!
BRACK.   No use, Mrs. Elvsted. No one's allowed in to see him.
MRS. ELVSTED.   Oh, but tell me, at least, what happened to him! What is it?
TESMAN.   Don't tell me he tried to—! Uh?
HEDDA.   Yes, he did, I'm sure of it.
TESMAN.   Hedda—how can you say—!
BRACK *(his eyes steadily on her)*.   Unhappily, you've guessed exactly right, Mrs. Tesman.
MRS. ELVSTED.   Oh, how horrible!
TESMAN.   Did it himself! Imagine!
HEDDA.   Shot himself!
BRACK.   Again, exactly right, Mrs. Tesman.
MRS. ELVSTED *(trying to control herself)*.   When did it happen, Mr. Brack?
BRACK.   This afternoon. Between three and four.
TESMAN.   But good Lord—where did he do it, then? Hm?
BRACK *(hesitating slightly)*.   Where? Why—in his room, I suppose.
MRS. ELVSTED.   No, that can't be right. I was there between six and seven.
BRACK.   Well, somewhere else, then. I don't know exactly. I only know he was found like that. Shot—in the chest.
MRS. ELVSTED.   What a horrible thought! That he should end that way!
HEDDA *(to BRACK)*.   In the chest, you say.
BRACK.   Yes—I told you.
HEDDA.   Not the temple?
BRACK.   In the chest, Mrs. Tesman.
HEDDA.   Well—well, the chest is just as good.
BRACK.   Why, Mrs. Tesman?
HEDDA *(evasively)*.   Oh, nothing—never mind.
TESMAN.   And the wound is critical, you say? Uh?
BRACK.   The wound is absolutely fatal. Most likely, it's over already.
MRS. ELVSTED.   Yes, yes, I can feel that it is! It's over! All over! Oh, Hedda—!
TESMAN.   But tell me now—how did you learn about this?
BRACK *(brusquely)*.   One of the police. Someone I talked to.
HEDDA *(in a clear, bold voice)*.   At last, something truly done!
TESMAN *(shocked)*.   My God, what are you saying, Hedda!
HEDDA.   I'm saying there's beauty in all this.
BRACK.   Hm, Mrs. Tesman—
TESMAN.   Beauty! What an idea!
MRS. ELVSTED.   Oh, Hedda, how can you talk about beauty in such a thing?
HEDDA.   Eilert Løvborg's settled accounts with himself. He's had the courage to do what—what had to be done.
MRS. ELVSTED.   Don't you believe it! It never happened like that. When he did this, he was in a delirium!
TESMAN.   In despair, you mean.

HEDDA.   No, he wasn't. I'm certain of that.

MRS. ELVSTED.   But he was! In delirium! The way he was when he tore up our book.

BRACK *(startled).*   The book? His manuscript, you mean? He tore it up?

MRS. ELVSTED.   Yes. Last night.

TESMAN *(in a low whisper).*   Oh, Hedda, we'll never come clear of all this.

BRACK.   Hm, that's very strange.

TESMAN *(walking about the room).*   To think Eilert could be gone like that! And then not to have left behind the one thing that could have made his name live on.

MRS. ELVSTED.   Oh, if it could only be put together again!

TESMAN.   Yes, imagine if that were possible! I don't know what I wouldn't give—

MRS. ELVSTED.   Perhaps it can, Mr. Tesman.

TESMAN.   What do you mean?

MRS. ELVSTED *(searching in the pockets of her dress).*   Look here. I've kept all these notes that he used to dictate from.

HEDDA *(coming a step closer).*   Ah—!

TESMAN.   You've kept them, Mrs. Elvsted! Uh?

MRS. ELVSTED.   Yes, here they are. I took them along when I left home. And they've stayed right here in my pocket—

TESMAN.   Oh, let me look!

MRS. ELVSTED *(hands him a sheaf of small papers).*   But they're in such a mess. All mixed up.

TESMAN.   But just think, if we could decipher them, even so! Maybe the two of us could help each other—

MRS. ELVSTED.   Oh yes! At least, we could try—

TESMAN.   We can do it! We *must*! I'll give my whole life to this!

HEDDA.   You, George. Your life?

TESMAN.   Yes. Or, let's say, all the time I can spare. My own research will have to wait. You can understand, Hedda. Hm! It's something I owe to Eilert's memory.

HEDDA.   Perhaps.

TESMAN.   And so, my dear Mrs. Elvsted, let's see if we can't join forces. Good Lord, there's no use brooding over what's gone by. Uh? We must try to compose our thoughts as much as we can, in order that—

MRS. ELVSTED.   Yes, yes, Mr. Tesman, I'll do the best I can.

TESMAN.   Come on, then. Let's look over these notes right away. Where shall we sit? Here? No, in there, in the back room. Excuse us, Judge. You come with me, Mrs. Elvsted.

MRS. ELVSTED.   Dear God—if only we can do this!

(TESMAN *and* MRS. ELVSTED *go into the inner room. She takes off her hat and coat. They both sit at the table under the hanging lamp and become totally immersed in examining the papers.* HEDDA *goes toward the stove and sits in the armchair. After a moment,* BRACK *goes over by her.)*

HEDDA *(her voice lowered).*   Ah, Judge—what a liberation it is, this act of Eilert Løvborg's.

BRACK.   Liberation, Mrs. Hedda? Well, yes, for him; you could certainly say he's been liberated—

HEDDA.   I mean for me. It's liberating to know that there can still actually be a free and courageous action in this world. Something that shimmers with spontaneous beauty.

BRACK *(smiling).*   Hm—my dear Mrs. Hedda—

HEDDA.   Oh, I already know what you're going to say. Because you're a kind of specialist too, you know, just like—Oh, well!

BRACK *(looking fixedly at her).*   Eilert Løvborg meant more to you than you're willing to admit, perhaps even to yourself. Or am I wrong about that?

HEDDA.   I won't answer that sort of question. I simply know that Eilert Løvborg's had the courage to live life after his own mind. And now—this last great act, filled with beauty! That he had the strength and the will to break away from the banquet of life—so young.

BRACK.   It grieves me, Mrs. Hedda—but I'm afraid I have to disburden you of this beautiful illusion.

HEDDA.   Illusion?

BRACK.   One that, in any case, you'd soon be deprived of.

HEDDA.   And what's that?

BRACK.   He didn't shoot himself—of his own free will.

HEDDA.   He didn't—!

BRACK.   No. This whole affair didn't go off quite the way I described it.

HEDDA *(in suspense).*   You've hidden something? What is it?

BRACK.   For poor Mrs. Elvsted's sake, I did a little editing here and there.

HEDDA.   Where?

BRACK.   First, the fact that he's already dead.

HEDDA.   In the hospital?

BRACK.   Yes. Without regaining consciousness.

HEDDA.   What else did you hide?

BRACK.   That the incident didn't occur in his room.

HEDDA.   Well, that's rather unimportant.

BRACK.   Not entirely. Suppose I were to tell you that Eilert Løvborg was found shot in—in Mademoiselle Diana's boudoir.

HEDDA *(half rises, then sinks back again).*   That's impossible, Judge! He wouldn't have gone there again today!

BRACK.   He was there this afternoon. He went there, demanding something he said they'd stolen from him. Kept raving about a lost child—

HEDDA.   Ah—so that was it—

BRACK.   I thought perhaps that might be his manuscript. But, I hear now, he destroyed that himself. So it must have been his wallet.

HEDDA.   I suppose so. Then, there—that's where they found him.

BRACK.   Yes, there. With a discharged pistol in his breast pocket. The bullet had wounded him fatally.

HEDDA.   In the chest—yes.

BRACK.   No—in the stomach—more or less.

HEDDA *(stares up at him with a look of revulsion).* That too! What is it, this—this curse—that everything I touch turns ridiculous and vile?

BRACK. There's something else, Mrs. Hedda. Another ugly aspect to the case.

HEDDA. What's that?

BRACK. The pistol he was carrying—

HEDDA *(breathlessly).* Well! What about it!

BRACK. He must have stolen it.

HEDDA *(springs up).* Stolen! That's not true! He didn't!

BRACK. It seems impossible otherwise. He must have stolen it—shh!

(TESMAN and MRS. ELVSTED have gotten up from the table in the inner room and come into the drawing room.)

TESMAN *(with both hands full of papers).* Hedda dear—it's nearly impossible to see in there under that overhead lamp. You know?

HEDDA. Yes, I know.

TESMAN. Do you think it would be all right if we used your table for a while? Hm?

HEDDA. Yes, I don't mind. *(Quickly.)* Wait! No, let me clear it off first.

TESMAN. Oh, don't bother, Hedda. There's plenty of room.

HEDDA. No, no, let me just clear it off, can't you? I'll put all this in by the piano. There!

(She has pulled out an object covered with sheet music from under the bookcase, adds more music to it, and carries the whole thing into the inner room and off left. TESMAN puts the scraps of paper on the writing table and moves the lamp over from the corner table. He and MRS. ELVSTED sit down and go on with their work. HEDDA comes back.)

HEDDA *(behind MRS. ELVSTED's chair, gently ruffling her hair).* Well, my sweet little Thea—how is it going with Eilert Løvborg's monument?

MRS. ELVSTED *(looking despondently up at her).* Oh, dear—it's going to be terribly hard to set these in order.

TESMAN. It's got to be done. There's just no alternative. Besides, setting other people's papers in order—it's exactly what I can do best.

(HEDDA goes over by the stove and sits on one of the taborets. BRACK stands over her, leaning on the armchair.)

HEDDA *(whispering).* What did you say about the pistol?

BRACK *(softly).* That he must have stolen it.

HEDDA. Why, necessarily, that?

BRACK. Because every other explanation would seem impossible, Mrs. Hedda.

HEDDA. I see.

BRACK *(glancing at her).* Of course, Eilert Løvborg was here this morning. Wasn't he?

HEDDA. Yes.

BRACK. Were you alone with him?

HEDDA. Yes, briefly.

BRACK. Did you leave the room while he was here?

HEDDA. No.

BRACK. Consider. You didn't leave, even for a moment.

HEDDA. Well, yes, perhaps, just for a moment—into the hall.

BRACK. And where did you have your pistol case?

HEDDA. I had it put away in—

BRACK. Yes, Mrs. Hedda?

HEDDA. It was lying over there, on the writing table.

BRACK. Have you looked since to see if both pistols are there?

HEDDA. No.

BRACK. No need to. I saw the pistol. Løvborg had it on him. I knew it immediately, from yesterday. And other days too.

HEDDA. Do you have it, maybe?

BRACK. No, the police have it.

HEDDA. What will they do with it?

BRACK. Try to trace it to the owner.

HEDDA. Do you think they'll succeed?

BRACK *(bending over her and whispering)*. No, Hedda Gabler—as long as I keep quiet.

HEDDA *(looking at him anxiously)*. And if you don't keep quiet—then what?

BRACK *(with a shrug)*. Counsel could always claim that the pistol was stolen.

HEDDA *(decisively)*. I'd rather die!

BRACK *(smiling)*. People *say* such things. But they don't *do* them.

HEDDA *(without answering)*. And what, then, if the pistol wasn't stolen. And they found the owner. What would happen?

BRACK. Well, Hedda—there'd be a scandal.

HEDDA. A scandal!

BRACK. A scandal, yes—the kind you're so deathly afraid of. Naturally, you'd appear in court—you and Mademoiselle Diana. She'd have to explain how the whole thing occurred. Whether it was an accident or homicide. Was he trying to pull the pistol out of his pocket to threaten her? Is that why it went off? Or had she torn the pistol out of his hand, shot him, and slipped it back in his pocket again? It's rather like her to do that, you know. She's a powerful woman, this Mademoiselle Diana.

HEDDA. But all that sordid business is no concern of mine.

BRACK. No. But you'll have to answer the question: why did you give Eilert Løvborg the pistol? And what conclusions will people draw from the fact that you did give it to him?

HEDDA *(her head sinking)*. That's true. I hadn't thought of that.

BRACK. Well, luckily there's no danger, as long as I keep quiet.

HEDDA. So I'm in your power, Judge. You have your hold over me from now on.

BRACK *(whispers more softly)*. My dearest Hedda—believe me—I won't abuse my position.

HEDDA.   All the same, I'm in your power. Tied to your will and desire. Not free. Not free, then! *(Rises impetuously.)* No—I can't bear the thought of it. Never!

BRACK *(looks at her half mockingly).*   One usually manages to adjust to the inevitable.

HEDDA *(returning his look).*   Yes, perhaps so. *(She goes over to the writing table. Suppressing an involuntary smile, she imitates* TESMAN's *intonation.)* Well? Getting on with it, George? Uh?

TESMAN.   Goodness knows, dear. It's going to mean months and months of work, in any case.

HEDDA *(as before).*   Imagine that! *(Runs her hand lightly through* MRS: ELVSTED's *hair.)* Don't you find it strange, Thea? Here you are, sitting now beside Tesman—just as you used to sit with Eilert Løvborg.

MRS. ELVSTED.   Oh, if I could only inspire your husband in the same way.

HEDDA.   Oh, that will surely come—in time.

TESMAN.   Yes, you know what, Hedda—I really think I'm beginning to feel something of the kind. But you go back and sit with Judge Brack.

HEDDA.   Is there nothing the two of you need from me now?

TESMAN.   No, nothing in the world. *(Turning his head.)* From now on, Judge, you'll have to be good enough to keep Hedda company.

BRACK *(with a glance at* HEDDA).   I'll take the greatest pleasure in that.

HEDDA.   Thanks. But I'm tired this evening. I want to rest a while in there on the sofa.

TESMAN.   Yes, do that, dear. Uh?

*(*HEDDA *goes into the inner room, pulling the curtains closed after her. Short pause. Suddenly she is heard playing a wild dance melody on the piano.)*

MRS. ELVSTED *(starting up from her chair).*   Oh—what's that?

TESMAN *(running to the center doorway).*   But Hedda dearest—don't go playing dance music tonight! Think of Auntie Rina! And Eilert, too!

HEDDA *(putting her head out between the curtains).*   And Auntie Julie. And all the rest of them. From now on I'll be quiet. *(She closes the curtains again.)*

TESMAN *(at the writing table).*   She can't feel very happy seeing us do this melancholy work. You know what, Mrs. Elvsted—you must move in with Aunt Julie. Then I can come over evenings. And then we can sit and work *there*. Uh?

MRS. ELVSTED.   Yes, perhaps that would be best—

HEDDA.   I can hear everything you say, Tesman. But what will I do evenings over here?

TESMAN *(leafing through the notes).*   Oh, I'm sure Judge Brack will be good enough to stop by and see you.

BRACK *(in the armchair, calling out gaily).*   I couldn't miss an evening, Mrs. Tesman! We'll have great times here together, the two of us!

HEDDA *(in a clear, ringing voice).*   Yes, you can hope so, Judge, can't you? You, the one cock of the walk—

(A shot is heard within. TESMAN, MRS. ELVSTED, *and* BRACK *start from their chairs.)*

TESMAN.   Oh, now she's fooling with those pistols again.

(He throws the curtains back and runs in. MRS. ELVSTED *follows.* HEDDA *lies, lifeless, stretched out on the sofa. Confusion and cries.* BERTA *comes in, bewildered, from the right.)*

TESMAN *(shrieking to* BRACK*).*   Shot herself! Shot herself in the temple! Can you imagine!
BRACK *(in the armchair, prostrated).*   But good God! People don't *do* such things!

QUESTIONS

1. Much occurs in this play before Hedda appears on stage. What is the point of the exchanges between Aunt Julie and the maid and then George and Aunt Julie? In what sense do these conversations establish a framework for the action to come? How do they begin to condition our view of Hedda and her dilemma?

2. More than in many of Ibsen's other plays, *Hedda Gabler* depends on the "supporting" characters. Discuss the role Mrs. Elvsted, Eilert Løvborg, and Judge Brack play in helping to introduce and resolve Hedda's dilemma.

3. Hedda says that Eilert Løvborg "has the courage to live according to his own principles." She says that she admires him because he is not afraid to "do something big . .. something beautiful." What is she talking about? How does such an act relate to her view of the society in which she lives. Is she correct about Løvborg? To what extent is she also trying to "do something big"? Does she succeed? How is your perception of her last act affected by Judge Brack's final comment, "People don't *do* such things"?

4. Ibsen's most famous play, A *Doll's House,* has been seen by feminists in our own day as a sort of manifesto for the women's liberation movement. Can the same be said for *Hedda Gabler*? At the end of A *Doll's House,* the heroine, Nora, decides to walk out on her husband and children because she feels they are suffocating her and preventing her from realizing her full individuality. In what sense might Hedda's end be seen as an even more profound insight into the dilemma women face?

5. Is Hedda a "tragic" figure in the same way that Hamlet is? Is her tragedy, like Hamlet's, a matter of adjusting her view of herself to her view of the world?

6. George Bernard Shaw once claimed that Ibsen's plays were "much more important to us" than Shakespeare's because the things that happen to his characters "are things that happen to us." Do you agree? Use examples from *Hamlet* and *Hedda Gabler* to support your conclusions.

5
THE DRAMA OF POST REALISM

R ealistic theater, as we have seen, arose in the nineteenth century, largely as a response to the aesthetic needs of the increasingly urbanized and middle-class culture of Europe and the United States. Realism is still a strong tradition in our own time. In fact, most of the serious drama premiered on and off Broadway every year is realist in inspiration and execution, as is most of what we see on television and in film. But drama, as we have pointed out earlier, has always been an art form especially sensitive to the tension between established convention and innovative approaches. And even though realism has continued to be dominant in the contemporary theater, modern playwrights have constantly experimented with new forms and perspectives that have challenged and modified the assumptions on which the realistic theater pioneered by Ibsen and others was based.

One important source of experimentation, coming from Berlin in the 1920s, was the so-called "Epic Theater" of Bertolt Brecht. An ardent Marxist, Brecht wanted to escape the confines of realism and to create a type of drama that would engage the minds, rather than the emotions, of his audience. In *Mother Courage* and other plays he produced a theater of argument rather than a theater of empathy. He didn't want his characters and their settings and situations to be reacted to as "real" people in "real" dilemmas, but to be seen as aspects of a dialogue about social justice and political responsibility. Moreover, he was impressed by popular theater—jugglers, mimes, clowns, street performers, and so on, who reveled in the theatricality of their exhibitions rather than trying to hide them behind a facade of realism. He used such figures in his plays as part of what he called an "alienation effect"—ways of reminding spectators that they were not seeing the "reality" most of his contemporaries worked so hard to capture, but rather a piece of theater to which they should first respond with their minds and then with their hearts.

If Brecht created a theater of ideas responding to the rise of fascism and other political developments, the French playwright Jean Genêt and others were interested in new attitudes toward human nature caused by the rise of Freudian theory and the barbarism of Nazi genocide. In a "theater of cruelty," they portrayed perversion and madness on the stage in an attempt to challenge audiences' assumptions about "civilization." Based on shocking vignettes and surreal episodes, the dramas they created often had characters who spoke directly to the audience, breaking the illusion of reality by insulting spectators and daring them to maintain their conventional morality in the face of the evidence about human depravity and amorality that was presented on the stage. One especially popular recent play drawing heavily on the theater of cruelty is *Marat/Sade* by the German playwright Peter Weiss (1965).

Perhaps the most influential of all forms of post-realist drama has been the *theater of the absurd*. This dramatic movement is an outgrowth of World War II and the deep skepticism it caused about the fate of humankind in an atomic age. Faith in religion, society, and history itself disappeared; the only demonstrable laws in the universe seemed to derive from blind fate, cosmic randomness, and chance. Language itself was no longer the sole medium for communicating truth, this part of its job taken over by the formulae of mathematics and science, while its remaining integrity was debased by advertising, government propaganda, and other mass communications. The theater of the absurd attempted to deal with all these developments, taking its rationale from the French existentialist philosopher Albert Camus in *The Myth of Sisyphus:* "In a universe that is suddenly deprived of illusion and of light, man feels a stranger . . . This divorce between man and his life, the actor and his setting, truly constitutes the feeling of Absurdity." In Camus' usage, *absurd* did not mean "incongruous" or "ridiculous," but rather "pointless" and "without purpose."

In *The Bald Soprano* (1950) Eugene Ionesco presents audiences with a group of people who repeat familiar sayings so frequently that human speech is reduced to inconsequential babble. His *Rhinoceros* (1960) shows all humanity, except for one solitary individual, turned into rhinos. And perhaps the most famous absurdist play is Samuel Beckett's *Waiting for Godot* (1952) a work in which two clownish figures (played as tramps) chatter wistfully on an almost completely bare stage while waiting for something to happen.

One of those avant garde movements whose radical views have been partly absorbed by the dominant culture, absurdism in the theater has parallels in other art forms—Kafka in fiction, Jackson Pollock and abstract expressionists in painting, John Cage and other atonal composers in music. Absurdism has been not so much a conscious artistic movement as a way of seeing things at a given moment in history. Just as a world whose central meanings were clear had dictated an art that was rational, linear, and realistic, so a world without clear consensus about those meanings dictated an art that was tentative and groping, individualistic to the point of eccentricity, and at times incomprehensible. While the "well-made play" of the realistic theater has a clear movement from exposition to conclusion, absurdist drama has had neither a beginning nor an end, only a middle. While realism presents characters who are "like us" in their self-conception and motivation, the characters of absurdist plays are one-dimensional bumblers, *anti-heroes* without ambitions we can identify with or grandeur which can awe us. While realistic plays attempt to create an illusion that the dramatic action on stage is "really happening," absurdist plays try to break that illusion and make us focus on the philosophical implications behind what is occurring. While realism is based on dialogue simulating actual speech, characters in absurdist plays speak in repetitious, partial, and inept phrases.

Absurdist plays, then, are not dramatic actions in the realist sense, but are akin to *ritual enactments.* However grotesque and difficult they can be at times, they nonetheless function somewhat like Greek drama. They raise ultimate questions about human destiny and the relationship of individual aspiration and universal law. And by forcing unacknowledged facts about the human dilemma to the surface, they provoke a kind of catharsis. We are liberated not from absurdity per se but from the dread of dealing with such absurdity. The absurdist play marries comedy and horror and makes us laugh even though we understand we are being confronted with the tragic dilemma of life emptied of its meaning and value.

The American Dream

One of the leading dramatists in America's theater of the absurd is Edward Albee. He is perhaps best known for *Who's Afraid of Virginia Woolf,* a longer work that was successful first on Broadway and later as a Hollywood film. But some of Albee's most interesting work has been done in his one-act plays, among them *The American Dream.*

The first thing that we notice about this work—and a fact which distinguishes it immediately from the generally more somber absurdist drama of Europe—is that it is extremely funny. The characters in *The American Dream,* Mommy, Daddy, Grandma, and the others seem almost to have stepped off the pages of the Sunday funny papers or out of the animation of a Saturday morning cartoon. Befuddled and oblique, they lack any sign of the depth and individuality that playwrights working in the realistic theater have tried so hard to instill in their characters. They talk in snappy non sequiturs. ("My what an unattractive apartment you have," Mrs. Barker says. "Yes," Mommy answers, "but you don't know what a trouble it is.") The zany conversation of the play, as much as the illogical plot, places this work not only in the absurdist tradition, but also in the mainstream of classic American theatrical comedy, a tradition stretching from the vaudeville stage to Marx Brothers movies and *Saturday Night Live* television skits.

Yet *The American Dream* has serious undertones as well. In a preface to this work Albee wrote: "The play is an examination of the American Scene, an attack on the substitution of artificial for real values in our society, a condemnation of complacency, cruelty, emasculation and vacuity; it is a stand against the fiction that everything in this slipping land of ours is peachy keen." From the moment we first see Mommy and Daddy talking at (rather than to) each other, we realize that the playwright intends to keep us at arm's length from what is happening on stage and wants us to view it as an object lesson rather than an imitation of life. The characters are mouthpieces for banal, "peachy keen" values. They trivialize each other through their infantile talk ("johnny," "bumble of joy," etc). This talk is also aggressive, allowing Albee to comment on the severely limited (and limiting) roles available to individuals living in the nuclear family, and on vulgarized attitudes toward love and marriage and youth and old age. Mommy says, "I have a right to live off you because I married you and because I used to let you get on top of me and bump your uglies; and I have a right to all your money when you die." A few moments later Grandma says to both Mommy and Daddy: "You don't have any feelings, that's what's wrong with you. . . . Old people whimper, and cry, and belch, and make great hollow rumbling sounds at the table; old people wake up in the middle of the night and find out they haven't been asleep, and when old people are asleep, they try to wake up, and they can't . . . not for the longest time."

The American Dream is both a skillful assault on the theater-goer's expectations and a parody of some of the conventions of the realistic theater. Mommy and Daddy's living room, focus of the action, is meant to recall the drawing rooms of traditional "serious" family drama. The "plot" of the play is a comic version of one of those highly-charged and suspenseful family dilemmas that realistic theater relished. There are moments when the characters announce some portentous revelation—as in Grandma's recollection of the fate of Mommy and Daddy's "bumble of joy"—yet these moments turn out to be absurd both in their dark humor and in their insight into the emptiness of such melodramatic confessions. What seem to be clues in this play turn out to be red herrings. We never learn exactly what Mommy and Daddy are waiting for; like the characters in Beckett's *Waiting for Godot* and other absurdist plays, they are simply waiting helplessly for whatever fate has in store for them.

The American dream of the play's title turns out to be a good-looking but vacuous young man; it is also that vision of eternal youth and genteel security that has exercised such an appeal for the American middle class, a vision which requires the suppression (Albee would say) of our individuality and humanity. The meaning of this play comes not from our empathy with Mommy, Daddy, and Grandma, but from our recognition of what they symbolize about contemporary American values. As with other absurdist drama, *The American Dream* is not an occasion for compelling interaction between characters, but rather a forum for making judgments about the quality of our lives.

Edward Albee (b. 1928)
The American Dream

CHARACTERS

MOMMY
DADDY
GRANDMA
MRS. BARKER
YOUNG MAN

THE SCENE: *A living room. Two armchairs, one toward either side of the stage, facing each other diagonally out toward the audience. Against the rear wall, a sofa. A door, leading out from the apartment, in the rear wall, far stage-right. An archway, leading to other rooms, in the side wall, stage-left.*
At the beginning, MOMMY *and* DADDY *are seated in the armchairs,* DADDY *in the armchair stage-left,* MOMMY *in the other.*
Curtain up. A silence. Then:

MOMMY.   I don't know what can be keeping them.

DADDY.   They're late, naturally.

MOMMY.   Of course, they're late; it never fails.

DADDY.   That's the way things are today, and there's nothing you can do about it.

MOMMY.   You're quite right.

DADDY.   When we took this apartment, they were quick enough to have me sign the lease; they were quick enough to take my check for two months' rent in advance . . .

MOMMY.   And one month's security . . .

DADDY.   . . . and one month's security. They were quick enough to check my references; they were quick enough about all that. But now! But now, try to get the icebox fixed, try to get the doorbell fixed, try to get the leak in the johnny fixed! Just try it . . . they aren't so quick about *that*.

MOMMY.   Of course not; it never fails. People think they can get away with anything these days . . . and, of course they can. I went to buy a new hat yesterday. (*Pause*) I said, I went to buy a new hat yesterday.

DADDY.   Oh! Yes . . . yes.

MOMMY.   Pay attention.

DADDY.   I *am* paying attention, Mommy.

MOMMY.   Well, be sure you do.

DADDY.   Oh, I am.

MOMMY.   All right, Daddy; now listen.

DADDY.   I'm listening, Mommy.

MOMMY.   You're sure!

DADDY.   Yes . . . yes, I'm sure, I'm all ears.

MOMMY (*Giggles at the thought; then*).   All right, now. I went to buy a
new hat yesterday and I said, "I'd like a new hat, please." And so, they showed
me a few hats, green ones and blue ones, and I didn't like any of them, not
one bit. What did I say? What did I just say?

DADDY.   You didn't like any of them, not one bit.

MOMMY.   That's right; you just keep paying attention. And then they
showed me one that I did like. It was a lovely little hat, and I said, "Oh, this is
a lovely little hat; I'll take this hat; oh my, it's lovely. What color is it?" And
they said, "Why, this is beige; isn't it a lovely little beige hat?" And I said,
"Oh, it's just lovely." And so, I bought it.

(Stops, looks at DADDY)

DADDY (*To show he is paying attention*).   And so you bought it.

MOMMY.   And so I bought it, and I walked out of the store with the hat
right on my head, and I ran spang into the chairman of our woman's club,
and she said, "Oh, my dear, isn't that a lovely little hat? Where did you get
that lovely little hat? It's the loveliest little hat; I've always wanted a wheat-
colored hat *myself.*" And, I said, "Why, no, my dear; this hat is beige; beige."
And she laughed and said, "Why no, my dear, that's a wheat-colored hat . . .
wheat. I know beige from wheat." And I said, "Well, my dear, I know beige
from wheat, too." What did I say? What did I just say?

DADDY (*Tonelessly*).   Well, my dear, I know beige from wheat, too.

MOMMY.   That's right. And she laughed, and she said, "Well, my dear,
they certainly put one over on you. That's wheat if I ever saw wheat. But it's
lovely, just the same." And then she walked off. She's a dreadful woman, you
don't know her; she has dreadful taste, two dreadful children, a dreadful
house, and an absolutely adorable husband who sits in a wheel chair all the
time. You don't know him. You don't know anybody, do you? She's just a
dreadful woman, but she *is* chairman of our woman's club, so naturally I'm
terribly fond of her. So, I went right back into the hat shop, and I said, "Look
here; what do you mean selling me a hat that you say is beige, when it's wheat
all the time . . . wheat! I can tell beige from wheat any day in the week, but
not in this artificial light of yours." They have artificial light, Daddy.

DADDY.   Have they!

MOMMY.   And I said, "The minute I got outside I could tell that it wasn't
a beige hat at all; it was a wheat hat." And they said to me, "How could you
tell that when you had the hat on the top of your head?" Well, that made me
angry, and so I made a scene right there; I screamed as hard as I could; I took
my hat off and I threw it down on the counter, and oh, I made a terrible
scene. I said, I made a terrible scene.

DADDY (*Snapping to*).   Yes . . . yes . . . good for you!

MOMMY.   And I made an absolutely terrible scene; and they became
frightened, and they said, "Oh, madam; oh, madam." But I kept right on, and
finally they admitted that they might have made a mistake; so they took my
hat into the back, and then they came out again with a hat that looked exactly
like it. I took one look at it, and I said, "This hat is wheat-colored; wheat."
Well, of course, they said, "Oh, no, madam, this hat is beige; you go outside
and see." So, I went outside, and lo and behold, it *was* beige. So I bought it.

DADDY (*Clearing his throat*).   I would imagine that it was the same hat they tried to sell you before.

MOMMY (*With a little laugh*).   Well, of course it was!

DADDY.   That's the way things are today; you just can't get satisfaction; you just try.

MOMMY.   Well, *I* got satisfaction.

DADDY.   That's right, Mommy. *You did* get satisfaction, didn't you?

MOMMY.   Why are they so late? I don't know what can be keeping them.

DADDY.   I've been trying for two weeks to have the leak in the johnny fixed.

MOMMY.   You can't get satisfaction; just try. *I* can get satisfaction, but you can't.

DADDY.   I've been trying for two weeks and it isn't so much for my sake; I can always go to the club.

MOMMY.   It isn't so much for my sake, either; I can always go shopping.

DADDY.   It's really for Grandma's sake.

MOMMY.   Of course it's for Grandma's sake. Grandma cries every time she goes to the johnny as it is; but now that it doesn't work it's even worse, it makes Grandma think she's getting feeble-headed.

DADDY.   Grandma *is* getting feeble-headed.

MOMMY.   Of course Grandma is getting feeble-headed, but not about her johnny-do's.

DADDY.   No; that's true. I must have it fixed.

MOMMY.   WHY are they so late? I don't know what can be keeping them.

DADDY.   When they came here the first time, they were ten minutes early; they were quick enough about it then.

(*Enter* GRANDMA *from the archway, stage left. She is loaded down with boxes, large and small, neatly wrapped and tied.*)

MOMMY.   Why Grandma, look at you! What *is* all that you're carrying?

GRANDMA.   They're boxes. What do they look like?

MOMMY.   Daddy! Look at Grandma; look at all the boxes she's carrying!

DADDY.   My goodness, Grandma; look at all those boxes.

GRANDMA.   Where'll I put them?

MOMMY.   Heavens! I don't know. Whatever are they for?

GRANDMA.   That's nobody's damn business.

MOMMY.   Well, in that case, put them down next to Daddy; there.

GRANDMA (*Dumping the boxes down, on and around* DADDY'S *feet*).   I sure wish you'd get the john fixed.

DADDY.   Oh, I do wish they'd come and fix it. We hear you . . . for hours . . . whimpering away. . . .

MOMMY.   Daddy! What a terrible thing to say to Grandma!

GRANDMA.   Yeah. For shame, talking to me that way.

DADDY.   I'm sorry, Grandma.

MOMMY.   Daddy's sorry, Grandma.

GRANDMA. Well, all right. In that case I'll go get the rest of the boxes. I suppose I deserve being talked to that way. I've gotten so old. Most people think that when you get so old, you either freeze to death, or you burn up. But you don't. When you get so old, all that happens is that people talk to you that way.

DADDY (*Contrite*). I said I'm sorry, Grandma.

MOMMY. Daddy said he was sorry.

GRANDMA. Well, that's all that counts. People being sorry. Makes you feel better; gives you a sense of dignity, and that's all that's important . . . a sense of dignity. And it doesn't matter if you don't care, or not, either. You got to have a sense of dignity, even if you don't care, 'cause, if you don't have that, civilization's doomed.

MOMMY. You've been reading my book club selections again!

DADDY. How dare you read Mommy's book club selections, Grandma!

GRANDMA. Because I'm old! When you're old you gotta do something. When you get old, you can't talk to people because people snap at you. When you get so old, people talk to you that way. That's why you become deaf, so you won't be able to hear people talking to you that way. And that's why you go and hide under the covers in the big soft bed, so you won't feel the house shaking from people talking to you that way. That's why old people die, eventually. People talk to them that way. I've got to go and get the rest of the boxes.

(GRANDMA *exits*)

DADDY. Poor Grandma, I didn't mean to hurt her.

MOMMY. Don't you worry about it; Grandma doesn't know what she means.

DADDY. She knows what she says, though.

MOMMY. Don't you worry about it; she won't know that soon. I love Grandma.

DADDY. I love her, too. Look how nicely she wrapped these boxes.

MOMMY. Grandma has always wrapped boxes nicely. When I was a little girl, I was very poor, and Grandma was very poor, too, because Grandpa was in heaven. And every day, when I went to school, Grandma used to wrap a box for me, and I used to take it with me to school; and when it was lunchtime, all the little boys and girls used to take out their boxes of lunch, and they weren't wrapped nicely at all, and they used to open them and eat their chicken legs and chocolate cakes; and I used to say, "Oh, look at my lovely lunch box; it's so nicely wrapped it would break my heart to open it." And so, I wouldn't open it.

DADDY. Because it was empty.

MOMMY. Oh no. Grandma always filled it up, because she never ate the dinner she cooked the evening before; she gave me all her food for my lunch box the next day. After school, I'd take the box back to Grandma, and she'd open it and eat the chicken legs and chocolate cake that was inside. Grandma used to say, "I love day-old cake." That's where the expression day-old cake came from. Grandma always ate everything a day late. I used to eat all the other little boys' and girls' food at school, because they thought my lunch box was empty. They thought my lunch box was empty, and that's why I wouldn't open it. They thought I suffered from the sin of pride, and since that made them better than me, they were very generous.

DADDY.   You were a very deceitful little girl.

MOMMY.   We were very poor! But then I married you, Daddy, and now we're very rich.

DADDY.   Grandma isn't rich.

MOMMY.   No, but you've been so good to Grandma she feels rich. She doesn't know you'd like to put her in a nursing home.

DADDY.   I wouldn't!

MOMMY.   Well, heaven knows, *I* would! I can't stand it, watching her do the cooking and the housework, polishing the silver, moving the furniture . . . .

DADDY.   She likes to do that. She says it's the least she can do to earn her keep.

MOMMY.   Well, she's right. You can't live off people. I can live off you, because I married you. And aren't you lucky all I brought with me was Grandma. A lot of women I know would have brought their whole families to live off you. All I brought was Grandma. Grandma is all the family I have.

DADDY.   I feel very fortunate.

MOMMY.   You should. I have a right to live off of you because I married you, and because I used to let you get on top of me and bump your uglies; and I have a right to all your money when you die. And when you do, Grandma and I can live by ourselves . . . if she's still here. Unless you have her put away in a nursing home.

DADDY.   I have no intention of putting her in a nursing home.

MOMMY.   Well, I wish somebody would do something with her!

DADDY.   At any rate, you're very well provided for.

MOMMY.   You're my sweet Daddy; that's very nice.

DADDY.   I love my Mommy.

(Enter GRANDMA *again, laden with more boxes)*

GRANDMA *(Dumping the boxes on and around* DADDY's *feet).*   There; that's the lot of them.

DADDY.   They're wrapped so nicely.

GRANDMA *(To* DADDY).   You won't get on my sweet side that way . . .

MOMMY.   Grandma!

GRANDMA.   . . . telling me how nicely I wrap boxes. Not after what you said: how I whimpered for hours. . . .

MOMMY.   Grandma!

GRANDMA *(To* MOMMY).   Shut up! *(To* DADDY*)* You don't have any feelings, that's what's wrong with you. Old people make all sorts of noises, half of them they can't help. Old people whimper, and cry, and belch, and make great hollow rumbling sounds at the table; old people wake up in the middle of the night screaming, and find out they haven't even been asleep; and when old people *are* asleep, they try to wake up, and they can't . . . not for the longest time.

MOMMY.   Homilies, homilies!

GRANDMA.   And there's more, too.

DADDY.   I'm really very sorry, Grandma.

GRANDMA.   I know you are, Daddy; it's Mommy over there makes all the trouble. If you'd listened to me, you wouldn't have married her in the first place. She was a tramp and a trollop and a trull to boot, and she's no better now.

MOMMY.   Grandma!

GRANDMA *(To* MOMMY*).*   Shut up! *(To* DADDY*)* When she was no more than eight years old she used to climb up on my lap and say, in a sickening little voice, "When I gwo up, I'm going to mahwy a wich old man; I'm going to set my wittle were end right down in a tub o' butter, that's what I'm going to do." And I warned you, Daddy; I told you to stay away from her type. I told you to. I did.

MOMMY.   You stop that! You're my mother, not his!

GRANDMA.   I am?

DADDY.   That's right, Grandma. Mommy's right.

GRANDMA.   Well, how would you expect somebody as old as I am to remember a thing like that? You don't make allowances for people. I want an allowance. I want an allowance!

DADDY.   All right, Grandma; I'll see to it.

MOMMY.   Grandma! I'm ashamed of you.

GRANDMA.   Humf! It's a fine time to say that. You should have gotten rid of me a long time ago if that's the way you feel. You should have had Daddy set me up in business somewhere . . . I could have gone into the fur business, or I could have been a singer. But no; not you. You wanted me around so you could sleep in my room when Daddy got fresh. But now it isn't important, because Daddy doesn't want to get fresh with you any more, and I don't blame him. You'd rather sleep with me, wouldn't you, Daddy?

MOMMY.   Daddy doesn't want to sleep with anyone. Daddy's been sick.

DADDY.   I've been sick. I don't even want to sleep in the apartment.

MOMMY.   You see? I told you.

DADDY.   I just want to get everything over with.

MOMMY.   That's right. Why are they so late? Why can't they get here on time?

GRANDMA *(An owl).*   Who? Who? . . . Who? Who?

MOMMY.   You know, Grandma.

GRANDMA.   No, I don't.

MOMMY.   Well, it doesn't really matter whether you do or not.

DADDY.   Is that true?

MOMMY.   Oh, more or less. Look how pretty Grandma wrapped these boxes.

GRANDMA.   I didn't really like wrapping them; it hurt my fingers, and it frightened me. But it had to be done.

MOMMY.   Why, Grandma?

GRANDMA.   None of your damn business.

MOMMY.   Go to bed.

GRANDMA.   I don't want to go to bed. I just got up. I want to stay here and watch. Besides . . .

MOMMY.   Go to bed.

DADDY.   Let her stay up, Mommy; it isn't noon yet.

GRANDMA.   I want to watch; besides . . .

DADDY.   Let her watch, Mommy.

MOMMY.   Well all right, you can watch; but don't you dare say a word.

GRANDMA.   Old people are very good at listening; old people don't like to talk; old people have colitis and lavender perfume. Now I'm going to be quiet.

DADDY.   She never mentioned she wanted to be a singer.

MOMMY.   Oh, I forgot to tell you, but it was ages ago.

(The doorbell rings)

Oh, goodness! Here they are!

GRANDMA.   Who? Who?

MOMMY.   Oh, just some people.

GRANDMA.   The van people? Is it the van people? Have you finally done it? Have you called the van people to come and take me away?

DADDY.   Of course not, Grandma!

GRANDMA.   Oh, don't be too sure. She'd have you carted off too, if she thought she could get away with it.

MOMMY.   Pay no attention to her, Daddy.

(An aside to GRANDMA*)*

My God, you're ungrateful!

(The doorbell rings again)

DADDY *(Wringing his hands)*.   Oh dear; oh dear.

MOMMY *(Still to* GRANDMA*)*.   Just you wait; I'll fix your wagon. *(Now to* DADDY*)* Well, go let them in Daddy. What are you waiting for?

DADDY.   I think we should talk about it some more. Maybe we've been hasty . . . a little hasty, perhaps.

(Doorbell rings again)

I'd like to talk about it some more.

MOMMY.   There's no need. You made up your mind; you were firm; you were masculine and decisive.

DADDY.   We might consider the pros and the . . .

MOMMY.   I won't argue with you; it has to be done; you were right. Open the door.

DADDY.   But I'm not sure that . . .

MOMMY.   Open the door.

DADDY.   Was I firm about it?

MOMMY.   Oh, so firm; so firm.

DADDY.   And was I decisive?

MOMMY.   SO decisive! Oh, I shivered.

DADDY.   And masculine? Was I really masculine?

MOMMY.   Oh, Daddy, you were so masculine; I shivered and fainted.

GRANDMA.   Shivered and fainted, did she? Humf!

MOMMY.   You be quiet.

GRANDMA.   Old people have a right to talk to themselves; it doesn't hurt the gums, and it's comforting.

(Doorbell rings again)

DADDY.   I shall now open the door.

MOMMY.   WHAT a masculine Daddy! Isn't he a masculine Daddy?

GRANDMA.   Don't expect me to say anything. Old people are obscene.

MOMMY.   Some of your opinions aren't so bad. You know that?

DADDY (*Backing off from the door*).   Maybe we can send them away.

MOMMY.   Oh, look at you! You're turning into jelly; you're indecisive; you're a woman.

DADDY.   All right. Watch me now; I'm going to open the door. Watch. Watch!

MOMMY.   We're watching; we're watching.

GRANDMA.   *I'm* not.

DADDY.   Watch now; it's opening. (*He opens the door*) It's open! (MRS. BARKER *steps into the room*) Here they are!

MOMMY.   Here they are!

GRANDMA.   Where?

DADDY.   Come in. You're late. But, of course, we expected you to be late; we were saying that we expected you to be late.

MOMMY.   Daddy, don't be rude! We were saying that you just can't get satisfaction these days, and we were talking about you, of course. Won't you come in?

MRS. BARKER.   Thank you. I don't mind if I do.

MOMMY.   We're very glad that you're here, late as you are. You do remember us, don't you? You were here once before. I'm Mommy, and this is Daddy, and that's Grandma, doddering there in the corner.

MRS. BARKER.   Hello, Mommy; hello, Daddy; and hello there, Grandma.

DADDY.   Now that you're here, I don't suppose you could go away and maybe come back some other time.

MRS. BARKER.   Oh no; we're much too efficient for that. I said, hello there, Grandma.

MOMMY.   Speak to them, Grandma.

GRANDMA.   I don't see them.

DADDY.   For shame, Grandma; they're here.

MRS. BARKER.   Yes, we're here, Grandma. I'm Mrs. Barker. I remember you; don't you remember me?

GRANDMA.   I don't recall. Maybe you were younger, or something.

MOMMY.   Grandma! What a terrible thing to say!

MRS. BARKER.   Oh now, don't scold her, Mommy; for all she knows she may be right.

DADDY.   Uh . . . Mrs. Barker, is it? Won't you sit down?

MRS. BARKER.   I don't mind if I do.

MOMMY.   Would you like a cigarette, and a drink, and would you like to cross your legs?

MRS. BARKER.   You forget yourself, Mommy; I'm a professional woman. But I will cross my legs.

DADDY.   Yes, make yourself comfortable.

MRS. BARKER.   I don't mind if I do.

GRANDMA.   Are they still here?

MOMMY.   Be quiet, Grandma.

MRS. BARKER.   Oh, we're still here. My, what an unattractive apartment you have!

MOMMY.   Yes, but you don't know what a trouble it is. Let me tell you . . .

DADDY.   I was saying to Mommy . . .

MRS. BARKER.   Yes, I know. I was listening outside.

DADDY.   About the icebox, and . . . the doorbell . . . and the . . .

MRS. BARKER.   . . . and the johnny. Yes, we're very efficient; we have to know everything in our work.

DADDY.   Exactly what do you do?

MOMMY.   Yes, what is your work?

MRS. BARKER.   Well, my dear, for one thing, I'm chairman of your woman's club.

MOMMY.   Don't be ridiculous. I was talking to the chairman of my woman's club just yester— Why, so you are. You remember, Daddy, the lady I was telling you about? The lady with the husband who sits in the *swing?* Don't you remember?

DADDY.   No . . . no . . .

MOMMY.   Of course you do. I'm so sorry, Mrs. Barker. I would have known you anywhere, except in this artificial light. And look! You have a hat just like the one I bought yesterday.

MRS. BARKER (*With a little laugh*).   No, not really; this hat is cream.

MOMMY.   Well, my dear, that may look like a cream hat to you, but I can . . .

MRS. BARKER.   Now, now; you seem to forget who I am.

MOMMY.   Yes, I do, don't I? Are you sure you're comfortable? Won't you take off your dress?

MRS. BARKER.   I don't mind if I do.

(She removes her dress)

MOMMY.   There. You must feel a great deal more comfortable.

MRS. BARKER.   Well, I certainly *look* a great deal more comfortable.

DADDY.   I'm going to blush and giggle.

MOMMY.   Daddy's going to blush and giggle.

MRS. BARKER (*Pulling the hem of her slip above her knees*).   You're lucky to have such a man for a husband.

MOMMY.   Oh, don't I know it!

DADDY.   I just blushed and giggled and went sticky wet.

MOMMY.   Isn't Daddy a caution, Mrs. Barker?

MRS. BARKER.   Maybe if I smoked . . . ?

MOMMY.   Oh, that isn't necessary.

MRS. BARKER.   I don't mind if I do.

MOMMY.   No; no, don't. Really.

MRS. BARKER.   I don't mind . . .

MOMMY.   I won't have you smoking in my house, and that's that! You're a professional woman.

DADDY.   Grandma drinks AND smokes; don't you, Grandma?

GRANDMA.   No.

MOMMY.   Well, now, Mrs. Barker; suppose you tell us why you're here.

GRANDMA (*As* MOMMY *walks through the boxes*).   The boxes . . . the boxes . . .

MOMMY.   Be quiet, Grandma.

DADDY.   What did you say, Grandma?

GRANDMA (*As* MOMMY *steps on several of the boxes*).   The boxes, damn it!

MRS. BARKER.   Boxes; she said boxes. She mentioned the boxes.

DADDY.   What about the boxes, Grandma? Maybe Mrs. Barker is here because of the boxes. Is that what you meant, Grandma?

GRANDMA.   I don't know if that's what I meant or not. It's certainly not what I *thought* I meant.

DADDY.   Grandma is of the opinion that . . .

MRS. BARKER.   Can we assume that the boxes are for us? I mean, can we assume that you had us come here for the boxes?

MOMMY.   Are you in the habit of receiving boxes?

DADDY.   A very good question.

MRS. BARKER.   Well, that would depend on the reason we're here. I've got my fingers in so many little pies, you know. Now, I can think of one of my little activities in which we are in the habit of receiving *baskets*; but more in a literary sense than really. We *might* receive boxes, though, under very special circumstances. I'm afraid that's the best answer I can give you.

DADDY.   It's a very interesting answer.

MRS. BARKER.   I thought so. But, does it help?

MOMMY.   No; I'm afraid not.

DADDY.   I wonder if it might help us any if I said I feel misgivings, that I have definite qualms.

MOMMY.   Where, Daddy?

DADDY.   Well, mostly right here, right around where the stitches were.

MOMMY.   Daddy had an operation, you know.

MRS. BARKER.   Oh, you poor Daddy! I didn't know; but then, how could I?

GRANDMA.   You might have asked; it wouldn't have hurt you.

MOMMY.   Dry up, Grandma.

GRANDMA.   There you go. Letting your true feelings come out. Old people aren't dry enough, I suppose. My sacks are empty, the fluid in my eyeballs is all caked on the inside edges, my spine is made of sugar candy, I breathe ice; but you don't hear me complain. Nobody hears old people complain because people think that's all old people do. And *that's* because old people are gnarled and sagged and twisted into the shape of a complaint. (*Signs off*) That's all.

MRS. BARKER.   What was wrong, Daddy?

DADDY.   Well, you know how it is: the doctors took out something that was there and put in something that wasn't there. An operation.

MRS. BARKER.   You're very fortunate, I should say.

MOMMY.   Oh, he is; he is. All his life, Daddy has wanted to be a United States Senator; but now . . . why now he's changed his mind, and for the rest of his life he's going to want to be Governor . . . it would be nearer the apartment, you know.

MRS. BARKER.   You *are* fortunate, Daddy.

DADDY.   Yes, indeed; except that I get these qualms now and then, definite ones.

MRS. BARKER.   Well, it's just a matter of things settling; you're like an old house.

MOMMY.   Why Daddy, thank Mrs. Barker.

DADDY.   Thank you.

MRS. BARKER.   Ambition! That's the ticket. I have a brother who's very much like you, Daddy . . . ambitious. Of course, he's a great deal younger than you; he's even younger than I am . . . if such a thing is possible. He runs a little newspaper. Just a little newspaper . . . but he runs it. He's chief cook and bottle washer of that little newspaper, which he calls *The Village Idiot*. He has such a sense of humor; he's so self-deprecating, so modest. And he'd never admit it himself, but he *is* the Village Idiot.

MOMMY.   Oh, I think that's just grand. Don' you think so, Daddy?

DADDY.   Yes, just grand.

MRS. BARKER.   My brother's a dear man, and he has a dear little wife, whom he loves, dearly. He loves her so much he just can't get a sentence out without mentioning her. He wants everybody to know he's married. He's really a stickler on that point; he can't be introduced to anybody and say hello without adding, "Of course, I'm married." As far as I'm concerned, he's the chief exponent of Woman Love in this whole country; he's even been written up in psychiatric journals because of it.

DADDY.   Indeed!

MOMMY.   Isn't that lovely.

MRS. BARKER.   Oh, I think so. There's too much woman hatred in this country, and that's a fact.

GRANDMA.   Oh, I don't know.

MOMMY.   Oh, I think that's just grand. Don't you think so, Daddy?

DADDY.   Yes, just grand.

GRANDMA.   In case anybody's interested . . .

MOMMY.   Be quiet, Grandma.

GRANDMA.   Nuts!

MOMMY.   Oh, Mrs. Barker, you *must* forgive Grandma. She's rural.

MRS. BARKER.   I don't mind if I do.

DADDY.   Maybe Grandma has something to say.

MOMMY.   Nonsense. Old people have nothing to say; and if old people *did* have something to say, nobody would listen to them. (*To* GRANDMA) You see? I can pull that stuff just as easy as you can.

GRANDMA.   Well, you got the rhythm, but you don't really have the quality. Besides, you're middle-aged.

MOMMY.   I'm proud of it!

GRANDMA.   Look. I'll show you how it's really done. Middle-aged people think they can do anything, but the truth is that middle-aged people can't do most things as well as they used to. Middle-aged people think they're special because they're like everybody else. We live in the age of deformity. You see? Rhythm *and* content. You'll learn.

DADDY.   I do wish I weren't surrounded by women; I'd like some men around here.

MRS. BARKER.   You can say that again!

GRANDMA.   I don't hardly count as a woman, so can I say my piece?

MOMMY.   Go on. Jabber away.

GRANDMA.   It's very simple; the fact is, these boxes don't have anything to do with why this good lady is come to call. Now, if you're interested in knowing why these boxes *are* here . . .

DADDY.   I'm sure that must be all very true, Grandma, but what does it have to do with why . . . pardon me, what is that name again?

MRS. BARKER.   Mrs. Barker.

DADDY.   Exactly. What does it have to with why . . . that name again?

MRS. BARKER.   Mrs. Barker.

DADDY.   Precisely. What does it have to do with why what's-her-name is here?

MOMMY.   They're here because we asked them.

MRS. BARKER.   Yes. That's why.

GRANDMA.   Now if you're interested in knowing why these boxes *are* here . . .

MOMMY.   Well, nobody *is* interested!

GRANDMA.   You can be as snippety as you like for all the good it'll do you.

DADDY.   You two will have to stop arguing.

MOMMY.   I don't argue with her.

DADDY.   It will just have to stop.

MOMMY.   Well, why don't you call a van and have her taken away?

GRANDMA.   Don't bother; there's no need.

DADDY.   No, now, perhaps I can go away myself. . . .

MOMMY.   Well, one or the other; the way things are now it's impossible. In the first place, it's too crowded in this apartment. (*To* GRANDMA) And it's you that takes up all the space, with your enema bottles, and your Pekinese, and God-only-knows-what-else . . . and now all these boxes. . . .

GRANDMA.   These boxes are . . .

MRS. BARKER.   I've never heard of enema *bottles* . . .

GRANDMA.   She means enema bags, but she doesn't know the difference. Mommy comes from extremely bad stock. And besides, when Mommy was born . . . well, it was a difficult delivery, and she had a head shaped like a banana.

MOMMY.   You ungrateful— Daddy? Daddy, you see how ungrateful she is after all these years, after all the things we've done for her? (*To* GRANDMA) One of these days you're going away in a van; that's what's going to happen to you!

GRANDMA.   Do tell!

MRS. BARKER.   Like a banana?

GRANDMA.   Yup, just like a banana.

MRS. BARKER.   My word!

MOMMY.   You stop listening to her; she'll say anything. Just the other night she called Daddy a hedgehog.

MRS. BARKER.   She didn't!

GRANDMA.   That's right, baby; you stick up for me.

MOMMY.   I don't know where she gets the words; on the television, maybe.

MRS. BARKER.   Did you really call him a hedgehog?

GRANDMA.   Oh look; what difference does it make whether I did or not?

DADDY.   Grandma's right. Leave Grandma alone.

MOMMY (*To* DADDY).   How dare you!

GRANDMA.   Oh, leave her alone, Daddy; the kid's all mixed up.

MOMMY.   You see? I told you. It's all those television shows. Daddy, you go right into Grandma's room and take her television and shake all the tubes loose.

DADDY.   Don't mention tubes to me.

MOMMY.   Oh! Mommy forgot! (*To* MRS. BARKER) Daddy has tubes now, where he used to have tracts.

MRS. BARKER.   Is that a fact!

GRANDMA.   I know why this dear lady is here.

MOMMY.   You be still.

MRS. BARKER.   Oh, I do wish you'd tell me.

MOMMY.   No! No! That wouldn't be fair at all.

DADDY.   Besides, she knows why she's here; she's here because we called them.

MRS. BARKER.   La! But that still leaves me puzzled. I know I'm here because you called us, but I'm such a busy girl, with this committee and that committee, and the Responsible Citizens Activities I indulge in.

MOMMY.   Oh my; busy, busy.

MRS. BARKER.   Yes, indeed. So I'm afraid you'll have to give me some help.

MOMMY.   Oh, no. No, you must be mistaken, I can't believe we asked you here to give you any help. With the way taxes are these days, and the way you can't get satisfaction in ANYTHING . . . no, I don't believe so.

DADDY.   And if you need help . . . why, I should think you'd apply for a Fulbright Scholarship . . .

MOMMY.   And if not that . . . why, then a Guggenheim Fellowship. . . .

GRANDMA.   Oh, come on; why not shoot the works and try for the Prix de Rome. (*Under her breath to* MOMMY *and* DADDY) Beasts!

MRS. BARKER.   Oh, what a jolly family. But let me think. I'm knee-deep in work these days; there's the Ladies' Auxiliary Air Raid committee, for one thing; how do you feel about air raids?

MOMMY.   Oh, I'd say we're hostile.

DADDY.   Yes, definitely; we're hostile.

MRS. BARKER.   Then, you'll be no help there. There's too much hostility in the world these days as it is; but I'll not badger you! There's a surfeit of badgers as well.

GRANDMA.   While we're at it, there's been a run on old people, too. The Department of Agriculture, or maybe it wasn't the Department of Agriculture—anyway, it was some department that's run by a girl—put out figures showing that ninety per cent of the adult population of the country is over eighty years old . . . or eighty per cent is over ninety years old . . .

MOMMY.   You're such a liar! You just finished saying that everyone is middle-aged.

GRANDMA.   I'm just telling you what the government says . . . that doesn't have anything to do with what . . .

MOMMY.   It's that television! Daddy, go break her television.

GRANDMA.   You won't find it.

DADDY (*Wearily getting up*).   If I must . . . I must.

MOMMY.   And don't step on the Pekinese; it's blind.

DADDY.   It may be blind, but Daddy isn't.

(He exits, through the archway, stage left)

GRANDMA.   You won't find *it*, either.

MOMMY.   Oh, I'm so fortunate to have such a husband. Just think; I could have a husband who was poor, or argumentative, or a husband who sat in a wheel chair all day . . . OOOOHHHH! *What* have I said? What *have* I said?

GRANDMA.   You said you could have a husband who sat in a wheel . . .

MOMMY.   I'm mortified! I could die! I could cut my tongue out! I could . . .

MRS. BARKER (*Forcing a smile*).   Oh, now . . . now . . . don't think about it . . .

MOMMY.   I could . . . why, I could . . .

MRS. BARKER.   . . . don't think about it . . . really. . . .

MOMMY.   You're quite right. I won't think about it, and that way I'll forget that I ever said it, and that way it will be all right. (*Pause*) There . . . I've forgotten. Well, now, now that Daddy is out of the room we can have some girl talk.

MRS. BARKER.   I'm not sure that I . . .

MOMMY.   You *do* want to have some girl talk, don't you?

MRS. BARKER.   I was going to say I'm not sure that I wouldn't care for a glass of water. I feel a little faint.

MOMMY.   Grandma, go get Mrs. Barker a glass of water.

GRANDMA.   Go get it yourself. I quit.

MOMMY.   Grandma loves to do little things around the house; it gives her a false sense of security.

GRANDMA.   I quit! I'm through!

MOMMY.   Now, you be a good Grandma, or you know what will happen to you. You'll be taken away in a van.

GRANDMA.   You don't frighten me. I'm too old to be frightened. Besides . . .

MOMMY.   WELL! I'll tend to you later. I'll hide your teeth . . . I'll . . .

GRANDMA.   Everything's hidden.

MRS. BARKER.   I *am* going to faint. I *am.*

MOMMY.   Good heavens! I'll go myself. (*As she exits, through the archway, stage-left*) I'll fix you, Grandma. I'll take care of you later. (*She exits*)

GRANDMA.   Oh, go soak your head. (*To* MRS. BARKER) Well, dearie, how do you feel?

MRS. BARKER.   A little better, I think. Yes, much better, thank you, Grandma.

GRANDMA.   That's good.

MRS. BARKER.   But . . . I feel so lost . . . not knowing why I'm here . . . and, on top of it, they say I was here before.

GRANDMA.   Well, you were. You weren't *here*, exactly, because we've moved around a lot, from one apartment to another, up and down the social ladder like mice, if you like similes.

MRS. BARKER.   I don't . . . particularly.

GRANDMA.   Well, then, I'm sorry.

MRS. BARKER (*Suddenly*).   Grandma, I feel I can trust you.

GRANDMA.   Don't be too sure; it's every man for himself around this place . . .

MRS. BARKER.   Oh . . . is it? Nonetheless, I really do feel that I can trust you. *Please* tell me why they called and asked us to come. I implore you!

GRANDMA.   Oh my; that feels good. It's been so long since anybody implored me. Do it again. Implore me some more.

MRS. BARKER.   You're your daughter's mother, all right!

GRANDMA.   Oh, I don't mean to be hard. If you won't implore me, then beg me, or ask me, or entreat me . . . just anything like that.

MRS. BARKER.   You're a dreadful old woman!

GRANDMA.   You'll understand some day. Please!

MRS. BARKER.   Oh, for heaven's sake! . . . I implore you . . . I beg you . . . I beseech you!

GRANDMA.   Beseech! Oh, that's the nicest word I've heard in ages. You're a dear, sweet woman . . . You . . . beseech . . . me. I can't resist that.

MRS. BARKER.   Well, then . . . please tell me why they asked us to come.

GRANDMA.   Well, I'll give you a hint. That's the best I can do, because I'm a muddleheaded old woman. Now listen, because it's important. Once upon a time, not too very long ago, but a long enough time ago . . . oh, about twenty years ago . . . there was a man very much like Daddy, and a woman very much like Mommy, who were married to each other, very much like Mommy and Daddy are married to each other; and they lived in an apartment very much like one that's very much like this one, and they lived there with an old woman who was very much like yours truly, only younger, because it was some time ago; in fact, they were all somewhat younger.

MRS. BARKER.   How fascinating!

GRANDMA.   Now, at the same time, there was a dear lady very much like you, only younger then, who did all sorts of Good Works . . . And one of the Good Works this dear lady did was in something very much like a volunteer capacity for an organization very much like the Bye-Bye Adoption Service, which is nearby and which was run by a terribly deaf old lady very much like the Miss Bye-Bye who runs the Bye-Bye Adoption Service nearby.

MRS. BARKER.   How enthralling!

GRANDMA.   Well, be that as it may. Nonetheless, one afternoon this man, who was very much like Daddy, and this woman who was very much like Mommy came to see this dear lady who did all the Good Works, who was very much like you, dear, and they were very sad and very hopeful, and they cried and smiled and bit their fingers, and they said all the most intimate things.

MRS. BARKER.   How spellbinding! What did they say?

GRANDMA.   Well, it was very sweet. The woman, who was very much like Mommy, said that she and the man who was very much like Daddy had never been blessed with anything very much like a bumble of joy.

MRS. BARKER.   A what?

GRANDMA.   A bumble; a bumble of joy.

MRS. BARKER.   Oh, like bundle.

GRANDMA.   Well, yes; very much like it. Bundle, bumble; who cares? At any rate, the woman, who was very much like Mommy, said that they wanted a bumble of their own, but that the man, who was very much like Daddy, couldn't have a bumble; and the man, who was very much like Daddy, said that yes, they had wanted a bumble of their own, but that the woman, who was very much like Mommy, couldn't have one, and that now they wanted to buy something very much like a bumble.

MRS. BARKER.   How engrossing!

GRANDMA.   Yes. And the dear lady, who was very much like you, said something that was very much like, "Oh, what a shame; but take heart . . . I think we have just the bumble *for* you." And, well, the lady, who was very much like Mommy, and the man, who was very much like Daddy, cried and smiled and bit their fingers, and said some more intimate things, which were totally irrelevant but which were pretty hot stuff, and so the dear lady, who was very much like you, and who had something very much like a penchant for pornography, listened with something very much like enthusiasm. "Whee," she said. "Whoooopeeeeee!" But that's beside the point.

MRS. BARKER.   I suppose *so.* But how gripping!

GRANDMA.   Anyway . . . they *bought* something very much like a bumble, and they took it away with them. But . . . things didn't work out very well.

MRS. BARKER.   You mean there was trouble?

GRANDMA.   You got it. (*With a glance through the archway*) But, I'm going to have to speed up now because I think I'm leaving soon.

MRS. BARKER.   Oh. Are you really?

GRANDMA.   Yup.

MRS. BARKER. But old people don't go anywhere; they're either taken places, or put places.

GRANDMA. Well, this old person is different. Anyway . . . things started going badly.

MRS. BARKER. Oh yes. Yes.

GRANDMA. Weeeeellll . . . in the first place, it turned out the bumble didn't look like either one of its parents. That was enough of a blow, but things got worse. One night, it cried its heart out, if you can imagine such a thing.

MRS. BARKER. Cried its heart out! Well!

GRANDMA. But that was only the beginning. Then it turned out it only had eyes for its Daddy.

MRS. BARKER. For its Daddy! Why, any self-respecting woman would have gouged those eyes right out of its head.

GRANDMA. Well, she did. That's exactly what she did. But then, it kept its nose up in the air.

MRS. BARKER. Ufggh! How disgusting!

GRANDMA. That's what they thought. But *then*, it began to develop an interest in its you-know-what.

MRS. BARKER. In its you-know-what! Well! I hope they cut its hands off at the wrists!

GRANDMA. Well, yes, they did that eventually. But first, they cut off its you-know-what.

MRS. BARKER. A much better idea!

GRANDMA. That's what they thought. But after they cut off its you-know-what, it *still* put its hands under the covers, *looking* for its you-know-what. So, finally, they *had* to cut off its hands at the wrists.

MRS. BARKER. Naturally!

GRANDMA. And it was such a resentful bumble. Why, one day it called its Mommy a dirty name.

MRS. BARKER. Well, I hope they cut its tongue out!

GRANDMA. Of course. And then, as it got bigger, they found out all sorts of terrible things about it, like: it didn't have a head on its shoulders, it had no guts, it was spineless, its feet were made of clay . . . just dreadful things.

MRS. BARKER. Dreadful!

GRANDMA. So you can understand how they became discouraged.

MRS. BARKER. I certainly can! And what did they do?

GRANDMA. What did they do? Well, for the last straw, it finally up and died; and you can imagine how *that* made them feel, their having paid for it, and all. So, they called up the lady who sold them the bumble in the first place and told her to come right over to their apartment. They wanted satisfaction; they wanted their money back. That's what they wanted.

MRS. BARKER. My, my, my.

GRANDMA. How do you like *them* apples?

MRS. BARKER. My, my, my.

DADDY (*Off stage*). Mommy! I can't find Grandma's television, and I can't find the Pekinese, either.

MOMMY (*Off stage*).   Isn't that funny! And I can't find the water.

GRANDMA.   Heh, heh, heh. I told them everything was hidden.

MRS. BARKER.   Did you hide the water, too?

GRANDMA (*Puzzled*).   No. No, I didn't do *that*.

DADDY (*Off stage*).   The truth of the matter is, I can't even find Grandma's room.

GRANDMA.   Heh, heh, heh.

MRS. BARKER.   My! You certainly did hide things, didn't you?

GRANDMA.   Sure, kid, sure.

MOMMY (*Sticking her head in the room*).   Did you ever hear of such a thing, Grandma? Daddy can't find your television, and he can't find the Pekinese, and the truth of the matter is he can't even find your room.

GRANDMA.   I told you. I hid everything.

MOMMY.   Nonsense, Grandma! Just wait until I get my hands on you. You're a troublemaker . . . that's what you are.

GRANDMA.   Well, I'll be out of here pretty soon, baby.

MOMMY.   Oh, you don't know how right you are! Daddy's been wanting to send you away for a long time now, but I've been restraining him. I'll tell you one thing, though . . . I'm getting sick and tired of this fighting, and I might just let him have his way. Then you'll see what'll happen. Away you'll go; in a van, too. I'll let Daddy call the van man.

GRANDMA.   I'm way ahead of you.

MOMMY.   How can you be so old and so smug at the same time? You have no sense of proportion.

GRANDMA.   You just answered your own question.

MOMMY.   Mrs. Barker, I'd much rather you came into the kitchen for that glass of water, what with Grandma out here, and all.

MRS. BARKER.   I don't see what Grandma has to do with it; and besides, I don't think you're very polite.

MOMMY.   You seem to forget that you're a guest in this house . . .

GRANDMA.   Apartment!

MOMMY.   Apartment! And that you're a professional woman. So, if you'll be so good as to come into the kitchen, I'll be more than happy to show you where the water is, and where the glass is, and then you can put two and two together, if you're clever enough.

(*She vanishes*)

MRS. BARKER (*After a moment's consideration*).   I suppose she's right.

GRANDMA.   Well, that's how it is when people call you up and ask you over to do something for them.

MRS. BARKER.   I suppose you're right, too. Well, Grandma, it's been very nice talking to you.

GRANDMA.   And I've enjoyed listening. Say, don't tell Mommy or Daddy that I gave you that hint, will you?

MRS. BARKER.   Oh, dear me, the hint! I'd forgotten about it, if you can imagine such a thing. No, I won't breathe a word of it to them.

GRANDMA.   I don't know if it helped you any . . .

MRS. BARKER.   I can't tell, yet. I'll have to . . . what *is* the word I want? . . . I'll have to relate it . . . that's it . . . I'll have to relate it to certain things that I *know* and . . . draw . . . conclusions . . . What I'll really have to do is to see if it applies to anything. I mean, after all, I *do* do volunteer work for an adoption service, but it isn't very much *like* the Bye-Bye Adoption Service . . . it *is* the Bye-Bye Adoption Service . . . and while I can remember Mommy and Daddy coming to see me, oh, about twenty years ago, about buying a bumble, I can't quite remember anyone very much *like* Mommy and Daddy coming to see me about buying a bumble. Don't you see? It really presents quite a problem . . . I'll have to think about it . . . mull it . . . but at any rate, it was truly first-class of you to try to help me. Oh, will you still be here after I've had my drink of water?

GRANDMA.   Probably . . . I'm not as spry as I used to be.

MRS. BARKER.   Oh. Well, I won't say good-by then.

GRANDMA.   No. Don't. (MRS. BARKER *exits through the archway*) People don't say good-by to old people because they think they'll frighten them. Lordy! If they only knew how awful "hello" and "my, you're looking chipper" sounded, they wouldn't say those things either. The truth is, there isn't much you *can* say to old people that doesn't sound just terrible. (*The doorbell rings*) Come on in! (*The* YOUNG MAN *enters.* GRANDMA *looks him over*) Well, now, aren't you a breath of fresh air!

YOUNG MAN.   Hello there.

GRANDMA.   My, my, my. Are you the van man?

YOUNG MAN.   The what?

GRANDMA.   The van man. The van man. Are you come to take me away?

YOUNG MAN.   I don't know what you're talking about.

GRANDMA.   Oh. (*Pause*) Well. (*Pause*) My, my, aren't you something!

YOUNG MAN.   Hm?

GRANDMA.   I said, my, my, aren't you something.

YOUNG MAN.   Oh. Thank you.

GRANDMA.   You don't sound very enthusiastic.

YOUNG MAN.   Oh, I'm . . . I'm used to it.

GRANDMA.   Yup . . . yup. You know, if I were about a hundred and fifty years younger I could go for you.

YOUNG MAN.   Yes, I imagine so.

GRANDMA.   Unh-hunh . . . will you look at those muscles!

YOUNG MAN (*Flexing his muscles*).   Yes, they're quite good, aren't they?

GRANDMA.   Boy, they sure are. They natural?

YOUNG MAN.   Well the basic structure was there, but I've done some work, too . . . you know, in a gym.

GRANDMA.   I'll bet you have. You ought to be in the movies, boy.

YOUNG MAN.   I know.

GRANDMA.   Yup! Right up there on the old silver screen. But I suppose you've heard that before.

YOUNG MAN.   Yes, I have.

GRANDMA.   You ought to try out for them . . . the movies.

YOUNG MAN.   Well, actually, I may have a career there yet. I've lived out on the West Coast almost all my life . . . and I've met a few people who . . .

might be able to help me. I'm not in too much of a hurry, though. I'm almost as young as I look.

GRANDMA.   Oh, that's nice. And will you look at that face!

YOUNG MAN.   Yes, it's quite good, isn't it? Clean-cut, midwest farm boy type, almost insultingly good-looking in a typically American way. Good profile, straight nose, honest eyes, wonderful smile . . .

GRANDMA.   Yup. Boy, you know what you are, don't you? You're the American Dream, that's what you are. All those other people, they don't know what they're talking about. You . . . *you* are the American Dream.

YOUNG MAN.   Thanks.

MOMMY (*Off stage*).   Who rang the doorbell?

GRANDMA (*Shouting off-stage*).   The American Dream!

MOMMY (*Off stage*).   What? What was that, Grandma?

GRANDMA (*Shouting*).   The American Dream! The American Dream! Damn it!

DADDY (*Off stage*).   How's that, Mommy?

MOMMY (*Off stage*).   Oh, some gibberish; pay no attention. Did you find Grandma's room?

DADDY (*Off stage*).   No. I can't even find Mrs. Barker.

YOUNG MAN.   What was all that?

GRANDMA.   Oh, that was just the folks, but let's not talk about them, honey; let's talk about you.

YOUNG MAN.   All right.

GRANDMA.   Well, let's see. If you're not the van man, what are you doing here?

YOUNG MAN.   I'm looking for work.

GRANDMA.   Are you! Well, what kind of work?

YOUNG MAN.   Oh, almost anything . . . almost anything that pays. I'll do almost anything for money.

GRANDMA.   Will you . . . will you? Hmmmm. I wonder if there's anything you could do around here?

YOUNG MAN.   There might be. It looked to be a likely building.

GRANDMA.   It's always looked to be a rather unlikely building to me, but I suppose you'd know better than I.

YOUNG MAN.   I can sense these things.

GRANDMA.   There *might* be something you could do around here. Stay there! Don't come any closer.

YOUNG MAN.   Sorry.

GRANDMA.   I don't mean I'd *mind*. I don't know whether I'd mind, or not . . . But it wouldn't look well; it would look just *awful*.

YOUNG MAN.   Yes; I suppose so.

GRANDMA.   Now, stay there, let me concentrate. What could you do? The folks have been in something of a quandary around here today, sort of a dilemma, and I wonder if you mightn't be some help.

YOUNG MAN.   I hope so . . . if there's money in it. Do you have any money?

GRANDMA.   Money! Oh, there's more money around here than you'd know what to do with.

YOUNG MAN.   I'm not so sure.

GRANDMA.   Well, maybe not. Besides, I've got money of my own.

YOUNG MAN.   You have?

GRANDMA.   Sure. Old people quite often have lots of money; more often than most people expect. Come here, so I can whisper to you . . . not too close. I might faint.

YOUNG MAN.   Oh, I'm sorry.

GRANDMA.   It's all right, dear. Anyway . . . have you ever heard of that big baking contest they run? The one where all the ladies get together in a big barn and bake away?

YOUNG MAN.   I'm . . . not . . . sure . . .

GRANDMA.   Not so close. Well, it doesn't matter whether you've heard of it or not. The important thing is—and I don't want anybody to hear this . . . the folks think I haven't been out of the house in eight years—the important thing is that I won first prize in that baking contest this year. Oh, it was in all the papers; not under my own name, though. I used a *nom de boulangère*; I called myself Uncle Henry.

YOUNG MAN.   Did you?

GRANDMA.   Why not? I didn't see any reason not to. I look just as much like an old man as I do like an old woman. And you know what I called it . . . what I won for?

YOUNG MAN.   No. What did you call it?

GRANDMA.   I called it Uncle Henry's Day-Old Cake.

YOUNG MAN.   That's a very nice name.

GRANDMA.   And it wasn't any trouble, either. All I did was go out and get a store-bought cake, and keep it around for a while, and then slip it in, unbeknownst to anybody. Simple.

YOUNG MAN.   You're a very resourceful person.

GRANDMA.   Pioneer stock.

YOUNG MAN.   Is all this true? Do you want me to believe all this?

GRANDMA.   Well, you can believe it or not . . . it doesn't make any difference to me. All *I* know is, Uncle Henry's Day-Old Cake won me twenty-five thousand smakerolas.

YOUNG MAN.   Twenty-five thou—

GRANDMA.   Right on the old loggerhead. Now . . . how do you like them apples?

YOUNG MAN.   Love 'em.

GRANDMA.   I thought you'd be impressed.

YOUNG MAN.   Money talks.

GRANDMA.   Hey! You look familiar.

YOUNG MAN.   Hm? Pardon?

GRANDMA.   I said, you look familiar.

YOUNG MAN.   Well, I've done some modeling.

GRANDMA.   No . . . no. I don't mean that. You look familiar.

YOUNG MAN.   Well, I'm a type.

GRANDMA.   Yup; you sure are. Why do you say you'd do anything for money . . . if you don't mind my being nosy?

YOUNG MAN.   No, no. It's part of the interviews. I'll be happy to tell you.

It's that I have no talents at all, except what you see . . . my person; my body, my face. In every other way I am incomplete, and I must therefore . . . compensate.

GRANDMA. What do you mean, incomplete? You look pretty complete to me.

YOUNG MAN. I think I can explain it to you, partially because you're very old, and very old people have perceptions they keep to themselves, because if they expose them to other people . . . well, you know what ridicule and neglect are.

GRANDMA. I do, child, I do.

YOUNG MAN. Then listen. My mother died the night that I was born, and I never knew my father; I doubt my mother did. But, I wasn't alone, because lying with me . . . in the placenta . . . there was someone else . . . my brother . . . my twin.

GRANDMA. Oh, my child.

YOUNG MAN. We were identical twins . . . he and I . . . not fraternal . . . identical; we were derived from the same ovum; and in *this,* in that we were twins not from separate ova but from the same one, we had a kinship such as you cannot imagine. We . . . we felt each other breathe . . . his heartbeats thundered in my temples . . . mine in his . . . our stomachs ached and we cried for feeding at the same time . . . are you old enough to understand?

GRANDMA. I think so, child; I think I'm nearly old enough.

YOUNG MAN. I hope so. But we were separated when we were still very young, my brother, my twin and I . . . inasmuch as you can separate one being. We were torn apart . . . thrown to opposite ends of the continent. I don't know what became of my brother . . . to the rest of myself . . . except that, from time to time, in the years that have passed, I have suffered losses . . . that I can't explain. A fall from grace . . . a departure of innocence . . . loss . . . loss. How can I put it to you? All right; like this: Once . . . it was as if all at once my heart . . . became numb . . . almost as though I . . . almost as though . . . just like that . . . it had been wrenched from my body . . . and from that time I have been unable to love. Once . . . I was asleep at the time . . . I awoke, and my eyes were burning. And since that time I have been unable to see anything, *anything,* with pity, with affection . . . with anything but . . . cool disinterest. And my groin . . . even there . . . since one time . . . one specific agony . . . since then I have not been able to *love* anyone with my body. And even my hands . . . I cannot touch another person and feel· love. And there is more . . . there are more losses, but it all comes down to this: I no longer have the capacity to feel anything. I have no emotions. I have been drained, torn asunder . . . disemboweled. I have, now, only my person . . . my body, my face. I use what I have . . . I let people love me . . . I let people touch me . . . I let them draw pleasure from my groin . . . from my presence . . . from the fact of me . . . but, that is all it comes to. As I told you, I am incomplete . . . I can feel nothing. I can feel nothing. And so . . . here I am . . . as you see me. I am . . . but this . . . what you see. And it will always be thus.

GRANDMA. Oh, my child; my child. (*Long pause; then*) I was mistaken . . . before. I don't know you from somewhere, but I knew . . . once . . . someone very much like you . . . or, very much as perhaps you were.

YOUNG MAN.   Be careful; be very careful. What I have told you may not be true. In my profession . . .

GRANDMA.   Shhhhhh.

(The YOUNG MAN *bows his head, in acquiescence)*

Someone . . . to be more precise . . . who might have turned out to be very much like you might have turned out to be. And . . . unless I'm terribly mistaken . . . you've found yourself a job.

YOUNG MAN.   What are my duties?

MRS. BARKER *(Off stage).*   Yoo-hoo! Yoo-hoo!

GRANDMA.   Oh-oh. You'll . . . you'll have to play it by ear, my dear . . . unless I get a chance to talk to you again. I've got to go into my act, now.

YOUNG MAN.   But, I . . .

GRANDMA.   Yoo-hoo!

MRS. BARKER *(Coming through archway).*   Yoo-hoo . . . . oh, there you are, Grandma. I'm glad to see somebody. I can't find Mommy or Daddy. *(Double takes)* Well . . . who's this?

GRANDMA.   This? Well . . . un . . . oh, this is the . . . uh . . . the van man. That's who it is . . . the van man.

MRS. BARKER.   So! It's true! They *did* call the van man. They *are* having you carted away.

GRANDMA *(Shrugging).*   Well, you know. It figures.

MRS. BARKER *(To* YOUNG MAN).   How dare you cart this poor old woman away!

YOUNG MAN *(After a quick look at* GRANDMA, *who nods).*   I do what I'm paid to do. I don't ask any questions.

MRS. BARKER *(After a brief pause).*   Oh. *(Pause)* Well, you're quite right, of course, and I shouldn't meddle.

GRANDMA *(To* YOUNG MAN).   Dear, will you take my things out to the van?

(She points to the boxes)

YOUNG MAN *(After only the briefest hesitation).*   Why certainly.

GRANDMA *(As the* YOUNG MAN *takes up half the boxes, exits by the front door).*   Isn't that a nice young van man?

MRS. BARKER *(Shaking her head in disbelief, watching the* YOUNG MAN *exit).*   Unh-hunh . . . some things have changed for the better. I remember when I had *my* mother carted off . . . the van man who came for her wasn't anything near as nice as this one.

GRANDMA.   Oh, did you have your mother carted off, too?

MRS. BARKER *(Cheerfully).*   Why certainly! Didn't you?

GRANDMA *(Puzzling).*   No . . . no, I didn't. At least, I can't remember. Listen dear; I got to talk to you for a second.

MRS. BARKER.   Why certainly, Grandma.

GRANDMA.   Now, listen.

MRS. BARKER.   Yes, Grandma. Yes.

GRANDMA.   Now listen carefully. You got this dilemma here with Mommy and Daddy . . .

MRS. BARKER.   Yes! I wonder where they've gone to?

GRANDMA.   They'll be back in. Now, LISTEN!

MRS. BARKER.   Oh, I'm sorry.

GRANDMA.   Now, you got this dilemma here with Mommy and Daddy, and I think I got the way out for you.

(The YOUNG MAN *re-enters through the front door)*

Will you take the rest of my things out now, dear?

(To MRS. BARKER, *while the* YOUNG MAN *takes the rest of the boxes, exits again by the front door)*

Fine. Now listen, dear.

(She begins to whisper in MRS. BARKER'S *ear)*

MRS. BARKER.   Oh! Oh! Oh! I don't think I could . . . do you really think I could? Well, why not? What a wonderful idea . . . what an absolutely wonderful idea!

GRANDMA.   Well, yes, I thought it was.

MRS. BARKER.   And you so old!

GRANDMA.   Heh, heh, heh.

MRS. BARKER.   Well, I think it's absolutely marvelous, anyway. I'm going to find Mommy and Daddy right now.

GRANDMA.   Good. You do that.

MRS. BARKER.   Well, now. I think I will say good-by. I can't thank you enough.

(She starts to exit through the archway)

GRANDMA.   You're welcome. Say it!

MRS. BARKER.   Huh? What?

GRANDMA.   Say good-by.

MRS. BARKER.   Oh. Good-by. *(She exits)* Mommy! I say, Mommy! Daddy!

GRANDMA.   Good-by. *(By herself now, she looks about)* Ah me. *(Shakes her head)* Ah me. *(Takes in the room)* Good-by.

(The YOUNG MAN *re-enters)*

GRANDMA.   Oh, hello, there.

YOUNG MAN.   All the boxes are outside.

GRANDMA *(A little sadly)*.   I don't know why I bother to take them with me. They don't have much in them . . . some old letters, a couple of regrets . . . Pekinese . . . blind at that . . . the television . . . my Sunday teeth . . . eighty-six years of living . . . some sounds . . . a few images, a little garbled by now . . . and, well . . . *(She shrugs)* . . . you know . . . the things one accumulates.

YOUNG MAN.   Can I get you . . . a cab, or something?

GRANDMA.   Oh no, dear . . . thank you just the same. I'll take it from here.

YOUNG MAN.   And what shall I do now?

GRANDMA.   Oh, you stay here, dear. It will all become clear to you. It will be explained. You'll understand.

YOUNG MAN.   Very well.

GRANDMA (*After one more look about*).   Well . . .

YOUNG MAN.   Let me see you to the elevator.

GRANDMA.   Oh . . . that *would* be nice, dear.

(They both exit by the front door, slowly)

(Enter MRS. BARKER, *followed by* MOMMY *and* DADDY)

MRS. BARKER.   . . . and I'm happy to tell you that the whole thing's settled. Just like that.

MOMMY.   Oh, we're so glad. We were afraid there might be a problem, what with delays, and all.

DADDY.   Yes, we're very relieved.

MRS. BARKER.   Well, now; that's what professional women are for.

MOMMY.   Why . . . where's Grandma? Grandma's not here! Where's Grandma? And look! The boxes are gone, too. Grandma's gone, and so are the boxes. She's taken off, and she's stolen something! Daddy!

MRS. BARKER.   Why, Mommy, the van man was here.

MOMMY (*Startled*).   The what?

MRS. BARKER.   The van man. The van man was here.

(The lights might dim a little, suddenly)

MOMMY (*Shakes her head*).   No, that's impossible.

MRS. BARKER.   Why, I saw him with my own two eyes.

MOMMY (*Near tears*).   No, no, that's impossible. No. There's no such thing as the van man. There is no van man. We . . . we made him up. Grandma? Grandma?

DADDY (*Moving to* MOMMY).   There, there, now.

MOMMY.   Oh Daddy . . . where's Grandma?

DADDY.   There, there, now.

(While DADDY *is comforting* MOMMY, GRANDMA *comes out, stage right, near the footlights)*

GRANDMA (*To the audience*).   Shhhhhh! I want to watch this.

(She motions to MRS BARKER *who, with a secret smile, tiptoes to the front door and opens it. The* YOUNG MAN *is framed therein. Lights up full again as he steps into the room)*

MRS. BARKER.   Surprise! Surprise! Here we are!

MOMMY.   What? What?

DADDY.   Hm? What?

MOMMY (*Her tears merely sniffles now*).   What surprise?

MRS. BARKER.   Why, I told you. The surprise I told you about.

DADDY.   You . . . you know, Mommy.

MOMMY.   Sur . . . prise?

DADDY (*urging her to cheerfulness*).   You remember, Mommy; why we asked . . . uh . . . what's-her-name to come here?

MRS. BARKER.   Mrs. Barker, if you don't mind.

DADDY.   Yes. Mommy? You remember now? About the bumble . . . about wanting satisfaction?

MOMMY (*Her sorrow turning into delight*).   Yes. Why yes! Of course! Yes! Oh, how wonderful!

MRS. BARKER (*To the* YOUNG MAN).   This is Mommy.

YOUNG MAN.   How . . . how do you do?

MRS. BARKER (*Stage whisper*).   Her name's Mommy.

YOUNG MAN.   How . . . how do you do, Mommy?

MOMMY.   Well! Hello there!

MRS. BARKER (*To the* YOUNG MAN).   And that is Daddy.

YOUNG MAN.   How do you do, sir?

DADDY.   How do you do?

MOMMY (*Herself again, circling the* YOUNG MAN, *feeling his arm, poking him*).   Yes, sir! Yes, sirree! Now this is more like it. Now this is a great deal more like it! Daddy! Come see. Come see if this isn't a great deal more like it.

DADDY.   I . . . I can see from here, Mommy. It does look a great deal more like it.

MOMMY.   Yes, sir. Yes sirree! Mrs. Barker, I don't know *how* to thank you.

MRS. BARKER.   Oh, don't worry about that. I'll send you a bill in the mail.

MOMMY.   What this really calls for is a celebration. It calls for a drink.

MRS. BARKER.   Oh, what a nice idea.

MOMMY.   There's some sauterne in the kitchen.

YOUNG MAN.   I'll go.

MOMMY.   Will you? Oh, how nice. The kitchen's through the archway there. (*As the* YOUNG MAN *exits: to* MRS. BARKER) He's very nice. Really top notch; much better than the other one.

MRS. BARKER.   I'm glad you're pleased. And I'm glad everything's all straightened out.

MOMMY.   Well, at least we know why we sent for you. We're glad that's cleared up. By the way, what's his name?

MRS. BARKER.   Ha! Call him whatever you like. He's yours. Call him what you called the other one.

MOMMY.   Daddy? What did we call the other one?

DADDY (*Puzzles*).   Why . . .

YOUNG MAN (*Re-entering with a tray on which are a bottle of sauterne and five glasses*).   Here we are!

MOMMY.   Hooray! Hooray!

MRS. BARKER.   Oh, good!

MOMMY (*Moving to the tray*).   So, let's— Five glasses? Why five? There are only four of us. Why five?

YOUNG MAN (*Catches* GRANDMA'S *eye;* GRANDMA *indicates she is not there*).   Oh, I'm sorry.

MOMMY.   You must learn to count. We're a wealthy family, and you must learn to count.

YOUNG MAN.   I will.

MOMMY.   Well, everybody take a glass. (*They do*) And we'll drink to celebrate. To satisfaction! Who says you can't get satisfaction these days!

MRS. BARKER.   What dreadful sauterne!

MOMMY.   Yes, isn't it? (*To* YOUNG MAN, *her voice already a little fuzzy from the wine*) You don't know how happy I am to see you! Yes sirree. Listen, that time we had with . . . with the other one. I'll tell you about it some time. (*Indicates* MRS. BARKER) After she's gone. She was responsible for all the trouble in the first place. I'll tell you all about it. (*Sidles up to him a little*) Maybe . . . maybe later tonight.

YOUNG MAN (*Not moving away*).   Why yes. That would be very nice.

MOMMY (*Puzzles*).   Something familiar about you . . . you know that? I can't quite place it . . .

GRANDMA (*Interrupting . . . to audience*).   Well, I guess that just about wraps it up. I mean, for better or worse, this is a comedy, and I don't think we'd better go any further. No, definitely not. So, let's leave things as they are right now . . . while everybody's happy . . . while everybody's got what he wants . . . or everybody's got what he thinks he wants. Good night, dears.

QUESTIONS

1. We have said that one of the hallmarks of absurdist drama is the way that playwrights purposely break the illusion that what is taking place on stage is "real." How does Albee do this in *The American Dream*? What does he achieve by preventing the audience from identifying with Mommy, Daddy, Grandma and the others as "real" characters of the kind Ibsen created?

2. Look back at the paragraph from Albee's preface to this play that we quoted in the introduction. Is this play too slender to bear the weight of the playwright's intention to provide "an examination of the American Scene"? Or is its streamlined comic form appropriate for such an inquiry? Is the play successful as "an attack on the substitution of artificial for real values in our society"?

3. Discuss the role of the Young Man in this play. Is he crucial to the meaning of the play? How does he figure in the conclusion of the dramatic action?

4. Grandma has the last lines: " . . . For better or worse, this is a comedy, and I don't think we'd better go any further. . . . Everybody's got what he wants . . . or everybody's got what he thinks he wants." Compare and contrast Albee's vision of what comedy can and should achieve with Molière's.

5. One critic has called *The American Dream* "a malignant fable for our time." What are the play's "fable-like" elements? In what sense are they "malignant"?

6

CLASSIC AMERICAN DRAMA

A merican theatergoers have had for decades a rich variety of plays available to them. Every kind of play, from ancient Greek drama (in excellent translations), to medieval drama (usually presented by university or church groups), to all of Shakespeare, to French comedy of Molière's time and later, to the drama of the great realists and absurdists of this century: all this and much more can be seen by people in this country who wish to appreciate the profusion of dramatic achievement that is their cultural legacy. Movies and television have brought such plays even closer, and today the theatergoer might need to go no further than his TV to be able to take advantage of the variety of dramatic possibility that the world has given him.

This fact might make it difficult to grasp the particular, even unique, characteristics of *American* drama. It might seem indistinguishable from all that surrounds it. But just as American literature differs in basic ways from English literature, and just as we know that the concerns of writers living on the European continent are not going to be identical to those of writers living on American soil, so we must recognize that in the most interesting and successful American plays, we will most likely see certain problems addressed which will be less prominent in the drama of other societies. These differences, of course, are not absolute. The themes of honesty, loyalty, betrayal, and self-knowledge tend to appear in all plays, indeed in all literature, but we should be able to note in the best American plays how these basic themes are given an American touch, how they are informed by the American sensibility, and how they help define the American character.

The three American plays that make up this section—Lillian Hellman's *The Little Foxes* (1939), Tennessee Williams' *The Glass Menagerie* (1944), Arthur Miller's *Death of a Salesman* (1947)—have each been given hundreds of productions and each has gained the stature of a classic American achievement. Audiences in this country and elsewhere have found in these plays a vision of problems and crises arising from this country's being what it is. The plays thus can remind Americans of their identity.

In each of the plays, for instance, one chief character or another is prompted to see, or to imagine, a "better," more "ideal," or "richer" life. In *The Little Foxes*, Birdie has a memory flowering constantly in her mind; she

889

thinks of the ancestral home, Lionnet, now no longer hers, where "the lawn was so smooth all the way down to the river, with the trims of zinnias and red-feather plush. And the figs and blue little plums and the scuppernongs. . . ." *The Glass Menagerie*, explicitly called a *memory play*, features a woman who dwells obsessively on her own romantic past, one she imagines was made madly successful by a constant round of "gentlemen callers" from the finest families in the Mississippi Delta. And in *Death of a Salesman*, Willy Loman is overwhelmed by fantasies of a land where he would be able to find immense success, and about which he would be able to say, as does his uncle Ben, " . . . when I walked into the jungle, I was seventeen. When I walked out I was twenty-one. And, by God, I was rich!"

Whether this land is in the past, as it is for Hellman's Birdie and Williams's Amanda Wingfield, or in the inaccessible future, as it is for Miller's Willy, it serves as the playwright's acknowledgment that much of the American dream is based on the belief that somewhere "out there" things will be much better for each of us, that Americans have as their destiny the progress toward a promised land, and that the frontier which we have yet to explore will give us the bountiful prospects that are rightfully ours. As his uncle tells Willy: "There's a new continent at your doorstep, William. You could walk out rich. Rich!" Willy wants to go forward into that continent but he is confined to his utterly dismal world of failure and disappointment. Birdie and Amanda each want to go backward to the world of the plantation, of "a great big place with white columns," but are prisoners in a world of utterly commonplace realities, vulgar striving and, in the case of Birdie at least, mean ambition. In each of these plays, one is brought face to face with people, strangely incomplete people, who have ideals or aspirations too large for life to accommodate.

Another prominent theme in the three plays is that of success and its costs. If the United States is, by reputation, the one place where anyone with initiative and courage can rise to prosperity, it is also, as a consequence, the place where a lack of personal achievement is most conspicuous. Not to triumph in a land where the advantages and possibilities are so great is truly to fail. Hence Willy Loman is bowed down by his sense that he has done nothing, that his two boys have done nothing, and that his family is encircled by people who have done everything. The importance of success to the Giddens family in *The Little Foxes* is so great that almost every member of that family is willing to sacrifice their collective sense of honor and their loyalties to each other for material gain. And in *The Glass Menagerie*, success is rendered either as fantasy—Amanda's notions of a constant stream of "gentlemen callers" for her desperately shy daughter Laura, who, wrapped in dreams of her own, retreats from the real world represented by a mediocre business school. Or success is rendered as all too real and demoralizing—Tom Wingfield, trapped in a ill-paying job in a warehouse. Where Amanda's successes are illusory and Laura's entirely internal and fragile, Tom's minimal successes give him neither joy nor satisfaction. Unlike his mother and his sister, Tom *can* see reality (just as can the wholly generous and wholly practical Jim O'Connor), but for him to grasp reality, Williams seems to say, is to take on a terrible burden. Tom must bear the responsibility of forcing truth and reality into the make-believe world of Amanda and Laura. In so doing, he causes them genuine pain. Williams, along with Hellman and Miller, prompts us to conclude that personal success (which in Tom's case consists of his having "to act without pity"), might be gained only at the expense of making others suffer.

Tom's own plight—knowing the truth but still being imprisoned in an unrewarding job and having no outlet for his own ambitious dreams save an endless round of moviegoing—should remind us of a fact about much of modern drama in general, and American drama in particular: that it is a drama without kings, without noble heroes. For all his honesty and intelligent understanding of the differences between fantasy and reality, Tom is hardly cut out of the same cloth as Hamlet (who also knew he had to be "cruel only to be kind"), nor is the perceptive and long-suffering Horace Giddens in *The Little Foxes* made of the same stuff as is Oedipus. And Willy Loman, although he suffers greatly and has high ambitions, would not be a hero recognizable to a Greek or Elizabethan audience. Indeed, Tennessee Williams himself once said that the theater is a place "where one has time for the problems of people to whom one would show the door if they came to one's office for a job." As we observed earlier in our discussions, modern drama is the drama of the common or ordinary individual. And American drama, written in a nation emphasizing the dignity of that common individual, is a drama in which heroism of the traditional kind is made virtually impossible.

If it is a drama written *about* the common individual, it is also a drama written *for* that individual. The great successes of the American theater are, by and large, commercial successes. They appeal to many Americans, often in many cities, and often for long periods of time. The plays in this section have been just such commercial successes. When they came to Broadway, their runs were long; production in other cities followed; each of the plays still enjoys popularity. These facts tell us something about the plays. They are not, in a technical sense, highly experimental. *Death of a Salesman* and *The Glass Menagerie* momentarily diverge from the rules and expectations of dramatic realism; these are the moments when Willy, looking back through his life from 1928 to 1942, comes into the presence of a figure from his past and speaks or listens to him, or the moments when Tom Wingfield steps out of his role as a character *in* the play and becomes a commentator *about* the play. Then the hard walls of the respective sets become permeable, and Willy can walk wherever he wants and Tom can say whatever he wants. But *The Glass Menagerie* takes place in only one location (an apartment and an alley in St. Louis), most of the action of *Death of a Salesman* occurs in Willy's house and yard, and the action of *The Little Foxes* is limited to the living room of the Giddens house.

In such drama, then, we are not being urged to concentrate on theatrical innovation, but on the play's engagement with life as we know it and on the moral significance of its action. Hence the function of plot is of extreme importance to such plays. We are made to want to know how Regina Giddens and Horace Giddens will struggle with each other and who will emerge the victor in their cruel contest of wills. We wait in horrible fascination as the mystery of Willy Loman's toying with suicide becomes at last a reality; we want to know how and when he will end his life. In *The Glass Menagerie* we await the arrival of the gentleman caller, somehow knowing that, when he comes, the world of dreams in which Amanda and Laura Wingfield have kept such an uneasy existence will be given a terrible jolt.

In sum, this kind of classic American drama does not stretch the traditional limits of dramatic convention (as does, for instance, Edward Albee's *The American Dream*). Indeed, in a play like *The Little Foxes*, the dramatist's skill wholly resides in bringing together, with efficiency and adroitness, a cast of very different characters and forcing them, through their differences, to reveal the crisis that will change or even destroy their lives. Such plays live for their climaxes: the death of Willy; the arrival of perfectly matter-of-fact Jim O'Connor and the consequent demolition of Amanda's dreams; the ruination of Regina.

One of the important features of traditional drama that is retained by each of the three playwrights is the conception and use of the tragic flaw. Although Willy Loman is everywhere choked by the city and weighed down by the routines of commercial life, his plight is not ultimately to be explained by social causes; he is no simple victim of capitalism and commercialism. Instead, he is a man who has never really reached the beginnings of self-knowledge. For him, as he pitiably admits, victory in life is "not just to be liked, but to be well-liked." His every act seems to be controlled by his desire for universal esteem. Around this desire accumulate all his illusions and confusions: he will not allow himself to see the true circumstances of his favored son Biff; he will not put the success of the fabulous Ben into perspective; he will not discard the many dreams he has of instant glory. The same debilitating lack of self-knowledge characterizes Amanda Wingfield and constantly threatens to overwhelm her daughter. The older woman never releases her hold on the dreams that keep her blind. The younger woman is able to retain her limited control of things only by holding on to the small and artificial world of her glass figurines. And the pathos of *The Little Foxes* stems from the collective resistance, on the part of the entire Giddens family, to the knowledge that what they are doing in their vicious struggle for money will destroy the only thing of true value that they have, namely the honor and dignity of that family. Horace knows what they are doing, but is powerless to stop the process; Regina is prevented by greed from seeing the consequence of her selfish and manipulative actions.

These three plays, then, grow out of concerns deep in the American consciousness: our fascination with success and failure, our sense that we have been providentially chosen to find a better and richer life somewhere else, and our deep-seated resistance to heroes who are not very much like ourselves. And, as plays, the three chosen for inclusion here reveal a crucial aspect of dramatic expression in America. That expression emphasizes the importance of plot and dispenses with more elaborate or experimental dramatic devices. It also emphasizes the belief that "character is destiny"—it says that people suffer the consequences of who they are and what their lack of self-knowledge dictates they shall be.

Lillian Hellman (1905–1984)
The Little Foxes

CHARACTERS

ADDIE
CAL
BIRDIE HUBBARD
OSCAR HUBBARD
LEO HUBBARD
REGINA GIDDENS
WILLIAM MARSHALL
BENJAMIN HUBBARD
ALEXANDRA GIDDENS
HORACE GIDDENS

SCENES

The scene of the play is the living room of the Giddens house, in a small town in the South.

Act I
The Spring of 1900, evening.

Act II
A week later, early morning.

Act III
Two weeks later, late afternoon.

There has been no attempt to write Southern dialect. It is to be understood that the accents are Southern.

ACT I

SCENE: *The living room of the Giddens home, in a small town in the deep South, the spring of 1900. Upstage is a staircase leading to the second story. Upstage, right, are double doors to the dining room. When these doors are open we see a section of the dining room and the furniture. Upstage, left, is an entrance hall with a coatrack and umbrella stand. There are large lace-curtained windows on the left wall. The room is lit by a center gas chandelier and painted china oil lamps on the tables. Against the wall is a large piano. Downstage, right, are a high couch, a large table, several chairs. Against the left back wall are a table and several chairs. Near the window there are a smaller couch and tables. The room is good-looking, the furniture expensive; but it reflects no particular taste. Everything is of the best and that is all.*

AT RISE: ADDIE, *a tall, nice-looking Negro woman of about fifty-five, is closing the windows. From behind the closed dining-room doors there is the sound of voices. After a second,* CAL, *a middle-aged Negro, comes in from the entrance hall carrying a tray with glasses and a bottle of port.* ADDIE *crosses, takes the tray from him, puts it on table, begins to arrange it.*

ADDIE (*pointing to the bottle*).   You gone stark out of your head?

CAL.   No, smart lady, I ain't. Miss Regina told me to get out that bottle. (*Points to bottle*) That very bottle for the mighty honored guest. When Miss Regina changes orders like that you can bet your dime she got her reason.

ADDIE (*points to dining room*).   Go on. You'll be needed.

CAL.   Miss Zan she had two helpings frozen fruit cream and she tell that honored guest, she tell him that you make the best frozen fruit cream in all the South.

ADDIE.   Did she? Well, see that Belle saves a little for her. She like it right before she go to bed. Save a few little cakes, too, she like—

(*The dining-room doors are opened and closed again by* BIRDIE HUBBARD. BIRDIE *is a woman of about forty, with a pretty, well-bred, faded face. Her movements are usually nervous and timid, but now, as she comes running into the room, she is gay and excited.* CAL *turns to* BIRDIE.)

BIRDIE.   Oh, Cal. I want you to get one of the kitchen boys to run home for me. He's to look in my desk drawer and— (*To* ADDIE) My, Addie. What a good supper! Just as good as good can be.

ADDIE.   You look pretty this evening, Miss Birdie, and young.

BIRDIE (*laughing*).   Me, young? (*Turns back to* CAL) Maybe you better find Simon and tell him to do it himself. He's to look in my desk, the left drawer, and bring my music album right away. Mr. Marshall is very anxious to see it because of his father and the opera in Chicago. (*To* ADDIE) Mr. Marshall is such a polite man with his manners and very educated and cultured and I've told him all about how my mama and papa used to go to Europe for the music— (*Laughs*) Imagine going all the way to Europe just to listen to music. Wouldn't that be nice, Addie? Just to sit there and listen— (*Turns*) *Left* drawer, Cal. Tell him that twice because he forgets. And tell him not to let any of the things drop out of the album and to bring it right in here when he comes back.

(*The dining-room doors are opened and quickly closed by* OSCAR HUBBARD. *He is a man in his late forties.*)

CAL.   Simon he won't get it right. But I'll tell him.

BIRDIE.   Left drawer, Cal, and tell him to bring the blue book and—

OSCAR (*sharply*).   Birdie.

BIRDIE (*turning nervously*).   Oh, Oscar. I was just sending Simon for my music album.

OSCAR (*to* CAL).   Never mind about the album. Miss Birdie has changed her mind.

BIRDIE.   But, really, Oscar. Really I promised Mr. Marshall. I— (CAL *exits.*)

OSCAR.   Why do you leave the dinner table and go running about like a child?

BIRDIE.   But, Oscar, Mr. Marshall said most specially he *wanted* to see my album. I told him about the time Mama met Wagner, and Mrs. Wagner gave her the signed program and the big picture. Mr. Marshall wants to see that. Very, very much. We had such a nice talk and—

OSCAR.   You have been chattering to him like a magpie. You haven't let him be for a second. I can't think he came South to be bored with you.

BIRDIE (*quickly, hurt*).   He wasn't bored. I don't believe he was bored. He's a very educated, cultured gentleman. (*Her voice rises*) I just don't believe it. You always talk like that when I'm having a nice time.

OSCAR (*turning to her, sharply*).   You have had too much wine. Get yourself in hand now.

BIRDIE (*drawing back, about to cry, shrilly*).   What am I doing? I am not doing anything. What am I doing?

OSCAR (*taking a step to her*).   I said get yourself in hand. Stop acting like a fool.

BIRDIE.   I don't believe he was bored. I just don't believe it. Some people like music and like to talk about it. That's all I was doing.

(LEO HUBBARD *comes hurrying through the dining-room door. He is a young man of twenty, with a weak kind of good looks.*)

LEO.   Mama! Papa! They are coming in now.

OSCAR (*softly*).   Sit down, Birdie. Sit down now. (BIRDIE *sits down, bows her head as if to hide her face.*)

(*The dining-room doors are opened by* CAL. *We see people beginning to rise from the table.* REGINA GIDDENS *comes in with* WILLIAM MARSHALL. REGINA *is a handsome woman of forty.* MARSHALL *is forty-five, pleasant-looking, self-possessed. Behind them comes* ALEXANDRA GIDDENS, *a pretty, rather delicate-looking girl of seventeen. She is followed by* BENJAMIN HUBBARD, *fifty-five, with a large jovial face and the light graceful movements that one often finds in large men.*)

REGINA.   Mr. Marshall, I think you're trying to console me. Chicago may be the noisiest, dirtiest city in the world but I should still prefer it to the sound of our horses and the smell of our azaleas. I should like crowds of people, and theaters, and lovely women—*Very* lovely women, Mr. Marshall?

MARSHALL.   In Chicago? Oh, I suppose so. But I can tell you this: I've never dined there with *three* such lovely ladies.

(ADDIE *begins to pass the port.*)

BEN.   Our Southern women are well favored.

LEO (*laughs*).   But one must go to Mobile for the ladies, sir. Very elegant worldly ladies, too.

BEN (*looks at him*).   Worldly, eh? *Worldly*, did you say?

OSCAR (*hastily, to* LEO).   Your Uncle Ben means that worldliness is not a mark of beauty in any woman.

LEO (*quickly*).   Of course, Uncle Ben. I didn't mean—

MARSHALL.   Your port is excellent, Mrs. Giddens.

REGINA.   Thank you, Mr. Marshall. We had been saving that bottle, hoping we could open it just for you.

ALEXANDRA (*as* ADDIE *comes to her with the tray*).   Oh. May I *really*, Addie?

ADDIE.   Better ask Mama.

ALEXANDRA.   May I, Mama?

REGINA (*nods, smiles*).   In Mr. Marshall's honor.

ALEXANDRA.   Mr. Marshall, this will be the first taste of port I've ever had.

MARSHALL.   No one ever had their first taste of a better port. (*He lifts his glass in a toast; she lifts hers; they both drink*) Well, I suppose it is all true, Mrs. Giddens.

REGINA.   What is true?

MARSHALL.   That you Southerners occupy a unique position in America. You live better than the rest of us, you eat better, you drink better. I wonder you find time, or want to find time, to do business.

BEN.   A great many Southerners don't.

MARSHALL.   Do all of you live here together?

REGINA.   Here with me? (*Laughs*) Oh, no. My brother Ben lives next door. My brother Oscar and his family live in the next square.

BEN.   But we are a very close family. We've always wanted it that way.

MARSHALL.   That is very pleasant. Keeping your family together to share each other's lives. My family moves around too much. My children seem never to come home. Away at school in the winter; in the summer, Europe with their mother—

REGINA (*eagerly*).   Oh, yes. Even down here we read about Mrs. Marshall in the society pages.

MARSHALL.   I dare say. She moves about a great deal. And all of you are part of the same business? Hubbard Sons?

BEN (*motions to* OSCAR).   Oscar and me. (*Motions to* REGINA) My sister's good husband is a banker.

MARSHALL (*looks at* REGINA, *surprised*).   Oh.

REGINA.   I am so sorry that my husband isn't here to meet you. He's been very ill. He is at Johns Hopkins. But he will be home soon. We think he is getting better now.

LEO.   I work for Uncle Horace. (REGINA *looks at him*) I mean I work for Uncle Horace at his bank. I keep an eye on things while he's away.

REGINA (*smiles*).   Really, Leo?

BEN (*looks at* LEO, *then to* MARSHALL).   Modesty in the young is as excellent as it is rare.

OSCAR (*to* LEO).   Your uncle means that a young man should speak more modestly.

LEO (*hastily, taking a step to* BEN).   Oh, I didn't mean, sir—

MARSHALL.   Oh, Mrs. Hubbard. Where's that Wagner autograph you promised to let me see? My train will be leaving soon and—

BIRDIE.   The autograph? Oh. Well. Really, Mr. Marshall, I didn't mean
to chatter so about it. Really I— (*Nervously, looking at* OSCAR) You must
excuse me. I didn't get it because, well, because I had—I—I had a little
headache and—

OSCAR.   My wife is a miserable victim of headaches.

REGINA (*quickly*).   Mr. Marshall said at supper that he would like you to
play for him, Alexandra.

ALEXANDRA (*who has been looking at* BIRDIE).   It's not I who play well,
sir. It's my aunt. She plays just wonderfully. She's my teacher. (*Rises. Eagerly*) May we play a duet? May we, Mama?

BIRDIE.   Thank you, dear. But I have my headache now. I—

OSCAR (*sharply*).   Don't be stubborn, Birdie. Mr. Marshall wants you to
play.

MARSHALL.   Indeed I do. If your headache isn't—

BIRDIE (*hesitates, then gets up, pleased*).   But I'd like to, sir. Very much.
(*She and* ALEXANDRA *go to the piano.*)

MARSHALL.   It's very remarkable how you Southern aristocrats have kept
together. Kept together and kept what belonged to you.

BEN.   You misunderstand, sir. Southern aristocrats have *not* kept
together and have *not* kept what belonged to them.

MARSHALL (*laughs, indicates room*).   You don't call this keeping what
belongs to you?

BEN.   But we are not aristocrats. (*Points to* BIRDIE *at the piano*) Our
brother's wife is the only one of us who belongs to the Southern aristocracy.

(BIRDIE *looks toward* BEN.)

MARSHALL (*smiles*).   My information is that you people have been here,
and solidly here, for a long time.

OSCAR.   And so we have. Since our great-grandfather.

BEN.   Who was *not* an aristocrat, like Birdie's.

MARSHALL.   You make great distinctions.

BEN.   Oh, they have been made for us. And maybe they are important
distinctions. Now you take Birdie's family. When my great-grandfather came
here they were the highest-tone plantation owners in this state.

LEO (*steps to* MARSHALL. *Proudly*).   My mother's grandfather was *governor* of the state before the war.

OSCAR.   They owned the plantation Lionnet. You may have heard of it,
sir?

MARSHALL (*laughs*).   No, I've never heard of anything but brick houses
on a lake, and cotton mills.

BEN.   Lionnet in its day was the best cotton land in the South. It still
brings us in a fair crop. Ah, they were great days for those people—even when
I can remember. They had the best of everything. (BIRDIE *turns to them*)
Cloth from Paris, trips to Europe, horses you can't raise anymore, niggers to
lift their fingers—

BIRDIE.   We were good to our people. Everybody knew that. We were
better to them than—

REGINA (*quickly*).   Why, Birdie. You aren't playing.

BEN.   But when the war comes these fine gentlemen ride off and leave the cotton, *and* the women, to rot.

BIRDIE.   My father was killed in the war. He was a fine soldier, Mr. Marshall. A fine man.

REGINA.   Oh, certainly, Birdie. A famous soldier.

BEN (*to* BIRDIE).   But that isn't the tale I am telling Mr. Marshall. (*To* MARSHALL) Well, sir, the war ends. Lionnet is almost ruined, and the sons finish ruining it. And there were thousands like them. Why? Because the Southern aristocrat can adapt himself to nothing. Too high-tone to try.

MARSHALL.   Sometimes it is difficult to learn new ways. (BIRDIE *and* ALEXANDRA *begin to play.* MARSHALL *leans forward, listening.*)

BEN.   Perhaps, perhaps. (*He sees that* MARSHALL *is listening to the music. Irritated, he turns to* BIRDIE *and* ALEXANDRA *at the piano, then back to* MARSHALL) You're right, Mr. Marshall. It is difficult to learn new ways. But maybe that's why it's profitable. *Our* grandfather and *our* father learned the new ways and learned how to make them pay. (*Smiles*) *They* were in trade. Hubbard Sons, Merchandise. Others, Birdie's family, for example, looked down on them. (*Settles back in chair*) To make a long story short, Lionnet now belongs to *us*. (BIRDIE *stops playing*) Twenty years ago we took over their land, their cotton, and their daughter. (BIRDIE *rises and stands stiffly by the piano.* MARSHALL, *who has been watching her, rises.*)

MARSHALL.   May I bring you a glass of port, Mrs. Hubbard?

BIRDIE (*softly*).   No, thank you, sir. You are most polite.

REGINA (*sharply, to* BEN).   You are boring Mr. Marshall with these ancient family tales.

BEN.   I hope not. I hope not. I am trying to make an important point— (*Bows to* MARSHALL) for our future business partner.

OSCAR (*to* MARSHALL).   My brother always says that it's folks like us who have struggled and fought to bring to our land some of the prosperity of your land.

BEN.   Some people call that patriotism.

REGINA (*laughs gaily*).   I hope you don't find my brothers too obvious, Mr. Marshall. I'm afraid they mean that this is the time for the ladies to leave the gentlemen to talk business.

MARSHALL (*hastily*).   Not at all. We settled everything this afternoon. (*He looks at his watch*) I have only a few minutes before I must leave for the train. (*Smiles at her*) And I insist they be spent with you.

REGINA.   And with another glass of port.

MARSHALL.   Thank you.

BEN.   My sister is right. (*To* MARSHALL) I am a plain man and I am trying to say a plain thing. A man ain't only in business for what he can get out of it. It's got to give him something here. (*Puts hand to his breast*) That's every bit as true for the nigger picking cotton for a silver quarter, as it is for you and me. (REGINA *gives* MARSHALL *a glass of port*) If it don't give him something here, then he don't pick the cotton right. Money isn't all. Not by three shots.

MARSHALL.   Really? Well, I always thought it was a great deal.

REGINA.   And so did I, Mr. Marshall.

MARSHALL (*pleasantly, but with meaning*).   Now you don't have to convince me that you are the right people for the deal. I wouldn't be here if you hadn't convinced me six months ago. You want the mill here, and I want it here. It isn't my business to find out why you want it.

BEN.   To bring the machine to the cotton, and not the cotton to the machine.

MARSHALL (*amused*).   You have a turn for neat phrases, Hubbard. Well, however grand your reasons are, mine are simple: I want to make money and I believe I'll make it on you. (*As* BEN *starts to speak, he smiles*) Mind you, I have no objections to more high-minded reasons. They are mighty valuable in business. It's fine to have partners who so closely follow the teachings of Christ. (*Gets up*) And now I must leave for my train.

REGINA.   I'm sorry you won't stay over with us, Mr. Marshall, but you'll come again. Anytime you like.

BEN (*motions to* LEO, *indicating the bottle*).   Fill them up, boy, fill them up. (LEO *moves around filling the glasses as* BEN *speaks*) Down here, sir, we have a strange custom. We drink the *last* drink for a toast. That's to prove that the Southerner is always still on his feet for the last drink. (*Picks up his glass*) It was Henry Frick, your Mr. Henry Frick, who said, "Railroads are the Rembrandts of investments." Well, *I* say, "Southern cotton mills *will be* the Rembrandts of investment." So I give you the firm of Hubbard Sons and Marshall, Cotton Mills, and to it a long and prosperous life. (*They all pick up their glasses.* MARSHALL *looks at them, amused. Then he, too, lifts his glass, smiles.*)

OSCAR.   The children will drive you to the depot. Leo! Alexandra! You will drive Mr. Marshall down.

LEO (*eagerly, looks at* BEN *who nods*).   Yes, sir. (*To* MARSHALL) Not often Uncle Ben lets *me* drive the horses. And a beautiful pair they are. (*Starts for hall*) Come on, Zan.

ALEXANDRA.   May I drive tonight, Uncle Ben, please? I'd like to and—

BEN (*shakes his head, laughs*).   In your evening clothes? Oh, no, my dear.

ALEXANDRA.   But Leo always— (*Stops, exits quickly.*)

REGINA.   I don't like to say good-bye to you, Mr. Marshall.

MARSHALL.   Then we won't say good-bye. You have promised that you would come and let me show you Chicago. Do I have to make you promise again?

REGINA (*looks at him as he presses her hand*).   I promise again.

MARSHALL (*moves to* BIRDIE).   Good-bye, Mrs. Hubbard.

BIRDIE.   Good-bye, sir.

MARSHALL (*as he passes* REGINA).   Remember.

REGINA.   I will.

(MARSHALL *exits, followed by* BEN *and* OSCAR. *For a second* REGINA *and* BIRDIE *stand looking after them. Then* REGINA *throws up her arms, laughs happily.*)

REGINA.   And there, Birdie, goes the man who has opened the door to our future.

BIRDIE *(surprised at the unaccustomed friendliness)*.   What?

REGINA.   *Our future.* Yours and mine, Ben's and Oscar's, the children— *(Looks at* BIRDIE'*s puzzled face, laughs)* Our future! *(Gaily)* You were charming at supper, Birdie. Mr. Marshall certainly thought so.

BIRDIE *(pleased)*.   Why, Regina! Do you think he did?

REGINA.   Can't you tell when you're being admired?

BIRDIE.   Oscar said I bored Mr. Marshall. But he admired *you.* He told me so.

REGINA.   What did he say?

BIRDIE.   He said to me, "I hope your sister-in-law will come to Chicago. Chicago will be at her feet." He said the ladies would bow to your manners and the gentlemen to your looks.

REGINA.   Did he? He seems a lonely man. Imagine being lonely with all that money. I don't think he likes his wife.

BIRDIE.   Not like his wife? What a thing to say.

REGINA.   She's away a great deal. He said that several times. And once he made fun of her being so social and high-tone. But that fits in all right. *(Sits back, stretches)* Her being social, I mean. She can introduce me. It won't take long with an introduction from her.

BIRDIE *(bewildered)*.   Introduce you? In Chicago? You mean you really might go? Oh, Regina, you can't leave here. What about Horace?

REGINA.   Don't look so scared about everything, Birdie. I'm going to live in Chicago. I've always wanted to. And now there'll be plenty of money to go with.

BIRDIE.   But Horace won't be able to move around. You know what the doctor wrote.

REGINA.   There'll be millions, Birdie, millions. You know what I've always said when people told me we were rich? I said I think you should either be a nigger or a millionaire. In between, like us, what for? *(Laughs)* But I'm not going away tomorrow, Birdie. There's plenty of time to worry about Horace when he comes home. If he ever decides to come home.

BIRDIE.   Will we be going to Chicago? I mean, Oscar and Leo and me?

REGINA.   You? I shouldn't think so. *(Laughs)* Well, we must remember tonight. It's a very important night and we mustn't forget it. We shall plan all the things we'd like to have and then we'll really have them. Make a wish, Birdie, any wish. It's bound to come true now. (BEN *and* OSCAR *enter.)*

BIRDIE *(laughs)*.   Well. Well, I don't know. Maybe. *(Regina turns to look at Ben)* Well, I guess I'd know right off what I wanted. (OSCAR *stands by the upper window, waves to the departing carriage.)*

REGINA *(looks up at Ben, smiles. He smiles back at her)*.   Well, you did it.

BEN.   Looks like it might be we did.

REGINA *(springs up)*.   Looks like it! Don't pretend. You're like a cat who's been licking the cream. *(Crosses to wine bottle)* Now we must all have a drink to celebrate.

OSCAR.   The children, Alexandra and Leo, make a very handsome couple, Regina. Marshall remarked himself what fine young folks they were. How well they looked together!

REGINA (*sharply*).   Yes. You said that before, Oscar.

BEN.   Yes, sir. It's beginning to look as if the deal's all set. I may not be a subtle man—but— (*Turns to them. After a second*) Now somebody ask me how I know the deal is set.

OSCAR.   What do you mean, Ben?

BEN.   You remember I told him that down here we drink the *last* drink for a toast?

OSCAR (*thoughtfully*).   Yes. I never heard that before.

BEN.   Nobody's ever heard it before. God forgives those who invent what they need. I already had his signature. But we've all done business with men whose word over a glass is better than a bond. Anyway it don't hurt to have both.

OSCAR (*turns to* REGINA).   You understand what Ben means?

REGINA.   Yes, Oscar. I understand. I understood immediately.

BEN (*looks at her admiringly*).   Did you, Regina? Well, when he lifted his glass to drink, I closed my eyes and saw the bricks going into place.

REGINA.   And *I* saw a lot more than that.

BEN.   Slowly, slowly. As yet we have only our hopes.

REGINA.   Birdie and I have just been planning what we want. I know what I want. What will you want, Ben?

BEN.   Caution. Don't count the chickens. (*Leans back, laughs*) Well, God would allow us a little daydreaming. Good for the soul when you've worked hard enough to deserve it. (*Pauses*) I think I'll have a stable. For a long time I've had my good eyes on Carter's in Savannah. A rich man's pleasure, the sport of kings, why not the sport of Hubbards? Why not?

REGINA (*smiles*).   Why not? What will you have, Oscar?

OSCAR.   I don't know. (*Thoughtfully*) The pleasure of seeing the bricks grow will be enough for me.

BEN.   Oh, of course. Our greatest pleasure will be to see the bricks grow. But we are all entitled to a little side indulgence.

OSCAR.   Yes, I suppose so. Well, then, I think we might take a few trips here and there, eh, Birdie?

BIRDIE (*surprised at being consulted*).   Yes, Oscar. I'd like that.

OSCAR.   We might even make a regular trip to Jekyll Island. I've heard the Cornelly place is for sale. We might think about buying it. Make a nice change. Do you good, Birdie, a change of climate. Fine shooting on Jekyll, the best.

BIRDIE.   I'd like—

OSCAR (*indulgently*).   What would you like?

BIRDIE.   Two things. Two things I'd like most.

REGINA.   Two! I should like a thousand. You are modest, Birdie.

BIRDIE (*warmly, delighted with the unexpected interest*).   I should like to have Lionnet back. I know you own it now, but I'd like to see it fixed up again, the way Mama and Papa had it. Every year it used to get a nice coat of paint—Papa was very particular about the paint—and the lawn was so smooth all the way down to the river, with the trims of zinnias and red-feather plush. And the figs and blue little plums and the scuppernongs— (*Smiles. Turns to* REGINA) The organ is still there and it wouldn't cost much to fix. We could have parties for Zan, the way Mama used to have for me.

BEN.   That's a pretty picture, Birdie. Might be a most pleasant way to live. (*Dismissing* BIRDIE) What do you want, Regina?

BIRDIE (*very happily, not noticing that they are no longer listening to her*).   I could have a cutting garden. Just where Mama's used to be. Oh, I do think we could be happier there. Papa used to say that *nobody* had ever lost their temper at Lionnet, and *nobody* ever would. Papa would never let anybody be nasty-spoken or mean. No, sir. He just didn't like it.

BEN.   What do you want, Regina?

REGINA.   I'm going to Chicago. And when I'm settled there and know the right people and the right things to buy—because I certainly don't now— I shall go to Paris and buy them. (*Laughs*) I'm going to leave you and Oscar to count the bricks.

BIRDIE.   Oscar. Please let me have Lionnet back.

OSCAR (*to* REGINA).   You are serious about moving to Chicago?

BEN.   She is going to see the great world and leave us in the little one. Well, we'll come and visit you and meet all the great and be proud you are our sister.

REGINA (*gaily*).   Certainly. And you won't even have to learn to be subtle, Ben. Stay as you are. You will be rich and the rich don't have to be subtle.

OSCAR.   But what about Alexandra? She's seventeen. Old enough to be thinking about marrying.

BIRDIE.   And, Oscar, I have one more wish. Just one more wish.

OSCAR (*turns*).   What is it, Birdie? What are you saying?

BIRDIE.   I want you to stop shooting. I mean, so much. I don't like to see animals and birds killed just for the killing. You only throw them away—

BEN (*to* REGINA).   It'll take a great deal of money to live as you're planning, Regina.

REGINA.   Certainly. But there'll be plenty of money. You have estimated the profits very high.

BEN.   I have—

BIRDIE (*Oscar is looking at her furiously*).   And you never let anybody else shoot, and the niggers need it so much to keep from starving. It's wicked to shoot food just because you like to shoot, when poor people need it so—

BEN (*laughs*).   I have estimated the profits very high—for myself.

REGINA.   What did you say?

BIRDIE.   I've always wanted to speak about it, Oscar.

OSCAR (*slowly, carefully*).   What are you chattering about?

BIRDIE (*nervously*).   I was talking about Lionnet and—and about your shooting—

OSCAR.   You are exciting yourself.

REGINA (*to* BEN). I didn't hear you. There was so much talking.

OSCAR (*to* BIRDIE). You have been acting very childish, very excited, all evening.

BIRDIE. Regina asked me what I'd like.

REGINA. What did you say, Ben?

BIRDIE. Now that we'll be so rich everybody was saying what they would like, so *I* said what *I* would like, too.

BEN. I said— (*He is interrupted by* OSCAR.)

OSCAR (*to* BIRDIE). Very well. We've all heard you. That's enough now.

BEN. I am waiting. (*They stop*) I am waiting for you to finish. You and Birdie. Four conversations are three too many. (BIRDIE *slowly sits down.* BEN *smiles, to* REGINA.) I said that I had, and I do, estimate the profits very high—for myself, and Oscar, of course.

REGINA. And what does that mean? (BEN *shrugs, looks toward* OSCAR.)

OSCAR (*looks at* BEN, *clears throat*). Well, Regina, it's like this. For forty-nine percent Marshall will put up four hundred thousand dollars. For fifty-one percent— (*Smiles archly*) a controlling interest, mind you—we will put up two hundred and twenty-five thousand dollars besides offering him certain benefits that our (*looks at* BEN) local position allows us to manage. Ben means that two hundred and twenty-five thousand dollars is a lot of money.

REGINA. I know the terms and I know it's a lot of money.

BEN (*nodding*). It is.

OSCAR. Ben means that we are ready with our two-thirds of the money. Your third, Horace's I mean, doesn't seem to be ready. (*Raises his hand as* REGINA *starts to speak*) Ben has written to Horace, I have written, and you have written. He answers. But he never mentions this business. Yet we have explained to him in great detail, and told him the urgency. Still he never mentions it. Ben has been very patient, Regina. Naturally, you are our sister and we want you to benefit from anything we do.

REGINA. And in addition to your concern for me, you do not want control to go out of the family. (*To* BEN) That right, Ben?

BEN. That's cynical. (*Smiles*) Cynicism is an unpleasant way of saying the truth.

OSCAR. No need to be cynical. We'd have no trouble raising the third share, the share that you want to take.

REGINA. I am sure you could get the third share, the share you were saving for me. But that would give you a strange partner. And strange partners sometimes want a great deal. (*Smiles unpleasantly*) But perhaps it would be wise for you to find him.

OSCAR. Now, now. Nobody says we *want* to do that. We would like to have you in and you would like to come in.

REGINA. Yes. I certainly would.

BEN (*laughs, puts up his hand*). But we haven't heard from Horace.

REGINA. I've given my word that Horace will put up the money. That should be enough.

BEN.   Oh, it was enough. I took your word. But I've got to have more than your word now. The contracts will be signed this week, and Marshall will want to see our money soon after. Regina, Horace has been in Baltimore for five months. I know that you've written him to come home, and that he hasn't come.

OSCAR.   It's beginning to look as if he doesn't want to come home.

REGINA.   Of course he wants to come home. You can't move around with heart trouble at any moment you choose. You know what doctors are like once they get their hands on a case like this—

OSCAR.   They can't very well keep him from answering letters, can they? (REGINA *turns to* BEN) They couldn't keep him from arranging for the money if he wanted to—

REGINA.   Has it occurred to you that Horace is also a good businessman?

BEN.   Certainly. He is a shrewd trader. Always has been. The bank is proof of that.

REGINA.   Then, possibly, he may be keeping silent because he doesn't think he is getting enough for his money. Seventy-five thousand he has to put up. That's a lot of money, too.

OSCAR.   Nonsense. He knows a good thing when he hears it. He knows that we can make *twice* the profit on cotton goods manufactured here than can be made in the North.

BEN.   That isn't what Regina means. May I interpret you, Regina? (*To* OSCAR) Regina is saying that Horace wants *more* than a third of our share.

OSCAR.   But he's only putting up a third of the money. You put up a third and you get a third. What else could he expect?

REGINA.   Well, *I* don't know. I don't know about these things. It would seem that if you put up a third you should only get a third. But then again, there's no law about it, is there? I should think that if you knew your money was very badly needed, well, you just might say, I want more, I want a bigger share. You boys have done that. I've heard you say so.

BEN (*after a pause, laughs*).   So you believe he has deliberately held out? For a larger share? Well, I don't believe it. But I do believe that's what *you* want. Am I right, Regina?

REGINA.   Oh, I shouldn't like to be too definite. But I could say that I wouldn't like to persuade Horace unless he did get a larger share. I must look after his interests. It seems only natural—

OSCAR.   And where would the larger share come from?

REGINA.   I don't know. That's not my business. (*Giggles*) But perhaps it could come off your share, Oscar. (REGINA *and* BEN *laugh.*)

OSCAR (*rises and wheels on both of them as they laugh*).   What kind of talk is this?

BEN.   I haven't said a thing.

OSCAR (*to* REGINA).   *You* are talking very big tonight.

REGINA (*stops laughing*).   Am I? Well, you should know me well enough to know that I wouldn't be asking for things I didn't think I could get.

OSCAR.   Listen. I don't believe you can even get Horace to come home, much less get money from him or talk quite so big about what you want.

REGINA.   Oh, I can get him home.

OSCAR. Then why haven't you?

REGINA. I thought I should fight his battles for him, before he came home. Horace is a very sick man. And even if *you* don't care how sick he is, I do.

BEN. Stop this foolish squabbling. How can you get him home?

REGINA. I will send Alexandra to Baltimore. She will ask him to come home. She will say that she wants him to come home, and that *I* want him to come home.

BIRDIE (*rises*). Well, of course she wants him here, but he's sick and maybe he's happy where he is.

REGINA (*ignores* BIRDIE, *to* BEN). You agree that he will come home if she asks him to, if she says that I miss him and want him—

BEN (*looks at her, smiles*). I admire you, Regina. And I agree. That's settled now and— (*Starts to rise.*)

REGINA (*quickly*). But before she brings him home, I want to know what he's going to get.

BEN. What do you want?

REGINA. Twice what you offered.

BEN. Well, you won't get it.

OSCAR (*to* REGINA). I think you've gone crazy.

REGINA. I don't want to fight, Ben—

BEN. I don't either. You won't get it. There isn't any chance of that. (*Roguishly*) You're holding us up, and that's not pretty, Regina, not pretty. (*Holds up his hand as he sees she is about to speak*) But we need you, and I don't want to fight. Here's what I'll do: I'll give Horace forty percent, instead of the thirty-three and a third he really should get. I'll do that, provided he is home and his money is up within two weeks. How's that?

REGINA. All right.

OSCAR. I've asked before: where is this extra share coming from?

BEN (*pleasantly*). From you. From your share.

OSCAR (*furiously*). From me, is it? That's just fine and dandy. That's my reward. For thirty-five years I've worked my hands to the bone for you. For thirty-five years I've done all the things you didn't want to do. And this is what I—

BEN (*turns to look at* OSCAR. OSCAR *breaks off*). My, my. I am being attacked tonight on all sides. First by my sister, then by my brother. And I ain't a man who likes being attacked. I can't believe that God wants the strong to parade their strength, but I don't mind doing it if it's got to be done. You ought to take these things better, Oscar. I've made you money in the past. I'm going to make you more money now. You'll be a very rich man. What's the difference to any of us if a little more goes here, a little less goes there—it's all in the family. And it will stay in the family. I'll never marry. (ADDIE *enters, begins to gather the glasses from the table*) So my money will go to Alexandra and Leo. They may even marry someday and— (ADDIE *looks at* BEN.)

BIRDIE (*rising*). Marry—Zan and Leo—

OSCAR (*carefully*). That would make a great difference in my feelings. If they married.

BEN. Yes, that's what I mean. Of course it would make a difference.

OSCAR (*carefully*).   Is that what *you* mean, Regina?

REGINA.   Oh, it's too far away. We'll talk about it in a few years.

OSCAR.   I want to talk about it now.

BEN (*nods*).   Naturally.

REGINA.   There's a lot of things to consider. They are first cousins, and—

OSCAR.   That isn't unusual. Our grandmother and grandfather were first cousins.

REGINA (*giggles*).   And look at us. (*Ben giggles.*)

OSCAR (*angrily*).   You're both being very gay with my money.

BEN (*sighs*).   These quarrels. I dislike them so. (*To* REGINA) A marriage might be a very wise arrangement, for several reasons. And then, Oscar has given up something for you. You should try to manage something for him.

REGINA.   I haven't said I was opposed to it. But Leo is a wild boy. There were those times when he took a little money from the bank and—

OSCAR.   That's all past history—

REGINA.   Oh, I know. And I know all young men are wild. I'm only mentioning it to show you that there are considerations—

BEN (*irritated because she does not understand that he is trying to keep* OSCAR *quiet*).   All right, so there are. But please assure Oscar that you will think about it very seriously.

REGINA (*smiles, nods*).   Very well. I assure Oscar that I will think about it seriously.

OSCAR (*sharply*).   That is not an answer.

REGINA (*rises*).   My, you're in a bad humor and you shall put me in one. I have said all that I am willing to say now. After all, Horace has to give his consent, too.

OSCAR.   Horace will do what you tell him to.

REGINA.   Yes, I think he will.

OSCAR.   And I have your word that you will try to—

REGINA (*patiently*).   Yes, Oscar. You have my word that I will think about it. Now do leave me alone. (*There is the sound of the front door being closed.*)

BIRDIE.   I—Alexandra is only seventeen. She—

LEO (*comes into the room*).   Mr. Marshall got off safe and sound. Weren't those fine clothes he had? You can always spot clothes made in a good place. Looks like maybe they were done in England. Lots of men in the North send all the way to England for their stuff.

BEN (*to* LEO).   Were you careful driving the horses?

LEO   Oh, yes, sir. I was. (ALEXANDRA *has come in on* BEN'S *question, hears the answer, looks angrily at* LEO.)

ALEXANDRA.   It's a lovely night. You should have come, Aunt Birdie.

REGINA.   Were you gracious to Mr. Marshall?

ALEXANDRA   I think so, Mama. I liked him.

REGINA.   Good. And now I have great news for you. You are going to Baltimore in the morning to bring your father home.

ALEXANDRA (*gasps, then delighted*).   Me? Papa said I should come? That must mean— (*Turns to* ADDIE) Addie, he must be well. Think of it, he'll be back home again. We'll bring him home.

REGINA. You are going alone, Alexandra.

ADDIE (ALEXANDRA *has turned in surprise*). Going alone? Going by herself? A child that age! Mr. Horace ain't going to like Zan traipsing up there by herself.

REGINA (*sharply*). Go upstairs and lay out Alexandra's things.

ADDIE. He'd expect me to be along—

REGINA. I'll be up in a few minutes to tell you what to pack. (ADDIE *slowly begins to climb the steps. To* ALEXANDRA) I should think you'd like going alone. At your age it certainly would have delighted me. You're a strange girl, Alexandra. Addie has babied you so much.

ALEXANDRA. I only thought it would be more fun if Addie and I went together.

BIRDIE (*timidly*). Maybe I could go with her, Regina. I'd really like to.

REGINA. She is going alone. She is getting old enough to take some responsibilities.

OSCAR. She'd better learn now. She's almost old enough to get married. (*Jovially, to* LEO, *slapping him on shoulder*) Eh, son?

LEO. Huh?

OSCAR (*annoyed with* LEO *for not understanding*). Old enough to get married, you're thinking, eh?

LEO. Oh, yes, sir. (*Feebly*) Lots of girls get married at Zan's age. Look at Mary Prester and Johanna and—

REGINA. Well, she's not getting married tomorrow. But she is going to Baltimore tomorrow, so let's talk about that. (*To* ALEXANDRA) You'll be glad to have Papa home again.

ALEXANDRA. I wanted to go before, Mama. You remember that. But you said *you* couldn't go, and that *I* couldn't go alone.

REGINA. I've changed my mind. (*Too casually*) You're to tell Papa how much you missed him, and that he must come home now—for your sake. Tell him that you *need* him home.

ALEXANDRA. Need him home? I don't understand.

REGINA. There is nothing for you to understand. You are simply to say what I have told you.

BIRDIE (*rises*). He may be too sick. She couldn't do that—

ALEXANDRA. Yes. He may be too sick to travel. I couldn't make him think he had to come home for me, if he is too sick to—

REGINA (*looks at her, sharply, challengingly*). You *couldn't* do what I tell you to do, Alexandra?

ALEXANDRA (*quietly*). No. I couldn't. If I thought it would hurt him.

REGINA (*after a second's silence, smiles pleasantly*). But you are doing this for Papa's own good. (*Takes* ALEXANDRA's *hand*) You must let me be the judge of his condition. It's the best possible cure for him to come home and be taken care of here. He mustn't stay there any longer and listen to those alarmist doctors. You are doing this entirely for his sake. Tell your papa that I want him to come home, that I miss him very much.

ALEXANDRA (*slowly*).   Yes, Mama.

REGINA (*to the others*).   I must go and start getting Alexandra ready now. Why don't you all go home?

BEN (*rises*).   I'll attend to the railroad ticket. One of the boys will bring it over. Good night, everybody. Have a nice trip, Alexandra. The food on the train is very good. The celery is so crisp. Have a good time and act like a little lady. (*Exits.*)

REGINA.   Good night, Ben. Good night, Oscar— (*Playfully*) Don't be so glum, Oscar. It makes you look as if you had chronic indigestion.

BIRDIE.   Good night, Regina.

REGINA.   Good night, Birdie. (*Exits upstairs.*)

OSCAR (*starts for hall*).   Come along.

LEO (*to Alexandra*).   Imagine your not wanting to go! What a little fool you are. Wish it were me. What I could do in a place like Baltimore!

ALEXANDRA.   Mind your business. I can guess the kind of things *you* could do.

LEO (*laughs*).   Oh, no, you couldn't. (*He exits.*)

REGINA (*calling from the top of the stairs*).   Come on, Alexandra.

BIRDIE (*quickly, softly*).   Zan.

ALEXANDRA.   I don't understand about my going. Aunt Birdie. (*Shrugs*) But anyway, Papa will be home again. (*Pats* BIRDIE's *arm*) Don't worry about me. I can take care of myself. Really I can.

BIRDIE (*shakes her head, softly*).   That's not what I'm worried about. Zan—

ALEXANDRA (*comes close to her*).   What's the matter?

BIRDIE.   It's about Leo—

ALEXANDRA (*whispering*).   He beat the horses. That's why we were late getting back. We had to wait until they cooled off. He always beats the horses as if—

BIRDIE (*whispering frantically, holding* ALEXANDRA's *hands*).   He's my son. My own son. But you are more to me—more to me than my own child. I love you more than anybody else—

ALEXANDRA.   Don't worry about the horses. I'm sorry I told you.

BIRDIE (*her voice rising*).   *I am not worrying about the horses.* I am worrying about *you.* You are *not* going to marry Leo. I am not going to let them do that to you—

ALEXANDRA.   Marry? To Leo? (*Laughs*) I wouldn't marry, Aunt Birdie. I've never even thought about it—

BIRDIE.   But they have thought about it. (*Wildly*) Zan, I couldn't stand to think about such a thing. You and— (*Oscar has come into the doorway on* ALEXANDRA'S *speech. He is standing quietly, listening.*)

ALEXANDRA (*laughs*).   But I'm not going to marry. And I'm certainly not going to marry Leo.

BIRDIE.   Don't you understand? They'll make you. They'll make you—

ALEXANDRA (*takes* BIRDIE's *hands, quietly, firmly*).   That's foolish, Aunt Birdie. I'm grown now. Nobody can make me do anything.

BIRDIE.   I just couldn't stand—

OSCAR (*sharply*).   Birdie. (BIRDIE *looks up, draws quickly away from* ALEXANDRA. *She stands rigid, frightened.*) Birdie, get your hat and coat.

ADDIE (*calls from upstairs*).   Come on, baby. Your mama's waiting for you, and she ain't nobody to keep waiting.

ALEXANDRA.   All right. (*Then softly, embracing* BIRDIE) Good night, Aunt Birdie. (*As she passes* OSCAR) Good night, Uncle Oscar. (BIRDIE *begins to move slowly toward the door as* ALEXANDRA *climbs the stairs.* ALEXANDRA *is almost out of view when* BIRDIE *reaches* OSCAR *in the doorway. As* BIRDIE *attempts to pass him, he slaps her hard, across the face.* BIRDIE *cries out, puts her hand to her face. On the cry,* ALEXANDRA *turns, begins to run down the stairs*) Aunt Birdie! What happened? What happened? I—

BIRDIE (*softly, without turning*).   Nothing, darling. Nothing happened. (*Anxious to keep* ALEXANDRA *from coming close*) Now go to bed. (OSCAR *exits*) Nothing happened. I only—I only twisted my ankle. (*She goes out.* ALEXANDRA *stands on the stairs looking after her.*)

ACT II

SCENE: *Same as Act One. A week later, morning.*

AT RISE: *The light comes from the open shutter of the right window; the other shutters are tightly closed.* ADDIE *is standing at the window, looking out. Near the dining-room doors are brooms, mops, rags, etc. After a second,* OSCAR *comes into the entrance hall, looks in the room, shivers, decides not to take his hat and coat off, comes into the room. At the sound of the door,* ADDIE *turns.*

ADDIE (*without interest*).   Oh, it's you, Mr. Oscar.

OSCAR.   What is this? It's not night. What's the matter here? (*Shivers*) Fine thing at this time of the morning. Blinds all closed. (ADDIE *begins to open shutters*) Where's Miss Regina? It's cold in here.

ADDIE.   Miss Regina ain't down yet.

OSCAR.   She had any word?

ADDIE.   No, sir.

OSCAR.   Wouldn't you think a girl that age could get on a train at one place and have sense enough to get off at another?

ADDIE.   Something must have happened. If Zan say she was coming last night, she's coming last night. Unless something happened. Sure fire disgrace to let a baby like that go all that way alone to bring home a sick man without—

OSCAR.   You do a lot of judging around here, Addie, eh? Judging of your white folks, I mean.

REGINA (*speaking from the upstairs hall*).   Who's downstairs, Addie? (*She appears in a dressing gown, peers down from the landing.* ADDIE *picks up broom, dustpan and brush and exits*) Oh, it's you, Oscar. What are you doing here so early? I haven't been down yet. I'm not finished dressing.

OSCAR (*speaking up to her*).   You had any word from them?

REGINA.   No.

OSCAR.   Then something certainly has happened. People don't just say they are arriving on Thursday night, and they haven't come by Friday morning.

REGINA.   Oh, nothing has happened. Alexandra just hasn't got sense enough to send a message.

OSCAR.   If nothing's happened, then why aren't they here?

REGINA.   You asked me that ten times last night. My, you do fret so, Oscar. Anything might have happened. They may have missed connections in Atlanta, the train may have been delayed—oh, a hundred things could have kept them.

OSCAR.   Where's Ben?

REGINA (*as she disappears upstairs*).   Where should he be? At home, probably. Really, Oscar, I don't tuck him in his bed and I don't take him out of it. Have some coffee and don't worry so much.

OSCAR.   Have some coffee? There isn't any coffee. (*Looks at his watch, shakes his head. After a second* CAL *enters with a large silver tray, coffee urn, small cups, newspaper.*) Oh, there you are. Is everything in this fancy house always late?

CAL (*looks at him, surprised*).   You ain't out shooting this morning, Mr. Oscar?

OSCAR.   First day I missed since I had my head cold. First day I missed in eight years.

CAL.   Yes, sir. I bet you. Simon he say you had a mighty good day yesterday morning. That's what Simon say. (*Brings* OSCAR *coffee and newspaper.*)

OSCAR.   Pretty good, pretty good.

CAL (*laughs, slyly*).   Bet you got enough bobwhite and squirrel to give every nigger in town a Jesus-party. Most of 'em ain't had no meat since the cotton picking was over. Bet they'd give anything for a little piece of that meat—

OSCAR (*turns his head to look at* CAL).   Cal, if I catch a nigger in this town going shooting, you know what's going to happen. (LEO *enters.*)

CAL (*hastily*).   Yes, sir, Mr. Oscar. It was Simon who told me and— Morning, Mr. Leo. You gentlemen having your breakfast with us here?

LEO.   The boys in the bank don't know a thing. They haven't had any message. (CAL *waits for an answer, gets none, shrugs, exits.*)

OSCAR (*peers at* LEO).   What you doing here, son?

LEO.   You told me to find out if the boys at the bank had any message from Uncle Horace or Zan—

OSCAR.   I told you if they had a message to bring it here. I told you that if they didn't have a message to stay at the bank and do your work.

LEO.   Oh, I guess I misunderstood.

OSCAR.   You didn't misunderstand. You just were looking for any excuse to take an hour off. (LEO *pours a cup of coffee*) You got to stop that kind of thing. You got to start settling down. You going to be a married man one of these days.

LEO.   Yes, sir.

OSCAR.   You also got to stop with that woman in Mobile. (*As* LEO *is about to speak*) You're young and I haven't got no objections to outside women. That is, I haven't got no objections so long as they don't interfere with serious things. Outside women are all right in their place, but *now* isn't their place. You got to realize that.

LEO (*nods*).   Yes, sir. I'll tell her. She'll act all right about it.

OSCAR.   Also, you got to start working harder at the bank. You got to convince your Uncle Horace you going to make a fit husband for Alexandra.

LEO.   What do you think has happened to them? Supposed to be here last night— (*Laughs*) Bet you Uncle Ben's mighty worried. Seventy-five thousand dollars worried.

OSCAR (*smiles happily*).   Ought to be worried. Damn well ought to be. First he don't answer the letters, then he don't come home— (*Giggles.*)

LEO.   What will happen if Uncle Horace don't come home or don't—

OSCAR.   Or don't put up the money? Oh, we'll get it from outside. Easy enough.

LEO (*surprised*).   But *you* don't want outsiders.

OSCAR.   What do I care who gets my share? I been shaved already. Serve Ben right if he had to give away some of his.

LEO.   Damn shame what they did to you.

OSCAR (*looking up the stairs*).   Don't talk so loud. Don't you worry. When I die, you'll have as much as the rest. You might have yours *and* Alexandra's. I'm not so easily licked.

LEO.   I wasn't thinking of myself, Papa—

OSCAR.   Well, you should be, you should be. It's every man's duty to think of himself.

LEO.   You think Uncle Horace don't want to go in on this?

OSCAR (*giggles*).   That's my hunch. He hasn't showed any signs of loving it yet.

LEO (*laughs*).   But he hasn't listened to Aunt Regina yet, either. Oh, he'll go along. It's too good a thing. Why wouldn't he want to? He's got plenty and plenty to invest with. He don't even have to sell anything. Eighty-eight thousand worth of Union Pacific bonds sitting right in his safe deposit box. All he's got to do is open the box.

OSCAR (*after a pause. Looks at his watch*).   Mighty late breakfast in this fancy house. Yes, he's had those bonds for fifteen years. Bought them when they were low and just locked them up.

LEO.   Yeah. Just has to open the box and take them out. That's all. Easy as easy can be. (*Laughs*) The things in that box! There's all those bonds, looking mighty fine. (OSCAR *slowly puts down his newspaper and turns to* LEO) Then right next to them is a baby shoe of Zan's and a cheap old cameo on a string, and, *and*—nobody'd believe this—a piece of an old violin. Not even a whole violin. Just a piece of an old thing, a piece of a violin.

OSCAR (*very softly, as if he were trying to control his voice*).   A piece of a violin! What do you think of that!

LEO.   Yes, sirree. A lot of other crazy things, too. A poem, I guess it is, signed with his mother's name, and two old schoolbooks with notes and— (LEO *catches* OSCAR'S *look. His voice trails off. He turns his head away.*)

OSCAR (*very softly*).   How do you know what's in the box, son?

LEO (*draws back, frightened, realizing what he has said*).   Oh, well. Well, er. Well, one of the boys, sir. It was one of the boys at the bank. He took old Manders' keys. It was Joe Horns. He just up and took Manders' keys and, and—well, took the box out. (*Quickly*) Then they all asked me if I wanted to see, too. So I looked a little, I guess, but then I made them close up the box quick and I told them never—

OSCAR (*looks at him*).   Joe Horns, you say? He opened it?

LEO.   Yes, sir, yes, he did. My word of honor. (*Very nervous now*) I suppose that don't excuse *me* for looking— (*Looking at* OSCAR) but I did make him close it up and put the keys back in Manders' drawer—

OSCAR (*leans forward, very softly*).   Tell me the truth, Leo. I am not going to be angry with you. Did you open the box yourself?

LEO.   No, sir, I didn't. I told you I didn't. No, I—

OSCAR (*irritated, patient*).   I am *not* going to be angry with you. (*Watching* LEO *carefully*) Sometimes a young fellow deserves credit for looking round him to see what's going on. Sometimes that's a good sign in a fellow your age. Many great men have made their fortune with their eyes. Did you open the box?

LEO (*very puzzled*).   No. I—

OSCAR (*moves to* LEO).   Did you open the box? It may have been—well, it may have been a good thing if you had.

LEO (*after a long pause*).   I opened it.

OSCAR (*quickly*).   Is that the truth? (LEO *nods*) Does anybody else know that you opened it? Come, Leo, don't be afraid of speaking the truth to me.

LEO.   No. Nobody knew. Nobody was in the bank when I did it. But—

OSCAR.   Did your Uncle Horace ever know you opened it?

LEO (*shakes his head*).   He only looks in it once every six months when he cuts the coupons, and sometimes Manders even does that for him. Uncle Horace don't even have the keys. Manders keeps them for him. Imagine not looking at all that. You can bet if I had the bonds, I'd watch 'em like—

OSCAR.   If you had them. *If* you had them. Then you could have a share in the mill, you and me. A fine, big share, too. (*Pauses, shrugs*) Well, a man can't be shot for wanting to see his son get on in the world, can he, boy?

LEO (*looks up, begins to understand*).   No, he can't. Natural enough. (*Laughs*) But I haven't got the bonds and Uncle Horace has. And now he can just sit back and wait to be a millionaire.

OSCAR (*innocently*).   You think your Uncle Horace likes you well enough to lend you the bonds if he decides not to use them himself?

LEO.   Papa, it must be that you haven't had your breakfast! (*Laughs loudly*) Lend me the bonds! My God—

OSCAR (*disappointed*).   No, I suppose not. Just a fancy of mine. A loan for three months, maybe four, easy enough for us to pay it back then. Anyway, this is only April— (*Slowly counting the months on his fingers*) and if he doesn't look at them until Autumn he wouldn't even miss them out of the box.

LEO.   That's it. He wouldn't even miss them. Ah, well—

OSCAR. No, sir. Wouldn't even miss them. How could he miss them if he never looks at them? (*Sighs as* LEO *stares at him*) Well, here we are sitting around waiting for him to come home and invest his money in something he hasn't lifted his hand to get. But I can't help thinking he's acting strange. You laugh when I say he could lend you the bonds if he's not going to use them himself. But would it hurt him?

LEO (*slowly looking at* OSCAR). No. No, it wouldn't.

OSCAR. People ought to help other people. But that's not always the way it happens. (BEN *enters, hangs his coat and hat in hall. Very carefully*) And so sometimes you got to think of yourself. (*As* LEO *stares at him*, BEN *appears in the doorway*) Morning, Ben.

BEN (*coming in, carrying his newspaper*). Fine sunny morning. Any news from the runaways?

REGINA (*on the staircase*). There's no news or you would have heard it. Quite a convention so early in the morning, aren't you all? (*Goes to coffee urn.*)

OSCAR. You rising mighty late these days. Is that the way they do things in Chicago society?

BEN (*looking at his paper*). Old Carter died up in Senateville. Eighty-one is a good time for us all, eh? What do you think has really happened to Horace, Regina?

REGINA. Nothing.

BEN. You don't think maybe he never started from Baltimore and never intends to start?

REGINA (*irritated*). Of course they've started. Didn't I have a letter from Alexandra? What is so strange about people arriving late? He has that cousin in Savannah he's so fond of. He may have stopped to see him. They'll be along today sometime, very flattered that you and Oscar are so worried about them.

BEN. I'm a natural worrier. Especially when I am getting ready to close a business deal and one of my partners remains silent *and* invisible.

REGINA (*laughs*). Oh, is that it? I thought you were worried about Horace's health.

OSCAR. Oh, that too. Who could help but worry? I'm worried. This is the first day I haven't been shooting since my head cold.

REGINA (*starts toward dining room*). Then you haven't had your breakfast. Come along. (OSCAR *and* LEO *follow her.*)

BEN. Regina. (*She turns at dining-room door*) That cousin of Horace's has been dead for years and, in any case, the train does not go through Savannah.

REGINA (*laughs, continues into dining room, seats herself*). Did he die? You're always remembering about people dying. (BEN *rises*) Now I intend to eat my breakfast in peace, and read my newspaper.

BEN (*goes toward dining room as he talks*). This is second breakfast for me. My first was bad. Celia ain't the cook she used to be. Too old to have taste anymore. If she hadn't belonged to Mama, I'd send her off to the country.

(OSCAR *and* LEO *start to eat.* BEN *seats himself.*)

LEO.   Uncle Horace will have some tales to tell, I bet. Baltimore is a lively town.

REGINA (*to* CAL).   The grits isn't hot enough. Take it back.

CAL.   Oh, yes'm. (*Calling into the kitchen as he exits*) Grits didn't hold the heat. Grits didn't hold the heat.

LEO.   When I was at school three of the boys and myself took a train once and went over to Baltimore. It was so big we thought we were in Europe. I was just a kid then—

REGINA.   I find it very pleasant (ADDIE *enters*) to have breakfast alone. I hate chattering before I've had something hot. (CAL *closes the dining-room doors*) Do be still, Leo.

(ADDIE *comes into the room, begins gathering up the cups, carries them to the large tray. Outside there are the sounds of voices. Quickly* ADDIE *runs into the hall. A few seconds later she appears again in the doorway, her arm around the shoulders of* HORACE GIDDENS, *supporting him. Horace is a tall man of about forty-five. He has been good looking, but now his face is tired and ill. He walks stiffly, as if it were an enormous effort, and carefully, as if he were unsure of his balance.* ADDIE *takes off his overcoat and hangs it on the hall tree. She then helps him to a chair.*)

HORACE.   How are you, Addie? How have you been?

ADDIE.   I'm all right, Mr. Horace. I've just been worried about you.

(ALEXANDRA *enters. She is flushed and excited, her hat awry, her face dirty. Her arms are full of packages, but she comes quickly to* ADDIE.)

ALEXANDRA.   Don't tell me how worried you were. We couldn't help it and there was no way to send a message.

ADDIE (*begins to take packages from* ALEXANDRA).   Yes, sir, I was mighty worried.

ALEXANDRA.   We had to stop in Mobile overnight. Papa didn't feel well. The trip was too much for him, and I made him stop and rest—(*As* ADDIE *takes the last package*) No, don't take that. That's Father's medicine. I'll hold it. It mustn't break. Now, about the stuff outside. Papa must have his wheelchair. I'll get that and the valises—

ADDIE (*very happy, holding* ALEXANDRA'S *arms*).   Since when you got to carry your own valises? Since when I ain't old enough to hold a bottle of medicine? (HORACE *coughs*) You feel all right, Mr. Horace?

HORACE (*nods*).   Glad to be sitting down.

ALEXANDRA (*opening package of medicine*).   He doesn't feel all right. He just says that. The trip was very hard on him, and now he must go right to bed.

ADDIE (*looking at him carefully*).   Them fancy doctors, they give you help?

HORACE.   They did their best.

ALEXANDRA (*has become conscious of the voices in the dining room*).   I bet Mama was worried. I better tell her we're here now. (*She starts for door.*)

HORACE.   Zan. (*She stops*) Not for a minute, dear.

ALEXANDRA.   Oh, Papa, you feel bad again. I knew you did. Do you want your medicine?

HORACE.   No, I don't feel that way. I'm just tired, darling. Let me rest a little.

ADDIE.   They're all in there eating breakfast.

ALEXANDRA.   Oh, are they all here? Why do they *always* have to be here? I was hoping Papa wouldn't have to see anybody, that it would be nice for him and quiet.

ADDIE.   Then let your papa rest for a minute.

HORACE.   Addie, I bet your coffee's as good as ever. They don't have such good coffee up North. Is it as good, Addie? (ADDIE *starts for coffee urn.*)

ALEXANDRA.   No. Dr. Reeves said not much coffee. Just now and then. I'm the nurse now, Addie.

ADDIE.   You'd be a better one if you didn't look so dirty. Now go take a bath. Change your linens, get out a fresh dress, give your hair a good brushing—go on—

ALEXANDRA.   Will you be all right, Papa?

ADDIE.   Go on.

ALEXANDRA (*on stairs, talks as she goes up*).   The pills Papa must take once every four hours. And the bottle only when—only if he feels very bad. Now don't move until I come back and don't talk much and remember about his medicine, Addie— (*As she disappears*) How's Aunt Birdie? Is she here?

ADDIE.   It ain't right for you to have coffee? It will hurt you?

HORACE (*slowly*).   Nothing can make much difference now. Get me a cup, Addie. (*She crosses to urn, pours a cup*) Funny. They can't make coffee up North. (ADDIE *brings him a cup*) They don't like red pepper, either. (*He takes the cup and gulps it greedily*) God, that's good. You remember how I used to drink it? Ten, twelve cups a day. So strong it had to stain the cup. (*Then slowly*) Addie, before I see anybody else, I want to know why Zan came to fetch me home. She's tried to tell me, but she doesn't seem to know herself.

ADDIE.   I don't know. All I know is big things are going on. Everybody going to be high-tone rich. Big rich. You too. All because smoke's going to start out of a building that ain't even up yet.

HORACE.   I've heard about it.

ADDIE.   And, er— (*Hesitates, steps to him*) And—well, Zan, maybe she going to marry Mr. Leo in a little while.

HORACE (*looks at her, then very slowly*).   What are you talking about?

ADDIE.   That's right. That's the talk, God help us.

HORACE (*angrily*).   What's the talk?

ADDIE.   I'm telling you. There's going to be a wedding—

HORACE (*after a second, quietly*).   Go and tell them I'm home.

ADDIE (*hesitates*).   Now you ain't to get excited. You're to be in your bed—

HORACE.   Go on, Addie. Go and say I'm back. (ADDIE *opens dining-room doors. He rises with difficulty, stands stiff, as if he were in pain, facing the dining room.*)

ADDIE.   Miss Regina. They're home. They got here—

REGINA.   Horace! (REGINA *quickly, rises, runs into the room. Warmly*) Horace! You've finally arrived. (*As she kisses him, the others come forward, all talking together.*)

BEN (*in doorway, carrying a napkin*).   Well, sir, you had us all mighty worried. (*He steps forward. They shake hands.* ADDIE *exits.*)

OSCAR.   You're a sight for sore eyes.

HORACE.   Hello, Ben.

(LEO *enters, eating a biscuit.*)

OSCAR.   And how you feel? Tip-top, I bet, because that's the way you're looking.

HORACE (*irritated with* OSCAR'S *lie*).   Hello, Oscar. Hello, Leo, how are you?

LEO (*shaking hands*).   I'm fine, sir. But a lot better now that you're back.

REGINA.   Now sit down. What did happen to you and where's Alexandra? I am so excited about seeing you that I almost forgot about her.

HORACE.   I didn't feel good, a little weak, I guess, and we stopped overnight to rest. Zan's upstairs washing off the train dirt.

REGINA.   Oh, I am so sorry the trip was hard on you. I didn't think that—

HORACE.   Well, it's just as if I had never been away. All of you here—

BEN.   Waiting to welcome you home.

(BIRDIE *bursts in. She is wearing a flannel kimono and her face is flushed and excited.*)

BIRDIE (*runs to him, kisses him*).   Horace!

HORACE (*warmly pressing her arm*).   I was just wondering where you were, Birdie.

BIRDIE (*excited*).   Oh, I would have been here. I didn't know you were back until Simon said he saw the buggy. (*She draws back to look at him. Her face sobers*) Oh, you don't look well, Horace. No, you don't.

REGINA (*laughs*).   Birdie, what a thing to say—

HORACE.   Oscar thinks I look very well.

OSCAR (*annoyed. Turns on* LEO).   Don't stand there holding that biscuit in your hand.

LEO.   Oh, well. I'll just finish my breakfast, Uncle Horace and then I'll give you all the news about the bank— (*He exits into the dining room.*)

OSCAR.   And what is that costume you have on?

BIRDIE (*looking at* HORACE).   Now that you're home, you'll feel better. Plenty of good rest and we'll take such fine care of you. (*Stops*) But where is Zan? I missed her so much.

OSCAR.   I asked you what is that strange costume you're parading around in?

BIRDIE (*nervously, backing toward stairs*).   Me? Oh! It's my wrapper. I was so excited about Horace I just rushed out of the house—

OSCAR.   Did you come across the square dressed that way? My dear Birdie, I—

HORACE (*to* REGINA, *wearily*).·   Yes, it's just like old times.

REGINA (*quickly to* OSCAR).   Now, no fights. This is a holiday.

BIRDIE (*runs quickly up the stairs*).   Zan! Zannie!

OSCAR.   Birdie! (*She stops.*)

BIRDIE.   Oh. Tell Zan I'll be back in a little while. (*Whispers*) Sorry, Oscar. (*Exits.*)

REGINA (*to* OSCAR *and* BEN).   Why don't you go finish your breakfast and let Horace rest for a minute?

BEN (*crossing to dining room with* OSCAR).   Never leave a meal unfinished. There are too many poor people who need the food. Mighty glad to see you home, Horace. Fine to have you back. Fine to have you back.

OSCAR (*to* LEO *as* BEN *closes dining-room doors*).   Your mother has gone crazy. Running around the streets like a woman—

(*The moment* REGINA *and* HORACE *are alone, they become awkward and self-conscious.*)

REGINA (*laughs awkwardly*).   Well. Here we are. It's been a long time. (*Horace smiles*) Five months. You know, Horace, I wanted to come and be with you in the hospital, but I didn't know where my duty was. Here, or with you. But you know how much I *wanted* to come.

HORACE.   That's kind of you, Regina. There was no need to come.

REGINA.   Oh, but there was. Five months lying there all by yourself, no kinfolks, no friends. Don't try to tell me you didn't have a bad time of it.

HORACE.   I didn't have a bad time. (*As she shakes her head, he becomes insistent*) No, I didn't, Regina. Oh, at first when I—when I heard the news about myself—but after I got used to that, I liked it there.

REGINA.   You *liked* it? Isn't that strange. You liked it so well you didn't want to come home?

HORACE.   That's not the way to put it. (*Then, kindly, as he sees her turn her head away*) But there I was and I got kind of used to it, kind of to like lying there and thinking. I never had much time to think before. And time's become valuable to me.

REGINA.   It sounds almost like a holiday.

HORACE (*laughs*).   It was, sort of. The first holiday I've had since I was a little kid.

REGINA.   And here I was thinking you were in pain and—

HORACE (*quietly*).   I was in pain.

REGINA.   And instead you were having a holiday! A holiday of thinking. Couldn't you have done that here?

HORACE.   I wanted to do it before I came here. I was thinking about us.

REGINA.   About us? About you and me? Thinking about you and me after all these years. You shall tell me everything you thought—someday.

HORACE (*there is silence for a minute*).   Regina. (*She turns to him*) Why did you send Zan to Baltimore?

REGINA.   Why? Because I wanted you home. You can't make anything suspicious out of that, can you?

HORACE.   I didn't mean to make anything suspicious about it. (*Hesitantly, taking her hand*) Zan said you wanted me to come home. I was so pleased at that and touched. It made me feel good.

REGINA (*taking away her hand*).   Touched that I should want you home?

HORACE.   I'm saying all the wrong things as usual. Let's try to get along better. There isn't so much more time. Regina, what's all this crazy talk I've been hearing about Zan and Leo? Zan and Leo marrying?

REGINA (*turning to him, sharply*).   Who gossips so much around here?

HORACE (*shocked*).   Regina!

REGINA (*anxious to quiet him*).   It's some foolishness that Oscar thought up. I'll explain later. I have no intention of allowing any such arrangement. It was simply a way of keeping Oscar quiet in all this business I've been writing you about—

HORACE (*carefully*).   What has Zan to do with any business of Oscar's? Whatever it is, you had better put it out of Oscar's head immediately. You know what I think of Leo.

REGINA.   But there's no need to talk about it now.

HORACE.   There is no need to talk about it ever. Not as long as I live. (HORACE *stops, slowly turns to look at her*) As long as I live. I've been in a hospital for five months. Yet since I've been here you have not once asked me about—about my health. (*Then gently*) Well, I suppose they've written you. I can't live very long.

REGINA.   I've never understood why people have to talk about this kind of thing.

HORACE (*there is a silence. Then he looks up at her, his face cold*).   You misunderstand. I don't intend to gossip about my sickness. I thought it was only fair to tell you. I was not asking for your sympathy.

REGINA (*sharply, turns to him*).   What do the doctors think caused your bad heart?

HORACE.   What do you mean?

REGINA.   They didn't think it possible, did they, that your fancy women may have—

HORACE (*smiles unpleasantly*).   Caused my heart to be bad? I don't think that's the best scientific theory. You don't catch heart trouble in bed.

REGINA (*angrily*).   I thought you might catch a bad conscience—in bed, as you say.

HORACE.   I didn't tell them about my bad conscience. Or about my fancy women. Nor did I tell them that my wife has not wanted me in bed with her for— (*Sharply*) How long is it, Regina? Ten years? Did you bring me home for this, to make me feel guilty again? That means you want something. But you'll not make me feel guilty anymore. My "thinking" has made a difference.

REGINA.   I see that it has. (*She looks toward dining-room door. Then comes to him, her manner warm and friendly*) It's foolish for us to fight this way. I didn't mean to be unpleasant. I was stupid.

HORACE (*wearily*).   God knows I didn't either. I came home wanting so much not to fight, and then all of a sudden there we were.

REGINA (*hastily*).   It's all my fault. I didn't ask about—about your illness because I didn't want to remind you of it. Anyway, I never believe doctors when they talk about— (*Brightly*) when they talk like that.

HORACE.   I understand. Well, we'll try our best with each other. (*He rises.*)

REGINA (*quickly*).   I'll try. Honestly, I will. Horace, Horace, I know you're tired but, but—couldn't you stay down here a few minutes longer? I want Ben to tell you something.

HORACE.   Tomorrow.

REGINA.   I'd like to now. It's very important to me. It's very important to all of us. (*Gaily, as she moves toward dining room*) Important to your beloved daughter. She'll be a very great heiress—

HORACE.   Will she? That's nice.

REGINA (*opens doors*).   Ben, are you finished breakfast?

HORACE.   Is this the mill business I've had so many letters about?

REGINA (*to* BEN).   Horace would like to talk to you now.

HORACE.   Horace would not like to talk to you now. I am very tired, Regina—

REGINA (*comes to him*).   Please. You've said we'll try our best with each other. I'll try. Really, I will. Please do this for me now. You will see what I've done while you've been away. How I watched your interests. (*Laughs gaily*) And I've done very well too. But things can't be delayed any longer. Every-thing must be settled this week— (HORACE *sits down*. BEN *enters*. OSCAR *has stayed in the dining room, his head turned to watch them*. LEO *is pretending to read the newspaper*) Now you must tell Horace all about it. Only be quick because he is very tired and must go to bed. (HORACE *is looking at her. His face hardens as she speaks*) But I think your news will be better for him than all the medicine in the world.

BEN (*looking at* HORACE).   It could wait. Horace may not feel like talking today.

REGINA.   What an old faker you are! You know it can't wait. You know it must be finished this week. You've been just as anxious for Horace to get here as I've been.

BEN (*very jovial*).   I suppose I have been. And why not? Horace has done Hubbard Sons many a good turn. Why shouldn't I be anxious to help him now?

REGINA (*laughs*).   Help him! Help him when you need him, that's what you mean.

BEN.   What a woman you married, Horace. (*Laughs awkwardly when* HORACE *does not answer*) Well, then I'll make it quick. You know what I've been telling you for years. How I've always said that every one of us little Southern businessmen had great things— (*Extends his arm*) —right beyond our fingertips. It's been my dream: my dream to make those fingers grow longer. I'm a lucky man, Horace, a lucky man. To dream and to live to get what you've dreamed of. That's *my* idea of a lucky man. For thirty years I've cried, bring the cotton mills to the cotton. (HORACE *opens the medicine bottle*) Well finally I got up nerve to go to Marshall Company in Chicago.

HORACE.   I know all this (*He takes the medicine.* REGINA *rises, steps to him.*)

BEN.   Can I get you something?

HORACE.   Some water, please.

REGINA (*turns quickly*).   Oh, I'm sorry. (*Brings him a glass of water. He drinks as they wait in silence*) You feel all right now?

HORACE.   Yes. You wrote me. I know all that.

(OSCAR *enters from dining room.*)

REGINA (*triumphantly*).   But you don't know that in the last few days Ben has agreed to give us—you, I mean—a much larger share.

HORACE.   Really? That's very generous of him.

BEN (*laughs*).   It wasn't so generous of me. It was smart of Regina.

REGINA (*as if she were signaling* HORACE).   I explained to Ben that perhaps you hadn't answered his letters because you didn't think he was offering you enough, and that the time was getting short and you could guess how much he needed you—

HORACE (*smiles at her, nods*).   And I could guess that he wants to keep control in the family.

REGINA (*triumphantly*).   Exactly. So I did a little bargaining for you and convinced my brothers they weren't the only Hubbards who had a business sense.

HORACE.   Did you have to convince them of that? How little people know about each other! (*laughs*) But you'll know better about Regina next time, eh, Ben? (BEN, REGINA, HORACE *laugh together.* OSCAR'S *face is angry*) Now let's see. We're getting a bigger share. (*Looking at* OSCAR) Who's getting less?

BEN.   Oscar.

HORACE.   Well, Oscar, you've grown very unselfish. What's happened to you?

(LEO *enters from dining room.*)

BEN (*quickly*).   Oscar doesn't mind. Not worth fighting about now, eh, Oscar?

OSCAR (*angrily*).   I'll get mine in the end. You can be sure of that. I've got my son's future to think about.

HORACE (*sharply*).   Leo? Oh, I see. (*Puts his head back, laughs.* REGINA *looks at him nervously*) I am beginning to see. Everybody will get theirs.

BEN.   I knew you'd see it. Seventy-five thousand, and that seventy-five thousand will make you a million.

REGINA.   It will, Horace, it will.

HORACE.   I believe you. (*After a second*) Now I can understand Oscar's self-sacrifice, but what did you have to promise Marshall Company besides the money you're putting up?

BEN.   They wouldn't take promises. They wanted guarantees.

HORACE.   Of what?

BEN.   Water power. Free and plenty of it.

HORACE.   You got them that, of course.

BEN.   Cheap. You'd think the Governor of a great state would make his price a little higher. From pride, you know. (HORACE *smiles.* BEN *smiles*) Cheap wages. "What do you mean by cheap wages?" I say to Marshall. "Less than Massachusetts," he says to me, "and that averages eight a week." "Eight a week! By God," I tell him, "I'd work for eight a week myself." Why, there ain't a mountain white or a town nigger but wouldn't give his right arm for three silver dollars every week, eh, Horace?

HORACE.   Sure. And they'll take less than that when you get around to playing them off against each other. You can save a little money that way, Ben. And make them hate each other just a little more than they do now.

REGINA.   What's all this about?

BEN (*laughs*).   There'll be no trouble from anybody, white or black. Marshall said that to me. "What about strikes? That's all we've had in Massachusetts for the last three years." I say to him, "What's a strike? I never heard of one. Come South, Marshall. We got good folks and we don't stand for any fancy fooling."

HORACE.   You're right. (*Slowly*) Well, it looks like you made a good deal for yourselves, and for Marshall, too. Your father used to say he made the thousands and you boys would make the millions. I think he was right. (*Rises.*)

REGINA (*as they look at* HORACE. *She laughs nervously*).   Millions for *us*, too.

HORACE.   Us? You and me? I don't think so. We've got enough money, Regina. We'll just sit by and watch the boys grow rich. (*They watch* HORACE *as he begins to move toward the staircase. He passes* LEO, *looks at him for a second*) How's everything at the bank, Leo?

LEO.   Fine, sir. Everything is fine.

HORACE.   How are all the ladies in Mobile? (HORACE *turns to* REGINA, *sharply*) Whatever made you think I'd let Zan marry—

REGINA.   Do you mean that you are turning this down? Is it possible that's what you mean?

BEN.   No, that's not what he means. Turning down a fortune. Horace is tired. He'd rather talk about it tomorrow—

REGINA.   We can't keep putting it off this way. Oscar must be in Chicago by the end of the week with the money and contracts.

OSCAR (*giggles, pleased*).   Yes, sir. Got to be there end of the week. No sense going without the money.

REGINA (*tensely*).   I've waited long enough for your answer. I'm not going to wait any longer.

HORACE (*very deliberately*).   I'm very tired now, Regina.

BEN (*quickly*).   Now, Horace probably has his reasons. Things he'd like explained. Tomorrow will do. I can—

REGINA (*turns to* BEN, *sharply*).   I want to know his reasons now!

HORACE (*as he climbs the steps*).   I don't know them all myself. Let's leave it at that.

REGINA.   We shall not leave it at that! We have waited for you here like children. Waited for you to come home.

HORACE.   So that you could invest my money. So that is why you wanted me home? Well, I had hoped— (*Quietly*) If you are disappointed, Regina, I'm sorry. But I must do what I think best. We'll talk about it another day.

REGINA.   We'll talk about it now. Just you and me.

HORACE (*looks down at her. His voice is tense*).   Please, Regina, it's been a hard trip. I don't feel well. Please leave me alone now.

REGINA (*quietly*).   I want to talk to you, Horace. (*He looks at her for a minute, then moves on, out of sight. She begins to climb the stairs.*)

BEN (*softly.* REGINA *turns to him as he speaks*).   Sometimes it is better to wait for the sun to rise again. (*She does not answer*) And sometimes, as our mother used to tell you, (REGINA *continues up stairs*) it's unwise for a good-looking woman to frown. (BEN *rises, moves toward stairs*) Softness and a smile do more to the heart of men— (*She disappears.* BEN *stands looking up the stairs. There is a long silence. Then* OSCAR *giggles.*)

OSCAR.   Let us hope she'll change his mind. Let us hope. (*After a second* BEN *crosses to table, picks up his newspaper.* OSCAR *looks at* BEN. *The silence makes* LEO *uncomfortable.*)

LEO.   The paper says twenty-seven cases of yellow fever in New Orleans. Guess the floodwaters caused it. (*Nobody pays attention*) Thought they were building the levees high enough. Like the niggers always say: a man born of woman can't build nothing high enough for the Mississippi. (*Gets no answer. Gives an embarrassed laugh.*)

(*Upstairs there is the sound of voices. The voices are not loud, but* BEN, OSCAR, LEO *become conscious of them.* LEO *crosses to landing, looks up, listens.*)

OSCAR (*pointing up*).   Now just suppose she don't change his mind? Just suppose he keeps on refusing?

BEN (*without conviction*).   He's tired. It was a mistake to talk to him today. He's a sick man, but he isn't a crazy one.

OSCAR.   But just suppose he is crazy. What then?

BEN (*puts down his paper, peers at* OSCAR).   Then we'll go outside for the money. There's plenty who would give it.

OSCAR.   And plenty who will want a lot for what they give. The ones who are rich enough to give will be smart enough to want. That means we'd be working for them, don't it, Ben?

BEN.   You don't have to tell me the things I told you six months ago.

OSCAR.   Oh, you're right not to worry. She'll change his mind. She always has. (*There is a silence. Suddenly* REGINA'S *voice becomes louder and sharper. All of them begin to listen now. Slowly* BEN *rises, goes to listen by the staircase.* OSCAR, *watching him, smiles. As they listen* REGINA'S *voice becomes very loud.* HORACE'S *voice is no longer heard*) Maybe. But I don't believe it. I never did believe he was going in with us.

BEN (*turning on him*).   What the hell do you expect me to do?

OSCAR (*mildly*).   Nothing. You done your almighty best. Nobody could blame you if the whole thing just dripped away right through our fingers. You can't do a thing. But there may be something I could do for us. (OSCAR *rises*) Or, I might better say, Leo could do for us. (BEN *turns, looks at* OSCAR. LEO *is staring at* OSCAR.) Ain't that true, son? Ain't it true you might be able to help your own kinfolks?

LEO (*nervously taking a step to him*).   Papa, I—

BEN (*slowly*).   How would he help us, Oscar?

OSCAR.   Leo's got a friend. Leo's friend owns eighty-eight thousand dollars in Union Pacific bonds. (BEN *turns to look at* LEO) Leo's friend don't look at the bonds much—not for five or six months at a time.

BEN (*after a pause*).   Union Pacific. Uh, huh. Let me understand. Leo's friend would—would lend him these bonds and he—

OSCAR (*nods*).   Would be kind enough to lend them to us.

BEN.   Leo.

LEO (*excited, comes to him*).   Yes, sir?

BEN.   When would your friend be wanting the bonds back?

LEO (*very nervously*).   I don't know. I—well, I—

OSCAR (*sharply. Steps to him*).   You told me he won't look at them until Autumn—

LEO.   Oh, that's right. But I—not till Autumn. Uncle Horace never—

BEN (*sharply*).   Be still.

OSCAR (*smiles at* LEO).   Your uncle doesn't wish to know your friend's name.

LEO (*starts to laugh*).   That's a good one. Not know his name—

OSCAR.   Shut up, Leo! (LEO *turns away*) He won't look at them again until September. That gives us five months. Leo will return the bonds in three months. And we'll have no trouble raising the money once the mills are going up. Will Marshall accept bonds?

(BEN *stops to listen to the voices from above. The voices are now very angry and very loud.*)

BEN (*smiling*).   Why not? Why not? (*Laughs*) Good. We are lucky. We'll take the loan from Leo's friend—I think he will make a safer partner than our sister. (*Nods toward stairs. Turns to* LEO) How soon can you get them?

LEO.   Today. Right now. They're in the safe-deposit box and—

BEN (*sharply*).   I don't want to know where they are.

OSCAR (*laughs*).   We will keep it secret from you. (*Pats* BEN'S *arm.*)

BEN.   Good. Draw a check for our part. You can take the night train for Chicago. Well, Oscar (*Holds out his hand*), good luck to us.

OSCAR.   Leo will be taken care of?

LEO.   I'm entitled to Uncle Horace's share. I'd enjoy being a partner—

BEN (*wheels on him*).   You would? You can go to hell, you little— (*Starts toward* LEO.)

OSCAR (*nervously*).   Now, now. He didn't mean that. I only want to be sure he'll get something out of all this.

BEN.   Of course. We'll take care of him. We won't have any trouble about that. I'll see you at the store.

OSCAR (*nods*).   That's settled then. Come on, son. (*Starts for door.*)

LEO (*puts out his hand*).   I was only going to say what a great day this was for me and—

BEN.   Go on.

(LEO *turns, follows* OSCAR *out. Again the voices upstairs can be heard.* REGINA'S *voice is high and furious.* BEN *looks up, smiles, winces at the noise.*)

ALEXANDRA (*upstairs*).   Mama—Mama—don't . . . (*The noise of running footsteps is heard and* ALEXANDRA *comes running down the steps, speaking as she comes.*) Uncle Ben! Uncle Ben! Please go up. Please make Mama stop. Uncle Ben, he's sick, he's so sick. How can Mama talk to him like that—please, make her stop. She'll—

BEN.   Alexandra, you have a tender heart.

ALEXANDRA (*crying*).   Go on up, Uncle Ben, please—

(*Suddenly the voices stop. A second later there is the sound of a door being slammed.*)

BEN.   Now you see. Everything is over. Don't worry. (*He starts for the door*) Alexandra, I want you to tell your mother how sorry I am that I had to leave. And don't worry so, my dear. Married folk frequently raise their voices, unfortunately.

(*He starts to put on his hat and coat as* REGINA *appears on the stairs.*)

ALEXANDRA (*furiously*).   How can you treat Papa like this? He's sick. He's very sick. Don't you know that? I won't let you.

REGINA.   Mind your business, Alexandra. (*To* BEN. *Her voice is cold and calm*) How much longer can you wait for the money?

BEN (*putting on his coat*).   He has refused? My, that's too bad.

REGINA.   He will change his mind. I'll find a way to make him. What's the longest you can wait now?

BEN.   I could wait until next week. But I can't wait until next week. (*He giggles, pleased*) I could but I can't. Could and can't. Well, I must go now. I'm very late—

REGINA (*coming downstairs toward him*).   You're not going. I want to talk to you.

BEN.   I was about to give Alexandra a message for you. I wanted to tell you that Oscar is going to Chicago tonight, so we can't be here for our usual Friday supper.

REGINA (*tensely*).   Oscar is going to Chi— (*Softly*) What do you mean?

BEN.   Just that. Everything is settled. He's going on to deliver to Marshall—

REGINA (*taking a step to him*).   I demand to know what—You are lying. You are trying to scare me. *You haven't got the money.* How could you have it? You can't have— (BEN *laughs*) You will wait until I—

(HORACE *comes into view on the landing.*)

BEN.   You are getting out of hand. Since when do I take orders from you?

REGINA.   Wait, you— (BEN *stops*) How *can* he go to Chicago? Did a ghost arrive with the money? (BEN *starts for the hall*) I don't believe you. Come back here. (REGINA *starts after him*) Come back here, you— (*The door slams. She stops in the doorway, staring, her fists clenched. After a pause she turns slowly.*)

HORACE (*very quietly*).   It's a great day when you and Ben cross swords. I've been waiting for it for years.

ALEXANDRA.   Papa, Papa, please go back! You will—

HORACE.   And so they don't need you, and so you will not have your millions, after all.

REGINA *(turns slowly)*.   You hate to see anybody live now, don't you? You hate to think that I'm going to be alive and have what I want.

HORACE.   I should have known you'd think that was the reason.

REGINA.   Because you're going to die and you know you're going to die.

ALEXANDRA *(shrilly)*.   Mama! Don't—Don't listen, Papa. Just don't listen. Go away—

HORACE.   Not to keep you from getting what you want. Not even partly that. I'm sick of you, sick of this house, sick of my life here. I'm sick of your brothers and their dirty tricks to make a dime. Why should I give you the money? *(Very angrily)* To pound the bones of this town to make dividends for you to spend? You wreck the town, you and your brothers, *you* wreck the town and live on it. Not me. Maybe it's easy for the dying to be honest. But it's not my fault I'm dying. I'll do no more harm now. I've done enough. I'll die my own way. And I'll do it without making the world any worse. I leave that to you.

REGINA *(looks up at him)*.   I hope you die. I hope you die soon. *(Smiles)* I'll be waiting for you to die.

ALEXANDRA *(shrieking)*.   Papa! Don't—Don't listen—Don't— (HORACE *turns slowly and starts upstairs.*)

ACT III

SCENE: *Same as Act One. Two weeks later. It is late afternoon and it is raining.*

AT RISE: HORACE *is sitting near the window in a wheelchair. On the table next to him is a safe-deposit box, and a small bottle of medicine.* BIRDIE *and* ALEXANDRA *are playing the piano. On a chair is a large sewing basket.*

BIRDIE *(counting for* ALEXANDRA*)*.   One and two and three and four. One and two and three and four. *(Nods—turns to* HORACE*)* We once played together, Horace. Remember?

HORACE *(has been looking out of the window)*.   What, Birdie?

BIRDIE.   We played together. You and me.

ALEXANDRA.   *Papa* used to play?

BIRDIE.   Indeed he did. (ADDIE *appears at the door in a large kitchen apron*) He played the fiddle and very well, too.

ALEXANDRA *(turns to smile at* HORACE*)*.   I never knew—

ADDIE.   Where's your mama?

ALEXANDRA.   Gone to Miss Safronia's to fit her dresses.

(ADDIE *nods, starts to exit.*)

HORACE.   Addie. Tell Cal to get on his things. I want him to go on an errand.

(ADDIE *nods, exits.* HORACE *moves nervously in his chair, looks out of the window.*)

ALEXANDRA (*who has been watching him*).   It's too bad it's been raining all day, Papa. But you can go out in the yard tomorrow. Don't be restless.

HORACE.   I'm not restless, darling.

BIRDIE.   I remember so well the time we played together, your papa and me. It was the first time Oscar brought me here to supper. I had never seen all the Hubbards together before, and you know what a ninny I am and how shy. (*Turns to look at* HORACE) You said you could play the fiddle and you'd be much obliged if I'd play with you. *I* was obliged to *you*, all right, all right. (*Laughs when he does not answer her*) Horace, you haven't heard a word I've said.

HORACE.   Birdie, when did Oscar get back from Chicago?

BIRDIE.   Yesterday. Hasn't he been here yet?

ALEXANDRA (*stops playing*).   No. Neither has Uncle Ben since—since that day.

BIRDIE.   Oh, I didn't know it was *that* bad. Oscar never tells me anything—

HORACE.   The Hubbards have had their great quarrel. I knew it would come someday. (*Laughs*) It came.

ALEXANDRA.   It came. It certainly came all right.

BIRDIE (*amazed*).   But Oscar was in such a good humor when he got home, I didn't—

HORACE.   Yes, I can understand that.

(ADDIE *enters carrying a large tray with glasses, a carafe of elderberry wine and a plate of cookies, which she puts on the table.*)

ALEXANDRA.   Addie! A party! What for?

ADDIE.   Nothing for. I had the fresh butter, so I made the cakes, and a little elderberry does the stomach good in the rain.

BIRDIE.   Isn't this nice! A party just for us. Let's play party music, Zan.

(ALEXANDRA *begins to play a gay piece.*)

ADDIE (*to* HORACE, *wheeling his chair to center*).   Come over here, Mr. Horace, and don't be thinking so much. A glass of elderberry will do more good.

(ALEXANDRA *reaches for a cake.* BIRDIE *pours herself a glass of wine.*)

ALEXANDRA.   Good cakes, Addie. It's nice here. Just us. Be nice if it could always be this way.

BIRDIE (*nods happily*).   Quiet and restful.

ADDIE.   Well, it won't be that way long. Little while now, even sitting here, you'll hear the red bricks going into place. The next day the smoke'll be pushing out the chimneys and by church time that Sunday every human born of woman will be living on chicken. That's how Mr. Ben's been telling the story.

HORACE.   They believe it that way?

ADDIE.   Believe it? They use to believing what Mr. Ben orders. There ain't been so much talk around here since Sherman's army didn't come near.

HORACE (*softly*).   They are fools.

ADDIE (*nods, sits down with the sewing basket*).   You ain't born in the South unless you're a fool.

BIRDIE (*has drunk another glass of wine*).   But we didn't play together after that night. Oscar said he didn't like me to play on the piano. (*Turns to* ALEXANDRA) You know what he said that night?

ALEXANDRA.   Who?

BIRDIE.   Oscar. He said that music made him nervous. He said he just sat and waited for the next note. (ALEXANDRA *laughs*) He wasn't poking fun. He meant it. Ah, well— (*She finishes her glass, shakes her head.* HORACE *looks at her, smiles*) Your papa don't like to admit it, but he's been mighty kind to me all these years. (*Running her hand along his sleeve*) Often he'd step in when somebody said something and once— (*She stops, turns away, her face still*) Once he stopped Oscar from— (*She stops, turns. Quickly*) I'm sorry I said that. Why, here I am so happy and yet I think about bad things. (*Laughs nervously*) That's not right, now, is it? (*She pours a drink.* CAL *appears in the door. He has on an old coat and is carrying a torn umbrella.*)

ALEXANDRA.   Have a cake, Cal.

CAL (*comes in, takes a cake*).   You want me, Mr. Horace?

HORACE.   What time is it, Cal?

CAL.   'Bout ten minutes before it's five.

HORACE.   All right. Now you walk yourself down to the bank.

CAL.   It'll be closed. Nobody'll be there but Mr. Manders, Mr. Joe Horns, Mr. Leo—

HORACE.   Go in the back way. They'll be at the table, going over the day's business. (*Points to the deposit box*) See that box?

CAL (*nods*).   Yes, sir.

HORACE.   You tell Mr. Manders that Mr. Horace says he's much obliged to him for bringing the box, it arrived all right.

CAL (*bewildered*).   He know you got the box. He bring it himself Wednesday. I opened the door to him and he say "Hello, Cal, coming on to summer weather."

HORACE.   You say just what I tell you. Understand?

(BIRDIE *pours another drink, stands at table.*)

CAL.   No, sir. I ain't going to say I understand. I'm going down and tell a man he give you something he already know he give you, and you say "understand."

HORACE.   Now, Cal.

CAL.   Yes, sir. I just going to say you obliged for the box coming all right. I ain't going to understand it, but I'm going to say it.

HORACE.   And tell him I want him to come over here after supper, and to bring Mr. Sol Fowler with him.

CAL (*nods*).   He's to come after supper and bring Mr. Sol Fowler, your attorney-at-law, with him.

HORACE.   That's right. Just walk right in the back room and say your piece. (*Slowly*) In front of everybody.

CAL.   Yes, sir. (*Mumbles to himself as he exits.*)

ALEXANDRA (*who has been watching* HORACE).   Is anything the matter, Papa?

HORACE.   Oh, no. Nothing.

ADDIE.   Miss Birdie, that elderberry going to give you a headache spell.

BIRDIE (*beginning to be drunk. Gaily*).   Oh, I don't think so. I don't think it will.

ALEXANDRA (*as* HORACE *puts his hand to his throat*).   Do you want your medicine, Papa?

HORACE.   No, no. I'm all right, darling.

BIRDIE.   Mama used to give me elderberry wine when I was a little girl. For hiccoughs. (*Laughs*) You know, I don't think people get hiccoughs anymore. Isn't that funny? (BIRDIE *laughs.* HORACE *and* ALEXANDRA *smile*) I used to get hiccoughs just when I shouldn't have.

ADDIE (*nods*).   And nobody gets growing pains no more. That is funny. Just as if there was some style in what you get. One year an ailment's stylish and the next year it ain't.

BIRDIE.   I remember. It was my first big party, at Lionnet I mean, and I was so excited, and there I was with hiccoughs and Mama laughing. (*Softly. Looking at carafe*) Mama always laughed. (*Picks up carafe*) A big party, a lovely dress from Mr. Worth in Paris, France, and hiccoughs. (*Pours drink*) My brother pounding me on the back and Mama with the elderberry bottle, laughing at me. Everybody was on their way to come, and I was such a ninny, hiccoughing away. (*Drinks*) You know, that was the first day I ever saw Oscar Hubbard. The Ballongs were selling their horses and he was going there to buy. He passed and lifted his hat—we could see him from the window—and my brother, to tease Mama, said maybe we should have invited the Hubbards to the party. He said Mama didn't like them because they kept a store, and he said that was old-fashioned of her. (*Her face lights up*) And then, and *then*, I saw Mama angry for the first time in my life. She said that wasn't the reason. She said she was old-fashioned, but not that way. She said she was old-fashioned enough not to like people who killed animals they couldn't use, and who made their money charging awful interest to ignorant niggers and cheating them on what they bought. She was very angry, Mama was. I had never seen her face like that. And then suddenly she laughed and said, "Look, I've frightened Birdie out of the hiccoughs." (*Her head drops. Then softly*) And so she had. They were all gone. (*Moves to sofa, sits.*)

ADDIE.   Yeah, they got mighty well-off cheating niggers. Well, there are people who eat the earth and eat all the people on it like in the Bible with the locusts. And other people who stand around and watch them eat it. (*Softly*) Sometimes I think it ain't right to stand and watch them do it.

BIRDIE (*thoughtfully*).   Like I say, if we could only go back to Lionnet. Everybody'd be better there. They'd be good and kind. I like people to be kind. (*Pours drink*) Don't you, Horace; don't you like people to be kind?

HORACE.   Yes, Birdie.

BIRDIE (*very drunk now*).   Yes, that was the first day I ever saw Oscar. Who would have thought—You all want to know something? Well, I don't like Leo. My very own son, and I don't like him. (*Laughs, gaily*) My, I guess I even like Oscar more.

ALEXANDRA.   Why did you marry Uncle Oscar?

ADDIE.   That's no question for you to be asking.

HORACE (*sharply*).   Why not? She's heard enough around here to ask anything.

BIRDIE.   I don't know. I thought I liked him. He was kind to me and I thought it was because he liked me too. But that wasn't the reason— (*Wheels on* ALEXANDRA) Ask why *he* married *me*. I can tell you that: he's told it to me often enough.

ADDIE.   Miss Birdie, don't—

BIRDIE (*speaking very rapidly*).   My family was good and the cotton on Lionnet's fields was better. Ben Hubbard wanted the cotton and Oscar Hubbard married it for him. He was kind to me, then. He used to smile at me. He hasn't smiled at me since. Everybody knew that's what he married me for. (ADDIE *rises*) Everybody but me. Stupid, stupid me.

ALEXANDRA (*to* HORACE, *softly*).   I see. (*Hesitates*) Papa, I mean—when you feel better couldn't we go away? I mean, by ourselves. Couldn't we find a way to go?

HORACE.   Yes, I know what you mean. We'll try to find a way. I promise you, darling.

ADDIE (*moves to* BIRDIE).   Rest a bit, Miss Birdie. You get talking like this you'll get a headache and—

BIRDIE (*sharply*).   I've never had a headache in my life. (*Begins to cry*) You know it as well as I do. (*Turns to* ALEXANDRA) I never had a headache, Zan. That's a lie they tell for me. I drink. All by myself, in my own room, by myself, I drink. Then, when they want to hide it, they say, "Birdie's got a headache again"—

ALEXANDRA (*comes to her*).   Aunt Birdie.

BIRDIE.   Even you won't like me now. You won't like me anymore.

ALEXANDRA.   I love you. I'll always love you.

BIRDIE (*angrily*).   Well, don't. Don't love me. Because in twenty years you'll just be like me. They'll do all the same things to you. (*Begins to laugh*) You know what? In twenty-two years I haven't had a whole day of happiness. Oh, a little, like today with you all. But never a single, whole day. I say to myself, if only I had one more *whole* day, then— (*The laugh stops*) And that's the way you'll be. And you'll trail after them, just like me, hoping they won't be so mean that day or say something to make you feel so bad—only you'll be worse off because you haven't got my Mama to remember— (*Turns away, her head drops. She stands quietly, swaying a little, holding to the sofa.*)

ALEXANDRA (*to* BIRDIE).   I guess we were all trying to make a happy day. You know, we sit around and try to pretend nothing's happened. We try to pretend we are not here. We make believe we are just by ourselves, someplace else, and it doesn't seem to work. (*Kisses* BIRDIE's *hand*) Come now, Aunt Birdie, I'll walk you home. You and me. (*She takes* BIRDIE's *arm. They move slowly out.*)

BIRDIE (*softly as they exit*).   You and me.

ADDIE (*after a minute*).   Well. First time I ever heard Miss Birdie say a word. Maybe it's good for her. I'm just sorry Zan had to hear it. (HORACE *moves his head as if he were uncomfortable*) You feel bad, don't you? (*He shrugs.*)

HORACE.   So you didn't want Zan to hear? It would be nice to let her stay innocent, like Birdie at her age. Let her listen now. Let her see everything. How else is she going to know that she's got to get away? I'm trying to show her that. I'm trying, but I've only got a little time left. She can even hate me when I'm dead, if she'll only learn to hate and fear this.

ADDIE.   Mr. Horace—

HORACE.   Pretty soon there'll be nobody to help her but you.

ADDIE.   What can I do?

HORACE.   Take her away.

ADDIE.   How can I do that? Do you think they'd let me just go away with her?

HORACE.   I'll fix it so they can't stop you when you're ready to go. You'll go, Addie?

ADDIE (*after a second, softly*).   Yes, sir. I promise. (*He touches her arm, nods.*)

HORACE (*quietly*).   I'm going to have Sol Fowler make me a new will. They'll make trouble, but you make Zan stand firm and Fowler'll do the rest. Addie, I'd like to leave you something for yourself. I always wanted to.

ADDIE (*laughs*).   Don't you do that, Mr. Horace. A nigger woman in a white man's will! I'd never get it nohow.

HORACE.   I know. But upstairs in the armoire drawer there's thirty-seven hundred-dollar bills. It's money left from my trip. It's in an envelope with your name. It's for you.

ADDIE.   It's mighty kind and good of you. I don't know what to say for thanks—

CAL (*appears in doorway*).   I'm back. (*No answer*) I'm back.

ADDIE.   So we see.

HORACE.   Well?

CAL.   Nothing. I just went down and spoke my piece. Just like you told me. I say, "Mr. Horace he thank you mightily for the safe box arriving in good shape and he say you come right after supper to his house and bring Mr. Attorney-at-law Sol Fowler with you." Then I wipe my hands on my coat. Every time I ever told a lie in my whole life, I wipe my hands right after. Well, while I'm wiping my hands, Mr. Leo jump up and say to me, "What box? What you talking about?"

HORACE (*smiles*).   Did he?

CAL.   And Mr. Leo say he got to leave a little early cause he got something to do. And then Mr. Manders say Mr. Leo should sit right down and finish up his work and stop acting like somebody made him Mr. President. So he sit down. Now, just like I told you, Mr. Manders was mighty surprised with the message because he knows right well he brought the box— (*Points to box, sighs*) But he took it all right. Some men take everything easy and some do not.

HORACE (*laughs*).   Mr. Leo was telling the truth; he *has* got something to do. I hope Manders don't keep him too long. (*Outside there is the sound of voices. Cal exits.* ADDIE *crosses quickly to* HORACE, *begins to wheel his chair toward the stairs*) No. Leave me where I am.

ADDIE.   But that's Miss Regina coming back.

HORACE (*nods, looking at door*).   Go away, Addie.

ADDIE (*hesitates*).   Mr. Horace. Don't talk no more today. You don't feel well and it won't do no good—

HORACE (*as he hears footsteps in the hall*).   Go on. (*She looks at him for a second, then picks up her sewing from table and exits as* REGINA *comes in from hall.* HORACE'S *chair is now so placed that he is in front of the table with the medicine.* REGINA *stands in the hall, shakes umbrella, stands it in the corner, takes off her cloak and throws it over the banister. She stares at* HORACE.)

REGINA (*as she takes off her gloves*).   We had agreed that you were to stay in your part of this house and I in mine. This room is *my* part of the house. Please don't come down here again.

HORACE.   I won't.

REGINA (*crosses toward bell cord*).   I'll get Cal to take you upstairs.

HORACE.   Before you do I want to tell you that after all, we have invested our money in Hubbard Sons and Marshall, Cotton Manufacturers.

REGINA (*stops, turns, stares at him*).   What are you talking about? You haven't seen Ben—When did you change your mind?

HORACE.   I didn't change my mind. *I* didn't invest the money. (*Smiles*) It was invested for me.

REGINA (*angrily*).   What—?

HORACE.   I had eighty-eight thousand dollars' worth of Union Pacific bonds in that safe-deposit box. They are not there now. Go and look. (*As she stares at him, he points to the box*) Go and look, Regina. (*She crosses quickly to the box, opens it*) Those bonds are as negotiable as money.

REGINA (*turns back to him*).   What kind of joke are you playing now? Is this for my benefit?

HORACE.   I don't look in that box very often, but three days ago, on Wednesday it was, because I had made a decision—

REGINA.   I want to know what you are talking about.

HORACE.   Don't interrupt me again. Because I had made a decision, I sent for the box. The bonds were gone. Eighty-eight thousand dollars gone. (*He smiles at her.*)

REGINA (*after a moment's silence, quietly*).   Do you think I'm crazy enough to believe what you're saying?

HORACE.   Believe anything you like.

REGINA (*slowly*).   Where did they go to?

HORACE.   They are in Chicago. With Mr. Marshall, I should guess.

REGINA.   What did they do? Walk to Chicago? Have you really gone crazy?

HORACE.   Leo took the bonds.

REGINA (*turns sharply, then speaks softly, without conviction*).   I don't believe it.

HORACE.   I wasn't there but I can guess what happened. This fine gentleman, with whom you were bargaining your daughter, took the keys and opened the box. You remember that the day of the fight Oscar went to Chicago? Well, he went with my bonds that his son Leo had stolen for him. (*Pleasantly*) And for Ben.

REGINA (*slowly, nods*).   When did you find out the bonds were gone?

HORACE.   Wednesday night.

REGINA.   I thought that's what you said. Why have you waited three days to do anything? (*Suddenly laughs*) This *will* make a fine story.

HORACE (*nods*).   Couldn't it?

REGINA.   A fine story to hold over their heads. How could they be such fools?

HORACE.   But I'm not going to hold it over their heads.

REGINA (*the laugh stops*).   What?

HORACE (*turns his chair to face her*).   I'm going to let them keep the bonds—as a loan from you. An eighty-eight-thousand-dollar loan; they should be grateful to you. They will be, I think.

REGINA (*slowly, smiles*).   I see. You are punishing me. But I won't let you punish me. If you won't do anything, I will. Now. (*She starts for door.*)

HORACE.   You won't do anything. Because you can't. (REGINA *stops*) It won't do you any good to make trouble because I shall simply say that I lent them the bonds.

REGINA (*slowly*).   You would do that?

HORACE.   Yes. For once in your life I am tying your hands. There is nothing for you to do. (*There is silence. Then she sits down.*)

REGINA.   I see. You are going to lend them the bonds and let them keep all the profit they make on them, and there is nothing I can do about it. Is that right?

HORACE.   Yes.

REGINA (*softly*).   Why did you say that I was making this gift?

HORACE.   I was coming to that. I am going to make a new will, Regina, leaving you eighty-eight thousand dollars in Union Pacific bonds. The rest will go to Zan. It's true that your brothers have borrowed your share for a little while. After my death I advise you to talk to Ben and Oscar. They won't admit anything and Ben, I think, will be smart enough to see that he's safe. Because I knew about the theft and said nothing. Nor will I say anything as long as I live. Is that clear to you?

REGINA (*nods, softly, without looking at him*).   You will not say anything as long as you live.

HORACE.   That's right. And by that time they will probably have replaced your bonds, and then they'll belong to you and nobody but us will ever know what happened. They'll be around any minute to see what I am going to do. I took good care to see that word reached Leo. They'll be mighty relieved to know I'm going to do nothing and Ben will think it all a capital joke on you. And that will be the end of that. There's nothing you can do to them, nothing you can do to me.

REGINA.   You hate me very much.

HORACE.   No.

REGINA.   Oh, I think you do. (*Puts her head back, sighs*) Well, we haven't been very good together. Anyway, I don't hate you either. I have only contempt for you. I've always had.

HORACE.   From the very first?

REGINA.   I think so.

HORACE.   I was in love with *you*. But why did *you* marry *me*?

REGINA.   I was lonely when I was young.

HORACE.   *You* were lonely?

REGINA.   Not the way people usually mean. Lonely for all the things I wasn't going to get. Everybody in this house was so busy and there was so little place for what I wanted. I wanted the world. Then, and then— (*Smiles*) Papa died and left the money to Ben and Oscar.

HORACE.   And you married me?

REGINA.   Yes, I thought— But I was wrong. You were a small-town clerk then. You haven't changed.

HORACE (*nods*).   And that wasn't what you wanted.

REGINA.   No. No, it wasn't what I wanted. (*Pleasantly*) It took me a little while to find out I had made a mistake. As for you— I don't know. It was almost as if I couldn't stand the kind of man you were— (*Smiles, softly*) I used to lie there at night, praying you wouldn't come near—

HORACE.   Really? It was as bad as that?

REGINA.   Remember when I went to Doctor Sloan and I told you he said there was something the matter with me and that you shouldn't touch me anymore?

HORACE.   I remember.

REGINA.   But you believed it. I couldn't understand that. I couldn't understand that anybody could be such a soft fool. That was when I began to despise you.

HORACE (*puts his hand to his throat, looks at the bottle of medicine on table*).   Why didn't you leave me?

REGINA.   I told you I married you for something. It turned out it was only for this. (*Carefully*) This wasn't what I wanted, but it was something. I never thought about it much, but if I had I'd have known that you would die before I would. But I couldn't have known that you would get heart trouble so early and so bad. I'm lucky, Horace. I've always been lucky. (HORACE *turns slowly to the medicine*) I'll be lucky again. (HORACE *looks at her. Then he puts his hand to his throat. Because he cannot reach the bottle he moves the chair closer. He reaches for the medicine, takes out the cork, picks up the spoon. The bottle slips and smashes on the table. He draws in his breath, gasps.*)

HORACE.   Please. Tell Addie— The other bottle is upstairs. (REGINA *has not moved. She does not move now. He stares at her. Then, suddenly as if he understood, he raises his voice. It is a panic-stricken whisper, too small to be heard outside the room.*) Addie! Addie! Come— (*Stops as he hears the softness of his voice. He makes a sudden, furious spring from the chair to the stairs, taking the first few steps as if he were a desperate runner. Then he slips, gasps, grasps the rail, makes a great effort to reach the landing. When he reaches the landing, he is on his knees. His knees give way, he falls on the landing, out of view.* REGINA *has not turned during his climb up the stairs. Now she waits a second. Then she goes below the landing, speaks up.*)

REGINA.   Horace. Horace. (*When there is no answer, she turns, calls*) Addie! Cal! Come in here. (*She starts up the steps.* ADDIE *and* CAL *appear. Both run toward the stairs*) He's had an attack. Come up here. (*They run up the steps quickly.*)

CAL.   My God. Mr. Horace—

(*They cannot be seen now.*)

REGINA (*her voice comes from the head of the stairs*).   Be still, Cal. Bring him in here.

(*Before the footsteps and the voices have completely died away,* ALEXANDRA *appears in the hall door, in her raincloak and hood. She comes into the room, begins to unfasten the cloak, suddenly looks around, sees the empty wheelchair, stares, begins to move swiftly as if to look in the dining room. At the same moment* ADDIE *runs down the stairs.* ALEXANDRA *turns and stares up at* ADDIE.)

ALEXANDRA.   Addie! What?

ADDIE (*takes* ALEXANDRA *by the shoulders*).   I'm going for the doctor. Go upstairs. (ALEXANDRA *looks at her, then quickly breaks away and runs up the steps.* ADDIE *exits. The stage is empty for a minute. Then the front doorbell begins to ring. When there is no answer, it rings again. A second later* LEO *appears in the hall, talking as he comes in.*)

LEO (*very nervous*).   Hello. (*Irritably*) Never saw any use ringing a bell when a door was open. If you are going to ring a bell, then somebody should answer it. (*Gets in the room, looks around, puzzled, listens, hears no sound*) Aunt Regina. (*He moves around restlessly*) Addie. (*Waits*) Where the hell— (*Crosses to the bell cord, rings it impatiently, waits, gets no answer, calls*) Cal! Cal! (CAL *appears on the stair landing.*)

CAL (*his voice is soft, shaken*).   Mr. Leo. Miss Regina says you stop that screaming noise.

LEO (*angrily*).   Where is everybody?

CAL.   Mr. Horace he got an attack. He's bad. Miss Regina says you stop that noise.

LEO.   Uncle Horace— What— What happened? (CAL *starts down the stairs, shakes his head, begins to move swiftly off.* LEO *looks around wildly*) But when— You seen Mr. Oscar or Mr. Ben? (CAL *shakes his head. Moves on.* LEO *grabs him by the arm*) Answer me, will you?

CAL.   No, I ain't seen 'em. I ain't got time to answer you. I got to get things. (CAL *runs off.*)

LEO.   But what's the matter with him? When did this happen— (*Calling after* CAL) You'd think Papa'd be someplace where you could find him. I been chasing him all afternoon.

(OSCAR *and* BEN *come quickly into the room.*)

LEO. Papa, I've been looking all over town for you and Uncle Ben—

BEN. Where is he?

OSCAR. Addie just told us it was a sudden attack, and—

BEN (*to* LEO). Where is he? When did it happen?

LEO. Upstairs. Will you listen to me, please? I been looking for you for—

OSCAR (*to* BEN). You think we should go up? (BEN, *looking up the steps, shakes his head.*)

BEN. I don't know. I don't know.

OSCAR. But he was all right—

LEO (*yelling*). *Will you listen to me?*

OSCAR. What is the matter with you?

LEO. I been trying to tell you. I been trying to find you for an hour—

OSCAR. Tell me what?

LEO. Uncle Horace knows about the bonds. He knows about them. He's had the box since Wednesday—

BEN (*sharply*). Stop shouting! What the hell are you talking about?

LEO (*furiously*). I'm telling you he knows about the bonds. Ain't that clear enough—

BEN (*grabbing* LEO's *arm*). You God-damn fool! Stop screaming! Now what happened? Talk quietly.

LEO. You heard me. Uncle Horace knows about the bonds. He's known since Wednesday.

BEN (*after a second*). How do you know that?

LEO. Because Cal comes down to Manders and says the box came okay and—

OSCAR (*trembling*). That might not mean a thing—

LEO (*angrily*). No? It might not, huh? Then he says Manders should come here tonight and bring Sol Fowler with him. I guess that don't mean a thing either.

OSCAR (*to* BEN). Ben— What— Do you think he's seen the—

BEN (*motions to the box*). There's the box. (*Both* OSCAR *and* LEO *turn sharply.* LEO *makes a leap to the box*) You ass. Put it down. What are you going to do with it, eat it?

LEO. I'm going to—

BEN (*furiously*). Put it down. Don't touch it again. Now sit down and shut up for a minute.

OSCAR. Since Wednesday. (*To* LEO) You said he had it since Wednesday. Why didn't he say something— (*To* BEN) I don't understand—

LEO (*taking a step*). I can put it back. I can put it back before anybody knows.

BEN (*who is standing at the table, softly*). He's had it since Wednesday. Yet he hasn't said a word to us.

OSCAR. *Why? Why?*

LEO. What's the difference why? He was getting ready to say plenty. He was going to say it to Fowler tonight—

OSCAR (*angrily*). Be still. (*Turns to* BEN, *looks at him, waits.*)

BEN (*after a minute*).   I don't believe that.

LEO (*wildly*).   *You* don't believe it? What do I care what *you* believe? I do the dirty work and then—

BEN (*turning his head to* LEO).   I'm remembering that. I'm remembering that, Leo.

OSCAR.   What do you mean?

LEO.   You—

BEN (*to* OSCAR).   If you don't shut that little fool up, I'll show you what I mean. For some reason he knows, but he don't say a word.

OSCAR.   Maybe he didn't know that *we*—

BEN (*quickly*).   That *Leo*— He's no fool. Does Manders know the bonds are missing?

LEO.   How could I tell? I was half crazy. I don't think so. Because Manders seemed kind of puzzled and—

OSCAR.   But we got to find out— (*He breaks off as* CAL *comes into the room carrying a kettle of hot water.*)

BEN.   How is he, Cal?

CAL.   I don't know, Mr. Ben. He was bad. (*Going toward stairs.*)

OSCAR.   But when did it happen?

CAL (*shrugs*).   He wasn't feeling bad early. (ADDIE *comes in quickly from the hall*) Then there he is next thing on the landing, fallen over, his eyes tight—

ADDIE (*to* CAL).   Dr. Sloan's over at the Ballongs. Hitch the buggy and go get him. (*She takes the kettle and cloths from him, pushes him, runs up the stairs*) Go on. (*She disappears.* CAL *exits.*)

BEN.   Never seen Sloan anywhere when you need him.

OSCAR (*softly*).   Sounds bad.

LEO.   He would have told *her* about it. Aunt Regina. He would have told his own wife—

BEN (*turning to* LEO).   Yes, he might have told her. But they weren't on such pretty terms and maybe he didn't. Maybe he didn't. (*Goes quickly to* LEO) Now listen to me. If she doesn't know, it may work out all right. If she does know, you're to say he lent you the bonds.

LEO.   Lent them to me! Who's going to believe that?

BEN.   Nobody.

OSCAR (*to* LEO).   Don't you understand? It can't do no harm to say it—

LEO.   Why should I say he lent them to me? Why not to you? (*Carefully*) Why not to Uncle Ben?

BEN (*smiles*).   Just because he didn't lend them to me. Remember that.

LEO.   But all he has to do is say he didn't lend them to me—

BEN (*furiously*).   But for some reason, he doesn't seem to be talking, does he?

(*There are footsteps above. They all stand looking at the stairs.* REGINA *begins to come slowly down.*)

BEN.   What happened?

REGINA.   He's had a bad attack.

OSCAR. Too bad. I'm sorry we weren't here when—when Horace needed us.

BEN. When *you* needed us.

REGINA. (*looks at him*). Yes.

BEN. How is he? Can we—can we go up?

REGINA (*shakes her head*). He's not conscious.

OSCAR (*pacing around*). It's that—it's that bad? Wouldn't you think Sloan could be found quickly, just once, just once?

REGINA. I don't think there is much for him to do.

BEN. Oh, don't talk like that. He's come through attacks before. He will now.

(REGINA *sits down. After a second she speaks softly.*)

REGINA. Well. We haven't seen each other since the day of our fight.

BEN (*tenderly*). That was nothing. Why, you and Oscar and I used to fight when we were kids.

OSCAR (*hurriedly*). Don't you think we should grow up? Is there anything we can do for Horace—

BEN. You don't feel well. Ah—

REGINA (*without looking at them*). No, I don't. (*Slight pause*) Horace told me about the bonds this afternoon. (*There is an immediate shocked silence.*)

LEO. The bonds. What do you mean? What bonds? What—

BEN (*looks at him furiously. Then to* REGINA). The Union Pacific bonds? *Horace's* Union Pacific bonds?

REGINA. Yes.

OSCAR (*steps to her, very nervously*). Well. Well what—what about them? What—what could he say?

REGINA. He said that Leo had stolen the bonds and given them to you.

OSCAR (*aghast, very loudly*). That's ridiculous, Regina, absolutely—

LEO. I don't know what you're talking about. What would I— Why—

REGINA (*wearily to* BEN). Isn't it enough that he stole them? Do I have to listen to this in the bargain?

OSCAR. You are talking—

LEO. I didn't steal anything. I don't know why—

REGINA (*to* BEN). Would you ask them to stop that, please? (*There is silence.* BEN *glowers at* OSCAR *and* LEO.)

BEN. Aren't we starting at the wrong end, Regina? What did Horace tell you?

REGINA (*smiles at him*). He told me that Leo had stolen the bonds.

LEO. I didn't steal—

REGINA. Please. Let me finish. Then he told me that he was going to pretend that he had lent them to you (LEO *turns sharply to* REGINA, *then looks at* OSCAR, *then looks back at* REGINA) as a present from me—to my brothers. He said there was nothing I could do about it. He said the rest of his money would go to Alexandra. That is all. (*There is a silence,* OSCAR *coughs,* LEO *smiles slyly.*)

LEO (*taking a step to her*).   I told you he had lent them—I could have told you—

REGINA (*ignores him, smiles sadly at* BEN).   So I'm very badly off, you see. Horace said there was nothing I could do about it as long as he was alive to say he had lent you the bonds.

BEN.   You shouldn't feel that way. It can all be explained, all be adjusted. It isn't as bad—

REGINA.   So you, at least, are willing to admit the bonds were stolen?

BEN (OSCAR *laughs nervously*).   I admit no such thing. It's possible that Horace made up that part of the story to tease you— (*Looks at her*) Or perhaps to punish you. Punish you.

REGINA (*sadly*).   It's not a pleasant story. I feel bad, Ben, naturally. I hadn't thought—

BEN.   Now you shall have the bonds safely back. That was the understanding, wasn't it, Oscar?

OSCAR.   Yes.

REGINA.   I'm glad to know that. (*Smiles*) Ah, I had greater hopes—

BEN.   Don't talk that way. That's foolish. (*Looks at his watch*) I think we ought to drive out for Sloan ourselves. If we can't find him we'll go over to Senateville for Doctor Morris. And don't think I'm dismissing this other business. I'm not. We'll have it all out on a more appropriate day.

REGINA.   I don't think you had better go yet. I think you had better stay and sit down.

BEN.   We'll be back with Sloan.

REGINA.   Cal has gone for him. I don't want you to go.

BEN.   Now don't worry and—

REGINA.   You will come back in this room and sit down. I have something more to say.

BEN (*turns, comes toward her*).   Since when do I take orders from you?

REGINA (*smiles*).   You don't—yet. (*Sharply*) Come back, Oscar. You too, Leo.

OSCAR (*sure of himself, laughs*).   My dear Regina—

BEN (*softly, pats her hand*).   Horace has already clipped your wings and very wittily. Do I have to clip them, too? (*Smiles at her*) You'd get farther with a smile, Regina. I'm a soft man for a woman's smile.

REGINA.   I'm smiling, Ben. I'm smiling because you are quite safe while Horace lives. But I don't think Horace will live. And if he doesn't live I shall want seventy-five percent in exchange for the bonds.

BEN (*steps back, whistles, laughs*).   Greedy! What a greedy girl you are! You want so much of everything.

REGINA.   Yes. And if I don't get what I want I am going to put all three of you in jail.

OSCAR (*furiously*).   You're mighty crazy. Having just admitted—

BEN.   And on what evidence would you put Oscar and Leo in jail?

REGINA (*laughs, gaily*).   Oscar, listen to him. He's getting ready to swear that it was you and Leo! What do you say to that? (OSCAR *turns furiously toward* BEN) Oh, don't be angry, Oscar. I'm going to see that he goes in with you.

BEN.   Try anything you like, Regina. (*Sharply*) And now we can stop all this and say good-bye to you. (ALEXANDRA *comes slowly down the steps.*) It's his money and he's obviously willing to let us borrow it. (*More pleasantly*) Learn to make threats when you can carry them through. For how many years have I told you a good-looking woman gets more by being soft and appealing? Mama used to tell you that. (*Looks at his watch*) Where the hell is Sloan? (*To* OSCAR) Take the buggy and— (*As* BEN *turns to* OSCAR, *he sees* ALEXANDRA. *She walks stiffly. She goes slowly to the lower window, her head bent. They all turn to look at her.*)

OSCAR (*after a second, moving toward her*).   What? Alexandra— (*She does not answer. After a second,* ADDIE *comes slowly down the stairs, moving as if she were very tired. At foot of steps, she looks at* ALEXANDRA, *then turns and slowly crosses to door and exits.* REGINA *rises.* BEN *looks nervously at* ALEXANDRA, *at* REGINA.)

OSCAR (*as* ADDIE *passes him, irritably to* ALEXANDRA).   Well, what is— (*Turns into room—sees* ADDIE *at foot of steps*) —what's? (*Ben puts up a hand, shakes his head*) My God, I didn't know—who *could* have known— I didn't know he was that sick. Well, well—I— (REGINA *stands quietly, her back to them.*)

BEN (*softly, sincerely*).   Seems like yesterday when he first came here.

OSCAR.   Yes, that's true. (*Turns to* BEN) The whole town loved him and respected him.

ALEXANDRA (*turns*).   Did you love him, Uncle Oscar?

OSCAR.   Certainly, I— What a strange thing to ask! I—

ALEXANDRA.   Did you love him, Uncle Ben?

BEN (*simply*).   Alexandra, I—

ALEXANDRA (*starts to laugh very loudly*).   And you, Mama, did you love him, too?

REGINA.   I know what you feel, Alexandra, but please try to control yourself.

ALEXANDRA.   I'm trying, Mama. I'm trying very hard.

BEN.   Grief makes some people laugh and some people cry. It's better to cry, Alexandra.

ALEXANDRA (*the laugh has stopped. She moves toward Regina*).   What was Papa doing on the staircase?

(BEN *turns to look at* ALEXANDRA.)

REGINA.   Please go and lie down, my dear. We all need time to get over shocks like this. (ALEXANDRA *does not move.* REGINA'S *voice becomes softer, more insistent.*) Please go, Alexandra.

ALEXANDRA.   No, Mama. I'll wait. I've got to talk to you.

REGINA.   Later. Go and rest now.

ALEXANDRA (*quietly*).   I'll wait, Mama. I've plenty of time.

REGINA (*hesitates, stares, makes a half shrug, turns back to* BEN).   As I was saying. Tomorrow morning I am going up to Judge Simmes. I shall tell him about Leo.

BEN (*motioning toward* ALEXANDRA).   Not in front of the child, Regina. I—

REGINA (*turns to him. Sharply*).   I didn't ask her to stay. Tomorrow morning I go to Judge Simmes—

OSCAR.   And what proof? What proof of all this—

REGINA (*turns sharply*).   None. I won't need any. The bonds are missing and they are with Marshall. That will be enough. If it isn't, I'll add what's necessary.

BEN.   I'm sure of that.

REGINA (*turns to* BEN).   You can be quite sure.

OSCAR.   We'll deny—

REGINA.   Deny your heads off. You couldn't find a jury that wouldn't weep for a woman whose brothers steal from her. And you couldn't find twelve men in this state you haven't cheated and who hate you for it.

OSCAR.   What kind of talk is this? You couldn't do anything like that! We're your own brothers. (*Points upstairs*) How can you talk that way when upstairs not five minutes ago—

REGINA.   Where was I? (*Smiles at* BEN) Well, they'll convict you. But I won't care much if they don't. Because by that time you'll be ruined. I shall also tell my story to Mr. Marshall, who likes me, I think, and who will not want to be involved in your scandal. A respectable firm like Marshall and Company. The deal would be off in an hour. (*Turns to them angrily*) And you know it. Now I don't want to hear any more from any of you. *You'll do no more bargaining in this house.* I'll take my seventy-five percent and we'll forget the story forever. That's one way of doing it, and the way I prefer. You know me well enough to know that I don't mind taking the other way.

BEN (*after a second, slowly*).   None of us has ever known you well enough, Regina.

REGINA.   You're getting old, Ben. Your tricks aren't as smart as they used to be. (*There is no answer. She waits, then smiles*) All right. I take it that's settled and I get what I asked for.

OSCAR (*furiously to* BEN).   Are you going to let her do this—

BEN (*turns to look at him, slowly*).   You have a suggestion?

REGINA (*puts her arms above her head, stretches, laughs*).   No, he hasn't. All right. Now, Leo, I have forgotten that you ever saw the bonds. (*Archly, to* BEN *and* OSCAR) And as long as you boys both behave yourselves, I've forgotten that we ever even talked about them. You can draw up the necessary papers tomorrow. (BEN *laughs.* LEO *stares at him, starts for door. Exits.* OSCAR *moves toward door angrily.* REGINA *looks at* BEN, *nods, laughs with him. For a second,* OSCAR *stands in the door, looking back at them. Then he exits.*)

REGINA.   You're a good loser, Ben. I like that.

BEN (*picks up his coat, turns to her*).   Well, I say to myself, what's the good? You and I aren't like Oscar. We're not sour people. I think that comes from a good digestion. Then, too, one loses today and wins tomorrow. I say to myself, years of planning and I get what I want. Then I don't get it. But I'm not discouraged. The century's turning, the world is open. Open for people like you and me. Ready for us, waiting for us. After all this is just the beginning. There are hundreds of Hubbards sitting in rooms like this throughout the country. All their names aren't Hubbard, but they are all Hubbards and they will own this country someday. We'll get along.

REGINA (*smiles*).   I think so.

BEN.   Then, too, I say to myself, things may change. (*Looks at* ALEXANDRA.) I agree with Alexandra. What is a man in a wheelchair doing on a staircase? I ask myself that.

REGINA (*looks up at him*).   And what do you answer?

BEN.   I have no answer. But maybe someday I will. Maybe never, but maybe someday. (*Smiles. Pats her arm*) When I do, I'll let you know. (*Goes toward hall.*)

REGINA.   When you do, write me. I will be in Chicago. (*Gaily*) Ah, Ben, if Papa had only left me his money.

BEN.   I'll see you tomorrow.

REGINA.   Oh, yes. Certainly. You'll be sort of working for me now.

BEN (*as he passes* ALEXANDRA).   Alexandra, you're turning out to be a right interesting girl. Well, good night all. (*He exits.*)

REGINA (*Sits quietly for a second, stretches*).   What do you want to talk to me about, Alexandra?

ALEXANDRA (*slowly*).   I've changed my mind. I don't want to talk.

REGINA.   You're acting very strange. Not like yourself. You've had a bad shock today. I know that. And you loved Papa, but you must have expected this to come someday. You knew how sick he was.

ALEXANDRA.   I knew. We all knew.

REGINA.   It will be good for you to get away from here. Good for me, too. Time heals most wounds, Alexandra. You're young, you shall have all the things I wanted. I'll make the world for you the way I wanted it to be for me. (*Uncomfortably*) Don't sit there staring. You've been around Birdie so much you're getting just like her.

ALEXANDRA (*nods*).   Funny. That's what Aunt Birdie said today.

REGINA.   Be good for you to get away from all this.

(ADDIE *enters.*)

ADDIE.   Cal is back, Miss Regina. He says Dr. Sloan will be coming in a few minutes.

REGINA.   We'll leave in a few weeks. A few weeks! That means two or three Saturdays, two or three Sundays. (*Sighs*) Well, I'm very tired. I shall go to bed. I don't want any supper. Put the lights out and lock up. (ADDIE *moves to the piano lamp, turns it out*) You go to your room, Alexandra. Addie will bring you something hot. You look very tired. (*Rises. To* ADDIE) Call me when Dr. Sloan gets here. I don't want to see anybody else. I don't want any condolence calls tonight. The whole town will be over.

ALEXANDRA.   Mama, I'm not coming with you. I'm not going to Chicago.

REGINA (*turns to her*).   You're very upset, Alexandra.

ALEXANDRA.   I mean what I say. With all my heart.

REGINA.   We'll talk about it tomorrow. The morning will make a difference.

ALEXANDRA.   It won't make any difference. And there isn't anything to talk about. I am going away from you. Because I want to. Because I know Papa would want me to.

REGINA (*careful, polite*).   You *know* your papa wanted you to go away from me?

ALEXANDRA.   Yes.

REGINA (*softly*).   And if I say no?

ALEXANDRA.   Say it Mama, say it. And see what happens.

REGINA (*softly, after a pause*).   And if I make you stay?

ALEXANDRA.   That would be foolish. It wouldn't work in the end.

REGINA.   You're very serious about it, aren't you? (*Crosses to stairs*) Well, you'll change your mind in a few days.

ALEXANDRA.   No.

REGINA (*going up the steps*).   Alexandra, I've come to the end of my rope. Somewhere there has to be what I want, too. Life goes too fast. Do what you want; think what you want; go where you want. I'd like to keep you with me, but I won't make you stay. Too many people used to make me do too many things. No, I won't make you stay.

ALEXANDRA.   You couldn't, Mama, because I want to leave here. As I've never wanted anything in my life before. Because now I understand what Papa was trying to tell me. All in one day: Addie said there were people who ate the earth and other people who stood around and watched them do it. And just now Uncle Ben said the same thing. Really, he said the same thing. (*Tensely*) Well, tell him for me, Mama, I'm not going to stand around and watch you do it. I'll be fighting as hard as he'll be fighting (*Rises*) someplace else.

REGINA.   Well, you have spirit, after all. I used to think you were all sugar water. We don't have to be bad friends. I don't want us to be bad friends, Alexandra. (*Starts, stops, turns to* ALEXANDRA) Would you like to come and talk to me, Alexandra? Would you—would you like to sleep in my room tonight?

ALEXANDRA (*takes a step toward the stairs*).   Are you afraid, Mama? (REGINA *does not answer. She moves up the stairs and out of sight.* ADDIE, *smiling, begins to put out the lamps.*)

QUESTIONS

1. In the introduction to this play we noted that it was "well made," with a series of plot complications leading inevitably to climax and resolution. Analyze these plot developments and the way in which they move the action forward.

2. One criticism sometimes leveled at this play is that the characters are one-dimensional, morally too black and white. Do you agree? Why might Hellman have decided not to create in-depth, subtle characterizations of figures like Oscar Hubbard and Horace Giddens?

3. What is the role of the black people in this play? To what extent is the treatment of and attitudes toward blacks a subtext for the larger social and economic world portrayed in *The Little Foxes?* How do Hellman's views on relations between the races relate to the historical and social themes at the core of her work?

4. At one point, Ben Hubbard says, "The century's turning, the world is open. Open for people like you and me." This comment, of course, has a different force for the audience than for Ben himself and is therefore ironic. What is his view of the future? How do we, on the other hand, see what lies in store for the region as a result of the dramatic conflict involving Ben and the others?

5. In the introduction, we compared this play to the section on Southern writers that concludes the fiction section of this volume. Take the comparison one step further by selecting one of those stories and discussing its themes and characters, as well as the implied world view of the writer, in relation to those of *The Little Foxes*.

Tennessee Williams (1911–1983)
The Glass Menagerie

CHARACTERS

AMANDA WINGFIELD, *the mother, a little woman of great but confused vitality clinging frantically to another time and place. Her characterization must be carefully created, not copied from type. She is not paranoiac, but her life is paranoia. There is much to admire in Amanda, and as much to love and pity as there is to laugh at. Certainly she has endurance and a kind of heroism, and though her foolishness makes her unwittingly cruel at times, there is tenderness in her slight person.*

LAURA WINGFIELD, *her daughter. Amanda, having failed to establish contact with reality, continues to live vitally in her illusions, but Laura's situation is even graver. A childhood illness has left her crippled, one leg slightly shorter than the other, and held in a brace. This defect need not be more than suggested on the stage. Stemming from this, Laura's separation increases till she is like a piece of her own glass collection, too exquisitely fragile to move from the shelf.*

TOM WINGFIELD, *her son and the narrator of the play. A poet with a job in a warehouse. His nature is not remorseless, but to escape from a trap he has to act without pity.*

JIM O'CONNOR, *the gentleman caller, a nice, ordinary, young man.*

SCENE *An alley in St. Louis.*

Part I. Preparation for a gentleman caller.

Part II. The gentleman calls.

Time: Now and the Past.

SCENE I

The Wingfield apartment is in the rear of the building, one of those vast hive-like conglomerations of cellular living-units that flower as warty growths in overcrowded urban centers of lower middle-class population and are symptomatic of the impulse of this largest and fundamentally enslaved section of American society to avoid fluidity and differentiation and to exist and function as one interfused mass of automatism.

The apartment faces an alley and is entered by a fire escape, a structure whose name is a touch of accidental poetic truth, for all of these huge buildings are always burning with the slow and implacable fires of human desperation. The fire escape is part of what we see—that is, the landing of it and steps descending from it.

The scene is memory and is therefore nonrealistic. Memory takes a lot of poetic license. It omits some details; others are exaggerated, according to the *emotional value of the articles it touches, for memory is seated predominantly in the heart. The interior is therefore rather dim and poetic.*

At the rise of the curtain, the audience is faced with the dark, grim rear wall of the Wingfield tenement. This building is flanked on both sides by dark, narrow alleys which run into murky canyons of tangled clotheslines, garbage cans, and the sinister latticework of neighboring fire escapes. It is up and down these side alleys that exterior entrances and exits are made during the play. At the end of TOM'S *opening commentary, the dark tenement wall slowly becomes transparent and reveals the interior of the ground-floor Wingfield apartment.*

Nearest the audience is the living room, which also serves as a sleeping room for LAURA, *the sofa unfolding to make her bed. Just beyond, separated from the living room by a wide arch or second proscenium with transparent faded portieres (or second curtain), is the dining room. In an old-fashioned whatnot in the living room are seen scores of transparent glass animals. A blown-up photograph of the father hangs on the wall of the living room, to the left of the archway. It is the face of a very handsome young man in a dough-boy's First World War cap. He is gallantly smiling, ineluctably smiling, as if to say "I will be smiling forever."*

Also hanging on the wall, near the photograph, are a typewriter keyboard chart and a Gregg shorthand diagram. An upright typewriter on a small table stands beneath the charts.

The audience hears and sees the opening scene in the dining room through both the transparent fourth wall of the building and the transparent gauze portieres of the dining-room arch. It is during this revealing scene that the fourth wall slowly ascends, out of sight. This transparent exterior wall is not brought down again until the very end of the play, during TOM'S *final speech.*

The narrator is an undisguised convention of the play. He takes whatever license with dramatic convention is convenient to his purposes.

TOM *enters, dressed as a merchant sailor, and strolls across to the fire escape. There he stops and lights a cigarette. He addresses the audience.*

TOM. Yes, I have tricks in my pocket, I have things up my sleeve. But I am the opposite of a stage magician. He gives you illusion that has the appearance of truth. I give you truth in the pleasant disguise of illusion.

To begin with, I turn back time. I reverse it to that quaint period, the thirties, when the huge middle class of America was matriculating in a school for the blind. Their eyes had failed them, or they had failed their eyes, and so they were having their fingers pressed forcibly down on the fiery Braille alphabet of a dissolving economy.

In Spain there was revolution. Here there was only shouting and confusion. In Spain there was Guernica. Here there were disturbances of labor, some-times pretty violent, in otherwise peaceful cities such as Chicago, Cleveland, Saint Louis . . .
This is the social background of the play.

(Music begins to play.)

The play is memory. Being a memory play, it is dimly lighted, it is sentimental, it is not realistic. In memory everything seems to happen to music. That explains the fiddle in the wings.

I am the narrator of the play, and also a character in it. The other characters are my mother, Amanda, my sister, Laura, and a gentleman caller who appears in the final scenes. He is the most realistic character in the play, being an emissary from a world of reality that we were somehow set apart from. But since I have a poet's weakness for symbols, I am using this character also as a symbol; he is the long-delayed but always expected something that we live for.

There is a fifth character in the play who doesn't appear except in this larger-than-life-size photograph over the mantel. This is our father who left us a long time ago. He was a telephone man who fell in love with long distances; he gave up his job with the telephone company and skipped the light fantastic out of town . . .

The last we heard of him was a picture postcard from Mazatlan, on the Pacific Coast of Mexico, containing a message of two words: "Hello—Goodbye!" and no address.
I think the rest of the play will explain itself. . . .

(AMANDA'S *voice becomes audible through the portieres.*)

(*Legend on screen:* "Ou sont les neiges.")

(TOM *divides the portieres and enters the dining room.* AMANDA *and* LAURA *are seated at a drop-leaf table. Eating is indicated by gestures without food or utensils.* AMANDA *faces the audience.* TOM *and* LAURA *are seated in profile. The interior has lit up softly and through the scrim we see* AMANDA *and* LAURA *seated at the table.*)

AMANDA (*calling*).   Tom?
TOM.   Yes, Mother.
AMANDA.   We can't say grace until you come to the table!
TOM.   Coming, Mother. (*He bows slightly and withdraws, reappearing a few moments later in his place at the table.*)
AMANDA (*to her son*).   Honey, don't *push* with your *fingers*. If you have to push with something, the thing to push with is a crust of bread. And chew—chew! Animals have secretions in their stomachs which enable them to digest food without mastication, but human beings are supposed to chew their food before they swallow it down. Eat food leisurely, son, and really enjoy it. A well-cooked meal has lots of delicate flavors that have to be held in the mouth for appreciation. So chew your food and give your salivary glands a chance to function!

(TOM *deliberately lays his imaginary fork down and pushes his chair back from the table.*)

TOM.   I haven't enjoyed one bite of this dinner because of your constant directions on how to eat it. It's you that make me rush through meals with your hawklike attention to every bite I take. Sickening—spoils my appetite—all this discussion of—animals' secretion—salivary glands—mastication!

AMANDA (*lightly*).   Temperament like a Metropolitan star!

(TOM *rises and walks toward the living room.*)

You're not excused from the table.

TOM.   I'm getting a cigarette.

AMANDA.   You smoke too much.

(LAURA *rises.*)

LAURA.   I'll bring in the blanc mange.

(TOM *remains standing with his cigarette by the portieres.*)

AMANDA (*rising*).   No, sister, no, sister—you be the lady this time and I'll be the darky.

LAURA.   I'm already up.

AMANDA.   Resume your seat, little sister—I want you to stay fresh and pretty—for gentlemen callers!

LAURA (*sitting down*).   I'm not expecting any gentlemen callers.

AMANDA (*crossing out to the kitchenette, airily*).   Sometimes they come when they are least expected! Why, I remember one Sunday afternoon in Blue Mountain—

(*She enters the kitchenette.*)

TOM.   I know what's coming!

LAURA.   Yes. But let her tell it.

TOM.   Again?

LAURA.   She loves to tell it.

(AMANDA *returns with a bowl of dessert.*)

AMANDA.   One Sunday afternoon in Blue Mountain—your mother received—*seventeen!*—gentlemen callers! Why, sometimes there weren't chairs enough to accommodate them all. We had to send the nigger over to bring in folding chairs from the parish house.

TOM (*remaining at the portieres*).   How did you entertain those gentlemen callers?

AMANDA.   I understood the art of conversation!

TOM.   I bet you could talk.

AMANDA.   Girls in those days *knew* how to talk, I can tell you.

TOM.   Yes?

(*Image on screen:* Amanda as a girl on a porch, greeting callers.)

AMANDA.   They knew how to entertain their gentlemen callers. It wasn't enough for a girl to be possessed of a pretty face and a graceful figure—although I wasn't slighted in either respect. She also needed to have a nimble wit and a tongue to meet all occasions.

TOM.   What did you talk about?

AMANDA.   Things of importance going on in the world! Never anything coarse or common or vulgar.

(She addresses TOM *as though he were seated in the vacant chair at the table though he remains by the portieres. He plays this scene as though reading from a script.)*

My callers were gentlemen—all! Among my callers were some of the most prominent young planters of the Mississippi Delta—planters and sons of planters!

*(*TOM *motions for music and a spot of light on* AMANDA. *Her eyes lift, her face glows, her voice becomes rich and elegiac.)*

(Screen legend: "Ou sont les neiges d'antan?")

There was young Champ Laughlin who later became vice-president of the Delta Planters Bank. Hadley Stevenson who was drowned in Moon Lake and left his widow one hundred and fifty thousand in government bonds. There were the Cutrere brothers, Wesley and Bates. Bates was one of my bright particular beaux! He got in a quarrel with that wild Wainwright boy. They shot it out on the floor of Moon Lake Casino. Bates was shot through the stomach. Died in the ambulance on his way to Memphis. His widow was also well provided-for, came into eight or ten thousand acres, that's all. She married him on the rebound—never loved her—carried my picture on him the night he died! And there was that boy that every girl in the Delta had set her cap for! That beautiful, brilliant young Fitzhugh boy from Greene County!

TOM.   What did he leave his widow?

AMANDA.   He never married! Gracious, you talk as though all of my old admirers had turned up their toes to the daisies!

TOM.   Isn't this the first you've mentioned that still survives?

AMANDA.   That Fitzhugh boy went North and made a fortune—came to be known as the Wolf of Wall Street! He had the Midas touch, whatever he touched turned to gold! And I could have been Mrs. Duncan J. Fitzhugh, mind you! But—I picked your *father!*

LAURA *(rising).*   Mother, let me clear the table.

AMANDA.   No, dear, you go in front and study your typewriter chart. Or practice your shorthand a little. Stay fresh and pretty!—It's almost time for our gentlemen callers to start arriving. *(She flounces girlishly toward the kitchenette.)* How many do you suppose we're going to entertain this afternoon?

*(*TOM *throws down the paper and jumps up with a groan.)*

LAURA *(alone in the dining room).*   I don't believe we're going to receive any, Mother.

AMANDA *(reappearing, airily).*   What? No one—not one? You must be joking!

*(*LAURA *nervously echoes her laugh. She slips in a fugitive manner through the half-open portieres and draws them gently behind her. A shaft of very clear*

light is thrown on her face against the faded tapestry of the curtains. Faintly the music of "The Glass Menagerie" is heard as she continues, lightly.)

Not one gentleman caller? It can't be true! There must be a flood, there must have been a tornado!

LAURA.   It isn't a flood, it's not a tornado, Mother. I'm just not popular like you were in Blue Mountain. . . .

(TOM utters another groan. LAURA glances at him with a faint, apologetic smile. Her voice catches a little.)

Mother's afraid I'm going to be an old maid.

(The scene dims out with the "Glass Menagerie" music.)

SCENE II

On the dark stage the screen is lighted with the image of blue roses. Gradually LAURA'S figure becomes apparent and the screen goes out. The music subsides.

LAURA *is seated in the delicate ivory chair at the small claw-foot table. She wears a dress of soft violet material for a kimono—her hair is tied back from her forehead with a ribbon. She is washing and polishing her collection of glass.* AMANDA *appears on the fire escape steps. At the sound of her ascent,* LAURA *catches her breath, thrusts the bowl of ornaments away, and seats herself stiffly before the diagram of the typewriter keyboard as though it held her spellbound. Something has happened to* AMANDA. *It is written on her face as she climbs to the landing: a look that is grim and hopeless and a little absurd. She has on one of those cheap or imitation velvety-looking cloth coats with imitation fur collar. Her hat is five or six years old, one of those dreadful cloche hats that were worn in the late Twenties, and she is clutching an enormous black patent-leather pocketbook with nickel clasps and initials. This is her full-dress outfit, the one she usually wears to the D.A.R. Before entering she looks through the door. She purses her lips, opens her eyes very wide, rolls them upward and shakes her head.Then she slowly lets herself in the door. Seeing her mother's expression* LAURA *touches her lips with a nervous gesture.*

LAURA.   Hello, Mother, I was— *(She makes a nervous gesture toward the chart on the wall.* AMANDA *leans against the shut door and stares at* LAURA *with a martyred look.)*

AMANDA.   Deception? Deception? *(She slowly removes her hat and gloves, continuing the sweet suffering stare. She lets the hat and gloves fall on the floor—a bit of acting.)*

LAURA *(shakily).*   How was the D.A.R. meeting?

(AMANDA slowly opens her purse and removes a dainty white handkerchief which she shakes out delicately and delicately touches to her lips and nostrils.)

Didn't you go to the D.A.R. meeting, Mother?

AMANDA (*faintly, almost inaudibly*).   —No.—No. (*then more forcibly.*) I did not have the strength—to go to the D.A.R. In fact, I did not have the courage! I wanted to find a hole in the ground and hide myself in it forever! (*She crosses slowly to the wall and removes the diagram of the typewriter keyboard. She holds it in front of her for a second, staring at it sweetly and sorrowfully—then bites her lips and tears it into two pieces.*)

LAURA (*faintly*).   Why did you do that, Mother?

(AMANDA *repeats the same procedure with the chart of the Gregg Alphabet.*)

Why are you—

AMANDA.   Why? Why? How old are you, Laura?

LAURA.   Mother, you know my age.

AMANDA.   I thought that you were an adult; it seems that I was mistaken. (*She crosses slowly to the sofa and sinks down and stares at* LAURA.)

LAURA.   Please don't stare at me, Mother.

(AMANDA *closes her eyes and lowers her head. There is a ten-second pause.*)

AMANDA.   What are we going to do, what is going to become of us, what is the future?

(*There is another pause.*)

LAURA.   Has something happened, Mother?

(AMANDA *draws a long breath, takes out the handkerchief again, goes through the dabbing process.*)

Mother, has—something happened?

AMANDA.   I'll be all right in a minute, I'm just bewildered—(*She hesitates.*)—by life. . . .

LAURA.   Mother, I wish that you would tell me what's happened!

AMANDA.   As you know, I was supposed to be inducted into my office at the D.A.R. this afternoon.

(*Screen image:* A swarm of typewriters.)

But I stopped off at Rubicam's Business College to speak to your teachers about your having a cold and ask them what progress they thought you were making down there.

LAURA.   Oh. . . .

AMANDA.   I went to the typing instructor and introduced myself as your mother. She didn't know who you were. "Wingfield," she said. "We don't have any such student enrolled at the school!"

I assured her she did, that you had been going to classes since early in January.

"I wonder," she said. "If you could be talking about that terribly shy little girl who dropped out of school after only a few days' attendance?"

"No," I said, "Laura, my daughter, has been going to school every day for the past six weeks!"

"Excuse me," she said. She took the attendance book out and there was your name, unmistakably printed, and all the dates you were absent until they decided that you had dropped out of school.
I still said, "No, there must have been some mistake! There must have been some mix-up in the records!"
And she said, "No—I remember her perfectly now. Her hands shook so that she couldn't hit the right keys! The first time we gave a speed test, she broke down completely—was sick at the stomach and almost had to be carried into the wash room! After that morning she never showed up any more. We phoned the house but never got any answer"—While I was working at Famous–Barr, I suppose, demonstrating those—

(*She indicates a brassiere with her hands.*)

Oh! I felt so weak I could barely keep on my feet! I had to sit down while they got me a glass of water! Fifty dollars' tuition, all of our plans—my hopes and ambitions for you—just gone up the spout, just gone up the spout like that.

(LAURA *draws a long breath and gets awkwardly to her feet. She crosses to the Victrola and winds it up.*)

What are you doing?
LAURA.   Oh! (*She releases the handle and returns to her seat.*)
AMANDA.   Laura, where have you been going when you've gone out pretending you were going to business college?
LAURA.   I've just been going out walking.
AMANDA.   That's not true.
LAURA.   It is. I just went walking.
AMANDA.   Walking? Walking? In winter? Deliberately courting pneumonia in that light coat? Where did you walk to, Laura?
LAURA.   All sorts of places—mostly in the park.
AMANDA.   Even after you'd started catching that cold?
LAURA.   It was the lesser of two evils, Mother.

(*Screen image:* Winter scene in a park.)

I couldn't go back there. I—threw up—on the floor!
AMANDA.   From half past seven till after five every day you mean to tell me you walked around in the park, because you wanted to make me think that you were still going to Rubicam's Business College?
LAURA.   It wasn't as bad as it sounds. I went inside places to get warmed up.
AMANDA.   Inside where?
LAURA.   I went in the art museum and the bird houses at the Zoo. I visited the penguins every day! Sometimes I did without lunch and went to the movies. Lately I've been spending most of my afternoons in the Jewel Box, that big glass house where they raise the tropical flowers.
AMANDA.   You did all this to deceive me, just for deception?

(LAURA *looks down.*) Why?

LAURA.   Mother, when you're disappointed, you get that awful suffering look on your face, like the picture of Jesus' mother in the museum!
AMANDA.   Hush!
LAURA.   I couldn't face it.

(There is a pause. A whisper of strings is heard. Legend on screen: "The Crust of Humility.")

AMANDA *(hopelessly fingering the huge pocketbook)*.   So what are we going to do the rest of our lives? Stay home and watch the parades go by? Amuse ourselves with the glass menagerie, darling? Eternally play those worn-out phonograph records your father left as a painful reminder of him? We won't have a business career— we've given that up because it gave us nervous indigestion! *(She laughs wearily.)* What is there left but dependency all our lives? I know so well what becomes of unmarried women who aren't prepared to occupy a position. I've seen such pitiful cases in the South— barely tolerated spinsters living upon the grudging patronage of a sister's husband or brother's wife!—stuck away in some little mousetrap of a room— encouraged by one in-law to visit another—little birdlike women without any nest—eating the crust of humility all their life!
Is that the future that we've mapped out for ourselves? I swear it's the only alternative I can think of! *(She pauses.)* It isn't a very pleasant alternative, is it? *(She pauses again.)* Of course—some girls *do marry.*

(LAURA twists her hands nervously.)

Haven't you ever liked some boy?
LAURA.   Yes. I liked one once. *(She rises.)* I came across his picture a while ago.
AMANDA *(with some interest)*.   He gave you his picture?
LAURA.   No, it's in the yearbook.
AMANDA *(disappointed)*.   Oh—a high school boy.

(Screen image: Jim as the high school hero bearing a silver cup.)

LAURA.   Yes. His name was Jim. *(She lifts the heavy annual from the claw-foot table.)* Here he is in *The Pirates of Penzance.*
AMANDA *(absently)*.   The what?
LAURA.   The operetta the senior class put on. He had a wonderful voice and we sat across the aisle from each other Mondays, Wednesdays and Fridays in the Aud. Here he is with the silver cup for debating! See his grin?
AMANDA *(absently)*.   He must have had a jolly disposition.
LAURA.   He used to call me—Blue Roses.

(Screen image: Blue roses.)

AMANDA.   Why did he call you such a name as that?
LAURA.   When I had that attack of pleurosis—he asked me what was the matter when I came back. I said pleurosis—he thought that I said Blue Roses! So that's what he always called me after that. Whenever he saw me, he'd holler, "Hello, Blue Roses!" I didn't care for the girl that he went out with. Emily Meisenbach. Emily was the best-dressed girl at Soldan. She never

struck me, though, as being sincere . . . It says in the Personal Section—
they're engaged. That's—six years ago! They must be married by now.

AMANDA.   Girls that aren't cut out for business careers usually wind up
married to some nice man. (*She gets up with a spark of revival.*) Sister, that's
what you'll do!

(LAURA *utters a startled, doubtful laugh. She reaches quickly for a piece of
glass.*)

LAURA.   But, Mother—
AMANDA.   Yes? (*She goes over to the photograph.*)
LAURA (*in a tone of frightened apology*).   I'm—crippled!
AMANDA.   Nonsense! Laura, I've told you never, never to use that word.
Why, you're not crippled, you just have a little defect—hardly noticeable,
even! When people have some slight disadvantage like that, they cultivate
other things to make up for it—develop charm—and vivacity—and—*charm!*
That's all you have to do! (*She turns again to the photograph.*) One thing your
father had *plenty of*—was *charm!*

(*The scene fades out with music.*)

SCENE III

Legend on screen: "After the fiasco—"
TOM *speaks from the fire escape landing.*

TOM.   After the fiasco at Rubicam's Business College, the idea of getting
a gentleman caller for Laura began to play a more and more important part in
Mother's calculations. It became an obsession. Like some archetype of the
universal unconscious, the image of the gentleman caller haunted our small
apartment. . . .

(*Screen image:* A young man at the door of a house with flowers.)

An evening at home rarely passed without some allusion to this image, this
specter, this hope. . . . Even when he wasn't mentioned, his presence hung in
Mother's preoccupied look and in my sister's frightened, apologetic
manner—hung like a sentence passed upon the Wingfields! Mother was a
woman of action as well as words. She began to take logical steps in the
planned direction. Late that winter and in the early spring—realizing that
extra money would be needed to properly feather the nest and plume the
bird—she conducted a vigorous campaign on the telephone, roping in sub-
scribers to one of those magazines for matrons called *The Homemaker's
Companion*, the type of journal that features the serialized sublimations of
ladies of letters who think in terms of delicate cuplike breasts, slim, tapering
waists, rich, creamy thighs, eyes like wood smoke in autumn, fingers that
soothe and caress like strains of music, bodies as powerful as Etruscan
sculpture.

(*Screen image:* The cover of a glamor magazine.)

(AMANDA *enters with the telephone on a long extension cord. She is spot-lighted in the dim stage.*)

AMANDA.   Ida Scott? This is Amanda Wingfield! We *missed* you at the D.A.R. last Monday! I said to myself: She's probably suffering with that sinus condition! How is that sinus condition?
Horrors! Heaven have mercy!—You're a Christian martyr, yes, that's what you are, a Christian martyr!
Well, I just now happened to notice that your subscription to the *Companion's* about to expire! Yes, it expires with the next issue, honey!—just when that wonderful new serial by Bessie Mae Hopper is getting off to such an exciting start. Oh, honey, it's something that you can't miss! You remember how *Gone with the Wind* took everybody by storm? You simply couldn't go out if you hadn't read it. All everybody *talked* was Scarlett O'Hara. Well, this is a book that critics already compare to *Gone with the Wind.* It's the *Gone with the Wind* of the post-World-War generation!—What?—Burning?—Oh, honey, don't let them burn, go take a look in the oven and I'll hold the wire! Heavens—I think she's hung up!

(*The scene dims out.*)

(*Legend on screen:* "You think I'm in love with Continental Shoemakers?")

(*Before the lights come up again, the violent voices of* TOM *and* AMANDA *are heard. They are quarreling behind the portieres. In front of them stands* LAURA *with clenched hands and panicky expression. A clear pool of light is on her figure throughout this scene.*)

TOM.   What in Christ's name am I—
AMANDA (*shrilly*).   Don't you use that—
TOM.   —supposed to do!
AMANDA.   —expression! Not in my—
TOM.   Ohhh!
AMANDA.   —presence! Have you gone out of your senses?
TOM.   I have, that's true, *driven* out!
AMANDA.   What is the matter with you, you—big—big—IDIOT!
TOM.   Look!—I've got *no thing*, no single thing—
AMANDA.   Lower your voice!
TOM.   —in my life here that I can call my OWN! Everything is—
AMANDA.   Stop that shouting!
TOM.   Yesterday you confiscated my books! You had the nerve to—
AMANDA.   I took that horrible novel back to the library—yes! That hideous book by that insane Mr. Lawrence.

(TOM *laughs wildly.*)

I cannot control the output of diseased minds or people who cater to them—

(TOM *laughs still more wildly.*)

BUT I WON'T ALLOW SUCH FILTH BROUGHT INTO MY HOUSE! No, no, no, no, no!

TOM.   House, house! Who pays rent on it, who makes a slave of himself to—

AMANDA *(fairly screeching).*   Don't you DARE to—

TOM.   No, no, I mustn't say things! *I've* got to just—

AMANDA.   Let me tell you—

TOM.   I don't want to hear any more!

(He tears the portieres open. The dining-room area is lit with a turgid smoky red glow. Now we see AMANDA; *her hair is in metal curlers and she is wearing a very old bathrobe, much too large for her slight figure, a relic of the faithless Mr. Wingfield. The upright typewriter now stands on the drop-leaf table, along with a wild disarray of manuscripts. The quarrel was probably precipitated by* AMANDA's *interruption of* TOM's *creative labor. A chair lies overthrown on the floor. Their gesticulating shadows are cast on the ceiling by the fiery glow.)*

AMANDA.   You *will* hear more, you—

TOM.   No, I won't hear more, I'm going out!

AMANDA.   You come right back in—

TOM.   Out, out, out! Because I'm—

AMANDA.   Come back here, Tom Wingfield! I'm not through talking to you!

TOM.   Oh, go—

LAURA *(desperately).*   —Tom!

AMANDA.   You're going to listen, and no more insolence from you! I'm at the end of my patience!

(He comes back toward her.)

TOM.   What do you think I'm at? Aren't I supposed to have any patience to reach the end of, Mother? I know, I know. It seems unimportant to you, what I'm *doing*—what I *want* to do—having a little *difference* between them! You don't think that—

AMANDA.   I think you've been doing things that you're ashamed of. That's why you act like this. I don't believe that you go every night .to the movies. Nobody goes to the movies night after night. Nobody in their right minds goes to the movies as often as you pretend to. People don't go to the movies at nearly midnight, and movies don't let out at two A.M. Come in stumbling. Muttering to yourself like a maniac! You get three hours' sleep and then go to work. Oh, I can picture the way you're doing down there. Moping, doping, because you're in no condition.

TOM *(wildly).*   No, I'm in no condition!

AMANDA.   What right have you got to jeopardize your job? Jeopardize the security of us all? How do you think we'd manage if you were—

TOM.   Listen! You think I'm crazy about the *warehouse*? *(He bends fiercely toward her slight figure.)* You think I'm in love with the Continental Shoemakers? You think I want to spend fifty-five *years* down there in that— *celotex interior!* with—*fluorescent*—*tubes!* Look! I'd rather somebody picked up a crowbar and battered out my brains—than go back mornings! I *go!* Every time you come in yelling that Goddamn *"Rise and Shine!" "Rise and Shine!"* I say to myself, "How *lucky dead* people are!" But I get up. I *go!* For sixty-five dollars a month I give up all that I dream of doing and being *ever!* And you say self—*self's* all I ever think of. Why, listen, if self is what I thought of, Mother, I'd be where he is—GONE! (*He points to his father's picture.*) As far as the system of transportation reaches! (*He starts past her. She grabs his arm.*) Don't grab at me, Mother!

AMANDA.   Where are you going?

TOM.   I'm going to the *movies!*

AMANDA.   I don't believe that lie!

(TOM *crouches toward her, overtowering her tiny figure. She backs away, gasping.*)

TOM.   I'm going to opium dens! Yes, opium dens, dens of vice and criminals' hangouts, Mother. I've joined the Hogan Gang, I'm a hired assassin, I carry a tommy gun in a violin case! I run a string of cat houses in the Valley! They call me Killer, Killer Wingfield, I'm leading a double-life, a simple, honest warehouse worker by day, by night a dynamic *czar* of the *underworld, Mother.* I go to gambling casinos, I spin away fortunes on the roulette table! I wear a patch over one eye and a false mustache, sometimes I put on green whiskers. On those occasions they call me—*El Diablo!* Oh, I could tell you many things to make you sleepless! My enemies plan to dynamite this place. They're going to blow us all sky-high some night! I'll be glad, very happy, and so will you! You'll go up, up on a broomstick, over Blue Mountain with seventeen gentlemen callers! You ugly—babbling old—*witch* . . . . (*He goes through a series of violent, clumsy movements, seizing his overcoat, lunging to the door, pulling it fiercely open. The women watch him, aghast. His arm catches in the sleeve of the coat as he struggles to pull it on. For a moment he is pinioned by the bulky garment. With an outraged groan he tears the coat off again, splitting the shoulder of it, and hurls it across the room. It strikes against the shelf of* LAURA'S *glass collection, and there is a tinkle of shattering glass.* LAURA *cries out as if wounded.*)

(*Music.*)

(*Screen legend:* "The Glass Menagerie.")

LAURA (*shrilly*).   My glass!—menagerie. . . . (*She covers her face and turns away.*)

(*But* AMANDA *is still stunned and stupefied by the "ugly witch" so that she barely notices this occurrence. Now she recovers her speech.*)

AMANDA (*in an awful voice*).   I won't speak to you—until you apologize!

(*She crosses through the portieres and draws them together behind her.* TOM *is left with* LAURA. LAURA *clings weakly to the mantel with her face averted.* TOM *stares at her stupidly for a moment. Then he crosses to the shelf. He drops awkwardly on his knees to collect the fallen glass, glancing at* LAURA *as if he would speak but couldn't.*)

(*"The Glass Menagerie" music steals in as the scene dims out.*)

SCENE IV

The interior of the apartment is dark. There is a faint light in the alley. A deep-voiced bell in a church is tolling the hour of five.

TOM appears at the top of the alley. After each solemn boom of the bell in the tower, he shakes a little noisemaker or rattle as if to express the tiny spasm of man in contrast to the sustained power and dignity of the Almighty. This and the unsteadiness of his advance make it evident that he has been drinking. As he climbs the few steps to the fire escape landing light steals up inside. LAURA appears in the front room in a nightdress. She notices that TOM's bed is empty. TOM fishes in his pockets for his door key, removing a motley assortment of articles in the search, including a shower of movie ticket stubs and an empty bottle. At last he finds the key, but just as he is about to insert it, it slips from his fingers. He strikes a match and crouches below the door.

TOM (*bitterly*).   One crack—and it falls through!

(LAURA *opens the door.*)

LAURA.   Tom! Tom, what are you doing?
TOM.   Looking for a door key.
LAURA.   Where have you been all this time?
TOM.   I have been to the movies.
LAURA.   All this time at the movies?
TOM.   There was a very long program. There was a Garbo picture and a Mickey Mouse and a travelogue and a newsreel and a preview of coming attractions. And there was an organ solo and a collection for the Milk Fund—simultaneously—which ended up in a terrible fight between a fat lady and an usher!
LAURA (*innocently*).   Did you have to stay through everything?
TOM.   Of course! And, oh, I forgot! There was a big stage show! The headliner on this stage show was Malvolio the Magician. He performed wonderful tricks, many of them, such as pouring water back and forth between pitchers. First it turned to wine and then it turned to beer and then it turned to whisky. I know it was whisky it finally turned into because he needed somebody to come up out of the audience to help him, and I came up—both shows! It was Kentucky Straight Bourbon. A very generous fellow, he gave souvenirs. (*He pulls from his back pocket a shimmering rainbow-colored scarf.*) He gave me this. This is his magic scarf. You can have it, Laura. You wave it over a canary cage and you get a bowl of goldfish. You wave it over the goldfish bowl and they fly away canaries. . . . But the wonderfullest trick of all was the coffin trick. We nailed him into a coffin and he got out of the coffin without removing one nail. (*He has come inside.*) There is a trick that would come in handy for me—get me out of this two-by-four situation! (*He flops onto the bed and starts removing his shoes.*)
LAURA.   Tom—shhh!
TOM.   What're you shushing me for?
LAURA.   You'll wake up Mother.

TOM.   Goody, goody! Pay 'er back for all those "Rise an' Shines." (*He lies down, groaning.*) You know it don't take much intelligence to get yourself into a nailed-up coffin, Laura. But who in hell ever got himself out of one without removing one nail?

(*As if in answer, the father's grinning photograph lights up. The scene dims out.*)

(*Immediately following, the church bell is heard striking six. At the sixth stroke the alarm clock goes off in* AMANDA'S *room, and after a few moments we hear her calling: "Rise and Shine! Rise and Shine!* LAURA, *Go tell your brother to rise and shine!"*)

TOM (*sitting up slowly*).   I'll rise—but I won't shine.

(*The light increases.*)

AMANDA.   Laura, tell your brother his coffee is ready.

(LAURA *slips into the front room.*)

LAURA.   Tom!—It's nearly seven. Don't make Mother nervous.

(*He stares at her stupidly.*)

(*beseechingly:*) Tom, speak to Mother this morning. Make up with her, apologize, speak to her!
TOM.   She won't to me. It's her that started not speaking.
LAURA.   If you just say you're sorry she'll start speaking.
TOM.   Her not speaking—is that such a tragedy?
LAURA.   Please—please!
AMANDA (*calling from the kitchenette*).   Laura, are you going to do what I asked you to do, or do I have to get dressed and go out myself?
LAURA.   Going, going—soon as I get on my coat!

(*She pulls on a shapeless felt hat with a nervous, jerky movement, pleadingly glancing at* TOM. *She rushes awkwardly for her coat. The coat is one of* AMANDA'S, *inaccurately made-over, the sleeves too short for* LAURA.)

Butter and what else?
AMANDA (*entering from the kitchenette*).   Just butter. Tell them to charge it.
LAURA.   Mother, they make such faces when I do that.
AMANDA.   Sticks and stones can break our bones, but the expression on Mr. Garfinkel's face won't harm us! Tell your brother his coffee is getting cold.
LAURA (*at the door*).   Do what I asked you, will you, will you, Tom?

(*He looks sullenly away.*)

AMANDA.   Laura, go now or just don't go at all!
LAURA (*rushing out*).   Going—going!

(*A second later she cries out.* TOM *springs up and crosses to the door.* TOM *opens the door.*)

TOM. Laura?

LAURA. I'm all right. I slipped, but I'm all right.

AMANDA (*peering anxiously after her*). If anyone breaks a leg on those fire-escape steps, the landlord ought to be sued for every cent he possesses! (*She shuts the door. Now she remembers she isn't speaking to* TOM *and returns to the other room.*)

(*As* TOM *comes listlessly for his coffee, she turns her back to him and stands rigidly facing the window on the gloomy gray vault of the areaway. Its light on her face with its aged but childish features is cruelly sharp, satirical as a Daumier print.*)

(*The music of "Ave Maria," is heard softly.*)

(TOM *glances sheepishly but sullenly at her averted figure and slumps at the table. The coffee is scalding hot; he sips it and gasps and spits it back in the cup. At his gasp,* AMANDA *catches her breath and half turns. Then she catches herself and turns back to the window.* TOM *blows on his coffee, glancing sidewise at his mother. She clears her throat.* TOM *clears his. He starts to rise, sinks back down again, scratches his head, clears his throat again.* AMANDA *coughs.* TOM *raises his cup in both hands to blow on it, his eyes staring over the rim of it at his mother for several moments. Then he slowly sets the cup down and awkwardly and hesitantly rises from the chair.*)

TOM (*hoarsely*). Mother. I—I apologize, Mother.

(AMANDA *draws a quick, shuddering breath. Her face works grotesquely. She breaks into childlike tears.*)

I'm sorry for what I said, for everything that I said, I didn't mean it.

AMANDA (*sobbingly*). My devotion has made me a witch and so I make myself hateful to my children!

TOM. No, you *don't*.

AMANDA. I worry so much, don't sleep, it makes me nervous!

TOM (*gently*). I understand that.

AMANDA. I've had to put up a solitary battle all these years. But you're my right-hand bower! Don't fall down, don't fail!

TOM (*gently*). I try, Mother.

AMANDA (*with great enthusiasm*). Try and you will *succeed!* (*The notion makes her breathless.*) Why, you—you're just *full* of natural endowments! Both of my children—they're *unusual* children! Don't you think I know it? I'm so—*proud!* Happy and—feel I've—so much to be thankful for but— promise me one thing, son!

TOM. What, Mother?

AMANDA. Promise, son, you'll—never be a drunkard!

TOM (*turns to her grinning*). I will never be a drunkard, Mother.

AMANDA. That's what frightened me so, that you'd be drinking! Eat a bowl of Purina!

TOM. Just coffee, Mother.

AMANDA. Shredded wheat biscuit?

TOM. No. No, Mother, just coffee.

AMANDA.   You can't put in a day's work on an empty stomach. You've got ten minutes—don't gulp! Drinking too-hot liquids makes cancer of the stomach. . . . Put cream in.

TOM.   No, thank you.

AMANDA.   To cool it.

TOM.   No! No, thank you, I want it black.

AMANDA.   I know, but it's not good for you. We have to do all that we can to build ourselves up. In these trying times we live in, all that we have to cling to is—each other. . . . That's why it's so important to— Tom, I—I sent out your sister so I could discuss something with you. If you hadn't spoken I would have spoken to you. (*She sits down.*)

TOM (*gently*).   What is it, Mother, that you want to discuss?

AMANDA.   *Laura!*

(TOM *puts his cup down slowly.*)

(*Legend on screen:* "Laura." *Music:* "The Glass Menagerie.")

TOM.   —Oh.—Laura . . .

AMANDA (*touching his sleeve*).   You know how Laura is. So quiet but— still water runs deep! She notices things and I think she—broods about them.

(TOM *looks up.*)

A few days ago I came in and she was crying.

TOM.   What about?

AMANDA.   You.

TOM.   Me?

AMANDA.   She has an idea that you're not happy here.

TOM.   What gave her that idea?

AMANDA.   What gives her any idea? However, you do act strangely. I—I'm not criticizing, understand *that!* I know your ambitions do not lie in the warehouse, that like everybody in the whole wide world—you've had to—make sacrifices, but—Tom—Tom—life's not easy, it calls for—Spartan endurance! There's so many things in my heart that I cannot describe to you! I've never told you but I—*loved* your father. . . .

TOM (*gently*).   I know that, Mother.

AMANDA.   And you—when I see you taking after his ways! Staying out late—and—well, you *had* been drinking the night you were in that— terrifying condition! Laura says that you hate the apartment and that you go out nights to get away from it! Is that true, Tom?

TOM.   No. You say there's so much in your heart that you can't describe to me. That's true of me, too. There's so much in my heart that I can't describe to *you!* So let's respect each other's—

AMANDA.   But, why—*why*, Tom—are you always so *restless?* Where do you *go* to, nights?

TOM.   I—go to the movies.

AMANDA.   Why do you go to the movies so much, Tom?

TOM.   I go to the movies because—I like adventure. Adventure is something I don't have much of at work, so I go to the movies.

AMANDA.   But, Tom, you go to the movies *entirely* too *much!*

TOM.   I like a lot of adventure.

(AMANDA *looks baffled, then hurt. As the familiar inquisition resumes,* TOM *becomes hard and impatient again.* AMANDA *slips back into her querulous attitude toward him.*)

(*Image on screen:* A sailing vessel with Jolly Roger.)

AMANDA.   Most young men find adventure in their careers.

TOM.   Then most young men are not employed in a warehouse.

AMANDA.   The world is full of young men employed in warehouses and offices and factories.

TOM.   Do all of them find adventure in their careers?

AMANDA.   They do or they do without it! Not everybody has a craze for adventure.

TOM.   Man is by instinct a lover, a hunter, a fighter, and none of those instincts are given much play at the warehouse!

AMANDA.   Man is by instinct! Don't quote instinct to me! Instinct is something that people have got away from! It belongs to animals! Christian adults don't want it!

TOM.   What do Christian adults want, then, Mother?

AMANDA.   Superior things! Things of the mind and the spirit! Only animals have to satisfy instincts! Surely your aims are somewhat higher than theirs! Than monkeys—pigs—

TOM.   I reckon they're not.

AMANDA.   You're joking. However, that isn't what I wanted to discuss.

TOM (*rising*).   I haven't much time.

AMANDA (*pushing his shoulders*).   Sit down.

TOM.   You want me to punch in red at the warehouse, Mother?

AMANDA.   You have five minutes. I want to talk about Laura.

(*Screen legend:* "Plans and Provisions.")

TOM.   All right! What about Laura?

AMANDA.   We have to be making some plans and provisions for her. She's older than you, two years, and nothing has happened. She just drifts along doing nothing. It frightens me terribly how she just drifts along.

TOM.   I guess she's the type that people call home girls.

AMANDA.   There's no such type, and if there is, it's a pity! That is unless the home is hers, with a husband!

TOM.   What?

AMANDA.   Oh, I can see the handwriting on the wall as plain as I see the nose in front of my face! It's terrifying! More and more you remind me of your father! He was out all hours without explanation!—Then *left! Goodbye!* And me with the bag to hold. I saw that letter you got from the Merchant Marine. I know what you're dreaming of. I'm not standing here blindfolded. (*She pauses.*) Very well, then. Then *do* it! But not till there's somebody to take your place.

TOM.   What do you mean?

AMANDA.   I mean that as soon as Laura has got somebody to take care of her, married, a home of her own, independent—why, then you'll be free to go wherever you please, on land, on sea, whichever way the wind blows you! But until that time you've got to look out for your sister. I don't say me because I'm old and don't matter! I say for your sister because she's young and dependent.

I put her in business college—a dismal failure! Frightened her so it made her sick at the stomach. I took her over to the Young People's League at the church. Another fiasco. She spoke to nobody, nobody spoke to her. Now all she does is fool with those pieces of glass and play those worn-out records. What kind of a life is that for a girl to lead?

TOM.   What can I do about it?

AMANDA.   Overcome selfishness! Self, self, self is all that you ever think of!

(TOM *springs up and crosses to get his coat. It is ugly and bulky. He pulls on a cap with earmuffs.*)

Where is your muffler? Put your wool muffler on!

(*He snatches it angrily from the closet, tosses it around his neck and pulls both ends tight.*)

Tom! I haven't said what I had in mind to ask you.

TOM.   I'm too late to—

AMANDA (*catching his arm—very importunately; then shyly*).   Down at the warehouse, aren't there some—nice young men?

TOM.   No!

AMANDA.   There *must* be—*some* . . .

TOM.   Mother— (*He gestures.*)

AMANDA.   Find out one that's clean-living—doesn't drink and ask him out for sister!

TOM.   What?

AMANDA.   For *sister!* To *meet!* Get *acquainted!*

TOM (*stamping to the door*).   Oh, my go-osh!

AMANDA.   Will you?

(*He opens the door. She says, imploringly:*)

Will you?

(*He starts down the fire escape.*)

Will you? *Will* you, dear?

TOM (*calling back*).   Yes!

(AMANDA *closes the door hesitantly and with a troubled but faintly hopeful expression.*)

(*Screen image:* The cover of a glamor magazine.)

(*The spotlight picks up* AMANDA *at the phone.*)

AMANDA.   Ella Cartwright? This is Amanda Wingfield!
How are you, honey?
How is that kidney condition?

(There is a five-second pause.)

Horrors!

(There is another pause.)

You're a Christian martyr, yes, honey, that's what you are, a Christian martyr! Well, I just now happened to notice in my little red book that your subscription to the *Companion* has just run out! I knew that you wouldn't want to miss out on the wonderful serial starting in this new issue. It's by Bessie Mae Hopper, the first thing she's written since *Honeymoon for Three*. Wasn't that a strange and interesting story? Well, this one is even lovelier, I believe. It has a sophisticated, society background. It's all about the horsey set on Long Island!

(The light fades out.)

SCENE V

Legend on the screen: "Annunciation."
Music is heard as the light slowly comes on.
It is early dusk of a spring evening. Supper has just been finished in the Wingfield apartment. AMANDA *and* LAURA, *in light-colored dresses, are removing dishes from the table in the dining room, which is shadowy, their movements formalized almost as a dance or ritual, their moving forms as pale and silent as moths.* TOM, *in white shirt and trousers, rises from the table and crosses toward the fire escape.*

AMANDA *(as he passes her).*   Son, will you do me a favor?
TOM.   What?
AMANDA.   Comb your hair! You look so pretty when your hair is combed!

(TOM *slouches on the sofa with the evening paper. Its enormous headline reads: "Franco Triumphs.")*

There is only one respect in which I would like you to emulate your father.
TOM.   What respect is that?
AMANDA.   The care he always took of his appearance. He never allowed himself to look untidy.

(He throws down the paper and crosses to the fire escape.)

Where are you going?
TOM.   I'm going out to smoke.
AMANDA.   You smoke too much. A pack a day at fifteen cents a pack. How much would that amount to in a month? Thirty times fifteen is how much, Tom? Figure it out and you will be astounded at what you could save.

Enough to give you a night-school course in accounting at Washington U.! Just think what a wonderful thing that would be for you, son!

(TOM *is unmoved by the thought.*)

TOM.   I'd rather smoke. (*He steps out on the landing, letting the screen door slam.*)

AMANDA (*sharply*).   I know! That's the tragedy of it. . . . (*Alone, she turns to look at her husband's picture.*)

(*Dance music: "The World Is Waiting for the Sunrise!"*)

TOM (*to the audience*).   Across the alley from us was the Paradise Dance Hall. On evenings in spring the windows and doors were open and the music came outdoors. Sometimes the lights were turned out except for a large glass sphere that hung from the ceiling. It would turn slowly about and filter the dusk with delicate rainbow colors. Then the orchestra played a waltz or a tango, something that had a slow and sensuous rhythm. Couples would come outside, to the relative privacy of the alley. You could see them kissing behind ash pits and telephone poles. This was the compensation for lives that passed like mine, without any change or adventure. Adventure and change were imminent in this year. They were waiting around the corner for all these kids. Suspended in the mist over Berchtesgaden, caught in the folds of Chamberlain's umbrella. In Spain there was Guernica! But here there was only hot swing music and liquor, dance halls, bars, and movies, and sex that hung in the gloom like a chandelier and flooded the world with brief, deceptive rainbows. . . . All the world was waiting for bombardments!

(AMANDA *turns from the picture and comes outside.*)

AMANDA (*sighing*).   A fire escape landing's a poor excuse for a porch. (*She spreads a newspaper on a step and sits down, gracefully and demurely as if she were settling into a swing on a Mississippi veranda.*) What are you looking at?
TOM.   The moon.
AMANDA.   Is there a moon this evening?
TOM.   It's rising over Garfinkel's Delicatessen.
AMANDA.   So it is! A little silver slipper of a moon. Have you made a wish on it yet?
TOM.   Um-hum.
AMANDA.   What did you wish for?
TOM.   That's a secret.
AMANDA.   A secret, huh? Well, I won't tell mine either. I will be just as mysterious as you.
TOM.   I bet I can guess what yours is.
AMANDA.   Is my head so transparent?
TOM.   You're not a sphinx.
AMANDA.   No, I don't have secrets. I'll tell you what I wished for on the moon. Success and happiness for my precious children! I wish for that whenever there's a moon, and when there isn't a moon, I wish for it, too.
TOM.   I thought perhaps you wished for a gentleman caller.

AMANDA.   Why do you say that?

TOM.   Don't you remember asking me to fetch one?

AMANDA.   I remember suggesting that it would be nice for your sister if you brought home some nice young man from the warehouse. I think that I've made that suggestion more than once.

TOM.   Yes, you have made it repeatedly.

AMANDA.   Well?

TOM.   We are going to have one.

AMANDA.   *What?*

TOM.   A gentleman caller!

(The annunciation is celebrated with music.)

*(*AMANDA *rises.)*

(Image on screen: A caller with a bouquet.)

AMANDA.   You mean you have asked some nice young man to come over?

TOM.   Yep. I've asked him to dinner.

AMANDA.   You really did?

TOM.   I did!

AMANDA.   You did, and did he—*accept?*

TOM.   He did!

AMANDA.   Well, well—well, well! That's—lovely!

TOM.   I thought that you would be pleased.

AMANDA.   It's definite then?

TOM.   Very definite.

AMANDA.   Soon?

TOM.   Very soon.

AMANDA.   For heaven's sake, stop putting on and tell me some things, will you?

TOM.   What things do you want me to tell you?

AMANDA.   *Naturally* I would like to know when he's *coming!*

TOM.   He's coming tomorrow.

AMANDA.   *Tomorrow?*

TOM.   Yep. Tomorrow.

AMANDA.   But, Tom!

TOM.   Yes, Mother?

AMANDA.   Tomorrow gives me no time!

TOM.   Time for what?

AMANDA.   Preparations! Why didn't you phone me at once, as soon as you asked him, the minute that he accepted? Then, don't you see, I could have been getting ready!

TOM.   You don't have to make any fuss.

AMANDA.   Oh, Tom, Tom, Tom, of course I have to make a fuss! I want things nice, not sloppy! Not thrown together. I'll certainly have to do some fast thinking, won't I?

TOM.   I don't see why you have to think at all.

AMANDA.   You just don't know. We can't have a gentleman caller in a pigsty! All my wedding silver has to be polished, the monogrammed table linen ought to be laundered! The windows have to be washed and fresh curtains put up. And how about clothes? We have to *wear* something, don't we?

TOM.   Mother, this boy is no one to make a fuss over!

AMANDA.   Do you realize he's the first young man we've introduced to your sister? It's terrible, dreadful, disgraceful that poor little sister has never received a single gentleman caller! Tom, come inside! (*She opens the screen door.*)

TOM.   What for?

AMANDA.   I want to ask you some things.

TOM.   If you're going to make such a fuss, I'll call it off, I'll tell him not to come!

AMANDA.   You certainly won't do anything of the kind. Nothing offends people worse than broken engagements. It simply means I'll have to work like a Turk! We won't be brilliant, but we will pass inspection. Come on inside.

(TOM *follows her inside, groaning.*)

Sit down.

TOM.   Any particular place you would like me to sit?

AMANDA.   Thank heavens I've got that new sofa! I'm also making payments on a floor lamp I'll have sent out! And put the chintz covers on, they'll brighten things up! Of course I'd hoped to have these walls re-papered. . . . What is the young man's name?

TOM.   His name is O'Connor.

AMANDA.   That, of course, means fish—tomorrow is Friday! I'll have that salmon loaf—with Durkee's dressing! What does he do? He works at the warehouse?

TOM.   Of course! How else would I—

AMANDA.   Tom, he—doesn't drink?

TOM.   Why do you ask me that?

AMANDA.   Your father *did*!

TOM.   Don't get started on that!

AMANDA.   He *does* drink, then?

TOM.   Not that I know of!

AMANDA.   Make sure, be certain! The last thing I want for my daughter's a boy who drinks!

TOM.   Aren't you being a little bit premature? Mr. O'Connor has not yet appeared on the scene!

AMANDA.   But will tomorrow. To meet your sister, and what do I know about his character? Nothing! Old maids are better off than wives of drunkards!

TOM.   Oh, my God!

AMANDA.   Be still!

TOM (*leaning forward to whisper*).   Lots of fellows meet girls whom they don't marry!

AMANDA.   Oh, talk sensibly, Tom—and don't be sarcastic! (*She has gotten a hairbrush.*)

TOM.   What are you doing?

AMANDA.   I'm brushing that cowlick down! (*She attacks his hair with the brush.*) What is this young man's position at the warehouse?

TOM (*submitting grimly to the brush and the interrogation*).   This young man's position is that of a shipping clerk, Mother.

AMANDA.   Sounds to me like a fairly responsible job, the sort of job *you* would be in if you just had more *get-up*. What is his salary? Have you any idea?

TOM.   I would judge it to be approximately eighty-five dollars a month.

AMANDA.   Well—not princely, but—

TOM.   Twenty more than I make.

AMANDA.   Yes, how well I know! But for a family man, eighty-five dollars a month is not much more then you can just get by on. . . .

TOM.   Yes, but Mr. O'Connor is not a family man.

AMANDA.   He might be, mightn't he? Some time in the future?

TOM.   I see. Plans and provisions.

AMANDA.   You are the only young man that I know of who ignores the fact that the future becomes the present, the present the past, and the past turns into everlasting regret if you don't plan for it!

TOM.   I will think that over and see what I can make of it.

AMANDA.   Don't be supercilious with your mother! Tell me some more about this—what do you call him?

TOM.   James D. O'Connor. The D. is for Delaney.

AMANDA.   Irish on *both* sides! *Gracious!* And doesn't drink?

TOM.   Shall I call him up and ask him right this minute?

AMANDA.   The only way to find out about those things is to make discreet inquiries at the proper moment. When I was a girl in Blue Mountain and it was suspected that a young man drank, the girl whose attentions he had been receiving, if any girl *was*, would sometimes speak to the minister of his church, or rather her father would if her father was living, and sort of feel him out on the young man's character. That is the way such things are discreetly handled to keep a young woman from making a tragic mistake!

TOM.   Then how did you happen to make a tragic mistake?

AMANDA.   That innocent look of your father's had everyone fooled! He *smiled*—the world was *enchanted!* No girl can do worse than put herself at the mercy of a handsome appearance! I hope that Mr. O'Connor is not too good-looking.

TOM.   No, he's not too good-looking. He's covered with freckles and hasn't too much of a nose.

AMANDA.   He's not right-down homely, though?

TOM.   Not right-down homely. Just medium homely, I'd say.

AMANDA.   Character's what to look for in a man.

TOM.   That's what I've always said, Mother.

AMANDA.   You've never said anything of the kind and I suspect you would never give it a thought.

TOM.   Don't be so suspicious of me.

AMANDA.   At least I hope he's the type that's up and coming.

TOM.   I think he really goes in for self-improvement.

AMANDA.   What reason have you to think so?

TOM.   He goes to night school.

AMANDA (*beaming*).   Splendid! What does he do, I mean study?

TOM.   Radio engineering and public speaking!

AMANDA.   Then he has visions of being advanced in the world! Any young man who studies public speaking is aiming to have an executive job some day! And radio engineering? A thing for the future! Both of these facts are very illuminating. Those are the sort of things that a mother should know concerning any young man who comes to call on her daughter. Seriously or—not.

TOM.   One little warning. He doesn't know about Laura. I didn't let on that we had dark ulterior motives. I just said, why don't you come and have dinner with us? He said okay and that was the whole conversation.

AMANDA.   I bet it was! You're eloquent as an oyster. However, he'll know about Laura when he gets here. When he sees how lovely and sweet and pretty she is, he'll thank his lucky stars he was asked to dinner.

TOM.   Mother, you mustn't expect too much of Laura.

AMANDA.   What do you mean?

TOM.   Laura seems all those things to you and me because she's ours and we love her. We don't even notice she's crippled any more.

AMANDA.   Don't say crippled! You know that I never allow that word to be used!

TOM.   But face facts, Mother. She is and—that's not all—

AMANDA.   What do you mean "not all"?

TOM.   Laura is very different from other girls.

AMANDA.   I think the difference is all to her advantage.

TOM.   Not quite all—in the eyes of others—strangers—she's terribly shy and lives in a world of her own and those things make her seem a little peculiar to people outside the house.

AMANDA.   Don't say peculiar.

TOM.   Face the facts. She is.

(*The dance hall music changes to a tango that has a minor and somewhat ominous tone.*)

AMANDA.   In what way is she peculiar—may I ask?

TOM (*gently*).   She lives in a world of her own—a world of little glass ornaments, Mother. . . .

(*He gets up.* AMANDA *remains holding the brush, looking at him, troubled.*)

She plays old phonograph records and—that's about all—(*He glances at himself in the mirror and crosses to the door.*)

AMANDA (*sharply*).   Where are you going?

TOM.   I'm going to the movies. (*He goes out the screen door.*)

AMANDA.   Not to the movies, every night to the movies! (*She follows quickly to the screen door.*) I don't believe you always go to the movies!

(*He is gone.* AMANDA *looks worriedly after him for a moment. Then vitality and optimism return and she turns from the door, crossing to the portieres.*)

Laura! Laura!

(LAURA *answers from the kitchenette.*)

LAURA.   Yes, Mother.

AMANDA.   Let those dishes go and come in front!

(LAURA *appears with a dish towel.* AMANDA *speaks to her gaily.*)

Laura, come here and make a wish on the moon!

(*Screen image:* The Moon.)

LAURA (*entering*).   Moon—moon?

AMANDA.   A little silver slipper of a moon. Look over your left shoulder, Laura, and make a wish!

(LAURA *looks faintly puzzled as if called out of sleep.* AMANDA *seizes her shoulders and turns her at an angle by the door.*)

Now! Now, darling, *wish!*

LAURA.   What shall I wish for, Mother?

AMANDA (*her voice trembling and her eyes suddenly filling with tears*).   Happiness! Good fortune!

(*The sound of the violin rises and the stage dims out.*)

SCENE VI

The light comes up on the fire escape landing. TOM *is leaning against the grill, smoking.*

(*Screen image:* The high school hero.)

TOM.   And so the following evening I brought Jim home to dinner. I had known Jim slightly in high school. In high school Jim was a hero. He had tremendous Irish good nature and vitality with the scrubbed and polished look of white chinaware. He seemed to move in a continual spotlight. He was a star in basketball, captain of the debating club, president of the senior class and the glee club and he sang the male lead in the annual light operas. He was always running or bounding, never just walking. He seemed always at the point of defeating the law of gravity. He was shooting with such velocity through his adolescence that you would logically expect him to arrive at nothing short of the White House by the time he was thirty. But Jim apparently ran into more interference after his graduation from Soldan. His speed had definitely slowed. Six years after he left high school he was holding a job that wasn't much better than mine.

(Screen image: The Clerk.*)*

He was the only one at the warehouse with whom I was on friendly terms. I was valuable to him as someone who could remember his former glory, who had seen him win basketball games and the silver cup in debating. He knew of my secret practice of retiring to a cabinet of the washroom to work on poems when business was slack in the warehouse. He called me Shakespeare. And while the other boys in the warehouse regarded me with suspicious hostility, Jim took a humorous attitude toward me. Gradually his attitude affected the others, their hostility wore off and they also began to smile at me as people smile at an oddly fashioned dog who trots across their path at some distance.

I knew that Jim and Laura had known each other at Soldan, and I had heard Laura speak admiringly of his voice. I didn't know if Jim remembered her or not. In high school Laura had been as unobtrusive as Jim had been astonishing. If he did remember Laura, it was not as my sister, for when I asked him to dinner, he grinned and said, "You know, Shakespeare, I never thought of you as having folks!"

He was about to discover that I did. . . .

(Legend on screen: "The accent of a coming foot.")

(The light dims on TOM *and comes up in the Wingfield living room—a delicate lemony light. It is about five on a Friday evening of late spring which comes "scattering poems in the sky.")*

*(*AMANDA *has worked like a Turk in preparation for the gentleman caller. The results are astonishing. The new floor lamp with its rose silk shade is in place, a colored paper lantern conceals the broken light fixture in the ceiling, new billowing white curtains are at the windows, chintz covers are on the chairs and sofa, a pair of new sofa pillows make their initial appearance. Open boxes and tissue paper are scattered on the floor.)*

*(*LAURA *stands in the middle of the room with lifted arms while* AMANDA *crouches before her, adjusting the hem of a new dress, devout and ritualistic. The dress is colored and designed by memory. The arrangement of* LAURA'S *hair is changed; it is softer and more becoming. A fragile, unearthly prettiness has come out in* LAURA: *she is like a piece of translucent glass touched by light, given a momentary radiance, not actual, not lasting.)*

AMANDA *(impatiently).*   Why are you trembling?
LAURA.   Mother, you've made me so nervous!
AMANDA.   How have I made you nervous?
LAURA.   By all this fuss! You make it seem so important!
AMANDA.   I don't understand you, Laura. You couldn't be satsified with just sitting home, and yet whenever I try to arrange something for you, you seem to resist it. *(She gets up.)* Now take a look at yourself. No, wait! Wait just a moment—I have an idea!
LAURA.   What is it now?

*(*AMANDA *produces two powder puffs which she wraps in handkerchiefs and stuffs in* LAURA'S *bosom.)*

LAURA. Mother, what are you doing?

AMANDA. They call them "Gay Deceivers"!

LAURA. I won't wear them!

AMANDA. You will!

LAURA. Why should I?

AMANDA. Because, to be painfully honest, your chest is flat.

LAURA. You make it seem like we were setting a trap.

AMANDA.   All pretty girls are a trap, a pretty trap, and men expect them to be.

(Legend on screen: "A pretty trap.")

Now look at yourself, young lady. This is the prettiest you will ever be! (*She stands back to admire* LAURA.) I've got to fix myself now! You're going to be surprised by your mother's appearance!

(AMANDA *crosses through the portieres, humming gaily.* LAURA *moves slowly to the long mirror and stares solemnly at herself. A wind blows the white curtains inward in a slow, graceful motion and with a faint, sorrowful sighing.*)

AMANDA (*from somewhere behind the portieres*).   It isn't dark enough yet.

(LAURA *turns slowly before the mirror with a troubled look.*)

(*Legend on screen:* "This is my sister: Celebrate her with strings!" *Music plays.*)

AMANDA (*laughing, still not visible*).   I'm going to show you something. I'm going to make a spectacular appearance!

LAURA. What is it, Mother?

AMANDA.   Possess your soul in patience—you will see! Something I've resurrected from that old trunk! Styles haven't changed so terribly much after all. . . . (*She parts the portieres.*) Now just look at your mother! (*She wears a girlish frock of yellowed voile with a blue silk sash. She carries a bunch of jonquils—the legend of her youth is nearly revived. Now she speaks feverishly:*) This is the dress in which I led the cotillion. Won the cakewalk twice at Sunset Hill, wore one Spring to the Governor's Ball in Jackson! See how I sashayed around the ballroom, Laura? (*She raises her skirt and does a mincing step around the room.*) I wore it on Sundays for my gentlemen callers! I had it on the day I met your father. . . . I had malaria fever all that Spring. The change of climate from East Tennessee to the Delta—weakened resistance. I had a little temperature all the time—not enough to be serious—just enough to make me restless and giddy! Invitations poured in—parties all over the Delta! "Stay in bed," said Mother, "you have a fever!"—but I just wouldn't. I took quinine but kept on going, going! Evenings, dances! Afternoons, long, long rides! Picnics—lovely! So lovely, that country in May—all lacy with dogwood, literally flooded with jonquils! That was the Spring I had the craze for jonquils. Jonquils became an absolute obsession. Mother said, "Honey, there's no more room for jonquils." And still I kept on bringing in more jonquils. Whenever, wherever I saw them, I'd say, "Stop! Stop! I see jonquils!" I made the young men help me gather the jonquils! It was a joke,

Amanda and her jonquils. Finally there were no more vases to hold them, every available space was filled with jonquils. No vases to hold them? All right, I'll hold them myself! And then I—(*She stops in front of the picture. Music plays.*) met your father! Malaria fever and jonquils and then—this—boy. . . . (*She switches on the rose-colored lamp.*) I hope they get here before it starts to rain. (*She crosses the room and places the jonquils in a bowl on the table.*) I gave your brother a little extra change so he and Mr. O'Connor could take the service car home.

LAURA (*with an altered look*).   What did you say his name was?

AMANDA.   O'Connor.

LAURA.   What is his first name?

AMANDA.   I don't remember. Oh, yes, I do. It was—Jim!

(LAURA *sways slightly and catches hold of a chair.*)

(*Legend on screen:* "Not Jim!")

LAURA (*faintly*).   Not—Jim!

AMANDA.   Yes, that was it, it was Jim! I've never known a Jim that wasn't nice!

(*The music becomes ominous.*)

LAURA.   Are you sure his name is Jim O'Connor?

AMANDA.   Yes. Why?

LAURA.   Is he the one that Tom used to know in high school?

AMANDA.   He didn't say so. I think he just got to know him at the warehouse.

LAURA.   There was a Jim O'Connor we both knew in high school—(*then, with effort.*) If that is the one that Tom is bringing to dinner—you'll have to excuse me, I won't come to the table.

AMANDA.   What sort of nonsense is this?

LAURA.   You asked me once if I'd ever liked a boy. Don't you remember I showed you this boy's picture?

AMANDA.   You mean the boy you showed me in the yearbook?

LAURA.   Yes, that boy.

AMANDA.   Laura, Laura, were you in love with that boy?

LAURA.   I don't know, Mother. All I know is I couldn't sit at the table if it was him!

AMANDA.   It won't be him! It isn't the least bit likely. But whether it is or not, you will come to the table. You will not be excused.

LAURA.   I'll have to be, Mother.

AMANDA.   I don't intend to humor your silliness, Laura. I've had too much from you and your brother, both! So just sit down and compose yourself till they come. Tom has forgotten his key so you'll have to let them in, when they arrive.

LAURA (*panicky*).   Oh, Mother—*you* answer the door!

AMANDA (*lightly*).   I'll be in the kitchen—busy!

LAURA.   Oh, Mother, please answer the door, don't make me do it!

AMANDA (*crossing into the kitchenette*).   I've got to fix the dressing for the salmon. Fuss, fuss—silliness!—over a gentleman caller!

(*The door swings shut.* LAURA *is left alone.*)

(*Legend on screen:* "Terror!")

(*She utters a low moan and turns off the lamp—sits stiffly on the edge of the sofa, knotting her fingers together.*)

(*Legend on screen:* "The Opening of a Door!")

(TOM *and* JIM *appear on the fire escape steps and climb to the landing. Hearing their approach,* LAURA *rises with a panicky gesture. She retreats to the portieres. The doorbell rings.* LAURA *catches her breath and touches her throat. Low drums sound.*)

AMANDA (*calling*).   Laura, sweetheart! The door!

(LAURA *stares at it without moving.*)

JIM.   I think we just beat the rain.

TOM.   Uh-huh. (*He rings again, nervously.* JIM *whistles and fishes for a cigarette.*)

AMANDA (*very, very gaily*).   Laura, that is your brother and Mr. O'Connor! Will you let them in, darling?

(LAURA *crosses toward the kitchenette door.*)

LAURA (*breathlessly*).   Mother—you go to the door!

(AMANDA *steps out of the kitchenette and stares furiously at* LAURA. *She points imperiously at the door.*)

LAURA.   Please, please!

AMANDA (*in a fierce whisper*).   What is the matter with you, you silly thing?

LAURA (*desperately*).   Please, you answer it, *please!*

AMANDA.   I told you I wasn't going to humor you, Laura. Why have you chosen this moment to lose your mind?

LAURA.   Please, please, please, you go!

AMANDA.   You'll have to go to the door because I can't!

LAURA (*despairingly*).   I can't either!

AMANDA.   *Why?*

LAURA.   I'm *sick!*

AMANDA.   I'm sick, too—of your nonsense! Why can't you and your brother be normal people? Fantastic whims and behavior!

(TOM *gives a long ring.*)

Preposterous goings on! Can you give me one reason— (*She calls out lyrically.*) Coming! *Just* one second!—why you should be afraid to open a door? Now you answer it, Laura!

LAURA.   Oh, oh, oh . . . (*She returns through the portieres, darts to the Victrola, winds it frantically and turns it on.*)

AMANDA.   Laura Wingfield, you march right to that door!

LAURA.   Yes—yes, Mother!

(*A faraway, scratchy rendition of "Dardanella" softens the air and gives her strength to move through it. She slips to the door and draws it cautiously open.* TOM *enters with the caller,* JIM O'CONNOR.)

TOM.   Laura, this is Jim. Jim, this is my sister, Laura.

JIM (*stepping inside*).   I didn't know that Shakespeare had a sister!

LAURA (*retreating, stiff and trembling, from the door*).   How—how do you do?

JIM (*heartily, extending his hand*).   Okay!

(LAURA *touches it hesitantly with hers.*)

JIM.   Your hand's *cold*, Laura!

LAURA.   Yes, well—I've been playing the Victrola. . . .

JIM.   Must have been playing classical music on it! You ought to play a little hot swing music to warm you up!

LAURA.   Excuse me—I haven't finished playing the Victrola. . . .

(*She turns awkwardly and hurries into the front room. She pauses a second by the Victrola. Then she catches her breath and darts through the portieres like a frightened deer.*)

JIM (*grinning*).   What was the matter?

TOM.   Oh—with Laura? Laura is—terribly shy.

JIM.   Shy, huh? It's unusual to meet a shy girl nowadays. I don't believe you ever mentioned you had a sister.

TOM.   Well, now you know. I have one. Here is the *Post Dispatch.* You want a piece of it?

JIM.   Uh-huh.

TOM.   What piece? The comics?

JIM.   Sports! (*He glances at it.*) Ole Dizzy Dean is on his bad behavior.

TOM (*uninterested*).   Yeah? (*He lights a cigarette and goes over to the fire-escape door.*)

JIM.   Where are *you* going?

TOM.   I'm going out on the terrace.

JIM (*going after him*).   You know, Shakespeare—I'm going to sell you a bill of goods!

TOM.   What goods?

JIM.   A course I'm taking.

TOM.   Huh?

JIM.   In public speaking! You and me, we're not the warehouse type.

TOM.   Thanks—that's good news. But what has public speaking got to do with it?

JIM.   It fits you for—executive positions!

TOM.   Awww.

JIM.   I tell you it's done a helluva lot for me.

(*Image on screen:* Executive at his desk.)

TOM. In what respect?

JIM. In every! Ask yourself what is the difference between you an' me and men in the office down front? Brains?—No!—Ability?—No! Then what? Just one little thing—

TOM. What is that one little thing?

JIM. Primarily it amounts to—social poise! Being able to square up to people and hold your own on any social level!

AMANDA (*from the kitchenette*). Tom?

TOM. Yes, Mother?

AMANDA. Is that you and Mr. O'Connor?

TOM. Yes, Mother.

AMANDA. Well, you just make yourselves comfortable in there.

TOM. Yes, Mother.

AMANDA. Ask Mr. O'Connor if he would like to wash his hands.

JIM. Aw, no—no—thank you—I took care of that at the warehouse. Tom—

TOM. Yes?

JIM. Mr. Mendoza was speaking to me about you.

TOM. Favorably?

JIM. What do you think?

TOM. Well—

JIM. You're going to be out of a job if you don't wake up.

TOM. I am waking up—

JIM. You show no signs.

TOM. The signs are interior.

(*Image on screen:* The sailing vessel with the Jolly Roger again.)

TOM. I'm planning to change. (*He leans over the fire-escape rail, speaking with quiet exhilaration. The incandescent marquees and signs of the first-run movie houses light his face from across the alley. He looks like a voyager.*) I'm right at the point of committing myself to a future that doesn't include the warehouse and Mr. Mendoza or even a night-school course in public speaking.

JIM. What are you gassing about?

TOM. I'm tired of the movies.

JIM. Movies!

TOM. Yes, movies! Look at them— (*a wave toward the marvels of Grand Avenue*) All of those glamorous people—having adventures—hogging it all, gobbling the whole thing up! You know what happens? People go to the *movies* instead of *moving!* Hollywood characters are supposed to have all the adventures for everybody in America, while everybody in America sits in a dark room and watches them have them! Yes, until there's a war. That's when adventure becomes available to the masses! *Everyone's* dish, not only Gable's! Then the people in the dark room come out of the dark room to have some adventures themselves—goody, goody! It's our turn now, to go to the South Sea Island—to make a safari—to be exotic, far-off! But I'm not patient. I don't want to wait till then. I'm tired of the *movies* and I am *about* to *move!*

JIM (*incredulously*).   Move?
TOM.   Yes.
JIM.   When?
TOM.   Soon!
JIM.   Where? Where?

(*The music seems to answer the question, while* TOM *thinks it over. He searches in his pockets.*)

TOM.   I'm starting to boil inside. I know I seem dreamy, but inside— well, I'm boiling! Whenever I pick up a shoe, I shudder a little thinking how short life is and what I am doing! Whatever that means, I know it doesn't mean shoes—except as something to wear on a traveler's feet! (*He finds what he has been searching for in his pockets and holds out a paper to Jim.*) Look—
JIM.   What?
TOM.   I'm a member.
JIM (*reading*).   The Union of Merchant Seamen.
TOM.   I paid my dues this month, instead of the light bill.
JIM.   You will regret it when they turn the lights off.
TOM.   I won't be here.
JIM.   How about your mother?
TOM.   I'm like my father. The bastard son of a bastard! Did you notice how he's grinning in his picture there? And he's been absent going on sixteen years!
JIM.   You're just talking, you drip. How does your mother feel about it?
TOM.   Shhh! Here comes Mother! Mother is not acquainted with my plans!
AMANDA (*coming through the portieres*).   Where are you all?
TOM.   On the terrace, Mother.

(*They start inside. She advances to them.* TOM *is distinctly shocked at her appearance. Even* JIM *blinks a little. He is making his first contact with girlish Southern vivacity and in spite of the night-school course in public speaking is somewhat thrown off the beam by the unexpected outlay of social charm. Certain responses are attempted by* JIM *but are swept aside by* AMANDA'S *gay laughter and chatter.* TOM *is embarassed but after the first shock* JIM *reacts very warmly. He grins and chuckles, is altogether won over.*)

(*Image on screen: Amanda as a girl.*)

AMANDA (*coyly smiling, shaking her girlish ringlets*).   Well, well, well, so this is Mr. O'Connor. Introductions entirely unnecessary. I've heard so much about you from my boy. I finally said to him, Tom—good gracious!—why don't you bring this paragon to supper? I'd like to meet this nice young man at the warehouse!—instead of just hearing him sing your praises so much! I don't know why my son is so stand-offish—that's not Southern behavior!
    Let's sit down and—I think we could stand a little more air in here! Tom, leave the door open. I felt a nice fresh breeze a moment ago. Where has it gone to? Mmm, so warm already! And not quite summer, even. We're going

to burn up when summer really gets started. However, we're having—we're having a very light supper. I think light things are better fo' this time of year. The same as light clothes are. Light clothes an' light food are what warm weather calls fo'. You know our blood gets so thick during th' winter—it takes a while fo' us to *adjust* ou'selves!—when the season changes . . . It's come so quick this year. I wasn't prepared. All of a sudden—heavens! Already summer! I ran to the trunk an' pulled out this light dress—terribly old! Historical` almost! But feels so good—so good an' co-ol, y'know. . . .

TOM. Mother—

AMANDA. Yes, honey?

TOM. How about—supper?

AMANDA. Honey, you go ask Sister if supper is ready! You know that Sister is in full charge of supper! Tell her you hungry boys are waiting for it. (*to* JIM) Have you met Laura?

JIM. She—

AMANDA. Let you in? Oh, good, you've met already! It's rare for a girl as sweet an' pretty as Laura to be domestic! But Laura is, thank heavens, not only pretty but also very domestic. I'm not at all. I never was a bit. I never could make a thing but angel-food cake. Well, in the South we had so many servants. Gone, gone, gone. All vestige of gracious living! Gone completely! I wasn't prepared for what the future brought me. All of my gentlemen callers were sons of planters and so of course I assumed that I would be married to one and raise my family on a large piece of land with plenty of servants. But man proposes—and woman accepts the proposal! To vary that old, old saying a little bit—I married no planter! I married a man who worked for the telephone company! That gallantly smiling gentleman over there! (*She points to the picture.*) A telephone man who—fell in love with long-distance! Now he travels and I don't even know where! But what am I going on for about my—tribulations? Tell me yours—I hope you don't have any! Tom?

TOM (*returning*). Yes, Mother?

AMANDA. Is supper nearly ready?

TOM. It looks to me like supper is on the table.

AMANDA. Let me look— (*She rises prettily and looks through the portieres.*) Oh, lovely! But where is Sister?

TOM. Laura is not feeling well and she says that she thinks she'd better not come to the table.

AMANDA. What? Nonsense! Laura? Oh, Laura!

LAURA (*from the kitchenette, faintly*). Yes, Mother.

AMANDA. You really must come to the table! We won't be seated until you come to the table! Come in, Mr. O'Connor. You sit over there, and I'll. . . . Laura? Laura Wingfield! You're keeping us waiting, honey! We can't say grace until you come to the table!

(*The kitchenette door is pushed weakly open and* LAURA *comes in. She is obviously quite faint, her lips trembling, her eyes wide and staring. She moves unsteadily toward the table.*)

(*Screen legend: "Terror!"*)

(Outside a summer storm is coming on abruptly. The white curtains billow inward at the windows and there is a sorrowful murmur from the deep blue dusk.)

(LAURA suddenly stumbles; she catches at a chair with a faint moan.)

TOM.   Laura!
AMANDA.   Laura!

(There is a clap of thunder.)

(Screen legend: "Ah!")

(despairingly) Why, Laura, you *are* ill, darling! Tom, help your sister into the living room, dear! Sit in the living room, Laura—rest on the sofa. Well! (*to* JIM *as* TOM *helps his sister to the sofa in the living room*) Standing over the hot stove made her ill! I told her that it was just too warm this evening, but—

(TOM comes back to the table.)

Is Laura all right now?
TOM.   Yes.
AMANDA.   What *is* that? Rain? A nice cool rain has come up! (*She gives* JIM *a frightened look.*) I think we may—have grace—now . . .

(TOM looks at her stupidly.) Tom, honey—you say grace!

TOM.   Oh . . . "For these and all thy mercies—"

(They bow their heads, AMANDA *stealing a nervous glance at* JIM. *In the living room* LAURA, *stretched on the sofa, clenches her hand to her lips, to hold back a shuddering sob.)*

God's Holy Name be praised—   *(The scene dims out.)*

SCENE VII

It is half an hour later. Dinner is just being finished in the dining room, LAURA *is still huddled upon the sofa, her feet drawn under her, her head resting on a pale blue pillow, her eyes wide and mysteriously watchful. The new floor lamp with its shade of rose-colored silk gives a soft, becoming light to her face, bringing out the fragile, unearthly prettiness which usually escapes attention. From outside there is a steady murmur of rain, but it is slackening and soon stops; the air outside becomes pale and luminous as the moon breaks through the clouds. A moment after the curtain rises, the lights in both rooms flicker and go out.*

JIM.   Hey, there, Mr. Light Bulb!

(AMANDA laughs nervously.)

(Legend on screen: "Suspension of a public service.")

AMANDA.   Where was Moses when the lights went out? Ha-ha. Do you know the answer to that one, Mr. O'Connor?

JIM.   No, Ma'am, what's the answer?
AMANDA.   In the dark!

(JIM *laughs appreciatively.*)

Everybody sit still. I'll light the candles. Isn't it lucky we have them on the table? Where's a match? Which of you gentlemen can provide a match?
JIM.   Here.
AMANDA.   Thank you, Sir.
JIM.   Not at all, Ma'am!
AMANDA (*as she lights the candles*).   I guess the fuse has burnt out. Mr. O'Connor, can you tell a burnt-out fuse? I know I can't and Tom is a total loss when it comes to mechanics.

(*They rise from the table and go into the kitchenette, from where their voices are heard.*)

Oh, be careful you don't bump into something. We don't want our gentleman caller to break his neck. Now wouldn't that be a fine howdy-do?
JIM.   Ha-ha! Where is the fuse-box?
AMANDA.   Right here next to the stove. Can you see anything?
JIM.   Just a minute.
AMANDA.   Isn't electricity a mysterious thing? Wasn't it Benjamin Franklin who tied a key to a kite? We live in such a mysterious universe, don't we? Some people say that science clears up all the mysteries for us. In my opinion it only creates more! Have you found it yet?
JIM.   No, Ma'am. All these fuses look okay to me.
AMANDA.   Tom!
TOM.   Yes, Mother?
AMANDA.   That light bill I gave you several days ago. The one I told you we got the notices about?

(*Legend on screen.* "Ha!")

TOM.   Oh—yeah.
AMANDA.   You didn't neglect to pay it by any chance?
TOM.   Why, I—
AMANDA.   Didn't! I might have known it!
JIM.   Shakespeare probably wrote a poem on that light bill, Mrs. Wingfield.
AMANDA.   I might have known better than to trust him with it! There's such a high price for negligence in this world!
JIM.   Maybe the poem will win a ten-dollar prize.
AMANDA.   We'll just have to spend the remainder of the evening in the nineteenth century, before Mr. Edison made the Mazda lamp!
JIM.   Candlelight is my favorite kind of light.
AMANDA.   That shows you're romantic! But that's no excuse for Tom. Well, we got through dinner. Very considerate of them to let us get through dinner before they plunged us into everlasting darkness, wasn't it, Mr. O'Connor?
JIM.   Ha-ha!

AMANDA.   Tom, as a penalty for your carelessness you can help me with the dishes.

JIM.   Let me give you a hand.

AMANDA.   Indeed you will not!

JIM.   I ought to be good for something.

AMANDA.   Good for something? (*Her tone is rhapsodic.*) You? Why, Mr. O'Connor, nobody, *nobody's* given me this much entertainment in years—as you have!

JIM.   Aw, now, Mrs. Wingfield!

AMANDA.   I'm not exaggerating, not one bit! But Sister is all by her lonesome. You go keep her company in the parlor! I'll give you this lovely old candelabrum that used to be on the altar at the Church of the Heavenly Rest. It was melted a little out of shape when the church burnt down. Lightning struck it one spring. Gypsy Jones was holding a revival at the time and he intimated that the church was destroyed because the Episcopalians gave card parties.

JIM.   Ha-ha.

AMANDA.   And how about you coaxing Sister to drink a little wine? I think it would be good for her! Can you carry both at once?

JIM.   Sure. I'm Superman!

AMANDA.   Now, Thomas, get into this apron!

(JIM *comes into the dining room, carrying the candelabrum, its candles lighted, in one hand and a glass of wine in the other. The door of the kitchenette swings closed on* AMANDA'S *gay laughter; the flickering light approaches the portieres.* LAURA *sits up nervously as* JIM *enters. She can hardly speak from the almost intolerable strain of being alone with a stranger.*)

(*Screen legend:* "I don't suppose you remember me at all!")

(*At first, before* JIM'S *warmth overcomes her paralyzing shyness,* LAURA'S *voice is thin and breathless, as though she had just run up a steep flight of stairs.* JIM'S *attitude is gently humorous. While the incident is apparently unimportant, it is to* LAURA *the climax of her secret life.*)

JIM.   Hello there, Laura.

LAURA (*faintly*).   Hello.

(*She clears her throat.*)

JIM.   How are you feeling now? Better?

LAURA.   Yes. Yes, thank you.

JIM.   This is for you. A little dandelion wine. (*He extends the glass toward her with extravagant gallantry.*)

LAURA.   Thank you.

JIM.   Drink it—but don't get drunk!

(*He laughs heartily.* LAURA *takes the glass uncertainly; she laughs shyly.*)

Where shall I set the candles?

LAURA.   Oh—oh, anywhere . . .

JIM.   How about here on the floor? Any objections?

LAURA.   No.

JIM.   I'll spread a newspaper under to catch the drippings. I like to sit on the floor. Mind if I do?

LAURA.   Oh, no.

JIM.   Give me a pillow?

LAURA.   What?

JIM.   A pillow!

LAURA.   Oh . . . (*She hands him one quickly.*)

JIM.   How about you? Don't you like to sit on the floor?

LAURA.   Oh—yes.

JIM.   Why don't you, then?

LAURA.   I—will.

JIM.   Take a pillow! (LAURA *does. She sits on the floor on the other side of the candelabrum.* JIM *crosses his legs and smiles engagingly at her.*) I can't hardly see you sitting way over there.

LAURA.   I can—see you.

JIM.   I know, but that's not fair, I'm in the limelight.

(LAURA *moves her pillow closer.*)

Good! Now I can see you! Comfortable?

LAURA.   Yes.

JIM.   So am I. Comfortable as a cow! Will you have some gum?

LAURA.   No, thank you.

JIM.   I think that I will indulge, with your permission. (*He musingly unwraps a stick of gum and holds it up.*) Think of the fortune made by the guy that invented the first piece of chewing gum. Amazing, huh? The Wrigley Building is one of the sights of Chicago—I saw it when I went up to the Century of Progress. Did you take in the Century of Progress?

LAURA.   No, I didn't.

JIM.   Well, it was quite a wonderful exposition. What impressed me most was the Hall of Science. Gives you an idea of what the future will be in America, even more wonderful than the present time is! (*There is a pause.* JIM *smiles at her.*) Your brother tells me you're shy. Is that right, Laura?

LAURA.   I—don't know.

JIM.   I judge you to be an old-fashioned type of girl. Well, I think that's a pretty good type to be. Hope you don't think I'm being too personal—do you?

LAURA (*hastily, out of embarrassment*).   I believe I *will* take a piece of gum, if you—don't mind. (*clearing her throat*) Mr. O'Connor, have you—kept up with your singing?

JIM.   Singing? Me?

LAURA.   Yes. I remember what a beautiful voice you had.

JIM.   When did you hear me sing?

(LAURA *does not answer, and in the long pause which follows a man's voice is heard singing offstage.*)

VOICE:

O blow, ye winds, heigh-ho,
A-roving I will go!
    I'm off to my love
    With a boxing glove—
Ten thousand miles away!

JIM.   You say you've heard me sing?

LAURA.   Oh, yes! Yes, very often . . . I—don't suppose—you remember me—at all?

JIM (*smiling doubtfully*).   You know I have an idea I've seen you before. I had that idea soon as you opened the door. It seemed almost like I was about to remember your name. But the name that I started to call you— wasn't a name! And so I stopped myself before I said it.

LAURA.   Wasn't it—Blue Roses?

JIM (*springing up, grinning*).   Blue Roses! My gosh, yes—Blue Roses! That's what I had on my tongue when you opened the door! Isn't it funny what tricks your memory plays? I didn't connect you with high school some- how or other. But that's where it was; it was high school. I didn't even know you were Shakespeare's sister! Gosh, I'm sorry.

LAURA.   I didn't expect you to. You—barely knew me!

JIM.   But we did have a speaking acquaintance, huh?

LAURA.   Yes, we—spoke to each other.

JIM.   When did you recognize me?

LAURA.   Oh, right away!

JIM.   Soon as I came in the door?

LAURA.   When I heard your name I thought it was probably you. I knew that Tom used to know you a little in high school. So when you came in the door—well, then I was—sure.

JIM.   Why didn't you *say* something, then?

LAURA (*breathlessly*).   I didn't know what to say, I was—too surprised!

JIM.   For goodness' sakes! You know, this sure is funny!

LAURA.   Yes! Yes, isn't it, though . . .

JIM.   Didn't we have a class in something together?

LAURA.   Yes, we did.

JIM.   What class was that?

LAURA.   It was—singing—chorus!

JIM.   Aw!

LAURA.   I sat across the aisle from you in the Aud.

JIM.   Aw.

LAURA.   Mondays, Wednesdays, and Fridays.

JIM.   Now I remember—you always came in late.

LAURA.   Yes, it was so hard for me, getting upstairs. I had that brace on my leg—it clumped so loud!

JIM.   I never heard any clumping.

LAURA (*wincing at the recollection*).   To me it sounded like—thunder!

JIM.   Well, well, well, I never even noticed.

LAURA.   And everybody was seated before I came in. I had to walk in front of all those people. My seat was in the back row. I had to go clumping all the way up the aisle with everyone watching!

JIM.   You shouldn't have been self-conscious.

LAURA.   I know, but I was. It was always such a relief when the singing started.

JIM.   Aw, yes, I've placed you now! I used to call you Blue Roses. How was it that I got started calling you that?

LAURA.   I was out of school a little while with pleurosis. When I came back you asked me what was the matter. I said I had pleurosis—you thought I said *Blue Roses*. That's what you always called me after that!

JIM.   I hope you didn't mind.

LAURA.   Oh, no—I liked it. You see, I wasn't acquainted with many—people. . . .

JIM.   As I remember you sort of stuck by yourself.

LAURA.   I—I—never have had much luck at—making friends.

JIM.   I don't see why you wouldn't.

LAURA.   Well, I—started out badly.

JIM.   You mean being—

LAURA.   Yes, it sort of—stood between me—

JIM.   You shouldn't have let it!

LAURA.   I know, but it did, and—

JIM.   You were shy with people!

LAURA.   I tried not to be but never could—

JIM.   Overcome it?

LAURA.   No, I—I never could!

JIM.   I guess being shy is something you have to work out of kind of gradually.

LAURA (*sorrowfully*).   Yes—I guess it—

JIM.   Takes time!

LAURA.   Yes—

JIM.   People are not so dreadful when you know them. That's what you have to remember! And everybody has problems, not just you, but practically everybody has got some problems. You think of yourself as having the only problems, as being the only one who is disappointed. But just look around you and you will see lots of people as disappointed as you are. For instance, I hoped when I was going to high school that I would be further along at this time, six years later, than I am now. You remember that wonderful write-up I had in *The Torch*?

LAURA.   Yes! (*She rises and crosses to the table.*)

JIM.   It said I was bound to succeed in anything I went into!

(LAURA *returns with the high school yearbook.*)

Holy Jeez! The Torch!

(*He accepts it reverently. They smile across the book with mutual wonder.* LAURA *crouches beside him and they begin to turn the pages.* LAURA'S *shyness is dissolving in his warmth.*)

LAURA.   Here you are in *The Pirates of Penzance!*
JIM (*wistfully*).   I sang the baritone lead in that operetta.
LAURA (*raptly*).   So—*beautifully!*
JIM (*protesting*).   Aw—
LAURA.   Yes, yes—beautifully—beautifully!
JIM.   You heard me?
LAURA.   All three times!
JIM.   No!
LAURA.   Yes!
JIM.   All three performances?
LAURA (*looking down*).   Yes.
JIM.   Why?
LAURA.   I—wanted to ask you to—autograph my program. (*She takes the program from the back of the yearbook and shows it to him.*)
JIM.   Why didn't you ask me to?
LAURA.   You were always surrounded by your own friends so much that I never had a chance to.
JIM.   You should have just—
LAURA.   Well, I—thought you might think I was—
JIM.   Thought I might think you was—what?
LAURA.   Oh—
JIM (*with reflective relish*).   I was beleaguered by females in those days.
LAURA.   You were terribly popular!
JIM.   Yeah—
LAURA.   You had such a—friendly way—
JIM.   I was spoiled in high school.
LAURA.   Everybody—liked you!
JIM.   Including you?
LAURA.   I—yes, I—did, too— (*She gently closes the book in her lap.*)
JIM.   Well, well, well! Give me that program, Laura.

(*She hands it to him. He signs it with a flourish.*)

There you are—better late than never!
LAURA.   Oh, I—what a—surprise!
JIM.   My signature isn't worth very much right now. But some day—maybe—it will increase in value! Being disappointed is one thing and being discouraged is something else. I am disappointed but I am not discouraged. I'm twenty-three years old. How old are you?
LAURA.   I'll be twenty-four in June.
JIM.   That's not old age!
LAURA.   No, but—
JIM.   You finished high school?
LAURA (*with difficulty*).   I didn't go back.
JIM.   You mean you dropped out?
LAURA.   I made bad grades in my final examinations. (*She rises and replaces the book and the program on the table. Her voice is strained.*) How is—Emily Meisenbach getting along?

JIM. Oh, that kraut-head!

LAURA. Why do you call her that?

JIM. That's what she was.

LAURA. You're not still—going with her?

JIM. I never see her.

LAURA. It said in the "Personal" section that you were—engaged!

JIM. I know, but I wasn't impressed by that—propaganda!

LAURA. It wasn't—the truth?

JIM. Only in Emily's optimistic opinion!

LAURA. Oh—

(Legend: "What have you done since high school?")

(JIM lights a cigarette and leans indolently back on his elbows smiling at LAURA with a warmth and charm which lights her inwardly with altar candles. She remains by the table, picks up a piece from the glass menagerie collection, and turns it in her hands to cover her tumult.)

JIM *(after several reflective puffs on his cigarette).* What have you done since high school?

(She seems not to hear him.)

Huh?

(LAURA looks up.)

I said what have you done since high school, Laura?

LAURA. Nothing much.

JIM. You must have been doing something these six long years.

LAURA. Yes.

JIM. Well, then, such as what?

LAURA. I took a business course at business college—

JIM. How did that work out?

LAURA. Well, not very—well—I had to drop out, it gave me—indigestion—

(JIM laughs gently.)

JIM. What are you doing now?

LAURA. I don't do anything—much. Oh, please don't think I sit around doing nothing! My glass collection takes up a good deal of time. Glass is something you have to take good care of.

JIM. What did you say—about glass?

LAURA. Collection I said—I have one— *(She clears her throat and turns away again, acutely shy.)*

JIM *(abruptly).* You know what I judge to be the trouble with you? Inferiority complex! Know what that is? That's what they call it when someone low-rates himself! I understand it because I had it, too. Although my case was not so aggravated as yours seems to be. I had it until I took up public speaking, developed my voice, and learned that I had an aptitude for science. Before that time I never thought of myself as being outstanding in any way whatsoever! Now I've never made a regular study of it, but I have a friend who says I can analyze people better than doctors that make a profession of it. I don't claim that to be necessarily true, but I can sure guess a person's psychology, Laura! (*He takes out his gum.*) Excuse me, Laura. I always take it out when the flavor is gone. I'll use this scrap of paper to wrap it in. I know how it is to get it stuck on a shoe. (*He wraps the gum in paper and puts it in his pocket.*) Yep—that's what I judge to be your principal trouble. A lack of confidence in yourself as a person. You don't have the proper amount of faith in yourself. I'm basing that fact on a number of your remarks and also on certain observations I've made. For instance that clumping you thought was so awful in high school. You say that you even dreaded to walk into class. You see what you did? You dropped out of school, you gave up an education because of a clump, which as far as I know was practically non-existent! A little physical defect is what you have. Hardly noticeable even! Magnified thousands of times by imagination! You know what my strong advice to you is? Think of yourself as *superior* in some way!

LAURA.   In what way would I think?

JIM.   Why, man alive, Laura! Just look about you a little. What do you see? A world full of common people! All of 'em born and all of 'em going to die! Which of them has one-tenth of your good points! Or mine! Or anyone else's, as far as that goes—gosh! Everybody excels in some one thing. Some in many! (*He unconsciously glances at himself in the mirror.*) All you've got to do is discover in *what!* Take me, for instance. (*He adjusts his tie at the mirror.*) My interest happens to lie in electro-dynamics. I'm taking a course in radio engineering at night school, Laura, on top of a fairly responsible job at the warehouse. I'm taking that course and studying public speaking.

LAURA.   Ohhhh.

JIM.   Because I believe in the future of television! (*turning his back to her.*) I wish to be ready to go up right along with it. Therefore I'm planning to get in on the ground floor. In fact I've already made the right connections and all that remains is for the industry itself to get under way! Full steam—(*His eyes are starry.*) Knowledge—Zzzzzp! Money—Zzzzzzp!—Power! That's the cycle democracy is built on!

(*His attitude is convincingly dynamic.* LAURA *stares at him, even her shyness eclipsed in her absolute wonder. He suddenly grins.*)

I guess you think I think a lot of myself!

LAURA.   No—o-o-o, I—

JIM.   Now how about you? Isn't there something you take more interest in than anything else?

LAURA.   Well, I do—as I said—have my—glass collection—

(*A peal of girlish laughter rings from the kitchenette.*)

JIM.   I'm not right sure I know what you're talking about. What kind of glass is it?

LAURA.   Little articles of it, they're ornaments mostly! Most of them are little animals made out of glass, the tiniest little animals in the world. Mother calls them a glass menagerie! Here's an example of one, if you'd like to see it! This one is one of the oldest. It's nearly thirteen.

(Music: "The Glass Menagerie.")

(He stretches out his hand.)

Oh, be careful—if you breathe, it breaks!

JIM.   I'd better not take it. I'm pretty clumsy with things.

LAURA.   Go on, I trust you with him! *(She places the piece in his palm.)* There now—you're holding him gently! Hold him over the light, he loves the light! You see how the light shines through him?

JIM.   It sure does shine!

LAURA.   I shouldn't be partial, but he is my favorite one.

JIM.   What kind of thing is this one supposed to be?

LAURA.   Haven't you noticed the single horn on his forehead?

JIM.   A unicorn, huh?

LAURA.   Mmmm-hmmm!

JIM.   Unicorns—aren't they extinct in the modern world?

LAURA.   I know!

JIM.   Poor little fellow, he must feel sort of lonesome.

LAURA *(smiling)*.   Well, if he does, he doesn't complain about it. He stays on a shelf with some horses that don't have horns and all of them seem to get along nicely together.

JIM.   How do you know?

LAURA *(lightly)*.   I haven't heard any arguments among them!

JIM *(grinning)*.   No arguments, huh? Well, that's a pretty good sign! Where shall I set him?

LAURA.   Put him on the table. They all like a change of scenery once in a while!

JIM.   Well, well, well, well— *(He places the glass piece on the table, then raises his arms and stretches.)* Look how big my shadow is when I stretch!

LAURA.   Oh, oh, yes—it stretches across the ceiling!

JIM *(crossing to the door)*.   I think it's stopped raining. *(He opens the fire-escape door and the background music changes to a dance tune.)* Where does the music come from?

LAURA.   From the Paradise Dance Hall across the alley.

JIM.   How about cutting the rug a little, Miss Wingfield?

LAURA.   Oh, I—

JIM.   Or is your program filled up? Let me have a look at it. *(He grasps an imaginary card.)* Why, every dance is taken! I'll just have to scratch some out.

(Waltz music: "La Golondrina.")

Ahhh, a waltz! *(He executes some sweeping turns by himself, then holds his arms toward LAURA.)*

LAURA *(breathlessly)*.   I—can't dance!

JIM.   There you go, that inferiority stuff!

LAURA.   I've never danced in my life!

JIM.   Come on, try!

LAURA.   Oh, but I'd step on you!

JIM.   I'm not made out of glass.

LAURA.   How—how—how do we start?

JIM.   Just leave it to me. You hold your arms out a little.

LAURA.   Like this?

JIM (*taking her in his arms*).   A little bit higher. Right. Now don't tighten up, that's the main thing about it—relax.

LAURA (*laughing breathlessly*).   It's hard not to.

JIM.   Okay.

LAURA.   I'm afraid you can't budge me.

JIM.   What do you bet I can't? (*He swings her into motion.*)

LAURA.   Goodness, yes, you can!

JIM.   Let yourself go, now, Laura, just let yourself go.

LAURA.   I'm—

JIM.   Come on!

LAURA.   —trying!

JIM.   Not so stiff—easy does it!

LAURA.   I know but I'm—

JIM.   Loosen th' backbone! There now, that's a lot better.

LAURA.   Am I?

JIM.   Lots, lots better! (*He moves her about the room in a clumsy waltz.*)

LAURA.   Oh, my!

JIM.   Ha-ha!

LAURA.   Oh, my goodness!

JIM.   Ha-ha-ha!

(*They suddenly bump into the table, and the glass piece on it falls to the floor.* JIM *stops the dance.*)

What did we hit on?

LAURA.   Table.

JIM.   Did something fall off it? I think—

LAURA.   Yes.

JIM.   I hope that it wasn't the little glass horse with the horn!

LAURA.   Yes. (*She stoops to pick it up.*)

JIM.   Aw, aw, aw. Is it broken?

LAURA.   Now it is just like all the other horses.

JIM.   It's lost its—

LAURA.   Horn! It doesn't matter. Maybe it's a blessing in disguise.

JIM.   You'll never forgive me. I bet that that was your favorite piece of glass.

LAURA.   I don't have favorites much. It's no tragedy, Freckles. Glass breaks so easily. No matter how careful you are. The traffic jars the shelves and things fall off them.

JIM.   Still I'm awfully sorry that I was the cause.

LAURA (*smiling*).   I'll just imagine he had an operation. The horn was removed to make him feel less—freakish!

(They both laugh.)

Now he will feel more at home with the other horses, the ones that don't have horns. . . .

JIM.   Ha-ha, that's very funny! *(Suddenly he is serious.)* I'm glad to see that you have a sense of humor. You know—you're—well—very different! Surprisingly different from anyone else I know! *(His voice becomes soft and hesitant with a genuine feeling.)* Do you mind me telling you that?

(LAURA is abashed beyond speech.)

I mean it in a nice way—

(LAURA nods shyly, looking away.)

You make me feel sort of—I don't know how to put it! I'm usually pretty good at expressing things, but—this is something that I don't know how to say!

(LAURA touches her throat and clears it—turns the broken unicorn in her hands. His voice becomes softer.)

Has anyone ever told you that you were pretty?

(There is a pause, and the music rises slightly. LAURA looks up slowly, with wonder, and shakes her head.)

Well, you are! In a very different way from anyone else. And all the nicer because of the difference, too.

(His voice becomes low and husky. LAURA turns away, nearly faint with the novelty of her emotions.)

I wish that you were my sister. I'd teach you to have some confidence in yourself. The different people are not like other people, but being different is nothing to be ashamed of. Because other people are not such wonderful people. They're one hundred times one thousand. You're one times one! They walk all over the earth. You just stay here. They're common as—weeds, but—you—well, you're—*Blue Roses!*

(Image on screen: Blue Roses.)

(The music changes.)

LAURA.   But blue is wrong for—roses. . . .
JIM.   It's right for you! You're—pretty!
LAURA.   In what respect am I pretty?
JIM.   In all respects—believe me! Your eyes—your hair—are pretty! Your hands are pretty! *(He catches hold of her hand.)* You think I'm making this up because I'm invited to dinner and have to be nice. Oh, I could do that! I could put on an act for you, Laura, and say lots of things without being very sincere. But this time I am. I'm talking to you sincerely. I happened to notice you had this inferiority complex that keeps you from feeling comfortable with people. Somebody needs to build your confidence up and make you proud instead of shy and turning away and—blushing. Somebody—ought to—*kiss* you, Laura!

(His hand slips slowly up her arm to her shoulder as the music swells tumultuously. He suddenly turns her about and kisses her on the lips. When he releases her, LAURA *sinks on the sofa with a bright, dazed look.* JIM *backs away and fishes in his pocket for a cigarette.)*

(Legend on screen: "A souvenir.")

Stumblejohn!

(He lights the cigarette, avoiding her look. There is a peal of girlish laughter from AMANDA *in the kitchenette.* LAURA *slowly raises and opens her hand. It still contains the little broken glass animal. She looks at it with a tender, bewildered expression.)*

Stumblejohn! I shouldn't have done that—that was way off the beam. You don't smoke, do you?

(She looks up, smiling, not hearing the question. He sits beside her rather gingerly. She looks at him speechlessly—waiting. He coughs decorously and moves a little farther aside as he considers the situation and senses her feelings, dimly, with perturbation. He speaks gently.)

Would you—care for a—mint?

(She doesn't seem to hear him but her look grows brighter even.)

Peppermint? Life Saver? My pocket's a regular drugstore—wherever I go. . . . *(He pops a mint in his mouth. Then he gulps and decides to make a clean breast of it. He speaks slowly and gingerly.)* Laura, you know, if I had a sister like you, I'd do the same thing as Tom. I'd bring out fellows and—introduce her to them. The right type of boys—of a type to—appreciate her. Only—well—he made a mistake about me. Maybe I've got no call to be saying this. That may not have been the idea in having me over. But what if it was? There's nothing wrong about that. The only trouble is that in my case—I'm not in a situation to—do the right thing. I can't take down your number and say I'll phone. I can't call up next week and—ask for a date. I thought I had better explain the situation in case you—misunderstood it and—I hurt your feelings. . . .

(There is a pause. Slowly, very slowly, LAURA'S *look changes, her eyes returning slowly from his to the glass figure in her palm.* AMANDA *utters another gay laugh in the kitchenette.)*

LAURA *(faintly)*. You—won't—call again?

JIM. No, Laura, I can't. *(He rises from the sofa.)* As I was just explaining, I've—got strings on me. Laura, I've—been going steady! I go out all the time with a girl named Betty. She's a home-girl like you, and Catholic, and Irish, and in a great many ways we—get along fine. I met her last summer on a moonlight boat trip up the river to Alton, on the *Majestic*. Well—right away from the start it was—love!

(Legend: Love!)

(LAURA *sways slightly forward and grips the arm of the sofa. He fails to notice, now enrapt in his own comfortable being.*)

Being in love has made a new man of me!

(*Leaning stiffly forward, clutching the arm of the sofa,* LAURA *struggles visibly with her storm. But* JIM *is oblivious; she is a long way off.*)

The power of love is really pretty tremendous! Love is something that— changes the whole world, Laura!

(*The storm abates a little and* LAURA *leans back. He notices her again.*)

It happened that Betty's aunt took sick, she got a wire and had to go to Centralia. So Tom—when he asked me to dinner—I naturally just accepted the invitation, not knowing that you—that he—that I— (*He stops awkwardly.*) Huh—I'm a stumblejohn!

(*He flops back on the sofa. The holy candles on the altar of* LAURA'S *face have been snuffed out. There is a look of almost infinite desolation.* JIM *glances at her uneasily.*)

I wish that you would—say something.

(*She bites her lip which was trembling and then bravely smiles. She opens her hand again on the broken glass figure. Then she gently takes his and raises it level with her own. She carefully places the unicorn in the palm of his hand, then pushes his fingers closed upon it.*)

What are you—doing that for? You want me to have him? Laura?

(*She nods.*)

What for?

LAURA.   A—souvenir. . . .

(*She rises unsteadily and crouches beside the Victrola to wind it up.*)

(*Legend on screen:* "Things have a way of turning out so badly!" *Or image:* "Gentleman caller waving goodbye—gaily.")

(*At this moment* AMANDA *rushes brightly back into the living room. She bears a pitcher of fruit punch in an old-fashioned cut-glass pitcher, and a plate of macaroons. The plate has a gold border and poppies painted on it.*)

AMANDA.   Well, well, well! Isn't the air delightful after the shower? I've made you children a little liquid refreshment. (*She turns gaily to* JIM.) Jim, do you know that song about lemonade?

> "Lemonade, lemonade
> Made in the shade and stirred with a spade—
> Good enough for any old maid!"

JIM (*uneasily*).   Ha-ha! No—I never heard it.

AMANDA.   Why, Laura! You look so serious!

JIM.   We were having a serious conversation.

AMANDA.   Good! Now you're better acquainted!

JIM (*uncertainly*).   Ha-ha! Yes.

AMANDA.   You modern young people are much more serious-minded than my generation. I was so gay as a girl!

JIM.   You haven't changed, Mrs. Wingfield.

AMANDA.   Tonight I'm rejuvenated! The gaiety of the occasion, Mr. O'Connor! (*She tosses her head with a peal of laughter, spilling some lemonade.*) Oooo! I'm baptizing myself!

JIM.   Here—let me—

AMANDA (*setting the pitcher down*).   There now. I discovered we had some maraschino cherries. I dumped them in, juice and all!

JIM.   You shouldn't have gone to that trouble, Mrs. Wingfield.

AMANDA.   Trouble, trouble? Why, it was loads of fun! Didn't you hear me cutting up in the kitchen? I bet your ears were burning! I told Tom how outdone with him I was for keeping you to himself so long a time! He should have brought you over much, much sooner! Well, now that you've found your way, I want you to be a very frequent caller! Not just occasional but all the time. Oh, we're going to have a lot of gay times together! I see them coming! Mmm, just breathe that air! So fresh, and the moon's so pretty! I'll skip back out—I know where my place is when young folks are having a—serious conversation!

JIM.   Oh, don't go out, Mrs. Wingfield. The fact of the matter is I've got to be going.

AMANDA.   Going, now? You're joking! Why, it's only the shank of the evening, Mr. O'Connor!

JIM.   Well, you know how it is.

AMANDA.   You mean you're a young workingman and have to keep workingmen's hours. We'll let you off early tonight. But only on the condition that next time you stay later. What's the best night for you? Isn't Saturday night the best night for you workingmen?

JIM.   I have a couple of time-clocks to punch, Mrs. Wingfield. One at morning, another one at night!

AMANDA.   My, but you *are* ambitious! You work at night, too?

JIM.   No, Ma'am, not work but—Betty!

(*He crosses deliberately to pick up his hat. The band at the Paradise Dance Hall goes into a tender waltz.*)

AMANDA.   Betty? Betty? Who's—Betty!

(*There is an ominous cracking sound in the sky.*)

JIM.   Oh, just a girl. The girl I go steady with!

(*He smiles charmingly. The sky falls.*)

(*Legend: "The Sky Falls."*)

AMANDA (*a long-drawn exhalation*).   Ohhhh . . . Is it a serious romance, Mr. O'Connor?

JIM.   We're going to be married the second Sunday in June.

AMANDA. Ohhhh—how nice! Tom didn't mention that you were engaged to be married.

JIM. The cat's not out of the bag at the warehouse yet. You know how they are. They call you Romeo and stuff like that. (*He stops at the oval mirror to put on his hat. He carefully shapes the brim and the crown to give a discreetly dashing effect.*) It's been a wonderful evening, Mrs. Wingfield. I guess this is what they mean by Southern hospitality.

AMANDA. It really wasn't anything at all.

JIM. I hope it don't seem like I'm rushing off. But I promised Betty I'd pick her up at the Wabash depot, an' by the time I get my jalopy down there her train'll be in. Some women are pretty upset if you keep 'em waiting.

AMANDA. Yes, I know—the tyranny of women! (*She extends her hand.*) Goodbye, Mr. O'Connor. I wish you luck—and happiness—and success! All three of them, and so does Laura! Don't you, Laura?

LAURA. Yes!

JIM (*taking* LAURA'S *hand*). Goodbye, Laura. I'm certainly going to treasure that souvenir. And don't you forget the good advice I gave you. (*He raises his voice to a cheery shout.*) So long, Shakespeare! Thanks again, ladies. Good night!

(*He grins and ducks jauntily out. Still bravely grimacing,* AMANDA *closes the door on the gentleman caller. Then she turns back to the room with a puzzled expression. She and* LAURA *don't dare to face each other.* LAURA *crouches beside the Victrola to wind it.*)

AMANDA (*faintly*). Things have a way of turning out so badly. I don't believe that I would play the Victrola. Well, well—well! Our gentleman caller was engaged to be married! (*She raises her voice.*) Tom!

TOM (*from the kitchenette*). Yes, Mother?

AMANDA. Come in here a minute. I want to tell you something awfully funny.

TOM (*entering with a macaroon and a glass of the lemonade*). Has the gentleman caller gotten away already?

AMANDA. The gentleman caller has made an early departure. What a wonderful joke you played on us!

TOM. How do you mean?

AMANDA. You didn't mention that he was engaged to be married.

TOM. Jim? Engaged?

AMANDA. That's what he just informed us.

TOM. I'll be jiggered! I didn't know about that.

AMANDA. That seems very peculiar.

TOM. What's peculiar about it?

AMANDA. Didn't you call him your best friend down at the warehouse?

TOM. He is, but how did I know?

AMANDA. It seems extremely peculiar that you wouldn't know your best friend was going to be married!

TOM. The warehouse is where I work, not where I know things about people!

AMANDA.   You don't know things anywhere! You live in a dream; you manufacture illusions!

(He crosses to the door.)

Where are you going?

TOM.   I'm going to the movies.

AMANDA.   That's right, now that you've had us make such fools of ourselves. The effort, the preparations, all the expense! The new floor lamp, the rug, the clothes for Laura! All for what? To entertain some other girl's fiancé! Go to the movies, go! Don't think about us, a mother deserted, an unmarried sister who's crippled and has no job! Don't let anything interfere with your selfish pleasure! Just go, go, go—to the movies!

TOM.   All right, I will! The more you shout about my selfishness to me the quicker I'll go, and I won't go to the movies!

AMANDA.   Go, then! Go to the moon—you selfish dreamer!

*(*TOM *smashes his glass on the floor. He plunges out on the fire escape, slamming the door.* LAURA *screams in fright. The dance-hall music becomes louder.* TOM *stands on the fire escape, gripping the rail. The moon breaks through the storm clouds, illuminating his face.)*

(Legend on screen: "And so goodbye . . .")

*(*TOM'S *closing speech is timed with what is happening inside the house. We see, as though through soundproof glass, that* AMANDA *appears to be making a comforting speech to* LAURA, *who is huddled upon the sofa. Now that we cannot hear the mother's speech, her silliness is gone and she has dignity and tragic beauty.* LAURA'S *hair hides her face until, at the end of the speech, she lifts her head to smile at her mother.* AMANDA'S *gestures are slow and graceful, almost dancelike, as she comforts her daughter. At the end of her speech she glances a moment at the father's picture—then withdraws through the portieres. At the close of* TOM'S *speech,* LAURA *blows out the candles, ending the play.)*

TOM.   I didn't go to the moon, I went much further—for time is the longest distance between two places. Not long after that I was fired for writing a poem on the lid of a shoe-box. I left Saint Louis. I descended the steps of this fire escape for a last time and followed, from then on, in my father's footsteps, attempting to find in motion what was lost in space. I traveled around a great deal. The cities swept about me like dead leaves, leaves that were brightly colored but torn away from the branches. I would have stopped, but I was pursued by something. It always came upon me unawares, taking me altogether by surprise. Perhaps it was a familiar bit of music. Perhaps it was only a piece of transparent glass. Perhaps I am walking along a street at night, in some strange city, before I have found companions. I pass the lighted window of a shop where perfume is sold. The window is filled with pieces of colored glass, tiny transparent bottles in delicate colors, like bits of a shattered rainbow. Then all at once my sister touches my shoulder. I turn around and look into her eyes. Oh, Laura, Laura, I tried to leave you behind me, but I am more faithful than I intended to be! I reach for a cigarette, I cross the street, I run into the movies or a bar, I buy a drink, I speak to the nearest stranger—anything that can blow your candles out!

(LAURA *bends over the candles.*)

For nowadays the world is lit by lightning! Blow out your candles, Laura—and so goodbye. . . .

(She blows the candles out.)

QUESTIONS

1. Tom Wingfield opens the play by saying ". . . I am the opposite of a stage magician. He gives you illusion that has the appearance of truth. I give you truth in the pleasant disguise of illusion." What is the nature of the "illusion" in *The Glass Menagerie?* In what ways are you prompted by Tennessee Williams to find it "pleasant"?

2. At the beginning of Scene Two, Amanda Wingfield says "Deception? Deception?" To what is she referring? Is what she has in mind a specific, or a general, deception?

3. In Scene Seven, Jim O'Connor tells Laura Wingfield that she has an "inferiority complex" and advises her to develop confidence in herself and to "think of yourself as *superior* in some way." How useful to Laura is this sort of advice? How penetrating is Jim's insight into her character?

4. Were you to take Amanda Wingfield's part in *The Glass Menagerie*, or were you to direct a production of the play, how attractive and admirable a person would you want her to be? What positive attributes of her character would you be tempted to emphasize?

5. Tom Wingfield closes the play by giving a speech that is at once poetic, rather noble, and mysterious. Is it an appropriate conclusion to the drama? In what ways does it bring the events and the problems of *The Glass Menagerie* to a fitting end?

Arthur Miller (b. 1915)
Death of a Salesman

CHARACTERS

WILLY LOMAN
LINDA
BIFF
HAPPY
BERNARD
THE WOMAN
CHARLEY
UNCLE BEN
HOWARD WAGNER
JENNY
STANLEY
MISS FORSYTHE
LETTA

The action takes place in Willy Loman's house and yard and in various places he visits in the New York and Boston of today.

Throughout the play, in the stage directions, left and right mean stage left and stage right.

ACT I

A melody is heard, played upon a flute. It is small and fine, telling of grass and trees and the horizon. The curtain rises.

Before us is the Salesman's house. We are aware of towering, angular shapes behind it, surrounding it on all sides. Only the blue light of the sky falls upon the house and forestage; the surrounding area shows an angry glow of orange. As more light appears, we see a solid vault of apartment houses around the small, fragile-seeming home. An air of the dream clings to the place, a dream rising out of reality. The kitchen at center seems actual enough, for there is a kitchen table with three chairs, and a refrigerator. But no other fixtures are seen. At the back of the kitchen there is a draped entrance, which leads to the living-room. To the right of the kitchen, on a level raised two feet, is a bedroom furnished only with a brass bedstead and a straight chair. On a shelf over the bed a silver athletic trophy stands. A window opens onto the apartment house at the side.

Behind the kitchen, on a level raised six and a half feet, is the boys' bedroom, at present barely visible. Two beds are dimly seen, and at the back of the room a dormer window. (This bedroom is above the unseen living-room.) At the left a stairway curves up to it from the kitchen.

The entire setting is wholly, or, in some places, partially transparent. The roof-line of the house is one-dimensional; under and over it we see the apartment buildings. Before the house lies an apron, curving beyond the forestage into the orchestra. This forward area serves as the back yard as well as the

*locale of all Willy's imaginings and of his city scenes. Whenever the action is in
the present the actors observe the imaginary wall-lines, entering the house only
through its door at the left. But in the scenes of the past these boundaries are
broken, and characters enter or leave a room by stepping "through" a wall onto
the forestage.*

From the right, WILLY LOMAN, *the Salesman, enters, carrying two large
sample cases. The flute plays on. He hears but is not aware of it. He is past
sixty years of age, dressed quietly. Even as he crosses the stage to the doorway of
the house, his exhaustion is apparent. He unlocks the door, comes into the
kitchen, and thankfully lets his burden down, feeling the soreness of his palms.
A word-sigh escapes his lips—it might be "Oh, boy, oh, boy." He closes the
door, then carries his cases out into the living-room, through the draped kitchen
doorway.*

LINDA, *his wife, has stirred in her bed at the right. She gets out and puts on
a robe, listening. Most often jovial, she has developed an iron repression of her
exceptions to Willy's behavior—she more than loves him, she admires him, as
though his mercurial nature, his temper, his massive dreams and little cruel-
ties, served her only as sharp reminders of the turbulent longings within him,
longings which she shares but lacks the temperament to utter and follow to
their end.*

LINDA (*hearing* WILLY *outside the bedroom, calls with some trepidation*).   Willy!

WILLY.   It's all right. I came back.

LINDA.   Why? What happened? (*Slight pause.*) Did something happen,
Willy?

WILLY.   No, nothing happened.

LINDA.   You didn't smash the car, did you?

WILLY (*with casual irritation*).   I said nothing happened. Didn't you hear
me?

LINDA.   Don't you feel well?

WILLY.   I'm tired to the death. (*The flute has faded away. He sits on the
bed beside her, a little numb.*) I couldn't make it. I just couldn't make it,
Linda.

LINDA (*very carefully, delicately*).   Where were you all day? You look
terrible.

WILLY.   I got as far as a little above Yonkers. I stopped for a cup of coffee.
Maybe it was the coffee.

LINDA.   What?

WILLY (*after a pause*).   I suddenly couldn't drive any more. The car kept
going off onto the shoulder, y'know?

LINDA (*helpfully*).   Oh. Maybe it was the steering again. I don't think
Angelo knows the Studebaker.

WILLY.   No, it's me, it's me. Suddenly I realize I'm goin' sixty miles an
hour and I don't remember the last five minutes. I'm—I can't seem to—keep
my mind to it.

LINDA.   Maybe it's your glasses. You never went for your new glasses.

WILLY.   No, I see everything. I came back ten miles an hour. It took me
nearly four hours from Yonkers.

LINDA (*resigned*). Well, you'll just have to take a rest, Willy, you can't continue this way.

WILLY. I just got back from Florida.

LINDA. But you didn't rest your mind. Your mind is overactive, and the mind is what counts, dear.

WILLY. I'll start out in the morning. Maybe I'll feel better in the morning. (*She is taking off his shoes.*) These goddam arch supports are killing me.

LINDA. Take an aspirin. Should I get you an aspirin? It'll soothe you.

WILLY (*with wonder*). I was driving along, you understand? And I was fine. I was even observing the scenery. You can imagine, me looking at scenery, on the road every week of my life. But it's so beautiful up there, Linda, the trees are so thick, and the sun is warm. I opened the windshield and just let the warm air bathe over me. And then all of a sudden I'm goin' off the road! I'm tellin' ya, I absolutely forgot I was driving. If I'd've gone the other way over the white line I might've killed somebody. So I went on again—and five minutes later I'm dreamin' again, and I nearly— (*He presses two fingers against his eyes.*) I have such thoughts, I have such strange thoughts.

LINDA. Willy, dear. Talk to them again. There's no reason why you can't work in New York.

WILLY. They don't need me in New York. I'm the New England man. I'm vital in New England.

LINDA. But you're sixty years old. They can't expect you to keep traveling every week.

WILLY. I'll have to send a wire to Portland. I'm supposed to see Brown and Morrison tomorrow morning at ten o'clock to show the line. Goddammit, I could sell them! (*He starts putting on his jacket.*)

LINDA (*taking the jacket from him*). Why don't you go down to the place tomorrow and tell Howard you've simply got to work in New York? You're too accommodating, dear.

WILLY. If old man Wagner was alive I'd a been in charge of New York now! That man was a prince, he was a masterful man. But that boy of his, that Howard, he don't appreciate. When I went north the first time, the Wagner Company didn't know where New England was!

LINDA. Why don't you tell those things to Howard, dear?

WILLY (*encouraged*). I will, I definitely will. Is there any cheese?

LINDA. I'll make you a sandwich.

WILLY. No, go to sleep. I'll take some milk. I'll be up right away. The boys in?

LINDA. They're sleeping. Happy took Biff on a date tonight.

WILLY (*interested*). That so?

LINDA. It was so nice to see them shaving together, one behind the other, in the bathroom. And going out together. You notice? The whole house smells of shaving lotion.

WILLY. Figure it out. Work a lifetime to pay off a house. You finally own it, and there's nobody to live in it.

LINDA. Well, dear, life is a casting off. It's always that way.

WILLY. No, no, some people—some people accomplish something. Did Biff say anything after I went this morning?

LINDA. You shouldn't have criticized him, Willy, especially after he just got off the train. You mustn't lose your temper with him.

WILLY. When the hell did I lose my temper? I simply asked him if he was making any money. Is that a criticism?

LINDA. But, dear, how could he make any money?

WILLY (*worried and angered*). There's such an undercurrent in him. He became a moody man. Did he apologize when I left this morning?

LINDA. He was crestfallen, Willy. You know how he admires you. I think if he finds himself, then you'll both be happier and not fight any more.

WILLY. How can he find himself on a farm? Is that a life? A farmhand? In the beginning, when he was young, I thought, well a young man, it's good for him to tramp around, take a lot of different jobs. But it's more than ten years now and he has yet to make thirty-five dollars a week!

LINDA. He's finding himself, Willy.

WILLY. Not finding yourself at the age of thirty-four is a disgrace!

LINDA. Shh!

WILLY. The trouble is he's lazy, goddammit!

LINDA. Willy, please!

WILLY. Biff is a lazy bum!

LINDA. They're sleeping. Get something to eat. Go on down.

WILLY. Why did he come home? I would like to know what brought him home.

LINDA. I don't know. I think he's still lost, Willy. I think he's very lost.

WILLY. Biff Loman is lost. In the greatest country in the world a young man with such—personal attractiveness, gets lost. And such a hard worker. There's one thing about Biff—he's not lazy.

LINDA. Never.

WILLY (*with pity and resolve*). I'll see him in the morning; I'll have a nice talk with him. I'll get him a job selling. He could be big in no time. My God! Remember how they used to follow him around in high school? When he smiled at one of them their faces lit up. When he walked down the street . . . (*He loses himself in reminiscences.*)

LINDA (*trying to bring him out of it*). Willy, dear, I got a new kind of American-type cheese today. It's whipped.

WILLY. Why do you get American when I like Swiss?

LINDA. I just thought you'd like a change—

WILLY. I don't want a change! I want Swiss cheese. Why am I always being contradicted?

LINDA (*with a covering laugh*). I thought it would be a surprise.

WILLY. Why don't you open a window in here, for God's sake?

LINDA (*with infinite patience*). They're all open, dear.

WILLY. The way they boxed us in here. Bricks and windows, windows and bricks.

LINDA. We should've bought the land next door.

WILLY. The street is lined with cars. There's not a breath of fresh air in the neighborhood. The grass don't grow any more, you can't raise a carrot in the back yard. They should've had a law against apartment houses. Remember those two beautiful elm trees out there? When I and Biff hung the swing between them?

LINDA.   Yeah, like being a million miles from the city.

WILLY.   They should've arrested the builder for cutting those down. They massacred the neighborhood. (*Lost.*) More and more I think of those days, Linda. This time of year it was lilac and wisteria. And then the peonies would come out, and the daffodils. What fragrance in this room!

LINDA.   Well, after all, people had to move somewhere.

WILLY.   No, there's more people now.

LINDA.   I don't think there's more people. I think—

WILLY.   There's more people! That's what's ruining this country! Population is getting out of control. The competition is maddening! Smell the stink from that apartment house! And another one on the other side . . . How can they whip cheese?

On WILLY'S *last line,* BIFF *and* HAPPY *raise themselves up in their beds, listening.*

LINDA.   Go down, try it. And be quiet.

WILLY (*turning to* LINDA *guiltily*).   You're not worried about me, are you, sweetheart?

BIFF.   What's the matter?

HAPPY.   Listen!

LINDA.   You've got too much on the ball to worry about.

WILLY.   You're my foundation and my support, Linda.

LINDA.   Just try to relax, dear. You make mountains out of molehills.

WILLY.   I won't fight with him any more. If he wants to go back to Texas, let him go.

LINDA.   He'll find his way.

WILLY.   Sure. Certain men just don't get started till later in life. Like Thomas Edison, I think. Or B.F. Goodrich. One of them was deaf. (*He starts for the bedroom doorway.*) I'll put my money on Biff.

LINDA.   And Willy—if it's warm Sunday we'll drive in the country. And we'll open the windshield, and take lunch.

WILLY.   No, the windshields don't open on the new cars.

LINDA.   But you opened it today.

WILLY.   Me? I didn't. (*He stops.*) Now isn't that peculiar! Isn't that a remarkable— (*He breaks off in amazement and fright as the flute is heard distantly.*)

LINDA.   What, darling?

WILLY.   That is the most remarkable thing.

LINDA.   What, dear?

WILLY.   I was thinking of the Chevvy. (*Slight pause.*) Nineteen twenty-eight . . . when I had that red Chevvy— (*Breaks off.*) That funny? I coulda sworn I was driving that Chevvy today.

LINDA.   Well, that's nothing. Something must've reminded you.

WILLY.   Remarkable. Ts. Remember those days? The way Biff used to simonize that car? The dealer refused to believe there was eighty thousand miles on it. (*He shakes his head.*) Heh! (*To* LINDA.) Close your eyes, I'll be right up. (*He walks out of the bedroom.*)

HAPPY (*to* BIFF).   Jesus, maybe he smashed up the car again!

LINDA (*calling after* WILLY).   Be careful on the stairs, dear! The cheese is on the middle shelf! (*She turns, goes over to the bed, takes his jacket, and goes out of the bedroom.*)

Light has risen on the boys' room. Unseen, WILLY *is heard talking to himself, "Eighty thousand miles," and a little laugh.* BIFF *gets out of bed, comes downstage a bit, and stands attentively.* BIFF *is two years older than his brother* HAPPY, *well built, but in these days bears a worn air and seems less self-assured. He has succeeded less, and his dreams are stronger and less acceptable than* HAPPY's. HAPPY *is tall, powerfully made. Sexuality is like a visible color on him, or a scent that many women have discovered. He, like his brother, is lost, but in a different way, for he has never allowed himself to turn his face toward defeat and is thus more confused and hard-skinned, although seemingly more content.*

HAPPY (*getting out of bed*).   He's going to get his license taken away if he keeps that up. I'm getting nervous about him, y'know, Biff?

BIFF.   His eyes are going.

HAPPY.   No, I've driven with him. He sees all right. He just doesn't keep his mind on it. I drove into the city with him last week. He stops at a green light and then it turns red and he goes. (*He laughs.*)

BIFF.   Maybe he's color-blind.

HAPPY.   Pop? Why he's got the finest eye for color in the business. You know that.

BIFF (*sitting down on his bed*).   I'm going to sleep.

HAPPY.   You're not still sour on Dad, are you, Biff?

BIFF.   He's all right, I guess.

WILLY (*underneath them, in the living-room*).   Yes, sir, eighty thousand miles—eighty-two thousand!

BIFF.   You smoking?

HAPPY (*holding out a pack of cigarettes*).   Want one?

BIFF (*taking a cigarette*).   I can never sleep when I smell it.

WILLY.   What a simonizing job, heh!

HAPPY (*with deep sentiment*).   Funny, Biff, y'know? Us sleeping in here again? The old beds. (*He pats his bed affectionately.*) All the talk that went across those two beds, huh? Our whole lives.

BIFF.   Yeah. Lotta dreams and plans.

HAPPY (*with a deep and masculine laugh*).   About five hundred women would like to know what was said in this room.

They share a soft laugh.

BIFF.   Remember that big Betsy something—what the hell was her name—over on Bushwick Avenue?

HAPPY (*combing his hair*).   With the collie dog!

BIFF.   That's the one. I got you in there, remember?

HAPPY.   Yeah, that was my first time—I think. Boy, there was a pig! (*They laugh, almost crudely.*) You taught me everything I know about women. Don't forget that.

BIFF.   I bet you forgot how bashful you used to be. Especially with girls.

HAPPY.   Oh, I still am, Biff.

BIFF.   Oh, go on.

HAPPY.   I just control it, that's all. I think I got less bashful and you got more so. What happened, Biff? Where's the old humor, the old confidence? (*He shakes* BIFF's *knee.* BIFF *gets up and moves restlessly about the room.*) What's the matter?

BIFF.   Why does Dad mock me all the time?

HAPPY.   He's not mocking you, he—

BIFF.   Everything I say there's a twist of mockery on his face. I can't get near him.

HAPPY.   He just wants you to make good, that's all. I wanted to talk to you about Dad for a long time, Biff. Something's—happening to him. He— talks to himself.

BIFF.   I noticed that this morning. But he always mumbled.

HAPPY.   But not so noticeable. It got so embarrassing I sent him to Florida. And you know something? Most of the time he's talking to you.

BIFF.   What's he say about me?

HAPPY.   I can't make it out.

BIFF.   What's he say about me?

HAPPY.   I think the fact that you're not settled, that you're still kind of up in the air . . .

BIFF.   There's one or two other things depressing him, Happy.

HAPPY.   What do you mean?

BIFF.   Never mind. Just don't lay it all to me.

HAPPY.   But I think if you just got started—I mean—is there any future for you out there?

BIFF.   I tell ya, Hap, I don't know what the future is. I don't know—what I'm supposed to want.

HAPPY.   What do you mean?

BIFF.   Well, I spent six or seven years after high school trying to work myself up. Shipping clerk, salesman, business of one kind or another. And it's a measly manner of existence. To get on that subway on the hot mornings in summer. To devote your whole life to keeping stock, or making phone calls, or selling or buying. To suffer fifty weeks of the year for the sake of a two-week vacation, when all you really desire is to be outdoors, with your shirt off. And always to have to get ahead of the next fella. And still—that's how you build a future.

HAPPY.   Well, you really enjoy it on a farm? Are you content out there?

BIFF (*with rising agitation*).   Hap, I've had twenty or thirty different kinds of jobs since I left home before the war, and it always turns out the same. I just realized it lately. In Nebraska when I herded cattle, and the Dakotas, and Arizona, and now in Texas. It's why I came home now, I guess, because I realized it. This farm I work on, it's spring there now, see? And they've got about fifteen new colts. There's nothing more inspiring or—beautiful than the sight of a mare and a new colt. And it's cool there now, see? Texas is cool now, and it's spring. And whenever spring comes to where I am, I suddenly get the feeling, my God, I'm not gettin' anywhere! What the hell am I doing, playing around with horses, twenty-eight dollars a week! I'm thirty-four years old, I oughta be makin' my future. That's when I come running home. And now, I get here, and I don't know what to do with myself. (*After a pause.*) I've always made a point of not wasting my life, and everytime I come back here I know that all I've done is to waste my life.

HAPPY.   You're a poet, you know that, Biff? You're a—you're an idealist!

BIFF.   No, I'm mixed up very bad. Maybe I oughta get married. Maybe I oughta get stuck into something. Maybe that's my trouble. I'm like a boy. I'm not married, I'm not in business, I just—I'm like a boy. Are you content, Hap? You're a success, aren't you? Are you content?

HAPPY.   Hell, no!

BIFF.   Why? You're making money, aren't you?

HAPPY (*moving about with energy, expressiveness*).   All I can do now is wait for the merchandise manager to die. And suppose I get to be merchandise manager? He's a good friend of mine, and he just built a terrific estate on Long Island. And he lived there about two months and sold it, and now he's building another one. He can't enjoy it once it's finished. And I know that's just what I would do. I don't know what the hell I'm workin' for. Sometimes I sit in my apartment—all alone. And I think of the rent I'm paying. And it's crazy. But then, it's what I always wanted. My own apartment, a car, and plenty of women. And still, goddammit, I'm lonely.

BIFF (*with enthusiasm*).   Listen, why don't you come out West with me?

HAPPY.   You and I, heh?

BIFF.   Sure, maybe we could buy a ranch. Raise cattle, use our muscles. Men built like we are should be working out in the open.

HAPPY (*avidly*).   The Loman Brothers, heh?

BIFF (*with vast affection*).   Sure, we'd be known all over the counties!

HAPPY (*enthralled*).   That's what I dream about, Biff. Sometimes I want to just rip my clothes off in the middle of the store and outbox that goddam merchandise manager. I mean I can outbox, outrun, and outlift anybody in that store, and I have to take orders from those common, petty sons-of-bitches till I can't stand it any more.

BIFF.   I'm tellin' you, kid, if you were with me I'd be happy out there.

HAPPY (*enthused*).   See, Biff, everybody around me is so false that I'm constantly lowering my ideals . . .

BIFF.   Baby, together we'd stand up for one another, we'd have someone to trust.

HAPPY.   If I were around you—

BIFF.   Hap, the trouble is we weren't brought up to grub for money. I don't know how to do it.

HAPPY.   Neither can I!

BIFF.   Then let's go!

HAPPY.   The only thing is—what can you make out there?

BIFF. But look at your friend. Builds an estate and then hasn't the peace of mind to live in it.

HAPPY. Yeah, but when he walks into the store the waves part in front of him. That's fifty-two thousand dollars a year coming through the revolving door, and I got more in my pinky finger than he's got in his head.

BIFF. Yeah, but you just said—

HAPPY. I gotta show some of those pompous, self-important executives over there that Hap Loman can make the grade. I want to walk into the store the way he walks in. Then I'll go with you, Biff. We'll be together yet, I swear. But take those two we had tonight. Now weren't they gorgeous creatures?

BIFF. Yeah, yeah, most gorgeous I've had in years.

HAPPY. I get that any time I want, Biff. Whenever I feel disgusted. The only trouble is, it gets like bowling or something. I just keep knockin' them over and it doesn't mean anything. You still run around a lot?

BIFF. Naa. I'd like to find a girl—steady, somebody with substance.

HAPPY. That's what I long for.

BIFF. Go on! You'd never come home.

HAPPY. I would! Somebody with character, with resistance! Like Mom, y'know? You're gonna call me a bastard when I tell you this. That girl Charlotte I was with tonight is engaged to be married in five weeks. (*He tries on his new hat.*)

BIFF. No kiddin'!

HAPPY. Sure, the guy's in line for the vice-presidency of the store. I don't know what gets into me, maybe I just have an overdeveloped sense of competition or something, but I went and ruined her, and furthermore I can't get rid of her. And he's the third executive I've done that to. Isn't that a crummy characteristic? And to top it all, I go to their weddings! (*Indignantly, but laughing.*) Like I'm not supposed to take bribes. Manufacturers offer me a hundred-dollar bill now and then to throw an order their way. You know how honest I am, but it's like this girl, see. I hate myself for it. Because I don't want the girl, and, still, I take it and—I love it!

BIFF. Let's go to sleep.

HAPPY. I guess we didn't settle anything, heh?

BIFF. I just got one idea that I think I'm going to try.

HAPPY. What's that?

BIFF. Remember Bill Oliver?

HAPPY. Sure, Oliver is very big now. You want to work for him again?

BIFF. No, but when I quit he said something to me. He put his arm on my shoulder, and said, "Biff, if you ever need anything, come to me."

HAPPY. I remember that. That sounds good.

BIFF. I think I'll go to see him. If I could get ten thousand or even seven or eight thousand dollars I could buy a beautiful ranch.

HAPPY. I bet he'd back you. 'Cause he thought highly of you, Biff. I mean, they all do. You're well liked, Biff. That's why I say to come back here, and we both have the apartment. And I'm tellin' you, Biff, any babe you want . . .

BIFF. No, with a ranch I could do the work I like and still be something. I just wonder though. I wonder if Oliver still thinks I stole that carton of basketballs.

HAPPY. Oh, he probably forgot that long ago. It's almost ten years. You're too sensitive. Anyway, he didn't really fire you.

BIFF. Well, I think he was going to. I think that's why I quit. I was never sure whether he knew or not. I know he thought the world of me, though. I was the only one he'd let lock up the place.

WILLY (*below*). You gonna wash the engine, Biff?

HAPPY. Shh!

BIFF *looks at* HAPPY, *who is gazing down, listening.* WILLY *is mumbling in the parlor.*

HAPPY. You hear that?

They listen. WILLY *laughs warmly.*

BIFF (*growing angry*). Doesn't he know Mom can hear that?

WILLY. Don't get your sweater dirty, Biff!

A look of pain crosses BIFF's *face.*

HAPPY. Isn't that terrible? Don't leave again, will you? You'll find a job here. You gotta stick around. I don't know what to do about him, it's getting embarrassing.

WILLY. What a simonizing job!

BIFF. Mom's hearing that!

WILLY. No kiddin', Biff, you got a date? Wonderful!

HAPPY. Go on to sleep. But talk to him in the morning, will you?

BIFF (*reluctantly getting into bed*). With her in the house. Brother!

HAPPY (*getting into bed*). I wish you'd have a good talk with him.

The light on their room begins to fade.

BIFF (*to himself in bed*). That selfish, stupid . . .

HAPPY. Sh . . . Sleep, Biff.

Their light is out. Well before they have finished speaking, WILLY's *form is dimly seen below in the darkened kitchen. He opens the refrigerator, searches in there, and takes out a bottle of milk. The apartment houses are fading out, and the entire house and surroundings become covered with leaves. Music insinuates itself as the leaves appear.*

WILLY. Just wanna be careful with those girls, Biff, that's all. Don't make any promises. No promises of any kind. Because a girl, y'know, they always believe what you tell 'em, and you're very young, Biff, you're too young to be talking seriously to girls.

Light rises on the kitchen. WILLY, *talking, shuts the refrigerator door and comes downstage to the kitchen table. He pours milk into a glass. He is totally immersed in himself, smiling faintly.*

WILLY.   Too young entirely, Biff. You want to watch your schooling first. Then when you're all set, there'll be plenty of girls for a boy like you. (*He smiles broadly at a kitchen chair.*) That so? The girls pay for you? (*He laughs.*) Boy, you must really be makin' a hit.

WILLY *is gradually addressing—physically—a point offstage, speaking through the wall of the kitchen, and his voice has been rising in volume to that of a normal conversation.*

WILLY.   I been wondering why you polish the car so careful. Ha! Don't leave the hubcaps, boys. Get the chamois to the hubcaps. Happy, use newspaper on the windows, it's the easiest thing. Show him how to do it, Biff! You see, Happy? Pad it up, use it like a pad. That's it, that's it, good work. You're doin' all right, Hap. (*He pauses, then nods in approbation for a few seconds, then looks upward.*) Biff, first thing we gotta do when we get time is clip that big branch over the house. Afraid it's gonna fall in a storm and hit the roof. Tell you what. We get a rope and sling her around, and then we climb up there with a couple of saws and take her down. Soon as you finish the car, boys, I wanna see ya. I got a surprise for you, boys.

BIFF (*offstage*).   Whatta ya got, Dad?

WILLY.   No, you finish first. Never leave a job till you're finished— remember that. (*Looking toward the "big trees."*) Biff, up in Albany I saw a beautiful hammock. I think I'll buy it next trip, and we'll hang it right between those two elms. Wouldn't that be something? Just swingin' there under those branches. Boy, that would be . . .

YOUNG BIFF *and* YOUNG HAPPY *appear from the direction* WILLY *was addressing.* HAPPY *carries rags and a pail of water.* BIFF, *wearing a sweater with a block "S," carries a football.*

BIFF (*pointing in the direction of the car offstage*).   How's that, Pop, professional?

WILLY.   Terrific. Terrific job, boys. Good work, Biff.

HAPPY.   Where's the surprise, Pop?

WILLY.   In the back seat of the car.

HAPPY.   Boy! (*He runs off.*)

BIFF.   What is it, Dad? Tell me, what'd you buy?

WILLY (*laughing, cuffs him*).   Never mind, something I want you to have.

BIFF (*turns and starts off*).   What is it, Hap?

HAPPY (*offstage*).   It's a punching bag!

BIFF.   Oh, Pop!

WILLY.   It's got Gene Tunney's signature on it!

HAPPY *runs onstage with a punching bag.*

BIFF.   Gee, how'd you know we wanted a punching bag?

WILLY.   Well, it's the finest thing for the timing.

HAPPY (*lies down on his back and pedals with his feet*).   I'm losing weight, you notice, Pop?

WILLY (*to* HAPPY).   Jumping rope is good too.

BIFF.   Did you see the new football I got?

WILLY (*examining the ball*).   Where'd you get a new ball?

BIFF.   The coach told me to practice my passing.

WILLY.   That so? And he gave you the ball, heh?

BIFF.   Well, I borrowed it from the locker room. (*He laughs confidentially.*)

WILLY (*laughing with him at the theft*).   I want you to return that.

HAPPY.   I told you he wouldn't like it!

BIFF (*angrily*).   Well, I'm bringing it back!

WILLY (*stopping the incipient argument, to* HAPPY).   Sure, he's gotta practice with a regulation ball, doesn't he? (*To* BIFF.) Coach'll probably congratulate you on your initiative!

BIFF.   Oh, he keeps congratulating my initiative all the time, Pop.

WILLY.   That's because he likes you. If somebody else took that ball there'd be an uproar. So what's the report, boys, what's the report?

BIFF.   Where'd you go this time, Dad? Gee we were lonesome for you.

WILLY (*pleased, puts an arm around each boy and they come down to the apron*).   Lonesome, heh?

BIFF.   Missed you every minute.

WILLY.   Don't say? Tell you a secret, boys. Don't breathe it to a soul. Someday I'll have my own business, and I'll never have to leave home any more.

HAPPY.   Like Uncle Charley, heh?

WILLY.   Bigger than Uncle Charley! Because Charley is not—liked. He's liked, but he's not—well liked.

BIFF.   Where'd you go this time, Dad?

WILLY.   Well, I got on the road, and I went north to Providence. Met the Mayor.

BIFF.   The Mayor of Providence!

WILLY.   He was sitting in the hotel lobby.

BIFF.   What'd he say?

WILLY.   He said, "Morning!" And I said, "You got a fine city here, Mayor." And then he had coffee with me. And then I went to Waterbury. Waterbury is a fine city. Big clock city, the famous Waterbury clock. Sold a nice bill there. And then Boston—Boston is the cradle of the Revolution. A fine city. And a couple of other towns in Mass., and on to Portland and Bangor and straight home!

BIFF.   Gee, I'd love to go with you sometime, Dad.

WILLY.   Soon as summer comes.

HAPPY.   Promise?

WILLY.   You and Hap and I, and I'll show you all the towns. America is full of beautiful towns and fine, upstanding people. And they know me, boys, they know me up and down New England. The finest people. And when I bring you fellas up, there'll be open sesame for all of us, 'cause one thing, boys: I have friends. I can park my car in any street in New England, and the cops protect it like their own. This summer, heh?

BIFF and HAPPY (*together*).   Yeah! You bet!

WILLY.   We'll take our bathing suits.

HAPPY.   We'll carry your bags, Pop!

WILLY.   Oh, won't that be something! Me comin' into the Boston stores with you boys carryin' my bags. What a sensation!

BIFF *is prancing around, practicing passing the ball.*

WILLY.   You nervous, Biff, about the game?

BIFF.   Not if you're gonna be there.

WILLY.   What do they say about you in school, now that they made you captain?

HAPPY.   There's a crowd of girls behind him everytime the classes change.

BIFF (*taking* WILLY's *hand*).   This Saturday, Pop, this Saturday—just for you, I'm going to break through for a touchdown.

HAPPY.   You're supposed to pass.

BIFF.   I'm takin' one play for Pop. You watch me, Pop, and when I take off my helmet, that means I'm breakin' out. Then you watch me crash through that line!

WILLY (*kisses* BIFF).   Oh, wait'll I tell this in Boston!

BERNARD *enters in knickers. He is younger than* BIFF, *earnest and loyal, a worried boy.*

BERNARD.   Biff, where are you? You're supposed to study with me today.

WILLY.   Hey, looka Bernard. What're you lookin' so anemic about, Bernard?

BERNARD.   He's gotta study, Uncle Willy. He's got Regents next week.

HAPPY (*tauntingly, spinning* BERNARD *around*).   Let's box, Bernard!

BERNARD.   Biff! (*He gets away from* HAPPY.) Listen, Biff, I heard Mr. Birnbaum say that if you don't start studyin' math he's gonna flunk you, and you won't graduate. I heard him!

WILLY.   You better study with him, Biff. Go ahead now.

BERNARD.   I heard him!

BIFF.   Oh, Pop, you didn't see my sneakers! (*He holds up a foot for* WILLY *to look at.*)

WILLY.   Hey, that's a beautiful job of printing!

BERNARD (*wiping his glasses*).   Just because he printed University of Virginia on his sneakers doesn't mean they've got to graduate him, Uncle Willy!

WILLY (*angrily*).   What're you talking about? With scholarships to three universities they're gonna flunk him?

BERNARD.   But I heard Mr. Birnbaum say—

WILLY.   Don't be a pest, Bernard! (*To his boys.*) What an anemic!

BERNARD.   Okay, I'm waiting for you in my house, Biff.

BERNARD *goes off. The Lomans laugh.*

WILLY.   Bernard is not well liked, is he?

BIFF.   He's liked, but he's not well liked.

HAPPY. That's right, Pop.

WILLY. That's just what I mean. Bernard can get the best marks in school, y'understand, but when he gets out in the business world, y'understand, you are going to be five times ahead of him. That's why I thank Almighty God you're both built like Adonises. Because the man who makes an appearance in the business world, the man who creates personal interest, is the man who gets ahead. Be liked and you will never want. You take me, for instance. I never have to wait in line to see a buyer. "Willy Loman is here!" That's all they have to know, and I go right through.

BIFF. Did you knock them dead, Pop?

WILLY. Knocked 'em cold in Providence, slaughtered 'em in Boston.

HAPPY (*on his back, pedaling again*). I'm losing weight, you notice, Pop?

LINDA *enters, as of old, a ribbon in her hair, carrying a basket of washing.*

LINDA (*with youthful energy*). Hello, dear!

WILLY. Sweetheart!

LINDA. How'd the Chevvy run?

WILLY. Chevrolet, Linda, is the greatest car ever built. (*To the boys.*) Since when do you let your mother carry wash up the stairs?

BIFF. Grab hold there, boy!

HAPPY. Where to, Mom?

LINDA. Hang them up on the line. And you better go down to your friends, Biff. The cellar is full of boys. They don't know what to do with themselves.

BIFF. Ah, when Pop comes home they can wait!

WILLY (*laughs appreciatively*). You better go down and tell them what to do, Biff.

BIFF. I think I'll have them sweep out the furnace room.

WILLY. Good work, Biff.

BIFF (*goes through wall-line of kitchen to doorway at back and calls down*). Fellas! Everybody sweep out the furnace room! I'll be right down!

VOICES. All right! Okay, Biff.

BIFF. George and Sam and Frank, come out back! We're hangin' up the wash! Come on, Hap, on the double! (*He and* HAPPY *carry out the basket.*)

LINDA. The way they obey him!

WILLY. Well, that's training, the training. I'm tellin' you, I was sellin' thousands and thousands, but I had to come home.

LINDA. Oh, the whole block'll be at that game. Did you sell anything?

WILLY. I did five hundred gross in Providence and seven hundred gross in Boston.

LINDA. No! Wait a minute, I've got a pencil. (*She pulls pencil and paper out of her apron pocket.*) That makes your commission . . . Two hundred— my God! Two hundred and twelve dollars!

WILLY. Well, I didn't figure it yet, but . . .

LINDA. How much did you do?

WILLY. Well, I—I did—about a hundred and eighty gross in Providence. Well, no—it came to—roughly two hundred gross on the whole trip.

LINDA (*without hesitation*). Two hundred gross. That's . . . (*She figures.*)

WILLY.   The trouble was that three of the stores were half closed for inventory in Boston. Otherwise I woulda broke records.

LINDA.   Well, it makes seventy dollars and some pennies. That's very good.

WILLY.   What do we owe?

LINDA.   Well, on the first there's sixteen dollars on the refrigerator—

WILLY.   Why sixteen?

LINDA.   Well, the fan belt broke, so it was a dollar eighty.

WILLY.   But it's brand new.

LINDA.   Well, the man said that's the way it is. Till they work themselves in, y'know.

They move through the wall-line into the kitchen.

WILLY.   I hope we didn't get stuck on that machine.

LINDA.   They got the biggest ads of any of them!

WILLY.   I know, it's a fine machine. What else?

LINDA.   Well, there's nine-sixty for the washing machine. And for the vacuum cleaner there's three and a half due on the fifteenth. Then the roof, you got twenty-one dollars remaining.

WILLY.   It don't leak, does it?

LINDA.   No, they did a wonderful job. Then you owe Frank for the carburetor.

WILLY.   I'm not going to pay that man! That goddam Chevrolet, they ought to prohibit the manufacture of that car!

LINDA.   Well, you owe him three and a half. And odds and ends, comes to around a hundred and twenty dollars by the fifteenth.

WILLY.   A hundred and twenty dollars! My God, if business don't pick up I don't know what I'm gonna do!

LINDA.   Well, next week you'll do better.

WILLY.   Oh, I'll knock 'em dead next week. I'll go to Hartford. I'm very well liked in Hartford. You know, the trouble is, Linda, people don't seem to take to me.

They move onto the forestage.

LINDA.   Oh, don't be foolish.

WILLY.   I know it when I walk in. They seem to laugh at me.

LINDA.   Why? Why would they laugh at you? Don't talk that way, Willy.

WILLY *moves to the edge of the stage.* LINDA *goes into the kitchen and starts to darn stockings.*

WILLY.   I don't know the reason for it, but they just pass me by. I'm not noticed.

LINDA.   But you're doing wonderful, dear. You're making seventy to a hundred dollars a week.

WILLY.   But I gotta be at it ten, twelve hours a day. Other men—I don't know—they do it easier. I don't know why—I can't stop myself—I talk too much. A man oughta come in with a few words. One thing about Charley. He's a man of few words, and they respect him.

LINDA. You don't talk too much, you're just lively.

WILLY (*smiling*). Well, I figure, what the hell, life is short, a couple of jokes. (*To himself.*) I joke too much! (*The smile goes.*)

LINDA. Why? You're—

WILLY. I'm fat. I'm very—foolish to look at, Linda. I didn't tell you, but Christmas time I happened to be calling on F. H. Stewarts, and a salesman I know, as I was going in to see the buyer I heard him say something about— walrus. And I—I cracked him right across the face. I won't take that. I simply will not take that. But they do laugh at me. I know that.

LINDA. Darling . . .

WILLY. I gotta overcome it. I know I gotta overcome it. I'm not dressing to advantage, maybe.

LINDA. Willy, darling, you're the handsomest man in the world—

WILLY. Oh, no, Linda.

LINDA. To me you are. (*Slight pause.*) The handsomest.

From the darkness is heard the laughter of a woman. WILLY *doesn't turn to it, but it continues through* LINDA's *lines.*

LINDA. And the boys, Willy. Few men are idolized by their children the way you are.

Music is heard as behind a scrim, to the left of the house, THE WOMAN; *dimly seen, is dressing.*

WILLY (*with great feeling*). You're the best there is, Linda, you're a pal, you know that? On the road—on the road I want to grab you sometimes and just kiss the life outa you.

The laughter is loud now, and he moves into a brightening area at the left, where THE WOMAN *has come from behind the scrim and is standing, putting on her hat, looking into a "mirror" and laughing.*

WILLY. 'Cause I get so lonely—especially when business is bad and there's nobody to talk to. I get the feeling that I'll never sell anything again, that I won't be making a living for you, or a business, a business for the boys. (*He talks through* THE WOMAN's *subsiding laughter;* THE WOMAN *primps at the "mirror."*) There's so much I want to make for—

THE WOMAN. Me? You didn't make me, Willy. I picked you.

WILLY (*pleased*). You picked me?

THE WOMAN (*who is quite proper-looking,* WILLY's *age*). I did. I've been sitting at that desk watching all the salesmen go by, day in, day out. But you've got such a sense of humor, and we do have such a good time together, don't we?

WILLY. Sure, sure. (*He takes her in his arms.*) Why do you have to go now?

THE WOMAN. It's two o'clock . . .

WILLY. No, come on in! (*He pulls her.*)

THE WOMAN. . . . my sisters'll be scandalized. When'll you be back?

WILLY. Oh, two weeks about. Will you come up again?

THE WOMAN. Sure thing. You do make me laugh. It's good for me. (*She squeezes his arm, kisses him.*) And I think you're a wonderful man.

WILLY.   You picked me, heh?

THE WOMAN.   Sure. Because you're so sweet. And such a kidder.

WILLY.   Well, I'll see you next time I'm in Boston.

THE WOMAN.   I'll put you right through to the buyers.

WILLY (*slapping her bottom*).   Right. Well, bottoms up!

THE WOMAN (*slaps him gently and laughs*).   You just kill me, Willy. (*He suddenly grabs her and kisses her roughly.*) You kill me. And thanks for the stockings. I love a lot of stockings. Well, good night.

WILLY.   Good night. And keep your pores open!

THE WOMAN.   Oh, Willy!

THE WOMAN *bursts out laughing, and* LINDA's *laughter blends in.* THE WOMAN *disappears into the dark. Now the area at the kitchen table brightens.* LINDA *is sitting where she was at the kitchen table, but now is mending a pair of her silk stockings.*

LINDA.   You are, Willy. The handsomest man. You've got no reason to feel that—

WILLY (*coming out of* THE WOMAN's *dimming area and going over to* LINDA).   I'll make it all up to you, Linda, I'll—

LINDA.   There's nothing to make up, dear. You're doing fine, better than—

WILLY (*noticing her mending*).   What's that?

LINDA.   Just mending my stockings. They're so expensive—

WILLY (*angrily, taking them from her*).   I won't have you mending stockings in this house! Now throw them out!

LINDA *puts the stockings in her pocket.*

BERNARD (*entering on the run*).   Where is he? If he doesn't study!

WILLY (*moving to the forestage, with great agitation*).   You'll give him the answers!

BERNARD.   I do, but I can't on a Regents! That's a state exam! They're liable to arrest me!

WILLY.   Where is he? I'll whip him, I'll whip him!

LINDA.   And he'd better give back that football, Willy, it's not nice.

WILLY.   Biff! Where is he? Why is he taking everything?

LINDA.   He's too rough with the girls, Willy. All the mothers are afraid of him!

WILLY.   I'll whip him!

BERNARD.   He's driving the car without a license!

THE WOMAN's *laugh is heard.*

WILLY.   Shut up!

LINDA.   All the mothers—

WILLY.   Shut up!

BERNARD (*backing quietly away and out*).   Mr. Birnbaum says he's stuck up.

WILLY.   Get outa here!

BERNARD.   If he doesn't buckle down he'll flunk math! (*He goes off.*)

LINDA.   He's right, Willy, you've gotta—

WILLY (*exploding at her*).   There's nothing the matter with him! You want him to be a worm like Bernard? He's got spirit, personality . . .

As he speaks, LINDA, *almost in tears, exits into the living-room.* WILLY *is alone in the kitchen, wilting and staring. The leaves are gone. It is night again, and the apartment houses look down from behind.*

WILLY.   Loaded with it. Loaded! What is he stealing? He's giving it back, isn't he? Why is he stealing? What did I tell him? I never in my life told him anything but decent things.

HAPPY *in pajamas has come down the stairs;* WILLY *suddenly becomes aware of* HAPPY's *presence.*

HAPPY.   Let's go now, come on.

WILLY (*sitting down at the kitchen table*).   Huh! Why did she have to wax the floors herself? Everytime she waxes the floors she keels over. She knows that!

HAPPY.   Shh! Take it easy. What brought you back tonight?

WILLY.   I got an awful scare. Nearly hit a kid in Yonkers. God! Why didn't I go to Alaska with my brother Ben that time! Ben! That man was a genius, that man was success incarnate! What a mistake! He begged me to go.

HAPPY.   Well, there's no use in—

WILLY.   You guys! There was a man started with the clothes on his back and ended up with diamond mines!

HAPPY.   Boy, someday I'd like to know how he did it.

WILLY.   What's the mystery? The man knew what he wanted and went out and got it! Walked into a jungle, and comes out, the age of twenty-one, and he's rich! The world is an oyster, but you don't crack it open on a mattress!

HAPPY.   Pop, I told you I'm gonna retire you for life.

WILLY.   You'll retire me for life on seventy goddam dollars a week? And your women and your car and your apartment, and you'll retire me for life! Christ's sake, I couldn't get past Yonkers today! Where are you guys, where are you? The woods are burning! I can't drive a car!

CHARLEY *has appeared in the doorway. He is a large man, slow of speech, laconic, immovable. In all he says, despite what he says, there is pity, and, now, trepidation. He has a robe over pajamas, slippers on his feet. He enters the kitchen.*

CHARLEY.   Everything all right?

HAPPY.   Yeah, Charley, everything's . . .

WILLY.   What's the matter?

CHARLEY.   I heard some noise. I thought something happened. Can't we do something about the walls? You sneeze in here, and in my house hats blow off.

HAPPY.   Let's go to bed, Dad. Come on.

CHARLEY *signals to* HAPPY *to go.*

WILLY.   You go ahead, I'm not tired at the moment.

HAPPY (*to* WILLY).   Take it easy, huh? (*He exits.*)

WILLY.   What're you doin' up?

CHARLEY (*sitting down at the kitchen table opposite* WILLY).   Couldn't sleep good. I had a heartburn.

WILLY.   Well, you don't know how to eat.

CHARLEY.   I eat with my mouth.

WILLY.   No, you're ignorant. You gotta know about vitamins and things like that.

CHARLEY.   Come on, let's shoot. Tire you out a little.

WILLY (*hesitantly*).   All right. You got cards?

CHARLEY (*taking a deck from his pocket*).   Yeah, I got them. Someplace. What is it with those vitamins?

WILLY (*dealing*).   They build up your bones. Chemistry.

CHARLEY.   Yeah, but there's no bones in a heartburn.

WILLY.   What are you talkin' about? Do you know the first thing about it?

CHARLEY.   Don't get insulted.

WILLY.   Don't talk about something you don't know anything about.

They are playing. Pause.

CHARLEY.   What're you doin' home?

WILLY.   A little trouble with the car.

CHARLEY.   Oh. (*Pause.*) I'd like to take a trip to California.

WILLY.   Don't say.

CHARLEY.   You want a job?

WILLY.   I got a job, I told you that. (*After a slight pause.*) What the hell are you offering me a job for?

CHARLEY.   Don't get insulted.

WILLY.   Don't insult me.

CHARLEY.   I don't see no sense in it. You don't have to go on this way.

WILLY.   I got a good job. (*Slight pause.*) What do you keep comin' in here for?

CHARLEY.   You want me to go?

WILLY (*after a pause, withering*).   I can't understand it. He's going back to Texas again. What the hell is that?

CHARLEY.   Let him go.

WILLY.   I got nothin' to give him, Charley, I'm clean, I'm clean.

CHARLEY.   He won't starve. None a them starve. Forget about him.

WILLY.   Then what have I got to remember?

CHARLEY.   You take it too hard. To hell with it. When a deposit bottle is broken you don't get your nickel back.

WILLY.   That's easy enough for you to say.

CHARLEY.   That ain't easy for me to say.

WILLY.   Did you see the ceiling I put up in the living-room?

CHARLEY.   Yeah, that's a piece of work. To put up a ceiling is a mystery to me. How do you do it?

WILLY. What's the difference?

CHARLEY. Well, talk about it.

WILLY. You gonna put up a ceiling?

CHARLEY. How could I put up a ceiling?

WILLY. Then what the hell are you bothering me for?

CHARLEY. You're insulted again.

WILLY. A man who can't handle tools is not a man. You're disgusting.

CHARLEY. Don't call me disgusting, Willy.

UNCLE BEN, *carrying a valise and an umbrella, enters the forestage from around the right corner of the house. He is a stolid man, in his sixties, with a mustache and an authoritative air. He is utterly certain of his destiny, and there is an aura of far places about him. He enters exactly as* WILLY *speaks.*

WILLY. I'm getting awfully tired, Ben.

BEN'*s music is heard.* BEN *looks around at everything.*

CHARLEY. Good, keep playing; you'll sleep better. Did you call me Ben?

BEN *looks at his watch.*

WILLY. That's funny. For a second there you reminded me of my brother Ben.

BEN. I only have a few minutes. (*He strolls, inspecting the place.* WILLY *and* CHARLEY *continue playing.*)

CHARLEY. You never heard from him again, heh? Since that time?

WILLY. Didn't Linda tell you? Couple of weeks ago we got a letter from his wife in Africa. He died.

CHARLEY. That so.

BEN (*chuckling*). So this is Brooklyn, eh?

CHARLEY. Maybe you're in for some of his money.

WILLY. Naa, he had seven sons. There's just one opportunity I had with that man . . .

BEN. I must make a train, William. There are several properties I'm looking at in Alaska.

WILLY. Sure, sure! If I'd gone with him to Alaska that time, everything would've been totally different.

CHARLEY. Go on, you'd froze to death up there.

WILLY. What're you talking about?

BEN. Opportunity is tremendous in Alaska, William. Surprised you're not up there.

WILLY. Sure, tremendous.

CHARLEY. Heh?

WILLY. There was the only man I ever met who knew the answers.

CHARLEY. Who?

BEN. How are you all?

WILLY (*taking a pot, smiling*). Fine, fine.

CHARLEY. Pretty sharp tonight.

BEN. Is Mother living with you?

WILLY.   No, she died a long time ago.

CHARLEY.   Who?

BEN.   That's too bad. Fine specimen of a lady, Mother.

WILLY (*to* CHARLEY).   Heh?

BEN.   I'd hoped to see the old girl.

CHARLEY.   Who died?

BEN.   Heard anything from Father, have you?

WILLY (*unnerved*).   What do you mean, who died?

CHARLEY (*taking a pot*).   What're you talkin' about?

BEN (*looking at his watch*).   William, it's half-past eight!

WILLY (*as though to dispel his confusion he angrily stops* CHARLEY'S *hand*).   That's my build!

CHARLEY.   I put the ace—

WILLY.   If you don't know how to play the game I'm not gonna throw my money away on you!

CHARLEY (*rising*).   It was my ace, for God's sake!

WILLY.   I'm through, I'm through!

BEN.   When did Mother die?

WILLY.   Long ago. Since the beginning you never knew how to play cards.

CHARLEY (*picks up the cards and goes to the door*).   All right! Next time I'll bring a deck with five aces.

WILLY.   I don't play that kind of game!

CHARLEY (*turning to him*).   You ought to be ashamed of yourself!

WILLY.   Yeah?

CHARLEY.   Yeah! (*He goes out.*)

WILLY (*slamming the door after him*).   Ignoramus!

BEN (*as* WILLY *comes toward him through the wall-line of the kitchen*).   So you're William.

WILLY (*shaking* BEN'S *hand*).   Ben! I've been waiting for you so long! What's the answer? How did you do it?

BEN.   Oh, there's a story in that.

LINDA *enters the forestage, as of old, carrying the wash basket.*

LINDA.   Is this Ben?

BEN (*gallantly*).   How do you do, my dear.

LINDA.   Where've you been all these years? Willy's always wondered why you—

WILLY (*pulling* BEN *away from her impatiently*).   Where is Dad? Didn't you follow him? How did you get started?

BEN.   Well, I don't know how much you remember.

WILLY.   Well, I was just a baby, of course, only three or four years old—

BEN.   Three years and eleven months.

WILLY.   What a memory, Ben!

BEN.   I have many enterprises, William, and I have never kept books.

WILLY.   I remember I was sitting under the wagon in—was it Nebraska?

BEN.   It was South Dakota, and I gave you a bunch of wild flowers.

WILLY.   I remember you walking away down some open road.

BEN (*laughing*).   I was going to find Father in Alaska.

WILLY.   Where is he?

BEN.   At that age I had a very faulty view of geography, William. I discovered after a few days that I was heading due south, so instead of Alaska, I ended up in Africa.

LINDA.   Africa!

WILLY.   The Gold Coast!

BEN.   Principally diamond mines.

LINDA.   Diamond mines!

BEN.   Yes, my dear. But I've only a few minutes—

WILLY.   No! Boys! Boys! (*Young* BIFF *and* HAPPY *appear.*) Listen to this. This is your Uncle Ben, a great man! Tell my boys, Ben!

BEN.   Why, boys, when I was seventeen I walked into the jungle, and when I was twenty-one I walked out. (*He laughs.*) And by God I was rich.

WILLY (*to the boys*).   You see what I been talking about? The greatest things can happen!

BEN (*glancing at his watch*).   I have an appointment in Ketchikan Tuesday week.

WILLY.   No, Ben! Please tell about Dad. I want my boys to hear. I want them to know the kind of stock they spring from. All I remember is a man with a big beard, and I was in Mamma's lap, sitting around a fire, and some kind of high music.

BEN.   His flute. He played the flute.

WILLY.   Sure, the flute, that's right!

New music is heard, a high, rollicking tune.

BEN.   Father was a very great and a very wild-hearted man. We would start in Boston, and he'd toss the whole family into the wagon, and then he'd drive the team right across the country; through Ohio, and Indiana, Michigan, Illinois, and all the Western states. And we'd stop in the towns and sell the flutes that he'd made on the way. Great inventor, Father. With one gadget he made more in a week than a man like you could make in a lifetime.

WILLY.   That's just the way I'm bringing them up, Ben—rugged, well liked, all-around.

BEN.   Yeah? (*To* BIFF). Hit that, boy—hard as you can. (*He pounds his stomach.*)

BIFF.   Oh, no, sir!

BEN (*taking boxing stance*).   Come on, get to me! (*He laughs.*)

WILLY.   Go to it, Biff! Go ahead, show him!

BIFF.   Okay! (*He cocks his fists and starts in.*)

LINDA (*to* WILLY).   Why must he fight, dear?

BEN (*sparring with* BIFF).   Good boy! Good boy!

WILLY.   How's that, Ben, heh?

HAPPY.   Give him the left, Biff!

LINDA.   Why are you fighting?

BEN.   Good boy! (*Suddenly comes in, trips* BIFF, *and stands over him, the point of his umbrella poised over* BIFF's *eye.*)

LINDA.   Look out, Biff!

BIFF.   Gee!

BEN (*patting* BIFF's *knee*).   Never fight fair with a stranger, boy. You'll never get out of the jungle that way. (*Taking* LINDA's *hand and bowing.*) It was an honor and a pleasure to meet you, Linda.

LINDA (*withdrawing her hand coldly, frightened*).   Have a nice—trip.

BEN (*to* WILLY).   And good luck with your—what do you do?

WILLY.   Selling.

BEN.   Yes. Well . . . (*He raises his hand in farewell to all.*)

WILLY.   No, Ben, I don't want you to think . . . (*He takes* BEN's *arm to show him.*) It's Brooklyn, I know, but we hunt too.

BEN.   Really, now.

WILLY.   Oh, sure, there's snakes and rabbits and—that's why I moved out here. Why, Biff can fell any one of these trees in no time! Boys! Go right over to where they're building the apartment house and get some sand. We're gonna rebuild the entire front stoop right now! Watch this, Ben!

BIFF.   Yes, sir! On the double, Hap!

HAPPY (*as he and* BIFF *run off*).   I lost weight, Pop, you notice?

CHARLEY *enters in knickers, even before the boys are gone.*

CHARLEY.   Listen, if they steal any more from that building the watchman'll put the cops on them!

LINDA (*to* WILLY).   Don't let Biff . . .

BEN *laughs lustily.*

WILLY.   You shoulda seen the lumber they brought home last week. At least a dozen six-by-tens worth all kinds a money.

CHARLEY.   Listen, if that watchman—

WILLY.   I gave them hell, understand. But I got a couple of fearless characters there.

CHARLEY.   Willy, the jails are full of fearless characters.

BEN (*clapping* WILLY *on the back, with a laugh at* CHARLEY).   And the stock exchange, friend!

WILLY (*joining in* BEN's *laughter*).   Where are the rest of your pants?

CHARLEY.   My wife bought them.

WILLY.   Now all you need is a golf club and you can go upstairs and go to sleep. (*To* BEN.) Great athlete! Between him and his son Bernard they can't hammer a nail!

BERNARD (*rushing in*).   The watchman's chasing Biff!

WILLY (*angrily*).   Shut up! He's not stealing anything!

LINDA (*alarmed, hurrying off left*).   Where is he? Biff, dear! (*She exits.*)

WILLY (*moving toward the left, away from* BEN).   There's nothing wrong. What's the matter with you?

BEN.   Nervy boy. Good!

WILLY (*laughing*).   Oh, nerves of iron, that Biff!

CHARLEY.   Don't know what it is. My New England man comes back and he's bleedin', they murdered him up there.

WILLY.   It's contacts, Charley, I got important contacts!

CHARLEY (*sarcastically*).   Glad to hear it, Willy. Come in later, we'll shoot a little casino. I'll take some of your Portland money. (*He laughs at* WILLY *and exits.*)

WILLY (*turning to* BEN).   Business is bad, it's murderous. But not for me, of course.

BEN.   I'll stop by on my way back to Africa.

WILLY (*longingly*).   Can't you stay a few days? You're just what I need, Ben, because I—I have a fine position here, but I—well, Dad left when I was such a baby and I never had a chance to talk to him and I still feel—kind of temporary about myself.

BEN.   I'll be late for my train.

They are at opposite ends of the stage.

WILLY.   Ben, my boys—can't we talk? They'd go into the jaws of hell for me, see, but I—

BEN.   William, you're being first-rate with your boys. Outstanding, manly chaps!

WILLY (*hanging on to his words*).   Oh, Ben, that's good to hear! Because sometimes I'm afraid that I'm not teaching them the right kind of—Ben, how should I teach them?

BEN (*giving great weight to each word, and with a certain vicious audacity*).   William, when I walked into the jungle, I was seventeen. When I walked out I was twenty-one. And, by God, I was rich! (*He goes off into the darkness around the right corner of the house.*)

WILLY.   . . . was rich! That's just the spirit I want to imbue them with! To walk into a jungle! I was right! I was right! I was right!

BEN *is gone, but* WILLY *is still speaking to him as* LINDA, *in nightgown and robe, enters the kitchen, glances around for* WILLY, *then goes to the door of the house, looks out and sees him. Comes down to his left. He looks at her.*

LINDA.   Willy, dear? Willy?

WILLY.   I was right!

LINDA.   Did you have some cheese? (*He can't answer.*) It's very late, darling. Come to bed, heh?

WILLY (*looking straight up*).   Gotta break your neck to see a star in this yard.

LINDA.   You coming in?

WILLY.   Whatever happened to that diamond watch fob? Remember? When Ben came from Africa that time? Didn't he give me a watch fob with a diamond in it?

LINDA.   You pawned it, dear. Twelve, thirteen years ago. For Biff's radio correspondence course.

WILLY.   Gee, that was a beautiful thing. I'll take a walk.

LINDA.   But you're in your slippers.

WILLY (*starting to go around the house at the left*).   I was right! I was! (*Half to* LINDA, *as he goes, shaking his head.*) What a man! There was a man worth talking to. I was right!

LINDA (*calling after* WILLY).   But in your slippers, Willy!

WILLY *is almost gone when* BIFF, *in his pajamas, comes down the stairs and enters the kitchen.*

BIFF.   What is he doing out there?

LINDA.   Sh!

BIFF.   God Almighty, Mom, how long has he been doing this?

LINDA.   Don't, he'll hear you.

BIFF.   What the hell is the matter with him?

LINDA.   It'll pass by morning.

BIFF.   Shouldn't we do anything?

LINDA.   Oh, my dear, you should do a lot of things, but there's nothing to do, so go to sleep.

HAPPY *comes down the stair and sits on the steps.*

HAPPY.   I never heard him so loud, Mom.

LINDA.   Well, come around more often; you'll hear him. (*She sits down at the table and mends the lining of* WILLY's *jacket.*)

BIFF.   Why didn't you ever write me about this, Mom?

LINDA.   How would I write to you? For over three months you had no address.

BIFF.   I was on the move. But you know I thought of you all the time. You know that, don't you, pal?

LINDA.   I know, dear, I know. But he likes to have a letter. Just to know that there's still a possibility for better things.

BIFF.   He's not like this all the time, is he?

LINDA.   It's when you come home he's always the worst.

BIFF.   When I come home?

LINDA.   When you write you're coming, he's all smiles, and talks about the future, and—he's just wonderful. And then the closer you seem to come, the more shaky he gets, and then, by the time you get here, he's arguing, and he seems angry at you. I think it's just that maybe he can't bring himself to—to open up to you. Why are you so hateful to each other? Why is that?

BIFF (*evasively*).   I'm not hateful, Mom.

LINDA.   But you no sooner come in the door than you're fighting!

BIFF.   I don't know why. I mean to change. I'm tryin', Mom, you understand?

LINDA.   Are you home to stay now?

BIFF.   I don't know. I want to look around, see what's doin'.

LINDA.   Biff, you can't look around all your life, can you?

BIFF.   I just can't take hold, Mom. I can't take hold of some kind of life.

LINDA.   Biff, a man is not a bird, to come and go with the springtime.

BIFF.   Your hair . . . (*He touches her hair.*) Your hair got so gray.

LINDA.   Oh, it's been gray since you were in high school. I just stopped dyeing it, that's all.

BIFF.   Dye it again, will ya? I don't want my pal looking old. (*He smiles.*)

LINDA.   You're such a boy! You think you can go away for a year and . . . You've got to get it into your head now that one day you'll knock on this door and there'll be strange people here—

BIFF.   What are you talking about? You're not even sixty, Mom.

LINDA.   But what about your father?

BIFF *(lamely)*.   Well, I meant him too.

HAPPY.   He admires Pop.

LINDA.   Biff, dear, if you don't have any feeling for him, then you can't have any feeling for me.

BIFF.   Sure I can, Mom.

LINDA.   No. You can't just come to see me, because I love him. *(With a threat, but only a threat, of tears.)* He's the dearest man in the world to me, and I won't have anyone making him feel unwanted and low and blue. You've got to make up your mind now, darling, there's no leeway any more. Either he's your father and you pay him that respect, or else you're not to come here. I know he's not easy to get along with—nobody knows that better than me—but . . .

WILLY *(from the left, with a laugh)*.   Hey, hey, Biffo!

BIFF *(starting to go out after WILLY)*.   What the hell is the matter with him? *(HAPPY stops him.)*

LINDA.   Don't—don't go near him!

BIFF.   Stop making excuses for him! He always, always wiped the floor with you. Never had an ounce of respect for you.

HAPPY.   He's always had respect for—

BIFF.   What the hell do you know about it?

HAPPY *(surlily)*.   Just don't call him crazy!

BIFF.   He's got no character—Charley wouldn't do this. Not in his own house—spewing out that vomit from his mind.

HAPPY.   Charley never had to cope with what he's got to.

BIFF.   People are worse off than Willy Loman. Believe me, I've seen them!

LINDA.   Then make Charley your father, Biff. You can't do that, can you? I don't say he's a great man. Willy Loman never made a lot of money. His name was never in the paper. He's not the finest character that ever lived. But he's a human being, and a terrible thing is happening to him. So attention must be paid. He's not to be allowed to fall into his grave like an old dog. Attention, attention must be finally paid to such a person. You called him crazy—

BIFF.   I didn't mean—

LINDA.   No, a lot of people think he's lost his—balance. But you don't have to be very smart to know what his trouble is. The man is exhausted.

HAPPY.   Sure!

LINDA.   A small man can be just as exhausted as a great man. He works for a company thirty-six years this March, opens up unheard-of territories to their trademark, and now in his old age they take his salary away.

HAPPY *(indignantly)*.   I didn't know that, Mom.

LINDA.   You never asked, my dear! Now that you get your spending money someplace else you don't trouble your mind with him.

HAPPY.   But I gave you money last—

LINDA.   Christmas time, fifty dollars! To fix the hot water it cost ninety-seven fifty! For five weeks he's been on straight commission, like a beginner, an unknown!

BIFF.   Those ungrateful bastards!

LINDA.   Are they any worse than his sons? When he brought them business, when he was young, they were glad to see him. But now his old friends, the old buyers that loved him so and always found some order to hand him in a pinch—they're all dead, retired. He used to be able to make six, seven calls a day in Boston. Now he takes his valises out of the car and puts them back and takes them out again and he's exhausted. Instead of walking he talks now. He drives seven hundred miles, and when he gets there no one knows him any more, no one welcomes him. And what goes through a man's mind, driving seven hundred miles home without having earned a cent? Why shouldn't he talk to himself? Why? When he has to go to Charley and borrow fifty dollars a week and pretend to me that it's his pay? How long can that go on? How long? You see what I'm sitting here and waiting for? And you tell me he has no character? The man who never worked a day but for your benefit? When does he get the medal for that? Is this his reward—to turn around at the age of sixty-three and find his sons, who he loved better than his life, one a philandering bum—

HAPPY.   Mom!

LINDA.   That's all you are, my baby! (*To* BIFF.) And you! What happened to the love you had for him? You were such pals! How you used to talk to him on the phone every night! How lonely he was till he could come home to you!

BIFF.   All right, Mom. I'll live here in my room, and I'll get a job. I'll keep away from him, that's all.

LINDA.   No, Biff. You can't stay here and fight all the time.

BIFF.   He threw me out of this house, remember that.

LINDA.   Why did he do that? I never knew why.

BIFF.   Because I know he's a fake and he doesn't like anybody around who knows!

LINDA.   Why a fake? In what way? What do you mean?

BIFF.   Just don't lay it all at my feet. It's between me and him—that's all I have to say. I'll chip in from now on. He'll settle for half my pay check. He'll be all right. I'm going to bed. (*He starts for the stairs.*)

LINDA.   He won't be all right.

BIFF (*turning on the stairs, furiously*).   I hate this city and I'll stay here. Now what do you want?

LINDA.   He's dying, Biff.

HAPPY *turns quickly to her, shocked.*

BIFF (*after a pause*).   Why is he dying?

LINDA.   He's been trying to kill himself.

BIFF (*with great horror*).   How?

LINDA.   I live from day to day.

BIFF.   What're you talking about?

LINDA.   Remember I wrote you that he smashed up the car again? In February?

BIFF.   Well?

LINDA.   The insurance inspector came. He said that they have evidence. That all these accidents in the last year—weren't—weren't—accidents.

HAPPY.   How can they tell that? That's a lie.

LINDA.   It seems there's a woman . . . (*She takes a breath as*)

⎰ BIFF (*sharply but contained*).   What woman?
⎱ LINDA (*simultaneously*).   . . . and this woman . . .

LINDA.   What?

BIFF.   Nothing. Go ahead.

LINDA.   What did you say?

BIFF.   Nothing. I just said what woman?

HAPPY.   What about her?

LINDA.   Well, it seems she was walking down the road and saw his car. She says that he wasn't driving fast at all, and that he didn't skid. She says he came to that little bridge, and then deliberately smashed into the railing, and it was only the shallowness of the water that saved him.

BIFF.   Oh, no, he probably just fell asleep again.

LINDA.   I don't think he fell asleep.

BIFF.   Why not?

LINDA.   Last month . . . (*With great difficulty.*) Oh, boys, it's so hard to say a thing like this! He's just a big stupid man to you, but I tell you there's more good in him than in many other people. (*She chokes, wipes her eyes.*) I was looking for a fuse. The lights blew out, and I went down the cellar. And behind the fuse box—it happened to fall out—was a length of rubber pipe—just short.

HAPPY.   No kidding?

LINDA.   There's a little attachment on the end of it. I knew right away. And sure enough, on the bottom of the water heater there's a new little nipple on the gas pipe.

HAPPY (*angrily*).   That—jerk.

BIFF.   Did you have it taken off?

LINDA.   I'm—I'm ashamed to. How can I mention it to him? Every day I go down and take away that little rubber pipe. But, when he comes home, I put it back where it was. How can I insult him that way? I don't know what to do. I live from day to day, boys. I tell you, I know every thought in his mind. It sounds so old-fashioned and silly, but I tell you he put his whole life into you and you've turned your backs on him. (*She is bent over in the chair, weeping, her face in her hands.*) Biff, I swear to God! Biff, his life is in your hands!

HAPPY (*to BIFF*).   How do you like that damned fool!

BIFF (*kissing her*).   All right, pal, all right. It's all settled now. I've been remiss. I know that, Mom. But now I'll stay, and I swear to you, I'll apply myself. (*Kneeling in front of her, in a fever of self-reproach.*) It's just—you see, Mom, I don't fit in business. Not that I won't try. I'll try, and I'll make good.

HAPPY.   Sure you will. The trouble with you in business was you never tried to please people.

BIFF.   I know, I—

HAPPY.   Like when you worked for Harrison's. Bob Harrison said you were tops, and then you go and do some damn fool thing like whistling whole songs in the elevator like a comedian.

BIFF (*against* HAPPY).   So what? I like to whistle sometimes.

HAPPY.   You don't raise a guy to a responsible job who whistles in the elevator!

LINDA.   Well, don't argue about it now.

HAPPY.   Like when you'd go off and swim in the middle of the day instead of taking the line around.

BIFF (*his resentment rising*).   Well, don't you run off? You take off sometimes, don't you? On a nice summer day?

HAPPY.   Yeah, but I cover myself!

LINDA.   Boys!

HAPPY.   If I'm going to take a fade the boss can call any number where I'm supposed to be and they'll swear to him that I just left. I'll tell you something that I hate to say, Biff, but in the business world some of them think you're crazy.

BIFF (*angered*).   Screw the business world!

HAPPY.   All right, screw it! Great, but cover yourself!

LINDA.   Hap, Hap!

BIFF.   I don't care what they think! They've laughed at Dad for years, and you know why? Because we don't belong in this nuthouse of a city! We should be mixing cement on some open plain, or—or carpenters. A carpenter is allowed to whistle!

WILLY *walks in from the entrance of the house, at left.*

WILLY.   Even your grandfather was better than a carpenter. (*Pause. They watch him.*) You never grew up. Bernard does not whistle in the elevator, I assure you.

BIFF (*as though to laugh* WILLY *out of it*).   Yeah, but you do, Pop.

WILLY.   I never in my life whistled in an elevator! And who in the business world thinks I'm crazy?

BIFF.   I didn't mean it like that, Pop. Now don't make a whole thing out of it, will ya?

WILLY.   Go back to the West! Be a carpenter, a cowboy, enjoy yourself!

LINDA.   Willy, he was just saying—

WILLY.   I heard what he said!

HAPPY (*trying to quiet* WILLY).   Hey, Pop, come on now . . .

WILLY (*continuing over* HAPPY's *line*).   They laugh at me, heh? Go to Filene's, go to the Hub, go to Slattery's, Boston. Call out the name Willy Loman and see what happens! Big shot!

BIFF.   All right, Pop.

WILLY.   Big!

BIFF.   All right!

WILLY.   Why do you always insult me?

BIFF.   I didn't say a word. (*To* LINDA.) Did I say a word?

LINDA.   He didn't say anything, Willy.

WILLY (*going to the doorway of the living-room*).   All right, good night, good night.

LINDA.   Willy, dear, he just decided . . .

WILLY (*to* BIFF).   If you get tired hanging around tomorrow, paint the ceiling I put up in the living-room.

BIFF.   I'm leaving early tomorrow.

HAPPY.   He's going to see Bill Oliver, Pop.

WILLY (*interestedly*).   Oliver? For what?

BIFF (*with reserve, but trying, trying*).   He always said he'd stake me. I'd like to go into business, so maybe I can take him up on it.

LINDA.   Isn't that wonderful?

WILLY.   Don't interrupt. What's wonderful about it? There's fifty men in the City of New York who'd stake him. (*To* BIFF.) Sporting goods?

BIFF.   I guess so. I know something about it and—

WILLY.   He knows something about it! You know sporting goods better than Spalding, for God's sake! How much is he giving you?

BIFF.   I don't know, I didn't even see him yet, but—

WILLY.   Then what're you talkin' about?

BIFF (*getting angry*).   Well, all I said was I'm gonna see him, that's all!

WILLY (*turning away*).   Ah, you're counting your chickens again.

BIFF (*starting left for the stairs*).   Oh, Jesus, I'm going to sleep!

WILLY (*calling after him*).   Don't curse in this house!

BIFF (*turning*).   Since when did you get so clean?

HAPPY (*trying to stop them*).   Wait a . . .

WILLY.   Don't use that language to me! I won't have it!

HAPPY (*grabbing* BIFF, *shouts*).   Wait a minute! I got an idea. I got a feasible idea. Come here, Biff, let's talk this over now, let's talk some sense here. When I was down in Florida last time, I thought of a great idea to sell sporting goods. It just came back to me. You and I, Biff—we have a line, the Loman Line. We train a couple of weeks, and put on a couple of exhibitions, see?

WILLY.   That's an idea!

HAPPY.   Wait! We form two basketball teams, see? Two water-polo teams. We play each other. It's a million dollars' worth of publicity. Two brothers, see? The Loman Brothers. Displays in the Royal Palms—all the hotels. And banners over the ring and the basketball court: "Loman Brothers." Baby, we could sell sporting goods!

WILLY.   That is a one-million-dollar idea!

LINDA.   Marvelous!

BIFF.   I'm in great shape as far as that's concerned.

HAPPY.   And the beauty of it is, Biff, it wouldn't be like a business. We'd be out playin' ball again . . .

BIFF (*enthused*).   Yeah, that's . . .

WILLY.   Million-dollar . . .

HAPPY.   And you wouldn't get fed up with it, Biff. It'd be the family again. There'd be the old honor, and comradeship, and if you wanted to go off for a swim or somethin'—well, you'd do it! Without some smart cooky gettin' up ahead of you!

WILLY.   Lick the world! You guys together could absolutely lick the civilized world.

BIFF.   I'll see Oliver tomorrow. Hap, if we could work that out . . .

LINDA.   Maybe things are beginning to—

WILLY (*wildly enthused, to* LINDA).   Stop interrupting! (*To* BIFF.) But don't wear sport jacket and slacks when you see Oliver.

BIFF.   No, I'll—

WILLY.   A business suit, and talk as little as possible, and don't crack any jokes.

BIFF.   He did like me. Always liked me.

LINDA.   He loved you!

WILLY (*to* LINDA).   Will you stop! (*To* BIFF.) Walk in very serious. You are not applying for a boy's job. Money is to pass. Be quiet, fine, and serious. Everybody likes a kidder, but nobody lends him money.

HAPPY.   I'll try to get some myself, Biff. I'm sure I can.

WILLY.   I see great things for you kids, I think your troubles are over. But remember, start big and you'll end big. Ask for fifteen. How much you gonna ask for?

BIFF.   Gee, I don't know—

WILLY.   And don't say "Gee." "Gee" is a boy's word. A man walking in for fifteen thousand dollars does not say "Gee!"

BIFF.   Ten, I think, would be top though.

WILLY.   Don't be so modest. You always started too low. Walk in with a big laugh. Don't look worried. Start off with a couple of your good stories to lighten things up. It's not what you say, it's how you say it—because personality always wins the day.

LINDA.   Oliver always thought the highest of him—

WILLY.   Will you let me talk?

BIFF.   Don't yell at her, Pop, will ya?

WILLY (*angrily*).   I was talking, wasn't I?

BIFF.   I don't like you yelling at her all the time, and I'm tellin' you, that's all.

WILLY.   What're you, takin' over this house?

LINDA.   Willy—

WILLY (*turning on her*).   Don't take his side all the time, goddammit!

BIFF (*furiously*).   Stop yelling at her!

WILLY (*suddenly pulling on his cheek, beaten down, guilt ridden*).   Give my best to Bill Oliver—he may remember me. (*He exits through the living-room doorway.*)

LINDA (*her voice subdued*).   What'd you have to start that for? (BIFF *turns away.*) You see how sweet he was as soon as you talked hopefully? (*She goes over to* BIFF.) Come up and say good night to him. Don't let him go to bed that way.

HAPPY.   Come on, Biff, let's buck him up.

LINDA.   Please, dear. Just say good night. It takes so little to make him happy. Come. (*She goes through the living-room doorway, calling upstairs from within the living-room.*) Your pajamas are hanging in the bathroom, Willy!

HAPPY (*looking toward where* LINDA *went out*).   What a woman! They broke the mold when they made her. You know that, Biff?

BIFF.   He's off salary. My God, working on commission!

HAPPY.   Well, let's face it: he's no hot-shot selling man. Except that sometimes, you have to admit, he's a sweet personality.

BIFF (*deciding*).   Lend me ten bucks, will ya? I want to buy some new ties.

HAPPY.   I'll take you to a place I know. Beautiful stuff. Wear one of my striped shirts tomorrow.

BIFF.   She got gray. Mom got awful old. Gee, I'm gonna go in to Oliver tomorrow and knock him for a—

HAPPY.   Come on up. Tell that to Dad. Let's give him a whirl. Come on.

BIFF (*steamed up*).   You know, with ten thousand bucks, boy!

HAPPY (*as they go into the living-room*).   That's the talk, Biff, that's the first time I've heard the old confidence out of you! (*From within the living-room, fading off.*) You're gonna live with me, kid, and any babe you want just say the word . . . (*The last lines are hardly heard. They are mounting the stairs to their parents' bedroom.*)

LINDA (*entering her bedroom and addressing* WILLY, *who is in the bathroom. She is straightening the bed for him*).   Can you do anything about the shower? It drips.

WILLY (*from the bathroom*).   All of a sudden everything falls to pieces! Goddam plumbing, oughta be sued, those people. I hardly finished putting it in and the thing . . . (*His words rumble off.*)

LINDA.   I'm just wondering if Oliver will remember him. You think he might?

WILLY (*coming out of the bathroom in his pajamas*).   Remember him? What's the matter with you, you crazy? If he'd've stayed with Oliver he'd be on top by now! Wait'll Oliver gets a look at him. You don't know the average caliber any more. The average young man today— (*he is getting into bed*) is got a caliber of zero. Greatest thing in the world for him was to bum around.

BIFF *and* HAPPY *enter the bedroom. Slight pause.*

WILLY (*stops short, looking at* BIFF).   Glad to hear it, boy.

HAPPY.   He wanted to say good night to you, sport.

WILLY (*to* BIFF).   Yeah. Knock him dead, boy. What'd you want to tell me?

BIFF.   Just take it easy, Pop. Good night. (*He turns to go.*)

WILLY (*unable to resist*).   And if anything falls off the desk while you're talking to him—like a package or something—don't you pick it up. They have office boys for that.

LINDA.   I'll make a big breakfast—

WILLY.   Will you let me finish? (*To* BIFF.) Tell him you were in the business in the West. Not farm work.

BIFF.   All right, Dad.

LINDA.   I think everything—

WILLY (*going right through her speech*).   And don't undersell yourself. No less than fifteen thousand dollars.

BIFF (*unable to bear him*).   Okay. Goodnight, Mom. (*He starts moving.*)

WILLY.   Because you got a greatness in you, Biff, remember that. You got all kinds a greatness . . . (*He lies back, exhausted.* BIFF *walks out.*)

LINDA (*calling after* BIFF).   Sleep well, darling!

HAPPY.   I'm gonna get married, Mom. I wanted to tell you.

LINDA.   Go to sleep, dear.

HAPPY (*going*).   I just wanted to tell you.

WILLY.   Keep up the good work. (HAPPY *exits.*) God . . . remember that Ebbets Field game? The championship of the city?

LINDA.   Just rest. Should I sing to you?

WILLY.   Yeah. Sing to me. (LINDA *hums a soft lullaby.*) When that team came out—he was the tallest, remember?

LINDA.   Oh, yes. And in gold.

BIFF *enters the darkened kitchen, takes a cigarette, and leaves the house. He comes downstage into a golden pool of light. He smokes, staring at the night.*

WILLY.   Like a young god. Hercules—something like that. And the sun, the sun all around him. Remember how he waved to me? Right up from the field, with the representatives of three colleges standing by? And the buyers I brought, and the cheers when he came out—Loman, Loman, Loman! God Almighty, he'll be great yet. A star like that, magnificent, can never really fade away!

The light on WILLY *is fading. The gas heater begins to glow through the kitchen wall, near the stairs, a blue flame beneath red coils.*

LINDA (*timidly*).   Willy dear, what has he got against you?

WILLY.   I'm so tired. Don't talk any more.

BIFF *slowly returns to the kitchen. He stops, stares toward the heater.*

LINDA.   Will you ask Howard to let you work in New York?

WILLY.   First thing in the morning. Everything'll be all right.

BIFF *reaches behind the heater and draws out a length of rubber tubing. He is horrified and turns his head toward* WILLY'S *room, still dimly lit, from which the strains of* LINDA'S *desperate but monotonous humming rise.*

WILLY (*staring through the window into the moonlight*).   Gee, look at the moon moving between the buildings!

BIFF *wraps the tubing around his hand and quickly goes up the stairs.*

ACT II

Music is heard, gay and bright. The curtain rises as the music fades away. WILLY, *in shirt sleeves, is sitting at the kitchen table, sipping coffee, his hat in his lap.* LINDA *is filling his cup when she can.*

WILLY.   Wonderful coffee. Meal in itself.

LINDA.   Can I make you some eggs?

WILLY.   No. Take a breath.

LINDA.   You look so rested, dear.

WILLY.   I slept like a dead one. First time in months. Imagine, sleeping till ten on a Tuesday morning. Boys left nice and early, heh?

LINDA.   They were out of here by eight o'clock.

WILLY.   Good work!

LINDA.   It was so thrilling to see them leaving together. I can't get over the shaving lotion in this house!

WILLY (*smiling*).   Mmm—

LINDA.   Biff was very changed this morning. His whole attitude seemed to be hopeful. He couldn't wait to get downtown to see Oliver.

WILLY.   He's heading for a change. There's no question, there simply are certain men that take longer to get—solidified. How did he dress?

LINDA.   His blue suit. He's so handsome in that suit. He could be a—anything in that suit!

WILLY *gets up from the table.* LINDA *holds his jacket for him.*

WILLY.   There's no question, no question at all. Gee, on the way home tonight I'd like to buy some seeds.

LINDA (*laughing*).   That'd be wonderful. But not enough sun gets back there. Nothing'll grow any more.

WILLY.   You wait, kid, before it's all over we're gonna get a little place out in the country, and I'll raise some vegetables, a couple of chickens . . .

LINDA.   You'll do it yet, dear.

WILLY *walks out of his jacket.* LINDA *follows him.*

WILLY.   And they'll get married, and come for a weekend. I'd build a little guest house. 'Cause I got so many fine tools, all I'd need would be a little lumber and some peace of mind.

LINDA (*joyfully*).   I sewed the lining . . .

WILLY.   I could build two guest houses, so they'd both come. Did he decide how much he's going to ask Oliver for?

LINDA (*getting him into the jacket*).   He didn't mention it, but I imagine ten or fifteen thousand. You going to talk to Howard today?

WILLY.   Yeah. I'll put it to him straight and simple. He'll just have to take me off the road.

LINDA.   And Willy, don't forget to ask for a little advance, because we've got the insurance premium. It's the grace period now.

WILLY.   That's a hundred . . . ?

LINDA.   A hundred and eight, sixty-eight. Because we're a little short again.

WILLY.   Why are we short?

LINDA.   Well, you had the motor job on the car . . .

WILLY.   That goddam Studebaker!

LINDA.   And you got one more payment on the refrigerator . . .

WILLY.   But it just broke again!

LINDA.   Well, it's old, dear.

WILLY.   I told you we should've bought a well-advertised machine. Charley bought a General Electric and it's twenty years old and it's still good, that son-of-a-bitch.

LINDA.   But, Willy—

WILLY.   Whoever heard of a Hastings refrigerator? Once in my life I would like to own something outright before it's broken! I'm always in a race with the junkyard! I just finished paying for the car and it's on its last legs. The refrigerator consumes belts like a goddam maniac. They time those things. They time them so when you finally paid for them, they're used up.

LINDA (*buttoning up his jacket as he unbuttons it*).   All told, about two hundred dollars would carry us, dear. But that includes the last payment on the mortgage. After this payment, Willy, the house belongs to us.

WILLY.   It's twenty-five years!

LINDA.   Biff was nine years old when we bought it.

WILLY.   Well, that's a great thing. To weather a twenty-five year mortgage is—

LINDA.   It's an accomplishment.

WILLY.   All the cement, the lumber, the reconstruction I put in this house! There ain't a crack to be found in it any more.

LINDA.   Well, it served its purpose.

WILLY.   What purpose? Some stranger'll come along, move in, and that's that. If only Biff would take this house, and raise a family . . . (*He starts to go.*) Good-by, I'm late.

LINDA (*suddenly remembering*).   Oh, I forgot! You're supposed to meet them for dinner.

WILLY.   Me?

LINDA.   At Frank's Chop House on Forty-eighth near Sixth Avenue.

WILLY.   Is that so! How about you?

LINDA.   No, just the three of you. They're gonna blow you to a big meal!

WILLY.   Don't say! Who thought of that?

LINDA.   Biff came to me this morning, Willy, and he said, "Tell Dad, we want to blow him to a big meal." Be there six o'clock. You and your two boys are going to have dinner.

WILLY.   Gee whiz! That's really somethin'. I'm gonna knock Howard for a loop, kid. I'll get an advance, and I'll come home with a New York job. Goddammit, now I'm gonna do it!

LINDA.   Oh, that's the spirit, Willy!

WILLY.   I will never get behind a wheel the rest of my life!

LINDA.   It's changing, Willy, I can feel it changing!

WILLY.   Beyond a question. G'by, I'm late. (*He starts to go again.*)

LINDA (*calling after him as she runs to the kitchen table for a handkerchief*).   You got your glasses?

WILLY (*feels for them, then comes back in*).   Yeah, yeah, got my glasses.

LINDA (*giving him the handkerchief*).   And a handkerchief.

WILLY.   Yeah, handkerchief.

LINDA.   And your saccharine?

WILLY.   Yeah, my saccharine.

LINDA.   Be careful on the subway stairs.

(*She kisses him, and a silk stocking is seen hanging from her hand. WILLY notices it.*)

WILLY.   Will you stop mending stockings? At least while I'm in the house. It gets me nervous. I can't tell you. Please.

LINDA *hides the stocking in her hand as she follows* WILLY *across the forestage in front of the house.*

LINDA.   Remember, Frank's Chop House.
WILLY (*passing the apron*).   Maybe beets would grow out there.
LINDA (*laughing*).   But you tried so many times.
WILLY.   Yeah. Well, don't work hard today. (*He disappears around the right corner of the house.*)
LINDA.   Be careful!

As WILLY *vanishes,* LINDA *waves to him. Suddenly the phone rings. She runs across the stage and into the kitchen and lifts it.*

LINDA.   Hello? Oh, Biff! I'm so glad you called, I just . . . Yes, sure, I just told him. Yes, he'll be there for dinner at six o'clock, I didn't forget. Listen, I was just dying to tell you. You know that little rubber pipe I told you about? That he connected to the gas heater? I finally decided to go down the cellar this morning and take it away and destroy it. But it's gone! Imagine? He took it away himself, it isn't there! (*She listens.*) When? Oh, then you took it. Oh—nothing, it's just that I'd hoped he'd taken it away himself. Oh, I'm not worried, darling, because this morning he left in such high spirits, it was like the old days! I'm not afraid any more. Did Mr. Oliver see you? . . . Well, you wait there then. And make a nice impression on him, darling. Just don't perspire too much before you see him. And have a nice time with Dad. He may have big news too! . . . That's right, a New York job. And be sweet to him tonight, dear. Be loving to him. Because he's only a little boat looking for a harbor. (*She is trembling with sorrow and joy.*) Oh, that's wonderful, Biff, you'll save his life. Thanks, darling. Just put your arm around him when he comes into the restaurant. Give him a smile. That's the boy . . . Good-by, dear . . . You got your comb? . . . That's fine. Good-by, Biff dear.

In the middle of her speech, HOWARD WAGNER, *thirty-six, wheels on a small typewriter table on which is a wire-recording machine and proceeds to plug it in. This is on the left forestage. Light slowly fades on* LINDA *as it rises on* HOWARD. HOWARD *is intent on threading the machine and only glances over his shoulder as* WILLY *appears.*

WILLY.   Pst! Pst!
HOWARD.   Hello, Willy, come in.
WILLY.   Like to have a little talk with you, Howard.
HOWARD.   Sorry to keep you waiting. I'll be with you in a minute.
WILLY.   What's that, Howard?
HOWARD.   Didn't you ever see one of these? Wire recorder.
WILLY.   Oh. Can we talk a minute?
HOWARD.   Records things. Just got delivery yesterday. Been driving me crazy, the most terrific machine I ever saw in my life. I was up all night with it.

WILLY.   What do you do with it?

HOWARD.   I bought it for dictation, but you can do anything with it. Listen to this. I had it home last night. Listen to what I picked up. The first one is my daughter. Get this. (*He flicks the switch and "Roll out the Barrel" is heard being whistled.*) Listen to that kid whistle.

WILLY.   That is lifelike, isn't it?

HOWARD.   Seven years old. Get that tone.

WILLY.   Ts, ts. Like to ask a little favor if you . . .

The whistling breaks off, and the voice of HOWARD's *daughter is heard.*

HIS DAUGHTER.   "Now you, Daddy."

HOWARD.   She's crazy for me! (*Again the same song is whistled.*) That's me! Ha! (*He winks.*)

WILLY.   You're very good!

The whistling breaks off again. The machine runs silent for a moment.

HOWARD.   Sh! Get this now, this is my son.

HIS SON.   "The capital of Alabama is Montgomery; the capital of Arizona is Phoenix; the capital of Arkansas is Little Rock; the capital of California is Sacramento . . ." (*and on, and on.*)

HOWARD (*holding up five fingers*).   Five years old, Willy!

WILLY.   He'll make an announcer some day!

HIS SON (*continuing*).   "The capital . . ."

HOWARD.   Get that—alphabetical order! (*The machine breaks off suddenly.*) Wait a minute. The maid kicked the plug out.

WILLY.   It certainly is a—

HOWARD.   Sh, for God's sake!

HIS SON.   "It's nine o'clock, Bulova watch time. So I have to go to sleep."

WILLY.   That really is—

HOWARD.   Wait a minute! The next is my wife.

They wait.

HOWARD'S VOICE.   "Go on, say something." (*Pause.*) "Well, you gonna talk?"

HIS WIFE.   "I can't think of anything."

HOWARD'S VOICE.   "Well, talk—it's turning."

HIS WIFE (*shyly, beaten*).   "Hello." (*Silence.*) "Oh, Howard, I can't talk into this . . ."

HOWARD (*snapping the machine off*).   That was my wife.

WILLY.   That is a wonderful machine. Can we—

HOWARD.   I tell you, Willy, I'm gonna take my camera, and my band-saw, and all my hobbies, and out they go. This is the most fascinating relaxation I ever found.

WILLY.   I think I'll get one myself.

HOWARD.   Sure, they're only a hundred and a half. You can't do without it. Supposing you wanna hear Jack Benny, see? But you can't be at home at that hour. So you tell the maid to turn the radio on when Jack Benny comes on, and this automatically goes on with the radio . . .

WILLY.   And when you come home you . . .

HOWARD.   You can come home twelve o'clock, one o'clock, any time you like, and you get yourself a Coke and sit yourself down, throw the switch, and there's Jack Benny's program in the middle of the night!

WILLY.   I'm definitely going to get one. Because lots of time I'm on the road, and I think to myself, what I must be missing on the radio!

HOWARD.   Don't you have a radio in the car?

WILLY.   Well, yeah, but who ever thinks of turning it on?

HOWARD.   Say, aren't you supposed to be in Boston?

WILLY.   That's what I want to talk to you about, Howard. You got a minute? (*He draws a chair in from the wing.*)

HOWARD.   What happened? What're you doing here?

WILLY.   Well . . .

HOWARD.   You didn't crack up again, did you?

WILLY.   Oh, no. No . . .

HOWARD.   Geez, you had me worried there for a minute. What's the trouble?

WILLY.   Well, tell you the truth, Howard, I've come to the decision that I'd rather not travel any more.

HOWARD.   Not travel! Well, what'll you do?

WILLY.   Remember, Christmas time, when you had the party here? You said you'd try to think of some spot for me here in town.

HOWARD.   With us?

WILLY.   Well, sure.

HOWARD.   Oh, yeah, yeah. I remember. Well, I couldn't think of anything for you, Willy.

WILLY.   I tell ya, Howard. The kids are all grown up, y'know. I don't need much any more. If I could take home—well, sixty-five dollars a week, I could swing it.

HOWARD.   Yeah, but Willy, see I—

WILLY.   I tell ya why, Howard. Speaking frankly and between the two of us, y'know—I'm just a little tired.

HOWARD.   Oh, I could understand that, Willy. But you're a road man, Willy, and we do a road business. We've only got a half-dozen salesmen on the floor here.

WILLY.   God knows, Howard, I never asked a favor of any man. But I was with the firm when your father used to carry you in here in his arms.

HOWARD.   I know that, Willy, but—

WILLY.   Your father came to me the day you were born and asked me what I thought of the name of Howard, may he rest in peace.

HOWARD.   I appreciate that, Willy, but there just is no spot here for you. If I had a spot I'd slam you right in, but I just don't have a single solitary spot.

He looks for his lighter. WILLY *has picked it up and gives it to him. Pause.*

WILLY (*with increasing anger*).   Howard, all I need to set my table is fifty dollars a week.

HOWARD.   But where am I going to put you, kid?

WILLY.   Look, it isn't a question of whether I can sell merchandise, is it?

HOWARD. No, but it's a business, kid, and everybody's gotta pull his own weight.

WILLY (*desperately*). Just let me tell you a story, Howard—

HOWARD. 'Cause you gotta admit, business is business.

WILLY (*angrily*). Business is definitely business, but just listen for a minute. You don't understand this. When I was a boy—eighteen, nineteen—I was already on the road. And there was a question in my mind as to whether selling had a future for me. Because in those days I had a yearning to go to Alaska. See, there were three gold strikes in one month in Alaska, and I felt like going out. Just for the ride, you might say.

HOWARD (*barely interested*). Don't say.

WILLY. Oh, yeah, my father lived many years in Alaska. He was an adventurous man. We've got quite a little streak of self-reliance in our family. I thought I'd go out with my older brother and try to locate him, and maybe settle in the North with the old man. And I was almost decided to go, when I met a salesman in the Parker House. His name was Dave Singleman. And he was eighty-four years old, and he'd drummed merchandise in thirty-one states. And old Dave, he'd go up to his room, y'understand, put on his green velvet slippers—I'll never forget—and pick up his phone and call the buyers, and without ever leaving his room, at the age of eighty-four, he made his living. And when I saw that, I realized that selling was the greatest career a man could want. 'Cause what could be more satisfying than to be able to go, at the age of eighty-four, into twenty or thirty different cities, and pick up a phone, and be remembered and loved and helped by so many different people? Do you know? when he died—and by the way he died the death of a salesman, in his green velvet slippers in the smoker of the New York, New Haven and Hartford, going into Boston—when he died, hundreds of salesmen and buyers were at his funeral. Things were sad on a lotta trains for months after that. (*He stands up.* HOWARD *has not looked at him.*) In those days there was personality in it, Howard. There was respect, and comradeship, and gratitude in it. Today, it's all cut and dried, and there's no chance for bringing friendship to bear—or personality. You see what I mean? They don't know me any more.

HOWARD (*moving away, to the right*). That's just the thing, Willy.

WILLY. If I had forty dollars a week—that's all I'd need. Forty dollars, Howard.

HOWARD. Kid, I can't take blood from a stone, I—

WILLY (*desperation is on him now*). Howard, the year Al Smith was nominated, your father came to me and—

HOWARD (*starting to go off*). I've got to see some people, kid.

WILLY (*stopping him*). I'm talking about your father! There were promises made across this desk! You mustn't tell me you've got people to see—I put thirty-four years into this firm, Howard, and now I can't pay my insurance! You can't eat the orange and throw the peel away—a man is not a piece of fruit! (*After a pause.*) Now pay attention. Your father—in 1928 I had a big year. I averaged a hundred and seventy dollars a week in commissions.

HOWARD (*impatiently*). Now, Willy, you never averaged—

WILLY (*banging his hand on the desk*).   I averaged a hundred and seventy dollars a week in the year of 1928! And your father came to me—or rather, I was in the office here—it was right over this desk—and he put his hand on my shoulder—

HOWARD (*getting up*).   You'll have to excuse me, Willy, I gotta see some people. Pull yourself together. (*Going out.*) I'll be back in a little while.

On HOWARD's *exit, the light on his chair grows very bright and strange.*

WILLY.   Pull myself together! What the hell did I say to him? My God, I was yelling at him! How could I! (WILLY *breaks off, staring at the light, which occupies the chair, animating it. He approaches this chair, standing across the desk from it.*) Frank, Frank, don't you remember what you told me that time? How you put your hand on my shoulder, and Frank . . . (*He leans on the desk and as he speaks the dead man's name he accidentally switches on the recorder, and instantly.*)

HOWARD'S SON.   ". . . of New York is Albany. The capital of Ohio is Cincinnati, the capital of Rhode Island is . . ." (*The recitation continues.*)

WILLY (*leaping away with fright, shouting*).   Ha! Howard! Howard! Howard!

HOWARD (*rushing in*).   What happened?

WILLY (*pointing at the machine, which continues nasally, childishly, with the capital cities*).   Shut it off! Shut it off!

HOWARD (*pulling the plug out*).   Look, Willy . . .

WILLY (*pressing his hands to his eyes*).   I gotta get myself some coffee. I'll get some coffee . . .

WILLY *starts to walk out.* HOWARD *stops him.*

HOWARD (*rolling up the cord*).   Willy, look . . .

WILLY.   I'll go to Boston.

HOWARD.   Willy, you can't go to Boston for us.

WILLY.   Why can't I go?

HOWARD.   I don't want you to represent us. I've been meaning to tell you for a long time now.

WILLY.   Howard, are you firing me?

HOWARD.   I think you need a good long rest, Willy.

WILLY.   Howard—

HOWARD.   And when you feel better, come back, and we'll see if we can work something out.

WILLY.   But I gotta earn money, Howard. I'm in no position to—

HOWARD.   Where are your sons? Why don't your sons give you a hand?

WILLY.   They're working on a very big deal.

HOWARD.   This is no time for false pride, Willy. You go to your sons and you tell them that you're tired. You've got two great boys, haven't you?

WILLY.   Oh, no question, no question, but in the meantime . . .

HOWARD.   Then that's that, heh?

WILLY.   All right, I'll go to Boston tomorrow.

HOWARD.   No, no.

WILLY.   I can't throw myself on my sons. I'm not a cripple!

HOWARD.   Look, kid, I'm busy this morning.

WILLY (*grasping* HOWARD's *arm*).   Howard, you've got to let me go to Boston!

HOWARD (*hard, keeping himself under control*).   I've got a line of people to see this morning. Sit down, take five minutes, and pull yourself together, and then go home, will ya? I need the office, Willy. (*He starts to go, turns, remembering the recorder, starts to push off the table holding the recorder.*) Oh, yeah. Whenever you can this week, stop by and drop off the samples. You'll feel better, Willy, and then come back and we'll talk. Pull yourself together, kid, there's people outside.

HOWARD *exits, pushing the table off left.* WILLY *stares into space, exhausted. Now the music is heard—*BEN's *music—first distantly, then closer, closer. As* WILLY *speaks,* BEN *enters from the right. He carries valise and umbrella.*

WILLY.   Oh, Ben, how did you do it? What is the answer? Did you wind up the Alaska deal already?

BEN.   Doesn't take much time if you know what you're doing. Just a short business trip. Boarding ship in an hour. Wanted to say good-by.

WILLY.   Ben, I've got to talk to you.

BEN (*glancing at his watch*).   Haven't the time, William.

WILLY (*crossing the apron to* BEN).   Ben, nothing's working out. I don't know what to do.

BEN.   Now, look here, William. I've bought timberland in Alaska and I need a man to look after things for me.

WILLY.   God, timberland! Me and my boys in those grand outdoors!

BEN.   You've a new continent at your doorstep, William. Get out of these cities, they're full of talk and time payments and courts of law. Screw on your fists and you can fight for a fortune up there.

WILLY.   Yes, yes! Linda, Linda!

LINDA *enters as of old, with the wash.*

LINDA.   Oh, you're back?

BEN.   I haven't much time.

WILLY.   No, wait! Linda, he's got a proposition for me in Alaska.

LINDA.   But you've got— (*To* BEN.) He's got a beautiful job here.

WILLY.   But in Alaska, kid, I could—

LINDA.   You're doing well enough, Willy!

BEN (*to* LINDA).   Enough for what, my dear?

LINDA (*frightened of* BEN *and angry at him*).   Don't say those things to him! Enough to be happy right here, right now. (*To* WILLY, *while* BEN *laughs.*) Why must everybody conquer the world? You're well liked, and the boys love you, and someday— (*to* BEN)—why, old man Wagner told him just the other day that if he keeps it up he'll be a member of the firm, didn't he, Willy?

WILLY.   Sure, sure. I am building something with this firm, Ben, and if a man is building something he must be on the right track, mustn't he?

BEN.   What are you building? Lay your hand on it. Where is it?

WILLY (*hesitantly*).   That's true, Linda, there's nothing.

LINDA.   Why? (*To* BEN.) There's a man eighty-four years old—

WILLY.   That's right, Ben, that's right. When I look at that man I say, what is there to worry about?

BEN.   Bah!

WILLY.   It's true, Ben. All he has to do is go into any city, pick up the phone, and he's making his living and you know why?

BEN (*picking up his valise*).   I've got to go.

WILLY (*holding* BEN *back*).   Look at this boy!

BIFF, *in his high school sweater, enters carrying suitcase.* HAPPY *carries* BIFF's *shoulder guards, gold helmet, and football pants.*

WILLY.   Without a penny to his name, three great universities are begging for him, and from there the sky's the limit, because it's not what you do, Ben. It's who you know and the smile on your face! It's contacts, Ben, contacts! The whole wealth of Alaska passes over the lunch table at the Commodore Hotel, and that's the wonder, the wonder of this country, that a man can end with diamonds here on the basis of being liked! (*He turns to* BIFF.) And that's why when you get out on that field today it's important. Because thousands of people will be rooting for you and loving you. (*To* BEN, *who has again begun to leave.*) And Ben! when he walks into a business office his name will sound out like a bell and all the doors will open to him! I've seen it, Ben, I've seen it a thousand times! You can't feel it with your hand like timber, but it's there!

BEN.   Good-by, William.

WILLY.   Ben, am I right? Don't you think I'm right? I value your advice.

BEN.   There's a new continent at your doorstep, William. You could walk out rich. Rich! (*He is gone.*)

WILLY.   We'll do it here, Ben! You hear me? We're gonna do it here!

Young BERNARD *rushes in. The gay music of the Boys is heard.*

BERNARD.   Oh, gee, I was afraid you left already!

WILLY.   Why? What time is it?

BERNARD.   It's half-past one!

WILLY.   Well, come on, everybody! Ebbets Field next stop! Where's the pennants? (*He rushes through the wall-line of the kitchen and out into the living-room.*)

LINDA (*to* BIFF).   Did you pack fresh underwear?

BIFF (*who has been limbering up*).   I want to go!

BERNARD.   Biff, I'm carrying your helmet, ain't I?

HAPPY.   No, I'm carrying the helmet.

BERNARD.   Oh, Biff, you promised me.

HAPPY.   I'm carrying the helmet.

BERNARD.   How am I going to get in the locker room?

LINDA.   Let him carry the shoulder guards. (*She puts her coat and hat on in the kitchen.*)

BERNARD. Can I, Biff? 'Cause I told everybody I'm going to be in the locker room.

HAPPY. In Ebbets Field it's the clubhouse.

BERNARD. I meant the clubhouse. Biff!

HAPPY. Biff!

BIFF (*grandly, after a slight pause*). Let him carry the shoulder guards.

HAPPY (*as he gives* BERNARD *the shoulder guards*). Stay close to us now.

WILLY *rushes in with the pennants.*

WILLY (*handing them out*). Everybody wave when Biff comes out on the field. (HAPPY *and* BERNARD *run off.*) You set now, boy?

The music has died away.

BIFF. Ready to go, Pop. Every muscle is ready.

WILLY (*at the edge of the apron*). You realize what this means?

BIFF. That's right, Pop.

WILLY (*feeling* BIFF's *muscles*). You're comin' home this afternoon captain of the All-Scholastic Championship Team of the City of New York.

BIFF. I got it, Pop. And remember, pal, when I take off my helmet, that touchdown is for you.

WILLY. Let's go! (*He is starting out, with his arm around* BIFF, *when* CHARLEY *enters, as of old, in knickers.*) I got no room for you, Charley.

CHARLEY. Room? For what?

WILLY. In the car.

CHARLEY. You goin' for a ride? I wanted to shoot some casino.

WILLY (*furiously*). Casino! (*Incredulously.*) Don't you realize what today is?

LINDA. Oh, he knows, Willy. He's just kidding you.

WILLY. That's nothing to kid about!

CHARLEY. No. Linda, what's goin' on?

LINDA. He's playing in Ebbets Field.

CHARLEY. Baseball in this weather?

WILLY. Don't talk to him. Come on, come on! (*He is pushing them out.*)

CHARLEY. Wait a minute, didn't you hear the news?

WILLY. What?

CHARLEY. Don't you listen to the radio? Ebbets Field just blew up.

WILLY. You go to hell! (CHARLEY *laughs. Pushing them out.*) Come on, come on! We're late.

CHARLEY (*as they go*). Knock a homer, Biff, knock a homer!

WILLY (*the last to leave, turning to* CHARLEY). I don't think that was funny, Charley. This is the greatest day of his life.

CHARLEY. Willy, when are you going to grow up?

WILLY. Yeah, heh? When this game is over, Charley, you'll be laughing out of the other side of your face. They'll be calling him another Red Grange. Twenty-five thousand a year.

CHARLEY (*kidding*). Is that so?

WILLY. Yeah, that's so.

CHARLEY. Well, then, I'm sorry, Willy. But tell me something.

WILLY.   What?

CHARLEY.   Who is Red Grange?

WILLY.   Put up your hands. Goddam you, put up your hands!

CHARLEY, *chuckling, shakes his head and walks away, around the left corner of the stage.* WILLY *follows him. The music rises to a mocking frenzy.*

WILLY.   Who the hell do you think you are, better then everybody else? You don't know everything, you big, ignorant, stupid . . . Put up your hands!

Light rises, on the right side of the forestage, on a small table in the reception room of CHARLEY's *office. Traffic sounds are heard.* BERNARD, *now mature, sits whistling to himself. A pair of tennis rackets and an overnight bag are on the floor beside him.*

WILLY (*offstage*).   What are you walking away for? Don't walk away! If you're going to say something say it to my face! I know you laugh at me behind my back. You'll laugh out of the other side of your goddam face after this game. Touchdown! Touchdown! Eighty thousand people! Touchdown! Right between the goal posts.

BERNARD *is a quiet, earnest, but self-assured young man.* WILLY's *voice is coming from right upstage now.* BERNARD *lowers his feet off the table and listens.* JENNY, *his father's secretary, enters.*

JENNY (*distressed*).   Say, Bernard, will you go out in the hall?

BERNARD.   What is that noise? Who is it?

JENNY.   Mr. Loman. He just got off the elevator.

BERNARD (*getting up*).   Who's he arguing with?

JENNY.   Nobody. There's nobody with him. I can't deal with him any more, and your father gets all upset everytime he comes. I've got a lot of typing to do, and your father's waiting to sign it. Will you see him?

WILLY (*entering*).   Touchdown! Touch— (*He sees* JENNY.) Jenny, Jenny, good to see you. How're ya? Workin'? Or still honest?

JENNY.   Fine. How've you been feeling?

WILLY.   Not much any more, Jenny. Ha, ha! (*He is surprised to see the rackets.*)

BERNARD.   Hello, Uncle Willy.

WILLY (*almost shocked*).   Bernard! Well, look who's here! (*He comes quickly, guiltily, to* BERNARD *and warmly shakes his hand.*)

BERNARD.   How are you? Good to see you.

WILLY.   What are you doing here?

BERNARD.   Oh, just stopped by to see Pop. Get off my feet till my train leaves. I'm going to Washington in a few minutes.

WILLY.   Is he in?

BERNARD.   Yes, he's in his office with the accountant. Sit down.

WILLY (*sitting down*).   What're you going to do in Washington?

BERNARD.   Oh, just a case I've got there, Willy.

WILLY.   That so? (*Indicating the rackets.*) You going to play tennis there?

BERNARD.   I'm staying with a friend who's got a court.

WILLY.   Don't say. His own tennis court. Must be fine people, I bet.

BERNARD.   They are, very nice. Dad tells me Biff's in town.

WILLY (*with a big smile*).   Yeah, Biff's in. Working on a very big deal, Bernard.

BERNARD.   What's Biff doing?

WILLY.   Well, he's been doing very big things in the West. But he decided to establish himself here. Very big. We're having dinner. Did I hear your wife had a boy?

BERNARD.   That's right. Our second.

WILLY.   Two boys! What do you know!

BERNARD.   What kind of a deal has Biff got?

WILLY.   Well, Bill Oliver—very big sporting-goods man—he wants Biff very badly. Called him in from the West. Long distance, carte blanche, special deliveries. Your friends have their own private tennis court?

BERNARD.   You still with the old firm, Willy?

WILLY (*after a pause*).   I'm—I'm overjoyed to see how you made the grade, Bernard, overjoyed. It's an encouraging thing to see a young man really—really—Looks very good for Biff—very— (*He breaks off, then.*) Bernard— (*He is so full of emotion, he breaks off again.*)

BERNARD.   What is it, Willy?

WILLY (*small and alone*).   What—what's the secret?

BERNARD.   What secret?

WILLY.   How—how did you? Why didn't he ever catch on?

BERNARD.   I wouldn't know that, Willy.

WILLY (*confidentially, desperately*).   You were his friend, his boyhood friend. There's something I don't understand about it. His life ended after that Ebbets Field game. From the age of seventeen nothing good ever happened to him.

BERNARD.   He never trained himself for anything.

WILLY.   But he did, he did. After high school he took so many correspondence courses. Radio mechanics; television; God knows what, and never made the slightest mark.

BERNARD (*taking off his glasses*).   Willy, do you want to talk candidly?

WILLY (*rising, faces* BERNARD).   I regard you as a very brilliant man, Bernard. I value your advice.

BERNARD.   Oh, the hell with the advice, Willy. I couldn't advise you. There's just one thing I've always wanted to ask you. When he was supposed to graduate, and the math teacher flunked him—

WILLY.   Oh, that son-of-a-bitch ruined his life.

BERNARD.   Yeah, but, Willy, all he had to do was go to summer school and make up that subject.

WILLY.   That's right, that's right.

BERNARD.   Did you tell him not to go to summer school?

WILLY.   Me? I begged him to go. I ordered him to go!

BERNARD.   Then why wouldn't he go?

WILLY.   Why? Why! Bernard, that question has been trailing me like a ghost for the last fifteen years. He flunked the subject, and laid down and died like a hammer hit him!

BERNARD.   Take it easy, kid.

WILLY.   Let me talk to you—I got nobody to talk to. Bernard, Bernard, was it my fault? Y'see? It keeps going around in my mind, maybe I did something to him. I got nothing to give him.

BERNARD.   Don't take it so hard.

WILLY.   Why did he lay down? What is the story there? You were his friend!

BERNARD.   Willy, I remember, it was June, and our grades came out. And he'd flunked math.

WILLY.   That son-of-a-bitch!

BERNARD.   No, it wasn't right then. Biff just got very angry, I remember, and he was ready to enroll in summer school.

WILLY (*surprised*).   He was?

BERNARD.   He wasn't beaten by it at all. But then, Willy, he disappeared from the block for almost a month. And I got the idea that he'd gone up to New England to see you. Did he have a talk with you then?

WILLY *stares in silence.*

BERNARD.   Willy?

WILLY (*with a stronge edge of resentment in his voice*).   Yeah, he came to Boston. What about it?

BERNARD.   Well, just that when he came back—I'll never forget this, it always mystifies me. Because I'd thought so well of Biff, even though he'd always taken advantage of me. I loved him, Willy, y'know? And he came back after that month and took his sneakers—remember those sneakers with "University of Virginia" printed on them? He was so proud of those, wore them every day. And he took them down in the cellar, and burned them up in the furnace. We had a fist fight. It lasted at least half an hour. Just the two of us, punching each other down the cellar, and crying right through it. I've often thought of how strange it was that I knew he'd given up his life. What happened in Boston, Willy?

WILLY *looks at him as at an intruder.*

BERNARD.   I just bring it up because you asked me.

WILLY (*angrily*).   Nothing. What do you mean, "What happened?" What's that got to do with anything?

BERNARD.   Well, don't get sore.

WILLY.   What are you trying to do, blame it on me? If a boy lays down is that my fault?

BERNARD.   Now, Willy, don't get—

WILLY.   Well, don't—don't talk to me that way! What does that mean, "What happened?"

CHARLEY *enters. He is in his vest, and he carries a bottle of bourbon.*

CHARLEY.   Hey, you're going to miss that train. (*He waves the bottle.*)

BERNARD.   Yeah, I'm going. (*He takes the bottle.*) Thanks, Pop. (*He picks up his rackets and bag.*) Good-by, Willy, and don't worry about it. You know, "If at first you don't succeed . . ."

WILLY.   Yes, I believe in that.

BERNARD.   But sometimes, Willy, it's better for a man just to walk away.

WILLY.   Walk away?

BERNARD.   That's right.

WILLY.   But if you can't walk away?

BERNARD (*after a slight pause*).   I guess that's when it's tough. (*Extending his hand.*) Good-by, Willy.

CHARLEY (*an arm on* BERNARD's *shoulder*).   How do you like this kid? Gonna argue a case in front of the Supreme Court.

BERNARD (*protesting*).   Pop!

WILLY (*genuinely shocked, pained, and happy*).   No! The Supreme Court!

BERNARD.   I gotta run. 'By, Dad!

CHARLEY.   Knock 'em dead, Bernard!

BERNARD *goes off.*

WILLY (*as* CHARLEY *takes out his wallet*).   The Supreme Court! And he didn't even mention it!

CHARLEY (*counting out money on the desk*).   He don't have to—he's gonna do it.

WILLY.   And you never told him what to do, did you? You never took any interest in him.

CHARLEY.   My salvation is that I never took any interest in anything. There's some money—fifty dollars. I got an accountant inside.

WILLY.   Charley, look . . . (*With difficulty.*) I got my insurance to pay. If you can arrange it—I need a hundred and ten dollars.

CHARLEY *doesn't reply for a moment; merely stops moving.*

WILLY.   I'd draw it from my bank but Linda would know, and I . . .

CHARLEY.   Sit down, Willy.

WILLY (*moving toward the chair*).   I'm keeping an account of everything, remember. I'll pay every penny back. (*He sits.*)

CHARLEY.   Now listen to me, Willy.

WILLY.   I want you to know I appreciate . . .

CHARLEY (*sitting down on the table*).   Willy, what're you doin'? What the hell is goin' on in your head?

WILLY.   Why? I'm simply . . .

CHARLEY.   I offered you a job. You can make fifty dollars a week. And I won't send you on the road.

WILLY.   I've got a job.

CHARLEY.   Without pay? What kind of a job is a job without pay? (*He rises.*) Now, look, kid, enough is enough. I'm no genius but I know when I'm being insulted.

WILLY.   Insulted!

CHARLEY.   Why don't you want to work for me?

WILLY.   What's the matter with you? I've got a job.

CHARLEY.   Then what're you walkin' in here every week for?

WILLY (*getting up*).   Well, if you don't want me to walk in here—

CHARLEY.   I am offering you a job.

WILLY.   I don't want your goddam job!

CHARLEY.   When the hell are you going to grow up?

WILLY (*furiously*).   You big ignoramus, if you say that to me again I'll rap you one! I don't care how big you are! (*He's ready to fight.*)

Pause.

CHARLEY (*kindly, going to him*).   How much do you need, Willy?

WILLY.   Charley, I'm strapped, I'm strapped. I don't know what to do. I was just fired.

CHARLEY.   Howard fired you?

WILLY.   That snotnose. Imagine that? I named him. I named him Howard.

CHARLEY.   Willy, when're you gonna realize that them things don't mean anything? You named him Howard, but you can't sell that. The only thing you got in this world is what you can sell. And the funny thing is that you're a salesman, and you don't know that.

WILLY.   I've always tried to think otherwise, I guess. I always felt that if a man was impressive, and well liked, that nothing—

CHARLEY.   Why must everybody like you? Who liked J.P. Morgan? Was he impressive? In a Turkish bath he'd look like a butcher. But with his pockets on he was very well liked. Now listen, Willy, I know you don't like me, and nobody can say I'm in love with you, but I'll give you a job because—just for the hell of it, put it that way. Now what do you say?

WILLY.   I—I just can't work for you, Charley.

CHARLEY.   What're you, jealous of me?

WILLY.   I can't work for you, that's all, don't ask me why.

CHARLEY (*angered, takes out more bills*).   You been jealous of me all your life, you damned fool! Here, pay your insurance. (*He puts the money in* WILLY's *hand.*)

WILLY.   I'm keeping strict accounts.

CHARLEY.   I've got some work to do. Take care of yourself. And pay your insurance.

WILLY (*moving to the right*).   Funny, y'know? After all the highways, and the trains, and the appointments, and the years, you end up worth more dead than alive.

CHARLEY.   Willy, nobody's worth nothin' dead. (*After a slight pause.*) Did you hear what I said?

WILLY *stands still, dreaming.*

CHARLEY.   Willy!

WILLY.   Apologize to Bernard for me when you see him. I didn't mean to argue with him. He's a fine boy. They're all fine boys, and they'll end up big—all of them. Someday they'll all play tennis together. Wish me luck, Charley. He saw Bill Oliver today.

CHARLEY.   Good luck.

WILLY (*on the verge of tears*).   Charley, you're the only friend I got. Isn't that a remarkable thing? (*He goes out.*)

CHARLEY.   Jesus!

CHARLEY *stares after him a moment and follows. All light blacks out. Suddenly raucous music is heard, and a red glow rises behind the screen at right.* STANLEY, *a young waiter, appears, carrying a table, followed by* HAPPY, *who is carrying two chairs.*

STANLEY (*putting the table down*).   That's all right, Mr. Loman, I can handle it myself. (*He turns and takes the chairs from* HAPPY *and places them at the table.*)

HAPPY (*glancing around*).   Oh, this is better.

STANLEY.   Sure, in the front there you're in the middle of all kinds a noise. Whenever you got a party, Mr. Loman, you just tell me and I'll put you back here. Y'know, there's a lotta people they don't like it private, because when they go out they like to see a lotta action around them because they're sick and tired to stay in the house by theirself. But I know you, you ain't from Hackensack. You know what I mean?

HAPPY (*sitting down*).   So how's it coming, Stanley?

STANLEY.   Ah, it's a dog's life. I only wish during the war they'd a took me in the Army. I coulda been dead by now.

HAPPY.   My brother's back, Stanley.

STANLEY.   Oh, he come back, heh? From the Far West.

HAPPY.   Yeah, big cattle man, my brother, so treat him right. And my father's coming too.

STANLEY.   Oh, your father too!

HAPPY.   You got a couple of nice lobsters?

STANLEY.   Hundred per cent, big.

HAPPY.   I want them with the claws.

STANLEY.   Don't worry, I don't give you no mice. (HAPPY *laughs.*) How about some wine? It'll put a head on the meal.

HAPPY.   No. You remember, Stanley, that recipe I brought you from overseas? With the champagne in it?

STANLEY.   Oh, yeah, sure. I still got it tacked up yet in the kitchen. But that'll have to cost a buck apiece anyways.

HAPPY.   That's all right.

STANLEY.   What'd you, hit a number or somethin'?

HAPPY.   No, it's a little celebration. My brother is—I think he pulled off a big deal today. I think we're going into business together.

STANLEY.   Great! That's the best for you. Because a family business, you know what I mean?—that's the best.

HAPPY.   That's what I think.

STANLEY.   'Cause what's the difference? Somebody steals? It's in the family. Know what I mean? (*Sotto voce.*) Like this bartender here. The boss is goin' crazy what kinda leak he's got in the cash register. You put it in but it don't come out.

HAPPY (*raising his head*).   Sh!

STANLEY.   What?

HAPPY.   You notice I wasn't lookin' right or left, was I?

STANLEY. No.

HAPPY. And my eyes are closed.

STANLEY. So what's the—?

HAPPY. Strudel's comin'.

STANLEY (*catching on, looks around*). Ah, no, there's no—

He breaks off as a furred, lavishly dressed girl enters and sits at the next table. Both follow her with their eyes.

STANLEY. Geez, how'd ya know?

HAPPY. I got radar or something. (*Staring directly at her profile.*) Oooooooo . . . Stanley.

STANLEY. I think that's for you, Mr. Loman.

HAPPY. Look at that mouth. Oh, God. And the binoculars.

STANLEY. Geez, you got a life, Mr. Loman.

HAPPY. Wait on her.

STANLEY (*going to the girl's table*). Would you like a menu, ma'am?

GIRL. I'm expecting someone, but I'd like a—

HAPPY. Why don't you bring her—excuse me, miss, do you mind? I sell champagne, and I'd like you to try my brand. Bring her a champagne, Stanley.

GIRL. That's awfully nice of you.

HAPPY. Don't mention it. It's all company money. (*He laughs.*)

GIRL. That's a charming product to be selling, isn't it?

HAPPY. Oh, gets to be like everything else. Selling is selling, y'know.

GIRL. I suppose.

HAPPY. You don't happen to sell, do you?

GIRL. No, I don't sell.

HAPPY. Would you object to a compliment from a stranger? You ought to be on a magazine cover.

GIRL (*looking at him a little archly*). I have been.

STANLEY *comes in with a glass of champagne.*

HAPPY. What'd I say before, Stanley? You see? She's a cover girl.

STANLEY. Oh, I could see, I could see.

HAPPY (*to the* GIRL). What magazine?

GIRL. Oh, a lot of them. (*She takes the drink.*) Thank you.

HAPPY. You know what they say in France, don't you? "Champagne is the drink of the complexion"—Hya, Biff!

BIFF *has entered and sits with* HAPPY.

BIFF. Hello, kid. Sorry I'm late.

HAPPY. I just got here. Uh, Miss—?

GIRL. Forsythe.

HAPPY. Miss Forsythe, this is my brother.

BIFF. Is Dad here?

HAPPY. His name is Biff. You might've heard of him. Great football player.

GIRL.   Really? What team?

HAPPY.   Are you familiar with football?

GIRL.   No, I'm afraid I'm not.

HAPPY.   Biff is quarterback with the New York Giants.

GIRL.   Well, that is nice, isn't it? (*She drinks.*)

HAPPY.   Good health.

GIRL.   I'm happy to meet you.

HAPPY.   That's my name. Hap. It's really Harold, but at West Point they called me Happy.

GIRL (*now really impressed*).   Oh, I see. How do you do? (*She turns her profile.*)

BIFF.   Isn't Dad coming?

HAPPY.   You want her?

BIFF.   Oh, I could never make that.

HAPPY.   I remember the time that idea would never come into your head. Where's the old confidence, Biff?

BIFF.   I just saw Oliver—

HAPPY.   Wait a minute. I've got to see that old confidence again. Do you want her? She's on call.

BIFF.   Oh, no. (*He turns to look at the* GIRL.)

HAPPY.   I'm telling you. Watch this. (*Turning to the* GIRL.) Honey? (*She turns to him.*) Are you busy?

GIRL.   Well, I am . . . but I could make a phone call.

HAPPY.   Do that, will you, honey? And see if you can get a friend. We'll be here for a while. Biff is one of the greatest football players in the country.

GIRL (*standing up*).   Well, I'm certainly happy to meet you.

HAPPY.   Come back soon.

GIRL.   I'll try.

HAPPY.   Don't try, honey, try hard.

The GIRL *exits.* STANLEY *follows, shaking his head in bewildered admiration.*

HAPPY.   Isn't that a shame now? A beautiful girl like that? That's why I can't get married. There's not a good woman in a thousand. New York is loaded with them, kid!

BIFF.   Hap, look—

HAPPY.   I told you she was on call!

BIFF (*strangely unnerved*).   Cut it out, will ya? I want to say something to you.

HAPPY.   Did you see Oliver?

BIFF.   I saw him all right. Now look, I want to tell Dad a couple of things and I want you to help me.

HAPPY.   What? Is he going to back you?

BIFF.   Are you crazy? You're out of your goddam head, you know that?

HAPPY.   Why? What happened?

BIFF (*breathlessly*).   I did a terrible thing today, Hap. It's been the strangest day I ever went through. I'm all numb, I swear.

HAPPY. You mean he wouldn't see you?

BIFF. Well, I waited six hours for him, see? All day. Kept sending my name in. Even tried to date his secretary so she'd get me to him, but no soap.

HAPPY. Because you're not showin' the old confidence, Biff. He remembered you, didn't he?

BIFF (*stopping* HAPPY *with a gesture*). Finally, about five o'clock, he comes out. Didn't remember who I was or anything. I felt like such an idiot, Hap.

HAPPY. Did you tell him my Florida idea?

BIFF. He walked away. I saw him for one minute. I got so mad I could've torn the walls down! How the hell did I ever get the idea I was a salesman there? I even believed myself that I'd been a salesman for him! And then he gave me one look and—I realized what a ridiculous lie my whole life has been! We've been talking in a dream for fifteen years. I was a shipping clerk.

HAPPY. What'd you do?

BIFF (*with great tension and wonder*). Well, he left, see. And the secretary went out. I was all alone in the waiting-room. I don't know what came over me, Hap. The next thing I know I'm in his office—paneled walls, everything. I can't explain it. I—Hap, I took his fountain pen.

HAPPY. Geez, did he catch you?

BIFF. I ran out. I ran down all eleven flights. I ran and ran and ran.

HAPPY. That was an awful dumb—what'd you do that for?

BIFF (*agonized*). I don't know, I just—wanted to take something, I don't know. You gotta help me, Hap, I'm gonna tell Pop.

HAPPY. You crazy? What for?

BIFF. Hap, he's got to understand that I'm not the man somebody lends that kind of money to. He thinks I've been spiting him all these years and it's eating him up.

HAPPY. That's just it. You tell him something nice.

BIFF. I can't.

HAPPY. Say you got a lunch date with Oliver tomorrow.

BIFF. So what do I do tomorrow?

HAPPY. You leave the house tomorrow and come back at night and say Oliver is thinking it over. And he thinks it over for a couple of weeks, and gradually it fades away and nobody's the worse.

BIFF. But it'll go on forever!

HAPPY. Dad is never so happy as when he's looking forward to something!

WILLY *enters.*

HAPPY. Hello, scout!

WILLY. Gee, I haven't been here in years!

STANLEY *has followed* WILLY *in and sets a chair for him.* STANLEY *starts off but* HAPPY *stops him.*

HAPPY. Stanley!

STANLEY *stands by, waiting for an order.*

BIFF (*going to* WILLY *with guilt, as to an invalid*).   Sit down, Pop. You want a drink?

WILLY.   Sure, I don't mind.

BIFF.   Let's get a load on.

WILLY.   You look worried.

BIFF.   N-no. (*To* STANLEY.) Scotch all around. Make it doubles.

STANLEY.   Doubles, right. (*He goes.*)

WILLY.   You had a couple already, didn't you?

BIFF.   Just a couple, yeah.

WILLY.   Well, what happened, boy? (*Nodding affirmatively, with a smile.*) Everything go all right?

BIFF (*takes a breath, then reaches out and grasps* WILLY's *hand*).   Pal . . . (*He is smiling bravely, and* WILLY *is smiling too.*) I had an experience today.

HAPPY.   Terrific, Pop.

WILLY.   That so? What happened?

BIFF (*high, slightly alcoholic, above the earth*).   I'm going to tell you everything from first to last. It's been a strange day. (*Silence. He looks around, composes himself as best he can, but his breath keeps breaking the rhythm of his voice.*) I had to wait quite a while for him, and—

WILLY.   Oliver?

BIFF.   Yeah, Oliver. All day, as a matter of cold fact. And a lot of— instances—facts, Pop, facts about my life came back to me. Who was it, Pop? Who ever said I was a salesman with Oliver?

WILLY.   Well, you were.

BIFF.   No, Dad, I was a shipping clerk.

WILLY.   But you were practically—

BIFF (*with determination*).   Dad, I don't know who said it first, but I was never a salesman for Bill Oliver.

WILLY.   What're you talking about?

BIFF.   Let's hold on to the facts tonight, Pop. We're not going to get anywhere bullin' around. I was a shipping clerk.

WILLY (*angrily*).   All right, now listen to me—

BIFF.   Why don't you let me finish?

WILLY.   I'm not interested in stories about the past or any crap of that kind because the woods are burning, boys, you understand? There's a big blaze going on all around. I was fired today.

BIFF (*shocked*).   How could you be?

WILLY.   I was fired, and I'm looking for a little good news to tell your mother, because the woman has waited and the woman has suffered. The gist of it is that I haven't got a story left in my head, Biff. So don't give me a lecture about facts and aspects. I am not interested. Now what've you got to say to me?

STANLEY *enters with three drinks. They wait until he leaves.*

WILLY.   Did you see Oliver?

BIFF.   Jesus, Dad!

WILLY.   You mean you didn't go up there?

HAPPY.   Sure he went up there.

BIFF.   I did. I—saw him. How could they fire you?

WILLY (*on the edge of his chair*).   What kind of a welcome did he give you?

BIFF.   He won't even let you work on commission?

WILLY.   I'm out! (*Driving.*) So tell me, he gave you a warm welcome?

HAPPY.   Sure, Pop, sure!

BIFF (*driven*).   Well, it was kind of—

WILLY.   I was wondering if he'd remember you. (*To* HAPPY.) Imagine, man doesn't see him for ten, twelve years and gives him that kind of welcome!

HAPPY.   Damn right!

BIFF (*trying to return to the offensive*).   Pop, look—

WILLY.   You know why he remembered you, don't you? Because you impressed him in those days.

BIFF.   Let's talk quietly and get this down to the facts, huh?

WILLY (*as though* BIFF *had been interrupting*).   Well, what happened? It's great news, Biff. Did he take you into his office or'd you talk in the waiting-room?

BIFF.   Well, he came in, see, and—

WILLY (*with a big smile*).   What'd he say? Betcha he threw his arm around you.

BIFF.   Well, he kinda—

WILLY.   He's a fine man. (*To* HAPPY.) Very hard man to see, y'know.

HAPPY (*agreeing*).   Oh, I know.

WILLY (*to* BIFF).   Is that where you had the drinks?

BIFF.   Yeah, he gave me a couple of—no, no!

HAPPY (*cutting in*).   He told him my Florida idea.

WILLY.   Don't interrupt. (*To* BIFF.) How'd he react to the Florida idea?

BIFF.   Dad, will you give me a minute to explain?

WILLY.   I've been waiting for you to explain since I sat down here! What happened? He took you into his office and what?

BIFF.   Well—I talked. And—and he listened, see.

WILLY.   Famous for the way he listens, y'know. What was his answer?

BIFF.   His answer was— (*He breaks off, suddenly angry.*) Dad, you're not letting me tell you what I want to tell you!

WILLY (*accusing, angered*).   You didn't see him, did you?

BIFF.   I did see him!

WILLY.   What'd you insult him or something? You insulted him, didn't you?

BIFF.   Listen, will you let me out of it, will you just let me out of it!

HAPPY.   What the hell!

WILLY.   Tell me what happened!

BIFF (*to* HAPPY).   I can't talk to him!

A single trumpet note jars the ear. The light of green leaves stains the house, which holds the air of night and a dream. Young BERNARD *enters and knocks on the door of the house.*

YOUNG BERNARD (*frantically*).   Mrs. Loman, Mrs. Loman!
HAPPY.   Tell him what happened!
BIFF (*to* HAPPY).   Shut up and leave me alone!
WILLY.   No, no! You had to go and flunk math!
BIFF.   What math? What're you talking about?
YOUNG BERNARD.   Mrs. Loman, Mrs. Loman!

LINDA *appears in the house, as of old.*

WILLY (*wildly*).   Math, math, math!
BIFF.   Take it easy, Pop!
YOUNG BERNARD.   Mrs. Loman!
WILLY (*furiously*).   If you hadn't flunked you'd've been set by now!
   BIFF.   Now, look, I'm gonna tell you what happened, and you're going to listen to me.
YOUNG BERNARD.   Mrs. Loman!
BIFF.   I waited six hours—
HAPPY.   What the hell are you saying?
   BIFF.   I kept sending in my name but he wouldn't see me. So finally he . . . (*He continues unheard as light fades low on the restaurant.*)
YOUNG BERNARD.   Biff flunked math!
LINDA.   No!
YOUNG BERNARD.   Birnbaum flunked him! They won't graduate him!
   LINDA.   But they have to. He's gotta go to the university. Where is he? Biff! Biff!
YOUNG BERNARD.   No, he left. He went to Grand Central.
LINDA.   Grand—You mean he went to Boston!
YOUNG BERNARD.   Is Uncle Willy in Boston?
   LINDA.   Oh, maybe Willy can talk to the teacher. Oh, the poor, poor boy!

Light on house area snaps out.

   BIFF (*at the table, now audible, holding up a gold fountain pen*).   . . . so I'm washed up with Oliver, you understand? Are you listening to me?
WILLY (*at a loss*).   Yeah, sure. If you hadn't flunked—
BIFF.   Flunked what? What're you talking about?
   WILLY.   Don't blame everything on me! I didn't flunk math—you did! What pen?
HAPPY.   That was awful dumb, Biff, a pen like that is worth—
WILLY (*seeing the pen for the first time*).   You took Oliver's pen?
BIFF (*weakening*).   Dad, I just explained it to you.
WILLY.   You stole Bill Oliver's fountain pen!
   BIFF.   I didn't exactly steal it! That's just what I've been explaining to you!
   HAPPY.   He had it in his hand and just then Oliver walked in, so he got nervous and stuck it in his pocket!
WILLY.   My God, Biff!
BIFF.   I never intended to do it, Dad!

OPERATOR'S VOICE. Standish Arms, good evening!

WILLY (*shouting*). I'm not in my room!

BIFF (*frightened*). Dad, what's the matter? (*He and* HAPPY *stand up.*)

OPERATOR. Ringing Mr. Loman for you!

WILLY. I'm not there, stop it!

BIFF (*horrified, gets down on one knee before* WILLY). Dad, I'll make good, I'll make good. (WILLY *tries to get to his feet.* BIFF *holds him down.*) Sit down now.

WILLY. No, you're no good, you're no good for anything.

BIFF. I am, Dad, I'll find something else, you understand? Now don't worry about anything. (*He holds up* WILLY's *face.*) Talk to me, Dad.

OPERATOR. Mr. Loman does not answer. Shall I page him?

WILLY (*attempting to stand, as though to rush and silence the* OPERATOR). No, no, no!

HAPPY. He'll strike something, Pop.

WILLY. No, no . . .

BIFF (*desperately, standing over* WILLY). Pop, listen! Listen to me! I'm telling you something good. Oliver talked to his partner about the Florida idea. You listening? He—he talked to his partner, and he came to me . . . I'm going to be all right, you hear? Dad, listen to me, he said it was just a question of the amount!

WILLY. Then you . . . got it?

HAPPY. He's gonna be terrific, Pop!

WILLY (*trying to stand*). Then you got it, haven't you? You got it! You got it!

BIFF (*agonized, holds* WILLY *down*). No, no. Look, Pop. I'm supposed to have lunch with them tomorrow. I'm just telling you this so you'll know that I can still make an impression, Pop. And I'll make good somewhere, but I can't go tomorrow, see?

WILLY. Why not? You simply—

BIFF. But the pen, Pop!

WILLY. You give it to him and tell him it was an oversight!

HAPPY. Sure, have lunch tomorrow!

BIFF. I can't say that—

WILLY. You were doing a crossword puzzle and accidentally used his pen!

BIFF. Listen, kid, I took those balls years ago, now I walk in with his fountain pen? That clinches it, don't you see? I can't face him like that! I'll try elsewhere.

PAGE'S VOICE. Paging Mr. Loman!

WILLY. Don't you want to be anything?

BIFF. Pop, how can I go back?

WILLY. You don't want to be anything, is that what's behind it?

BIFF (*now angry at* WILLY *for not crediting his sympathy*). Don't take it that way! You think it was easy walking into that office after what I'd done to him? A team of horses couldn't have dragged me back to Bill Oliver!

WILLY. Then why'd you go?

BIFF.   Why did I go? Why did I go! Look at you! Look at what's become of you!

Off left, THE WOMAN *laughs.*

WILLY.   Biff, you're going to go to that lunch tomorrow, or—
BIFF.   I can't go. I've got no appointment!
HAPPY.   Biff, for . . . !
WILLY.   Are you spiting me?
BIFF.   Don't take it that way! Goddammit!

WILLY (*strikes* BIFF *and falters away from the table*).   You rotten little louse! Are you spiting me?
THE WOMAN.   Someone's at the door, Willy!
BIFF.   I'm no good, can't you see what I am?
HAPPY (*separating them*).   Hey, you're in a restaurant! Now cut it out, both of you! (*The girls enter.*) Hello girls, sit down.

THE WOMAN *laughs, off left.*

MISS FORSYTHE.   I guess we might as well. This is Letta.
THE WOMAN.   Willy, are you going to wake up?
BIFF (*ignoring* WILLY).   How're ya, miss, sit down. What do you drink?
MISS FORSYTHE.   Letta might not be able to stay long.
LETTA.   I gotta get up very early tomorrow. I got jury duty. I'm so excited! Were you fellows ever on a jury?
BIFF.   No, but I been in front of them! (*The girls laugh.*) This is my father.
LETTA.   Isn't he cute? Sit down with us, Pop.
HAPPY.   Sit him down, Biff!
BIFF (*going to him*).   Come on, slugger, drink us under the table. To hell with it! Come on, sit down, pal.

On BIFF's *last insistence*, WILLY *is about to sit.*

THE WOMAN (*now urgently*).   Willy, are you going to answer the door!

THE WOMAN's *call pulls* WILLY *back. He starts right, befuddled.*

BIFF.   Hey, where are you going?
WILLY.   Open the door.
BIFF.   The door?
WILLY.   The washroom . . . the door . . . where's the door?
BIFF (*leading* WILLY *to the left*).   Just go straight down.

WILLY *moves left.*

THE WOMAN.   Willy, Willy, are you going to get up, get up, get up, get up?

WILLY *exits left.*

LETTA.   I think it's sweet you bring your daddy along.
MISS FORSYTHE.   Oh, he isn't really your father!

BIFF (*at left, turning to her resentfully*).   Miss Forsythe, you've just seen a prince walk by. A fine, troubled prince. A hardworking, unappreciated prince. A pal, you understand? A good companion. Always for his boys.

LETTA.   That's so sweet.

HAPPY.   Well, girls, what's the program? We're wasting time. Come on, Biff. Gather round. Where would you like to go?

BIFF.   Why don't you do something for him?

HAPPY.   Me!

BIFF.   Don't you give a damn for him, Hap?

HAPPY.   What're you talking about? I'm the one who—

BIFF.   I sense it, you don't give a good goddam about him. (*He takes the rolled-up hose from his pocket and puts it on the table in front of* HAPPY.) Look what I found in the cellar, for Christ's sake. How can you bear to let it go on?

HAPPY.   Me? Who goes away? Who runs off and—

BIFF.   Yeah, but he doesn't mean anything to you. You could help him—I can't! Don't you understand what I'm talking about? He's going to kill himself, don't you know that?

HAPPY.   Don't I know it! Me!

BIFF.   Hap, help him! Jesus . . . help him . . . Help me, help me, I can't bear to look at his face! (*Ready to weep, he hurries out, up right.*)

HAPPY (*starting after him*).   Where are you going?

MISS FORSYTHE.   What's he so mad about?

HAPPY.   Come on, girls, we'll catch up with him.

MISS FORSYTHE (*as* HAPPY *pushes her out*).   Say, I don't like that temper of his!

HAPPY.   He's just a little overstrung, he'll be all right!

WILLY (*off left, as* THE WOMAN *laughs*).   Don't answer! Don't answer!

LETTA.   Don't you want to tell your father—

HAPPY.   No, that's not my father. He's just a guy. Come on, we'll catch Biff, and, honey, we're going to paint this town! Stanley, where's the check! Hey, Stanley!

They exit. STANLEY *looks toward left.*

STANLEY (*calling to* HAPPY *indignantly*).   Mr. Loman! Mr. Loman!

STANLEY *picks up a chair and follows them off. Knocking is heard off left.* THE WOMAN *enters, laughing.* WILLY *follows her. She is in a black slip; he is buttoning his shirt. Raw, sensuous music accompanies their speech.*

WILLY.   Will you stop laughing? Will you stop?

THE WOMAN.   Aren't you going to answer the door? He'll wake the whole hotel.

WILLY.   I'm not expecting anybody.

THE WOMAN.   Whyn't you have another drink, honey, and stop being so damn self-centered?

WILLY.   I'm so lonely.

THE WOMAN.   You know you ruined me, Willy? From now on, whenever you come to the office, I'll see that you go right through to the buyers. No waiting at my desk any more, Willy. You ruined me.

WILLY.   That's nice of you to say that.

THE WOMAN.   Gee, you are self-centered! Why so sad? You are the saddest, self-centeredest soul I ever did see-saw. (*She laughs. He kisses her.*) Come on inside, drummer boy. It's silly to be dressing in the middle of the night. (*As knocking is heard.*) Aren't you going to answer the door?

WILLY.   They're knocking on the wrong door.

THE WOMAN.   But I felt the knocking. And he heard us talking in here. Maybe the hotel's on fire!

WILLY (*his terror rising*).   It's a mistake.

THE WOMAN.   Then tell him to go away!

WILLY.   There's nobody there.

THE WOMAN.   It's getting on my nerves, Willy. There's somebody standing out there and it's getting on my nerves!

WILLY (*pushing her away from him*).   All right, stay in the bathroom here, and don't come out. I think there's a law in Massachusetts about it, so don't come out. It may be that new room clerk. He looked very mean. So don't come out. It's a mistake, there's no fire.

The knocking is heard again. He takes a few steps away from her, and she vanishes into the wing. The light follows him, and now he is facing YOUNG BIFF, *who carries a suitcase.* BIFF *steps toward him. The music is gone.*

BIFF.   Why didn't you answer?

WILLY.   Biff! What are you doing in Boston?

BIFF.   Why didn't you answer? I've been knocking for five minutes, I called you on the phone—

WILLY.   I just heard you. I was in the bathroom and had the door shut. Did anything happen home?

BIFF.   Dad—I let you down.

WILLY.   What do you mean?

BIFF.   Dad . . .

WILLY.   Biffo, what's this about? (*Putting his arm around* BIFF.) Come on, let's go downstairs and get you a malted.

BIFF.   Dad, I flunked math.

WILLY.   Not for the term?

BIFF.   The term. I haven't got enough credits to graduate.

WILLY.   You mean to say Bernard wouldn't give you the answers?

BIFF.   He did, he tried, but I only got a sixty-one.

WILLY.   And they wouldn't give you four points?

BIFF.   Birnbaum refused absolutely. I begged him, Pop, but he won't give me those points. You gotta talk to him before they close the school. Because if he saw the kind of man you are, and you just talked to him in your way, I'm sure he'd come through for me. The class came right before practice, see, and I didn't go enough. Would you talk to him? He'd like you, Pop. You know the way you could talk.

WILLY.   You're on. We'll drive right back.

BIFF.   Oh, Dad, good work! I'm sure he'll change it for you!

WILLY.   Go downstairs and tell the clerk I'm checkin' out. Go right down.

BIFF. Yes, sir! See, the reason he hates me, Pop—one day he was late for class so I got up at the blackboard and imitated him. I crossed my eyes and talked with a lithp.

WILLY (*laughing*). You did? The kids like it?

BIFF. They nearly died laughing!

WILLY. Yeah? What'd you do?

BIFF. The thquare root of thixthy twee is . . . (WILLY *bursts out laughing*; BIFF *joins him*.) And in the middle of it he walked in!

WILLY *laughs and* THE WOMAN *joins in offstage.*

WILLY (*without hesitation*). Hurry downstairs and—

BIFF. Somebody in there?

WILLY. No, that was next door.

THE WOMAN *laughs offstage.*

BIFF. Somebody got in your bathroom!

WILLY. No, it's the next room, there's a party—

THE WOMAN (*enters, laughing. She lisps this*). Can I come in? There's something in the bathtub, Willy, and it's moving!

WILLY *looks at* BIFF, *who is staring open-mouthed and horrified at* THE WOMAN.

WILLY. Ah—you better go back to your room. They must be finished painting by now. They're painting her room so I let her take a shower here. Go back, go back . . . (*He pushes her.*)

THE WOMAN (*resisting*). But I've got to get dressed, Willy, I can't—

WILLY. Get out of here! Go back, go back . . . (*Suddenly striving for the ordinary.*) This is Miss Francis, Biff, she's a buyer. They're painting her room. Go back, Miss Francis, go back . . .

THE WOMAN. But my clothes, I can't go out naked in the hall!

WILLY (*pushing her offstage*). Get outa here! Go back, go back!

BIFF *slowly sits down on his suitcase as the argument continues offstage.*

THE WOMAN. Where's my stockings? You promised me stockings, Willy!

WILLY. I have no stockings here!

THE WOMAN. You had two boxes of size nine sheers for me, and I want them!

WILLY. Here, for God's sake, will you get outa here!

THE WOMAN (*enters holding a box of stockings*). I just hope there's nobody in the hall. That's all I hope. (*To* BIFF.) Are you football or baseball?

BIFF. Football.

THE WOMAN (*angry, humiliated*). That's me too. G'night. (*She snatches her clothes from* WILLY, *and walks out.*)

WILLY (*after a pause*). Well, better get going. I want to get to the school first thing in the morning. Get my suits out of the closet. I'll get my valise. (BIFF *doesn't move.*) What's the matter? (BIFF *remains motionless, tears falling.*) She's a buyer. Buys for J. H. Simmons. She lives down the hall—they're painting. You don't imagine—(*He breaks off. After a pause.*) Now listen, pal, she's just a buyer. She sees merchandise in her room and they have to keep it looking just so . . . (*Pause. Assuming command.*) All right, get my suits. (BIFF *doesn't move.*) Now stop crying and do as I say. I gave you an order, Biff, I gave you an order! Is that what you do when I give you an order? How dare you cry! (*Putting his arm around* BIFF.) Now look, Biff, when you grow up you'll understand about these things. You mustn't—you mustn't overemphasize a thing like this. I'll see Birnbaum first thing in the morning.

BIFF. Never mind.

WILLY (*getting down beside* BIFF).   Never mind! He's going to give you those points. I'll see to it.

BIFF. He wouldn't listen to you.

WILLY.   He certainly will listen to me. You need those points for the U. of Virginia.

BIFF. I'm not going there.

WILLY. Heh? If I can't get him to change that mark you'll make it up in summer school. You've got all summer to—

BIFF (*his weeping breaking from him*). Dad . . .

WILLY (*infected by it*). Oh, my boy . . .

BIFF. Dad . . .

WILLY. She's nothing to me, Biff. I was lonely, I was terribly lonely.

BIFF. You—you gave her Mama's stockings! (*His tears break through and he rises to go.*)

WILLY (*grabbing for* BIFF). I gave you an order!

BIFF. Don't touch me, you—liar!

WILLY. Apologize for that!

BIFF. You fake! You phony little fake! You fake! (*Overcome, he turns quickly and weeping fully goes out with his suitcase.* WILLY *is left on the floor on his knees.*)

WILLY. I gave you an order! Biff, come back here or I'll beat you! Come back here! I'll whip you!

STANLEY *comes quickly in from the right and stands in front of* WILLY.

WILLY (*shouts at* STANLEY). I gave you an order . . .

STANLEY. Hey, let's pick it up, pick it up, Mr. Loman. (*He helps* WILLY *to his feet.*) Your boys left with the chippies. They said they'll see you home.

A second waiter watches some distance away.

WILLY. But we were supposed to have dinner together.

Music is heard, WILLY's *theme.*

STANLEY. Can you make it?

WILLY. I'll—sure, I can make it. (*Suddenly concerned about his clothes.*) Do I—I look all right?

STANLEY. Sure, you look all right. (*He flicks a speck off* WILLY's *lapel.*)

WILLY. Here—here's a dollar.

STANLEY. Oh, your son paid me. It's all right.

WILLY (*putting it in* STANLEY's *hand*). No, take it. You're a good boy.

STANLEY.   Oh, no, you don't have to . . .

WILLY.   Here—here's some more, I don't need it any more. (*After a slight pause.*) Tell me—is there a seed store in the neighborhood?

STANLEY.   Seeds? You mean like to plant?

As WILLY *turns,* STANLEY *slips the money back into his jacket pocket.*

WILLY.   Yes. Carrots, peas . . .

STANLEY.   Well, there's hardware stores on Sixth Avenue, but it may be too late now.

WILLY (*anxiously*).   Oh, I'd better hurry. I've got to get some seeds. (*He starts off to the right.*) I've got to get some seeds, right away. Nothing's planted. I don't have a thing in the ground.

WILLY *hurries out as the light goes down.* STANLEY *moves over to the right after him, watches him off. The other waiter has been staring at* WILLY.

STANLEY (*to the waiter*).   Well, whatta you looking at?

The waiter picks up the chairs and moves off right. STANLEY *takes the table and follows him. The light fades on this area. There is a long pause, the sound of the flute coming over. The light gradually rises on the kitchen, which is empty.* HAPPY *appears at the door of the house, followed by* BIFF. HAPPY *is carrying a large bunch of long-stemmed roses. He enters the kitchen, looks around for* LINDA. *Not seeing her, he turns to* BIFF, *who is just outside the house door, and makes a gesture with his hands, indicating "Not here, I guess." He looks into the living-room and freezes. Inside,* LINDA, *unseen, is seated,* WILLY's *coat on her lap. She rises ominously and quietly and moves toward* HAPPY, *who backs up into the kitchen, afraid.*

HAPPY.   Hey, what're you doing up? (LINDA *says nothing but moves toward him implacably.*) Where's Pop? (*He keeps backing to the right, and now* LINDA *is in full view in the doorway to the living-room.*) Is he sleeping?

LINDA.   Where were you?

HAPPY (*trying to laugh it off*).   We met two girls, Mom, very fine types. Here, we brought you some flowers. (*Offering them to her.*) Put them in your room, Ma.

She knocks them to the floor at BIFF's *feet. He has now come inside and closed the door behind him. She stares at* BIFF, *silent.*

HAPPY.   Now what'd you do that for? Mom, I want you to have some flowers—

LINDA (*cutting* HAPPY *off, violently to* BIFF).   Don't you care whether he lives or dies?

HAPPY (*going to the stairs*).   Come upstairs, Biff.

BIFF (*with a flare of disgust, to* HAPPY).   Go away from me! (*To* LINDA.) What do you mean, lives or dies? Nobody's dying around here, pal.

LINDA.   Get out of my sight! Get out of here!

BIFF.   I wanna see the boss.

LINDA.   You're not going near him!

BIFF.   Where is he? (*He moves into the living-room and* LINDA *follows.*)

LINDA (*shouting after* BIFF).   You invite him for dinner. He looks forward to it all day— (BIFF *appears in his parents' bedroom, looks around, and exits.*) —and then you desert him there. There's no stranger you'd do that to!

HAPPY.   Why? He had a swell time with us. Listen, when I— (LINDA *comes back into the kitchen.*) —desert him I hope I don't outlive the day!

LINDA.   Get out of here!

HAPPY.   Now look, Mom . . .

LINDA.   Did you have to go to women tonight? You and your lousy rotten whores!

BIFF *re-enters the kitchen.*

HAPPY.   Mom, all we did was follow Biff around trying to cheer him up! (*To* BIFF.) Boy, what a night you gave me!

LINDA.   Get out of here, both of you, and don't come back! I don't want you tormenting him any more. Go on now, get your things together! (*To* BIFF.) You can sleep in his apartment. (*She starts to pick up the flowers and stops herself.*) Pick up this stuff, I'm not your maid any more. Pick it up, you bum, you!

HAPPY *turns his back to her in refusal.* BIFF *slowly moves over and gets down on his knees, picking up the flowers.*

LINDA.   You're a pair of animals! Not one, not another living soul would have had the cruelty to walk out on that man in a restaurant!

BIFF (*not looking at her*).   Is that what he said?

LINDA.   He didn't have to say anything. He was so humiliated he nearly limped when he came in.

HAPPY.   But, Mom, he had a great time with us—

BIFF (*cutting him off violently*).   Shut up!

Without another word, HAPPY *goes upstairs.*

LINDA.   You! You didn't even go in to see if he was all right!

BIFF (*still on the floor in front of* LINDA, *the flowers in his hand; with self-loathing*).   No. Didn't. Didn't do a damned thing. How do you like that, heh? Left him babbling in a toilet.

LINDA.   You louse. You . . .

BIFF.   Now you hit it on the nose! (*He gets up, throws the flowers in the wastebasket.*) The scum of the earth, and you're looking at him!

LINDA.   Get out of here!

BIFF.   I gotta talk to the boss, Mom. Where is he?

LINDA.   You're not going near him. Get out of this house!

BIFF (*with absolute assurance, determination*).   No. We're gonna have an abrupt conversation, him and me.

LINDA.   You're not talking to him!

Hammering is heard from outside the house, off right. BIFF *turns toward the noise.*

LINDA (*suddenly pleading*).   Will you please leave him alone?

BIFF.   What's he doing out there?
LINDA.   He's planting the garden!
BIFF (*quietly*).   Now? Oh, my God!

BIFF *moves outside*, LINDA *following. The light dies down on them and comes up on the center of the apron as* WILLY *walks into it. He is carrying a flashlight, a hoe, and a handful of seed packets. He raps the top of the hoe sharply to fix it firmly, and then moves to the left, measuring off the distance with his foot. He holds the flashlight to look at the seed packets, reading off the instructions. He is in the blue of night.*

WILLY.   Carrots . . . quarter-inch apart. Rows . . . one-foot rows. (*He measures it off.*) One foot. (*He puts down a package and measures off.*) Beets. (*He puts down another package and measures again.*) Lettuce. (*He reads the package, puts it down.*) One foot— (*He breaks off as* BEN *appears at the right and moves slowly down to him.*) What a proposition, ts, ts. Terrific, terrific. 'Cause she's suffered, Ben, the woman has suffered. You understand me? A man can't go out the way he came in, Ben, a man has got to add up to something. You can't, you can't— (BEN *moves toward him as though to interrupt.*) You gotta consider, now. Don't answer so quick. Remember it's a guaranteed twenty-thousand-dollar proposition. Now look, Ben, I want you to go through the ins and outs of this thing with me. I've got nobody to talk to, Ben, and the woman has suffered, you hear me?

BEN (*standing still, considering*).   What's the proposition?

WILLY.   It's twenty thousand dollars on the barrelhead. Guaranteed, gilt-edged, you understand?

BEN.   You don't want to make a fool of yourself. They might not honor the policy.

WILLY.   How can they dare refuse? Didn't I work like a coolie to meet every premium on the nose? And now they don't pay off? Impossible!

BEN.   It's called a cowardly thing, William.

WILLY.   Why? Does it take more guts to stand here the rest of my life ringing up a zero?

BEN (*yielding*).   That's a point, William. (*He moves, thinking, turns.*) And twenty thousand—that *is* something one can feel with the hand, it is there.

WILLY (*now assured, with rising power*).   Oh, Ben, that's the whole beauty of it! I see it like a diamond, shining in the dark, hard and rough, that I can pick up and touch in my hand. Not like—like an appointment! This would not be another damned-fool appointment, Ben, and it changes all the aspects. Because he thinks I'm nothing, see, and so he spites me. But the funeral— (*Straightening up.*) Ben, that funeral will be massive! They'll come from Maine, Massachusetts, Vermont, New Hampshire! All the old-timers with the strange license plates—that boy will be thunder-struck, Ben, because he never realized—I am known! Rhode Island, New York, New Jersey—I am known, Ben, and he'll see it with his eyes once and for all. He'll see what I am, Ben! He's in for a shock, that boy!

BEN (*coming down to the edge of the garden*).   He'll call you a coward.

WILLY (*suddenly fearful*).   No, that would be terrible.

BEN.   Yes. And a damned fool.

WILLY.   No, no, he mustn't, I won't have that! (*He is broken and desperate.*)

BEN.   He'll hate you, William.

The gay music of the Boys is heard.

WILLY.   Oh, Ben, how do we get back to all the great times? Used to be so full of light, and comradeship, the sleigh-riding in winter, and the ruddiness on his cheeks. And always some kind of good news coming up, always something nice coming up ahead. And never even let me carry the valises in the house, and simonizing, simonizing that little red car! Why, why can't I give him something and not have him hate me?

BEN.   Let me think about it. (*He glances at his watch.*) I still have a little time. Remarkable proposition, but you've got to be sure you're not making a fool of yourself.

BEN *drifts off upstage and goes out of sight.* BIFF *comes down from the left.*

WILLY (*suddenly conscious of* BIFF, *turns and looks up at him, then begins picking up the packages of seeds in confusion*).   Where the hell is that seed? (*Indignantly.*) You can't see nothing out here! They boxed in the whole goddam neighborhood!

BIFF.   There are people all around here. Don't you realize that?

WILLY.   I'm busy. Don't bother me.

BIFF (*taking the hoe from* WILLY).   I'm saying good-by to you, Pop. (WILLY *looks at him, silent, unable to move.*) I'm not coming back any more.

WILLY.   You're not going to see Oliver tomorrow?

BIFF.   I've got no appointment, Dad.

WILLY.   He put his arm around you, and you've got no appointment?

BIFF.   Pop, get this now, will you? Everytime I've left it's been a fight that sent me out of here. Today I realized something about myself and I tried to explain it to you and I—I think I'm just not smart enough to make any sense out of it for you. To hell with whose fault it is or anything like that. (*He takes* WILLY's *arm.*) Let's just wrap it up, heh? Come on in, we'll tell Mom. (*He gently tries to pull* WILLY *to left.*)

WILLY (*frozen, immobile, with guilt in his voice*).   No, I don't want to see her.

BIFF.   Come on! (*He pulls again, and* WILLY *tries to pull away.*)

WILLY (*highly nervous*).   No, no, I don't want to see her.

BIFF (*tries to look into* WILLY's *face, as if to find the answer there*).   Why don't you want to see her?

WILLY (*more harshly now*).   Don't bother me, will you?

BIFF.   What do you mean, you don't want to see her? You don't want them calling you yellow, do you? This isn't your fault; it's me, I'm a bum. Now come inside! (WILLY *strains to get away.*) Did you hear what I said to you?

WILLY *pulls away and quickly goes by himself into the house.* BIFF *follows.*

LINDA (*to* WILLY).   Did you plant, dear?

BIFF.   What's he doing out there?
LINDA.   He's planting the garden!
BIFF (*quietly*).   Now? Oh, my God!

BIFF *moves outside,* LINDA *following. The light dies down on them and comes up on the center of the apron as* WILLY *walks into it. He is carrying a flashlight, a hoe, and a handful of seed packets. He raps the top of the hoe sharply to fix it firmly, and then moves to the left, measuring off the distance with his foot. He holds the flashlight to look at the seed packets, reading off the instructions. He is in the blue of night.*

WILLY.   Carrots . . . quarter-inch apart. Rows . . . one-foot rows. (*He measures it off.*) One foot. (*He puts down a package and measures off.*) Beets. (*He puts down another package and measures again.*) Lettuce. (*He reads the package, puts it down.*) One foot— (*He breaks off as* BEN *appears at the right and moves slowly down to him.*) What a proposition, ts, ts. Terrific, terrific. 'Cause she's suffered, Ben, the woman has suffered. You understand me? A man can't go out the way he came in, Ben, a man has got to add up to something. You can't, you can't— (BEN *moves toward him as though to interrupt.*) You gotta consider, now. Don't answer so quick. Remember it's a guaranteed twenty-thousand-dollar proposition. Now look, Ben, I want you to go through the ins and outs of this thing with me. I've got nobody to talk to, Ben, and the woman has suffered, you hear me?

BEN (*standing still, considering*).   What's the proposition?

WILLY.   It's twenty thousand dollars on the barrelhead. Guaranteed, gilt-edged, you understand?

BEN.   You don't want to make a fool of yourself. They might not honor the policy.

WILLY.   How can they dare refuse? Didn't I work like a coolie to meet every premium on the nose? And now they don't pay off? Impossible!

BEN.   It's called a cowardly thing, William.

WILLY.   Why? Does it take more guts to stand here the rest of my life ringing up a zero?

BEN (*yielding*).   That's a point, William. (*He moves, thinking, turns.*) And twenty thousand—that *is* something one can feel with the hand, it is there.

WILLY (*now assured, with rising power*).   Oh, Ben, that's the whole beauty of it! I see it like a diamond, shining in the dark, hard and rough, that I can pick up and touch in my hand. Not like—like an appointment! This would not be another damned-fool appointment, Ben, and it changes all the aspects. Because he thinks I'm nothing, see, and so he spites me. But the funeral— (*Straightening up.*) Ben, that funeral will be massive! They'll come from Maine, Massachusetts, Vermont, New Hampshire! All the old-timers with the strange license plates—that boy will be thunder-struck, Ben, because he never realized—I am known! Rhode Island, New York, New Jersey—I am known, Ben, and he'll see it with his eyes once and for all. He'll see what I am, Ben! He's in for a shock, that boy!

BEN (*coming down to the edge of the garden*).   He'll call you a coward.

WILLY (*suddenly fearful*).   No, that would be terrible.

BEN.   Yes. And a damned fool.

WILLY.   No, no, he mustn't, I won't have that! (*He is broken and desperate.*)

BEN.   He'll hate you, William.

The gay music of the Boys is heard.

WILLY.   Oh, Ben, how do we get back to all the great times? Used to be so full of light, and comradeship, the sleigh-riding in winter, and the ruddiness on his cheeks. And always some kind of good news coming up, always something nice coming up ahead. And never even let me carry the valises in the house, and simonizing, simonizing that little red car! Why, why can't I give him something and not have him hate me?

BEN.   Let me think about it. (*He glances at his watch.*) I still have a little time. Remarkable proposition, but you've got to be sure you're not making a fool of yourself.

BEN *drifts off upstage and goes out of sight.* BIFF *comes down from the left.*

WILLY (*suddenly conscious of* BIFF, *turns and looks up at him, then begins picking up the packages of seeds in confusion*).   Where the hell is that seed? (*Indignantly.*) You can't see nothing out here! They boxed in the whole goddam neighborhood!

BIFF.   There are people all around here. Don't you realize that?

WILLY.   I'm busy. Don't bother me.

BIFF (*taking the hoe from* WILLY).   I'm saying good-by to you, Pop. (WILLY *looks at him, silent, unable to move.*) I'm not coming back any more.

WILLY.   You're not going to see Oliver tomorrow?

BIFF.   I've got no appointment, Dad.

WILLY.   He put his arm around you, and you've got no appointment?

BIFF.   Pop, get this now, will you? Everytime I've left it's been a fight that sent me out of here. Today I realized something about myself and I tried to explain it to you and I—I think I'm just not smart enough to make any sense out of it for you. To hell with whose fault it is or anything like that. (*He takes* WILLY's *arm.*) Let's just wrap it up, heh? Come on in, we'll tell Mom. (*He gently tries to pull* WILLY *to left.*)

WILLY (*frozen, immobile, with guilt in his voice*).   No, I don't want to see her.

BIFF.   Come on! (*He pulls again, and* WILLY *tries to pull away.*)

WILLY (*highly nervous*).   No, no, I don't want to see her.

BIFF (*tries to look into* WILLY's *face, as if to find the answer there*).   Why don't you want to see her?

WILLY (*more harshly now*).   Don't bother me, will you?

BIFF.   What do you mean, you don't want to see her? You don't want them calling you yellow, do you? This isn't your fault; it's me, I'm a bum. Now come inside! (WILLY *strains to get away.*) Did you hear what I said to you?

WILLY *pulls away and quickly goes by himself into the house.* BIFF *follows.*

LINDA (*to* WILLY).   Did you plant, dear?

BIFF (*at the door, to* LINDA).   All right, we had it out. I'm going and I'm not writing any more.

LINDA (*going to* WILLY *in the kitchen*).   I think that's the best way, dear. 'Cause there's no use drawing it out, you'll just never get along.

WILLY *doesn't respond.*

BIFF.   People ask where I am and what I'm doing, you don't know, and you don't care. That way it'll be off your mind and you can start brightening up again. All right? That clears it, doesn't it? (WILLY *is silent, and* BIFF *goes to him.*) You gonna wish me luck, scout? (*He extends his hand.*) What do you say?

LINDA.   Shake his hand, Willy.

WILLY (*turning to her, seething with hurt*).   There's no necessity to mention the pen at all, y'know.

BIFF (*gently*).   I've got no appointment, Dad.

WILLY (*erupting fiercely*).   He put his arm around . . . ?

BIFF.   Dad, you're never going to see what I am, so what's the use of arguing? If I strike oil I'll send you a check. Meantime forget I'm alive.

WILLY (*to* LINDA).   Spite, see?

BIFF.   Shake hands, Dad.

WILLY.   Not my hand.

BIFF.   I was hoping not to go this way.

WILLY.   Well, this is the way you're going. Good-by.

BIFF *looks at him a moment, then turns sharply and goes to the stairs.*

WILLY (*stops him with*).   May you rot in hell if you leave this house!

BIFF (*turning*).   Exactly what is it that you want from me?

WILLY.   I want you to know, on the train, in the mountains, in the valleys, wherever you go, that you cut down your life for spite!

BIFF.   No, no.

WILLY.   Spite, spite, is the word of your undoing! And when you're down and out, remember what did it. When you're rotting somewhere beside the railroad tracks, remember, and don't you dare blame it on me!

BIFF.   I'm not blaming it on you!

WILLY.   I won't take the rap for this, you hear?

HAPPY *comes down the stairs and stands on the bottom step, watching.*

BIFF.   That's just what I'm telling you!

WILLY (*sinking into a chair at the table, with full accusation*).   You're trying to put a knife in me—don't think I don't know what you're doing!

BIFF.   All right, phony! Then let's lay it on the line. (*He whips the rubber tube out of his pocket and puts it on the table.*)

HAPPY.   You crazy—

LINDA.   Biff! (*She moves to grab the hose, but* BIFF *holds it down with his hand.*)

BIFF.   Leave it there! Don't move it!

WILLY (*not looking at it*).   What is that?

BIFF.   You know goddam well what that is.

WILLY (*caged, wanting to escape*). I never saw that.

BIFF. You saw it. The mice didn't bring it into the cellar! What is this supposed to do, make a hero out of you? This supposed to make me sorry for you?

WILLY. Never heard of it.

BIFF. There'll be no pity for you, you hear it? No pity!

WILLY (*to* LINDA). You hear the spite!

BIFF. No, you're going to hear the truth—what you are and what I am!

LINDA. Stop it!

WILLY. Spite!

HAPPY (*coming down toward* BIFF). You cut it now!

BIFF (*to* HAPPY). The man don't know who we are! The man is gonna know! (*To* WILLY.) We never told the truth for ten minutes in this house!

HAPPY. We always told the truth!

BIFF (*turning on him*). You big blow, are you the assistant buyer? You're one of the two assistants to the assistant, aren't you?

HAPPY. Well, I'm practically—

BIFF. You're practically full of it! We all are! And I'm through with it. (*To* WILLY.) Now hear this, Willy, this is me.

WILLY. I know you!

BIFF. You know why I had no address for three months? I stole a suit in Kansas City and I was in jail. (*To* LINDA, *who is sobbing.*) Stop crying. I'm through with it.

LINDA *turns away from them, her hands covering her face.*

WILLY. I suppose that's my fault!

BIFF. I stole myself out of every good job since high school!

WILLY. And whose fault is that?

BIFF. And I never got anywhere because you blew me so full of hot air I could never stand taking orders from anybody! That's whose fault it is!

WILLY. I hear that!

LINDA. Don't, Biff!

BIFF. It's goddam time you heard that! I had to be boss big shot in two weeks, and I'm through with it!

WILLY. Then hang yourself! For spite, hang yourself!

BIFF. No! Nobody's hanging himself, Willy! I ran down eleven flights with a pen in my hand today. And suddenly I stopped, you hear me? And in the middle of that office building, do you hear this? I stopped in the middle of that building and I saw—the sky. I saw the things that I love in this world. The work and the food and time to sit and smoke. And I looked at the pen and said to myself, what the hell am I grabbing this for? Why am I trying to become what I don't want to be? What am I doing in an office, making a contemptuous, begging fool of myself, when all I want is out there, waiting for me the minute I say I know who I am! Why can't I say that, Willy? (*He tries to make* WILLY *face him, but* WILLY *pulls away and moves to the left.*)

WILLY (*with hatred, threateningly*). The door of your life is wide open!

BIFF. Pop! I'm a dime a dozen, and so are you!

WILLY (*turning on him now in an uncontrolled outburst*). I am not a dime a dozen! I am Willy Loman, and you are Biff Loman!

BIFF *starts for* WILLY, *but is blocked by* HAPPY. *In his fury,* BIFF *seems on the verge of attacking his father.*

BIFF. I am not a leader of men, Willy, and neither are you. You were never anything but a hard-working drummer who landed in the ash can like all the rest of them! I'm one dollar an hour, Willy! I tried seven states and I couldn't raise it. A buck an hour! Do you gather my meaning? I'm not bringing home any prizes any more, and you're going to stop waiting for me to bring them home!

WILLY (*directly to* BIFF). You vengeful, spiteful mut!

BIFF *breaks from* HAPPY. WILLY, *in fright, starts up the stairs.* BIFF *grabs him.*

BIFF (*at the peak of his fury*). Pop, I'm nothing! I'm nothing, Pop. Can't you understand that? There's no spite in it any more. I'm just what I am, that's all.

BIFF's *fury has spent itself, and he breaks down, sobbing, holding on to* WILLY, *who dumbly fumbles for* BIFF's *face.*

WILLY (*astonished*). What're you doing? What're you doing? (*To* LINDA.) Why is he crying?

BIFF (*crying, broken*). Will you let me go, for Christ's sake? Will you take that phony dream and burn it before something happens? (*Struggling to contain himself, he pulls away and moves to the stairs.*) I'll go in the morning. Put him—put him to bed. (*Exhausted,* BIFF *moves up the stairs to his room.*)

WILLY (*after a long pause, astonished, elevated*). Isn't that—isn't that remarkable? Biff—he likes me!

LINDA. He loves you, Willy!

HAPPY (*deeply moved*). Always did, Pop.

WILLY. Oh, Biff! (*Staring wildly.*) He cried! Cried to me. (*He is choking with his love, and now cries out his promise.*) That boy—that boy is going to be magnificent!

BEN *appears in the light just outside the kitchen.*

BEN. Yes, outstanding, with twenty thousand behind him.

LINDA (*sensing the racing of his mind, fearfully, carefully*). Now come to bed, Willy. It's all settled now.

WILLY (*finding it difficult not to rush out of the house*). Yes, we'll sleep. Come on. Go to sleep, Hap.

BEN. And it does take a great kind of a man to crack the jungle.

In accents of dread, BEN's *idyllic music starts up.*

HAPPY (*his arm around* LINDA). I'm getting married, Pop, don't forget it. I'm changing everything. I'm gonna run that department before the year is up. You'll see, Mom. (*He kisses her.*)

BEN.   The jungle is dark but full of diamonds, Willy.

WILLY *turns, moves, listening to* BEN.

LINDA.   Be good. You're both good boys, just act that way, that's all.

HAPPY.   'Night, Pop. (*He goes upstairs.*)

LINDA (*to* WILLY).   Come, dear.

BEN (*with greater force*).   One must go in to fetch a diamond out.

WILLY (*to* LINDA, *as he moves slowly along the edge of the kitchen, toward the door*).   I just want to get settled down, Linda. Let me sit alone for a little.

LINDA (*almost uttering her fear*).   I want you upstairs.

WILLY (*taking her in his arms*).   In a few minutes, Linda. I couldn't sleep right now. Go on, you look awful tired. (*He kisses her.*)

BEN.   Not like an appointment at all. A diamond is rough and hard to the touch.

WILLY.   Go on now. I'll be right up.

LINDA.   I think this is the only way, Willy.

WILLY.   Sure, it's the best thing.

BEN.   Best thing!

WILLY.   The only way. Everything is gonna be—go on, kid, get to bed. You look so tired.

LINDA.   Come right up.

WILLY.   Two minutes.

LINDA *goes into the living-room, then reappears in her bedroom.* WILLY *moves just outside the kitchen door.*

WILLY.   Loves me. (*Wonderingly.*) Always loved me. Isn't that a remarkable thing? Ben, he'll worship me for it!

BEN (*with promise*).   It's dark there, but full of diamonds.

WILLY.   Can you imagine that magnificence with twenty thousand dollars in his pocket?

LINDA (*calling from her room*).   Willy! Come up!

WILLY (*calling into the kitchen*).   Yes! Yes. Coming! It's very smart, you realize that, don't you, sweetheart? Even Ben sees it. I gotta go, baby. 'By! 'By! (*Going over to* BEN, *almost dancing.*) Imagine? When the mail comes he'll be ahead of Bernard again!

BEN.   A perfect proposition all around.

WILLY.   Did you see how he cried to me? Oh, if I could kiss him, Ben!

BEN.   Time, William, time!

WILLY.   Oh, Ben, I always knew one way or another we were gonna make it, Biff and I!

BEN (*looking at his watch*).   The boat. We'll be late. (*He moves slowly off into the darkness.*)

WILLY (*elegiacally, turning to the house*).   Now when you kick off, boy, I want a seventy-yard boot, and get right down the field under the ball, and when you hit, hit low and hit hard, because it's important, boy. (*He swings around and faces the audience.*) There's all kinds of important people in the stands, and the first thing you know . . . (*Suddenly realizing he is alone.*) Ben! Ben, where do I . . . ? (*He makes a sudden movement of search.*) Ben, how do I . . . ?

LINDA (*calling*).   Willy, you coming up?

WILLY (*uttering a gasp of fear, whirling about as if to quiet her*).   Sh! (*He turns around as if to find his way; sounds, faces, voices, seem to be swarming in upon him and he flicks at them, crying*) Sh! Sh! (*Suddenly music, faint and high, stops him. It rises in intensity, almost to an unbearable scream. He goes up and down on his toes, and rushes off around the house.*) Shhh!

LINDA.   Willy?

There is no answer. LINDA *waits.* BIFF *gets up off his bed. He is still in his clothes.* HAPPY *sits up.* BIFF *stands listening.*

LINDA (*with real fear*).   Willy, answer me! Willy!

There is the sound of a car starting and moving away at full speed.

LINDA.   No!

BIFF (*rushing down the stairs*).   Pop!

As the car speeds off, the music crashes down in a frenzy of sound, which becomes the soft pulsation of a single cello string. BIFF *slowly returns to his bedroom. He and* HAPPY *gravely don their jackets.* LINDA *slowly walks out of her room. The music has developed into a dead march. The leaves of day are appearing over everything.* CHARLEY *and* BERNARD, *somberly dressed, appear and knock on the kitchen door.* BIFF *and* HAPPY *slowly descend the stairs to the kitchen as* CHARLEY *and* BERNARD *enter. All stop a moment when* LINDA, *in clothes of mourning, bearing a little bunch of roses, comes through the draped doorway into the kitchen. She goes to* CHARLEY *and takes his arm. Now all move toward the audience, through the wall-line of the kitchen. At the limit of the apron,* LINDA *lays down the flowers, kneels, and sits back on her heels. All stare down at the grave.*

REQUIEM

CHARLEY.   It's getting dark, Linda.

LINDA *doesn't react. She stares at the grave.*

BIFF.   How about it, Mom? Better get some rest, heh? They'll be closing the gate soon.

LINDA *makes no move. Pause.*

HAPPY (*deeply angered*).   He had no right to do that. There was no necessity for it. We would've helped him.

CHARLEY (*grunting*).   Hmmm.

BIFF.   Come along, Mom.

LINDA.   Why didn't anybody come?

CHARLEY.   It was a very nice funeral.

LINDA.   But where are all the people he knew? Maybe they blame him.

CHARLEY.   Naa. It's a rough world, Linda. They wouldn't blame him.

LINDA.   I can't understand it. At this time especially. First time in thirty-five years we were just about free and clear. He only needed a little salary. He was even finished with the dentist.

CHARLEY.   No man only needs a little salary.

LINDA.   I can't understand it.

BIFF.   There were a lot of nice days. When he'd come home from a trip; or on Sundays, making the stoop; finishing the cellar; putting on the new porch; when he built the extra bathroom; and put up the garage. You know something, Charley, there's more of him in that front stoop than in all the sales he ever made.

CHARLEY.   Yeah. He was a happy man with a batch of cement.

LINDA.   He was so wonderful with his hands.

BIFF.   He had the wrong dreams. All, all, wrong.

HAPPY (*almost ready to fight* BIFF).   Don't say that!

BIFF.   He never knew who he was.

CHARLEY (*stopping* HAPPY's *movement and reply. To* BIFF).   Nobody dast blame this man. You don't understand: Willy was a salesman. And for a salesman, there is no rock bottom to the life. He don't put a bolt to a nut, he don't tell you the law or give you medicine. He's a man way out there in the blue, riding on a smile and a shoeshine. And when they start not smiling back—that's an earthquake. And then you get yourself a couple of spots on your hat, and you're finished. Nobody dast blame this man. A salesman is got to dream, boy. It comes with the territory.

BIFF.   Charley, the man didn't know who he was.

HAPPY (*infuriated*).   Don't say that!

BIFF.   Why don't you come with me, Happy?

HAPPY.   I'm not licked that easily. I'm staying right in this city, and I'm gonna beat this racket! (*He looks at* BIFF, *his chin set.*) The Loman Brothers!

BIFF.   I know who I am, kid.

HAPPY.   All right, boy. I'm gonna show you and everybody else that Willy Loman did not die in vain. He had a good dream. It's the only dream you can have—to come out number-one man. He fought it out here, and this is where I'm gonna win it for him.

BIFF (*with a hopeless glance at* HAPPY, *bends toward his mother*).   Let's go, Mom.

LINDA.   I'll be with you in a minute. Go on, Charley. (*He hesitates.*) I want to, just for a minute. I never had a chance to say good-by.

CHARLEY *moves away, followed by* HAPPY. BIFF *remains a slight distance up and left of* LINDA. *She sits there, summoning herself. The flute begins, not far away, playing behind her speech.*

LINDA.   Forgive me, dear. I can't cry. I don't know what it is, but I can't cry. I don't understand it. Why did you ever do that? Help me, Willy, I can't cry. It seems to me that you're just on another trip. I keep expecting you.

Willy, dear, I can't cry. Why did you do it? I search and search and I search, and I can't understand it, Willy. I made the last payment on the house today. Today, dear. And there'll be nobody home. (*A sob rises in her throat.*) We're free and clear. (*Sobbing more fully, released.*) We're free. (BIFF *comes slowly toward her.*) We're free . . . We're free . . .

BIFF *lifts her to her feet and moves out up right with her in his arms.* LINDA *sobs quietly.* BERNARD *and* CHARLEY *come together and follow them, followed by* HAPPY. *Only the music of the flute is left on the darkening stage as over the house the hard towers of the apartment buildings rise into sharp focus, and*

The Curtain Falls

QUESTIONS

1. One critic has said that Willy Loman is "merely pathetic" and "lacks the tragic grandeur Miller imagines for him." In what sense is "merely pathetic" different from "tragic"? Do you agree with this assessment of the play?

2. At one point in *Death of a Salesman*, Linda says, "Life is a casting off." Willy argues with her, saying, "No . . . some people accomplish something." To what extent is Willy's fate a result of this desire to "accomplish something"? Is this his "tragic flaw"? How would you compare his fate to that of Oedipus and Hamlet? To Hedda Gabler's?

3. By letting the walls of the present dissolve and thus allowing Ben to appear on stage, along with scenes of the Loman family in earlier and better times, Miller has departed fairly significantly from the conventions of the realistic theater. Yet these little experiments in the play seem to add to the psychological realism of the portrait of Willy. How exactly does this process work? Would we react differently to Willy if his dilemma were conveyed to us exclusively through the more conventional expository techniques of a play like *The Little Foxes*?

4. In some sense it could be said that selling is a symbolic American occupation. Could a play titled "Death of a Lawyer" or "Death of a Doctor" have the same impact as one titled "Death of a Salesman"? Select and analyze points in the play where you think Miller is trying to use Willy's job and all its implications to elevate him into the status of a representative American.

5. The past plays a major role in this play. In fact, the past is centrally involved in its suspense. That is, the issue is less whether Willy will kill himself, than whether his imaginative encounters with his past will lead him to see what his life has really been about. Look over the play once again, paying special attention to the flashbacks. Does Willy become more realistic about his life as a result of these scenes? Analyze the scene in which his infidelity in the hotel room is revealed to Biff. What role does this moment play in the creation of suspense? To what degree might it be seen as a climactic moment in the play? Is it a sufficient explanation for the tension between Willy and Biff?

WRITING ESSAYS ABOUT LITERATURE

O ne of the first facts to accept about the writing of an essay about a literary topic is that, in all likelihood, it is an *artificial* or *arranged* act. The writer of such an essay has been asked to do something that she or he would not have done without being asked. The writing of a formal essay about something one has read is usually done as the result of an assignment, a request, a classroom activity.

Other kinds of writing, like poems in the springtime or letters to a friend or entries in a diary, spring directly from personal needs and pleasures. One writes in those cases because one must release emotional pressures; one is answering to oneself or to someone very close. The writing comes because it must and there is, in such cases, no public response, no official reader. It is otherwise with most assigned essays on literary topics.

To recognize this important fact gives the writer of a literary essay a substantial advantage over the person who blindy proceeds to labor under the impression that what she or he is doing, when writing about literature, is just putting down on paper immediate impressions and random thoughts. The person who knows from the start that a literary essay is a *deliberate* act, that it involves *strategy* and *planning*, is already in a good position to succeed with any assignment that comes from a teacher. Keep in mind that the very word *essay* comes from the French word *essayer* (to try or to attempt) and its source thus tells you that the word, and hence the act, is a challenge and that it involves labor. One witty but nonetheless truthful way of summing up all of this comes from the writer Gene Fowler: "Writing is easy. All you do is stare at a blank sheet of paper until drops of blood form on your forehead." Another truth about writing, however, is that recognizing how hard it can be makes it much easier.

One of the first questions you will want to ask of yourself as a writer is: what kind of essay is appropriate to the specific occasion with which I have been presented? That is, given a particular kind of assignment or problem, how can the essay I am to write best engage my skills and the literary material I am to work with? Your first response should be to *consider carefully the nature of the assignment* and determine what it is really asking you to produce. If, for instance, the assignment asks you to describe the kind of prose style that Ernest Hemingway uses in one of his short stories, you would be correct in imagining that your job will be to act as something of a surveyor or scientist. You are being asked to *observe*, to *name*, and to *characterize*. Engaged in such a mission, your eye should, of course, be on details and your writing should be as careful as a doctor's report on the appearance of a patient. In the case of "The Killers," for instance, you would want to concentrate on Hemingway's purposefully sparse and unemotional diction as well as the tone of objectivity and non-involvement.

Another kind of essay, an *analytical explication*, would be appropriate if you had been asked to write on, for instance, the argument that forms the basis of Andrew Marvell's poem "To His Coy Mistress." In that case, you would want to lay out (*explicate* comes from the Latin word *explicare*, which means to unfold) the poem so that a reader can see and inspect its structure. Once again, your prose should be scalpel clean and should allow you (and then your reader) to see the poem part by part, section after section, in a clear and utterly objective way. Your eye should be trained on the many particular things, large and small, that constitute the poem. You would, with such an assigment, probably note the usefulness of beginning where the poem begins ("Had we but world enough, and time, / This coyness, lady, were no crime") and would trace the poem's movement to its last lines ("Thus, though we cannot make our sun / Stand still, yet we will make him run"). In your essay, you and your skills as a writer should be as unobtrusive as possible but the poem should loom large in the reader's awareness. If that happens, you will be successful.

An explication, then, is best seen as a service, an act meant to assist someone else (your reader) in seeing more precisely and accurately the object before him or her. Such service, to sum up, should be clean, thorough, efficient, and, by and large, impersonal.

Full-scale explications, however, are not always the appropriate means to respond to some writing occasions. Should you be asked, for instance, to comment on the respective characteristics of two, or perhaps three or even more, long poems or short stories, you would be overwhelmed were you patiently to delineate the properties of each. In your attention to detail and in your thoroughness, you would risk losing the reader's attention and you might wind up drowning in your evidence. Another strategy is needed. The first thing to do would be to select very carefully those passages in each of the works that seem most indicative of the works in their entirety. Is it a particular piece of narrative description in the short story? Is it one central stanza in the poem? To make these choices is to take chances and to exercise judgment, but good essays depend on the skill, even the artfulness, that the writer has in exercising such judgment.

Once the selections are made, it is wise to pause for a moment and to consider if, in your job as someone who has been asked to make comparisons between several literary works, you wish to extend your task and to make evaluative judgments among them. Is your essay to be a perfectly neutral description of the various characteristics you have carefully noted, or can you show that one poem or one story is superior to another on the basis of the evidence you have gathered? Both kinds of essays can be written, and both involve considerable skill, but it is important not to confuse them. The first

—the *neutral description or explication*—involves the craft of careful selection and accurate observation. The second—the *evaluative comparison*—draws on selection and observaton, to be sure, but also asks the essayist to be judgmental, to offer opinions about the respective merits of the different works of literary art under consideration.

If you have decided, in the light of the assignment you have been given or which you have given yourself, that your real mission in writing is to make evaluative judgments between various literary works, to decide what is weak or strong in each, then you should recognize that you have embarked on a task that will draw on your argumentative skills. You will first have to make sure that you know clearly what your main *thesis* is. The essay in its entirety should relate cogently and comfortably to that thesis. Secondly, you will have to recognize that your own good taste alone will not guarantee that your essay will be persuasive. You will have to show, with specific pieces of evidence drawn from the works under consideration, *how* you have reached your judgments and comparative evaluations. And, thirdly, you should formulate your essay in such a way that anyone who might want to differ with your findings will discover that you have anticipated the arguments opposing your own and have done everything within your power to answer them even before they can be asked. These three rules, appropriate to every kind of argument, are: (1) establish your thesis, (2) enforce any judgments you make by using quotations or other specific evidence, and (3) anticipate your opposition.

Suppose, for instance, that you find yourself faced with the interesting challenge of comparing the respective poetic properties and merits of, for example, Thomas Hardy's "I look into my glass" and John Milton's "How soon hath Time" (pp. 443–44 and 523) as two poems concerned with the wasting power of time as it passes in a person's life. You would want to deliberate a while about the appropriate bases for comparing the two poems. Although they both take up the subject of aging, Milton's poem seems to be written by a young man concerned about the ways in which his promise might or might not be realized with the passage of time. On the other hand, the poem by Hardy seems to be about an older man with much of his life over and his possibilities exhausted who is pained by memories of his youth. With that major difference in mind, you might note a major similarity: that both poems seem to consider time as something of an enemy, an opposing force. For Hardy, time makes men grieve; for Milton, time robs them of their youth, and thus of the years in which they might prosper and achieve success. This correspondence seen, you might then propose to yourself, on a tentative basis, a *thesis*:

Time is the Enemy in these works by John Milton and Thomas Hardy.

With your thesis in place as a means to guide your thoughts, you would want to review the two poems carefully, noting to yourself (and perhaps with the help of note cards, underlinings, or some other simple memory device) how the two poems differ. (The terms used for the poetry discussion in this book—under the headings of "words," "rhetoric," and "technique"—cover a wide range of poetic devices and strategies customarily used by poets and you might wish to refer to those sections for help in finding just the right terms for your own discussion.) Suppose, for instance, that one of the first notable differences to which you wish to draw attention is the visual difference between the two poems. One, a sonnet, is made up of rather long lines that together comprise four sentences, the first two short and the third and fourth becoming considerably longer. Milton's poem seems to stretch out as one reads it, beginning compactly and ending with extensive, long breaths. Hardy's poem, by contrast, is three quatrains, each making up a complete sentence. His poem ends as it begins: short, clipped, and restrained. With this observation in mind, and with the particular evidence noted, you might find yourself jotting down one central difference between the two poems, a difference that you might wish to develop as you compose your essay:

Form as a key to differences between Milton and Hardy.

Another aspect of the two poems that you might wish to note, and then develop, is the respective presences of Hardy's "God" and Milton's "great task-master." Are these two forces the same, or are they different in some important way? Does Milton relate to his "task-master" in the same way as Hardy relates to his "God"? What is the tone of each poem as it addresses that apparently important force? And what is the relationship of each such force to the force of time? These relationships seem important, and hence must be understood. Once you believe you are on the way to doing so, you might have established for your essay another crucial subheading:

Divinity and Time in the two poems.

If you have been keeping track of what you have thus far done, you will note, first of all, that you have done a good deal. Although writing might have its difficulties, they are not insuperable. By going at the job in an organized way, and by doing it bit by bit, you might surprise yourself by how much can be accomplished. It is a good practice never to overwhelm yourself by dwelling on how many words and pages you have to write; consider rather that you will inevitably reach your destination in writing by proceeding as you have always proceeded in other journeys: step by step. What you have done thus far is to begin with a working thesis which has gained support by certain evidence drawn from the formal or technical distinctions between the two poems under consideration. Then the thesis has been developed and enriched by remarks you have made about the respective presences of "God" and the "great task-master" in the two poems. You are now treating both time as an enemy and time in its relationship to the divinity. You have, in short, found that thinking about your writing, and doing the writing itself, have allowed you to expand your understanding of the two poems. This is an important discovery, for it demonstrates an old truth about the exercise of writing: *It is a means to comprehension.* By the very act of writing, you discover things.

Your work, however, is not yet over. You are close to being finished, but you must now guard against letting the essay collapse. There must continually be a sense of quiet excitement as it nears its conclusion. Your reader must be made to feel that you are taking him or her to a final destination that is not just a recap of everything you have said so far. With this in mind, you might wish to consider an ending that would be seen to grow naturally out of everything you have said but is yet fresh and arresting. One step to take is to offer a qualitative judgment about the two poems, to argue that either Milton or Hardy, faced with the same problem of time and divinity, does the *better* job as a poet in dramatically illustrating that problem. Much literary discussion, after all, does come down to preferences and taste. Your essay could take on genuine dramatic coloration were you to make your own preference known and to defend it.

But other compelling ways to end the essay are also open to you. You might wish to conclude by suddenly reversing your direction a bit by saying that while time certainly *appears* to be the enemy in both poems, and while you yourself began your investigation by noting the similarity between Milton and Hardy in this important respect, you now wish to announce that Milton is somehow at ease in his poem, while Hardy is not, and this crucial difference between them can be explained by Milton's perfect reliance upon his "task-master," a reliance apparently not available to Hardy. You would then be in a position to conclude your essay by saying that John Milton might have time as an enemy, but such an enemy can be thwarted by faith in God's will. Thomas Hardy, on the other hand, faces the enemy time without any such reliance or any such faith. With this thought in mind, your last sentence might go: "Time is indeed John Milton's enemy, but it is an enemy a belief in God can help overcome; time is also Thomas Hardy's enemy, but it is an enemy over whom even God cannot triumph."

In whatever way you conclude, you should try to provide your essay with one of the qualities that has been mentioned in several discussions in this book, namely the sense of *development*. The essay should be felt by you and by the reader to be going somewhere. It should not be simply a raw list of observations and remarks. To say this is to touch on one of the secrets of all good essay-writing. It is, finally, an art, one something like the art of literature we have described in the previous pages. The very best essays have the same qualities of all good writing: deftness, surprise, elegance, organization, and the charm of genuine intelligence. All of these wonderful qualities, however, cannot instantly be created by anyone. In all likelihood, the essays you first write will disappoint you in some respects. They might indeed not have all the deftness and elegance of which you are capable. But do not resign yourself to feeling that since writing an essay is an art, and you do not feel yourself to be an artist, you will never be a great success as a writer in this particular form. The fact of the matter is that most success in writing is not a function of being a genius. It is a result of practice. The way to be a good writer is to write, write, write. And the way to be an even better writer is to write more.

In any case, what you will have done thus far with Milton and Hardy will not, at this stage, be a finished draft: it will just be a draft. The proper treatment for such an item is benign neglect. Put it away for a while and think about something else. Then, having allowed yourself enough time before the essay is due, extract it from its place of safekeeping and read it over. Do so (this is important) with the eye of the toughest editor and critic you know or can imagine. Read it as if it were the work of someone you did not know.

Read it without mercy. And begin now to add, correct, and change. This second draft should, upon completion, feel fuller and richer. It should make you feel slightly embarrassed at your first attempt, but also good about the new strength you have been able to bring to your basic ideas and judgments.

If you have sufficient time, repeat this process. But (and this also is important) do not think that the process can be repeated forever without some real danger to your writing. The essay you finally deliver to your instructor should retain some of the freshness and electricity you originally brought to the assignment. If that freshness is gone, all you will have left is stale labor and it will show.

What, then, is writing an essay about a literary topic? It is an artificial act, like many other things that people do with their brains. It involves labor, planning, strategy, and a touch of art. It is a skill that improves over time. It is writing for an audience—first and most importantly yourself and then someone else who needs to be convinced and pleased. At its very best it partakes of the same qualities possessed by the work of art it is written about. Finally, it is a means of discovery. It is one of the best ways humans have of finding out for themselves what it is that they really know, feel, and think. Beginning only as just another classroom assignment, an essay can be a memorable, and eminently valuable, document teaching you who you are.

GLOSSARY

absurdism A twentieth century literary movement most intimately associated with drama in the theater of the absurd. Absurdism emphasizes the meaninglessness of life and assaults the conventions of realism in presentation.

allegory A narrative in which abstract concepts are represented by persons, objects, or events. (The medieval play *Everyman* is a noted example of allegory, for instance, as is John Bunyan's *Pilgrim's Progress*.) Many poems have allegorical overtones. However, in a strict allegory such as Edmund Spenser's *The Faerie Queen*, there is no possibility of an interpretation other than the one intended by the author.

alliteration The repetition of consonant sounds at the beginning of words in a line of verse ("sessions of sweet silent thought," for instance).

allusion A figure of speech based on a reference to history, classical mythology, another work of literature, and so forth, which has certain built-in emotional associations. (The Roman goddess Diana, for instance, suggests remoteness and virginity.)

ambiguity In the positive sense of the word, the multiple possibilities of meaning or interpretation in a work which complicate and enrich the reader's experience. In the negative, unintended sense, a verbal confusion obscuring meaning.

anapestic A metrical pattern involving two weak or unaccented syllables followed by a strong or accented one.

apostrophe A figure of speech in which the speaker of a poem directly addresses a person, idea, or object (for example, John Donne begins his famous poem, "Death, be not proud . . .").

approximate rhyme A pattern of rhyme in which the sounds of the rhyming words are similar but not identical (for example, "dizzy" and "easy" in Theodore Roethke's "My Papa's Waltz"). Sometimes referred to as "slant rhyme."

aside In drama, a brief remark which a character addresses directly to the audience. Far briefer than a soliloquy, the aside is a device which allows a dramatist to indicate what a character is thinking.

assonance   The repetition of vowel sounds in a line of verse ("Blind eyes could blaze *like* meteors and be gay," for instance).

ballad   A form of poetry telling a story. The earliest ballads in English were the folk ballads of the thirteenth century, sung or chanted at ceremonial occasions, and handed down from one generation to another.

blank verse   A sequence of unrhymed iambic pentameter poetry. During the Elizabethan era, blank verse was thought to be the poetic form most closely approximating the spoken word.

caesura   A natural pause in a line of verse.

catharsis   Aristotle's term defining the sense of release (and relief) an audience experiences at the conclusion of a tragedy.

chorus   In drama, especially Greek drama, a group of actors speaking or chanting in unison, and expressing sentiments which comment on the main action of the work.

climax   The point of greatest intensity and complication in the plot of a story or drama. Also referred to as the "turning point."

comedy   A form of drama which generally has a happy ending and emphasizes human folly rather than human grandeur.

complication   That part of the plot of a story or drama which makes relationships more complex and leads directly to the climax. Also referred to as the "rising action."

conclusion   The finale of a story or play which reestablishes stability and brings the plot to an end.

confessional poem   A form of poetry generally associated with the twentieth century in which the author explores his or her turbulent emotions, often using them as a way of characterizing the chaos of the surrounding world.

conflict   The antagonism within a character, between one character and another, or between a character and some aspect of the outer world which creates tension in a plot.

connotation   The implied meanings and multiple associations of a word.

consonance   The repetition of consonant sounds in a line of verse (for instance, Milton's "Of man's *f*irst disobedience, and the *f*ruit/ of that *f*orbidden tree . . ."). Unlike alliteration, consonance can occur internally within words rather than only at their beginnings.

convention   A characteristic of a literary genre which has, over time, become expected of it. In poetry, for instance, rhyme was a convention which was rarely challenged until the end of the nineteenth century.

couplet   Two lines which rhyme ("'Tis hard to say, if greater want of skill/ Appear in writing or in judging ill," for instance).

dactylic   A metrical pattern involving one strong or accented syllable followed by two weak or unaccented ones.

denotation   The exact, dictionary meaning of a word.

denouement   A French term indicating the "unravelling" of a plot. See also *climax*.

diction   The author's choice of words or of patterns of words. "Levels" of diction refers to the choices an author has ranging from the pompous to the vulgar.

didactic   In literature, referring to works which openly espouse certain causes or points of view and seek to "teach" the reader something. At its most extreme, the didactic work becomes propagandistic.

dimeter   A poetic line with two feet.

dramatic irony   See *irony*.

dramatic monologue   A poetic form featuring a speaker in a specific situation, usually one with conflict, addressing one or more listeners and frequently revealing, in some unwitting way, an aspect of his character. In poetry, the dramatic monologue is similar to the soliloquy in drama.

dramatic poetry   Poetry whose primary emphasis is on a situation involving character and conflict, even if it is no more than the dramatization of inner doubts on the part of the speaker.

elegy   A lyric poem celebrating a dead person or persons.

enjambment   The continuation of a poetic phrase past the rhyming words at the end of a line of verse.

exact rhyme   Duplication or near duplication of sounds at the ends of lines of verse.

exposition   The beginning situation in a drama or story, i.e., the time when characters and conflicts are introduced.

figurative language   Language that cannot be taken literally, i.e., language using metaphor, simile and other figures of speech.

first person narrator   See *point of view*.

fixed form   In poetry, any form (sonnet, villanelle, etc.) whose basic form is prescribed by convention.

foot   In poetry, the unit of measurement for meter. A foot consists of patterns of stressed and unstressed syllables.

foreshadowing   In fiction and drama, a hint of what is to come as the plot develops.

free verse   Poetry without definitely established metrical patterns. These patterns are frequently replaced with other devices such as the repetition of words and ideas, the recurrence of certain sounds, and so forth.

genre   The different "kinds" of literature, such as fiction, poetry, and drama.

hexameter   A poetic line with six feet.

hubris   The overweening pride which the Greeks saw as a tragic hero's greatest flaw.

iambic   A metrical pattern involving a weak or unaccented syllable followed by a strong or accented one.

imagery   The "word pictures" drawn from the senses by which a poet makes the reader "see," "feel," and "hear" the scenes and situations of a poem.

internal rhyme   Rhyme which occurs within a line of verse.

intimate observer   See *point of view.*

irony   The result of a disparity between the apparent and actual meanings in a work of literature. Three types of irony are discussed in this book. In *dramatic irony* the author intends a different meaning than that understood by the speaker or narrator. *Situational irony* involves a discrepancy between what is and what should be. *Verbal irony* involves the use of words to indicate that what is said is different from what is meant.

lyric poetry   The word "lyrical" comes from lyre, a musical instrument, thus suggesting the relationship between lyric and song. This genre of poetry is distinguished by the presence of deep emotion. Most often the lyric is about love or death, although it may be about almost any subject or mood.

melodrama   A presentation characterized by sensational episodes, cloying sentiment, and forced happy endings.

metaphor   A comparison between two dissimilar elements or areas of experience.

meter   The "beat" of a poem. Meter is the pattern of stressed and unstressed sounds in lines of verse that can be analyzed, syllable by syllable, through scansion.

metonymy   An event, idea, object, and so forth, referred to by closely alluding to some quality associated with it. In his history plays, for instance, Shakespeare typically uses the word "crown" as a synonym for "king."

narrative poetry   Poetry which tells a story or reports events.

objective observer   See *point of view.*

octave   The first eight lines of a sonnet. Also, an eight-line stanza in any poem.

ode   A lengthy lyrical poem, often addressed to some praiseworthy person, object, or quality.

omniscient narrator   See *point of view.*

onomatopoeia   In poetry, the use of words whose sounds ("whip," "flop," "buzz," etc.) seem to echo the actions they describe.

overstatement   A rhetorical device, often comic in intent, in which poets make readers question the surface meanings of assertions or interpretations of situations. Also called *hyperbole.*

oxymoron   Two or more words which apparently contradict each other (as in W. B. Yeats' "a terrible beauty") but actually join to make a new meaning.

paradox A statement or situation which seems absurd or contradictory but may actually represent a more profound level of truth.

paraphrase The restatement in one's own words of what a poem says. A step-by-step translation of poetic sentiments into prose.

pentameter A poetic line with five feet.

peripety In drama, the abrupt change in a course of events brought about by a sudden revelation or insight.

persona The speaker or narrator in a work of literature. The persona is the writer's mask, the posture he or she adopts to tell a story and make points more effectively.

plot The chronology or sequence of events in a work of literature. More significantly, the inner logic which gives a story or play meaning.

point of view In fiction, the narrator's level of involvement in the action and relative closeness to the characters and their dilemmas. Four different possible points of view are discussed in this book. The *first person narrator* is a named person (or simply the unnamed "I") who tells the story. Close to events, the first person narrator is frequently an "unreliable witness" whose version the reader doubts. The *intimate observer* has unlimited access to the hearts and minds of the characters of a story. The *objective observer* knows and says nothing more than can be gathered by "objectively" witnessing the scene being described. The *omniscient narrator* stands above the story, unlimited in his knowledge of what will happen and intruding at will into the minds and motives of the characters.

prosody The study of sound and rhythm in poetry.

protagonist The main character in a work of literature.

quatrain A four-line stanza of poetry.

quintet A five-line stanza of poetry.

refrain A phrase or line of poetry repeated at regular intervals.

resolution That part of the plot of a story or play which links the climax and conclusion. The point at which the complex issues of the plot begin to "unravel."

rhetoric In literature generally, the strategies a writer employs to move readers toward certain conclusions. In poetry some of these strategies involve such devices as overstatement and allusion, which are part of the art of rhetoric as developed in ancient Rome.

rhyme The repetition of sounds within or at the ends of lines of verse.

rhyme scheme The pattern of end rhymes in a poem or in its stanzas.

rhythm The recurring stresses and pauses in a line of verse and in whole poems.

satire Literature which ridicules what the writer regards as human folly.

scansion The process of marking the alternating accented and unaccented syllables that make up a poem's meter.

simile   A comparison between two essentially different ideas or areas of experience using words such as "like" or "as" (Wordsworth's "I wandered lonely as a cloud," for instance).

situational irony   See *irony*.

soliloquy   In drama a speech in which a character reveals his or her inner thoughts to the audience by appearing to "think out loud."

sonnet   A form with a carefully defined structure and rhyme scheme. Sonnets consist of fourteen lines of iambic pentameter verse usually rhymed according to either the Petrarchan (Italian) or Shakespearean tradition. The first eight lines (the octave) tend to pose a dilemma or problem which the concluding six lines (or sestet) typically resolve.

spondaic   A somewhat unusual metrical pattern involving two stressed syllables.

stanza   A pattern of lines which is repeated throughout a poem.

symbol   A word standing for something else. Certain words (the Cross, the dove, etc.) have a range of meanings beyond their literal definition and writers sometimes use these words because of their manifold and far-reaching associations.

synecdoche   A figure of speech in which part of something is made to stand for the whole. For instance, in Shakespeare's line, "If you read this line, remember not that hand that wrote it," the word "hand" stands for "writer" or "poet."

syntax   The ordering of words into distinctive grammatical patterns.

tetrameter   A poetic line with four feet.

tone   The general atmosphere of a piece of writing; the particular pitch or "sound" of a word or passage.

tragedy   In drama, a work showing a protagonist engaged in a morally significant struggle ending in ruin.

tragic flaw   That extreme quality in a protagonist—pride, sensitivity, intelligence, and so forth—that may be the cause of his or her appeal and is certainly the cause of his or her ultimate downfall.

trimeter   A poetic line with three feet.

trochaic   A metrical pattern involving one strong or accented syllable followed by a weak or unaccented one.

understatement   A rhetorical device which can intensify a work by forcing the reader to supply the full insight and meaning of a situation. In understatement the poet says less than he or she means, or less than the occasion seems to warrant. Also called *meiosis*.

verbal irony   See *irony*.

villanelle   A French-inspired poetic form involving five three-line stanzas and a final stanza of four lines. Only two rhyming sounds are permitted in the entire poem. The first and third lines are repeated in the third line of each succeeding stanza.

voice   A writer's unmistakably personal way of addressing subject matter and giving his or her work a distinctive feel and shape.

1081

INDEX OF AUTHORS, TITLES, AND FIRST LINES

D E F G H I J 0 1 2 3 4

Allegory + Symb.   Justraretion

Faith (double meaning)
Goodman
Pink ribbon
Brown - (Dark + Dreary)

"Faith kept me back awhile"
        — he is a simple man of faith

" My Faith is gone" — wife + his faith.
        His belief in the basic goodness of man is gone

Fact or dream?

Hamlet   Dialectic
    Underlying meanings

Verbal attack on Queen
killing Polonius - acc. but just.
Ophelia
fooling G + R
fighting w/ Laertes

Psych Cit

Innocence Betrayed
    village — superego
    Forest — id
    Brown — ego

    Satan — B's alter ego
        — projection of psyche
        — Faithless.